Hong Kong Chronicles
Overview & Chronology

by

Hong Kong Chronicles Institute

Chung Hwa Book Co., (H.K.) Ltd

Hong Kong Chronicles: Overview & Chronology

Duty Editors: Wang Bo, Wei Lingcha, Yang Anqi
Design: Circle Communications Ltd., Mo Mok
Production: Chung Hwa Book Co., (H.K.) Ltd

Compiled &
Translated by: Hong Kong Chronicles Institute
25/F Fortis Tower
77-79 Gloucester Road, Wan Chai, H.K.
Tel: 852 2603 3500   Fax: 852 2603 0031
E-mail: info@hkchronicles.org.hk
Website: www.hkchronicles.org.hk

Published by: Chung Hwa Book Co., (H.K.) Ltd.
Flat B, 1/F, North Point Industrial Building,
499 King's Road, North Point, H.K.
E-mail: info@chunghwabook.com.hk
Website: www.chunghwabook.com.hk

Distributed by: SUP Publishing Logistics (H.K.) Ltd.
16/F, Tsuen Wan Industrial Centre,
220-248 Texaco Road, Tsuen Wan, N.T., H.K.
Tel: 852 2150 2100   Fax: 852 2407 3062
E-mail: info@suplogistics.com.hk

Printed by: C & C Joint Printing Co., (H.K.) Ltd.
14/F, C&C Building, 36 Ting Lai Road, Tai Po, H. K.

First Edition July 2022

Specifications: 285mm×210mm

ISBN   978-988-8807-32-1

衷心感謝以下機構及人士的慷慨支持，
讓《香港志》能夠付梓出版，永留印記。

*Hong Kong Chronicles has been made possible with the
generous contributions of the following benefactors:*

首席惠澤機構
Principal Benefactor

香港賽馬會慈善信託基金
The Hong Kong Jockey Club Charities Trust
同心同步同進 *RIDING HIGH TOGETHER*

惠澤機構
Benefactors

香港董氏慈善基金會

The Tung Foundation

黃廷方慈善基金

Ng Teng Fong Charitable Foundation

恒隆地產

Hang Lung Properties Limited

太古集團

John Swire & Sons

怡和管理有限公司

Jardine Matheson Limited

信德集團何鴻燊博士基金會有限公司

Shun Tak Holdings – Dr. Stanley Ho Hung Sun Foundation Limited

恒基兆業地產集團

Henderson Land Group

滙豐

HSBC

中國銀行(香港)有限公司

Bank of China (Hong Kong) Limited

COUNCIL AND EXECUTIVE COMMITTEE

Lee Kam-keung

Leung Cho-nga

David Lung Ping-yee

Siu Kwok-kin

Wong Siu-lun

Victor Zheng Wan-tai

Dick Lee Ming-kwan

Liu Shuyong

Poon Yiu-ming

Tang Chung

Emilie Yeh Yueh-yu

EDITORIAL TEAM

Maps 1 and 2

The region of Hong Kong on the "Coastal Map of Guangdong" in *Yue daji*, an official record of Guangdong compiled by Guo Fei (郭棐). Published in 1598 (25th year of the reign of Emperor Wanli [萬曆] of the Ming Dynasty).

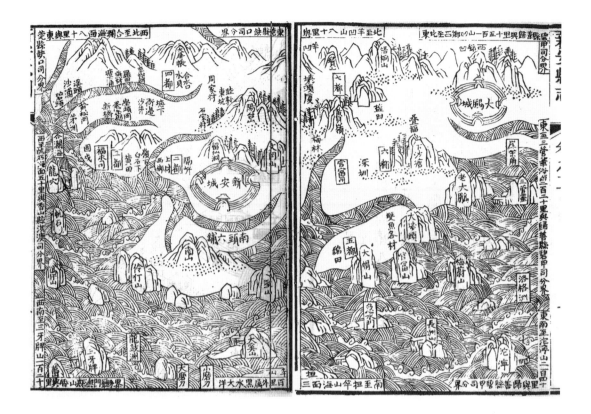

Maps 3 and 4
The maps of Xin'an County in Xin'an County Local Chronicles compiled by Shu Maoguan (舒懋官) and Wang Chongxi (王崇熙). Published in 1819 (24th year of the reign of Emperor Jiaqing [嘉慶] of the Qing Dynasty).

新安縣圖

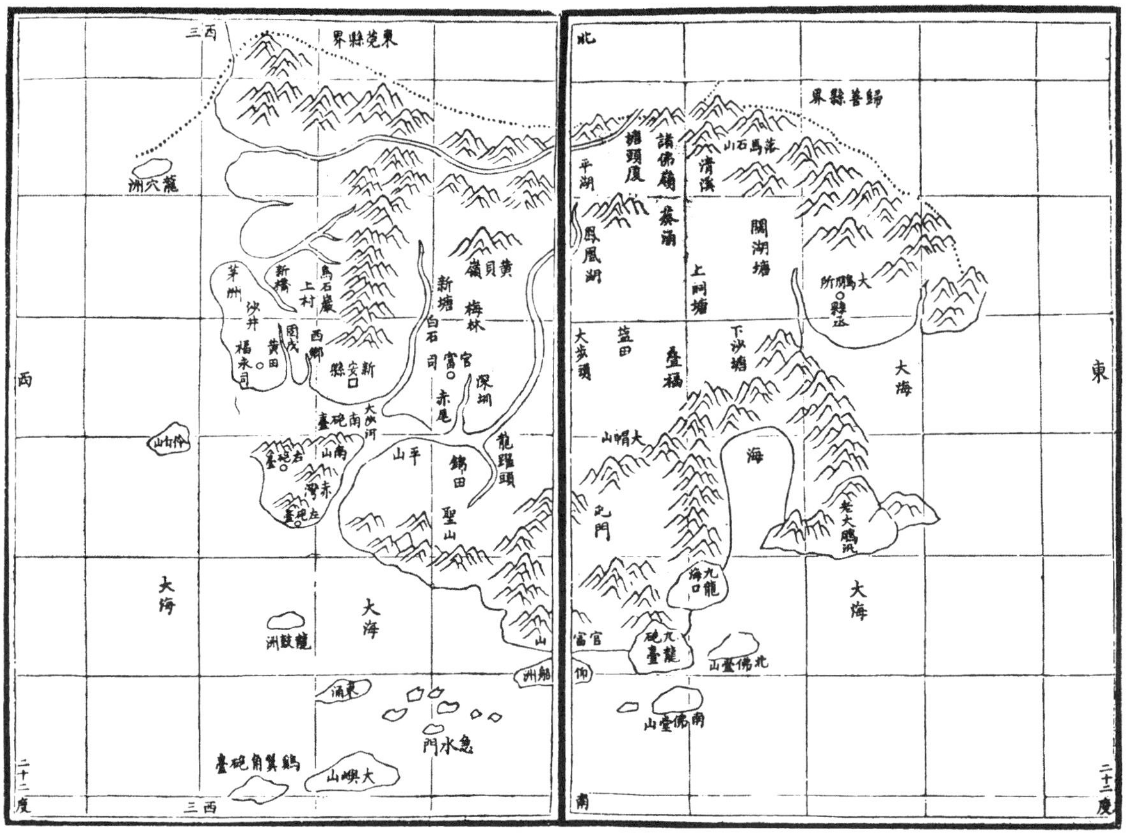

Map 5
"Map of Xin'an County" in *Guangdong Tongzhi* (Gazetteer of Guangdong Province) compiled by Ruan Yuan (阮元) and Chen Changqi (陳昌齊). Published in 1822 (2nd year of the reign of Emperor Daoguang [道光] of the Qing Dynasty).

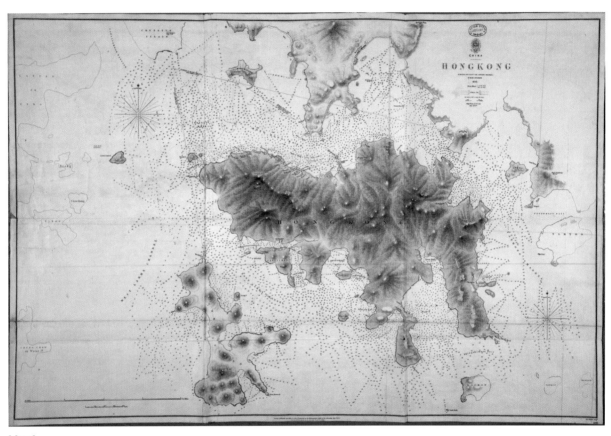

Map 6
The map of Hong Kong Island based on surveys conducted by Captain Sir Edward Belcher of HMS *Sulphur* in 1841. (Courtesy of The National Archives of the United Kingdom, ref. FO925/2293)

Map 7

"Map of the San-On District, Kwangtung Province"—a map of Xin'an County with keys in Chinese and English and drawn from actual observations by Italian missionary Simeone Volonteri in 1866. The map was engraved by F. A. Brockhaus in Leipzig, Germany. (Provided by the National Library of Australia, MAP RM 279)

新安縣全圖

MAP OF THE

SAN-ON-DISTRICT,

(KWANGTUNG PROVINCE,)

DRAWN FROM ACTUAL OBSERVATIONS MADE BY

AN ITALIAN MISSIONARY OF THE

PROPAGANDA

In the Course of his Professional Labors During a Period

OF

FOUR YEARS.

Being the first and only map hitherto published.

May 1866.

REFERENCES.

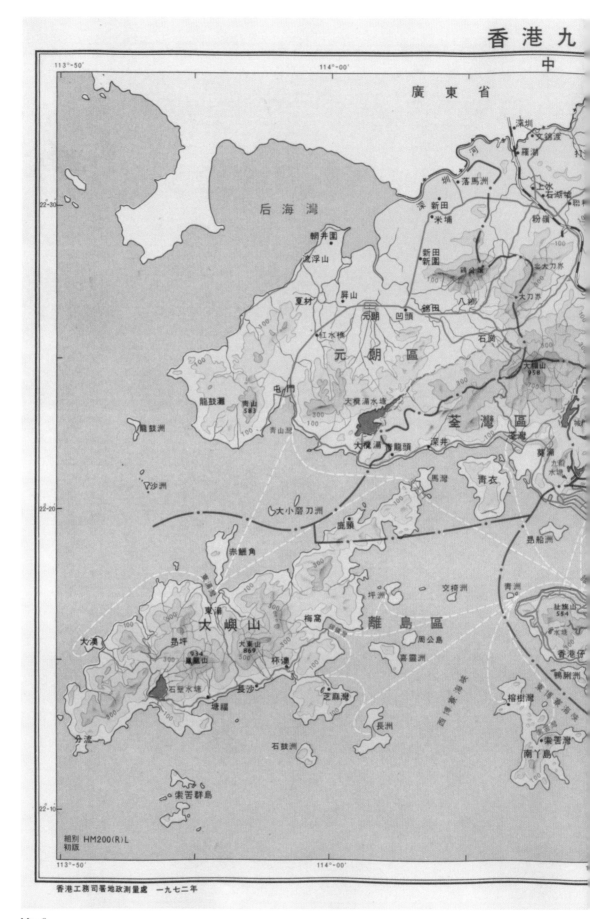

Map 8
The map of Hong Kong, Kowloon and the New Territories, 1972. (Courtesy of Public Records Office,
Government Records Service)

新界

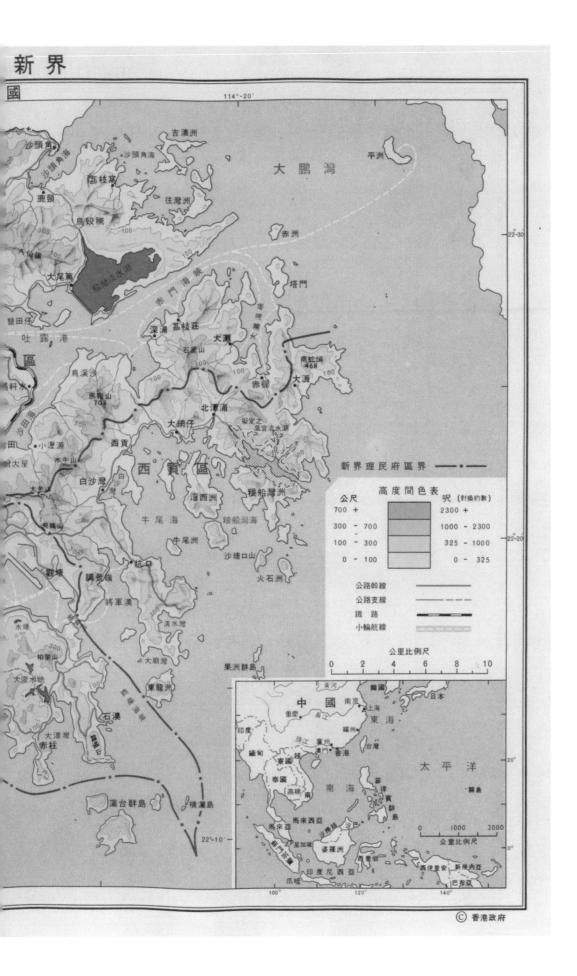

國

114°-20'

大鵬灣

沙頭角
沙頭角海
荔枝窩
鹿頸
烏蛟騰
仙嶺
大尾篤
船灣淡水湖

吉澳洲
沙頭角海
住灣洲
平洲
赤洲
塔門

赤門海峽

鹽田仔
吐露港
深涌 荔枝莊
大灘
石屋山
南蛇嶺
468
赤徑 大浪

區
科水
烏溪沙
馬鞍山
703
大網仔
北潭涌
擬定之
萬宜淡水湖

沙田海
田
小瀝源
大水屋
大圍

西貢
水牛山
白沙灣
西貢區
溶西洲
糧船灣洲

牛尾海
糧船灣海
牛尾洲
沙塘口山
火石洲

新界理民府區界 ——·—

高度間色表

公尺	呎 (對換約數)
700 +	2300 +
300 - 700	1000 - 2300
100 - 300	325 - 1000
0 - 100	0 - 325

公路幹線 ————
公路支線 — — —
鐵路 ▬▬▬▬
小輪航線 ░░░░

公里比例尺
0 2 4 6 8 10

22°-30

22°-20

飛鵝山
坑口
調景嶺
將軍澳
清水灣

水塘
柏架山
銀線灣
大頭洲
大潭水塘
石澳
大潭灣
赤柱

果洲群島

蒲台群島
橫瀾島

22°-10'

100°

中國 南京
黃河 韓國
重慶 長江 上海 日本
印度 福州 東海
珠江 廣州 台灣
緬甸 澳門 香港
越南
寮國 太平洋
泰國
高棉 南海 菲律賓群島
關島
馬來西亞
星加坡 沙巴
馬來亞 沙撈越
汶萊
婆羅洲
西里伯
西伊里安 新畿內亞
蘇門答臘
印度尼西亞
爪哇 帝汶島 巴布亞

公里比例尺
0 1000 2000

120° 140°

20°

0°

Ⓒ 香港政府

ix

Map 9
The map of the territory of Hong Kong, 1985. (Reproduced with permission of the Director of Lands.
© The Government of the HKSAR. Licence No. 81/2021)

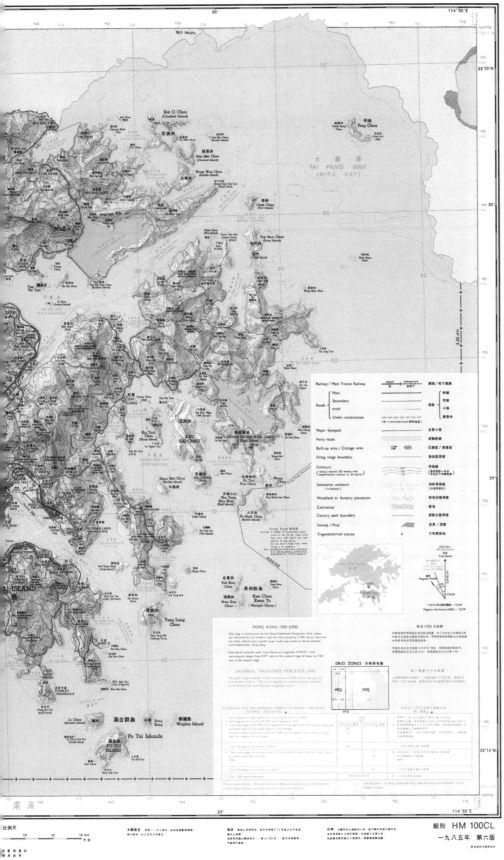

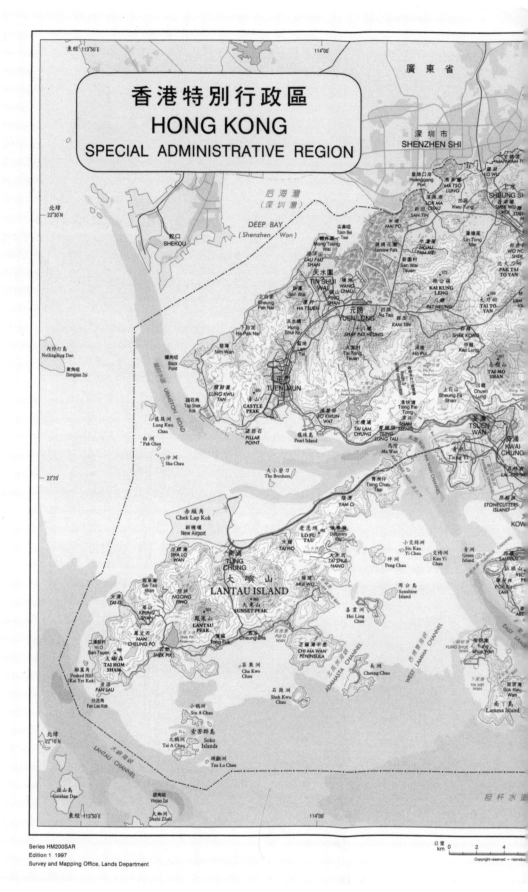

Map 10
Topographic map of the Hong Kong Special Administrative Region, 1997.
(Courtesy of Public Records Office, Government Records Service)

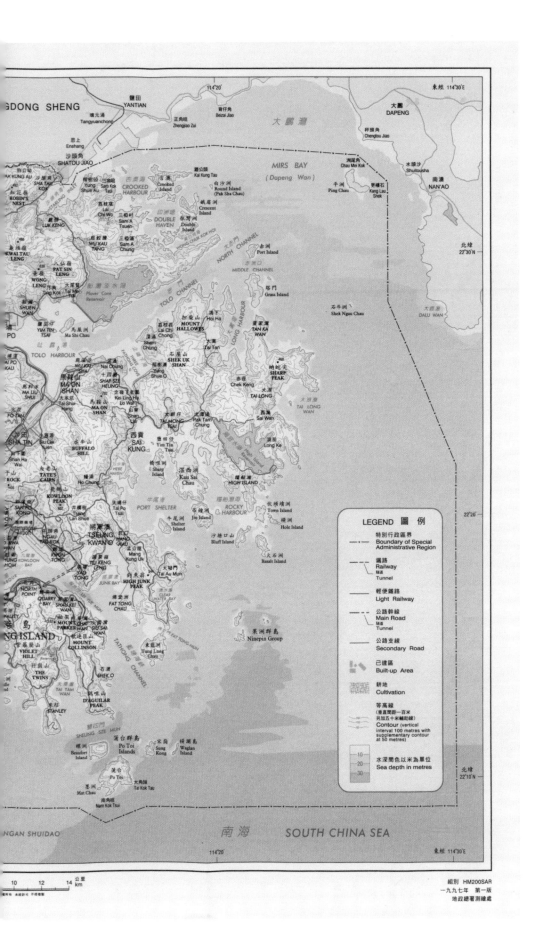

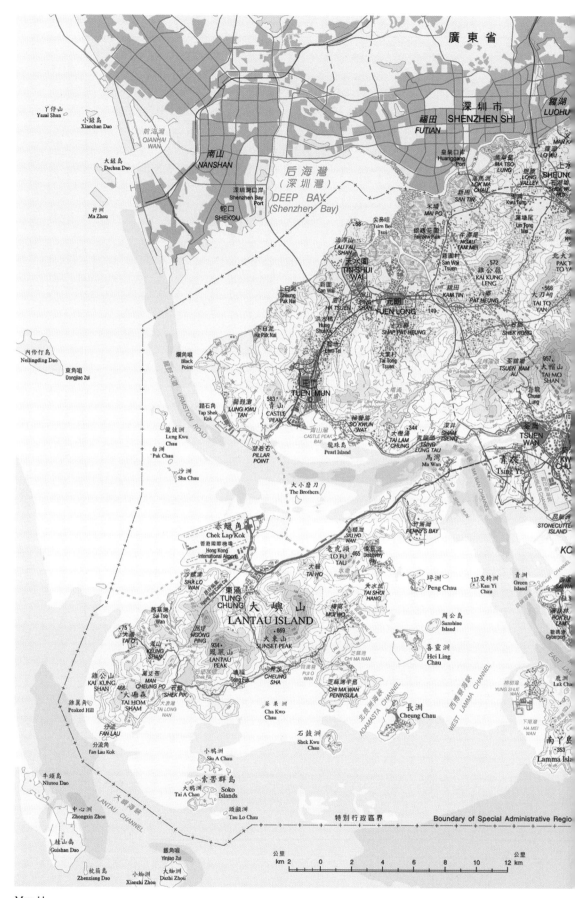

Map 11
Topographic map of the Hong Kong Special Administrative Region, 2017.
(Courtesy of HKSAR Government and DATA.GOV.HK)

ANGDONG SHENG
鹽田 YANTIAN

背仔角 Beizai Jiao
大鵬 DAPENG

塘元涌 Tangyuenchong
正角咀 Zhengjiao Zui
大亞灣 DAYA WAN

恩上 Enshang
沙頭角 SHATOUJIAO
大鵬灣 MIRS BAY (Dapeng Wan)

秤頭角 Chengtou Jiao
洲尾角 Chau Mei Kok
水頭沙 Shuitousha
南澳 NAN'AO

蓮麻坑 Lin Ma Hang
492 紅花嶺 ROBIN'S NEST
長排頭 Ledge Point
雞公頭 Kai Kung Tau
白沙洲 Round Island
更樓石 Kang Lau Shek
平洲 Ping Chau

沙頭 SHA TAU KOK
橫崗門 Yung Shue Au
三角咀 Sam Kok Tsui
吉澳海 CROOKED HARBOUR
吉澳 Crooked Island
娥眉洲 Crescent Island

鹿頸 LUK KENG
荔枝窩 Lai Chi Wo
印洲塘 DOUBLE HAVEN
往灣洲 Double Island

亀頭嶺 KWAI TAU LENG
486
烏蛟騰 WU KAU TANG
三椏村 Sam A Tsuen
三椏涌 Sam A Chung
黃竹角海 WONG CHUK KOK HOI

八仙嶺 PAT SIN LENG
639 黃嶺 WONG LENG
赤門 NORTH CHANNEL
大赤門
131 赤洲 Port Island

鹽灣仔 YIM TIN TSAI
河頭 Ting Kok
大尾篤 Tai Mei Tuk
船灣淡水湖 Plover Cove Reservoir
赤洲口 MIDDLE CHANNEL

大埔 TAI PO
馬屎洲 Ma Shi Chau
塔門 Grass Island

大埔滘 TAI PO KAU
吐露港 TOLO HARBOUR
擔柴山 MOUNT HALLOWES
海下 Hoi Ha

石牛洲 Shek Ngau Chau
大鹿灣 DALU WAN

烏溪沙 WU KAI SHA
西沙 Sai O
荔枝莊 Lai Chi Chong
深涌 Sham Chung
石屋山 SHEK UK SHAN
468 蚺蛇尖 SHARP PEAK

馬鞍山 MA ON SHAN
十四鄉 SHAP SZE HEUNG
梅子林 Yung Shue O
企嶺下老圍 Kei Ling Ha Lo Wai
赤徑 Chek Keng
大浪 TAI LONG

702
大水坑 Tai Shui Hang
馬鞍山 MA ON SHAN
大網仔 TAI MONG TSAI
北潭涌 Pak Tam Chung
西灣 Sai Wan
大浪灣 TAI LONG WAN

沙田 SHA TIN
西貢 SAI KUNG
鹽田仔 Yim Tin Tsai

606 水牛山 BUFFALO HILL
278 滘西洲 Kau Sai Chau
浪茄 Long Ke

大老山 TATE'S CAIRN
495
黃麖仔 Ho Chung
橋咀島 Sharp Island
217
糧船灣 HIGH ISLAND

九龍坳 KOWLOON PEAK
602
大埔仔 Tai Po Tsai
伏頭墳洲 Town Island

九龍 KOWLOON
將軍澳 TSEUNG KWAN O
281
孟公屋 Mang Kung Uk
吊鐘洲 Jin Island
牛尾洲 Shelter Island
糧船灣海 ROCKY HARBOUR
橫洲 Wang Chau

調景嶺 TIU KENG LENG
344 魷魚灣 High Junk Bay
大坳門 Tai Au Mun
沙塘口山 Bluff Island

北角 NORTH POINT
鰂魚涌 QUARRY BAY
筲箕灣 SHAU KEI WAN
清水灣 CLEAR WATER BAY
火石洲 Basalt Island

香港島 HONG KONG ISLAND
532 柏架山 MOUNT PARKER
小西灣 SIO SAI WAN
佛堂洲 FAT TONG CHAU

跑馬地 HAPPY VALLEY
紫羅蘭山 VIOLET HILL
歌連臣山 MOUNT COLLINSON
232 東龍洲 Tung Lung Chau
果洲群島 Ninepin Group

淺水灣 Middle Island
386
石澳 SHEK O
鶴咀山 D'AGUILAR PEAK

銀洲 Round Island
赤柱 STANLEY
大潭灣 TAI TAM BAY

雙四門 SHEUNG SZE MUN
蒲台群島 Po Toi Islands
宋崗 Sung Kong
橫瀾島 Waglan Island

螺洲 Beaufort Island
蒲台 Po Toi
墨洲 Mat Chau
大角頭 Tai Kok Tau
南角咀 Nam Kok Tsui

香 港 特 別 行 政 區
HONG KONG SPECIAL ADMINISTRATIVE REGION

南海
SOUTH CHINA SEA

地政總署測繪處繪製
Cartography by Survey and Mapping Office, Lands Department

Foreword

Preservation of Our History Through Hong Kong Chronicles

It is said that "A mighty tree grows from its roots just as a great river flows from its source." As part of human civilisation and of Chinese tradition, we in Hong Kong have long aspired to trace our roots and preserve our history.

Since ancient times, our ancestors have lived and thrived on the land of Hong Kong, leaving behind traces of their lives and of an evolution spanning thousands of years. However, for over 200 years since the compilation of Xin'an County Local Chronicles in 1819, no other Chinese local chronicles with reference to Hong Kong had been published.

Yet, these two centuries were a significant period witnessing the remarkable growth of Hong Kong into a cosmopolitan city through the hard work and dedication of its people. During the same period, Hong Kong's unbroken bond and its shared future with the Mainland were manifest. The British occupation of Hong Kong since 1841 ushered in 150 years of dramatic ups and downs. The return of Hong Kong in 1997 set the stage for a new era of rejuvenation alongside the motherland.

Hong Kong, frequently looked askance as a "borrowed place" on "borrowed time" in the past, has transformed since 1997 into a Special Administrative Region within the framework of "One Country, Two Systems." We, the people of Hong Kong, should no longer see ourselves as transients but should strive to deepen our understanding and strengthen our ties with the Mainland. That way, we shall be able to take on the responsibility as masters of our own house and find the right direction toward building a brighter future.

Local chronicles have the important functions of preserving history, providing reference for policymaking and educating the people. Through the compilation of local chronicles, it serves to seek out, preserve and promote the stories of people, their socio-economic development and way of life as well as political structure. It plays an important role of cultural significance in driving the future by reflecting on the past.

At Hong Kong Chronicles Institute, our goal is to compile a comprehensive record of Hong Kong's past, with detailed materials on its natural environment, politics, economy, society, culture and people. We hope Hong Kong Chronicles as a book series will become an enduring body of information and a source of wisdom in support of Hong Kong's continued development.

C. H. Tung

Vice Chairman, Chinese People's Political Consultative Conference

Chairman, Our Hong Kong Foundation

Chairman, Hong Kong Chronicles Institute

General Rules

1. As a Special Administrative Region of the People's Republic of China under the framework of "One Country, Two Systems," Hong Kong has adopted a unique approach in compiling its first-ever series of local chronicles. Instead of being a government project as in the Mainland, Hong Kong Chronicles are initiated and compiled by Our Hong Kong Foundation, a non-profit organisation, with support from the Chinese Central Government and HKSAR Government, community-wide participation and academic authorship.

2. Hong Kong Chronicles are published as a comprehensive, systematic and objective historical record of social and natural developments in Hong Kong. While they are based on the tradition of historical Chinese local chronicles, innovative approaches to the content and format are used to highlight the unique characteristics of Hong Kong.

3. Hong Kong Chronicles cover a timeframe spanning from ancient times to 01 July 2017. In certain volumes, historical events beyond 01 July 2017 are also included when it is necessary to present them in their entirety.

4. Geographically, Hong Kong Chronicles cover events in locations within the jurisdiction of the Hong Kong Special Administrative Region as of 01 July 1997. Those occurring outside of the territory are also covered if deemed relevant to Hong Kong.

5. The first book, *Overview*, gives an overall account of Hong Kong's history, providing readers with an all-around impression of the structural cohesion underlying the different component parts of the book series. In subsequent books, prefaces and summaries serve to sustain the unity of the series.

6. The volume *People* does not include persons still living; names of people are listed in chronological order according to their dates of birth. Persons still living are included when relevant to specific events, with the emphasis being on the events themselves.

7. The names of dynasties, institutions and places, names of people, titles and units of measurement are written in their original form and historical context. For events before 1840, dates are indicated in both the Chinese Era and the Common Era; for events in 1841 or after, dates are indicated in the Common Era only.

8. Statistical data published in Hong Kong Chronicles come mainly from official sources released by the government of Hong Kong.

9. For terms used repeatedly throughout the book series, abbreviations or short forms are provided when they first appear and are used exclusively thereafter.

10. Sources of historical materials used in Hong Kong Chronicles are included in footnotes or in the bibliography section for easy reference.

11. Other matters to note in each book are listed in its "Publication Notes."

Table Of Contents

Foreword

General Rules

Overview

Introduction 3
(1) Superior Geographic Location and Natural Environment 4
(2) A Highly Open Economic System 8
(3) Migration and the Growth of an Immigrant City 17
(4) British Colonial Rule 22
(5) Hong Kong's Unique Position in Modern Chinese History 30
(6) From "Long-Term View" to "One Country, Two Systems" 37
(7) A Place of Cultural Diversity 45

Chronology

Publication Notes 59
Prior to the Qin Dynasty 60
Qin, Han, Wei, Jin 60
Sui, Tang and Five Dynasties &
Ten Kingdoms 62
Song, Yuan 63
Ming 69
Qing (1644–1840) 77
1841 93
1842 96
1843 98
1844 99
1845 102
1846 103
1847 104
1848 106
1849 107
1850 108
1851 108
1852 109

1853 110
1854 110
1855 111
1856 112
1857 113
1858 114
1859 115
1860 116
1861 117
1862 118
1863 119
1864 120
1865 121
1866 122
1867 124
1868 124
1869 125
1870 126
1871 127
1872 128

1873	129	1919	181
1874	130	1920	182
1875	131	1921	183
1876	132	1922	185
1877	133	1923	188
1878	134	1924	190
1879	134	1925	190
1880	135	1926	193
1881	135	1927	194
1882	137	1928	196
1883	137	1929	198
1884	138	1930	199
1885	140	1931	200
1886	140	1932	203
1887	142	1933	204
1888	143	1934	206
1889	144	1935	207
1890	146	1936	210
1891	147	1937	211
1892	148	1938	214
1893	148	1939	218
1894	149	1940	220
1895	150	1941	222
1896	151	1942	228
1897	152	1943	233
1898	153	1944	236
1899	154	1945	238
1900	158	1946	242
1901	160	1947	247
1902	160	1948	252
1903	161	1949	256
1904	162	1950	263
1905	163	1951	268
1906	164	1952	273
1907	165	1953	278
1908	167	1954	283
1909	168	1955	287
1910	169	1956	292
1911	170	1957	296
1912	172	1958	300
1913	175	1959	304
1914	176	1960	308
1915	177	1961	312
1916	178	1962	315
1917	179	1963	320
1918	180	1964	326

1965	332	1992	500
1966	337	1993	507
1967	344	1994	516
1968	351	1995	523
1969	355	1996	529
1970	360	1997	539
1971	365	1998	558
1972	370	1999	568
1973	378	2000	576
1974	386	2001	585
1975	390	2002	592
1976	395	2003	599
1977	402	2004	611
1978	408	2005	619
1979	415	2006	628
1980	422	2007	636
1981	428	2008	645
1982	433	2009	651
1983	441	2010	658
1984	447	2011	664
1985	454	2012	670
1986	461	2013	678
1987	468	2014	685
1988	474	2015	693
1989	481	2016	701
1990	487	2017	709
1991	495		

Appendices 718
I   Glossary of Personal Names and Their Chinese Equivalents............................718
II   Glossary of Official Institutions and Titles..724
III Glossary of Ordinances and Documents 728
IV   Miscellaneous Terms..738
V   Abbreviations..745

Bibliography 747

Overview

Introduction

Hong Kong is located between latitude 22°08' and 22°35' North and longitude 113°49' and 114°31' East. It lies on the southern edge of China just outside the Pearl River estuary. Adjacent to Shenzhen of Guangdong Province, it is bounded by the Shenzhen River in the north and surrounded at its southern border by the vast South China Sea.

Hong Kong consists of Hong Kong Island, Kowloon and the New Territories (including 262 outlying islands). Hong Kong has a total land area of 1,106.42 square kilometres, including 80.72 square kilometres on Hong Kong Island, 46.94 square kilometres in Kowloon and 978.76 square kilometres in the New Territories.

According to official statistics, Hong Kong has a population of about 7,391,700 as of mid-2017, including 7,172,800 "usual" (permanent) residents and 218,900 "mobile" (temporary) residents. The vast majority are of Chinese descent and mostly of Cantonese ancestry; foreign nationals account for approximately 8% of the population. The overall population density is 6,830 per square kilometre.

Prior to the Qin Dynasty, Hong Kong was inhabited by the Yue people, who were indigenous to the Lingnan region. The first emperor of a unified China, Qin Shi Huang (秦始皇), introduced an administrative system of prefectures and counties. In the 33rd year of his reign (214 B.C.), Qin Shi Huang conquered Lingnan and assumed control of the area, establishing the three prefectures of Nanhai, Guilin and Xiang, thus starting the jurisdiction of ensuing Chinese dynasties over Hong Kong. For more than 500 years during the Qin Dynasty, Han Dynasty, Three Kingdoms and early Eastern Jin Dynasty, Hong Kong was part of Panyu County (now Guangzhou). For more than 400 years (331 A.D.–756 A.D.) from the 6th year of Xianhe (咸和) of the Eastern Jin Dynasty to the 1st year of Zhide (至德) of the Tang Dynasty, Hong Kong was part of Bao'an County. For more than 800 years (757 A.D.–1572 A.D.) from the 2nd year of Zhide to the periods of Five Dynasties, Song and Yuan until the 6th year of Emperor Longqing (隆慶) of the Ming Dynasty, Hong Kong was part of Dongguan County.

At one point during the reign of Emperor Jiajing (嘉靖) (1521–1567) of the Ming Dynasty, turmoil erupted in Nantou due to a famine and the looting of rice. Wu Zuo (吳祚), a member of the local gentry who took part in quelling the riots, suggested to Deputy Commander of Guangdong Coastal Defence Liu Wen (劉 穩) that a county should be established in the area. Many officials and village elites seconded the proposal, given that the region was over 100 *li* (approximately 30 miles) from the seat of Dongguan County and was frequently harassed by pirates. Liu Wen then referred the proposition to the governor of Guangdong. As a result, in the first year of the reign of Emperor Wanli (萬曆) (1573), Xin'an County, with seat in Nantou, was established. It was believed that this land could "bring change by discarding the old and make peace by mitigating risks." An area 56 miles to the north of southern coastline of Dongguan County, together with 33,971 residents from 7,608 households, were allocated to the newly established Xin'an County by the authorities of Guangzhou. From the first year of the reign of Emperor Wanli (1573) of the Ming Dynasty to the 19th century prior to British colonisation, Hong Kong had been mostly under the jurisdiction of Xin'an County, Guangzhou. The exception was the period of county reincorporation from the fifth to the seventh year of the reign of the Qing Emperor Kangxi (康熙) (1666–1668). The jurisdiction of Xin'an County included both present-day Shenzhen and Hong Kong.

Opinions vary as to the origin of the name "Hong Kong." One account is that it was named after the sweetness of local spring water; another account suggests that it referred to the existence of agarwood in Hong Kong and the ensuing lucrative trade of incense wood. The earliest recorded use of the name "Hong Kong" is found in the historical document *Yue daji,* an official record of Guangdong written by Guo Fei (郭棐) in 1595 during the reign of Emperor Wanli (萬曆) of the Ming Dynasty. In this book, names for what we now know in English as Hong Kong, Stanley, Wong Nai Chung and Tsim Sha Tsui were included in the "Coastal Map of Guangdong," with "Hong Kong" marked near today's Aberdeen.

1 Superior Geographic Location and Natural Environment

Sitting next to the Mainland of China in the north and between the Pacific Ocean and Indian Ocean, Hong Kong boasts significant geographic advantages. It has an easily accessible deep-water harbour and a world-class airport, making it a global shipping and aviation hub where numerous global sea lanes and air traffic routes converge.

Hong Kong features a rich and varied geological landscape. The current geological structure is the outcome of upward displacement of the earth's crust presumably through volcanic activity and erosion over multiple geological ages. For its unique geological landform, Hong Kong Geopark was selected to be a member of the Global Geopark Network by the United Nations Educational, Scientific and Cultural Organization (UNESCO).

Benefiting from a sub-tropical climate, as well as mountainous landscape and extensive coastline, Hong Kong is home to a rich variety of flora and fauna, with many endemic terrestrial animal species, such as Romer's tree frog, Bogadek's burrowing lizard, the Hong Kong Tusktail and Hong Kong Clubtail dragonflies. The best-known marine animals are the Indo-Pacific humpback dolphins, also called the Chinese white dolphin. Numerous country parks, marine parks, and other protected areas help preserve the biodiversity of Hong Kong.

1.1 Geographic Location

Hong Kong's Tuen Mun was once an important port along the ancient Maritime Silk Road. During the Tang Dynasty (618 A.D.–907 A.D.), a maritime trade commissioner was appointed in Guangzhou to handle relations with other countries and overseas trade. The maritime route was connected to Guangzhou on the east bank of the Pearl River estuary and included the waypoints of Fat Tong Mun, Kap Shui Mun, Tuen Mun, Nam Shan, Nantou and Humen. Castle Peak Bay in Tuen Mun was the largest deep-water port along the route serving local and foreign vessels, making it one of the more prominent ports on the ancient Maritime Silk Road.

In modern times, Hong Kong's favourable geographic location is even more significant in support of rapid economic development. Today, Hong Kong is not only the most important port in southern China but also the centre of maritime transport in Asia. Hong Kong is a shipping hub centrally located along the sea routes linking Europe, Africa and South Asia to East Asia. It is also a transit point linking the Americas to Southeast Asia and South Asia, and a part of the route from Australia and New Zealand to East Asia. These factors play a large role in Hong Kong's position as an important aviation hub regionally and internationally. As of the end of 2016, Hong Kong hosts more than 100 airlines providing over 1,100 daily flights to and from approximately 190 airports worldwide.

1.2 Natural Environment

1.2.1 Climate

Hong Kong has a sub-tropical climate and is frequently affected by warm and humid maritime tropical air masses. As such, temperatures are relatively high throughout the year. In winter, the temperature falls due to cold, dry northerly winds, caused by continental anticyclones. Temperatures occasionally fall below freezing at higher altitudes, but rarely fall below 5°C at sea level.

Seasons in Hong Kong are generally distinct, with a humid and foggy spring, a hot and rainy summer, a short and breezy autumn, and a moderately cold winter. In March and April, it can be extremely humid, with reduced visibility from foggy and drizzly weather. From May to August, it is hot and humid with occasional showers and thunderstorms. In July, it is usually sunny for one to two weeks, and sometimes longer. The best weather comes in November and December, with a gentle breeze, plenty of sunshine and moderate temperature. In January and February, it is mostly cloudy, with occasional cold fronts sweeping through and bringing dry northerly winds.

The average annual rainfall varies considerably across Hong Kong—from about 1,400 millimetres in Tung Ping Chau to over 3,000 millimetres in the vicinity of Tai Mo Shan. About 80% of rainfall take place between May and September; June and August are usually the rainiest months while December and January are the driest.

Because of its climatic conditions, Hong Kong is affected by tropical cyclones of varying intensity from May to November, with typhoons being especially frequent between July and September. Hong Kong has experienced numerous occasions of severe natural disasters, usually typhoons and severe rainstorms, and has suffered from significant human casualties and economic losses as a result. The catastrophic typhoon of 1874 caused thousands of deaths and the loss of many ships, prompting the construction of typhoon shelters for boats and the founding of the Hong Kong Observatory. The typhoon of 1906 claimed tens of thousands of lives, left 1,319 people missing and 2,785 vessels damaged. The Great Typhoon of 1937 led to an estimated 11,000 deaths. In 1962, Typhoon Wanda caused 130 deaths, 53 missing and 46,000 homeless.

When a tropical cyclone approaches Hong Kong, heavy rain may last for days, often leading to landslides and floods. In 1925, rainstorms caused a serious landslide in Po Hing Fong, a high-class residential area at Mid-Levels on Hong Kong Island, killing 75 people, mostly wealthy merchants from the Chinese community. On 11 June 1966, another severe rainstorm and landslide killed 64 people, with 48 people missing and 6,183 people affected. The June 18 rainstorm in 1972 led to the most severe landslides in the history of colonial Hong Kong. The Hong Kong Observatory recorded a total rainfall measuring 652.3 millimetres from 16 to 18 June. This heavy rain caused 71 deaths in Sau Mau Ping of East Kowloon and 67 deaths on Po Shan Road at Mid-Levels on Hong Kong Island.

1.2.2 Topography, Geology and Landforms

Hong Kong consists of many islands and peninsulas and is marked by unique geological landforms and coastal areas, including sea cliffs, sea caves, sea arches, sea inlets, tombolos, wave-cut platforms, sea stacks, sea chasms, blowholes, etc. Hong Kong has a 1,180-km-long twisting coastline, forming a scenic landscape. Due to its hilly terrain, Hong Kong relies heavily on coastal areas for urban development; its coastal areas have been repeatedly extended through reclamation.

Like the southeast coastal areas of neighbouring Guangdong Province, the geological environment of Hong Kong is the result of violent movements of the earth's crust and erosion over multiple geological ages. Hong Kong has steep and undulating mountains and hills. Tai Mo Shan, located in the central New Territories, is the tallest mountain, measuring 957 metres above sea level. The deepest seabed, located in Lo Chau Mun, north of Po Toi Island, is 66 metres below sea level.

Sedimentary rocks are the oldest outcrops, laid down by river sediments about 400 million years ago. The limestone (also known as marble) and siltstone in the central and western New Territories were formed from rocks and sediments accumulating in shallow seas between 350 million and 290 million years ago. Between 170 and 140 million years ago, there were multiple violent volcanic eruptions, resulting in layers of volcanic ash. Volcanic activity ceased after a major eruption involving the High Island supervolcano located in the southeast. The supervolcano emerged due to uplift in the earth's crust and soil erosion. Its top was in Sai Kung and its magma reservoir was beneath Kowloon and the northern part of Hong Kong Island. The younger rock strata on Tung Ping Chau were formed by sediments from a lake at the edge of a desert about 50 million years ago.

For its unique geological landforms, Hong Kong National Geopark was established and became a member of the National Geoparks of China in 2009. In 2011, it became a member of the Global Geoparks Network and was renamed the Hong Kong Global Geopark of China. In 2015, it was renamed Hong Kong UNESCO Global Geopark.

Hong Kong Geopark comprises two interconnected regions: the Sai Kung Volcanic Rock Region and the Northeast New Territories Sedimentary Rock Region. The former consists of four geo-areas. The High Island Geo-Area and Ninepin Group Geo-Area have globally rare rhyolitic hexagonal rock columns. Up to 100 metres tall, these structures are far larger than the basalt rock columns of the Giant's Causeway in Northern Ireland. The peculiar and majestic hexagonal columns along the coast of the Ung Kong Group Geo-Area are characterised by sea caves and sea arches, while the Sharp Island Geo-Area is marked by geological remains characteristic of craters.

The Northeast New Territories Sedimentary Rock Region consists of four geo-areas which form a beautiful landscape of significant scientific value. The Port Island–Bluff Head Geo-Area is home to the oldest sedimentary rocks in Hong Kong, dating back to the Devonian period (about 400 million years ago). The Tung Ping Chau Geo-Area is a famous rock-viewing scenic spot and has the youngest sedimentary rocks in Hong Kong, formed about 55 million years ago. The coast is made up of straticulate rocks, forming a unique geomorphologic landscape. Lai Chi Chong, located in the Tolo Channel Geo-Area, has very rare volcanic sedimentary rocks, displaying distinctive folds, faults and bedding structures, making it a great location for geological study. Ma Shi Chau is another notable site for ecological research. A geo-site from the Permian period, Ma Shi Chau has distinctive outcrops of colourful mudstone and siltstone, as well as rich geological structures, such as faults and folds.

Hong Kong has undergone significant changes in landform. Hong Kong Island, Lantau Island and other islands were once part of the mainland. During the Ice Age, the sea level was 120 metres lower than the current level, and the coastline was about 100 kilometres to the south of Hong Kong Island. By the end of the last Ice Age, about 11,000 years ago, the sea level began to rise rapidly, reaching its present height about 8,000 years ago. Many coastal areas were submerged due to rising seawater, leaving the mountain ridges above water, thereby forming Hong Kong Island, Lantau Island and other islands. These islands are separated from the mainland by only a strip of water, displaying similarity in form, structure and alignment with those on the mainland.

1.2.3 Flora and Fauna

Hong Kong, located at the northern edge of the Southeast Asian tropical plant distribution, shares similarities with Guangdong Province in flora species and structures. Though Hong Kong is a small place, it has approximately 3,300 vascular plant species, including 2,100 native species.

Forests account for about one-fifth of the land area of Hong Kong; they are important habitats for wildlife and help prevent water loss and soil erosion in catchment areas. Remnants of old forests can be found in deep ravines or behind traditional rural villages. These forests have been largely preserved due to the difficulty of access, abundant moisture in the area and the culture of preservation stemming from traditional *feng shui.*

Feng shui woodlands are common in many villages across the New Territories, and although small in scale, they are dense and luxuriant. They are also the only remaining lowland evergreen broad-leaf woods in Hong Kong, often containing rare plant and animal species of great ecological value.

To protect native plants effectively, the Forests and Countryside Ordinance 2007 was enacted by the HKSAR government. It prohibits any acts of damage to the forests and plantations on government land, including the use of fire. In addition, the Agriculture, Fisheries and Conservation Department (AFCD) has added to the number and diversity of plants by cultivating rare or endangered plant species in the countryside, such as *Keteleeria fortune, Camellia crapnelliana* and *Camellia granthamiana*. For conservation and education purposes, approximately 300 species of native plants, including rare and protected species, were planted in the Shing Mun Arboretum. In 2009, the Country Parks Plantation Enrichment Programme was introduced by the HKSAR government, replacing withering exotic tree species with native saplings to promote the healthy growth of forests and the diversity of flora and fauna species.

The unique climate and geographic environment have created habitats for a wide variety of animals. As of 2016, over 540 species of birds, 57 species of terrestrial mammals, 24 species of amphibians, 86 species of reptiles, 236 species of butterflies, and 124 species of dragonflies have been observed in Hong Kong. Hong Kong has various endemic species, such as Romer's tree frog, Bogadek's burrowing lizard, and the Hong Kong Tusktail and Hong Kong Clubtail dragonflies, as well as endangered terrestrial species, including the three-striped box turtle, yellow-breasted bunting, short-legged toad, green turtle, and pangolin.

The Mai Po Marshes area is one of the major avian and nature conservations regions in Asia and an important stopover for migratory birds. The Mai Po Marshes and Inner Deep Bay areas have been designated as "Wetlands of International Importance" under the Ramsar Convention. These wetlands, an area of about 1,500 hectares, consisting of intertidal mudflats, fishponds, marshes, reedbeds and dwarf mangroves, provide a rich habitat for migratory and resident birds, particularly wading birds. There are about 400 species of birds in the area, including 50 globally threatened or endangered species, such as black-faced spoonbills, Baer's pochards, Nordmann's greenshanks and spoon-billed sandpipers. The traditional *feng shui* woodlands and secondary forests near old villages and temples are important habitats for many woodland birds, including various species of warblers, flycatchers, robins, thrushes, bulbuls and tits.

Before and during the Second World War, traces of tigers were found in Castle Peak near Tuen Mun, in Sha Tau Kok and in Sheung Shui, indicating that South China tigers resided in Hong Kong. These tigers disappeared from Hong Kong as urbanisation accelerated after the Second World War. Mammals, such as the Indian muntjac, and wild boars are common in the countryside, but other mammals, such as leopard cats, ferret badgers and masked palm civets, are rarely seen. Bats, including Himalayan leaf-nosed bats, Pomona roundleaf bats and Chinese rufous horseshoe bats, often live in caves and water diversion tunnels. Rare animal species, such as the Eurasian otter, crab-eating mongoose and pangolins, are also occasionally found.

There are over 100 species of amphibians and reptiles in Hong Kong. Of the 24 species of amphibians, Hong Kong cascade frogs, Hong Kong newts and Romer's tree frogs are protected under the Wild Animals Protection Ordinance. Romer's tree frogs, as small as a thumb, are the smallest amphibians in Hong Kong. Most of the 52 species of snakes in Hong Kong are non-venomous, and reports of venomous snake bites are rare. Among the 10 native species of turtles found in Hong Kong, green sea turtles are of conservation value because it is the only species of sea turtle that breeds locally.

Fresh water from the Pearl River flows into waters west of Hong Kong, while water on the east is largely unaffected by the Pearl River. This special hydrographic condition provides a suitable eco-environment for a wide variety of marine life. Hong Kong waters are home to many species of fish, crustaceans, molluscs and other marine life; at least 150 species are of fishery significance. The red sea bream is common in eastern waters as schools of snapper fry are abundant along the shore of Mirs Bay in early spring. Hong Kong waters are also close to the northern boundary of stony coral reefs and are home to 84 stony coral species, hence a diverse mix by international standards.

Two marine mammal species, namely the Indo-Pacific humpback dolphin (commonly known as the Chinese white dolphin) and the finless porpoise, can be seen in Hong Kong throughout the year. Chinese white dolphins prefer the estuarine environment in the west of Hong Kong, while finless porpoises live predominantly in oceanic waters to the east and south.

1.2.4 Country Parks, Marine Parks and Protected Areas

About three-quarters of Hong Kong's landmass is considered the countryside, including 24 country parks and 22 special areas. Country parks are designated for nature and water conservation and serve the public with recreational and educational facilities, while special areas are mainly for nature conservation. Country parks include: Shing Mun, Kam Shan, Lion Rock, Aberdeen, Tai Tam, Sai Kung East, Sai Kung West, Plover Cove, Lantau South, Lantau North, Pat Sin Leng, Tai Lam, Tai Mo Shan, Lam Tsuen, Ma On Shan, Kiu Tsui, Shek O, Pok Fu Lam, Clear Water Bay, Lung Fu Shan, etc. They cover mountains, woodlands, reservoirs and waterfront areas in all parts of Hong Kong. Altogether, country parks and special areas occupy 44,312 hectares, representing approximately 40% of Hong Kong's landmass.

In addition to country parks and special areas, there are five marine parks and one marine reserve in Hong Kong, covering an area of 3,400 hectares along coastal areas, seascapes and biological habitats. Marine reserves are dedicated to nature conservation, education and scientific research. Fishing is limited in marine parks under a government permit system and is prohibited in the marine reserve.

Besides these protected areas, areas of special geology and habitats of rare plants and animals are protected by rigorous land development plans and restrictions by the government. As of 2016, 67 locations have been designated "Sites of Special Scientific Interest."

2 A Highly Open Economic System

Hong Kong is a unique city, having grown from an unknown, traditional fishing village in pre-colonial times to a prestigious international metropolis. It has taken a development path with historical opportunities different from other Chinese cities. Hong Kong has progressed through various phases of economic development—from a traditional economy to an entrepot and an industrial city, from a diversified economy to a service-oriented and later a high value-added service-based economy.

As one of the world's freest economies, Hong Kong grew more rapidly than other emerging economies in the decades after the Second World War. In terms of GDP per capita, Hong Kong was a leading member of the Four Asian Tigers.

During the 20 years from 1977 to 1997, Hong Kong's GDP grew at an average annual rate of about 7% in real terms, which was twice the average growth rate of the overall global economy during the same period. In 1997, Hong Kong's GDP per capita reached US$26,400, second only to Japan and Singapore in Asia, and ahead of some economies of the Organisation for Economic Co-operation and Development (OECD), including Canada, the United Kingdom and Australia.

With China's reform and opening-up, Hong Kong has been provided with unprecedented economic opportunities. The people of Hong Kong are participants, contributors, and beneficiaries of this endeavour. Especially in the last 50 years, Hong Kong and the Mainland have complemented each other's strengths and worked towards the common goal of development.

2.1 Traditional Economy

Major economic activities of ancient Hong Kong included agriculture, fishery, salt-making, pearl-mining, agarwood-harvesting and ceramics. Prior to the British colonial era, family-based agriculture and fishing were key sectors of livelihood. In addition to the large tracts of farmland in the New Territories, plots of land on Hong Kong Island were also owned and leased to tenant farmers by prominent families from the New Territories. The *General Report of Taxable Land in Hong Kong,* kept by the Tang clan of Kam Tin, contains reports submitted by their ancestors to the Guangdong government, claiming land ownership across all parts of Hong Kong Island. Urban development in the late Qing Dynasty led to a shift away from traditional agriculture, as some farmers in the New Territories sought to make a living overseas. After the Second World War, rapid urbanisation and industrialisation drove more farmers in the New Territories towards urban areas or overseas, leaving behind deserted farmlands and a gradually declining agricultural sector.

Fishing was an important traditional industry in Hong Kong. In the early days of British rule, Stanley was a prosperous fishing town, providing anchorage for more than 350 boats of different sizes. Additionally, Hong Kong Village was a large fishing port with about 200 people, while Kwan Tai Lo was another fishing village populated by about 50 people. Hong Kong Island also had as many as 2,000 Tanka people; many of them worked as fishermen.

From the Han Dynasty to the Southern Song Dynasty, salt-making was a local industry of considerable scale. As late as the reign of Emperor Gaozong (高宗) (1127–1162) of the Song Dynasty, officials and soldiers were dispatched by the government to build and manage a saltern named Kwun Fu Cheung in northwest Kowloon Bay. A saltern also existed on Lantau Island, which harboured illegal salt-making activities. During the reign of Emperor Ningzong (寧宗) (1194–1224) of the Song Dynasty, Commissioner of Guangdong Tea and Salt Supervisorate Xu Anguo (徐安國) ordered a crackdown on salt smugglers. This gave rise to a rebellion on the island among salt farmers, who fought all the way by boat to the city wall of Guangzhou by availing themselves of high tide.

Pearl-mining started early in Hong Kong. In the 6th year of Dabao (大寶) (963 A.D.), Liu Chang (劉鋹) who was the last ruler of the Southern Han Dynasty, recruited thousands of soldiers from Hepu, Haimen, Dongguan and Tai Po Hoi (present-day Tolo Harbour in the New Territories) as a group known as "Mei Chuan Dou" for pearl-mining.

During the Ming Dynasty, varieties of Chinese eaglewood, such as agarwood, were major products of Hong Kong and were in high demand on the markets of Guangdong, Jiangsu and Zhejiang. According to the *Yu di lue er: Wu chan* (records of products) as kept in Volume III of *Xin'an County Local Chronicles* compiled by Wang Chongxi (王崇熙), Hong Kong's best areas for producing agarwood were Lek Yuen in Shatin and Sha Lo Wan on the west side of Lantau Island.

In the 400–500 years between the mid-Ming Dynasty and the 1920s, blue-and-white porcelain objects were produced in Tai Po Wun Yiu in the New Territories. Initially owned by the Man and Tse clans, Tai Po Wun Yiu was later managed and operated by Ma Choi Yuen (馬彩淵), originally from Changle of Guangdong, and his descendants. The kiln in Tai Po Wun Yiu, long and wide, was better known as dragon kiln, a rectangle-shaped kiln commonly seen in southern China. It had a producing capacity of 10,000 pieces. Products from Tai Po Wun Yiu were sold mainly in Jiangmen, Guangzhou, Dongguan and Shilong in Guangdong Province, but also sometimes in Southeast Asian countries.

2.2 Modern Economic Development

In January 1841, British troops landed on Hong Kong Island. In June, Charles C. Elliot, Plenipotentiary and Chief Superintendent of British Trade in China and Lieutenant Governor of Hong Kong, declared that Hong Kong was a free port to further British trade interests. In the next century, especially in the decades after the Second World War, Hong Kong gradually adapted to a changing global economic and political landscape, becoming the world's freest and most open commercial port.

Hong Kong's free port status continued after 1997 and was maintained through provisions clearly stated in Chapter Five of the Basic Law. The Hong Kong Special Administrative Region (HKSAR), for example, shall "maintain the status of a free port and shall not impose any tariff unless otherwise prescribed by law," "pursue the policy of free trade and safeguard the free movement of goods, intangible assets and capital," "safeguard the free operation of financial business and financial markets. Markets for foreign exchange, gold, securities, futures and the like shall continue." The HKSAR shall "safeguard the free flow of capital within, into and out of the Region" and "taking the low tax policy previously pursued in Hong Kong as reference, enact laws on its own concerning types of taxes, tax rates, tax reductions, allowances and exemptions, and other matters of taxation."

Modern economic development in Hong Kong can be divided roughly into six stages.

2.2.1 The Early Days of Entrepot Trade (1841—1860)

After the British declared Hong Kong a free port, foreign businesses arrived here for business opportunities. During this period, British merchants in Hong Kong and Guangzhou were significantly engaged in the opium trade, making Hong Kong the largest hub for opium trafficking in the Far East. According to a 24 July 1844 report by Colonial Treasurer Robert Montgomery Martin, re-export of opium was a key business among major foreign firms including Jardine Matheson and Dent & Co. In 1850, a memorandum by William Henry Mitchell, Deputy Magistrate of Hong Kong, showed that three-quarters of the opium shipped from India to China between 1845 and 1849 was distributed through Hong Kong.

In the early British colonial days, Hong Kong was a centre for the profitable business of transporting Chinese people abroad. Chinese labourers became a source of highly valued cheap labour as huge demand for miners came as gold was discovered in California in 1848 and in Australia four years later. It was a time of a shifting landscape of labour upon the decline of slavery. After the Qing government imposed an overseas travel ban, Hong Kong and Macao became the only ports from which Chinese people could go abroad upon recruitment by foreign companies and governments. From 1851 to 1872, as many as 320,000 Chinese labourers took passage from Hong Kong to countries around the world. Besides Chinese labourers, Chinese small business owners, artisans, and seamen also travelled widely abroad. This mass migration proved to be a very profitable business for Hong Kong-based shipowners; it spurred the early development of Hong Kong's shipping, import and export trade and financial sectors.

2.2.2 The Entrepot Period (1861—1950)

Following the Second Opium War, Britain gained control of the Kowloon Peninsula, including the strategically significant Victoria Harbour. Victoria Harbour, located between Kowloon and Hong Kong Island, provided a safe berth for British ships as well as ships from other countries. From 1750 onwards, Britain undertook a process of rapid industrialisation with an emphasis on manufacturing. The 1879 opening of the Suez Canal and the construction of submarine cables between Europe and Asia for rapid communication further spurred trade between the West and China. As a result, Hong Kong became an entrepot. Statistics show that goods imported by China through Hong Kong in 1867 accounted for 20% of total imports, while goods exported by China via Hong Kong accounted for 14% of total exports. In 1880, 37% of China's imports and 21% of its exports in value were transported via Hong Kong.

When the New Territories was leased to Britain in 1898, Hong Kong's land area increased 11-fold and its total population increased by more than one-third; it facilitated continued economic development. In 1900, Hong Kong accounted for 42% and 40% of Chinese exports and imports, respectively, while the tonnage of ships passing through Hong Kong exceeded 14.02 million tons, double the amount 15 years earlier. In 1911, as the Kowloon-Canton Railway began operation, transhipment became more viable. Despite the impact of two world wars, entrepot trade continued to develop in Hong Kong.

Britain was the first Western country to recognise the founding of the People's Republic of China in 1949, largely because of the British national interest in the Mainland of China and Hong Kong. From then on, commercial exchange between Hong Kong and the Mainland increased. Hong Kong's foreign trade exceeded HK$7.5 billion in 1950 and reached HK$9.3 billion in 1951. In the same year, Hong Kong's exports to China exceeded HK$1.6 billion, accounting for 36.2% of the total exports of Hong Kong.

2.2.3 The Industrialisation Period (1951—1970)

Following the outbreak of the Korean War in 1950, the United States in conjunction with the United Nations imposed a trade embargo on China. This had an adverse impact on the entrepot trade of Hong Kong. In 1952, Hong Kong's foreign trade volume declined to HK$6.6 billion, and its exports to the Mainland fell to HK$500 million. Hong Kong had little choice but to undergo economic restructuring and focus on the development of viable industries.

The civil war in the Mainland led to massive flow of capital, equipment and technical and managerial personnel from Shanghai and Guangzhou into Hong Kong. Between 1946 and 1950, commodities, negotiable securities, gold and foreign currencies with a total value of no less than US$500 million moved from the Mainland to Hong Kong, providing sufficient capital for industrial development. The relocation of textile, rubber, metal, chemical and match-making industries from the Mainland to Hong Kong also played an important role in the industrialisation of Hong Kong. From the 1950s to the 1960s, Hong Kong had basically completed the transition from entrepot trade to manufacturing. For instance, Hong Kong had 961 factories with over 47,000 workers in 1947 and 4,541 factories with more than 170,000 workers in 1959. Locally made products accounted for 69.6% of Hong Kong's exports in 1959, surpassing the amount of re-exported goods. In the 1960s, the rapid growth of textile and apparel industries, coupled with the emerging sectors of electronics, watch and toy making, gave rise to an economic boom in Hong Kong.

2.2.4 Industrial Diversification (1971—1985)

In the late 1960s, a growing number of economies were shifting towards export-oriented growth; by the early 1970s, Taiwan and South Korea were nearing Hong Kong in terms of exports. Meanwhile, developed countries were showing signs of economic recession, and protectionist sentiments were on the rise. The 1974 Multi-fibre Arrangement Regarding International Trade in Textiles imposed strict quotas on textile trade. In 1977, a blanket restriction was imposed on Hong Kong by the European Economic Community, expanding the scope of restrictions from fabrics to garments made of cotton, synthetic fibre, wool and mixed fabrics. In late 1983, textiles and clothing from Hong Kong came under further US restrictions and arbitrary suspension. Amid an increasingly challenging global market, Hong Kong began an economic transition towards diversification and effected a significant economic restructuring.

As Hong Kong moved towards industrial modernisation and diversification, it had a focus on high value-added products. The number of registered factories in Hong Kong increased from 15,285 in 1970 to 45,409 in 1980, and the number of workers employed in manufacturing increased from 569,000 to 892,000, an increase of 1.97 times and 0.57 times, respectively. Exports of goods made in Hong Kong totalled HK$68.171 billion in 1980, accounting for 69.4% of total exports. About 40% of employment came from manufacturing. Following the launch of China's reform and opening-up, Hong Kong's manufacturing sector moved north to the Pearl River Delta, where low-cost production made its manufactured products more competitive. Foreign trade, transportation, finance, construction and tourism were all growing rapidly and becoming the backbone of Hong

Kong's economy. By 1984, Hong Kong's GDP per capita had reached US$5,316, ranking the third highest in Asia, below Japan and Brunei and slightly above Singapore.

Between 1969 and 1979, Hong Kong's financial institutions and financial markets were becoming increasingly international. In 1969, only 30 foreign banks were registered in Hong Kong. By 1979, this number had increased to 71, and foreign banks accounted for 67.6% of all banking institutions in Hong Kong. The insurance, fund management, foreign exchange, bullion and securities markets in Hong Kong were also becoming internationalised. By the late 1970s, Hong Kong had emerged as an international financial centre within the Asia Pacific region.

In 1981, Western countries were caught in an economic crisis amid rising unemployment, unacceptably high levels of inflation and negative economic growth. This led to the implementation of even more stringent protectionist measures. Exacerbated by uncertainty arising from the Sino-British negotiation in 1982 regarding the future of Hong Kong, Hong Kong experienced extreme economic volatility with plummeting stocks, sinking investor confidence, massive capital outflows and the freefall of the Hong Kong dollar. On 17 October 1983, the government announced a currency board arrangement and introduced the Linked Exchange Rate System (LERS), a pegged exchange rate at HK$7.8 to US$1. The LERS provided a stable Hong Kong dollar and a foundation for Hong Kong's continued economic development.

2.2.5 Transition from Manufacturing to Services (1985—1997)

In May 1985, instruments of ratification of the Sino-British Joint Declaration were exchanged between the Chinese and British governments. This was not only a period of political transition; Hong Kong was also transforming from a trade- and manufacturing-based economy into a service-based economy.

Hong Kong's economic structure experienced its first transformation in the period of industrialisation between the 1960s and the mid-1970s. The second transition towards a service economy, which began in the late 1970s, gained impetus in the mid-1980s and lasted until the end of the 1990s. During this period, Hong Kong emerged as an international financial centre within the Asia Pacific region. At the same time, by riding the crest of China's reform and opening-up, it became a transit port and a support centre for global trade with the Mainland, especially in southern China. This was the hallmark of Hong Kong's second economic transformation.

Manufacturing as a share of Hong Kong's GDP during this period decreased year by year, from 23% in 1987 to 9.3% in 1994, due to the large-scale northward migration of the manufacturing sector. Services became a key component of the local economy as reflected in the growth and increasing output of the export/import trade, finance, real estate and transportation sectors. The service industry accounted for 84% of Hong Kong's GDP in 1996 following an average annual growth rate of 16% by market value between 1984 and 1996 that far exceeded any other national markets. As one of the most service-oriented economies, Hong Kong's shipping, trade and related services, financial and business services and tourism were highly competitive and among the world's best.

Import/Export: The rapid growth in trade was a key driver of the rise of the service industry. In the decade from 1986 to 1995, total trade volume jumped from HK$552.5 billion to HK$2,835.2 billion, an increase of 4.13 times. In 1996, Hong Kong's foreign trade totalled HK$2,933.5 billion, ranking eighth in the world. Hong Kong also benefited from the economic growth driven by the national reform and opening-up policy. In 1985, China became Hong Kong's largest trading partner for the first time since 1959. In 1988, Hong Kong's entrepot trade exceeded exports of locally made goods, accounting for 56% of the total exports. The percentage continued to rise, reaching 81% in 1994.

Financial Services: The financial industry grew at a rapid pace in the mid and late 1980s and became the third largest sector after the import/export trade and real estate. The Banking Ordinance was revised in 1986 to better address the modern financial environment, and Hong Kong's banking sector enjoyed a period of sustained and steady development. By the 1990s, a sound and efficient banking system was well established. In 1998, banks in Hong Kong earned an additional HK$88.2 billion, equivalent to 7.5% of GDP and three times as much as the level in 1990. By the end of 1996, Hong Kong had 182 licenced banks, while 80 of the world's top 100 banks had operations in Hong Kong.

Hong Kong's well-developed and active foreign-exchange market became an integral part of the global market. A survey conducted by the Bank for International Settlements showed that Hong Kong's average daily foreign-exchange turnover in April 1995 was US$91 billion, equivalent to 6% of the world's total, the fifth largest globally. In 1996, Hong Kong was the world's tenth largest stock market and the second largest in Asia, just behind Tokyo. Its bond and futures markets were also increasingly active. The trading of Hang Seng Index Futures contracts introduced by the Hong Kong Futures Exchange in May 1986 marked a new phase of market development. In the first half of 1987, the Hang Seng Index Futures ranked second highest in the world by trading volume, behind only the S&P 500 Index Futures market.

Real Estate: The real estate industry developed in parallel with Hong Kong's economy, becoming most active following the transition from manufacturing to services. Real estate has often been regarded as a barometer for economic development. In the early 1980s, it accounted for 13.6% of Hong Kong's GDP; it then fell to 6.4% in 1984 before rebounding gradually. In 1996, it accounted for 8.2% of GDP and added an economic value of HK$98,464 million, employing 64,028 people in 8,298 agencies—an increase of 92% and 101%, respectively, in comparison with 1987. During this time, real estate was the second largest industry in Hong Kong, behind the import and export sector and ahead of the manufacturing and financial industries.

Tourism: In the 1980s, Hong Kong was among the highest in the world in terms of tourist arrivals, spending per tourist and total revenue. In 1990, Hong Kong had 5.93 million tourist arrivals and a total revenue of HK$38 billion. In 1992 and 1993, Hong Kong was named World's Top Destination for Long-Haul Travel. In 1995, it received 10.2 million tourist visits, with revenue from tourism reaching HK$72.9 billion. In 1996, Hong Kong's tourism revenue was HK$84.54 billion, or 6.9% of GDP, ranking eighth place in the global tourism market and becoming the top market in Asia.

Shipping: Hong Kong is an important shipping and air transportation centre in the Far East. In the peak years, it had a worldwide network of more than 460 ports in over 100 countries and regions across the world and was the world's busiest by the throughput of twenty-foot equivalent units (TEUs). In 1996, Hong Kong received 41,056 arrivals of ocean-going vessels and 112,000 arrivals of river cargo vessels with a total of 13.3 million TEUs of container cargo. Hong Kong is also one of the world's busiest aviation hubs. In 1996, it handled 158,797 flights, 1.56 million metric tonnes of air cargo and 23.48 million passengers.

Trade and finance were most prominent during Hong Kong's second economic transformation. By 1987, manufacturing was outpaced by the macro trade sector comprising wholesale, retail, import/export, restaurants and hotels. The sector's GDP share rose from 22.3% in 1986 to a peak of 26.7% in 1996, in a period of economic prosperity driven by port-related commerce. The transportation, warehouse and telecommunication sectors grew from 8.2% in 1986 to 9.8% in 1996 along with the continued development of entrepot trade. Following a decline during the real estate and financial crises of the early 1980s, the GDP share of the macro finance sector (finance, insurance, real estate and commercial services) began to recover in 1987 and accounted for 25.1% of GDP by 1996.

2.2.6 A High Value-added Service Economy (1997—2017)

As an export-oriented open economy, Hong Kong is relatively susceptible to the impact of external volatility. Since 1997, Hong Kong had suffered setbacks successively in the wake of the Asian financial crisis in 1997, followed by the 9/11 attacks in 2001, SARS epidemic in 2003, and the global financial crisis triggered by US subprime mortgages in 2008. The Asian financial crisis in 1997, combined with internal structural issues, caused Hong Kong to plunge into an economic recession in 1998. Hong Kong's GDP returned to pre-1997 levels in 2005 and had achieved a record-high GDP and GDP per capita by 2008. However, Hong Kong was hit by another recession in 2009, following the 2008 global financial crisis, but began to recover by 2010. In the aftermath of the economic crises of 1998 and 2009, Hong Kong experienced negative growth rate of 5.9% and 2.5%, respectively, forming a W-shaped development trajectory in the years after 1997.

In the 20 years following the return to China in 1997, Hong Kong went through a third industrial restructuring to become a high value-added service economy. Developments in four key industries—finance, logistics and trade, professional services and tourism—made up an increasing share of the GDP. The financial industry performed best, followed by tourism. Services accounted for a GDP share of 91%–92% and began to expand offshore, while manufacturing continued to decline.

The "Six Industries"—cultural and creative industries, education services, medical services, environmental services, innovation and technology, and testing and certification services—have yet to become the key industries of Hong Kong despite efforts (and some progress) made by the HKSAR government.

The rapid economic development of China has had a positive influence on the Hong Kong economy. The 2003 Mainland and Hong Kong Closer Economic Partnership Arrangement (CEPA) and its supplementary agreements helped facilitate the economic recovery and subsequent growth of Hong Kong. Through trade liberalisation in goods and services, promotion of investment, and elimination of tariff and non-tariff barriers, CEPA provided a foundation of economic integration between Hong Kong and the Mainland. This relationship helped Hong Kong's economy to recover from the 2008 financial crisis by the fourth quarter of 2009, ahead of other economies under similar circumstances. Conversely, whenever China was in a period of economic adjustment, particularly concerning foreign trade, Hong Kong tended to experience an economic slowdown and sluggish trade in goods and services with China.

With the rapid economic development of China amid political and economic reforms and opening-up policies, many corporations in Hong Kong expanded their businesses into the Mainland, especially after the return of Hong Kong in 1997, by investing in port facilities, infrastructure, real estate, public utilities and retail businesses. These Hong Kong conglomerates included CK Hutchison, CK Asset Holdings, Henderson Land, Hang Lung Properties, The Wharf Holdings, New World Development, Kerry Properties, Hopewell, and Lee Kam Kee. Chinese state-owned enterprises in Hong Kong, including China Resources, China Travel Service, and China Merchants were largely focused on business development in China. Supported by substantial national investments, these Hong Kong-based corporations and Chinese state-owned enterprises grew into national giants. British companies such as HSBC, Standard Chartered, Jardine Matheson and Swire also made substantial investments in banking, property and hotel development in China.

After its return to China in 1997, Hong Kong became a high-income economy, with its GDP per capita reaching HK$339,478 (US$43,700) in 2016. However, with diminishing economic drivers, sustainable growth remained a concern. Unlike other developed economies where knowledge-based industries typically make up over 50% of GDP, these industries only represented 25% of Hong Kong's GDP in 2013. In other words, new economic drivers were lacking while traditional strengths had become less relevant in a changing global environment.

Hong Kong has been ranked top for its economic freedom and favourable business environment by various international rating institutions. According to the *World Competitiveness Yearbook*, published by the International Institute for Management Development, Hong Kong is globally competitive, taking fourth place in 2014, second place in 2015 and first place in 2016. According to the *2016 Doing Business Report*, released by the World Bank, Hong Kong is fourth in the world and one of the best places to do business.

Although Hong Kong is globally competitive in economic terms, it is limited by a homogenous economic structure, its heavy reliance on the service industry, and weak links in innovative technology and high-end manufacturing. It lacks economic vitality and is susceptible to volatility driven by external factors. The continued efforts by the HKSAR government to expand scientific research and industrial restructuring have faced various obstacles. As such, Hong Kong lacks long-term drivers of economic growth. To encourage sustainable development and remain competitive, many believe Hong Kong should take advantage of opportunities presented by the Belt and Road Initiative to kickstart another round of economic transformation.

2.3 Land System and Economic Development

Hong Kong's land system and related policies are a product of British colonial rule. Following the occupation of Hong Kong Island by Britain, Henry Pottinger, Plenipotentiary and Chief Superintendent of British Trade in China and Administrator of Hong Kong, declared that the British Crown owned all the land in Hong Kong. Under British rule, one could purchase the right to use land from the Hong Kong government (i.e. by leasehold), but one could not acquire permanent ownership (i.e. by freehold).

All land acquired by Britain with the lease of the New Territories in 1898 was also declared government property. By means of land registration, all indigenous land was placed under a Block Crown Lease. The original form of permanent ownership was annulled. Indigenous landowners were granted a leasehold by the Hong Kong government for a 75-year term, renewable for another 24 years.

Under British colonial rule, a leasehold system was put in place; land was sold to the highest bidder. Hong Kong, a free trade economy with low tax rates, relied heavily on the sale of land as a major source of government revenue. This was especially true in the decades after the Second World War, when substantial funding was required to support population growth and social development.

For a steady source of government revenue, a land policy was formulated to maintain prices by limiting the supply of sellable land. This led to the high price of land in Hong Kong. Revenue from land sales amounted to HK$46,637 million, or 10.1% of total government revenue, between 1971 and 1989; in 1980, land sales amounted to 35.6% of total government revenue. The proportion of government revenue from land sales was unmatched by any other developed economies.

The land system remained largely unchanged after the return of Hong Kong in 1997. Various government departments have proposed adjustments to land supply policies but have not achieved significant changes because of political, social and economic considerations. Land expansion slowed down after the 2000s and lagged far behind the needs generated by Hong Kong's population growth and economic development. This has served to keep the land prices high.

Land prices have had a direct impact on property prices and rents. The average price of a residence in Hong Kong was the most expensive in the world (US$1,616 per square foot in 2017). Hong Kong also had the highest house price-to-income ratio of 19.4, followed by a ratio of 12.9 in Sydney, Australia. Office rents in Central District were the world's most expensive (US$302.51 per square foot in 2017), surpassing West London (US$213.85), Midtown Manhattan (US$203), and West Kowloon in Hong Kong (US$190).

The high prices of land and property have dampened economic development and undermined the quality of life in Hong Kong. The issues of land supply and housing prices have been a source of continuing concern for the HKSAR government and have remained largely unresolved.

2.4 Participation in National Reform and Opening-Up

During the Third Plenary Session of the Eleventh Central Committee of the Communist Party of China in December 1978, under the leadership of Deng Xiaoping (鄧小平), China decided to implement new policies of reform and opening-up. This created many new opportunities for Hong Kong.

The abundance of low-wage labour and low-cost land in the Mainland complemented well with the availability of funding, technology, management experience and a global sales network in Hong Kong. During the initial stage, businesses in Hong Kong invested heavily and created many "firsts in China," including the first joint venture, the first jointly constructed highway, the first jointly run five-star hotel and the opening of the first branch of a foreign bank.

Since the introduction of reform and opening-up, Hong Kong has been the largest source of foreign investment in the Mainland. From 1979 to 1996, Hong Kong's direct investment there totalled US$99.297 billion, or 56.8% of the US$174.887 billion in total inbound investment. By the end of 2016, Hong Kong's investment in the Mainland amounted to US$914.79 billion, or more than half of the total from sources outside the Mainland. These investments were mutually beneficial for both economies.

Hong Kong has played a key role in supporting the initial growth of a market economy in the Mainland. Professionals in Hong Kong not only introduced the global market and the rules of international commerce to the Mainland, but also took part in the establishment of special economic zones in the Mainland by providing expertise on planning, making rules and regulations as well as launching various undertakings.

Initial investments by Hong Kong businesses in the Mainland focused largely on manufacturing and services, such as hotels, tourist facilities and taxis, in the southern Chinese provinces of Guangdong and Fujian, where connections were easiest to establish due to geographic and historical closeness. These projects were generally small in scale, requiring minimal technology and producing high returns in a short investment period.

Confidence among overseas investors grew substantially following Deng Xiaoping's (鄧小平) southern tour in 1992. Investments in the Mainland made by Hong Kong businesses were growing larger in total sum, longer in length, wider in scope and at a faster pace.

By then, Hong Kong's manufacturing sector had begun to decline, exacerbated by a mixture of rising labour costs, high rents, insufficient space, poor economies of scale and low output. In response, manufacturing began moving to the Mainland in pursuit of lower manufacturing costs. These reduced costs allowed Hong Kong to retain a competitive edge amid global competition. In Guangdong Province, for example, in 1997, more than five million workers were regularly employed by Hong Kong companies, saving about $200 billion in yearly wages alone. In turn, Hong Kong brought to the Mainland advanced technology, management expertise, employment opportunities and technical training, and helped foster the industrialisation, urbanisation and modernisation of the Chinese economy.

In the years following the reform and opening-up, Hong Kong became a base from which China established overseas economic ties. Representative businesses from different ministries, provinces and municipalities were established in Hong Kong where Chinese businesses already in place continued to grow. According to the 1996 government statistics, Mainland was the second largest investor in Hong Kong with US$14.8 billion, 18.7% of Hong Kong's total. This was below the United Kingdom (27.7%) and above the United States (18.2%) and Japan (15.5%). Chinese-funded enterprises served as a link connecting the Mainland with Hong Kong and the rest of the world in terms of capital inflow, technology and management expertise. These enterprises were important platforms for developing talent, gathering timely information on the global economy and earning foreign exchange. Hong Kong has played a vital role as an investor and an intermediary for foreign investment in the Mainland.

A new type of securities, known as red chips, emerged in the 1980s as part of the ongoing financial reform policies umder implementation in China. These are shares of Chinese enterprises registered outside the Mainland and listed on the Hong Kong Stock Exchange. In the 1990s, Chinese state-owned enterprises (SOEs) began listing in the Hong Kong stock exchange as H-Shares. By the end of 1997, stocks of 39 SOEs were being traded on the Hong Kong Stock Exchange with a capitalisation of HK$59 billion. The introduction of red chips and H-Shares changed the structure, variety, and scope of product offerings in the Hong Kong securities market, contributing to the diversification of the basic, financial and high-tech industries.

3 Migration and the Growth of an Immigrant City

Hong Kong is a city of immigrants. Most people in Hong Kong have ancestors who moved, over the centuries, from the Mainland to Hong Kong. The first large-scale migration on record began in the Song Dynasty. The Hakka people began arriving in Hong Kong in the early Qing Dynasty when the coastal evacuation order was rescinded; they continued to migrate to Hong Kong until the end of the dynasty. Under the early British colonial rule in the 1850s, waves of migrants moved from Guangdong and took refuge in Hong Kong. These immigrants formed a local Chinese community indispensable to the urban and commercial development of Hong Kong. After the Second World War, an influx of immigrants, both legal and illegal, helped accelerate the industrialisation of Hong Kong with their capital, expertise and labour, creating an economic boom supported most prominently by entrepreneurs from Jiangsu and Zhejiang. Additionally, non-Chinese immigrants despite their small numbers have also made significant contribution to the prosperity and development of Hong Kong.

3.1 Early Inhabitants in Ancient Times

There is evidence of people living in Hong Kong as early as the mid-Neolithic period, or about 7,000 years ago. This period is known as the Big Bay (Tai Wan) Culture by some historians after the historical site of Tai Wan on Lamma Island. The early inhabitants of Tai Wan made a living by fishing, hunting, gathering and making cloth from tree bark. They were skilled in making pottery-based cooking utensils, which were sometimes painted in coloured patterns prior to firing. Similar cultural relics were also found at the Neolithic Jinlan Temple site in Zengcheng and other places in Guangdong, including Houshawan in Zhuhai and Xiantouling in Shenzhen. Scholars believe that the round-footed pottery, painted pottery and white pottery of the Big Bay Culture found in the Pearl River Delta region were influenced by the Daxi culture in the region of the Yangtze River.

Around 4,000 to 5,000 years ago, settlements in Hong Kong were relatively larger and became more active, as indicated by traces of human lives found in the coastal areas of Hong Kong. Archaeological findings show that they were influenced by the Liangzhu Culture in the lower reaches of the Yangtze River. The penannular rings, battle axes and bracelets discovered at the Yung Long site in Tuen Mun had an origin from the Yangtze River basin. The bracelets were the known artefacts of the Liangzhu Culture that had spread to the southernmost places.

In 1997, a prehistoric burial ground of 20 tombs dating to the late Neolithic period was discovered at Tung Wan Tsai North on Ma Wan Island; it was one of China's top 10 archaeological finds of the year. Study of the human bones revealed common characteristics with people of southern China, particularly of those from the Pearl River basin of the late Neolithic period. Traces of tooth extraction found on the skull of a 40-year-old female reflected the customary methods of tooth extraction commonly found in the Neolithic human bones excavated from the Hedang Beiqiu site in Foshan. Because of these physical and cultural similarities, inhabitants of Hong Kong in the late Neolithic period and inhabitants of the Pearl River Delta are thought to share similar origins.

Relics of the Bronze Age discovered in Hong Kong included axes, daggers, swords, hewing axes and arrowheads. These shared the same characteristics as bronze relics found in Guangdong. Most of them were weapons, with a few ritual vessels and containers. A bronze sword with the pattern of a human face discovered at Shek Pik on Lantau Island was nearly identical to those found in a tomb of the Eastern Zhou Dynasty in Sankeng, Qingyuan, Guangdong Province and on the upper layer of the Shixia excavation site in Qujiang, Guangdong Province. Relics commonly found in Hong Kong, such as pottery with a double-F pattern and a spiral pattern from the Spring and Autumn period, or pottery marked with the Chinese character for rice from the Warring States period, shared features similar to relics found in some 200 historic sites and 50–60 tombs in Guangdong. Similar relics were also found at historic sites in Guangxi, Fujian, Hunan and Jiangxi.

In the tomb cluster of the Shang Dynasty, discovered in 1989 at the Tai Wan site on Lamma Island, a jade *yazhang* blade and a complete string ornament unearthed from Tomb No. 6 were deemed national treasures by relic experts. The *yazhang* blade was a ritual object of the late Neolithic period from the middle and lower basins of the Yellow River. The *yazhang* blade found in Tai Wan, featuring a similar style of micro-engraving as those found in the tombs of Erlitou and those of the Shang Dynasty, proved that the civilisations and rituals of northern China expanded southwards.

The prehistoric relics found in Hong Kong are closely correlated to the ancient culture of Lingnan and of the civilisations of the Yangtze and Yellow River basins, suggesting that there was a prehistoric movement of people and cultures.

3.2 Indigenous People of the New Territories

Large-scale migration to Hong Kong on record began in the Song Dynasty. In 973 A.D., Tang Hon-fat (鄧漢黻), a Gentleman for Rendering Service and a native of Jishui, Jiangxi Province, travelled south to Guangdong and settled in Sham Tin at the foot of the Guijiao Mountain in Dongguan (present-day Kam Tin in the New Territories). He founded the Tang clan—one of the most distinguished and powerful family groups in Hong Kong up until the early Qing Dynasty. Members of the clan owned farmland in the New Territories and some land in Kowloon and on Hong Kong Island. In the Northern Song Dynasty, Hau Ng-long (侯五郎), an imperial examination scholar, relocated from Panyu, Guangdong to present-day Sheung Shui, where his descendant Hau Cheuk-fung (侯卓峰) established a family estate in Ho Sheung Heung during the early Ming Dynasty. In the Song Dynasty, Pang Kwei (彭桂) settled in present-day Fanling where his descendants grew into a large family. Also in the Song Dynasty, Lam Cheung-shing (林長勝) and his entire family moved from Putian, Fujian to Pang Po Wai near present-day Wong Tai Sin. In the late Southern Song Dynasty, Tao Man-chat (陶文質) relocated from Yuling, Guangxi to present-day San Tin, Yuen Long before moving to Tuen Mun with his son Tao Chu-si (陶處斯). In the late Yuan Dynasty, Liu Chung-kit (廖仲傑) moved from Tingzhou, Fujian and settled in Sheung Shui. In the early Ming Dynasty, the descendants of Wen Tianrui (文天瑞), a relative of statesman Wen Tianxiang (文 天 祥), settled in Tai Hang and later in San Tin. Since then, other families have arrived in Hong Kong where they established new villages and became indigenous inhabitants of the New Territories.

The population of Hong Kong in the Qing Dynasty could be classified into four major groups, namely the "Punti," "Hakka," Tanka" and "Hoklo." The Punti, meaning local or aboriginal, lived in the area north of Nanling and later moved southward to Guangdong and Hong Kong in the Song Dynasty. They spoke a form of Cantonese called the Weitou dialect, which was quite distinct from the dialect of Guangzhou. According to an 1898 survey by James Haldane Stewart Lockhart, Colonial Secretary of Hong Kong, there was a Punti population of 64,140 across 161 villages in the New Territories, mainly near the Shenzhen River and in the Yuen Long valley. They made a living primarily by farming and doing business.

The Hakka ancestors were said to be Han Chinese who had moved from the Central Plain to various parts of southern China across different ancient periods. They spoke the Hakka dialect and had a distinct architectural culture and other unique customs. Many Hakka people moved to Hong Kong in the early Qing Dynasty when the coastal evacuation order was rescinded. During the years of Emperor Jiaqing (嘉慶) (1796–1820), Hakka villages in Xin'an County were so large in number that they were registered in a separate category called "Hakka Villages" under the jurisdiction of Kwun Fu Inspectorate in the Xin'an County Local Chronicles. According to the Xin'an County Local Chronicles, there were at least 86 Hakka villages in Hong Kong at the time, including Lin Ma Hang, Kowloon Tong and Man Uk Pin. Hakka families continued to move to Hong Kong until the late Qing Dynasty.

The Tanka people were traditionally boat dwellers and were not considered part of the Guangdong group of Han Chinese people. They spoke the Tanka dialect which was phonetically comparable to the Cantonese spoken in Guangzhou but based on different vocabulary. The Tanka people lived near waters—streams, harbours, waterways and islands—and were known to be skilled swimmers, fishermen, and operators of small, wooden boats. Living on water, they often faced discrimination from their counterparts living onshore; many gradually moved ashore.

The Hoklo people were also known as "Fuklo" or "Holo." Their ancestors came from Fujian and settled in Chaoshan and Hailufeng in eastern Guangdong before moving to Cheung Chau, Peng Chau and Sha Tau Kok in a cluster of fishermen communities in Hong Kong. They spoke the Fuklo dialect, a form of Hokkien with an eastern Guangdong accent.

3.3 Mobility and the Chinese Community in the 19th Century

In the 1840s, following the British occupation of Hong Kong Island, some Chinese people, mostly men, came here to make a living. The early migrants mainly worked as labourers, stonemasons, hawkers and servants.

In the 1850s, Guangdong endured a series of conflicts, including the Red Turban Rebellion initiated by the fraternal organisation Tiandihui, the Punti–Hakka Clan Wars and the Second Opium War. A large number of Chinese migrants began taking refuge in Hong Kong. Unlike their predecessors, these migrants included many wealthy businessmen as well as some craftsmen.

These early businessmen and craftsmen were engaged in trade and retail by virtue of their wealth and craftsmanship. They were key to the rapid growth of stores and shops in Hong Kong. In 1858, Hong Kong Island only had 75,000 residents, but there were more than 2,000 stores run by Chinese people. These included 287 grocery stores, 49 foreign goods stores, 35 traders, 30 compradors, 17 money changers, 51 rice dealers, 53 shipbuilding sheds, 12 printing houses, 116 metalsmiths' shops and 92 carpenters. The Chinese population of Hong Kong grew from 85,330 in 1859 to 121,825 in 1865, an increase of over 36,000 people, comprising mostly new migrants.

Between the late 1870s and early 1880s, Chinese businessmen—most prominently Nam Pak Hong-affiliated businessmen and compradors—became a hugely influential social group. On 03 June 1881, Governor of Hong Kong John Pope Hennessy remarked in the Legislative Council that a significant majority of Hong Kong's tax revenue came from Chinese businesses. Among the top 20 taxpayers in 1876 were 12 Europeans who contributed a total of HK$62,523 (an average of HK$5,210 each) and eight Chinese persons who contributed a total of HK$28,267 (an average of HK$3,533 each). By 1881, among the top 20 taxpayers were three Europeans with a total contribution of HK$16,038 (an average of HK$5,346 each) and 17 Chinese persons with a total contribution of HK$99,110 (an average of HK$5,830 each). The wealthiest Chinese businessmen and merchants had exceeded their foreign counterparts in total and individual tax payments by 1881. In just 40 years since the British occupation of Hong Kong, Chinese businesses had become the major economic pillars of Hong Kong.

Amid the growing influence of Chinese businesses, a number of Chinese social groups and networks began to emerge. Nam Pak Hong Union, established in 1868, was one of the earliest, largest and most influential social groups. In 1870, Chinese businessmen Leung On（梁安）, Li Sing（李陞）, Wong Shing（黃勝）and Ko Mun-wo（高滿華）, with the support of the Hong Kong government, founded the Tung Wah Hospital. This hospital became a leading social organisation that brought together Chinese magnates in support of the development of the Chinese community in Hong Kong. Following the establishment of Tung Wah Hospital, other social organisations were formed by Chinese businessmen to address the needs of the Chinese community at large. In 1878, Lo Kang-yeung（盧賡揚）and his associates founded the charitable group Po Leung Kuk; in 1896, Ku Fai-shan（古輝山）and others established the Chinese Chamber of Commerce in 1900, Fung Wah-chuen（馮華川）and Chan Kang-yu（陳賡虞）formed the Chinese Commercial Union of Hong Kong; in 1913, Lau Chu-pak（劉鑄伯）restructured the Chinese Commercial Union into the Hong Kong Chinese Merchants' Guild, rivalling the 50-year-old Hong Kong General Chamber of Commerce (which was renamed the Chinese General Chamber of Commerce in 1952 and remains in operation to date).

Except the indigenous people of the New Territories, few Chinese settled in Hong Kong before the Second World War; many were here to make a living and return home after some years. It was customary for chambers of commerce and hometown associations to prefix their names with *Lue Kong* (sojourning in Hong Kong) or *Kiu Kong* (residing overseas in Hong Kong) as an indication of the temporary status of migrants.

3.4 Post-WW II Immigration and Economic Development

The instability inflicted by the Second World War, the Chinese Civil War and the subsequent change of regime led to an influx of legal and illegal immigrants to Hong Kong from the Mainland. Due to the political circumstances, many were unable to return home and simply chose to stay, thereby making Hong Kong an immigrant city. According to the census in March 1961, Hong Kong had a population of 3,133,131. About 827,000 of these people were immigrants who had arrived after 1949. Together with 244,000 of their children born in Hong Kong, they formed an immigrant population of 1,071,000.

Amongst the post-war immigrants, entrepreneurs from Jiangsu and Zhejiang played a key role in the industrialisation of Hong Kong at a time of uncertainty during the 1950s embargo on China. Among the pioneers were cotton and textile entrepreneurs, including Tang Hsiang-chien（唐翔千）, Tang Ping-yuan（唐炳源）, Chao Kuang-piu（曹光彪）, Wong Toong-yuen（王統元）, Lee Chen-che（李震之）, Vincent V. C. Woo（吳文政）, Fang Chao-chow（方肇周）, Kuo Cheng-dai（郭正達）, Yeung Yuen-lung（楊元龍）, Ann Tse-kai (T. K. Ann)（安子介）, Yung Hung-ching（榮鴻慶）, Cha Chi-ming（查濟民）, Chen Din-hwa（陳廷驊）, Lau Hon-kwan（劉漢堃）, Song Vung-ji（宋文傑）and Chou Wen-hsien（周文軒）. They brought to Hong Kong their vast production capacity, expertise, capital and marketing networks. Combined with the influx of cheap labour into Hong Kong, it allowed Hong Kong to undergo rapid industrialisation. Likewise, Pao Yue-kong (Y. K. Pao)（包玉剛）, Tung Chao-yung (C. Y. Tung)（董浩雲）, T. Y. Chao（趙從衍）and Tsao Wen-king（曹文錦）, also from Jiangsu and Zhejiang, became international shipping tycoons and made Hong Kong a global logistics hub.

After the Second World War, immigrants to Hong Kong came mostly from the Mainland, including those of Chinese descent with a Southeast Asian background previously living in the Mainland. A small number of immigrants came directly from Southeast Asia; among the most notable were entrepreneurs Robin Chan Yau-hing（陳有慶）, Tin Ka-ping（田家炳）and Robert Kuok Hock-nien（郭鶴年）.

Waves of refugees fled to Hong Kong in 1957, 1962, 1972, and between 1978–1979. From November 1974, under the "Touch Base" policy, illegal immigrants were given formal Hong Kong residency once they reached the urban centre and registered with the government. This lenient approach was adopted at a time of labour shortages and led to a surge of immigrants who were escaping from the Mainland. In October 1980, Governor Murray MacLehose met with Guangdong officials in Guangzhou and reached an agreement on a daily quota of legal immigrants. Under the agreement, the "Touch Base" policy was replaced with the "Repatriation Upon Arrest" policy under which illegal immigrants were subject to immediate deportation. A daily immigration quota of 75 "one-way" permits was agreed upon in 1982 and was increased to 150 in 1995. The waves of immigrants were largely due to the wide gap in living standards at the time between Hong Kong and the Mainland. With rapid economic development and rising living standards under the national reform and opening-up policy, Hong Kong-bound immigrants from the Mainland gradually decreased in the 1980s.

3.5 The Impact of Non-Chinese on Social Development

Hong Kong has always had a predominant population of ethnic Chinese. The non-Chinese communities of Hong Kong, however, have commanded significant economic power, especially before the Second World War. They have played a vital role in making Hong Kong a cosmopolitan city in the last century.

Jardine, Matheson & Co. and Butterfield & Swire were among the British trading houses in Hong Kong and were renowned with a long history. Jardine, Matheson & Co., founded by Scotsmen William Jardine and James Matheson in 1832, began in Guangzhou as a trading firm, including in the trade of opium. Butterfield & Swire was established by John Samuel Swire and Richard Butterfield in Shanghai in 1866 and expanded to Hong Kong in 1870. In colonial Hong Kong, both companies were synonymous with the development of various industrial sectors, including foreign trade, finance, shipping and aviation. Lane Crawford, founded by British businessmen Thomas Lane and Ninian Crawford in Hong Kong in 1850, began as a provider of ship supplies and became the oldest and most prestigious department store in Hong Kong. Renowned British professional services, such as the legal firm Deacons and architecture firms P&T Architects and Engineers as well as Leigh & Orange, helped advance the development of Hong Kong.

Among the other non-Chinese groups in Hong Kong were the Portuguese from Macao as the earliest Europeans to settle in Hong Kong after the British. They were well known in the printing industry. In 1844, Noronha & Co., Hong Kong's first printing house, was founded by a Portuguese from Macao named Delfino Noronha. In 1859, it became the official printer of government publications and continued for three generations before it was acquired by the government and became the Printing Department. American Joseph Whittlesey Noble was a dentist, a medical doctor, an educator, an entrepreneur and a newspaper publisher. He co-founded the Hong Kong College of Medicine and, in the late 19th century, purchased the Dairy Farm Co. His other investments included the Hongkong Hotel, Peak Tramways, Hongkong Electric, and Green Island Cement. In 1895, Jebsen & Co. was founded in Hong Kong by Germans Jacob Jebsen and Henrich Jessen; it started in shipping and gradually diversified to become active in various markets in Hong Kong and the Mainland. Upon the arrival of the Sisters of St. Paul de Chartres of France in 1848, an orphanage named Asile de la Sainte Enfance was founded, followed by the establishment of St. Paul's Hospital and a boarding school on Hong Kong Island, as well as St. Teresa's Orphanage and St. Teresa's Hospital in Kowloon. Schools, orphanages and hospitals were also established by a group of six nuns from Italy's Canossian Daughters of Charity following their arrival in 1860.

High-achieving individuals throughout the history of Hong Kong came from diverse backgrounds. The Kadoorie family, of Jewish descent, arrived in the 19th century and founded the China Light & Power Company in 1901, one of Hong Kong's two power companies. The Kadoorie Agricultural Aid Association was formed in 1951 by brothers Horace and Lawrence to provide low-income farmers with training, supplies and interest-free loans. Parsi businessman Sir Hormusjee Naorojee Mody made a significant financial contribution to the construction of The University of Hong Kong's main building. Armenian merchant Catchick Paul Chater cultivated a new landscape through his reclamation project in Central District. The work and dedication of immgrants from India, Pakistan, the Philippines, Indonesia, Malaysia and other places have also made Hong Kong a place of diversity and cultural vibrancy.

4 British Colonial Rule

The Opium Wars marked a turning point in Chinese history and the beginning of Hong Kong's modern history. Following the wars, as China gradually opened its door to the world, Hong Kong became a place of historical significance in a short period of time.

4.1 British Occupation of Hong Kong

From the 1840s and onwards, Britain annexed Hong Kong Island, Kowloon and the New Territories under the Treaty of Nanking, Convention of Peking, and Convention Between Great Britain and China Respecting an Extension of Hong Kong Territory, respectively, following a series of military campaigns, including two Opium Wars, and diplomatic coercion against the backdrop of colonial expansionism.

4.1.1 The Cession of Hong Kong Island

Britain was an established colonial power and had aimed to expand its empire by taking possession of islands in the Chinese coastal areas and establishing British trading hubs.

In the 1820s, British opium barges frequently made Hong Kong an anchorage. In March 1839, Imperial Commissioner Lin Zexu (林則徐) was dispatched to crack down on the opium trade in Guangdong; batches of crude opium were seized from British and American traders and destroyed on the beach of Humen. It led to a skirmish with British vessels, under the command of Chief Superintendent of British Trade Charles Elliot, in the waters near Tsim Sha Tsui. The conflict soon escalated and resulted in a series of battles in Kowloon, Chuenpi and Kwun Chung. Two of the three battles in the ensuing opium war were fought in Hong Kong.

The First Opium War began when the British expeditionary force arrived in China in June 1840. British forces subsequently headed north to Xiamen, captured Dinghai and reached Baihekou in Tianjin by the end of July. Under pressure, Imperial Commissioner Qishan (琦善) was dispatched by the Qing government in a negotiation with the British in Guangzhou. On 25 January 1841, Hong Kong Island was seized by British naval forces before negotiations were concluded.

On 30 April 1841, Britain halted the negotiation in Guangdong, intensified its military campaign against China, and appointed Henry Pottinger in place of Charles Elliot as Plenipotentiary and Chief Superintendent of British Trade in China. Under the command of Henry Pottinger, British troops and vessels moved northward and launched attacks on cities along the coast and nearby rivers, arriving in Nanking on 04 August 1842. Emperor Daoguang (道光) surrendered as the Qing army came under repeated defeat.

On 29 August 1842, the Treaty of Nanking was signed between Britain and China on the British warship *Cornwallis*. It was known as the first of many unequal treaties in modern China. Under Article 3, Hong Kong Island was ceded to Britain in perpetuity. The cession of Hong Kong Island in the First Opium War was a watershed moment in Chinese history.

4.1.2 The Annexation of Kowloon

The Kowloon peninsula, located across from Hong Kong Island, was deemed vital to British interest because it meant complete control over Victoria Harbour and additional land resources ideal for barracks, trading firms and warehouses. Following the outbreak of the Second Opium War in 1856, Colonial Secretary of Hong Kong

William Thomas Mercer and British military advisors suggested the Kowloon peninsula and Stonecutters Island be annexed. On 18 March 1860, with British government approval and without a formal declaration of war on China, British troops landed at Tsim Sha Tsui near the tip of the Kowloon peninsula under Commander of British Troops in China and Hong Kong James Hope Grant. They camped onshore and prepared to launch an attack northward. On 21 March, Governor-General of Guangdong and Guangxi Lao Chongguang (勞崇光) was forced to sign a lease agreement on Kowloon, drafted by British envoy to Guangzhou Harry Parkes, in Guangzhou under the control of British and French forces.

In September 1860, Emperor Xianfeng (咸豐) escaped to Rehe after the Anglo-French forces invaded Beijing and defeated the Qing army in the Battle of Palikao. On 13 October, Anglo-French forces breached the city gate of Andingmen in Peking, placed cannons along the city wall and aimed directly at the Forbidden City. On 18 and 19 October, Anglo-French forces looted the Old Summer Palace and set it on fire. Under intense military and diplomatic pressure, Prince Gong Yixin (奕訢), a plenipotentiary representative of the Qing government, accepted all the conditions put forward by Britain and France. The Convention of Peking between China and Britain was subsequently signed on 24 October. Under Article 6 of the Convention, the land south of Boundary Street in Kowloon, originally under the jurisdiction of Xin'an County, along with Stonecutters Island, were ceded to Britain.

4.1.3 The New Territories Lease

By the end of the 19th Century, China had been carved up by foreign powers into their respective spheres of influence. The Qing army was severely weakened after the First Sino-Japanese War which broke out in July 1894. Britain felt emboldened to annex more Chinese territories. On 09 November 1894, Sir William Robinson, the 11th Governor of Hong Kong, made a recommendation to Britain's Colonial Office that Hong Kong be further expanded to include Mirs Bay and Shenzhen Bay. In March 1898, as France had been granted a lease on Guangzhou Bay, Britain also made a demand for more territory with the Qing government. On 02 April, negotiation began. Under pressure from British Minister to China Sir Claude Maxwell Macdonald, Chinese senior official Li Hongzhang (李鴻章) accepted the British proposal with the condition that the Kowloon Walled City be retained under Chinese jurisdiction.

The Convention between Great Britain and China Respecting an Extension of Hong Kong Territory was signed in Peking on 09 June 1898 and came into force on 01 July. Britain was granted a 99-year lease on the area north of Boundary Street and south of a border defined by the shortest straight line between Starling Inlet on the seafront of Sha Tau Kok and Shenzhen Bay. Britain also gained access to 235 surrounding islands and the waters of Mirs Bay and Shenzhen Bay. The Delimitation of the Northern Frontier of the New Territories, signed on 19 March 1899, moved the border further north, giving Britain control of the Shenzhen River.

4.2 The System of Government

British colonial rule came in different forms, including direct rule in Crown colonies and self-governance in dominions. In colonial Hong Kong, where British officials were concerned about retaining control over a majority population of Chinese, a centralised government system was adopted, putting executive and legislative powers in the hands of government officials who were legally bound to the British government through the governor of Hong Kong.

The constitutional structure of Hong Kong under British rule was formally established by Queen Victoria on 05 April 1843 in the Letters Patent, also known as the Charter of the Colony of Hong Kong. As stipulated in the charter, a governor was to be appointed and granted exclusive power. The charter also made general provisions for establishing an Executive Council and a Legislative Council.

On 06 April 1843, Sir Henry Pottinger, Hong Kong's first governor, was issued the Royal Instructions of 1843. It outlined the organisational structure, jurisdiction and protocol of the Executive Council and the Legislative

Council, including the role of the governor, as well as the appointment and dismissal of councillors and the process by which resolutions and laws were made.

By the Letters Patent and Royal Instructions, the governor was the sole representative of the British monarch in Hong Kong with direct authority over colonial officials, military personnel and civilians. The governor, by default, was Chairman of the Executive Council and President of the Legislative Council. Legislative bills must be approved by the governor before they became law. The governor was also Commander-in-Chief of British forces stationed in Hong Kong and was empowered to appoint judges and officials and to grant official pardons and amnesties. The power of the governor, although extensive in nature, could only be exercised to safeguard British national interests. The governor was required to report directly to the British government and consult with the British government on major issues. Public opinion, especially that of British businessmen and Chinese elites, was taken into consideration in policymaking to avoid public discontent and parliamentary scrutiny.

The Executive Council and Legislative Council, comprising senior government officials, were the two most important bodies in support of the governor regarding policymaking and governance. The Executive Council was empowered to approve any bills before adoption by the Legislative Council and to be consulted by the governor in exercising the Letters Patent, except matters deemed urgent, trivial or highly confidential. However, only the governor had the right to raise issues directly while councillors had to first seek the governor's consent in writing before raising an issue. The governor had absolute discretion even in cases of disagreement with a majority of councillors as long as records were made and passed onto the British government.

The Legislative Council was established to play a supporting role in law-making and public finances as the governor had decisive influence on the legislature. According to the Royal Instructions, the governor was empowered to preside over the Legislative Council and cast regular and tie-breaking votes. The Finance Committee of the Legislative Council by protocol could accept, reject or reduce—but not increase—the annual government budget.

The Legislative and Executive Councils in the early days consisted solely of senior government officials. Business elites began serving as unofficial members (non-ex-officio) of the Legislative Council and Executive Council in 1850 and 1896, respectively. Chinese people were excluded until Ng Choy (伍才), also known as Wu Tingfang (伍廷芳), became the first unofficial member of the Legislative Council in 1880 and Chow Shou-son (周壽臣) became the first unofficial member of the Executive Council in 1926. From 1844 to 1984, members of both councils were appointed exclusively by the British government. On 26 September 1985, 24 councillors—comprising 12 members selected by the electoral college and another 12 by functional constituencies—were elected in the first Legislative Council election. The governor's ex-officio presidency in the Legislative Council ended on 19 February 1993.

4.3 Legal Development and The Rule of Law

Continental law and common law are the world's two major legal systems. The common law, also called the Anglo-American law or case law, originates in England and is the basis of Hong Kong's legal system by reason of British colonial rule.

The laws of colonial Hong Kong had their origins in both common law and statutory law. The statutory laws of Hong Kong derived from three sources: (1) laws enacted by the British government for Hong Kong, (2) British domestic laws applicable to Hong Kong and (3) Hong Kong legislation enacted by the Hong Kong government. The legal instruments of Hong Kong, including the Letters Patent, were enacted by the British monarch as the constitutional basis of the government structure of Hong Kong. Hong Kong's legal system follows the common law principle of *stare decisis,* under which courts must follow legal precedents set by previous court decisions. Before 1997, the *stare decisis* was applied to cases from Britain and Hong Kong. The British Judicial Committee of the Privy Council was Hong Kong's final court of Appeal; Hong Kong courts were required to follow the precedent set by the Privy Council, while judgements from other British courts served as a reference. Lower courts in colonial Hong Kong were subordinate to the Supreme Court. The principle of *stare decisis* in common law has played a critical role in the uniformity and predictability of the legal system of Hong Kong.

The laws of Hong Kong are built upon the common law principle of due process, by which trials must follow a clear, well-established legal process, and any conclusion reached in a trial must be accepted as an impartial decision. The principle of due process is based on the following precepts: 1) no penalty without a law; 2) everything which is not forbidden is allowed; 3) presumption of innocence; 4) law-based administration and 5) sufficiency of evidence.

The laws of Hong Kong in the early days had clear colonial undertones. For example, the Regulation of the Chinese Ordinance of 1888 discriminated against Chinese people. Certain behaviours considered criminal in Britain were permitted or even protected by the Hong Kong government. The most notable example was the statement by the Hong Kong Legislative Council explicitly permitting businesses to legally import and sell opium upon paying the government for a licence.

Hong Kong has had a long-standing emphasis on economic legislation. A series of economic laws were enacted by the Hong Kong government as early as the 1850s and 1860s. These included the Market Ordinance 1854, Lis Pendens and Purchasers Ordinance 1856, Bankers Cheques-False Pretence Ordinance 1860, Fraudulent Trustees, and etc. Ordinance 1860, Patents Ordinance 1862, Merchandise Marks Ordinance 1863, Bankruptcy Ordinance 1864, Personal Property Security Ordinance 1864, Mercantile Law Amendment Ordinance 1864, and Coinage Offences Ordinance 1865. An initial count in the early 1990s suggested that about 40% of over 500 chapters of statutory law in Hong Kong were related to the economy, essentially regulating all aspects of economic activity.

The development of Hong Kong's legal system was driven by economic, political and social factors throughout the colonial period. As the size and complexity of Hong Kong's economy increased throughout the 1960s, previous colonial legislations concerning the economy became outdated. Thus, new statutory laws were enacted to fill the gap. The rise of civil and commercial litigation expanded Hong Kong's case law in relation to property law, contract law and company law. Political factors, especially in the fight against corruption, led to the Corrupt and Illegal Practices Ordinance 1955, Prevention of Bribery Ordinance 1970, and Independent Commission against Corruption Ordinance 1974. Social factors, including a shift in gender equality in the 1970s, led to legislative reforms in gender relations, marriage and property inheritance.

Hong Kong's legislative system is supported by a culture of respect and compliance with the rule of law. The rule of law has played a critical role in facilitating law and order in Hong Kong and in the broad development of Hong Kong as a core value highly prized by the people of Hong Kong.

4.4 Direct and Indirect Rule

Early British rule in Hong Kong was characterised by colonialist ideas of a racial hierarchy. To control the Chinese population, a curfew was implemented by the government in October 1842, requiring Chinese people to carry a lantern at night. Those without a permit for going out at night were required to stay at home once dusk fell; offenders were arrested and punished. It was estimated that more than 1,000 Chinese were arrested by the police for curfew violations each year between 1878 and 1882. A total of 2,196 arrests were made in 1895, and as many as 3,477 in 1896. An official report in 1879 found that 99% of those arrested were innocent pedestrians or carriage bearers. The discriminatory policy was abolished in June 1897.

Racial discrimination was common in early colonial Hong Kong. For instance, a residential policy of racial segregation was implemented in the early 1940s, making the district of Victoria in Central an exclusively European residential area. Chinese residents were subsequently forced to relocate to Tai Ping Shan. In 1888, under the European District Reservation Ordinance adopted by Governor William Des Voeux, only European-style houses were allowed in the area between Wellington Street and Caine Road. A cap was also placed on the number of residents as a measure to prevent Chinese people from moving to the area. In 1904, under the Peak District Reservation Ordinance, Chinese people were prohibited from residential occupancy at Victoria Peak (other than servants), making the area exclusively for Westerners. Robert Ho Tung (何東) and his family were the only Chinese granted permission to live on the Peak but often faced rejection and exclusion; they were once asked to leave the area. It was not until 1946 that these laws were completely repealed.

The British, who were a minority in Hong Kong, used a combination of direct and indirect rule to govern the Chinese population. Direct rule was administered through the law, the judiciary and the police. In 1844, the Registrar-General of Hong Kong was appointed to keep track of the population through a registry and periodic censuses. In late 1846, by Ordinance No. 7 of the Legislative Council, the Registrar-General also carried the titles "Protector of the Chinese," "Superintendent of Police," and "Justice of the Peace," and was authorised to enter any house or boat inhabited or manned by Chinese people. In the 1850s, the Registrar-General was officially renamed as the Protector of the Chinese (later known as the Secretary for Chinese Affairs).

On 01 February 1841, following the occupation of Hong Kong Island, British Plenipotentiary Sir Charles Elliot and Commander of British Forces in the First Opium War Gordon Bremer proclaimed that "all heads of villages are held responsible that commands [emanating from the colonial authorities] are duly respected and observed." This policy of using high-ranking Chinese to subdue the Chinese population was a form of indirect rule. In 1844, under the Chinese Peace Officers Regulation Ordinance, a community-based system of law enforcement called *Baojia* was implemented. Selected Chinese peace officers were appointed by the governor at the recommendation of each village. The peace officers, called "Paouchong" and "Paoukea," were essentially police officers commanded by the Chief Magistrate of Police. In 1853, under Ordinance No. 3 of the Legislative Council, selection of local constables (known as Tepos) was specified by the government. Tepos were under the payroll of the Chinese community and were authorised to preside over civil disputes amongst the local population. During the Second Opium War, under the Regulation of Chinese and Census Ordinance of 1857, all homes and individual residents were required to be registered; units of 10 households were formed with a self-elected unit head appointed by the governor. Each household had a duty to report any suspicious activities to the unit head who was responsible for notifying the Registrar-General. The *Baojia* system was abolished in June 1861.

The Chinese upper class were encouraged to help support local governance through a policy of conciliation. In exchange, members of the Chinese elite were conferred British knighthoods, appointed as Justices of the Peace, and offered formal positions in non-government organisations, such as the District Watch Force and the Sanitary Board of Hong Kong. The Hong Kong government also exerted influence through Chinese charitable organisations, including Tung Wah Hospital and Po Leung Kuk.

The government policy of direct and indirect rule continued after the acquisition of the New Territories in 1899. The government headquarters of the New Territories was established in Tai Po and headed by Colonial Secretary James Stewart Lockhart. When Lockhart left office, officials were appointed to maintain public order and handle land affairs, giving rise to a new governing structure. In 1907, a District Office headed by a District Officer was established as the governing body in the New Territories. The District Officer was renamed as District Commissioner in 1948 but retained the same authority and power.

Under British rule, police stations were established in various locations in the New Territories. By 1911, a group of 164 police officers was deployed in 17 police stations across the New Territories. These police stations, combined with the District Office, allowed the government to oversee and take direct control of the area.

From the resistance against British rule in New Territories, British officials recognized the important role of village heads and elites in supporting effective governance and directing their fellow villagers. They were ultimately recruited to become members of the rural committees across the New Territories, including three anti-British leaders Tse Heung-po（謝香圃）of Sheung Tsuen, Tang Tsing-wan（鄧青雲）of Ping Shan and Man Tsam-chuen（文湛泉）of Tai Hang. With the gradual expansion of British direct rule, traditional leaders in the New Territories became less influential as indicated in the *Report on the New Territories 1899–1912*, a government document presented to the Legislative Council in 1912.

4.5 Social Tension and Upheaval

Hong Kong was occupied by Japanese forces for three years and eight months from 25 December 1941 to 15 August 1945. In late August 1945, British colonial rule was restored amid a new era of post-war decolonisation.

In the 1950s and 1960s, Hong Kong's economy grew rapidly in the era of industrialisation and social stability. However, social tensions gradually intensified as ordinary citizens were unable to reap the benefits of economic development. The government failed to address systemic problems, such as low wages, inadequate housing supply, limited health care, little schooling for children from poor families and widespread corruption. These issues only exacerbated social tensions; a slight dispute or change in policy could easily spark negative sentiments and trigger further social unrest.

4.5.1 The Riots in Kowloon and Tsuen Wan

The first major post-war social conflict, known as the Double Ten Riots, took place in Kowloon and Tsuen Wan. On 10 October 1956, a "Double Ten" emblem and a "Blue Sky, White Sun and a Wholly Red Earth" flag were raised outside Block G of Lei Cheng Uk Resettlement Area in Kowloon. They were removed by the management office in compliance with Urban Council regulations. The incident precipitated a riot by pro-Kuomintang (Chinese Nationalist Party) activists. The rioters threw stones at the riot police, burned cars, ransacked Chinese department stores, destroyed a Garden bakery factory, and looted and burned down Heung To Middle School, a pro-left establishment. Riots also took place in the industrial town of Tsuen Wan where assaults on local factories, leftist unions and homes caused many deaths and injuries. It included the death of four leftist workers following the brawls at the Federation of Trade Unions Medical Clinic, Hong Kong & Kowloon Spinning, Weaving & Dyeing Trade Workers Union Club, and HK & Kowloon Silk Workers Union Club.

When the police force was unable to control the riots for lack of proper training, British troops were deployed by the Hong Kong government. The three-day riots resulted in 59 deaths—15 were killed by rioters and 44 were shot by the military or police. Of the 6,000 people arrested, 1,241 people were convicted.

These riots were deemed politically motivated as pro-Kuomintang unions and associated triad groups took part in provoking the protests. A government report later found that post-war refugees in Hong Kong had difficulty making a living and were discontented with their conditions. These social challenges, combined with the political frustration and economic hardship amongst the pro-KMT groups, were the root causes of the riots.

4.5.2 The Star Ferry Fare Hike

In the 1960s, economic inflation caused the price of everyday necessities in Hong Kong to soar considerably. In 1965, public confidence in the Hong Kong economy was rocked by an economic slowdown, a bank run and a sluggish property market. On 01 October, the Star Ferry company applied to the government for a fare increase as a result of rising wages and operating costs. The public was deeply concerned about the spiral effect of the proposed fare increases.

In April 1966, a young man named So Sau-chung（蘇守忠）went on a two-day hunger strike outside the Star Ferry Terminal on Hong Kong Island in protest of the fare increases. Following his arrest by the police, young supporters presented a petition at the Government House and staged a rally in Kowloon chanting "we oppose fare hikes." The demonstration quickly turned into a riot; demonstrators threw rocks, bricks and empty bottles at police officers and police cars and vandalized buses with bamboo poles. Bus stop signs, police traffic posts and other vehicles were set on fire. The government imposed a curfew in Kowloon and New Kowloon (north of Boundary Street and south of the mountain ranges of Lion Rock, Beacon Hill, Tate's Cairn and Kowloon Peak). During the four-day riot, 10 police officers were injured, including seven hit with stones from the rioters. One civilian died of a gunshot to the chest; eight were hospitalised for gunshot wounds or other injuries. Some 905 people were arrested, 323 of whom were sentenced to imprisonment.

Following the incident, a Commission of Inquiry was set up by the government to identify the cause. The report concluded that most protesters were driven by economic hardship and were bitter over the wealth disparity in Hong Kong. Most protesters also felt strongly resentful over British colonial rule and the lack of respect for Chinese people among officials, as well as government bureaucracy. The report recommended that the government should promote better public communication and engagement.

4.5.3 The 1967 Riots

In 1967, given the persistent social conflict against the backdrop of the Cultural Revolution in the Mainland, Hong Kong endured its longest and largest social unrest in the post-war colonial period. It was generally known as the 1967 Hong Kong Riots and sometimes also called the Anti-British Colonial Rule movement by the leftists.

In April 1967, a labour dispute broke out at an artificial flower factory in San Po Kong. In early May, upon police intervention, workers were injured while some were arrested in what was a prelude to the 1967 Hong Kong riots. Starting 19 May 1967, thousands of leftists demonstrated outside the Government House; hundreds of protest banners were placed on the gates and walls at the premise. In June, labour unions launched a strike. In mid-July, the leftists began planting bombs and decoys across the city, while the Hong Kong police squads and British soldiers scrambled to remove them. Public fear was widespread, and there were calls to restore order. The riots ended in December after the last bomb was found and removed on Christmas Day.

The 1967 riots were an extremely volatile time in Hong Kong, causing 51 deaths and 832 injuries. Between 11 May 1967 and 01 June 1968, a total of 4,498 people were arrested and tried; 2,077 were convicted.

At the time, many leftist groups believed in fighting colonial rule and resisting heavily armed police. The public, however, largely disagreed and resented their tactics, leaving the leftists with a tainted reputation for a long time afterwards. The Hong Kong government seized the opportunity to strengthen its publicity campaign for greater public support.

4.6 Transformation of Government Relations in the Community

The public outcry stemming from the Star Ferry fare hike and riots in 1967 led to the realisation amongst government officials that young people had a mindset vastly different from that of the previous generation. It also revealed that the traditional model of governance was no longer effective. The Hong Kong government came to understand the importance of improved relations with the community through better communication and engagement.

In office from 1971 to 1982, Sir Murray MacLehose was the longest-serving governor of Hong Kong. He had had a career in foreign affairs and diplomacy, and his appointment marked a change in the British political and diplomatic strategy regarding Hong Kong—which was now to be largely defined by the expiry of the lease on the New Territories in 1997. As he said: "My object in Hong Kong must be to ensure that conditions in Hong Kong are so superior in every way to those in China that the CPG (Central People's Government) will hesitate before facing the problems of absorption." To improve the living standards of people in Hong Kong, Governor MacLehose implemented a series of radical reforms in housing, education, health care and social welfare in Hong Kong, while promoting further development through industrialisation and urbanisation.

4.6.1 Improved Relationship between Government and Civil Society

Government initiatives for a constructive relationship with the public began under the administration of Governor Sir David Trench. In May 1968, City District Offices were set up in urban areas, resembling the District Office in the New Territories, supported by the District Officer Scheme to serve as a bridge between the government and the public. In 1969, for the first time, a summary of the *Hong Kong Yearbook* was published in Chinese to facilitate further dissemination of information on the state of government affairs.

To bridge the gap between the government and civil society and improve public relations, Governor MacLehose continued to rely on a network of non-governmental advisors, appointing unofficial members to the Legislative Council and Executive Council and officers to the Urban Council and District Offices. Platforms of consultative democracy were developed to solicit public views through the publication of green papers (discussion documents outlining proposed government policies) and through public debates. The administration of Governor MacLehose proactively reached out to the community through a series of local initiatives, including the Clean Hong Kong and Fight Violent Crime campaigns.

4.6.2 Ten-Year Housing Programme

In the early 1970s, housing shortages remained persistent. In post-war Hong Kong, hundreds of thousands of people settled in squatter huts near or on the hillside; living conditions were often appalling. Governor MacLehose proposed a Ten-year Housing Programme to provide 1.8 million people with public housing within a decade. Despite falling short of the public housing target, as many as 960,000 people were accommodated with the establishment of six new towns, 33 public housing estates, 16 subsidised estates and 11 revamped complexes under his administration.

4.6.3 Land in the New Territories and New Town Development

In the 1970s, with the Ten-Year Housing Programme and development of new towns, Hong Kong entered a phase of rapid urban development, particularly in the New Territories, where there was sufficient land to develop new towns under a government plan. To address the longstanding issue of land rights in the New Territories, a land resumption and compensation agreement was made between the MacLehose administration and indigenous inhabitants. The government agreed to implement a New Territories Small House Policy, which granted male villagers of proven indigenous descent the right to build one "small house" without paying government premium, thereby resolving a half-a-century-old dispute concerning the transfer of land rights in the New Territories.

4.6.4 Independent Commission Against Corruption (ICAC)

Widespread corruption was one of the most serious social issues in Hong Kong. In 1973, Police Chief Superintendent Peter Fitzroy Godber, who was under investigation for corruption, fled to Taiwan. It led to massive outrage and two public demonstrations, calling on the government to "fight corruption and arrest Godber." Governor MacLehose understood that it was essential to establish an independent and effective anti-corruption agency. On February 1974, the Independent Commission Against Corruption (ICAC) was founded. The ICAC was one of the most significant developments in the post-war era and had a far-reaching impact on Hong Kong's system and culture of anti-corruption.

4.6.5 Labour Rights and Social Welfare Policy

A social safety net and protective labour standards were virtually non-existent in Hong Kong. As late as the 1950s and 1960s, labour rights were uncommon—other than the occasional public holiday, it was common to work all year round. Working conditions were generally appalling and industrial safety regulations were missing.

The Employment Ordinance 1968 fell short on worker protection and labour rights in its original form. It was further amended to provide workers with rest days, paid annual leave, statutory holidays, paid sick leave, maternity benefits, and protection against anti-union discrimination. The Labour Tribunal, established in 1973, supported workers in recovering outstanding wages and settling disputes with employers.

Prior to 1971, Hong Kong lacked a comprehensive social welfare policy; programmes provided by the government merely involved temporary shelter and short-term food assistance. To a large degree, people in need relied on assistance provided by charitable, non-governmental organisations. The Public Assistance Scheme in 1971 marked the beginning of social assistance in the form of cash payments, subject to the fluctuation of consumer prices. The Disability and Infirmity Allowance Scheme was introduced in 1973 to give the disabled and disadvantaged some financial help. The Criminal and Law Enforcement Injuries Compensation Scheme, also introduced in 1973, aimed to compensate victims of violent crimes as well as law enforcement officers injured on duty.

4.6.6 Nine Years of Free and Compulsory Education

The shortage of school places, coupled with low enrolment rates among school-age children, was a long-standing issue, exacerbated by the post-war population boom and prevalence of child labour at the time. Following the introduction of six years of free education in 1971, Governor MacLehose pushed to extend universal education by including junior secondary schools in the mandatory scheme. In 1978, with the introduction of nine years of compulsory education, all primary school graduates were provided three years of junior high school curriculum free of charge in a public or subsidised school. In 1980, compulsory education was extended to minors under the age of 15 who had not completed junior secondary education.

Hong Kong experienced its most significant transformation in the era of British colonial rule during the 11-year administration of Governor Murray MacLehose. The transformation came largely from the rise of decolonisation and progressivism in the post-war period. After the 1967 riots in Hong Kong, social activism continued to spread with campaigns to make Chinese an official government language, assert Chinese sovereignty on the Diaoyu Islands, and fight widespread corruption through protest such as the Golden Jubilee Secondary School incident. In a wave of social reform, MacLehose strengthened community relations and gained public support by improving the living standards of people and fighting corruption. Under his administration, Hong Kong industrialised and urbanised at a much faster rate than the Mainland; it led to a Hong Kong with distinct characteristics.

5 Hong Kong's Unique Position in Modern Chinese History

Hong Kong, a Chinese territory once under foreign colonial rule, is a place where Chinese and foreign cultures collide and intermingle. Under the unique political circumstances, combined with its geographic location and sense of patriotism towards the Mainland, Hong Kong has played an important role in the development of modern China. Hong Kong was at the forefront of Chinese contemporary history through its involvement in a series of historic events, including the Hundred Days' Reform, 1911 Revolution, Labour Movement, War of Resistance against Japanese Aggression and the decades of national reform and opening-up.

5.1 Hong Kong and the Hundred Days' Reform

Hong Kong was home to several key figures of the Hundred Days' Reform, including Hong Rengan (Hung Jen-kan) (洪仁玕), Wang Tao (王韜), Ho Kai (何啟) and Woo Lai-woon (胡禮垣). Hong Rengan, a clan brother of the Taiping leader Hong Xiuquan (洪秀全), was a missionary and counsellor of the London Missionary Society and lived in Hong Kong for more than four years. In 1859, Hong Rengan left Hong Kong for Tianjing (capital of the Taipings in Nanjing), where he was granted the title Prince Gan by Hong Xiuquan for whom he outlined a capitalist-leaning policy agenda in a document titled *New Theory for Assisting the Management of State Affairs*. On politics, he emphasised the rule of law and the importance of public sentiment. For the economy, he proposed a focus on the manufacturing of trains, ships and various equipment while further expanding the mining, banking and postal sectors. In doing so, he stressed that "the wealthy should hire workers, rather than buy slave labour." For diplomacy, he believed that China should pursue trade relations with other nations on equal grounds. These ideas were influenced by his life experiences, especially from the time he spent in Hong Kong. Although unrealised, his ideas of saving the nation and its people through the adoption of Western learning were inspirational for the thinkers after the Opium War.

Wang Tao (王韜), a scholar from Suzhou who had lived in Hong Kong for nearly 20 years and had visited the West, including Britain and France, was a strong proponent of the self-strengthening movement. He founded the newspaper *Universal Circulating Herald* and published numerous articles in support of the Hundred Days' Reform. He pushed for reform regarding China's civil service, military training, education and law; he advocated for growing China's industrial and commercial capabilities with respect to mining iron, coal, metals and other minerals, developing machinery and textile industries, building railways and establishing private companies to develop a shipping industry, in addition to abolishing internal tariff known as *likin*. A proponent of constitutional monarchy, Wang Tao was widely read in newspapers and was able to exert much greater influence than Hong Rengan (Hung Jen-kan)(洪仁玕).

Ho Kai (何啟) and Woo Lai-woon (胡禮垣) were outstanding intellectuals educated in Western-style schools in Hong Kong. They co-authored a series of political works, including *Review of Zeng Jize's Article*, *Discourse on the New Government*, *Foundations of the New Government*, *Review of Kang Youwei's Speech*, *Practice of the New Government*, *Review of the Exhortation to learning* and *Accommodations of the New Government*. These were published in daily newspapers and books before they were released as an advocacy series on politics, ideology, economy and culture, collectively known as the *True Interpretation of the New Policies*.

Ho Kai (何 啟) and Woo Lai-woon (胡 禮 垣) proposed that officials be appointed based on their level of support with the Hundred Days' Reform and suggested that officials be paid a higher salary so as to mitigate bribery. They called for a change in political structure with the establishment of an electoral and parliamentary system, stressing the importance of civil rights in saving the country. They pressed for economic reform with the construction of a rail system across China's provinces, prefectures, municipalities and counties and the acquisition of large ships through commercial partnerships to support greater business activities. They pushed for cultural education with a focus on nurturing talent in schools and promoting public discourse through newspapers. These policy proposals were meant to strengthen China and guard against the risk of invasion by foreign powers.

The political writings of Ho Kai (何啟) and Woo Lai-woon (胡禮垣) were an attempt by patriotic intellectuals in Hong Kong to tackle the problems of Chinese society with Western political and economic ideas. They were leading thinkers of the time and had a large impact on future reformers such as Kang Youwei (康有為) and his disciples, who devoured every idea presented in these writings. Likewise, while studying at the Hong Kong College of Medicine, Sun Yat-sen (孫 中 山) was a student of Ho Kai and was inspired by his enlightening thoughts.

5.2 Hong Kong and the 1911 Revolution

Hong Kong was the birthplace of Sun Yat-sen's（孫中山）revolutionary ideas. His comrades converged here to form various groups, solicit funding, promote a revolutionary agenda and plan for an armed rebellion.

Sun Yat-sen（孫中山）studied in Hong Kong, including two years of secondary school and five years of tertiary education. As he recalled, "after a year of medical training in Guangzhou, I chose to complete my studies in Hong Kong given a new school with an English curriculum and more freedom to promote a revolution." The new school mentioned was the Hong Kong College of Medicine. On 20 February 1923, in his speech at The University of Hong Kong, Sun Yat-sen reiterated that his political philosophy had indeed originated in Hong Kong.

Many of Sun Yat-sen's organisations were founded in Hong Kong which served as the base of the revolutionary movement. On 21 February 1895, Sun Yat-sen（孫中山）, in association with Yeung Ku-wan（楊衢雲）and Tse Tsan-tai（謝纘泰）of the Furen Literary Society, established the Revive China Society with its headquarters at 13 Staunton Street in Central, Hong Kong. In August 1905, Sun Yat-sen and others founded the Chinese United League in Tokyo; in October, he formed a branch of the Chinese United League at the newspaper bureau of *China Daily* in Hong Kong. In 1909, as momentum continued, Sun Yat-sen set up a southern branch of the Chinese United League on Wong Nai Chung Road in Hong Kong.

Based in Hong Kong, Sun Yat-sen（孫中山）and his comrades had launched several armed uprisings to overthrow the autocratic rule of the Qing Dynasty. Over a period of 16 years—from the founding of the Revive China Society in Hong Kong in 1895 to the Wuchang Uprising in 1911—six of the 10 uprisings were initiated in Hong Kong under Sun Yat-sen. Among these were the First Guangzhou Uprising, Huizhou Uprising, Huanggang Uprising, Qinühu Uprising, Guangzhou Xinjun Uprising, and Second Guangzhou Uprising. The Hong Quanfu Uprising in Guangzhou was launched in Hong Kong by Tse Tsan-tai（謝纘泰）, a member of the Revive China Society. In the seven uprisings, Hong Kong was a command post during the planning, financing and execution stages, an intermediary for arms procurement and production, and a centre for recruitment, liaison and refuge with revolutionaries locally and abroad. Although the uprisings were largely unsuccessful, they created a sense of awakening among the Chinese people inspired by the undaunted heroism and sacrifice of the revolutionaries in Hong Kong.

Hong Kong was a place of major publicity campaigns in support of the 1911 Revolution. On 25 January 1900, *China Daily* (Hong Kong edition) was founded as the first official newspaper of the revolutionaries who disseminated their ideas through articles such as "The True Solution of the Chinese Question" in which Sun Yat-sen（孫中山）, in 1904, described the failures of the Qing government. *China Daily* (Hong Kong edition) was a platform for political debates and often refuted fallacies laid upon the revolution while providing detailed coverage on the armed uprisings. The newspaper was a propaganda machine of the Revive China Society, Chinese United League and Kuomintang in the early days.

Hong Kong also played a pivotal role in financing the revolutionary agenda through fundraisers and transfer of funds. The revolutionaries were generously supported by Hong Kong businessmen, such as Wong Wing-sheung（黃詠商）, Yu Yuk-chi（余育之）, Li Ki-tong（李紀堂）and Li Yuk-tong（李煜堂）, and some donors even fell into financial hardship. Li Ki-tong was particularly notable for his unparalleled financial support.

Among the early supporters of the 1911 Revolution was Ip Ting-sz（葉定仕）, a Hakka farmer in Lin Ma Hang Village and an indigenous resident of the New Territories. He was known for making substantial contribution to the cause. Following his relocation to Thailand, he became a leader of Chinese overseas and served as President of the Siamese Branch of Chinese United League; he also donated much of his personal assets to support the armed uprisings.

5.3 The Seamen's Strike and the Canton—Hong Kong Strike

A greater sense of Chinese national identity and cultural pride emerged following the May Fourth Movement. The Hong Kong Seamen's Strike and Canton–Hong Kong Strike both erupted against the backdrop of growing cultural identity.

5.3.1 The Seamen's Strike of 1922

Seamen were some of the earliest industrial workers of Hong Kong. For many years, exploited by foreign shipowners, they had been contractors working a heavy workload for a meagre salary.

In March 1921, a mutual aid group for seamen in Hong Kong known as the Chinese Seamen's Charitable Association was reorganised into a modern labour union; it was renamed Chinese Seamen's Union by Sun Yat-sen (孫 中 山). Upon establishment, it tried to seek higher wages on behalf of seamen in three consecutive negotiations with shipowners but to no avail. Endorsed by a large majority of Hong Kong-based seamen, a labour strike was staged on 13 January 1922, and seamen on strike were arranged to return to Guangzhou. The Hong Kong government subsequently declared the union an illegal group, launched a crackdown with the use of police force and attempted to seize the union's signboard.

The public was angered by the government's handling of the seamen's strike, while an increasing number of workers from other industries joined the strike, reaching 120,000 by the end of February. On 03 March, police were dispatched to suppress the workers on strike, including those who decided to return to Guangzhou on foot; shots were fired at workers in Shatin by the police, killing five and injuring seven in what became known as the Shatin Massacre. The massacre only exacerbated public resistance and sparked further protests, bringing the local economy to a standstill.

On 05 March, following the mediation by the Guangzhou government, an agreement was reached between the Chinese Seamen's Union and the Hong Kong government. The Hong Kong government endorsed a 15%–30% wage increase proposed by the Seamen's Union, followed by a communiqué renouncing the order of outlawing the Seamen's Union and the return of its signboard. The 52-day Seamen's Strike was a victory for the workers.

5.3.2 The Canton—Hong Kong Strike

A nationwide anti-imperialist movement erupted after the killing of 13 labour demonstrators in Shanghai on 30 May 1925. As public outcry ensued in Hong Kong, a labour strike in protest was urged by the All-China Federation of Trade Unions following a joint meeting with other trade unions. A large-scale strike began on the evening of 19 June with seamen, tram workers and printing press workers, quickly followed by workers of other trades. The workers on strike took to the plan of action with the Seamen's Strike and began departing for Guangzhou by train and ship.

On 23 June, workers on strike were joined by the public of Guangdong in a mass protest in Guangzhou, totalling 100,000 people. As protesters marched near Shaji (also known as Shakee), British and French sailors stationed in the foreign concession area of Shamian on the opposite bank opened fire with machine guns, killing 52 people instantly and seriously injuring more than 170 people. The Shaji Massacre provoked further public anger and sparked more labour strikes by some 250,000 workers in Hong Kong.

The Canton–Hong Kong Strike Committee was established in Guangzhou by the All-China Federation of Trade Unions to command labour strikes in Guangdong and Hong Kong for greater effect and impose an economic blockade on Hong Kong. A picket line of more than 2,000 workers was formed to maintain order, stop traffic between Hong Kong and Shamian, and guard against smugglers. As a result of the massive strike, combined with an economic blockade, Hong Kong suffered from a severe socioeconomic decline and a drastic drop in trade with the Mainland. Hong Kong's exports to the Mainland accounted for 24% of China's total imports in 1924 and dropped to 18.6% in 1925 and 11.1% in 1926. The Hong Kong government had to borrow £3 million from the British government amid a fiscal deficit of more than HK$5 million in 1925. The economic life of Hong Kong came to a halt while streets were buried under piles of garbage; public transport ceased to operate while soaring food prices resulted from a short supply.

In July 1926, as a military campaign to reunify China was launched by the National Revolutionary Army, many workers on strike in Guangdong and Hong Kong joined the forces in support of the Northern Expedition. To minimise any burden on the military campaign, with support from the Canton–Hong Kong Strike Committee, negotiations aiming to resolve the strike were held between the Chinese Nationalist government and the Hong Kong government. The Canton–Hong Kong Strike Committee also decided to lift the blockade and end the strike in September 1926, followed by an official announcement on 10 October that picket lines blocking access to the seaports were to withdraw effective noon.

The Canton-Hong Kong Strike was unprecedented in the history of labour movement in China, lasting for 16 months between June 1925 and October 1926. It was part of China's nationalist movement of the 1920s; it reflected China's resistance after facing more than half a century of foreign aggression, oppression and exploitation. The support of more than 200,000 people in the labour strike was a testament to a strong identity with the Chinese nation among the people of Hong Kong. The strike was a contributing factor supporting the Northern Expedition and China's recovery of the British-occupied territory in Hankow. The Canton-Hong Kong Strike, above all, highlighted the close political and economic relationship between Guangdong and Hong Kong.

5.4 Hong Kong and War of Resistance against Japanese Aggression

During the War of Resistance against Japanese Aggression, Hong Kong was an important hub of supplies and served as a centre of the Anti-Japanese National Salvation Movement. The Hong Kong–Kowloon Brigade, comprising anti-Japanese guerrillas led by the Communist Party of China, supported allied forces in the fight against the Japanese army in Japanese-occupied Hong Kong.

5.4.1 A Channel for Transport of War Supplies

Chinese resistance against the Japanese invasion began in July 1937. In late August, the Japanese army started taking the coastal areas of China—from the island of Qinhuangdao in the north to the boundary of French Indochina in the south. As such, Hong Kong became a vital channel of war supplies for the Chinese government. According to statistics, 130,000 tonnes of supplies—including bombs, aircraft and aircraft parts, machine guns, detonators, dynamites, anti-aircraft guns, torpedoes, search lights and gas masks—were transported by the Kowloon-Canton Railway between February and October 1938. The military supplies made their way from Hong Kong to the central, southwestern as well as the coastal regions of China, giving Chinese forces some relief in the war effort.

5.4.2 China Defence League and Office of the Eighth Route Army

The China Defence League (CDL), founded by Soong Ching-ling (Song Qingling) (宋 慶 齡) on 14 June 1938 in Hong Kong, aimed to recruit international supporters and Chinese overseas in assisting China against Japanese aggression.

The China Defence League, by making use of Hong Kong's global connections, appealed for international support with news about the calamity of war in China through the *China Defence League Newsletter*. Particularly, it enabled China's Eighth Route Army and New Fourth Army with substantial funding and supplies. In the first year, it raised HK$250,000 and obtained donations of goods, including clothes, daily essentials, medical equipment, medicine and canned food, from international supporters and Chinese overseas. Fundraisers in the form of film screenings, theatrical and musical performances were also held to rally public support in Hong Kong for China's war efforts. Relief supplies were shipped to many places across China, including the wartime capital of Chongqing, remote areas in Yan'an and as far as the International Peace Hospital in Wutaishan of northeastern Shanxi.

In January 1938, a branch office of the Eighth Route Army under the command of Liao Chengzhi (廖承志) and Pan Hannian (潘漢年) was established in Hong Kong. The primary objective was to support China's Eighth Route Army and New Fourth Army by fundraising and seeking donation of supplies. In October 1939, a large quantity of Western medicines donated by Chinese in Latin America, as well as 20 trucks and two cars donated by Chinese in Southeast Asia made their way to Hong Kong and were transferred to the Eighth Route Army in Guilin. The Hong Kong office also facilitated the return of Chinese overseas to China where they could join the war effort.

5.4.3 Hong Kong in Support of China's War Efforts

The people of Hong Kong had been highly supportive of China's War of Resistance since the early stage. After the Marco Polo Bridge Incident on 07 July 1937, dozens of social groups were founded in Hong Kong to provide China with monetary assistance by means of fundraising. The Hong Kong Students Relief Association raised more than HK$20,000 from September 1937 to May 1938 through sales of flowers and other charity bazaars, benefit concerts and shows, as well as hunger strikes. The donation drive on 13 August 1938 began with hawkers in Sham Shui Po and rapidly gained momentum in raising over a million dollars. In October 1938, funding earmarked for a celebration of the National Day was donated to purchase 360,000 pieces of winter clothing by 76 business groups as part of the war efforts in Hong Kong. Likewise, other groups, including the academic community, supported China by providing winter clothes and gas masks with money raised throvgh flag days. In late 1938, ambulatory vehicles and supplies were purchased with a donation of HK$4,000 and delivered to the Eighth Route Army in Guilin by members of the Hong Kong–Kowloon–New Territories Drivers Union. In May 1941, people of Hong Kong bought more than HK$4.1 million worth of war bonds as Huang Yanpei (黃炎培), Secretary of China's War Bond Committee, made an appeal for public support in person.

5.4.4 Japanese Occupation of Hong Kong and a Secret Rescue Operation

By June 1940, Japanese troops had taken control of southern China. The Chiefs of Staff Committee of Great Britain believed Hong Kong was not a vital interest and was undefendable. As the British government contemplated a complete withdrawal, Hong Kong was in jeopardy.

On 07 December 1941, war broke out in the Pacific while Japanese troops marched across the Shenzhen River into the New Territories in the morning of 08 December (Hong Kong time). In the fierce fighting on Hong Kong Island, Japanese commander Wakamatsu was seriously injured while Canadian Brigadier John Kelburne Lawson was killed in action. After 18 days of battle, British troops were defeated following the overwhelming attacks on land, at sea and in the air by Japanese forces. On 25 December, hours before Governor Sir Mark Young surrendered, Japanese troops invaded the field hospital at St. Stephen's College in Stanley, killing 70 unarmed and wounded British soldiers and raping and mutilating many of the nurses in what became known as the St. Stephen's College Massacre.

As Hong Kong was quickly overrun by the Imperial Japanese army, outspoken local intellectuals in opposition to the Japanese aggression fell into grave danger. Under the instruction of Chinese leader Zhou Enlai (周恩來) and the Secretariat of the Chinese Communist Party's Central Committee, a large-scale covert rescue operation was devised by the local Chinese communist groups and East River (Dongjiang) guerrillas in early 1942. The intellectuals were smuggled out of the strictly Japanese-occupied areas into safe zones controlled by the guerrillas. More than 800 people, mostly freedom fighters, cultural figures and intellectuals along with their families, were saved. These individuals included He Xiangning (何香凝), Liu Yazi (柳亞子), Liang Shuming (梁漱溟), Zou Taofen (鄒韜奮), Mao Dun (茅盾), Hu Sheng (胡繩), Qian Jiaju (千家駒), Li Shu (黎澍), Fan Changjiang (范長江), Qiao Guanhua (喬冠華), Xia Yan (夏衍) and Hu Feng (胡風). Among those who managed to escape from Hong Kong included members of the Kuomintang, British officers and soldiers, and other foreign nationals.

5.4.5 Three Years and Eight Months of Hardship

Hong Kong was plundered by the Japanese troops upon their capture of the city. The Japanese occupation government forcibly took over Hong Kong's shipyards, key companies, factories and mines. Chinese-owned factories labelled as "enemy facilities" were disbanded and confiscated, including Chiap Hua Steelworks with assets totalling HK$7 million and Sam Sam Weaving Factory, a branch of Sam Hsing Weaving Factory and a government contractor of military supplies, with assets of more than HK$2 million.

The military yen issued by the Japanese government without a currency peg was forced upon the local population of Hong Kong at an arbitrary exchange rate. It was one Hong Kong dollar for one Japanese military yen at the time when Japanese troops occupied Guangzhou. After the fall of Hong Kong, a huge amount of Japanese yen was shipped from Guangzhou; it became two Hong Kong dollars for one military yen; by July 1942, it was four for one. Nearly $2 billion in Japanese military notes were issued as Hong Kong was being stripped of its wealth.

Amid a severe shortage of food and supplies, a repatriation policy was implemented by the Japanese troops in an attempt to downsize the local population from over 1.6 million to about 500,000 by sending them back to China. The drive to discharge a large part of the population began with incentives but largely turned into a forced expulsion. Most were deported under coercion and violence, while many of the old, weak, sick and disabled died as they were drowned, killed or left on deserted islands in the hands of the Japanese soldiers. Repatriation was essentially a death sentence.

Many in Hong Kong died from torture and abuse inflicted by the military police arm of the Imperial Japanese Army known as Kenpeitai. Methods of torture included burning, electrocution, feet crushing, hanging, kneeling, whipping and decapitation. Violence and torture on ordinary citizens continued to take place even after Japan's unconditional surrender on 15 August 1945. On 19 August, while searching for guerrillas at Chung Hau in Silver Mine Bay on Lantau Island, Japanese troops arrested 300 people, including the village leader and his fellow villagers; 11 people were killed, many were wounded, and houses were burned down in what became known as the Silver Mine Bay Massacre.

5.4.6 Anti-Japanese Militia in Hong Kong

Although Hong Kong was not deemed a frontline by the Chinese national government in the fight against the Imperial Japanese Army, it remained a place of strategic importance and military intelligence for which Chinese agents were dispatched; 33 of them were executed upon capture by the Japanese troops.

In February 1942, the Hong Kong–Kowloon Brigade was formed in Wong Mo Ying Village, Sai Kung, New Territories. Choi Kwok-leung (蔡國樑), formerly a worker in the factory of Hong Kong Amoy Canning, was brigade commander; Chan Tat-ming (陳達明), a young intellectual, was political commissar. Led by the Chinese Communist Party, the brigade consisted mainly of local farmers, fishermen, workers and young intellectuals, and was nearly 1,000-strong as the only established local armed group throughout the Japanese occupation of Hong Kong.

The Hong Kong–Kowloon Brigade launched attacks on Japanese troops and adversaries with guerrilla tactics. More than 100 Japanese soldiers and over 70 traitors, "puppet" policemen and enemy spies were killed or wounded; more than 600 Japanese "puppet" soldiers were captured; four Japanese vessels were sunk; one Japanese aircraft was destroyed; more than 550 rifles and pistols, 60 machine guns, six cannons, 40 vehicles and vessels and a large amount of ammunition were seized. The guerrillas also took part in the rescue of allied pilots and provided allied forces with timely intelligence. During the Japanese occupation, 115 members of the Hong Kong–Kowloon Brigade sacrificed their lives in defence of Hong Kong.

6 From "Long-Term View" to "One Country, Two Systems"

The Chinese Communist Party's policy and guiding principles towards Hong Kong were shaped by many years of experience. Party leaders Zhou Enlai（周恩來）and Deng Xiaoping（鄧小平）visited Hong Kong in their early years, taking advantage of its special status to carry out revolutionary work. The party's top leader Mao Zedong（毛澤東）began making plans for the future of Hong Kong during the Chinese Civil War. After the founding of the People's Republic of China, Mao Zedong and Zhou Enlai summarized their policy as "taking a long-term view and making full use of Hong Kong" to ensure its political stability and economic prosperity.

In the 1980s, Deng Xiaoping（鄧小平）put forward the concept of "One Country, Two Systems" in dealing with the question regarding Hong Kong, forming a policy basis leading to the Sino-British Joint Declaration. It was also proposed that the system of governance be defined in the Basic Law and ratified by the National People's Congress (NPC) with the establishment of the Hong Kong Special Administrative Region.

6.1 Chinese Communist Party's Strategies and Measures on Hong Kong

The British occupation of Hong Kong was a legacy of the unequal treaties between Britain and the Qing government. After the fall of the Qing Dynasty, demands for returning the New Territories were successively made by the Beiyang government and the national government of the Republic of China but were largely ignored by the British government.

The Chinese Communist Party took a long-term strategic approach to the issue of Hong Kong. On 09 December 1946, in his reply to an American journalist regarding Hong Kong, Mao Zedong（毛澤東）said, "We won't seek the return of Hong Kong immediately. China is a big place where many regions are not well managed yet. Why should we rush to retrieve such a small territory? We can solve the problem through future negotiations." In February 1949, when meeting with a USSR delegation in Xibaipo, Mao Zedong commented, "It doesn't make much sense to focus on the return of Hong Kong and Macao. On the contrary, it is more beneficial for China to foster diplomatic relationships and expand international trade by leveraging these places, especially Hong Kong."

When the People's Liberation Army arrived in Guangdong in October 1949, troops were forbidden by the Chinese government from crossing the boundary line of Zhangmutou about 40 kilometres north of Lo Wu; instead, security forces were deployed to preserve order along the border. To avoid causing social unrest in Hong Kong, political and military authorities in southern China and Guangdong took a prudent approach to the border issues with the objectives of "maintaining a peaceful border," "avoiding border disputes," and "staying away from provocation while holding ground." The People's Republic of China had a clear stance that Hong Kong has always been a part of China. It did not accept the three unequal treaties imposed by the imperialist powers; it favoured addressing the issue through negotiation and maintaining the status quo until then. The interim policy of "taking a long-term view and making full use of Hong Kong" was hence adopted.

Tensions between the communist and capitalist blocs escalated at the outbreak of the Korean War in the early 1950s. As the United States imposed an economic blockade on China, Hong Kong under British administration was at the forefront of US sanctions. The Chinese government's policy towards Hong Kong, however, remained unchanged.

On 28 April 1957, speaking at a business seminar in Shanghai, Premier Zhou Enlai（周恩來）elaborated on "leveraging" Hong Kong for economic development: "We will regain sovereignty over Hong Kong as Britain may also realise…Chinese policy on Hong Kong must be different from that on the Mainland. Applying the same policy will not work well because Hong Kong is a capitalist market under British rule. It could not and should not become socialist. Hong Kong could only exist and develop under a capitalist system. It is an arrangement beneficial to us…Our enterprises in Hong Kong should adapt to the local environment so that we could make Hong Kong work for us…Hong Kong could be our economic bridge with other countries for foreign investment and foreign exchange reserves."

The trade exhibition in Canton, supply of fresh water from the East River (Dongjiang) and triple daily freight express trains were some of the schemes implemented by the Chinese government conducive to Hong Kong's economic development. These reflected a mutually beneficial relationship between Hong Kong and the Mainland. From October 1955 to May 1956, three product exhibitions were held in Guangdong Province, promoting Chinese foreign trade and export industries in close proximity to Hong Kong. The China Import & Export Fair, also known as the Canton Fair, hosted by the Ministry of Commerce of China in association with the provincial government of Guangdong, has been held in the spring and autumn each year since 1957.

For a lack of sustainable fresh water supply, water crises were a repeated occurrence in Hong Kong. It was particularly problematic in the post-war period as Hong Kong's population and economy grew rapidly. A severe shortage took place in 1963 and was the worst drought in 60 years when Hong Kong's water reserve dropped to a level enough for only 43 days. On 01 June, a water rationing system was put in place by the Hong Kong government, supplying water only once every four days for four hours. The measure of limited water supply lasted a full year and became a norm of daily life in Hong Kong.

The Chinese General Chamber of Commerce and Hong Kong Federation of Trade Unions had repeatedly tried to address the issue of water shortage with the provincial government of Guangdong. The British government had also approached the Central People's Government through diplomacy with a request for water supply from the East River (Dongjiang). As a result, Premier Zhou Enlai (周恩來) ordered the launch of the East River-Shenzhen Water Supply Project to supply Hong Kong with freshwater at a cost of RMB10 cents per tonne. The British government was reassured by the pragmatism of the Chinese government with a solution to the water crisis. Governor Sir Robert Black in one of his regular reports to the British government earnestly commended the Chinese government for de-politicizing and resolving an urgent issue in a joint effort.

When construction first began under the East River-Shenzhen Water Supply Project in 1964, despite economic hardship, China remained keen to proceed with the project and allocated RMB 38 million of foreign aid funding to ensure successful completion. The first phase was completed on 27 February 1965; in the same year Hong Kong was supplied with 68.2 million cubic metres (m^3) of water, roughly a third of Hong Kong's annual water consumption at the time. To meet increasing demand, the East River-Shenzhen Water Supply Project was expanded three times in the 1970s, 1980s and 1990s at a total cost of over RMB 2 billion. Since the mid-1960s, Hong Kong has relied mostly on the Mainland for water supply. The Mainland in 1995, for example, supplied 690 million m^3 of water, about 75% of the 919 million m^3 consumed in Hong Kong in the same year; in 1996, it supplied 720 million m^3 of water, about 78% of the 928 million m^3 consumed during the year; in 1997, it supplied 750 million m^3 of water, about 82% of the 913 million m^3 consumed in the year. In 2017, it supplied Hong Kong with 651 million m^3 of water, a considerable amount as in previous years.

In the early days, fresh food exported to Hong Kong from the Mainland took a long time to arrive. Due to a complex supply chain and the lack of designated routes, food products were often damaged during transport, causing significant losses. In 1962, arranged by China's Ministry of Railways and Ministry of Foreign Economic Relations and Trade, three daily freight-dedicated express trains (train numbers 751, 753 and 755) began service in shipping refrigerated goods from Shanghai, Zhengzhou, Wuhan/Changsha to Shenzhen where goods were transhipped to Hong Kong. They were in operation year-round except on the first day of Chinese New Year. These express trains had been running uninterrupted since operation began despite three years of hardship from natural disasters in the Mainland; they remained operational during the Cultural Revolution, the floods in southern China, the collapse of a tunnel, and the travel rush among migrant workers in each Spring Festival. Between 1962 and 1995, over 80 million live pigs, five million live cattle, 810 million live poultry, 1.35 million tonnes of frozen food, and large quantities of other commodities were transported to Hong Kong and Macao by these express trains. The low-cost, stable supply of food from the Mainland to Hong Kong, coupled with the public housing policy of the Hong Kong government, helped keep Hong Kong's inflation and labour cost below those of developed countries, boosting Hong Kong's competitiveness in the global market.

6.2 The Return of Hong Kong to China

Beginning in the 1970s, the Chinese government began taking a closer look at the issue of Hong Kong and its long-term political future. On 08 March 1972, Huang Hua (黃華), China's permanent representative to the United Nations, in a letter to the chairman of the UN Special Committee on Decolonization, stated that "The questions of Hong Kong and Macau belong to the category of questions resulting from the series of unequal treaties left over by history, treaties which the imperialists imposed on China. Hong Kong and Macau are part of Chinese territory occupied by the British and Portuguese authorities. The settlement of the questions of Hong Kong and Macau is entirely within China's sovereign right and does not at all fall under the ordinary category of colonial territories. Consequently, they should not be included in the list of colonial territories covered by the Declaration on the Granting of Independence to Colonial Countries and Peoples."

On 15 June of the same year, the United Nations Special Committee on Decolonization passed a resolution recommending to the United Nations General Assembly that Hong Kong and Macao be removed from the list of colonies. On 08 November 1972, this proposal was passed with an overwhelming majority of 99-5 votes at the 27th UN General Assembly. The resolution made legitimate China's claim over the sovereignty of Hong Kong, ruled out the possibility of either international condominium or independence with Hong Kong, and provided a foundation to address the issue of Hong Kong through international law.

6.2.1 The Concept of "One Country, Two Systems"

Since the founding of the People's Republic of China, particularly in the years of reform and opening-up, Chinese foreign relations were under rapid change amid a shifting international diplomatic landscape. With the 99-year lease of the New Territories due to expire in 1997, Hong Kong's future was an issue awaiting a resolution as first raised by the British government. In a meeting with Deng Xiaoping (鄧小平) in Beijing on 29 March 1979, Governor Murray MacLehose pointed out the legal issues in extending land leases in the New Territories beyond 1997 due to the uncertain future of Hong Kong. With only 18 years to go before 1997, it was proving problematic.

Deng Xiaoping (鄧小平) made clear that China did not support MacLehose's proposal to extend British rule in Hong Kong after June 1997. He pointed out: "We have long maintained that Hong Kong's sovereignty belongs to the People's Republic of China, but Hong Kong also has a special status. Hong Kong is a part of China; it is not up for discussion. But it can be certain that when this is resolved in 1997, we will respect the special status of Hong Kong…For a long time to come in the current and early next century, Hong Kong could remain capitalist while socialism continues in the Mainland." The concept of "One Country, Two Systems" was conceived in his remarks before the term was coined.

6.2.2 Sino-British Joint Declaration

The Chinese government, in consideration of a constructive relationship between China and Britain, as well as a stable and prosperous Hong Kong, took measures to resolve the issue of Hong Kong through diplomacy and negotiation with the British government; talks were held between September 1982 and September 1984. In the first phase of negotiation from September 1982 to June 1983, beginning with British Prime Minister Margaret Thatcher's visit to China, principles and procedures were outlined; in the second phase from July 1983 to September 1984, a series of 22 rounds of negotiation was held on substantive issues.

In September 1982, following UK Prime Minister Margaret Thatcher's meetings in Beijing with Premier of the State Council Zhao Ziyang (趙紫陽) and Chairman of the Communist Party of China (CPC) Central Advisory Commission Deng Xiaoping (鄧小平), China officially notified Britain of its decision to recover Hong Kong in 1997 and to adopt special policies after the return of Hong Kong. These included the establishment of a special administrative region administered by Hong Kong people while retaining Hong Kong's social and economic systems and its way of life. Margaret Thatcher insisted that the three unequal treaties should remain in effect, adding that if China agreed to British administration in Hong Kong after 1997, Britain would take into consideration China's claim to sovereignty.

Deng Xiaoping (鄧小平) replied: "China will take back Hong Kong in 1997. That is, China will not only take back the New Territories, but also Hong Kong Island and Kowloon...Hong Kong's prosperity will depend on the implementation of policies suitable for Hong Kong after the resumption of sovereignty. The current political and economic system of Hong Kong, and largely most of its laws, can be retained."

Despite Britain's attempt to preserve its administration in Hong Kong in exchange for recognition of Chinese sovereignty over Hong Kong after 1997, China made it clear that "it is not possible for Britain to exchange sovereignty for governance." As China insisted on Chinese sovereignty over Hong Kong where sovereignty and governance were inseparable, Britain no longer sought to retain the right to govern solely or jointly. As the issue was resolved, negotiations proceeded more smoothly and a final agreement was reached.

In the afternoon of 19 December 1984 at the West Hall of the Great Hall of the People in Beijing, a joint declaration between China and Britain on the future of Hong Kong was formally signed by Zhao Ziyang (趙紫陽) and Margaret Thatcher in the presence of Deng Xiaoping (鄧小平), Chairman of the CPC Central Advisory Commission, and Li Xiannian (李先念), President of the People's Republic of China.

In the Sino-British Joint Declaration, People's Republic of China declared to resume the exercise of sovereignty over Hong Kong with effect from 01 July 1997, while the United Kingdom declared to restore Hong Kong to the People's Republic of China. The Chinese government also declared the basic policies of China regarding Hong Kong, including the following: upholding national unity and territorial integrity and taking account of the history of Hong Kong and its realities; establishment of a Hong Kong Special Administrative Region (HKSAR) upon resuming the exercise of sovereignty over Hong Kong in accordance with the provisions of Article 31 of the Constitution of the People's Republic of China; a high degree of autonomy, except in foreign and defence affairs, under the authority of the Central People's Government, and vested with executive, legislative and independent judicial power, including that of final adjudication; maintaining Hong Kong's current social and economic systems as well as its lifestyle, in addition to the status of a free port and of a separate customs territory and of an international financial centre, etc.

6.2.3 Formulation of the Basic Law

During the Sino-British negotiation, a legal framework by the Chinese government was also underway to support the exercise of sovereignty over Hong Kong. At the Fifth Session of the Fifth National People's Congress on 04 December 1982, the Constitution of the People's Republic of China was amended with Article 31, stipulating that "the state may establish special administrative regions when necessary. The systems instituted in special administrative regions shall, in light of specific circumstances, be prescribed by laws enacted by the National People's Congress." Article 62 was also amended to include Clause 13, granting the National People's Congress the authority to "approve the establishment of provinces, autonomous regions and cities directly under central government jurisdiction." These provisions were significant in that the principle of "One Country, Two Systems" was enshrined in the Constitution and made an integral part of China's system of governance.

Upon the signing of the Sino-British Joint Declaration, groundwork concerning the return of Hong Kong under the Chinese government began immediately, in particular, with the formulation of the Basic Law of the Hong Kong Special Administrative Region of the People's Republic of China.

The Basic Law Drafting Committee was formed on 01 July 1985, comprising 59 members (36 from the Mainland and 23 from Hong Kong). In the spirit of democracy and openness, members were engaged in frank discussion during the plenary and special group meetings where controversial issues were resolved through debate and compromise. Objections could be raised by individual members and tabled for a resolution in committee plenary meetings. The first and second drafts in full, upon approval from the National People's Congress Standing Committee, were published in newspapers for public consultation and suggestion. Each provision and annex in the draft, as well as the design of HKSAR's flag and emblem, were adopted by a two-thirds majority in a secret ballot with all committee members. In the end, more than 100 amendments, including over 80 substantive revisions, were made to the initial draft by the committee members.

The Hong Kong Basic Law Consultative Committee, headed by local community and business leaders, was a key channel to express public views on the drafts with the Basic Law through meetings and forums. Suggestions from the public were submitted for consideration of the Drafting Committee; many were adopted in the Basic Law. For a greater understanding in the Mainland regarding Hong Kong and the concept of "One Country, Two Systems," officials of the Hong Kong and Macao Affairs Office under the direction of the Central People's Government went on a nationwide tour to spell out China's policy on Hong Kong and cultivate support from local governments. The Chinese government also made it clear on multiple occasions that the British government was welcome to share its perspective on the Basic Law, even though it was part of China's internal affairs.

In February 1990, after four years and eight months of efforts, the final draft of the Basic Law was completed by the Drafting Committee; the design of HKSAR's flag and emblem had also taken shape with input from the public. On 4 April 1990, HKSAR's Basic Law and three annexes—(1) Method for the Selection of the Chief Executive of the HKSAR, (2) Method for the Formation of the Legislative Council of the HKSAR and Its Voting Procedures, and (3) National Laws to be Applied in the HKSAR—as well HKSAR's flag and emblem among other items—were ratified at the Third Session of the Seventh National People's Congress.

The principle of "One Country, Two Systems" was officially authorised and institutionalised in the Basic Law, providing a legal framework in the HKSAR as a national law adopted by the National People's Congress in accordance with the Chinese Constitution. The Basic Law, along with the Chinese Constitution, has formed the constitutional basis of the HKSAR.

6.2.4 Pre-1997 Talks between China and Britain

From late 1984 to early 1989, China and Britain maintained a cooperative relationship based on the Sino-British Joint Declaration. The June Fourth Incident of 1989 in the Mainland detrimentally affected both the Sino-British relationship and the settlement of the Hong Kong issue. The people of Hong Kong became more critical of Chinese rule as they were concerned about the future of Hong Kong. Amid Western sanctions on China, Britain was increasingly unaccommodating on the issue of Hong Kong. Subsequently, four legislative proposals were put forward: (1) OMELCO (Office of Members of the Executive and Legislative Councils) Consensus, (2) British Nationality Selection Scheme, (3) Hong Kong Bill of Rights Ordinance, and (4) Construction of a New Airport.

Political reform was a major issue between China and Britain in the years prior to mid-1997. Colonial Hong Kong under British administration was far from a democracy as democratic reform was opposed by the Hong Kong government. As stated in the *Hong Kong Annual Report 1978*, it was the government's position that "no major change to the constitutional principle of Hong Kong should be made." That was until Britain confirmed its restoration of Hong Kong in the Sino-British Joint Declaration and began pushing for "decolonisation" with democratic reform and representative governance.

Upon China's confirmation to resume sovereignty over Hong Kong, UK Prime Minister Margaret Thatcher immediately brought forward democratic reform in Hong Kong. In her memoir, she stated that given the lack of progress in the negotiation, a democratic structure in Hong Kong ought to be established to achieve independence or autonomy soon, as in the case with Singapore." The Thatcher proposal was implemented until the return of Hong Kong in 1997.

In April 1992, Chris Patten, Chairman of the Conservative Party in the United Kingdom, was appointed as the last governor of Hong Kong under Prime Minister John Major and continued with the political agenda of democratic reform. On 07 October 1992, in his first policy address at the Legislative Council (LegCo), he outlined his plan for constitutional reform. He first made a change in the legislature by decoupling his governorship from the presidency of the Legislative Council and calling for an election to select a new president amongst members of LegCo. In 1995, directly elected LegCo members increased from 18 to 20, while the voting age was lowered from 21 to 18; a single representative was elected in each electoral district based on a new "single-seat, single-vote" system. The functional constituencies were broadened to include 2.7 million voters while all forms of corporate voting were replaced with individual voting. It was also in 1995 when an Election Committee comprising members of District Boards was established to return 10 members to the Legislative Council. The District Boards were given additional political power and functions, including direct elections starting from 1994 in all districts except those in the New Territories.

On the eve of the confirmation of the Basic Law, the Chinese and British foreign ministers discussed how the last Legislative Council elected in 1995 could transit beyond 1997. Following the exchange of seven diplomatic letters, they arrived at an agreement to ensure a smooth political transition and conformity with the Basic Law. Simply put, it was agreed that legislative members might continue to serve after 1997 and beyond in the HKSAR provided they were qualified under the Basic Law which they needed to pledge to uphold with allegiance to the HKSAR government, and were subject to confirmation by the Preparatory Committee. It was known as the "through train" arrangement to which China and Britain agreed.

China therefore objected strongly to the political reform proposed by Governor Chris Patten as it was deemed a deviation from the "through train" agreement. From China's perspective, it was in violation of the Sino-British Joint Declaration, of the principles of transition to the Basic Law, and of the mutual understanding and agreement between China and Britain (collectively known as the "triple violations"). Thus, Chinese government officials strongly demanded that their British counterparts stay on track according to the principles set forth in previous agreements.

6.2.5 Towards a New Era

The political reform proposed by Governor Chris Patten was gazetted and submitted to the Legislative Council. China saw it an act of revocation of the bilateral arrangement intended to provide a coherent transition of sovereignty. The Chinese government decided to make a fresh start in preparation for the return of Hong Kong in 1997.

In March 1993, following the First Session of the Eighth National People's Congress, a Preliminary Working Committee was authorised to be established by the NPC Standing Committee. The Preliminary Committee was preceded by the Preparatory Committee established in Beijing on 26 January 1996 in the final preparation stage of the establishment of the Hong Kong Special Administrative Region.

Given the British contravention in the "through train" scheme, members of the Legislative Council, Urban Council and District Boards were ineligible for office in the HKSAR and must step down on 30 June 1997. To ensure continuity of government operation under the Basic Law, a Provisional Legislative Council was founded by the Preparatory Committee in March 1996; 60 members were elected in December of the same year.

Before midnight on 30 June 1997, a ceremony marking the return of Hong Kong was held in the Grand Hall on the fifth floor of the Hong Kong Convention and Exhibition Centre in the presence of Chinese President Jiang Zemin (江澤民), Premier of the State Council Li Peng (李鵬), Prince Charles and UK Prime Minister Tony Blair, among more than 4,000 Chinese and foreign dignitaries and guests. At 11:59 p.m. on 30 June, the national flag of the United Kingdom and the colonial flag of Hong Kong were slowly lowered to the British national anthem. At midnight on 01 July, the national flag of China and the regional flag of the HKSAR were raised to the national anthem of the People's Republic of China. Jiang Zemin（江澤民）then solemnly announced the resumption of China's exercise of sovereignty over Hong Kong.

At 1:30 a.m. on 01 July 1997, under the HKSAR government, Chief Executive Tung Chee-hwa（董建華）, principal government officials, members of the Executive Council and Provisional Legislative Council, and judges of the Court of Final Appeal and the High Court took the oath of office, marking the start of a new era in Hong Kong.

6.3 Implementation of "One Country, Two Systems"

Following the return to China in 1997, Hong Kong was reintegrated into the Chinese national system of government as a special administrative region began under the Basic Law of Hong Kong. The Central People's Government has supported the HKSAR in accordance with the Basic Law with respect to the duty of constitutional responsibility and the faithful execution of office of the HKSAR government and its chief executive.

The HKSAR Chief Executive reports to the Central People's Government annually on the implementation of the Basic Law and other matters of national relevance and is supported in the exercise of authority under the guidance of top Chinese leadership.

The NPC Standing Committee is empowered by the Chinese Constitution and Hong Kong Basic Law to review legislation passed in the HKSAR, amend national laws applicable to the HKSAR as prescribed in Annex III of the Basic Law, confer governmental power upon the HKSAR, and provide legal interpretation of the Basic Law. Interpretations of the Basic Law and its related articles as well as decisions on matters of governance in the HKSAR were made in 1999, 2004, 2005, 2011 and 2016 on issues regarding 1) the right of abode for children of Chinese descent born outside of Hong Kong to permanent residents, 2) the procedure by which the Chief Executive and members of the Legislative Council are elected, 3) the term of office of a Chief Executive from a by-election, 4) the jurisdiction over state immunity, and 5) the requirements of lawful oaths with public officials.

The Basic Law of Hong Kong explicitly stipulates that HKSAR residents are entitled to taking part lawfully in the national affairs of China. From the HKSAR, 36 deputies are elected to the National People's Congress in each session since 1997 under the Election Council. The people of Hong Kong, including community leaders and representatives of different sectors, are encouraged to join the Chinese People's Political Consultative Conference.

Electoral reform with the election of the Chief Executive and composition of the Legislative Council is promoted by the Central People's Government and HKSAR Government under the principle of gradual and orderly progress in democratic procedures according to the Basic Law and requirements of the National People's Congress Standing Committee. The government and legislature of the HKSAR are composed of local inhabitants. The chief executive is elected and then appointed by the Central People's Government; members of the Legislative Council are also elected. The Chief Executive election has become increasingly democratic by means of an expanding Election Committee. The first Chief Executive was elected by a committee of 400 electors; the second Chief Executive by a committee of 800 electors; and the third and fourth by a committee of 1,200 electors. The Chief Executive is responsible for implementing the Basic Law, signing bills and budgets, promulgating laws, deciding on government policies and issuing executive orders, and is supported in policymaking by the Executive Council. The first four chief executives of the HKSAR are Tung Chee-hwa（董建華）, Donald Tsang Yam-kuen（曾蔭權）, Leung Chun-ying（梁振英）and Carrie Lam Cheng Yuet-ngor（林鄭月娥）.

The Legislative Council is the legislature of the HKSAR. In recent years, legislators are elected through an increasing number of direct elections. Of the 70 members in the sixth Legislative Council in 2016, 35 were directly elected through geographical constituencies and 35 were elected through interest-group-based functional constituencies. In addition to the function of law-making, members of the Legislative Council engage in debate on issues of public interest, examine and approve government budgets, raise questions on the work of the government, such as the annual policy address, and endorse the appointment and removal of the judges of the Court of Final Appeal and the chief judge of the High Court.

The laws in force before the return of Hong Kong, including the common law, rules of equity, ordinances, subordinate legislation and customary law, are maintained, except for any that contravene the Basic Law or are amended by the Legislative Council of the HKSAR. The national laws listed in Annex III of the Basic Law are promulgated or implemented in Hong Kong through legislation. The power of final adjudication is vested in the HKSAR Court of Final Appeal. The Basic Law is the foundation of a sound judicial system, including the appointment and removal of judges so that judicial power may be exercised independently and free from any interference.

The principle of "One Country, Two Systems" is in the interest of the people in the Mainland and Hong Kong, as well as foreign investors. The implementation of such policy is a milestone in the history of Hong Kong.

Since July 1997, Hong Kong has witnessed complex changes in the internal and external environment. The stalling economic reform, exacerbated by two financial crises, has made it difficult for young people to move up the socioeconomic ladder. The shortage of land and housing beginning in the colonial era has been a long-running issue yet to be addressed effectively. History learning and civic education in Hong Kong have had little impact on a generation of young people, leading to a weak sense of national identity and cultural belonging. The world has been reshaped by the rise of populist ideas, including anti-elitism, anti-authoritarianism and anti-globalisation. The implementation of "One Country, Two Systems" has run against turbulent times as a result.

Article 23 of the Basic Law of Hong Kong stipulates that the HKSAR must enact its own laws to prohibit any act that endangers national security. The *Consultation Document on the Proposal to Implement Article 23 of the Basic Law* was released on 24 September 2002, followed by the first reading of the National Security (Legislative Provisions) Bill in the Legislative Council on 26 February 2003. In opposition to the proposed bill, a public demonstration took place on 01 July; it was estimated by the organisers that 500,000 people participated while the police put the number of participants at 350,000. On 06 July, Liberal Party Chairman James Tien Pei-chun（田北俊）resigned from the Executive Council, expressing his objection to the government's hasty attempts to legislate a national security law. On 05 September, it was announced by the government that the proposed legislation had been shelved. Without a bill on the agenda in the years following, Article 23 of the Basic Law was yet to be implemented.

In April 2012, a curriculum reform was brought forward through the release of the *Moral and National Education Curriculum Guide* by the Education Bureau. It triggered an anti-national education movement. On 30 August, a student group called Scholarism assembled a demonstration outside the Central Government Offices and demanded that the new curriculum be withdrawn. In the evening of 07 September, crowds dressed in black took part in another rally outside the Central Government Offices. On 08 October, introduction of "moral and national education" was put on hold by the government.

In June 2014, a white paper titled *The Practice of the "One Country, Two Systems" Policy in the Hong Kong Special Administrative Region* was issued by the Information Office of the State Council of the People's Republic of China. The white paper pointed out: "The system of the special administrative region, as prescribed in the Constitution of the People's Republic of China and the Basic Law of the HKSAR, is a special administrative system developed by the state for certain regions. Under this system, the central government exercises overall jurisdiction over the HKSAR, including the powers directly exercised by the central government, and the powers delegated to the HKSAR by the central government to enable it to exercise a high degree of autonomy in accordance with the law. The central government has the power of oversight over the exercise of a high degree of autonomy in the HKSAR."

On 31 August 2014, the Decision of the Standing Committee of the National People's Congress on Issues Relating to the Selection of the Chief Executive of the HKSAR by Universal Suffrage and on the Method for Forming the Legislative Council of the Hong Kong Special Administrative Region in the Year 2016 was promulgated. In the early hours of 28 September, an "Occupy" protest was mobilised by the founders of the "Occupy Central" movement, including Benny Tai Yiu-ting (戴耀廷), Chan Kin-man (陳健民) and Chu Yiu-ming (朱耀明), opposing the "August 31 Decision" and demanding the implementation of universal suffrage. The protests began on the premises outside the Central Government Offices and later spread to major traffic sections, including Harcourt Road. Police officers attempted to disperse protesters with tear gas and pepper spray. On the same day, a spokesperson of the Hong Kong and Macao Affairs Office of the State Council condemned the illegal acts which undermined the rule of law and social order, showing full support in the efforts of the HKSAR government to maintain social stability and protect lives and property. The spokesperson emphasised the legitimacy of the NPC Standing Committee's decision as it was made in accordance with the Basic Law and the current circumstances of Hong Kong upon a full account of public views.

The illegal protests intensified as protesters began to occupy the streets of Admiralty, Causeway Bay, Mong Kok and other areas, bringing traffic to a standstill on Hong Kong Island and in Kowloon. The protests ended after 79 days following a police operation on 15 December. On the same day, a spokesperson of the Liaison Office of the Central People's Government in the HKSAR said that the illegal protests had harmed the rule of law, social order and vital interests of Hong Kong, causing much tangible and latent harm. The Chinese government also reiterated its support for the HKSAR government to implement political reform, including on the issue of universal suffrage in accordance with the Basic Law, and approach the illegal protests according to the laws of Hong Kong. It was also noted that only by holding lawbreakers accountable could Hong Kong safeguard its core values, stability and prosperity.

The framework of "One Country, Two Systems" is a constitutional order supported by the Chinese Constitution and Hong Kong Basic Law; it is a principle of significant political and legal implication. A consensus on the principle is key to the implementation of "One Country, Two Systems" and leading Hong Kong out of its political gridlock in recent years.

7 A Place of Cultural Diversity

Hong Kong is a diverse, multicultural city with many Chinese traditions. Traditional Chinese values, such as the culture of charity, are endured within Hong Kong. At the same time, Hong Kong is also supportive of diverse cultures as exemplified by the peaceful coexistence of many religions. Hong Kong is a place where East meets West and where northern and southern Chinese cultures mix, making it culturally inclusive, dynamic and, in many ways, unique.

7.1 The Continuity of Cultural Traditions

Hong Kong rests on the foundation of Chinese culture. Most Hong Kong people can trace their ancestry back to the Mainland, especially in the Pearl River Delta region. Their ancestors brought with them Chinese cultural traditions, including folk customs, intangible cultural heritage, as well as dramatic and literary arts.

The folk customs of Hong Kong in the Ming Dynasty and Qing Dynasty, such as the worship of ancestors and gods during the *Da Jiao* festival and Yu Lan ghost festival, remain today. Some of these traditions are named on the National List of Intangible Cultural Heritage. Traditional festivals, such as the Spring Festival, Ching Ming Festival, Dragon Boat Festival, Mid-Autumn Festival and Chung Yeung Festival, continue to be observed in Hong Kong.

Hong Kong residents attach great importance to filial piety and are accustomed to worshipping their ancestors. Twice a year, in the spring and autumn, the indigenous inhabitants of the New Territories pay respect to their ancestors by sweeping ancestral graves and presenting offerings. In addition to the memorial shrines at home, ancestral halls are built in the village for the purpose of worshipping ancestors. The traditional Chinese culture of showing reverence for ancestors is represented in these practices.

Like other coastal residents in China, Hong Kong fishermen and farmers regard the god Tin Hau as their guardian spirit. There are over 50 large Tin Hau temples in Hong Kong, despite a shrinking population of fishermen. Tin Hau's birthday, on the 23rd day of the third month of the lunar calendar, is celebrated as a major festival across Hong Kong, particularly amongst the indigenous residents of the New Territories.

Da Jiao means holding sacrificial rituals. The *Jiao* Festival is also known as "Tai Ping Ching Chiu" (Tai Ping Qing Jiao) in Hong Kong, except in Kat O in Sha Tau Kok and Ko Lau Wan and Tap Mun in Sai Kung where it is called "On Lung Ching Chiu." These festivals offer prayers for peace and stability. The *Jiao* Festival in Cheung Chau, commonly called the Bun Festival, is well known for street parades and its bun-scrambling competition. This has gradually become a major folk custom in recent decades, enjoyed by foreigners and Chinese alike. *Da Jiao* is one of the local customs that reflects and strengthens the cohesion of a community as a long-standing Chinese cultural tradition in Hong Kong.

Hong Kong's intangible cultural heritage is extremely rich. In 2014, 480 local items of culture were included in the list of intangible cultural heritage compiled by the HKSAR government. Following three rounds of nominations, 10 items were included in the Representative National List of the Intangible Cultural Heritage by the National Cultural Heritage Administration. These were: Cantonese opera, Chinese herbal tea, Cheung Chau *Jiao* Festival (Cheung Chau Bun Festival), Dragon Boat Water Parade of Tai O, Yu Lan Ghost Festival of the Hong Kong Chiu Chow community, Tai Hang Fire Dragon Dance, Quanzhen Temples Taoist Ritual Music, *Guqin* (Qin-crafting), Hakka Unicorn Dance at Hang Hau in Sai Kung, and rituals of offering at Wong Tai Sin Temple. On 14 August 2017, in addition to these 10 items, 10 more cultural items were included on the first Representative List of the Intangible Cultural Heritage of Hong Kong by the Leisure and Cultural Services Department. These included traditional Nan Yin music, Spring and Autumn Ancestral Worship, Tin Hau Festival, Pok Fu Lam Fire Dragon Dance during the Mid-Autumn Festival, Taoist rituals of the Zhengyi School, basin feasts, Hong Kong-style milk tea, paper-crafting, cheongsam dresses, traditional Chinese wedding dresses, and bamboo scaffold techniques for temporary theatres. In 2009, Cantonese opera was added to the Representative List of the Intangible Cultural Heritage of Humanity by the United Nations Educational, Scientific and Cultural Organisation (UNESCO) as a world-class cultural asset of Guangdong, Hong Kong and Macao.

Originating in Guangzhou and Foshan, Cantonese opera—locally known as Tai Hei—is very popular in Hong Kong. After the 1911 Revolution, Hong Kong became a central site of the development of Cantonese opera. The four best opera troupes from Guangzhou and Hong Kong were renowned for their long-term presence in Hong Kong. In later years, celebrated singers included Ma Si-tsang (馬師曾), Sit Kok-sin (薛覺先) and Hung Sin-nui (紅線女), followed by Sun Ma Sze-tsang (新馬師曾), Fong Yim-fan (芳艷芬), Yam Kim-fai (任劍輝) and Bak Sheut-sin (白雪仙).

The Barwo Artists Association of Guangdong is a Cantonese opera guild. It was established more than 100 years ago during the reign of Emperor Guangxu (光緒) of the Qing Dynasty between 1875 and 1908. Its branch in Hong Kong was re-named the Chinese Artists Association of Hong Kong in 1953 as a support organisation which has played a critical role in the development of Cantonese opera in Hong Kong.

Martial arts novels are a unique genre of Chinese literature. These novels were popularised after the 1911 Revolution but waned in popularity thereafter. The genre was resurrected by Hong Kong-based writers Leung Yue-sang (梁羽生) and Louis Cha Leung-yung (查良鏞) who created a modern form of martial arts novels. Together with Taiwan-based writer Gu Long (古龍), who also rose to fame, they were known as the "three masters of martial arts novels." Their novels became highly popular among Chinese readers all over the world and have stood the test of time. Other Hong Kong-based authors have also created transformative work by drawing on traditional Chinese literature, including the best-sellers in science fiction by Ni Kuang (倪匡) and Huang Yi (黃易) and romance novels by Yi Shu (亦舒) and Eunice Lam (林燕妮).

7.2 Coexistence of Multiple Religions

There are many religions currently practiced in Hong Kong, including Buddhism, Taoism, *Kongjiao* (Confucianism), Protestantism, Catholicism, Islam, Hinduism, Sikhism, Judaism, Mormonism, Zoroastrianism (Mazdaizm) and Eastern Orthodoxy.

7.2.1 Buddhism

Buddhism is one of the major religions in Hong Kong. It was introduced to Hong Kong in the Northern Dynasty and Southern Dynasty more than 1,570 years ago. The Tsing Shan Monastery in Tuen Mun and Ling To Monastery in Ha Tsuen, Yuen Long are ancient temples built at the end of the Eastern Jin Dynasty. The Ling Wan Monastery in Kam Tin was built in the early Ming Dynasty. Other notable Buddhist sites include the Po Lin Monastery, Chi Lin Nunnery, and Tsz Shan Monastery. There are more than 400 Buddhist temples and viharas and approximately one million followers of Buddhism in Hong Kong.

7.2.2 Taoism

Taoism is a Chinese indigenous religion. According to a 2010 survey by the Hong Kong Taoist Association, there are more than one million followers and more than 300 Taoist monasteries and temples in Hong Kong. The Ching Chung Koon in Tuen Mun and Fung Ying Seen Koon in Fanling belong to the Quanzhen school originating from Guangzhou. Among the Taoist monasteries, Wong Tai Sin Temple in Kowloon is the most well-known in Hong Kong.

7.2.3 Kongjiao

Kongjiao, also known as Confucianism, enshrines Confucius as its founder and promulgates Confucian ideas. There is no initiation rite with *Kongjiao*. People who respect and accept the teachings of Confucius can be regarded as disciples of *Kongjiao*. Founded in the turbulent 1920s, Confucius Hall is one of the most representative *Kongjiao* organisations in Hong Kong. The Confucian Academy was founded in 1930 with the goal of incorporating *Kongjiao* ideas into the curriculum of primary schools, secondary schools and universities.

7.2.4 Protestantism

Protestantism, known locally as Christianity, is one of the three major denominations of the Christian faith. It was introduced to Hong Kong in 1841. Today there are more than 70 denominations and about 500,000 Protestant Christians in Hong Kong, with at least 1,500 Protestant Christian churches in Hong Kong, of which approximately 1,300 preach in Chinese. Local churches include the Church of Christ in China, True Jesus Church, and Christian Assembly.

7.2.5 Catholicism

Catholicism, also known as Roman Catholicism, is the earliest and largest of the three major denominations of Christianity. The Catholic Church established a missionary district in Hong Kong in 1841 and made it a diocese in 1946 with its own Catholic bishop since then. The Catholic Diocese of Hong Kong is the largest Chinese

Catholic diocese in the world. As of 2017, there are approximately 389,000 local Catholics, along with 292 priests, 58 friars and 469 nuns in Hong Kong. There are 52 parishes in Hong Kong, comprising 40 churches, 31 chapels and 26 halls for religious services.

7.2.6 Islam

There are about 300,000 Muslims in Hong Kong, including 150,000 Indonesians, 50,000 Chinese and 30,000 Pakistanis, as well as followers from India, Malaysia, the Middle East, Africa and elsewhere. The Incorporated Trustees of the Islamic Community Fund of Hong Kong is a charitable organisation responsible for coordinating all Islamic activities in Hong Kong and managing five mosques, two Islamic cemeteries and a kindergarten. The Chinese Muslim Cultural and Fraternal Association is the main group representing Chinese Muslims in Hong Kong.

7.2.7 Hinduism

There are about 100,000 Hindus in Hong Kong, mainly from India, Nepal, Sri Lanka, and Thailand. The Hindu Association of Hong Kong manages the Happy Valley Hindu Temple, which is a place for its followers to conduct social and religious activities. At the temple, followers may meditate, participate in spiritual seminars, practice yoga, and take part in other community activities.

7.2.8 Sikhism

There are approximately 12,000 Sikhs in Hong Kong. The earliest Sikhs hailed from Punjab in India and arrived in Hong Kong as part of the British armed forces in the 19th century. The first Sikh temple in Hong Kong was built on Queen's Road East in Wan Chai in 1901. It was named the Siri Guru Singh Sabha and was later renamed Khalsa Diwan. It is currently listed as a Grade II historic building.

7.2.9 Judaism

Judaism was first introduced to Hong Kong in the 1840s, following the cession of Hong Kong to Great Britain. Today, Hong Kong's Jewish population comes from around the world. There are three main synagogues in Hong Kong: Ohel Leah Synagogue, United Jewish Congregation of Hong Kong, and Chabad Lubavitch. The Hong Kong Jewish community is very active. In addition to setting up educational centres, it has also established several charitable organisations and cultural associations, including the Jewish Women's Association of Hong Kong, United Israel Appeal, Israeli Chamber of Commerce, and Jewish Historical Society.

The influence of religion can be felt all over Hong Kong. Different religions offer diverse perspectives on life and the world and are part of the spiritual life of many people in Hong Kong. Festivals closely related to Western religions, such as Easter and Christmas, are well integrated into the lives of Hong Kong. Furthermore, different religious groups in Hong Kong have mobilised their followers and made significant contributions to Hong Kong's education, health care and social welfare sectors.

The harmonious coexistence of different faiths has long been a normal part of social life in Hong Kong.

7.3 Cultural Exchange between China and the World

Hong Kong is a major hub for cultural exchange between China and the rest of the world; it is a place where the West can learn about the East, and vice versa. Missionaries, businessmen and local people have all made vital contributions towards the cultural exchange between China and the world.

In the 19th century, with the assistance of Wang Tao (王韜) and others, James Legge, a missionary from the London Missionary Society, spent more than 20 years translating *Four Books and Five Classics* into English. His work, *Chinese Classics*, was published in Hong Kong and London in both English and Chinese with English annotations. Although missionaries arriving in the East had been translating parts of the Chinese classics since the end of the 16th century, James Legge was the only one who translated in full the *Four Books and Five Classics* into English and introduced them to the Western world. In the 20th century, Lau Din-cheuk (劉殿 爵) came to the fore as a famous translator and sinologist in Hong Kong. His translations of works, including *Lao Tzu*, *Mencius* and the *Analects of Confucius*, are highly celebrated and deemed authoritative works among Western scholars studying Chinese philosophy.

Newspapers and publications founded by Westerners in Hong Kong have had a great influence on the local media, and even on the media of modern China. The *Chinese Serial*, which made its debut in Hong Kong on 01 August 1853, was the first Chinese newspaper in Hong Kong and the Mainland; it had a print run of 3,000 per issue. It was available in Hong Kong, Guangzhou, Xiamen, Fuzhou, Ningbo, Shanghai and other trading ports. Walter Henry Medhurst was its first editor, followed by Charles Batten Hillier in 1854 and James Legge in 1855. The *Chinese Serial* published numerous articles introducing Western social sciences and natural sciences to the Chinese population. These articles would go on to influence the Meiji Restoration in Japan. The *Chinese and Foreign Gazette* was the first Chinese newspaper with movable type printing in the world and a pioneer in the modern Chinese newspaper industry. Its predecessor, known as the *Hong Kong Shipping Gazette*, was first published circa 03 November 1857. Wong Shing (黃勝), who served as the first editor of the *Chinese and Foreign Gazette*, was one of the first Chinese students to study in the United States. The *Chinese Mail* was founded in 1872 by Chan Oi-ting (陳藹廷) who was a translator of the English-language newspaper *China Mail*. The *Chinese Mail* was described in the *China Mail* as the first Chinese newspaper "fully managed by local people," but in the early years, it published mostly translated articles from *China Mail*. The printing and distribution of *Chinese Mail* was also managed by *China Mail*.

Many private and public Western-style schools were established following the British occupation of Hong Kong. At the end of the 19th century, included in secondary school curriculums were Latin, reading, writing, dictation, translation, Shakespeare, arithmetic, algebra, Euclidean geometry, trigonometry, surveying, general knowledge, history and geography. The diverse curriculum provided students with basic knowledge, an understanding of natural sciences, and familiarity with Western socio-political ideas. Many Chinese reformers of the 20th century such as Yung Wing (容閎), Wu Tingfang (伍廷芳), Ho Kai (何啟), Woo Lai-woon (胡禮垣), Sun Yat-sen (孫 中山) and Tse Tsan-tai (謝纘泰) were shaped as students by the Western education available in Hong Kong.

Hong Kong was an important place of knowledge exchange in the medical field. To promote Western medicine and train Chinese medical professionals, a group of doctors, including Dr Patrick Manson and Ho Kai (何啟), initiated a medical school in Hong Kong. The Hong Kong College of Medicine for Chinese, founded on 01 October 1887, ran a five-year programme with a British-based curriculum; it was more advanced than the South China Medical College (as a part of the Canton Hospital) established in Guangzhou by an American medical missionary in 1866 and was ahead of the medical school in Tianjin founded by Li Hongzhang (李鴻章) in 1881.

The University of Hong Kong, established in 1912, was Hong Kong's first tertiary institution and a key learning centre of Western knowledge among Chinese students. In the early days, it adopted the slogan "established for China" and was an institution where students sponsored by the Beiyang government and other provincial governments came to study. Upon graduation, many of these students pursued further studies overseas before returning to China where they became leaders in their respective fields. Notable individuals included mechanical engineer Liu Hsien-Chou (Liu Xianzhou) (劉仙洲), bacteriologist Lin Chung-yang (C. E. Lim) (林宗揚), aesthetic theorist Zhu Guangqian (朱光潛), psychologist Gao Juefu (高覺敷), railway engineer Shi Zhiren (石 志仁) and port engineer Zhao Jinsheng (趙今聲).

Some of the most internationally renowned scientists, including Charles Kao Kuen (高 錕), Yau Shing-tung (丘成桐), Daniel Tsui Chee (崔琦), Che Chi-ming (支志明) and Dennis Lo Yuk-ming (盧煜明) were students in Hong Kong. Charles Kao Kuen attended high school in Hong Kong and was Vice Chancellor of

The Chinese University of Hong Kong. In 1966, Kao published a paper on the application of optical fibre technology in communications, laying the foundation of the Internet. He was dubbed the "Father of Fibre Optics" and was awarded the Nobel Prize in Physics in 2009.

After high school and undergraduate studies in Hong Kong, Yau Shing-tung（丘成桐）obtained his PhD in the US under the guidance of Professor Chern Shiing-shen（陳省身）. In 1982, Yau Shing-tung was awarded the Fields Medal in Mathematics, an honour considered equivalent to the Nobel Prize by mathematicians, for proving the Calabi's Conjecture proposed a quarter of a century earlier.

Daniel Tsui Chee（崔琦）pursued his studies in the United States after secondary school in Hong Kong. He received a PhD from The University of Chicago in 1967 and became a professor of electrical engineering at Princeton University in 1982. In 1998, Robert Laughlin, Horst Störmer and Daniel Tsui were awarded the Nobel Prize in Physics for their discovery of the Fractional Quantum Hall Effect. Tsui was listed in the *American Men and Women of Science* and in 2000 was elected a foreign academician of the Chinese Academy of Sciences.

After receiving his undergraduate and PhD degrees from The University of Hong Kong, Che Chi-ming（支志明）conducted research in photochemistry and bio-inorganic chemistry at the California Institute of Technology from 1980 to 1983, before returning to his alma mater as a professor of chemistry. He was the first Hong Kong member of the Chinese Academy of Sciences and won a first-class State Natural Science Award in 2006. Up until 2017, he was the only scientist from Hong Kong to have received this award. In 2013, Che was elected a foreign associate of the US National Academy of Sciences. He has contributed extensively to the research and commercialisation of organometallic chemistry and photochemistry.

Dennis Lo Yuk-ming（盧煜明）, a professor of medicine at The Chinese University of Hong Kong, is a pioneer of non-invasive prenatal diagnosis through his research on deoxyribonucleic acid (DNA) and ribonucleic acid (RNA) in human plasma. His published works include a report titled *Fetal Nucleic Acids in Maternal Plasma*. He became a foreign associate of the US National Academy of Sciences in 2013.

7.4 Philanthropy and Hong Kong–Mainland Ties

Hong Kong has inherited the Chinese philanthropic culture of "almsgiving for the poor and the needy." Public social services are provided by a multitude of non-governmental charitable organisations in Hong Kong, including the Tung Wah Group of Hospitals, Po Leung Kuk, Lok Sin Tong, Chung Sing Benevolent Society, Yan Chai Hospital, Pok Oi Hospital, Yan Oi Tong, Community Chest of Hong Kong, and Oxfam Hong Kong. Fundraising activities are regularly held and well recognised locally, including the flag days and TV charity concerts such as *Tung Wah Charity Gala*, *Gala Spectacular* and *Yan Chai Charity Show*, as well as annual events such as the "Community Chest Walk for Millions" and "Oxfam Trailwalker."

In addition to the relief efforts in times of war and natural disasters, a wide range of education, healthcare and social services are provided daily by charitable organisations, partially supported in most cases by the government. The Tung Wah Group of Hospitals and Po Leung Kuk are Hong Kong's oldest and largest non-government welfare providers. The Tung Wah Group of Hospitals had some 303 service units with over 10,000 staff members and a total recurrent expenditure of HK$4 billion in 2016, covering 32 medical and health service units, 53 education service units, and 218 social service units (62 for the elderly, 71 for children and youth, 44 for rehabilitation, 23 for social enterprises and 18 for public services). Po Leung Kuk had over 301 service units in the same year.

The Hong Kong Jockey Club (HKJC), founded in 1884, is not only a world-class horse-racing organisation but also the largest charity in Hong Kong. The HKJC is a non-profit organisation from which profits are donated to support charitable causes and community projects. In the fiscal year 2015 and 2016, donations totalled more than HK$3.9 billion. From 2005 to 2015, it funded more than 1,000 projects in 10 fields: arts and culture, education and training, elderly services, poverty alleviation and emergency relief, environmental protection, family services, medical and health, rehabilitation services, sports and recreation, and youth development.

The philanthropic culture of Hong Kong has also been demonstrated in the care shown by the people of Hong Kong towards their compatriots in the Mainland. In the late Qing Dynasty and early Republican period, Tung Wah Hospital repeatedly provided relief in times of floods, droughts and military calamities. Its efforts were recognised through commendation plaques from emperors of the Qing Dynasty and presidents of the Republic of China. For relief provided during the Northern Chinese Famine of 1876–1879, Tung Wah Hospital was awarded a plaque titled *Shen Wei Pu You* (blessed by the gods) by Emperor Guangxu (光緒); in 1885, for relief following floods in Guangdong in 1884, it was awarded a plaque titled *Wan Wu Xian Li* (compassion for all) by Emperor Guangxu; in 1918, for relief provided for floods in the Beijing and Zhili regions, it was awarded a plaque titled *Shan Yu Ren Tong* (benevolence bountiful) by President Feng Guozhang (馮國璋); for relief in the devastation wrought by droughts in the provinces of Zhili, Shandong, Henan, Shaanxi and Shanxi from 1919 to 1920, it was awarded a plaque titled *Ji Gong Hao Yi* (timely charity) by President Xu Shichang (徐世昌).

Throughout the 1990s, disaster relief efforts in the forms of donation and on-site support by the people of Hong Kong continued with each major natural disaster in the Mainland. In 1991, following a severe flood in eastern China which affected more than 200 million people, a record HK$107.2 million was raised in a seven-hour live charity concert in Happy Valley supported by hundreds of performing artists from Hong Kong, Taiwan and the Mainland and a participating audience of 100,000; more than HK$400 million in donation was made through the Hong Kong Branch of Xinhua News Agency. After the Wenchuan, Sichuan earthquake in 2008, more than HK$2 billion in donation was raised in Hong Kong over a period of less than two months.

The modernisation of China was driven partly by the growth in education, technology and sports. The development of education, science, culture and sports in China has been supported by prominent businesses and individuals in Hong Kong since the early years of reform. Donations were made by Sir Run Run Shaw (邵逸夫) to support China's Ministry of Education for school improvements. Shantou University and Ningbo University were founded with the financial support of tycoons Li Ka-shing (李嘉誠) and Pao Yue-kong (包玉剛), respectively. Other supporters included Wong Kwan-cheng (王寬誠), Lee Shau-kee (李兆基), Henry Fok Ying-tung (霍英東), Tsang Hin-chi (曾憲梓), Tin Ka-ping (田家炳), Cheng Yu-tung (鄭裕彤), Chiang Chun (蔣震) and the Sun Hung Kai Foundation. Many people in Hong Kong also supported education development in China by contributing to charitable initiatives, including Project Hope, Sowers Action and *Wu Zhi Qiao* (Bridge to China).

The Ho Leung Ho Lee Foundation, co-founded by the S. H. Ho Foundation, Wei Lun Foundation of Mr. and Mrs. Lee Quo-wei (利國偉夫婦) and philanthropists Leung Kau-kui (梁銶鋸) and Ho Tim (何添), was established to support the development of science and technology in China. The Qiu Shi Foundation, established by entrepreneur Cha Chi-ming (查濟民), was also founded to accomplish a similar mission.

Henry Fok Ying-tung (霍英東) was particularly well known for his contributions toward the development of sports in China, including his sponsorship of sporting events through the Fok Ying Tung Sports Foundation. Sir Run Run Shaw was an early leader in heritage preservation with notable contribution to the conservation of the Mogao Caves. Stanley Ho Hung-sun (何鴻燊) repurchased and donated many ancient Chinese cultural relics stolen in the 19th century by foreign troops at the Old Summer Palace, including the bronze pig- and horse-head statues. In recent years, Ronnie Chan Chi-chung (陳啟宗) and Hui Wing-mau (許榮茂) have donated to the conservation of the Hall of Mental Cultivation of the Imperial Palace.

Conversely, Hong Kong has received Chinese support in times of crisis. In November 1951 when more than 10,000 people were rendered homeless in a fire at Tung Tau Tsuen in Kowloon City, food and financial aid were immediately provided by the Guangzhou branch of the Chinese People's Relief Association. In December 1953 when a fire broke out in Shek Kip Mei and Sham Shui Po, it again provided victims with similar relief support. In August 1971 when Typhoon Rose claimed more than 20,000 homes and over 120 lives in Hong Kong, financial aid was provided by the Red Cross Society of China.

7.5 Cultural Exchange between Northern and Southern China

Hong Kong is where East meets West and where cultures of northern and southern China converge. Many Chinese intellectuals from all over China moved south in four major influxes and were instrumental in the cultural development of Hong Kong.

The 1911 Revolution marked the first wave of Chinese intellectuals who relocated to Hong Kong from the Mainland. These included renowned academics of the Qing Dynasty, including Chen Botao (陳伯陶), Lai Tsi-hsi (賴際熙), Ou Ta-tian (區大典), Wu Daorong (吳道鎔) and Zhu Ruzhen (朱汝珍), who brought with them their rich knowledge of Chinese cultural studies. In Kowloon, Chen Botao compiled the Dongguan County Local Chronicles and reworked a nostalgic poem series titled *Song Tai Qiu Chang* (Autumn Chants on the Terrace of Song Emperors). Lai Tsi-hsi and Ou Ta-tian became lecturers at The University of Hong Kong and promoted Chinese literature and history. Lai Tsi-hsi travelled across Southeast Asia with Vice Chancellor William Woodward Hornell for a fundraiser in 1926 and helped establish and run the School of Chinese in 1927. Earlier, in 1923, Lai Tsi-hsi, with the financial support of businessmen Robert Ho Tung (何東), Kwok Chun-yeung (郭春秧), Lee Hy-san (利希慎) and Lee Hoi-tung (李海東), established Hong Kong's first non-government library. Located on Bonham Road, it was known as the Hok Hoi. In addition to a collection of books, it was equipped with a reading room dedicated to academic research and lectures.

The second wave of intellectuals came during the War of Resistance against Japanese Aggression. In the autumn of 1935, Xu Dishan (許地山), upon introduction by Hu Shih (胡適), was appointed Chair Professor of HKU's School of Chinese. Xu Dishan, a charismatic leader in the academic and cultural sectors, served in many associations and became a driver of education reform in Hong Kong. At the invitation of Xu Dishan, renowned historiographer Chen Yinke (陳寅恪) became a visiting professor at The University of Hong Kong; his one-year stay in Hong Kong left behind a remarkable legacy.

In November 1937, following the outbreak of the War of Resistance against Japananese Aggression, Cai Yuanpei (蔡元培) took refuge in Hong Kong. On February 28 of the following year, he chaired the Academia Sinica's General Assembly in Hong Kong. He was also a supporter of the Hong Kong New Etymology Society and China Defence League. Cai Yuanpei died of illness in Hong Kong on 05 March 1940 and was buried at the Aberdeen Chinese Permanent Cemetery.

The Hong Kong Chapter of the All-China Resistance Association of Writers and Artists was founded by a group of intellectuals following their relocation to Hong Kong. Among them were Xu Dishan (許地山), Dai Wangshu (戴望舒), Yang Gang (楊剛), Lin Huanping (林煥平), Xu Chi (徐遲), Ma Er (Ye Junjian) (馬耳 [葉君健]), Yu Feng (郁風), Ye Lingfeng (葉靈鳳), Feng Yidai (馮亦代) and Huang Yaomian (黃藥眠). They kept alive the spirit of young cultural enthusiasts and reinvigorated Hong Kong's literary community amidst difficult times.

The literary landscape of Hong Kong was shaped by Chinese migrant writers in two ways. Firstly, they boosted the development of literary arts and the growth of literary periodicals, newspapers and publications. Among these publications were *Literary and Arts Front* under the editorship of Mao Dun (茅盾), *Supplement of Li Pao* under the editorship of Mao Dun and Ye Lingfeng (葉靈鳳), *Supplement of Sing Tao Daily* under the editorship of Dai Wangshu (戴望舒), *Modern Critique* under the editorship of Chow Ching-wen (周鯨文), *Da Feng* under the editorship of Lu Danlin (陸丹林), and *Chinese Writers* under the editorship of Dai Wangshu and Ye Junjian (葉君健). Secondly, Chinese writers and their patriotic concern of national welfare inspired a generation of young writers in Hong Kong to achieve high literary standards intellectually and artistically. Under the influence of writers hailing from the north, the first generation of local writers, including Lui Lun (侶倫), Lee Yuk-chung (李育中), Ah Ning (阿寧), Ha Yik (夏易) and Shu Hong-shing (舒巷城), focused on real-life perspectives, using realism to express the patriotism of the people of Hong Kong.

The third wave took place in the early post-war period, beginning in the summer of 1946. Many left-leaning writers from Shanghai, Beiping (present-day Beijing), Guangzhou and Nanjing headed south to escape the civil war and persecution by the Kuomintang authorities. These writers founded newspapers and magazines, established schools and publishing houses, organised literary societies and book clubs, and taught in training courses. These initiatives provided young people in Hong Kong with career opportunities in the literary and culture sectors.

The fourth wave began in the early 1950s. After moving to Hong Kong, Xu Xu (徐訏) and Cao Juren (曹聚仁) co-founded the Chuangken Publishing Company and published the prose periodicals *Humour* and *Hot Wind*. Moreover, Xu Xu authored the novel *The Other Shore*; Cao Juren wrote the novel *Hotel*; and Li Huiying (李輝英) compiled *A History of Chinese Fiction* and *Twenty Years of New Literature*. Xu Su (徐速) as a new litterateur wrote the novel *Sun, Moon and Star* based on a story of three women during the Second Sino-Japanese War. The book was highly acclaimed in Southeast Asia. Liu Yichang (劉以鬯), who came from Shanghai and worked as an editor for several newspapers, released China's first stream-of-consciousness novel *The Drunkard* in 1963. Eileen Chang (張愛玲), following her arrival in Hong Kong for the second time in the early 1950s, wrote two long novels *The Rice Sprout Song* and *Love in Redland*, addressing the political issues of the time. In 1952, painter Chan Hoi-ying (陳海鷹) fulfilled the wishes of his teacher, Li Tiefu (李鐵夫), and founded the Hong Kong Academy of Fine Arts as Hong Kong's first art school for which he was the first principal. The name of the school was inscribed by Qi Baishi (齊白石).

Among the intellectuals who came to Hong Kong were many renowned historians who helped promote the study of Hong Kong's local history. *Hong Kong and Its External Communications Before 1842: The History of Hong Kong Prior to British Arrival,* written by Lo Hsiang-lin (羅香林) and his students, remains a standard reference guide to the ancient history of Hong Kong, as is his book *The Role of Hong Kong in the Cultural Interchange Between East and West*. The escape journey and tales of the imperial family of the Song Dynasty are depicted in the books *Song mo er di nan qian nian lu kao* (A study of the routes taken by the last two emperors of the Song Dynasty) and *Song huang tai ji nian ji* (A commemorative collection on Sung Wong Toi) by Jian Youwen (簡又文). The history of Hong Kong in the late Song Dynasty is described in *Kowloon and Historical Records of Song Dynasty* by Jao Tsung-i (饒宗頤), a historian widely recognised for a wealth of published works. Jao Tsung-i of the South and Ji Xianlin (季羨林) of the North are well known for their mastery of Chinese culture and studies of contemporary China.

The founding of The Chinese University of Hong Kong was closely related to the influx of Chinese intellectuals. New Asia College, originally named Asia Evening College of Arts and Commerce, was founded in October 1949 by former northern residents Ch'ien Mu (錢穆) and Tsui Shu-chin (崔書琴), together with Lau Sheung-yee (劉尚義) of Hong Kong, later joined by Tang Chun-i (唐君毅) and Tchang Pi-kai (張丕介). Their intention was to honour the academic spirit of the Song Danasty and Ming Danasty and help preserve traditional Chinese humanism. New Asia College was regarded as a major centre of Confucianism in the 20th century. The influence of Ch'ien Mu, Tang Chun-i, Mou Tsung-san (牟宗三) and Hsu Fu-kuan (徐復觀) had a great impact on the Chinese and global academic circles. In early 1951, Anglican bishop Ronald Owen Hall, following a discussion with former President of Lingnan University Lee Ying-lam (李應林) and former President of St. John's University in Shanghai Au Wai-kwok (歐偉國), established Chung Chi College, a Christian institution for higher education in Hong Kong. United College was founded in 1956 through the amalgamation of five colleges: Wah Kiu, Canton Overseas, Wen Hua, Kwang Hsia, and Ping Jing. These were relocated from Guangzhou to Hong Kong between 1947 and 1950. In June 1959, it was announced by the Hong Kong government that Chung Chi College, New Asia College and United College be merged into a new, publicly-funded university. The Chinese University of Hong Kong was officially established in October 1963 and has since become a world-class institution upon the founding principles of emphasising Chinese culture, integrating Eastern and Western knowledge, and linking by the heritage of Chinese culture.

Conversely, northward movement of intellectuals and culture from Hong Kong to China was scarce in the past. In 1962, at the invitation of Premier Zhou Enlai (周恩來), Professor Emeritus Hou Pao-chang (侯寶璋)

of The University of Hong Kong became Vice President of the China Medical University (presently known as Peking Union Medical College) in Beijing. An enormous turn in cultural exchange took place upon the national reform and opening-up policy. The popular culture of Hong Kong in the forms of films, TV dramas and pop music has brought a wider range of cultural offerings and a greater understanding of Hong Kong's cultural make-up.

In filmmaking, *The Shaolin Temple* in 1982, directed by Hong Kong's Cheung Sing-yim（張鑫炎）and starring Mainland actor Jet Li Lianjie（李連杰）, was a local box office hit and internationally acclaimed. *The Burning of Yuan Ming Yuan* and *Reign Behind a Curtain*, adaptations of Chinese history by Hong Kong director Li Han-hsiang（李 翰 祥）under a Mainland partnership, achieved huge market success. Other celebrated films were *Boat People* in 1982 directed by Ann Hui（許鞍華）, *Little Heroes* in 1983 directed by Mou Tun-fei（牟敦芾）and *Homecoming* in 1984 directed by Yim Ho（嚴浩）. These were produced by Bluebird Movie Enterprises, a production company founded by Xia Meng（夏夢）. Hong Kong's film industry not only offered a greater choice of movies but also raised the level of expertise in movie production in the Mainland.

In 1983, TV dramas produced by Asia Television, starting with the series *The Legendary Fok*, began airing in some locations in the Mainland. The drama series aired on prime-time television with China Central Television (CCTV) every Sunday evening starting 06 May 1984 and became an instant sensation. In the following 10 years, *Love and Passion*, *The Legend of the Condor Heroes*, *The Bund* and *Fatherland* made their debut. Hong Kong television stars, including Patrick Tse Yin（謝賢）, Adam Cheng Siu-chow（鄭少秋）, Chow Yun-fat（周潤發）, Carol Cheng Yu-ling（鄭裕玲）, Tony Leung Chiu-wai（梁朝偉）, Andy Lau Tak-wah（劉德華）, Leslie Cheung Kwok-wing（張國榮）, Angie Chiu Ngar-chi（趙雅芝）, Elizabeth Wang Ming-chun（汪明荃）, Felix Wong Yat-wah（黃日華）, Barbara Yung Mei-ling（翁美玲）, Alex Man Chi-leung（萬梓良）, Carina Lau Kar-ling（劉嘉玲）, Simon Yam Tat-wah（任達華）and Stephen Chow Sing-chi（周星馳）became household names in the Mainland.

Hong Kong's pop music was first carried and made popular through Hong Kong TV dramas aired in the Mainland where a generation of young fans emerged with the debut of Hong Kong singers Alan Tam Wing-lun（譚詠麟）, Leslie Cheung Kwok-wing（張國榮）, Anita Mui Yim-fong（梅艷芳）, Roman Tam Pak-sin（羅文）and Sam Hui Koon-kit（許冠傑）. Throughout the 1980s, Chinese pop charts were dominated by artists of Hong Kong and Taiwan. In the 1990s, Jacky Cheung Hok-yau（張學友）, Andy Lau Tak-wah（劉德華）, Leon Lai Ming（黎明）and Aaron Kwok Fu-shing（郭富城）—collectively known as the Four Heavenly Kings—were Hong Kong's leading artists and were immensely popular as singers, actors and dancers in the Mainland. Among renowned songwriters and lyricists in Hong Kong were James Wong Jum-sum（黃霑）and Joseph Koo Kar-fai（顧嘉煇）.

During this period, many Chinese intellectuals came to Hong Kong to advance their academic exposure and knowledge in support of national development and modernisation. In 1991, an alumni group in Beijing was established by former students at The University of Hong Kong, aiming to promote further cultural exchange between Hong Kong and the Mainland. The Hong Kong Institute for the Promotion of Chinese Culture (HKIPCC) and Beijing–Hong Kong Academic Exchange Centre (BHKAEC) in Hong Kong were established earlier in 1985 to do the same.

The success story of Wang Tao（汪滔）is a prime example of the impact of academic exchange between Hong Kong and the Mainland. In 2006, he and his associates founded SZ DJI Technology Co., Ltd, a leading global developer and manufacturer of unmanned aerial vehicle control systems and drone solutions. It now has customers in more than 100 countries. Born in Hangzhou, Zhejiang, Wang Tao enrolled in the Department of Electronic & Computer Engineering at the Hong Kong University of Science and Technology. During his time there, he used the university's scientific resources to establish his start-up company. "I wouldn't have achieved so much if I hadn't come to Hong Kong," he said.

*　　　　　*　　　　　*

Hong Kong is a unique city that has undergone a developmental path distinct from its counterparts in the Mainland. With a history spanning 7,000 years, Hong Kong has transformed from a little-known traditional fishing and farming community into a prestigious cosmopolitan city.

Hong Kong is an immigrant city with a long history. The ancestors of most people in Hong Kong were settlers from the Mainland over many different historical periods. Through dedication and perseverance, Hong Kong has become the dynamic and prosperous city that it is today.

Hong Kong is culturally diverse. Influenced by both Chinese and Western cultures from the mid-19th century onwards, Hong Kong took on a distinctive and important role in the development of modern China. By heritage and geography, many aspects of Chinese culture have deep roots here and continue to thrive, while Western cultures have helped form parts of Hong Kong. Hong Kong is a multi-cultural platform of Western systems and ideas, combined with Chinese northern and southern sub-cultures; it has been—and still is—China's window to the world and a global gateway to China.

Hong Kong is the freest economy in the world. The economic miracle of Hong Kong was born out of an excellent geographical location, a unique deep-water harbour, a free port policy initiated by Britain and the agility, talent and high spirit of the people of Hong Kong, as well as the national policy making Hong Kong a stable and prosperous place, coupled with unmatched economic opportunities in the decades of national reform and opening-up in the Mainland.

The "One Country, Two Systems" framework is a unique characteristic of Hong Kong and is instrumental in ensuring the successful return of Hong Kong in 1997. Under the jurisdiction of the National People's Congress and in accordance with the Basic Law, Hong Kong Special Administrative Region (HKSAR) enjoys a high degree of autonomy and is given executive, legislative and judicial power, including the power of final adjudication. Hong Kong's way of life, including its capitalist system, is to remain in place up until 2047.

The "One Country, Two Systems" policy has made significant strides and has received full recognition since its inception, despite some challenges. Under the Chinese Constitution and the Basic Law, collaborative efforts by the Central People's Government, HKSAR Government and its local community are focused on building social consensus and addressing socioeconomic issues, thereby ensuring a brighter prospect for Hong Kong through the successful implementation of "One Country, Two Systems."

Chronology

Publication Notes

I. This volume consists of the first two books, namely *Overview* and *Chronology* of Hong Kong Chronicles and is compiled mostly in chronological order and occasionally by events.

II. This volume mainly focuses on natural, political, economic, cultural and social events occurring in Hong Kong within the specified timeframe. Events which take place outside of Hong Kong but have historic significance are also introduced.

III. The Gregorian calendar is adopted for the chronological system of this book. "B.C." is used to indicate the years before the common era. "A.D." is used to indicate the years of the common era and is omitted in all four-digital years. Chinese dynasties and regnal years are included to indicate periods of Chinese imperial rule.

IV. The day, month and year of each historical event are included when specific dates are identified; events without an identifiable date are placed at the end of the month or year of occurrence.

V. When the ancient and modern names of places are the same, modern names are not repeated. Conversely, where the ancient and modern names of places are different, their modern names are listed.

VI. Chinese translation of foreign names, including names of persons, official institutions and titles, regulations and documents, foreign-funded institutions and foreign organisations, books and periodicals can be found in the Glossary.

VII. Names and official titles of institutions and organisations are presented in full form initially and are abbreviated thereafter.

VIII. Historical events are mainly based on primary sources with a small number deriving from verified research work. While sources are not indicated individually, key references are provided.

5000 B.C.–4000 B.C. (New Stone Age, or Neolithic)

Traces of human activity in Hong Kong from this period have been found, indicating clusters of very early inhabitants in the coastal areas of present-day Lung Kwu Chau in Tuen Mun, Chung Hom Wan on Hong Kong Island and Tai Wan on Lamma Island. Inhabitation was likely on a seasonal and migratory basis. Usually crafted from a type of stone known as flint, tools for daily use included adzes, choppers, spatulas and bone tools. Life was sustained by foraging, fishing and hunting. Clothing was made from bark cloth. Coloured and white pottery were used in ceremonial rituals; cooking utensils were made from less-fine clay mixed with sand. Remains of round- and square-shaped houses from this period have been found on a sandbank near Tai Wan on Lamma Island. (Figure 001)

4000 B.C.–3000 B.C. (New Stone Age)

Large stone houses were built during this period. Sites in Hong Kong indicating early settlement included the coastal areas of Kwo Lo Wan in Chek Lap Kok, Tung Wan on Lantau Island and Lung Kwu Chau in Tuen Mun. Round-bottom pottery utensils were characterised by the etching of a stylised phoenix engraved at the mouth rim. Flint tools, made from flakes chipped from a larger stone with ground stone tools, including adzes, demonstrated a developed state of craftsmanship involving both stone and woodwork. The use of large stone sinkers indicated relatively advanced fishing techniques.

3000 B.C.–2000 B.C. (New Stone Age)

During this period, humans settled in relatively large clusters in the coastal areas of Hong Kong. Clan cemeteries also appeared at Sha Ha in Sai Kung and Yung Long in Tuen Mun. People continued to survive by foraging, fishing and hunting. Bark clothing was replaced with textiles spun and woven using spinning wheels. While round-bottomed pottery pots remained, cooking techniques were improved with the use of fire grates. Jade replaced earthenware vessels as objects of religious significance. Flint tools, such as adzes and cutting blades, as well as arrowheads and large axes dating back to the Yangtze River Valley culture, have also been found. (Figure 002)

2000 B.C.–1000 B.C. (New Stone Age to Bronze Age)

Evidence that Hong Kong had entered the early Bronze Age post-1500 B.C. can be seen at Pa Tau Kwu and Pak Mong on Lantau Island, Tung Wan Tsai in Ma Wan and Tai Wan on Lamma Island. The pattern of houses from this period at Pa Tau Kwu suggests settlements moving from sand dunes to headlands before moving to highlands as a form of defence. Relics include dagger-axes, spears and arrowheads. In the graveyards at Tung Wan Tsai and Tai Wan were more than 30 tombs with grave goods, including thin-body penannular ornaments and collared bracelets characteristic of the Shang Dynasty. The production, form and pattern of jade daggers and blades of this period were also influenced by the Shang Dynasty and Erlitou culture. (Figure 003)

1000 B.C.–221 B.C. (Bronze Age to Iron Age)

During this period, Hong Kong is known for the use and production of bronze to make dagger-axes, swords, spears, axes, knives, arrowheads and fishing hooks. Stone moulds and traces of advanced bronzeware casting have been found in the areas of Kwo Lo Wan in Chek Lap Kok, So Kwun Wat in Tuen Mun and Sha Lo Wan on Lantau Island. The early inhabitants of Pak Mong on Lantau Island used advanced winch-like rotary mechanisms in the mass production of ornaments, including crystal and quartz penannular rings.

214 B.C. (33rd year of the reign of Qin Shi Huang [秦始皇] of the Qin Dynasty)

The prefectures of Nanhai, Guilin and Xiang were formed by Qin Shi Huang (秦始皇) after his victory in Lingnan. The Nanhai Prefectural office was located in Panyu. Hong Kong was placed under the jurisdiction of Panyu County (present-day Guangzhou) in Nanhai Prefecture.

204 B.C. (3rd year of Emperor Gaozu [高祖] of the Western Han Dynasty)

The County Magistrate of Longchuan County, Zhao Tuo (趙佗), succeeded the Commander of the Nanhai Prefecture, Ren Xiao (任囂), who died in 206 B.C. Zhao mobilised his troops and consolidated the prefectures of Nanhai, Guilin and Xiang. He then declared himself Martial King of the newly founded Kingdom of Nanyue with its capital in Panyu. Hong Kong came under the jurisdiction of Panyu County for 93 years.

Figure 001
A painted pottery basin of the Neolithic period, featuring an incised pattern and perforated ring-foot, excavated from a site at Chung Hom Wan in Stanley. (Photo courtesy of Antiquities and Monuments Office)

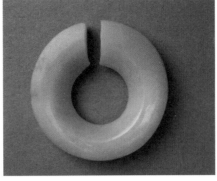

Figure 002
A slotted stone ring of the Neolithic period excavated from a site at Yung Long in Tuen Mun. (Photo courtesy of Antiquities and Monuments Office)

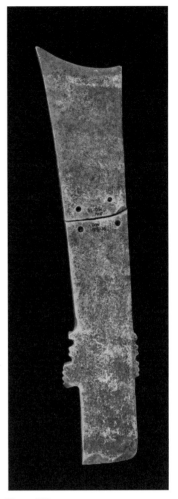

Figure 005
The inscription "Daji Panyu" (Great fortune to Panyu) on the brick wall of Lei Cheng Uk Han Tomb—indicating the jurisdiction of Panyu County over Hong Kong during the Han Dynasty. (Illustration by Hong Kong Chronicles Institute; photo courtesy of Hong Kong Museum of History)

Figure 004
Inside the Lei Cheng Uk Han Tomb—built in the Eastern Han Dynasty. (Photo courtesy of HKSAR Government)

Figure 003
A *yazhang* blade of the Bronze Age excavated from a site at Tai Wan on Lamma Island. (Photo courtesy of Antiquities and Monuments Office)

111 B.C. (6th year of Yuanding [元鼎] of the Western Han Dynasty)

The Nanyue Kingdom was defeated by General Lu Bode (路博德) and Admiral Yang Pu (楊僕) known by their official titles of *fubo jiangjun* and *louchuan jiangjun*, respectively, under Emperor Wu of the Han Dynasty (漢武帝). Nine prefectures, namely Nanhai, Cangwu, Hepu, Yulin, Jiaozhi, Jiuzhen, Rinan, Zhuya and Dan'er, were placed under a provincial administration. Hong Kong became part of Panyu County of Nanhai Prefecture.

Post-111 B.C. (6th year of Yuanding of the Western Han Dynasty)

Salt farms in the Hong Kong area were placed under the jurisdiction of the Panyu Bureau of Salt Affairs, an office established by the Han government after defeating the House of Zhao of Nanyue. A nationwide monopoly on salt and iron had been implemented nationwide since the 4th year of Yuanshou (元狩) of the Han Dynasty (119 B.C.).

206 B.C.–8 A.D. (The Western Han Dynasty)

Relics of stamped hard-paste porcelain vases, three-legged jars, boxes, and tools such as iron shovels and hoes, possibly from the Nanyue Kingdom, were found at the site of Pak Mong on Lantau Island. These give some indication of the cultural development of Hong Kong between the Nanyue and Western Han periods.

25 A.D.–220 A.D. (The Eastern Han Dynasty)

Hong Kong remained under the administration of Panyu County of Nanhai Prefecture. The phrases "Peace to Panyu" and "Fortune to Panyu" were inscribed on the bricks of Lei Cheng Uk Han Tomb in Kowloon. (Figures 004 and 005)

265 A.D. (1st year of Ganlu [甘露] of the Eastern Wu Dynasty)

Salt farms in the area of Dongguanchang, including Hong Kong, came under the Bureau of Salt Affairs in Nantou. Its commissioner was appointed by the Wu Dynasty.

331 A.D. (6th year of Xianhe [咸和] of the Eastern Jin Dynasty)

Hong Kong became part of Bao'an County, one of six counties under the Dongguan Prefecture which was one of the two administrations formed in the reorganisation of the Nanhai Prefecture. The salt farm of Dongguanchang in Hong Kong was administered by the commissioner of the Dongguan Bureau of Salt Affairs.

May–Jun 411 A.D. (4th month of the 7th year of Yixi [義熙] of the Eastern Jin Dynasty)

After joining a rebellion known as the Way of the Five Pecks of Rice against the Jin Dynasty, Lu Xun (盧循) was defeated and killed in Jiaozhou by Provincial Governor Du Huidu (杜慧度). Lu Xun's remaining supporters, known as Luyu or Luting, reportedly retreated to Tai Hai Shan (present-day Lantau Island).

428 A.D. (5th year of Yuanjia [元嘉] of the Liu Song Dynasty)

Buddhist master Pui To (杯渡) reportedly stayed in Tuen Mun on his southbound trip to Jiaozhou and Guangzhou. Ling To Monastery in Yuen Long and Pui To Monastery in Pui To Shan (present-day Tsing Shan Monastery in Castle Peak) were built by monks in his memory. The monasteries are two of Hong Kong's Three Oldest Temples. (Figure 006)

590 A.D. (10th year of Kaihuang [開皇] of the Sui Dynasty)

Bao'an County, in which Hong Kong was included, came under the jurisdiction of Guangzhou after the Dongguan Prefecture was abolished.

Feb–Mar 736 A.D. (1st month of the 24th year of Kaiyuan [開元] of the Tang Dynasty)

The Tang Dynasty established Tuen Mun Garrison (as part of Bao'an County, Guangzhou) under the command of the "Protectorate General Assigned to Defend the South." Headquartered at Nantou, the garrison had 2,000 soldiers deployed in defence of the maritime routes (near the present-day Pearl River Estuary).

Feb–Mar 744 A.D. (2nd month of the 3rd year of Tianbao [天寶] of the Tang Dynasty)

Soldiers from Tuen Mun Garrison were dispatched by the Prefect of the Nanhai Prefecture, Liu Julin (劉巨鱗), to move northward and quell the pirate Wu Lingguang (吳令光) of Zhejiang.

Oct–Nov 757 A.D. (9th month of the 2nd year of Zhide [至德] of the Tang Dynasty)

Bao'an County was renamed Dongguan County as part of Guangzhou.

Jun–Jul 815 A.D. (5th month of the 10th year of Yuanhe [元和] of the Tang Dynasty)

In the poem "Song of Riding the Wave," Liu Yuxi (劉禹錫) wrote that "Tuen Mun is battered with wave upon wave despite a lack of strong wind." This is the earliest literary description of Hong Kong. In 819 A.D., Han Yu (韓愈) described in the last poem of "Six Poems for Sending Off Yuan Shiba" that "rough waves are distinct despite the elevation of Tuen Mun."

Aug–Sep 917 A.D. (7th month of the 1st year of Qianheng [乾亨] of the Southern Han Dynasty)

Liu Yan (劉龑) established a new kingdom called "Dayue" with its capital in Panyu and assumed the regnal name of Qianheng (乾亨) (The kingdom was to be renamed Han the following year). Guangzhou was elevated in status and renamed Xingwang Prefecture; Hong Kong became part of Dongguan County of Xingwang Prefecture.

954 A.D. (12th year of Qianhe [乾和] of the Southern Han Dynasty)

Vice Commander of Kaiyi military station, Chen Xun (陳巡), who was also Inspector General and Guard-in-Command of Tuen Mun Garrison, ordered the construction of a statue of Buddhist Master Pui To (杯渡) at the site of Pui To Rock in Pui To Shan (present-day Castle Peak). (Figures 007 and 008)

Figure 006
The Ling To Monastery located at Ha Tsuen in Yuen Long in 1982. Its present size and form are the result of rebuilding during the Qing Dynasty. It is said to have been inhabited by Buddhist Master Pui To (杯渡) from the late Eastern Jin Dynasty to the early Liu Song Dynasty. (Photo courtesy of Hong Kong Museum of History)

Figure 007
The statue of Buddhist Master Pui To (杯渡) at Tsing Shan Monastery's Pui To Rock in Tuen Mun. (Photo taken in 2020 by Hong Kong Chronicles Institute)

Figure 008
Tsing Shan Monastery, also known as Tsing Shan Temple, one of the three oldest temples in Hong Kong. (Photo taken in 2020 by Hong Kong Chronicles Institute)

963 A.D. (6th year of Dabao [大寶] of the Southern Han Dynasty)

The last emperor of the Southern Han Dynasty, Liu Chang (劉鋹), established Mei Chuan Dou ("dou" being a sub-county administrative division) where 2,000 soldiers were stationed to oversee pearl fishing in Tai Po Hoi (present-day Tolo Harbour). This was the earliest record of pearl fishing in Hong Kong. At the time, men diving for pearls went as deep as 500 feet, weighed down with rocks; many drowned.

08 Mar 969 A.D. (18th of the 2nd month of the 12th year of Dabao of the Southern Han Dynasty)

The last emperor of the Southern Han dynasty, Liu Chang (劉鋹), renamed Pui To Shan as Sui Ying Shan with a monument to mark the occasion.

23 Jun 972 A.D. (10th of the 5th month of the 5th year of Kaibao [開寶] of the Northern Song Dynasty)

The Song court, seeing pearl fishing as harmful, issued a ban on the practice and abolished Mei Chuan Dou. The young and healthy were assigned to the army unit of Jingjiang while the old and weak were sent away. Pearl fishing was resumed shortly thereafter.

973 A.D. (6th year of Kaibao of the Northern Song Dynasty)

Tang Hon-fat (鄧漢黻), a government official and a native of Jishui of Jiangxi Province, travelled to Guangdong and lived in Sham Tin (present-day Kam Tin). He was the founder of the Tang clan in Guangdong.

Dec 984 A.D.–Jan 985 A.D. (12th month of the 1st year of Yongxi [雍熙] of the Northern Song Dynasty)

The Song court abolished pearl farms in Lingnan and issued a ban on pearl fishing.

1008 (1st year of Dazhongxiangfu [大中祥符] of the Northern Song Dynasty)

Lam Chung-kin (林松堅) and his brother relocated with their clan from Putian, Fujian to Pang Po Wai, Kowloon (present-day Tai Hom in Diamond Hill) and later to Po Kong Village (present-day Choi Hung Road Playground in Wong Tai Sin).

1012 (5th year of Dazhongxiangfu of the Northern Song Dynasty)

The Nam Tong Stone Pagoda was built at South Fat Tong Mun (present-day Tung Lung Chau).

1023–1085 (1st year of Tiansheng [天聖]–8th year of Yuanfeng [元豐] of the Northern Song Dynasty)

Hau Ng-long (侯五郎), a holder of of *jinshi* (the highest degree in the imperial examination), relocated from Panyu, Guangdong to Dongguan County (present-day Sheung Shui) where he became a founding ancestor of Ho Sheung Heung. The area was further developed by his 11th-generation descendent Hau Cheuk-fung (侯卓峰) in the early Ming Dynasty.

Jul 1060 (6th month of the 5th year of Jiayou [嘉祐] of the Northern Song Dynasty)

The *New Book of Tang* was completed, describing a "sailing distance of 200 *li* (an ancient Chinese unit equivalent to 0.31 mile) southeast from Guangzhou to Tuen Mun Shan" in its geography section. This is the first acknowledgement of a place in the Hong Kong region in an official record.

Pre-1078 (1st year of Yuanfeng [元豐] of the Northern Song Dynasty)

Hainanshan was established in Tai Hai Shan (present-day Lantau Island) by the Song court for the production of salt.

1089 (4th year of Yuanyou [元祐] of the Northern Song Dynasty)

Jiang Zhiqi (蔣之奇), Prefect of Guangzhou, wrote *The History of Pui To Shan*, a depiction of the legend of Buddhist master Pui To (杯渡)—who was said to have made a journey south during the Yuanjia (元嘉) period (424 A.D.–453 A.D.) of the Liu Song Dynasty—and a description of the origin of the name Pui To Shan.

Post-1105 (4th year of Chongning [崇寧] of the Northern Song Dynasty)

Deng Fuxie (鄧符協) of Jishui, Jiangxi Province relocated to Kwai Kok Shan in Sham Tin (present-day Kam Tin) where he established the first school on record in Hong Kong called Li Ying College.

15 Jan 1115 (18th of the 12th month of the 4th year of Zhenghe [政和] of the Northern Song Dynasty)

The Song court ordered the resumption of pearl fishing and instructed the Customs Officer of Guangnan to send pearls to the imperial court as tribute.

Post-1127 (1st year of Jianyan [建炎] of the Southern Song Dynasty)

The Tao clan of Jiangxi moved from Yulin in Guangxi to Ngau Tam Mei in Yuen Long in the period between the Northern Song Dynasty and Southern Song Dynasty. The clan then relocated to Tuen Mun and founded the village of Tuen Mun Tai Tsuen (present-day Tuen Tsz Wai) during the late Yuan Dynasty and early Ming Dynasty.

As late as 1127–1161 (1st year of Jianyan–31st year of Shaoxing [紹興] of the Southern Song Dynasty)

The Song court established an administrative unit named Kwun Fu Cheung (Guanfuchang) on the northwest coast of present-day Kowloon Bay to manage salt production.

Figure 009
The Kun Lung Gate Tower, circa early 20th century, located at Lung Yeuk Tau in Fanling. The poem inscribed on the tower refers to an imperial marriage between a member of the Southern Song Dynasty and a member of the Tang clan. (Photo courtesy of Special Collections, The University of Hong Kong Libraries)

1129 (3rd year of Jianyan of the Southern Song Dynasty)

Tang Yuen-leung (鄧元亮) of Sham Tin (present-day Kam Tim), then Gan County Magistrate in Jiangxi, organised an armed rescue of a Song princess during the invasion of Jin troops. His son Tang Wai-kap (鄧惟汲) later married the princess. During the period of Shaoxi (紹熙) (1190–1194) of the Song Dynasty, Emperor Guangzong (光宗) was reunited with the princess and called her Royal Aunt. Tang Wai-kap was conferred the imperial title *shui yuan jun ma* and was granted land in Dongguan. This was one case of marriage between the imperial family and a local clan. (Figure 009)

Dec 1154–Jan 1155 (12th month of the 25th year of Shaoxing [紹興] of the Southern Song Dynasty)

The Song court abolished the annual tribute of pearls and authorised private pearl fishing.

1131–1162 (Shaoxing of the Southern Song Dynasty)

The Song court subdued Zhu You (朱祐) and others in Tai Hai Shan by enlisting the strongest members of his forces. The local ban on fishing and salt-making was lifted.

The salt administrative unit of Hainanshan was upgraded in status to Hainanchang.

30 Nov 1164 (15th of the 11th month of the 2nd year of Longxing [隆興] of the Southern Song Dynasty)

Guangdong Province's Bureau of Tea and Salt ordered the closure of Kwun Fu Cheung due to its low salt production and remote location; it decreed a merger with another administrative unit called Tip Fuk Cheung (Diefuchang) (present-day northeast Sha Tau Kok). Kwun Fu Cheung would be re-established in the late Southern Song Dynasty.

20 Jun 1183 (29th of the 5th month of the 10th year of Chunxi [淳熙] of the Southern Song Dynasty)

The Song court issued a strict ban on illegal salt making in Tai Hai Shan.

1183 (10th year of Chunxi of the Southern Song Dynasty)

Pang Kwei (彭桂) of Luling, Jiangxi Province relocated his clan from Jieyang to Longshan, Dongguan County (present-day Lung Yeuk Tau in Fanling). He was the founder of today's Pang clan in Fanling.

15 Mar 1185 (12th of the 2nd month of the 12th year of Chunxi of the Southern Song Dynasty)

The Song court mobilised Guangdong's Bureau of Salt and Tea and marine forces to crack down on salt smuggling in Tai Hai Shan.

1191 (2nd year of Shaoxi [紹熙] of the Southern Song Dynasty)

A drought occurred in Dongguan County.

Jul–Aug 1197 (Leap 6th month of the 3rd year of Qingyuan [慶元] of the Southern Song Dynasty)

Xu Anguo (徐安國), Inspector of Guangdong Province's Bureau of Salt and Tea, moved to arrest salt smugglers in Tai Hai Shan. Local people resisted by forcing Gao Deng (高登), Deputy Security Controller, to lead their uprising; they advanced as far as Guangzhou by boat. In the 8th month (Sep–Oct), Qian Zhiwang (錢之望) was appointed as Guangzhou Prefect; he dispatched soldiers based in Yanxiangzhai of Fuzhou, bringing an end to the revolts through a massacre in the 10th month (Nov–Dec).

1197 (3rd year of Qingyuan of the Southern Song Dynasty)

The Song court stationed 300 soldiers in Tai Hai Shan on a quarterly rotational basis.

1200 (6th year of Qingyuan of the Southern Song Dynasty)

The number of soldiers stationed in Tai Hai Shan was reduced to 150. They were later transferred to Kwun Fu Cheung until full dismissal at the end of the Southern Song Dynasty.

May–Jun 1245 (5th month of the 5th year of Chunyou [淳祐] of the Southern Song Dynasty)

A typhoon hit Dongguan County; the sea level rose enormously and more than 2,000 households were overwhelmed by seawater.

Dec 1245–Jan 1246 (12th month of the 5th year of Chunyou of the Southern Song Dynasty)

Three consecutive days of heavy snowfall left more than a foot of snow in Dongguan County.

1254 (2nd year of Baoyou [寶祐] of the Southern Song Dynasty)

Li Maoying (李昴英) was given the noble title of *kaiguo nan* (dynasty founding baron) of Panyu and was granted feudal control of 300 households by the Song court. Part of his land, called Shiyishuishan (mountain of fief tax), was located in Tai Hai Shan (present-day Lantau Island). Two boundary stones inscribed with the characters "Shiyishuishan of the Li Family" are still extant. (Figure 010)

1258 (6th year of Baoyou of the Southern Song Dynasty)

Tang Yim-lung (鄧炎龍) of Lung Yeuk Tau took the provincial imperial examination and ranked first. Two years later, he passed another special session of the imperial examination called *Caoshi*.

Circa 1266 (2nd year of Xianchun [咸淳] of the Southern Song Dynasty)

Lam Tao-yi (林道義) of Po Kong built a temple near northern Fat Tong (present-day Joss House Bay) in Sai Kung. Rebuilt several times and renamed Tin Hau Temple, also known as the Big Temple, it is the oldest and largest temple still extant in Hong Kong. (Figure 011)

20 Jul 1274 (15th of the 6th month of the 10th year of Xianchun of the Southern Song Dynasty)

Yan Yizhang (嚴益彰), Superintendent of Kwun Fu Cheung, commemorated his visit to southern and northern Fat Tong in Sai Kung with an engraved stone in northern Fat Tong. The stone is thought to be the oldest with a marked date in Hong Kong. (Figure 012)

Mar–Apr 1277 (2nd month of the 2nd year of Jingyan [景炎] of the Southern Song Dynasty)

All Song troops in Guangdong surrendered upon the capture of Guangzhou by soldiers of the Yuan Dynasty. Song Emperor Duanzong (端宗), also known as Di Shi (帝昰), formed a seaborne court sailing through Dapeng to Mui Wai Shan (present-day Mui Wo) and began construction of a temporary palace.

May–Jun 1277 (4th month of the 2nd year of Jingyan of the Southern Song Dynasty)

Emperor Duanzong (端宗) and his entourage moved to Kwun Fu Cheung in Kowloon. An engraved rock named Sung Wong Toi (Terrace of the Song Emperor) was later placed to commemorate this occasion. (Figure 013)

Figure 011
The Tin Hau Temple, also known as the Tin Hau Temple of North Fat Tong, located at Joss House Bay in Sai Kung and built during the Song Dynasty. (Photo taken in 2020 by Hong Kong Chronicles Institute)

Figure 012
The rock inscription located at Tei Tong Tsui of Joss House Bay in Sai Kung, dating back to 20 July 1274, was declared a monument in 1979. (Illustration by Hong Kong Chronicles Institute; photo courtesy of Antiquities and Monuments Office)

Figure 013
The engraved rock (upper right) at Sung Wong Toi in the 1920s–1930s. The gate (centre) was built in 1915. (Photo courtesy of Hong Kong Museum of History)

Figure 010
The "Shiyishuishan of the Li Family" boundary stone on display at Hong Kong Museum of History. (Photo taken in 2019 and courtesy of Po Choi Siu-tsun)

Jul 1277 (6th month of the 2nd year of Jingyan of the Southern Song Dynasty)

Emperor Duanzong (端宗) and his entourage travelled to Nam Tong Pagoda at Fat Tong Mun and stayed in Kwun Fu Cheung.

Sep–Oct 1277 (9th month of the 2nd year of Jingyan of the Southern Song Dynasty)

The Song imperial family living in Kwun Fu Cheung was pursued by generals of the Yuan Dynasty, including Meng Gudai (蒙固岱), Suo Duo (索多), Pu Shougeng (蒲壽庚) and Liu Shen (劉深). Emperor Duanzong (端宗) and his entourage fled to Tsin Wan (present-day Tsuen Wan) by boat.

Nov–Dec 1277 (11th month of the 2nd year of Jingyan of the Southern Song Dynasty)

In Tsin Wan, Emperor Duanzong (端宗) was attacked by General Liu Shen (劉深). He and his general Zhang Shijie (張世傑) retreated to Xiu Shan.

Mar–Apr 1278 (3rd month of the 3rd year of Jingyan of the Southern Song Dynasty)

Emperor Duanzong (端宗) relocated to Gangzhou. This is a part of Lantau Island according to historians Jian Youwen (簡又文) and Lo Hsiang-lin (羅香林) but is said to be part of Zhanjiang in Guangdong by scholar Jao Tsung-i (饒宗頤).

08 May 1278 (15th of the 4th month of the 3rd year of Jingyan of the Southern Song Dynasty)

Emperor Duanzong (端宗) died of an illness in Gangzhou at the age of 11.

10 May 1278 (17th of the 4th month of the 3rd year of Jingyan of the Southern Song Dynasty)

The eight-year-old Prince of Wei Bing (昺) succeeded to the throne in Gangzhou and became Emperor Bing (宋帝昺). On the 1st day of the 5th month (23 May), his reign was named Xiangxing (祥興). Gangzhou was renamed Xianglong County.

22 Jun 1278 (1st of the 6th month of the 1st year of Xiangxing [祥興] of the Southern Song Dynasty)

A solar eclipse was observed in Dongguan County.

Jun–Jul 1278 (6th month of the 1st year of Xiangxing of the Southern Song Dynasty)

Emperor Bing (宋帝昺), escorted by General Zhang Shijie (張世傑), fled to Mount Ya. The Song Dynasty was overthrown after multiple defeats in the following year. Hong Kong came under the rule of the Yuan Dynasty.

Circa 1279 (16th year of Zhiyuan [至元] of the Yuan Dynasty)

Tang Fung-shun (鄧馮遜) of the fifth generation of his clan in Ping Shan built an ancestral hall—which is the oldest hall still standing in Hong Kong. (Figure 014)

Figure 014
The Tang Ancestral Hall in Ping Shan. (Photo taken in 2020 by Hong Kong Chronicles Institute)

1280 (17th year of Zhiyuan of the Yuan Dynasty)

The Yuan court issued a directive to restart pearl fishing in Tai Po Hoi under the Guangzhou administration.

Jul–Aug 1282 (6th month of the 19th year of Zhiyuan of the Yuan Dynasty)

Crops in Dongguan County were damaged as a result of swelling seawater.

1293 (30th year of Zhiyuan of the Yuan Dynasty)

The Yuan court abolished the salt administration based in Kwun Fu Cheung. Salt management records were transferred to Wong Tin Cheung (present-day Bao'an District in Shenzhen).

1297 (1st year of Dade [大德] of the Yuan Dynasty)

Under the direct order of the Yuan court, over 700 Tanka households were instructed to resume pearl fishing in Tai Po Hoi and Huizhou at three-year intervals.

1304 (8th year of Dade of the Yuan Dynasty)

The Yuan court established a sub-county magistracy in Tuen Mun in the Hong Kong region. It came under the jurisdiction of Dongguan County of Guangzhou Prefecture. The office was situated in Tuen Mun Garrison Fort where a sub-county magistrate and 150 soldiers were stationed. A sub-county magistracy was also established at Kwun Fu.

Jan–Feb 1318 (12th month of the 4th year of Yanyou [延祐] of the Yuan Dynasty)

The Yuan court established the Guangzhou Pearl Inspectorate to oversee pearl fishing in Guangzhou. It included Tai Po Hoi, a key production base.

Jul–Aug 1320 (6th month of the 7th year of Yanyou of the Yuan Dynasty)

The Yuan court banned pearl fishing in Tai Po Hoi following a complaint submitted by Cheung Wai-yan (張惟寅), a member of the Dongguan gentry, citing public inconvenience.

Mar–Apr 1337 (2nd month of the 3rd year of Zhiyuan [至元] of the Yuan Dynasty)

The Yuan court re-established the Pearl Inspectorate for pearl fishing in Tai Po Hoi.

1350 (10th year of Zhizheng [至正] of the Yuan Dynasty)

Liu Chung-kit (廖仲傑) of Tingzhou, Fujian relocated to Dongguan, Guangdong, settling near Sheung Yue River in Fung Shui Heung (present-day Sheung Shui Heung). He was the founder of today's Liu clan in Sheung Shui.

1352 (12th year of Zhizheng of the Yuan Dynasty)

After moving from Dongguan to present-day Wong Tai Sin, Ng Shing-tat (吳成達) established Nga Tsin Village as a founder of the Ng clan in Nga Tsin Wai Tsuen.

1359 (19th year of Zhizheng of the Yuan Dynasty)

Amid widespread revolts in the late Yuan Dynasty, He Zhen (何真) of Dongguan led his villagers to defend his hometown, occupying Dongguan and Huizhou. He assigned his subordinates Ou Mengsu (歐孟素), Lin Yishi (林一石) and Zou Zineng (鄒子能) to defend Lidong (present-day Loi Tung in Sha Tau Kok), Lam Village and Sham Tin (present-day Kam Tin), respectively.

Circa 1362–1368 (22nd–28th year of Zhizheng of the Yuan Dynasty)

Tang Kwai-sau (鄧季琇) of Dongguan relocated to Lung Yeuk Tau in Fanling and established Lo Wai Village. He was the founder of the Tang clan in Lung Yeuk Tau.

18 Apr 1368 (1st of the 4th month of the 1st year of Hongwu [洪武] of the Ming Dynasty)

Hong Kong came under the rule of the Ming Dynasty. He Zhen (何 真), Councillor of Jiangxi of the Yuan Dynasty, surrendered Dongguan and Huizhou. Earlier, on the 2nd day of the 2nd month (20 February), Ming General Liao Yongzhong (廖永忠) and Colonel Zhu Liangzu (朱亮祖) were both dispatched to Guangdong.

Post-1368 (1st year of Hongwu of the Ming Dynasty)

The Man clan of Jiangxi relocated from Ping Shan to Tai Hang in Tai Po.

1370 (3rd year of Hongwu of the Ming Dynasty)

The Tuen Mun Garrison Fort was incorporated as part of Gushu Garrison Fort (present-day Bao'an in Shenzhen).

The Ming court established the Kwun Fu Sub-county Magistracy—for which a sub-county magistrate, a clerk and 50 archers were assigned. The office was situated in Kwun Fu Garrison Fort (present-day Kowloon City) with similar jurisdictional power as Tuen Mun Sub-county Magistracy.

Oct–Nov 1374 (9th month of the 7th year of Hongwu of the Ming Dynasty)

The Ming court abolished pearl fishing in Tai Po Hoi. Before that, between the 4th and 8th months (May–Oct), only half a catty of pearls had been harvested from Tai Po Hoi under the command of Dongguan Magistrate Zhan Xun (詹勛). Pearl fishing was resumed between 1573 and 1620 during the reign of Emperor Wanli (萬曆).

1381 (14th year of Hongwu of the Ming Dynasty)

The Nanhai Military Station was established south of Dongguan County by the Ming court to protect the area including Hong Kong.

27 Apr 1382 (14th of the 3rd month of the 15th year of Hongwu of the Ming Dynasty)

Nobleman Zhao Yong (趙庸) of Nanxiong enlisted 10,000 Tanka persons in Dongguan and Xiangshan into the navy as a way to prevent Tanka people from becoming bandits and also to defend the locality.

1382 (15th year of Hongwu of the Ming Dynasty)

Tang Tung-sou (鄧通叟) of Ping Shan was appointed as Prefect of Ningguo Prefecture after passing a special examination.

1384 (17th year of Hongwu of the Ming Dynasty)

The Ming court restored coastal defences and ordered the construction of signal stations—which covered Hong Kong.

1394 (27th year of Hongwu of the Ming Dynasty)

Dongguan Garrison in Nantou and Dapeng Garrison on Dapeng Peninsula were formed under the command of the Nanhai Military Station.

1368–1398 (Hongwu of the Ming Dynasty)

Tang Tung-sou (鄧彥通) of Ping Shan built the Tsui Sing Lau Pagoda—which became the only ancient pagoda in Hong Kong. (Figures 015 and 016)

1415 (13th year of Yongle [永樂] of the Ming Dynasty)

Dongguan County was hit by a typhoon and flooded in the autumn.

A snowfall occurred in Dongguan County.

1403–1424 (Yongle of the Ming Dynasty)

To evade military service, Man Sai-ko (文世歌), a seventh-generation descendent of the Man clan in Yongxin of Jiangxi Province relocated to Lo Fu Hang in Tuen Mun. He then settled in San Tin where he became a clan founder.

1426–1435 (Xuande [宣德] of the Ming Dynasty)

The Ling Wan Retreat House was built by Tang Yam (鄧欽) of Kam Tin in honour of his stepmother. Known as Ling Wan Nunnery, it is the only nunnery amongst Hong Kong's three remaining oldest temples.

1444 (9th year of Zhengtong [正統] of the Ming Dynasty)

The Man clan of San Tin built an ancestral hall named Tun Yue Tong in Fan Tin Village.

Figure 015
The Tsui Sing Lau Pagoda, also known as the Pagoda of Gathering Stars and Wenchang Tower, in the 1950s. It was built by the Tang clan of Ping Shan. (Photo courtesy of Hong Kong Museum of History)

Figure 016
The present-day Tsui Sing Lau Pagoda. (Photo courtesy of Antiquities and Monuments Office)

Figure 017
An aerial view of the walled villages of Kat Hing Wai (lower) and Tai Hong Wai (upper) in Kam Tin, Yuen Long. (Photo taken in the 1960s and courtesy of Special Collections, The University of Hong Kong Libraries)

06 Sep 1453 (4th of the 8th month of the 4th year of Jingtai [景泰] of the Ming Dynasty)

The Kwun Fu Sub-county Magistracy was moved to a more strategic location in Tuen Mun Village.

1461 (5th year of Tianshun [天順] of the Ming Dynasty)

Dongguan County was hit by drought and famine. In a disaster relief effort organised by Magistrate Wu Zhong (吳中), among the donors were 50 people who contributed more than 7,000 *qian* (ancient Chinese dollar) each.

In the autumn, flooding in Dongguan County led to crop damage, causing a famine the following spring.

1471 (7th year of Chenghua [成化] of the Ming Dynasty)

Tang Ting-ching (鄧廷貞) of Kam Tin was appointed as a lecturer in Wan'an County of Jiangxi Province after passing a provincial civil service examination based on his treatise on the *Book of Documents*.

1475 (11th year of Chenghua of the Ming Dynasty)

In the autumn, a typhoon hit Dongguan County. Nearly half of all crops were damaged by floods.

1465–1487 (Chenghua of the Ming Dynasty)

The Tang clan in Kam Tin constructed the walled villages of Kat Hing Wai and Tai Hong Wai. (Figure 017)

1500–1520 (13th year of Hongzhi [弘治]–15th year of Zhengde [正德] of the Ming Dynasty)

The Tang clan in Ping Shan built an ancestral hall named Yu Kiu.

Sep–Oct 1503 (9th month of the 16th year of Hongzhi of the Ming Dynasty)

Crops were destroyed amid swelling seal level in Dongguan County.

1488–1505 (Hongzhi of the Ming Dynasty)

The Kwan Tai Temple in Tai O was built. It is the oldest Kwan Tai temple still in existence in Hong Kong.

1514 (9th year of Zhengde [正德] of the Ming Dynasty)

Jorge Álvares, a Portuguese explorer, arrived in Tuen Mun from Melaka (present-day Malacca) with two ships. He erected a monument with the Portuguese coat of arms to signal occupation and attempted to trade with China. This was followed by seven years of Portuguese occupation of Tuen Mun and Kwai Chung.

15 Aug 1517 (28th of the 7th month of the 12th year of Zhengde of the Ming Dynasty)

The Governor of Portuguese India, Captain Fernão Peres de Andrade, ordered Jorge Álvares and Tomé Pires to sail on a fleet of four ships from Melaka to Tuen Mun. They arrived on 17 June, carrying gifts and letters certifying their credentials. At the end of September, they entered Guangzhou ostensibly to pay tribute; their proposal for trade was turned down. Upon returning to Tuen Mun, the mission attempted without success to use bribery as a means of arranging a meeting with Emperor Wuzong (武宗) of the Ming Dynasty. In 1521, members of the mission were imprisoned in Guangzhou for crimes of killing and plundering committed by the Portuguese in Tuen Mun.

Aug 1518 (6th–7th month of the 13th year of Zhengde of the Ming Dynasty)

Following the orders of the Governor of Portuguese India, Captain Simão de Andrade arrived in Tuen Mun with three ships in the name of "searching for Tomé Pires." Simão de Andrade set up barracks and execution grounds and produced firelocks without permission from the Ming court, while his men engaged in looting, human trafficking and ravaging women.

27 Jun 1521 (23rd of the 5th month of the 16th year of Zhengde of the Ming Dynasty)

Wang Hong (汪鋐), Deputy Commander of the Guangdong Maritime Circuit, launched an attack on more than 10 Portuguese ships in Tuen Mun with a fleet of over 50 Ming naval vessels. On the night of 07 September, three Portuguese ships escaped under the cover of a rainstorm. It marked the first sea battle between China and a European power known as the Battle of Tuen Mun. Ming forces later recovered Tuen Mun after a three-month siege and no Portuguese remained in the vicinity thereafter.

Aug 1522 (7th–8th month of the 1st year of the reign of Emperor Jiajing [嘉靖] of the Ming Dynasty)

By the order of King Manuel I of Portugal, Martim Afonso de Melo Coutinho and Pedro Homem arrived in Tuen Mun from Melaka on a fleet of six ships. Portuguese envoys, accompanied by 300 soldiers, attempted to establish peace with the Ming court, build a fort and conduct trade, but to no avail. Instead, Wang Hong (汪鋐), Deputy Commander of the Guangdong Maritime Circuit, launched an attack on the Portuguese mission with soldiers of Nantou Garrison under his command. The Portuguese suffered losses in Sai Tso Wan and Shaozhou; Pedro Homem was killed. The Ming army captured two Portuguese ships with cannons, beheaded 35 Portuguese soldiers and took away 42 Portuguese leaders, including Bartholameu Soarez. All the Portuguese leaders were later executed on 23 September on charges of piracy. During the night, Martim Afonso de Melo Coutinho fled to Melaka with the remaining soldiers. The Portuguese turned their focus to Fujian and Zhejiang and later succeeded in occupying Macao from 1557 to 1999.

1525 (4th year of the reign of Emperor Jiajing of the Ming Dynasty)

The Tang clan in Lung Yeuk Tau built an ancestral hall named Tang Chung Ling.

Mar–Apr 1526 (2nd month of the 5th year of the reign of Emperor Jiajing of the Ming Dynasty)

Dongguan County was hit by thunderstorms, lightning and heavy rainfall.

1531 (10th year of the reign of Emperor Jiajing of the Ming Dynasty)

Feng Tili (馮體立) of Wudu (present-day Hong Kong) in Dongguan passed a provincial civil service examination based on his treatise on the *Classic of Poetry* and was appointed as Director of Schools in Haizhou, South Zhili. He later served as Magistrate of Ziyang County of Shandong, Luocheng County of Guangxi and Mengzhi County of Yunnan.

1533 (12th year of the reign of Emperor Jiajing of the Ming Dynasty)

Dongguan was attacked by pirates Xu Zegui (許折桂) and Wen Zongshan (溫宗善). Battalion Commander Gu Sheng (顧晟) died in the line of duty while trying to hunt down pirates in Chun Fa Yeung (waters near present-day Tsing Yi Island).

1535–1550 (14th–29th year of the reign of Emperor Jiajing of the Ming Dynasty)

Villages and ships along the coast of Hong Kong were frequently threatened with robbery and extortion by pirates including Lin Daoqian (林道乾). Fishermen were afraid to go out to sea.

1540 (19th year of the reign of Emperor Jiajing of the Ming Dynasty)

The Ming court set up coastal defences with the three-route patrol units against Japanese pirates along the coast of Guangdong. The middle route ran from Nantou of Dongguan County to coastal points such as Fat Tong Mun, Shap Tsz Moon and Leng Shui Kwok, covering today's Hong Kong region.

1542 (21st year of the reign of Emperor Jiajing of the Ming Dynasty)

The salt administration of Wong Tin Cheung (present-day Bao'an in Shenzhen) was reorganised by the Ming court and became part of Dongguanchang.

1551 (30th year of the reign of Emperor Jiajing of the Ming Dynasty)

The Dongguan Battalion was invaded by pirate He Yaba (何亞八) and his accomplices in the autumn. Battalion Commander Wan Li (萬里) died in defence of the Nanshan Signal Station. He Yaba continued his assault into the Hong Kong region, killing Liu Chung-shan (廖重山) and a couple surnamed Hou (侯) in Sheung Shui, before he and his forces were annihilated by Commander Li Maocai (李茂材).

1558 (37th year of the reign of Emperor Jiajing of the Ming Dynasty)

Dongguan County was hit by a drought.

1563 (42nd year of the reign of Emperor Jiajing of the Ming Dynasty)

Governor of Fujian Tan Lun (譚綸) and Brigade General Qi Jiguang (戚繼光) petitioned the Ming court to reinstate the former system of naval stations. Six stations were established in Guangdong, including four in the Hong Kong region (Fat Tong Mun, Lung Shuen Wan, Tai O and Long To Wan). Each guard station had around 200 soldiers.

Apr–May 1565 (4th month of the 44th year of the reign of Emperor Jiajing of the Ming Dynasty)

The price of rice soared to 100 copper cash (0.1 tael of silver) per *dou* following a famine in Dongguan County.

30 Dec 1567 (1st of the 12th month of the 1st year of the reign of Emperor Longqing [隆慶] of the Ming Dynasty)

Dongguan County was struck by an earthquake in the winter.

1567–1572 (The reign of Emperor Longqing of the Ming Dynasty)

Tang Hung-lun (鄧孔麟) of Dabu (present-day Tai Po) offered himself as ransom for his father when his father was kidnapped by pirate Lin Feng (林鳳). Tang Hung-lun ultimately managed to escape. Another Dabu man, Tang Sze-mang (鄧師孟), also offered himself as ransom for his father and drowned. In 1595, the Hall of the Tang Family Filial Son in Tai Po was constructed by the Tang clan of Lung Yeuk Tau in commemoration of Tang Sze-mang. The temple no longer exists.

May–Jun 1573 (5th month of the 1st year of the reign of Emperor Wanli [萬曆] of the Ming Dynasty)

Xin'an County, headquartered in Nantou under the administration of Guangzhou, was established by the Ming court at the request of the local gentry of Nantou. It was formed with 56 *li* (an ancient unit equivalent to 0.31 mile) of land and 7,608 households with a population of 33,971 from Dongguan County, covering the areas of present-day Hong Kong and Shenzhen. The name "Xin'an" means "bring change by discarding the old and make peace by mitigating risks."

11 Feb 1574 (20th of the 1st month of the 2nd year of the reign of Emperor Wanli of the Ming Dynasty)

The Chan, Wai, Tong, Ng, Hui, Choi, Yuan, Lee, Yeung and Wong clans jointly established a walled village called Chik Chuen Wai, commonly known as Tai Wai, near the Shing Mun River in Sha Tin.

1574 (2nd year of the reign of Emperor Wanli of the Ming Dynasty)

Lin Yunlong (林雲龍) of Fujian was appointed as the first Kwun Fu Sub-county Magistrate of the newly established Xin'an County.

1578 (6th year of the reign of Emperor Wanli of the Ming Dynasty)

A comet was observed in Xin'an County.

1581 (9th year of the reign of Emperor Wanli of the Ming Dynasty)

Cang wu zong du jun men zhi (Military Gazetteer of Guangdong and Guangxi), compiled by Ying Jia (應檟) and revised by Liu Yaohui (劉堯誨), appeared with the "Complete Chart of Guangdong and Guangxi"—which was the first map to mention Kowloon.

1583 (11th year of the reign of Emperor Wanli of the Ming Dynasty)

Xin'an County was hit by a severe drought in the summer and autumn.

1587 (15th year of the reign of Emperor Wanli of the Ming Dynasty)

Xin'an County Magistrate Qiu Tiqian (邱體乾) led the compilation of the first official Xin'an County Local Chronicles— of which only the preface remains today.

During a drought in Xin'an County, 2,000 *dan* (an ancient unit equivalent to 2.75 bushels) of grain were donated by Deng Yuanxun (鄧元勳) of Sham Tin. "Sham Tin" was later renamed "Kam Tin" by County Magistrate Qiu Tiqian (邱體乾) as a tribute to the "fertile land like a piece of rich brocade."

1591 (19th year of the reign of Emperor Wanli of the Ming Dynasty)

A lieutenant-colonel was assigned to Nantou by the Ming court to guard the waters around Fat Tong Mun, Kowloon, Tuen Mun and Kap Shui Mun in the Hong Kong region.

1596 (24th year of the reign of Emperor Wanli of the Ming Dynasty)

Following a severe drought in Xin'an County, rice was priced at 160 copper cash per *dou* (an ancient unit equivalent to 2.2 gallons), Chen Xi (陳禧) of Tsing Yi Island donated 1,000 *dan* (an ancient unit equivalent to 2.75 bushels) of grain and was honoured as a "Distinguished Guest in a Township Ceremony."

1598 (26th year of the reign of Emperor Wanli of the Ming Dynasty)

Guo Fei (郭棐) of Panyu published a Guangdong chronicle called *Yue daji* with the "Coastal Map of Guangdong"— on which more than 70 Hong Kong locations were marked. The name "Hong Kong," marked near present-day Aberdeen, is the earliest known identification of Hong Kong on an ancient map. (Maps 1 and 2)

1600–1644 (28th year of the reign of Emperor Wanli–17th year of the reign of Emperor Chongzhen [崇 禎] of the Ming Dynasty)

The Hau Ku Shek Ancestral Hall at Ho Sheung Heung in Sheung Shui was built. (Figure 018)

Figure 018
The Hau Ku Shek Ancestral Hall located at Ho Sheung Heung in Sheung Shui, New Territories. (Photo courtesy of Antiquities and Monuments Office)

Figure 019
Remains of an animal-driven grinder complete with a groove and wheel made of granite as a tool for production of porcelain powder in Sheung Wun You Village. (Photo courtesy of Antiquities and Monuments Office)

Figure 020
The present-day village of Fanling Wai with three ancient cannons and a *feng shui* pond. (Photo taken in 2020 by Hong Kong Chronicles Institute)

26 Sep 1603 (22nd of the 8th month of the 31st year of the reign of Emperor Wanli of the Ming Dynasty)

Xin'an County was struck by an earthquake in the autumn.

15 Sep 1605 (3rd of the 8th month of the 33rd year of the reign of Emperor Wanli of the Ming Dynasty)

Xin'an County was struck by an earthquake in the autumn.

1605 (33rd year of the reign of Emperor Wanli of the Ming Dynasty)

The Ming court banned pearl farming and private pearl fishing, given the diminishing stocks of mussels and clams in Guangdong. The pearl farming industry in Hong Kong subsequently declined.

1610 (38th year of the reign of Emperor Wanli of the Ming Dynasty)

Tang Leung-sze (鄧良仕) of Kam Tin was admitted to the Imperial Academy and later appointed as a Sub-director of Schools.

16 Jul 1620 (17th of the 6th month of the 48th year of the reign of Emperor Wanli of the Ming Dynasty)

Xin'an County was struck by an earthquake.

1573–1620 (The reign of Emperor Wanli of the Ming Dynasty)

The Man and Tse clans relocated to Dapu where they established a village and built kilns for the production of blue-and-white porcelain, a vital economic sector of Hong Kong during the Ming Dynasty and Qing Dynasty. (Figure 019)

Liu Nam-sa (廖南沙), a seventh-generation descendent of the Liu clan in Sheung Shui, worked with other members of his clan to establish a village (present-day Wai Nei Village) between the Ng Tung River and the Sheung Yue River. The area was later developed into Sheung Shui Heung.

The Pang clan of Lung Shan moved into Fan Pik Leng and established the village of Fanling Wai after an earlier relocation from Lung Shan to Fan Leng Lau. (Figure 020)

1623 (3rd year of Tianqi [天啟] of the Ming Dynasty)

Two large Dutch ships arrived in Anxia through Fat Tong Mun. They retreated after a militia, under Xin'an County Magistrate Tao Xuexiu (陶學修), was organised for defence.

May–Jun 1624 (4th month of the 4th year of Tianqi of the Ming Dynasty)

The price of rice in Xin'an County further rose to 150 copper cash per *dou* (an ancient unit equivalent to 2.2 gallons) .

1629 (2nd year of the reign of Emperor Chongzhen of the Ming Dynasty)

A pandemic broke out in Xin'an County, causing large numbers of deaths.

1630 (3rd year of the reign of Emperor Chongzhen of the Ming Dynasty)

Led by Li Kuiqi (李魁奇), over 100 pirate ships invaded Fat Tong Mun and plundered coastal villages. Troops of Nantou Fort, led by Lieutenant Colonel Chen Gong (陳拱), were mobilised in retaliation; Chen was killed in battle at Nantouhai (present-day Deep Bay).

May 1631 (4th month of the 4th year of Emperor Chongzhen of the Ming Dynasty)

The price of rice in Xin'an County rose even higher to 160 copper cash per *dou* (an ancient unit equivalent to 2.2 gallons).

1633 (6th year of the reign of Emperor Chongzhen of the Ming Dynasty)

Pirate Liu Xiang (劉香) attacked the coastal areas of Xin'an (including present-day Hong Kong) and was repelled by Zheng Zhilong (鄭芝龍), Major General of Fujian. Liu Xiang mounted another attack on Xin'an and invaded Nantou with over 200 pirate ships on 15 June 1634. A third attack in 1635 followed before Liu and his fellow pirates were defeated at sea by Zheng Zhilong in June-July 1635.

Apr–Jul 1636 (4th–5th month of the 9th year of Emperor Chongzhen of the Ming Dynasty)

Xin'an County was hit by drought and famine. The County Magistrate ordered disaster relief as the price of rice again hit 160 copper cash per *dou* (an ancient unit equivalent to 2.2 gallons).

1637 (10th year of the reign of Emperor Chongzhen of the Ming Dynasty)

Following the orders of King Charles I of England, Captain John Weddell of the Courteen Association arrived in southern China, accompanied by armed merchant ships. He and his fleet ignored the order to anchor near Lantau Island and continued up the Pearl River estuary towards Guangzhou but soon retreated. This is known to be Britain's first official mission to China.

Xin'an County Magistrate Li Xuan (李鉉) resumed the compilation of the Xin'an County Local Chronicles. The text is now lost.

Circa 1640–1644 (13th–17th year of the reign of Emperor Chongzhen of the Ming Dynasty)

According to Xin'an County Magistrate Zhou Xiyao (周希曜), armed disputes over market and land share were frequent among the villages of Xin'an County, including Hong Kong.

Dec 1641 (11th month of the 14th year of the reign of Emperor Chongzhen of the Ming Dynasty)

In Huizhou, Mianhua Wang (綿花王) of Yinpingzui led a group of bandits in an attack on Lung Yeuk Tau Village. Xin'an County Magistrate Zhou Xiyao (周希曜) commanded troops to capture Mianhua Wang and 30 other culprits, beheading 300 others along the way.

10 Jun 1643 (24th of the 4th month of the 16th year of the reign of Emperor Chongzhen of the Ming Dynasty)

A typhoon hit Xin'an County, causing significant damage to trees, houses and boats.

1643 (16th year of the reign of Emperor Chongzhen of the Ming Dynasty)

Xin'an County Magistrate Zhou Xiyao (周希曜) revised the Xin'an County Local Chronicles. The original text is lost today; only the preface published in the 1688 and 1819 editions has remained.

Pre—1644 (17th year of the reign of Emperor Chongzhen of the Ming Dynasty)

King Law Ka Shuk, a village academy in Dapu Tau, was established; it later became known as the Tang Ancestral Hall.

The Che Kung Temple at Ho Chung in Sai Kung was built. It is the oldest existing Che Kung temple in Hong Kong.

1644–1736 (1st year of the reign of Emperor Shunzhi [順治]–the 1st year of the reign of Emperor Qianlong [乾隆] of the Qing Dynasty)

An earlier iteration of the Kang Yung Study Hall was built by the Lee clan of Wo Hang Village in Sha Tau Kok.

11 Oct 1646 (3rd of the 9th month of the 3rd year of the reign of Emperor Shunzhi of the Qing Dynasty)

The Liu clan of Sheung Shui began construction of the village of Sheung Shui Wai; it was completed a year later.

1646 (3rd year of the reign of Emperor Shunzhi of the Qing Dynasty)

A bandit from Huizhou named Chen Yao (陳耀) invaded the areas of San Tin, Kowloon and Kwun Fu and launched a nine-day siege on Lung Yeuk Tau but retreated empty-handed.

Wu Qiwei (吳起渭) of Jiangxi Province became the first Sub-county Magistrate of Kwun Fu in the Qing Dynasty.

Apr–May 1647 (3rd month of the 4th year of the reign of Emperor Shunzhi of the Qing Dynasty)

Ming loyalist Lieutenant Colonel Li Wanrong (李萬榮) seized Kei Po Shan (present-day Devil's Peak) between the southeast side of Kowloon Garrison and northern Lei Yue Mun. He blocked the channel and extorted money from merchant ships near Haimen. He surrendered in 1656, following a siege by Qing Brigade General Huang Yingjie (黃應傑) at Dapeng Mountain.

1648 (5th year of the reign of Emperor Shunzhi of the Qing Dynasty)

Xin'an County was struck by a severe famine; rice was priced at 1.2 taels of silver per *dou* (an ancient unit equivalent to 2.2 gallons). Simultaneously, Xin'an County was struck by a pandemic, which caused many deaths and a streak of looting.

1653 (10th year of the reign of Emperor Shunzhi of the Qing Dynasty)

Xin'an County was stricken with another famine. The price of rice increased to 800 copper cash per *dou* (an ancient unit equivalent to 2.2 gallons); many died from starvation.

08 Dec 1655 (24th of the 10th month of the 12th year of the reign of Emperor Shunzhi of the Qing Dynasty)

Xin'an County experienced a severe hail storm; houses were damaged and some people were hurt.

27 Jul 1656 (16th of the 6th month of the 13th year of the reign of Emperor Shunzhi of the Qing Dynasty)

The Qing court issued the first-ever proclamation banning travel by sea—a decree which affected Zhejiang, Fujian, Guangdong, Jiangnan (present-day Jiangsu), Shandong and Tianjin. Earthen dams and wooden fences were ordered to be erected to prevent coastal residents from providing relief to Ming loyalist Zheng Chenggong (鄭成功), also known to Westerners as Koxinga.

23 Dec 1660 (8th of the 11th month of the 17th year of the reign of Emperor Shunzhi of the Qing Dynasty)

Xin'an County was struck by thunder, lightning and seven days of continuous rain.

Sep–Oct 1661 (8th month of the 18th year of the reign of Emperor Shunzhi of the Qing Dynasty)

The Qing court issued an evacuation order for four provinces, namely Jiangnan, Zhejiang, Fujian and Guangdong. The order was for people to move inland away from the coast. (Figure 021)

Apr–May 1662 (3rd month of the 1st year of the reign of Emperor Kangxi [康熙] of the Qing Dynasty)

The Qing court implemented a policy to withdraw the boundary 30–50 *li* (an ancient unit equivalent to 0.31 mile) from the coast, accompanied by an order to all coastal residents to evacuate the area. Brigade General Cao Zhi (曹志) was sent to make people move inland. Habitation in the coastal areas was totally demolished. This first-ever evacuation affected the entire region of Hong Kong.

1662 (1st year of the reign of Emperor Kangxi of the Qing Dynasty)

An unusually high tide occurred in Xin'an County.

Sep 1663 (8th month of the 2nd year of the reign of Emperor Kangxi of the Qing Dynasty)

The Qing court conducted a survey of the boundary of Guangdong in preparation for a second evacuation, involving a total of 24 villages to the east and west of Xin'an County.

Feb–Mar 1664 (2nd month of the 3rd year of the reign of Emperor Kangxi of the Qing Dynasty)

A comet was observed in the southwest of Xin'an County. A drought occurred during the spring and summer.

Mar–Apr 1664 (3rd month of the 3rd year of the reign of Emperor Kangxi of the Qing Dynasty)

The Qing court ordered a second, 30-*li* (an ancient unit equivalent to 0.31 mile) inward evacuation of people living on or near the coast. Garrison Commander Jiang Kongrun (蔣孔閏) and County Magistrate Zhang Pu (張璞) supervised the demolition of homes and the building of barriers and fences. All forms of residence, farming and fishing in the restricted areas were prohibited; offenders were executed. Coastal residents were suddenly rendered homeless.

Sep–Oct 1664 (8th month of the 3rd year of the reign of Emperor Kangxi of the Qing Dynasty)

Bandit Yuan Rui (袁瑞) seized the areas of Kwun Fu (present-day Kowloon City) and Lek Yuen (present-day Shatin) and was later killed by Major Liang Youcai (梁有才).

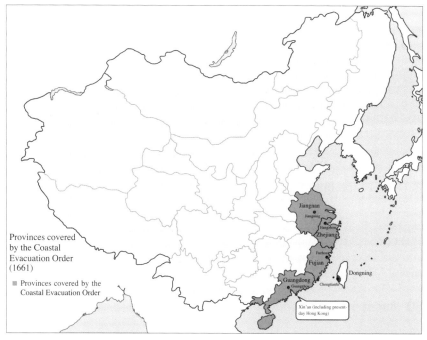

Figure 021
The Coastal Evacuation Order issued by the Qing court in 1661, covering provinces highlighted in green. (Illustration by Hong Kong Chronicles Institute. Source of reference: *Zhongguo shi gao di tu ji xia ce* [historical maps of China, volume 2])

18 Mar 1665 (2nd of the 2nd month of the 4th year of the reign of Emperor Kangxi of the Qing Dynasty)

In Xin'an County, white circles were seen gathering around the sun before dissipating a few hours later.

20 Nov 1666 (24th of the 10th month of the 5th year of the reign of Emperor Kangxi of the Qing Dynasty)

A comet with a tail several *zhang* (an ancient unit equivalent to 3.65 yards) in length like a long rainbow was observed in the southeast of Xin'an County.

1666 (5th year of the reign of Emperor Kangxi of the Qing Dynasty)

Xin'an County was dissolved and merged with Dongguan County by an order of the Qing court.

Spring of 1667 (6th year of the reign of Emperor Kangxi of the Qing Dynasty)

The former Xin'an County was struck by a drought.

Aug–Sep 1667 (7th month of the 6th year of the reign of Emperor Kangxi of the Qing Dynasty)

The former Xin'an County was hit by heavy thunderstorms.

Feb–Mar 1668 (1st month of the 7th year of the reign of Emperor Kangxi of the Qing Dynasty)

Guangdong Governor Wang Lairen (王來任) appealed to the Qing court for the reinstatement of coastal occupation, explaining the ills of inland evacuation in two memorials to the throne, but to no avail.

Jun–Jul 1668 (5th month of the 7th year of the reign of Emperor Kangxi of the Qing Dynasty)

Houses and crops in the former Xin'an County were damaged by rain and hail.

Nov–Dec 1668 (10th month of the 7th year of the reign of Emperor Kangxi of the Qing Dynasty)

After surveying the border areas, Zhou Youde (周有德), Governor-General of Guangdong and Guangxi, asked the Qing court to allow residents to return to their villages on the coast while continuing the ban on sea travel.

1668 (7th year of the reign of Emperor Kangxi of the Qing Dynasty)

The Qing court installed barriers in Hong Kong and assigned troops to guard Tuen Mun, Kowloon, Tai Po Tau and Ma Tseuk Leng (all part of today's Hong Kong) to prevent residents from returning to the areas subject to the inward evacuation order.

Feb–Mar 1669 (1st month of the 8th year of the reign of Emperor Kangxi of the Qing Dynasty)

Extremely high tides were observed in the former Xin'an County.

The Qing court reinstated the original coastal boundary at the recommendation of Wang Lairen (王來任) and Zhou Youde (周有德), allowing some residents to return to the Hong Kong region. The ban on sea travel and on the return to outlying islands continued.

28 Jul 1669 (1st of the 8th year of the reign of Emperor Kangxi of the Qing Dynasty)

Many houses were damaged when three tornadoes struck the western and southern parts of the former Xin'an County.

Jul–Aug 1669 (7th month of the 8th year of the reign of Emperor Kangxi of the Qing Dynasty)

Xin'an County was re-established by the Qing court; Hong Kong remained part of the county. The new County Magistrate, Li Kecheng (李可成) of Tieling of Liaodong Province, arranged for the return of residents and for the cultivation of abandoned farmland.

20 Sep 1669 (26th of the 8th month of the 8th year of the reign of Emperor Kangxi of the Qing Dynasty)

A typhoon hit Xin'an County, destroying almost all of the houses.

1669 (8th year of the reign of Emperor Kangxi of the Qing Dynasty)

The Tai Kiu Tun Market on the west bank of present-day Yuen Long Creek was re-established as Yuen Long Market on the east bank (present-day Yuen Long Old Market) by Tang Man-wai (鄧文蔚) of Kam Tin. The Tai Wong Temple was later built there to worship both Hung Shing (洪聖) (a highly revered sea god) and Yeung Hau (楊侯) (popularly believed to be Yeung Leung-jit [楊亮節] who was a marquis loyal to the Southern Song Dynasty).

Post-1669 (8th year of the reign of Emperor Kangxi of the Qing Dynasty)

The Tin Kong Hui market (near present-day Tin Kwong Po in Sheung Shui) was jointly established by the Liu clan of Sheung Shui, Hau clan of Ho Sheung Heung and Tang clan of Lung Yeuk Tau. The market was later relocated to Shek Wu Hui.

1671 (10th year of the reign of Emperor Kangxi of the Qing Dynasty)

The Office of the Sub-county Magistracy of Kwun Fu was relocated to Chiwei Village (present-day Futian in Shenzhen) with jurisdiction over Hong Kong.

Oct–Nov 1672 (9th month of the 11th year of the reign of Emperor Kangxi of the Qing Dynasty)

Taiwanese pirate Li Qi (李奇) looted the villages at Ho Chung in Sai Kung during his attack on the coastal areas of Hong Kong. All the pirates were caught or killed near Lek Yuen by a militia under the command of County Magistrate Li Kecheng (李可成) and Major Cai Chang (蔡昶).

1672 (11th year of the reign of Emperor Kangxi of the Qing Dynasty)

Xin'an County Magistrate Li Kecheng (李可成) led the compilation of a revised Xin'an County Local Chronicles—which is now lost.

Tang Cheung (鄧祥) and Tang Tim-cheong (鄧天章) of Lung Yeuk Tau were granted permission to build a market in Tai Po Tau (present-day Tai Po Old Market) adjacent to the Tang Ancestral Hall (Hall of the Tang Family Filial Son). Rental proceeds were offered to the ancestral hall.

05 Jul 1673 (21st of the 5th month of the 12th year during the reign of Emperor Kangxi of the Qing Dynasty)

Xin'an County was struck by a typhoon; rising seawater swamped houses and crops. Magistrate Li Kecheng (李可成) composed and offered an appeal *Ji feng wen* (Ode to the Wing) and conducted sacrificial rituals.

1676 (15th year of the reign of Emperor Kangxi of the Qing Dynasty)

Taiwan pirates entered the coastal areas of Xin'an via Huiyang plundering all the way. The walled village of Pang Po Wai in Kowloon (present-day Tai Hom in Diamond Hill) fell to the invasion of more than 100 pirate ships. Only a few young children, students and cattle herders, who were away at the time, survived.

26 Jun 1680 (1st of the 6th month of the 19th year during the reign of Emperor Kangxi of the Qing Dynasty)

The coastal area around Ha Tsuen was looted after pirates landed at Sha Kong in Pak Shek Hoi (present-day Sha Kong Wai). After several days of resistance, soldiers and the people of Kai Pak Ling Fort (present-day Kai Pak Ling) were defeated and killed.

Jul–Aug 1680 (7th month of the 19th year of the reign of Emperor Kangxi of the Qing Dynasty)

Comets were sighted on the west side of Xin'an County for several months.

1680 (19th year of the reign of Emperor Kangxi of the Qing Dynasty)

The Cheng clan of Yong'an in Fujian relocated to Shing Mun Wai in Tsuen Wan.

Frequent encounters with tigers resulted in a great number of injuries in Xin'an County. The incidents diminished only after more than a year later.

Figure 022
The present-day Chou Wong Yi Kung Study Hall in Kam Tin, Yuen Long. (Photo taken in 2020 by Hong Kong Chronicles Institute)

Circa 1681 (20th year of the reign of Emperor Kangxi of the Qing Dynasty)

The Chou Wong Yi Kung Study Hall, also known as Baode (repaying for good deeds) Temple, located in Shek Wu Hui in Sheung Shui was jointly established by the Liu clan of Sheung Shui, Tang clan of Lung Yeuk Tau, Hou clan of Ho Sheung Heung and Man clan of Tai Hang. It honoured Wang Lairen (王來任) (who was Governor of Guangdong) and Zhou Youde (周有德) (who was Governor-General of Guangdong and Guangxi) for their efforts in ending the coastal evacuation order. The study hall was destroyed during the Shek Wu Hui fire in 1955.

1682 (21st year of the reign of Emperor Kangxi of the Qing Dynasty)

The Tuen Mun Signal Station was reorganized as Tuen Mun Garrison. This fort was guarded by a lieutenant and 30 soldiers. Four guard posts were set up in Mong Tseng, Kowloon, Tai Po Tau and Ma Tseuk Leng.

1683 (22nd year of the reign of Emperor Kangxi of the Qing Dynasty)

The Qing court lifted its ban on sea travel after conciliation with the Zheng clan of Taiwan, thereby allowing the resumption of sailing and fishing as well as the return of former residents to Tai Hai Shan (present-day Lantau Island).

The British merchant ship *Carolina* of the East India Company sailed from Macao and stayed near Lantau Island for two months to conduct unauthorised trade.

16 Feb 1684 (2nd of the 1st month of the 23rd year of the reign of Emperor Kangxi of the Qing Dynasty)

Ministers were appointed to conduct a survey on boundaries. Following an order issued by the Qing court, land formerly belonging to displaced residents was returned with a three-year tax exemption in an effort to cultivate abandoned farmland.

1684 (23rd year of the reign of Emperor Kangxi of the Qing Dynasty)

The Tang clan of Kam Tin began building the Chou Wong Yi Kung Study Hall in commemoration of the efforts of Zhou Youde (周有德), Governor-General of Guangdong and Guangxi, and Wang Lairen (王來任), Governor of Guangdong, for bringing about the repeal of the coastal evacuation order. The construction was completed in the following year. (Figure 022)

1684 (23rd year of the reign of Emperor Kangxi of the Qing Dynasty)

The Tin Hau Temple at Fung Chi Village in Ping Shan was built.

1685 (24th year of the reign of Emperor Kangxi of the Qing Dynasty)

Tang Man-wai (鄧文蔚) of Kam Tin, upon ranking third in the imperial palace examination, was appointed as Magistrate of Longyou County of Quzhou Prefecture in Zhejiang.

The *Jiao* Festival, consisting of purification rituals to bring peace and harmony, was inaugurated by the Tang clan of Kam Tin in commemoration of Wang Lairen (王來任) and Zhou Youde (周有德). The festival has been held once every ten years in Kam Tin since then and is the oldest of its kind in Hong Kong.

Figure 023
The Ngo Yeung Waterfall—one of the eight scenic features of Xin'an depicted in the Kangxi (康熙) edition of Xin'an County Local Chronicles.

Figure 024
Waterfall at Aberdeen, an oil painting by William Havell in 1816. (Photo courtesy of HKSAR Government)

Figure 025
Waterfall Bay in Aberdeen. (Photo taken in 2020 and courtesy of Samson Wong Chu-shing)

1686 (25th year of the reign of Emperor Kangxi of the Qing Dynasty)

Crop failure resulted from a severe autumn drought in Xin'an County.

1688 (27th year of the reign of Emperor Kangxi of the Qing Dynasty)

Xin'an County Magistrate Jin Wenmo (靳文謨) revised the Xin'an County Local Chronicles with the assistance of scholar Tang Man-wai (鄧文蔚) of Kam Tin. This edition comprising 13 chapters is preserved to date.

The Ngo Yeung Waterfall (present-day Waterfall Bay) and Pui To Trail (in present-day Castle Peak) in Hong Kong were named two of the eight best scenic features of Xin'an in the Kangxi (康熙) edition of Xin'an County Local Chronicles. (Figures 023, 024 and 025)

Three of Hong Kong's markets, namely Tai Kiu Tun Market (on the present-day west bank of Yuen Long Creek and relocated to Yuen Long Market in 1669), Tin Kong Market (near present-day Sheung Shui) and Tai Po Tau Market (present-day Tai Po Old Market) were listed in the Kangxi (康熙) edition of Xin'an County Local Chronicles.

1691 (30th year of the reign of Emperor Kangxi of the Qing Dynasty)

The Tin Hau Temple at Tai Po Tau Market (present-day Tai Po Old Market) was built.

1692 (31st year of the reign of Emperor Kangxi of the Qing Dynasty)

The Yuen Kwan Tai Temple at Mong Tseng Wai in Yuen Long was built.

1695 (34th year of the reign of Emperor Kangxi of the Qing Dynasty)

The Tin Hau Temple at Lung Yeuk Tau in Fanling was built.

1699 (38th year of the reign of Emperor Kangxi of Qing Dynasty)

The Yeung Hau Temple in Tai O was built.

1700–1750 (39th year of the reign of Emperor Kangxi–15th year of the reign of Emperor Qianlong of the Qing Dynasty)

The village of Lo Uk Tsuen in Chai Wan on Hong Kong Island was established by the Lo clan of Jinan, Shandong Province.

1704 (43rd year of the reign of Emperor Kangxi of the Qing Dynasty)

The Dapeng Marine Battalion, equipped with three batteries and nine guard posts, was formed by the Qing court. The eighth guard post named Hung Heung Lo was located on Hong Kong Island.

1708 (47th year of the reign of Emperor Kangxi of the Qing Dynasty)

Xin'an County was struck by a severe famine.

1710 (49th year of the reign of Emperor Kangxi of Qing Dynasty)

The filial act of Tang Tsun-yuen (鄧俊元) of Kam Tin in building the Bin Mo Bridge for his mother was recorded in the Jiaqing (嘉慶) edition of Xin'an County Local Chronicles. (Figure 026)

1710–1775 (49th year of the reign of Emperor Kangxi–40th year of the reign of Emperor Qianlong of the Qing Dynasty)

The Yeuk Hui Study Hall was founded by the Tang clan of Ping Shan. Equestrian training was available for fellow villagers seeking to take the imperial military degree examination.

1714 (53rd year of the reign of Emperor Kangxi of the Qing Dynasty)

The Yuen Kwan Yi Tai Temple at Yuen Long Old Market was built; it also functioned as the ancestral hall of the Tang clan of Sai Pin Wai.

1718 (57th year of the reign of Emperor Kangxi of the Qing Dynasty)

An ancestral hall known as the Hall of Five Willows was built by the Tao clan of Tuen Tsz Wai in Tuen Mun.

The I Shing Temple, dedicated to the worship of the gods Hung Shing and Che Kung, was built in Wang Chau (part of Ping Shan).

Pre-1722 (61st year of the reign of Emperor Kangxi of the Qing Dynasty)

The Nam Tong Battery (present-day Tung Lung Chau) in Fat Tong Mun was established by the Qing court. It was manned by a sub-lieutenant and 25 soldiers under the command of the Dapeng Marine Battalion. The battery was relocated to the waterfront of Kowloon Walled City in 1810. (Figure 027)

1724 (2nd year of the reign of Emperor Yongzheng [雍正] of the Qing Dynasty)

Liu Kau-ngo (廖九我) of Sheung Shui donated farmland—large enough to produce 50 *dan* (an ancient unit equivalent to 2.75 bushels) of grain per year—in Soo Kun Poo (present-day So Kon Po on Hong Kong Island) to the Man Kong Study Hall (in present-day Nantou, Shenzhen) for communal purposes.

The village of Nga Tsin Wai was jointly formed by the Ng, Chan and Lee clans of Nga Tsin Village in Kowloon upon redevelopment; a wall was put up around the village. A Tin Hau Temple was also built in the same year.

1726 (4th year of the reign of Emperor Yongzheng of the Qing Dynasty)

The first *Jiao* Festival at the village of Nga Tsin Wai in Kowloon was held and was also scheduled to repeat once every 10 years.

Hakka farmers in Huizhou, Chaozhou and Jiayingzhou of Guangdong as well as Jiangxi and Fujian were recruited to establish farmlands in Xin'an County and were offered a tax exemption until 1736 by the Qing court.

Figure 026
The present-day Bin Mo Bridge located at Shui Tau Village in Kam Tin. (Photo taken in 2020 by Hong Kong Chronicles Institute)

Figure 027
The site of Tung Lung Fort on the island of Tung Lung Chau in Sai Kung. (Photo courtesy of Antiquities and Monuments Office)

1728 (6th year of the reign of Emperor Yongzheng of the Qing Dynasty)

Tang Siu-kee (鄧肇基) of Lung Yeuk Tau was admitted to the Imperial Academy and was later appointed as Sub-director of Schools of Guishan County.

1729 (7th year of the reign of Emperor Yongzheng of the Qing Dynasty)

The Kai Yat Kok Battery in Fan Lau on Lantau Island was constructed under an order of the Qing court.

1730 (8th year of the reign of Emperor Yongzheng of the Qing Dynasty)

The Hau Wong Temple in Kowloon City was built.

1735 (13th year of the reign of Emperor Yongzheng of the Qing Dynasty)

Pirate brothers Cheng Lin-fuk (鄭連福) and Cheng Lin-cheong (鄭連昌) led an invasion of the coastal areas of Guangdong and captured Lantau Island and Demon's Peak (present-day Devil's Peak) north of Lei Yue Mun in Hong Kong.

1723–1735 (The reign of Emperor Yongzheng of the Qing Dynasty)

The walled village of Tsin Wan Wai (present-day Lo Wai in Tsuen Wan), jointly established by the Cheung, Tsang, Wong, Hui and Tang clans, was the first village in Tsuen Wan to be constructed after the coastal evacuation order in the early Qing Dynasty was rescinded.

1736 (1st year of the reign of Emperor Qianlong [乾隆] of the Qing Dynasty)

Tang Yu-cheung (鄧與璋) of Kam Tin passed a provincial-level imperial examination based on the *Book of Documents*; he was appointed as Director of Schools in Deqingzhou after earning degrees under a special quota in 1737 and 1742.

Tang Siu-chou (鄧紹周) of Kam Tin was admitted to the Imperial Academy and was later appointed as Director of Schools of Yingde County (and later of other counties including Lianshan, Renhua and Yangshan) of Shaozhou Prefecture.

1739–1767 (4th–32nd year of the reign of Qianlong of the Qing Dynasty)

The villages of So Uk Tsuen and Lee Uk Tsuen in Cheung Sha Wan were established by the So and Lee clans, respectively, of Xin'an County.

1740 (5th year of the reign of Emperor Qianlong of the Qing Dynasty)

Tang Ping (鄧炳) of Lung Yeuk Tau was admitted to the Imperial Academy and was later appointed as Director of Schools of Guangning County.

1744 (9th year of the reign of Emperor Qianlong of the Qing Dynasty)

The walled village of Kun Lung Wai, also known as San Wai, was established by the Tang clan of Lung Yeuk Tau.

1747 (12th year of the reign of Emperor Qianlong of the Qing Dynasty)

The Tin Hau Temple in Causeway Bay was built.

1750 (15th year of the reign of Emperor Qianlong of the Qing Dynasty)

An ancestral hall named Yau Kung Tong was built by two sub-clans of the Tang clan of Kam Tin to enshrine their founding ancestors Tang Hung-wai (鄧洪惠) and Deng Hongchi (鄧洪贄). The sub-clans merged to become the Tang clan of Ha Tsuen.

1751 (16th year of the reign of Emperor Qianlong of the Qing Dynasty)

The Liu clan of Sheung Shui built an ancestral hall named Liu Man Shek Tong in commemoration of ancestor Liu Kong (廖剛), a senior Northern Song official, and his four sons who were known for a high collective salary of 10,000 *dan* (an ancient unit equivalent to 2.75 bushels) of grain per year. (Figure 028)

Figure 028
The ancestral hall of Liu Man Shek Tong in Sheung Shui. (Photo taken in 2020 by Hong Kong Chronicles Institute)

Post-1751 (16th year of the reign of Emperor Qianlong of the Qing Dynasty)

The market of Ha Tsuen Hui was founded by the Tang clan of Ha Tsuen in Yuen Long and was later developed into Ha Tsuen Market.

1753 (18th year of the reign of Emperor Qianlong of the Qing Dynasty)

In the spring, pirate Cheng Lin-cheong (鄭連昌) built a Tin Hau temple on the shore of Lei Yue Mun.

04 Mar 1757 (15th day of the 1st month of the 22nd year of the reign of Emperor Qianlong of the Qing Dynasty)

More than a foot of snowfall accumulated overnight in Xin'an County.

1757 (22nd year of the reign of Emperor Qianlong of the Qing Dynasty)

Chen Rensheng (陳任盛) of Ninghua of Fujian Province relocated to Lo Uk Cheung in Tsuen Wan where he was founder of the Chan clan.

The price of rice in Xin'an County remained high.

1759 (24th year of the reign of Emperor Qianlong of the Qing Dynasty)

The Lung Kai Temple (present-day Lung Shan Temple) in Lung Yeuk Tau was renovated.

17 Sep 1760 (9th of the 8th month of the 25th year of the reign of Emperor Qianlong of the Qing Dynasty)

Xin'an County was hit by a typhoon.

08 Sep 1761 (10th of the 8th month of the 26th year of the reign of Emperor Qianlong of the Qing Dynasty)

Xin'an County was hit by a typhoon.

1762 (27th year of the reign of Emperor Qianlong of the Qing Dynasty)

Tang Fong (鄧晃) of Kam Tin passed a provincial-level imperial examination based on the *Book of Documents* and later became a lecturer at Man Kong Study Hall.

21 Jun 1768 (7th of the 5th month of the 33rd year of the reign of Emperor Qianlong of the Qing Dynasty)

Xin'an County experienced heavy rainfall for seven consecutive days.

02 Sep 1770 (13th of the 7th month of the 35th year of the reign of Emperor Qianlong of the Qing Dynasty)

Xin'an County was struck by an earthquake.

1771 (36th year of the reign of Emperor Qianlong of the Qing Dynasty)

Names of places, including Fan Chin Chow (present-day Hong Kong Island), were included on the *Chart of the China Sea* drawn by British hydrographer Alexander Dalrymple in the oldest Western map of Hong Kong known to exist. (Figure 029)

1772 (37th year of the reign of Emperor Qianlong of the Qing Dynasty)

People were attacked by packs of wolves and tigers in Xin'an County.

1773 (38th year of the reign of Emperor Qianlong of the Qing Dynasty)

The Hung Shing Temple in Ap Lei Chau was built.

Circa 1775–1786 (40th–51st year of the reign of Emperor Qianlong of the Qing Dynasty)

The *Prohibition of Illicit Salt Trade* was carved on a stone tablet at Tai Wong Temple in Yuen Long Market (present-day Yuen Long Old Market) by the order of the Inspector of Salt of Guangdong.

1775–1800 (40th year of the reign of Emperor Qianlong–5th year of the reign of Emperor Jiaqing [嘉慶] of the Qing Dynasty)

So Lau Yuen, also known as Chi Ka Tong, was built at Shui Tau Village in Kam Tin. It was used as a place for arbitration but was later converted into a private school in the mid-19th century.

1777–1778 (42nd–43rd year of the reign of Emperor Qianlong of the Qing Dynasty)

Xin'an County suffered from a two-year drought, resulting in both high rice prices and a high death toll.

1779 (44th year of the reign of Emperor Qianlong of the Qing Dynasty)

Tang Fei-hung (鄧飛鴻) of Ping Shan passed a provincial-level imperial military degree examination.

1780 (45th year of the reign of Emperor Qianlong of the Qing Dynasty)

In addition to the English names for Lamma Island and Kowloon, present-day Hong Kong Island was marked "Fan-Chin-Cheo" and "He-ong-Kong" on the *Chart of the China Sea* drawn by British captain George Hayter based on earlier maps from Portugal and China. It was known to be the first time that Hong Kong Island appeared in English translation on a Western map, albeit under a slightly different spelling.

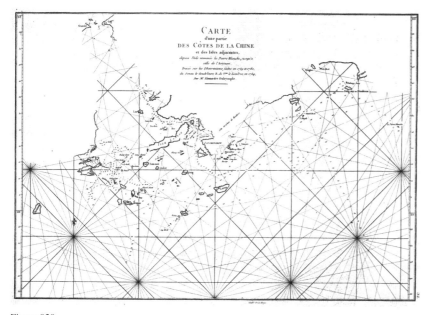

Figure 029
The 1775 edition of the *Chart of the China Sea* drawn by British hydrographer Alexander Dalrymple in 1771 is known to be the oldest Western map of Hong Kong. (Image courtesy of Wattis Fine Art)

Figure 030
The Hakka village of Sam Tung Uk in Tsuen Wan (and currently the Sam Tung Uk Museum). (Photo taken on 03 September 1979 and courtesy of Yau Tin-kwai/South China Morning Post via Getty Images)

1783 (48th year of the reign of Emperor Qianlong of the Qing Dynasty)

Fundraising was held by residents of the island of Cheung Chau for the renovation of Yuk Hui Temple dedicated to the Taoist god Pak Tai.

1786 (51st year of the reign of Emperor Qianlong of the Qing Dynasty)

Xin'an County Magistrate Li Dagen (李大根) was assigned by the Governor-General of Guangdong and Guangxi to resolve a rental dispute between the landowners from the Tang clan of Kam Tin and tenants from Shap Pat Heung in Yuen Long. To settle the dispute, he issued standard grain measuring equipment which everyone had to use; notices to that effect were erected at Tai Wong Temple in Yuen Long and Tin Hau Temple in Shap Pat Heung.

The village of Sam Tung Uk was established by the Chan clan of Tsuen Wan. (Figure 030)

1786 (51st year of the reign of Emperor Qianlong of the Qing Dynasty)

Xin'an County was struck by a plague of locusts, causing major losses of harvest. This was followed by a severe drought in the autumn and winter months, leading to severe famine.

1787 (52nd year of the reign of Emperor Qianlong of the Qing Dynasty)

A *dou* (an ancient unit equivalent to 2.2 gallons) of rice was priced at one silver dollar during a severe drought in Xin'an County where many died.

1788 (53rd year of the reign of Emperor Qianlong of the Qing Dynasty)

Hau Cheuk-wan (侯倬雲) of Kam Tsin (present-day Kam Tsin Village in Sheung Shui) passed a provincial-level imperial examination based on the *Classic of Poetry* and was appointed as Director of Schools of Lingshan County.

Pirate Tan A-che (譚阿車) remained on the run after two years of looting coastal areas.

1789 (54th year of the reign of Emperor Qianlong of the Qing Dynasty)

Tang Ying-yuen (鄧英元) of Kam Tin passed a provincial-level imperial military degree examination; in 1819, he sponsored the publication of Xin'an County Local Chronicles.

The Cheung Shan Monastery (present-day Cheung Shan Kwu Tsz) at Wo Keng Shan in Ping Che was built.

1790 (55th year of the reign of Emperor Qianlong of the Qing Dynasty)

The Fan Sin Temple at Sheung Wun Yiu in Tai Po was built in honour of an early pottery master named Fan Sin (樊仙).

1791 (56th year of the reign of Emperor Qianlong of the Qing Dynasty)

Xin'an County was repeatedly hit by typhoons.

1736–1795 (The reign of Emperor Qianlong of the Qing Dynasty)

The Cheung Chau Market was established by residents on the island of Cheung Chau.

Jul–Aug 1797 (The intercalary 6th month of the 2nd year of the reign of Emperor Jiaqing of the Qing Dynasty)

Xin'an County was hit by four consecutive typhoons; many houses and trees were destroyed.

04 Apr 1802 (3rd of the 3rd month of the 7th year of the reign of Emperor Jiaqing of the Qing Dynasty)

A solar halo was observed in Xin'an County.

1802 (7th year of the reign of Emperor Jiaqing of the Qing Dynasty)

Admission to Guangzhou Academy was made available to Hakka students with special quotas implemented by the Qing court; Hakka students of Xin'an County were now eligible to take the imperial examination.

1803 (8th year of the reign of Emperor Jiaqing of the Qing Dynasty)

Fundraising was held by residents of Pui O on Lantau Island for a walled village as a defensive measure again pirate Tan A-che (譚阿車). The village, known today as Pui O Lo Wai, was completed in 1805.

Feb–Apr 1804 (1st–2nd month of the 9th year of the reign of Emperor Jiaqing of the Qing Dynasty)

Price of salt rose due to heavy rainfall in Xin'an County, reaching 12 silver dollars per 100 catties (one *catty* equivalent to 1.33 pounds).

1804 (9th year of the reign of Emperor Jiaqing of the Qing Dynasty)

Pirates Guo Podai (郭婆帶), Wu Shier (鄔石二) and Zheng Yi (鄭一) led a group of more than 1,000 pirate boats of varying sizes in a siege against coastal villages including Ping Shan. They were repulsed by the strong defence of Ping Shan.

Tang Shui-tai (鄧瑞泰) of Ping Shan passed a provincial-level imperial military degree examination.

23 Sep 1805 (1st of the 8th month of the 10th year of the reign of Emperor Jiaqing of the Qing Dynasty)

Severe floods resulted from heavy rainfall in Xin'an County.

1806 (11th year of the reign of Emperor Jiaqing of the Qing Dynasty)

The East India Company appointed hydrographer James Horsburgh to conduct a years-long survey in the South China Sea and draw a coastal map covering the waters of Hong Kong.

18 Mar 1807 (10th of the 2nd month of the 12th year of the reign of Emperor Jiaqing of the Qing Dynasty)

Herds of cattle were killed in Kowloon and in Ho Chung following two consecutive days of rain and hail.

1807 (12th year of the reign of Emperor Jiaqing of the Qing Dynasty)

Liu Yau-chup (廖有執) of Sheung Shui passed a provincial-level imperial examination.

The re-carving of the inscription on the memorial rock Sung Wong Toi was completed. The rock was erected to commemorate the passage of the last two Song emperors through the Hong Kong region as they sought refuge from Mongol troops. The inscription is still extant today.

11 Sep 1808 (21st of the 7th month of the 13th year of the reign of Emperor Jiaqing of the Qing Dynasty)

Colonel Lin Guoliang (林國良) of Humen Regiment sailed with 25 ships in an attempt to capture pirate Cheung Po (張保), also named Cheung Po Tsai (張保仔). Lin was defeated, captured and killed at Ma Chau Yeung (present-day Ma Chau, Soko Islands).

20 Nov 1809 (13th of the 10th month of the 14th year of the reign of Emperor Jiaqing of the Qing Dynasty)

Admiral of the Guangdong Squadron Sun Quanmou (孫全謀) and Xiangshan County Magistrate Peng Zhaolin (彭 昭麟), in conjunction with a fleet of Portuguese ships from Macao, launched an attack on pirate Cheung Po (張保) at Chek Lek Kok (present-day Chek Lap Kok on Lantau Island). Cheung Po was surrounded at Tung Chung Bay but escaped under favourable wind conditions on 29 November.

Nov–Dec 1809 (10th month of the 14th year of the reign of Emperor Jiaqing of the Qing Dynasty)

Hundreds of pirate ships led by Guo Podai (郭婆帶), anchored at Chek Lek Kok on Lantau Island, remained at large despite eradication attempts by a naval fleet under the command of Xin'an County Magistrate Zheng Yulun (鄭 域輪) and later by hundreds of warships under Governor-General of Guangdong and Guangxi Bai Ling (百齡).

Jan–Feb 1810 (12th month of the 14th year of the reign of Emperor Jiaqing of the Qing Dynasty)

Pirate Guo Podai (郭婆帶), along with his 8,000 followers and 128 ships, surrendered to the Qing court. Guo Podai was awarded the title of a sub-lieutenant under his new name Xuexian (學顯).

04 Apr 1810 (1st of the 3rd month of the 15th year of the reign of Emperor Jiaqing of the Qing Dynasty)

Pirates Zheng Yi Sao (鄭一嫂) and Cheung Po (張保), along with 16,000 followers, over 270 ships of all sizes and more than 1,000 cannons, surrendered to the Qing court.

1810 (15th year of the reign of Emperor Jiaqing of the Qing Dynasty)

Captain Daniel Ross, commissioned by the East India Company to make a hydrographic survey, drew the *Chart of the Different Passages Leading to Macao Roads*. In this map, present-day Hong Kong Island was marked as "Hong Kong" and translated as "Red River" in Chinese (pronounced in Cantonese as "Hung Kong" resembling Hong Kong). This is the earliest Western map known to exist where Hong Kong Island is labelled as Hong Kong.

1811 (16th year of the reign of Emperor Jiaqing of the Qing Dynasty)

The Qing court converted all signal stations in Hong Kong into guard posts. Guard posts existed in Tuen Mun, Tai Po Tau, Kowloon, Mong Tseng, Shing Mun Au, Wang Chau, Kwun Chung, Tsiu Keng, Ma Tseuk Leng, Lantau Island, Hung Heung Lo and Tung Chung Hou. All guard posts were under the direct command of Tuen Mun Military Post .

The Yeung Hau Temple at Tung Tau Village of Ha Tsuen in Yuen Long, dedicated to Yeung Leung-jit (楊亮節), was renovated.

1812 (17th year of the reign of Emperor Jiaqing of the Qing Dynasty)

The east side of Xin'an County was struck by a plague of locusts.

1813 (18th year of the reign of Emperor Jiaqing of the Qing Dynasty)

Tang Tai-hung (鄧大雄) of Kam Tin passed a provincial-level imperial military degree examination and sponsored the revision and compilation of Xin'an County Local Chronicles in 1819.

1816 (21st year of the reign of Emperor Jiaqing of the Qing Dynasty)

The delegation of British diplomat William Pitt Amherst arrived at Waterfall Bay in Aberdeen and conducted a general survey of Hong Kong Island and its harbour. He joined British commissioner George Thomas Staunton on a special mission to Beijing in the second British mission to China (following the Macartney mission in 1793).

Sep–Oct 1817 (8th month of the 22nd year of the reign of Emperor Jiaqing of the Qing Dynasty)

The Qing court built another eight guard posts in Tung Chung Hou, as well as two batteries, seven barracks and an arsenal at the foot of the Stone Lion Hill at Tung Chung Hou.

Figure 031
The Tung Chung Battery, also known as Tung Chung Fort and Tung Chung Walled City, in the 1970s (formerly a naval headquarters of the Dapeng Right Battalion during the Qing Dynasty and currently a declared monument in Hong Kong). (Photo courtesy of HKSAR Government)

1819 (24th year of the reign of Emperor Jiaqing of the Qing Dynasty)

The Xin'an County Local Chronicles comprising 24 chapters was completed; Xin'an County Magistrate Shu Maoguan (舒懋官) was Chief Editor and Wang Chongxi (王崇熙) was Chief Compiler.

Four markets in Hong Kong were listed in the Jiaqing (嘉慶) edition of Xin'an County Local Chronicles, namely Yuen Long Market (relocated from Tai Kiu Tun Market to present-day Yuen Long Old Market), Shek Wu Market (relocated from Tin Kong Market to present-day Sheung Shui), Tai Po Market (Tai Po Tau Market known today as Tai Po Old Market) and Cheung Chau Market.

The Lantau Guard Post and Tung Chung Hou Guard Post on Lantau Island, as well as the Hung Heung Lo Guard Post on Hong Kong Island, were established. Troops were also stationed at Chek Chu (present-day Stanley.)

1821 (1st year of the reign of Emperor Daoguang [道光] of the Qing Dynasty)

The Qing court assigned a sub-lieutenant, a sergeant and 16 soldiers to Tuen Mun Military Station and sent 60 soldiers to man the guard posts of Mong Tseng, Wang Chau, Kwun Chung, Tsiu Keng, Tai Po Tau and Shing Mun Au—all of which were under the Tuen Mun command.

Governor General of Guangdong and Guangxi Ruan Yuan (阮元) issued a ban on opium under an imperial order and ordered foreign vessels engaged in opium trading depart from the Pearl River Delta. Since then, over 10 British armed opium-smuggling barges would enter Kap Shui Mun, return to Lingding Channel in September and anchor in the waters of Lantau Island each year. The smuggling of opium was extremely lucrative and drained the Chinese economy of silver.

1829 (9th year of the reign of Emperor Daoguang of the Qing Dynasty)

At least six opium barges (floating warehouses) were anchored in Hong Kong waters during the year. These were part of a fleet owned by the East India Company and used for trafficking opium into China. They would take anchorage near Lingding Channel and retreat to Kumsing Moon in Zhongshan County or Hong Kong waters during typhoon seasons.

1830 (10th year of the reign of Emperor Daoguang of the Qing Dynasty)

The Yau Sin Study Hall at the San Wai village of Ha Tsuen in Yuen Long was founded by Tang Man-chung (鄧萬鍾) of Ha Tsuen.

04 Jul 1831 (25th of 5th month of 11th year of the reign of Emperor Daoguang of the Qing Dynasty)

Emperor Daoguang (道光) of the Qing Dynasty ordered a crackdown on opium. He assigned Governor General of Guangdong and Guangxi Li Hongbin (李鴻賓) to eradicate opium near Lantau Island and in Humen where barges carrying opium were anchored.

1831 (11th year of the reign of Emperor Daoguang of the Qing Dynasty)

The Dapeng Battalion was rearranged into the "left" and "right" units by the Qing court. The "right" unit was stationed at the new Tung Chung Battery for strengthened defence of Lantau Island. (Figure 031)

21 Aug 1834 (17th of 7th month of 14th year of the reign of Emperor Daoguang of the Qing Dynasty)

The first Chief Superintendent of the Trade of British Subjects in China, William John Napier, suggested in a dispatch that Hong Kong Island be seized by force. He was the first British official to propose such a measure. He arrived in Macao on 15 July and moved to enter Guangzhou without authorisation. He attempted to expand trade but failed after a two-month stalemate; he died in Macao on 11 October.

11 Sep 1835 (19th of the 7th month of the 15th year of the reign of Emperor Daoguang of the Qing Dynasty)

Governor General of Guangdong and Guangxi Lu Kun (盧坤) issued an order banning the requisition of fishing boats by soldiers in the name of hunting pirates. The order was inscribed onto a stone tablet at the Tin Hau Temple on Peng Chau.

31 Oct 1835 (10th of the 9th month of the 15th year of the reign of Emperor Daoguang of the Qing Dynasty)

Director of the Court of State Ceremonial Huang Juezi (黃爵滋) submitted a report to the throne concerning British collusion with local merchants and naval personnel. It involved the smuggling of opium into Guangzhou, Nanhai, Panyu and other coastal areas by means of fast galleys launched from barges and floating warehouses anchored near Lantau Island.

Feb–Mar 1836 (1st month of the 16th year of the reign of Emperor Daoguang of the Qing Dynasty)

Xin'an County was issued an order to arrest Chan Ya-sun (陳亞辛), owner of Tung Hop Shop in Tai O Chung. He was found to have illegally built four cannons upon investigation by the subordinates of Admiral of the Guangdong Squadron Guan Tianpei (關天培).

1836 (16th year of the reign of Emperor Daoguang of the Qing Dynasty)

Admiral Charles Elliot became Chief Superintendent of the Trade of British Subjects in China.

04 Aug 1837 (4th of the 7th month of the 17th year of the reign of Emperor Daoguang of the Qing Dynasty)

Governor General of Guangdong and Guangxi Deng Tingzhen (鄧廷楨) demanded in an official order to Chief Superintendent of the Trade of British Subjects in China Admiral Charles Elliot that British barges be withdrawn from Lingding Channel.

23 Aug 1838 (4th of the 7th month of the 18th year of the reign of Emperor Daoguang of the Qing Dynasty)

French painter Auguste Borget arrived in Hong Kong for a three-day stay. He made many landscape drawings on the local temples, fishermen, farmlands and graves, depicting the rich cultural life of Hong Kong prior to British colonisation.

03 Jun 1839 (22nd of the 4th month of the 19th year of the reign of Emperor Daoguang of the Qing Dynasty)

In Humen, Imperial Commissioner Lin Zexu (林則徐) started publicly destroying opium seized from foreign traders. From 03–25 June, a total of 2,376,254 catties of opium in 19,179 boxes and 2,119 bags was destroyed.

07 Jul 1839 (27th of the 5th month of the 19th year of the reign of Emperor Daoguang of the Qing Dynasty)

Lin Wei-hsi (林維喜), a villager of Tsim Sha Tsui Village in Kowloon, was beaten and killed by British sailors. The incident, coupled with the destruction of opium in Humen, triggered the First Opium War.

02 Aug 1839 (23rd of the 6th month of the 19th year of the reign of Emperor Daoguang of the Qing Dynasty)

Imperial Commissioner Lin Zexu (林則徐) issued a proclamation forbidding any contact between local residents and foreigners. He demanded that the sailors responsible for the murder of Lin Wei-hsi (林維喜) be turned over to Chinese authorities. Admiral Charles Elliot refused; instead he tried the suspects himself and issued light sentences. Chinese authorities viewed the use of extraterritorial jurisdiction as an infringement of sovereignty.

04 Sep 1839 (27th of the 7th month of the 19th year of the reign of Emperor Daoguang of the Qing Dynasty)

Five British armed vessels, under the command of Admiral Charles Elliot, opened fire on Qing naval vessels in the waters near Kowloon after being denied the purchase of food supplies. The British vessels retreated to Tsim Sha Tsui after Lieutenant Colonel of Dapeng Lai Enjue (賴恩爵) returned fire with the support of batteries onshore in what became known as the Battle of Kowloon.

04 Nov 1839 (29th of the 9th month of the 19th year of the reign of Emperor Daoguang of the Qing Dynasty)

British warships anchored near the waters of Tsim Sha Tsui launched an attack on Kwun Chung (present-day Jordan in Kowloon) in a 10-day conflict. British forces tried six times to storm Chinese bases at Kwun Chung Hill but were repelled; British warships and opium ships were forced to retreat from Tsim Sha Tsui in what became known as the Battle of Kwun Chung.

20 Feb 1840 (18th of the 1st month of the 20th year of the reign of Emperor Daoguang of the Qing Dynasty)

Admirals George Elliot and Charles Elliot were appointed as Joint Plenipotentiary. George Elliot also became Commander-in-Chief of the East Indies and China Station. In a confidential memo, British Foreign Secretary Lord Palmerston devised plans for an invasion of China and a draft treaty with China.

29 Feb 1840 (27th of the 1st month of the 20th year of the reign of Emperor Daoguang of the Qing Dynasty)

Imperial Commissioner Lin Zexu (林則徐) and Admiral Guan Tianpei (關天培) sent men to set on fire 23 fishing boats involved in smuggling opium and supplying British ships anchored in Cheung Sha Wan. They also destroyed six encampments onshore.

27 Apr 1840 (26th of the 3rd month of the 20th year of the reign of Emperor Daoguang of the Qing Dynasty)

Imperial Commissioner Lin Zexu (林則徐), upon a survey of Hong Kong's topography, suggested that defences be strengthened. He provided a detailed description of implementation in two memorials to the throne—*Dapeng Battalion Reform with Coastal Defence* and *Battery Installation in Kwun Chung*. The Qing court immediately authorised a status upgrade of Dapeng Battalion to brigade status to be located in Kowloon with an additional colonel. Batteries were constructed in Ching Ying (Tsim Sha Tsui) and Kwun Chung (Jordan) and were equipped with 56 cannons and manned by two battalions deployed from Dapeng. The Hung Heung Lo Guard Post was also reinstated.

May–Jun 1840 (5th month of the 20th year of the reign of Emperor Daoguang of the Qing Dynasty)

The First Opium War officially broke out. More than 40 warships and 4,000 soldiers of the British Expeditionary Force gathered north of Hong Kong Island. They moved north to attack Xiamen and captured Dinghai. On 11 August, British forces arrived at Baihekou in Tianjin and delivered a peace treaty prepared by Lord Palmerston—which included demands for war reparation of opium destroyed and cession of islands. The Qing court assigned Imperial Commissioner Qishan (琦善) for negotiation with the British. (Figure 032)

29 Nov 1840 (6th of the 11th month of the 20th year of the reign of the Emperor Daoguang of Qing Dynasty)

George Elliot fell ill and returned to Britain; Charles Elliot became the sole Plenipotentiary while Rear Admiral Gordon Bremer became Commander-in-Chief of British Forces.

Figure 032
The First Opium War of 1841 depicted by Edward Duncan in a painting preserved at the National Army Museum of the United Kingdom. (Photo courtesy of Niday Picture Library/Alamy Stock Photo)

Figure 033
On 25 January 1841, British troops landed on Hong Kong Island and forced the Qing army to withdraw. (Drawing published in the *Illustrated London News* on 07 February 1903 and courtesy of Three Lions/Hulton Archive via Getty Images)

19 Dec 1840 (26th of the 11th month of the 20th year of the reign of Emperor Daoguang of the Qing Dynasty)

Imperial Commissioner Qishan (琦善) presented a memorial to the throne with a request to accept British demand for six million silver dollars in war reparation for lost opium. He suggested a concessionary policy of opening up the ports of Xiamen and Fuzhou (in addition to the ports in Guangzhou) for foreign trade so as to circumvent the British possession of Lantau Island or Hong Kong Island.

1840 (20th year of the reign of Emperor Daoguang of the Qing Dynasty)

The Shin Shut Study Hall was founded by the Tang clan of Lung Yeuk Tau to support civil and martial arts education among villagers.

1821–1850 (The reign of Emperor Daoguang of the Qing Dynasty)

The Yi Tai Study Hall, enshrining Man Cheong (God of Literature) and Kwan Tai (God of Martial Arts), was built at Shui Tau Village of Kam Tin in Yuen Long.

The Hip Tin Temple, enshrining Kwan Tai, was built at Shan Tsui Village in Sha Tau Kok.

16 Jan 1841

Charles Elliot, Chief Superintendent of the Trade of British Subjects in China, Envoy Extraordinary and Minister Plenipotentiary to Imperial China, demanded with Qing Imperial Commissioner Qishan (琦善) that Hong Kong Island be ceded to Britain for lodging and conducting trade.

20 Jan 1841

In a Circular to Her Britannic Majesty's subjects, Charles Elliot claimed that he had reached a "conclusion of preliminary arrangements" with Qishan (琦善), including "the cession of the island and harbour of Hong Kong to the British crown."

25 Jan 1841

Soldiers from the British surveying vessel *Sulphur* landed on Hong Kong Island and conducted a land survey, becoming the first foreign occupiers of the island. (Map 6)

26 Jan 1841

British warships arrived at Possession Point on Hong Kong Island, carrying British troops led by Commander-in-Chief of British forces in the First Anglo-Chinese War Gordon Bremer. After the troops had landed, they declared formal occupation of the island by hoisting the British flag and firing a royal salute, 19 months before the signing of the Sino-British Treaty of Nanking. (Figure 033)

29 Jan 1841

Charles Elliot, Chief Superintendent of the Trade of British Subjects in China, Envoy Extraordinary and Minister Plenipotentiary to Imperial China, was concurrently appointed as Administrator of Hong Kong and made responsible for the British administration of Hong Kong.

30 Jan 1841

Charles Elliot, Chief Superintendent of the Trade of British Subjects in China, Envoy Extraordinary and Minister Plenipotentiary to Imperial China and Administrator of Hong Kong, demanded with Qing Imperial Commissioner Qishan (琦善) that Chinese soldiers be withdrawn from the Tsim Sha Tsui Battery; Qishan complied.

01 Feb 1841

Charles Elliot and Gordon Bremer issued a joint proclamation, stating that they had obtained written proof of Qishan's (琦善) agreement to cede Hong Kong Island to Britain. They asked that the inhabitants of Hong Kong Island "...must pay duty and obedience" to the administration of British officials and promised that the inhabitants "...will be governed...according to the laws, customs, and usages of the Chinese." However, inhabitants should not break British laws and were governed by British magistrates.

21 Feb 1841

Several members of the gentry in Dongguan, led by Deng Chun (鄧淳), submitted a written statement to Governor-General of Guangdong and Guangxi Lin Zexu (林則徐) in protest of "false proclamation" issued by Charles Elliot and Gordon Bremer, who claimed that "the island of Hong Kong had been ceded to the British crown under the seal of the Imperial Commissioner Qishan (琦善)."

06 Mar 1841

Emperor Daoguang (道光) of the Qing Dynasty condemned Britain for "outrageously occupying Hong Kong, issuing false proclamations without authorisation, and committing all kinds of unlawful acts." He ordered military officials Yang Fang (楊芳) and Yishan (奕山) to recapture Hong Kong Island with troops from Guangzhou.

23 Mar 1841

The British army took over the batteries in Kwun Chung and Tsim Sha Tsui in Kowloon. In May, the British demolished the barracks of the batteries from which bricks and stones were shipped to Hong Kong Island for building roads and houses.

22 Apr 1841

The Roman Catholic Church officially established an apostolic prefecture within a six-mile vicinity on Hong Kong Island, which was directly governed by the central missionary agency in Rome and became independent from the Diocese De Macau. Father Theodore Joset, Sacred Congregation of Propaganda Fide's representative in Macao, was appointed as the first Prefect Apostolic of Hong Kong.

01 May 1841

Captain William Caine was appointed as Chief Magistrate by Charles Elliot and was authorised to manage Chinese affairs according to Chinese laws and customs and to invoke punishment on Chinese offenders. Caine was also authorised to apply the British Police Law and customs in law enforcement and issue sentences to non-Chinese people.

The *Hong Kong Gazette* was inaugurated to announce orders, public notices and reports issued by the British government and Hong Kong government. Charles Elliot published a notice in the first issue of the *Hong Kong Gazette*, announcing the principles and conditions for dealing with land issues. Each piece of land would be auctioned publicly (leasehold in substance), with the highest bidder receiving the land.

14 May 1841

British Foreign Secretary Lord Palmerston wrote to Charles Elliot, criticising Elliot for prematurely issuing a proclamation of the cession of Hong Kong Island to Britain, even though no formal treaty had been signed with Qing Imperial Commissioner Qishan (琦善) to finalise the cession of Hong Kong.

15 May 1841

The second issue of the *Hong Kong Gazette* published the results of Hong Kong's first census. The population of Hong Kong Island totalled 7,450; Stanley (a district on Hong Kong Island) had a population of 2,000.

26 May 1841

Emperor Daoguang（道光）of the Qing Dynasty explained that because "Hong Kong should not be occupied by treacherous barbarians for a prolonged period," he ordered Imperial Commissioner Qiying（耆英）"to recapture Hong Kong by overt or covert attack at an opportune time, for asserting imperial authority" if Qiying was prepared to do so.

07 Jun 1841

Charles Elliot declared Hong Kong a free port.

14 Jun 1841

The Hong Kong government held the first public auction of land, selling a total of 34 plots of land between East Point in the east and Sheung Wan in the west.

22 Jun 1841

Deputy Superintendent of the Trade of British Subjects in China Alexander Robert Johnston was appointed as Administrator of Hong Kong; he remained in office until 12 August.

21 Jul 1841

Hong Kong was hit by a typhoon, which caused serious damage to ships, houses and piers around Kwan Tai Lo and Tsim Sha Tsui. A sailboat carrying Charles Elliot and his party was wrecked on their way back to Hong Kong and they were rescued by nearby ships and returned to Macao.

31 Jul 1841

Navy Lieutenant William Pedder was appointed as the first Harbour Master and Marine Magistrate.

09 Aug 1841

Victoria Prison (Gaol), Hong Kong's first modern prison, became operational.

12 Aug 1841

Henry Pottinger was appointed as Administrator of Hong Kong before becoming the first Governor of Hong Kong on 26 June 1843.

20 Aug 1841

Newly appointed Administrator of Hong Kong Henry Pottinger arrived in Hong Kong; on the following day he led 14 warships with 2,519 soldiers travelling north in a new campaign to invade China.

Nov 1841

Hong Kong's first post office was established on Garden Road.

1841

The Hong Kong Dispensary, forerunner of the A.S. Watson Group (Hong Kong) Limited, was founded.

British-owned enterprise Gibb, Livingston & Co. set up a Hong Kong branch to engage in shipping, import and export trade, etc. In the same year, Union Insurance Society of Canton Limited, a joint venture of Gibb, Livingston & Company, relocated its headquarters to Hong Kong, becoming the first foreign insurance company headquartered in Hong Kong.

Richard James Gilman established Gilman & Company Limited, a British-owned enterprise, for export trade, shipping and insurance brokerage.

16 Feb 1842

Henry Pottinger reasserted Hong Kong's position as a free port, laying the foundation for Hong Kong not to levy tariffs on imported goods.

27 Feb 1842

Henry Pottinger officially moved the office of the Chief Superintendent of the Trade of British Subjects in China from Macao to Hong Kong and began handling Hong Kong's administrative affairs directly.

Feb 1842

Queen's Road was completed, becoming one of the modern roads in the early years of Hong Kong. (Figure 034)

17 Mar 1842

The Friend of China, the first English newspaper in Hong Kong, started publication; on 24 March, it was merged with the *Hong Kong Gazette* to form *The Friend of China and Hong Kong Gazette*.

29 Mar 1842

Henry Pottinger announced Hong Kong's provisional currency system, which stipulated various currencies be used as Hong Kong's legal tender, including the Spanish silver dollar, Mexican silver dollar and other silver dollars as well as the East India Company rupee and Chinese copper coins, with established exchange rates. British silver coins could be used in fairs and markets at their market value. On April 27, Pottinger announced that the silver dollar from Mexico and other republics would be adopted as the standard currency pertaining to government revenue and business transactions in Hong Kong and other British-occupied regions in China.

15 May 1842

Hong Kong's first Baptist church, located on Queen's Road, was founded by John Lewis Shuck, a missionary from the American Baptist Churches in the US, and his wife, Henrietta Hall. On July 19, a dedication ceremony was held; both English and Chinese worshipping services were available.

Figure 034
A view of Central and Western districts on northern Hong Kong Island the Harbour Office with its flagstaff was located on Queen's Road West in the mid-19th century. (Painting composed on 29 November 1846 and courtesy of Special Collections, The University of Hong Kong Libraries)

Figure 035
A depiction of the signing of the Treaty of Nanking between the Qing government and Britain in 1842. (Image courtesy of Anne S. K. Brown Military Collection, Brown Digital Repository, Brown University Library)

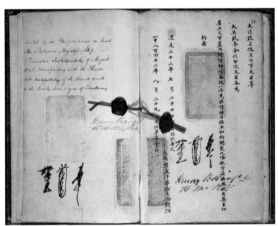

Figure 036
Text of the Treaty of Nanking of 1842. (Photo courtesy of CPA Media Pte Ltd/Alamy Stock Photo)

16 May 1842

The Central Market opened as the first public market in Hong Kong.

07 Jun 1842

The cornerstone was laid for The Cathedral of the Immaculate Conception, the first Catholic church in Hong Kong, at the junction of today's Wellington Street and Pottinger Street in Central.

Jun 1842

Henry Pottinger assembled British reinforcements dispatched from India and once again sailed north to enter the Yangtze River. By attacking and successfully occupying Shanghai and Zhenjiang, he cut off the north-south transport lane of grain to the capital. The troops reached the city of Nanjing on 04 August, leaving Emperor Daoguang (道光) of the Qing Dynasty no choice but to start negotiations.

29 Aug 1842

The Treaty of Nanking was signed by Qing government representatives Qiying (耆英) and Yilibu (伊里布) and British representative Henry Pottinger on the British warship *Cornwallis*, anchored in the Xiaguan River in Nanjing. The treaty stipulated that "… the Island of Hongkong, to be possessed in perpetuity by Her Britannic Majesty, Her Heirs and Successors, and to be governed by such Laws and Regulations as Her Majesty the Queen of Great Britain, etc., shall see fit to direct." Hong Kong Island was formally ceded to Britain. (Figures 035 and 036)

04 Oct 1842

Chief Magistrate William Caine decreed that, except for district watchmen on night patrol, all Chinese be prohibited from going out after 11 p.m.; it was the first curfew in Hong Kong.

01 Nov 1842

Morrison Memorial School was relocated from Macao to Morrison Hill on Hong Kong Island, making it the first English-language school in Hong Kong. Principal Pastor Samuel Robbins Brown and eleven students, including Wong Shing (黃勝), Yung Wing (容閎) and Wong Fun (黃寬), also moved to the new campus.

1842

Abdoolally Ebrahim & Company was founded by an Indian businessman.

04 Jan 1843

The British government issued an Order in Council to move the Criminal and Admiralty Courts, established in 1833 in Guangzhou, to Hong Kong, where it would be responsible for hearing criminal cases involving British subjects located on Hong Kong Island, in the Mainland and within one hundred miles from its coastlines. On 04 March 1844, the court heard its first case.

05 Apr 1843

Letters Patent (i.e. the Hong Kong Charter) was promulgated by Britain's Queen Victoria, declaring the establishment of the Colony of Hong Kong and confirming the status of Hong Kong as a British colonial regime. The charter also stipulated that the Governor of Hong Kong would be granted extensive authority, as well as the general provisions for the establishment of the Executive Council and the Legislative Council.

06 Apr 1843

Queen Victoria issued the Royal Instructions pertaining to the compositions, powers and procedures of the Executive Council and the Legislative Council of Hong Kong, as well as the functions of the Governor in relation to the councils, appointment and removal of council members, and council protocols for bills and resolutions.

19 Apr 1843

Anglican priest Vincent John Stanton was appointed by the British government to serve as the first Colonial Chaplain of Hong Kong.

May 1843

Fever was rampant in Hong Kong from May to October, killing 24% of British troops and 10% of European civilians. Henry Pottinger and key officials of the Hong Kong government took refuge in Macao and did not return to Hong Kong until November when the epidemic, known as the Hong Kong Fever, had subsided.

01 Jun 1843

The Medical Missionary Hospital on Morrison Hill, the first hospital in Hong Kong, was established by the Medical Missionary Society.

26 Jun 1843

After the exchange ceremony for the Treaty of Nanking between Qiying (耆英) and Henry Pottinger, Hong Kong officially became a British Crown Colony. Pottinger was sworn in as the first Governor of Hong Kong and served in the position until 07 May 1844. (Figure 037)

Governor Henry Pottinger announced that Queenstown—developed area along the north coast of Hong Kong Island—had been renamed the City of Victoria.

27 Jun 1843

Governor Henry Pottinger appointed George Alexander Malcolm as Hong Kong's first Colonial Secretary.

27 Jun 1843

Governor Henry Pottinger appointed the first Justices of Peace with a group of 44 gentlemen, including William Caine and businessman Andrew Jardine.

Figure 037
Portrait of Henry Pottinger by Samuel Robbins Brown. (Image courtesy of Hong Kong Museum of Art Collection)

21 Jul 1843

Thomas Westbrook Waldron was appointed as the first Consul of the United States in Hong Kong.

22 Jul 1843

Qing Imperial Commissioner Qiying (耆英) and Governor of Hong Kong Henry Pottinger signed the General Regulations (under which the British Trade is to be conducted at the Five Ports of Canton, Amoy, Foochow, Ningpo, and Shanghai). As a supplement to the 1842 Treaty of Nanking, it recognised British consular jurisdiction in China and set the Chinese customs duty rate at five percent.

24 Aug 1843

Governor Henry Pottinger appointed former Administrator of Hong Kong Alexander Robert Johnston, Chinese Secretary and Interpreter to the Superintendent of Trade John Robert Morrison and Chief Magistrate William Caine to the Executive Council and the Legislative Council.

12 Oct 1843

The Hong Kong government appointed Alexander Anderson as the first Colonial Surgeon.

13 Dec 1843

The Qing government moved the Guanfu Assistant Magistrate's Office from Xin'an County to Kowloon and renamed it the Kowloon Assistant Magistrate's Office, an "important office governing coastal areas and territorial seas." Xu Wenshen (許文深) was appointed as the first Assistant Magistrate of Kowloon. The Office's jurisdiction roughly covered present-day Kowloon and the New Territories.

1843

Chief Magistrate William Caine appointed Hong Kong's first 28 police officers.

The Peninsular and Oriental Steam Navigation Company (P&O) set up an office in Hong Kong.

The Stanley Military Cemetery—the earliest known military cemetery in Hong Kong—was built.

Yuen Fat Hong, the first Nam Pak Hong (south-north trading company) and the first modern Chinese-owned firm in Hong Kong, was founded by Chaozhou businessman Ko Yuen-sing (高元盛) in Sheung Wan.

The London Missionary Society relocated its headquarters and its affiliated printing house from Malacca to Central, Hong Kong. During the same time, Anglo-Chinese College (presently known as Ying Wa College), founded in 1818, was also relocated to Hong Kong.

11 Jan 1844

The first meeting of the Legislative Council, chaired by the Governor, was held. The first Commander of British forces in Hong Kong, Major General George Charles D'Aguilar, was appointed as a councillor to fill the vacancy left by deceased councillor John Robert Morrison.

13 Jan 1844

Major General George Charles D'Aguilar was concurrently appointed as Lieutenant Governor of Hong Kong.

14 Feb 1844

Chinese Secretary of the Hong Kong government Charles Gützlaff established the Chinese Union—a subdivision of the Foreign Christian Missionary Society whose mission was to train Chinese missionaries for service in the Mainland.

28 Feb 1844

The Legislative Council passed its first four bills on slavery, publications, land registration and the regulation of merchant ships.

02 Mar 1844

The Slavery Ordinance 1844 and Printing Regulation Ordinance 1844 were promulgated. The former stipulated that the British anti-slavery legislation was applicable to Hong Kong but was vetoed by Queen Victoria. The latter required newspapers and books to be registered before publication.

09 Mar 1844

The Land Registration Ordinance 1844 was promulgated, requiring the registration of all documents regarding amended deeds for land and real estate with the Land Office.

Chief Magistrate William Caine announced that all Chinese must apply for a licence with his assistant, Charles Gützlaff, in order to become district watchmen who were trained to maintain public order in the Chinese community together with the police.

12 Mar 1844

The Merchant Shipping Ordinance 1844 was promulgated, stipulating owners of British commercial vessels should not abandon any crew members or refuse to bring them back to Britain. The Ordinance was subsequently vetoed by Queen Victoria.

14 Mar 1844

British-owned company Jardine, Matheson & Co. moved its headquarters to Hong Kong and set up an office in the East Point area—a site it had acquired during the first land auction of Hong Kong.

20 Mar 1844

The Legislative Council passed the Good Order and Cleanliness Ordinance 1844, which prohibited discarding rubbish in public areas and disrupting order in the community.

02 Apr 1844

Dent & Co. moved from Macao to Hong Kong, setting up its office and warehouse on Queen's Road Central and engaging in the import and export trade, shipping and insurance industries.

24 Apr 1844

The Hong Kong government announced that all Chinese residing in Hong Kong must register with Charles Gützlaff, Assistant to the Chief Magistrate, to prevent Hong Kong from becoming a gathering place for unscrupulous elements.

01 May 1844

The Legislative Council passed the Justices of the Peace—Summary Jurisdiction Ordinance 1844, specifying that the Justices of the Peace should try cases with summary procedures and ensure that they would adopt measures required to perform their duties.

The Legislative Council passed the Police Force Regulation Ordinance 1844, establishing the Hong Kong Police Force with police officers' inauguration procedures, security measures, and management systems.

01 May 1844

The Legislative Council passed the Licencing Public Houses & c. Ordinance 1844, effective 01 July, stipulating that any retailer of alcoholic beverages exceeding two gallons must apply for a licence in advance.

07 May 1844

John Walter Hulme was appointed as the first Chief Justice of Hong Kong.

08 May 1844

John Francis Davis was sworn in as the second Governor of Hong Kong; he remained in office until 18 March 1848.

15 May 1844

Robert Montgomery Martin was appointed as the first Colonial Treasurer of Hong Kong to oversee financial affairs.

12 Jun 1844

The Chinese Peace Officers Regulation Ordinance 1844 was promulgated, authorising the Governor to appoint Chinese men as Peace Officers to assist in the government administration of the villages on Hong Kong Island in accordance with traditional Chinese customs.

26 Jun 1844

The Public Gaming Ordinance 1844 was promulgated, stipulating that operating a gambling venue or taking part in gambling was illegal.

01 Oct 1844

The Supreme Court of Hong Kong was established and held its first criminal session the following day under the auspices of the Chief Justice. It was Hong Kong's first trial by a permanent court with a jury.

Paul Ivy Sterling and Henry Charles Sirr were admitted as barristers by the Supreme Court, becoming the first group of barristers in Hong Kong. Edward Farncomb, having obtained the qualification to practise as a lawyer, was the first lawyer in Hong Kong.

19 Oct 1844

The Registration of Inhabitants Ordinance 1844 was promulgated, specifying that from 01 November onwards, all male residents of Hong Kong Island who were aged 21 or above or capable of earning a living, including boat dwellers, must register with the Registrar General every year and pay a registration fee (known as a "head tax").

31 Oct 1844

Chinese residents went on strike in protest of the Registration of Inhabitants Ordinance 1844 one day before it came into effect. The strike lasted until 13 November, when the Legislative Council passed an amendment to the Ordinance (promulgated in the *Gazette* on 20 November), stipulating exemptions from registration for certain persons and cancellation of registration fees.

04 Nov 1844

The Hong Kong government hung a camp follower who was convicted of murdering a police officer of European descent in Stanley; it marked the first documented case of execution by hanging in Hong Kong.

Nov 1844

The Hong Kong government made the British pound and the Indian silver dollar as legal tender in accordance with a directive from London.

28 Dec 1844

The Salt, Opium Licencing & c. Ordinance 1844 was promulgated, empowering the Governor-in-Council to issue licences—obtained in the form of public auctions or bids—for the sale of salt, opium, marijuana, and tuber leaves. This was the beginning of Hong Kong's opium monopoly.

1844

The Union Chapel (present-day Union Church) in Hong Kong was founded by James Legge, a pastor from the London Missionary Society.

Noronha Printers & Writers Co. was founded by Delfino Noronha, a Portuguese in Macao, as the first printing company in Hong Kong; it started printing the Gazette and other official publications in 1859.

D'Aguilar Hospital, located in Central, was completed and became the first hospital for the British forces in Hong Kong.

The Chinese Repository, founded on 31 May 1832, was relocated from Guangzhou to Hong Kong; it ceased publication in December 1851.

15 Jan 1845

The Triad and Secret Societies Ordinance 1845 was promulgated, stipulating that it was a felony for any Chinese to join a triad or secret society, punishable by imprisonment for not more than three years and subject to hard labour. After serving their sentences, they would receive a tattoo on the right cheek and be expelled from Hong Kong.

20 Feb 1845

English-language newspaper *The China Mail* was founded by British publisher Andrew Shortrede. It remained in business until 1974, making it the longest-running English-language newspaper in Hong Kong as of 01 July 2017.

07 Mar 1845

The Executive Council adopted the first Rules and Regulations for the Executive and Legislative Councils, which set a general framework for handling matters of the two councils.

Apr 1845

The Oriental Bank opened a branch in Hong Kong and in 1846 issued Hong Kong's first batch of notes, with a face value of five dollars each. It was the first bank in Hong Kong and the first bank to issue banknotes in Hong Kong. On 30 August 1851, it was granted a Royal Charter; its banknotes could be used to pay government accounts. The banknotes were in circulation until the bank's reorganisation in February 1884. The bank was closed in 1892.

03 May 1845

The Hong Kong government promulgated an Order from the Privy Council, stipulating that gold mohur of the East India Company, silver dollars from Spain, Mexico and other South American countries, and copper coins of China were considered legal tender of Hong Kong as with the British gold, silver and copper coins. The official exchange rate was fixed at one silver dollar to four shillings and two pence; one rupee to one shilling and ten pence; and one shilling to 288 copper coins.

02 Jun 1845

The Supreme Court heard the first libel case in Hong Kong, in which John Carr, Editor of *The Friend of China*, was accused of defaming British Rear Admiral Thomas Cochrane in an article published on 13 July 1844. The court ruled in favour of John Carr.

07 Jun 1845

The Rating Ordinance 1845 was promulgated, stipulating the collection of quarterly rates according to a certain percentage of the annual valuation of land and property to pay for police operating expenses.

01 Aug 1845

The British Peninsular and Oriental Steam Navigation Company launched a regular postal route between Hong Kong and London.

19 Aug 1845

The Jurors Ordinance 1845 was promulgated, specifying the number (six) and qualifications of jurors. The Supreme Court–Summary Jurisdiction Ordinance 1845 was also promulgated, stipulating that the Supreme Court could hold a trial without a jury for disputes involving debts and claims of not more than HK$100.

1845

The Murray Battery in Central was completed and became the first permanent fortification of the British forces in Hong Kong.

The Happy Valley Racecourse, Hong Kong's first racecourse, was completed. Its first race was held in 1846. (Figure 038)

American Tudor Ice Company established the first icehouse in Hong Kong as a supplier primarily for the British forces hospital.

The Hong Kong government completed construction of three berthing piers along the coast of the City of Victoria.

The Hong Kong Cemetery in Happy Valley was opened upon completion. It was Hong Kong's first public cemetery and known as the Colonial Cemetery in the early days.

04 Feb 1846

The Admiralty Court was established in Hong Kong, and Chief Justice of Hong Kong John Walter Hulme was appointed as Judge of Admiralty Court by the British government. On 14 January 1847, the Court heard its first case.

12 May 1846

Headquarters House (also known as Flagstaff House) was completed; it was the first building at Victoria Barracks in present-day Central District.

26 May 1846

The Hong Kong Club, a high-end gathering place of social activities for Europeans in Hong Kong, was established at the junction of present-day Queen's Road Central and Wyndham Street. Women and Chinese people were denied membership. (Figure 039)

Figure 038
The Happy Valley Racecourse circa 1858—showing a memorial to the sailors who died in the line of duty on board the British naval vessel *Vestal* in March 1847. The memorial was relocated to Hong Kong Cemetery in the 1950s. (Image courtesy of adoc-photos/Corbis via Getty Images)

Figure 039
The Hong Kong Club Building in 1903, located on Queen's Road Central. (Photo courtesy of Public Records Office, Government Records Service)

Figure 040
Murray House in Central (centre)—it was dismantled in the early 1980s and later reconstructed on the seafront of Stanley. (Image courtesy of Universal History Archive/Universal Images Group via Getty Images)

May 1846

Murray House, located at the first fixed barracks of British forces in Hong Kong called Murray Barracks, was completed in present-day Central District. (Figure 040)

28 Dec 1846

Reverend Samuel Robbins Brown, the first principal of Morrison Memorial School, left Hong Kong for the US, taking with him his students Yung Wing (容閎), Wong Fun (黃寬) and Wong Shing (黃勝), making them the first Chinese students to study in the US.

1846

The General Post Office was relocated to the Registrar General Office building at the corner of Queen's Road and Pedder Street.

British-owned Douglas Lapraik & Co. was founded in Hong Kong, initially dealing in timepieces but later expanded into other sectors, including real estate, shipping and trading.

Li Chy (李濟), founder of the Chy Loong Ginger Factory in Guangzhou, relocated the factory to Hong Kong, making it the first preserved ginger factory in Hong Kong.

The London Missionary Society appointed Ho Fuk-tong (何福堂) as pastor, making him the first Chinese pastor in Hong Kong and the second Chinese pastor in China.

14 Jan 1847

Chun Teen-soong (陳天宋) was convicted of robbery of the opium merchant ship *Privateer* and murder of its captain in a trial at the Admiralty Court, making him the first Chinese pirate to be sentenced to death in Hong Kong.

20 Jan 1847

The Registration and Census Ordinance 1846 was promulgated, granting the Registrar General with the additional titles of Protector of Chinese Inhabitants, Justice of the Peace, and Captain Superintendent of Police. It stipulated that all Chinese in Hong Kong were subject to the full supervision of the Registrar General.

Jan 1847

The Hong Kong Branch of the Royal Asiatic Society was founded; it ceased operation in 1859 but was re-established in 1959.

10 Apr 1847

The Prevention of Piracy Ordinance 1847 was promulgated, stipulating that the captains of British warships and merchant ships were empowered to search Chinese ships and consider them as pirates if they were carrying weapons. It was vetoed by the Queen of England on 01 January of the following year.

31 May 1847

The Kowloon Walled City, where the Deputy Magistrate of Kowloon and Commodore of the Dapeng Brigade were based along with 32 cannons, was built by the Qing government as a military stronghold to fend off attacks from British troops. (Figures 041 and 042)

Jun 1847

Chief Magistrate William Caine was accused of instructing his Chinese comprador Lo A-king (Lo Aqui) (盧亞景) to extort bribes from businesses at the Central Market; Caine was found innocent in a following investigation.

Sep 1847

Deputy Magistrate of Kowloon Xu Wenshen (許文深) and Commodore of Dapeng Brigade Wang Pengnian (王鵬年) made a donation in the establishment of Lung Tsun Free School at the Kowloon Walled City. (Figure 043)

Figure 041
Kowloon Walled City against the backdrop of Lion Rock, with its wall stretching over the top of White Crane Hill. (Photo taken circa 1906 and courtesy of HKSAR Government)

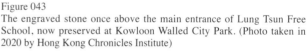

Figure 043
The engraved stone once above the main entrance of Lung Tsun Free School, now preserved at Kowloon Walled City Park. (Photo taken in 2020 by Hong Kong Chronicles Institute)

Figure 042
The wall of Kowloon Walled City. (Photo taken circa 1930 and courtesy of HKSAR Government)

22 Nov 1847

Chief Justice John Walter Hulme appeared before the Executive Council in defence of his alcohol abuse alleged by Governor John Francis Davis in Hong Kong's first disciplinary hearing of a judge. On 30 November, he was convicted and suspended from his duties effective immediately; on 16 June 1848, the British Colonial Office overturned the ruling and reinstated his official position following an appeal.

1847

A British House of Commons special committee issued a report condemning the extravagant spending of the Hong Kong government. It demanded a decrease in expenditure and suggested a reduction in the annual allocation of funds to £25,000 starting the following year and no further allocation in 1855. Since the establishment as a free port, Hong Kong had fallen short on government revenue and tackled fiscal deficits with funding allocated by the British Parliament.

The German Barmen Mission began sending missionaries to China and made Hong Kong a base for learning Chinese.

The Hong Kong government began importing a large amount of shillings from Britain and issuing them under the gold standard. It differentiated from the local currency under the silver standard and the local common practice by the actual weight of silver. As such, shillings were used in Hong Kong at a discount and limited in circulation.

The Man Mo Temple on Hollywood Road, where the Chinese god of literature (Man Cheong) and god of martial arts (Kwan Tai) were enshrined, was completed and then expanded in 1851. It also served as an important venue for communal discussion and dispute resolution in the Chinese community. (Figure 044)

Residents in Stanley rebuilt the Sin On Communal Hall, where local affairs were handled.

Missions Etranges de Paris was relocated from Macao to Hong Kong, making it the first Catholic religious order to come to Hong Kong for missionary work.

The Hung Shing Temple in Wan Chai was built.

04 Feb 1848

The Admiralty Court found twelve Chinese men who robbed a ship in December the previous year guilty of piracy; four of them were hanged on the same day.

21 Mar 1848

George Bonham was sworn in as the third Governor of Hong Kong; he remained in office until 12 April 1854.

Figure 044
Man Mo Temple on Hollywood Road in Sheung Wan. (Photo taken circa 1890 and courtesy of Hong Kong Museum of History)

Figure 045
St. John's Cathedral, a Victorian Gothic building, on Garden Road in Central. (Photo taken in 1870 and courtesy of Hong Kong Museum of History)

12 Sep 1848

The first four nuns sent by the Sisters of St. Paul de Chartres arrived; they were the first Catholic sisters to come to Hong Kong for missionary work.

19 Oct 1848

The Hong Kong and Canton Steam Packet Company, the first steamship company in Hong Kong, was established by Jardine, Matheson & Co., Dent & Co. and other foreign firms in Hong Kong and Guangzhou. A regular service between Hong Kong and Guangzhou began in the spring of 1849 and ended in 1854 when the company was closed.

Nov 1848

Governor George Bonham ordered the construction of all public works to be halted because of the Hong Kong government's financial concerns. The government recorded £25,072 in local fiscal revenue and £40,302 in allocations from Britain, totalling £65,374 in revenue and £62,309 in expenditure during the year.

1848

The Government Civil Hospital was established as the first public hospital in Hong Kong.

The St. Michael's Catholic Cemetery in Happy Valley was completed.

22 Feb 1849

The Petty Sessions Court Ordinance 1849 was promulgated to establish Petty Sessions and give the Chief Magistrate jurisdiction over minor criminal cases.

25 Feb 1849

Pirate Chui A-poo (徐亞保) killed two British military officers in Stanley who were molesting women and attacking others.

03 Mar 1849

The Hong Kong government announced that the lease term of land sold in auctions would be extended from 75 to 999 years to increase revenue from land sales.

11 Mar 1849

St. John's Cathedral, the Anglican Cathedral of the Diocese of Victoria founded in the same year, was opened upon completion. (Figure 045)

28 Sep 1849

The Royal Navy fought pirate Chui A-poo (徐亞保) in waters near Hong Kong; by 03 October, the navy had destroyed most of Chui's ships.

25 Oct 1849

The Victoria Regatta Club was established; in 1872, it merged with other sports organisations, including the Hong Kong Swimming Club, and was renamed the Victoria Recreation Club, the oldest sporting club in Hong Kong.

1849

The Peninsular and Oriental Steam Navigation Company launched a regular route between Hong Kong and Shanghai.

By decree of the Letters Patent, the Diocese of Victoria of the Anglican Church was established in Hong Kong to administer missionary affairs in Hong Kong, the Mainland and Japan; George Smith was appointed as the first Bishop.

The Jamia Mosque, the first mosque in Hong Kong, was completed on Shelley Street.

Liao Ruyi (廖汝翼) from Sheung Shui passed the Chinese imperial examination at provincial level.

14 Feb 1850

The British ship *Lady Montagu* carried 450 Chinese workers from Hong Kong to Peru; 300 workers died during the voyage.

20 Mar 1850

The Rendition of Chinese Ordinance 1850 was promulgated, stipulating that any Chinese person who violated the laws of the Qing government and was hiding in Hong Kong must be deported to the Mainland upon investigation and confirmation by the Magistrate.

14 Jun 1850

With the approval of the British Colonial Office, David Jardine of Jardine, Matheson & Co. and Joseph Frost Edger of Jamieson, How & Co.—two nominated representatives of the Justices of the Peace—assumed office as the first two Unofficial Members of the Legislative Council.

07 Sep 1850

The French ship *Albert* carried hundreds of Chinese workers from Hong Kong to Peru. Some workers started a riot, killing five persons—the captain, first mate, second mate, cook and tally clerk—and then forced the sailors to return to China. On 02 October, when the ship arrived at Lo Man Shan in the Pearl River Estuary, about 140 people escaped in fishing boats, while the rest were arrested by the Hong Kong police.

1850

The US-owned Russell & Co. opened a branch in Hong Kong.

Lane Crawford opened for business in Central. At first, it was just a temporary store selling daily necessities to the Royal Navy and their families. Later, it developed into Hong Kong's oldest department store.

1850

Four representatives of the Muslim community formed a trustee organisation to manage the mosques and Muslim cemeteries in Hong Kong. The organisation, the first Muslim group in Hong Kong, later developed into the Incorporated Trustees of the Islamic Community Fund of Hong Kong.

10 Mar 1851

A special hearing was held in the Criminal Court to try the case of pirate Chui A-poo (徐亞保), who was accused of killing two British military officers on 25 February 1849. Chui was sentenced to indefinite deportation; on 02 April, he hung himself in prison.

15 Apr 1851

William Thomas Bridges was appointed as a barrister by the Supreme Court; in the same year, he established Hong Kong's first law firm—the predecessor of the law firm Deacons—specialising in assisting clients with litigation matters.

Jun 1851

A popular venue for British people to relax and hold events, the Hong Kong Cricket Club was established opposite the parade ground of the Murray Barracks.

08 Sep 1851

Portuguese Consul General in Macao Manuel Pereira took office as the first Portuguese Consul in Hong Kong.

28 Dec 1851

A night fire broke out at Sheung Wan Lower Bazaar (present-day Jervois Street); British forces in Hong Kong blew up houses to stop the spread of the fire. Two British soldiers died, 200 Chinese were missing, and 450 houses were destroyed.

1851

St. Paul's College was established by Anglican pastor Vincent John Stanton; it initially accepted mainly Chinese boys who were taught English.

Chaozhou merchant Chen Wun-wing (陳煥榮) established a trading company called Kin Tye Lung in Sai Wan.

The Hakka Congregation in Sheung Wan was founded by Reverend Theodore Hamberg of the Basel Mission. It was the first Hakka church in Hong Kong.

Kwong Fook I Tsz, also known as Pak Shing Temple, was built in Sheung Wan to house the ancestral tablets of Chinese people without relatives or friends who died in Hong Kong. The temple was rebuilt in 1895.

Hong Kong had a population of 32,983, including 31,463 Chinese and 1,520 foreigners, according to government statistics.

05 Jan 1852

The Criminal Court found British national William Fenton not guilty of ship hijacking and accessory to murder, but three of his Chinese subordinates were sentenced to death for piracy; on 15 April, in a retrial, Fenton was sentenced to three years in prison for consorting with pirates.

16 Mar 1852

The Legislative Council passed the Marriages Ordinance 1852, stipulating that if one or both of the parties was or were a person or persons professing the Christian religion, they could choose to register their marriage according to the ceremonies and procedures of this ordinance.

17 Apr 1852

Ten Portuguese sailors were convicted of murder and piracy and sentenced to death by the Supreme Court of Hong Kong for robbing the British merchant ship *Herald* and killing seven crew members in Dutch East Indies (present-day Indonesia), making them the first foreign pirate crew to be convicted of piracy. Four of them were granted amnesty on 26 April and instead sentenced to lifelong exile; the remaining six were executed on 03 May.

1852

The Peninsular and Oriental Steam Navigation Company (commonly known as P&O) launched a regular route between Hong Kong and Calcutta, India.

Parsi Dorabjee Naorojee Mithaiwala came to Hong Kong and later founded Naorojee & Co. He was also the founder of Kowloon Ferry (predecessor of Star Ferry).

The Zoroastrian Cemetery in Happy Valley was completed.

The Hong Kong government filled in the area between present-day Jervois Street and present-day Morrison Street with rubble from the 1851 Sheung Wan Lower Bazaar fire and hillside stones. The new praya was the first official reclamation project in Hong Kong and was named Bonham Strand.

03 Feb 1853

The Judicial Committee of the Privy Council in Britain heard the first civil appeal case from Hong Kong, involving the encashment of a bill of exchange.

27 Apr 1853

The British Crown announced that British currency would begin circulation in Hong Kong with immediate effect.

Governor Samuel George Bonham visited Tianjing (present-day Nanjing). On 30 April, he wrote to the Taiping Heavenly Kingdom, stating British neutrality in the war between the Qing government and the Taiping Heavenly Kingdom and reiterating Britain's rights to trade in five ports in accordance with the Treaty of Nanking.

Apr 1853

The ship *Emigrant*, chartered by Turner & Co., left the port of Whampoa (Huangpu) in Guangzhou for Hong Kong on 14 April; some of the 250 Chinese labourers on board died. The Hong Kong government placed the ship under quarantine upon its arrival and transferred the sick to an onshore hospital where 63 patients had a high fever and three patients died. On 18 May, the hospital received two new patients. A government committee concluded that the outbreak of disease on board was due to overcrowding, poor ventilation and the lack of knowledge in sanitation among the Chinese.

01 Aug 1853

The *Chinese Serial* was published as the first Chinese periodical in Hong Kong by British missionary Walter Henry Medhurst; it ceased publication in May 1856. (Figure 046)

24 Sep 1853

The Hong Kong government began publishing the *Gazette* independently.

1853

The Hong Kong government expenditure fell from £62,309 in 1848 to £36,419 in 1853.

13 Apr 1854

John Bowring was sworn in as the fourth Governor of Hong Kong; he remained in office until 02 May 1859.

30 May 1854

The Hong Kong Volunteers was founded with 99 European members; it was disbanded in the same year.

19 Aug 1854

Luo Yatian (羅亞添), from a fraternal organisation called Tiandihui, and his followers captured the Kowloon Walled City. On 31 August, the Qing government recaptured it with the assistance of foreign mercenaries in Hong Kong.

02 Sep 1854

The Market Ordinance 1854 was promulgated, stipulating that any transaction conducted without permission from the government would be considered a public nuisance, invalidated and penalised. Thus, a system of government licensing was established.

16 Sep 1854

The Hong Kong government issued an order temporarily banning the trafficking of coolies to the Chincha Islands of Peru.

28 Oct 1854

The Hongkong Law Society was established as the first professional lawyers' association in Hong Kong by lawyer William Gaskell.

Figure 046
Front cover of the first issue of *Chinese Serial*, printed and distributed by Ying Wa College in 1853. (Image courtesy of Ying Wa College and Bodleian Libraries, University of Oxford)

Figure 047
The Government House on Upper Albert Road in Central. (Photo taken circa 1875 and courtesy of Hong Kong Museum of History)

1854

During the 1850s, Guangdong experienced the Red Turban Rebellion and then the massive Punti–Hakka Clan Wars, causing a mass migration of Chinese refugees to Hong Kong. According to government statistics, the total population of Hong Kong increased from 39,017 in 1853 to 55,715 in 1854, of which the Chinese population increased from 37,536 to 54,072, representing a year-on-year increase of 44%.

Wellington Barracks and Wellington Battery in Central District were built; the Barracks later became the headquarters of the British forces in Hong Kong.

The French Convent School (present-day St. Paul's Convent School) was founded. The first Catholic school for girls in Hong Kong, it was later run by the Sisters of St. Paul de Chartres. The school moved to its current location in Causeway Bay in 1914.

A book on the Taiping Rebellion, *The Visions of Hung-Siu-Tshuen and Origin of the Kwang-Si Insurrection*, was published. Written in English by Reverend Theodore Hamberg of the Basel Mission, the book was based on the verbal account of Hong Rengan (洪仁玕), a clan brother of Hung Siu-Tshuen (Hong Xiuquan) (洪秀全), King of the Taiping Heavenly Kingdom. Hong Rengan took refuge and recounted his experiences with Reverend Hamberg in Hong Kong in April 1852.

20 Jan 1855

The Neutrality Ordinance 1855 was promulgated, under which the Hong Kong government remained neutral in the war between the Qing government and the Taiping Heavenly Kingdom.

10 Mar 1855

The Registration of Vessels Ordinance 1855 was promulgated, stipulating that unregistered British vessels were not allowed to trade in the port of Hong Kong.

01 Oct 1855

The Government House on Upper Albert Road, which commenced construction in October 1851, was completed and subsequently became the official residence of the governors of Hong Kong. (Figure 047)

1855

The German-owned Siemssen & Co. set up a branch in Hong Kong, engaging mainly in the import and export trade; it later played a part in establishing The Hongkong and Shanghai Banking Corporation.

1855

A total of 14,683 Chinese, mainly from Guangdong and Fujian, travelled abroad via Hong Kong.

The Sassoon family of Jewish merchants purchased land in Happy Valley to build the Jewish Cemetery; it was opened in 1855.

02 Feb 1856

The Chinese Passengers Act 1855, enacted by the British Parliament, was promulgated, stipulating that any ocean-going vessel departing from the port of Hong Kong on a journey longer than seven days and carrying more than 20 passengers of Asian descent would be subject to inspection by immigration officers. Otherwise, they would not be allowed to leave Hong Kong.

13 Feb 1856

The British ship *John Calvin*, carrying 301 Chinese coolies, docked in Hong Kong in preparation for a voyage to Cuba. On 11 March, it left Hong Kong with the 289 Chinese passengers and crew members as 89 people refused to stay on board. When the ship arrived in Cuba on 23 September, 114 Chinese labourers and eleven crew members had died. The case was heard by the Supreme Court of Hong Kong by order of the British government; it was ruled that £1,000 paid in deposit by Steele & Co., the ship's agent in Hong Kong, should be confiscated. Later, Governor John Bowring agreed to revoke the confiscation following appeals by Steele & Co. and pleas from several other foreign firms, including Jardine, Matheson & Co. and Dent & Co.

23 Feb 1856

Chief Justice John Walter Hulme promulgated the first set of professional rules to be observed by barristers in Hong Kong.

14 Jun 1856

The Victoria (Lighting) Ordinance 1856 was promulgated to install streetlights and collect a streetlight tax levied at 1.5% of the rateable value.

The Chinese Burials and Nuisances Ordinance 1856 was promulgated, authorising the Governor-in-Council to designate the locations of Chinese cemeteries and impose penalties for burials in non-designated locations and for damage to trees and public places caused by unauthorised burials. On 21 June, the Hong Kong government designated two Chinese public cemeteries, one in Mount Davis and one in Wong Nai Chung, as the first two public Chinese cemeteries in Hong Kong.

22 Jul 1856

The British Army in Hong Kong transferred part of its land on Hong Kong Island to the Board of Admiralty; it was subsequently developed into the Naval Dockyard in Admiralty.

25 Aug 1856

During the criminal session in which a policeman of European descent was accused of extortion, Attorney General Thomas Chisholm Anstey suggested that police officers' identification numbers be shown on their uniforms in addition to wearing caps embedded with the Crown emblem. The proposal was subsequently adopted by Chief Justice John Walter Hulme.

08 Oct 1856

The trading ship *Arrow*, registered in Hong Kong with a largely Hong Kong Chinese crew and flying the British flag, was detained in Huangpu, Guangzhou on suspicion of smuggling opium. Britain used the *Arrow* Incident as a pretext for attacking Guangzhou, triggering the Second Opium War. (Figure 048)

21 Nov 1856

All Chinese-run shops in Hong Kong went on strike to protest a decree issued by the Hong Kong government on 16 November which mandated that all windows, doors and layouts of Chinese buildings be in accordance with the specifications of European buildings.

Figure 048
The Anglo-French fleet assembled at Victoria Harbour in preparation for an invasion of Peking. (Photo taken in March 1860 and courtesy of Wellcome Library no. 569627i)

Figure 049
A map of the City of Victoria, Hong Kong; ① to ⑥ were locations with boundary stones put in place by the Hong Kong government in 1903 to mark the city limits. (Illustration by Hong Kong Chronicles Institute. Source of reference: *City of Victoria: A Selection of the Museum's Historical Photographs*)

22 Nov 1856

The Registration and Census Ordinance 1846 was implemented, stipulating that any Chinese who failed to register with local authorities would be deported.

07 Jan 1857

The Peace of the Colony Ordinance 1857 was promulgated, requiring Chinese to carry a Night Pass (commonly known as a Night Paper) issued by the police for leaving home between 8 p.m. and dawn the following day.

15 Jan 1857

Over 400 European residents in Hong Kong, including Governor John Bowring's wife, suffered from poisoning with arsenic after eating bread from Esing Bakery; no one died as the arsenic content was low. On 02 February, the case was heard in the Supreme Court; staff of Esing Bakery were given a light sentence of deportation due to insufficient evidence.

21 Apr 1857

British troops attacked the Kowloon Walled City and captured Commodore of Dapeng Brigade Zhang Yutang (張 玉堂) for refusing to hand over anti-British individuals; he was taken to Hong Kong Island but was later released.

09 May 1857

The Hong Kong government announced that Hong Kong Island would be divided into nine regions: Victoria, Shau Kei Wan, Sai Wan, Shek O, Tai Tam Tuk, Stanley, Hong Kong, Aberdeen and Pok Fu Lam. The City of Victoria was divided into seven "yeuks" (districts), namely Sai Wan, Sheung Wan, Central, Ha Wan (present-day Wan Chai)— which were collectively known as the Four Circuits) in addition to Victoria Peak, Wong Nai Chung and Soo Kun Poo (So Kon Po). The seven yeuks were later expanded to nine yeuks and 11 yeuks. (Figure 049)

12 May 1857

William Lobscheid, a missionary from the Rhenish Mission Society, was appointed as Hong Kong's first Inspector of Government Schools.

Jun 1857

Agra & United Service Bank Limited opened a branch in Hong Kong and was granted a Royal Charter in the same year. Initially issued in October 1863, its banknotes remained in circulation until May 1866, when they were recalled and invalidated because of a financial crisis; on 31 December 1872, the branch was shut down.

04 Jul 1857

American Eli Boggs, associated with several piracy cases, was convicted of piracy and sentenced to life imprisonment by the Supreme Court of Hong Kong.

11 Jul 1857

Antonie Kup assumed office as the first Consul of the Netherlands in Hong Kong.

01 Oct 1857

English-language newspaper *Hong Kong Daily Press* started publication in Hong Kong with Yorick Murrow as the first editor-in-chief; it ceased publication in 1941.

07 Nov 1857

The Emigration Passage Brokers Ordinance 1857 was promulgated, stipulating that emigration passage brokers could legally transport Chinese labourers abroad for trade after paying a licence fee.

28 Nov 1857

The Venereal Diseases Ordinance 1857 was promulgated, requiring that all brothels be registered and kept in three districts: east of Spring Garden in Wan Chai, west of the junction of Hollywood Road and Queen's Road West in Sai Ying Pun, and the Victoria Peak except areas facing Queen's Road. The Ordinance stipulated residents of the brothels should provide their names and undergo health checks.

1857

The Chartered Mercantile Bank of India, London and China (later known as the Mercantile Bank Limited) opened a branch in Hong Kong. In August 1857, the bank started issuing banknotes, making it the second banknote-issuing bank in Hong Kong, and was granted a Royal Charter in the same year. In 1858, banknotes issued by Mercantile Bank Limited were recognised as legal tender by the Hong Kong government.

The Rules and Regulations for Government Schools was enacted by the Government School Committee; Chinese students were offered free admission. The new regulations also set the rules for teachers, examinations and the keeping of teaching records in government schools; these were the first regulations for government schools.

St. Francis' Hospital was founded by the Hong Kong Catholic Church; it was closed after only one year of operation.

Guangdong businessman Li Sing (李陞) founded the "gold mountain" firm Wo Hing and Co. in Sai Wan for businesses in ship chartering.

09 Jan 1858

The Hong Kong government gazetted an excerpt of the Legislative Council meeting minutes for the first time.

24 Feb 1858

The Legislative Council approved the appointment of Wong Shing (黃勝) as the first Chinese juror.

20 Mar 1858

The Prepared Opium Ordinance 1858 was promulgated to auction off the licence to manufacture and sell prepared opium to the highest bidder.

11 Apr 1858

Father Paolo Mem Reina from Italy's Pontifical Institute for Foreign Missions (*Pontificio Istituto Missioni Estere* or PIME) arrived in Hong Kong to engage in educational and missionary work.

02 Jun 1858

British Secretary of State for Foreign Affairs James Harris ordered Envoy Extraordinary and Minister Plenipotentiary to Imperial China James Bruce to seek cession of the Kowloon peninsula and Stonecutters Island during negotiations with the Chinese authorities.

17 Jul 1858

Attorney General Thomas Chisholm Anstey had previously charged Registrar General Daniel Richard Caldwell for collusion with pirate Wong Ma-chow (黃墨洲) in a corruption and malfeasance case. In a report submitted on this day to Governor John Bowring, the Commission of Inquiry ruled that it was no longer appropriate for Caldwell to be a Justice of the Peace, but it did not propose removing him from his post as Registrar General.

31 Jul 1858

Governor John Bowring issued an statement in Chinese and English, denouncing the Qing government for an order to withdraw all Chinese people from Hong Kong and a ban on food supply to Hong Kong. Bowring declared the Qing government an enemy of Britain and emphasised that the Qing government would be subject to harsh consequences.

Jul 1858

The first Standing Rules and Orders 1858 of the Legislative Council took effect, setting out the manner of speaking in meetings, committee quorum, voting method, duties of the clerk as well as the procedures for handling petitions, ordinances and witnesses. Councillors were also allowed to submit petitions to the Governor (who was also Council chairman by virtue of office). A petition, once read in public, could be followed up by the Council or handled by an ad hoc committee whereby witnesses could be summoned.

09 Aug 1858

José de Aguilar assumed office as the first Consul of Spain in Hong Kong.

08 Nov 1858

Following the signing of the Treaty of Tientsin between China and Britain on 26 June, representatives of the two countries signed the Agreement Containing Rules of Trade (made in pursuance of Article XXVI of the Treaty of Tientsin) in Shanghai. Paragraph 5 stipulated that British businessmen were permitted to import duty-paid opium, officially legalising the opium trade in Hong Kong.

08 Dec 1858

The Hong Kong government's financial budget was passed in a vote by the Legislative Council for the first time; it set a precedent giving the Council the power to control public expenditure.

1858

Captain William King-Hall of the Royal Navy ship *Calcutta* and Major General Charles van Straubenzee (Commander of the British Troops in Guangzhou) successively proposed occupying the headland of the Kowloon peninsula and Stonecutters Island. The proposal was approved by the British government.

The Hong Kong government extended the City of Victoria to Soo Kun Poo in the east and Shek Tong Tsui in the west, and added the Shek Tong Tsui yeuk, thus forming eight yeuks (districts). The eight yeuks were Shek Tong Tsui, Sai Ying Pun, Sheung Wan, Victoria Peak, Central, Ha Wan, Wong Nai Chung and Soo Kun Poo.

The Legislative Council permitted for the first time that citizens could sit in its meetings upon introduction by councillors and the Governor.

The South Block of Western Market, located on Queen's Road Central, was completed.

06 Jun 1859

Colonial Secretary William Thomas Mercer completed the Memorandum on the Kowloon Peninsula Question, in which he analysed how the occupation of the Kowloon peninsula would contribute to the colony of Hong Kong.

09 Sep 1859

Hercules Robinson was sworn in as the fifth Governor of Hong Kong; he remained in office until 15 March 1865.

Nov 1859

Club Germania, initially located on Queen's Road East and relocated to Kennedy Road on 31 December 1902, was founded.

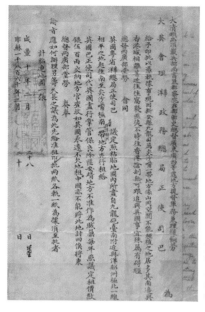

Figure 050
The Chinese edition of the Deed of Lease of Kowloon,
signed by Harry Smith Parkes and Lao Chongguang
(勞崇光) in 1860. (Image courtesy of Public Records
Office, Government Records Service)

1859

The Chartered Bank of India, Australia and China (present-day Standard Chartered Bank) opened a branch in Hong Kong; in 1862, it became the third banknote-issuing bank in Hong Kong.

21 Jan 1860

The Hong Kong government reorganised the Government School Committee into the Board of Education for management of all government schools in Hong Kong.

18 Mar 1860

Lieutenant General James Hope-Grant, Commander of British Troops in China and Hong Kong, ordered the 44th (East Essex) Regiment of Foot to land at Tsim Sha Tsui, Kowloon and unilaterally occupy the southern tip of the Kowloon peninsula where a British camp could be established.

20 Mar 1860

British Consul in Guangzhou Harry Smith Parkes and Governor-General of Guangdong and Guangxi Lao Chongguang (勞崇光) signed the Deed of Lease of Kowloon, under which the British could lease part of the Kowloon peninsula (from the south end of the Kowloon Battery to the north end of Stonecutters Island, along with Stonecutters Island) for an annual rent of 500 taels of silver. (Figure 050)

12 Apr 1860

Six sisters from the Italian Canossian Daughters of Charity arrived in Hong Kong to engage in missionary and educational work. In May, they established the Italian Convent School (present-day Sacred Heart Canossian College) at Mid-Levels to offer Chinese, English and Portuguese lessons to Chinese girls.

12 May 1860

The Fraudulent Trustees, and Etc. Ordinance 1860 was promulgated, stipulating that any trustee of an estate who took possession of the estate or misappropriated the estate for his/her own benefit was guilty of a misdemeanour and was subject to trial by the Supreme Court.

11 Jul 1860

James Legge submitted an education reform plan to the Board of Education, suggesting that the Hong Kong government establish a model government school for the Chinese, with English as the main language of instruction. On 23 March 1861, the Legislative Council agreed to provide the project with a funding of HK$20,500.

25 Aug 1860

William Henry Adams was appointed as Chief Justice of Hong Kong.

24 Oct 1860

The Convention of Peking was signed by the British and Chinese governments. Article 6 stipulated that the Qing government would cede to Britain the southern part of the Kowloon peninsula (south of present-day Boundary Street) along with Stonecutters Island. Prior to this, the British army laid siege to Peking (Beijing) where Yuanmingyuan (Old Summer Palace) was looted and burned.

15 Dec 1860

The Hong Kong government published the full text of the Convention of Peking and the Treaty of Tientsin in the *Gazette*. (Figure 051)

1860

The Diocesan Native Female Training School, located at Mid-Levels, was founded by Lady Lydia Smith as the first girls' school managed by the Anglican Church in Hong Kong; it was closed in 1868. The Diocesan School and Orphanage (present-day Diocesan Girls' School) was established in 1899 with the mission of the original school.

Bowrington Canal, Hong Kong's first man-made waterway, was built. (Figure 052)

19 Jan 1861

Envoy Extraordinary and Minister Plenipotentiary to Imperial China James Bruce and Governor of Hong Kong Hercules Robinson, along with the District Magistrate of Xin'an County, Commodore of the Dapeng Brigade and Assistant Magistrate of Kowloon of the Qing government, attended a government ceremony to mark the annexation of Kowloon.

04 Feb 1861

The Kowloon Order-in-Council was promulgated by the British monarch, stating that the leased land in the southern part of the Kowloon peninsula became an official part of the Colony of Hong Kong. On 30 March, the Hong Kong government gazetted the order, and Kowloon began to implement the same legal system as that of Hong Kong Island.

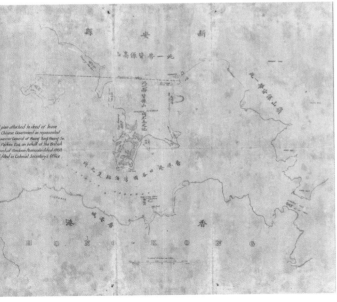

Figure 051
A replica of the map affixed to the Treaty of Peking of 1860, indicating a "Proposed Boundary" at the location of present-day Boundary Street. (Image courtesy of Public Records Office, Government Records Service)

Figure 052
The Bowrington Canal located in Wan Chai on Hong Kong Island. (Photo taken circa 1910 and courtesy of Hong Kong Museum of History)

09 Feb 1861

The Hong Kong government announced the results of a census. As of 31 December 1860, Hong Kong had a population of 94,917, including 90,691 Chinese residents and boat dwellers and 2,476 foreign nationals.

Apr 1861

Lady Lechler of the Basel Mission founded a charity school in Sai Ying Pun as the first girls' school supervised by the Hakka-language church in Hong Kong.

29 May 1861

The Hong Kong General Chamber of Commerce, consisting of foreign business entities in Hong Kong, was founded. Alexander Percival, a partner at Jardine, Matheson & Co., was the first chairman.

30 Jun 1861

The Hong Kong government abolished the system of Chinese Peace Officers in place since the promulgation of the Chinese Peace Officers Regulation Ordinance 1844.

24 Sep 1861

The Executive Council accepted the investigation report of the Civil Service Abuses Inquiry appointed by Governor Hercules Robinson. The report found Registrar General Daniel Richard Caldwell guilty of corruption, dereliction of duty, and collusion with pirates. The Council expelled Caldwell from office.

12 Oct 1861

The Hong Kong government announced in the *Gazette* that the British government would launch an examination to recruit cadet officers (later called administrative officers) for assignment in Hong Kong. In September 1862, the first group of cadet officers, including Walter Meredith Dean, Cecil Clementi Smith and Malcolm Struan Tonnochy, arrived in Hong Kong.

1861

The Dominican Order of Spain moved the headquarters of the Dominican Church of the Rosary from Macao to Hong Kong. The new monastery was established on Caine Road on 01 July of the same year.

The Commercial Bank Corporation of India and the East set up a branch in Hong Kong. In 1866, it began issuing banknotes in Hong Kong but ceased in the same year after the company was liquidated.

James Legge's English translations of *Analects of Confucius*, *Great Learning*, *Doctrine of Mean* and *Mencius* were published in Hong Kong as Volumes I and II of *The Chinese Classics*.

04 Jan 1862

The Hong Kong government commissioned the publication of a Chinese version of the *Gazette* that was originally released in English.

04 Mar 1862

Frederick Stewart took office as the first Principal of Government Central School (present-day Queen's College), which was established in Sheung Wan following the merger of four government schools and renowned for many outstanding Chinese alumni, including Sun Yat-sen (孫中山), Ho Kai (何啟) and Wei Yuk (韋玉). (Figure 053)

22 Mar 1862

The Volunteers Ordinance 1862 was promulgated, becoming the first ordinance regarding the enlistment of volunteer soldiers in Hong Kong.

Jun 1862

The Hong Kong and China Gas Company Limited was registered in London. It began supplying gas in 1864 as the first public utility company in Hong Kong.

Figure 053
Queen's College on Aberdeen Street in Sheung Wan. (Photo taken circa 1903 and courtesy of Hong Kong Museum of History)

Figure 054
A blue definitive stamp with a portrait of Queen Victoria issued in 1862, with a face value of 12 cents. (Image courtesy of Hong Kong Museum of History)

01 Jul 1862

The Hong Kong government replaced the British pound with "yuen" (dollar) as the unit of financial accounting and formally adopted the silver standard, ushering in a silver-based monetary system that lasted for 73 years.

05 Jul 1862

The Patents Ordinance 1862 was promulgated, stipulating that any inventor who had obtained a patent right in Britain could apply to the Governor for the same right in Hong Kong.

28 Jul 1862

Napoleon-Ernest Godeaux took office as the first French Consul in Hong Kong.

08 Dec 1862

Hong Kong Post issued the first batch of stamps in seven denominations, ranging from two cents to 96 cents. (Figure 054)

1862

John Heard took office as the first Russian Consul in Hong Kong.

The Hong Kong Police Force set up the first floating police station for the Water Police division (later renamed Marine Police).

01 Jan 1863

The Compagnie des Messageries Maritimes established a branch in Hong Kong to operate routes between Hong Kong and Europe.

Jan 1863

McGregor & Co. built Hong Kong's first modern pier, allowing for the direct berthing of ships near its warehouse at Spring Garden in Wan Chai.

Jul 1863

The Hong Kong and Whampoa Dock Company Limited was established in Guangzhou; Hong Kong Superintendent of the Peninsular and Oriental Steam Navigation Company Thomas Sutherland served as its chairman; operations in Hong Kong commenced in 1866.

01 Oct 1863

The Hong Kong Branch of the Bank of Hindustan, China and Japan Limited commenced operations.

26 Dec 1863

The Merchandise Marks Ordinance 1863 was promulgated, stipulating that forgery of trademarks or false description of goods with fraudulent intent were subject to criminal and civil liabilities.

1863

Pokfulam Reservoir was built and became the first reservoir in Hong Kong with an initial storage capacity of two million gallons; its capacity was increased to 68 million gallons in 1877 after two expansions.

A floating prison, converted from a ship and berthed at Stonecutters Island, was completed to relieve overcrowding at Victoria Prison.

Wheelock Marden Co. and Shanghai Tug & Lighter Co. were merged into Wheelock and Company Limited.

Gustave Overback took office as the first Austrian Consul in Hong Kong.

Jardine, Matheson & Co. laid the first telegraph line in Hong Kong, connecting its head office in East Point with its branch in Central.

The Lin Fa Kung (Lotus Temple) in Tai Hang was built for the worship of Kwun Yum (Guanyin) (Goddess of Mercy). Its front hall was in half-octagonal shape with a double-eaves-tended roof, making it architecturally unique.

The Yuk Hui Temple (Pak Tai Temple) in Wan Chai was built to enshrine a bronze statue of Pak Tai (God of the North) cast in 1603, which was the 31st year of the reign of Emperor Wanli (萬曆) of the Ming Dynasty.

30 Apr 1864

The Bankruptcy Ordinance 1864 was promulgated, granting the Supreme Court jurisdiction over bankruptcy petitions and providing comprehensive procedures for handling bankruptcy petitions.

17 Sep 1864

The Mercantile Law Amendment Ordinance 1864 was promulgated, stipulating that a commercial guarantee commitment would not be deemed invalid simply because it was not made in writing.

12 Nov 1864

Hong Kong and China Gas Company Limited installed a gas storage system at the junction of Whitty Street and Queen's Road West in Sai Wan, with a capacity of 3,400 cubic metres per day.

16 Nov 1864

The Union Dock Company, formed in a merger of Dent & Co. and Whampoa and Heard, acquired a site at Hung Hom in Kowloon for the construction of a dockyard that could accommodate warships.

03 Dec 1864

Hong Kong and China Gas Company Limited inaugurated its service of supplying gas for 500 streetlights in Central through a 24-kilometre gas pipeline.

1864

Francis Chomley assumed office as the first Italian Consul in Hong Kong.

The Barrack Block of the Central Police Station was completed, marking the official opening of the station.

The first Hong Kong coins were minted by the Hong Kong government. Denominations included a 10-cent silver coin, a one-cent copper coin and a one-mil copper coin. (Figure 055)

The Hong Kong government sold 26 waterfront sites and 39 non-waterfront sites at its first public auction of land on the Kowloon peninsula.

Father Timoleone Raimondi from the Pontifical Institute for Foreign Missions of Milan established St. Saviour's College, a commercial school, on Wellington Street in Central. On 07 November 1875, the college was renamed St. Joseph's College and came under the management of the De La Salle Brothers.

1864

The Hong Kong Botanical Garden was partially completed and opened to the public. In 1871, it was fully completed, making it the first public park in Hong Kong. (Figure 056)

The West Point Reformatory was established, making it the first reformatory and industrial school in Hong Kong. The school was taken over by the Salesians of Don Bosco in 1927 and renamed St Louis Industrial School. In 1936, it was expanded and renamed St. Louis School.

03 Mar 1865

The Hongkong and Shanghai Banking Corporation was established as a British-owned bank, with its headquarters at 1 Queen's Road Central. It became a note-issuing bank and was the only bank headquartered in Hong Kong at that time. On 18 August 1866, the Hongkong and Shanghai Banking Corporation Ordinance 1866 was promulgated to regulate banknote issuance and operations of the bank. (Figure 057)

Figure 055
A Hong Kong one-mil copper coin minted in 1865.
(Image courtesy of Hong Kong Museum of History)

Figure 057
The second-generation HSBC building. (Photo taken circa 1895 and courtesy of Hong Kong Museum of History)

Figure 056
A group photo of young Chinese at Hong Kong Botanical Garden.
(Photo taken circa 1875-1880 and courtesy of Special Collections,
The University of Hong Kong Libraries)

09 Mar 1865

The Privy Council issued an order to divide the judicial jurisdiction between the Supreme Court of Hong Kong and the British Consul in China. The Supreme Court would focus more on cases arising within the jurisdiction of the Hong Kong government.

18 Mar 1865

The Companies Ordinance of 1865 was promulgated, stipulating that any banking institution of ten or more persons and any other business organisation of more than 20 people must be registered.

30 Jun 1865

The Education (Educational) Department was established to replace the Board of Education and take charge of education-related affairs in Hong Kong.

01 Jul 1865

The Coinage Offences Ordinance 1865 was promulgated, stipulating that it was a criminal offence to sell, buy, use, transport and possess knowingly counterfeit currency. Those convicted of currency counterfeiting could be sentenced to life imprisonment.

20 Oct 1865

The Hongkong, Canton and Macao Steamboat Company was incorporated for ferry services between Guangzhou, Hong Kong and Macao.

1865

Tai Fu Tai Mansion was completed, becoming the residence of Man Chung-luen (文頌鑾), a 21st-generation descendant of the Man clan in San Tin, Yuen Long.

St. Stephen's Church was founded as the first Chinese-language Anglican Church in Hong Kong.

A Tin Hau temple was built on Second Street (now Pak Hoi Street) in Yau Ma Tei; it moved to its present location on Temple Street in 1876. Adjoining the temple were a communal hall, a temple for the earth god, and two study halls. The Tin Hau Temple and the adjoining buildings served as a multi-functional place for worship, arbitration and study.

01 Feb 1866

During a Sai Wan neighbourhood meeting, it was decided that a proposal should be submitted to the Hong Kong government to establish a District Watch Force for night watches and assist the police in maintaining peace and order in the Chinese community. On 16 August, the proposal was adopted by the Legislative Council and put into force. (Figure 058)

Figure 058
The conical hat issued to district watchmen in the early 20th century. The district watchmen were a civilian security force supplementary to the Hong Kong police. (Photo courtesy of Hong Kong Museum of History)

Figure 059
The Hong Kong Mint located at East Point. (Painting composed in the 1860s and courtesy of Hong Kong Museum of Art Collection)

12 Mar 1866

Richard Graves MacDonnell was sworn in as the sixth Governor of Hong Kong; he remained in office until 11 April 1872.

07 May 1866

The Hong Kong Mint was established in East Point (present-day Causeway Bay) and began minting silver coins with denominations of five cents, 10 cents, 20 cents, 50 cents and one dollar until its closure in 1868. (Figure 059)

May 1866

The first bilingual map of Xin'an County was published. The map took Italian Father Simeone Volonteri four years to complete with the help of Chinese Father Andreas Leong Chi-hing (梁子馨). (Map 7)

01 Jul 1866

The German-owned Carlowitz & Co. opened a branch in Hong Kong for businesses in shipping, import and export trade, and insurance.

08 Sep 1866

The Stamp Ordinance 1866 was promulgated, under which the stamp duty was officially enforced.

24 Oct 1866

John Jackson Smale took office as Chief Justice of Hong Kong.

17 Dec 1866

Club Lusitano, a Portuguese Club in Hong Kong on Shelley Street, was inaugurated by Governor of Macao José Maria da Ponte e Horta.

1866

Securities trading began in Hong Kong.

The German-owned Melchers & Co. set up its first Asian branch in Hong Kong for import-export trade. In 1887, it began serving as an agent for shipping lines run by Norddeutscher Lloyd in the Mainland and in Hong Kong.

The Hong Kong Fire Insurance Company was founded by Jardine, Matheson & Co. as the first fire insurance company in Hong Kong where it also owned the first fire engine.

23 Jan 1867

The Registrar General's Office received instruction from the Hong Kong government to become an open communication platform between Chinese residents and the government.

31 Jan 1867

The *Colorado*, owned by the Pacific Mail Steamship Company, arrived in Hong Kong from San Francisco, US, marking the maiden voyage of the first regular passenger line connecting the two places.

15 Jun 1867

The Hope Dock in Aberdeen, the first large-scale dry dock in Hong Kong, was inaugurated.

22 Jun 1867

The Order and Cleanliness Ordinance 1867 was promulgated, bringing gambling under government control.

The Hongkong Emigration Ordinance 1867 was issued, appointing medical officers to inspect the facilities on ships carrying emigrants in a bid to improve the health condition of Chinese emigrants on board ships departing from Hong Kong.

1867

The German-owned Arnhold Karberg & Co. opened a branch in Hong Kong, engaging mainly in machinery trading, shipping and insurance.

Tsang Tai Uk, a Hakka walled village in Sha Tin, was completed. It was built over a period of 20 years by Tsang Koon-man (曾貫萬), a businessman who ran a quarry in Shau Kei Wan. (Figure 060)

The first group of Sikh policemen were recruited to perform duties in Hong Kong.

29 Feb 1868

The Hongkong Hotel was opened at the junction of Queen's Road and Pedder Street in Central as the first high-class hotel in Hong Kong. (Figure 061)

23 May 1868

The Fire Brigade Ordinance 1868 was promulgated, under which volunteers and officers from the police force were selected to form the Hong Kong Fire Brigade. Charles May, who served concurrently as Captain Superintendent of Police and Warden of Victoria Prison, was appointed as the first Brigade Superintendent. In 1961, it was renamed the Hong Kong Fire Services Department.

01 Jul 1868

Governor-General of Guangdong and Guangxi Ruilin (瑞麟) imposed a blockade on Hong Kong to crack down on tax evasion and capture opium smugglers. The Qing government set up checkpoints at the eastern and western exits of sea lanes in Hong Kong, such as Lei Yue Mun, Kap Shui Mun and Kowloon City, and sent patrol ships to intercept privately owned Chinese boats travelling between Hong Kong and the Guangdong coast. A *likin* (a tax on goods in transit) of 16 taels of silver was charged per box of opium.

Figure 060
An aerial view of Tsang Tai Uk in Sha Tin. (Photo taken in 2006 and courtesy of Felix Wong/South China Morning Post via Getty Images)

Figure 061
The six-storey Hongkong Hotel. (Photo taken circa 1890-1895 and courtesy of Hong Kong Museum of History)

1868

Tang Tinggui（唐廷桂）and William McGregor Smith set up a joint-venture sugar refinery in East Point as the first sugar refinery in Hong Kong with modern machinery.

Chiu Yu-tin（招雨田）, Chan Woon-wing（陳煥榮）and other Nam Pak Hong businessmen established the Nam Pak Hong Association on Bonham Strand to formulate industry rules and settle disputes. It was the most important Chinese business association in Hong Kong.

22 Apr 1869

Acting Registrar General Alfred Lister inspected the Kwong Fook I Tsz (Temple of Common Benevolence), which provided refuge and medical services for the homeless and elderly. He found the sanitary conditions to be poor as the sick and the dead shared the same rooms; it led to extensive coverage in Hong Kong newspapers. The Hong Kong government found in an investigation that it was inhumane and subsequently ordered the temple to close down by the end of the month.

Figure 062
The first-generation Hong Kong City Hall, funded by community donation. (Photo taken circa 1875 and courtesy of Hong Kong Museum of History)

Figure 063
The Tung Wah Board of Directors in official uniform at the Assembly Hall of Tung Wah Hospital upon conferment of official titles by the Qing government in recognition of their efforts in disaster relief. (Photo taken circa 1885 and courtesy of Hong Kong Museum of History)

01 Jun 1869

A hospital committee for the establishment of a Chinese hospital was set up, comprising 20 leaders and businessmen in the Chinese community, including comprador of Gibb, Livingston & Company Leung On (梁安) and owner of Kin Nam Rice Company Ho Pui-yin (何裴然). In November, Governor Richard Graves MacDonnell assigned a plot of land on Po Yan Street in Sheung Wan for the hospital and provided a HK$115,000 subsidy for its construction.

Sep 1869

The Diocesan Home and Orphanage (present-day Diocesan Boys' School) was established to provide education for boys and girls of British, Chinese and Eurasian descent.

01 Oct 1869

The first training school for Hong Kong police officers was opened.

02 Oct 1869

The Public Assemblages (Regulation of Traffic) Ordinance 1869 was promulgated, empowering the Captain Superintendent of Police to formulate regulations on the use of roads in connection with all public events and authorising the Harbour Master to come up with similar regulations for ships travelling in the waters of Hong Kong.

03 Nov 1869

During his visit to Hong Kong, Prince Alfred attended an opera as the first public performance held in the first-generation Hong Kong City Hall. (Figure 062)

1869

The Great Northern Telegraph Co. Limited established a branch in Hong Kong, making it the first local telegraph office.

02 Apr 1870

The Chinese Hospital Incorporation Ordinance 1870 was promulgated, confirming the establishment of Tung Wah Hospital, which had 13 founding directors. Founding Chairman Leung On (梁安) was responsible for preparatory work to build the hospital. On 02 April, Governor Richard Graves MacDonnell officiated at the hospital's ground-breaking ceremony. (Figure 063)

27 Aug 1870

The Crown Rights (Re-entry, etc.) Ordinance 1870 was promulgated, empowering the Hong Kong government to repossess land or property found to be in violation of government leases.

1870

British trading company Butterfield & Swire opened an office in Hong Kong.

1870

The first synagogue in Hong Kong was established on Hollywood Road.

The Kun Ting Study Hall, built by the Tang clan of Hang Mei Tsuen in Ping Shan, was completed.

The Muslim Cemetery in Happy Valley, Hong Kong's first Islamic cemetery, was completed.

11 Mar 1871

The *Chinese and Foreign Weekly News*, a Chinese-language weekly newspaper published by *The China Mail*, was launched.

01 Apr 1871

The Great Northern Telegraph Company launched a submarine cable connecting Hong Kong and Shanghai, making it the first telegraph line beyond Hong Kong and the first of its kind in East Asia.

06 May 1871

According to a government census, as of 02 April 1871, Hong Kong had a population of 124,198, including 115,444 Chinese and 8,754 foreign nationals.

03 Jun 1871

The Legal Practitioners Ordinance 1871 was promulgated, consolidating and amending the laws related to legal practitioners, including barristers, solicitors, attorneys and proctors.

14 Jun 1871

At 9:45 a.m., the Governor received a telegraph from London, marking the official opening of the telegraph line between Hong Kong and London.

27 Jun 1871

Superintendent of the Canton Maritime Customs of the Qing government set up four regular customs checkpoints in Kap Shui Mun, Kowloon City, Fat Tau Chau and Cheung Chau to collect customs duties from vessels carrying opium passing through Hong Kong waters.

27 Jul 1871

The Hongkong Pier and Godown Company Limited was established in Wan Chai and opened the first commercial godown in Hong Kong; it also built a pier in March 1873.

02 Sep 1871

The Banishment of Dangerous Characters Ordinance of 1871 was promulgated, stipulating that any person naturalised as a British subject or anyone who was British not by descent could be refused entry or deported by the Governor-in-Council with validity of up to five years.

09 Sep 1871

The Hong Kong government announced that Chinese people must carry a light when going out from 7 p.m. to 5 a.m. the next day or they would be detained.

16 Sep 1871

The Auxiliary Police Force Ordinance 1871 was promulgated, giving the Governor the power to appoint auxiliary police constables on special terms in order to strengthen the manpower of the Hong Kong Police Force. (Figure 064)

23 Sep 1871

The Hong Kong government announced that the Queen had approved the appointment of Adolph Theodor Eimbcke as the first German Consul in Hong Kong following a unified Germany.

18 Nov 1871

The Hongkong Pier and Godown Company Ordinance 1871 was promulgated, establishing a company to build a public pier and godown in Victoria Harbour for loading, unloading and storing goods.

1871

The first-generation Standard Chartered Bank building was completed at the junction of Queen's Road Central and Duddell Street.

13 Jan 1872

The Hong Kong government announced that, effective 20 January, the gambling rules and regulations mandated by the Governor under the Order and Cleanliness Ordinance 1867 would be abolished; the gambling industry was once again banned.

14 Jan 1872

St. Peter's Church, dedicated to serving seafarers, was opened upon completion.

14 Feb 1872

Governor Richard Graves MacDonnell officiated at the opening ceremony of Tung Wah Hospital, which cost HK$45,000 to build and could accommodate 80–100 patients. It was the first Chinese hospital in Hong Kong and offered traditional Chinese medicine and therapeutics.

Figure 064
Sikh and Chinese constables at the Central Police Station on Hollywood Road in Central. (Photo taken in 1906 and courtesy of Public Records Office, Government Records Service)

16 Apr 1872

Arthur Kennedy was sworn in as the seventh Governor of Hong Kong; he remained in office until 01 March 1877.

17 Apr 1872

The Chinese Mail started publication. Its predecessor was the *Chinese and Foreign Weekly News,* which was shut down on 06 April.

26 Jun 1872

The Governor's authorisation to issue one-dollar banknotes through The Hongkong and Shanghai Banking Corporation as a remedy for depreciation of worn-out silver dollars was endorsed by the Executive Council upon notification. The Colonial Secretary strongly opposed the measure but suggested to keep in circulation HK$226,000 worth of unrecallable one-dollar banknotes.

20 Jul 1872

The Hong Kong government required all workers' dormitories to be registered for an annual fee of HK$5 per 10 beds. With the additional cost laid upon tenants by their landlords, about 10,000 workers went on a five-day strike beginning 25 July and 60 labour leaders were arrested. The Nam Pak Hong Association met with labour representatives and agreed to negotiate with the government. The fees were subsequently lowered by the Registrar General.

27 Jul 1872

The Births and Deaths Registration Ordinance 1872 was promulgated, authorising the Registrar General's Office to register births and deaths in Hong Kong.

Jul 1872

The Legislative Council established a Finance Committee as its first Standing Committee responsible for all public expenditure proposals, except the government budget.

24 Sep 1872

Several Chinese businessmen in Hong Kong jointly made a request with Governor Arthur Kennedy to punish people for forcing women into prostitution.

15 Oct 1872

Hayashi Michisaburō was appointed as the first Vice-Consul of Japan in Hong Kong. On 20 April 1873, Japan officially set up a consulate in Hong Kong to manage Japanese affairs with Britain and China within Hong Kong; it also regulated affairs with China in Guangzhou, Shantou, Qiongzhou, etc.

20 Nov 1872

The construction of St. Joseph's Church, which commenced in 1871, was completed; it was opened for worship.

21 Dec 1872

The Foreign Offenders Detention Ordinance 1872 was promulgated, stipulating arrangements for temporary detention in Hong Kong for foreigners accused or convicted of crimes in China or Japan while being deported to their home countries.

19 Jan 1873

China Merchants Steam Navigation Company's cargo vessel *Aden* made its maiden voyage with a Shanghai–Hong Kong route.

20 Feb 1873

The first Hong Kong Derby was held at the Happy Valley Racecourse, becoming one of Hong Kong's longest-standing horse racing championships.

26 Apr 1873

The Hong Kong government announced the implementation of the subsidised school programme to help five types of subsidised schools; it set the qualifications for participating schools and the standards for annual grants-in-aid. The subsidised schools would be supervised by the government.

03 May 1873

The Chinese Emigrant Ship Fittings Ordinance of 1873 was promulgated, forbidding all emigrant vessels departing from Hong Kong from using any facilities or structures prohibited by the Ordinance, including fences in the cabin to restrict passenger activities.

10 May 1873

The Protection of Women-Emigration Abuses Ordinance 1873 was promulgated, prohibiting the trading, abduction and unlawful detention of Chinese women and female children for the purpose of prostitution and of decoying Chinese into or away from Hong Kong.

01 Jun 1873

The *Galley of Lorne* of the British-owned China Pacific Steamship Company, with 641 Chinese passengers on board, embarked on its maiden voyage from Hong Kong to San Francisco. The ship completed the journey in 26 days, setting a record with the fastest voyage from Hong Kong to San Francisco.

02 Jul 1873

The Legislative Council passed the Standing Rules and Orders 1873, which contained a section titled "Progress of Bills" that set out the procedure for taking a bill through the various stages of the legislative process, including the committal of a bill to a Special Committee for examination. The Rules also covered how members should handle each stage in the progress of a bill and required announcements about the bills to be published in the *Gazette*.

12 Jul 1873

The Dangerous Goods Ordinance 1873 was promulgated, stipulating the requirements for the transport and storage of specified dangerous goods.

06 Aug 1873

Weather information on Xiamen, Shanghai and Hong Kong was telexed to Hong Kong readers for the first time under the heading "China Coast Meteorological Register" in *The China Mail*.

Sep 1873

The British navy bought a building on a hill in Wan Chai from Jardine, Matheson & Co. and converted it into the Royal Naval Hospital.

04 Oct 1873

The Hong Kong Code of Civil Procedure Ordinance 1873 was promulgated, amending and consolidating previous civil litigation procedures along with a uniform code of civil litigation procedure.

1873

The Kwun Yum Temple on Station Lane in Hung Hom, Kowloon, was completed, becoming the biggest temple of its kind in Kowloon.

04 Feb 1874

The *Universal Circulating Herald* was founded by Wang Tao (王韜) as the first newspaper financed and edited by Chinese people in Hong Kong. (Figure 065)

14 Feb 1874

The passenger ship *Wan Loong* sunk in Hong Kong waters, causing about 100 deaths.

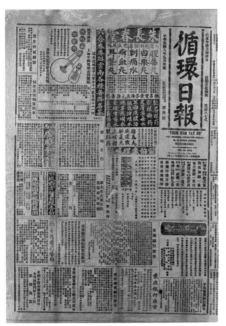

Figure 065
The newspaper *Universal Circulating Herald* dated 03 May 1919. (Image courtesy of Hong Kong Museum of History)

Figure 066
The aftermath of a typhoon in 1874 at the Kowloon waterfront where many boats were destroyed. (Photo courtesy of Hong Kong Museum of History)

09 May 1874

The Chinese Emigration Consolidation Ordinance 1874 was promulgated, amending and consolidating previous requirements related to ferries and ships used for carrying Chinese passengers and emigrants.

22 Sep 1874

Hong Kong was hit by a catastrophic typhoon, causing thousands of deaths in one of the worst typhoons in the history of Hong Kong. In 1880, human remains of 399 victims killed in the disaster and over 100 corpses found on Stonecutters Island were collected by Tung Wah Hospital and buried at Kellett Bay Cemetery's Public Graves for Typhoon Victims. The hospital built a pavilion in the cemetery in memory of the typhoon victims. (Figure 066)

17 Nov 1874

The Prefecture Apostolic of Hong Kong was raised to Vicariate Apostolic, extending its jurisdiction to Xin'an County, Guishan County (present-day Huiyang) and Haifeng County in Guangdong Province.

1874

The Hongkong Ice Company Limited with an ice-making plant in Causeway Bay was founded by Scottish engineers John Kyle and William Neish Bain.

The Tang clan of Ping Shan built the Shut Hing Study Hall at Tong Fong Tsuen in memory of member Tang Shut-hing (鄧述卿), but it was demolished in 1977, leaving only the entrance hall and a plaque.

The first rickshaw was introduced to Hong Kong from Japan.

02 Jan 1875

The Hong Kong government announced the Chinese translations of its major departments and officials' titles for the first time.

10 Apr 1875

The Marriage Ordinance of 1875 was promulgated, stipulating that all previous official records of marriages must be submitted to the Registrar General and that all future marriages in Hong Kong should be registered.

16 Apr 1875

The Cape D'Aguilar Lighthouse, Hong Kong's first lighthouse, was inaugurated in an opening ceremony; it was taken out of service in 1896.

01 Jul 1875

The Green Island Lighthouse was opened to assist ships arriving from the west of Victoria Harbour.

19 Jul 1875

Copper coins minted in London were issued in Hong Kong for the first time. On 20 June 1876, newly minted 5-, 10- and 20-cent silver coins also began to circulate.

07 Nov 1875

At the invitation of Bishop Timoleon Raimondi, six friars from the Institute of the Brothers of the Christian Schools (also known as De La Salle Brothers) came to Hong Kong on an educational mission and took over West Point Reformatory and St. Saviour's College.

1875

The 192-metre Lung Tsun Stone Bridge was completed. The bridge, which connected Kowloon Walled City with Victoria Harbour and served as a berth for loading and unloading cargo, commenced construction in 1873. (Figure 067)

The Man Mo Temple made a donation for constructing a coffin home in Sai Wan to temporarily store the remains of Chinese people awaiting burial in their hometowns. Subsequently administered by Tung Wah Hospital, it moved to its present location in Sandy Bay in 1899 and was renamed the Tung Wah Coffin Home.

15 Jan 1876

The Hong Kong government instructed Chinese residents to present their views to the government through the Registrar General, who also served as Protector of Chinese Inhabitants, in a bid to encourage direct communications between Chinese residents and the government.

Figure 067
The Pavilion for Greeting Officials (centre) and Lung Tsun Stone Bridge (bottom), built by the Qing government, at Kowloon Walled City. (Photo taken circa 1898 and courtesy of HKSAR Government)

01 Mar 1876

The Cape Collinson Lighthouse was commissioned to assist the navigation of vessels arriving from the south and east into Victoria Harbour.

1876

A. S. Watson Co., Limited established the first soft drink plant in Hong Kong, which mainly produced soft drinks for medical use; it was then one of the largest soft drink plants in Asia.

01 Apr 1877

Hong Kong joined the Universal Postal Union, resulting in a significant decrease in postage rates.

09 Apr 1877

Britain amended the Letters Patent promulgated in 1843, stipulating that if the Governor of Hong Kong died or was unable to perform his duties, the Lieutenant Governor, Officer Administering the Government, Colonial Secretary or Acting Colonial Secretary would administer Hong Kong in an acting capacity, following the above order of priority.

Amendments to the Royal Instructions by Britain were gazetted, stipulating that three of the ex-officio members of the Executive Council would be the Commander of British Forces in Hong Kong, the Colonial Secretary, and the Attorney General. At the same time, the Governor would be allowed to appoint temporary official members to fill temporary vacancies in the Executive Council.

23 Apr 1877

John Pope Hennessy was sworn in as Lieutenant Governor of Hong Kong. On 06 June, he was pronounced the eighth Governor of Hong Kong in the *Gazette*; he resigned on 07 March 1882.

18 May 1877

Ng Choy (伍才), also known as Wu Tingfang (伍廷芳), was called to the Bar by the Supreme Court, making him the first Chinese barrister in Hong Kong. (Figure 068)

Figure 068
Ng Choy (伍才), also known as Wu Tingfang (伍廷芳), in a court dress. (Photo taken in 1880 and courtesy of HKSAR Government)

19 May 1877

Chinese businessmen Li Sing (李陞) and Ho Kwan-shan (何崑山), also known as Ho A-mei (何阿美), incorporated On Tai Insurance Company as the first wholly Chinese-owned insurance company in Hong Kong.

07 Jun 1877

The first public examination for the recruitment of government clerks was held. Successful candidates were to serve in the Registrar General's Office.

The first Chinese couple to marry according to the new Hong Kong marriage law registered their marriage in the presence of Hong Kong's Registrar of Marriages.

22 Sep 1877

The Hong Kong Apostolic Vicariate founded the *Hong Kong Catholic Register* as the first English Catholic weekly newspaper in Hong Kong and the Mainland.

1877

The Hong Kong government abolished the practice of public flogging.

The Hong Kong branch of Mitsui & Co. Limited was opened for business, making it the first Japanese enterprise to expand to Hong Kong; it was shut down in January 1882.

British-owned Boyd & Co. started business in Hong Kong, engaging primarily in the import and export trade.

07 May 1878

Governor John Pope Hennessy donated 5,000 silver dollars and Chinese businessman Leung On (梁安) raised about 30,000 taels of silver in Hong Kong and Southeast Asia to help the victims of drought and famine in northern China.

25 Sep 1878

A group of pirates robbed a private Chinese bank at 52 Wing Lok Street. One pirate was shot dead while two were arrested by the police; the rest escaped by boat with HK$250 worth of stolen money and goods. The incident raised public concern over safety in Hong Kong.

08 Nov 1878

Four Hong Kong businessmen, namely Lo Kang-yeung (盧賡揚), Fung Po-hei (馮普熙), Shi Shang-kai (施笙階) and Tse Tat-shing (謝達盛), submitted a joint petition to Governor John Pope Hennessy, asking for approval to raise funds for rescuing kidnapped women and children. This became the official founding date of Po Leung Kuk.

14 Dec 1878

Ng Choy (伍才), also known as Wu Tingfang (伍廷芳), was appointed as the first Chinese Justice of the Peace by Governor John Pope Hennessy.

25 Dec 1878

A fire broke out on Hing Lung Street in Central and spread to Queen's Road Central, Stanley Street and Wellington Street; 368 houses were affected, with property losses amounting to HK$1 million.

1878

The Hongkong and Shanghai Banking Corporation offered a loan of 3.5 million taels of silver to the Qing government to settle the expenses incurred by General Zuo Zongtang (左宗棠) in quelling the Dungan Revolt (Tongzhi Hui Revolt) in northwestern China.

08 Jan 1879

The bilingual (English and Chinese) edition of the notices in the Gazette that were directly related to Chinese affairs was made available. The English version would prevail in case of any discrepancy.

22 Mar 1879

The Sacred Heart Church in Sai Wan was completed and began holding services; it was renamed St. Anthony's Church in 1892.

06 Aug 1879

Ernst Johann Eitel became Inspector of Schools, succeeding Frederick Stewart who had assumed the position of Acting Colonial Secretary.

04 Oct 1879

Yubinkisen Mitsubishi Kaisha, predecessor of Nippon Yusen Kabushiki Kaisha, began operating a route between Yokohama and Hong Kong as the first direct sea route connecting Japan and Hong Kong.

19 Nov 1879

The Hong Kong government announced that any fines and brothel licence fees levied under the Contagious Diseases Ordinance 1867 would be separated from the general stream of government revenue and used to subsidise expenses in treating venereal diseases in a hospital exclusively serving police officers and civil servants.

1879

The Hong Kong government amended the Grant-in-Aid Scheme 1873, dropping the required four-hour daily session of secular education in church schools.

The *Reform Daily News* (or Wai San Yat Po) was founded by Luk Kei-shun (陸 驥 純) as a local newspaper in support of the Hundred Days' Reform; it was renamed *National News* in 1909.

Emperor Guangxu (光緒) of the Qing Dynasty bestowed a plaque with the inscription "Shen Wei Pu You" (blessed by the gods) to Tung Wah Hospital in commendation of a donation of about HK$665,000 for disaster relief with victims from several provinces in the Northern Chinese Famine of 1875–1878.

21 Jan 1880

At Governor John Pope Hennessy's request, Ng Choy (伍才), also known as Wu Tingfang (伍廷芳), accepted an appointment to deputise for Hugh Bold Gibb, who was on leave in Britain, making Ng the first Chinese Unofficial Member of the Legislative Council.

04 Apr 1880

The first Synod of the Fifth Region of the Catholic Church in China was held in Hong Kong; it lasted eight days.

17 May 1880

The establishment of Po Leung Kuk was approved by Governor John Pope Hennessy. The Po Leung Kuk Ordinance 1882 was promulgated on 05 August 1882. It had a temporary office at Tung Wah Hospital in the early days and was committed to protecting vulnerable women and children from being kidnapped as well as supporting the Protector of Chinese in the mediation of disputes among Chinese families and married couples.

1880

The total value of Chinese export and import trans-shipments through Hong Kong rose from 14% and 20% in 1867 to 21% and 37% in 1880, respectively.

Sun Yee Opium Company, Lai Hing Hong and the private Chinese bank Tak On Ngan Ho successfully joined the Hong Kong General Chamber of Commerce as its first Chinese-owned corporate members.

Lok Sin Tong Benevolent Society, a charitable organisation, was established in the Kowloon Walled City.

The Man Mo Temple Free School was established to provide free education for students from low-income families.

18 Jan 1881

The Commission of Independent Examiners held a meeting chaired by Inspector of Schools Ernst Johann Eitel. It was decided that examinations would be conducted by designated individuals other than school teachers; it marked the beginning of Hong Kong's public examination system.

19 Mar 1881

The Census Ordinance 1881 was promulgated, authorising population census to be taken in Hong Kong.

02 Apr 1881

The Stonecutters East Battery was built, making it the first fortification on Stonecutters Island.

03 Jun 1881

Governor John Pope Hennessy addressed members of the Legislative Council, stating that in Hong Kong "…where so much of the commercial life is conducted by the Chinese—where the wealthiest merchants are Chinese—where the Chinese possess so much property—where they are permanent inhabitants, and where nine-tenths of the Government revenues are contributed by them."

11 Jun 1881

The Hong Kong government announced results of a census. As of 03 April 1881, Hong Kong had a population of 160,402, including 150,690 Chinese and 9,712 foreign nationals.

15 Jun 1881

Robert Fraser-Smith founded the *Hong Kong Telegraph* and became its first editor-in-chief. The newspaper continued until 01 April 1951.

25 Jun 1881

Five naturalisation ordinances, each named after five Chinese individuals in Hong Kong who were approved for British naturalisation, were promulgated, marking the first group of British-naturalised Chinese.

12 Sep 1881

The Government Normal School was opened in Wan Chai as the first full-time teacher training school in Hong Kong. The first group of 12 students was enrolled; it was closed in 1883.

1881

Taikoo Sugar was established by Butterfield & Swire; its sugar refinery in Quarry Bay started production in 1884 and became the world's largest and most sophisticated refinery. (Figure 069)

The Nethersole Clinic was set up in Tai Ping Shan, primarily providing medical services for Chinese people.

Appointed by the British government, former Royal Engineers officer Osbert Chadwick arrived in Hong Kong for a study on the local sanitary situation. In 1882, he released a highly critical report titled *Mr. Chadwick's Reports on the Sanitary Condition of Hong Kong*.

Figure 069
The Taikoo Sugar Refinery in Quarry Bay. (Photo taken circa 1895 and courtesy of Hong Kong Museum of History)

18 Feb 1882

The Tramways Ordinance 1882 was promulgated, establishing Hongkong and China Tramways Company Limited for the planning and construction of six tram routes, including that of the Peak Tram.

13 Mar 1882

George Phillippo was appointed as Chief Justice of Hong Kong; he remained in office until 05 October 1888.

1882

Eleven Methodist Church followers from Guangzhou and Foshan set up a school on Wellington Street in Central; it became a Methodist gospel church in 1884 and was known as the Wesleyan Church.

Oriental Telephone and Electric Company introduced a public telephone service to Hong Kong; the company was later renamed China and Japan Telephone and Electric Company.

Butterfield & Swire was granted a quarry permit for operation in Quarry Bay, becoming the only British-owned company with such a licence in Hong Kong.

02 Mar 1883

The Hong Kong Observatory was established with four primary responsibilities, namely meteorological observations, magnetic observations, a time service based on astronomical observations and a tropical cyclone warning service. William Doberck was the first Director.

30 Mar 1883

George Bowen was sworn in as the ninth Governor of Hong Kong; he remained in office until 19 December 1885.

31 Mar 1883

Reverend Charles Robert Hager, from the American Board of Commissioners for Foreign Missions, arrived in Hong Kong and began to preach in Guangdong and Hong Kong. He later set up a Protestant gospel church on Bridges Street on Hong Kong Island.

A contract between Eastern Extension Telegraph Company and Imperial Chinese Telegraph Administration was signed for telegraph cables running from Shanghai and Guangdong to Hong Kong, marking the beginning of telegraph communication between Hong Kong and Mainland cities.

21 Apr 1883

The Sanitary Board, which later became the Urban Council, was established to manage municipal sanitation matters.

23 May 1883

Governor George Bowen issued a notice in the *Gazette*, stating that no judicial proceedings should be taken against Chinese hawkers accused of violating cleanliness and public order regulations without first consulting the Registrar General.

May 1883

The Causeway Bay Typhoon Shelter was built, making it the first typhoon shelter in Hong Kong; the breakwater across from Causeway Road was about 426 metres long.

28 Jul 1883

The British-owned Douglas Steamship Company was established and registered in Hong Kong.

07 Aug 1883

Governor George Bowen's proposal to expand the Legislative Council with the addition of five Unofficial Members and six Official Members was accepted by Secretary of State for the Colonies Edward Henry Stanley, 15th Earl of Derby. Among the Unofficial Members, at least one should be of Chinese descent, while two others should be nominated by the Hong Kong General Chamber of Commerce and the Justices of the Peace.

08 Oct 1883

The Hong Kong Rope Manufacturing Company, with a factory in Kennedy Town, was established by Shewan, Tomes & Co.; it was the first rope factory in Hong Kong.

1883

Lui King-fai (呂景輝), an elderly man from Lantau Island, established two monasteries—Shun Yeung Sin Yuen and Po Wan Sin Yuen—at Luk Wu Tung on Fung Wong Shan, Lantau Island.

The Chinese Christian Cemetery was completed in Pok Fu Lam and became the earliest extant permanent Chinese Christian cemetery in Hong Kong.

The young Sun Yat-sen (孫中山) arrived in Hong Kong from his hometown, Cuiheng Village in Xiangshan County; he entered the Diocesan Home and Orphanage (later renamed the Diocesan School and Orphanage). He began attending the Government Central School in 1884 and graduated in 1886.

26 Feb 1884

The first-generation Marine Police Headquarters, built in 1869, was destroyed in a fire. The second-generation Marine Police Headquarters was later built on the Tsim Sha Tsui coast.

28 Feb 1884

Governor George Bowen appointed Wong Shing (黃 勝) as an Unofficial Member of the Legislative Council to succeed Wu Tingfang (伍廷芳), making him the first Chinese member to be officially appointed to the Council.

05 Apr 1884

An amended Royal Instructions from the British monarch was promulgated, marking a total of four ex-officio members of the Executive Council with the additional membership of the Colonial Treasurer.

10 Apr 1884

The Medical Registration Ordinance 1884 was promulgated, stipulating that all doctors, other than Chinese medicine practitioners, were prohibited from practising if they were not formally registered with the Hong Kong government.

16 Aug 1884

The Hong Kong government announced a visual structure with drum-, ball- and cone-shape signals to be adopted by the Hong Kong Observatory in the first tropical cyclone warning system for vessels departing from Hong Kong.

11 Sep 1884

The Chinese workers of Whampoa Dock in Hung Hom refused to repair the French warship La Galissonnière, which arrived in Hong Kong for dry-docking, in protest of her role in the invasion of Taiwan during the Sino-French War.

17 Sep 1884

A proclamation titled Notice to the Chinese in Hong Kong and Macao by Governor-General of Guangdong and Guangxi Zhang Zhidong (張之洞) was published in four Chinese newspapers in Hong Kong. He accused the French military of luring Chinese workers in Hong Kong and Macao for labour on warships, warned that Chinese workers were deceived into serving on the frontline in the Sino-French War, and called for a revolt among Chinese workers onboard warships.

18 Sep 1884

Chinese workers attempted to detonate explosives to the French warship at Whampoa Dockyard but were discovered by French soldiers and detained by the Hong Kong police.

Figure 070
Spectators gathered to watch horse racing on a race day at Black Rock near Happy Valley Racecourse before a grandstand became available. (Photo taken circa 1890 and courtesy of Hong Kong Museum of History)

Figure 071
A horse racing event in 1894. (Photo courtesy of Hong Kong Museum of History)

22 Sep 1884

Cargo boat operators began boycotting the French by refusing to carry goods for their merchant ships. As a result, several were prosecuted and fined HK$5 by the Hong Kong government.

30 Sep 1884

Cargo boat operators went on strike, extending their boycott of French warships to vessels of other countries and refusing to carry passengers. Consequently, port services came to a near standstill. The next day, the boycott spread to other industries.

03 Oct 1884

Strikers held a demonstration at Kennedy Town Praya in protest of cargo boat operators who started working again. The police were attacked with stones when heading to the area of Gap Road (present-day Hollywood Road) to disperse crowds of strikers. Indian mounted police, armed with swords, were then sent in to disperse the crowd, resulting in the death of one Chinese, multiple injuries, and the arrest of about 30 people. The Hong Kong government tried the arrestees the same day; six were sentenced to one year of hard labour.

05 Oct 1884

In the early morning, notices were found along the waterfront of Hong Kong Island, stating that several industries had held meetings and decided that all cargo boat operators and coolies should return to work that morning while other anti-French actions would continue.

09 Oct 1884

The Peace Preservation Ordinance 1884 was promulgated; it remained in force until 01 April 1885 in the hope of restoring peace and order to the community of Hong Kong.

04 Nov 1884

The Hong Kong Jockey Club as a permanent organisation for horse-racing was initiated by 34 foreign businessmen and members of the Legislative Council in a meeting at City Hall. (Figures 070 and 071)

1884

The Hong Kong General Chamber of Commerce and Unofficial Justices of the Peace could each nominate one person to be an Unofficial Member of the Legislative Council.

The Standing Rules and Orders for the Legislative Council of Hong Kong 1884 was adopted. For the first time, it established a committee system in the Legislative Council, including Special Committees and Standing Committees. Special Committees were responsible for specific tasks assigned by the Council; Standing Committees (including the Finance Committee, Law Committee and Public Works Committee) took charge of specific matters related to the functions of the Council. In addition, procedures for enquiries submitted to the Hong Kong government by the Council, including meeting notices and enquiries on public affairs, were established in accordance with the Standing Rules.

The Hong Kong St. John Ambulance Association was founded—under which St. John Ambulance Brigade was set up in 1916.

The construction of Lo Pan Temple on Ching Lin Terrace in Kennedy Town—dedicated to the God of Carpenters and Builders—was completed by the Contractors' Guild.

01 Jan 1885

The Hong Kong Observatory set up a time ball at the second-generation Marine Police Headquarters in Tsim Sha Tsui so that vessels in the harbour could tell the exact time. In 1907, the Time Ball was relocated to the Signal Tower on Signal Hill.

07 Mar 1885

The Weights and Measures Ordinance 1885 was promulgated, specifying Chinese and British standard weights and measures, as well as standardised conversion ratios.

09 May 1885

The Bill of Exchange Ordinance 1885 was promulgated, specifying the type and use of bills of exchange, etc.

23 May 1885

The Married Women's Disposition of Property Ordinance 1885 was promulgated, stipulating that married women, with the consent of their husbands, could act on the land and property they owned through deeds.

Nov 1885

Emperor Guangxu (光緒) of the Qing Dynasty bestowed a plaque with the inscription "Wan Wu Xian Li" (compassion for all) to Tung Wah Hospital in recognition of a contribution of approximately 46,000 silver dollars for relief with victims of floods across the Pearl River Delta in June 1885. (Figure 072)

1885

The European Lunatic Asylum, also known as the Victoria Mental Hospital, was completed and started operations on Bonham Road. The nearby Chinese Lunatic Asylum was completed in 1891.

The Hong Kong government set up the first public mortuary.

12 Feb 1886

The Hong Kong Football Club as the first football club in Hong Kong was established by Colonial Secretary James Stewart Lockhart and a group of British expatriate residents and soldiers.

27 Mar 1886

The Printers and Publishers Ordinance 1886 was promulgated, regulating the printing and publication of newspapers, books and other published works.

Mar 1886

The Hong Kong government issued £200,000 worth of bonds in London at an interest rate of 4.5% per annum in a bid to cover the construction cost of infrastructure projects in Hong Kong.

Figure 072
Tung Wah Hospital was awarded a plaque titled "Wan Wu Xian Li" (compassion for all) by Emperor Guangxu (光緒) of the Qing Dynasty in 1885; presently on display at the Assembly Hall of Tung Wah Hospital. (Photo courtesy of the Collection of Tung Wah Museum)

Figure 073
Hong Kong & Kowloon Wharf and Godown Company in Tsim Sha Tsui, Kowloon. (Photo taken circa 1900–1910 and courtesy of Hong Kong Museum of History)

Figure 074
Kowloon Wharf in the 1930s. (Photo courtesy of H. Armstrong Roberts/Retrofile via Getty Images)

08 May 1886

The Sale of Land by Auction Ordinance 1886 was promulgated, introducing the provisions of English land auction laws in Hong Kong.

The Bill of Sale Ordinance 1886 was promulgated, consolidating and amending the laws on prevention of frauds.

11 Sep 1886

The Hong Kong and Qing governments signed the Management of Hong Kong Opium Affairs Statute in Hong Kong, authorising the Inspector General of Chinese Maritime Customs to establish the Kowloon Customs to collect tariffs and *likin* on opium transported through Hong Kong.

18 Dec 1886

The Wills Act Amendment Ordinance 1886 was promulgated, stipulating conformity with amendments to the Wills Act made by the British Parliament.

1886

The Hong Kong (Submarine Mining) Company was established by the British army as the first Hong Kong-based Chinese regular army unit whose members consisted mainly of Hakka people and boat dwellers from Hong Kong and the Pearl River Delta region.

The Fairlea Girls' School, located at Mid-Levels, was founded by Margaret Elizabeth Johnstone, a missionary of the Church Missionary Society. In 1936, it merged with the Victoria Home and Orphanage to form the present-day Heep Yunn School in To Kwa Wan.

The Hong Kong and Kowloon Wharf and Godown Company Limited, predecessor of The Wharf (Holdings) Limited, was jointly established by Catchick Paul Chater and Jardine, Matheson & Co. (Figures 073 and 074)

Figure 075
The Dairy Farm Company on Wyndham Street in Central on Hong Kong Island. (Photo taken circa 1908 and courtesy of HKSAR Government)

1886

The Dairy Farm Co. with Hong Kong's first herd of dairy cattle in Pok Fu Lam was incorporated by Scottish surgeon Patrick Manson and five businessmen. (Figure 075)

The Tien Wah Mining Company, founded by Ho Kwan-shan (何崑山), received approval for silver mining at Mui Wo on Lantau Island.

03 Jan 1887

Green Island Cement Company Limited from Macao underwent reincorporation in Hong Kong, becoming the first local cement company. In 1900, it set up a factory at Hok Yuen in Hung Hom.

16 Feb 1887

Alice Memorial Hospital on Hollywood Road was inaugurated in an opening ceremony; it was operational the following day, providing Chinese residents of Hong Kong with Western-style medical care.

26 Feb 1887

The Defamation and Libel Ordinance 1887 was promulgated. Introduced by Hong Kong independently, it was the first ordinance to decree that acts of defamation were liable to civil and criminal prosecution.

02 Apr 1887

The Kowloon Customs, under the command of the Inspector General of Chinese Maritime Customs, was established, with Englishman Frank Arthur Morgan as the first Customs Commissioner. Headquartered on the second floor of the Bank Building on Queen's Road Central, the Kowloon Customs took over the four neighbouring customs houses originally set up by the Canton Customs of the Qing government.

01 Jun 1887

The Imports and Exports Office under the Harbour Department was established to keep the Kowloon Customs informed of opium imports. In 1888, the Office submitted its first annual report on Hong Kong opium imports and exports.

11 Aug 1887

The coastal fortification system in Lei Yue Mun, which included several underground tunnels connecting the central redoubt with its nearby gun batteries, was completed.

Figure 076
The "Four Desperados" (Front row, from left to right): Yeung Hok-ling (楊鶴齡), Sun Yat-sen (孫中山), Chan Siu-bak (陳少白) and Yau Lit (尢列), with Kwan King-leung (關景良) (standing at the back) on the third floor of the Hong Kong College of Medicine. (Photo taken circa 1888 and courtesy of Hong Kong Museum of History)

23 Aug 1887

Ho Wyson (何渭臣) became the first Chinese solicitor in Hong Kong.

01 Oct 1887

The Hong Kong College of Medicine for Chinese was established with a campus at Alice Memorial Hospital to train Chinese doctors in Western-style medical services, with Patrick Manson as the founding President and Sun Yat-sen (孫中山) as one of its earliest graduates. The college was renamed the Hong Kong College of Medicine in 1907 and was incorporated into The University of Hong Kong in 1911. (Figure 076)

06 Oct 1887

William Des Voeux was sworn in as the 10th Governor of Hong Kong; he remained in office until 07 May 1891.

15 Nov 1887

The passenger ship *Wah Yeung* caught fire and sank on its way from Hong Kong to Guangzhou, causing over 300 deaths.

1887

The Canadian Pacific Steamship Company launched the first route between Hong Kong and Canada; in 1891, it also offered regular services linking Vancouver, Japan and Hong Kong.

19 Jan 1888

Britain added two clauses to the Letters Patent and Royal Instructions, which outlined constitutional provisions for the administration of Hong Kong. First, succeeding governors would not be allowed to execute duties unless they had taken an oath in the presence of judges of the Supreme Court and members of the Executive Council. Second, when formulating ordinances, governors should seek advice and obtain consent from the Legislative Council. For the first time, the Legislative Council was given law-making power.

04 Feb 1888

The Vaccination Ordinance 1888 was promulgated, requiring children (six months to 14 years old) who have lived in Hong Kong for more than six months to be vaccinated for smallpox. It became Hong Kong's first ordinance on disease prevention.

18 Feb 1888

The Colonial Books (Preservation and Registration) Ordinance 1888 was promulgated, stipulating that a copy of all locally printed books and journals should be submitted to the Hong Kong government for registration and preservation.

24 Mar 1888

The Regulation of Chinese Ordinance 1888 was promulgated, requiring all residents to register household information. Any appointed district watchman was given the same power as a constable. Noise was prohibited in certain areas, and Chinese people must carry a pass when going out at night. In addition, Chinese people were not allowed to publish notices or assemble in public places without permission.

05 May 1888

The European District Reservation Ordinance 1888 was promulgated, stipulating that only Western-style houses were allowed to be built in the European areas designated by the Ordinance.

30 May 1888

The Peak Tram commenced operations, marking the beginning of rail services in Hong Kong. (Figure 077)

02 Jun 1888

The Public Health Ordinance 1887 was promulgated, stipulating the composition of the Sanitary Board with the Surveyor General, Registrar General, Captain Superintendent of Police, Colonial Surgeon, and not more than six Unofficial Members. Four of the Unofficial Members (two of whom were Chinese) were to be appointed by the Governor and the other two to be elected by taxpayers on the jury roster.

11 Jun 1888

The Sanitary Board held its first election for the positions of two Unofficial Members. John David Humphreys and John Joseph Francis won with 71 and 55 votes, respectively.

05 Oct 1888

James Russell was appointed as Chief Justice of Hong Kong.

01 Nov 1888

Tai Tam Reservoir became operational as the second reservoir in Hong Kong.

07 Dec 1888

The Cathedral of the Immaculate Conception was completed at its new location on Caine Road at Mid-Levels. The cathedral was open to the public the following day after its first Mass was held. (Figure 078)

1888

Kowloon No. 1 Dock at Hung Hom, owned by the Hong Kong and Whampoa Dock Company Limited, was completed; it was one of shipyard facilities capable of building the largest ships in the world at that time.

24 Jan 1889

The Hongkong Electric Company Limited was incorporated; it started supplying electricity to certain areas of Hong Kong Island the following year. (Figure 079)

02 Mar 1889

The Hongkong Land Investment and Agency Company Limited was founded by Catchick Paul Chater and James Johnstone Keswick, making it the longest-standing real estate conglomerate in Hong Kong.

16 Mar 1889

The Stone Cutters' Island Ordinance 1889 was promulgated, designating Stonecutters Island as a restricted military zone.

05 Apr 1889

The China and Japan Telephone and Electric Company published the first 62 telephone numbers in *The China Mail*. The numbers 1 to 62 were held by companies and individuals; telephone operators were responsible for connecting users at both ends of a telephone conversation.

10 May 1889

The Hong Kong Golf Club was established as the first golf organisation in Hong Kong.

11 May 1889

The Praya Reclamation Ordinance 1889 was promulgated, stipulating commencement of reclamation works in Central while addressing the impact of sediment accumulation along the waterfront on deep-water piers and the lack of open space for commercial development on the north shore of Hong Kong Island. The reclamation project was completed in 1903.

18 May 1889

The Protection of Women and Girls Ordinance 1889 was promulgated, prohibiting forced prostitution.

Figure 077
The Peak Tram Terminus on Garden Road in Central on Hong Kong Island. (Photo taken circa 1890 and courtesy of Hong Kong Museum of History)

Figure 078
The Gothic-like Cathedral of The Immaculate Conception in Hong Kong; it became the cathedral of the Catholic Diocese of Hong Kong. (Photo taken circa 1910 and courtesy of Hong Kong Museum of History)

Figure 079
Early electric streetlights and utility poles on Des Voeux Road Central on Hong Kong Island outside the first-generation City Hall (left). (Photo taken circa 1890 and courtesy of HKSAR Government)

29 May 1889

The Hong Kong Observatory recorded 581 millimetres of rainfall, which resulted in a landslide that destroyed part of the rail track of the Peak Tram. It was the earliest recorded landslide in Hong Kong.

29 Jun 1889

The Crown Lands Resumption Ordinance 1889 was promulgated, stipulating that the Governor could reclaim crown land on the grounds of public interest if negotiations with land owners were unsuccessful. An arbitration board was to be set up to determine the value of the land and the amount of compensation.

06 Jul 1889

The Chinese Extradition Ordinance 1889 was promulgated, implementing Article 21 of a treaty signed between the British and the Qing governments in Tianjin on 26 June 1858. This ordinance set out the procedures and conditions for the surrender of fugitives.

01 Mar 1890

Ho Kai (何啟) was appointed as an Unofficial Member of the Legislative Council. He remained in office until 02 March 1914, making him the longest-serving Chinese Unofficial Member of the Council. (Figure 080)

The Central School for Girls was founded in Central. In 1893, it was relocated to a new campus donated by Emanuel Raphael Belilios and was renamed Belilios Public School.

25 Jul 1890

The Colonial Courts of Admiralty Act 1890 of the United Kingdom was promulgated, abolishing all Colonial Courts of Admiralty, including the one in Hong Kong whose jurisdiction was transferred to the Supreme Court.

01 Dec 1890

Hongkong Electric commenced operations at 6 p.m., switching on Hong Kong's first electric streetlights in Central.

Figure 080
Ho Kai (何啟) in his university graduation gown.
(Photo courtesy of HKSAR Government)

Figure 081
A two-cent definitive stamp with a portrait of Queen Victoria and markings "Hong Kong Jubilee" in commemoration of Hong Kong's 50th anniversary as a British colony. (Image courtesy of Hong Kong Museum of History)

10 Dec 1890

The steamship *Namoa*, sailing from Hong Kong to Shantou, was attacked by over 40 armed pirates, who killed the captain and two other people on the ship and stole HK$55,000 worth of property. In 1891, the Qing government captured 19 of the pirates, who were sent to Kowloon City for decapitation.

1890

During this year, Hong Kong accounted for 56.7% of China's total imports and 38.9% of its total exports.

The first buildings of Lei Yue Mun Barracks were completed; the main barracks were finished in 1939.

The Hong Kong Corinthian Sailing Club was founded; it was granted permission to use name Royal Hong Kong Yacht Club in May 1894.

01 Jan 1891

The British-owned Dodwell, Carlill & Co. opened a branch in Hong Kong, engaging in the shipping business and import and export trade.

22 Jan 1891

Hong Kong Post Office issued its first set of special stamps, the Golden Jubilee commemorative stamps, which were created by overprinting on the Queen Victoria definitive stamps (with a face value of two cents) with the English words "1841 Hong Kong Jubilee 1891." A total of 50,000 stamps went on sale. They were also the world's first set of commemorative stamps issued as definitive stamps. (Figure 081)

03 Feb 1891

The Stockbrokers' Association of Hong Kong was established; it became the first official stock exchange.

09 May 1891

The Gambling Ordinance 1891 was promulgated, outlawing venues for public gambling and lottery sales.

27 Jun 1891

The Forts Protection Ordinance 1891 was promulgated, prohibiting unauthorised access to batteries, fortifications and military fieldworks.

15 Aug 1891

As of 20 May 1891, Hong Kong had a population of 221,441, including 210,995 Chinese and 10,446 foreign nationals, according a government census.

07 Nov 1891

The Bankruptcy Ordinance 1891 was promulgated, providing comprehensive regulations on the legal procedures and matters relating to bankruptcy. The Ordinance came into effect on 31 December.

10 Dec 1891

William Robinson was sworn in as the 11th Governor of Hong Kong; he remained in office until 01 February 1898.

1891

The National Bank of China Limited commenced operations in Hong Kong as a Chinese-foreign joint venture. It started issuing banknotes in Hong Kong in 1894 and remained in operation until 1911.

The Mount Caroline Cemetery, located on Broadwood Road in Soo Kun Poo, was opened as a public cemetery for the Chinese in Hong Kong.

13 Mar 1892

The Furen Literary Society, located on Pak Tsz Lane in Central, was founded by seven people, including Yeung Ku-wan (楊衢雲), who was also President, and Tse Tsan-tai (謝纘泰). The society was dedicated to promoting Western studies and Chinese patriotism; it became one of the most important organisations in Hong Kong for bringing together aspiring Chinese revolutionaries.

01 Apr 1892

The Gap Rock Lighthouse, located in Chinese waters, became operational; it was then the only lighthouse built by a Hong Kong contractor in the Mainland.

11 Jun 1892

Fielding Clarke was appointed as Chief Justice of Hong Kong.

29 Aug 1892

Tai Po New Market (present-day Tai Wo Market), established by the Tai Po Tsat Yeuk community, was opened for business. (Yeuk refers to an oath-sworn inter-clan and inter-village mutual defence alliance; Tsat Yeuk means seven yeuks.)

10 Oct 1892

The British passenger ship *Bokhara* was travelling from Shanghai to Hong Kong when it was hit by a typhoon and sank near Gupo Island in Penghu. A total of 125 people died, including 11 members of the Hong Kong cricket team.

1892

The first buildings of the Whitfield Barracks in Tsim Sha Tsui as the first permanent British army barracks in Kowloon were completed.

The Man Mo Yee Tai Temple, built by the Tai Po Tsat Yeuk community, was completed.

18 Jan 1893

The Hong Kong Observatory recorded a temperature of zero degrees Celsius in the morning, marking the lowest on record as of 01 July 2017. From 15 January onwards, ice appeared in several hilly areas, including The Peak. Some ships even reported snowfall in the northern waters of Hong Kong.

Feb 1893

The Chartered Mercantile Bank of India, London and China was reorganised due to financial problems and was renamed Mercantile Bank Limited. As the bank gave up its Royal Charter, its banknotes were no longer in circulation in Hong Kong; it resumed issuing banknotes in 1912.

Figure 082
A cleaning crew sanitised Market Street (later called Po Hing Fong) near Po Yan Street in Tai Ping Shan District as part of the epidemic prevention against the bubonic plague in 1894. The exterior wall of the left building was marked "Done" to indicate disinfection completed. (Photo courtesy of Hong Kong Museum of History)

Figure 083
A glass factory in Kennedy Town requisitioned by the Hong Kong government for use as a temporary hospital where patients had to lie on the ground amid a lack of equipment during the bubonic plague of 1894. (Photo courtesy of Hong Kong Museum of History)

05 Sep 1893

Nethersole School of Nursing (affiliated with the Nethersole Hospital) as the first nurse training school in Hong Kong was opened next to the Alice Memorial Hospital on Bonham Road.

10 May 1894

Government medical authorities discovered the first case of bubonic plague. A local epidemic subsequently broke out, affecting mostly the Chinese community. By 31 December, hospitals recorded 2,447 plague-related deaths and a mortality rate of 93.4%.

11 May 1894

The Hong Kong government announced the creation of a standing committee in the Sanitary Board and enacted 12 by-laws to control the outbreak of the bubonic plague. Measures included the deployment of the medical ship *Hygeia* moored in the middle of Victoria Harbour for quarantine purposes; Sanitary Board staff were authorised to enter the residences of infected persons for disinfection. (Figure 082)

20 May 1894

A glass factory in Kennedy Town was requisitioned under the administration of Tung Wah Hospital for isolating and treating patients infected with the bubonic plague. (Figure 083)

31 May 1894

Another six by-laws were promulgated to control the spread of the bubonic plague, requiring residents to move out of their homes within 24 hours after a medical officer determined that their residence did not meet sanitary standards.

14 Jun 1894

Japanese bacteriologist Kitasato Shibasaburō discovered that infectious rod-shaped bacteria (bacillus) were the pathogen directly responsible for the bubonic plague in Hong Kong.

15 Jun 1894

French bacteriologist Alexandre Yersin arrived in Hong Kong where he established the pathogen of the bubonic plague from a bacillus carried by rats and transmitted to humans by fleas. In 1896, Yersin developed an antiserum treatment for the plague; the bacillus was later named *Yersinia pestis* in his honour.

15 Aug 1894

Acting Superintendent of the Government Civil Hospital James Alfred Lowson reported to the Hong Kong government that the plague outbreak was closely related to the lack of toilet sanitation.

09 Nov 1894

Governor William Robinson wrote to the British Colonial Office, proposing to expand the boundary of Hong Kong. He believed that such demands should be imposed on China before it could recover from previous defeats.

1894

The Brennan Torpedo Station in Lei Yue Mun commenced operations.

The French-owned Banque de l'Indochine opened a branch in Hong Kong.

Japanese entrepreneur Umeya Shōkichi came to Hong Kong where he opened the Umeya Photo Studio. Over the next 20 years, Umeya provided financial support to Sun Yat-sen's (孫中山) revolutionary cause.

21 Feb 1895

Sun Yat-sen (孫中山) and others joined efforts with the Furen Literary Society in establishing the revolutionary group Revive China Society. Yeung Ku-wan (楊衢雲) was its president. Its headquarters was located on Staunton Street in Central, behind the storefront of Kuen Hang Club, a fake business created as a cover for revolutionary activities.

01 Mar 1895

Acting Superintendent of the Government Civil Hospital James Alfred Lowson submitted a plague investigation report to the Hong Kong government, expressing doubts about the effectiveness of the treatment provided by Tung Wah Hospital and suggesting that the hospital needed government regulation.

The German-owned Jebsen & Co. established its headquarters in Central and started its business in shipping, import and export trade, and sales; it began selling Blue Girl Beer in 1906.

09 Mar 1895

The Defences Sketching Prevention Ordinance 1895 was promulgated, prohibiting unauthorised persons from describing, surveying or photographing military facilities.

13 Mar 1895

Sun Yat-sen (孫中山), Yeung Ku-wan (楊衢雲), Tse Tsan-tai (謝纘泰) and Wong Wing-sheung (黃詠商) secretly met at the Kuen Hang Club on 13, 16 and 21 March to devise a plan to capture Guangzhou.

14 Mar 1895

The Hong Kong government ordered that all "common lodging houses" must be registered within 48 hours or face severe punishment. On 23 March, hundreds of dockyard workers went on strike to protest the order. By 29 March, they were joined by coal carriers and dock labourers, exceeding 10,000 strikers in all. On 03 April, after mediation by Chinese compradors, owners of workers' dormitories proceeded with registration at the Sanitary Board, ending the 12-day strike the following day.

23 Mar 1895

The Bank Notes Issue Ordinance 1895 was promulgated, stipulating that banks in Hong Kong must have the sanction of the relevant British government minister signified through the Governor before they could issue banknotes. The National Bank of China Limited was prohibited from issuing new banknotes. In 1911, the bank closed down, and its banknotes in circulation were withdrawn and destroyed by the Hong Kong government.

30 Mar 1895

The Hong Kong government announced an order issued by the Privy Council on 02 February 1895, stipulating that Hong Kong's legal currencies included the Mexican silver dollar, British silver dollar, Hong Kong silver dollar and Hong Kong coins, among which Hong Kong coins had a payment limit. The order was implemented on 01 April.

13 Apr 1895

The Chinese Immigration Regulation Ordinance 1895 was promulgated, stipulating that if bubonic plague, cholera, smallpox or any other epidemics occurred outside Hong Kong, the Governor-in-Council had the right to prohibit or regulate the entry of Chinese people from those places into Hong Kong.

13 May 1895

The British Colonial Defence Committee submitted a report to the British government, proposing the permanent lease of parts of Xin'an County.

01 Jun 1895

The Uniform Ordinance 1895 was promulgated, prohibiting non-military personnel, other than stage performers, from wearing British military uniforms.

27 Aug 1895

The Hong Kong government ordered Kuen Hang Club to shut down since it was partially responsible for a planned uprising in the Mainland.

31 Oct 1895

Sun Yat-sen（孫中山）left Hong Kong for Japan with Chan Siu-bak（陳少白）and Cheng Si-leung（鄭士良）to avoid being extradited to the Mainland by the Hong Kong government. Previously, on 29 October, Sun returned to Hong Kong following the failure of the first Guangzhou Uprising.

12 Nov 1895

The Hong Kong Football Club organised the first Hong Kong Football Challenge Cup, which was also the first football championship in Asia and was renamed the Hong Kong Football Challenge Shield in 1896.

24 Dec 1895

The pumping station in Yau Ma Tei commenced operations to supply the Kowloon peninsula with groundwater.

1895

The American-owned Standard Oil Company (later renamed Exxon Mobil) opened a branch in Hong Kong to sell kerosene.

Lam Woo & Co. was founded by brothers Lam Woo（林護）and Lam Kau-mow（林裘謀）as one of the earliest Chinese-owned construction companies.

17 Jan 1896

Chun Wah Wui Koon was inaugurated as the first modern Chinese chamber of commerce in Hong Kong founded by dozens of prominent businessmen, including Fung Wah-chuen（馮華川）who was comprador of the National Bank of China.

18 Jan 1896

A foundation stone-laying ceremony was held at the new location of Po Leung Kuk on Tai Ping Shan Street.

Feb 1896

The Commission to Inquire into the Working and Organisation of Tung Wah Hospital was appointed by Governor William Robinson to examine the hospital's role in tackling the plague of 1894. The report suggested that the hospital should hire Chinese doctors who practised Western medicine.

04 Mar 1896

The Hong Kong government issued a banishment order against Sun Yat-sen (孫 中 山) on the grounds that he was "…dangerous to the peace and good order of the Colony," forbidding him from "…residing or being within the Colony for the space of five years from the date hereof upon the grounds hereinafter appearing." Another two five-year banishment orders against Sun were issued on 30 January 1902 and 11 June 1907.

16 May 1896

John Worrell Carrington was appointed as Chief Justice of Hong Kong.

28 May 1896

A bronze statue of Queen Victoria was unveiled in the square in front of the HSBC building in Central to celebrate the Queen's birthday and the 60th anniversary of her accession to the throne.

24 Oct 1896

The Hong Kong government announced that Catchick Paul Chater and James Jardine Bell-Irving were appointed as the first two Unofficial Members of the Executive Council.

Wei Yuk (韋玉) became an Unofficial Member of the Legislative Council.

1896

The Royal Navy decided to expand the Naval Dockyard in present-day Admiralty and designated the coast north of Queen's Road as a naval zone.

Yokohama Specie Bank Limited of Japan opened a branch in Hong Kong.

Lee Leung-yik (利良奕), upon his return to Hong Kong after working for some years in the US, set up Lai Cheong Lung Company on Queen's Road in Central.

The first-generation Kwong Fuk Bridge was built across the Lam Tsuen River, connecting Tai Po Tsat Yeuk and Tai Po New Market (present-day Tai Wo Market).

03 Apr 1897

Captain Superintendent of Police Francis Henry May was concurrently appointed as Superintendent of Victoria Gaol.

29 May 1897

The Regulation of Chinese Ordinance 1888 was amended, repealing the compulsory curfew measures imposed on the Chinese in Section 30. The Governor-in-Council retained the power to impose a curfew on Chinese persons. (Figure 084)

The Flogging Ordinance 1897 was promulgated, specifying the maximum number of strokes allowed to be inflicted.

21 Jun 1897

The Hong Kong Police Force exposed illegal gambling and corruption involving 128 police officers, including a European acting deputy superintendent, 13 European police officers, 37 Indian police officers and 76 Chinese police officers. One was sentenced to imprisonment while 77 resigned, retired, were dismissed or did not have their contracts renewed.

23 Jun 1897

The 60th anniversary of Queen Victoria's accession to the throne was marked with a two-day celebration, including street parades.

16 Sep 1897

The pier on Murray Road in Central was opened after reconstruction; the original wooden structures were replaced with stone structures.

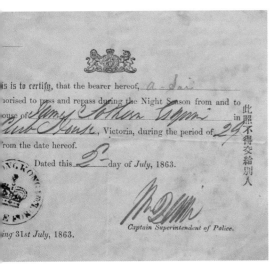

Figure 084
A night pass issued in 1863. Chinese residents were required to carry it when going out during curfew hours. (Image courtesy of Police Museum, Hong Kong Police Force)

Figure 085
An outpost at the border (present-day Boundary Street) on Kowloon peninsula where customs officers and armed guards of the Qing government were stationed. It moved northward to Shenzhen River upon the signing of the Convention Between Great Britain and China Respecting an Extension of Hong Kong Territory. (Photo taken circa 1898 and courtesy of Public Records Office, Government Records Service)

1897

Kowloon introduced a water meter-based fresh water charging system.

The Hong Kong Exchange Banks' Association, predecessor of the Hong Kong Association of Banks, was established to codify rules for conducting banking business and set exchange rates for foreign currency trading.

The Manufacturers Life Insurance Company from Canada began operating an insurance business in Hong Kong.

The German Hildesheim mission opened a nursing home in Hong Kong to house and teach blind girls. The home was the predecessor of the present-day Ebenezer School & Home for the Visually Impaired.

The Chiu Yuen Cemetery in Mount Davis, a public cemetery for local Eurasians, was established under the initiative of businessman Robert Ho Tung (何東).

05 Mar 1898

The Misdemeanors Punishment Ordinance 1898 was promulgated, stipulating that those guilty of bribery could be sentenced to not more than two years' imprisonment or a fine of not more than HK$500, or both. It was the first anti-corruption ordinance in Hong Kong.

02 Apr 1898

Representatives of China and Britain held talks on the topic of expanding the territory of Hong Kong. On 24 April, the British representative proposed extending the territory to the area south of the line from Shenzhen Bay to Dapeng Bay, which included the Kowloon Walled City.

May 1898

Hong Kong and Kowloon Wharf and Godown Company Limited acquired the ferries of Kowloon Ferry Company and established the Star Ferry Company. Star Ferry became a major mode of transport between Tsim Sha Tsui and Hong Kong Island.

09 Jun 1898

The Convention between Great Britain and China Respecting an Extension of Hong Kong Territory was signed in Beijing. Under the Convention, which came into force on 01 July for a term of 99 years, Great Britain would lease the vast area south of the shortest straight-line distance from Sha Tau Kok Hoi (Starling Inlet) to Shenzhen Bay and north of the present-day Boundary Street, as well as 235 surrounding islands and the waters of Dapeng Bay and Shenzhen Bay. These territories and waters, originally owned by China, became additional areas under the administration of Hong Kong and became known as the New Territories. (Figure 085)

13 Aug 1898

The Kellet Island Ordinance 1898 was promulgated, prohibiting any non-military boats from entering within 50 yards of the high-tide line of the island and forbidding anyone to access the island without authorisation.

29 Sep 1898

Kang Youwei (康有為), a prominent leader of the Hundred Days' Reform, arrived in Hong Kong by ship with British assistance; he was arranged to stay at the Central Police Station. Later, Robert Ho Tung (何東) invited Kang to stay at his residence Idlewild. On 19 October, Kang left Hong Kong for Japan.

08 Oct 1898

The *Report by Mr. Stewart Lockhart on the Extension of the Colony of Hong Kong* was submitted to the British government by Colonial Secretary James Stewart Lockhart. It included general information about the New Territories and his proposals for governance, including the addition of Shenzhen to the leased territory. Attached to the report was an appendix titled "List Containing the Name and Population of Each Village in the New Territories," which became the first official record of the population and distribution of the villages in the New Territories.

20 Oct 1898

Britain issued an Order in Council making the New Territories a part of the Colony of Hong Kong; all Hong Kong laws were to be applied. Officials of the Qing government stationed at the Kowloon Walled City, were allowed to exercise jurisdiction within the premise on the condition of non-interference with the armed forces defending Hong Kong.

25 Nov 1898

Henry Arthur Blake was sworn in as the 12th Governor of Hong Kong; he remained in office until 21 November 1903.

1898

The first lift in Hong Kong, powered by the first substation of Hongkong Electric Company Limited, was installed in Queen's Building, Central.

China Provident Company Limited, operated by Shewan, Tomes & Company, was established.

The Hongkong Cotton-spinning, Weaving and Dyeing Company was founded by Jardine, Matheson & Co., establishing Hong Kong's first textile and dyeing mill with 50,000 spindles in Causeway Bay.

The French Sisters of St. Paul de Chartres opened a hospital called the Asile de la Sainte Enfance (The Refuge of the Holy Childhood) in Wan Chai to provide medical services to the underprivileged. In 1916, the hospital was relocated to Causeway Bay and was later re-established as St. Paul's Hospital.

18 Feb 1899

The Sung Wong T'oi Reservation Ordinance 1899 was promulgated, prohibiting any construction around or damage to Sacred Hill of Sung Wong Toi as proposed by Legislative Councillor Ho Kai (何啟) and adopted by the Hong Kong government.

16 Mar 1899

Alternate Circuit Intendant of Guangdong Wang Cunshan (王存善) and Colonial Secretary James Stewart Lockhart determined the land boundary for the northern part of the New Territories and erected wooden boundary marks. (Figure 086)

19 Mar 1899

Wang Cunshan (王存善) and James Stewart Lockhart signed the Delimitation of the Northern Frontier of the New Territories to determine the boundary of the northern part of the New Territories (which included the entire Shenzhen River) and to put it under British jurisdiction.

Figure 086
A boundary inspection of northern New Territories in March 1899 by Chinese representative Wang Cunshan (王存善) (second from left) and British representative James Stewart Lockhart (third from left); a wooden boundary marker "Boundary of Xin'an County of the Qing Dynasty" was erected near the shore of Sha Tau Kok Hoi (Starling Inlet). (Photo courtesy of Public Records Office, Government Records Service)

28 Mar 1899

Jardine, Matheson & Co. and Minister of Railways of the Qing government Sheng Xuanhuai (盛宣懷) signed a preliminary agreement on the Canton–Kowloon Railway with respect to the construction of a railway between Guangzhou and Kowloon.

The Hong Kong government put up a mat-shed on a hill near Tai Po Market as a temporary police station and for flag-raising ceremonies. On the same day, the gentry in Ping Shan, Ha Tsuen and Kam Tin put up a notice announcing the organisation of armed resistance to the British.

03 Apr 1899

Captain Superintendent of Police Francis Henry May entered Tai Po New Market (present-day Tai Wo Market) with four Sikh policemen and was besieged by Tai Po villagers. At night, the mat-shed used as a temporary police station was burnt down, and the British troops were forced to evacuate. On 04 April, Colonial Secretary James Stewart Lockhart and Commander of British Forces in Hong Kong Major General William Julius Gascoigne arrived in Tai Po by boat with 125 British soldiers to quell the unrest.

09 Apr 1899

Governor Henry Arthur Blake announced that the official takeover of the New Territories would come into effect on 17 April. Notices in Chinese were posted across the New Territories to outline the government policy on the New Territories.

10 Apr 1899

The gentry of the New Territories established the Tai Ping Kung Kuk (Great Peace Public Council) at Tung Ping Social School in Yuen Long, calling on all village fighters to resist the British troops by force. This alliance was funded by the local villages.

14 Apr 1899

Tai Po villagers once again burnt down the mat-shed used for flag-raising ceremonies near Tai Po New Market (present-day Tai Wo Market).

15 Apr 1899

On their way to Tai Po New Market, 122 Indian soldiers were intercepted by more than 1,000 village fighters armed with jingals (a type of matchlock gun) and cannons at Mui Shue Hang. In the afternoon, the British warship *Fame* arrived and opened fire on the fortifications set up by the village fighters, whose defence eventually collapsed in disorder.

Figure 087
The entrance of the village of Kat Hing Wai along with the chained-ring iron gate returned in 1925. (Photo taken in 1977 and courtesy of HKSAR Government)

16 Apr 1899

The British flag was raised in a ceremony in Tai Po, marking the formal takeover of the New Territories in the presence of Colonial Secretary James Stewart Lockhart, Major General William Julius Gascoigne and Commodore Francis Powell.

17 Apr 1899

The village fighters in the New Territories fought several battles against British troops in the area around Lam Tsuen Valley in Tai Po but were defeated; their artillery positions at Lam Tsuen Au were destroyed.

18 Apr 1899

About 1,200 village fighters in the New Territories were defeated following a counterattack on British troops near Shek Tau Wai Village in Pat Heung.

British troops bombed the walls of villages Kat Hing Wai and Tai Hong Wai in Kam Tin. The chain iron gate of Kat Hing Wai was seized and shipped to Britain as a trophy. (Figure 087)

19 Apr 1899

British reinforcements landed in Tuen Mun and Tsuen Wan. On the same day, villages in the New Territories, including Kam Tin, Ha Tsuen and Ping Shan, successively surrendered to the British troops.

21 Apr 1899

Villagers in Kam Tin, Ha Tsuen and other villages were forced to hand in petitions for submission under the direction of Colonial Secretary James Stewart Lockhart, ending the armed resistance of New Territories villagers. Resistance to British troops claimed the lives of 500 village fighters and injured two British soldiers.

16 May 1899

British troops in conjunction with the Hong Kong Volunteers were deployed to capture the Kowloon Walled City from which officials and soldiers of the Qing government were to be expelled on the grounds that officials of Xin'an County took part in mobilising New Territories villagers to resist British authority.

27 May 1899

The Hong Kong government promulgated the provision of administrative regions in the New Territories for the first time. It established seven districts (yeuks) and 41 sub-districts. On 08 July, the government revised the administrative regions in the New Territories by adding Tung Hoi District and dividing the New Territories into eight districts and 46 sub-districts.

03 Jun 1899

The Hong Kong government's Land Office seized the title deeds of New Territories villagers submitted under the pretext of registering for land titles.

Figure 088
Governor Henry Arthur Blake in a meeting at Tai Po Market with the gentry and village elites of the New Territories on the principles of governance with respect to the newly leased territories. (Photo taken on 02 August 1899 and courtesy of Hong Kong Museum of History)

Jun 1899

Queen's College began publishing *The Yellow Dragon*; it was the oldest journal published by a secondary school in Hong Kong.

08 Jul 1899

The Hong Kong government appointed a group of New Territories gentry as members of various Sub-District Committees. These members served as middlemen in helping the government convey policies to the villagers and presenting the villagers' views to the government.

02 Aug 1899

Governor Henry Arthur Blake went to Tai Po and explained to the villagers the principles of governance of the New Territories. (Figure 088)

04 Oct 1899

Following Governor-General of Guangdong and Guangxi Tan Zhonglin's (譚鍾麟) instructions, the customs stations at Kap Shui Mun, Cheung Chau and Fat Tau Chau, previously under the jurisdiction of the Kowloon Customs, were closed at midnight while the newly built customs stations at Taishan, Lingding, Sha Yu Chong and Samun were opened. The Kowloon Customs was renamed Kowloon New Customs.

Nov 1899

The Hong Kong government began to survey the land in the New Territories. The survey, covering 40,737.95 acres, was completed in May 1903.

27 Dec 1899

Britain issued an Order in Council declaring Kowloon Walled City a part of the Colony of Hong Kong to which the laws of Hong Kong were applicable. It claimed that the exercise of jurisdiction by Qing government officials in Kowloon Walled City hindered the ability of the armed forces to defend Hong Kong.

30 Dec 1899

The Summoning of Chinese Ordinance 1899 was promulgated. The Registrar General, as directed by the Governor, was assigned to investigate and report on matters related to the Chinese population (whether British subjects or otherwise) in the New Territories. The Registrar General had the right to summon Chinese to provide information in person.

1899

The Tai Po Police Station was constructed as the first permanent police station in the New Territories.

Figure 089
An advertisement of the Sincere Department Store in 1910. (Image courtesy of Hong Kong Museum of History)

08 Jan 1900

The Sincere Department Store was founded by Chinese-Australian Ma Ying-piu (馬應彪) as the first Chinese-owned department store in Hong Kong. The store was a pioneer of modern retail practices, such as employing saleswomen, offering genuine products exactly for marked prices, and issuing receipts to customers. (Figure 089)

24 Jan 1900

Yeung Ku-wan (楊衢雲) returned to Hong Kong from Japan and resigned as President of the Revive China Society. The position was filled by Sun Yat-sen (孫中山).

25 Jan 1900

The Revive China Society launched its official newspaper *China Daily* with the appointment of Chan Siu-bak (陳少白) as the first president. The newspaper continued running until 1913.

23 Feb 1900

Zhongguo xun bao (China Ten-day Report), a magazine published every 10 days, was founded to publicise the Chinese revolution. Each issue covered a selection of news from the newspaper *China Daily*.

26 Feb 1900

President of the Tien Tsu Hui (Natural Foot Society) Archibald Little (Alicia Ellen Neve Bewicke) gave a speech at the Hong Kong Chinese Club on the harm caused by foot-binding. More than 100 people attended the lecture.

17 Jun 1900

On 17 June and 17 July, Sun Yat-sen (孫中山) travelled from Singapore to the waters surrounding Hong Kong to plan an uprising in Huizhou with his revolutionary comrades.

18 Jul 1900

Governor-General of Guangdong and Guangxi Li Hongzhang (李鴻章) visited Hong Kong and made it clear to Governor Henry Arthur Blake that he could not disobey the Qing government's imperial order instructing him to return to the north. This ended Blake's attempt to seek independence for Guangdong and Guangxi by forging an alliance between Li and the revolutionary leaders.

28 Jul 1900

The New Territories (Land Court) Ordinance 1900 was promulgated, stipulating that all land in the New Territories was owned by the Hong Kong government and could not be used without permission, and that New Territories villagers must register their land with the government. The Governor-in-Council had the power to fix land rates; and the Governor could terminate the operation of the Land Court.

04 Aug 1900

The Kowloon Bowling Green Club was founded as the first lawn bowling organisation in Hong Kong.

Aug 1900

Sun Yat-sen (孫中山) submitted to Governor Henry Arthur Blake a written statement authored by Ho Kai (何啟), a respected and influential Hong Kong gentleman, and asked Blake to forward this statement to other countries. The statement listed the crimes of the Qing government and proposed six articles of state governance.

10 Nov 1900

The New Territories (Extension of Laws) Ordinance 1900 was promulgated, under which New Kowloon was set up and would be governed by the laws applicable to Hong Kong Island and Kowloon.

The Hong Kong Observatory fired a typhoon shot to alert citizens to the impending danger amid a typhoon which claimed over 200 lives and sank ten steamers and 110 sailing boats. It was rare for a typhoon to hit Hong Kong in November.

22 Nov 1900

Hei Loi Garden on Hollywood Road in Sheung Wan was opened for the screening of foreign scenery films, which were then called "Tricks of Lights" by the local people of Hong Kong. The Garden was the first mobile venue for showing films in Hong Kong.

29 Nov 1900

An inauguration ceremony for Blake Pier, officiated by Governor Henry Arthur Blake, was held. (Figure 090)

Nov 1900

The Ellis Kadoorie School for Boys in Western District was founded by Jewish businessman Ellis Kadoorie, Chinese businessman Lau Chu-pak (劉鑄伯) and others. In 1916, the school was taken over by the Hong Kong government and renamed Sir Ellis Kadoorie Secondary School.

1900

The Chinese Commercial Union was founded by Fung Wah-chuen (馮華川) and Chan Gung-yu (陳賡如) as a liaison with Chinese merchants in Hong Kong. On 22 November 1913, it was renamed the Hong Kong Chinese Merchants' Guild and relocated to a new office on Connaught Road in Central; in 1952, it was renamed the Chinese General Chamber of Commerce, Hong Kong.

Pottinger Battery and Gough Battery were built on Devil's Peak; they were the first fortifications in the area.

The German-owned, Shanghai-based Deutsch-Asiatische Bank opened a branch in Hong Kong.

Figure 090
Blake Pier in Central. (Photo taken in 1905 and courtesy of Special Collections, The University of Hong Kong Libraries)

10 Jan 1901

Yeung Ku-wan (楊衢雲), who was the first President of the Revive China Society, was shot in his apartment on Gage Street in Central by an assassin under the Qing government; he died the following day.

23 Jan 1901

The Hong Kong government announced that Queen Victoria had passed away.

25 Jan 1901

The China Light & Power Company Syndicate was incorporated. Its first power station on Des Voeux Road (present-day Chatham Road) in Hung Hom began supplying electricity to the Kowloon peninsula in 1903.

14 Aug 1901

The collapse of buildings at 32–34 Cochrane Street in Central caused 43 deaths.

15 Aug 1901

As of 20 January 1901, Hong Kong had a population of 283,975, including 274,543 Chinese and 9,432 foreign nationals, according to a government census.

1901

The Yuen On Steamship Company and Shiu On Steamship Company were established to jointly run a midnight ferry service between Hong Kong and Guangzhou.

The Chinese YMCA of Hong Kong was founded.

The construction of Sri Guru Singh Sabha in Wan Chai was completed as the first Sikh temple in Hong Kong.

A True Interpretation of the New Policies, a collection of essays on political reforms co-authored by Ho Kai (何啟) and Woo Lai-woon (胡禮垣), was published by a Chinese press in Shanghai.

15 Jan 1902

A foundation stone-laying ceremony was held in the expansion of the Naval Dockyard in Admiralty. The expansion project began in 1901 and was completed in 1909.

07 Feb 1902

The Hongkong Tramway Electric Company Limited was established in London for building and operating trams in Hong Kong. It was taken over by Electric Traction Company of Hongkong Limited in the same year. In 1910, it was renamed Hong Kong Tramways Company Limited (currently in operation).

27 Mar 1902

William Meigh Goodman was appointed as Chief Justice of Hong Kong; he remained in office until 30 April 1905.

11 Apr 1902

The Committee on Education, formed by Arthur Winbolt Brewin, Ho Kai (何啟) and Edward Alexander Irving, conducted a comprehensive survey of various schools in Hong Kong and published a report proposing a school for advanced Chinese studies.

19 Apr 1902

The Kowloon British School (present-day King George V School) in Tsim Sha Tsui was completed and inaugurated; classes began on 05 May.

Apr 1902

The Kowloon Waterworks was completed and started supplying water.

02 Aug 1902

The Hong Kong Observatory fired typhoon shots to alert citizens to impending danger amid a typhoon which claimed 21 lives.

19 Dec 1902

The Employers and Servants Ordinance of 1902 was promulgated to regulate employment relations and contracts.

1902

The American-owned National City Bank of New York opened a branch in Hong Kong. The branch, later known as Citibank, was the first American-owned bank in Hong Kong.

The Hong Kong government put up three marine boundary stones—one in Heiyanjiao, Shenzhen, one in Cheung Shan, and one in Kau Ling Chung, Lantau Island.

The Tai O Police Station was completed, making it the first permanent police station on an outlying island.

The Ohel Leah Synagogue, located on Robinson Road, was completed.

10 Feb 1903

The Pak Sha Wan Battery in Lei Yue Mun was completed. Later in the same month, the Sai Wan Battery in Lei Yue Mun was also completed.

Feb 1903

The China and Japan Telephone and Electric Company completed the installation of a mile-long Hong Kong–Kowloon submarine telephone cable between Bayview Hotel in North Point and Whampoa Dock in Hung Hom.

06 Jun 1903

The Tung Wah Hospital Infectious Disease Hospital was inaugurated at Kennedy Town. The hospital, which could accommodate up to 68 patients, was established in light of the smallpox epidemic in 1897. The foundation stone of the hospital was laid on 18 November 1901.

03 Jul 1903

The newly revised Code of Regulations for Educational Grants-in-Aid, effective from 01 January 1904, was issued. According to the Code, an inspection report prepared by an inspector would replace the test scores of students as the basis of eligibility for school subsidies.

17 Jul 1903

The Wireless Telegraphy Ordinance 1903 was promulgated, authorising the Governor to implement licensing system for wireless telegraph stations; it was the first law on wireless telegraphy in Hong Kong.

25 Sep 1903

The Water-works Ordinance 1903 was promulgated, installing water metres across Hong Kong to assess water charges, following a report on the fresh water supply in Hong Kong submitted by Osbert Chadwick in 1902.

06 Nov 1903

The English newspaper *South China Morning Post* was founded by Tse Tsan-tai (謝纘泰) and British journalist Alfred Cunningham. The Chinese name was changed from *South Qing Morning Post* to *South China Morning Post* in 1913. The newspaper remains in circulation today.

24 Dec 1903

The Public Health and Buildings Ordinance 1903 was promulgated to provide comprehensive requirements for public health and building construction.

1903

A. S. Watson & Co., Limited founded the first distilled water manufacturing plant in Hong Kong to improve the quality of fresh water.

Dutched-owned Java-China-Japan Lijn opened a branch in Hong Kong as a headquarters in East Asia and operated a shipping route between Java and Hong Kong.

St. Stephen's College was founded on Bonham Road in Sai Ying Pun, providing English-language education for Chinese children from wealthy families. It was relocated to Pok Fu Lam in 1924 and to its present address in Stanley in 1928.

The Chinese Insurance Association of Hong Kong was established by 12 local Chinese-owned insurance companies.

15 Mar 1904

Li Shing Scientific and Industrial College, located in Central, began classes for its first cohort of 40 students. It was the first industrial college in Hong Kong and funded by Li Ki-tong (李紀堂), the third son of Li Sing (李陞); Reverand Walter Ngon Fong (鄺金龍) was the first principal.

29 Apr 1904

The Peak District Reservation Ordinance 1904 was promulgated, designating the Peak District (which included Mount Cameron, Mount Gough, Mount Kellett and Victoria Peak) as an area in which Chinese persons were not permitted to reside.

May 1904

The first-generation Alexandra House was opened upon completion.

07 Jun 1904

The Alice Memorial Maternity Hospital was opened upon completion. Funded by Ho Kai (何啟), it was the first maternity hospital in Hong Kong.

24 Jun 1904

The Hong Kong government, following the Headmen of the Four Hills system implemented by the Qing government in Kowloon East, announced the appointments of Wu Tam (胡譚) of Ngau Tau Kok, Lo Fui (盧魁) of Sai Tso Wan, Lo Fun (羅寬) of Cha Kwo Ling and Lau Fat (劉發) of Lei Yue Mun as Headmen of the Four Hills. In addition to collecting tax payments, they were responsible for maintaining order in quarries and solving housing problems for labourers.

29 Jul 1904

Matthew Nathan was sworn in as the 13th Governor of Hong Kong; he remained in office until 20 April 1907.

13 Aug 1904

The tramway line between Kennedy Town and Shau Kei Wan, run by Electric Traction Company of Hongkong Limited, was officially opened. (Figure 091)

1904

Brothers Jian Zhaonan (簡照南) and Jian Yujie (簡玉階) founded Nanyang Tobacco Co. Limited in Wan Chai, later renamed Nanyang Brothers Tobacco Co. Limited. Its products were widely sold across China and Southeast Asia.

Butterfield & Swire built living quarters for Chinese labourers in Lai Chi Kok, providing temporary accommodation for more than 2,000 Chinese workers.

Reformist Kang Youwei (康有為) delegated his follower Xu Qin (徐勤) to establish a newspaper called *Commercial Newspaper* in Hong Kong to promote constitutional monarchy.

Figure 091
The first-generation single-deck tram on Des Voeux Road in Central. (Photo taken in 1904 and courtesy of Alan Cheung Shun-kwong)

Figure 092
The Kowloon–Canton Railway under construction. (Photo taken in 1908 and courtesy of Hong Kong Museum of History)

20 Feb 1905

"Poetry Talks at a Mountain Spring" was serialised by Pan Feisheng (潘飛聲) in *The Chinese Mail*'s supplement called *Record of Popular Wisdom* until 20 August 1906. It was later collectively published into Hong Kong's first work of poetry.

08 May 1905

The Rosary Church in Tsim Sha Tsui was completed, making it the first Catholic church on the Kowloon peninsula.

25 May 1905

Francis Taylor Piggott was appointed as Chief Justice of Hong Kong.

04 Jun 1905

Weiyi qu bao yousuowei (Only Interesting Newspaper That Matters) started publication as the first vernacular Cantonese newspaper in China under the editorship of Zheng Guangong (鄭貫公); it was renamed *Eastern Press* in July 1906 before ceasing publication in 1907.

01 Aug 1905

Two District Land Offices, with defined jurisdiction in the southern and northern districts of the New Territories, was established by Governor Matthew Nathan in conjunction with the Executive Council. The Southern District covered New Kowloon and three islands, namely Tung Lung Chau, Fat Tong Chau and Tit Cham Chau (Slope Island); the Northern District covered the inland areas of the New Territories (excluding New Kowloon) and all islands north of latitude 22.15° N and east of longitude 114.1° E in the New Territories (apart from the aforesaid islands).

Hong Kong Huaqi Match Co., a Sino-US joint venture, suspended operations following the Shanghai Chamber of Commerce's call for a nationwide anti-American boycott campaign in protest of the unequal treatment of Chinese labourers by Americans.

07 Sep 1905

The Legislative Council approved funding for rail surveys in the construction of the Kowloon-Canton Railway (British Section). The railway project began construction in 1906. (Figure 092)

09 Sep 1905

The Hong Kong government signed a treaty with Governor-General of Hunan and Hubei Zhang Zhidong (張之洞), agreeing to provide the Qing government with a loan of £1.1 million for redeeming the Canton-Hankow Railway.

Sep 1905

Lane Crawford opened its flagship store on Ice House Street in Central; the six-storey building had a retail space of 19,000 square metres.

16 Oct 1905

Sun Yat-sen (孫中山) officiated at the inauguration of the Hong Kong branch of the Tongmenghui of China (Chinese United League) on a steamer. Located at the office of *China Daily* on Des Voeux Road Central, it was the first branch to be established outside of its headquarters in Tokyo.

15 Dec 1905

An editorial titled "An Imperial University for Hong Kong" was published in *The China Mail*, advising the British government to establish a university in Hong Kong to attract students from southern China.

1905

The Director of Public Works erected a permanent stone monument to replace the temporary wooden marker between Sha Tau Kok and Lin Ma Hang, signifying the land boundary between Guangdong and Hong Kong.

The Pinewood Battery in Lung Fu Shan on Hong Kong Island was completed and was later converted into an anti-aircraft battery. In 1941, it was destroyed by the Japanese during the Battle of Hong Kong.

Guangzhou's Kwong Sang Hong opened a branch in Central. Its registered trademark, Two Girls, was the first cosmetics brand in Hong Kong.

The Imperial Brewing Company was founded by Portuguese-owned Barretto & Co.; it opened the first brewery in Hong Kong on Wong Nai Chung Road in December 1907.

The Hongkong Milling Company Limited was founded by Canadian merchant Alfred Herbert Rennie. Located in Junk Bay (present-day Tseung Kwan O), it was then the largest flour mill in East Asia; it was shut down in 1908.

01 Mar 1906

Nederlandsche Handel-Maatschappij opened a branch in Hong Kong, making it the first Dutch-owned bank in Hong Kong.

01 Apr 1906

The first-generation Tsim Sha Tsui Star Ferry Pier was opened upon completion. (Figure 093)

20 Jul 1906

The Ho Miu Ling Hospital on Breezy Path was opened upon completion with a donation from Ho Miu-ling (何妙齡), daughter of Ho Fuk-tong (何福堂) and wife of Wu Tingfang (伍廷芳).

Figure 093
The first-generation Star Ferry Pier located in Tsim Sha Tsui, Kowloon. (Photo taken circa 1910 and courtesy of Hong Kong Museum of History)

18 Sep 1906

The Hong Kong Observatory failed to give a timely warning amid a typhoon, resulting in an untold number of deaths. About 1,500 bodies were recovered within a few days after the typhoon. The typhoon caused damage to 670 ocean-going vessels and 2,983 fishing boats. It was known as the 1906 Hong Kong Typhoon. In the same month, the Hong Kong government established a typhoon relief fund to assist victims.

04 Oct 1906

Queen's College began offering evening classes in business, engineering and applied sciences. In 1907, these were placed under the Hong Kong Technical Institute.

14 Oct 1906

At 3 a.m., a fire broke out in the cargo vessel *Hankow* at a ferry pier in Sheung Wan and raged on for six hours, by which time the vessel had been completely burnt down, resulting in 111 deaths and property losses of HK$550,000.

21 Nov 1906

The Sze Hai Tong Banking and Insurance Company Limited, headquartered in Singapore, opened a branch in Hong Kong.

1906

The construction of an extended Robinson Road, a main thoroughfare on the Kowloon peninsula, was completed; it was renamed Nathan Road on 19 March 1909.

The Western Market (North Block) was completed. Located on Des Voeux Road Central, it became the oldest surviving market building in Hong Kong.

The Netherlands-owned Asiatic Petroleum Company opened a branch in Hong Kong; it became its company headquarters in southern China in 1913.

Connaught Aerated Water Factory was founded, making it the first Chinese-owned soft drink manufacturing plant in Hong Kong.

The Bacteriological Institute (renamed Pathological Institute after the Second World War) on Caine Lane in Sheung Wan commenced operations upon completion.

The Victoria Recreation Club hosted the first Cross Harbour Race—which became an annual event until 1942; it was resumed in 1947.

Buddhist masters Da Yue (大悦), Dun Xiu (頓修) and Yue Ming (悦明) built a Bodhimaṇḍa (retreat) on Lantau Island called Tai Mao Pung (The Big Thatched Hut) which was renamed Po Lin Monastery in 1924.

British company Thomas Cook & Son opened a branch on Des Voeux Road to provide services such as tourist consultation, foreign currency exchange, and passage ticket reservation.

Jan 1907

The *Novel World Weekly*, which became the earliest literary journal in Hong Kong, started publication of novels in the Mandarin Ducks and Butterfly School genre.

31 May 1907

The Hong Kong government announced new typhoon warning measures established by the Hong Kong Observatory. Marine police would set off explosive bombs at intervals of ten seconds; light signals would also be displayed at night from flagstaffs at the Water Police Station in Tsim Sha Tsui and at the Harbour Office.

29 Jul 1907

Frederick Lugard was sworn in as the 14th Governor of Hong Kong; he remained in office until 16 March 1912.

02 Aug 1907

The Life Insurance Companies Ordinance 1907 was promulgated, regulating life insurance companies; it was the first ordinance on the insurance industry in Hong Kong.

Aug 1907

Wing On Company, a department store founded by overseas Chinese brothers from Australia Kwok Lok (Gock Lock) (郭樂) and Kwok Chuen (Gock Chin) (郭泉) with HK$160,000 in capital, was opened on Queen's Road Central. (Figure 094)

The Taikoo Dockyard in Quarry Bay commenced operations; it was then the largest dockyard in Hong Kong. (Figure 095)

27 Sep 1907

The offices of the Assistance Superintendent of Police and Police Magistrate in the New Territories were merged to become a District Office responsible for all government affairs in the New Territories. Edwin Richard Hallifax was the first District Officer.

11 Oct 1907

The Seditious Publications Ordinance 1907 was promulgated, stipulating that any person who printed, published, sold or distributed newspapers, books or texts which could cause civil strife or crime in China would be subject to two years' imprisonment or a fine of not more than HK$500, or both. This was the first time that the Hong Kong government enacted a law to restrict content in Chinese books and newspapers.

01 Nov 1907

The Victoria Cinematograph on Des Voeux Road Central was opened, making it one of the first fixed venues for screening films in early Hong Kong.

03 Dec 1907

The Hong Kong government dispatched six warships from Hong Kong to the West River to combat piracy.

05 Dec 1907

The Hong Kong Theatre, founded by brothers Li Zhang (李璋) and Li Qi (李琪), was opened, making it the first wholly Chinese-owned movie theatre in Hong Kong.

1907

The British Military Hospital on Bowen Road at Mid-Levels was opened, replacing the D'Aguilar Hospital.

Ip Ting-sz (葉定仕) was elected as Head of the Siamese (Thailand) Branch of the Tongmenghui of China. Born to an indigenous Hakka farming family at Lin Ma Hang Village in the New Territories, Ip later became one of the overseas Chinese leaders in Thailand and an active participant of the 1911 Revolution.

Figure 094
A poster of Hong Kong Wing On Company Limited circa 1920s–1930s. (Image courtesy of the Collection of Hong Kong Heritage Museum)

Figure 095
Taikoo Dockyard in Quarry Bay on Hong Kong Island. (Photo taken circa 1909 and courtesy of Hong Kong Museum of History)

17 Jan 1908

Governor Frederick Lugard gave a speech at St. Stephen's College, proposing publicly for the first time the idea of building a university in Hong Kong that would provide Western education and become a top academy in the Far East.

03 Feb 1908

The Hong Kong Football Club co-hosted a friendly match with the Shanghai Football Association in which the Hong Kong Football Club claimed a 3–0 home victory. It was named the first Hong Kong–Shanghai Cup. After the second match in 1913, the game officially became an interport competition.

18 Mar 1908

Governor Frederick Lugard convened the first meeting of a preparatory committee for The University of Hong Kong. He announced that Parsi merchant Hormusjee Naorojee Mody intended to donate to the cause and discussed matters concerning fundraising and construction.

05 Apr 1908

The first boycott against Japanese goods and ships in Hong Kong took place in protest of the Qing government's weak attitude in dealing with the incident involving arms smuggling by Japanese cargo vessel *Daini Tatsumaru*.

06 Apr 1908

A group of Chinese mechanics founded a labour organisation in Hong Kong. In 1919, it was renamed the Chinese Engineers' Institute.

06 May 1908

The British government asked the Hong Kong government to close all opium dens by 1910, in accordance with an agreement signed between the Chinese and British governments in 1907 on gradually reducing opium imports from India to China over the next 10 years.

23 May 1908

The Taikoo Dockyard and Engineering Company of Hong Kong was incorporated in London. On 03 October, *Sungkiang* became the first ship to use the services of Taikoo Dockyard.

05 Jun 1908

The Man Mo Temple Ordinance 1908 was promulgated, putting the assets of Man Mo Temple under the management of the Tung Wah Hospital.

11 Jul 1908

The clubhouse of Kowloon Cricket Club on Cox's Road was opened; Hormusjee Naorojee Mody served as president.

27 Jul 1908

The Hong Kong Observatory set off three signal bombs at 11:30 p.m. and hoisted Black Typhoon Signal No. 10 amid a typhoon that resulted in the collapse of a building and killed 59 people. The typhoon sank the British steamer *Ying King* in the waters between Pillar Point and Castle Peak, claiming 423 lives and leaving 42 survivors, making it the deadliest shipwreck on record in Hong Kong.

Jul 1908

Cheung Chau Government Primary School was opened as the first government school on an outlying island.

05 Dec 1908

The Hong Kong First Division Football League was initiated at the Army Sports Ground in Happy Valley, making it the first football league in Hong Kong.

1908

Ng Tung-kai (吳東啟) founded Li Man Hing Kwok Weaving and Manufacturing Co., one of Hong Kong's earliest garment manufacturing plants, which provided greater job opportunities for women.

The first car appeared on the streets of Hong Kong; it was imported from Britain by a dentist.

Chinese students from several English-language schools in Hong Kong formed a football team as the first all-Chinese local football team. In 1910, it was renamed the South China Football Club.

Bauhinia blakeana was identified as a new species by Superintendent of the Botanical and Afforestation Department Stephen Troyte Dunn; his findings were published in the *Journal of Botany, British and Foreign*. The new species was discovered on the shore of Pok Fu Lam by a father from Missioni Etrangeres de Paris in the late 19th century; its Latin name was given to commemorate former Governor Henry Arthur Blake and his wife for supporting the Hong Kong Botanical Garden.

16 Jan 1909

Governor Frederick Lugard spoke on the progress of establishment of The University of Hong Kong, noting Parsi merchant Hormusjee Naorojee Mody had donated HK$150,000 to cover the cost of construction and another HK$30,000 for setting up a foundation. On 16 February, a statement calling on the Chinese community for financial contribution was issued by Lugard; it was shared with Governor-General of Guangdong and Guangxi Zhang Renjun (張人駿) via Acting British Consul in Guangzhou Harry Fox. In April, Zhang issued a notice on the statement to officials and the public in Guangdong.

01 Mar 1909

American-owned Oriental Brewery Limited was founded in Lai Chi Kok. It had an annual production capacity of 100,000 barrels.

09 Jun 1909

Governor-General of Guangdong and Guangxi Zhang Renjun (張人駿) sent a letter to Governor Frederick Lugard, pledging to donate 200,000 silver dollars in his own name to support the establishment of The University of Hong Kong.

02 Jul 1909

The Hong Kong government appointed Edward Alexander Irving as the first Director of Education to coordinate all school matters in Hong Kong.

01 Sep 1909

Muneei Matsushima founded the Japanese newspaper *Hong Kong News* (*Honkon Nippō*), which catered mainly to the Japanese nationals in Hong Kong. The Chinese and English editions were published in June 1938 and June 1939, respectively, making it the only trilingual newspaper in Hong Kong.

03 Sep 1909

The Opium Ordinance of 1909 was promulgated, prohibiting the export of prepared opium to China and the sale of opium to women or persons under the age of 16, while also ordering the closing of all opium dens.

17 Sep 1909

The Preventive Service, predecessor of the Customs and Excise Department, was established under the Harbour Department by the Hong Kong government for collection of duties on alcoholic beverages.

12 Nov 1909

The Harbour of Refuge Ordinance 1909 was promulgated, authorising the construction of typhoon shelters in Tai Kok Tsui, Mong Kok and Yau Ma Tei.

1909

The Southern Branch of Tongmenghui (united allegiance society) was established on Wong Nai Chung Road. It was headed by Hu Hanmin (胡漢民); Wang Jingwei (汪精衞) and Lin Zhimian (林直勉) served as secretary and accountant, respectively. The branch was responsible only for the affairs of Hong Kong and Macao; work in the southwestern provinces was transferred to the Southern Branch.

Traditional Chinese medicine company Eu Yan Sang, established in Malaysia, opened its first branch in Hong Kong.

The Hong Kong Lawn Tennis Association (present-day Hong Kong Tennis Association) was established, making it the first tennis organisation in Hong Kong.

The Hong Kong Confucian Society was founded by Chinese businessmen Lau Chu-pak (劉鑄伯) and Yeung Bik-chi (楊碧池).

The Pu Ming Zen Monastery as the earliest retreat house on Lantau Island was established by Buddhist nun Gosho (果修), a disciple of Master Miao Tsan (妙參).

The Hong Kong Sze Yap Commercial & Industrial Association was established by Chinese from Taishan, Xinhui, Kaiping and Enping with a mission to connect with fellow villagers for protection of rights and interests. In 1951, it revised its constitution and amended its Chinese name.

07 Jan 1910

The Portuguese in Hong Kong established a recreational sports club called Club de Recreio.

16 Mar 1910

Governor Frederick Lugard officiated at the ground-breaking ceremony of the main building of The University of Hong Kong and conferred Hormusjee Naorojee Mody with the title of Knight Bachelor for his donation to the university. (Figure 096)

07 May 1910

The Hong Kong government announced the death of King Edward VII.

Figure 096
The ground-breaking ceremony dedicated to The University of Hong Kong's main building. (Photo taken on 16 March 1910 and courtesy of Hong Kong Museum of History)

Figure 097
The opening day of Kowloon–Canton Railway at Tsim Sha Tsui Station. (Photo taken on 01 October 1910 and courtesy of Hong Kong Museum of History)

01 Oct 1910

The 22-mile British Section of the Kowloon-Canton Railway became operational upon completion; it later became an important land transport link between Kowloon, the New Territories and Guangzhou. (Figure 097)

15 Oct 1910

Kwan Sum-yin (關心焉) and Chan Chi-kau (陳子裘) called on Chinese people in a movement to "end the queue, keep the attire" by cutting their queues but rejecting Western-style clothing.

1910

The Kowloon Reservoir was completed for fresh water supply to New Kowloon and the southern part of the New Territories; it was the first reservoir in the New Territories.

The Chinese Gold and Silver Exchange Society was established in Central for trading gold, silver, and foreign currencies.

27 Mar 1911

Belgian aviator Charles Van den Born made a demonstration flight in Sha Tin; it was the first-ever powered flight in Hong Kong.

31 Mar 1911

The University Ordinance 1911 was promulgated, establishing The University of Hong Kong and finalising the regulations on governance, operation and organisation.

08 Apr 1911

The revolutionaries held a preparatory meeting in Hong Kong for the anti-Qing uprising in Guangzhou and decided to launch an offensive in Guangzhou from ten directions, led by Zhao Sheng (趙聲) as Commander-in-Chief and Huang Xing (黃興) as his deputy. This was called the Huanghuagang Uprising, which started in Guangzhou on the 29th day of the third lunar month (27 April).

19 Jun 1911

The third-generation General Post Office Building on Pedder Street in Central was opened. (Figure 098)

04 Oct 1911

The Kowloon–Canton Railway became operational. Qing and British representatives travelled to Lo Wu Station in Shenzhen on the first trains from Guangzhou and Tsim Sha Tsui, respectively. A ceremony was then held at Lo Wu Bridge, officially connecting the British and Chinese sections.

09 Oct 1911

Kwong Wah Hospital in Yau Ma Tei started admitting patients upon completion, making it the first hospital in the Kowloon.

Figure 098
The third-generation General Post Office building located at the junction of Pedder Street and Des Voeux Road (present-day World-Wide House) on Hong Kong Island. (Photo courtesy of HKSAR Government)

18 Oct 1911

Eight days after the Wuchang Uprising broke out, the Ta-Ching Government Bank, Bank of Communications, and China Merchants Group in Hong Kong hoisted yellow dragon flags of the Qing Empire in celebration of Confucius' Birthday. In response, some members of the public threw stones at their offices. The flags were later withdrawn to calm the situation.

28 Oct 1911

St. Paul's Church in Central, designed and built by Chinese architect Lam Woo (林護) and Reverend Arthur Dudley Stewart of the Anglican Church, was inaugurated upon completion.

06 Nov 1911

Firecrackers were set off by various organisations and residents in Hong Kong to celebrate the success of the 1911 Revolution.

09 Nov 1911

Guangdong declared independence; Hu Hanmin (胡漢民) was selected as Governor by the gentry. Hu, who was in Hong Kong together with Li Yuk-tong (李煜堂), Lam Woo (林護) and other key members of the Southern Branch of Tongmenghui, returned to Guangzhou to assume his duties.

17 Nov 1911

The Societies Ordinance 1911 was promulgated, stipulating that any group or organisation with more than 10 members, unless exempt, should register with the Registrar General. Otherwise, they would be considered illegal.

23 Nov 1911

As of 20 May 1911, Hong Kong had a population of 456,739, including 444,664 Chinese and 12,075 foreign nationals, according to a government census.

21 Dec 1911

Sun Yat-sen (孫中山) arrived in Hong Kong on the British passenger ship *Devonshire* for a stay of eight hours, before leaving for Shanghai to prepare for the organisation of the Republic of China. During his stay, he met with Liao Chung-kai (Liao Zhongkai) (廖仲愷), Chan Siu-bak (陳少白), Hu Hanmin (胡漢民) and Miyazaki Torazō.

1911

The United Services Recreation Club was established.

The Hong Kong Golf Club constructed a golf course in Fanling, which became a popular destination for European golf lovers then.

15 Jan 1912

The Supreme Court Building—of which construction began in late 1899 and took 12 years to complete—was inaugurated. The cornerstone was laid on 12 November 1903. (Figure 099)

02 Mar 1912

The Chinese Recreation Club, Hong Kong was founded by Ho Kai (何啟), Wei Yuk (韋玉), Yuen Hiu-fan (阮曉繁) and Wong Po-ning (王保寧). It was the first club with a swimming pool.

11 Mar 1912

The main building of The University of Hong Kong was inaugurated; Charles Norton Edgecumbe Eliot was appointed as the first president. The first group of about 50 students were enrolled in September. (Figure 100)

23 Mar 1912

Li Yuk-tong (李煜堂), an overseas Chinese from the US, proposed the establishment of the Bank of Canton with a head office in Central. It was the first wholly Chinese-owned commercial bank in Hong Kong.

Figure 099
The Supreme Court and a bronze statue of Queen Victoria at Statue Square in Central on Hong Kong Island, taken in 1924. (Photo taken in 1924 and courtesy of Public Records Office, Government Records Service)

Figure 100
The University of Hong Kong main building. (Photo taken in 1912 and courtesy of Hong Kong Museum of History)

01 Apr 1912

The Fanling-Sha Tau Kok line of the Kowloon–Canton Railway was commissioned; it continued operations until 01 April 1928.

19 Apr 1912

The Foreign Copper Coin Ordinance 1912 was promulgated, prohibiting the import and circulation of foreign copper coins, except for copper coins prescribed by the Privy Council Order issued on 2 February 1895 and Chinese copper coins. The Ordinance took effect on 01 July.

William Rees-Davies was appointed as Chief Justice of Hong Kong.

18 May 1912

Sun Yat-sen (孫中山) arrived in Hong Kong from Guangzhou for a four-day stay; he attended banquets with Hong Kong businessmen and visited the Government House at the invitation of the Officer Administering the Government Claud Severn. (Figure 101)

04 Jul 1912

On his way from Blake Pier to the inauguration ceremony at City Hall, Governor-appoint Francis Henry May was shot by Lee Hon-hung (李漢雄) on Pedder Street. May was not injured; Lee was arrested by the police and sentenced to life imprisonment. This was the only assassination attempt targeting a governor in the history of Hong Kong.

Francis Henry May was sworn in as the 15th Governor of Hong Kong; he remained in office until 12 September 1918.

Figure 101
Sun Yat-sen (孫中山) (front row, right), Ho Kai (何啟) (back row, first from left), Officer Administering the Government Claud Severn (front row, left) and others in 1912. (Photo courtesy of Hong Kong Museum of History)

19 Aug 1912

In the evening, about 40 pirates attacked the Cheung Chau Police Station, taking munitions and more than HK$1,000 in cash. They then robbed a pawn shop on the island, taking a large amount of jewellery and more than HK$2,000 in cash before fleeing by boat to Macao. Three Indian constables were killed in the incident.

24 Nov 1912

Hong Kong Tramways Company Limited refused to accept Chinese coins (minted in Guangdong) in accordance with the Foreign Copper Coin Ordinance of 1912, causing public discontent and triggering a tramway boycott. It marked a significant spontaneous protest by the Chinese with respect to government policies.

1912

The Mount Davis Fortress was completed.

Mercantile Bank Limited resumed issuing banknotes. Even though it became a wholly owned subsidiary of The Hongkong and Shanghai Banking Corporation in 1959, it retained the right to issue banknotes until 1974.

The Overseas Chanting Society was founded by Lau Pok-tuen (劉博端), Lau Yau-wan (劉筱雲) and Ho Bing-foo (何冰甫) as the first poetry society in Hong Kong since the founding of the Republic of China.

28 Apr 1913

Films with synchronised sound were shown for the first time at Hong Kong City Hall.

14 Jun 1913

The collapse of two buildings located at 7–9, Upper Station Street on Victoria Peak resulted in 18 deaths and 25 injuries.

16 Jun 1913

A plot of land in Aberdeen was allocated by the Hong Kong government for the Chinese-funded construction of the Chinese Permanent Cemetery in Aberdeen, which was opened on 17 October 1915. The Board of Management of the Chinese Permanent Cemetery was also established to manage the cemetery. It was the first permanent cemetery in Hong Kong for Chinese people without religious backgrounds.

11 Jul 1913

The Foreign Silver and Nickel Coin Ordinance 1913 was promulgated, effective 01 March 1914, forbidding the unauthorised import of foreign silver and nickel coins and their circulation in Hong Kong.

08 Aug 1913

The Education Ordinance 1913 was promulgated, stipulating that all schools, except government schools, military schools and those exempted by the Governor-in-Council, must be registered and were subject to government supervision.

Sep 1913

The first scout troop in Hong Kong, known as The First Hong Kong Troop, was formed. It was officially registered with the Scout Association based in Britain the following year. In July 1915, the Hong Kong Branch of The Boy Scouts Association (present-day Scout Association of Hong Kong) was formed to co-ordinate the training and activities of scouts.

1913

The Tai Po Market Railway Station was completed.

The Government Vegetable Market in Yau Ma Tei was built as a wholesale market for fruits and vegetables.

Hong Kong athletes represented China in the first Far Eastern Championship Games in Manila, the Philippines.

Lai Man-wai (黎民偉) made the first Hong Kong film *Zhuangzi Tests His Wife*.

06 Mar 1914

The British Judicial Committee of the Privy Council heard the first criminal appeal case from the Supreme Court of Hong Kong, involving an Indian soldier accused of murdering his superior in Guangzhou. British extraterritorial jurisdiction in China was the legal basis to support the Supreme Court of Hong Kong's decision to hear the case.

28 Apr 1914

A fire broke out at Standard Oil's Kowloon No. 5 oil storage tank. It burnt for days, destroying 1.5 million gallons of oil.

May 1914

The Hong Kong Chinese Civil Servants' Association was established, making it the oldest civil service union in Hong Kong.

06 Jul 1914

The Legislative Council appropriated HK$50,000 from recurrent revenue for relief efforts in the floods of the West River in Guangdong.

05 Aug 1914

Britain declared war on Germany and joined what later became The First World War. The Hong Kong government declared martial law in Hong Kong and implemented the Military Stores (Prohibition of Exportation) Ordinance 1862 to regulate the export of military supplies.

12 Aug 1914

British troops in Hong Kong mistook the Japanese merchant ship *Shikoku Maru* for a hostile vessel and opened fire, killing one of its crew.

06 Oct 1914

The Trading with the Enemy Ordinance 1914 was promulgated, forbidding Hong Kong merchants from trading with citizens of enemy states.

23 Oct 1914

The Hong Kong Police Reserve Ordinance 1914 was promulgated, establishing the Special Police Reserve, predecessor of the Hong Kong Auxiliary Police Force.

27 Oct 1914

The Alien Enemies (Winding Up) Ordinance 1914 was promulgated, empowering the Hong Kong government to wind up and liquidate businesses of citizens of enemy states who had been expelled, detained or imprisoned.

Oct 1914

The Hong Kong government began detaining German men stranded in Hong Kong at the Hung Hom internment camp.

1914

The Stockbrokers' Association of Hong Kong was renamed Hong Kong Stock Exchange.

Kom Tong Hall, a Mid-Levels mansion owned by businessman Ho Kom-tong (何甘棠), was completed.

The Commercial Press opened a branch in Hong Kong, one of its first branches to be established outside Shanghai.

The Hong Kong government established an anti-piracy force (comprising Indians led by police inspectors on secondment) to protect the coastal and inland waterways, while large ocean-going vessels were escorted by the British military—a task assumed by the Hong Kong police in 1930. In May 1930, the first members of Hong Kong Police's Anti-piracy Guard were recruited, including Chinese from Weihaiwei, Russians and Indians.

The Hong Kong Football Association was established.

Figure 102
Assistant Superintendent of Police in the New Territories Donald Burlingham (in uniform, centre) in a group photo after he shot a tiger in Sheung Shui. (Photo taken on 08 March 1915 and courtesy of HKSAR Government)

08 Mar 1915

Residents of Wa Shan in Sheung Shui reported the sighting of a tiger in the nearby woods. Two British police officers were dispatched but failed to kill the tiger. Subsequently, Assistant Superintendent of Police in the New Territories Donald Burlingham, together with six Indian constables, rounded up the tiger and shot it. The incident resulted in the deaths of two police officers and a Chinese civilian. (Figure 102)

12 Jul 1915

The Sincere Insurance & Investment Co. Limited was incorporated with registered capital of HK$1.2 million.

17 Jul 1915

The Legislative Council approved a government allocation of HK$50,000 for a relief fund set up by Tung Wah Hospital to help victims of the West River floods in Guangdong and a fire in Guangzhou.

04 Aug 1915

The Lee Garden Tai Pak Lau was opened in Sai Wan, featuring a Chinese opera theatre, a stage, and Chinese and Western restaurants. It was a key entertainment venue in the Western District of Hong Kong Island.

15 Sep 1915

The government announced the establishment of the Board of Chinese Vernacular Primary Education to promote Chinese-language education in Hong Kong and fill the gap of government funding by raising additional money.

16 Dec 1915

The Yau Ma Tei Typhoon Shelter was built for boats sailing in the waters of the New Territories and West Kowloon.

17 Dec 1915

The Importation and Exportation Ordinance 1915 was promulgated, regulating all import and export of goods and authorising the Hong Kong Imports and Exports Office to conduct inspections.

31 Dec 1915

The Wing On Fire and Marine Insurance Co. Limited was incorporated by Wing On Company, marking an entry into the insurance business.

1915

The Anglican Church founded St. Paul's Girls' College at Mid-Levels; it was relocated to McDonald Road in 1927. In 1945, it was merged with St. Paul's College to form St. Paul's School, the first co-educational secondary school in Hong Kong. In 1950, St. Paul's College was reinstated while St. Paul's School was renamed St. Paul's Co-educational College.

Chinese businessman Loke Yew (陸佑) offered an interest-free loan of HK$500,000 to The University of Hong Kong to meet its shortfall in operating funds.

The *Hong Kong Morning Post,* founded by revolutionaries in Hong Kong, was renamed the *Xiangjiang Morning Post* in 1919. Later, it became the official newspaper of the Kuomintang in Hong Kong.

The Chung Sing Drama Club was founded to provide study and exchange opportunities in music and drama. In 1919, it was renamed the Chung Sing Benevolent Society; its services were extended to the charity sector.

The Hong Kong Chinese Christian Churches Union was established as advocated by seven Christian churches: Anglican Church, London Missionary Society, Basel Mission, Wesleyan Church (Methodist Church), Chinese Rhenish Church, Congregational Church and Baptist Church.

28 Mar 1916

The Tsim Sha Tsui Terminus of the Kowloon–Canton Railway began providing full rail services upon completion. (Figure 103)

10 Apr 1916

Au Tak (區德) established the Kai Tak Land Investment Company Limited and continued Ho Kai's (何啟) efforts to promote a reclamation project in Kowloon Bay.

14 Jul 1916

The Tobacco Ordinance 1916 was promulgated, introducing duties on tobacco imported into Hong Kong.

16 Aug 1916

The Hong Kong government issued an order to prohibit ships carrying Chinese people from coming to Hong Kong from Macao, in view of the epidemic of cholera in Macao in early August.

20 Oct 1916

The War Loan Ordinance 1916 was promulgated, authorising the Governor to loan not more than HK$3 million in the form of "colonial bonds" to the British government for the war in Europe.

Figure 103
The building and platform of Kowloon–Canton Railway's Tsim Sha Tsui Terminus. (Photo taken in 1917 and courtesy of Hong Kong Museum of History)

1916

Britain began recruiting Chinese workers in Hong Kong. They were dispatched to the battlefront in Mesopotamia (present-day Iraq) as part of the Chinese Labour Corps to build railways and drive transport vessels. By October 1918, about 6,000 Chinese workers, mostly from Hong Kong, had worked as support staff; 384 had died of diseases or accidents.

American Express Company set up a branch in Hong Kong. In addition to its banking business, it was also a travel and shipping agency.

The Koon Yick Food Factory registered a trademark for its chili sauce and was the first sauce manufacturer to be incorporated in Hong Kong.

The Chinese Amateur Athletic Federation of Hong Kong was established to organise local competitions and select Chinese athletes for international events.

The South China Recreation Club was founded, with Lo Hap-fu (盧俠父) as its first chairman. It joined the Hong Kong Football Association and was renamed the South China Athletic Association in 1920.

The Hong Kong Art Club, the oldest surviving art group in Hong Kong, was established by foreign nationals residing in Hong Kong and held its first annual exhibition.

The Ka Ying Chow Commercial Association was established to liaise with the Meizhou business community in Hong Kong (Ka Ying or Jiaying is another name for Meizhou located in northeastern Guangdong.) On 26 August 2016, it was renamed the Hong Kong Meizhou General Chamber of Commerce.

Several distinguished members of the Chinese community in Hong Kong formed a Buddhist sermon society, marking the beginning of the urban Buddhist community in modern Hong Kong. In July 1931, it was reorganised as the Hong Kong Buddhist Studies Association.

The first Girl Guide unit in Hong Kong was formed at Victoria British School. In 1919, a Hong Kong branch of the Girl Guides Association was established; in 1978, it was separated from the Girl Guide Association in Britain and became The Hong Kong Girl Guides Association.

03 May 1917

The Constitutional Reform Association of Hong Kong was formed by foreign nationals who were interested in Hong Kong affairs, specifically the constitutional reform of the Hong Kong government; Henry Pollock was its president.

07 Jun 1917

The Legislative Council passed a proposal to set a special war rate of 7% as part of Hong Kong's contribution in support of the British war effort in Europe.

01 Jul 1917

The Hong Kong Observatory began using a visual tropical cyclone warning system to replace the gun-firing local storm signal system. The new system featured the numbers one to seven indicating the intensity of typhoons.

31 Aug 1917

The Military Service Ordinance 1917 was promulgated, stipulating that, unless exempt, any British male between the ages of 18 and 54 who usually resided in Hong Kong was obligated to serve. The Governor was also given the power to recruit anyone into the military.

24 Sep 1917

The Bank of China opened a subsidiary on Bonham Strand in Sheung Wan; it was upgraded to a branch in February 1919 with Pei Tsu-yee (貝祖詒) serving as manager.

12 Oct 1917

The Deportation Ordinance 1917 was promulgated, amending and consolidating deportation-related ordinances enacted between 1912 and 1915.

22 Nov 1917

The Legislative Council approved a donation of HK$10,000 to aid flood-affected areas in northern China.

1917

The Hong Kong branch of the Fukien Chamber of Commerce was founded; it was renamed the Hong Kong Fukien Chamber of Commerce in 2017.

The Indian Recreation Club was established.

22 Jan 1918

A gunfight broke out between police officers and bandits during the search of a flat on Gresson Street in Wan Chai. The Hong Kong government dispatched British forces stationed in Hong Kong for reinforcement; Governor Francis Henry May appeared on the scene to persuade the bandits to surrender. Eight people, including five policemen, were killed.

02 Feb 1918

A ceremony was held to mark the completion of the Tai Tam Tuk Reservoir. The reservoir's dam was the first one built by the Department of Public Works of Hong Kong without the guidance of engineering consultants from London.

13 Feb 1918

After an earthquake with a magnitude of 7.3 hit Shantou's Nan'ao Island, Hong Kong also experienced an earthquake that lasted for 30 seconds and caused cracks in the external walls of many buildings in Kowloon and on Hong Kong Island.

26 Feb 1918

During the second day of the annual Derby Day races at the Happy Valley Racecourse, the bamboo scaffolding on the upper deck of the grandstand collapsed and knocked over a food cooker on the lower deck. It set the bamboo matting on fire, killing 570 people and leaving 135 missing. (Figure 104)

24 Mar 1918

Businessman Ho Kom-tong (何甘棠) invited eminent monks and Taoist priests to perform Buddhist rituals for seven days and nights to chant sutras for the victims of the Happy Valley Racecourse fire.

Apr 1918

The Hong Kong government accused two Chinese persons of building an illegal wireless station on Des Voeux Road Central. The prosecution argued that the two were simply experimenting with radio technology; because the equipment had a receiving range of 50 miles, it was in breach of the law. The magistrate eventually imposed on each defendant a HK$25 fine and a HK$100 good behaviour bond for one year. Their radio equipment was also confiscated.

Figure 104
A fire broke out at Happy Valley Racecourse on Derby Day on 26 February 1918. (Photo courtesy of Hong Kong Museum of History)

14 Jun 1918

The Hong Kong Automobile Association was founded by David Landale, a senior executive of Jardine Matheson. It became involved in motor racing in the 1950s and was the only recognised organisation in Hong Kong to issue racing certificates.

10 Aug 1918

War Drummer, Hong Kong's first wartime standard cargo ship, was completed and launched at the Whampoa Dock. The vessel was 325 feet long and 45 feet wide and had a load capacity of 5,080 tonnes.

10 Oct 1918

The headquarters and central clubhouse of the Chinese YMCA of Hong Kong commenced operations upon completion. The clubhouse had an indoor swimming pool with both cool and hot water supply, as well as an elevated wok-shaped running track; it was the first indoor sports complex in Hong Kong.

14 Nov 1918

The Bank of East Asia Limited was incorporated by Chinese businessmen Kan Tong-po (簡東浦), Li Koon-chun (李冠春), Li Tse-fong (李子方), Chow Shou-son (周壽臣) and others. It started operations on 04 January 1919.

29 Dec 1918

The Hong Kong government held a memorial service for the soldiers who died in the First World War.

1918

The Chinese Muslim Cultural and Fraternal Association was established.

Advised by Buddhist Gao Henian (高鶴年), businessman Chan Chun-ting (陳春亭) went to the Guanzong Temple in Ningbo to study under Great Master Dixian (諦閑). After completing the Triple Platform Ordination, Chan was given the monastic name Tak Chun (得真) and the courtesy name Hin Ki (顯奇). Master Hin Ki later presided over the restoration of the Tsing Shan Monastery.

14 Mar 1919

The Fire Brigade started providing an ambulance service on 24-hour stand-by in shifts with a driver and three paramedics at a time.

28 Apr 1919

The Chinese delegation submitted a memorandum during the Paris Peace Conference, requesting the return of all foreign concessions, including the New Territories. The request was rejected on 14 May.

03 Jun 1919

Nine students from To Ying School were arrested for marching in the streets with oil-paper umbrellas written with the words "Chinese goods." It was the first street protest in Hong Kong related to the May Fourth Movement.

26 Jul 1919

About 300 coolies refused to work during a typhoon and looted rice shops in Wan Chai before moving onto Causeway Bay, Central and Sai Wan.

22 Aug 1919

The Hong Kong Observatory hoisted Hurricane Signal No. 7 (the highest back then) amid a typhoon that caused many ships to run aground and about 500 to 600 Chinese sailboats to sink.

07 Sep 1919

Tung Wah Hospital purchased rice from Wuhu and sold it at a low price in an attempt to solve the rice shortage in Hong Kong. The purchase lasted until early October of the same year.

19 Sep 1919

The Rice Ordinance 1919 was promulgated, authorising the Governor to take possession of any rice in Hong Kong and regulate the operations of rice merchants when necessary.

30 Sep 1919

Reginald Edward Stubbs was sworn in as the 16th Governor of Hong Kong; he left office on 31 October 1925.

1919

The Imports and Exports Office began to publish detailed annual import and export statistics.

The Chinese Banks' Association, initiated by Pei Tsu-yee (貝祖詒) of the Bank of China, was formed.

The China Brothers Hat Manufacturing Company was founded by brothers Hui Lap-sam (許立三), Hui Pee-kook (許庇縠) and Hui Ngok (許岳). The company was known for wool felt hats under its Three Lions brand and was then the largest hat manufacturer in Hong Kong.

Wah Yan College was established in Central, making it the first English-language school run by the Chinese in Hong Kong. In 1924, it opened a Kowloon branch (Wah Yan College, Kowloon). The two schools were placed under the care of the Jesuit Order in 1932.

Mo Dunmei (莫敦梅) set up a private school on Heard Street in Wan Chai, teaching ancient Chinese prose and Confucianism. In 1934, it was renamed Dunmei School.

Ying Wa College launched a student newspaper, *Ying Wa Echo*, in which students could exchange views and share knowledge. The newspaper also reported on school activities and events of the Young Men's Association.

20 Jan 1920

The Kowloon Residents' Association was established to put forward proposals to the government for improving the living conditions of Kowloon residents. B. L. Frost was the first chairman.

03 Feb 1920

At 11:30 p.m., a fire broke out in the warehouse of Nam Wah Company at 26 Kennedy Town in Sai Wan; it spread to eight other buildings, killing 34 people.

10 Mar 1920

The Hong Kong Young Women's Christian Association was founded and held its first meeting.

09 Apr 1920

The Hong Kong government appointed representatives from the Education Department and local communities to a Board of Education for the purpose of developing Hong Kong's education policy, replacing the Board of Chinese Vernacular Primary Education (established in 1911).

18 Apr 1920

The employers of Chinese mechanical workers agreed to a 20%–32.5% pay rise, ending a month-long strike initiated by members of the Chinese Engineers' Institute. This was the first successful trade union-led industrial movement in Hong Kong; it set a precedent of Hong Kong's Chinese workers receiving assistance from Guangzhou during strikes.

25 Jun 1920

The Societies Ordinance 1920 was promulgated, repealing the requirement of registration with all societies. Triad societies and groups whose purposes were contrary to the peace and order of Hong Kong were deemed unlawful. The Governor-in-Council was given absolute discretion to declare a society unlawful on the conditions specified in the Ordinance.

Sep 1920

The Hong Kong government agreed to provide The University of Hong Kong with funding of HK$1 million for establishing a solid financial base for the university.

28 Oct 1920

The Legislative Council approved a grant of HK$100,000 to help famine victims in the Mainland.

14 Nov 1920

Pok Oi Hospital in Yuen Long commenced operations.

31 Dec 1920

The Prisons Department was separated from the Hong Kong police, becoming an independent government agency responsible for the administration of prisons and prisoners.

1920

The Police Training School was established inside the Central Police Station. Henceforth, Hong Kong police officers would receive comprehensive police training.

The Kai Tak Company completed the first phase of reclamation on the west shore of Kowloon Bay. The new triangular-shaped reclaimed area was called the Kai Tak Bund.

Garden City in Ho Man Tin, the first residential project in Hong Kong to utilise the garden city concept in urban planning, was completed.

The Hong Kong Construction Association was established as an accredited representative for key contractors in Hong Kong; Lam Yam-chuen（林蔭泉）was its first president.

Wong Chung-yik（王寵益）became the first professor of pathology and the first professor of Chinese descent at The University of Hong Kong.

The Vernacular Normal School for Men and Vernacular Normal School for Women were established by the government for training male and female teachers, respectively, in Chinese. The former was incorporated into the Government Vernacular Middle School in 1926, and the latter was closed in 1941.

The Hong Kong Chinese Medical Association, predecessor of the Hong Kong Medical Association, was founded.

25 Feb 1921

An explosion at Hoy Sun Fire Cracker Factory in Yau Ma Tei killed 32 people, making it the deadliest firecracker accident in the history of Hong Kong.

03 Mar 1921

The Singaporean vessel *Hong Moh*, carrying about 800 Chinese from Hong Kong to Xiamen, sank after hitting a rock near Shantou. Only 250 people were rescued; most of the Chinese passengers were rubber plantation coolies.

27 Mar 1921

The Chinese Seamen's Union was established; it was the first seamen's union in China and the predecessor of the Hong Kong Seamen's Union.

Apr 1921

The Chin Woo Athletic Federation was established in Hong Kong.

04 May 1921

The Secretary for Chinese Affairs issued an order to prohibit Chinese people in Hong Kong from celebrating the establishment of the National Government of the Republic of China in Guangzhou. On 06 May, the Secretary issued another notice, warning Hong Kong residents not to raise funds for the Guangzhou government. On 23 May, Governor Reginald Edward Stubbs apologised for issuing the notice but maintained that the Hong Kong government would only recognise the Beijing government of the Republic of China.

23 Jun 1921

The Hong Kong branch of the Society for the Prevention of Cruelty to Animals was founded; Governor Reginald Edward Stubbs was its president and patron.

28 Jun 1921

The University of Hong Kong began admitting female students for the first time, including Rachel Irving, daughter of Edward Alexander Irving (then Director of Education), and Irene Ho Tung (何艾齡), daughter of Robert Ho Tung (何東).

30 Jul 1921

Legislative Council Unofficial Members Lau Chu-pak (劉鑄伯) and Ho Fook (何福) initiated a meeting to study the issue of *mui tsai* (young female bondservants) and subsequently set up the Society for the Protection of the Mui Tsai to assist Po Leung Kuk in monitoring the abuse of Chinese servant girls.

01 Aug 1921

Chiu Chow Pat Yap Chamber of Commerce was established, with Wong Siu-ping (王少平) and Chan Chun-chuen (陳春泉) officiating at the opening ceremony; it was renamed the Hong Kong Chiu Chow Chamber of Commerce in 1945.

08 Aug 1921

The first meeting of the Anti-Mui Tsai Society was held by 26 staunch opponents of the *mui tsai* system. The Manifesto of the Anti-Mui Tsai Society was adopted.

Sep 1921

The Wan Chai waterfront reclamation scheme was launched; it was completed in 1930.

Oct 1921

The first issue of the literary magazine *Dual Voices* was published, featuring fiction in both vernacular and classical Chinese. Of the 25 pieces, two were in classical Chinese and 23 were in vernacular Chinese.

26 Nov 1921

The Kowloon Motor Bus Company was established, providing two bus routes between Tsim Sha Tsui and Sham Shui Po and between Tsim Sha Tsui and Kowloon City.

04 Dec 1921

At the Washington Naval Conference, foreign powers including Britain, France and Japan expressed their willingness to return Weihaiwei, Guangzhou Bay and Jiaozhou Bay to China. The British representatives stressed that the New Territories was of defensive significance to Hong Kong, so it would not be returned.

10 Dec 1921

The *Hongkong Evening News* was founded as the first evening newspaper in Hong Kong.

15 Dec 1921

Hong Kong had a population of 625,166, including 610,368 Chinese and 14,798 foreign nationals, according to a government census.

1921

The Hong Kong Stockbrokers Association was established as the second stock exchange in Hong Kong.

The New World Cinema, founded by brothers Lai Hoi-shan (黎海山), Lai Pak-hoi (黎北海) and Lai Man-wai (黎民偉), was opened in Sheung Wan.

The Five Districts Business Welfare Association was established and held its inauguration ceremony on 15 January 1923.

The Tsik Chung Sin Koon, located at Chuk Yuen Village in Kowloon, was founded by Taoist priest Leung Ren-yan (梁仁庵) for worshipping Wong Tai Sin under an administrative institute called Sik Sik Yuen; it was renamed Chik Chung Wong Sin Hall in 1925. (Figure 105)

Figure 105
Wong Tai Sin Temple in the early days at Chuk Yuen Village in Kowloon. (Photo taken in 1925 and courtesy of HKSAR Government)

12 Jan 1922

The Chinese Seamen's Union announced the start of a strike after three unsuccessful requests for a pay rise. The strikers went back to Guangzhou and published the declaration and rules for the strike.

01 Feb 1922

The Hong Kong government declared that the Chinese Seamen's Union was an illegal organisation on the grounds that it endangered the peace and order of Hong Kong. The police were ordered to inspect the premises; the union was closed and its signboard was removed.

24 Feb 1922

The Chinese Engineers' Institute held a trade union meeting to discuss the mediation strategies of all parties involved in the seamen's strike (including labourers, employers and the government). More than 400 representatives from 113 trade unions attended the meeting.

28 Feb 1922

The Executive Council held a meeting to draft an emergency bill at noon; it was passed by the Legislative Council in the afternoon. The Emergency Regulations Ordinance 1922 was promulgated in the evening, specifying that in cases of emergency or danger to public order, the Governor-in-Council could make any regulations in the interest of the public.

03 Mar 1922

More than 2,000 striking workers tried to leave Hong Kong on foot but were stopped by the police along Tai Po Road near Sha Tin. Deputy Superintendent of Police Thomas Henry King ordered shots to be fired, resulting in five deaths and seven injuries. It became known as the Shatin Massacre.

The Hong Kong government announced that under the amended Royal Instructions, the terms of office for Executive Council and Legislative Council's Unofficial Members were changed to five and four years, respectively.

05 Mar 1922

The Hong Kong government, shipping companies and the Chinese Seamen's Union reached an agreement under which shipowners would offer a 15%–30% pay rise. The seamen returned to work.

06 Mar 1922

The Hong Kong government announced in the *Gazette* a decision to revoke the illegal status of the Chinese Seamen's Union. The following day, the government returned the signboard to the union and released many arrestees. (Figure 106)

07 Mar 1922

The Chinese Seamen's Union announced the resumption of work, ending the seamen's strike.

24 Mar 1922

The Crown Lands Resumption Amendment Ordinance 1922 was promulgated, allowing government compensation at market value for land resumption.

26 Mar 1922

Over 600 people attended a meeting of the Anti-Mui Tsai Society. The Society's writing on the subject and the reasons for its formation were compiled into a book, which was sent to Clara Blanche Haslewood in London who financed the printing of the book for public distribution. British public opinion began to turn against keeping *mui tsai* (young female bondservant) in Hong Kong.

06 Apr 1922

Prince Edward (later King Edward VIII) was the first British Crown Prince to visit Hong Kong, staying for two days on his way from India to Japan. On 07 April, he laid the foundation stone of St. Stephen's College (present-day St. Stephen's Girls College) at its Mid-Levels campus.

19 Jul 1922

The Chinese Sisters of the Precious Blood was established. Approved by the Holy See in 1929, it was the first Chinese congregation of the Hong Kong Apostolic Vicariate.

29 Sep 1922

The Industrial Employment of Children Ordinance 1922 was promulgated, authorising the Governor-in-Council to declare an industry dangerous and to stipulate the minimum age with respect to the employment of children in a specific industry, as well as the requirements of employment of children for industrial operation, and the responsibilities of employers.

15 Oct 1922

Peking opera master Mei Lanfang (梅蘭芳) arrived in Hong Kong with a troupe of more than 100 people and premiered with a show at Tai Ping Theatre on 24 October; the performances lasted for nearly a month.

17 Oct 1922

Tsan Yuk Hospital, a maternity hospital in Sai Ying Pun, was opened as the first maternity hospital for Chinese in Hong Kong; it was founded by the London Missionary Society.

Oct 1922

The Tsung Tsin Association was established; Lai Tsi-hsi (賴際熙) was its first President. Its headquarters office commenced services upon completion in 1929.

09 Nov 1922

The Yeung Wo Nursing Home, established by the Chinese community in Hong Kong, was opened in Happy Valley to provide medical services; it was the predecessor of the Hong Kong Sanatorium & Hospital.

1922

The Education Department significantly reduced the number of subsidised schools under the Grant Code, retaining only 15 secondary schools whose education quality met the official requirements.

The Chinese Estates Limited was founded by Fung Ping-shan (馮平山) and Li Koon-chun (李冠春).

Figure 106
On 06 March 1922, a union signboard confiscated earlier was returned by the Hong Kong government upon the success of the Hong Kong Seamen's Strike. (Photo courtesy of Lai Man-wai's descendants)

15 Feb 1923

The Female Domestic Service Ordinance 1923 was promulgated, prohibiting the employment of *mui tsai* (young female bondservants) under the age of ten and forbidding the transfer of *mui tsai.*

18 Feb 1923

The Hong Kong Synod of Basel Mission was established, becoming a statutory body in 1956 as the Tsung Tsin Mission of Hong Kong.

20 Feb 1923

Sun Yat-sen (孫中山) delivered an English speech at the Great Hall of The University of Hong Kong, stating that Hong Kong was the cradle of his revolutionary ideas.

20 Mar 1923

The first group of Chinese police officers recruited from Weihaiwei in Shandong Province arrived in Hong Kong on the ship *Kueichow*. The Weihaiwei police, known by the initial letter "D" in their service numbers, operated as an independent contingent of the Hong Kong Police Force until 01 April 1964.

24 May 1923

The Cenotaph in Central was unveiled to commemorate the soldiers who perished in the First World War. It later also served as a memorial to those who died defending Hong Kong in the Second World War. (Figure 107)

May 1923

Kai Tack Motor Bus Company Limited started services between Tsim Sha Tsui and Yau Ma Tei, Hung Hom and Kowloon City.

Figure 107
A commemoration ceremony underway at the Cenotaph on Chater Road in Central. (Photo taken in 1930 and courtesy of HKSAR Government)

Jun 1923

The Hongkong & Kowloon Taxicab Company began operations with 80 French Citroën saloons as the first taxi company in Hong Kong.

14 Jul 1923

The Minxin Film Company was founded by brothers Lai Man-wai (黎民偉), Lai Hoi-shan (黎海山) and Lai Pak-hoi (黎北海) as the first film production company in Hong Kong.

17 Aug 1923

The Hong Kong Observatory hoisted Hurricane Signal No. 7 for nearly 96 hours until 22 August amid a typhoon which killed 100 people and damaged 11 ocean-going vessels and 10 fishing boats.

02 Sep 1923

The China Motor Bus Company Limited was founded by Ngan Shing-kwan (顏成坤) for bus services on the Kowloon peninsula and in the New Territories. In 1933, he acquired a franchise for bus services on Hong Kong Island.

05 Oct 1923

The Dangerous Drugs Ordinance 1923 was promulgated, empowering the Imports and Exports Office to regulate dangerous drugs.

18 Oct 1923

A controller was appointed by the Canadian government to coordinate its Chinese immigration matters in Hong Kong.

05 Nov 1923

The Hongkong and Yaumati Ferry Company Limited was incorporated and began operating passenger ferry services between Central and Sham Shui Po, Mong Kok and Yau Ma Tei on 01 January 1924.

27 Nov 1923

The Lee Hysan Estate Company Limited was founded by Lee Hy-san (利希慎) who acquired plots of land in East Point from Jardine Matheson the following year for the development of Lee Garden Amusement Park and Lee Theatre.

02 Dec 1923

The Radio Communications Co. (Oriental) Limited recorded the opera performances at Star Theatre in Tsim Sha Tsui for transmission to a receiver at Kowloon Hotel. The signals could be clearly received by a ship of the Peninsular and Oriental Steam Navigation Company 60 miles away, marking the first broadcast of its kind in Hong Kong and the Far East.

1923

The second-generation Yau Ma Tei Police Station, located at the junction of Canton Road and Public Square Street in Kowloon, was opened upon completion; it became the oldest police station building (which remains) on the Kowloon peninsula.

The District Office promulgated regulations on land premium for construction of village houses in any district of Hong Kong. It was strongly opposed by villagers of the New Territories who made repeated appeals with the Hong Kong and British governments.

The Pedder Building, designed by Palmer & Turner, was opened upon completion (it is the only existing pre-Second World War building on Pedder Street in Central).

The establishment of Hok Hoi Library on Bonham Road in Sai Ying Pun was initiated by Lai Tsi-hsi (賴際熙) with support from fellow merchants Robert Ho Tung (何東), Kwok Chun-yeung (郭春秧), Lee Hy-san (利希慎) and Lee Hoi-tung (李海東). It had a reading room and a book collection in place to support academic research.

Lee Kung Man Knitting Factory (HK) Limited, a producer of knitted underwear and socks located on Nam Cheong Street in Sham Shui Po, was founded by Fung Sau-yu (馮壽如).

07 Apr 1924

Indian poet Rabindranath Tagore stopped by Hong Kong during a visit to the Mainland and received a warm welcome from the local Indian community.

22 May 1924

Chinese athletes in Hong Kong participated in the third National Games of the Republic of China in Wuchang; it was the first time Hong Kong athletes took part in the Games.

31 May 1924

US pilot Harry Abbott completed a trial flight in the airspace over the Kai Tak Bund, marking the first documented flight at Kai Tak.

16 Aug 1924

The Foolish Old Man's Hut Poetry Club, later known as North Hill Poetry Club, was established by Mok Hok-ming (莫鶴鳴) and Choi Jit-fu (蔡哲夫) at the residence of a deputy manager on Lee Garden Hill borrowed from Lee Hy-san (利希慎); it was disbanded in 1925.

24 Aug 1924

The gentry of the New Territories held a meeting at Man Mo Temple in Tai Po, opposing the District Office's land premium regulation of 1923. After the meeting, a commission was formed to protect the residents' land rights; it was later registered as the New Territories Association of Agricultural, Industrial and Commercial Research.

29 Aug 1924

The Novel Weekly was founded to publish articles in classical Chinese as well as serials and short stories in vernacular Chinese. "The Status of New Poetry" by Hui Man-lau (許夢留) as the the first commentary on modern Chinese poetry in Hong Kong was published in the first two issues of 1925.

17 Oct 1924

Henry Cowper Gollan was appointed as Chief Justice of Hong Kong.

Dec 1924

Ka Wah Ngan Ho relocated its head office from Guangzhou to a location on Des Voeux Road Central in Hong Kong and was registered as Ka Wah Savings Bank.

1924

The US Equitable Eastern Banking Corporation, later known as Chase Bank, opened a branch in Hong Kong.

The first storm drain in Hong Kong was completed, connecting Wan Chai Road to the waterfront outfall.

24 Jan 1925

The Abbott School of Aviation, founded by US pilot Harry Abbott at the Kai Tak Bund, held its opening ceremony.

13 Mar 1925

The Chinese newspapers in Hong Kong suspended publication for one day while trade unions, including the Chinese Seamen's Union, flew their flags at half-mast in memory of Sun Yat-sen (孫中山) who passed away on 12 March.

26 May 1925

Governor Reginald Edward Stubbs officiated at a ceremony marking the return of an iron gate, taken by British troops in 1899 during the local resistance to British occupation, from Britain to the Tang clan of Kat Hing Wai at Kam Tin in the New Territories.

05 Jun 1925

Wah Kiu Yat Po, also known as Overseas Chinese Daily News, was founded as the first newspaper with a Sunday edition in Hong Kong; it ceased publication on 13 January 1995.

18 Jun 1925

All trade union organisations in Hong Kong held a joint meeting, establishing the Federation of Hong Kong Trade Unions and resolving to stage a general strike in support of the victims of the May Thirtieth Massacre in Shanghai. Workers in the shipping, printing, and tram industries were among the first to go on strike, followed by other industries, totalling about 250,000 strikers. The strikers left their jobs and returned to Guangzhou. (Figure 108)

22 Jun 1925

The Hong Kong government promulgated several regulations in the *Gazette*, imposing restrictions on the export of designated grains, gold and silver currencies, as well as censoring mail and telegrams sent from Hong Kong. On 25 June, it announced the authorisation of the Secretary for Chinese Affairs to review the publication of Chinese news. On 06 July, it stipulated that the Commissioner of Police could deport unemployed persons.

23 Jun 1925

Morrison Brown Yung (容覲彤), son of Yung Wing (容閎), was granted a mining lease by the government for Mining Lot No. 3 at Lin Ma Hang, where he ran a mining operation for eight years and was in charge of the excavation of six mine tunnels, totalling about 2,100 metres long.

26 Jun 1925

The Telephone Ordinance 1925 was promulgated, issuing a 50-year franchise to the Hong Kong Telephone Company Limited to start operation with the local telephone network on 01 July. The franchise under the China and Japan Telephone and Electric Company, which began on 01 February 1905, ended on 30 June upon non-renewal by the government.

Figure 108
Crowds raised the banner "Canton–Hong Kong Strike Committee" during the 1925 Canton–Hong Kong Strike. (Photo courtesy of Hong Kong Museum of History)

Jun 1925

The Queen's Pier, where official welcome and farewell ceremonies for governors were conducted, was inaugurated. Originally known as the Queen's Statue Wharf, it was rebuilt in 1921. On 31 July, 1924, it was renamed Queen's Pier following an announcement in the Legislative Council by the Colonial Secretary.

06 Jul 1925

The American Club Hong Kong, an American fraternity organisation, was founded.

08 Jul 1925

The Kung Sheung Daily News was founded by lawyer Hung Hing-kam (洪興錦); it ceased publication on 01 December 1984.

10 Jul 1925

The Canton–Hong Kong Strike Committee, set up in Guangzhou, announced an immediate economic blockade of Hong Kong, banning the export of goods to Hong Kong.

16 Jul 1925

The Hong Kong Trade Maintenance Association, an importer of food from Shanghai, Macao, Vietnam, Penang and Singapore, was formed by a group of Chinese business leaders, together with The Hongkong and Shanghai Banking Corporation comprador Ho Saikwong (何世光) and Chairman of the Chinese Merchants' Guild Li Yau-tsun (李右泉).

17 Jul 1925

A landslide at Po Hing Fong in Sheung Wan caused the collapse of a retaining wall and buried five houses, killing 75 people, including former Legislative Councillor Chau Siu-ki (周少岐) and his family, and injuring 20.

01 Aug 1925

The Medical Officer for Schools was created by the Hong Kong government to provide regular medical examination and treatment for students in government and subsidised schools.

21 Aug 1925

Tung Wah Hospital, in conjunction with the Hong Kong Chinese Merchants' Guild and a business chamber called 24 Hong Association, jointly sent a telegram to Chinese associations in China and overseas, calling for a halt to the remittance of monetary aid to striking workers leaving Hong Kong for Guangzhou.

23 Sep 1925

The Hong Kong government made a request with the British government for a loan of £3 million in light of an annual deficit of over HK$5 million following the strikes and economic blockade imposed by the Canton–Hong Kong Strike Committee.

01 Nov 1925

Cecil Clementi was sworn in as the 17th Governor of Hong Kong; he left office on 01 February 1930.

02 Dec 1925

Governor Cecil Clementi met with Yang Xiyan (楊西岩), a representative of the Guangzhou National Government, at the Government House and expressed his willingness to resolve the Canton–Hong Kong Strike through negotiation.

21 Dec 1925

The Kowloon Hospital in Kowloon City was completed and started admission of patients.

1925

The Hong Kong government's revenue decreased from HK$24,209,600 in 1924 to HK$23,244,400 in 1925 and HK$21,416,000 in 1926 as a result of the Canton–Hong Kong Strike. It was not until 1928 that it returned to the pre-strike level.

The government's first proposal to develop the Kai Tak Bund into an airport was rejected by Britain's Committee of Imperial Defence for violating the provisions of the Washington Naval Treaty 1922, which prohibited the establishment of new air bases in East Asia.

The Fung Keong Rubber Manufactory, a manufacturer of rubber shoes and rubber products located in Shau Kei Wan, was founded by Fung Keong (馮強); it was the largest rubber factory in Hong Kong before the Second World War.

01 Jan 1926

A large fire broke out at Hong Kong Hotel in Central, destroying HK$2.5 million worth of property and killing a navy sailor who was fighting the blaze.

01 Mar 1926

The Government Vernacular Middle School was founded, making it the first Chinese-language school founded by the Hong Kong government. It was renamed Clementi Middle School (present-day Clementi Secondary School) in 1951 to commemorate the active contribution of Governor Cecil Clementi in promoting Chinese-language education during his term of office.

08 Mar 1926

The junior secondary boys' section of Munsang College at the Kai Tak Bund was formally opened. The school was initiated by Ts'o Seen-wan (曹善允) and built with donations from Au Chak-mun (區澤民) and Mok Kon-sang (莫幹生). A kindergarten and primary school were added the following year.

Mar 1926

The Hong Kong government opened a Government Vernacular Normal School in Tai Po; it was the first teacher training school in the New Territories.

03 Apr 1926

Hong Kong government representatives travelled to Guangzhou where they joined the British Consul-General of Guangzhou in negotiation with representatives of the Guangzhou National Government over the issue of strikes. By 23 July, five meetings had been held without successful outcomes.

16 Apr 1926

Trade unions in various sectors of Hong Kong held a nine-day meeting in Guangzhou and resolved to set up the Hong Kong Federation of Unions in support of the Canton–Hong Kong Strike.

May 1926

Governor Cecil Clementi proposed that the New Territories Association of Agricultural, Industrial and Commercial Research be renamed as Heung Yee Kuk.

01 Jul 1926

The Hong Kong Observatory began broadcast of weather reports and forecasts on the 600-metre wavelength from the VPS channel of Cape D'Aguilar Wireless Station at noon and 8 p.m. daily, followed by a rebroadcast on the 2,800-metre wavelength at 1 p.m. and 9 p.m. everyday. Typhoon information was broadcast at noon and rebroadcast every two hours until early morning.

Figure 109
Chow Shou-son (周壽臣) was the first Chinese to become an Unofficial Member of the Executive Council. (Photo taken in 1937 and courtesy of Special Collections, The University of Hong Kong Libraries)

09 Jul 1926

To "…disarm anti-British sentiment in China and encourage local Chinese loyalty in Hong Kong," Governor Cecil Clementi appointed Chow Shou-son (周壽臣) as the first Chinese Unofficial Member of the Executive Council. (Figure 109)

19 Jul 1926

The Hong Kong Observatory recorded 534.1 millimetres of rainfall in a single day.

27 Aug 1926

The Wireless Telegraphy Ordinance 1926 was promulgated, requiring owners of radios and other wireless equipment to apply for a licence. Offenders were liable to a maximum fine of HK$1,000 or 12 months' imprisonment.

27 Sep 1926

A typhoon with the highest wind speed reaching 100 miles per hour hit Hong Kong, causing many ships to run aground. As of 30 September, the typhoon killed at least 36 people.

10 Oct 1926

The Canton–Hong Kong Strike Committee announced the lifting of the economic blockade on Hong Kong, ending the 16-month strike.

1926

The Central Fire Station in Central entered service upon completion.

The Garden Company Limited was founded by Cheung Tze-fong (張子芳) and his cousin Wong Wah-ngok (黃華岳) in Kowloon to produce biscuits and bread.

King's College, formerly the West Point Government School founded in 1857, was established at Mid-Levels.

The Hong Kong Society for the Protection of Children was established.

The Mahavira Hall and other buildings of the Tsing Shan Monastery in Tuen Mun were completed.

18 Feb 1927

Chinese writer Lu Xun (魯迅) visited Hong Kong for two days and was invited to deliver two speeches "Silent China" and "The Old Tune Has Come to an End" at the YMCA on Hong Kong Island.

Feb 1927

The Hong Kong Radio Society in conjunction with the government conducted a trial broadcast on the 355-metre wavelength (which has been in use by the government ever since).

10 Mar 1927

Royal Air Force Kai Tak, the first military airfield in Hong Kong, commenced operations. It was upgraded to a Station in 1930.

01 Apr 1927

The Factory (Accidents) Ordinance 1927 was promulgated, stipulating that the Governor had the power to appoint Inspectors of Factories to ensure factory safety and that the Governor-in-Council was authorised to formulate regulations to prevent factory accidents.

11 Apr 1927

The Nanking and Hankow Barracks, developed by the Department of Public Works in Sham Shui Po, were formally handed over to the British army. The barracks were used as prisoner-of-war camps during the Japanese occupation.

09 May 1927

The passenger steamer *Leung Kwong*, owned by Chiat Woo Company, was sailing from Hong Kong to Jiangmen in Guangdong when it collided with the passenger trawler *Moonshine* and sank in the waters of Kap Shui Mun. Some 126 people on board were rescued; 105 lost their lives.

27 May 1927

The government declared the Hong Kong Branch of the Chinese Seamen's Union as an illegal organisation in the *Gazette*.

May 1927

The Chung Hwa Book Company set up a branch in Hong Kong.

08 Jul 1927

The Illegal Strikes and Lock-outs Ordinance 1927 was promulgated, outlawing all strikes other than those involving labour disputes and prohibiting all Hong Kong trade unions from being affiliated with trade unions or organisations outside Hong Kong without the consent of the Governor-in-Council.

15 Sep 1927

The Legislative Council approved a HK$5 million government loan for public works programmes, such as water conservation projects, airport construction and port development.

Oct 1927

After the unsuccessful Nanchang Uprising, Chinese Communist leaders Zhou Enlai (周恩來), Ye Ting (葉挺) and Nie Rongzhen (聶榮臻) arrived in Hong Kong. While recuperating in a residence located on Canton Road in Yau Ma Tei, Zhou attended a meeting convened in Hong Kong by the Guangdong Provincial Committee of the Communist Party of China for planning the Guangzhou Uprising.

10 Dec 1927

The Joint Planning Sub-committee of the Chiefs of Staff Committee in Britain submitted its first *Defence of Hong Kong: Report of Joint Planning Sub-Committee*, stating that Hong Kong was a strategic location for the Royal Navy in Asia and should be defended at all costs. It recommended that a line of defence be established between the New Territories and Kowloon.

16 Dec 1927

The Hong Kong Police Reserve Ordinance 1927 was promulgated, re-establishing the Hong Kong Police Reserve as a standing disciplined force that supported the regular police force.

Figure 110
Ho Tung Gardens, including a Chinese-style mansion and a private garden, on Peak Road on Hong Kong Island. It was developed by and for Sir Robert Ho Tung（何東）in 1927 and was demolished in 2015. (Photo taken in 2011 and courtesy of HKSAR Government)

1927

The first Police Emergency Unit on Hong Kong Island was established to deal with both minor disturbances and serious crimes.

The main building of Robert Ho Tung's（何東）private villa, The Falls, located at 75 Peak Road, was completed. Ho Tung was the first non-European person allowed to live on the Peak since the Peak District Reservation Ordinance 1904 took effect. In 1938, the villa was renamed Hiu Kok Yuen, also known as Ho Tung Gardens. (Figure 110)

Yuen Hing Weaving & Dyeing Works was founded with a factory in Kowloon.

The University of Hong Kong set up a Chinese Department (present-day School of Chinese), making it the first tertiary institute in Hong Kong to promote Chinese-language education. Lai Tsi-hsi（賴際熙）was the first head of department.

The Hong Kong Journalism Studies Institute (Sun Mun Hok Se) was established to offer a two-year programme as the first educational organisation dedicated to journalism in Hong Kong; it was closed in 1931.

The Labour Advisory Board was founded as an advisory body on labour policies, comprising government officials, representatives from the British Armed Forces in Hong Kong and major employers.

09 Mar 1928

Governor Cecil Clementi visited Guangzhou for three days; he met with Chairman of Guangdong Province Li Jishen（李濟深）. It was the highest-level meeting between the Hong Kong government and the Guangzhou National Government of the Republic of China since the Canton–Hong Kong Strike.

Mar 1928

Chen Yu（陳郁）became Secretary of the Hong Kong Municipal Committee of the Communist Party of China and Chairman of the Chinese Seamen's Union.

Chinese Communist leader Zhou Enlai（周恩來）presided over the Enlarged Meeting of the Guangdong Provincial Committee in Hong Kong, which dealt with the aftermath of the Guangzhou Uprising. He also instructed the Committee to rescue Secretary Deng Zhongxia（鄧中夏）, who was arrested in Hong Kong.

01 Apr 1928

The Hong Kong Branch of China Travel Service was established, making it the first Chinese-owned travel agency in Hong Kong.

09 Apr 1928

Twenty-one Japanese warships, including the *Nagato*, *Mutsu* and *Fusō*, visited Hong Kong for six days.

30 Apr 1928

Businessman Lee Hy-san (利希慎) was shot dead on Wellington Street in Central; the murderer disappeared without a trace.

18 May 1928

Japanese shops in Wan Chai were vandalised with stones; fines were imposed on the culprits in a bid to contain the rise of anti-Japanese sentiment in the Chinese community following the Jinan Incident on 03 May.

20 Jun 1928

The Government Broadcasting Station began trial broadcast under the station code G.O.W., following the establishment of the Hongkong Radio Society in 1923. On 08 October 1929, G.O.W. was officially opened, becoming Hong Kong's first public broadcasting station.

15 Aug 1928

The semi-monthly *Companion* released its first issue as the first modern vernacular Chinese literary magazine in Hong Kong; it ceased publication less than a year later.

11 Dec 1928

The seven-storey Peninsula Hotel in Kowloon was opened to the public upon completion. It was the tallest building on the Kowloon peninsula until the 1950s. (Figure 111)

1928

A concrete slipway was built for seaplanes at the Kai Tak Airport.

The Hong Kong government leased the land behind the Hindu Temple in Happy Valley at a nominal rent to provide a burial ground for Indians in Hong Kong. It became the only Hindu cemetery in Hong Kong.

Geologist Charles Montague Heanley published the first report on archaeological excavations in Hong Kong in Volume 7 of the *Bulletin of the Geological Society of China*.

The Eastern Sports Club, formerly known as the China Building Football Team, was founded on Johnston Road in Wan Chai.

Chinese literary magazine *Le Péle-méle* was launched to publish literary works on subject matters related to Guangzhou and Hong Kong, as well as paintings, sketches, cartoons, photographs and other illustrations; it ceased publication in 1932.

Figure 111
Kowloon–Canton Railway's Tsim Sha Tsui Terminus and an adjacent Clock Tower; located to the right side was the seven-storey Peninsula Hotel. (Photo taken in the 1930s and courtesy of Hong Kong Museum of History)

01 Jan 1929

The Hong Kong Chinese Merchants' Guild Library was opened as the first modern library established by the Chinese community in Hong Kong,

16 Jan 1929

The China Merchants Steam Navigation Company's steamship *Hsin Wah* sank after hitting rocks near Waglan Island; over 400 people died.

11 Mar 1929

The King Edward Hotel caught fire and collapsed, resulting in 11 deaths and three injuries, including Chairman of the Guangdong Provincial Government Chen Mingshu (陳銘樞) and his wife.

04 Jun 1929

The Hong Kong government established a Wireless School; it was closed on 31 March 1930. On 02 January 1935, it was reopened and renamed Government Wireless Telegraph School.

29 Jun 1929

The newly built swimming shed under the South China Athletic Association at Tsat Tsz Mui in Eastern District on Hong Kong Island was opened; it was damaged in a typhoon the same year. It was rebuilt and reopened on 01 May 1930.

Jul 1929

Britain planned to offer Weihaiwei in Shangdong Province to the National Government of the Republic of China in exchange for a permanent lease on the New Territories. As the National Government remained firm in upholding China's territorial integrity, the plan was never proposed.

15 Sep 1929

Chinese magazine *Tie Ma* was founded for publication of fiction, prose, poetry, translated poems and other works. Due to poor sales and printing costs, only one issue of the magazine was published.

Sep 1929

Deng Xiaoping (鄧小平) visited Hong Kong early in the month and learnt about the situation in Guangxi from the Guangdong Provincial Committee of the Communist Party of China. Deng discussed with Nie Rongzhen (聶榮臻) and others on starting party works in Guangxi.

01 Nov 1929

The Female Domestic Service Amendment Ordinance 1929 was promulgated, stipulating that any *mui tsai* (young female bondservants) who had not been in Hong Kong previously or was not registered under the Ordinance should not be brought to Hong Kong.

The Industrial Employment of Women, Young Persons and Children Amendment Ordinance 1929 was promulgated, providing additional protection for women and people aged 15 to 18 under industrial employment. This was based on the protection of children provided by the Industrial Employment of Children Ordinance 1922.

27 Nov 1929

Tung Wah Eastern Hospital at Soo Kun Poo in Causeway Bay commenced operations with a full range of Western medical facilities for the public.

19 Dec 1929

Based on the Draft Code of Model Standing Orders for Colonial Legislatures promulgated by Britain in 1928, the Legislative Council of Hong Kong passed amendments to the Standing Orders to regulate the conduct of members in meetings, including: the relevancy of speeches to the subject of debate; the avoidance of preliminaries; the termination of debates; the right of the President of the Legislative Council to speak without interruption; and the withdrawal and suspension of members for gross disorderly conduct. The scope of the petition was extended to cover concerns outside of legislative jurisdiction, but the petition still required the Governor of Hong Kong's consent to be executed. The Standing Orders also abolished special committees, instead designating an ad hoc committee to see to matters assigned by the Legislative Council and to dissolve itself upon submitting the relevant report.

1929

The airport infrastructure of the Kai Tak Bund became operational upon completion for both military and civil purposes. In the same year, the Harbour Master was also made the Director of Air Services by the Hong Kong government.

Canossa Hospital was founded by the Canossian Daughters of Charity.

The Hong Kong government proposed a standard curriculum for Chinese primary and secondary schools, setting out the subjects to be taught in each grade with designated textbooks.

The Welfare League, a support organisation for mixed race people in need, was founded by several Eurasian families in Hong Kong; Robert Ho Tung (何東) was the founding president.

District Officer (North) John Alexander Fraser and 19 members of the Chinese gentry, including Chow Shou-son (周壽臣), Robert Kotewall, Fung Ping-shan (馮平山) and Tang Shiu-kin (鄧肇堅), erected a Memorial Archway inscribed with the Chinese characters "Heung Hoi Ming Shan" (Famous Mountain of Hong Kong) in front of the Tsing Shan Temple to commemorate the visit of Governor Cecil Clementi to Castle Peak.

Communist leader Zhou Enlai (周恩來) dispatched personnel to establish an underground radio substation in Hong Kong. In January 1930, the substation secured contacts with the Central Committee of the Communist Party of China and party organisations in southern China.

The Harbour Department and Directorate of Air Services were established to manage Kai Tak Airport. On 11 September the following year, Albert James Robert Moss became the first Superintendent of the Civil Aerodrome.

Businessman Ho Kam-tong (何甘棠) became the first Chinese owner of a racehorse that won the Hong Kong Derby.

Jan 1930

Deng Xiaoping (鄧小平) attended a discussion session organised by the Central Military Commission in Hong Kong concerning work arrangements for the Red Army in Guangxi. He also presented a supplementary report on the work in Guangxi and the preparations for the Baise Uprising and the Longzhou Uprising.

01 Feb 1930

The *South China Daily News*, which later became the official newspaper in Hong Kong under the regime of Wang Jingwei (汪精衞), was founded by Lin Bosheng (林柏生).

31 Mar 1930

The opening ceremony for the first submarine pipeline built under Victoria Harbour was held at Queen's Pier, marking the beginning of the water supply from reservoirs in Kowloon to Hong Kong Island.

01 Apr 1930

Literary magazine *On the Island* was launched to publish novels, prose, translated literature and other works; it ceased publication in 1931.

28 Apr 1930

A six-day international academic conference on the unification of meteorological signals in the Far East was held in Hong Kong.

09 May 1930

William Peel was sworn in as the 18th Governor of Hong Kong; he remained in office until 17 May 1935.

31 May 1930

The Joint Planning Sub-committee of the Chiefs of Staff Committee in Britain released the *Defence of Hong Kong: Report of Joint Planning Sub-Committee of 1930*, recommending that a range of concrete pillboxes be built from Sha Tin Hoi to Gin Drinkers Bay, known as the Gin Drinkers Line. In December 1935, the first pillbox was completed.

01 Aug 1930

Joseph Horsford Kemp was appointed as Chief Justice of Hong Kong.

11 Aug 1930

All scaffolding workers went on strike, demanding higher wages along with the abolition of the labour contract system, in addition to the provision of proper food and accommodation. On 21 August, following negotiation under the mediation of merchant Li Yau-tsun（李右泉）and Chairman of the Hong Kong Chinese Merchants' Guild Li Yick-mui （李亦梅）, a consensus was reached on the issues of wage increase and accommodation. The scaffolding workers resumed their work.

Oct 1930

The United Photoplay Service Company (later known as the Lianhua Film Production and Processing Company Limited) was established by film industry professionals, including Lo Ming-yau（羅明佑）, Lai Man-wai（黎民偉） and Lai Pak-hoi（黎北海）, in a bid to revive the Chinese film industry in Hong Kong.

05 Dec 1930

The District Watch Force Ordinance 1930 was promulgated, establishing the legal status of the District Watch Force.

1930

Kowloon Tong Garden City Estate was completed, making it the second estate of its kind in Hong Kong. (Figure 112)

The National City Bank of New York Building on Queen's Road Central was completed.

Amoy Canning of Xiamen opened a branch in Hong Kong with a factory located in Ngau Chi Wan for production of soya sauce and other sauces.

Hong Kong Brewers and Distillers Limited was founded by Parsi merchant Jehangir Hormusjee Ruttonjee; its plant at Sham Tseng in Tsuen Wan went into operation in 1933.

The Hong Kong Salvation Army was established. Its centre, initially on Prince Edward Road, provided shelter for homeless women and girls.

The Tao Fung Shan Christian Centre in Sha Tin was founded by Norwegian missionary Karl Ludvig Reichelt; its temple with Chinese architectural features was completed in September 1934.

The Yau Ma Tei (Yaumati) Theatre, the only existing pre-Second World War theatre in Hong Kong, was completed.

The Lo Family House, located at Shek Chung Au in Sha Tau Kok was developed by Lo Yick-fai（羅奕輝）. During the Japanese occupation, 11 Lo family members took part in guerrilla activities against the Japanese while the Lo Family House became an important base for the Hong Kong–Kowloon Independent Brigade.

01 Mar 1931

The Hong Kong Observatory expanded the scale of the Tropical Cyclone Warning Signal to Hurricane Signal No. 10, with Typhoon Signals 5 to 8 indicating wind direction. In 1973, Signals 5 to 8 were changed to No. 8 Northeast Gale or Storm Signal, No. 8 Southeast Gale or Storm Signal, No. 8 Southwest Gale or Storm Signal, and No. 8 Northwest Gale or Storm Signal. The other signals are still in use today.

Figure 112
The Garden City Estate in Kowloon Tong. (Photo taken in the 1930s and courtesy of Hong Kong Museum of History)

Figure 113
A Kowloon–Canton Railway train derailed at Ma Liu Shui (near present-day University Station) in the New Territories. (Photo taken in 1931 and courtesy of Hong Kong Museum of History)

19 Apr 1931

The first literati gathering of the Zheng Sheng Poetry Society, founded during the year by Zhang Qiuqin (張秋琴), Tan Liyuan (譚荔垣) and Zhang Yunfei (張雲飛), was held. In the following year, the society published the *Zheng sheng yin she shi zhong ji*, a poetry collection of classical Chinese poems.

20 Apr 1931

Heavy rainfall caused subsidence on parts of the Kowloon–Canton Railway track near Ma Liu Shui in the New Territories. When a Kowloon-bound train passed over it, the defective railway track collapsed, causing the derailment of the train's engine and four carriages, leaving 12 people dead and 32 injured. (Figure 113)

06 Jun 1931

Hồ Chí Minh, who founded the Communist Party of Vietnam in Hong Kong on 03 February 1930, was arrested and imprisoned at Victoria Prison. After several trials, he was expelled from Hong Kong in January 1933 and went to Xiamen.

10 Jun 1931

Secretary of the Guangdong Provincial Committee of the Communist Party of China Cai Hesen（蔡和森）was arrested by the Hong Kong police while attending a seamen's meeting in Hong Kong. He was handed over to Guangdong Provincial Government Chairman Chen Jitang（陳濟棠）and was executed.

01 Sep 1931

Long-distance telephone services were established between Hong Kong and Guangdong Province. The Governor of Hong Kong and the Chairman of Guangdong Province made their first call to each other.

23 Sep 1931

People from all walks of life in Hong Kong held rallies to commemorate their compatriots who died in northeast China during the 9.18 Incident (Mukden Incident or Manchurian Incident). Flags flew at half-mast in shops and associations. A Japanese businessman taunted the Chinese in front of the Yamakawa Store in Wan Chai and beat one of them to death, triggering a riot that lasted for several days and resulted in six deaths and 25 injuries.

16 Oct 1931

The Liquors Amendment Ordinance 1931 was promulgated; on 22 October, the Legislative Council decided to impose taxes on cosmetics and medicinal alcohol with an alcohol concentration of more than 10%.

Oct 1931

The China Zhi Gong Party, led by Chen Jiongming（陳炯明）and others, held its second congress in Hong Kong and moved its central party headquarters to Hong Kong.

10 Nov 1931

The Hong Kong Red Swastika Society was established as a religious charity to help refugees who had fled over the border into Hong Kong.

10 Dec 1931

The Hong Kong government announced the results of the last pre-Second World War census. As of 07 March 1931, excluding military personnel, Hong Kong had a population of 840,473, an increase by 34.43% from a population of 625,166 in the 1921 census.

1931

Brothers Kwok Lok（郭樂）and Kwok Chuen（郭泉）founded Wing On Commercial and Saving Bank Limited (later known as Wing On Bank), which was opened on 19 September 1934.

International Assurance Company (present-day AIA Group) from the US opened its Hong Kong branch on Queen's Road Central, engaging in life insurance businesses.

Hongkong Land completed the nine-storey Gloucester Hotel in Central on the site of Hong Kong Hotel's North Wing, which was damaged in a fire in 1926; it was the tallest building in Hong Kong at the time.

The New Territories Mining Co. Ltd. was granted a 50-year licence by the Hong Kong government and began operating the Ma On Shan Iron Mine in 1932. In its heyday, the mine's output accounted for half of Hong Kong's total production.

Shanghai's China Can Company opened a branch factory in Hong Kong to design and produce metal cans and boxes. It subsequently became the first factory in Hong Kong to manufacture metal toys.

Tung Wah Hospital, Kwong Wah Hospital and Tung Wah Eastern Hospital were amalgamated into the Tung Wah Group of Hospitals, managed by a single Board of Directors.

The Rotary Club of Hong Kong was established.

06 Jan 1932

La Salle College, located on Boundary Street in Kowloon, was opened.

10 Feb 1932

The Tung Wah Group of Hospitals held a fundraising rally to help victims of the January 28 Incident in Shanghai and remitted donations of HK$33,000 on 11 February.

12 Feb 1932

The Juvenile Offenders Ordinance 1932 was promulgated, establishing a Juvenile Court for the trial of offences committed by juveniles and children under the age of 16.

Feb 1932

A Hong Kong medical team of more than 20 people, including Sze Tsung-sing (施正信) and Fung Hing-yau (馮慶友), went to Shanghai on a mission to treat wounded soldiers of the 19th Route Army.

10 Mar 1932

The Hong Kong Nudist Society, founded by a Latvian, Herbert Edward Lanepart, was incorporated with 18 men and three women as members. In 1948, it was renamed the Hong Kong Sunbathing Society.

23 May 1932

The first Empire Products Fair was held at the Peninsula Hotel for two days, selling agricultural and industrial products from various British colonies and dominions.

27 Jun 1932

General Cai Tingkai (蔡廷鍇), Commander of the 19th Route Army who fought against the Japanese during the January 28 Incident, came to Hong Kong and received an enthusiastic welcome.

19 Aug 1932

The Factories and Workshops Ordinance 1932 was promulgated, consolidating previous ordinances relating to the employment of women, youths and children in the industrial sector and accidents in factories. The Ordinance authorised the Governor to appoint Protectors of Labour and enabled the Governor-in-Council to develop regulations for labour protection.

28 Oct 1932

The Empire Preference Ordinance 1932 was promulgated to facilitate the implementation of the Ottawa Agreement 1932. Hong Kong had to charge a duty equal to 20% of the total value of the motor vehicle if it was not manufactured within the Commonwealth.

04 Nov 1932

The Hong Kong Post Office launched an experimental airmail service in which mail was transported by air to Marseille in France and then forwarded by surface mail to London.

04 Dec 1932

The Yung Sheh Hiking Club was established by Ng Bar-ling (吳灞陵) as the first hiking organisation in Hong Kong.

14 Dec 1932

Fung Ping Shan Library was opened at The University of Hong Kong as the first university library dedicated exclusively to collecting Chinese classics. The library was established with a contribution of HK$150,000 from Hong Kong businessman Fung Ping-shan (馮平山).

18 Dec 1932

St. Teresa's Church in Kowloon Tong was officially opened with a consecration ceremony.

1932

Lee Kum Kee moved from Macao to Hong Kong where its office was established on Queen's Road Central as a brand of oyster sauce and shrimp paste.

The Hong Kong Jockey Club started organising its own sweepstakes. Combining horse races and raffles, sweepstakes were then highly popular but were discontinued in 1977.

Chinese businessman Aw Boon-haw (胡文虎) moved the head office of Eng Aun Tong from Singapore to Hong Kong and set up a pharmaceutical factory in Hong Kong.

Charles Montague Heanley and Joseph Lexden Shellshear delivered a paper titled *A Contribution to the Prehistory of Hong Kong and the New Territories* at a conference held in Hanoi, Vietnam. It was the first paper to describe the discovery of a quartz penannular workshop from the Spring and Autumn period at an archaeological site in So Kwun Wat, Tuen Mun.

13 Jan 1933

China Motor Bus and Kowloon Motor Bus were granted 15-year franchises for bus services on Hong Kong Island and in Kowloon and the New Territories, respectively, effective from 11 June 1934.

11 Feb 1933

Nobel Laureate in Literature and famous British playwright George Bernard Shaw visited Hong Kong; he gave a speech at The University of Hong Kong on 13 February.

25 Feb 1933

Wing Lung Ngan Ho, founded by Wu Yee-sun (伍宜孫) and Wu Jieh-yee (伍絜宜), was opened. In 1960, the bank was reorganised and became the Wing Lung Bank.

Feb 1933

The Junior Technical School (present-day Tang Shiu Kin Victoria Government Secondary School) was established, with an initial intake of 40 students. It was the first government school to provide full-time vocational training for young people aged 12 to 16.

03 Mar 1933

Hang Seng Ngan Ho, founded by Lam Bing-yim (林炳炎), Ho Sin-hang (何善衡), Leung Chik-wai (梁植偉) and Sheng Tsun-lin (盛春霖), was opened. It was reorganised into the Hang Seng Bank on 07 February 1960.

06 Mar 1933

Man Kung, Hongkong and Yaumati Ferry's car ferry, made its maiden voyage at 7:30 a.m., marking the beginning of cross-harbour vehicular ferry service in Hong Kong.

13 Apr 1933

The Places of Public Entertainment Regulation Ordinance 1919 were promulgated to censor films and posters.

Apr 1933

The Hong Kong Branch of the Kuomintang Central News Agency was established.

04 May 1933

The Hong Kong Playground Association was established with the aim of building and managing children's recreation facilities in Hong Kong; Colonial Secretary Wilfrid Thomas Southorn was the first president.

07 May 1933

The *Spring Thunder Semimonthly*, edited and published by the Hong Kong Association of Literary and Art Study, launched its first issue.

May 1933

Father Daniel Finn conducted archaeological excavations on Lamma Island and successively published 13 papers pertaining to the archaeological discoveries on Lamma Island in the *Hong Kong Naturalist* between May 1933 and December 1936.

10 Jun 1933

The residents of Kowloon Walled City were notified by the District Office (South) that they would be resettled by September and that Kau Shat Ling outside the city was designated for housing redevelopment. The residents sought help from the National Government of the Republic of China and the Guangdong Provincial Government on the grounds that Kowloon Walled City was under China's jurisdiction. The National Government tried to interfere through diplomatic channels, whereas Britain preferred avoiding any head-on confrontation with China.

22 Jun 1933

The Hong Kong Hockey Association was established.

20 Sep 1933

Hong Kong's first film with fully synchronised dialogue *The Idiot's Wedding Night*, directed by Lai Pak-hoi (黎北海), was released.

Sep 1933

Pui Ching Middle School, a private school from Guangzhou, opened a branch in Hong Kong, initially providing primary and the first year of secondary school education. In 1935, a secondary school section was added.

06 Oct 1933

The seven-storey Luk Kwok Hotel in Wan Chai was opened as the first hotel in Hong Kong with a Chinese restaurant.

10 Oct 1933

Hong Kong female swimmer Yeung Sau-king (楊秀瓊) won five champion titles in the Republic of China's Fifth National Games held in Nanjing.

25 Oct 1933

The Hong Kong government lifted the ban on male and female Cantonese opera singers appearing together in the same performance. From then on, female actresses were hired to play female roles, while male actors playing female roles were gradually phased out. Previously, Cantonese opera troupes in Hong Kong were divided into all-male or all-female troupes. The all-male casts were more popular, with male performers in the roles of females.

20 Nov 1933

The Juvenile Court, set up in accordance with the Juvenile Offenders Ordinance 1932, held its first court session at the Central Magistracy.

15 Dec 1933

The first issue of the monthly poetry and prose magazine *Red Beans* was published; it ceased publication on 16 August 1936.

1933

Singapore's Overseas-Chinese Banking Corporation Limited set up a branch on Queen's Road Central.

The Chung Hwa Department Store was opened on Queen's Road Central.

The Jubilee Street Pier in Central began providing passenger and vehicular ferry services; it was later renamed the United Pier.

06 Feb 1934

Return from the Battleground, Hong Kong's first anti-Japanese and patriotic film, was released.

23 Feb 1934

Atholl MacGregor was appointed as Chief Justice of Hong Kong.

26 Feb 1934

Tak Ming Secondary School, founded by Hu Hanmin (胡漢民) and Chen Jitang (陳濟棠), was inaugurated in an opening ceremony.

17 Mar 1934

South China Athletic Association's clubhouse at Caroline Hill was opened to the public upon completion.

14 May 1934

42 people were killed and 46 were injured when Gasholder No. 1 in Shek Tong Tsui exploded and caused a fire.

18 May 1934

Hong Kong female swimmer Yeung Sau-king (楊秀瓊) won four gold medals for China at the 10th Far Eastern Championship Games held in Manila.

03 Aug 1934

The Places of Public Entertainment Regulations 1934 was promulgated, allowing the Hong Kong government to exercise complete control over the registration, construction, safety and hygiene of places of entertainment.

04 Aug 1934

Hong Kong sent a lawn bowls delegation to participate in the Second British Empire Games (later known as the Commonwealth Games) in London, marking the first time that Hong Kong delegates participated in the Games.

10 Aug 1934

The Births and Deaths Registration Ordinance 1934 was promulgated, requiring all births and deaths in Hong Kong to be registered with the Hong Kong government within 14 days and 24 hours, respectively.

01 Sep 1934

The Chinese Manufacturers' Association of Hong Kong was established; Ip Lan-chuen (葉蘭泉) was the first president.

Sep 1934

Jin ryh shy ge (Poetry Today), a modern Chinese poetry magazine, published its first and only issue.

16 Oct 1934

The Hong Kong Badminton Association was established.

21 Nov 1934

St. John Hospital (Haw Par Hospital) on Cheung Chau, funded by Aw Boon-haw (胡文虎) and Ip Kwai-chung (葉貴松), commenced services upon completion; it was the first hospital on an outlying island.

1934

The Stonecutters Island Barracks was built.

Sheung Shui Revenue Station of the Hong Kong government went into operation; it was the first outstation of the Preventive Service.

1934

The first overseas branch of Beijing's Bank of Communications was set up in Hong Kong.

The Kitchee Sports Club was established on Johnston Road in Wan Chai; Yuen Yau-chun (阮有進) was the first president.

Shanghai's Tianyi Film Company set up a branch in Hong Kong, ushering the Shaw family's film-making business in Hong Kong. In 1937, it was renamed Nanyang Film Company.

02 Jan 1935

Hong Kong and Swatow Commercial Bank, predecessor of the Public Bank, was opened.

05 Jan 1935

Scholar Hu Shi (胡適) visited Hong Kong. On 06 January, he spoke at the Overseas Chinese Education Association, criticising the outdated Chinese education in Hong Kong; on 07 January, he received an honorary doctorate from The University of Hong Kong.

16 Feb 1935

The Commission Appointed by His Excellency the Governor of Hong Kong to Inquire into the Causes and Effects of the Present Trade Depression in Hong Kong released a report. It concluded that Hong Kong was not an independent economic entity and would be affected by the strengths and weaknesses of neighbouring regions. It was roughly estimated that four-fifths of transit goods in Hong Kong's foreign trade were re-exported from overseas or northern China to southern China, then re-shipped from Hong Kong to northern China or overseas.

01 Mar 1935

The Urban Council Ordinance 1935 was promulgated, reorganising the Sanitary Board into the Urban Council. On 01 January 1936, the Urban Council was established; William James Carrie was the first chairman.

12 Apr 1935

The Buildings Ordinance 1935 was promulgated, specifying the required length, height and thickness of building walls to improve lighting and ventilation.

17 May 1935

Tung Lin Kok Yuen in Happy Valley, funded by Robert Ho Tung's (何東) wife, Clara Ho Cheung Lin-kok (何張蓮覺), was opened, making it the first Buddhist monastery on Hong Kong Island.

27 May 1935

Edmund Burney (His Majesty's Inspector of Schools) published a report, suggesting that the bilingual curriculum in Chinese and English in government and subsidised schools in Hong Kong was ineffective. He recommended that schools should improve their English curriculum to meet future social development, while the Chinese curriculum should be reassessed.

07 Jun 1935

The Importation and Exportation Ordinance 1915 were promulgated. From midnight on 15 June, unless authorised by the Imports and Exports Office, export of silver coins minted in the Mainland or silver ingots (unless the ingots were made outside Hong Kong and the Mainland) was prohibited. On 09 November, the Governor-in-Council amended this regulation, stipulating that from noon on the same day all people, except the Colonial Treasurer and designated person, were prohibited from exporting British silver dollars, Mexican silver dollars, Hong Kong silver coins or silver ingots.

28 Jun 1935

The rebuilt headquarters of the Hong Kong Gold and Silver Exchange Society on Mercer Street in Sheung Wan was opened to the public.

Jun 1935

The University of Hong Kong held its first secondary school certificate examination; it was taken by 691 students of whom 243 passed.

01 Jul 1935

The Hong Kong government announced a total ban on prostitution with effect from midnight and ordered all brothels to close. The brothels in Shek Tong Tsui were closed overnight, although some brothels continued to operate under the name "tourist guide agencies."

02 Jul 1935

The Bank of East Asia opened its new building at 10 Des Voeux Road Central.

01 Sep 1935

Xu Dishan (許地山) was appointed as Head of The University of Hong Kong's Faculty of Arts. He devoted himself to teaching reforms, participating in social and cultural activities, and publishing literary works. He died of illness on 04 August 1941.

02 Sep 1935

Part of the Shing Mun Reservoir, of which construction began in 1932, was opened upon completion. It was renamed Jubilee Reservoir in celebration of the Silver Jubilee of King George V's accession to the throne. The main dam was completed on 30 January 1937 and was over 86 metres high; it was the first reservoir in the New Territories to supply water to Hong Kong Island.

04 Sep 1935

The Bank of Canton announced that it would stop payments pending restructuring, triggering a bank run. The nearby National Commercial & Savings Bank Limited also experienced a bank run and announced its closure on 16 September.

13 Sep 1935

The Deportation of Aliens Ordinance 1935 was promulgated, stipulating that the Governor-in-Council could, through summarily procedure, expel any foreigner who had been deported from the United Kingdom or any British possessions, or had been convicted of an offence in Hong Kong, or whose deportation was in the public interest of Hong Kong.

Sep 1935

The Hong Kong School for the Deaf (present-day Chun Tok School) was jointly established by British Anglican Church missionaries Beatrice Pope and Winifred Griffin and Canadian General Secretary of Hong Kong Young Women's Christian Association Nell E. Elliott; it was the first school for deaf children in Hong Kong.

10 Oct 1935

The third-generation HSBC building, located at 1 Queen's Road Central, was completed; the cornerstone was laid on 17 October 1934. (Figure 114)

19 Oct 1935

The Hong Kong Football Team, which included Lee Wai-tong (李惠堂), won the football final of the Sixth National Games of the Republic of China held in Shanghai, beating Guangdong 3–1.

09 Nov 1935

The Dollar Currency Notes Ordinance 1935 was promulgated, stipulating that the Colonial Treasurer had the right to issue HK$1 banknotes as legal tender. The Colonial Treasurer was also required to set up a note security fund as a reserve for the issuance of banknotes.

Figure 114
The third-generation HSBC building on Queen's Road Central in Central. (Photo taken circa 1945 and courtesy of Hong Kong Museum of History)

Nov 1935

The Hong Kong government agreed to the Proposal of Issuance of Permits for All Territories to Transport Foreign Munitions to China, formulated by the National Government of the Republic of China, allowing the importation of foreign arms with permits issued by the National Government.

10 Dec 1935

Confucius Hall Hong Kong, located on Caroline Hill Road in Causeway Bay, was opened to the public upon completion; it was one of the few Chinese assembly halls in the early days of Hong Kong.

12 Dec 1935

Andrew Caldecott took office as the 19th Governor of Hong Kong; he remained in office until 16 April 1937.

13 Dec 1935

The Currency Ordinance 1935 was promulgated, stipulating that only banknotes issued by Chartered Bank of India, Australia & China, HSBC and Mercantile Bank Limited were legal tender. The Exchange Fund was set up to replace silver with certificates of indebtedness as collateral for the issuance of notes and was responsible for the purchase and recovery of private silver dollars. By then, Hong Kong's currency had abandoned the silver standard and was pegged to the British pound at HK$16 to £1.

1935

The Chinese Manufacturers' Association of Hong Kong participated in the first Chinese Products Exhibition in Singapore to expand overseas markets.

Chong Ching-um (莊靜庵) and his wife established Chung Nam Watch Co., Limited as a manufacturer of wristbands for famous European and American watch brands.

The True Light Seminary in Guangzhou (founded by the Presbyterian Church of the United States) established a branch school called True Light Primary School at Mid-Levels in Hong Kong. In 1947, a secondary section was established, which was renamed the True Light Middle School of Hong Kong in 1948.

21 Jan 1936

The Hong Kong government announced the death of King George V after a long illness.

15 Feb 1936

The Chinese YMCA of Hong Kong held its first group wedding ceremony, officiated by Chow Shou-son (周壽臣) and attended by 11 couples, at its central clubhouse on Bridges Street.

Feb 1936

Kai Tak Airport opened a new hangar and office building.

24 Mar 1936

Dorado, a British Imperial Airways aircraft, arrived in Hong Kong from Penang and became the first civilian airliner to land at Kai Tak Airport using a civilian hangar.

07 Jun 1936

Zou Taofen (鄒韜奮) and Hu Yuzhi (胡愈之) established the newspaper *Life Daily News* in Hong Kong.

10 Jun 1936

The Hong Kong Eugenics League was established according to its charter; it was the predecessor of the Family Planning Association of Hong Kong.

21 Jul 1936

Haw Par Mansion, developed by businessman Aw Boon-haw (胡文虎) in Tai Hang, was inaugurated. The inauguration ceremony was attended by more than 1,000 guests from various political, economic and cultural circles, including Governor Andrew Caldecott. (Figure 115)

Figure 115
Haw Par Mansion located in Tai Hang on Hong Kong Island; adjacent was a private garden owned by businessman Aw Boon-haw (胡文虎); on the right was the seven-storey Tiger Pagoda. (Photo courtesy of Special Collections, The University of Hong Kong Libraries)

17 Aug 1936

The Hong Kong Observatory hoisted Hurricane Signal No. 10 amid a typhoon which caused 20 deaths, 179 injuries and financial losses of HK$10 million.

23 Oct 1936

Philippine Clipper, a seaplane of Pan American World Airways (Pan Am), landed at Kai Tak Airport after making its first flight across the Pacific Ocean.

04 Nov 1936

Chairman of the Guangdong Provincial Government Huang Musong (黃慕松) and Mayor of Guangzhou Special City Zeng Yangfu (曾養甫) arrived in Hong Kong for a three-day visit and were received by Governor Andrew Caldecott.

05 Nov 1936

The China National Aviation Corporation opened its business in Hong Kong, operating routes between Shanghai, Guangzhou and Hong Kong.

15 Nov 1936

The South China Film Association held a press conference to call on the National Government of the Republic of China to lift the ban on the production of films in dialects, actively initiating the Cantonese Film Salvation Movement.

Nov 1936

Diao Zuoqian (Philip K. C. Tyau) (刁作謙), Special Commissioner of the National Government of the Republic of China for Foreign Affairs in Kwangtung and Kwangsi, negotiated with the Hong Kong government over its forced eviction of residents from Kowloon Walled City in June 1933. The Hong Kong government insisted on relocating the residents and demolishing their dwellings.

12 Dec 1936

The Hong Kong government announced the abdication of King Edward VIII.

1936

General Officer Commanding British Troops in China Arthur Wollaston Bartholomew drew up the Hong Kong Defence Scheme 1936. Taking the Japanese forces as a hypothetical enemy, the defence scheme relied on the Gin Drinkers Line as the frontline to defend the Kowloon peninsula until the arrival of reinforcement and believed the Gin Drinkers Line could hold off the Japanese for 54 days.

Chiaphua Manufactory Company opened a branch in Hong Kong to produce and sell steel products and metal utensils; later, it also manufactured military supplies.

The Boys' & Girls' Clubs Association of Hong Kong was founded.

The Hong Kong Table Tennis Association was founded.

01 Jan 1937

The Presbyterian Church of the United States opened a primary section of the Hong Kong branch of Guangzhou's Pui Ying Secondary School on Bonham Road in Sai Ying Pun and a junior secondary section in autumn of the same year.

Jan 1937

Walter Schofield conducted a two-month field excavation at the Tung Wan site on Lantau Island and discovered tombs and human bones dating to the Shang Dynasty (approx. 1600 B.C. to 1046 B.C. or 3,500 years ago). World-renowned archaeologist Johan Gunnar Andersson came to Hong Kong to join the excavations.

01 Apr 1937

The second-generation Wanchai Market, in German Bauhaus style, was opened upon completion.

13 Apr 1937

Queen Mary Hospital was established and began admission of patients.

18 Apr 1937

Macao beat Hong Kong 2–1 in the first Hong Kong–Macao Interport Football Championship in Macao.

12 May 1937

Military troops review and carnival parade were held in Hong Kong to celebrate the coronation of King George VI.

17 May 1937

An explosion occurred on the *Dojima Maru*, a ferry owned by Osaka Shosen Kaisha (Osaka Mercantile Steamship Co., Ltd.), near Queen's Pier, causing 34 deaths and 20 injuries.

25 Jun 1937

The Currency Amendment Ordinance 1937 was promulgated, stipulating that before 01 August, all British silver dollars must be handed over to the Colonial Treasurer in exchange for the same face value of Hong Kong dollars. The section in the Currency Notes Ordinance 1935 that allowed anyone to apply for a licence to hold silver dollars was repealed.

26 Jun 1937

The Education Department held its first secondary school certificate examination. Of the 721 students who sat for the exam, 423 obtained the certificate.

29 Jun 1937

The Eurasia Aviation Corporation began operating a route between Hong Kong and Beijing.

15 Jul 1937

The Stanley Battery was completed.

16 Jul 1937

The Hong Kong government changed the title of Colonial Treasurer to Financial Secretary following the practice of the restructured British government. Sydney Caine was appointed as the first Financial Secretary.

20 Jul 1937

The Seamen's and Foreign Service Association changed its name to Sojourning Seamen's and Foreign Service Relief Association for Compatriots in the War Zone, combining the labour movement with anti-Japanese work.

22 Jul 1937

Hong Kong's first case of cholera was diagnosed, followed by an epidemic of the disease. A total of 1,690 people were infected with a death toll of 1,082 during the year.

31 Jul 1937

Major social groups, including the Hong Kong Chinese Merchants' Guild, Tung Wah Group of Hospitals and Chinese Manufacturers' Association of Hong Kong, organised a joint meeting to raise funds for war victims in northern China after the Marco Polo Bridge Incident.

15 Aug 1937

The Hong Kong Seamen's Union was founded, formerly known as the Chinese Seamen's Union. On 21 January 1938, it was closed by the Governor-in-Council in accordance with Section 16 of the Emergency Regulations Ordinance 1931; it was reinstated by the Hong Kong government on 06 January 1946.

17 Aug 1937

The Kowloon–Canton Railway was connected to the Canton–Hankow Railway, allowing trains departing from Tsim Sha Tsui to reach Hubei Province directly. These railways were important channels for the Mainland to obtain military supplies after the coastal areas of China fell to the Japanese milltary.

02 Sep 1937

A typhoon directly hit Hong Kong, resulting in a storm surge that flooded Tolo Harbour and inundated large areas of Sha Tin and Tai Po, causing about 11,000 deaths, the highest death toll ever recorded in Hong Kong. It became known as the Great Hong Kong Typhoon of 1937. (Figure 116)

A fire broke out on Connaught Road West in Sheung Wan, affecting buildings from numbers 131 to 137 and causing 41 deaths.

22 Sep 1937

The Legislative Council approved an appropriation of HK$50,000 for the establishment of the Air Raid Precautions Department, which was responsible for building air raid facilities and training air raid wardens.

Sep 1937

The Hong Kong branch of the National Salvation Bonds Advisory Committee was established to issue National Salvation Bonds in response to the appeal by the National Government of the Republic of China. Chow Shou-son (周 壽臣) served as Chairman; it raised HK$5.35 million by February 1938.

28 Oct 1937

Geoffrey Northcote was sworn in as the 20th Governor of Hong Kong; he left office on 06 September 1941.

26 Nov 1937

Yang Hucheng (楊虎城), one of the instigators of the Xi'an Incident, arrived in Hong Kong after visiting Europe. He gave a speech on the significance of uniting the whole nation to wage a war of resistance against the Japanese invaders.

Figure 116
A typhoon destroyed part of a rail in the Sha Tin section of Kowloon–Canton Railway. (Photo taken in 1937 and courtesy of Public Records Office, Government Records Service)

Nov 1937

The filming of the Cantonese-dialect anti-war film *Zuihou guantou* (The Last Stand), featuring actors from Hong Kong under the South China Film Industry Relief Association, was complete. The master film along with copies were donated to the Chinese Relief Association on 03 January 1938 for fundraising efforts nationwide. The South China Film Industry Relief Association, initiated by Lam Kwan-san (林坤山) and Kwong Shan-ha (鄺山夏) and comprising six film companies—Quan Qiu, Naam Yuet, Da Guan, Nan Yang, He Zhong and Qi Ming—aimed to support China with fundraising through anti-war and patriotic films.

01 Dec 1937

Pan American World Airways (Pan Am) launched a direct flight from Hong Kong to San Francisco.

09 Dec 1937

A large-scale blackout drill was held in the urban districts on Hong Kong Island and in Kowloon.

28 Dec 1937

Li & Fung Limited of Guangzhou established a branch in Hong Kong for businesses in the export trade. After the Japanese surrender in 1945, the company resumed its business in Hong Kong; its headquarters was relocated to Hong Kong the following year.

1937

Hong Kong's import and export trade volume began increasing from £66.9 million to reach £69.3 million in 1939; its volume of smuggled goods also increased from US$50 million before the outbreak of the Sino-Japanese War to reach a post-war level of US$80 million.

The pillboxes, observation post and command post at Shing Mun Redoubt were completed, forming a stronghold on the Gin Drinkers Line south of the Shing Mun Reservoir.

The Stanley Post Office commenced operations; it became the oldest post office in Hong Kong still in operation today.

Chaozhou businessman Ma Kam-chan (馬錦燦) founded Tai Sang Ngan Ho in Hong Kong; it became Tai Sang Bank in 1961.

Yin Chi-chung (C. C. Yin) (尹致中) founded Dah Chung Industrial Co., Limited, a manufacturer of steel needles and buttons; it was renamed Dah Chung Holding Limited in 1947.

Sam Yuk Secondary School, founded by the Seventh-day Adventist Church, was relocated from Guangzhou to Hong Kong. It was initially located in Sha Tin and was relocated to Clear Water Bay Road in 1939.

The Hong Kong Prison in Stanley was completed with a capacity of 1,559 inmates; it was then Hong Kong's most fortified prison.

The International News Service, founded by Hu Yuzhi (胡愈之) and Fan Changjiang (范長江), moved from Shanghai to Hong Kong. In 1938, it moved its headquarters to Guilin, Guangxi while the Hong Kong office became a branch.

Jan 1938

The office of the Eighth Route Army Hong Kong, officially known as the Yue Hwa Company, was set up at 18 Queen's Road Central; Liao Chengzhi (廖承志) served as Office Director.

03 Feb 1938

Japanese warships blocked the waters of Humen; all ships running between Guangdong and Hong Kong were suspended the following day.

04 Feb 1938

The four-day Exhibition of Chinese Products, co-organised by the Chinese Manufacturers' Association of Hong Kong and the Hong Kong Young Women's Christian Association, began at St. Paul's College in Mid Levels; it was the first Hong Kong Brands and Products Expo.

Feb 1938

From February to October, 130,000 tonnes of military supplies, including bombs, aircraft and aircraft parts, machine guns, detonators, safety fuses, TNT, anti-aircraft guns, field guns, torpedoes, searchlights and gas masks were transported via the Kowloon–Canton Railway from Hong Kong to major war zones in central, eastern coastal and southwestern China.

01 Mar 1938

Shen Bao (*Shun Pao*) (Shanghai News) was relocated from Shanghai to Hong Kong; it ceased publication on 31 July 1939.

18 Mar 1938

The Central Bank of China opened a correspondence office in Hong Kong. According to the Ministry of Finance of the National Government of the Republic of China, banks in China must apply to the head office or the Hong Kong office of the Central Bank of China to purchase foreign exchange.

22 Mar 1938

The Canton–Kowloon Highway between Guangdong and Hong Kong was opened. Kowloon Customs enacted regulations to set up the Man Kam To control point at the boundary between Hong Kong and Shenzhen to control the passage of vehicles.

27 Mar 1938

The Baptist Convention of Hong Kong was inaugurated at the Hong Kong Baptist Church on Caine Road, Central.

12 Apr 1938

The Government Trade School, predecessor of Hong Kong Polytechnic University, was inaugurated in Wan Chai. It was the first government-funded educational institution to provide post-secondary engineering education in Hong Kong; it was renamed the Hong Kong Technical College in 1947.

28 May 1938

Lai Chi Kok Hospital began accepting an overflow of pulmonary tuberculosis patients from the Tung Wah Group of Hospitals. The hospital, formerly known as Lai Chi Kok Prison, was rebuilt by the Hong Kong government and managed by the Tung Wah Group of Hospitals.

14 Jun 1938

Soong Ch'ing-ling (Song Qingling) (宋慶齡) founded the China Defence League in Hong Kong and became its Chairperson; Soong Tse-vung (Song Ziwen) (宋子文) served as its President. The League aimed to unite foreign friends and overseas Chinese who supported China's War of Resistance against Japanese Aggression. After the fall of Hong Kong in December 1941, the League was relocated to Chongqing.

13 Jul 1938

The Chinese Art Association and the Chinese Poetry Society co-organised the first symposium for poets in Hong Kong to develop Hong Kong into a frontline of anti-Japanese literature.

Jul 1938

The British Chiefs of Staff Committee decided to narrow the range of defence of the Hong Kong Garrison and changed its target to protecting Hong Kong Island and preventing Japanese forces from controlling the harbours.

01 Aug 1938

Aw Boon-haw (胡文虎) founded *Sing Tao Daily* and began to promote China's War of Resistance against Japanese Aggression. On 13 August, *Sing Tao Evening Post* started publication.

Figure 117
A confrontation between Japanese and British troops at Lo Wu Bridge. (Photo taken in late 1938 and courtesy of Public Records Office, Government Records Service)

10 Aug 1938

In response to donation activities commemorating the August 13 Incident held by the Hong Kong Relief Association for South China Refugees, the Hong Kong Chinese Merchants' Guild and 12 banks set up donation platforms and boxes. As of 19 August, more than HK$200,000 were raised for national salvation.

13 Aug 1938

The Hong Kong edition of the newspaper *Ta Kung Pao* was founded by Hu Zhengzhi（胡政之）; *Ta Kung Wan Pao*, the evening edition, started publication on 15 November.

29 Sep 1938

The Hong Kong Chinese Women's Club was founded to unite women in Hong Kong to participate in charity work for national salvation. Madame Lo Man-kam（羅文錦夫人）and Madame Li Shu-pui（李樹培夫人）served as President and Chairperson, respectively.

07 Oct 1938

The Governor-in-Council formulated 33 regulations for maintaining security and order in accordance with the Emergency Regulations Ordinance 1922. These included the regulation that without the permission of the local authorities, nobody could provide fuel or maintenance for Chinese or Japanese ships for either military or civil use so that Hong Kong could remain neutral during the Sino-Japanese War. (Figure 117)

11 Oct 1938

The Housing Commission published the *Report of the Housing Commission 1935*, pointing out that residential overcrowding in Hong Kong was the result of unaffordable rent prices. The Commission recommended that the Hong Kong government set up committees and departments for urban planning and housing to address these issues.

12 Oct 1938

In accordance with regulations formulated under the Emergency Regulations Ordinance 1922, the Hong Kong government set up camps for aliens—Chinese and Japanese soldiers and refugees with no regular work or place of residence in Hong Kong—so that they could be under centralised management. The move was intended to help manage the large numbers of refugees swarming into Hong Kong after the fall of Guangzhou.

28 Oct 1938

The Hong Kong government announced four refugee camps to be established in North Point, Ma Tau Chung, King's Park and Pat Heung for arriving refugees.

31 Oct 1938

The China State Bank Limited of Shanghai opened a branch in Hong Kong.

14 Nov 1938

Lingnan University in Guangzhou was relocated to Hong Kong and resumed classes in school buildings borrowed from The University of Hong Kong.

18 Nov 1938

The Hong Kong government appointed Henry Robert Butters as the first Labour Officer in charge of the new Labour Department under the Secretariat for Chinese Affairs. The Department was responsible for inspecting workplaces, improving labour laws and mediating labour disputes. In 1946, it became an independent department.

21 Nov 1938

Hon Wah College was founded by Cheng Hung-nien (Zheng Hongnian) (鄭洪年).

08 Dec 1938

South China Film Association for Supporting the War Refugees was founded to raise funds for refugees driven to Hong Kong by the Japanese invasion of China.

31 Dec 1938

On 29 December, Hong Kong's *South China Daily News* published a telegram from Wang Jingwei (汪精衞) to Chairman of the National Government of the Republic of China Chiang Kai-shek (蔣介石), in which he expressed support for a compromise with Japan. The next day, the Hong Kong press blasted Wang for his telegram.

Dec 1938

The Cape Collinson Battery in the east part of Hong Kong Island was completed.

1938

The Hong Kong government estimated a population of 1,028,600 in Hong Kong.

Smallpox broke out in Hong Kong, claiming 1,920 lives by 30 May.

The pillboxes in Wong Nai Chung Gap were completed.

The Chung Hom Kok Battery in the west of Stanley on Hong Kong Island was built.

The Eighth Route Army's Hong Kong Office commissioned Yang Lin (楊琳), also known as Qin Bangli (秦邦禮), to set up Liow & Co. on Connaught Road Central to procure military supplies. In 1948, Liow & Co. was restructured as China Resources Company.

Leung Kwai-yee (梁季彝) founded Kwong On Ngan Ho. In 1954, it was granted a banking licence and renamed Kwong On Bank.

Young Brothers Banking Corporation of Chongqing opened a branch in Hong Kong, engaging mainly in the remittance business.

1938

Three brothers Tse Yee-chee (謝汝池), Tse Lai-sang (謝麗生) and Tse Yee-hung (謝汝雄) founded Kwong Hing Tai Garments Factory, which grew into one of the largest garment factories in Hong Kong in the 1950s.

Pun Jong-sau (潘壯修) founded the Hing Wah Battery Factory in Hong Kong; it became a major battery manufacturer and created the Five Rams brand.

The Barwo Association for Cantonese opera artists in Guangzhou was relocated to Hong Kong; Sit Kok-sin (薛覺先) remained as President. It was the predecessor of the Barwo Artists Association of Hong Kong.

The Pooi To Girls' School, founded by the Women's Missionary Union of Southern Baptist Convention, was relocated from Zhaoqing in Guangdong to Kwong Wah Street in Mong Kok.

Chen Kung-che (陳公哲) carried out an eight-month archaeological investigation and excavation along the coast of Hong Kong. He unearthed pottery, jades, bronzes and bone tools, including the first jade *yazhang* blade ever found in a Chinese field excavation. He also discovered cliff carvings near Sha Kong Pui (present-day Shek Pik); Chen was the first Chinese scholar to engage in archaeological work in Hong Kong.

The Social Service Centre of the Churches was founded to provide services for residents. On 01 January 1949, it was transformed into an independent non-governmental family service for underprivileged families and was renamed the Hong Kong Family Welfare Society.

17 Jan 1939

Lam Pak-sang (林柏生), Editor-in-Chief of *South China Daily News* in Hong Kong, was seriously injured by two workers, who attacked him with a hammer and an iron rod on Des Voeux Road Central. In December 1938, Lam helped Wang Jingwei (汪精衛) released a telegraph that advocated peaceful negotiation with Japan.

21 Feb 1939

Japanese military aircraft bombed a train of the Kowloon–Canton Railway near Lo Wu in Hong Kong, killing at least 12 people and injuring 12.

25 Feb 1939

The Hong Kong Fukienese Association was founded; Aw Boon-haw (胡文虎) was its chairman.

10 Mar 1939

The Jubilee Battery in Mount Davis was completed.

26 Mar 1939

Members of the All China Literary and Artistic Circles' Association sojourning in Hong Kong held their first gathering and announced the establishment of a correspondence office, which was subsequently reorganised as the Hong Kong Branch of the Association, an important literary organisation gathering men of letters arriving in Hong Kong from the north.

11 Apr 1939

The *Report on Labour and Labour Conditions in Hong Kong* (Butters Report) was released by Labour Officer Henry Robert Butters. It reviewed the labour conditions in Hong Kong and put forward suggestions for improvement.

23 Apr 1939

The Institute of Journalism was founded and inaugurated in Hong Kong.

01 May 1939

Sing Pao Daily News was founded; its forerunner was the semi-weekly *Sing Pao Newspaper*, founded on 05 August 1938.

03 May 1939

The new Central Market was opened upon completion.

31 May 1939

The Hong Kong Branch of the Sino-British Cultural Association was founded; Xu Dishan (許地山) and Robert Kotewall served as Chairman and Vice-Chairman, respectively.

06 Jun 1939

The *National Times* (Guo min ri bao), Kuomintang's official newspaper in Hong Kong, began publication. It was renamed *Hong Kong Times* on 04 August 1949 and ceased publication on 17 February 1993.

23 Jun 1939

The Town Planning Ordinance 1939 was promulgated, authorising the Governor-in-Council, as advised by the Town Planning Board, to systematically prepare and review plans for the development of existing or potential urban areas and to improve the overall welfare of Hong Kong. On 30 June, the Town Planning Board was set up and put in charge of urban planning.

28 Jul 1939

The Compulsory Service Ordinance 1939 was promulgated, requiring all British males aged between 18 and 55 residing in Hong Kong to serve in the local defence reserve. Most of the conscripts were enlisted in the Hong Kong Volunteer Defence Corps or the Hong Kong Royal Naval Volunteer Reserve.

Jul 1939

The Chinese Kuomintang General Branch in Hong Kong and Macao was established; Central Executive Committee member Wu Tiecheng (吳鐵城) was Chairman. Four branches were subsequently and successively founded in Hong Kong, Kowloon, Macao and Guangzhou Bay.

06 Aug 1939

The English publication *Chinese Writers* was co-founded by the Hong Kong Branch and Chongqing Headquarters of the All-China Resistance Association of Writers and Artists in a bid to introduce Chinese literary works to foreign countries.

23 Aug 1939

The Hong Kong government demolished the Kowloon–Canton Railway bridge across the boundary at the Shenzhen River to prevent the Japanese army from invading Hong Kong.

24 Aug 1939

The Royal Navy blocked the waters of Lei Yue Mun in the east of Victoria Harbour and placed obstacles to fend off Japanese warships.

25 Aug 1939

The Hong Kong government began persuading foreign women and children to leave Hong Kong, triggering a rush of bank withdrawals and a currency exchange boom. On 28 August, the rush of withdrawals began to gradually subside.

26 Aug 1939

With the authorisation of the British government under the Emergency Powers (Colonial Defence) Order in Council 1939, the Hong Kong government promulgated the Defence Regulations 1939, giving itself the authority to examine all telegrams, letters, newspapers and other publications. On 04 September, the Hong Kong government revised the Regulations, enabling the requisition of any assets, including ships and aircraft.

03 Sep 1939

The Hong Kong government announced that Britain has declared war on Germany, ordered German nationals living in Hong Kong be detained at La Salle College and seized German assets in Hong Kong.

08 Sep 1939

The Defence (Finance) Regulations 1939 was promulgated, prohibiting the trading of foreign currency and gold, as well as the export of foreign currency, gold and securities, except for legal tender and banknotes issued by designated banks in Hong Kong.

Sep 1939

The Teachers Training College was established in the temporary premises on Hospital Road in Sai Ying Pun as the first full-time teacher training institution in Hong Kong, On 23 April 1941, permanent school buildings on Bonham Road were inaugurated; it was renamed Northcote Training College.

23 Nov 1939

The Hong Kong Observatory hoisted Increasing Gale or Storm Signal No. 9 amid a typhoon; it marked the rearmost typhoon signal hoisted in a calendar year.

03 Dec 1939

A fire broke out in a building at 480 Shanghai Street in Mong Kok; it spread to two nearby buildings, causing 46 deaths and 11 injuries.

1939

Informal census results showed a Hong Kong population of 1.8 million, including 1.05 million permanent residents and 750,000 refugees.

A Chinese merchant association was formed by Jiangsu, Zhejiang and Shanghai residents living in Hong Kong; in 1946, it was renamed the Kiangsu and Chekiang Residents (H.K.) Association.

Chow Tai Fook Jewellery of Guangdong opened a first branch on Queen's Road Central in Hong Kong.

The Grant Schools Council, with a membership of 22 secondary schools, was founded to promote cooperation and policymaking with the Education Department. It was the earliest professional association of schools in Hong Kong.

The Hong Kong Branch of the All-China Resistance Association of Writers and Artists called on writers of newspaper articles to donate their royalties in commemoration of the Marco Polo Bridge Incident of 1937; many did so in support of China's War of Resistance against Japanese Aggression.

03 Feb 1940

A fire broke out at Shek Kip Mei Village in Sham Shui Po, destroying over 700 houses destroyed and displacing some 5,000 residents.

22 Feb 1940

The Chinese Culture Association began a five-day Guangdong Heritage Exhibition at The University of HongKong's Fung Ping Shan Library, putting on display more than 5,000 cultural artefacts (paintings, handwritings and inscriptions of different historical periods) from Guangdong. Huang Bore (Huang Banruo) (黃般若), Executive Committee Member and Chief of General Affairs, loaned out his collection. Together with Ye Gongchuo (葉恭綽), Jian Youwen (簡又文), Huang Cibo (黃慈博), Xu Dishan (許地山) and Li Jingkang (K. H. Li) (李景康), he compiled the *Guangdong Heritage* following the exhibition.

26 Feb 1940

CLP Power's Hok Un (also called Hok Yuen) Power Station, located in Hung Hom, was inaugurated.

04 Mar 1940

The areas of Kowloon and the City of Victoria were hit by a hailstorm, breaking more than 1,000 glass windows; it was the first hailstorm on record under the Hong Kong Observatory.

05 Mar 1940

Cai Yuanpei (蔡元培), President of Academia Sinica and former President of Peking University, passed away in Hong Kong and was buried on 10 March at the Aberdeen Chinese Permanent Cemetery. On 25 March, The University of Hong Kong held a memorial.

06 Mar 1940

Hong Kong Soya Bean Products Co., Limited was founded by Lo Kwee-seong (羅桂祥) as a manufacturer of soya milk drinks under the brand Vitasoy with a factory in Causeway Bay.

26 Apr 1940

The Summary Offences Amendment Ordinance 1940 was promulgated, prohibiting spitting in public places and on public transport.

01 Jun 1940

The Hong Kong government summoned a volunteer force formed by dozens of foreign veterans to prevent enemy sabotage in Hong Kong. The force, known as the Hughesliers, was led by Lieutenant Colonel Arthur William Hughes, who was General Manager of Hong Kong-based Union Insurance Society of Canton.

11 Jun 1940

The Hong Kong government announced that Italy had declared war on Britain; it proceeded to arrest Italian nationals and seize Italian assets in Hong Kong and put the Italian consulate, churches and schools under surveillance.

26 Jun 1940

The British army blew up two bridges of the Shenzhen River at the boundary between Guangdong and Hong Kong, defending Hong Kong against Japanese troops assembled in Shenzhen. (Figure 118)

01 Jul 1940

The Hong Kong government began to evacuate British women and children from Hong Kong, arranging for the first group of 1,640 women and children to leave Hong Kong for Australia via Manila.

Figure 118
The Japanese army's blockade of Hong Kong and prohibition of train traffic. (Photo taken in August 1940 and courtesy of adoc-photos/Corbis via Getty Images)

19 Jul 1940

Britain's Chiefs of Staff Committee submitted *The Situation in the Far East in the Event of Japanese Intervention Against Us*, pointing out that Hong Kong was "not a vital interest [of Great Britain] and the garrison could not long withstand Japanese attack…Militarily our position in the Far East would be stronger without this unsatisfactory commitment," but also reiterating that Britain should not give up Hong Kong immediately to avoid "an incalculable loss of prestige."

05 Aug 1940

A landslide at the Tai Po Tunnel of the Kowloon–Canton Railway resulted in over 20 deaths and more than 10 injuries.

01 Sep 1940

Writer Xiao Hong (蕭紅) began serialising her novel *Hulan he zhuan (Tales of Hulan River)* in a supplement to *Sing Tao Daily*; it was completed on 27 December.

16 Sep 1940

Wen yi qing nian (Literary and Artistic Youth) started publication to serve the anti-Japanese cause. Its content included literary and artistic works, translations, reviews, and news of events and activities; it ceased publication in September 1942.

09 Oct 1940

Brothers Aw Boon-haw (胡文虎) and Aw Boon-par (胡文豹) opened the Tiger Balm Garden, located beside Haw Par Mansion, for public access.

29 Nov 1940

The Immigration Control Ordinance 1940 was promulgated, requiring that foreigners carry a passport issued by their government or an immigration certificate issued by the Hong Kong government to settle in (or transit through) Hong Kong. Hong Kong residents must carry a pass issued by the Hong Kong government to enter Hong Kong. The measures came into effect on 15 January 1941.

1940

A cholera epidemic broke out again in Hong Kong, causing 543 deaths in 815 confirmed cases by the end of September, representing a mortality rate of 66.6%.

The first vehicular bridge in Hong Kong was completed on Bowen Road at Mid-Levels.

07 Jan 1941

British Prime Minister Winston Churchill denied reinforcement in Hong Kong requested by Air Chief Marshall Robert Brooke-Popham, Commander-in-Chief of the Far East Command, reasserting that "we must avoid frittering away our troops on untenable positions."

14 Feb 1941

The Essential Commodities Board was formed to manage the supply of daily necessities, including food. On 21 February, the Food and Firewood Control Board was set up to manage the supply of food and firewood.

15 Mar 1941

The Japanese army in Sha Tau Kok tightly blockaded the border between Guangdong and Hong Kong with sandbags and electrified wire fences, completely cutting off travel lines for travelling merchants.

19 Mar 1941

The Chinese Maritime Trust (1941) Limited was incorporated by Tung Chao-yung (C. Y. Tung) (董浩雲) to conduct shipping businesses in the coastal areas of China and Southeast Asia.

08 Apr 1941

China Commercial Daily, a Chinese newspaper issued by the Communist Party of China, began publication; it was suspended on 30 November due to the outbreak of the Pacific War.

14 Apr 1941

The Japanese army in Guangzhou blocked the Pearl River on 09 April, cutting off traffic between Guangdong and Hong Kong.

03 May 1941

Huang Yanpei (黃炎培), Standing Director and Secretary General of the National Government of the Republic of China's War Bond Subscription Committee, arrived in Hong Kong from Chongqing to call on Hong Kong people to buy Chinese war bonds.

17 May 1941

Writer Mao Dun (茅 盾) serialised his novel *Putrefaction* in *Popular Life*, a Chinese publication that resumed operations in Hong Kong. The serialisation was completed in September.

23 May 1941

The Government Rice Monopoly Board was set up for a stable supply of rice in Hong Kong.

19 Jun 1941

The Tsuen Wan Chinese Permanent Cemetery was opened upon completion.

20 Jun 1941

John Alexander Fraser assumed office as the first Defence Secretary.

Jun 1941

The first issue of *Literary Times* was published under the editorship of Duanmu Hongliang (端 木 蕻 良) and authorship of Dai Wangshu (戴望舒).

01 Jul 1941

The China Defence League held the inaugural ceremony of the One Bowl of Rice initiative to raise funds for the Chinese Industrial Co-operatives to support China's anti-Japanese war and provide relief for refugees. A total of HK$25,000 was raised in the month of August.

26 Jul 1941

An order was promulgated to freeze the assets in Hong Kong owned by all persons from Japan and Japanese-occupied areas.

11 Aug 1941

The Hong Kong government set up a committee under the chairmanship of Puisne Judge Paul Cressall to investigate allegations of corruption in the procurement of construction materials and military supplies by the Air Raid Precautions Department.

13 Aug 1941

Overseas Chinese in Hong Kong organised fund-raising and charity sale activities at the Astor Theatre in commemoration of the fourth anniversary of the Battle of Shanghai (8.13 Incident).

10 Sep 1941

Sir Mark Young became the 21st Governor of Hong Kong. After the fall of Hong Kong, Young was captured and imprisoned. Following the Japanese surrender, Young was released and resumed his role as Governor.

12 Sep 1941

Wu Chongqing (Foggy Chungking), a play by Song Zhidi (宋之的), was performed in Hong Kong for two days in a row and caused a sensation.

18 Sep 1941

Overseas Chinese delegations in Hong Kong held an extended commemoration and the one-dollar aircraft donation campaign to mark the 10th anniversary of the 9.18 Incident.

The Chinese newspaper *Kwong Min Pao* was founded in Hong Kong by the China Democratic Political League (predecessor of the China Democratic League). On 10 October, the newspaper published the League's founding declaration and vision on China's current affairs; it ceased publication on 14 December.

24 Oct 1941

The Special Branch of the Hong Kong Police Force in a discussion with Director of the Eighth Route Army's Office in Hong Kong Liao Chengzhi (廖承志) suggested an offer of munitions and radio equipment in exchange for deployment of Chinese communist guerrillas to destroy the Japanese military airfield on Hainan Island. Liao sent a telegram to the Party Central Committee for instructions on the plan, which was approved by Mao Zedong (毛澤東) on 26 October but was never realised.

31 Oct 1941

The Hong Kong government established a commission to investigate corruption in the Civil Service.

03 Nov 1941

The Hong Kong Chinese Regiment was formed, and the first batch of 50 Chinese non-commissioned officers were recruited at the Wellington Barracks; this was the first Hong Kong Chinese infantry troop.

06 Nov 1941

The Army Division of Japanese Imperial General Headquarters drew up the Operational Outline for the Occupation of Hong Kong and the Central Agreement between the Army and the Navy on the Operation of Hong Kong. The plan aimed to achieve a quick and direct occupation of the Kowloon peninsula and Hong Kong Island by coordinating army and navy personnel and rapid seizure of air control over Hong Kong.

13 Nov 1941

At the close of the Legislative Council meeting, Governor Mark Young adjourned the session for an indefinite period.

16 Nov 1941

Canadian troops, comprising the Winnipeg Grenadiers and the Royal Rifles of Canada, arrived in Hong Kong to reinforce the defence.

30 Nov 1941

The Commander of the Japanese 23rd Army Lieutenant General Sakai Takashi issued a battle order aiming to capture Hong Kong.

06 Dec 1941

British troops received confirmation that three divisions of the Japanese army were within 13 kilometres of the border.

07 Dec 1941

The Pacific War broke out. Governor Mark Young ordered all officers and men of the regular forces and the Volunteer Defence Corps to report for duty immediately. On the same day, the *Gazette* published a supplement declaring a state of emergency in Hong Kong.

Figure 119
The Japanese army landed at North Point. (Photo taken in 1941 and courtesy of Apic/Hulton Archive via Getty Images)

08 Dec 1941

At 8 a.m., the Japanese army launched an attack on Hong Kong by sending 36 warplanes to bombard Kai Tak Airport, destroying 12 aircraft at the airport and paralysing British air capabilities. At the same time, the Japanese army crossed the border via a pontoon bridge set up in haste over the Shenzhen River. The main force broke through the border at noon. After entering Hong Kong, the Japanese army marched southward in two columns: east and west.

The Third and Fifth Brigades of the Guangdong People's Anti-Japanese Guerrilla Force sent several teams to the New Territories to carry out guerrilla warfare behind enemy lines.

09 Dec 1941

The 38th Division of the Japanese army attacked the Gin Drinkers Line at night and captured the Shing Mun Redoubt. The following day, British troops retreated to Golden Hill (Kam Shan) in Sha Tin.

The Japanese 23rd Army Command formulated the Guidance Plans for Military Rule in Hong Kong Island and Kowloon, which outlined plans for the occupation of Hong Kong, including reducing the general population and running operations with the Japanese military yen.

11 Dec 1941

The Gin Drinkers Line was lost, and the British troops retreated to Kowloon. At noon, Commander of British Forces in Hong Kong Major General Christopher Michael Maltby ordered the troops to abandon Kowloon and retreat to Hong Kong Island.

12 Dec 1941

The remnants of the British troops retreating from the Gin Drinkers Line withdrew from Sam Ka Tsuen in Lei Yue Mun to Hong Kong Island by boat. The Japanese army began occupying Kowloon.

13 Dec 1941

Governor Mark Young refused Japanese army's demands to surrender.

14 Dec 1941

The Japanese army began to shell the British positions on Hong Kong Island. On that night, the Royal Navy destroyer *Thracian* launched a raid and sank two Japanese ships berthed in Victoria Harbour.

16 Dec 1941

The Japanese army launched a massive air attack on Hong Kong Island, dropping 114 bombs on the British positions in Lei Yue Mun and Mount Davis.

18 Dec 1941

The Japanese army began to land at North Point, Tai Koo and Aldrich Bay in the east of Hong Kong Island at night and repelled a counterattack by British troops. (Figure 119)

19 Dec 1941

The Japanese army advanced into Wong Nai Chung Gap while moving south along the Sir Cecil's Ride trail and fought a fierce battle with British troops. (Figure 120)

21 Dec 1941

From 19 December to this day, the Japanese army repelled three counterattacks by British troops in Wong Nai Chung Gap and seized the high ground of Hong Kong Island. More than 800 Japanese soldiers were wounded or killed, and 461 British soldiers lost their lives. Canadian Army Brigadier John Kelburne Lawson, Commander of the West Brigade, was also killed during the battle.

22 Dec 1941

The Japanese army attacked Mount Cameron at night and advanced to Repulse Bay. In the meantime, they massacred over 50 British prisoners of war near Eucliffe at Repulse Bay.

23 Dec 1941

In the early morning, the Japanese army successively took possession of the Repulse Bay Hotel and Mount Cameron, and the British counterattack on Mount Cameron failed. In the morning, the Japanese army continued to attack Stanley Peninsula and advanced towards Aberdeen, while marching upon Wan Chai at the same time.

24 Dec 1941

At 5 p.m., the British position at Leighton Hill fell.

The Japanese 23rd Army formulated the Implementation Guidelines for the Evacuation of the Population in Hong Kong and Kowloon Regions for evacuating the so-called "lower class" and "vagrants" immediately after taking over Hong Kong but retained those whose jobs were related to military functions, such as factory workers, shipbuilders and farmers.

25 Dec 1941

In the early morning, the Japanese army captured St. Stephen's College in Stanley, which was being made as a temporary hospital, slaughtering about 70 wounded British soldiers and raping and killing the medical staff. This was known as the St. Stephen's College Massacre.

In the afternoon, the Japanese army captured Wan Chai. At dusk, Governor Mark Young and Commander of British Forces in Hong Kong Major General Christopher Michael Maltby went to the Peninsula Hotel in Tsim Sha Tsui. On behalf of Britain, Young signed an armistice agreement with Commander of the Japanese 23rd Army Lieutenant General Sakai Takashi, formally surrendering to the Japanese army. (Figures 121, 122 and 123)

Military representatives of the National Government of the Republic of China in Hong Kong, including Chan Chak (陳策), together with 70 British officers and soldiers, breached the Japanese naval siege and escaped from Hong Kong on five British torpedo boats.

26 Dec 1941

In the early morning, British troops in Stanley ceased fire and surrendered, marking the formal end to the Battle of Hong Kong, in which 1,679 defenders were killed and 10,818 were captured; 692 Japanese soldiers were killed.

The Japanese army abolished the Combat Command at the Peninsula Hotel in Tsim Sha Tsui and established the Military Administration Board (Gunseichō). On 30 December, the Military Administration Board issued the Provisional Rules for the Conduct of Business of the Military Administration Board of Hong Kong, according to which Lieutenant General Sakai Takashi and Vice Admiral Niimi Masaichi would jointly serve as Chief Officers of the Military Administration Board.

28 Dec 1941

The Japanese army ceremonially entered Hong Kong by holding a victory parade along Nathan Road in Kowloon and Hennessy Road on Hong Kong Island.

Figure 120
A Japanese bombardment on the Peak of Hong Kong Island. (Photo taken on 19 December 1941 and courtesy of National Diet Library)

Figure 121
Japanese bombers on a flight to Hong Kong. (Photo taken on 25 December 1941 and courtesy of National Diet Library)

Figure 122
The Japanese army marched into the urban centre of Hong Kong on 25 December 1941. (Photo courtesy of National Diet Library)

Figure 123
Governor Mark Young signed an armistice agreement at the Peninsula Hotel in a formal surrender of Hong Kong to the Japanese army. Sitting second from right in the back row was Japanese commander Sakai Takashi; on his right was Commander of British Forces in Hong Kong Christopher Michael Maltby. Governor Mark Young, not pictured, was seated at the far left. (Photo courtesy of Peter Horree/Alamy Stock Photo)

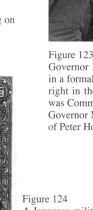

Figure 124
A Japanese military note with a face value of 100 yen—issued without serial numbers and non-convertible for Japanese yen. (Image courtesy of Hong Kong Museum of History)

29 Dec 1941

The Military Administration Board promulgated the Outline of the Public Policy of the Exchange Market, stipulating an exchange rate of one military yen for two Hong Kong dollars available at the military yen exchange office with a daily limit of 10 Hong Kong dollars for each person. The following day, the Military Administration Board announced that Hong Kong currencies worth less than ten dollars at par value could continue to circulate. On 31 December 1941 and 05 January 1942, the Military Administration Board set up a military yen exchange office in Kowloon and another on Hong Kong Island, respectively. (Figure 124)

1941

The Hong Kong government estimated a population of 1,640,000 in Hong Kong, including about 750,000 refugees.

During the year, 80 films were produced in Hong Kong, including 13 patriotic films, such as the Mandarin film *Glorious Future* (Ten Thousand Li Ahead) written and directed by Cai Chusheng（蔡楚生）and produced by the San Sang Film Company.

In light of the tensions in the Asia-Pacific region, the Hong Kong government decided to add four member seats in the Executive Council, which were filled by Commander of the Royal Navy in Hong Kong Alfred Creighton Collinson, Vice-Chancellor of The University of Hong Kong Duncan John Sloss, Defence Secretary John Alexander Fraser and Director of The Hongkong and Shanghai Banking Corporation Stanley Hudson Dodwell.

The Bokhara Battery, located at Cape D'Aguilar in the southeast corner of Hong Kong Island, was completed.

03 Jan 1942

The Military Administration Board formulated the Outline for an Emergency Response to Economic Recovery in Hong Kong and Kowloon and the Outline for a Financial Emergency Response in Hong Kong and Kowloon. The former proposed restoring the naval and army facilities in Hong Kong, making military yen the basic currency, and prohibiting the circulation of Hong Kong dollars. The latter suggested seizing assets of banks and financial institutions belonging to "enemy states" and maintaining the circulation value of the military yen.

06 Jan 1942

The Military Administration Board started implementing its repatriation policy to evacuate the population in Hong Kong. Later, the occupation government set up the Department of Repatriation Affairs to handle related matters. Most of the Chinese in Hong Kong were forced to return to the Mainland on foot or by sea. By the end of 1943, a total of 993,326 people had been forced out of Hong Kong.

09 Jan 1942

Arranged by Liu Shaowen（劉少文）and Pan Jing'an（潘靜安）of the Eighth Route Army's Office in Hong Kong, intellectuals including He Xiangning（何香凝）, Liu Yazi（柳亞子）, Zou Taofen（鄒韜奮）and Mao Dun（茅盾）were evacuated from Hong Kong with support from the Guangdong People's Anti-Japanese Guerrilla Force. By May, an estimated 800 people had been evacuated during the Great Secret Rescue.

Lieutenant Colonel Lindsay Tasman Ride of the Hong Kong Volunteer Defence Corps, together with Lance Corporal Francis Lee Yiu-piu（李耀標）, as well as Lieutenant Denys Warwick Morley and Sub-Lieutenant David Davis of the Hong Kong Royal Naval Volunteer Reserve, escaped from the prisoner of war camp in Sham Shui Po and left Hong Kong with the help of the Guangdong People's Anti-Japanese Guerrilla Force. In May, Ride set up the British Army Aid Group in Qujiang, Guangdong, to help the Allied forces collect military intelligence and rescue British soldiers and civilians detained in Hong Kong concentration camps.

10 Jan 1942

The Military Administration Board summoned 158 influential Hong Kong people and appointed nine as members of the Rehabilitation Advisory Committee. These included Robert Kotewall, Chow Shou-son（周壽臣）, Lo Man-kam（羅文錦）and William Ngartse Thomas Tam（譚雅士）. The committee was set up on 12 January and was dissolved on 20 February.

19 Jan 1942

The Japanese army announced the formation of the Governor's Office of the Captured Territory of Hong Kong in place of the Military Administration Board. The handover began on 20 February, changing military rule to civilian governance.

21 Jan 1942

The Military Administration Board announced the implementation of a district system, under which Hong Kong and Kowloon were divided into several districts with a district office and a Chinese chief each.

22 Jan 1942

Writer Xiao Hong（蕭紅）died of an illness at a temporary ambulance post at St. Stephen's College.

28 Jan 1942

The Ministry of Finance of the Japanese government enacted the Temporary Measures for Hong Kong Finance Ordinance, which specified that Hong Kong dollars with a large face value could continue to circulate and that the Japanese military yen should be used for other amounts. This restricted the circulation of fiat money issued by the Government of the Republic of China in Hong Kong. Non-cooperative financial institutions were forced to give their businesses over to the Yokohama Specie Bank Limited or the Bank of Taiwan.

Jan 1942

British and American expatriates were sent to the Stanley Internment Camp. (Figure 125)

The Military Administration Board began implementing a food rationing system, under which each person was given a quota of only four taels of rice per day.

03 Feb 1942

The Hong Kong–Kowloon Independent Brigade of Guangdong People's Anti-Japanese Guerrilla Force, led by the Communist Party of China, was established at Wong Mo Ying Village in Sai Kung, New Territories. Cai Guoliang (蔡國樑), formerly a worker of the Hong Kong Amoy Canning Factory, was its commander; Chen Daming (陳達明), leader of the student movements in Hong Kong, was political commissar; and Huang Gaoyang (黃高陽) was head of the political training office.

13 Feb 1942

The first batch of 483 labourers recruited in Hong Kong by Hop Kee Company founded by the Japanese navy arrived at Hainan Island. From this month to July 1943, 20,565 labourers were transported from Hong Kong to Hainan Island and were forced to work in severe conditions; many of these labourers lost their lives on Hainan Island.

20 Feb 1942

The Governor's Office of the Captured Territory of Hong Kong was established; it was under the direct command of Tokyo's Imperial General Headquarters headed by the Japanese Emperor, the Chief of the Imperial Japanese Army General Staff and the Chief of the Imperial Japanese Navy General Staff. Lieutenant General Isogai Rensuke was appointed as Governor.

Figure 125
British prisoners of war at Stanley Internment Camp. (Photo taken in 1945 and courtesy of Public Records Office, Government Records Service)

Feb 1942

The occupation government conducted a census, indicating a population of 1,129,308 in Hong Kong, including 602,566 on Hong Kong Island, 440,542 in Kowloon and 86,200 in the New Territories.

Lieutenant Colonel Noma Kennosuke served as Head of the Japanese Gendarmerie (Kempeitai) in Hong Kong. He was sentenced to death for war crimes by the British War Crimes Court in Hong Kong after the Second World War.

The occupation government allowed 10 Chinese-owned banks controlled by Japanese or pro-Japanese parties, including the Bank of East Asia and Wing On Bank, to resume business. Nine banks, including the Bank of Canton and the China & South Sea Bank, were ordered to close on the grounds of operational difficulties; their assets were controlled or seized by the Japanese.

15 Mar 1942

The occupation government increased the ration of rice from one *ge* (equivalent to 0.1 litre) to one *ge* and six *shao* (one *shao* equivalent to one centilitre); that is, six taels and four maces (one mace equivalent to 0.1 tael), commonly known as "six taels and four." A total of 98 rice ration houses were set up in Hong Kong, including 57 on Hong Kong Island and 41 in Kowloon.

21 Mar 1942

With the closure of the military yen exchange offices in mid-February, the occupation government ordered the establishment of a military yen clearing house with the Yokohama Specie Bank and the Bank of Taiwan, keeping the exchange rate of two Hong Kong dollars to one military yen.

28 Mar 1942

The occupation government promulgated the Governor's Order No. 9—Order for the Control of Entry and Exit, Residence, Removal and Movement of Goods and the Conduct of Enterprises, Businesses and Commerce in the Area Controlled by the Governor of the Captured Territory of Hongkong—to strictly control economic activities in Hong Kong. Any person entering, leaving, residing or conducting business in Hong Kong must seek approval from the Governor.

The occupation government promulgated the Governor's Order No. 10—Regulations for the Chinese Representative Council of the Governor's Office of the Captured Territory of Hongkong—and the Governor's Order No. 11— Regulations for the Chinese Cooperative Council. These laws set up the Chinese Representative Council and the Chinese Cooperative Council (collectively known as the "Two Chinese Councils"). The hope was that filling up these councils with influential Chinese people would help legitimise military rule in Hong Kong.

07 Apr 1942

The occupation government authorised Yokohama Specie Bank Limited to liquidate the assets of four banks: The Hongkong and Shanghai Banking Corporation, Standard Chartered Bank, Mercantile Bank and Belgian Bank.

10 Apr 1942

The Governor's Office of the occupation government was relocated from Peninsula Hotel to The Hongkong and Shanghai Banking Corporation building.

16 Apr 1942

The occupation government promulgated the Governor's Order No. 14 of 1942—Regulations for the Bureau dealing with the governing of Hongkong—according to which an Area Bureau was established in each of the three main areas of Hong Kong Island, Kowloon and the New Territories. Each Area Bureau was staffed with three Chiefs, three Deputy Chiefs, nine Subordinate Chiefs and 126 Officials.

The occupation government promulgated the Governor's Order No. 15 of 1942—Regulations for Private Classes in Nipponese Language. Private Japanese language institutes were set up for promoting enslaving education.

20 Apr 1942

The occupation government launched a Japanisation campaign, changing the name of Hong Kong Island to "Heung Tao" and changing street names with British overtones to names with Japanese overtones. For example, Queen's Road Central was renamed Nakameiji-dori; Des Voeux Road Central was renamed Higashishōwa-dori; the Peninsula Hotel was renamed Toa Hoteru.

Figure 126
Front page of *Heung Tao Daily* dated 24 July 1942, with the headline "one military yen was equivalent to four Hong Kong dollars." Hong Kong residents were stripped of their assets through devaluation of the local currency during the Japanese occupation. (Image courtesy of Hong Kong Museum of History)

27 Apr 1942

Poet Dai Wangshu (戴望舒) wrote the modern poem "Written on a Prison Wall" inside Victoria Prison, having been arrested and imprisoned by the Japanese army.

Apr 1942

The occupation government implemented stringent regulations that prohibited anyone leaving Hong Kong from taking more than 200 military yen or 500 Hong Kong dollars. The size of suitcases should not exceed four square feet.

The Hong Kong Jockey Club was renamed the Hongkong Race Club. On 25 April, it held its first horse race following the Japanese occupation of Hong Kong.

15 May 1942

The occupation government formulated the Guidelines for the Regulation of Currency in the Captured Territory of Hong Kong, which proposed abandoning the fixed rate of exchanging two Hong Kong dollars for one military yen and lowering the value of the Hong Kong dollar. The guidelines recommended enforcing the circulation of military yen as the only currency in Hong Kong.

30 May 1942

The occupation government implemented a sugar rationing system.

05 Jun 1942

The occupation government promulgated the Governor's Order No. 22 of 1942—Regulations for Censoring Films and Plays—stipulating that all films and plays screened or staged in Hong Kong must first be submitted for censorship by the Press Section of the Governor's Office.

11 Jul 1942

The Hong Kong Economic Committee, established by the Japanese army in June, formulated the Temporary Measures for Currency in the Captured Territory of Hong Kong, according to which the exchange rate of the Hong Kong dollar to military yen was changed from 2:1 to 4:1. (Figure 126)

16 Jul 1942

The occupation government implemented a ration system for edible oil.

20 Jul 1942

The occupation government promulgated the Governor's Order No. 26 of 1942—Regulations for the Organisation of the District Government of the Captured Territory of Hongkong. A district administration system would be implemented, with 12 districts under the jurisdiction of Hong Kong Island, nine districts under Kowloon, and seven districts under the New Territories. Each District Bureau would have one District Chief, one District Deputy Chief and 5–10 Secretaries.

24 Jul 1942

The occupation government promulgated the Governor's Order No. 32 of 1942—Regulations for Currency and Exchange in the Area controlled by the Governor of the Captured Territory of Hongkong. Under this order, Hong Kong dollar banknotes must be handed over to the military yen exchange offices in exchange for military yen at the rate of four Hong Kong dollars to one military yen.

Jul 1942

The Ministry of Foreign Affairs of the National Government of the Republic of China contacted British Ambassador to China Horace James Seymour, asking if the British government would hand over Hong Kong after the war, but the British government did not give a positive reply; this was the first time that China contacted Britain regarding the future of Hong Kong.

04 Aug 1942

Captain David Ronald Holmes of the British Army Aid Group entered Hong Kong secretly to get in touch with the Hong Kong–Kowloon Independent Brigade. He and Brigade commander Cai Guoliang (蔡國樑) discussed cooperation between the two sides.

10 Aug 1942

Rice, edible oil, firewood, sugar and other rationed goods could only be purchased with military yen. Rice stations would accept only military yen, and oil stations and firewood stations took military yen as the base currency. The Hong Kong dollar was still in use in other general stores.

Aug 1942

The occupation government announced that Wan Chai would be set aside as a place of residence for the Japanese and ordered more than 2,000 residents to move out within three days. Lieutenant Governor Hirano Shigeru instructed the Japanese army to set up 500 "comfort stations" in the vicinity of Lockhart Road.

The occupation government began allowing the public to apply for the return of goods detained by the Japanese army; most of the goods had already been sent to Japan or shipped to the frontline by the occupation government.

10 Sep 1942

The occupation government held a ground-breaking ceremony in Ngau Chi Wan for the expansion of Kai Tak Airport. The airport was intended to serve as a major civilian and military airport in East and Southeast Asia.

13 Sep 1942

The occupation government promulgated the Governor's Order No. 40 of 1942—Regulations for the Population—obliging Hong Kong residents to register births, deaths, relocation, emigration and naturalisation details with the Governor's Office within 10 days of their occurrence to facilitate the formulation of a population evacuation policy by the Governor's Office.

18 Sep 1942

The occupation government enacted Governor's Order No. 43 of 1942—Order for Trade Control—announcing the establishment of the Hongkong Trade Syndicate, which was founded on 08 October. From then on, only members of the Association or merchants licenced by the Governor were allowed to trade outside Guangdong Province, Xiamen, Macao and Guangzhou Bay.

According to a census by the occupation government, Hong Kong's population had decreased from 1,640,000 in 1941 to 980,000.

Sep 1942

About 2,500 British prisoners of war in Hong Kong were sent to Japan; nearly 1,100 of them died on the way.

The Japanese army surrounded Wu Kau Tang in the New Territories and forced the villagers to surrender their weapons and give the names of anti-Japanese guerrillas. Village head Li Sai-fan (李世藩) was tortured to death.

01 Oct 1942

The Japanese passenger and cargo ship *Lisbon Maru*, with 1,834 British prisoners of war and 778 Japanese officers and soldiers on board, was sunk by an American submarine in the sea off Zhoushan, Zhejiang. The Japanese sent ships and warships to rescue the Japanese soldiers but refused to rescue the prisoners of war, causing about 800 deaths. Chinese fishermen from nearby islands rescued 384 British prisoners of war.

25 Oct 1942

Twelve US bombers attacked the Kowloon Docks, marking the first air raid on Hong Kong by Allied forces.

30 Oct 1942

The occupation government promulgated the Governor's Order No. 46 of 1942—Regulations for the Prohibition of Shortwave Broadcasting—prohibiting the public from listening to short wave broadcasts and from owning radio sets that could receive short wave broadcasts. The Order came into effect on 01 November.

Oct 1942

The occupation government forced Chief Manager of The Hongkong and Shanghai Banking Corporation Vandeleur Molyneux Grayburn to sign some of the bank's unissued banknotes. A total of HK$113.5 million, signed under duress, were in circulation during the Japanese occupation.

09 Jan 1943

The occupation government detorated explosives at Sacred Hill in Kowloon City and discarded the boulder engraved with three Chinese characters "Sung Wong Toi" (Terrace of the Song emperors) to expand Kai Tak Airport. In 1956, the boulder was moved to its present site on Sung Wong Toi Road in Kowloon City.

11 Jan 1943

The Sino-British Treaty for the Relinquishment of Extra-Territorial Rights in China was signed by China and Britain in Chongqing, under which Britain renounced all of its privileges and concessions in China but refused to make a commitment on its leasehold in the New Territories. The Chinese delegates said China reserved the right to discuss the issue in the future.

25 Jan 1943

The occupation government implemented a salt rationing system, allowing 0.5 kilogram of salt per month for each person at a price of 20 maces (a Chinese currency unit) per catty.

Feb 1943

The occupation government instituted rations of 12 catties of brown rice and six taels of flour per month for each person at double the previous price.

03 Mar 1943

More than 100 Japanese soldiers raided the base of the political training office of the Hong Kong–Kowloon Independent Brigade at Yen Tai Shan in Lo Lung Tin of Sha Tau Kok. Three guerrillas were killed in action; three were captured and executed. This event became known as the March Third Incident.

The occupation government promulgated the Governor's Order No. 11 of 1943—Regulations for the Establishment of Government-run Hong Kong East Asia Academy. On 01 May, the East Asia Academy was opened at St. Stephen's College; Kobayashi Munechi was the Dean. The college was intended for implementing enslaving education.

16 Mar 1943

The occupation government announced that Hong Kong had a population of 979,994, comprising 967,868 Chinese, 4,784 Japanese and 7,342 foreign nationals.

10 Apr 1943

The occupation government promulgated the Governor's Order No. 17 of 1943—Regulations for Restrictions on the Trading of Essential Goods and Materials—stipulating that approval must be obtained for the trade of essential goods and materials, such as steel, copper and mercury.

May 1943

The Hong Kong–Kowloon Independent Brigade's Lantau Island Detachment leader Lau Chun-cheung (劉春祥) sailed with guerrillas at night on a wooden boat across the waters to Lantau Island and were ambushed by two Japanese gunboats in the waters near Sha Chau and Lung Kwu Chau. After a fierce battle, the boat was sunk; 11 guerrillas, including Tsang Ho-sung (曾可送), Lam Yung (林容), Wong Sung (汪送), Tam Kam-fo (譚金火), Wan Fat (溫發), Lau Kai (劉佳) and boat operator Leung Hak (梁克) died heroically.

The Kempeitai arrested former Hong Kong Defence Secretary John Alexander Fraser, Chief of Staff of British Forces in Hong Kong Colonel Lanceray Arthur Newnham and over 100 others who were imprisoned in war camps, including the Stanley Internment Camp. They were accused of secretly cooperating with the British Army Aid Group to plan an escape. Fraser, Newnham and more than 30 others were executed by the Japanese army.

01 Jun 1943

The occupation government banned the circulation of Hong Kong dollars and made Japanese military yen the only legal currency in Hong Kong. The military yen in circulation increased from 25.34 million yen in April 1943 to 1,962.75 million yen in August 1945 when the Japanese surrendered.

01 Aug 1943

Those without a household registration were forcibly repatriated to their hometowns by the Japanese army, effective immediately.

18 Aug 1943

The Bureau of Electricity announced a further reduction in electricity consumption effective 01 September. To save electricity, decorative electric lights, neon signs and ice cream-making machines were banned.

Aug 1943

The Hong Kong Planning Unit was set up in Britain. Subordinate to the British Colonial Office and headed by former Colonial Secretary of Hong Kong Norman Lockhart Smith, it was responsible for studying specific tasks and long-term reform measures necessary upon the return of Hong Kong to Britain. In September 1944, the unit was reorganised and headed by former Cadet Officer (later called an Administrative Officer) of the Hong Kong government David Mercer MacDougall.

02 Sep 1943

An air raid by Allied forces destroyed the oil depot in Lai Chi Kok.

05 Sep 1943

Cars were banned in downtown Hong Kong and Kowloon to save gasoline.

Sep 1943

According to Japanese statistics, since the Japanese occupation, 973,000 people had left Hong Kong—of whom 381,000 left voluntarily; 576,000 were "persuaded" to leave; and 16,000 were forcibly repatriated.

09 Oct 1943

The Kempeitai in Sha Tau Kok arrested over 70 villagers from Lin Ma Hang accused of hiding Allied prisoners of war and guerrillas. Villager Yip Tin-cheong (葉天祥) was tortured to death.

19 Oct 1943

Chairman of the Hong Kong Chinese Representative Council Robert Kotewall and three representatives met with the Governor of the occupation government, putting forward multiple requests and suggestions for improvement; none of them were adopted.

Oct 1943

The occupation government announced the results of a population survey, indicating Hong Kong had a population of 855,888, including 390,137 on Hong Kong Island, 373,941 in Kowloon and 91,810 in the New Territories.

22 Nov 1943

During a dinner with Chairman of the National Government of the Republic of China Chiang Kai-shek (蔣 介 石) at the Cairo Conference, US President Franklin Roosevelt noted that he would support the return of Hong Kong to the Mainland and help put pressure on the British government if Chiang were willing to join the efforts of the Communist Party of China in the fight against Japan.

Dec 1943

The Guangdong People's Anti-Japanese Guerrilla Force was reorganised into the East River (Dongjiang) Column of the Guangdong People's Anti-Japanese Guerrilla Force. From then on until the East River Column's evacuation to the north, because of geographical and historical peculiarities, the Hong Kong–Kowloon Independent Brigade was twice called the Hong Kong–Kowloon Independent Brigade of the East River Column and placed under the Column's direct command.

1943

The occupation government stipulated that Hong Kong residents must apply for a Resident's Certificate and that those without a job, beggars and vagrants would be deported.

Figure 127
US fighter pilot Lieutenant Donald W. Kerr (left), who was rescued after his plane was shot down, in a picture with East River (Dongjiang) Column commander Zeng Sheng (曾生) on 18 March 1944. (Photo courtesy of the Family of Lt. Donald W. Kerr)

11 Feb 1944

Lieutenant Donald W. Kerr of the Chinese–American Composite Wing was commanding a bombing mission of Kai Tak Airport when his plane was hit. He parachuted to Kwun Yam Shan, north of the airport. The Hong Kong–Kowloon Independent Brigade broke through the Japanese army's encirclement and escorted him to the base of the Hong Kong-Kowloon Independent Brigade at Tai Long Sai Village in Sai Kung. From there, he was taken to the headquarters of the East River Column at To Yang Village on Dapeng Peninsula. (Figure 127)

15 Apr 1944

The occupation government implemented a rice rationing policy under which rice rations were only given to people and their families who cooperated with the Japanese army and government. In December, the policy limited its beneficiaries only to the collaborators, not their families.

21 Apr 1944

The Urban Detachment of the Hong Kong–Kowloon Independent Brigade blew up the Railway Bridge No. 4 on Waterloo Road in Kowloon.

Apr 1944

For 21 days, the Japanese forces deployed more than 2,600 soldiers, 40 warships and gunboats and four aircraft to sweep the stronghold of the Hong Kong–Kowloon Independent Brigade's Lantau Island Detachment but failed to find any trace of the guerrillas. During this period, Abbot Fat Ho (筏可) of the Po Lin Monastery on Lantau Island hid and protected Deputy Commander of the Brigade Lu Feng (魯風), who was recovering from an illness in the temple. Abbot Fat Ho was tortured by the Japanese but refused to divulge any information.

Jul 1944

The Kempeitai sent hundreds of refugees to Lo Chau, an uninhabited island southeast of Hok Tsui (Cape D'Aguilar) on Hong Kong Island, where many drowned or starved to death. In April 1945, fishermen found human bones all over the beach.

12 Aug 1944

The bronze statue of Queen Victoria from the Statue Square in Central, the pair of bronze lions in front of The Hongkong and Shanghai Banking Corporation (HSBC) building and the full-length statue of former HSBC Chief Manager Thomas Jackson were removed by the Japanese military and sent back to Tokyo as war trophies.

16 Aug 1944

The Marine Detachment of the Hong Kong–Kowloon Independent Brigade attacked the mobile marine unit of the Japanese military at sea near Wong Chuk Kok, sinking at least one enemy boat, killing 25 Japanese soldiers, capturing 13 crew members, and seizing a large amount of munitions.

20 Aug 1944

The electricity and gas supply in Hong Kong was suspended due to the lack of fuel.

08 Sep 1944

The Kempeitai in Sha Tau Kok arrested about 60 villagers from Lin Ma Hang accused of helping the guerrillas to steal explosives from a nearby mine. Villager Yip Tin-sung（葉天送）and miner Yip Sang（葉生）were tortured to death.

Sep 1944

Taiwanese interpreter for the Kempeitai in Kowloon, Lin Taiyi（林台宜）, was captured by guerrillas in Sai Kung. In response, the Kempeitai conducted extensive searches in the villages of Sai Kung, including Tai Lam Wu, Kai Ham, Ho Chung, Tai Tung and Nam Wai. Many villagers were arrested; some were beaten to death.

The Kempeitai set up a secret police force under the Political Affairs Section to monitor all Japanese, Chinese and nationals of neutral countries.

16 Oct 1944

The Allied forces sent 30 bombers in an attack on the Whampoa Dock in Kowloon; some of the bombs hit downtown Hung Hom by mistake. (Figure 128)

Figure 128
B-24 bombers of the Allied forces in an air raid over Kowloon Docks. (Photo taken on 16 October 1944 and courtesy of HKSAR Government)

08 Nov 1944

In response to a question in the House of Commons, British Deputy Prime Minister Clement Attlee said the British government would encourage investment in Hong Kong after the war. This was the first time a British government official publicly stated that Britain would take back Hong Kong.

24 Dec 1944

The passenger ship *Lingnan Maru* was attacked by US warplanes in the vicinity of Mo To Chau (The Brothers Islands), off Castle Peak Bay, on its way from Hong Kong to Macao, killing 349 people, including Chan Lim-pak (陳 廉伯), a member of the Chinese Representative Council who had been collaborating with Japan.

28 Dec 1944

Cheng Po (鄭保), chief of Nam Wa Po Village in Tai Po, and others were taken to the Kempeitai in Tai Po and were questioned under torture about the whereabouts of the guerrillas. Cheng and two others refused to provide information and died from torture.

1944

The Hong Kong Volunteer Company was formed in India; its members were mostly Chinese from Hong Kong.

At the beginning of the year, Lau Kam-chun (劉錦進), also known as Darkie Lau (劉黑仔), Captain of the Pistol Unit of the Hong Kong–Kowloon Independent Brigade, led a raid on Kai Tak Airport, blowing up the oil depot and an aircraft. Japanese troops immediately returned from Sai Kung (where the Hong Kong–Kowloon Independent Brigade was based) to defend Kowloon.

The occupation government issued military notes with a face value of 100 yen, which were printed in large quantities at the printing house in the basement of the China Building in Hong Kong.

11 Jan 1945

Lieutenant General Tanaka Hisakazu, Commander of the Japanese 23rd Army in Guangzhou, arrived in Hong Kong and took over from Isogai Rensuke as the second Governor of the occupation government starting 01 February.

15 Jan 1945

The Allied forces launched a massive air raid on Hong Kong for two consecutive days, flying a total of 471 sorties and dropping about 150 tonnes of bombs, destroying 21 Japanese transport ships and warships; it was the largest air raid on Hong Kong by the Allied forces.

21 Jan 1945

The Allied forces dispatched 30 warplanes to attack Hong Kong.

Jan 1945

The Japanese occupation government was incorporated under the 23rd Army; possession of Hong Kong dollars was again banned by decree.

Kuomintang member So Kuen (蘇權) assisted in hiding a downed American pilot. The two were beheaded by the Japanese army after they were discovered by an Indian policeman.

08 Feb 1945

At the Yalta Conference, US President Franklin Roosevelt proposed that Hong Kong be returned to China and made an international free port. The proposal was firmly opposed by British Prime Minister Winston Churchill.

24 Mar 1945

The occupation government announced that Hong Kong residents aged 10 and above must apply for a Resident Certificate issued by the Deputy Commissioner of Police in the period of 09–19 April and must carry it at all times. (Figure 129)

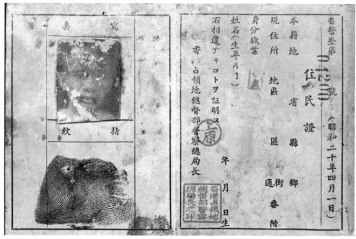

Figure 129
A resident permit issued in April 1945 by the Japanese occupation government. (Image courtesy of Hong Kong Museum of History)

Figure 130
Colonel Tokunaga Isao of the Japanese army, who took charge of all internment camps in Hong Kong during the Japanese occupation, was detained at Stanley Prison. (Photo taken in 1945 and courtesy of PNA Rota/Hulton Archive via Getty Images)

01 May 1945

Head of Hong Kong Planning Unit David Mercer MacDougall, Director of Butterfield & Swire George Warren Swire, Hongkong and Shanghai Banking Corporation Chairman Arthur Morse and Assistant Under-Secretary of the Colonial Office Edward Gent met to discuss political reform in Hong Kong, including the establishment of a municipal council and the reorganisation of the Legislative Council. This later became the blueprint for the constitutional reform instituted by Mark Young when he became Governor of Hong Kong.

16 May 1945

The occupation government promulgated the Governor's Order No. 37 of 1945—Rules and Regulations for the Maintenance of Law and Order by the Governor's Office of the Captured Territory of Hongkong. Anyone who was found to have committed disorderly conduct would be tried by a special court.

12 Jun 1945

The Allied forces sent 62 US warplanes to attack the north shore of Hong Kong Island; it was the last raid on Hong Kong by the Allied forces during the Second World War.

13 Aug 1945

British Ambassador to China Horace James Seymour notified the National Government of the Republic of China that Britain would reoccupy Hong Kong. The National Government opposed the proposition on the grounds that Hong Kong was a part of the China theatre.

15 Aug 1945

Japanese Emperor Hirohito announced his acceptance of the Potsdam Declaration and Japan's unconditional surrender following the atomic bombs on Japanese cities Hiroshima and Nagasaki. In the afternoon, Hong Kong's JPHA Radio read out the imperial edict on the Japanese surrender in both Japanese and Cantonese.

17 Aug 1945

US President Harry S. Truman approved General Order No. 1, demanding the Japanese military within China to surrender to Supreme Allied Commander of China Theatre Chiang Kai-shek (蔣介石). On 19 Aug, Truman decided to remove Hong Kong from the China theatre for surrender purposes, and the Japanese military in Hong Kong would surrender to Britain instead. (Figure 130)

19 Aug 1945

The Japanese army launched a search in the area of Chung Hau at Silver Mine Bay on Lantau Island for guerrillas who attacked a military camp at Mui Wo; 300 villagers were arrested. Japanese military officer Kishi Yasuo beheaded the village chief and tortured the villagers; 11 villagers were killed while many sustained injuries, in addition to many burned houses, in what became known as the Silver Mine Bay Massacre.

20 Aug 1945

Chairman of the National Government of the Republic of China Chiang Kai-shek (蔣介石) called US President Harry S. Truman, demanding that Britain should not accept the Japanese surrender in Chinese territory or in Hong Kong.

23 Aug 1945

Chiang Kai-shek (蔣介石) called US President Harry S. Truman again, saying that as Supreme Allied Commander of China Theatre he agreed to let a British officer accept the surrender of the Japanese in Hong Kong on his behalf.

Commander-in-Chief of the Army of the Republic of China Ho Ying-chin (何應欽) appointed Zhang Fakui (張發奎) as a representative to accept the Japanese surrender in Hong Kong, Guangdong, Kowloon and Hainan Island.

24 Aug 1945

Chiang Kai-shek (蔣介石) said publicly at a joint meeting between the Kuomintang Central Standing Committee and the Supreme National Defence Council that he would negotiate with Britain over the issue of Hong Kong through diplomatic channels.

27 Aug 1945

Former Colonial Secretary of Hong Kong Franklin Gimson left the Stanley Internment Camp and announced to the public on government radio channel (ZBW) that British troops would arrive to accept the Japanese surrender. On the same day, General Luo Zhuoying (羅卓英) was ordered by the National Government of the Republic of China to lead the 13th Army into Kowloon but was ordered to retreat two days later.

31 Aug 1945

The British Pacific Fleet's Task Group 111.2, under the command of Rear Admiral Cecil Harcourt, entered Victoria Harbour and took over the Naval Dockyard.

01 Sep 1945

Admiral Cecil Harcourt announced the establishment of the British Military Administration in Hong Kong on government radio, replacing the provisional government set up by former Colonial Secretary Franklin Gimson after the Japanese surrender.

13 Sep 1945

The British Military Administration in Hong Kong announced that the Hong Kong dollar would become legal tender again the following day and suspended the use of all Japanese military notes with a face value of over 10 yen as well as Hong Kong dollar notes signed under duress. Military notes with a face value of less than 10 yen remained valid because of the shortage of Hong Kong dollar notes at that time.

16 Sep 1945

The Japanese surrender ceremony was held at the Government House. Major General Okada Umekichi and Vice Admiral Fujita Ruitarō signed the instrument of surrender in the presence of Rear Admiral Cecil Harcourt, representing Britain as Supreme Allied Commander of China Theatre. The Chinese side dispatched Major General Pan Huaguo (潘華國) to observe the ceremony. Britain officially regained control of Hong Kong. (Figure 131)

20 Sep 1945

The British Military Administration in Hong Kong announced in a statement that it had abolished the opium monopoly, listed opium as a dangerous drug and banned the sale and consumption of opium.

Figure 131
On 16 September 1945, Japanese troops formally surrendered at the Government House. Imperial Japanese Army Major General Okada Umekichi handed over his sword to British Rear Admiral Cecil Harcourt (Flag Officer Commanding Eleventh Aircraft Carrier Squadron). (Photo taken by Jack Hawes and courtesy of Jack Hawes/Department of National Defence of Canada/Library and Archives Canada/PA-114815)

28 Sep 1945

The Hong Kong–Kowloon Independent Brigade declared its withdrawal from Hong Kong. According to incomplete statistics, during the guerrilla war that lasted for three years and eight months, the Brigade killed or wounded more than 100 Japanese soldiers and more than 70 Chinese collaborators, puppet policemen and spies; captured and accepted the surrender of more than 600 Chinese puppet soldiers; sank four Japanese ships; destroyed a Japanese aircraft; and captured more than 550 handguns and rifles, more than 60 machine guns, six cannons, more than 40 vehicles and vessels and a large amount of munitions.

Sep 1945

Towards the end of the month, at the request of the British Military Administration in Hong Kong, a village guard unit was established by the East River Column with 96 members of the Hong Kong–Kowloon Independent Brigade. The unit was to assist the British in maintaining public order in the New Territories and was disbanded the following year.

The British Military Administration in Hong Kong established the Public Relations Office, predecessor of the Information Services Department.

The Military Administration estimated that Hong Kong had a total population of about 600,000.

28 Oct 1945

The passenger ship *Ching Cheung*, on its way from Shantou to Hong Kong, sank near Kwo Chau Kwan To (Ninepin Islands), killing about 220 people on board. Fishing boats rescued 123 survivors the following day and sent them back to Hong Kong.

Oct 1945

A Chinese military mission began to take over Japanese supplies and navy vessels in Hong Kong. According to an agreement, Hong Kong was re-taken by Britain. However, since Hong Kong was a part of the China theatre, enemy supplies were deemed property of China.

The British Military Administration in Hong Kong established the Fisheries Department and its subsidiary statutory authority, the Fish Marketing Organization. New regulations were also announced, requiring fish caught (in fresh water or in the sea) to be auctioned at designated wholesale fish markets, thus establishing a fish market system in Hong Kong.

13 Nov 1945

The Communist Party of China launched *Zheng Bao*, its first newspaper in Hong Kong.

15 Nov 1945

The Kowloon–Canton Railway restored full service.

Nov 1945

The Catholic Diocese of Hong Kong established the Catholic Centre as the first organisation of the Diocese to offer diversified services.

19 Dec 1945

The Tenancy Tribunal held its first trial in the Supreme Court.

26 Dec 1945

Special Commissioner of the Naval Department of the National Government Liu Yonggao (劉永誥) came to Hong Kong to collect 35 Japanese navy vessels.

1945

Hiram's Highway, constructed by the British Forces in Hong Kong from a dirt road initially built by the Japanese army during the Japanese occupation, was opened to traffic.

Wing Hang Ngan Ho was established on Bonham Strand by Fung Yiu-king (馮堯敬); it was registered as Wing Hang Bank and was granted a banking licence in 1960.

The Hong Kong Buddhist Association was established.

01 Jan 1946

The China Democratic League established a South China General Branch in Hong Kong; it established a Hong Kong–Kowloon Branch on 28 February.

04 Jan 1946

The Chinese newspaper *Hwa Shang Pao* resumed publication; it ceased publication on 16 October 1949.

07 Jan 1946

The British Military Administration in Hong Kong introduced a modified system of rice ration, requiring people to register at a nearby depot.

20 Jan 1946

Chinese mechanics of three major dockyards demanded higher salary. After a week of negotiations, an increase by 25 cents in hourly wage (about 56% higher than that of 1941) was agreed upon on 27 January 1946.

Jan 1946

The United Nations Relief and Rehabilitation Administration established an office in Kowloon for distribution of relief supplies.

11 Feb 1946

The Hong Kong Chinese Fishermen's Guild issued a report, claiming the destruction of 1,121 large fishing boats by the Japanese in Hong Kong between 1937 and 1941 and a death toll of 14,415. The report was submitted to the National Government of the Republic of China for seeking compensation from Japan.

15 Feb 1946

Anglo-Portuguese John Vincent Braga submitted to the British Foreign Office a memorandum titled Anti-British Feeling in China, recommending improved relations between the Chinese and British people in Hong Kong.

19 Feb 1946

The British Military Administration in Hong Kong arraigned the first group of suspects accused of wartime collaboration with the Japanese, including four Chinese and two foreign nationals.

21 Mar 1946

An explosion in a British army ammunition dump at A Kung Ngam in Lei Yue Mun resulted in dozens of casualties and numerous sunken boats.

28 Mar 1946

The British War Crimes Courts in Hong Kong began hearings on Japanese war crimes, starting with atrocities committed at Silver Mine Bay on Lantau Island between 18 and 26 August 1945.

01 Apr 1946

Under the British government's Colonial Development and Welfare Act 1945, Hong Kong received a grant of £1 million (about HK$16 million) for post-Second World War development and social welfare spending in the next 10 years.

02 Apr 1946

The Hongkong and Shanghai Banking Corporation announced that all duress notes issued during the Japanese occupation were recognised as legal tender with immediate effect. The Bank Notes and Certificates of Indebtedness Ordinance 1946 was promulgated on 16 August, authorising all note-issuing banks to recognise duress notes.

11 Apr 1946

The Hong Kong Apostolic Vicariate was raised to a Diocese by the Roman Catholic Church. Father Enrico Valtorta was named the first Bishop of the Diocese on 31 October 1948.

13 Apr 1946

The British Military Administration in Hong Kong began compiling compensation claims for wartime losses. Businesses, organisations and individuals could file reports with the War Claims Commission for future claims.

01 May 1946

Vice Admiral Cecil Harcourt, Head of the British Military Administration in Hong Kong, announced the conclusion of the Administration. Mark Young took an oath at the Government House and resumed his duties as Governor of Hong Kong; he remained in office until 17 May 1947.

The Legislative Council resumed its duties and held its first post-Second World War meeting.

The Civil Aviation Department was established, replacing the Harbour Department for matters relating to civil aviation administration at Kai Tak Airport.

07 May 1946

The first post-Second World War list of members of the Executive Council was announced; it included six Official Members and one Unofficial Member.

10 May 1946

Heung To Middle School was founded on Waterloo Road in Kowloon.

17 May 1946

Chinese employees of Hongkong Electric Company appealed for greater compensation and benefits with eight specific requests. As negotiation turned unsuccessful, workers of North Point Power Station walked off at 4 p.m., leading to a power outage and suspension of tram service in parts of Hong Kong Island. On 31 May, an agreement was reached to provide a 38% pay rise among skilled workers; operation resumed at 11 p.m.

28 May 1946

The Urban Council held its first post-Second World War meeting; there were no elected members yet.

06 Jun 1946

The Hong Kong government launched a food conservation campaign to tackle food shortages; public talks, including a Chinese radio programme, were held to provide information, share agricultural techniques and promote vegetable gardening.

12 Jun 1946

More than 1,000 representatives of Chinese community groups held a service at the Confucius Hall in Causeway Bay to commemorate those killed in Hong Kong during the War of Resistance against Japanese Aggression.

23 Jun 1946

The first Miss Hong Kong beauty contest—an event that was part of the Grand International Charity Swimming Gala (organised by the Royal Air Force Recreation Club in conjunction with the Chinese Amateur Swimming Team)—was held at Ritz Night Club in North Point. Lee Lan (李蘭) won first place; Pak Kwong (白光) and Poon Kong-fung (潘江楓) were the first and second runners-up, respectively.

02 Jul 1946

The Piece-Goods (Control) Order 1946 was promulgated, effective 01 July 1946, stipulating government control on all imported textiles.

06 Jul 1946

Henry Blackall was appointed as Chief Justice of Hong Kong.

07 Jul 1946

Representatives of the National Government of the Republic of China in Hong Kong, along with local Chinese organisations, held a memorial service at King's Theatre in Central to commemorate those who died during the War of Resistance against Japanese Aggression.

10 Jul 1946

The Canton–Kowloon Highway was reopened.

12 Jul 1946

The Price Control Order 1946 was promulgated, controlling the prices of several types of food and other daily necessities.

18 Jul 1946

The Hong Kong Observatory hoisted the first post-Second World War Hurricane Signal No. 10 amid a typhoon—which destroyed two ships and two fishing boats, caused 11 deaths and seven injuries, and damaged many houses, particularly on Hong Kong Island.

26 Jul 1946

The Peak District (Residence) Ordinance 1918 and Cheung Chau (Residence) Ordinance 1919 were abolished, outlawing residential restrictions on Chinese and other ethnic groups on the Peak and Cheung Chau Island.

Following the workers of the Hongkong and Yaumatei Ferry, workers of Star Ferry also went on strike. The Royal Navy assumed cross-harbour ferry service between Hong Kong Island and Kowloon temporarily.

28 Aug 1946

Governor Mark Young announced a constitutional reform proposal known as the Young Plan, calling for a municipal council with 48 members—nominated by professional bodies and elected by Chinese and European residents—for local affairs on Hong Kong Island, in Kowloon and New Kowloon.

Figure 132
The first DC-3 aircraft of Cathay Pacific Airways *Betsy* flying over Hong Kong. (Photo taken circa late 1940s and courtesy of Cathay Pacific Airways Limited and Swire HK Archive Service)·

30 Aug 1946

The government held its first Liberation Day ceremony at the Cenotaph in Central and made 30 August an annual public holiday.

01 Sep 1946

Pui Kiu Middle School—a school recruiting the children of overseas Chinese in Southeast Asia—was founded in Happy Valley.

The Education Advancement Society for the Children of Workers in Hong Kong and Kowloon—later known as the Education Advancement Society for Workers in Hong Kong and Kowloon—was established. In the same month, it founded its first Workers' Children School at the Naval Dockyard Workers' Union Office on Lockhart Road in Wan Chai. The Mongkok Workers' Children School in Kowloon was established on 21 February 1947.

06 Sep 1946

The Wholesale (Kowloon) Marketing (Vegetables) Order 1946 was promulgated, establishing a government department for centralised distribution of vegetables through a wholesale market in Yau Ma Tei—which began to operate on 15 September in a regulated market.

New Life Evening Post reported in a news article "Planned Governance of Kowloon City by Our Government" that the National Government of the Republic of China had reaffirmed its jurisdiction over the Kowloon Walled City and its plan to station a Chinese official assigned from the government of Bao'an County.

14 Sep 1946

A Hong Kong government spokesperson asserted in a statement that Chinese jurisdiction over the Kowloon Walled City ended in 1899 in consideration of British military interests, adding that Hong Kong had exercised its right to govern the Kowloon Walled City just as it had in Kowloon and the New Territories in the past 50 years.

The Hong Kong government banned the re-export of cotton yarn originating from China in a bid to crack down on the smuggling and resale of supplies intended as aid for China.

The Rural Training College was established to prepare teachers for rural schools in the New Territories; it was closed in 1954.

16 Sep 1946

In a meeting with Governor Mark Young, Special Commissioner of the National Government of the Republic of China for Foreign Affairs in Kwangtung and Kwangsi T. W. Kwok (郭德華) reiterated Chinese sovereignty over the Kowloon Walled City in response to the statement issued by the Hong Kong government on 14 September.

24 Sep 1946

Cathay Pacific Airways Limited was incorporated, becoming Hong Kong's first provider of civil aviation services. (Figure 132)

25 Sep 1946

A Royal Air Force transport aircraft crashed into Lion Rock shortly after take-off from Kai Tak Airport, killing all 19 people on board.

Sep 1946

The Fish Marketing Organization Loan Fund was established with HK$250,000 in government funding; it provided fishermen with low-interest loans for motorised fishing boats and other fishing equipment.

10 Oct 1946

The Ta Teh Institute in Tuen Mun—a tertiary institution founded by the Communist Party of China and left-wing democratic activists in Hong Kong—was established; it was shut down on 23 February 1949 following a government ban. (Figure 133)

16 Oct 1946

The *Far Eastern Economic Review*—an English-language magazine on political and economic topics—was founded; it ceased publication in December 2009.

17 Oct 1946

Two bronze lion statues—taken by Japanese troops during the Second World War—arrived from Tokyo and were returned to their original positions at the HSBC headquarters in Central. The bronze statue of Queen Victoria was also returned and was later relocated to Victoria Park upon its opening in 1955.

21 Oct 1946

The University of Hong Kong resumed classes.

26 Oct 1946

Chinese hawker Wong Shui-cheong (王水祥) was kicked to death by an Indian police constable of the Emergency Unit during a crackdown on unlicenced hawkers on Portland Street in Yau Ma Tei. It led to a riot in which British troops were deployed to confront the public. More than 10 people were injured; 35 people were arrested.

27 Oct 1946

An anti-civil war league was formed in Hong Kong, calling for an end to the Chinese Civil War.

07 Nov 1946

South China Textiles Limited was founded by Lee Chen-che (李震之) as the first cotton mill in Hong Kong following the end of the Second World War.

09 Dec 1946

Mao Zedong (毛澤東) noted at a meeting with Western journalists in the town of Wangjiaping that he would not demand the immediate return of Hong Kong, suggesting a future resolution through negotiation.

Dec 1946

The Prisons Department established its first institution for delinquent boys aged 8 to 16.

The first batch (10 boxes) of a book collection of the National Central Library in China—placed in temporary storage at The University of Hong Kong's Fung Ping Shan Library before getting stolen by the Japanese during the Second World War—was flown back to Hong Kong from Japan, followed by the second batch (107 boxes) on 08 February 1947.

1946

The London Office of the Hong Kong Government was established for commercial matters with the United Kingdom. It was replaced with the HKSAR Economic and Trade Office in London on 17 July 1997.

The Hong Kong Police Force Anti-Corruption Branch was established; Frederick Frank Walter Shaftain served as its first commissioner.

Figure 133
The school campus of Ta Teh Institute in 1947. (Photo courtesy of Lau Chi-pang)

Figure 134
The Japanese War Memorial was demolished on 26 February 1947. (Photo courtesy of HKSAR Government)

1946

The Development Secretariat—comprising four departments in agriculture, forestry, fisheries and gardens—was formed; Geoffrey Herklots served as the first Secretary for Development.

The District Office arranged elections in 21 rural districts of the New Territories for a Senior Advisory Council in support of management of rural affairs.

The Medical Department's Relief Branch began providing food for the poor—a policy replaced with cash assistance in 1971.

The Accident Insurance Association of Hong Kong was established.

Tai Lin Radio Service Limited—Hong Kong's first electrical appliance retail chain—was established; it was closed on 17 October 2008.

The *Jiao* Festival in Sheung Shui Heung of the New Territories—a festival of its kind with the longest interval (once every 60 years) in Hong Kong—was held.

01 Jan 1947

The *Economic Bulletin*—Hong Kong's oldest Chinese-language financial magazine—began publication.

Hong Kong's first 16mm full-colour Cantonese film *White Powder and Neon Lights* was screened.

25 Jan 1947

A Philippine Airlines cargo plane, carrying US$15 million worth of gold, crashed near Mount Parker on Hong Kong Island, killing four people onboard.

30 Jan 1947

The Hong Kong edition of the Chinese Communist Party publication *Chuin Chung Weekly* began publication; it ceased on 20 October 1949.

04 Feb 1947

A fire broke out on the passenger ship *Sai On*—moored at Tung On Pier in Sheung Wan—in the early morning, killing about 200 people.

21 Feb 1947

The Hong Kong War Memorial Fund Ordinance 1947 was promulgated, establishing a voluntary fund to support family members of military personnel killed or injured in Hong Kong during the Second World War.

26 Feb 1947

The Hong Kong government blew up the Japanese War Memorial on Mount Cameron (present-day Bowen Hill). It was put in place by the Japanese military during the Second World War. (Figure 134)

04 Mar 1947

Hong Kong Airways Limited was incorporated by the British Overseas Airways Corporation; it was acquired by Cathay Pacific Airways in 1958.

31 Mar 1947

The Hong Kong government held the first Health Week in a campaign to promote public hygiene.

Mar 1947

A radio communication centre was established at the Central Police Station to improve efficiency in commanding district police stations in times of emergency.

01 Apr 1947

The Inland Revenue Department was established for collecting taxes on properties, profits and salaries.

The Harcourt Health Centre was established as a government clinic for tuberculosis.

12 Apr 1947

British Lieutenant General Neil Ritchie presented villagers in Sai Kung with a banner of commendation bearing the Chinese characters "loyalty," "bravery," "honesty" and "love" in recognition of their efforts in assisting the Allied forces during the Japanese occupation.

14 Apr 1947

The Bank of China acquired the site of the first-generation Hong Kong City Hall for HK$3,745,000; it planned to build the Bank of China building on the site.

18 Apr 1947

Tai Yau Bank was founded.

24 Apr 1947

The Hong Kong government announced a ban on gold imports with immediate effect. The public could only sell gold to the government at a price fixed by the government.

Apr 1947

The Chinese Music Institute in Hong Kong was established by members of the Southern Bureau of the Central Committee of the Communist Party of China; Ma Sicong (馬思聰) served as its president. The institute was dissolved in 1950.

01 May 1947

The China Zhi Gong Party held its third congress in Hong Kong where it resolved to join the People's Democratic United Front under the Communist Party of China.

Dah Sing Bank was incorporated; it was opened for business on 30 October.

03 May 1947

The Inland Revenue Ordinance 1947 was promulgated, authorising tax collection on salaries and profits.

15 May 1947

The Hong Kong Branch of Xinhua News Agency—an institution of the Communist Party of China in Hong Kong—was established; Qiao Guanhua (喬冠華) served as its first director. It was located in the former office of the East River Column at 172 Nathan Road in Kowloon.

18 May 1947

The Landlord and Tenant Ordinance 1947 was promulgated, allowing landlords to increase rents above the levels set before the Second World War.

30 May 1947

Sin Hua Bank was incorporated in Hong Kong.

May 1947

The Hong Kong Branch of the Communist Party of China's Central Committee was founded; Fang Fang（方方） and Yin Linping（尹林平）served as Secretary and Deputy Secretary, respectively.

05 Jun 1947

Ye Lingfeng（葉靈鳳）founded *Hong Kong History and Geography*—a weekly publication under the newspaper *Sing Tao Daily* with coverage on local anecdotes. In 1953, he established Tai Ping Shan Naturography—a special column in the newspaper *Ta Kung Pao* on Hong Kong's culture, customs, plants and animals. In 1958, his articles were compiled in the book *Hong Kong Naturography*.

14 Jun 1947

The Import Control Order 1947 was promulgated, introducing a system of licences for import of goods, unless otherwise exempt.

28 Jun 1947

The Hong Kong government announced an open tender for beach operation at Repulse Bay, Stanley, Big Wave Bay and Shek O.

01 Jul 1947

Raymond Wong Chok-mui（黃作梅）, former Head of Hong Kong–Kowloon Independent Brigade's International Liaison Unit, was made a Member of the Order of the British Empire in recognition of his assistance to the Allied forces during the Japanese occupation.

05 Jul 1947

The Hong Kong government granted HK$50,000 to help flood victims in Guangdong Province.

15 Jul 1947

Chiyu Banking Corporation Limited, founded by overseas Chinese businessman Tan Kah-kee (陳嘉庚), was opened for business.

24 Jul 1947

The Hong Kong government announced limited approval by the British Colonial Office with respect to Governor Mark Young's constitutional reform proposal.

25 Jul 1947

Alexander Grantham was sworn in as the 22nd Governor of Hong Kong. He left office on 31 December 1957.

01 Aug 1947

The Jury Amendment Ordinance 1947 was promulgated, making women eligible for jury duty.

06 Aug 1947

Tsen Ho Bank closed after 10 months of operation; it marked the first collapse of a bank in Hong Kong after the Second World War.

Figure 135
The Nanyang Cotton Mill in Hong Kong in 1948. (Photo courtesy of HKSAR Government)

16 Aug 1947

Chinese machine operators began a large labour strike, demanding a 150% pay rise. Workers from various sectors, including private dockyards, cement plants and piers as well as workers of the Naval Dockyard and Kowloon–Canton Railway, joined the 27-day strike. On 11 September, labour agreements were reached to provide higher pay, including a 20% increase for dockyard workers.

27 Aug 1947

The Social Welfare Office—predecessor of the Social Welfare Department—was established under the Secretariat for Chinese Affairs.

23 Sep 1947

The first pair of fishing boats refitted with motors—financed through a loan scheme under the Fish Marketing Organization—passed a sea trial.

02 Oct 1947

Nanyang Cotton Mill Limited was founded by Wang Yuncheng (王雲程); it was the second largest textile mill in Hong Kong. (Figure 135)

15 Oct 1947

Wyler Textiles Limited was founded by Wu Kunsheng (吳昆生); it became the third largest textile mill in Hong Kong.

18 Oct 1947

The first post-Second World War cross-harbour swimming race was held; it ran from the pier of Tsim Sha Tsui Rail Station to Victoria Recreation Club in Central.

12 Nov 1947

The Taiwan Democratic Self-Government League was founded in Hong Kong.

14 Nov 1947

Author Huang Guliu (黃谷柳) began to publish his novel *The Tale of Shrimpball*—a depiction of daily life of Hong Kong—as a series in the newspaper *Hwa Shang Pao*.

24 Nov 1947

Hong Kong participated in a meeting of the United Nations (UN) Economic Commission for Asia and the Far East in the Philippines as an Associate Member. It was the first time Hong Kong was represented as an entity at a UN meeting.

27 Nov 1947

The Hong Kong government ordered residents of Kowloon Walled City to vacate from their wooden shacks before 11 December.

06 Dec 1947

The National Government of the Republic of China issued a statement regarding the demolition of wooden shacks in Kowloon Walled City by the Hong Kong government, reiterating its jurisdiction over Kowloon Walled City.

18 Dec 1947

The Hong Kong (Rehabilitation) Loan Ordinance 1947 was promulgated, issuing HK$150 million in government bonds to support post-Second World War reconstruction.

1947

The Hong Kong government estimated a local population of 1.8 million amid an influx of refugees following the outbreak of the Chinese Civil War.

The Hong Kong government established a Statistical Branch.

The District Office (North) was split into two offices: Yuen Long District Office (responsible for Yuen Long and Castle Peak) and Tai Po District Office (responsible for Tai Po, Sha Tin, Sheung Shui, Fanling, Sha Tau Kok and Ta Kwu Ling).

Ng Tor-tai（吳多泰）proposed the concept of land co-ownership for property owners; buildings were sold by the floor, with a different owner for each floor of a building. (Figure 136)

Figure 136
The brochure on the by-the-floor sale of Universal Mansion located on Hillwood Road in Tsim Sha Tsui during the 1960s and 1970s. (Courtesy of Hong Kong Museum of History)

1947

Lai Sun Garment Factory was founded by Lim Por-yen (林百欣) as a manufacturer of shirts and trousers.

Wellington College, a private secondary school, was founded by Chang Pui-chung (張沛松).

The Hong Kong Council of Social Service was established as a federation of non-governmental organisations to promote social services; it became a statutory body in 1951.

The Fuyu Poetry Society in Hong Kong was founded by Liu Yazi (柳亞子) along with leftist literati in support of the Communist Party of China's call for "Liberation of China" by "promoting new poetry" and "liberating old poetry."

The Fisheries Department opened schools in Tai Po, Sha Tau Kok, Shau Kei Wan, Stanley, Aberdeen, Cheung Chau and Tai O in a bid to promote education among children of fishermen.

The Wah Yan Dramatic Society—a pioneer of Cantonese opera performed in English—was co-founded by Father Terence Sheridan, Wong Chin-wah (黃展華) and others in association with Wah Yan College, Hong Kong.

The Hong Kong Stock Exchange (formerly known as the Stockbrokers' Association of Hong Kong) and Hong Kong Stockbrokers' Association merged to form The Hong Kong Stock Exchange Limited.

China Plastics Company was founded by Chieng Han-chow (錢涵洲) as Hong Kong's first plastics factory.

The Employers' Federation of Hong Kong was established.

01 Jan 1948

The Revolutionary Committee of the Chinese Kuomintang held its inaugural meeting at 52 Kennedy Road on Hong Kong Island. Soong Ching-ling (Song Qingling) (宋慶齡) and Li Jishen (李濟深) served as Honorary Chairman and Chairman, respectively.

05 Jan 1948

The China Democratic League held its third plenary session in Hong Kong where it established a temporary headquarters and announced its cooperation with the Communist Party of China.

The Hong Kong government deployed more than 200 police officers and more than 100 workers to demolish houses in Kowloon Walled City.

07 Jan 1948

Governor Alexander Grantham and Special Commissioner of the National Government of the Republic of China for Foreign Affairs in Kwangtung and Kwangsi T. W. Kwok (郭德華) met at the Government House regarding the demolition of houses in Kowloon Walled City. A delegation led by the head of Bao'an County also met with affected residents.

11 Jan 1948

A delegation of the Guangdong Provincial Assembly arrived in Hong Kong to meet with residents of the Kowloon Walled City.

12 Jan 1948

The Hong Kong government deployed 150 police officers in another attempt to forcibly demolish houses in Kowloon Walled City, resulting in a clash with residents. The police opened fire and deployed tear gas, causing several injuries.

The Ministry of Foreign Affairs of the National Government of the Republic of China summoned the British Ambassador to the Republic of China in a protest regarding the bloodshed in the Kowloon Walled City caused by the Hong Kong government.

14 Jan 1948

The Harbour Department was renamed the Marine Department—responsible for port operation and shipping traffic management.

24 Jan 1948

The Chinese Ambassador in London sent a diplomatic note to the British government and reiterated China's sovereignty over the Kowloon Walled City.

30 Jan 1948

The Banking Ordinance 1948 was promulgated, marking the first banking legislation in Hong Kong. It stipulated that all banking institutions must obtain a government licence, pay certain registration fees and provide annual financial reports. It also specified the establishment of the Banking Advisory Committee.

01 Mar 1948

The *Literature and Art for the Masses* Series—with a focus on art and literature under the editorship of Feng Naichao (馮乃超), Shao Quanlin (邵荃麟) and Hu Sheng (胡繩)—began publication; it ceased publication in 1949.

03 Mar 1948

Hong Kong was struck by a minor earthquake for the first time after the Second World War.

12 Mar 1948

The Hong Kong Bar Association was established as a professional organisation of barristers in Hong Kong.

The Trade Unions and Trade Disputes Ordinance 1948 was promulgated, requiring trade unions to register with the government.

16 Mar 1948

South Sea Textile Manufacturing Company in Tsuen Wan—a manufacturer of yarn and textiles founded by Tang Ping-yuan (唐炳源)—was incorporated.

30 Mar 1948

Hong Kong Cotton Mills was founded by Wong Toong-yuen (王統元). In 1954, it merged with Peninsula Spinners (relocated from Shanghai to Hong Kong in 1949), forming HKS Group International Limited.

Mar 1948

Paul Tsui Ka-cheung (徐家祥) was appointed as the first Chinese Cadet Officer (later known as Administrative Officer).

01 Apr 1948

Her Majesty's Treasury began to loosen its control over Hong Kong government's finances. The Secretary of State for the Colonies still retained certain power, including the right to review Hong Kong's annual budget.

09 Apr 1948

The Hong Kong government provided authorised retailers with 10,000 sacks of rice to be sold at an affordable price of 72 cents per catty in a bid to fight black market speculation.

15 Apr 1948

Chinese and British officials began restoration of boundary stones at Sha Tau Kok. The Memorandum on the Replacement of Certain Boundary Stones on the Anglo-Chinese Border at Sha Tau Kok was signed on 17 April.

17 Apr 1948

The Hong Kong and Kowloon Federation of Trade Unions was founded; it was renamed The Hong Kong Federation of Trade Unions in 1986 (currently the largest trade union federation in Hong Kong).

Anglican Church Bishop Ronald Owen Hall formed a special committee under the Hong Kong Social Welfare Council and held an inaugural meeting. The committee was funded with a donation of £14,000 from the Air Raid Distress Fund endorsed by the Lord Mayor of London—and later became the Hong Kong Housing Society. On 18 May 1951, it became a statutory body on housing matters.

05 May 1948

Li Jishen (李濟深), He Xiangning (何香凝), Shen Junru (沈鈞儒), Zhang Bojun (章伯鈞) and other democratic supporters in Hong Kong sent a telegram to Mao Zedong (毛澤東). They expressed support for the Communist Party of China's May 1st Slogans, calling for a new political consultative conference and a democratic coalition government.

May 1948

Kai Tak Airport's new control tower was completed.

08 Jun 1948

A Lingnan-style art exhibition began at St John's Cathedral in Central, putting on display more than 100 paintings and calligraphy works by Gao Jianfu (高劍父), Chao Shao-an (趙少昂), Yang Shanshen (楊善深), Guan Shanyue (關山月) and Li Gemin (黎葛民).

12 Jun 1948

The Hong Kong government approved Broadcast Relay Service (Hong Kong)'s application for operation of Radio Rediffusion and issued Hong Kong's first cable radio licence.

Jun 1948

The Hong Kong government began publishing data collected by the Statistical Branch in a monthly edition of the *Gazette.*

16 Jul 1948

Cathay Pacific Airways' flying boat *Miss Macao* that offered regular service between Hong Kong and Macao was hijacked and crashed into the sea, killing all 26 on board. One of the hijackers survived. This was the first airplane hijack in Hong Kong's aviation history.

19 Jul 1948

The Maurine Grantham Nursery, located on Un Chau Street in Kowloon and run by the Young Women's Christian Association, was opened as the first nursery in Hong Kong.

30 Jul 1948

The Prevention of Corruption Ordinance 1948 was promulgated, authorising the Attorney-General to give written permission to police officers above the rank of an assistant superintendent to conduct investigations on corruption.

Jul 1948

The Police Training School in Wong Chuk Hang was opened as Hong Kong's first permanent police academy.

06 Aug 1948

Leslie Bertram Gibson was appointed as Chief Justice of Hong Kong.

13 Aug 1948

The Police Force Ordinance 1948 was promulgated, defining Hong Kong's police force in terms of its organisation, discipline, mission, management, welfare and delegation of powers.

17 Aug 1948

Anglican Church Bishop Ronald Owen Hall proposed establishing the Hong Kong Juvenile Care Centre as a temporary shelter for problem children.

Aug 1948

The Hong Kong Broadcasting Station announced cancellation of its callsigns ZBW and ZEK; it was renamed Radio Hong Kong (later known as Radio Television Hong Kong).

Liow & Company was renamed China Resources Company; it was registered on 18 December. Since the early 1950s, it had been serving as the agent in Hong Kong for all Chinese import/export companies. In 1983, it was reorganised as China Resources Company (Holdings) Limited.

09 Sep 1948

The Hong Kong and Kowloon Trades Union Council was established as a pro-Kuomintang trade union federation.

The Hong Kong edition of the newspaper *Wen Wei Po* began publication.

20 Sep 1948

The drivers of eight taxi companies in Hong Kong demanded a rise in their daily wage from HK$6 to HK$8. When the request was rejected by the employers and the Employers' Federation, drivers employed by Star Taxicab Company went on strike. The next day, drivers of seven other taxi companies held a "go-slow" protest. On 21 January 1949, an agreement on wages was reached, ending the 124-day labour action.

22 Sep 1948

A fire broke out at night in the warehouse of Wing On Company in Sai Wan, resulting in 176 people dead or missing, 69 injured and over HK$20 million losses in property.

Sep 1948

The *Hong Kong Preliminary Planning Report 1948*, prepared by British architect Patrick Abercrombie, was released. It identified three long-term goals: 1) an improved domestic and international transport network with port facilities, railways and tunnels; 2) development of new towns to ease overcrowded urban areas; and 3) enhanced regulation and mechanism in support of urban planning and zoning.

12 Oct 1948

The Justice of the Peace Court began its first trial, setting a precedence of judicial duties in the courts of law and allowing full-time judges to focus on criminal cases.

18 Oct 1948

The British Ambassador to China (on behalf of the Hong Kong government) signed an anti-smuggling agreement with the Ministry of Foreign Affairs of the National Government of the Republic of China, allowing Chinese customs officials to carry out enforcement in the waters of Hong Kong.

22 Oct 1948

The Hong Kong Anti-Tuberculosis Association—founded by Jehangir Hormusjee Ruttonjee, Chau Sik-nin (周錫年) and Seaward Woo (胡兆熾)—was established as a statutory body; it began before the Second World War and was later renamed Hong Kong Tuberculosis, Chest and Heart Diseases Association.

26 Oct 1948

Joint Publishing in Hong Kong was formed through a merger of Life Bookstore, Dushu Publishing House, and Xinzhi Book Company. In 1949, it moved its headquarters to Beijing with a branch in Hong Kong.

29 Oct 1948

The Public Order Ordinance 1948 was promulgated, prohibiting political attires in public places during public assemblies. It also specified penalties for disorderly public conduct.

The Diplomatic Privileges Ordinance 1948 was promulgated, granting diplomatic immunity to international organisations (and their staff) of which the United Kingdom was a member.

15 Nov 1948

The Sanitary Department began a two-week clean-up campaign in which people were prosecuted for urinating, defecating or littering on the streets. It marked the beginning of the Clean Hong Kong Campaign.

14 Dec 1948

The Hong Kong Observatory became a member of the World Meteorological Organization.

16 Dec 1948

The Sixth Exhibition of Chinese Products, organised by the Chinese Manufacturers' Association of Hong Kong, began in an 18-day expo in Tsim Sha Tsui following the end of the Second World War. In 1951, it was renamed Exhibition of Hong Kong Products.

20 Dec 1948

The British War Crimes Court in Hong Kong held its final trial of Japanese war criminals, concluding a run of 46 trials in more than two years and eight months. Of 122 suspects, 21 were sentenced to death, two to life imprisonment, and 85 to imprisonment from six months to 20 years; 14 were acquitted.

21 Dec 1948

A China National Aviation Corporation airliner flying from Shanghai to Hong Kong crashed near Basalt Island in Sai Kung, killing all 35 people onboard.

30 Dec 1948

An investiture was held at the Government House. Lo Man-kam (羅文錦) was knighted for his efforts in helping to rebuild Hong Kong after the Second World War; 18 soldiers and Chinese civilians, including Chan Kwan-po (陳君葆), were awarded the Order of the British Empire in recognition of their contribution in aiding the Allied forces during the Japanese occupation.

Dec 1948

The New Territories District Office was established to oversee district offices in Tai Po, Yuen Long and Southern District for greater governance in the New Territories (and outlying islands); John Barrow was appointed as the first District Commissioner, New Territories.

1948

The British Council set up a headquarters in Hong Kong.

Liu Chong Hing Savings Bank was founded; it became Liu Chong Hing Bank on 17 March 1955 and was renamed Chong Hing Bank in 2006.

The San Miguel Brewery of the Philippines opened a brewery at Sham Tseng in Tsuen Wan.

Hotel Miramar in Tsim Sha Tsui was opened for business. In 1957, it was acquired by Young Chi-wan (楊志雲). On 26 August of the same year, he and Ho Sin-hang (何善衡) jointly established Miramar Hotel and Investment Company Limited.

20 Jan 1949

The Hong Kong Bottlers Federal Incorporation was founded by American businessman Anker B. Henningsen with the exclusive right to bottle Coca-Cola in Hong Kong. It was acquired by Swire Group in 1965 and renamed Swire Bottler Limited in 1974.

22 Jan 1949

The Immigrants Control Ordinance 1949 was promulgated, introducing control measures on the entry, exit and movement of persons not born in Hong Kong.

01 Feb 1949

Mao Zedong (毛澤東) noted during a three-day meeting in Xibaipo with a delegation of the Communist Party of the Soviet Union that it would not make much sense to address the issues of Hong Kong and Macao in a rush and that it would be more beneficial to develop international relations and trade by leveraging these regions, especially Hong Kong.

09 Feb 1949

The newspaper *Wen Wei Po* published an editorial "New China and Hong Kong" in which it announced a decision by the Communist Party of China to retain the status quo of Hong Kong for the time being.

17 Feb 1949

The newspaper *Ta Kung Pao* published an editorial "Promising Future for Hong Kong" in which it highlighted a good Sino-British relationship and a promising future in Hong Kong.

24 Feb 1949

The Ruttonjee Sanatorium—refitted from the former Royal Naval Hospital and managed by the Hong Kong Anti-Tuberculosis Association—was opened for tuberculosis patients.

A Cathay Pacific Airways airliner flying from Manila to Hong Kong crashed near Choi Sai Woo (present-day Braemer Hill) in North Point, killing all 23 people on board.

25 Feb 1949

The Reform Club of Hong Kong was founded under the chairmanship of Brook Antony Bernacchi; it was dissolved in March 1998.

01 Mar 1949

The Hong Kong Defence Force—comprising the newly reorganised Hong Kong Regiment, Hong Kong Royal Naval Volunteer Reserve, and Hong Kong Auxiliary Air Force—was formed; it was granted a Royal title in 1951.

The English newspaper *Hong Kong Tiger Standard* was founded by Aw Boon-haw (胡文虎).

22 Mar 1949

Radio Rediffusion—launched by the Broadcast Relay Services (Hong Kong) Limited and sponsored by the British Broadcast Relay Services Limited—made its debut as the first commercial radio station in Hong Kong. (Figure 137)

Figure 137
The first-generation Rediffusion House in Wan Chai showcased in *Rediffusion Weekly* published on 09 April 1950. (Courtesy of Hong Kong Museum of History)

01 Apr 1949

The Registrar General's Department was established for the registration of land, incorporation, trademark, bankruptcy and marriage; William Aneurin Jones was the first Registrar General.

08 Apr 1949

The Hong Kong Schools Music and Speech Association held its first Hong Kong Schools' Music Festival.

The Declaration on the Cleaning Movements Towards Cantonese Films—endorsed by 164 Cantonese film practitioners in Hong Kong—was published in the newspaper *Ta Kung Pao*, calling on producers to stop making films deemed harmful to national interest and social morality.

16 Apr 1949

The Lai Chi Kok Amusement Park, later known as Lai Yuen, was opened. (Figures 138 and 139)

17 Apr 1949

Kowloon Motor Bus began service with its first double-decker on bus route No.1 running between Tsim Sha Tsui and Kowloon City.

25 Apr 1949

Kuomintang officials and wealthy businessmen travelling on a dozen aircraft arrived at Kai Tak Airport in Hong Kong from Shanghai between 4:00 p.m. and 8:05 p.m. amid the Chinese Civil War.

Figure 138
The male Asian elephant Tino—the only elephant domesticated in Hong Kong and a "Treasure of the Zoo" of Lai Chi Kok Amusement Park. (Photo taken in 1964 and courtesy of Sing Tao News Corporation Limited)

Figure 139
The roundabout boat ride at Lai Chi Kok Amusement Park in 1964. (Photo courtesy of Sing Tao News Corporation Limited)

29 Apr 1949

The Illegal Strikes and Lockouts Ordinance 1949 was promulgated, prohibiting strikes and lockouts for reasons other than labour disputes.

08 May 1949

The Hong Kong Chinese Reform Association was founded by Ma Man-fai (馬文輝), Mok Ying-kwai (莫應溎) and Percy Chen (陳丕士), aiming for moderate democratic reform.

24 May 1949

China Dyeing Works Limited was founded by Cha Chi-ming (查濟民); in the same year, a bleaching and dyeing plant was established on Castle Peak Road in Tsuen Wan.

25 May 1949

Workers of Mayar Silk Mills went on strike in protest of a new unfavourable employment contract. On 11 May, Lau Chung-ping (樓頌平), Chairman of Hong Kong & Kowloon Silk Factories Workers Association and a representative of the workers, was dismissed by his employer. On 14 August, a labour agreement (5% pay rise) was reached upon mediation by the Labour Department; workers returned to work after an 81-day strike. On 04 January 1950, Lau Chung-ping was deported for instigating a labour strike.

27 May 1949

The Education Department announced its plan to open two schools in Wan Chai and Hung Hom, aiming to replace all Workers' Children Schools. It triggered a campaign in the Chinese labour community to save the schools. On 12 July, the Education Department proposed reorganising the Workers' Children Schools Management Committee and keeping only five Workers' Children Schools through re-registration. On 15 September, two new government-run schools for workers' children were opened.

The Societies Ordinance 1949 was promulgated, stipulating that all societies established in Hong Kong (unless exempt or not required according to the Ordinance) must be registered with the Registrar of Societies, otherwise they would be deemed unlawful.

May 1949

Mount Davis Cottage Area, also known as Kung Man Village since 1952, was completed with the first group of wooden huts designed to accommodate the poor whose homes were demolished or burnt down. It was the first public resettlement project for the poor—designated by the Hong Kong government and built by Chung Sing Benevolent Society under a loan scheme.

01 Jun 1949

The Hong Kong government imposed a three-month curfew along the border as the Chinese Civil War gradually spread to areas south of the Yangtze River.

10 Jun 1949

The Education Department resolved to reorganise the committees of two schools for fishermen's children in Aberdeen and on Cheung Chau in a bid to improve the quality of education. The committee chairmen and school principals were appointed by the Education Department under the new system.

22 Jun 1949

Unofficial Members of the Legislative Council commenced a debate on the Young Plan. A motion—proposed by Councillor David Fortune Landale on 27 April—was passed to increase the number of Legislative Council Unofficial Members; it replaced the original plan of forming a municipal council.

10 Jul 1949

A fraternity among Chinese filmmakers was established as the first professional filmmaking organisation in Hong Kong; it was later renamed South China Film Industry Workers Union.

18 Jul 1949

A group of five—including representatives from the Chinese Manufacturers Association of Hong Kong and the Hong Kong Chinese Reform Association—presented Governor Alexander Grantham with a petition (co-signed by 138 Chinese organisations) on constitutional reform.

Jul 1949

Governor Alexander Grantham highlighted in a pamphlet that Hong Kong was "…one of the largest entrepot trading centres in the world…40% of Hong Kong's trade [was] with China, and the Colony serve[d] as the principal doorway whereby our goods reach[ed] the vast potential market of the Chinese interior."

14 Aug 1949

Huang Shaohong (黃紹竑) and other Kuomintang members in Hong Kong, totalling 44, declared their withdrawal from the party and cooperation with the Communist Party of China.

19 Aug 1949

The Registration of Persons Ordinance 1949 was promulgated, requiring all Hong Kong residents aged 12 and above to register for an identity card. The Registration of Persons Office was established on the same day and began handling registration and issuance of identity cards in October. It marked the first time Hong Kong identity cards were issued.

29 Aug 1949

British Secretary of State for Foreign Affairs Ernest Bevin and Secretary of State for the Colonies Arthur Creech Jones filed a memorandum with the Cabinet, noting that Britain should retain Hong Kong but refrain from discussing Hong Kong's future with the Chinese government in the foreseeable future and from making statements that might provoke China.

Aug 1949

Raymond Wong Chok-mui (黃作梅) assumed office as the second Director of the Hong Kong Branch of Xinhua News Agency.

Chow Shou-son (周壽臣) and more than 2,000 community leaders, including Executive and Legislative Councillors, made an appeal with Governor Alexander Grantham for a ban on the butchering of dogs.

02 Sep 1949

The Expulsion of Undesirables Ordinance 1949 was promulgated, authorising deportation of any person who was a non-British alien or resided in Hong Kong for less than 10 years if deemed "undesirable" by the authority.

19 Sep 1949

China Merchants' ship *Hai Liao*—en route from Hong Kong to Shantou—renounced the National Government of the Republic of China and changed course; it arrived at the port of Dalian on 28 September.

General Yang Jie (楊杰)—a faction leader (southwestern area) of the Kuomintang Revolutionary Committee who denounced Chiang Kai-shek (蔣介石) for his military tactics and corruption—was assassinated in his flat on Hennessy Road in Wan Chai.

24 Sep 1949

The Hong Kong government designated all reservoirs as restricted areas, prohibiting any persons from reaching within 300 yards based on the highest water level without permission of the Commissioner of Police.

28 Sep 1949

The Pharmaceutical Society of Hong Kong, comprising pharmacists and industry professionals, was established as a trade platform.

02 Oct 1949

Banquets at Jinling Restaurant were organised by trade unions and journalists in celebration of the founding of the People's Republic of China on 01 October. Newspapers *Hwa Shang Pao*, *Ta Kung Pao* and *Wen Wei Po* took turns taking holidays from 01 to 03 October and released commemorative issues.

08 Oct 1949

The film *Wong Fei-hung's Whip that Smacks the Candle* as the first part of *The Story of Wong Fei-hung* starring Kwan Tak-hing (關德興) and Walter Tso Tat-wah (曹達華) premiered as the first Hong Kong film on Chinese martial artist Wong Fei-hung (黃飛鴻).

10 Oct 1949

The Asia Evening College of Arts and Commerce—co-founded by Ch'ien Mu (Qian Mu) (錢穆), Tang Chun-i (唐君毅) and Tchang Pi-kai (張丕介)—was opened for classes at Wah Nam Middle School. On 01 March 1950, it was renamed New Asia College and relocated to Sham Shui Po, becoming a day school.

23 Oct 1949

The Sham Shui Po Kaifong Welfare Advancement Association—one of the earliest Kaifong (people living in the same neighbourhood) welfare associations in Hong Kong—was established. Others in various districts later emerged with support from the Social Welfare Office.

Oct 1949

The People's Liberation Army arrived in Guangdong Province. By the order of the Chinese government, it refrained from crossing Cheung Muk Tau—about 40 kilometres north of Lo Wu, Hong Kong—so as to prevent any disputes with the Hong Kong government.

Chu Hai University was renamed Chu Hai College after its relocation from Guangzhou to Hong Kong with a temporary campus in Mong Kok, Kowloon.

The Education Department announced its implementation of the Joint Primary 6 Examination starting from the 1949 academic year as part of a selection process for secondary school education among primary school graduates. The examination was replaced with the Academic Aptitude Test in early 1978.

04 Nov 1949

The Air Transport (Licencing of Air Services) Regulations 1949 was promulgated, introducing a regulatory regime regarding licences and permits for scheduled and non-scheduled flights.

08 Nov 1949

The Tung Wah Group of Hospitals began receiving Chinese refugees as well as wounded Kuomintang soldiers.

09 Nov 1949

Staff of China National Aviation Corporation and Central Air Transport Corporation in Hong Kong announced an uprising and flew 12 aircraft from Hong Kong to Tianjin and Beijing in what became known as the Two Airlines Uprising.

11 Nov 1949

Lo Hin-shing (羅顯勝) and William Ngar-tse Thomas Tam (譚雅士) became the first Chinese appointed as Permanent Magistrates.

14 Nov 1949

Great South Fishing Industries Limited—Hong Kong's largest and longest-running Chinese-owned commercial fishing company—was incorporated.

17 Nov 1949

Governor Alexander Grantham announced that no aircraft of China National Aviation Corporation and Central Air Transport Corporation were to move until a Sino-British air agreement was further clarified; 71 aircraft were stranded in Hong Kong.

24 Nov 1949

Tai An-go (戴安國) and Shen Teh-hsieh (沈德燮), on behalf of the Taiwan authority, applied to freeze assets of China National Aviation Corporation (CNAC) and Central Air Transport Corporation (CATC) in Hong Kong through an interim injunction with the Supreme Court of Hong Kong. The next day, CNAC and CATC staff in Hong Kong filed an objection. The court placed all CNAC and CATC assets in Hong Kong under temporary government custody.

04 Dec 1949

The Shantou-bound passenger ship *Yu On* sank in the waters near Lei Yue Mun, claiming 80 lives; only four people survived.

09 Dec 1949

The Essential Services Corps Ordinance 1949 was promulgated, allowing voluntary auxiliary forces to be established to maintain basic services and public order in times of emergency.

14 Dec 1949

Nanyang Commercial Bank—incorporated on 02 February 1948—was opened for business.

19 Dec 1949

Americans Claire Lee Chennault and Whiting Willauer filed a petition with the Supreme Court of Hong Kong for transfer of assets from China National Aviation Corporation and Central Air Transport Corporation to US-registered Civil Air Transport Incorporated.

24 Dec 1949

About 1,500 workers of Hong Kong Tramways joined a "go slow" strike and operated trams without collecting fares, calling for higher wages. On 28 December, the tram depot on Russell Street in Causeway Bay was locked following an order issued by the management. Services were suspended and all tram conductors were dismissed. The strike ended in January 1950.

30 Dec 1949

The Emergency (Principal) Regulations Ordinance 1949 was promulgated, consolidating the emergency powers previously conferred by the Emergency Regulations Ordinance 1922.

1949

The Hong Kong government estimated a population of 1.86 million amid an influx of refugees resulting from the Chinese Civil War.

The United Nations concluded its role in food ration in Hong Kong.

The police started construction of observation posts (commonly known as the MacIntosh Forts) along the border by the Shenzhen River; seven posts were in place by 1953.

Star Industrial Company Limited was founded; it was known for its iconic plastics brand Red A.

Yangtzekiang Garment Manufacturing Company was founded by Chan Sui-kau (陳瑞球) as owner of famous brands DOCTOR and Michel Rene.

The Institute of Chartered Secretaries and Administrators approved the establishment of Hong Kong Institute of Chartered Secretaries.

The New Method English Tutorial School, predecessor of the New Method College, was established on Electric Road in North Point. It became the first private school to join the Education Department's Direct Subsidy Scheme in 1997; it was closed in September 2012.

1949

The Hong Kong branch of an association dedicated to promoting Chinese Islamic culture was reinstituted as Hong Kong Chinese Islamic Federation.

The Alliance Bible Institute, led by Reverend William C. Newbern, was relocated from Wuzhou, Guangxi to Cheung Chau, Hong Kong. It resumed classes the following year and was renamed Alliance Bible Seminary in 1955.

The Foreign Correspondents' Club—founded in Chongqing—was relocated to Hong Kong. In 1982, it moved to a premise on Lower Albert Road in Central.

01 Jan 1950

The Hong Kong Observatory launched a Local Strong Wind Signal alert system—which was renamed Strong Monsoon Signal on 15 April 1956.

06 Jan 1950

The British government officially recognised the People's Republic of China and appointed a Chargés d'Affaires ad interim in China. On 17 June 1954, it established diplomatic relations with China at the level of Chargé d'Affaires.

The Dogs and Cats Ordinance 1950 was promulgated, requiring dog owners to obtain a licence and vaccinate their dogs to prevent the spread of rabies.

07 Jan 1950

The Hong Kong office of Special Commissioner of the former National Government of the Republic of China for Foreign Affairs in Kwangtung and Kwangsi was closed. The Chinese government made a request for a similar official institution in Hong Kong but was denied.

09 Jan 1950

Premier Zhou Enlai (周恩來) of the Government Administration Council instructed personnel of the former National Government of the Republic of China in Hong Kong to protect state property and await official orders from the Central People's Government.

More than 400 rice shops in Hong Kong and Kowloon began selling low-price rice distributed by the Hong Kong government.

The Chase Bank branch on Queen's Road Central was robbed HK$400,000 and US$4,000 by six armed robbers, marking the first robbery at a foreign bank in Hong Kong.

10 Jan 1950

The Hong Kong government announced that it would stop recognising travel documents issued by the former National Government of the Republic of China.

11 Jan 1950

A fire broke out in the squatter area of Tung Tau Village in Kowloon City, destroying 2,500 huts and leaving over 17,000 residents homeless.

The Dairy Farm Company rejected labour demands and sought for arbitration during a negotiation mediated by the Labour Department. In the evening, some 1,200 workers joined a Dairy Farm Workers' Union rally in Causeway Bay. On 16 January, workers agreed to arbitration upon instruction from the Hong Kong Federation of Trade Unions. On 02 February, an arbitration tribunal was established under the Trade Unions and Trade Disputes Ordinance 1948; it held its first hearing on 09 February. On 24 March, an agreement—including an extra monthly allowance $30 for male workers—was announced.

14 Jan 1950

Staff of China Merchants Group and crew members of its 13 ships in Hong Kong declared an uprising. The national flag of the People's Republic of China was flown on vessels the next day. The vessels arrived in Guangzhou on 24 October.

17 Jan 1950

The Hong Kong branches of Bank of China, Bank of Communications, Farmers Bank of China, Central Trust of China, Postal Remittance and Savings Banks, Kwangtung Provincial Bank and Kwangsi Bank, as well as the procurement offices of the Ministry of Communications, also declared an uprising.

27 Jan 1950

The Military Installations Closed Areas Order 1950 were promulgated, effective 01 February, designating 55 British military sites as restricted zones.

30 Jan 1950

Over 2,000 tram workers clashed with the police during a rally on Russell Street in Causeway Bay. After 10 p.m., the police opened fire and used tear gas, causing more than 40 injuries in what became known as the Russell Street Incident. At 1 a.m., the police closed the Tramway Workers' Union office and deported the union leaders, including its chairman Lau Fat (劉法).

10 Feb 1950

The Interpretation Ordinance 1950 was promulgated, providing better interpretations of legal terms and specialised vocabulary.

23 Feb 1950

The Hong Kong Dental Society (present-day Hong Kong Dental Association) was founded.

24 Feb 1950

The Government Administration Council dispatched its representatives to open an office in Hong Kong and take over assets of the former National Government of the Republic of China. On 01 April, it was renamed Office of the Commissioner of the Government Administration Council for Taking Over Kuomintang Governmental Agencies in Hong Kong and Kowloon.

10 Mar 1950

The Legal Officers Ordinance 1950 was promulgated, outlining the rights and responsibilities of legal officers.

15 Mar 1950

The foundation stone laying ceremony was held for the 17-storey Bank of China building; it was the highest building in Hong Kong upon completion in the following year. On 19 November 1951, it was officially occupied. (Figures 140)

Figure 140
The Bank of China building in central in 1953. It was then the tallest building in Hong Kong—6.5 metres higher than the neighbouring third-generation HSBC Building. (Photo courtesy of HKSAR Government)

28 Mar 1950

The Matriculation Board of The University of Hong Kong announced that Chinese Language would no longer be a compulsory subject in the Hong Kong School Certificate Examination starting in the following year.

02 Apr 1950

Seven China National Aviation Corporation and Central Air Transport Corporation aircraft stranded in Hong Kong were blown up by Kuomintang agent Song Xiangyun (宋祥雲).

03 Apr 1950

Premier Zhou Enlai (周恩來) of the Government Administration Council said in a statement that the Hong Kong government should take full responsibility of the destruction of China National Aviation Corporation and Central Air Transport Corporation aircraft.

04 Apr 1950

The Hong Kong government eased restrictions on rice import, allowing a small quantity of rice from Thailand (re-export was prohibited). The import of rice from other places was still prohibited.

06 Apr 1950

The police established two special units known as the Flying Squad—one on Hong Kong Island and another in Kowloon—dedicated to handling major incidents.

26 Apr 1950

The Hong Kong government began requiring police registration of Chinese residents in Macao for entry into Hong Kong. The Immigration Department also announced required inspection of inbound ships in a designated area before they were allowed to dock.

28 Apr 1950

The Immigrants Control (Amendment) (No. 2) Regulations 1950 was promulgated, effective 01 May, revoking the exemption that allowed the entry of Chinese people from the Mainland without valid travel documents or visas. The Hong Kong government also established a control point at Lo Wu and began building a wire fence at the border with Guangdong Province, ending the free flow of people.

02 May 1950

The office of newspaper *Sing Tao Daily* was attacked with a grenade, leaving one girl dead and nine people injured. The police offered a reward for information leading to the arrest of the perpetrators.

03 May 1950

The Emergency (Principal) Regulations Ordinance 1949 was implemented, introducing life imprisonment for illegal possession or carriage of arms, ammunitions or explosive substances.

10 May 1950

The British Privy Council issued an order freezing the assets (including the aircraft) of China National Aviation Corporation and Central Air Transport Corporation; it also delegated the Supreme Court of Hong Kong to issue a ruling on ownership.

20 May 1950

The Exploration of Lantau Island Development Committee—chaired by the District Office (South) and comprising 17 organisations and institutions, including the Kowloon Chamber of Commerce and several Kaifong Welfare Associations—held its first meeting.

01 Jun 1950

Aw Boon-haw (胡文虎) was made an Associate Knight of the Order of St. John by the British monarch.

18 Jun 1950

A tour group of about 150 people, organised by leftist unions and schools, went on an excursion on Hong Kong Island. While passing a refugee area at Mount Davis, they performed the Yangko dance at its outskirts, causing a clash with the pro-Kuomintang refugees in what became known as the Yangko Dance Incident during which more than 60 people were injured. On 26 June, the government began relocating refugees from Mount Davis to Rennie's Mill (present-day Tiu Keng Leng).

23 Jun 1950

The Vehicle and Road Traffic (Amendment) (No. 2) Regulations 1950 was promulgated, placing a limit on vehicle loads and prohibiting private cars from carrying fee-paying passengers.

30 Jun 1950

The Export Control Order 1950 was promulgated, prohibiting goods from being exported without permits and banning 11 specified types of goods (such as copper alloy, petroleum products and rubber) from being exported to the Mainland, Taiwan and Macao.

The Public Services Commission Ordinance 1950 was promulgated, establishing a Public Services Commission.

03 Jul 1950

The first Workers' Medical Clinic—founded by the Hong Kong Federation of Trade Unions—was opened.

08 Jul 1950

The Exportation (Prohibition) (North Korea) Order 1950 was promulgated, imposing a broad embargo on North Korea.

12 Jul 1950

The British Red Cross Society established a branch in Hong Kong.

01 Aug 1950

The Great Wall Pictorial was established by Great Wall Movie Enterprises Limited; it was the first monthly movie magazine in Southeast Asia.

11 Aug 1950

The Hong Kong government announced a new list of more than 100 prohibited items for export, including hardware and machinery, chemical materials and instruments, petroleum and related equipment, radio devices as well as land and sea traffic devices.

21 Sep 1950

The US Department of Commerce announced a ban on the export of unlicenced items of strategic value to Hong Kong and Macao.

30 Sep 1950

The Education Department announced in a quarterly report that a 10-year government programme would be launched to build five new schools annually in a step to meet the growing demand for school places starting in 1951.

Sep 1950

Civics for Hong Kong—a compulsory primary school textbook on civic education designated by the Education Department—went on sale.

01 Oct 1950

Trade unions and various organisations in Hong Kong celebrated the first National Day of the People's Republic of China at China Restaurant.

05 Oct 1950

The *New Evening Post*—a subsidiary of the newspaper *Ta Kung Pao*—began publication.

The Hong Kong Observatory hoisted Increasing Gale or Storm Signal No. 9 for six hours amid Typhoon Ossia. The next day, a landslide near Chun Shing Street in Happy Valley buried two huts, killing nine people.

11 Oct 1950

The Emergency Principal (Amendment) (No. 2) Regulations 1950 was promulgated, effective 20 October, imposing a maximum penalty of a death sentence for carrying explosive substances or using arms without legal authorisation. It was in response to a rise in armed robberies.

15 Oct 1950

Cable & Wireless began trans-Pacific wireless call service from Hong Kong to Hawaii.

17 Oct 1950

The Lepers' Home in Sandy Bay—under the Tung Wah Group of Hospitals—was opened as the first care centre dedicated to treating leprosy in Hong Kong with a capacity of 160 patients.

Oct 1950

The Department of Agriculture, Fisheries and Forestry was formed in a merger with the Agriculture Department, Forestry Department and Fisheries Department.

01 Nov 1950

The Hong Kong Aircraft Engineering Company Limited—headquartered at Kai Tak Airport—was established in a merger between Pacific Air Maintenance and Supply Company Limited and Jardine Aircraft Maintenance Company Limited; it became the largest aircraft maintenance engineering company in Hong Kong.

15 Nov 1950

The Sanitary Department took down three squatter areas in Causeway Bay and Fortress Hill under the escort of over 300 riot police officers.

24 Nov 1950

The Amateur Sports Federation of Hong Kong was established; Arthur Morse served as its first president.

25 Nov 1950

Electra House—constructed on the site of the former Mercury House on Connaught Road Central in Sheung Wan—became the new headquarters of Cable & Wireless.

29 Nov 1950

Tai Shing Secondary School was founded by Confucius Hall as the first Confucian secondary school in Hong Kong; it was renamed Confucius Hall Secondary School in 1953.

Nov 1950

The "999" emergency call system established by the police became operational.

The Auxiliary Fire Services was formed under the Essential Services Corps Ordinance 1949; it was disbanded in 1975.

01 Dec 1950

Wo Hop Shek Cemetery in Fanling was opened as Hong Kong's largest public cemetery. The Kowloon–Canton Railway Wo Hop Shek Spur Line (for carriage of bodies) was completed on 11 September.

03 Dec 1950

The US Department of Commerce announced a permit system for goods exported to Hong Kong, Macao and the Mainland effective immediately, prohibiting the export of war supplies to the Mainland.

04 Dec 1950

A fire broke out in the squatter area of Lei Cheng Uk in Sham Shui Po, destroying about 1,500 homes and leaving thousands of people homeless. The Sham Shui Po Kaifong Welfare Advancement Association registered a total of 2,419 victims.

08 Dec 1950

The Exportation (Prohibition) (Specific Articles) (No. 2) Order 1950 was promulgated, prohibiting the export of arms, mechanical parts and military supplies without a licence.

22 Dec 1950

The Auxiliary Medical Service was established under the Essential Services Corps Ordinance 1949.

1950

The Sek Kong Camp and its military airfield were put into service.

The Hong Kong government estimated a local population of 2,060,000.

The Hong Kong Model Housing Society, a voluntary organisation, was founded to provide low-income people with low-cost housing.

The Family Planning Association of Hong Kong—successor to the Hong Kong Eugenics League established in 1936—was founded to provide birth control services. In 1952, it was one of the eight founding members of the International Planned Parenthood Federation.

Cheung Kong Plastics Company was founded by Li Ka-shing (李嘉誠).

The China Christian Sacred Music School, predecessor of Hong Kong Music Institute, was established.

05 Jan 1951

The Protection of Women and Juveniles Ordinance 1951 was promulgated, strengthening the protection of women and girls and extending such protection to boys.

21 Jan 1951

Luen Wo Hui in Fan Ling was inaugurated as the first modern market in Hong Kong since the end of the Second World War.

28 Jan 1951

The Police Special Branch raided several locations, including Heung To Middle School, Hung Hom Workers' Children School and Hong Kong Match Factory; many were detained for questioning.

16 Feb 1951

The Kowloon Tuberculosis Clinic—built by the Hong Kong government with support from the United Nations— was opened to serve the public with free screening and treatment; it was the first government-built clinic after the Second World War.

02 Mar 1951

The Education Department's Evening School of Higher Chinese Studies was founded, offering courses in literature, commerce and journalism. In 1975, it was renamed Chinese Evening Institute; in 1982, it became the Institute of Language in Education.

07 Mar 1951

Financial Secretary Geoffrey Follows released the 1951/52 Budget and proposed that the total fiscal reserves should be no less than that of the estimated revenues of the same financial year.

11 Mar 1951

A Pacific Overseas Airline (Siam) airliner crashed between Mount Parker and Mount Butler in the eastern part of Hong Kong Island upon take-off from Kai Tak Airport, killing all 24 people on board.

15 Mar 1951

Gerard Lewis Howe took office as Chief Justice of Hong Kong.

The China People's Navigation Corporation agreed to the continued operation of China Merchants Steam Navigation Company in Hong Kong.

04 Apr 1951

Radio Hong Kong moved to Electra House, where Cable & Wireless was headquartered, and continued to operate under the government's Public Relations Office. In April 1954, it was made an independent unit led by the Director of Broadcasting.

09 Apr 1951

A Siamese Airway airliner flying from Bangkok to Hong Kong crashed into the waters between Shek O and Waglan Island amid severe weather conditions, killing all 16 people on board.

12 Apr 1951

The Hong Kong government requisitioned *Yung Hao*—an oil tanker owned by China Tanker Company Limited under the Chinese Ministry of Transport—which it turned over to the Royal Navy at a Marine Department pier under marine police escort.

27 Apr 1951

The Emergency (Exportation) (Miscellaneous Provisions) Regulations 1951 was promulgated, authorising the Director of Commerce and Industry to seize any embargoed goods being exported to the Mainland and any transport used for conveying those goods.

Apr 1951

The Education Department began implementation of a health service programme in schools.

02 May 1951

Shu Hong-sing (舒巷城), also known by his pen name Chun Ho (秦可), published his short story "The Fog of Lei Yue Mun" in the magazine *Skyline Weekly*.

17 May 1951

A group of 70 Japanese war criminals—convicted and sentenced to prison by the British War Crimes Courts in Hong Kong—were repatriated to Japan to continue serving their sentences.

18 May 1951

The Control of Publications Consolidation Ordinance 1951 was promulgated, requiring all local newspapers and news agencies to register with the government. The government was authorised to de-register them, suspend their publications and ban them from publishing content found to be treasonous, seditious, libellous, obscene or in contempt of court.

23 May 1951

The Amateur Sports Federation of Hong Kong was recognised as a member of the International Olympic Committee. On 11 July, it was renamed Amateur Sports Federation and Olympic Committee of Hong Kong. In 1952, Hong Kong competed in a Summer Olympic Games for the first time.

26 May 1951

The first group of 10 female police cadets in Hong Kong began training; on 08 September 1952, the first 17 female police officers were put on duty.

01 Jun 1951

The Hong Kong government announced a land acquisition and compensation scheme with respect to the expansion of Kai Tak Airport, including HK$2.25 per square foot of residential land and HK$0.45 per square foot of arable land.

05 Jun 1951

The Southorn Stadium in Wan Chai—managed by the Hong Kong Playground Association—was opened.

15 Jun 1951

The Hong Kong government tightened border control with Guangdong by establishing a closed area which included Chung Ying Street (where special permits were required for public access) in Sha Tau Kok under the Frontier Closed Area Order 1951. (Figure 141)

22 Jun 1951

The Exportation (Prohibition) (Specific Articles) Order 1951 and Importation (Prohibition) (Specific Articles) Order 1951 were promulgated, effective 25 June, forbidding the import/export of 13 specified items (unless authorised by the Director of Commerce and Industry) in compliance with the embargoes imposed on China by the United Nations and Britain.

The Diamond Hill Crematorium became operational as the first crematorium built after the Second World War.

29 Jun 1951

The Subsidised Schools Council was established as an advisory body on government policy in education. In 1993, it became the Subsidized Primary School Council.

Figure 141
An inflow of Mainland refugees. (Photo taken circa 1950s and courtesy of HKSAR Government)

01 Aug 1951

The Hong Kong Observatory hoisted Increasing Gale or Storm Signal No. 9 for five hours amid Typhoon Louise—which caused one death.

05 Aug 1951

The Hong Kong Auxiliary of the Mission to Lepers (later renamed as The Leprosy Mission Hong Kong Auxiliary) began construction of Hong Kong's first permanent leprosy hospital on Hei Ling Chau.

09 Aug 1951

Hong Kong's first Vegetable Marketing Cooperative Society was founded in Fanling.

18 Aug 1951

A landslide struck the squatter area of Tai Hang Sai, commonly known as Kowloon Tsai (an area between Kowloon Tong and Kowloon City), destroying three houses and killing 12 people.

29 Aug 1951

The Diocese of Hong Kong and Macao was established as a separate entity of the Holy Catholic Church of China.

Aug 1951

The Hong Kong Cascade Frog—an endangered species on the International Union for Conservation of Nature's Red List of Threatened Species—was first discovered in Tai Mo Shan.

01 Sep 1951

The Chinese government introduced new immigration control regulations on Chinese citizens travelling to Hong Kong and Macao, marking the end of free flow of people between the Mainland and Hong Kong/Macao.

The Hong Kong government implemented a unified school system, prescribing a six-year curriculum in both primary and secondary schools, a secondary school admission system based on the Joint Primary 6 Examination. Examinees were awarded a certificate of primary education (issued by the Education Department) upon passing.

08 Sep 1951

The Treaty of Peace with Japan (also known as the Treaty of San Francisco) was officially signed by Britain and 47 other countries along with Japan. The British government thereafter would no longer make reparation claims (including for losses from the exchange of the Japanese military yen during the Second World War) on behalf of Hong Kong.

14 Sep 1951

The Compulsory Service Ordinance 1951 was promulgated, corresponding with Britain's National Service. British citizens residing in Hong Kong (males aged 18 or above but under 60 and females aged 21 or above but under 50) were subject to compulsory military service, unless exempt otherwise. Over 1,800 people (half of whom were British Chinese) signed up in the first enlistment.

Sep 1951

Grantham Training College was established; it adopted a one-year curriculum of teacher training to cope with the growing demand for primary school teachers.

03 Oct 1951

Chung Chi College—co-founded by Hong Kong Anglican Church Bishop Ronald Owen Hall, former President of Lingnan University in Guangzhou Lee Ying-lin (李應林) and former Chairman of the Board of St. John's University in Shanghai Au Wai-kwok (歐偉國)—was opened in a ceremony.

12 Oct 1951

The Chinese Manufacturers' Association of Hong Kong held its first Exhibition of Hong Kong Products in Singapore, displaying industrial products from over 150 manufacturers.

25 Oct 1951

The Chinese Reform Association launched a signature campaign to support the continuation of seeking reparations from Japan for losses suffered by Hong Kong residents during the Japanese occupation. The campaign document was submitted to the British government for its assistance.

29 Oct 1951

The Hong Kong government formed a Committee on Higher Education for planning the future development of higher education.

09 Nov 1951

The Motor Vehicles Insurance (Third Party Risks) Ordinance 1951 was promulgated, effective 01 June 1952, stipulating that all motor vehicle drivers must purchase insurance covering third-party risks according to the requirements of the Ordinance.

21 Nov 1951

A fire broke out at Tung Tau Tsuen in Kowloon City, destroying 3,000 houses and leaving over 15,000 people homeless.

25 Nov 1951

West Point, a publication on translated literary works founded in Shanghai, resumed in Hong Kong under the editorship of Liu Yichang (劉以鬯).

10 Dec 1951

Patrick Yu Shuk-siu (余叔韶) became the first Chinese to be appointed as Crown Counsel of the Legal Department.

14 Dec 1951

The nineth Exhibition of Hong Kong Products (previously known as the Exhibition of Chinese Products) began for a 21-day expo. The slogan "Hong Kong people use Hong Kong goods" was later adopted at the 15th Exhibition of Hong Kong Products in 1957.

19 Dec 1951

The Hong Kong government released its *Report on Government Expenditure on Education in Hong Kong* (also called the *Fisher Report)*—prepared by Chief Education Officer of Manchester (UK) Norman George Fisher—proposing further government support in primary education and training of teachers. (Figure 142)

Figure 142
One of the rooftop primary schools in 1964 established to accommodate children of the large numbers of immigrants from the Mainland after the Second World War as existing schools were unable to provide more places. (Photo courtesy of the Public Records Office, Government Records Service)

21 Dec 1951

The Immigration Department announced a new immigration policy, requiring residents of Guangdong Province bound for Hong Kong (bypassing Macao) to present a valid document for returning to the Mainland and those via Macao to present a valid document issued by Hong Kong or Macao.

1951

The Hong Kong government launched a fire-fighting scheme under which seawater tanks were placed across Hong Kong for fire-fighting purposes.

The Kadoorie Agricultural Aid Association was founded by Jewish businessmen and brothers Lawrence and Horace Kadoorie, together with Norman Wright and Woo Ting-sang (胡挺生). It aimed to provide farmers with tools and seeds. In 1956, it developed an experimental farm at Pak Ngau Shek in Tai Po; on 20 January 1995, it was renamed the Kadoorie Farm & Botanic Garden.

Pak Fah Yeow Manufactory, founded in Singapore, was relocated to Hong Kong.

Tseng Lan Shue Village in Sai Kung held a "On Lung Ching Chiu"—a *Jiao* festival organised once every 30 years.

Jian She was established; it became the longest-running classical poetry club in Hong Kong.

04 Jan 1952

The Civil Aid Services was established in accordance with the Essential Services Corps Ordinance 1949.

11 Jan 1952

The Venereal Disease Ordinance 1952 was promulgated, requiring medical practitioners—who received information from a patient as found by the patient to be suffering from a venereal disease—to notify the Deputy Director of Health Services. If a patient was a suspected source of a venereal disease having infected two or more other patients, compulsory medical examinations or treatments would be required.

Jan 1952

The Printing Department was established to provide government departments with printing services and publication advice.

01 Feb 1952

Cable & Wireless began offering radio facsimile services between Hong Kong and Singapore as well as Britain.

04 Feb 1952

Hong Kong's table tennis team won a bronze medal in the men's team competition at the 19th World Table Tennis Championships in Mumbai, marking its first medal in an international tournament.

07 Feb 1952

King George VI died of lung cancer. Flags were flown at half-mast across Hong Kong where the local stock market was suspended for the day.

10 Feb 1952

Otto Marling Lund, Chief Commissioner of the St. John Ambulance Brigade, conducted a ceremonial inspection and unveiled the St. John War Memorial at Wong Nai Chung Gap, paying tribute to the 55 cadets who died in the Second World War.

29 Feb 1952

The Exportation (Prohibition) (Specific Articles) Order 1951 was amended, adding seven articles to the original list of 13 categories of commodities prohibited from import/export without approval.

01 Mar 1952

More than 1,000 people gathered at the Kowloon–Canton Railway terminus in Tsim Sha Tsui and clashed with the police on Jordan Road in protest of the Hong Kong government's decision to ban a Guangdong comfort mission from visiting victims of the Tung Tau Tsuen fire in Kowloon City. A protester attempting to take down the Union Jack from a police station was shot dead by a police officer. More than 30 people were injured and over 100 were arrested—12 of whom were later deported. It became known as the March 1st Incident.

05 Mar 1952

The newspaper article "Protest Against British Imperialist's Killing of Our Residents in Hong Kong"—a commentary on the March 1st Incident originally published by the *People's Daily*—was reprinted in the newspapers *Ta Kung Pao*, *Wen Wei Po* and the *New Evening Post*. Ten people in charge of the three newspapers were later charged on suspicion of publishing seditious materials.

07 Mar 1952

The Tenancy (Prolonged Duration) Ordinance 1952 was promulgated, forbidding landlords of post-Second World War residential buildings from evicting tenants within three years of their taking occupation of the premise. It also stipulated that payable rent should be based on the agreement between landlord and tenant; landlords were also required to provide a written notification three months prior to any rent increase.

09 Mar 1952

Lam Kam Road, a major link between Yuen Long and Tai Po, was opened to traffic.

17 Mar 1952

The Hong Kong Federation of Trade Unions began a four-day relief campaign supported by the community for distribution of rice for fire victims of Tung Tau Tsuen. The Chinese General Chamber of Commerce provided victims with HK$10 each—donated by compatriots in Guangdong Province.

Mar 1952

The Hong Kong Model Housing Society completed its first low-cost housing estate located in North Point, providing 100 residential units.

Apr 1952

The Bacille Calmette-Guerin vaccination campaign was launched with funding from the United Nations International Children's Emergency Fund (present-day United Nation's Children's Fund).

The Chinese Drama Group of the Sino-British Club was established; it made its debut with *Scarlet Flower Saga* in May.

02 May 1952

The Agricultural Products (Marketing) Ordinance 1952 was promulgated, providing a comprehensive wholesale system of agricultural products.

The Hong Kong Settlers Housing Corporation—founded by Chau Sik-nin（周錫年）, Ngan Shing-kwan（顏成坤） and Dhun Jehangir Ruttonjee as a private company aiming to provide the poor with affordable housing—was announced.

05 May 1952

The Supreme Court ruled that newspaper *Ta Kung Pao* must suspend publication for six months for reprinting a commentary of the *People's Daily* on 05 March. Senior newspaper staff Fei Yi-ming（費彝民）and Li Tsung-ying（李宗瀛）were also found guilty—a verdict upheld in a following appeal at the Full Court of the Supreme Court. The suspension ended on 17 May upon negotiation between Premier Zhou Enlai（周恩來）of the Government Administration Council and British Chargé d'Affaires to the People's Republic of China.

06 May 1952

The Hong Kong Anti-Tuberculosis Association began a free public vaccination campaign at Ruttonjee Sanatorium in a continued effort to prevent the spread of tuberculosis.

15 May 1952

The United Nations International Children's Emergency Fund announced its contribution of US$87,000 to a Hong Kong government fund of US$145,000, formally established in April 1952 for four children health-related projects: tuberculosis vaccination, diphtheria vaccination, a children's hospital, and medical facilities for children in resettlement areas.

16 May 1952

The Business Regulation Ordinance 1952 was promulgated, requiring all business organisations to register and pay a business registration fee within three months after commencement. Registration began on 19 May.

30 May 1952

The Urban Council held its first post-Second World War elections for two Unofficial Members amongst nine candidates. William Sui-tak Louey (雷瑞德) and Brook Bernacchi were elected.

13 Jun 1952

The Emergency (Resettlement Areas) Regulations 1952 was promulgated, designating 19 parcels of crown land as resettlement areas for residents of various squatter areas.

16 Jun 1952

The Education Department held its first Hong Kong Chinese School Certificate Examination.

27 Jun 1952

The General Loan and Stock Ordinance 1952 was promulgated, declaring the terms and procedures applicable to loans authorised to be raised by the Hong Kong government.

19 Jul 1952

Hong Kong participated in the 15th Olympic Games in Helsinki, Finland where Hong Kong was represented for the first time in a Summer Games.

25 Jul 1952

The *Chinese Student Weekly* was founded, becoming an important platform of literary works in Hong Kong. It ceased publication on 21 July 1974.

28 Jul 1952

The Judicial Committee of the Privy Council overruled a decision by the Supreme Court of Hong Kong on China National Aviation Corporation (CNAC) and Central Air Transport Corporation (CATC), affirming ownership of CNAC and CATC assets by Civil Air Transport Incorporated. The police immediately took hold of the airlines' aircraft and facilities at Kai Tak Airport.

Aug 1952

Amateur herpetologist John Romer discovered a previously unknown variety of tree frog in a cave on Lamma Island. It was a species unique to Hong Kong and was named Romer's tree frog.

11 Sep 1952

Sheung Li Uk was opened as the first public housing estate built by Hong Kong Housing Society and as one of the two earliest public housing projects.

25 Sep 1952

The passenger ship *Takshing*, bound for Macao from Hong Kong, was intercepted by a People's Liberation Army patrol boat and diverted to Garbage Tail Island. A passenger accused of spying in Guangdong Province was discovered and taken away. The ship later returned to Hong Kong under British naval escort.

30 Sep 1952

The Chinese General Chamber of Commerce's official name in Chinese was amended.

Sep 1952

The Hong Kong government was told by Britain to shelve all constitutional reform plans as they were not deemed an urgent issue.

08 Oct 1952

The Supreme Court of Hong Kong, in accordance with the British Privy Council's ruling, awarded the ownership of China National Aviation Corporation (CNAC) and Central Air Transport Corporation (CATC) aircraft to Civil Air Transport Incorporated. The remaining CNAC and CATC aircraft at Kai Tak Airport were later transported away in batches.

10 Oct 1952

The Hong Kong government announced that 21 April would be designated a public holiday in celebration of the birthday of Queen Elizabeth II, starting in the following year. In 1983, following the British tradition, it was scheduled for the second Saturday of June each year.

11 Oct 1952

Hong Kong Commercial Daily began publication under one of its founders and first editor-in-chief Cheung Hok-hung (張學孔) who was previously with the newspaper *Ta Kung Pao*.

17 Oct 1952

Osamu Itagaki arrived in Hong Kong to assume office as the first Consul-General of Japan in Hong Kong since the end of the Second World War. He publicly apologised for Japan's invasion and occupation of Hong Kong between 1941 and 1945.

20 Oct 1952

In response to a question in the House of Commons on Hong Kong's constitutional development, Secretary of State for the Colonies Oliver Lyttelton noted that Hong Kong was not prepared for large-scale political reforms and could only make limited reforms to its Urban Council. On 22 October, Governor Alexander Grantham announced in the Legislative Council that the Young Plan would be shelved.

29 Oct 1952

A fire broke out in a squatter area in Kowloon Tsai, burning down 104 houses, killing one baby and injuring three people.

12 Nov 1952

The Hong Kong & Kowloon Licenced Hawkers Association was established.

15 Nov 1952

Ng Cho-fan (吳楚帆), Pak Yin (白燕) and Chun Kim (秦劍) co-founded Union Film Enterprise Limited, aiming to promote high-quality Cantonese films dedicated to social reality and artistic dignity. Its first film was an adaptation of Chinese writer Ba Jin's (巴金) *The Family*. The company was closed in 1967.

24 Nov 1952

Post-Second World War reclamation in central Victoria Harbour commenced in a four-phase project. The first phase was completed in August 1955 while the last phase was completed in January 1986. (Figure 143)

Figure 143
An aerial view of Victoria Harbour off the shore of Central under the first phase of reclamation in 1953. (Photo courtesy of HKSAR Government)

27 Nov 1952

The Bank of Korea established a branch in Hong Kong; it was officially opened on 03 February 1953, marking the first Korean bank in Hong Kong.

28 Nov 1952

A fire broke out in Shek Kip Mei Village, destroying more than 300 houses and affecting more than 4,000 people; one died and more than 40 sustained injuries.

11 Dec 1952

The Empire Theatre in North Point was opened; it was renamed State Theatre in 1959.

19 Dec 1952

The Education Ordinance 1952 was promulgated, establishing a Board of Education with provisions on school personnel (supervisors, managers, principals and teachers) as well as school facilities and curricula in a bid to prevent schools from becoming platforms of political propaganda. The Syllabus and Textbook Committee was also established in the same year.

25 Dec 1952

The Danemann Watch Case Factory in Tsuen Wan was established; it became the largest and most advanced factory in Hong Kong during the mid-1950s, capable of producing waterproof watch cases.

1952

The Asian Games Federation approved Hong Kong's application for membership, allowing participation in the Asian Games.

The Hong Kong Red Cross launched its voluntary, non-remunerated blood donation programme to provide hospitals with a supply of blood free of charge.

The Joint Office of Joint Public-Private Banks was established for centralised leadership of nine Chinese-owned banks in Hong Kong. These included 1) Yien Yieh Commercial Bank, 2) Kincheng Banking Corporation, 3) China & South Sea Bank Limited, 4) Sin Hua Trust, Savings and Commercial Bank Limited, 5) China State Bank Limited, 6) The National Commercial Bank Limited, 7) National Industrial Bank of China, 8) Young Brothers Banking Corporation and 9) Wo Sang Bank. In 1958, six remaining banks came under the Bank of China; the Joint Office was abolished.

Wah Kwong Shipping was founded by Chao Tsong-yea (趙從衍).

A group of 23 Hong Kong students were awarded scholarships by the British Colonial Development and Welfare Fund in support of further education in Britain.

The Church World Service (based in New York) and Lutheran World Federation (based in Geneva) began community works in Hong Kong. They established the Hong Kong Church World Service and the Lutheran World Service, Hong Kong, respectively. The Hong Kong Christian Welfare and Relief Council was also established in the same year. Following two mergers of the three services, they became the service arm of Hong Kong Christian Council in 1976.

Author Eileen Chang (張愛玲), who studied in Hong Kong from 1939 to 1942, returned to Hong Kong and wrote the novels *The Rice Sprout Song* and *Love in Redland* between 1952 and 1955.

Everyman's Literature began publication under the editorship of Huang Sicheng (黃思騁); it ceased publication in 1954.

The Hong Kong Academy of Fine Arts, located in Yau Ma Tei, was founded by Chan Hoi-ying (陳海鷹) as the first private art school to promote art education after the Second World War.

Cao Juren (曹聚仁) released his novel *The Hotel*—a depiction of Chinese refugees in Hong Kong from a humanistic perspective.

13 Jan 1953

A fire broke out in the squatter area of Ho Man Tin, destroying 1,600 houses and leaving more than 16,000 residents homeless.

15 Jan 1953

Children's Paradise, Hong Kong's first full-colour children's magazine, began publication; 1,006 issues were published before it was closed on 16 December 1994.

20 Jan 1953

The United Nations Association of Hong Kong, founded by Ma Man-fai (馬文輝) on 01 January, held its inaugural meeting.

25 Jan 1953

The Preventive Service in conjunction with the Royal Naval Police seized 3,000 taels of gold worth over HK$900,000 aboard a British warship.

Jan 1953

China Weekly was founded as a publication on current affairs as well as literary and artistic works; it established the Li Bai Platinum Award for Short Stories. It became a monthly magazine in April 1964, was rebranded as *China Monthly* in 1973 and ceased publication in 1975.

11 Feb 1953

The Department of Agriculture, Fisheries and Forestry held its first Fisheries Exhibition at Aberdeen Wholesale Fish Market in a showcase of new mechanised fishing boats and fishing techniques.

18 Feb 1953

The Victoria and Kowloon District Courts were established in place of the Summary Court of the Supreme Court.

21 Feb 1953

The first post-Second World War Agricultural Show of the New Territories was held at Yuen Long Middle School. (Figure 144)

04 Mar 1953

The Hong Kong government announced a Revenue Equalization Fund—established to tackle future budget deficits with an allocation of HK$10 million from the financial budget.

06 Mar 1953

The Stanley Training Centre, reinstituted from the Stanley Reformatory School, was formed as Hong Kong's first Training Centre to provide teenage offenders aged 14 to 18 with educational and vocational training.

15 Mar 1953

The Yuen Yuen Institute in Tsuen Wan, established by Chiu Lut-sau (趙聿修) and Lui Chung-tak (呂重德) in 1950, was opened as a monastery of Confucianism, Buddhism and Taoism.

09 Apr 1953

A patient with male and female sexual characteristics underwent a second surgery to remove the female organ; it marked the first sex reassignment surgery in Hong Kong.

15 Apr 1953

The Hong Kong government accepted a new scheme of rent increases as proposed in a report prepared by the Rent Control Committee. It allowed an initial 50% increase from pre-Second World War levels and another 50% increase after one year with commercial and residential buildings. It further allowed another 100% increase after two years and a complete deregulation after three years with commercial buildings as well as a review on deregulation with residential buildings after two years.

Figure 144
An Agricultural Show billboard on a road towards Yuen Long in January 1957. (Photo courtesy of The Hong Kong Heritage Project)

29 Apr 1953

The Committee on Chinese Custom and Law in Hong Kong, appointed by Governor Alexander Grantham, released its report in the Legislative Council. It disagreed with the government's reliance on the Qing legal code and recommended that the government should take into consideration the modern Chinese Civil Code as well as the Chinese customs and social condition in Hong Kong when formulating laws on marriage and inheritance in order to establish monogamy as the only legal form of marriage.

Apr 1953

The British Colonial Development and Welfare Fund awarded a grant of £13,000 to support small-scale irrigation projects in the New Territories.

01 May 1953

The Sanitary Department was renamed the Urban Services Department as agency responsible for public hygiene, resettlement areas and park management.

The Prisons Department introduced an Earnings Scheme, allowing inmates to earn wages for their work, in place of a scheme of gratuities upon release.

04 May 1953

The International Women's League in Hong Kong held an inaugural meeting on ending the concubine system. On 24 July, Hong Kong Young Women's Christian Association held a joint meeting with other women's organisations— and agreed to abolish such customs. The International Women's League in Hong Kong raised the issue with the Colonial Secretary in March 1954.

20 May 1953

The Public Services Commission released its first report in the Legislative Council, urging the government to hire local qualified talent as public servants.

02 Jun 1953

The Hong Kong government held several celebratory events as Queen Elizabeth II was crowned.

25 Jun 1953

Queen Mary Hospital began employing radiotherapy as a form of treatment for cancer patients, making it the first medical institution in the Commonwealth to do so.

29 Jun 1953

Route Twisk, a road linking Tsuen Wan and Shek Kong, was opened for military and government vehicles; it was opened to the public on 25 May 1961.

06 Jul 1953

The Chinese Manufacturers' Association of Hong Kong in conjunction with the Kowloon Chamber of Commerce started a petition in protest of the government decision to allow rent increases and abolish rent controls in the next two to three years. The petition was presented to the Colonial Secretary as well as Chinese representative Chau Sik-nin (周 錫年) the following day.

17 Jul 1953

The Chinese Artists Association of Hong Kong (formerly known as the Hong Kong Branch of Guangdong Professional Union for Cantonese Opera Performers) became a registered professional organisation of Cantonese opera practitioners in Hong Kong.

20 Jul 1953

The Secretariat for Chinese Affairs established a Tenancy Inquiry Bureau for public enquiries as well as investigation and prosecution for violations of the tenancy law.

27 Jul 1953

A Royal Air Force transport aircraft veered off the runway upon landing at Kai Tak Airport, crashing into the houses nearby. The ensuing fire killed one person and injured two.

Jul 1953

The Catholic Diocese of Hong Kong's Catholic Centre established a welfare office to provide civilian relief and support community recovery from the Second World War. The office became an affiliate of Caritas Internationalis in 1955 and was renamed Caritas Hong Kong in 1961 (with a corresponding Chinese name in 1974) as the largest social welfare organisation in the Catholic Diocese of Hong Kong.

07 Sep 1953

The Queen Elizabeth II Youth Centre, sponsored by The Hong Kong Jockey Club and the Princess Elizabeth Wedding Fund, was opened to the public. Located next to MacPherson Playground in Mong Kok, it was also known as MacPherson Stadium and was the first indoor stadium in Kowloon.

08 Sep 1953

A building collapsed on Wuhu Street in Hung Hom, causing 12 deaths and 25 injuries.

09 Sep 1953

The Royal Navy minesweeper *H.M.M.L. 1323* was shelled by a People's Liberation Army gunboat in the waters near Hong Kong, killing the captain and five crew members while injuring five.

25 Sep 1953

The Workmen's Compensation Ordinance 1953 was promulgated, requiring employers to compensate employees injured at work.

16 Oct 1953

The Bank of Tokyo's branch in Hong Kong was opened as the first Japanese-owned bank to commence business in Hong Kong after the Second World War.

22 Oct 1953

The United States relaxed restrictions on exports to Hong Kong, allowing 13 categories of non-strategic materials, including food, paper and cosmetics, without special approval from the US Department of Commerce.

26 Oct 1953

The Hong Kong government began allowing the re-export of gold; re-exporters must apply for a licence beforehand.

27 Nov 1953

The Film Censorship Regulations 1953 was promulgated, requiring all films to be reviewed by one or more members of a panel appointed by the governor before public screening. A board of review was also established, consisting of members appointed by the Secretary for Chinese Affairs, Director of Education, Commissioner of Police and Governor of Hong Kong, to handle appeal against initial rulings.

25 Dec 1953

On Christmas night, a fire broke out in the squatter area of Shek Kip Mei; it burnt for six hours across 41 acres of land, killing three people, injuring 51, destroying 2,580 huts and leaving more than 50,000 homeless. (Figures 145 and 146)

29 Dec 1953

The Emergency (Immediate Resumption) (Application) Regulations 1953 was promulgated, setting aside 8.5 hectares of land to resettle 58,203 fire victims of Shek Kip Mei who had registered with the government.

31 Dec 1953

The Urban Council (Amendment) (No. 2) Ordinance 1953 was promulgated, allowing certain groups of people to vote in the Urban Council elections. These included teachers, members of the Hong Kong Defence Force and the Essential Services Corps, civil servants (except police officers), as well as taxpayers who had paid Income Tax or Profits Tax for four years or more.

The British government donated £200,000 to Hong Kong for the resettlement of victims in the Shek Kip Mei fire.

Figure 145
The Shek Kip Mei fire in 1953—which destroyed all of Pak Tin Village. (Photo courtesy of Public Records Office, Government Records Service)

Figure 146
The reconstruction of Shek Kip Mei Estate where seven-storey resettlement blocks were built to replace the temporary two-storey bungalows. (Photo taken in June 1957 and courtesy of Public Records Office, Government Records Service)

Figure 147
Refugees climbing over a barbed wire fence at the border between Guangdong and Hong Kong in the 1970s. (Photo courtesy of Hong Kong Museum of History)

Figure 148
The Chinese General Chamber of Commerce and Hong Kong Federation of Trade Unions, on behalf of the Guangdong branch of the Chinese People's Relief Association, provided victims of the Shek Kip Mei fire with cash and rice through relief efforts at the Army Sports Ground on Boundary Street and Cheung Sha Wan Sports Ground on Maple Street in January 1954. (Photo courtesy of Hong Kong Federation of Trade Unions)

Dec 1953

The Hong Kong Telephone Company installed the first 15 public phone booths in the urban centres of Hong Kong Island and Kowloon.

1953

The police completed a chain-link fence at the border to tackle illegal immigration and cross-border crimes. The fence was reinforced with additional barbed wire in 1962. (Figure 147)

The Sisters Announcers of the Lord, an order of nuns founded in 1936 in Shaozhou (present-day Shaoguan) of Guangdong, was relocated to Hong Kong where a general motherhouse was established.

Henry Fok Ying-tung (霍英東) launched the first "off-plan" sale of property—requiring deposits and payment instalments prior to construction—in Hong Kong for a building on Public Square Street in Yau Ma Tei.

Chun Au Knitting Factory, established in the 1930s, founded Chicks—a famous underwear brand in Hong Kong.

Alliance Française de Hong Kong was founded.

The Hindu Temple in Happy Valley was opened to the public upon completion.

01 Jan 1954

Henry Fong Yik-fai (方奕輝) became the first Chinese Chief Inspector of Police.

04 Jan 1954

The US government donated US$150,000 to help victims of the Shek Kip Mei fire.

05 Jan 1954

The Guangdong and Guangzhou branches of the Chinese People's Relief Association donated 700,000 market catties of rice and RMB 1 billion (HK$100,000 equivalent in 1955) to help victims of the Shek Kip Mei fire. (Figure 148)

07 Jan 1954

The Hong Kong government abolished the ration of sugar and butter.

14 Jan 1954

Women's organisations in Hong Kong began a HK$1-voucher relief campaign, raising over HK$40,000 to help victims of the Shek Kip Mei fire.

18 Jan 1954

The Hong Kong Christian Council was established.

20 Jan 1954

Liang Yusheng (梁羽生) began publishing his first serialised novel *Dragon and Tiger Fight in the Capital* in the *New Evening Post*, marking the start of a new school of martial arts novels.

12 Feb 1954

The J. E. Joseph Trust Fund Ordinance 1954 was promulgated, providing farmers' cooperatives and individual farmers with loans in support of agricultural production.

16 Feb 1954

The Public Works Department completed the first two-storey bungalows to accommodate victims of the Shek Kip Mei fire at a nearby site. The first eight Mark I resettlement blocks were built on the original fire site in the same year.

18 Feb 1954

Local contemporary Chinese ink painter Lui Shou-kwan (呂壽琨) held his first solo exhibition in a three-day event at Hong Kong Hotel.

25 Feb 1954

The fourth Junior Chamber International Asia-Pacific Conference was held in Hong Kong with representatives from 11 Asian countries.

Feb 1954

Both Chinese and Hong Kong government authorities reinforced border defences and began frequent inspection on passers-by in Sha Tau Kok where Chung Ying Street became a restricted area in which people, other than local residents, were not allowed to enter or leave without permission.

The first-generation Queen's Pier was demolished for the purpose of reclamation in Central District.

16 Mar 1954

The Hong Kong Buddhist Association held the first exhibition of Buddha's relics (en route from India to Japan via Hong Kong) with a one-hour public worship ceremony at Tung Lin Kok Yuen—a Buddhist nunnery in Hong Kong.

01 Apr 1954

The Literary World, a publication on novels and translated literary works, was founded by Huang Tianshi (黃天石). It suspended publication on 21 July after 12 issues and resumed in May 1956 as a journal of the Hong Kong Chinese PEN Centre, covering Chinese and foreign literature, drama, literary theory and creation. Following the 46th issue in June 1965, it became a supplement of the newspaper *Sing Tao Daily* in the form of a biweekly called Literary World.

30 Apr 1954

The Urban Council (Commissioner for Resettlement) Ordinance 1954 was promulgated, establishing a Resettlement Department. David Ronald Holmes was the first Commissioner for Resettlement. The Commissioner, responsible for resettlement construction projects, would also be an Official Member of the Urban Council.

The Housing Ordinance 1954 was promulgated, establishing the Hong Kong Housing Authority which was a quasi-governmental organisation responsible for managing public housing estates.

01 May 1954

Hong Kong took part in the second Asian Games in Manila, The Philippines, marking its first-time participation in the Asian Games. On 05 May, Stephen Xavier won a bronze medal in the 200-metre race, becoming Hong Kong's first Asian Games medallist.

10 May 1954

The Newspaper Society of Hong Kong was jointly founded by newspapers *Kung Sheung Daily News*, *Wah Kiu Yat Po*, *Sing Tao Daily* and *South China Morning Post*.

13 May 1954

Rose, Rose I Love You, a film in Putonghua, premiered as Hong Kong's first film shown on Cinerama.

21 May 1954

The fishing vessel *Southern Glory* was marked in a hand-over ceremony; it was the first locally designed and built modern fishing trawler by Kwong Cheung Hing Shipyard in Cheung Sha Wan, Kowloon.

10 Jun 1954

The Hong Kong branch of China Travel Service was reorganised and registered independently as China Travel Service (Hong Kong) Limited. It was the only China-owned travel agency in Hong Kong before the 1980s.

14 Jul 1954

A fire broke out at a papaya farm located in Kam Shan near Tai Po Market Railway Station in the New Territories, destroying five huts, killing 14 people and injuring eight.

22 Jul 1954

A fire broke out in the squatter area of Tai Hang Tung (commonly known as Kowloon Tsai) in Sham Shui Po. It destroyed 3,800 huts, killed nine people and affected more than 14,000 people.

23 Jul 1954

A Cathay Pacific Airways Douglas C-54 Skymaster airliner, en route from Bangkok to Hong Kong, was mistaken for a Taiwan authority's military aircraft and shot down by two People's Liberation Army warplanes near Hainan Island, killing 10 people. The Chinese government assumed responsibility through diplomatic channels and paid £367,000 in compensation.

27 Jul 1954

National Investment Company Limited, founded by Henry Fok Ying-tung (霍英東), was incorporated. It was the first real estate developer to accept loan payment in instalments.

06 Aug 1954

The Hong Kong Lawn Bowls Team won a silver medal in the Men's Fours at the fifth Commonwealth Games in Vancouver, Canada. It was Hong Kong's first Commonwealth Games medal.

12 Aug 1954

The Sun Ngai Art Academy in Central District was raided by the police; three people in charge, as well as two models, were arrested on suspicion of illegally operating a vice establishment. The following day, people in charge of life drawing schools across Hong Kong were taken to police stations for questioning.

13 Aug 1954

The Rating (Amendment) Ordinance 1954 was promulgated, effective 01 April 1955, making rates (property tax) in the New Territories on par with those of Hong Kong Island and Kowloon.

15 Aug 1954

The Young Companion, a pictorial publication founded in Shanghai in 1926, resumed in Hong Kong. *Magnificent China*, published in January 1966 by the same magazine press, was the first publication to describe sea trade routes between China and the rest of the world with the term "The China [Porcelain] Road."

29 Aug 1954

The Hong Kong Observatory hoisted Increasing Gale or Storm Signal No. 9 for more than six hours amid Typhoon Ida—which resulted in one death and 12 injuries.

06 Sep 1954

Heung Yee Kuk, in protest of the government imposition of rates in the New Territories, held a meeting with 600 representatives from various districts. On 07 October, a petition signed by more than 600 people was presented to the government for a rates exemption with houses in the rural area and a tax reduction with houses in the Extended Urban region.

15 Sep 1954

The Hong Kong Police Headquarters was relocated to its new premises on Arsenal Street in Wan Chai.

20 Sep 1954

Arnaldo de Oliveira Sales was named President of the Amateur Sports Federation and Olympic Committee of Hong Kong. He was praised for supporting Hong Kong athletes to compete in international events; he retired from office in 1999.

21 Sep 1954

Hong Kong Flour Mills in Shek Tong Tsui was established by David Sung Ling-fang (孫麟方). It was the largest mill in Hong Kong after the Second World War.

Sep 1954

An agency of China News Service was established in Hong Kong. It was replaced by the China News Service Hong Kong Office in 1975 and renamed the China News Service HK Branch in 1985.

01 Oct 1954

Fires broke out in the squatter areas of Lei Cheng Uk Village in Kowloon and on Tin Hau Temple Road on Hong Kong Island, destroying nearly 600 huts and leaving around 6,600 people homeless.

11 Oct 1954

The US-based Cooperative for Assistance and Relief Everywhere held its Far East regional conference in Hong Kong.

15 Oct 1954

The Mining Ordinance 1954 was promulgated, regulating minerals prospecting, industrial mining and minerals trading in addition to establishing a Mines Department.

18 Oct 1954

The Medical Department launched a diphtheria prevention campaign, urging vaccination among infants and children under the age of two.

26 Oct 1954

The Hong Kong Civic Association was established under the chairmanship of French Reverend Brigant Cassian.

06 Nov 1954

The Hong Kong Observatory hoisted Increasing Gale or Storm Signal No. 9 for nearly five hours amid Typhoon Pamela—which resulted in three deaths and 13 injuries.

20 Nov 1954

A fire broke out in a squatter village on Tai Po Road in Shek Kip Mei, destroying more than 500 houses, killing five people, injuring more than 20 and affecting more than 3,000.

1954

Government departments began moving into the first building (East Wing) of the Central Government Offices Complex upon completion.

The Hong Kong Chinese Importers' and Exporters' Association was established.

Nan Fung Textiles Limited in Tsuen Wan was founded by Chen Din-hwa (陳廷驊). It became operational two years later with the highest output in Hong Kong.

The Hong Kong Council of the Church of Christ in China was established, marking its formal separation from the Guangdong Synod of the Church of Christ in China.

Hong Kong Telephone Company introduced its first batch of six-digit telephone numbers (770-000 to 770-999) for Eastern District on Hong Kong Island, marking an expansion from five to six digits.

The Hong Kong Economic and Trade Office in Tokyo was established to promote economic ties and cultural exchange between Hong Kong and Japan.

01 Jan 1955

The Hong Kong government began deregulating the rice trade by establishing a franchise of 29 rice merchants.

06 Jan 1955

The Subcommittee on Trade of the United Nations Economic Commission for Asia and the Far East held a meeting with representatives from 27 countries in Hong Kong for the first time.

08 Feb 1955

Louis Cha Leung-yung (查良鏞), best known by his pen name Jin Yong (金庸), began publishing his first serial novel *The Book and the Sword* in the *New Evening Post*.

20 Feb 1955

The Sai Wan Memorial, located at the Sai Wan War Cemetery, was unveiled in commemoration of fallen soldiers in the Battle of Hong Kong in 1941.

21 Feb 1955

A fire broke out at Shek Wu Hui in Sheung Shui early in the morning, destroying 80% of houses (approximately 300 units) across eight streets in the market town; 4,000 people were affected and HK$2 million worth of property losses were incurred. One person died and six sustained injuries. The Bo Tak Temple, located in the centre of the old market, was also destroyed.

04 Mar 1955

The Grantham Scholarships Fund Ordinance 1955 was promulgated, establishing a trust fund for scholarships for full-time students in need of financial aid.

07 Mar 1955

Norwegian scholar Edvard Hambro released his research report commissioned by the United Nations High Commissioner for Refugees, noting some 667,000 refugees arriving in Hong Kong from the Mainland during 1954.

15 Mar 1955

Former Kuomintang general Wei Lihuang (衛立煌) secretly left Hong Kong for Guangzhou and published the "Letter to Fellow Officers in Taiwan."

Mar 1955

Buddhist and Taoist temples in Hong Kong performed solemn services for rain, praying for an end to a two-month drought.

The Hongkong Electric Company began installing electricity metres in subdivided flats on Hong Kong Island so as to prevent disputes over electricity bills amongst tenants of the same flat.

01 Apr 1955

A waterspout near Cheung Chau sank three large ships and capsized 36 fishing boats, killing 14 people.

02 Apr 1955

The first Hong Kong Festival of the Arts, organised by the British Council, was opened. The last festival was held in 1962.

05 Apr 1955

A radiofacsimile service between Hong Kong and London was introduced, enabling transmission of messages and images in minutes.

11 Apr 1955

Kashmir Princess, an Air India charter plane, exploded and crashed while en route from Hong Kong to Jakarta, Indonesia. It killed 16 people, including Director of the Hong Kong Branch of Xinhua News Agency Raymond Wong Chok-mui (黃作梅) and several Chinese and Vietnamese diplomats on the way to the Asian-African Conference in Bandung. Only three crew members survived.

12 Apr 1955

The Ministry of Foreign Affairs of the People's Republic of China issued a statement on the bombing of *Kashmir Princess*, emphasising its pre-incident alert for enhanced security with the Hong Kong government and its demand for accountability from the British government. It demanded the arrest of Kuomintang and American secret agents involved in the incident.

A fin whale was stranded in Victoria Harbour near Connaught Road West in Sheung Wan.

14 Apr 1955

A Chinese tenement building located at 64 Staunton Street in Central collapsed, killing seven people, including a pregnant woman, and injuring 27.

07 May 1955

Victoria Park in Causeway Bay was opened as the largest public park in Hong Kong. (Figure 149)

13 May 1955

The Hong Kong Exporters' Association was incorporated.

May 1955

Cottages of Wai Man Village at Butterfly Valley in Lai Chi Kok were completed in the first housing project by Hong Kong Settlers Housing Corporation. These were sold to victims of fire who lost their homes in squatter areas.

06 Jun 1955

The Medical Department began providing free typhoid vaccine in four designated centres.

10 Jun 1955

The Corrupt and Illegal Practices Ordinance 1955 was promulgated, prohibiting fraudulent practices in elections.

Figure 149
The first public swimming pool in Hong Kong at Victoria Park in Causeway Bay in 1967. (Photo courtesy of South China Morning Post Publishers Limited)

Figure 150
Onlookers near an Eastern Han Dynasty tomb discovered at Lei Cheng Uk Village in 1955. (Photo courtesy of Hong Kong Museum of History)

11 Jun 1955

The Education Department issued a guideline on Chinese language education in primary schools for a standardised curriculum with a focus on vernacular Chinese among junior primary students and some classical Chinese among senior primary students. The *Four Books and Five Classics* were no longer taught.

13 Jun 1955

The new Tsan Yuk Hospital building on Hospital Road in Sai Ying Pun was opened.

08 Jul 1955

The Kadoorie Agricultural Aid Loan Fund Ordinance 1955 was promulgated, establishing a government fund of HK$500,000 in collaboration with the Kadoorie family in support of farmers for agricultural development through interest-free loans.

18 Jul 1955

Hong Kong's first Lions Club was established. In 1960, Lions Clubs International District 303 of Hong Kong and Macao was established with approval from Lions Clubs International.

Jul 1955

The World-Wide Steamship Company Limited was founded by Pao Yue-kong (包玉剛).

02 Aug 1955

The Hongkong Chinese Bank was opened for business. On 10 December, it was incorporated as a limited company.

05 Aug 1955

The Education Department announced a seven-year programme for an additional 182,000 primary school places in Hong Kong.

09 Aug 1955

An Eastern Han Dynasty tomb was discovered at the site of a resettlement building in Lei Cheng Uk Village. A group of students of The University of Hong Kong, led by Head of Chinese Department Frederick Seguier Drake, later unearthed various relics of the Eastern Han Dynasty, including 58 pieces of ancient pottery and bronze objects. (Figure 150)

19 Aug 1955

The Factories and Industrial Undertakings Ordinance 1955 was promulgated, regulating the operation of factories to ensure the safety of workers.

28 Aug 1955

A group of primary school teachers and students were swept away in a flash flood during a picnic in Tai Po Kau, causing 28 deaths. A memorial park and a monument were later established at the site.

03 Sep 1955

The police offered a reward for the capture of Chow Tse-ming (周梓銘), an employee of Hong Kong Aircraft Engineering Company Limited and a suspect in the explosion of airliner *Kashmir Princess*, who had fled to Taiwan.

05 Sep 1955

The first two diesel-electric locomotives, *Sir Alexander* and *Lady Maurine,* were officially put into service with Kowloon–Canton Railway.

08 Oct 1955

A group of 39 Chinese scholars, including aerospace engineer Qian Xuesen (錢學森), returned from the US to the Mainland via Hong Kong where 24 of them issued a joint statement titled Salute to the Motherland.

24 Oct 1955

Queen Elizabeth School's campus in Mong Kok was opened as the first public co-educational secondary school facility in Hong Kong.

01 Nov 1955

A fire broke out in the squatter area of Fa Hui Village near Prince Edward Road, destroying 400 houses, killing five people and leaving nearly 6,000 people homeless.

Figure 151
The Government Stadium in So Kon Po on Hong Kong Island. (Photo courtesy of Sing Tao News Corporation Limited)

12 Nov 1955

A British battle tank collided with a train during a military exercise in the New Territories, causing four deaths and 20 injuries.

22 Nov 1955

Michael Joseph Hogan succeeded Gerard Lewis Howe as Chief Justice of Hong Kong after Howe passed away in Britain during his term of office.

The ocean liner *Ruys* set sail for South Africa and South America with an exhibition of Hong Kong export products in a new promotion campaign by the Hong Kong government in collaboration with Koninklijke Java-China-Paketvaart Lijnen.

02 Dec 1955

The 13th Exhibition of Hong Kong Products began for a 32-day expo; it set a record with more than a million visitors.

03 Dec 1955

The Government Stadium with a capacity of 28,000 was inaugurated with an opening football match between Hong Kong League XI and Clube Ferroviário of Mozambique. Hong Kong won 2–1. (Figure 151)

1955

The Hong Kong government completed an outline plan to develop Kwun Tong into a satellite town; it marked the beginning of new town development in Hong Kong. (Figure 152)

The Hong Kong Jockey Club began to allocate its annual surplus for charity causes and community projects.

K. Wah Group was founded by Lui Che-woo (呂志和).

The Hoh Kai-Wing (何啟榮) family founded Kong Ngee Motion Picture Production Company in Singapore; Chun Kim (秦劍) served as General Manager. The company produced mainly Cantonese films.

 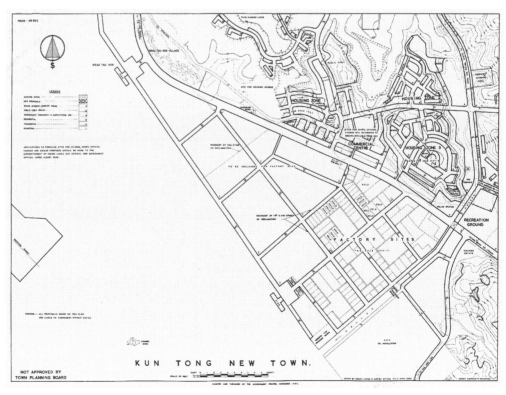

Figure 152
The zoning plan of Kwun Tong as a satellite town outlining an industrial area along the waterfront of Kowloon Bay and residential and commercial areas inland. (Courtesy of Public Records Office, Government Records Service)

11 Jan 1956

The Hong Kong government released an investigative report on the bombing of airliner *Kashmir Princess*, pointing out a time bomb planted by a Kuomintang agent during a stopover at Kai Tak Airport as part of an assassination attempt directed at Premier Zhou Enlai (周恩來) who was scheduled to take the flight.

27 Jan 1956

The Urban Council (Amendment) Ordinance 1956 was promulgated, increasing the number of Unofficial Members in the Urban Council by six (four were elected seats), for an extended office term of four years. The Urban Council, after reorganisation, consisted of 22 members, including six Official Members, eight Unofficial Members and eight Elected Members.

The Gambling (Amendment) Ordinance 1956 was promulgated, effective 01 March, stipulating that commercial gaming houses (fees charged), including facilities for Mahjong, Tin Kau or any games with Mahjong tiles, dominoes or playing cards, must apply for a licence with the Commissioner of Police.

30 Jan 1956

The Royal Academy of Dance began its first graded examination period in Hong Kong—which ended on 07 February.

10 Feb 1956

Hong Kong and the Mainland adjusted their immigration policies by lifting the quota on Guangdong residents allowed to enter Hong Kong. On 03 September, the Hong Kong government reinstated the entry quota system, stipulating an equal number of entries and exits of people. Between February and September, 54,000 people entered Hong Kong from the Mainland.

15 Feb 1956

The first silk fabrics exhibition in Hong Kong began for a three-day show on locally made silk products.

17 Feb 1956

The Hong Kong Life Guard Club (present-day Hong Kong Life Saving Society) was founded. In the same year, Henri Kwok Hon-ming (郭漢銘), one of the founding members, became the first person in Hong Kong to receive the highest diploma from the Royal Life Saving Society, UK.

18 Feb 1956

The *Literary Current Monthly Magazine* began publication as a key platform for Hong Kong writers. The last issue was published on 01 May 1959.

22 Feb 1956

The Legislative Council passed a motion to improve the broadcasting industry. It opposed the commercialisation of Radio Hong Kong (e.g. sponsored programmes) and suggested commercial radio stations be established through private investment.

05 Mar 1956

Hong Kong Baptist College was founded with funding from the Southern Baptist Convention. Lam Chi-fung (林子豐) served as its first President; it was opened on 11 September.

07 Mar 1956

The Urban Council held its first election since reorganisation. Four members of the Reform Club and two members of the Hong Kong Civic Association were elected. Alison Bell of the Reform Club became the first woman councillor in Hong Kong.

15 Mar 1956

Overseas Trust Bank, founded by Chinese-Malaysian businessman Chang Ming-thien (張明添), was opened for business in Hong Kong.

21 Mar 1956

The Motion Picture & General Investment Company Limited was incorporated by International Films Distributing Agency and Yung Hwa Motion Picture Industries Limited. Dato Loke Wan-tho (陸運濤) was Chairman; Chung Kai-man (鍾啟文) was General Manager; and Sung Kei (宋淇) was Production Manager. Its first production was *Golden Lotus*. On 07 June 1965, it was reorganised as Cathay Organisation (Hong Kong) Limited.

26 Mar 1956

Two British fighter planes collided during a military exercise under heavy fog and crashed into Devil's Peak near Yau Tong, destroying several civilian houses. Two pilots were killed; an elderly woman died of severe burns.

29 Mar 1956

The Immigration Department began issuing Re-entry Permits, replacing Frontier Passes. Hong Kong residents were required to carry a Re-entry Permit upon return.

03 Apr 1956

The Department of Agriculture, Fisheries and Forestry held its first Annual Tree Planting Day.

14 Apr 1956

Youths' Garden began publication as a journal on new knowledge, school life as well as artistic and literary works. It ceased publication under a government order on 22 November 1967 amid riots.

28 Apr 1956

The Health Department in collaboration with the Medical Department concluded a two-week pest control campaign with 66 inspectors and cleaners to clear more than 750 locations known for infestation of mosquitos. It was the first campaign of its kind organised by the government.

10 May 1956

The Hong Kong government said in response to Heung Yee Kuk's petition regarding rates that it would not reduce the rates specified in the bill but would temporarily suspend the collection of rates on land in the New Territories.

11 May 1956

The Adoption Ordinance 1956 was promulgated, specifying the conditions under which a court of law could issue adoption orders, as well as the qualification requirements of child adopters.

18 May 1956

New Territories villagers gathered at Tai Po Theatre in support of Heung Yee Kuk's opposition to the government collection of rates and charges of land premiums for construction of residential houses on farmland.

08 Jun 1956

An installation ceremony of the Sung Wong Toi inscription stone was held. The stone was relocated from Kowloon City's Sacred Hill to its present location on Sung Wong Toi Road in Kowloon City to accommodate the expansion of Kai Tak Airport. The new location—named Sung Wong Toi Garden—was officially opened in November 1959.

23 Jun 1956

Five private post-secondary colleges—Canton Overseas, Kwang Hsia, Wah Kiu, Wen Hua and Ping Jing (all relocated from Guangzhou and Shanghai to Hong Kong)—were amalgamated into United College where classes began in September.

Figure 153
A "Blue Sky, White Sun, and a Wholly Red Earth" flag on top and a large "Double Tenth" emblem hanging at Block G of Lei Cheng Uk Resettlement Estate where police officers were on guard. (Photo taken on 16 October 1956 and courtesy of Bettmann/Bettmann via Getty Images)

Figure 154
An armoured police vehicle on patrol on Tai Po Road during the Double Tenth Riots in 1956. (Photo courtesy of Sing Tao News Corporation Limited)

03 Jul 1956

Kowloon City Ferry Pier was opened for ferry services between Kowloon City and Wan Chai.

23 Jul 1956

The Gold Network of Radio Rediffusion began its broadcast of primarily Cantonese programmes 17 hours a day.

14 Aug 1956

A landslide occurred in a stone quarry at A Kung Ngam in Shau Kei Wan, causing two deaths and 10 injuries.

Aug 1956

Wah Kiu Film Company was founded by Cheung Ying (張瑛) and Tse Yik-chi (謝益之). Its first production was an adaptation of Cao Yu's (曹禺) *Thunderstorm*.

01 Sep 1956

The first Asian Cup, a tournament organised by the Asian Football Confederation, began at the Government Stadium in Hong Kong, ending on 15 September. Team Hong Kong came in third place.

03 Sep 1956

The Hong Kong Society of Architects was established; it was renamed The Hong Kong Institute of Architects in 1972.

24 Sep 1956

The Urban Council launched Hong Kong's first Anti-mosquito Campaign in a six-day programme, aiming to raise public awareness on mosquito control.

28 Sep 1956

Superintendent of Mines William Murray Keay was found guilty of accepting HK$25,000 in bribes and was sentenced to two years in prison.

10 Oct 1956

In the morning, two staff members of the Resettlement Department removed a "Blue Sky, White Sun, and a Wholly Red Earth" flag and a large "Double Tenth" emblem displayed illegally on Block G of Lei Cheng Uk Resettlement Estate during the "Double Tenth Day." The removal triggered strong resentment among pro-Kuomintang residents who surrounded the Resettlement Department's office while demanding an apology and compensation. It escalated into three days of disturbances in what become known as the Riots in Kowloon and Tsuen Wan or Double Tenth Riots. (Figures 153 and 154)

The Chinese Culture Association was established.

11 Oct 1956

During a noon government meeting, Edgeworth Beresford David, who was the Officer Administering the Government, authorised the deployment of the British garrison forces to assist the police in restoring order amid riots in Kowloon.

Riots continued in Sham Shui Po, Mong Kok and Yau Ma Tei. In the afternoon, a taxi carrying Vice Consul and Chancellor of the Swiss Consulate Fritz Ernst and his wife was blocked and attacked by rioters on Tai Po Road. The taxi was overturned and burnt, injuring the Vice Consul and killing his wife and two other people.

Pao Hsing Cotton Mill, South Sea Textile Manufacturing Company and several other cotton mills in Tsuen Wan were stormed by a large number of pro-Kuomintang workers in the afternoon. Employers were forced to hoist the "Blue Sky, White Sun, and a Wholly Red Earth" flag and asked to dismiss leftist workers. Leftist trade unions were attacked and looted. Riot police quelled the riots in the early hours on the following day with the assistance of British forces.

Curfew was declared on Kowloon Peninsula, shutting down all ferries and public transport, including the Kowloon–Canton Railway (British Section). The following day, curfew was also imposed in Tsuen Wan and Sham Tseng.

12 Oct 1956

The police and British garrison forces began a large-scale, two-day manhunt for participants in the Double Tenth Riots, arresting about 2,870 people.

13 Oct 1956

Premier Zhou Enlai (周恩來) of the State Council met with British Chargé d'Affaires to the People's Republic of China Con Douglas Walter O'Neill regarding the Double Tenth Riots, noting that the riots were provoked by agents of the Taiwan authority rather than a result of factional struggles between leftists and rightists as claimed by the Hong Kong government.

14 Oct 1956

The Emergency (Detention Orders) Regulations 1956 was promulgated, allowing the police to detain and interrogate persons arrested in connection with the Double Tenth Riots for up to 14 days. The Governor could authorise extended detention for a further period or periods of 14 days if necessary.

16 Oct 1956

Traffic and public services resumed as curfews were terminated. The Double Tenth Riots caused 59 deaths and 384 injuries, making it the deadliest riot in Hong Kong. At least 6,000 people were arrested—1,455 were charged with defying the curfews and 1,241 were convicted; 740 others were charged with serious crimes, including rioting and looting, and 291 were convicted.

31 Oct 1956

The Standing Committee on Corruption was formed as an advisory body on curbing and preventing the prevalence of corruption. It was chaired by a Principal Crown Counsel nominated by the Attorney General; members included the Establishment Officer and Superintendent of Hong Kong Police Force's Anti-Corruption Branch. On 16 March 1960, it was reorganised and came under the chairmanship of the Attorney General; members included the Establishment Officer, Deputy Commissioner of Police and three Unofficial Members of the Executive Council.

23 Nov 1956

The buildings of Chung Chi College, located at Ma Liu Shui in Sha Tin, were completed.

Nov 1956

Arthur Hodgson, Head of the Orthopaedic and Trauma Unit at The University of Hong Kong, and his team published a research paper titled *Anterior Spinal Fusion* on the treatment of spinal tuberculosis caused by pulmonary tuberculosis in the *British Journal of Surgery*. This medical procedure, known as the Hong Kong Operation, received international acclaims.

23 Dec 1956

A fire broke out at Shek Wu Hui in Sheung Shui, destroying 300 huts, killing three people and injuring three others. (Figure 155)

1956

The first sewage screening plant in Hong Kong was commissioned on Anchor Street in Kowloon.

The Resettlement Department issued guidelines to 12 voluntary organisations regarding their plan to establish schools on the rooftops of resettlement buildings so as to ensure compliance with facility requirements set forth by the Education Department.

01 Jan 1957

The *Report on the Riots in Kowloon and Tsuen Wan* was released. It called the riot in Kowloon a criminal act instigated by a group of pro-Kuomintang triad members—not an act of political premeditation—and attributed the riots in Tsuen Wan to a conflict between left-wing and right-wing trade unions.

21 Jan 1957

A fire broke out in the squatter area of Tai Hang Sai in Kowloon, destroying more than 20 huts, causing two deaths and leaving around 100 people homeless.

22 Jan 1957

Staff of the Resettlement Department were sent to Chuk Yuen Village where household residents were registered and asked to move out within a month. It led to a protest among residents of Chuk Yuen Village and other villages in Nga Tsin Wai Tsuen affected by land resumption.

13 Feb 1957

Fire broke out in four wooden tenement buildings on Canton Road in Mong Kok, claiming 33 lives.

15 Feb 1957

The first Exhibition of Watches and Clocks was held in front of the Tsim Sha Tsui clock tower.

Figure 155
The aftermath of a fire at the market town of Shek Wu Hui in Sheung Shui. (Photo courtesy of HKSAR Government)

22 Feb 1957

The Hong Kong government announced in the *Gazette* its recovery of more than 200 lots of land in Chuk Yuen District where resettlement buildings were to be built.

23 Feb 1957

New Asia College launched a two-year Fine Arts Specialised Training Programme for students of Chinese and Western-style painting. It marked the first fine art degree course offered in Hong Kong.

01 Mar 1957

The Dutiable Commodities (Amendment) Ordinance 1957 was promulgated, stipulating that methanol containers must be conspicuously labelled with the warning "Poison" and that importers, wholesalers and retailers of methanol must add colouring or flavouring substance to methanol in possession. All liquor distillers, importers and retailers were also prohibited from storing methanol without the written permission of the Director of Commerce and Industry.

11 Mar 1957

A committee representing 10 indigenous villages near Kowloon Walled City was formed to oppose the government's plan to relocate residents of Chuk Yuen Village. In a press conference at the Village Office of Chuk Yuen United Village, it presented a petition to halt the relocation plan. On 13 April, it was expanded to include three more villages and was later known as the Kowloon Thirteen Villages in support of Chuk Yuen Villagers Committee.

17 Mar 1957

The new Star Ferry Pier in Tsim Sha Tsui was opened for service.

22 Mar 1957

The Housing Department was established as a government body on public housing in place of Urban Services Department's Housing Division. George Tippett Rowe was appointed as the first Commissioner for Housing.

28 Mar 1957

Hung Shui Hang Reservoir and Lam Tei Reservoir in Tuen Mun became operational for dozens of villages between Yuen Long and Tuen Mun, marking the first group of reservoirs dedicated to irrigation purposes in Hong Kong.

28 Apr 1957

Premier Zhou Enlai (周恩來) of the State Council spoke on the special role of Hong Kong for future economic development during a Shanghai business seminar. He noted 1) China would regain sovereignty over Hong Kong one day, 2) Chinese policy towards Hong Kong would be different from those regarding the Mainland; simply copying [the policy used in the Mainland] would not bring a good outcome and 3) Hong Kong could serve as a platform for China to create international economic ties, attract foreign investment and build up foreign exchange reserves.

21 May 1957

The University of Hong Kong's (HKU) Department of Extra-Mural Studies was formally instituted to provide access among secondary school graduates who had not been admitted to the university and young people without higher education. It was renamed the School of Professional and Continuing Education (SPACE) in 1992. HKU was the first institution in Hong Kong to offer a continued learning programme.

24 May 1957

The Medical Registration (Amendment) Ordinance 1957 was promulgated, establishing the Medical Council of Hong Kong while prohibiting any practitioner of Western medicine not registered with the Council from practice, unless exempt otherwise.

A 30-member Hong Kong film delegation, led by Dato Loke Wan-tho (陸運濤), attended the 4th Asian Film Festival in Tokyo. Linda Lin Dai (林黛) won Best Actress for her performance in the film *Golden Lotus*.

29 May 1957

Rediffusion Television, established by Radio Rediffusion, made its debut as the first television station in Hong Kong.

31 May 1957

The Tai Po Jockey Club Clinic, managed by the Medical Department, became operational. It was the first public clinic donated by The Hong Kong Jockey Club.

01 Jun 1957

Literature Century began publication as a journal focused on literary realism under the chief editorship of Xia Guo (夏果). It ceased publication in 1969 and was one of the longest-running literary journals in Hong Kong.

07 Jun 1957

The Hong Kong Airport (Control of Obstructions) Ordinance 1957 was promulgated, improving aviation safety by restricting the height of buildings within the area of air routes.

21 Jun 1957

The Hong Kong Tourism Board Ordinance 1957 was promulgated, establishing the Hong Kong Tourist Association as a statutory body to promote Hong Kong and attract overseas tourists internationally.

The Lei Cheng Uk Han Tomb Museum was opened. Modified from the Eastern Han tomb discovered in Lei Cheng Uk village in 1955, it was the first museum on a historical site in Hong Kong.

24 Jul 1957

The Ministry of Foreign Affairs of the People's Republic of China requested in a diplomatic note to the British government that the Hong Kong government abolish its relocation of Chuk Yuen Village and properly resettle and compensate residents already evicted. On 06 August, the British Foreign Office noted in a reply that China had misunderstood the actions of the Hong Kong government, stressing that new housing units in Lo Fu Ngam (present-day Lok Fu) had been built to accommodate affected residents.

Jul 1957

The US Policy on Hong Kong (NSC 5717)—a proposal to leverage Hong Kong as a centre of cultural propaganda and intelligence on China—was approved by US President Dwight Eisenhower. It was the first official guiding document of US policy on Hong Kong.

03 Aug 1957

The first section of South Lantau Road, linking Mui Wo and Cheung Sha, was opened as the first motorway on Lantau Island.

31 Aug 1957

A mass grave dating back to the Japanese occupation was discovered at Morrison Hill in Wan Chai where remains of more than 200 civilians massacred by Japanese soldiers were found.

05 Sep 1957

The eighth World Health Organization West Pacific Regional Conference was held in Hong Kong with representatives from 14 countries.

06 Sep 1957

The Radiation Ordinance 1957 was promulgated, establishing a Radiation Board for regulation on the import, export, possession and use of radioactive substances and irradiating apparatus.

22 Sep 1957

The Hong Kong Observatory hoisted the only Hurricane Signal No. 10 of the 1950s amid Typhoon Gloria—which killed nine people, injured 10 and affected 10,367.

26 Sep 1957

Maryknoll Fathers' School in Sham Shui Po was founded by Maryknoll Fathers and Brothers.

Sep 1957

Hong Kong-made industrial products were exhibited at the Frankfurt International Trade Fair in West Germany; orders worth hundreds of thousands of British pounds were secured.

14 Oct 1957

The Education Department's first evening secondary school founded after the Second World War began for classes.

16 Oct 1957

The Victoria Park Swimming Pool in Causeway Bay was opened as the first public swimming pool in Hong Kong.

21 Oct 1957

The first factory estate in Hong Kong, located in Cheung Sha Wan and managed by the Resettlement Department, was completed as part of a government resettlement programme intended to provide manufacturers (unable to afford their own workshops) with low-cost production space.

25 Nov 1957

The North Point Estate, located on Java Road in North Point, was completed by the Hong Kong Housing Authority. It was the first government-funded public housing estate, aiming to provide 600 units initially. (Figure 156)

07 Dec 1957

Tai Lam Chung Reservoir was completed; it was then the largest reservoir in Hong Kong with a total capacity of about 20 million cubic metres of freshwater. The project began in 1952 when Tai Lam Chung was designated an afforestation area.

08 Dec 1957

The first public multi-storey car park in Hong Kong, located opposite to the new Star Ferry Pier in Central, was opened.

15 Dec 1957

The new Star Ferry Pier in Central was opened.

Figure 156
An aerial view of North Point Estate in 1968 dubbed a deluxe residence among low-income families. (Photo courtesy of HKSAR Government)

1957

Grantham Hospital in Wong Chuk Hang on Hong Kong Island was completed. Managed by the Hong Kong Anti-Tuberculosis Association, it was dedicated to treating tuberculosis patients in the early years.

China Light and Power Company installed a power network on Lantau Island for a stable supply of electricity.

The Ministry of Foreign Trade and the People's Government of Guangdong Province were granted permission by the State Council to co-host a China Import and Export Fair in Guangzhou on behalf of the China Council for the Promotion of International Trade. The fair—which Premier Zhou Enlai (周恩來) of the State Council called the Canton Fair—was held in the spring and autumn of each year to the present day.

The Hong Kong Association of Travel Agents was founded to promote professionalism among travel agencies and tour guides.

The Mongkok Workers' Night School was opened as the first private school for vocational education in Hong Kong.

The Sino-British Orchestra, founded in 1947, was renamed the Hong Kong Philharmonic Orchestra and became an independent group from the Sino British Club.

The Ten Thousand Buddhas Monastery in Sha Tin was opened. The Venerable Yuet Kai (月溪) served as its first abbot.

The Hong Kong Chinese Arts Club in collaboration with the British Council began a two-year Southeast Asian Touring Exhibition of Chinese Paintings, featuring over 100 paintings and calligraphy works of 91 Hong Kong-based painters, including Bao Shaoyou (鮑少遊), Lui Shou-kwan (呂壽琨) and Ding Yanyong (丁衍庸). It marked the first overseas collective exhibition of Hong Kong painters across Southeast Asian countries, including Malaya, Thailand and Singapore.

The Hong Kong Artists Association was founded by Lui Shou-kwan (呂壽琨), Kwong Yeu-ting (鄺耀鼎) and Douglas Bland for promotion of modern arts in Hong Kong.

The 17-storey Empire Court in Causeway Bay was completed; it became the tallest building in place of the Bank of China building.

01 Jan 1958

The Social Welfare Office, formerly under the Secretary for Chinese Affairs, became an independent department and was renamed the Social Welfare Department.

05 Jan 1958

Hong Kong's first automatic traffic light system was installed at the junction of Arbuthnot Road, Caine Road, Upper Albert Road and Glenealy in Central, replacing the manually operated light system.

10 Jan 1958

The Education (Amendment) Ordinance 1958 was promulgated, introducing strengthened regulations on school facilities to ensure the safety of teachers and students.

23 Jan 1958

Robert Black was sworn in as the 23rd Governor of Hong Kong. He remained in office until 01 April 1964.

Jan 1958

Tang Chun-i (唐君毅), Hsu Fu-kuan (徐復觀), Chang Chun-mai (張君勱) and Mou Tsung-san (牟宗三) jointly published "A Manifesto on the Reappraisal of Chinese Culture: Our Joint Understanding of the Sinological Study Relating to World Cultural Outlook" in the January 1958 issue of *Democratic Critique*. It was dubbed the New Confucian Manifesto.

01 Feb 1958

The Amateur Sports Federation and Olympic Committee of Hong Kong and 11 affiliated sports associations co-organised the first Festival of Sport at Queen Elizabeth II Youth Centre in Kowloon in a bid to promote sports for all.

01 Mar 1958

A group of 500 Naval Dockyard workers surrounded the dockyard office in protest of the dismissal of 12 employees as part of a closedown plan. The police were called in to mediate the dispute.

03 Mar 1958

The first pair of cross-harbour submarine gas pipelines between Hung Hom and Causeway Bay were installed to supply petroleum gas from a plant in Kowloon to Hong Kong Island. The plant in Sai Wan was subsequently closed.

06 Mar 1958

Governor Robert Black announced in the Legislative Council that the Hong Kong government could decide on its financial budget and issue bonds and loans without having to consult the British government starting from the following year.

Mar 1958

The Police Training Contingent was established at Fanling Camp as a paramilitary force capable of handling riots. In 1968, it became the Police Tactical Unit.

04 Apr 1958

The Urban Council introduced a cartoon character called Miss Ping On (meaning "wellbeing") in an education campaign on mosquito control and practice of hygiene such as handwashing. The Council also crowned the most hygienic residents of each resettlement area. (Figure 157)

22 Apr 1958

A fire in the squatter area of Kai Tak New Village near Kowloon City killed five people, including two pregnant women, and injured nine.

25 Apr 1958

The Hong Kong police implemented a new immigration rule, requiring Hong Kong residents returning from Macao to hold a Re-entry Permit. The measure, announced on 17 March 1958, was originally scheduled for implementation on 01 April but was postponed twice.

Figure 157
A poster of Miss Ping On in 1959 reminding the public to "maintain hygiene by cleaning gutters" in a government campaign. (Courtesy of HKSAR Government)

Apr 1958

Liang Weilin (梁威林) arrived in Hong Kong to serve as Director of the Hong Kong Branch of Xinhua News Agency. He remained in office until December 1977, making him the longest-serving director of the agency to date.

01 May 1958

The Education Department banned eight leftist schools in Hong Kong from flying the national flag of China on Labour Day. On 10 June, the Ministry of Foreign Affairs of the People's Republic of China issued a statement, condemning the Hong Kong government for imposing the ban.

05 May 1958

The clinic ship *Chee Hong*, donated by The Hong Kong Jockey Club and managed by the Medical Department, became operational. It served various rural and fishing villages along the east coast of Hong Kong.

17 May 1958

The Alhambra Theatre in Yau Ma Tei collapsed during demolition, causing six deaths and 13 injuries.

24 May 1958

Hong Kong participated in the third Asian Games held in Tokyo, Japan, winning for the first time a silver and a bronze medal in table tennis and shooting events, respectively.

30 May 1958

The Resettlement Ordinance 1958 was promulgated, empowering the Governor to appoint public officers for squatter clearance and resettlement functions, such as removing unlawful structures, reviewing applicants' eligibility for resettlement, as well as erecting buildings in resettlement estates and cottage areas.

May 1958

The Hong Kong Federation of Students was established.

Jul 1958

The Hong Kong police set up checkpoints on several major roads in the New Territories to combat smuggling.

06 Aug 1958

Principal of Pui Kiu Middle School To Pak-fui (杜伯奎) was deported on the grounds that he continued to manage the school after being removed from his position as Supervisor.

10 Aug 1958

The Hong Kong Chinese Arts Club was founded; members included Li Yanshan (李研山), Chao Shao-an (趙少昂), Chang Chun-shih (張君實) and Lui Shou-kwan (呂壽琨).

11 Aug 1958

Kwan Shan (關山) won a Silver Sail for Best Actor at the 12th Locarno International Film Festival in Switzerland for his role in *The True Story of Ah Q*. He was the first male actor from Hong Kong to win an international film award.

26 Aug 1958

The campus of Chung Wah Middle School was sequestered by the police on the grounds of structural safety, resulting in a clash with teachers and students, as well as journalists on the scene. The Ministry of Foreign Affairs of the People's Republic of China later lodged a protest to the British government regarding the incident.

12 Sep 1958

The 13/31 runway at Kai Tak Airport became operational at a construction cost of HK$90 million. The airport was renamed Hong Kong International Airport on the same day. (Figure 158)

Figure 158
Kai Tak Airport's Runway 13/31 in 1958 following a redevelopment in which 1.5 miles of runway was reclaimed in the waters off Kowloon Bay. (Photo courtesy of HKSAR Government)

03 Oct 1958

The Immigration (Control and Offences) Ordinance 1958 was promulgated, consolidating the laws on immigration control for comprehensive regulations on entry/exit enforcement and travel documents.

25 Nov 1958

The Hong Kong Rice Dealers United Association was founded.

27 Nov 1958

The Family Planning Association of Hong Kong established two marriage guidance centres (on Hong Kong Island and in Kowloon) for free-of-charge counselling service on marriage and birth control.

Nov 1958

Tai Lam Prison was opened as a centre primarily for drug addicts.

09 Dec 1958

The Hong Kong police prohibited 10 leftist schools, including Pui Kiu Middle School and Heung To Middle School, from holding a joint sport exhibition at South China Athletic Association Stadium.

12 Dec 1958

The Modern Literature and Art Association Hong Kong was founded by Quanan Shum (崑南), Wucius Wong (王無 邪), Yip Wai-lim (葉維廉) and others. In May 1959, they established *The New Currents*—a magazine on literature, art review and commentary, book recommendation and other literature-related news.

27 Dec 1958

Shaw Brothers (Hong Kong) Limited, a film production company, was incorporated. (Figures 159 and 160)

1958

Banque Nationale pour le Commerce et l'Industrie (present-day BNP Paribas) of France began banking services in Hong Kong.

Chen Hsong Machinery was established by Chiang Chen (蔣震). Initially a machine maintenance workshop, it began producing injection moulding machines in 1965 onwards and became a leading manufacturer of such machines.

Hong Kong's first steel rolling mill, located at Tiu Keng Leng in Tseung Kwan O, was founded by Shiu Wing Steel Limited. Products included steel bars made with iron from ship plates.

02 Jan 1959

The Judiciary established Hong Kong's first evening court at the Kowloon Magistracy.

08 Jan 1959

The Hong Kong Diocesan Council for the Lay Apostolate was founded by Bishop Lorenzo Bianchi.

23 Jan 1959

The Hong Kong Auxiliary Police Force Ordinance 1959 was promulgated, forming the Hong Kong Auxiliary Police Force through a merger of the Hong Kong Police Reserve and the Special Constabulary.

Mercantile Bank Limited became a subsidiary of The Hongkong and Shanghai Banking Corporation.

01 Feb 1959

The Lancashire Pact—signed by the Hong Kong government and British Board of Trade in December 1958—came into effect, with Hong Kong self-imposing an annual maximum export of 164 million square yards of cotton goods to Britain for three years. It was the first bilateral agreement since the US and Europe had imposed textile quotas on Hong Kong.

The first Hong Kong Open was held at Fanling Golf Course as the first international golf tournament in Hong Kong. Taiwanese golfer Lu Liang-huan (呂良煥) won the championship.

Figure 159
Run Run Shaw (邵逸夫), left, and Michael Hui Koon-man (許冠文) at a press conference on the movie
The Warlord. (Photo taken on 18 April 1972 and courtesy of South China Morning Post Publishers
Limited)

Figure 160
An aerial view of Shaw Studio in Clear Water Bay. (Photo taken in November 1971 and courtesy of South China Morning Post
Publishers Limited)

04 Feb 1959

The Far East Qianzhuang (native bank) was opened in Tsuen Wan as the first banking institution operating in the New Territories. It was renamed the Far East Bank the following year.

06 Feb 1959

The Business Registration Ordinance 1959 was promulgated, stipulating that all persons doing business in Hong Kong, unless exempt otherwise, must apply for a business registration certificate from the Companies Registry of the Registrar General's Department.

02 Apr 1959

The first pedestrian subway in Hong Kong was opened under Connaught Road Central.

The Archbishop of Canterbury of the Anglican Church, Geoffrey Fisher, arrived in Hong Kong for a five-day visit.

05 Apr 1959

Hong Kong table tennis player Jung Kuo-tuan (容國團), representing China, won the men's singles title at the 25th World Table Tennis Championships in Dortmund, West Germany. He was the first sport world champion of the People's Republic of China.

Apr 1959

Knightly World—a magazine featuring local martial arts novels—was founded by publisher Law Bun (羅斌). It ceased publication in January 2019, making it the longest-running martial arts magazine in Hong Kong.

The Hong Kong government began funding the installation of seawater toilet flushing systems at resettlement areas in Kowloon in a bid to improve sanitation by replacing the use of aqua privies.

11 May 1959

The New Territories General Chamber of Commerce was established to promote business development and cooperation among chambers of commerce in the New Territories.

17 May 1959

The first Hong Kong Pharmaceutical Products Display, organised by the Hong Kong and Kowloon Western Drug Trade Employees' Welfare Association, began in an exhibition of new drugs from Hong Kong and other countries.

20 May 1959

Ming Pao—a newspaper founded by Louis Cha Leung-yung (查良鏞) and Shen Pao-sing (沈寶新)—began publication.

22 May 1959

The Clean Air Ordinance was promulgated, introducing control of emissions caused by the combustion of industrial fuels.

12 Jun 1959

Four days of heavy rain caused serious damage in the New Territories. On 18 June, the Hong Kong government allocated HK$500,000 to help the farmers affected by floods.

19 Jun 1959

Wong Ying-kau (黃應求), a business and sports celebrity and son of businessman Wong Sik-pun (黃錫彬), was kidnapped and killed, marking the beginning of the Three Wolves Case.

29 Jun 1959

The Hong Kong Jockey Club (Charities) Limited was incorporated to administer donations by The Hong Kong Jockey Club. The Hong Kong Jockey Club Charities Trust was founded in 1993.

15 Jul 1959

The Hong Kong Society for Rehabilitation was established to provide rehabilitation services for people with disabilities.

17 Jul 1959

A runway lighting system for night navigation was installed at Hong Kong International (Kai Tak) Airport, enabling aircraft take-off and landing at night to facilitate 24-hour operations.

01 Aug 1959

The Standard Chartered Bank unveiled its new 19-storey building on Des Voeux Road Central in Central. It was then the tallest building in Hong Kong.

26 Aug 1959

Commercial Radio, operated by Hong Kong Commercial Broadcasting Corporation Limited, made its debut.

23 Sep 1959

The Hong Kong government announced a new general order requiring civil servants whose wealth and living standards exceeded their official income to submit a reasonable explanation to the Governor. The Governor could appoint a three-person tribunal (chaired by a Judiciary representative) for further investigation; civil servants would be dismissed upon confirmation of violation.

05 Oct 1959

Hong Kong Daily News, founded by publisher Law Bun (羅斌), began publication; it ceased on 12 July 2015.

09 Oct 1959

The Agreement between the Government of Hong Kong and the Admiralty was promulgated, requiring Hong Kong to pay the Royal Navy £7 million for reclaiming the Naval Dockyard in Admiralty.

01 Nov 1959

Hong Kong's first radio-equipped taxi fleet, owned by the Blue Taxicab Limited, began to operate.

11 Nov 1959

The Hong Kong government released a white paper titled *Problem of Narcotic Drugs in Hong Kong*, indicating dangerous drugs as one of the biggest social and economic problems. Solutions proposed in the paper included legislative amendments to strengthen the powers of the Preventive Services and the police in detaining and prosecuting drug traffickers, as well as the establishment of a voluntary drug treatment centre in Castle Peak Hospital.

26 Nov 1959

The Colony Armorial Bearings (Protection) Ordinance 1959 was promulgated, prohibiting anyone, without the written permission of the Colonial Secretary, from making, displaying, selling or using replicas of (or anything closely resembling) the Coat of Arms of Hong Kong for business, trade or profession purposes.

27 Nov 1959

The Hong Kong police launched a scheme for special taxi services in the New Territories and began recruiting operators. Operators with no fewer than six taxis could apply for an operation licence in the New Territories. These taxis were also allowed to carry passengers to and from designated taxi stands in Kowloon.

28 Nov 1959

The Hong Kong government took over the Naval Dockyard in Admiralty to facilitate the construction of a road between Central District and Eastern District on Hong Kong Island.

11 Dec 1959

The Heung Yee Kuk Ordinance 1959 was promulgated, making Heung Yee Kuk a statutory advisory body for handling affairs in the New Territories.

31 Dec 1959

Hang Seng Ngan Ho, a native bank, was renamed and incorporated as Hang Seng Bank. The Hang Seng Bank Headquarters building on Des Voeux Road Central was subsequently built.

1959

Hong Kong-made products rose to 69.9% of all exports, surpassing the share of re-export trade. The growing proportion of locally made products for export suggested Hong Kong had successfully industrialised.

The Public Relations Office was renamed the Information Services Department.

The Medical Department was renamed the Medical and Health Department.

Johnson Electric Industrial Manufactory was founded by Wang Seng-liang (汪松亮) and his wife Koo Yik-chun (顧亦珍). It was incorporated as a limited company on 25 April 1960.

Bridget O'Rorke was appointed Hong Kong's first female Cadet Officer (later known as an Administrative Officer).

Four Seasons Estate—Hong Kong Housing Society's first public housing estate in Tsuen Wan New Town—was completed.

Daily Pictorial, also known as *Ngan Tang Yat Po,* began publication as the first full-colour entertainment newspaper in Hong Kong. (Figure 161)

Wan Li Bookstore (present-day Wan Li Book Company Limited) was founded.

01 Jan 1960

The one-dollar coin became a legal tender in Hong Kong; it went into circulation the following day in place of the one-dollar note—of which printing production ended in the late 1960s. (Figure 162)

Figure 161
Daily Pictorial, also known as *Ngan Tang Yat Po,* dated 03 June 1965. (Courtesy of Hong Kong Museum of History)

Figure 162
The one-dollar coin issued in 1960—designed with the head of Queen Elizabeth II on one side and a lion holding a pearl along the characters "Hong Kong One Dollar" on the other side. The lion symbolised the British Monarchy while the pearl signified Hong Kong as the Pearl of the Orient. (Courtesy of Hong Kong Museum of History)

15 Jan 1960

Hong Kong's second vehicular ferry service, operated by The Hongkong and Yaumati Ferry Company, commenced with a route between Reclamation Street in Sheung Wan on Hong Kong Island and Jordan Road Ferry Pier in Kowloon.

24 Jan 1960

The Hong Kong government conducted a pilot survey on boat dwellers in Yau Ma Tei, western Victoria Harbour, Aberdeen and Tai Po in association with the 1961 census. On 24 February 1961, results were released and indicated a boat dweller population of around 150,000.

Jan 1960

The Hong Kong government established a HK$2 million Fisheries Development Loan Fund as a revolving loan facility to help local fishermen develop deep-sea fishing capabilities. In December 1961, it was granted an additional HK$3 million by the government.

12 Feb 1960

A fire broke out in the squatter area of Lei Cheng Uk Village, destroying 642 huts, killing four children, injuring five others and affecting 2,397 people.

21 Feb 1960

The Castle Peak Psychiatric Hospital began admitting the first group of patients from Victoria Mental Hospital in Sai Ying Pun. It was officially opened on 27 March 1961 and later renamed Castle Peak Hospital.

27 Feb 1960

The *Children's Weekly* began publication, featuring cartoons and comic strips adapted from fairy tales and articles submitted by students, as well as book reviews and student news. It ceased publication in September 1966.

15 Mar 1960

An armed conflict involving dozens of villagers broke out in the villages of Tin Liu and Muk Kiu Tau at Shap Pat Heung in Yuen Long, causing three serious injuries and more than 10 minor injuries.

Mar 1960

Cadet Officers were retitled as Administrative Officers in a significant reform of the Civil Service by the Hong Kong government.

John Fulton, Vice Chancellor of the University of Sussex in the UK, submitted his *Report on the Development of Post-Secondary Colleges* to the Hong Kong government. Based on his assessment during an earlier visit to Hong Kong, he suggested that Chinese should be made the medium of instruction at a new university which the government was planning to establish. In 1962, Fulton arrived in Hong Kong to chair a commission of international scholars formed to assess the education standards of New Asia College, Chung Chi College and United College, and to determine the organisational structure of the new university. In April 1963, *Report of the Fulton Commission* was released, stating that the new university should adopt a federal system, incorporating the three colleges. The report became a blueprint and basis for the establishment of The Chinese University of Hong Kong.

16 Apr 1960

The Hongkong and Shanghai Banking Corporation (HSBC) opened a branch in Tsuen Wan. It was the first HSBC branch and the first modern foreign-owned bank in the New Territories.

06 May 1960

Heavy rain in the New Territories caused widespread devastation in Tai Po, Yuen Long and Sheung Shui. At least seven people were killed; 5,300 acres of rice fields and 1,300 acres of vegetable fields were flooded, resulting in property losses of HK$3 million.

13 May 1960

The Hong Kong government released a draft of the *North-east Kowloon Development Scheme* in a public consultation. The Scheme called for a plan to accommodate over 600,000 residents through the development of 1,300 acres of land, including the area of Kowloon Walled City.

20 May 1960

The Registration of Persons Ordinance 1960 was promulgated, effective 01 June, requiring all Hong Kong residents to renew their identity cards in batches.

29 May 1960

The Air Mail Centre at Hong Kong International (Kai Tak) Airport began operations with express mail and parcels.

May 1960

The Registration of Persons Office's official Chinese name was amended.

The Drug Regulations 1960 was enforced in the New Territories, requiring livestock farms to obtain a licence for purchase of antibiotics or drugs intended for animals.

09 Jun 1960

The Hong Kong Observatory hoisted Hurricane Signal No. 10 for nine hours amid Typhoon Mary—which left 45 people dead, 11 missing and 127 injured, damaged 814 fishing boats and six ocean-going vessels, and destroyed 330 squatter huts.

30 Jun 1960

The Federation of Hong Kong Industries Ordinance 1960 was promulgated, establishing the Federation of Hong Kong Industries—a statutory body aiming to protect the interests of local manufacturers. It was officially formed on 22 November 1960; Chau Sik-nin（周錫年）served as its first Chairman.

Jun 1960

The Suicide Prevention Society was founded by Tu Hok-fui（杜學魁）and Elsie Elliott as the first organisation of its kind in Asia; a telephone counselling service was established in the same year. It was officially registered as The Hong Kong Samaritans in 1963 and was renamed The Samaritan Befrienders Hong Kong in 1976.

12 Jul 1960

The community centre at Wong Tai Sin Resettlement Area—funded by the US government with a donation of US$200,000—was inaugurated as the first community centre in Hong Kong. It was jointly run by the Social Welfare Department and private welfare institutions.

05 Sep 1960

The Queen Elizabeth Hospital School of General Nursing was established.

07 Sep 1960

Chinachem Investment Company Limited was incorporated by Wang Din-shin（王廷歆）and his son Teddy Wang Teh-huei（王德輝）.

09 Sep 1960

The Mental Health Ordinance 1962 was promulgated, regulating the admission, supervision and treatment of mentally incapacitated persons.

17 Sep 1960

A fire broke out in the squatter area of Tai Hang Tung in Kowloon, destroying over 300 huts, killing four people, including a pregnant woman, and leaving over 4,500 people homeless.

19 Sep 1960

The Third Teachers' Training College, initially a branch of Grantham Teachers' Training College, began offering courses at Lo Fu Ngam Government Primary School. On 27 October 1961, it was renamed Sir Robert Black College of Education.

Sep 1960

The Hong Kong government formed a diving unit (under the Fire Brigade) to support underwater rescue missions. It later became known as the Fire Services Department Diving Unit.

21 Oct 1960

The Chinese Gold and Silver Exchange suspended trading of gold in response to extreme price fluctuations in Europe. The suspension was extended to 24 October.

01 Nov 1960

Tin Tin Daily News was founded as the first full-colour newspaper in Hong Kong; it ceased publication on 08 September 2000.

03 Nov 1960

The Hong Kong Daimaru Department Store was opened in Causeway Bay; it began for business operation the following day as the first Japanese-owned department store in Hong Kong. It was closed on 31 December 1998. (Figure 163)

11 Nov 1960

The Road Traffic (Amendment) Ordinance 1960 was promulgated, exempting police vehicles, fire engines and ambulances from traffic light control.

Figure 163
The Japanese-owned Daimaru Department Store in Causeway Bay. (Photo taken in 1976 and courtesy of South China Morning Post Publishers Limited)

Figure 164
Cheung Chi-doy (張子岱) (left) of Happy Valley Athletic Association upon scoring a second goal in a Football Association First Division League match with Seiko Sports Association. (Photo taken on 13 April 1975 and courtesy of South China Morning Post Publishers Limited)

15 Nov 1960

The Hong Kong government reached its first agreement on water supply with the Guangdong authorities, specifying an annual import of 22.7 million cubic metres of fresh water from Shenzhen Reservoir.

1960

Secondary schools were formally categorised as grammar schools, prevocational schools and secondary technical schools. Grammar schools offered a traditional curriculum towards university education while the three-year programmes of technical and prevocational secondary schools were geared towards industry- and commerce-related applied subjects.

Hong Kong became a member of the International Criminal Police Organization (Interpol).

The Target Committee on Corruption was formed by the police. Members included a Deputy Commissioner of Police, Director of Criminal Investigation, Superintendent of the Anti-Corruption Branch and, later, a representative of the Establishment Officer.

The Hong Kong Jockey Club was granted a Royal title by Queen Elizabeth II at the end of the year. In January 1961, an amended official Chinese title bearing the honour was announced by the Secretary for Chinese Affairs.

The Gin Drinkers Bay Landfill became operational. When it was closed in 1979, it had accumulated 3.5 million tonnes of waste. In 1993, restoration works began at the site to be designated as Kwai Chung Park. In 2000, it was completed; its 3.9-hectare BMX park was opened.

14 Jan 1961

Hong Kong footballer Cheung Chi-doy (張子岱) made his debut for Blackpool Football Club in the First Division of the English Football League. He was the first Chinese player to play in the top tier of English football. On 25 November, he scored a goal for Blackpool, becoming the first Chinese player to score in the league. (Figure 164)

16 Jan 1961

A fire broke out in the squatter area on Valley Road in Hung Hom, destroying about 1,200 huts, claiming six lives and affecting over 10,000 people.

01 Feb 1961

Hong Kong began receiving a daily supply of 22 million gallons of water from Shenzhen Reservoir.

10 Feb 1961

Businessman Wong Sik-pun (黃錫彬) was kidnapped near his home at Jardine's Lookout; he was released after 17 days in what was part of the Three Wolves Case.

11 Feb 1961

The Hong Kong government began its first post-Second World War census in accordance with the Census Ordinance 1931; it ended on 07 March. Results showed a total population of 3,133,131 in Hong Kong, about 3.7 times that of 1931.

22 Feb 1961

British Secretary of State for Foreign Affairs Alexander Douglas-Home said in a secret note to Britain's Minister of Defence and Prime Minister that if China were to take over Hong Kong by force, "nuclear strikes against China would be the only alternative to complete abandonment of the colony." He also suggested that the British government should discuss with the United States about the possibility of using nuclear weapons to defend Hong Kong and "encourage the Chinese to believe that an attack on Hong Kong would involve nuclear retaliation."

Feb 1961

The Education Department announced a five-year Chinese-language secondary school programme with an amended curriculum.

Mar 1961

The Hong Kong government began applying fluoride to drinking water for improving public dental health.

19 Apr 1961

A US Air Force transport aircraft carrying 16 military personnel and their families crashed into Mount Parker on the eastern part of Hong Kong Island after taking off from Hong Kong International (Kai Tak) Airport under heavy fog, killing 14 people on board.

15 May 1961

A fire broke out in three adjacent buildings on Lai Chi Kok Road in Sham Shui Po, causing 29 deaths and 50 injuries.

19 May 1961

The Hong Kong Observatory hoisted Hurricane Signal No. 10 for two and a half hours amid Typhoon Alice—which caused four deaths and 20 injuries.

01 Jun 1961

The third-generation Hong Kong–Macau Ferry Terminal in Sheung Wan became operational.

02 Jun 1961

The Hong Kong government announced that Tiu Keng Leng, an area originally used for refugee housing, would be designated a resettlement area where 1) government permission was required to build or expand houses; 2) residents could stay indefinitely upon registration and 3) new accommodation must be arranged for existing residents should they be asked to relocate by the government.

09 Jun 1961

Dozens of Taoist groups in Hong Kong jointly announced the establishment of the Hong Kong Taoist Association—which received government approval for registration in March 1962.

15 Jun 1961

Rumours emerged that Liu Chong Hing Bank Limited's chairman had fled Hong Kong amid a police investigation and led to a bank run. On 16 June, Hongkong and Shanghai Banking Corporation and Standard Chartered Bank issued a joint statement reassuring the bank's integrity, putting an end to the bank run.

24 Jun 1961

Lung Cheung Road—between Kai Tak Airport and Tai Po Road—was opened to traffic, linking eastern Kowloon with eastern New Territories. Upon joining Ching Cheung Road in west Kowloon, it formed a strategic route between east and west Kowloon.

21 Jul 1961

The second-generation Queen's Theatre, located at Luk Hoi Tung Building in Central, was opened; it was closed on 30 September 2007.

26 Jul 1961

Renowned comedian Charlie Chaplin and his entourage arrived in Hong Kong on a world tour and gave a press interview.

04 Aug 1961

The Immigration Service Ordinance 1961 was promulgated, making the Immigration Department an independent agency from the Hong Kong Police Force with an amended Chinese name—which was again amended on 01 July 1997.

18 Aug 1961

The Medical and Health Department confirmed an outbreak of cholera in Hong Kong—which was declared an infected area in the *Gazette.* Two government committees were formed for emergency measures to prevent further spread of the disease. On 12 October, an end to the pandemic was pronounced by the Hong Kong government. A total of 129 people were infected and 15 people died.

01 Sep 1961

The Town Planning Board's *Tsuen Wan and District Outline Development Plan* was released as the first statutory plan for a Tsuen Wan New Town—a self-sufficient satellite town to be developed in a 15-year period for a population of 640,000.

05 Sep 1961

The Education Department announced its implementation of the Secondary School Entrance Examination starting 1962 in place of the Joint Primary 6 Examination.

07 Sep 1961

The Society for the Aid and Rehabilitation of Drug Abusers was established, followed by the establishment of a drug rehabilitation centre on the island of Shek Kwu Chau.

28 Sep 1961

In a meeting of Heung Yee Kuk, representatives of 24 Rural Committees unanimously voted to oppose the existing land policy of the government, making 21 October an Anti-Land Policy Day on which a meeting with all 27 Rural Committees of the New Territories was to be held to gather the views of villagers for submission to the government.

03 Oct 1961

The Hong Kong government, in accordance with the Deportation of Aliens Ordinance 1935, detained John Tsang Siu-fo (曾 昭 科), Assistant Superintendent of Police and Deputy Commandant of the Police Training School, on suspicion of espionage. On 30 November, he and four others were deported to the Mainland via Lo Wu.

27 Oct 1961

Audrey Chau Shuet-yeng (周雪瑩) became the first Chinese female appointed as an Administrative Officer in Hong Kong.

03 Nov 1961

Tung Wah Hospital successfully performed Hong Kong's first cornea transplant.

11 Nov 1961

Chungking Mansions, located at Tsim Sha Tsui in Kowloon, was opened for occupancy upon receipt of a government permit.

06 Dec 1961

The Shaw House, along with the first phase of Shaw Studios, located at Clear Water Bay in Kowloon and owned by Shaw Brothers, was opened.

07 Dec 1961

A fire broke out at the 19th Exhibition of Hong Kong Products three days after opening; it destroyed more than 30 stands in what became the most destructive incident in the exhibition's history. It was closed until 20 December and was extended to 21 January 1962, marking the first extended exhibition.

10 Dec 1961

The police, while handling a brawl on Lung Cheung Road, unexpectedly found out two of the arrested were involved in kidnapping Wong Ying-kau (黃應求) and Wong Sik-pun (黃錫彬). On 13 December, human remains of Wong Ying-kau and Tang Tin-fuk (鄧天福), victims of the Three Wolves Case, were recovered at Repulse Bay.

22 Dec 1961

Fok Ying Tung Group acquired plots of land in Tsim Sha Tsui for HK$30 million from Hong Kong and Kowloon Wharf and Godown Company Limited. The Star House was later built on the site.

1961

The people of Hong Kong sent HK$124 million worth of food and daily supplies to their relatives and friends in the Mainland during its period of economic hardship. The number of two-pound food packages from Hong Kong to the Mainland increased from 870,000 in 1959 to 13.3 million in 1961.

The Hong Kong Buddhist Sangha Association was established.

The Duke of Edinburgh's Award, founded in 1956, was launched in Hong Kong to cultivate young people's self-enriching and community-serving spirits. The first Gold Award in Hong Kong was given to a male participant in 1963. The scheme was renamed The Hong Kong Award for Young People on 01 April 1997.

The Hong Kong Amateur Drama Society was founded as a non-profit organisation dedicated to original and translated foreign plays. Members included Chung King-fai (鍾景輝), Chung Wai-ming (鍾偉明) and Lily Leung Shun-yin (梁舜燕). The Society was dissolved in 1977.

15 Jan 1962

The Oxfam Hostel, located at Mount Davis, was opened for cancer patients.

18 Jan 1962

The 11th Pacific Air Travel Association Conference was held in Hong Kong, bringing together 550 delegates from 32 countries in the Asia Pacific region.

29 Jan 1962

The Hong Kong Country Club, located at Deep Water Bay, was opened as the first country club in Hong Kong and the first club accessible to people of all nationalities and racial backgrounds.

28 Feb 1962

The Hong Kong government released its 1962/63 Budget—which specified its general revenue account as recurrent and capital accounts separately for the first time. It placed an emphasis on having a surplus in the recurrent account so as to ensure sufficient reserves for more public services.

02 Mar 1962

The new Hong Kong City Hall, located in Central District, was inaugurated as the first multi-purpose leisure and cultural complex built after the Second World War. The City Hall Museum and Art Gallery (predecessor of the Hong Kong Museum of Art and Hong Kong Museum of History) was opened on the same day. The City Hall Public Library was opened on 05 March. (Figure 165)

14 Mar 1962

The Supreme Court of Hong Kong convicted three defendants of the Three Wolves Case. Lee Wai（李渭）, Ma Kwong-tsan（馬廣燦）and Ngai Ping-kin（倪秉堅）were found guilty of murdering Wong Ying-kau（黃應求）and Tang Tin-fuk（鄧天福）and sentenced to death. On 28 November, they were executed by hanging.

19 Mar 1962

A strong earthquake of magnitude five on the Richter scale struck Hong Kong where tremors lasted for nearly an hour noticeable across different districts.

The Hong Kong government ordered residents of Kowloon Walled City to register for relocation and move out by a deadline so as to allow the implementation of the Northeast Kowloon Development Scheme. The residents formed a committee to oppose demolition and eviction by the government.

Mar 1962

The Ministry of Railways and Ministry of Foreign Trade of the People's Republic of China jointly launched three daily express trains—from Shanghai, Zhengzhou, Wuhan or Changsha to Hong Kong—for delivery of fresh foods and other goods. From 1962 to 1995, over 80 million live hogs, over 5 million live cattle, over 810 million live poultry, 1.35 million tons of frozen food, among other products, were transported to Hong Kong. (Figure 166)

01 Apr 1962

The US quota on cotton goods from Hong Kong came into effect.

09 Apr 1962

Hua Chiao Commercial Bank was established. It merged with Bank of China (Hong Kong) in 2001.

05 May 1962

Bao'an County of Guangdong Province relaxed control on public travel to Hong Kong. According to its estimates, about 80,000 people fled between 27 April and 08 July. About 58,810 were later repatriated by the Hong Kong government.

12 May 1962

Governor Robert Black visited the border where he inspected a refugee escape route (into Hong Kong) and an internment camp in Fanling. On the same day, the Hong Kong government announced that around 10,000 illegal immigrants were arrested from 01 May to 11 May.

15 May 1962

More than 6,000 illegal immigrants were arrested, marking the highest number on a single day in the first two weeks of May. On 18 May, the Hong Kong government erected barbed wire fences along the border between Guangdong and Hong Kong to deter illegal immigrants.

21 May 1962

The first Government Lottery—established in accordance with the Government Lotteries Ordinance 1962—went on sale. The first prize of $684,800 was drawn on 07 July. The last Lottery was held on 14 October 1975.

15 Jun 1962

A newt captured by amateur herpetologist John Romer was identified as a new species in a paper published by American biologists George Sprague Myers and Alan E. Leviton. It was named the Hong Kong newt.

Figure 165
The High Block of the second-generation Hong Kong City Hall in Central. (Photo taken in 1976 and courtesy of Public Records Office, Government Records Service)

Figure 166
Livestock of hogs and cattle were selected from 60 suburban farms by Shanghai Foodstuffs Import & Export Corporation and shipped to Hong Kong on express trains. (Photo courtesy of Xinhua News Agency)

Jun 1962

Wah Kui Literature—a journal of literary theories, novels, poetries and works by young authors—began publication. It was renamed *Man Ngai Monthly Literature* in July 1963; it ceased publication in January 1965.

01 Jul 1962

The Commonwealth Immigrants Act 1962, enacted by the British government, came into effect. It restricted the rights of abode in Great Britain for residents from all British colonies, including Hong Kong.

27 Jul 1962

The Emergency (Deportation and Detention) Regulations 1962 was promulgated, establishing a Deportation and Detention Advisory Tribunal to support the Governor on whether a deportation or detention order should be issued in different cases.

01 Aug 1962

A devastating fire broke out in a Chinese tenement building on Un Chau Street in Sham Shui Po, destroying five houses, killing 44 (including four pregnant women) and injuring 21.

03 Aug 1962

The Hong Kong police intercepted a boat carrying illegal immigrants in Shenzhen Bay (also known as Deep Bay). Two illegal immigrants were killed; one was injured. About 80 people were detained.

17 Aug 1962

The Emergency (Immigration (Control and Offences) Ordinance 1958) (Amendment) Regulations 1962 was promulgated, increasing the maximum penalty from two to three years of imprisonment for aiding or abetting illegal immigrants.

24 Aug 1962

The Hong Kong government confirmed four cholera carriers in Hong Kong and set up five temporary stations to provide vaccination to the public.

Hong Kong participated in the fourth Asian Games held in Jakarta, Indonesia and won two silver medals, including the first-ever medal in tennis.

30 Aug 1962

The City Hall Memorial Garden was inaugurated in remembrance of combatants and civilians who died during the Battle of Hong Kong in 1941.

01 Sep 1962

The Hong Kong Observatory hoisted Hurricane Signal No. 10 for eight hours amid Typhoon Wanda—which triggered a severe storm surge and a record tide level of 5.03 metres at Tai Po Kau. The typhoon left 130 people dead, 53 missing and over 46,000 affected; it damaged 36 ocean-going vessels and 2,053 fishing boats. (Figures 167 and 168)

18 Sep 1962

Hong Kong Society for Rehabilitation's medical centre in Lam Tin was completed as the first in-patient rehabilitation and the first barrier-free facility in Hong Kong. In 1971, it was renamed Margaret Trench Medical Rehabilitation Centre. In 2000, it merged with Kowloon Hospital and was renamed Hong Kong Society for Rehabilitation Lam Tin Complex.

21 Sep 1962

The Building (Planning) (Amendment) (No. 2) Regulations 1962 was promulgated, effective 19 October, introducing tightened restrictions on plot ratio and floor area under the Building Ordinance.

02 Oct 1962

The Impresarios Association of the Far East inaugurated its first Asian Music Festival for a six-day event at City Hall.

06 Oct 1962

A total of 52 pieces of jewellery worth HK$400,000, as well as US$66,000, CHF 25,000 and ITL 250,000 in cash, were stolen from a Western-style mansion on Cooper Road at Jardine's Lookout on Hong Kong Island. It was then the largest burglary in Hong Kong.

Figure 167
A large cargo ship ran aground and overturned at the waterfront of Sai Wan during Typhoon Wanda. (Photo taken in 1962 and courtesy of HKSAR Government)

Figure 168
Typhoon Wanda caused severe damage, including the destruction of houses and vehicles in the seaside section of Percival Street in Causeway Bay. (Photo taken in September 1962 and courtesy of Public Records Office, Government Records Service)

20 Oct 1962

Writer Liu Yichang (劉以鬯) began publishing his novel *The Drunkard* as a series in *Sing Tao Evening Post*. It was the first stream-of-consciousness novel in China.

31 Oct 1962

The film *Sun, Moon and Star*, produced by Motion Picture & General Investment Company Limited, won Best Feature Film at the first Golden Horse Awards. Lucilla You Min (尤敏) won Best Leading Actress for her role in the film.

02 Nov 1962

Hong Kong International (Kai Tak) Airport's new passenger terminal was completed; it became operational on 12 November.

05 Nov 1962

The 17th World Congress of the Junior Chamber International began at City Hall; it was a seven-day meeting with over 2,000 representatives from 67 countries and regions.

15 Nov 1962

The Cape Collinson Crematorium in Chai Wan, built by the government and equipped with three prayer halls, was opened as the first crematorium with such facilities in the world.

28 Nov 1962

A human-smuggling ship sank in the waters off Chai Wan where 32 bodies were retrieved by 07 December.

24 Dec 1962

The new Hang Seng Bank Headquarters, a 22-storey building (73.45 metres tall) designed by Yuen Tat-cho (阮達祖), was opened.

1962

The Hong Kong government estimated a local population increase from 3,209,500 in 1961 to 3,442,700 in 1962, a growth by nearly 240,000.

The Hong Kong government began construction of a nullah—running from Ma Tin Tsuen in Yuen Long to Deep Bay—as a measure to protect the Yuen Long area from floods; it was completed in 1967.

Wong Chak (王澤) began publishing his comic strip *Old Master Q* in newspapers *Ming Pao* and *Sing Tao Daily*.

Jao Tsung-i (饒宗頤) was awarded the Prix Stanislas Julien by the Académie des Inscriptions et Belles-Lettres (France) for his book *Oracle Bone Diviners of the Yin Dynasty*. He was the first Hong Kong scholar to receive such an honour.

Hou Pao-chang (侯寶璋), a renowned pathologist and Professor Emeritus of The University of Hong Kong, became Vice President of Chinese Medical College, Peking (present-day Peking Union Medical College) at the invitation of Premier Zhou Enlai (周恩來) of the State Council.

Teacher Walter Chu Wai-tak (朱維德) discovered fragments of a stone inscription at Fat Tau Chau in Sai Kung. The Antiquities and Monuments Office during a nearby archaeological survey in 1979 discovered other fragments and parts of the stone pillar base, confirming the area as a former Chinese customs station. Additional blue-and-white porcelain pieces and stone pillars were discovered in 2004.

17 Jan 1963

The Ministry of Foreign Affairs of the People's Republic of China strongly protested to the British government regarding the demolition of houses in Kowloon Walled City between March 1962 and 07 January 1963. It reiterated China's jurisdiction in the area and requested an immediate stop to the demolition. On 21 January, Britain ordered the Hong Kong government to suspend demolition but refused to recognise China's jurisdiction.

Sun Hung Kai Enterprises Company Limited was established by Lee Shau-kee (李兆基), Kwok Tak-seng (郭得 勝) and Fung King-hey (馮景禧). They also founded Sun Hung Kai (Holdings) Limited (present-day Sun Hung Kai Properties Limited) on 14 July 1972 and made it a publicly listed company on 23 August 1972.

22 Jan 1963

China Motor Bus Company's first double-decker began running on Route No. 2 between Shau Kei Wan and Sheung Wan. It was also the first double-deck bus in regular service on Hong Kong Island.

Jan 1963

The Juvenile Liaison Section, responsible for curbing and preventing youth crime, was inaugurated at several police stations. In October 1965, a section headquarters was established as a central coordinator.

12 Feb 1963

The Hong Kong government announced a Low-Cost Housing Scheme—established by the Hong Kong Housing Authority under the Urban Council with a government loan of HK$260 million—aiming to accommodate 300,000 people over a period of 10 years.

22 Feb 1963

The Hong Kong government announced a comprehensive development plan for Central District with a focus on the Naval Dockyard in Admiralty and reclamation projects in Central.

Feb 1963

The Hong Kong Working Committee for Equal Pay, dedicated to gender equality across government agencies, was jointly formed by the Hong Kong Council of Women, Hong Kong Association of University Women, Hong Kong Chinese Women's Club, Hong Kong Toastmistresses' Club and other women's organisations.

01 Mar 1963

Express News, founded and operated by Chairman of Sing Tao Holdings Limited Sally Aw Sian (胡 仙), began publication; it ceased on 16 March 1998.

Modern Edition, a publication on poetry, fiction, essay, literary criticism with a focus on existentialist literature, philosophy, as well as modernist literature and theory, was founded. It hosted a literary award in 1963/64 before ceasing publication in December.

08 Mar 1963

The *People's Daily* in Beijing published an editorial titled "A Comment on the Statement of the Communist Party of the USA," pointing out issues arising from the status quo of Hong Kong and Macao as a result of historical unequal treaties. It indicated that China would maintain the current status quo until a time when these issues could be resolved peacefully through negotiation.

11 Mar 1963

Ni Kuang (倪匡) began publishing his science fiction *Diamond Flower* as part of a series in the newspaper *Ming Pao*, marking the beginning of the Wisely Series.

30 Mar 1963

The Rent Increases (Domestic Premises) Control Ordinance 1963 was promulgated; it remained effective until 30 June 1965, restricting rent increase on post-Second World War domestic premises within provision on resolving related disputes. It also stipulated landlords were not allowed to increase rent within two years without tenant consent following a rent increase.

15 Apr 1963

Hong Kong Hilton Hotel on Garden Road in Central was opened for business. Its Chinese restaurant/nightclub named Eagle's Nest was highly popular during the 1970s. The hotel was demolished in 1994 and replaced by Cheung Kong Center.

23 Apr 1963

The Hong Kong government officially recognised diplomas awarded by Chung Chi College, New Asia College and United College. However, graduates were required to pass an English proficiency examination through the University of London's General Certificate of Examination or University of Hong Kong's matriculation examination for civil service posts.

02 May 1963

The Hong Kong government implemented a measure to ration water, limiting supply to three hours a day. It was changed to four hours every other day starting 16 May. (Figure 169)

19 May 1963

The Taoist community held a seven-day special prayer for rain at Yuen Yuen Institute in Tsuen Wan.

23 May 1963

Governor Robert Black visited Tung Ping Chau for an inspection of a batch of five water storage tanks upon completion. These were built to tackle the shortage of fresh water on the island with government funding allocated in January 1962.

24 May 1963

Director of the Hong Kong Branch of Xinhua News Agency Liang Weilin (梁威林) made several proposals with the Hong Kong government for fresh water import from the Mainland, including a pipeline for water from East River (Dongjiang) to Hong Kong via Shenzhen Reservoir.

26 May 1963

About 300 monks and 3,000 Buddhist worshippers held a three-day solemn service for rain at Happy Valley Racecourse.

31 May 1963

The Hong Kong government in conjunction with the Hong Kong Auxiliary Air Force tried to induce rainfall through cloud-seeding in the sky above west of Cheung Chau, but to no avail.

01 Jun 1963

The Hong Kong government implemented further measures in water rations by dividing Hong Kong into six water supply zones and limiting the hours during which water was available. Household supply was restricted to two hours every four days while public supply on the street was restricted to two hours every two days.

04 Jun 1963

The Hong Kong government reached an agreement with Guangdong Province, allowing water supply from the Pearl River to Hong Kong by ship as a temporary relief measure.

10 Jun 1963

The Asian-Pacific Science Information Centres Conference began for a five-day meeting in Hong Kong. It was co-sponsored by the US National Academy of Sciences, Institute of Advanced Projects of the East-West Center in Hawaii and The University of Hong Kong.

13 Jun 1963

Governor Robert Black wrote in a memo to the Colonial Office that imported water from East River (Dongjiang) was key to a stable supply of water for Hong Kong. He requested such message be conveyed to the People's Republic of China by the British Chargé d'Affaires—who reached out to the Chinese government on 18 June regarding water supply to Hong Kong.

18 Jun 1963

The first footbridge above a carriageway in Hong Kong, located at the junction of Yee Wo Street and Leighton Road in Causeway Bay, was opened upon completion.

Figure 169
People in queue for fresh water from public standpipes in 1963 amid water rationing imposed by the Hong Kong government during a water shortage. (Photo courtesy of Sing Tao News Corporation Limited)

Figure 170
The Mandarin Hotel (centre) developed on the former site of Queen's Building in Central. (Photo taken in 1963 and courtesy of HKSAR Government)

27 Jun 1963

Ianthe, the first tanker chartered by the Hong Kong government to transport fresh water from the Pearl River, arrived at Hong Kong Oil and Caltex Terminal in Tsuen Wan and unloaded 3.1 million gallons of fresh water.

01 Aug 1963

The Cape Collinson Chinese Permanent Cemetery—located at Cape Collinson in Chai Wan and under the Board of Management of the Chinese Permanent Cemeteries—was opened.

Aug 1963

The Office of the Unofficial Members of the Executive and Legislative Councils was established at Union House in Central, enabling the public to express their views on matters of public interest and lodge complaints against government departments.

01 Sep 1963

The new North Point Ferry Pier became operational with routes from North Point to Hung Hom and Kowloon City.

The Mandarin Hotel (present-day Mandarin Oriental, Hong Kong) in Central was inaugurated in a soft opening; it was fully opened in October. A 27-storey hotel developed by Hongkong Land, it was then the tallest building in Hong Kong. (Figure 170)

06 Sep 1963

The Preventive Service Ordinance 1963 was promulgated, formally establishing the Preventive Service as a statutory government department under the jurisdiction of the Commerce and Industry Department.

The Demolished Buildings (Re-development of Sites) (Amendment) Ordinance 1963 was promulgated, stipulating compensation for owners and tenants via Lands Tribunal in cases of redevelopment. On 29 September, a building at 257 Des Voeux Road Central in Sheung Wan became the first one eligible for government compensation.

06 Sep 1963

The Medical Clinics Ordinance 1963 was promulgated, effective 01 January 1964, mandating the registration, supervision and inspection of clinics, as well as forbidding unregistered doctors from practising in clinics.

The Dutiable Commodities (Marking and Colouring of Hydrocarbon Oils) Regulations 1963 was promulgated, prohibiting light diesel oil from being sold for marine or industrial use before colouring substances were added.

10 Sep 1963

Queen Elizabeth Hospital in Yau Ma Tei, constructed at a cost HK$70.3 million, became operational with a capacity of 1,338 beds. It was then the largest general hospital in the British Commonwealth. (Figure 171)

01 Oct 1963

A sub-committee on reparation of the United Nations Association of Hong Kong began to re-register for losses in connection with the Japanese occupation, ending on 31 October, as a precursor to compensation claims with the Japanese government.

17 Oct 1963

The Chinese University of Hong Kong held its inauguration ceremony at City Hall in celebration of its official establishment by combining New Asia College, Chung Chi College and United College. In November, Li Choh-ming (李卓敏) became the first Vice Chancellor. (Figure 172)

The Hong Kong Democratic Self-Government Party was founded and registered as a legitimate society under the chairmanship of Ma Man-fai (馬文輝). It was the first political association in Hong Kong.

27 Nov 1963

The Hongkong Booksellers' and Stationers' Association held its first major expo at City Hall's High Block where 40 exhibitors participated in the seven-day exhibition.

28 Nov 1963

Shek Pik Reservoir on Lantau Island became operational after eight years of construction at a cost of HK$200 million. It was then the largest reservoir in Hong Kong with a capacity of 5.4 billion gallons of water.

Figure 171
Queen Elizabeth Hospital located at King's Park in Kowloon. (Photo taken on 11 December 1963 and courtesy of Public Records Office, Government Records Service)

Figure 172
An aerial view of The Chinese University of Hong Kong campus at Ma Liu Shui in Sha Tin. (Photo taken in 1975 and courtesy of HKSAR Government)

08 Dec 1963

Premier Zhou Enlai (周恩來) of the State Council noted in a meeting with Liu Zhaolun (劉兆倫), Head of Guangdong Province Water Conservancy and Hydro-electric Bureau, that Dongjiang–Shenzhen water supply should be free of political implications since 95% of Hong Kong residents were compatriots, proposing a project of water supply to Hong Kong for RMB 10 cents per tonne, without further bargaining, as a way to defray construction expenses.

1963

The Hong Kong Standards and Testing Centre was established as the first not-for-profit testing, inspection and certification organisation in Hong Kong.

The Hong Kong Anti-Cancer Society was founded by John Ho Hung-chiu (何鴻超) to raise public awareness of cancer and support patients and their families.

10 Jan 1964

The Hong Kong government announced a registration and pricing system for sale of well water as a solution to support small industrial companies amid water shortages.

11 Jan 1964

The Hong Kong Nurses Association was incorporated to provide training courses in nursing. It was renamed the College of Nursing, Hong Kong in 1992.

16 Jan 1964

A double-deck bus crashed into a two-storey arcade on Kweilin Street in Sham Shui Po, killing three people and injuring 11 others.

17 Jan 1964

The Hong Kong Eye Bank and Research Foundation was co-founded by the Lions Club of Hong Kong and Hong Kong Ophthalmological Society as the first non-profit distribution centre of corneas for transplantation in Hong Kong.

22 Jan 1964

The Hong Kong government released its *Report of the Education Commission 1963* (also known as the *Marsh-Sampson Report*), proposing 1) a code of aids be established on government assistance for schools, 2) the number of subsidised schools be increased, and 3) and subsidised places in not-for-profit schools be expanded.

24 Jan 1964

Two British experts arrived in Hong Kong for a feasibility study on seawater desalination proposed by China Light and Power Company and Hongkong Electric Company. On 05 February, a report was presented to Director of Public Works Alec Michael John Wright.

The Societies (Amendment) Ordinance 1964 was promulgated, plugging a loophole that office bearers previously convicted of a violation under the Societies Ordinance 1961 were free from prosecution for holding an office without approval of the Registrar of Societies.

30 Jan 1964

King Baudouin of Belgium and his wife arrived in Hong Kong for a four-day visit.

31 Jan 1964

The Fung Ping Shan Museum of Chinese Art and Archaeology under The University of Hong Kong was inaugurated. In 1994, it was renamed the University Museum and Art Gallery.

03 Feb 1964

The Hong Kong Buddhist Cemetery, located at Cape Collinson in Chai Wan, was opened.

12 Feb 1964

The Hong Kong government released a white paper titled *The 1963–1972 Development of Medical Services in Hongkong*. It proposed an improved ratio of hospital facilities to the population of Hong Kong through a substantial increase of hospital beds.

19 Feb 1964

Hong Kong was designated an infected area upon confirmation of its first case of cholera. The World Health Organization was notified.

20 Feb 1964

Construction of Plover Cove Reservoir commenced.

02 Mar 1964

The ship *Ceylon* departed for Europe with a maritime exhibition of Hong Kong-made products—a promotional campaign jointly sponsored by the Hong Kong General Chamber of Commerce, Federation of Hong Kong Industries, and Swedish East Asia Company Limited.

06 Mar 1964

The Chor Fung Ming Opera Troupe, led by Yam Kim-fai (任劍輝) and Pak Suet-sin (白雪仙), made its debut in a fundraiser for Hong Kong Anti-Cancer Society at Lee Theatre with a one-act opera titled *Loyalty unto Death*.

14 Mar 1964

Coloane, Hong Kong's first hydrofoil vessel, made its maiden voyage from Hong Kong–Macau Ferry Terminal. The vessel, operated by Shun Tak Shipping Company Limited, began ferry services between Hong Kong and Macao the following day.

15 Mar 1964

Shek Wu Hui, a market town in Sheung Shui, was unveiled with a parade by the local community upon renovation.

20 Mar 1964

The letter-pressed *Chen Feng Yi Pu* began publication as a B4-size newspaper. In February 1967, it adopted the B6-size format and was renamed *Chen Feng*.

25 Mar 1964

Ellen Li Shu-pui (李曹秀群) became the first Chinese female member of the Urban Council of Hong Kong. (Figure 173)

Figure 173
Ellen Li Shu-pui (李曹秀群) (front left) and Elsie Elliott (second right), who were elected in 1963, at an Urban Council meeting in 1964. (Photo courtesy of HKSAR Government)

12 Apr 1964

A tram overturned on Queen's Road East in Wan Chai, killing one person and injuring 59. It was the first tram flip-over accident in Hong Kong.

14 Apr 1964

David Trench was sworn in as the 24th governor of Hong Kong. He remained in office until 19 October 1971.

22 Apr 1964

The Agreement between the People's Council of Kwangtung Province and the Hongkong Authorities on the Supply of Water to Hongkong and Kowloon from the East River was signed in Guangzhou for an annual supply of 68.2 million cubic metres of water from Guangdong to Hong Kong at a cost of RMB 10 cents per cubic metre, effective 01 March 1965. (Figures 174 and 175)

14 May 1964

The Circle Art Group began its first group exhibition in a six-day event at Hong Kong City Hall.

24 May 1964

Lam Kei-ping (林紀平), a villager of Lam Tsuen in Tai Po, resisted arrest after shooting police corporal Lam Yik-yan (林奕仁) dead with a shotgun; he was subsequently shot dead in a gun battle where some 170 police officers were deployed. A superintendent of police, a police corporal and a constable were killed; 12 police officers were injured.

Figure 174
Cao Ruoming (曹若茗) (right) of Bao'an County of Guangdong Province and Dermont Barty (left) of the Hong Kong government signed the first agreement on water supply from East River (Dongjiang) to Hong Kong. (Photo taken on 15 November 1960 and courtesy of HKSAR Government)

Figure 175
Large pipes near the entrance of the new Lion Rock Tunnel for water supply from East River (Dongjiang) in Guangdong Province to Plover Cove Reservoir in Hong Kong. (Photo taken in 1964 and courtesy of HKSAR Government)

Figure 176
The Beatles arrived in Hong Kong in June 1964, setting a new trend in hair and clothing style among local youngsters. (Courtesy of South China Morning Post Publishers Limited)

29 May 1964

The Hong Kong government eased its limit on water supply from four hours every four days to four hours every two days upon rainfall from Typhoon Viola. On 01 July, water supply was increased to eight hours per day.

01 Jun 1964

The first successful treatment for foetus-in-foetu in Hong Kong took place at Queen Mary Hospital where three foetuses were removed from a three-month-old male infant via laparotomy.

05 Jun 1964

The Kowloon Tsai Swimming Pool was unveiled as the first public swimming pool in Kowloon; it was officially opened the following day.

08 Jun 1964

The Beatles arrived in Hong Kong and were welcomed by 5,000 people at the airport. They performed at Princess Theatre in Tsim Sha Tsui the following day and left Hong Kong on 10 June. (Figure 176)

12 Jun 1964

The Hong Kong government announced an expanded Legislative Council with the addition of five Unofficial Members and three Official Members. It marked the first time that the number of Unofficial Members was greater than that of Official Members. The Governor retained the power to give an original vote and a casting vote.

19 Jun 1964

Ivy Ling Po (凌波), an actress with Shaw Brothers (Hong Kong) Limited, won Best Actress at the 11th Asian Film Festival for her role in the film *Lady General Hua Mu-lan*.

20 Jun 1964

A Hong Kong-bound aircraft of Taiwan's Civil Air Transport Incorporated crashed in Taiwan, killing all 57 people on board. These included Dato Loke Wan-tho (陸運濤), founder of Motion Picture and General Investment Company Limited, and his wife, as well as senior executives Wong Chih-Po (王植波) and Harry Chow Hai-loong (周海龍). They were returning to Hong Kong after attending the 11th Asian Film Festival in Taiwan.

29 Jun 1964

The Institute of Radiology of Queen Elizabeth Hospital, established with a HK$6 million donation from The Hong Kong Jockey Club, was inaugurated to provide cancer patients with radiological service.

Jun 1964

An electronics factory in Hong Kong started the first local production of portable televisions and began exporting to the US in the same year.

01 Jul 1964

The Department of Agriculture and Fisheries was formed in a merger between the Agriculture and Forestry Department and the Co-operative Development and Fisheries Department; Jack Cater served as its director.

The Hong Kong government approved an agreement between the Hong Kong Association of Banks and licenced banks on a fixed deposit interest rate, effective until March 1965, by setting a maximum and minimum interest rate among participating banks.

17 Jul 1964

Linda Lin Dai (林黛), a four-time winner of Asian Film Festival's Best Actress award, committed suicide in her flat by drug overdose at the age of 29.

22 Jul 1964

A nursery, located at Wang Tau Hom in Wong Tai Sin and founded by the Hong Kong branch of British Commonwealth Save the Children Fund, was opened for children with intellectual disabilities.

31 Jul 1964

The Hang Seng Index was first published by Hang Seng Bank for internal reference with a base of 100 points.

Jul 1964

Photo Pictorial began publication; it ceased in 2005 and was the longest-running publication on photography in Hong Kong.

The first corneal transplant surgery with a local donor was successfully performed at Hong Kong Baptist Hospital.

The Hong Kong Ballet Group was founded as the first ballet troupe in Hong Kong.

08 Aug 1964

The Hong Kong Observatory hoisted Increasing Gale or Storm Signal No. 9 for about three and a half hours amid Typhoon Ida—which left five people dead, four missing, 56 injured and damaged three ocean-going vessels and 67 fishing boats. A landslide near Kwun Tong Resettlement Estate left about 5,600 people homeless.

18 Aug 1964

Yuen Sang Enterprises Limited was established as a manufacturer and seller of stainless-steel watches and watch cases.

31 Aug 1964

The Hong Kong Repertory Theatre (unrelated to Hong Kong Repertory Theatre established by the Urban Council) was established; its first performance was *The House of 72 Tenants* in December.

01 Sep 1964

The Hong Kong government announced equal treatment of married female civil servants as their unmarried counterparts, effective 01 January retroactively.

04 Sep 1964

The XVIII Olympiad Tokyo 1964 torch arrived in Hong Kong. It was the first Olympic flame passing through Hong Kong. (Figure 177)

The Buildings (Amendment) (No. 2) Ordinance 1964 was promulgated, empowering the Building Authority to ban demolition, excavation or piling works for reasons of safety of nearby buildings. By November, more than 300 construction projects were halted.

Figure 177
Cheung Kin-man (張乾文), a swimmer who represented Hong Kong in several Olympic Games, on the last leg of the XVIII Olympiad Tokyo 1964 torch relay in Hong Kong passing through Queen's Road Central. (Photo taken on 04 September 1964 and courtesy of South China Morning Post Publishers Limited)

05 Sep 1964

The Hong Kong Observatory hoisted Hurricane Signal No. 10 for about four hours amid Typhoon Ruby—which left 38 people dead, six missing, over 300 injured and damaged 20 ocean-going vessels and 314 fishing boats.

14 Sep 1964

The Waterworks Office announced normalisation of full-day water supply in Hong Kong after a two-week trial run.

Hong Kong reached an agreement with Canada for an annual quota on the export of six types of cotton fabric to Canada effective 01 October.

17 Sep 1964

The Hong Kong branch of US-based Rainier International Bank was opened for business.

18 Sep 1964

The Inland Revenue (Amendment) Ordinance 1964 was promulgated, stipulating expenses incurred in generating profits were not deductible in cases where such profits were not subject to taxation.

28 Sep 1964

The Federation of Hong Kong Garment Manufacturers was incorporated.

30 Sep 1964

The Hong Kong government released a white paper titled *Review of Policies for Squatter Control, Resettlement and Government Low-Cost Housing*. It outlined the criteria of eligibility for resettlement and specified which type of residents had priority.

13 Oct 1964

The Hong Kong Observatory hoisted Hurricane Signal No. 10 for about eight hours amid Typhoon Dot—which left 26 people dead, 10 missing, 85 injured and damaged two ocean-going vessels and 90 fishing boats.

16 Oct 1964

The Banking Ordinance 1964 was promulgated, stipulating that all licenced banks must have a sufficient level of reserves. The Office of the Commissioner of Banking was also established to regulate banking institutions.

27 Oct 1964

The British government announced a 15% duty on all imports, including those from Hong Kong, effective 28 October.

05 Nov 1964

Ten drug traffickers were sentenced to six to seven years' imprisonment in a trial of a drug syndicate located in Yau Ma Tei. The trial began on 01 September after it took the police three months to crack the case.

06 Nov 1964

The Television Ordinance 1964 was promulgated, requiring a government licence for television broadcast.

10 Nov 1964

The Hong Kong government introduced an assistance scheme with a one-off, interest-free loan for low-income households forced to move out of houses built prior to the Second World War and deemed unsafe.

18 Nov 1964

The Central Harbour Services Pier in Central became operational upon completion.

23 Nov 1964

The Hong Kong government increased the limit on the gross floor area of village houses in the New Territories from 700 to 1,000 square feet.

Nov 1964

The Union Bank of Hong Kong was incorporated.

05 Dec 1964

The Hong Kong police uncovered large numbers of handguns, bullets and time bombs in a penthouse at 26–28 King's Road in Causeway Bay. It was then the largest case of illegal weapons.

08 Dec 1964

The Federation of Motion Film Producers of Hong Kong was incorporated. In addition to promoting the local film industry, it represented Hong Kong through its selection of local films for entry in the Asia Pacific Film Festival and in the Academy Awards for Best Foreign Language Film.

10 Dec 1964

The Chinese Merchandise Emporium Limited was established.

17 Dec 1964

Caritas Medical Centre in Cheung Sha Wan became operational. On 22 February 1967, a lift tower in the centre called the Montini Tower, donated by Pope Paul VI, was opened.

Toppan Printing Company (H.K.) Limited was co-founded by Toppan Printing Company of Japan and Hong Kong businesswoman Sally Aw Sian (胡仙), making the most advanced letterpress printing technology available in Hong Kong.

Golden Eagle, a film by Feng Huang (Phoenix) Motion Picture Company, was released. It was the first locally produced film to gross more than HK$1 million at the box office.

1964

The Hong Kong Association of the Heads of Secondary Schools was established to promote interactions among secondary school principals and to enhance professional leadership and education quality.

19 Jan 1965

The Hong Kong government accepted a recommendation by the Urban Council to make *Bauhinia blakeana* the floral emblem of Hong Kong.

Figure 178
Ming Tak Bank was hit by a bank run. (Photo taken on 27 January 1965 and courtesy of South China Morning Post Publishers Limited)

22 Jan 1965

The Urban Council (Amendment) Ordinance 1965 was promulgated, effective 01 April, expanding the Urban Council with the addition of four Unofficial Members (two appointed and two elected).

27 Jan 1965

The Office of the Commissioner of Banking announced a takeover of Ming Tak Bank following a bank run. The bank was closed for an audit on assets, liabilities and real estate holdings; on 04 February, its application for bankruptcy was approved by the Supreme Court of Hong Kong. (Figure 178)

06 Feb 1965

The Aberdeen branch of Canton Trust and Commercial Bank was struck by a bank run; nearly 1,000 people waited outside to withdraw money. On 08 February, the Office of the Commissioner of Banking announced its takeover of the bank.

07 Feb 1965

The police seized about HK$2.25 million worth of drugs, including 3,500 pounds of crude opium and 180 pounds of morphine, at Kang Sang Farm in Ngau Tam Mei, San Tin. It was the largest volume of narcotics found by the police in 20 years after the Second World War.

08 Feb 1965

Several Chinese-owned banks in Hong Kong, including Hang Seng Bank, Dao Heng Bank, Far East Bank and Wing Lung Bank, were struck by a bank run. The Hongkong and Shanghai Banking Corporation (HSBC) announced in the evening its full support of Hang Seng Bank. The following day, HSBC announced its full support of Wing Lung Bank and Far East Bank; Standard Chartered Bank announced its unlimited support of Kwong On Bank and Dao Heng Bank.

09 Feb 1965

The Emergency (Bank Control) Regulations 1965 was promulgated, placing a daily limit of HK$100 on withdrawal from bank accounts. On 13 February, the Executive Council announced the limit would be lifted on 16 February.

10 Feb 1965

The Hong Kong government implemented two measures to stabilise the supply of Hong Kong banknotes: 1) all banks were required to provide the Commissioner of Banking with a report on the amount of cash on deposit at the end of each business day, and 2) all banks were required to return surplus banknotes on deposit to the three note-issuing banks, namely Standard Chartered Bank, Hongkong and Shanghai Banking Corporation and Mercantile Bank Limited.

The Hong Kong Association for the Mentally Handicapped, Children and Young Persons was established for school children with learning disabilities. It was renamed the Hong Chi Association in 1997.

11 Feb 1965

The first batch of £5 million banknotes arrived in Hong Kong by air and were place in deposit with The Hongkong and Shanghai Banking Corporation for circulation at a rate of £1 to HK$16, followed by another £20 million later. On the same day, it was confirmed by the Hong Kong government that HK$50 million worth of banknotes had arrived from London on 10 February.

26 Feb 1965

The Chinese edition of *Reader's Digest* began publication in Hong Kong and went into circulation across Asia.

27 Feb 1965

The first phase of the Dongjiang-Shenzhen Water Supply Scheme was completed in Tangxia, Dongguan. Under the scheme, 60 million cubic metres of water—one-third of Hong Kong's annual water consumption—was supplied to Hong Kong in 1965. On 01 March, Shenzhen Reservoir began to supply water from the East River (Dongjiang) to Hong Kong; a ceremony was held to mark the occasion.

07 Mar 1965

The Catholic Diocese of Hong Kong began holding Masses in Cantonese.

31 Mar 1965

Cable & Wireless completed the installation of a submarine telephone line between Hong Kong and Singapore.

Mar 1965

The Commerce and Industry Department's Industry Inspection Branch was established to ensure compliance with quotas on cotton-based textiles through inspection of factories under the Certificate of Preference or Certificate of Origin system.

01 Apr 1965

The Chinese University of Hong Kong Department of Extramural Studies was established to provide adult workers with programmes for continued learning. In 2006, it became the School of Continuing and Professional Studies.

09 Apr 1965

The Hongkong and Shanghai Banking Corporation (HSBC) acquired 51% of Hang Seng Bank's controlling interests for HK$51 million; Hang Seng Bank became a member of the HSBC Group.

12 Apr 1965

The Hong Kong government released its *Household Expenditure Survey and Consumer Price Index 1963/64* and *Cost of Living Survey 1958–1963/64*. It marked the first government release of the Consumer Price Index of Hong Kong.

28 Apr 1965

The Hong Kong government published a white paper titled *Education Policy* in which it sought to restore a six-year primary school system and lower the enrolment age of primary school students from seven to six, and proposed a universal primary education scheme.

Apr 1965

The first batch of Mark IV resettlement blocks were completed at Tung Tau Estate in Kowloon City. Each flat was equipped with a bathroom and a balcony to improve the living condition of public housing.

American ecologists Lee Merriam Talbot and Martha Talbot, commissioned by the Department of Agriculture and Fisheries, published a paper titled *Conservation of the Hong Kong Countryside: Summary Report and Recommendation*. They put forward nine recommendations (including a council on country parks and nature conservancy, a system of parks, reserves and recreational areas, a network of conservation zones and a scheme to preserve marine habitats and wildlife) and 10 suggestions regarding the establishment of country parks. The report became a blueprint for nature conservation and country parks in Hong Kong.

10 May 1965

More than 100 people appealed in a demonstration at the Government House that Canton Trust and Commercial Bank not to be liquidated so that withdrawal of deposits could be made. It turned into a disturbance in which nine demonstrators were arrested.

13 May 1965

The Legislative Council approved a white paper titled *Aims and Policy for Social Welfare in Hong Kong*. It was a proposal for multiple social security and welfare schemes focused on young people.

14 May 1965

The Grand Substitution, produced by Shaw Brothers Studio, won Best Film at the 12th Asian Film Festival; Li Ching (李菁) of Shaw Brothers Studio won Best Actress for her role in *The Mermaid.*

28 May 1965

The Miscellaneous Licences (Amendment) Ordinance 1965 was promulgated, requiring all dancing schools to be licenced and equipped with adequate lighting to prevent immoral behaviour.

01 Jun 1965

The Star Ferry made its maiden voyage with a new Central–Hung Hom service; it ended the route in April 2011.

03 Jun 1965

The first Hong Kong Chinese School Certificate Examination under a five-year curriculum began; it was concluded on 16 June. Results were released on 06 August. A total of 7,085 students were registered for the examination; 4,476 of 6,990 examinees passed.

08 Jun 1965

The Cheung Sha Wan Wholesale Vegetable Market was opened; it became operational on 10 June and replaced the market on Canton Road in Yau Ma Tei.

11 Jun 1965

The Limitation Ordinance 1965 was promulgated, consolidating and amending laws with respect to the limitation of legal actions and arbitrations.

16 Jun 1965

The Action Committee Against Narcotics began with its first meeting as an intra-governmental coordinator on measures regarding anti-drug trafficking and drug rehabilitation.

23 Jun 1965

Ellen Li Shu-pui (李曹秀群) was sworn in as the first female member of the Legislative Council.

30 Jun 1965

The Legislative Council approved a Lotteries Fund in support of social welfare services with proceeds from government lotteries and auctions of special vehicle licence plates. It was allocated HK$7.4 million initially.

Jun 1965

The Family Planning Association introduced intrauterine-based birth control in Hong Kong.

15 Jul 1965

The Real Estate Developers Association of Hong Kong was founded; Henry Fok Ying-tung (霍英東) served as President.

28 Jul 1965

The Advisory Committee on Gambling Policy submitted a report to the Legislative Council. It recommended the prohibition of illegal gambling, dissemination of information about illegal gambling, suspension of new licences for mahjong houses, and opposition to a proposed dog racing track in Hong Kong.

09 Aug 1965

The Medical and Health Department launched a diphtheria prevention campaign to provide children with vaccination.

12 Aug 1965

The Tsz Wan Shan Resettlement Estate began for occupancy. By September 1971, 63 buildings had been built in what was then the largest resettlement area in Hong Kong.

16 Aug 1965

The Kowloon Public Library was inaugurated as the first library in Kowloon under the Urban Council; it was opened to the public the following day.

Kestrel, Hong Kong's first motorised stern trawler, made its maiden voyage from Aberdeen. It was the first motorised fishing boat under the Government Development Loan Fund.

24 Aug 1965

A US military transport aircraft crashed into the sea near Kowloon Bay; 59 were killed while 12 were rescued.

02 Sep 1965

The Hong Kong government released a main report prepared by the Salaries Commission, rejecting a request for greater benefits by the Hong Kong Chinese Civil Servants' Association.

07 Sep 1965

The Supreme Court of Hong Kong found five defendants guilty of robbing a jewellery shop on 08 March with prison terms ranging from eight to 15 years. Two of the defendants, who wounded police officers with snatched firearms during a trial at South Kowloon Magistracy on 03 June, were also sentenced to 10 strokes of flogging each.

Sep 1965

The Educational Department started two special education classes for children with intellectual disabilities.

05 Oct 1965

The Urban Council passed a motion proposed by Councillor Henry Hu Hung-lick (胡鴻烈) to make government correspondence available in Chinese following the implementation of the Urban Council.

12 Oct 1965

The Shau Kei Wan Rotary Training Centre for the Visually Impaired opened a braille library. Run by the Hong Kong Society for the Blind, it was Hong Kong's first library for the blind.

14 Oct 1965

The Anne Black Red Cross Headquarters on Harcourt Road in Admiralty was inaugurated.

26 Oct 1965

The University Grants Committee was established as a non-statutory advisory body on funding local institutions, namely The University of Hong Kong and The Chinese University of Hong Kong. Michael Alexander Robert Young-Herries was the first chairman.

04 Nov 1965

The Star Ferry announced its application to the government for fare increase with effect from 01 January 1966. Urban Councillor Elsie Elliott launched a signature drive against the fare increase on 10 November and made a request with the Governor to reject the application by presenting a petition, signed by 23,272 members of the public, on 23 November.

05 Nov 1965

The Hong Kong government announced in the *Gazette* that the Industrial Training Advisory Committee was established, mainly responsible for nurturing industrial talent and studying issues related to industrial education and vocational training.

01 Dec 1965

Current Literature, a Chinese-language monthly journal, was founded by Xu Su (徐速); it ceased publication in April 1979.

03 Dec 1965

Hong Kong League XI hosted Australia's national team in a football match at the Government Stadium. The rough style among Australian players coupled with unfair referee decisions triggered a riot; hundreds of police officers were deployed and nine people were arrested.

1965

The first six residential blocks of Tai Hang Sai Estate in Shek Kip Mei began for occupancy. Developed by Hong Kong Settlers Housing Corporation Limited, it was the only private low-cost housing estate in Hong Kong.

The Hong Kong Economic and Trade Office (ETO) in Brussels was established as a representative office in the European Economic Community (present-day European Union). In 2006, it became a regional office in coordination with other ETOs in Europe, representing Hong Kong in bilateral relations with 15 European countries.

04 Jan 1966

The Urban Council passed a gentlemen's agreement into by-law, allowing cooked food vendors to operate legally with two tables and eight chairs.

07 Jan 1966

The Explosive Substances (Amendment) Ordinance 1966 was promulgated, stipulating that any persons convicted of making or possessing explosive substances without legal justification would be liable to imprisonment of up to 14 years, with the burden of proof on the defendant. In addition, prosecutors might request a closed trial in consideration of public safety.

The Application of English Law Ordinance 1966 was promulgated, declaring the extent to which English common law, rules of equity and UK parliamentary enactment were applied in Hong Kong.

An amended Royal Instructions was promulgated, stipulating that the Commander of British Forces in Hong Kong would cease to be an ex-officio member of the Legislative Council while increasing the maximum number of Official Members from seven to eight.

26 Jan 1966

The Hong Kong government granted Television Broadcasts Limited a 15-year wireless television franchise.

Jan 1966

Ming Pao Monthly, established by Louis Cha Leung-yung (查良鏞), founder of the newspaper *Ming Pao*, began publication. It was the oldest comprehensive cultural monthly in Hong Kong.

Hai Kwang Literature Monthly began publication as a monthly journal on the arts, novels, prose, poems and other works; it ceased publication in January 1967.

01 Feb 1966

Rediffusion Television launched the first actor training programme in Hong Kong.

10 Feb 1966

Thomas P, a large oil tanker, ran aground and spilt oil in the Lamma Channel.

22 Feb 1966

The British government published its *1966 Defence White Paper*, suggesting a defence policy under which a British garrison be maintained in Hong Kong.

02 Mar 1966

The Hong Kong government refused the entry of Soviet crew members of the Soviet passenger ship *M. Uritskiy*. It later allowed the group of 50 seamen to disembark during daytime over the next two days.

04 Mar 1966

A Canadian Pacific Airlines flight en route from Hong Kong to Japan crashed while landing at Tokyo's Haneda Airport under poor weather conditions; 64 people died and eight survived.

14 Mar 1966

A fire broke out at Chung Kiu Chinese Products Emporium on Nathan Road in Mong Kok, causing four deaths and 17 injuries.

19 Mar 1966

The Transport Advisory Committee in a report approved Star Ferry's application to increase fare by five cents for first-class tickets.

22 Mar 1966

The Ocean Terminal in Tsim Sha Tsui was completed as Hong Kong's first cruise terminal.

28 Mar 1966

The American Express Company announced the establishment of a regional headquarters in Hong Kong from which to expand its banking business in Southeast Asia and Australia.

Mar 1966

The Hong Kong government began its first-phase development of Castle Peak New Town—which included a residential area for 100,000 people and other areas for industrial development through reclamation of 220 acres of land.

01 Apr 1966

Chung Hwa Travel Service Hong Kong began handling passport and visa applications from Hong Kong and Macao residents for travel to Taiwan.

The Hong Kong government rolled out a density-based zoning policy for categorisation of urban, suburban and rural areas, outlining the extent to which residential buildings could be developed.

03 Apr 1966

Urban Councillor Elsie Elliott called on the public to object to Star Ferry's fare increase by sending 200 letters addressed to Kaifong associations, clan associations and other organisations.

04 Apr 1966

So Sau-chung (蘇守忠), a 25-year-old, went on a hunger strike outside the Star Ferry Pier on Hong Kong Island in protest of a fare increase; he was arrested the next day. Protests sprang up in Kowloon and escalated into a violent disturbance by 06 April. On 07 April, Governor David Trench ordered a curfew and deployed British forces to assist the police in crowd dispersal. It caused one death and 26 injuries; 1,465 people were arrested while 905 were charged and 323 were sentenced to prison in what became known as the Star Ferry Riots. (Figure 179)

04 Apr 1966

The Princess Margaret Road Flyover was opened to traffic; it was the first flyover in Kowloon.

12 Apr 1966

The Hong Kong government launched an anti-cholera campaign in which fixed and mobile stations were set up to provide the public with vaccination. (Figure 180)

Figure 179
So Sau-chung (蘇守忠), in sunglasses, on the second day of his hunger strike at Star Ferry Pier in 1966. (Photo courtesy of Sing Tao News Corporation Limited)

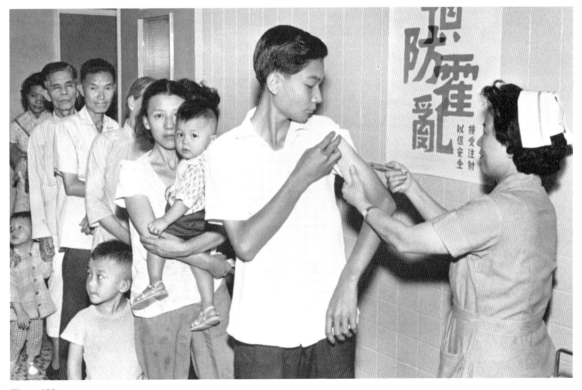

Figure 180
Residents in queue for cholera vaccines. (Photo taken in 1964 and courtesy of Public Records Office, Government Records Service)

19 Apr 1966

The Harcourt Road Flyover in Admiralty was officially opened to traffic, making it the first flyover on Hong Kong Island.

23 Apr 1966

The Committee to Examine the Law and Practice Relating to Corporal Punishment in Hong Kong released a report, proposing a three-year trial of abolishing corporal punishment among children under the age of 14.

26 Apr 1966

The Hong Kong government and Star Ferry Company reached an agreement on fare adjustment, raising the price of first-class tickets from 20 cents to 25 cents and monthly adult passes from HK$8 to HK$10, effective 02 May.

03 May 1966

The Hong Kong government established an inquiry for an investigation on the Star Ferry Riots (Kowloon Disturbances). On 21 February 1967, a commission report was released, citing socio-economic problems and youth problems as root causes while noting the importance of public communication by the government.

05 May 1966

Urban Councillor Elsie Elliott, speaking at a press conference in London, put forward five proposals for reform of the Hong Kong government, including the addition of elected members in the Legislative Council.

06 May 1966

The Urban Council (Amendment) Ordinance 1966 was promulgated, increasing the number of residents eligible to vote in Urban Council elections. It revoked the requirement of proficiency in English, introduced new voter categories based on social contribution, professional qualification and education level, and enacted a voter eligibility requirement of at least three years of residency in Hong Kong.

09 May 1966

The Blue and the Black, a film produced by Shaw Brothers Studio, won Best Film at the 13th Asian Film Festival.

14 May 1966

Cable & Wireless established a branch in Tsuen Wan as the first telegraph station in the New Territories.

16 May 1966

The Hong Kong government began voter registration for upcoming Urban Council elections in 1967. The number of categories of eligible voters was increased to 23, covering those with an education level attained through the General Certificate of Education Examination (UK) or Hong Kong School Certificate Examinations, as well as monks, nuns and missionaries.

17 May 1966

The Hong Kong government began demolition of houses known to have existed for a hundred years at Ngau Tau Kok Village in Kowloon.

26 May 1966

The Statue Square in Central was officially inaugurated by Governor David Trench.

27 May 1966

The Hong Kong government announced a new list of Executive Councillors. Unofficial Members increased from six to eight in total number, including four ethnic Chinese, while Official Members remained at six in total number.

10 Jun 1966

The Chinese newspaper *People's Daily* published an editorial criticising Britain for an act of hostility towards China by allowing entry of US naval vessels into Hong Kong waters.

Figure 181
A flash flood swept away dozens of cars on Ming Yuen Western Street in North Point. (Photo taken in June 1966 and courtesy of HKSAR Government)

11 Jun 1966

A three-day heavy rainstorm began and caused severe landslides and collapse of houses, leaving 64 people dead, 48 missing, 29 injured and 6,183 affected. Total rainfall reached 495 millimetres, including 383 millimetres in a single day in what became known as the 6.12 Rainstorm. (Figure 181)

15 Jun 1966

The Educational Department announced suspension of classes (all public, private and subsidised schools) until 20 June amid landslides and traffic congestions following several days of heavy rainstorm.

30 Jun 1966

The Rent Increases (Domestic Premises) Control Ordinance 1963—which was due to expire on 30 Jun 1965—came to an end after it was extended by a year through an amendment in 1965.

Jun 1966

Gertrude Rosenblum Williams, a professor at the University of London who was commissioned by the Hong Kong government, published her *Report on the Feasibility of a Survey into Social Welfare Provision and Allied Topics in Hong Kong*. She recommended that an independent body be established to provide the government with advice on the formulation of social policy.

07 Jul 1966

The Hong Kong government adopted recommendations by the Advisory Committee on Gambling Policy with respect to strictly prohibiting illegal gambling, including those with horse and dog racing, and permitting an additional racecourse to be operated by The Hong Kong Jockey Club.

18 Jul 1966

The first Chinese Language Conference, chaired by Lo Hsiang-lin (羅香林) of The University of Hong Kong's (HKU) Department of Chinese, under the theme "Teaching and Learning of Chinese as a First and a Second Language" began at HKU's Loke Yew Hall; it was concluded on 22 July.

01 Aug 1966

The Commonwealth Office of the United Kingdom, established through a consolidation of the Colonial Office and the Commonwealth Relations Office, assumed the responsibility of Hong Kong affairs. On 17 October 1968, it merged with the Foreign Office to form the Foreign and Commonwealth Office.

25 Aug 1966

The Paris Theatre at San Po Kong was opened for business. It had a capacity of over 3,000 seats and was then the largest theatre in Hong Kong; it closed in March 1992.

28 Aug 1966

Frederick Lee, Britain's Secretary of State for the Colonies, arrived in Hong Kong for a seven-day visit to discuss the political system, military expenditure, economic development and social welfare issues of Hong Kong with local politicians and merchants. He departed on 03 September.

01 Sep 1966

The Public Relations Association of Hong Kong was established.

06 Sep 1966

The first Hong Kong Festival began in London as a showcase of Hong Kong-made products and trade promotion between Hong Kong and Britain.

15 Sep 1966

The Hong Kong government, in accordance with the Banking Ordinance 1964, ordered the takeover of Yau Yue Commercial Bank and its debts by The Hongkong and Shanghai Banking Corporation.

28 Sep 1966

Tung Chung Road, running between Tung Chung on northern Lantau Island and Cheung Sha on southern Lantau Island, was opened to traffic. It took two and a half years and HK$4.5 million to construct the road.

30 Sep 1966

The Hong Kong Trade Development Council Ordinance 1966 was promulgated, establishing Hong Kong Trade Development Council as a statutory body to develop foreign trade.

04 Oct 1966

The *Report of the Ad Hoc Committee on the Future Scope and Operation of the Urban Council* was published, recommending a municipal council with substantial powers on local affairs. The report was approved by 16 Unofficial Members of the Urban Council.

30 Oct 1966

Chao Lei (趙雷) won Best Leading Actor at the fourth Golden Horse Awards for his role in the film *Hsi-Shih, Beauty of Beauties*.

16 Nov 1966

Chinese-Vietnamese Wong Kai-kei (黃啟基), convicted of murder and sentenced to death by hanging, was executed. It marked the last execution in Hong Kong.

17 Nov 1966

A foundation stone ceremony was held at Mei Foo Sun Chuen in Lai Chi Kok—Hong Kong's first large-scale private housing estate. The first phase was completed two years later.

21 Nov 1966

A wildfire broke out at Tai Po Tsai in Clear Water Bay and destroyed a backlot of Shaw Brothers Studio.

25 Nov 1966

The Legal Aid Ordinance 1966 was promulgated, making legal aid available to eligible parties in civil cases at the Full Court, Supreme Court or District Court. In January 1967, a sub-department of the Judiciary called the Legal Aid Section was established by the Hong Kong government to provide legal assistance in civil cases.

01 Dec 1966

Urban Councillor Elsie Elliott presented a Declaration of Rights for Hongkong Citizens and proposed the adoption of 13 civil and political rights, including those regarding fair interrogation and free education, at the annual debate.

04 Dec 1966

The Macao government declared martial law amid the 12.3 Incident. Many Macao residents fled to Hong Kong by ferry.

09 Dec 1966

Hong Kong participated in the fifth Asian Games in Bangkok, Thailand, winning a bronze medal.

15 Dec 1966

Arnaldo de Oliveira Sales, President of the Amateur Sports Federation and Olympic Committee of Hong Kong, was elected as Vice-President of the Asian Games Federation. On 14 December 1970, he became Honorary Life Vice-President.

20 Dec 1966

Governor David Trench announced an agreement with the British government on an annual increase of defence spending from HK$40 million to HK$80 million provided by Hong Kong in the next four years. The increased amount was about one-third of total defence spending on Hong Kong.

23 Dec 1966

The Hong Kong Export Credit Insurance Corporation was established as a statutory body for protection against non-payment risks with an initial liability of HK$300 million.

28 Dec 1966

The Po Yick General Chinese and Foreign Goods Import and Export Commercial Society of Hong Kong inaugurated its first Cosmopolitan Merchandise Exhibition at Hong Kong City Hall for a nine-day expo of daily necessities, apparel, stationery and other commodities from all over the world.

Dec 1966

Residents of six villages (Kam Chuk Pai, Chung Pui, Chung Mei, Wang Tau Ling, Tai Kau and Siu Kau), affected by the construction of Plover Cove Reservoir, were relocated to the reclaimed land at Tai Po Market. On 30 January 1967, a ceremony was held to mark the opening of the new village.

1966

The first Hong Kong Commercial Counsellor was assigned to the British Embassy in Washington DC as an official correspondent on US policy regarding Hong Kong and a facilitator of US–Hong Kong economic and trade relations. It later became the Hong Kong Economic and Trade Office, Washington DC.

01 Jan 1967

The Hong Kong Shippers' Council was established to promote the interests of Hong Kong importers and exporters in the area of transportation and logistics.

04 Jan 1967

Plover Cove Reservoir's main dam was completed. On 25 September, desalination began by pumping out seawater.

15 Jan 1967

Ma Sicong (馬思聰), a professor of the Central Conservatory of Music, escaped to Hong Kong.

20 Jan 1967

The Hong Kong Productivity Council was established as a statutory body to promote productivity excellence by offering advanced technologies and innovative services to local enterprises.

The Matrimonial Causes Ordinance 1966 was promulgated, enacting comprehensive provisions on matrimonial proceedings and related matters in place of the Divorce Ordinance 1933.

Jan 1967

The milestone with Chinese inscription "Kwan Tai Lo" dating back to early Hong Kong was discovered near Aberdeen.

03 Feb 1967

The Pensions (Amendment) Ordinance 1967 was promulgated, requiring civil servants' pensions and retirement benefits to be calculated based on their full substantive salary upon retirement (instead of 90% as stipulated in 1959).

13 Feb 1967

The Hong Kong government released its *Report of the Working Party on Local Administration*, also known as *The Dickinson Report*, recommending the establishment of first-level administrative bodies (Municipal Councils, Urban District Councils and District Councils), determined by population sizes, with appointed and elected council members responsible for district affairs relating to public health, education, welfare, licensing and estate management, etc.

16 Feb 1967

The Hong Kong government imposed new immigration controls, requiring Macao residents to fill out a white card on arrival and a yellow card on departure as with other foreign passport holders.

17 Feb 1967

The English Schools Foundation Ordinance 1967 was promulgated, establishing an English Schools Foundation in charge of English-language international schools in Hong Kong.

20 Feb 1967

The Provisional Council for the Use and Conservation of the Countryside was established as an advisor to the Governor of Hong Kong on conservation programmes and preservation of countryside parks.

20 Feb 1967

The Hong Kong Commercial Counsellor of UK Mission Geneva was inaugurated to safeguard Hong Kong's commercial interests under the General Agreement on Tariffs and Trade. It later became the Hong Kong Economic and Trade Office, Geneva; it began representing Hong Kong at the World Trade Organization as well as the Organisation for Economic Cooperation & Development's Trade Committee upon the establishment of the HKSAR.

12 Mar 1967

Pan Ku Magazine was founded as a periodical on current affairs, literature, art, drama and philosophy; it ceased publication in 1978.

21 Mar 1967

The Hong Kong Archaeological Society was established as an organisation dedicated to the study of archaeology and preservation of archaeological artefacts and sites in Hong Kong.

22 Mar 1967

A Heung Yee Kuk sub-committee rejected the government proposal to establish a municipal council in charge of Tsuen Wan, citing the need to preserve the traditional political system of the New Territories as a whole.

28 Mar 1967

The Central Taxicab Company was embroiled in a labour dispute over the termination of a taxi driver. It triggered a "go slow" industrial action among its drivers and those of the Hongkong and Shanghai Taxicab Company, followed by rounds of unsuccessful negotiations. On 15 April, the two companies announced they would cease operations and divest more than 150 taxis.

31 Mar 1967

A submarine telephone line running between Hong Kong and Commonwealth nations in Southeast Asia became operational at a project cost of £23.6 million.

01 Apr 1967

China Airlines began daily flights between Taipei and Hong Kong.

04 Apr 1967

The Hong Kong Observatory launched a thunderstorm and heavy rainfall alert system, allowing the public to receive warning signals after signing up through a telephone company.

13 Apr 1967

Hong Kong Artificial Flower Works was struck by a labour dispute following the refusal to meet employee demands; 658 workers, including several worker representatives, were dismissed on 28 and 29 April on the grounds of a drop in business.

14 Apr 1967

The Hong Kong Fire Services Department's new headquarters on Java Road in North Point went into service.

01 May 1967

More than 100 workers of Green Island Cement Company gathered in the office with the *Quotations from Chairman Mao Tse-Tung* in their hands, demanding an apology from the company for the beating of two workers by two foreign engineers and calling for the engineers to be fired. The company agreed to a meeting with the workers on the following day; on 04 May, it announced it would close the next day.

Figure 182
Police firing tear gas on workers engaged in a labour strike near Tung Tau Village in Kowloon City on 12 May 1967. (Photo courtesy of Robin Lam Kit/South China Morning Post via Getty Images)

06 May 1967

Hong Kong Artificial Flower Works was blocked from sending out shipment of products by workers on strike; police intervened, arresting 21 workers and injuring many in what became known as the Tai Yau Street Incident. Leftist unions and media came out in support of the workers—an event which turned into a series of riots over a period of seven months generally known as the 1967 Riots or, among leftists, Anti-British and Counter-Violence Movement. (Figure 182)

16 May 1967

The Committee of Hongkong–Kowloon Chinese Compatriots of All Circles for the Struggle against Persecution by the British Authorities in Hong Kong, or simply known as the Struggle Committee, was established at the Workers' Club headquarters of the Hong Kong Federation of Trade Unions; it had 102 members.

The Hong Kong Stock Exchange suspended trading for two weeks, resuming on 29 May. On 06 June, it suspended trading again before resuming on 21 June.

17 May 1967

The Hong Kong government released its *White Paper on Chinese Marriage in Hong Kong*, announcing an intent to make monogamy as the only legitimate form of marriage through legislation and make concubinage illegal. All marriages were to be registered.

18 May 1967

Thousands of leftists demonstrated at the Government House with big-character posters in a four-day protest condemning the "persecution of Hong Kong compatriots." On 22 May, many protesters were injured following a police crackdown in what became known as the Garden Road Bloodshed.

24 May 1967

The Emergency (Prevention of Inflammatory Speeches) Regulations 1967 was promulgated, prohibiting broadcasts of inflammatory content with a maximum penalty of HK$50,000 in fine and ten years of imprisonment.

In a meeting (and another on 27 May) with the Ministry of Foreign Affairs and the Hong Kong and Macau Works Committee, Premier Zhou Enlai (周恩來) of the State Council emphasised that the leftist movement in Hong Kong should proceed in accordance with the policy of the Chinese Central Government and should be on just grounds and made to the leftists' advantage with restraint.

01 Jun 1967

The Emergency (Prevention of Inflammatory Posters) Regulations 1967 was promulgated, prohibiting the spreading of slogans with inflammatory content with a maximum penalty of $5,000 in fine and two years of imprisonment.

10 Jun 1967

Leftist unions, including the Government, Armed Forces and Hospital Chinese Workers Union, launched a joint labour strike, followed by a larger one of the Motor Transport Workers General Union and others on 24 June. On 27 June, nearly 20,000 students in 32 leftist schools walked out of classes for a day. From 29 June to 02 July, a four-day strike was staged by those in the grain, oil, food, merchandise sectors.

17 Jun 1967

The first Hong Kong International Karting Prix began for a two-day event at Shek Kong Airfield in the New Territories.

29 Jun 1967

The local supply of water was shortened from eight hours per day to four hours every other day due to below-average rainfall since 01 May and a pending commitment to additional water from the Mainland.

30 Jun 1967

A Thai Airways International airliner crashed into the sea at Kowloon Bay while attempting to land in heavy rain; 24 people on board were killed and 56 were rescued.

13 Jul 1967

The Hong Kong government imposed further measures on water rations, limiting the supply to four hours every four days in households and four hours a day in industrial areas.

14 Jul 1967

The Factories and Industrial Undertakings (Amendment) Ordinance 1967 was promulgated, authorising the Commissioner of Labour to impose a gradual reduction of maximum work hours among female and young workers. On 29 November, regulations were approved by the Legislative Council for implementation of eight-hour days and 48-hour weeks over a period of four years starting 01 December.

20 Jul 1967

The Hong Kong government implemented nine regulations in accordance with the Emergency (Principal) Regulations Ordinance 1949, prohibiting dissemination of false information and sabotage and authorising the police to seize weapons and disperse assemblies, among other powers.

22 Jul 1967

The Emergency (Principal) (Amendment) Regulations 1967 was promulgated, making it an offence to deny police access to—or stay in—premises found to have offensive weapons. It also empowered the police to search for and seize weapons without a warrant.

28 Jul 1967

Leftists began planting both real and fake bombs bearing such messages as "compatriots stay away" in urban centres across Hong Kong.

31 Jul 1967

British aircraft carrier *Hermes* arrived in Hong Kong to help maintain public order.

01 Aug 1967

The Emergency (Principal) (Amendment) (No. 2) Regulations 1967 was promulgated, eliminating the sentence limitation of no more than five years imposed by the District Court for offences specified in the Emergency (Principal) Regulations.

04 Aug 1967

The Hong Kong police in conjunction with the British garrison conducted a joint air-and-land operation, raiding Kiu Kwan Mansion, New Metropole Building and Ming Yuen Mansion in North Point with helicopters launched from the British aircraft carrier *Hermes*. Among the 30 people arrested were Wong Kin-lap (黃建立), Principal of Hon Wah College, and Ng Lun-wah (吳麟華), Manager of Chinese Goods Centre Limited.

The Chinese Manufacturers' Association of Hong Kong became the first Chinese industrial association authorised to issue Certificates of Origin.

09 Aug 1967

Five persons-in-charge and over 30 staff members of local leftist newspapers were arrested, including Wu Tai-chow (胡棣周), Director of *Hong Kong Evening News* and Publisher of *Afternoon News*, and Poon Wai-wai (潘懷偉), Director of *Tin Fung Yat Pao*. On 17 August, a Central Magistracy court order was issued to suspend the three newspapers—which were allowed to resume publication on 18 February 1968. The persons-in-charge of the three newspapers were sentenced by the Central Magistracy to three years in prison on 29 August, 04 and 07 September.

24 Aug 1967

Commercial Radio commentator Lam Bun (林彬), a critic of the leftists, and his cousin Lam Kwong-hoi (林光海) sustained serious injuries in an arson attack by rioters and died the following day and on 29 August, respectively.

28 Aug 1967

A second line of barbed wire fences was installed at the border to prevent illegal immigrants from entering Hong Kong.

01 Sep 1967

The Education Department implemented a "1.1 system"—which mandated a 1:1.1 class-to-teacher ratio, reduced class sizes from 45 to 40 students in all public and subsidised primary schools, and required teachers to provide moral education.

03 Sep 1967

The In Tao Art Association—dedicated to promoting the modern ink painting movement—was established by Laurence Tam Chi-sing (譚志成), Irene Chou (周綠雲) and Ng Yiu-chung (吳耀忠), who were students in a Chinese Ink Painting course under The Chinese University of Hong Kong's Department of Extramural Studies. On 01 November 1968, it held its first exhibition in a five-day event at City Hall. In 1971, some members of the association formed the One Art Group, a modern painting and calligraphy group.

06 Sep 1967

The Hong Kong government temporarily restored the unlimited supply of water following an announcement that reservoirs were overflowing.

08 Sep 1967

The Emergency (Firework) Regulations 1967 was promulgated, confiscating all fireworks and firecrackers—regardless of whether they were licenced—except those designated for re-export on cargo ships. It aimed to prevent explosive substances from being used for bombs and provided compensation on any losses incurred from confiscation.

21 Sep 1967

The Hong Kong police seized a batch of antibiotics, valued between HK$20,000 and HK$50,000, and some 10,000 LSD tablets from four pharmacies in Tsim Sha Tsui; four men were arrested. It was the first seizure of LSD by the police.

01 Oct 1967

Guangdong Province began supplying water to Hong Kong at 10 a.m. in accordance with the 1964 water supply agreement. Hong Kong resumed unlimited water supply at 4 p.m.

03 Oct 1967

The Plover Cove Reservoir in Tai Po was completed, followed by a trial run in water-pumping.

07 Oct 1967

Morse Park, funded by The Hong Kong Jockey Club with a donation of HK$1.7 million and named in honour of the late HKJC chairman Arthur Morse, was inaugurated as the largest park in Kowloon.

17 Oct 1967

Northcote Training College, Grantham Training College and Sir Robert Black Training College—all founded by the government—were reinstituted as Teachers' Training Colleges.

26 Oct 1967

Governor David Trench officiated at a ceremony at Shek Pai Wan Resettlement Estate to mark its one millionth resident being rehoused to a resettlement estate.

30 Oct 1967

The first Hong Kong Week, organised by the Federation of Hong Kong Industries in conjunction with the Hong Kong Trade Development Council, began at City Hall in a promotional campaign of local products. It included music performances, Cantonese operas, acrobatic performances, fashion shows, ball games and funfairs. On 29 April 1969, it was renamed the Festival of Hong Kong by the Executive Council.

05 Nov 1967

A Cathay Pacific Airways Convair 880M aircraft en route from Hong Kong to Saigon, South Vietnam, veered off the runway during take-off at Kai Tak Airport and crashed into the sea, killing one person and injuring 28.

08 Nov 1967

The first International Book Exhibition began at City Hall with 142 publishers from 14 countries.

14 Nov 1967

The 1.43-km Lion Rock Tunnel, a link between Kowloon and eastern New Territories, was opened to traffic as the first vehicular tunnel in Hong Kong at a cost of HK$22 million. (Figure 183)

Figure 183
The entrance/exit point of Lion Rock Tunnel in Sha Tin in one-tube, two-way operation. (Photo taken on 07 November 1967 and courtesy of South China Morning Post Publishers Limited)

Figure 184
Governor David Trench speaking at the opening ceremony of Television Broadcasts Limited (TVB).
Back row, from left: Run Run Shaw (邵逸夫), Harold Lee Hsiao-wo (利孝和), Douglas Clague and
Tang Ping-yuan (唐炳源). (Photo courtesy of South China Morning Post Publishers Limited)

15 Nov 1967

Television Broadcasts Limited started publishing the *TV Week* magazine. The last issue was released on 27 August 1997.

17 Nov 1967

Juno Revolving Restaurant was opened at Wu Sang House in Mong Kok; it was the first of its kind in Hong Kong.

The amended Letters Patent and Royal Instructions were promulgated. The Letters Patent stipulated that an Acting Governor be appointed by the British monarch in the absence of the Governor or should he become unable to perform official duty. The Colonial Secretary would be Acting Governor if no designated individuals were specified.

The Public Order Ordinance 1967 was promulgated, stipulating that all public meetings and processions must be approved in advance by the Commissioner of Police. The police were empowered to disperse those without authorisation while officers at the rank of an Inspector or above were also allowed to ban any public display of flags and insignias.

19 Nov 1967

Television Broadcasts Limited (TVB) became the first local station to broadcast full-colour programmes with the debut of its channels TVB Jade and TVB Pearl in Chinese and English, respectively. (Figure 184)

Lingnan College was inaugurated in Hong Kong. It originated from Lingnan University in Guangzhou—established as Christian College in 1888 before closing for restructuring in 1952—and was conceived by alumnus Edward Chan Tak-tai (陳德泰) in 1966. On 17 October 1978, it became a registered post-secondary institution.

20 Nov 1967

The Hong Kong government announced a 14.3% depreciation of the Hong Kong dollar corresponding to the British pound in a bid to maintain an exchange rate of HK$16 to £1.

01 Dec 1967

Lau Nai-keung (劉迺強) published his article "The Riots, Public Opinions and the Adoption of Chinese as an Official Language" in *Undergrad* (magazine of the Hong Kong University Students' Union), calling on the government to recognise Chinese as one of Hong Kong's official languages.

04 Dec 1967

The Census and Statistics Department—responsible for government statistical work and population surveys—was formed in a merger of the Office of the Commissioner for Census and Statistical Planning (under the Government Secretariat) and the Statistical Branch (under the Commerce and Industry Department).

05 Dec 1967

The 25th Exhibition of Hong Kong Products (also named the Silver Jubilee Exhibition of Hong Kong Products) began; it marked the first time a government booth was organised.

09 Dec 1967

The Chinese University of Hong Kong held a ground-breaking and tree-planting ceremony on its new campus in Sha Tin.

27 Dec 1967

The Hong Kong government began providing infants and children six months to four years old with measles vaccines available at 33 maternal and child health centres.

Dec 1967

The 1967 Riots gradually subsided. These marked the largest social unrest in Hong Kong after the Second World War, resulting in 51 deaths, 832 injuries and 4,979 arrests.

Wah On House was opened for occupancy; it was the first building of Wah Fu Estate Phase I in Aberdeen. Wah Fu Estate, a low-cost public housing estate developed in phases by the Hong Kong Housing Authority, consisted of 25 buildings with a housing capacity of 54,000 residents upon completion in 1978.

1967

The University of Hong Kong's Centre of Asian Studies was established to promote the study of humanities and social sciences with respect to Asian cultures.

11 Jan 1968

Attorney General Denys Roberts announced that from midnight on 14 January to midnight on 29 January, an amnesty would be granted to those in illegal possession of explosives, arms and offensive weapons if they turned themselves in and surrendered such possessions to a police station, excluding those who had caused bodily harm with these firearms.

17 Jan 1968

Ming Pao Weekly began publication. As of 01 July 2017, it was the longest-running entertainment leisure magazine in Hong Kong.

20 Jan 1968

The Student Union of Chung Chi College of The Chinese University of Hong Kong held a two-day seminar on "Including Chinese as an Official Language" with about 100 representatives from local tertiary institutions. Deputy Colonial Secretary Denis Campbell Bray, Urban Councillors Henry Hu Hung-lick (胡鴻烈) and Denny Huang Mong-hwa (黃夢花) also attended in support of making Chinese an official language. A communiqué was issued after the seminar, calling for government support in making Chinese and English official languages of equal status along with a proposal for a committee on implementation.

24 Jan 1968

The Hong Kong government established a total of 10 District Offices (Central District, Western District, Wan Chai, North Point, Wong Tai Sin, Kowloon City, Yau Ma Tei, Mong Kok, Sham Shui Po and Kwun Tong), each headed by a District Officer, under the City District Officer Scheme designed to provide direct communication and improve government relations with the public. The first group of four District Officers took office on 10 May; all 10 District Officers were named by 24 January 1969.

02 Feb 1968

The Hong Kong Psychological Society was established as a professional group of Hong Kong-based psychologists, aiming to maintain professionalism amongst members and promote psychology as an academic and professional discipline in Hong Kong.

14 Feb 1968

A report titled *Hong Kong Mass Transport Study,* prepared by British firm Freeman, Fox, Wilbur Smith and Associates, was submitted to the Legislative Council by the government, recommending an underground railway system with a Tsuen Wan Line, a Kwun Tong Line, an Island Line and a Sha Tin Line. The *Hong Kong Mass Transport Study: Supplementary Report* was subsequently released by the firm on 22 March, followed by a revised supplementary report in June, advising against the Sha Tin Line. The *Hong Kong Mass Transit Further Studies: Final Report* was released in August 1970, proposing a detailed plan for a $4.4 billion underground system with 48 stations and 52.6 km of railways, including lines between Tsuen Wan and Central, Kwun Tong and Central, Kennedy Town and Chai Wan, as well as Diamond Hill and Sheung Wan.

11 Mar 1968

The Police Public Relations Branch was formed to disseminate police-related information and improve relations with the public, taking over a role previously supported by the Information Services Department.

01 Apr 1968

The Hong Kong Journalists Association was established to promote a healthy work environment, uphold press freedom, and safeguard journalistic integrity.

10 Apr 1968

The Hong Kong police uncovered a counterfeit banknotes syndicate and seized 1.5 million Philippine pesos and American Express Travellers Cheques, totalling about HK$5 million. It was known to be largest case in Hong Kong and the Far East at the time. On 15 July, five defendants were sentenced to 10 years in prison.

The Hong Kong government proposed an old-age allowance scheme and a universal healthcare programme in the *Report of the Working Party on Social Security*.

20 Apr 1968

More than 2,000 people attended the first dance party organised by the Urban Council at the rooftop garden of Blake Pier.

A three-day celebration of the Tin Hau Festival began at Shap Pat Heung in Yuen Long. In a parade, 108 members of the Chiuchow Fraternity Floral Tribute Society were dressed in the folktale characters from the novel *Water Margin.* It was also the first time the Chiuchow "Ying song and dance" routine was performed at the Tin Hau Festival in Yuen Long.

29 Apr 1968

About 4,000 sea- and land-based logistics workers attended a rally "Work Resumption, Factory Transfer and Career Change" at the Hong Kong Federation of Trade Unions Workers' Club, ending a 10-month strike.

22 May 1968

The Hong Kong government approved a proposal by The University of Hong Kong to establish a law department offering a three-year law degree programme within the Faculty of Social Sciences, marking the first law programme in Hong Kong. The programme began on 29 September 1969 and became an independent faculty as the School of Law on 01 July 1978, making it the first law school in Hong Kong.

24 May 1968

Over 46,000 people made a visit to the garden at the Government House. It was the first time since 1855 that the public was invited onto the premises.

01 Jun 1968

Her Majesty's Treasury (UK) issued bonds denominated in Hong Kong dollars for purchase by the Hong Kong government in British pound sterling. Capped at half of Hong Kong's total non-local official assets or £150 million, it was to ensure a stable exchange rate with the Hong Kong dollar. The bonds were held as non-transferable reserves in Britain and could be converted to British pounds by the Hong Kong government should the need arise.

04 Jun 1968

The Sandy Bay Children's Orthopaedic Hospital, founded and operated by the Society for the Relief of Disabled Children, was opened as the first children's hospital in Hong Kong and the first children's hospital dedicated to orthopaedic services in Southeast Asia. Formerly known as the Sandy Bay Children's Convalescent Home founded in October 1956, it was renamed the Duchess of Kent Children's Hospital in 1974.

13 Jun 1968

Several landslides in Hong Kong and Kowloon resulted from heavy morning rains, claiming at least 22 lives and affecting more than 200 others. Ma Shan Village in Shau Kei Wan and Tai Hang Sun Chun in Causeway Bay were the worst affected areas.

19 Jun 1968

The Industrial Relations Institute was established to train workers, promote industrial relations, and encourage participation in the trade union movement.

Jun 1968

The Hong Kong government required that all government public documents, including replies, notices and forms, be available in Chinese.

The Provisional Council for the Use and Conservation of the Countryside released a study on the requirements of recreational facilities and nature conservation in a report titled *The Countryside and the People*.

03 Jul 1968

A programme under Commercial Radio Hong Kong known as *Eighteenth Floor Block C* made its debut, featuring a storyline about the daily life of Hong Kong with various perspectives on social issues; it became the longest-running Chinese radio drama in the world.

12 Jul 1968

The Commissions of Inquiry Ordinance 1968 was promulgated, authorising a Commission of Inquiry appointed by the Governor-in-Council to investigate the operation and management of public institutions, conduct of public officials, and matters of great significance to public interest. The commission was granted the authority to summon anyone to testify as each inquiry was a judicial proceeding.

20 Jul 1968

The Fire Services Training School at Pat Heung was opened as a training base for all firemen in Hong Kong and as the headquarters of the Hong Kong Fire Services Department in the New Territories.

Jul 1968

The novel influenza A (H3N2) began spreading in Hong Kong. On 17 July, an official report to the World Health Organization (WHO) was made by the Medical and Health Department, followed by a WHO estimate of 500,000 infections in Hong Kong by the end of this month. The virus caused the third global influenza pandemic of the 20th century.

21 Aug 1968

The Hong Kong Observatory hoisted Hurricane Signal No. 10 for about six and a half hours amidst Typhoon Shirley. The hurricane caused three deaths, four injured, and damage to one ocean-going vessel and three fishing boats.

02 Sep 1968

The fourth Pan-Pacific Conference on Rehabilitation was held at Hong Kong City Hall. During the seven-day session, over 1,000 representatives from more than 30 countries took part in the exchange on rehabilitation of people with disabilities and clinical experience.

14 Sep 1968

The 1968/69 Hong Kong First Division League began with the first football match between Kowloon Motor Bus and South China. Professional players were allowed to compete for the first time under a new rule of the Hong Kong Football Association and were registered with five of the 12 participating teams, marking the first professional football league in Asia.

27 Sep 1968

The Employment Ordinance 1968 was promulgated, governing the conditions of employment in Hong Kong with respect to employment contracts, employee welfare and benefits, as well as remunerations and job placements.

30 Sep 1968

The third Indo-Pacific Council of the International Committee of Scientific Management, hosted by the Hong Kong Management Association, was held at Hong Kong City Hall as the first high-level meeting of its type in Hong Kong.

Sep 1968

Wen she xian began publication as a twice-a-week supplement in the weekly magazine *Zhong bao zhoukan*, covering literature and student social movement. It ceased publication after releasing a collection of 23 essays and reports compiled as a *Special Issue on Defending the Diaoyu Islands* in the 60th issue published in 1971.

09 Oct 1968

Construction of Mei Foo Sun Chuen Phase I on the former site of Mobil (Mei Foo) Oil Depot was completed. It was the first of eight phases of a residential complex comprising 99 blocks and 13,115 apartment units as Hong Kong's first large-scale private housing estate. The project was completed on 03 May 1978. (Figure 185)

The Legislative Council amended the rules of procedure by passing the Standing Orders of the Legislative Council of Hong Kong 1968, stipulating a session period be scheduled each year and a protocol of meeting minutes undersigned by the president for distribution to fellow legislators prior to the next meeting. The practice remains today.

Figure 185
The soon-to-be-completed Mei Foo Sun Chuen behind Lai Chi Kok Bridge. (Photo taken in 1968 and courtesy of South China Morning Post Publishers Limited)

09 Oct 1968

The Hong Kong government put forward a long-term plan on the local transportation network along with a proposed route numbering system across Hong Kong in a strategic paper titled *Hong Kong Long-Term Road Study*, prepared by British consultancy Freeman, Fox, Wilbur Smith and Associates.

22 Oct 1968

The Education Department initiated a consultation process with primary and secondary schools through the *Report of the Working Party on the Teaching of Chinese*, suggesting an emphasis on Chinese reading and comprehension and proposing a dual-track curriculum of Chinese Language and Chinese Culture for students in Form 4 and 5.

29 Oct 1968

The Lai Chi Kok Bridge, connecting downtown Kowloon with the industrial areas of Tsuen Wan and Kwai Chung in the New Territories, was opened as Hong Kong's first harbour-crossing bridge measuring 790 metres in total length.

Oct 1968

The Café de Coral Group was founded by Victor Lo Tang-seong (羅騰祥) and Lo Kai-muk (羅開睦). The first shop was opened for business in the following year on Sugar Street, Causeway Bay, serving mainly hamburgers and light refreshments. The fast-food chain opened its first branch on Jordan Road, Kowloon, in February 1972.

04 Nov 1968

Caritas House, located at Mid-Levels on Hong Kong Island, was inaugurated as a community welfare centre in Hong Kong.

08 Nov 1968

The Community Chest of Hong Kong Ordinance 1968 was promulgated, establishing the Community Chest as a non-profit, non-government charity dedicated to fundraising in support of community projects. It was the first of its kind in Asia.

09 Nov 1968

More than 100 people were injured in the collapse of a bamboo spectator stand at the Shek Kong Barracks during a fundraising performance of the 48th Gurkha Infantry Brigade (British Forces Overseas Hong Kong). A Commission of Inquiry was appointed by the governor on 27 November, followed by a Commission report released on 09 April 1969 which identified design flaws in the spectator stand and recommended further regulation on spectator stands.

18 Nov 1968

The Chinese Language Press Institute was inaugurated in a ceremony, promoting further cooperation, exchange and industrywide operation among Chinese-language newspapers around the world. Sally Aw Sian(胡仙), proprietor of *Sing Tao Daily*, was the first chairperson; executive committee members included representatives of 15 different newspapers from Hong Kong, Taiwan, Southeast Asia, and the US.

Nov 1968

The Hong Kong Observatory established a frost warning system in anticipation of frost in the mountains or inland areas of the New Territories. The first frost warning was issued on 28 December 1991.

1968

Hong Kong became a correspondent member of the International Organization for Standardization, a global non-governmental standard-setting body.

09 Jan 1969

The first kidney transplant surgery in Hong Kong took place at Queen Mary Hospital.

20 Jan 1969

The Plover Cove Reservoir was put into use upon completion with a water storage capacity of 37–39 billion gallons, or three times the combined capacity of all reservoirs at the time. It was the world's first freshwater reservoir built in the sea and increased Hong Kong's total storage capacity to 46 billion gallons. (Figure 186)

22 Jan 1969

The *Oriental Daily News* was founded by Ma Sik-chun（馬惜珍）.

08 Feb 1969

The Hong Kong government announced the repeal of the Emergency (Prevention of Inflammatory Speeches) Regulations 1967, Emergency (Prevention of Inflammatory Posters) Regulations 1967, Emergency (Closed Areas) Regulations 1967 and Emergency (General Holiday) Regulations 1967.

11 Feb 1969

The Hong Kong Association for Natural Scenery Protection was established. Founders included John H. Pain, a British employee of the Hong Kong Tourist Association, and Agnes Black, a professor of Zoology at The University of Hong Kong. It became the first local environmental group in Hong Kong and was renamed the Conservancy Association in 1971.

Figure 186
The Plover Cove Reservoir under construction as the first reservoir in the world with a dam (measuring approximately two kilometres in length) in the sea. (Photo taken in 1968 and courtesy of HKSAR Government)

26 Feb 1969

The Hong Kong government announced the 1969/70 Budget and estimated a surplus of HK$64 million. It was the first budget surplus since the Second World War.

28 Feb 1969

The Registrar General's Office was renamed the City District Office to help improve government engagement with the public. In 1973, the City District Office became part of the Home Affairs Department established by the Government Secretariat.

An amended Royal Instructions was promulgated, stipulating protocols regarding appointment, reprimand and discharge of civil servants at the discretion of the governor without having to consult the Executive Council.

An amended Royal Instructions was promulgated, increasing the minimum number of legislators required to convene a meeting from five to 10. The Legislative Council had 26 members at the time.

The waste incinerator built in Lai Chi Kok at a cost of HK$22 million began operations with a daily capacity of 750 tons. The incinerator was decommissioned on 13 December 1990.

04 Mar 1969

The Urban Council released a *Report on the Reform of Local Government*, prepared by the Local Government Committee, recommending gradual expansion in representation and independence of the Urban Council by increasing the number of elected members and granting financial independence.

28 Mar 1969

Hong Kong became an official member of the Asian Development Bank with a capital contribution of US$8 million by the government. The bank is a regional financial institution consisting of member countries in the Asia-Pacific region. It promotes economic and social development by providing financial and technical support to member countries.

Mar 1969

The American Chamber of Commerce in Hong Kong was incorporated. It was an observer at the first meeting of the Asia Pacific Council of American Chambers of Commerce on 06 October.

09 Apr 1969

The Hong Kong Children's Choir was founded as Hong Kong's first children's choir and immediately began to arrange its first practice.

15 Apr 1969

Tang Shiu Kin Hospital in Wan Chai was opened; it became operational the following day. Half of the construction cost was borne by businessman Tang Shiu-kin (鄧肇堅). A key provider of emergency services in the eastern part of Hong Kong Island, it became Hong Kong's first training centre of emergency medicine in 1994.

22 Apr 1969

The Peninsula Electric Power Company's power station in Tsing Yi Power became operational under a joint venture between Hong Kong's China Light & Power Company and its US partner Standard Oil Company. Equipped with six and four oil-fired generators in two power plants, respectively, by 1977, it had a total power capacity of 1,520 megawatts as a supplier for Kowloon and the New Territories before it was decommissioned in 1998.

Apr 1969

Nan Yang College was incorporated as Hong Kong's first Buddhist post-secondary institution, co-founded by the Hong Kong Buddhist Sangha Association and Hong Kong Buddhist Association. Enrolment began in May; classes started in September. It was renamed Hong Kong Nan Yang College in May 1970.

29 May 1969

Francis Hsu Chen-ping (徐誠斌) was appointed the third bishop (and the first Chinese bishop) of the Catholic Diocese of Hong Kong by the Roman Curia.

16 Jun 1969

An exhibition game between the English Football Association and Hong Kong Football Association was held at the Government Stadium and attended by some 20,000 spectators. Following the match, a riot broke out in protest of the English players' unsportsmanlike conduct; it was brought under control by midnight by riot police.

26 Jun 1969

The Cross-Harbour Tunnel Company in collaboration with the Cross-Harbour Tunnel International Associated Group signed a HK$270 million contract to construct the Cross-Harbour Tunnel in Hung Hom under a "Build-Operate-Transfer" project model adopted by the government.

11 Jul 1969

Ann Tse-kai (T. K. Ann) (安子介) incorporated Winsor Industrial Corporation Limited as a manufacturer of textile products. On 24 October, it became a publicly listed company in Hong Kong; it was one of Hong Kong's largest textile companies.

21 Jul 1969

The Hong Kong Chinese Civil Servants' Association held an all-female member meeting and announced an agenda to fight for equal pay among teachers, nurses and social workers. On 20 September, it held a special meeting and called on the government for a policy on gender equality and equal pay, followed by an appeal to the Queen in the same month.

Jul 1969

The Social Welfare Department launched Hong Kong's first Summer Youth programme, aiming to provide teenagers with a range of recreational activities, including outdoor activities and leadership training.

06 Aug 1969

The Hong Kong government announced details of a financial assistance scheme with an annual allocation of HK$5.5 million over a period of five years to support university undergraduate students. A grant of up to HK$2,000 to cover tuition and related expenses and a loan of up to HK$4,000 to cover living expenses were available under the scheme.

18 Aug 1969

The Asian Workshop on Higher Education was held at The Chinese University of Hong Kong under the theme "A New Man for a New Society." Over 100 representatives from 22 universities in Asia took part in the two-week conference for an exchange of views among educators.

01 Sep 1969

The Road Traffic (Amendment) Ordinance 1969, Public Transport Services (Hong Kong Island) (Amendment) Ordinance 1969 and Public Transport Services (Kowloon and New Territories) (Amendment) Ordinance 1969 came into effect. Fourteen-seat public light buses (minibuses) became operational and a mode of public transport in Hong Kong. Vehicles registered as minibuses must be labelled as such with a specified number of seats available and be painted yellow. (Figure 187)

A ground-breaking ceremony was held to begin construction of the Cross-Harbour Tunnel. The tunnel, measuring 1.9 km in length across Victoria Harbour between Hung Hom in Kowloon and Causeway Bay on Hong Kong Island, was designed as an immersed tube composed of 15 caissons. The first caisson was successfully installed on 08 October 1970; an opening ceremony upon completion was held on 20 February 1972.

15 Sep 1969

Dozens of students from various colleges staged a two-day sit-in outside Chu Hai College of Higher Education in protest of the expulsion of 12 students on 23 August for publishing articles critical of Chu Hai College.

24 Sep 1969

Hong Kong's first satellite station in Stanley, managed by Cable & Wireless, became operational. It could transmit and receive signals for colour and black-and-white TVs and communication with telefax and satellite telephone.

Figure 187
Minibuses were allowed to operate as a legal means of public transport starting 01 September 1969. (Photo taken in 1979 and courtesy of Yau Tin-kwai/South China Morning Post via Getty Images)

26 Sep 1969

The United Federation of Travel Agents' Associations held its third meeting at Hong Kong City Hall with 800 international representatives over a period of six days. It was the first time such a meeting was held in Hong Kong.

27 Sep 1969

In protest of a traffic ticket for an unlawful passenger pickup/drop-off, a group of drivers parked about 40 minibuses outside the Yuen Long Police Station, blocking traffic and attracting more than 1,000 onlookers before police arrived to disperse the crowd with tear gas. By 6 p.m., 14 people were arrested as the area returned to normal.

Sep 1969

The Morrison Hill Technical Institute under the Education Department was established, offering apprenticeship programmes, part-time and full-time courses in construction, mechanical and electrical engineering, as well as business management, in support of a growing industrial sector.

06 Oct 1969

The Hong Kong government reached an agreement with three civil service associations on the implementation of equal pay in phases starting retroactively from 01 April in the same year to April 1975.

24 Nov 1969

The Hang Seng Index (HSI) made its debut, closing at 158.5 points on the first day. On 17 December, an agreement between Hang Seng Bank and Hong Kong Stock Exchange was reached to apply HSI to the stock market's operations in Hong Kong. Prior to a merger forming the HKEx Group in April 1986, HSI was based on the median price quoted by the Hong Kong Stock Exchange, Far East Exchange and Kam Ngan Stock Exchange.

Nov 1969

Orient Overseas Container Line launched a regular container service route between Hong Kong and North America, becoming Asia's first shipping company with containerised cargo. In 1973, it became a publicly traded company listed in Hong Kong and as the first shipping company to do so.

Hong Kong's first experimental fish culture zone, covering a 0.4-hectare area at Tiger Cave in Tolo Harbour, came into operation. The fish farm was founded by Ho Hung-tai (何鴻帶), a fisherman and head of Sam Mun Tsai Village in Tai Po.

Figure 188
The neon sign of the first Festival of Hong Kong on display at Victoria Harbour. (Photo taken in 1969 and courtesy of Public Records Office, Government Records Service)

08 Dec 1969

The Festival of Hong Kong made its debut in an opening ceremony at Hong Kong City Hall. Over 470 cultural and recreational programmes, including exhibitions, sports and music performances, were featured. (Figure 188)

14 Dec 1969

Hong Kong's first International Marathon was held by the Hong Kong Amateur Athletic Association as part of the Festival of Hong Kong. A total of 28 international runners from nine locations took part in the competition starting at Yuen Long Stadium which was opened on the same day; a South Korean athlete took the win.

17 Dec 1969

The Far East Exchange Limited, founded by Ronald Li Fook-shiu (李福兆), was opened for business. It was Hong Kong's second stock exchange, breaking a monopoly in existence since 1891, before merging with Hong Kong Stock Exchange.

01 Jan 1970

The Sun Yat-sen Library on Boundary Street in Kowloon was unveiled. The three-storey private library with a collection of 75,000 books and various facilities, including an exhibition room for displaying Chinese cultural relics, was founded by the Chinese Culture Association.

07 Jan 1970

Senior Puisne Judge Ivo Rigby was appointed as Chief Justice of Hong Kong.

09 Jan 1970

The Employment (Amendment) Ordinance 1970 was promulgated, mandating 10 weeks of unpaid maternity leave (four and six weeks before and after childbirth) for pregnant women. Employees shall not be dismissed during maternity leave.

19 Jan 1970

The police uncovered a counterfeit banknote syndicate in North Point, seized a batch of counterfeit Philippine pesos and US dollars totalling HK$7.7 million, and put five people under arrest. On 19 March, three male defendants charged with producing and possessing counterfeit notes were sentenced to two years in prison. On 23 March, a female defendant was convicted of possessing counterfeit notes and sentenced to one and a half years in prison.

23 Jan 1970

Jardine Fleming & Company Ltd was incorporated under a joint venture between Jardine Matheson and Robert Fleming & Co. It was the first merchant (investment) bank in Hong Kong, providing investment management and financial advisory services.

13 Feb 1970

The Sir David Trench Trust Fund for Recreation Ordinance 1970 was promulgated, establishing an eponymous fund in support of recreational, sports, cultural and social activities.

Feb 1970

The Seventies, a monthly magazine founded by Lee Yee (李怡), made its debut. It was renamed *The Nineties* in May 1984 before ceasing publication in May 1998.

13 Mar 1970

The Wills Ordinance 1970 was promulgated to consolidate existing legislations on wills, regulate the making and revocation of wills, and expand the scope of wills to all assets and property.

14 Mar 1970

Hong Kong made its debut at the World Exposition in Osaka, Japan. On 19 March, a celebration day took place at the Hong Kong Pavilion; by the closing day on 13 September a total of 9.19 million visits were made to the Hong Kong Pavilion.

26 Mar 1970

Hong Kong Baptist College was authorised to become a post-secondary college under government approval. Its Chinese name was slightly amended to reflect a higher status in April 1972.

03 Apr 1970

The World Buddhist Conference, organised by the Hong Kong Buddhist Association, began at Hong Kong City Hall with 262 Buddhist leaders from more than 26 countries and regions on religions issues. It was the first international Buddhist conference in Hong Kong.

04 Apr 1970

The seabed of Kwai Chung was allocated by the Hong Kong government for a container terminal to be funded, built and operated by a private enterprise.

11 Apr 1970

A PanAm Boeing 747 airliner arrived at Kai Tak Airport from Tokyo, marking the first arrival of the largest airliner in the world. The airliner set off for San Francisco via Japan the next day with the first group of passengers from Hong Kong.

20 Apr 1970

The Hong Kong Computer Society was founded, becoming the first professional body dedicated to the development and application of information technology in Hong Kong.

21 Apr 1970

A semi-final of the Hong Kong Senior Challenge Shield between South China and Fire Services was held at the Government Stadium. In protest of the game ended prematurely by the referee, about 1,000 spectators refused to leave the stadium in a riot for which police officers were dispatched.

04 May 1970

The 24th Congress of the Federation of Commonwealth Chambers of Commerce began at Hong Kong City Hall. Some 200 delegates of the Commonwealth joined the five-day session.

08 May 1970

The film production company Golden Harvest, founded by Raymond Chow Man-wai (鄒文懷), a former production manager at Shaw Brothers, was incorporated.

18 May 1970

The 19th Congress of the International Press Institute began in Hong Kong over three days with representatives from 37 countries.

22 May 1970

The Metrication Committee under the chairmanship of Legislative Councillor Sir Chung Sze-yuen (鍾士元) was appointed by the government to explore the adoption and implementation of the metric system. Committee recommendations were adopted on 26 May 1971, putting in use the metric system within the government domain and allowing the private sector to decide on adoption.

29 May 1970

The New World Development Company Limited, founded by Cheng Yu-tung (鄭裕彤), was incorporated. The property developer was first listed on the Hong Kong Stock Exchange on 23 November 1972.

May 1970

Panorama, a magazine of short stories and articles on literature, history and art, was founded under the sponsorship of artist Zhang Daqian (張 大 千) whose paintings were regularly featured on the cover. It ceased publication in October 1973; it resumed publication two months later under an amended Chinese name, running until September 1995.

01 Jun 1970

The 11-storey carpark building with a capacity of 900 spaces across eight floors, located on Rumsey Street in Central, was opened as the largest government carpark in Hong Kong.

19 Jun 1970

The Multi-Storey Buildings (Owners Incorporation) Ordinance 1970 was promulgated, facilitating joint management of residential buildings and units by their respective owners as a group. On 01 December 1971, Mei King Mansion in To Kwa Wan became the first owners' incorporation of a multi-storey building in Hong Kong.

The Inland Revenue (Amendment) Ordinance 1970 was promulgated, introducing tax exemptions with dependent parent allowance and charitable donations.

24 Jun 1970

The Kowloon Park, located on the former site of the Whitfield Barracks, made its opening. On 1 February 1989, Kowloon Park was re-opened after it was renovated to include the largest gymnasium in Kowloon at the time and the first depth-adjustable indoor swimming pool in Hong Kong.

26 Jun 1970

The Government Secretariat created an Establishment Officer, responsible for civil servants in terms of their assignment, compensation and training, in place of the Personnel Director. Samuel Tedford Kidd, who was Principal Assistant Colonial Secretary (Land Affairs), became the first Establishment Officer.

01 Jul 1970

The Legal Aid Department, originally under the Judiciary, became independent and was expanded to include criminal litigation along with civil litigation, as well as assignment of solicitors and barristers for eligible persons unable to afford legal representation.

The Urban Council put into force a new hawker management policy, stipulating the withdrawal of hawker licences upon the death of licencees and government discretion to grant a transfer of licence to widows/widowers with respect to fixed food stalls of non-cooked food. On the same day, hawkers held a rally in protest.

10 Jul 1970

The Marriage Reform Ordinance 1970 was promulgated (effective date to be determined by the Governor), implementing monogamy with post-registration or dissolution of customary marriages and validated marriages. The law was made effective from 07 October 1971 by the authority of the Governor.

12 Jul 1970

A public forum on making Chinese an official language was held by 17 students with support from various cultural organisations. It was concurred by more than 350 people at the forum, followed by a joint statement to seek endorsement from the president of the World Assembly of Youth. On 19 July, the Campaign for Chinese as an Official Language was officially formed by 13 student publications and organisations.

18 Jul 1970

The Hong Kong Lawn Bowls Team won a gold medal at the nineth Commonwealth Games in Edinburgh, United Kingdom, making it Hong Kong's first gold medal in a Commonwealth Games.

22 Jul 1970

The Hong Kong government announced that it would implement equal pay among nurses in seven phases from 01 April 1969 to 01 April 1975 as the first batch of civil servants under such policy.

Jul 1970

The First Institute of Art and Design was founded by Lui Lup-fan (呂立勳). It initially only offered evening classes but gradually added diploma courses in fashion design, interior design, 3D animation and photography.

Aug 1970

Founder of Orient Overseas Container Line, Tung Chao-yung (C. Y. Tung) (董浩雲), was named the world's leading shipping magnate in a *Forbes* magazine article "Oceans of Wealth." In December 1980, *Seawise Giant*, a super tanker under an affiliated company, Island Navigation Corporation, was launched in a ceremony in Japan. With a deadweight of 564,763 tons and powered by a 50,000-horsepower engine, it was a top tanker with the largest capacity in the world.

01 Sep 1970

The Islamic College, founded by the Chinese Muslim Cultural and Fraternal Association, held its inauguration. It was Hong Kong's first Islamic school and was renamed Islamic Kasim Tuet Memorial College in 1997.

07 Sep 1970

A group of 36 officials from the District Office and Squatter Control Branch, escorted by two teams of riot police comprising 248 officers, were dispatched to demolish a facility dedicated to teaching Mao Zedong Thought in Lau Fau Shan, New Territories.

24 Sep 1970

An alliance, along with a theme song, was formed by several groups, including the All-Hong Kong Working Party to Promote Chinese as an Official Language, Campaign for Chinese as an Official Language, and Committee on the Problem of the Official Status of the Chinese Language in Hong Kong of the Hong Kong Federation of Students.

25 Sep 1970

The International Markets Advertising Conference was held in Hong Kong for the first time and attended by representatives from eight countries of the Asia-Pacific region.

02 Oct 1970

The fortnightly women's magazine *Sisters* was launched, featuring articles on fashion, beauty, cooking and family life. In 2005, *Sisters* was relaunched as a monthly beauty magazine named *Sisters Beauty Pro*.

06 Oct 1970

Urban Councillor Henry Hu Hung-lick (胡鴻烈) proposed a motion to swiftly amend Section 45 of the Urban Council Ordinance to facilitate council meetings in English and Chinese simultaneously. The motion was passed with 17 affirmative votes and five abstentions.

21 Oct 1970

Daiwa Securities International (HK) was established and subsequently registered on 28 December, specialising in brokerage, underwriting and proprietary businesses of Japanese and global securities.

The Chinese Language Committee on the question of making Chinese an official language in Hong Kong under the chairmanship of Sir Kenneth Fung Ping-fan (馮秉芬), Unofficial Member of the Executive Council, was established by the government. On 05 February 1971, the committee submitted its first report, recommending the use of the Chinese language in the Legislative Council, Urban Council and government units and committees.

04 Dec 1970

Pope Paul VI arrived in Hong Kong in the afternoon and hosted a Mass with 40,000 people at the Government Stadium before departing after a three-hour stay in the first visit by a pope to Hong Kong. (Figure 189)

09 Dec 1970

World-class footballer Pelé arrived in Hong Kong with the national team of Brazil for a 10-day visit, appearing in four exhibition games with Team Hong Kong and Hong Kong League XI for a total of 78,000 spectators. (Figure 190)

18 Dec 1970

The Prevention of Bribery Ordinance 1970 was promulgated, outlining the description of offences and the powers of investigation and evidence in relation to bribery and corruption.

Figure 189
Pope Paul VI met with worshippers at the Government Stadium on 04 December 1970 during his visit to Hong Kong. (Photo courtesy of HKSAR Government)

Figure 190
World-class footballer Pelé (in white) played in an exhibition match with Team Hong Kong at the Government Stadium. (Photo taken on 13 December 1970 and courtesy of South China Morning Post Publishers Limited)

18 Dec 1970

The Royal Hong Kong Regiment Ordinance 1970 and Royal Hong Kong Auxiliary Air Force Ordinance 1970 were promulgated, establishing the Royal Hong Kong Regiment (The Volunteers) and Royal Hong Kong Auxiliary Air Force in place of the Royal Hong Kong Defence Force. The Volunteers were disbanded on 03 September 1995.

27 Dec 1970

Angry with the prison guards for unjustified beating, nearly 500 inmates in Tong Fuk Prison on Lantau Island staged a riot at breakfast, vandalising prison cells and taking a prison guard hostage. Marine and riot police were dispatched while officials of the Prisons Department mediated the situation with a promise to investigate and provide improved food services.

Dec 1970

The Keep Hong Kong Clean Committee, chaired by Urban Councillor Denny Huang Mong-hwa (黃夢花), was established by the Urban Council. On 12 June 1971, it was renamed the Keep Hong Kong Clean Campaign Committee as a government advisor on improving the urban environment, related publicity and education campaigns.

1970

The *Colony Outline Plan*, a proposal of city planning, was completed by the government, specifying the functional purpose of each district according to demographic and land usage. Statutory zoning plans were drafted by the Town Planning Board upon review and approval by the Committee on Planning & Land Development, Governor-in-Council, and Executive Council.

Radio Television Hong Kong's Public Affairs Television Unit was established. In the following year, it began producing programmes on current affairs, culture and education, as well as shows on social realities.

The comic strip *Little Rascals* created by Tony Wong Yuk-long (黃玉郎) was launched. Starting from issue no. 99 in 1975, it was renamed *Oriental Heroes*; it ended with issue no. 1280 on 26 May 2000 and was published under the name *New Dragon Tiger Gate* starting from 03 June of the same year as the longest-running martial arts comic strip in Hong Kong as of 2017.

The Hong Kong Archaeological Society uncovered chipped and ground stone tools, white pottery and painted pottery basins from the Neolithic period during an excavation at the Chung Hom Wan site on Hong Kong Island.

A rock carving at Big Wave Bay on Hong Kong Island was discovered, revealing geometric designs and abstract forms of animal motif, and became Hong Kong's first declared monument on 20 October 1978.

Curved rock carvings on Cheung Chau were discovered and in 1982 became a declared monument by the government.

15 Jan 1971

US-based Chase Bank announced the establishment of its Southeast Asian headquarters in Hong Kong.

British investment bank Schroders, in collaboration with Standard Chartered Bank and the Kadoorie family, established Schroders & Chartered Limited as a service provider of investment management and corporate finance. The Schroder Trust Fund, launched in the following year, was the first global fund managed in Hong Kong.

22 Jan 1971

The Intestates' Estates Ordinance 1971 was promulgated, eliminating gender inequality with respect to inheritance and putting in place an expedited process with inheritance cases in the absence of an apparent heir.

26 Jan 1971

Enjoy Yourself Tonight, a variety show originally in black-and-white produced by Television Broadcasts Limited, became the first colour TV programme in Hong Kong on Chinese New Year's Eve. A total of 6,613 episodes were aired between 20 November 1967 and 07 October 1994.

07 Feb 1971

The Community Chest of Hong Kong held its first "Walk for A Million" on Hong Kong Island and its second in Kowloon on 21 February, raising a total of HK$979,734. It was later renamed "Walk for Millions."

14 Feb 1971

Upon US–Japan negotiation on the sovereignty of Okinawa and Diaoyu Islands, the Hong Kong Action Committee for Defending the Diaoyu Islands was established to support the Baodiao (Protect Diaoyu Islands) Movement globally.

26 Feb 1971

The student unions of three colleges of education, namely Northcote, Grantham and Sir Robert Black, issued a joint statement in protest of a new pay scale with lower starting salaries for graduate-qualified and certificate-qualified teachers under the 1970/71 Budget, demanding to retain the old system among existing teachers. On 18 October, another statement was issued, condemning the lack of progress and disregard for educators while an agreement with nurses on similar issues had been reached.

27 Feb 1971

A government census began in Hong Kong; it was concluded on 09 March. It showed a population of 3,948,179, including 3,936,630 permanent residents and 11,549 mobile (non-permanent) residents.

Feb 1971

Experimental operation began with Hong Kong's first desalination plant located on the coast near the Tai Lam Chung Reservoir with a daily production capacity of 50,000 gallons of fresh water through a vacuum distillation process.

01 Mar 1971

The government-sponsored Public Assistance Scheme was launched for residents having lived in Hong Kong for at least one year with a monthly savings of less than HK$50 after all living expenses. Disbursement began on 01 April.

03 Mar 1971

Elsie Elliott, Hilton Cheong-Leen (張有興), Denny Huang Mong-hwa (黃夢花), Charles Sin Cho-chiu (冼祖昭) and Cecilia Yeung Lai-yin (楊勵賢) were directly elected to the Urban Council.

15 Mar 1971

The Kam Ngan Stock Exchange Ltd, founded by Woo Hon-fai (胡漢輝), was opened for business as Hong Kong's third stock exchange before it was later merged with Hong Kong Stock Exchange.

16 Mar 1971

The Hong Kong Jockey Club in a special meeting passed a motion to professionalise horse racing and allow professional jockeys to compete beginning from the 1971/72 season.

17 Mar 1971

Sponsored by Chase Bank, a symposium on global finance and US-HK economic relations was held in Hong Kong.

18 Mar 1971

The three-day Central Committee meeting of the Asian Catholic Bishops' Conference began in Hong Kong; it established the Federation of the Asian Bishops' Conferences with an office in Hong Kong.

10 Apr 1971

A protest at the Japanese Cultural and Information Centre on D'Aguilar Street in Central, organised by the Hong Kong Action Committee for Defending the Diaoyu Islands, was stopped as police cordoned off the area, dispersed the protesters and arrested 21 people for unlawful assembly and obstructing traffic.

12 Apr 1971

Five young female prisoners escaped from Tai Lam Chung Prison; a female guard died from serious injuries in an attack. All five were captured on the same day and later charged with murder. On 05 August, following a trial, two had their charges dropped while three were given sentences between nine months and three years in a detention-training centre.

15 Apr 1971

Members of a Chinese delegation to the 31st World Table Tennis Championships arrived at the invitation of Hong Kong Table Tennis Association, appearing in exhibition games with their Hong Kong counterparts at Southorn Stadium in Wan Chai on 15, 16 and 18 April.

06 Jun 1971

The Heung Yee Kuk N.T. Special Committee held a meeting at the New Territories Heung Yee Kuk Yuen Long District Secondary School with 800 village representatives, demanding four items with respect to their rights to land use and announcing there would be public demonstration across the New Territories if demands were not met by the government.

08 Jun 1971

Cheung Kong (Holdings) Limited, a real estate conglomerate founded by Li Ka-shing (李嘉誠), was incorporated, becoming a listed company in Hong Kong on 01 November 1972 under the name CK Asset Holdings Limited.

07 Jul 1971

Upon the escalation on the issue of defending the Diaoyu Islands following the US–Japan Okinawa Reversion Agreement signed on 17 June, Hong Kong Federation of Students (HKFS) held a demonstration (which was originally permitted by government to be held at the Government Stadium) at Victoria Park with over 1,000 participants and 3,000–4,000 onlookers. The crowds were dispersed by the police using batons and 21 people were arrested for unlawful assembly. There was a HKFS press conference demanding the release of those arrested.

23 Jul 1971

The Hong Kong Polytechnic Ordinance 1971 was promulgated, effective 24 March 1972, reorganising the Hong Kong Technical College into the Hong Kong Polytechnic with a focus on industrial and business training. On 01 August 1972, Hong Kong Polytechnic was formally opened with departments in engineering, business administration, math and science, navigation and textiles under the directorship of Charles Old.

Jul 1971

The first Hong Kong Yearbook in Chinese *Report for the Year 1970* was released as a stand-alone publication translated, printed and distributed by *Tin Tin Daily News*.

12 Aug 1971

The police, making an exception, approved a Defend the Diaoyu Islands assembly at Victoria Park, organised by the Hong Kong Defend Diaoyutai United Front, on the condition that certain rules were to be observed. On the following day, more than 3,000 people participated in the assembly after which letters of protest were presented to the consulates-general of the United States and Japan in Hong Kong. (Figure 191)

Figure 191
A rally in defence of Diaoyu Islands on Hong Kong Island on 12 August 1971. (Photo courtesy of Hong Kong Museum of History)

16 Aug 1971

Typhoon Signal No. 10 was hoisted for nearly six hours amid Typhoon Rose—which left 110 people dead, five missing and 286 injured; 34 ocean-going vessels and 303 fishing boats sustained damage; and 88 passengers drowned as the Hong Kong–Macao passenger ship *Fat Shan* sank.

20 Aug 1971

Apollo Telephone Answering Services Ltd introduced the first paging service in Hong Kong.

22 Aug 1971

Four groups dedicated to defending the Diaoyu Islands held an assembly at The University of Hong Kong and issued a joint statement reiterating their stance. More than 50 participants then staged a rally at the US Consulate General to protest against America's attempt to use the "One China, One Taiwan" and "Two China" ideas to split China.

23 Aug 1971

The Red Cross Society of China donated RMB 3 million through the Bank of China to the Hong Kong Federation of Trade Unions and the Chinese General Chamber of Commerce in a relief effort for families of victims in Typhoon Rose.

03 Sep 1971

The Education Ordinance 1971 was promulgated, implementing free and compulsory primary education for children aged 6–11. The Director of Education was empowered to issue an attendance order to parents who refused to send their children to school without acceptable reasons.

06 Sep 1971

With the opening of the Educational Television Centre, educational television programmes began airing on Television Broadcasts Limited Pearl and Rediffusion Television Channel 1 and 2 at different times.

20 Sep 1971

Hong Kong Shue Yan College on Shing Woo Road in Happy Valley, founded by Henry Hu Hung-lick (胡 鴻 烈) and his wife Chung Chi-yung (鍾期榮), was inaugurated. Henry Hu Hung-lick was Supervisor; Chung Chi-yung was Principal. On 29 January 1976, it became an officially approved post-secondary college registered with the government.

Sep 1971

The Castle Peak Resettlement Estate, built by the Resettlement Department, was opened for occupancy. The first public housing estate in Castle Peak (in Tuen Mun), it was renamed Castle Peak Estate in 1973 and then San Fat Estate in 1974.

10 Oct 1971

The Hong Kong Post-Secondary Students Association was established as a centre of education and career information as well as a platform of academic research and cultural exchange. Ng Yat-po (吳日波) was appointed as its first president.

15 Oct 1971

Joyce Mary Bennett was ordained as a pastor by Bishop John Gilbert Hindley Baker of the Diocese of Hong Kong and Macao, becoming the first British female pastor of the Anglican Church in the world and the first non-Chinese female pastor of the Hong Kong Anglican Church (Episcopal).

22 Oct 1971

The Immigration Ordinance 1971 was promulgated, effective 01 April 1972, stipulating the right of entry for people born in Hong Kong, British citizens naturalised in Hong Kong, and Chinese residents of not less than seven years in Hong Kong, in addition to immigration control on British citizens living and working in Hong Kong.

27 Oct 1971

Governor-designate Murray MacLehose told the British Foreign and Commonwealth Office: "My object in Hong Kong must be to ensure that conditions in Hong Kong are so superior in every way to those of China that the CPG [Central People's Government] will hesitate before facing the problems of absorption."

30 Oct 1971

An alarm-four fire broke out at the Jumbo Floating Restaurant, moored in Aberdeen Typhoon Shelter and scheduled to open on 15 November. The fire lasted an hour and a half before it was brought under control, killing 34 people, injuring another 42 and destroying the restaurant. On 09 November, a Commission of Inquiry was appointed for an investigation on the cause of the accident; on 24 May 1972, it was concluded in a report that the welders on site and their employer, as well as the ship builder, should be held responsible, while criticising the Marine Department, Labour Department and Hong Kong Fire Services for lack of supervision. It was recommended in the report that the relevant ordinance be revised for stringent oversight to prevent similar occurrences. (Figure 192)

03 Nov 1971

Attorney General Denys Roberts proposed an amendment to the Standing Orders of the Legislative Council of Hong Kong 1968, allowing English or Cantonese be spoken in the Legislative Council. The motion was passed.

15 Nov 1971

The Big Boss grossed over HK$3 million, marking a box office record in Hong Kong. This was the first film in which Hollywood star Bruce Lee Jun-fan (李小龍) appeared after returning to Hong Kong.

19 Nov 1971

Sir Murray MacLehose took office as the 25th Governor of Hong Kong. Leaving office on 08 May 1982, he was the longest-serving governor in colonial Hong Kong.

25 Nov 1971

The seventh Bowling World Cup was held at the Four Seas Bowling Centre in Kowloon, marking the first such event in Hong Kong. American bowler Roger Dalkin won the championship.

Figure 192
A four-alarm fire with heavy smoke broke out at the Jumbo Floating Restaurant, located in the Aberdeen Typhoon Shelter, on 30 October 1971. (Photo courtesy of South China Morning Post Publishers Limited)

27 Nov 1971

The second Festival of Hong Kong was opened at Edinburgh Place, featuring over 600 cultural programmes, including exhibitions, musical, sports and school events.

01 Dec 1971

The Factories and Industrial Undertakings (Amendment) Regulations 1967 was promulgated, reducing the work hours of women and young industrial workers to no more than eight hours a day for a total of 48 hours per week.

03 Dec 1971

The Antiquities and Monuments Ordinance 1971 was promulgated, effective 01 January 1976, allowing the Antiquities Authority to declare historic monuments based on the recommendation of the Antiquities Advisory Board. It also prohibited any person from demolishing or destroying a declared monument to ensure preservation of Hong Kong's cultural relics of historical, archaeological or palaeontological value.

09 Dec 1971

The first China Homecoming Tour, organised by The Hong Kong University Students' Union, arrived in China for a 29-day trip visiting government agencies, factories, schools and historical sites and meeting with provincial and municipal officials in eight cities.

1971

The Hong Kong Subsidized Secondary Schools Council was established, aiming to promote the rights and independence of all subsidised secondary schools and the welfare and interest of staff and students in member schools.

The Hong Kong government in association with the Sir David Trench Fund for Recreation launched a pilot scheme for an expansion of outdoor facilities, including tables, seats and barbecue pits, at Shing Mun Reservoir.

William Meacham and Solomon Matthew Bard, both of the Hong Kong Archaeological Society, led an exploration at the Sham Wan site on Lamma Island. The five excavations between 1971 and 1976 unearthed iterative cultural deposits from the Neolithic period, Bronze Age and later historical periods, establishing the sequence of ancient human cultural development in Hong Kong.

05 Jan 1972

The Kowloon Stock Exchange Limited, founded by Peter Chan Po-fun (陳普芬), was opened for business as the fourth stock exchange in Hong Kong before it later merged with Hong Kong Stock Exchange.

20 Jan 1972

It was announced that the Governor in conjunction with the Executive Council had accepted in principle the recommendation outlined in the second report prepared by the Hong Kong Chinese Language Committee regarding the use of Chinese in verbal and written government communications with the public. The Director of Home Affairs was assigned to oversee the implementation of Chinese and English bilingualism.

31 Jan 1972

Jardine, Matheson & Company issued US$15 million Eurodollar warrants, tradable between February 1972 and November 1978, marking the first time that warrants were traded in Hong Kong.

Feb 1972

Construction began with the water tunnel system of High Island Reservoir under a joint venture among Hong Kong, Swedish, French and West German companies. In October, an Italian company began building the main dam, auxiliary dam and other structures.

08 Mar 1972

Huang Hua (黃華), China's permanent representative to the United Nations, wrote a letter to the Chairman of the UN Special Committee on Decolonization, stating: "Hong Kong and Macau are part of Chinese territory occupied by the British and Portuguese authorities. The settlement of the questions of Hong Kong and Macau is entirely within China's sovereign right and does not at all fall under the ordinary category of 'colonial Territories.' Consequently, they should not be included in the list of colonial Territories covered by the Declaration on the Granting of Independence to Colonial Countries and Peoples."

14 Mar 1972

The Hong Kong Immigration Department began the process of visa applications from Taiwan residents, Commonwealth of Nations citizens in Taiwan, and foreigners coming from Taiwan to Hong Kong and travelling to the United Kingdom, in place of the British Consulate in Taipei which closed on the same day. On 13 March, an agreement was reached between the United Kingdom and China in Beijing, recognising the government of the People's Republic of China as the sole legitimate government representing China, and Taiwan as a province of China. Diplomatic representatives of each side were upgraded from chargé d'affaires to ambassadors.

30 Mar 1972

The Labour Tribunal Ordinance 1972 was promulgated, effective 01 March 1973, establishing a Labour Tribunal to hear civil cases between employers and employees regarding non-payment of wages, severance payments, vacation allowances, etc. The Tribunal was designed in a way that it did not have to follow the rigorous procedures of a court; attorneys were not allowed to appear on behalf of the litigant parties.

The Offences against the Person (Amendment) Ordinance 1972 was promulgated, stipulating that a pregnant woman may have a legal abortion if two doctors agreed on the threat of mental or physical harm with continued pregnancy, followed by a government announcement on 20 October listing 11 hospitals legally allowed to perform abortions under the conditions laid out in the Ordinance.

20 Apr 1972

The government gazetted the Chinese version of the Labour Tribunal Ordinance 1972; it was the first bilingual ordinance enacted in Hong Kong. The English version was to prevail in case of any doubt or discrepancy in the two versions.

23 Apr 1972

Seawise University, founded by Tung Chao-yung (C. Y. Tung) (董浩雲), as the world's first university at sea, arrived in Hong Kong for the first time with 57 professors and 420 students on board. It fulfilled C. Y. Tung's vision of operating a university at sea and took the place of *Queen Elizabeth* which caught fire in January. (Figure 193)

Figure 193
Seawise University—the world's first university at sea. (Photo courtesy of Tung Group)

10 May 1972

The government accepted the motion passed by the Legislative Council to reconsider the revaluation policy for the renewal of government land leases. On 24 May, the government reduced the revaluation tax of land lease renewals by 20%.

13 May 1972

At 9:30 a.m., a protest in Victoria Park was held by the Hong Kong Defend Diaoyutai United Front in conjunction with the Hong Kong Action Committee for Defending the Diaoyu Islands, involving about 400 people. At 11:00 a.m., another protest organised by the Hong Kong Federation of Students took place at Edinburgh Place, involving more than 600 people who marched to the US and Japanese consulates-general with their letters of protest.

26 May 1972

The Hongkong and Shanghai Banking Corporation founded Wardley Limited to manage its business portfolio of investment banking, investment funds, corporate finance, underwriting, and mergers and acquisitions.

01 Jun 1972

Hong Kong's first detention centre for young delinquents was opened at Sha Tsui on Lantau Island. Young offenders in the centre were subject to strict discipline and manual labour to develop a sense of respect for the law and the rights of others.

The journal *Poetry* started publishing traditional and modern Chinese poetry, alongside poetry reviews; it ceased publication in June 1984.

09 Jun 1972

The Hong Kong government appointed McKinsey & Company for a special study on improving government organisation and administrative performance. The first report, submitted in November, pinpointed the lack of skilled manpower in the government as a key obstacle and emphasised the need for greater administrative efficiency. Suggestions for improvement were proposed, including strengthening the existing structure, introducing a new structure, and improving personnel management.

13 Jun 1972

The Hang Seng Bank launched its Initial Public Offering (IPO) at HK$100 per share. It closed at HK$165 on the first day in what was the first IPO of a bank in Hong Kong after the Second World War.

15 Jun 1972

A Cathay Pacific airliner en route from Singapore to Hong Kong exploded and crashed in the central part of the Republic of Vietnam (South Vietnam), killing all 81 people on board.

18 Jun 1972

The Hong Kong Observatory recorded 232.6 millimetres of rainfall on this day amid heavy thunderstorms. A total of 652.3 millimetres of rainfall were recorded between 16 and 18 June as the highest in three days on record since 1889, causing floods and landslides across Hong Kong. In the morning, 78 huts in Sau Mau Ping Grade B Licenced Area were buried in a landslide, while Blocks 8 and 9 of the Kwun Tong Resettlement Estate were also affected in a landslide, causing 71 deaths and 60 injuries. In the evening, landslides caused severe damage at multiple locations on Po Shan Road at Mid-Levels of Hong Kong Island, including the collapse of Kotewall Court and destruction of the top four floors of the newly constructed but unoccupied Greenview Gardens, resulting in 67 deaths and 20 injuries. A total of 149 people died from the single deadliest day of rainstorm on record during what became known as the June 18 Rainstorm or 1972 Rainstorm Disaster. (Figures 194 and 195)

20 Jun 1972

Tsim Sha Tsui Properties Limited, founded by Ng Teng-fong (黃廷方), was incorporated as a business in real estate development. It became a publicly listed company in Hong Kong on 20 July.

Figure 194
Severe landslides resulted from the rainstorms on 18 June 1972, flooding Kotewall Court at Mid-Levels on Hong Kong Island. (Photo courtesy of HKSAR Government)

Figure 195
Dweller huts in Sau Mau Ping were buried under mud after the rainstorms on 18 June 1972. (Photo courtesy of Post Staff Photographer/ South China Morning Post via Getty Images)

22 Jun 1972

A Commission of Inquiry, chaired by District Court judge Yang Ti-liang (T. L. Yang) (楊鐵樑), was appointed by the government to launch an investigation into the loss of lives and injuries sustained during the rainstorms of 16–18 June, particularly in Sau Mau Ping and on Po Shan Road. On 28 November, a report was submitted by the commission with a review on the causes and a list of recommendations on improvement in civil engineering, land policy, building development, and rescue operation.

23 Jun 1972

Hopewell Holdings Limited, founded by Gordon Wu Ying-sheung (胡應湘), was incorporated as a business in infrastructure and property development. It became a publicly listed company in Hong Kong on 08 August.

24 Jun 1972

At 8 p.m., Television Broadcasts Limited began a 12-hour charity show for victims of the June 18 Rainstorm, raising a record HK$9 million for disaster relief. It marked the beginning of disaster fundraisers on television.

28 Jun 1972

Amendments to the Royal Instructions were promulgated, increasing the maximum number of official members of the Legislative Council from eight to 10 (inclusive of the Governor of Hong Kong and four ex-officio members) and of unofficial members from 13 to 15. On 30 June, the government further increased the number by one official member and one unofficial member, increasing the number of seats of the Legislative Council from 26 to 28.

Siu Lam Hospital was opened as Hong Kong's first hospital for people with intellectual disabilities with a capacity of 200 patients.

06 Jul 1972

The government, following a delink of the Hong Kong dollar with the British pound, announced a link to the US dollar at an official exchange rate of HK$5.65 to US$1, followed by an updated rate of HK$5.085 to US$1 beginning February 1973.

23 Jul 1972

The Police Special Branch arrested two Chinese businessmen on suspicion of involvement in Soviet espionage. Ho Hung-yan (何鴻恩) was put into custody at Victoria Detention Centre while the other was released. On 25 August, two Soviet nationals were arrested when an espionage operation was identified by the police. The British Foreign Office immediately lodged a formal complaint with the Soviet authority. On 14 November, Ho Hung-yan was deported on a Soviet cargo vessel.

Figure 196
The Cross-Harbour Tunnel in Hung Hom was opened to traffic on 02 August 1972 in a ceremony with actress Lydia Shum Tin-ha (沈殿霞) as grand marshal in a vintage car. (Photo courtesy of Sing Tao News Corporation Limited)

02 Aug 1972

At 6 p.m., Governor of Hong Kong Sir Murray MacLehose unveiled the Cross-Harbour Tunnel, Hong Kong's first harbour-crossing tunnel, which was officially opened to traffic at 11:30 p.m. on 03 August. Drivers who drove through the tunnel that day were given a commemorative sticker. (Figure 196)

03 Aug 1972

The Hong Kong delegation participated in the fourth Paralympic Games in Heidelberg, West Germany. It was the first time Hong Kong took part in the Paralympic Games. In table tennis, Leslie Lam (林龍) won a silver medal in the men's singles and a bronze medal with Lee Koon-hung (李冠雄) in the men's doubles.

16 Aug 1972

The Keep Hong Kong Clean campaign held its opening ceremony at Hong Kong City Hall, introducing the mascot, Lap Sap Chung, a litterbug cartoon character. (Figure 197)

21 Aug 1972

The Association of Government Land & Engineering Surveying Officers was incorporated. On 24 August, it filed its first petition with the government demanding reform of the promotion system in the Public Works Department.

24 Aug 1972

The Secretary for Information as a principal coordinator of government information and public affairs was created. Director of Commerce and Industry Jack Cater was reassigned to the new post.

29 Aug 1972

The Peak Tower (with a restaurant), standing above the Peak Tram terminus on Victoria Peak, was unveiled. It was redeveloped in 1993 and was re-opened to the public on 28 May 1997. (Figure 198)

01 Sep 1972

The Public Health and Municipal Services (Amended) (No. 4) Ordinance 1972 was promulgated, allowing seizure of articles belonging to unlicenced hawkers and further confiscation under a court order. A government plan was simultaneously formulated to relocate all hawkers to designated bazaars, public markets and cooked food centres.

Figure 197
"Lap Sap Chung" (litterbug) was a feature highlight of the Keep Hong Kong Clean campaign. (Photo taken in 1975 and courtesy of Public Records Office, Government Records Service)

Figure 198
The Peak Tower was unveiled as a third-generation structure on Victoria Peak. (Photo taken in 1973 and courtesy of HKSAR Government)

Figure 199
An aerial view of Kwai Chung Container Terminals. (Photo taken in 1978 and courtesy of HKSAR Government)

05 Sep 1972

Kwai Chung Container Terminal 1 became operational as Hong Kong's first modern port of standardised container shipping. It was constructed at a cost of HK$150 million and operated by Modern Terminals Limited (founded in 1969). On the same day, the mega container ship *Tokyo Bay* arrived at Terminal 1 as the first container ship to berth at the port. In 1973, Terminals 2 and 3 were also opened. (Figure 199)

In 1972, West Germany's Munich Olympic Games came under attack by an armed Palestinian terrorist group called Black September, who took members of the Israeli Olympic team hostage at the Olympic Village. Two Hong Kong athletes were also taken but were released after Arnaldo de Oliveira Sales, Head of the Hong Kong Delegation, negotiated with the terrorists.

06 Sep 1972

A joint statement was issued by 16 groups in the education sector in protest of the government implementation of a new pay scale starting from April 1973 without prior agreement. It also called for fair remuneration and advancement for Certificated Masters and Mistresses (diploma-qualified teachers). On 16 September, a statement of objection was jointly issued by 2,000 teachers from public, subsidized and grant schools.

18 Sep 1972

A 10-day Shippers Cooperation Conference, sponsored by the UN Economic Commission for Asia and the Far East, began at Hong Kong City Hall with industry representatives from 19 countries.

Sep 1972

Rayson Huang (黃麗松) was appointed as Vice Chancellor of The University of Hong Kong, becoming the first Chinese to head the university.

02 Oct 1972

The telephone area code system was amended. Area codes originally in alphabets were replaced with numbers, namely from "O" to "12" in the New Territories, "H" to "5" on Hong Kong Island, and "K" to "3" in Kowloon. Besides the addition of area codes, telephone numbers were assigned six digits. The area code of the New Territories was changed from "12" to "0" starting 01 July 1981.

06 Oct 1972

Shun Tak Enterprises Corporation Limited, founded by Stanley Ho Hung-sun (何鴻燊), was incorporated as a conglomerate in the hotel, property and transport businesses. It became a publicly listed company in Hong Kong on 25 January 1973.

09 Oct 1972

The Hong Kong Observatory (HKO) introduced a Fire Danger Warning system to provide precautionary indication of dry conditions in two levels of risk—Yellow and Red—jointly issued by the HKO and Hong Kong Fire Services Department.

14 Oct 1972

A gas leak was found at Daimaru Department Store in Causeway Bay; an explosion occurred during an inspection by fire fighters, killing a fire fighter and a store cashier and injuring 211 passers-by and rescuers.

16 Oct 1972

Chak Nuen-fai (翟暖暉) established the monthly magazine *Wide Angle*, which was initially a journal on culture, arts, sciences and current affairs. By the mid-1970s, it became an economic and political journal on Hong Kong, Taiwan and the Mainland.

18 Oct 1972

The government released a white paper titled *Social Welfare in Hong Kong: The Way Ahead* and a proposal called *The Five-Year Plan for Social Welfare Development in Hong Kong 1973-78*, suggesting financial assistance for the elderly and people with disabilities, in addition to building more community and social services centres serving the elderly.

Governor Murray MacLehose delivered his first Policy Address in which a Ten-Year Housing Programme was put forward to improve the living environment and facilitate home ownership. The programme aimed to provide 1.8 million people with self-contained housing units at a cost of HK$3.34 billion between 1973 and 1982, in conjunction with the development of new towns in Tsuen Wan, Sha Tin and Tuen Mun. By 1987, 1.5 million people were accommodated, despite falling short of the original target by 300,000 people.

For the first time, simultaneous interpretation between English and Cantonese became available at meetings of the Legislative Council (LegCo). Legislator Chung Sze-yuen (鍾士元) was the first member to speak in Cantonese on the floor of LegCo since its establishment in 1843.

27 Oct 1972

Barclays Bank International was approved for a branch in Hong Kong by the government, marking the first banking licence issued since the Banking Ordinance 1965 was enacted to tighten restrictions.

29 Oct 1972

The TV series *Below the Lion Rock*, produced by Radio Television Hong Kong, made its debut, depicting the hard life and resilience of people in the resettlement area of Wang Tau Hom located at the southern foot of Lion Rock in Kowloon. A theme song released in 1979 bearing the name of the series by Cantopop singer Roman Tam (羅文) became a classic hit.

30 Oct 1972

Hongkong Land announced a stock-for-stock exchange with Dairy Farm Ice and Cold Storage Company Limited in an acquisition under which two shares of Hongkong Land with a par value of HK$5 were exchanged for one share of Dairy Farm Ice and Cold Storage with a par value of HK$7.50. On 14 December, Hongkong Land announced a 90% stake and acquisition of the remaining shares in accordance with the Companies Ordinance 1932. The Pokfulam Ranch under Hongkong Land was remodelled as a private housing estate named Chi Fu Fa Yuen.

06 Nov 1972

The fifth Annual Conference of the Chinese Language Press Institute began in a three-day event with a total of 110 representatives of international press associations. Sally Aw Sian (胡仙) of *Sing Tao Daily* was elected to serve as Chairman (1972–1974).

08 Nov 1972

The United Nations Resolution 2908 was adopted at the 27th General Assembly, removing Hong Kong and Macao from the list of countries in the Declaration on the Granting of Independence to Colonial Countries and Peoples as suggested by the UN Special Committee on Decolonization. On 14 December, the Permanent Representative of the United Kingdom to the UN stated in an official letter that information on Hong Kong would no longer be provided to the UN Secretariat by the United Kingdom.

The Hong Kong University Students' Union began an 11-day cultural festival. Five winners from over 300 entries were selected in a Youth Literary Competition under an adjudicating panel with Koo Siu-sun (古兆申), Li Huiying (李輝英), Xu Xu (徐訏) and Wong Kai-chee (黃繼持), etc. In 1978, a bi-monthly magazine called *Youth Literature* was co-launched by The University of Hong Kong, The Chinese University of Hong Kong, and the Youth Literary Awards Committee. It was a journal dedicated to poetry, essays, fiction and literary review and reports.

14 Nov 1972

The New Territories Small House Policy was adopted by the Governor-in-Council. Effective 01 December, indigenous male villagers over the age of 18 were made eligible for a one-time permission to build a small house no larger than 700 square feet and no taller than 25 feet in a designated village. From 29 August 1975, small houses of up to three floors were allowed.

Nov 1972

The Legislative Council was expanded to 30 members, including 15 official members and 15 unofficial members.

The journal *Ocean Literary* began publication with articles, essays, stories and literary note. It ceased publication in October 1980.

01 Dec 1972

The Medical and Health Department launched a three-year Methadone Treatment Programme at the Methadone Clinic in Sai Ying Pun under a plan to treat 550 drug abusers on a budget of HK$2.1 million.

15 Dec 1972

The Companies (Amendment) Ordinance 1972 was promulgated, effective 01 March 1973, stipulating that the prospectus of listed companies must be written in English and must be accompanied with a Chinese translation.

1972

The Curriculum Development Committee was established to formulate a syllabus for primary and secondary school, with support from a Textbook Committee and a number of Subject Committees.

01 Jan 1973

The Hong Kong Society of Accountants was established under the Professional Accountants Ordinance 1972 as a professional organisation responsible for accreditation, professional development and standards of accountants.

06 Jan 1973

The Securities Advisory Council was formed to support the formulation and enforcement of securities-related legislations and provide regulatory oversight in the stock market. John Joseph Swaine was the first Commissioner of Securities.

11 Jan 1973

The Office of the Commissioner of Banking issued a directive for a limit on stock-related bank loans.

20 Jan 1973

A group of about 40 Americans of the Vietnam Peace Committee, together with over 100 local academics, marched from Victoria Park to the US Consulate General on Garden Road in protest of the US invasion of Vietnam.

26 Jan 1973

A Board of Education, chaired by Senior Unofficial Member of the Legislative Council Woo Pak-chuen (胡百全), was established by the government in a study of secondary education over the next decade. In August, it released the *Report of the Board of Education on the Proposed Expansion of Secondary School Education in Hong Kong over the Next Decade*; public consultation on the proposal began on 01 November 1974.

02 Feb 1973

The Television (Amendment) Ordinance 1973 was promulgated, outlining detailed requirements in applying for television broadcast licences. It also required licenced TV stations to broadcast educational and government-produced news and public announcement programmes in a more regulated industry.

20 Feb 1973

The 34-storey, 1,003-room Excelsior Hotel in Causeway Bay was opened for business as the largest hotel then in Hong Kong.

26 Feb 1973

The first Hong Kong Arts Festival was opened at Hong Kong City Hall for 27 days of performances with orchestras, theatrical groups and dance troupes from all over the world.

27 Feb 1973

The three colleges of education in Hong Kong went on a one-day strike with 2,000 people to oppose a new pay scale for certificated masters and mistresses (diploma-qualified teachers). Under the Hong Kong Education Bodies' Joint Secretariat, a one-day strike took place with about 10,000 certificated masters and mistresses of government, subsidised and grant schools on 04 April; another boycott took place with 80% of primary schools on 13 April. The Joint Secretariat on 29 April decided to cancel the strike scheduled for 04 and 05 May in view of the Secondary School Entrance Examination, following the mediation of three religious leaders.

Sun Hung Kai Securities Limited, founded by Fung King-hey (馮景禧), was incorporated. It was then known as Sun Hung Kai (Private) Limited.

01 Mar 1973

The Stock Exchange Control Ordinance 1973 was promulgated, prohibiting unlicenced stock exchanges except those approved by the Governor-in-Council. Offenders were liable to a fine of HK$500,000 and an additional HK$50,000 for each day of unauthorised operation.

12 Mar 1973

Upon discovery of three counterfeit 1000-share certificates, Hopewell Holdings requested temporary suspension of trading of its shares, causing a selling run for fear of abrogation of shares. The Hang Seng Index dropped to 1,301.13 points from a peak of 1,774.96 points on 09 March. On 10 December 1974, the Hang Seng Index fell to 150.11 points, the lowest since its public debut in November 1969. It was Hong Kong's first stock market crash and known as the Crash of 1973.

13 Mar 1973

World-Wide Shipping Group and Wheelock Maritime International Limited issued a statement, announcing a joint venture forming World-Wide Wheelock Shipping Inc.

Mar 1973

The Fight Crime Committee, chaired by Secretary for Information Jack Cater, was established. Comprising senior members of the Police Force, City District Office, Government Secretariat, New Territories District Office, and Information Services Department, it was responsible for tackling the problem of violent crimes. The Fight Violent Crime campaign was launched on 14 May.

01 Apr 1973

The Urban Council was restructured and given further autonomy and financial independence. Ex-officio members by virtue of office were replaced with members of the public through election (50%) and appointment (50%); chairmen and vice chairmen were elected within the Council. Responsibilities in public sanitation, recreational and cultural services remained unchanged, funded by revenue from rental of facilities and from government rates (taxes on occupancy of property). On 10 April, an inaugural general meeting was held; Arnaldo de Oliveira Sales was elected as Chairman.

The Old Age and Disability Allowance scheme was launched for persons aged 75 or above and persons with disabilities. The monthly allowances were HK$55 and up to HK$110 for the elderly and those with disabilities, respectively.

The Hong Kong Housing Authority responsible for public housing development was reorganised under a different Chinese name. The Housing Department was formed as its executive arm to support the Ten-Year Housing Programme by merging the Resettlement Department and the Building Section of Urban Services Department. All resettlement areas and low-cost housing estates were henceforth collectively known as public housing estates.

12 Apr 1973

The Asian Composers League held its inaugural ceremony at Hong Kong City Hall.

19 Apr 1973

Nearly 400 inmates in Stanley Prison staged a protest over food and welfare issues. The Commissioner of Prisons arrived at the scene for meditation. On 20 April, in another disturbance with over 300 inmates, prison cells were vandalised; three prison guards were taken hostage. It was resolved in the evening after riot police were dispatched, followed by a meeting between the Commissioner of Prisons and prisoners.

27 Apr 1973

Cony Electronic Products Ltd, founded by Alex Au Yan-din (柯俊文), was incorporated. On 25 August 1981, it became a publicly listed company as Conic Investment Company Limited; it was one of the largest electronics companies in Hong Kong.

28 Apr 1973

The Connaught Centre in Central held its topping-out ceremony. With 50 floors and circular windows, it was Asia's tallest building upon opening. Construction under Hongkong Land began on 07 October 1971; occupancy began in December 1972. It was renamed Jardine House on 01 January 1989. (Figure 200)

03 May 1973

The last two offenders convicted in the 1967 Hong Kong Riots were released from prison.

09 May 1973

The government resumed negotiation with Hong Kong Education Bodies' Joint Secretariat regarding the pay scale of certificate-qualified teachers. It proposed that salaries be increased from HK$1,250 to HK$1,750 over a seven-year period, followed by a further increase to a maximum of HK$2,050 over the next seven-year period, in addition to shortening the timespan between starting and maximum salaries from 18 to 14 years. The proposal was accepted in a general meeting on 20 May, ending the teachers' strike.

14 May 1973

The Anti-Corruption Branch of the Police Force began an investigation of Chief Superintendent Peter Fitzroy Godber in accordance with the Prevention of Bribery Ordinance 1970. Canadian intelligence reports in April indicated suspicious movement with Godber's overseas bank account. On 11 May, Godber's request for early retirement and departure from Hong Kong was denied by the police commissioner.

23 May 1973

The second proposal by McKinsey & Company was adopted by the government with respect to establishing six policy units (economy, environment, home affairs, housing, security, and social welfare) within the Government Secretariat. Jack Cater was appointed as Director of Home Affairs; James Jeavons Robson as Secretary for the Environment; and Ian MacDonald Lightbody as Secretary for Housing.

Figure 200
The Connaught Centre became the tallest building in Central District in the 1970s. (Photo courtesy of South China Morning Post Publishers Limited)

Figure 201
Elaine Sun Wing-yan (孫泳恩) (third from right) was crowned winner in the first Miss Hong Kong Pageant. (Photo courtesy of South China Morning Post Publishers Limited)

26 May 1973

Puisne judge Geoffrey Briggs was appointed as Chief Justice of Hong Kong.

30 May 1973

The Good Citizen Award, supported by corporate donations, was established as part of the Fight Violent Crime campaign with rewards for solving crimes. The first awards were presented to three citizens on 22 June.

04 Jun 1973

The police conducted a search at the apartment of Chief Superintendent Peter Fitzroy Godber for evidence of corruption. On 08 June, Godber fled to England via Singapore on a Singapore Airlines flight.

08 Jun 1973

Gilda Fashions Limited, a wig manufacturer, announced its forthcoming closure on 08 July and terminated 1,300 workers. On 14 June, workers were denied access to the factory and sought assistance from the Labour Department. On 27 June, an agreement on a total severance package of HK$390,000 was reached.

13 Jun 1973

A Commission of Inquiry, headed by Senior Puisne Judge William Alexander "Alastair" Blair-Kerr, was established by the government to launch an investigation of Peter Fitzroy Godber's escape. He was able to leave Hong Kong just before he was to be charged with corruption. On 26 July, it was revealed in the first commission report that Godber had HK$4,377,248 in assets, roughly six times his net income between August 1952 and May 1973.

20 Jun 1973

The Secretary for Defence was renamed Secretary for Security and was put in charge of policies regarding security, emergency response, law & order, immigration, prison management, anti-narcotics and fire services. George Peter Lloyd was appointed as Acting Secretary for Security.

24 Jun 1973

Television Broadcasts Limited (TVB) hosted its first Miss Hong Kong Pageant. The final round was held at Lee Theatre and broadcast on TV for the first time. Elaine Sun Wing-yan (孫泳恩) took the crown. (Figure 201)

29 Jun 1973

The American fast-food chain Kentucky Fried Chicken opened its first branch in Mei Foo Sun Chuen as the first major foreign fast-food chain in Hong Kong.

01 Jul 1973

Zhang Shizhao (章士釗), a member of the National People's Congress Standing Committee and the Chinese People's Political Consultative Conference who was also President of the Central Research Institute of Culture and History, died of illness in Hong Kong at the age of 92. On 07 July, a public funeral service was held at the Hong Kong Funeral Home with 1,400 people in attendance. On 11 July, a special flight was arranged by the Chinese government to carry his ashes back to Beijing.

03 Jul 1973

The *Hong Kong Economic Journal,* founded by Lam Shan-muk (林山木) and his wife Lok Yau-mui (駱友梅), began publication as Hong Kong's first daily financial newspaper.

10 Jul 1973

Henderson Development Limited, a property development company founded by Lee Shau-kee (李兆基), was incorporated; it was opened for business on 21 November.

16 Jul 1973

The Hong Kong Observatory hoisted Storm Signal No. 9 for about five and a half hours amid Typhoon Dot—which caused one death and at least 30 injuries.

20 Jul 1973

Martial arts movie star Bruce Lee Jun-fan (李小龍) died unexpectedly at the age of 33. On 25 July, about 30,000 movie fans took part in a public memorial service at Kowloon Funeral Parlour. On 24 September, upon completion of an inquest, it was ruled in a magistrates' court that he died of a cerebral oedema, induced by an allergy. (Figure 202)

22 Jul 1973

A bus running between Ngong Ping and Mui Wo rolled down a slope in a crash on Keung Shan Road, Lantau Island, causing 17 deaths and 39 injuries. Helicopters were dispatched by the British Forces Overseas Hong Kong in a rescue effort.

01 Aug 1973

The Commodity Exchanges (Prohibition) Ordinance 1973 was promulgated, prohibiting the establishment of further commodity exchanges and trading of any goods specified in the Schedule, other than wet markets, wholesale marine fish markets and wholesale vegetable markets.

07 Aug 1973

Police Superintendent Ernest Hunt was formally charged with maintaining a standard of living incompatible with his remuneration between 1971 and 1973, in violation of Section 10 of the Prevention of Bribery Ordinance 1970. On 09 August, he was arraigned in the Victoria District Court; on 01 November, he was convicted and sentenced to one year in prison, becoming the first police superintendent found guilty under Section 10 of the Ordinance.

09 Aug 1973

The police uncovered a counterfeit operation of share certificates in Causeway Bay. Equipment, including offset printing presses, and more than 200 counterfeit Jardine Matheson & Co share certificates (worth about HK$3 million) were found. On 21 August, trading of Jardine, Matheson & Company shares was suspended in all four stock exchanges for 48 hours amid a police investigation. On 18 September, other counterfeit share certificates of listed companies, including Lee Hing Development, Mai Hon Enterprises, and Orient Overseas, appeared on the market.

Figure 202
Crowds of fans gathered in mourning for the death of Hollywood star Bruce Lee Jun-fan (李小龍) outside the Kowloon Funeral Parlour on 25 July 1973. (Photo courtesy of Sing Tao News Corporation Limited)

Figure 203
About 300 people held a rally to "fight corruption and arrest Godber" at Morse Park, Kowloon. (Photo taken on 02 September 1973 and courtesy of South China Morning Post Publishers Limited)

10 Aug 1973

Rediffusion Television and Commercial Television were granted 15-year wireless television licences to operate bilingual (Chinese and English) channels and Chinese channels, respectively.

16 Aug 1973

The expansion of Plover Cove Reservoir was completed, raising the height of the main dam and two auxiliary dams from 27 feet to 44 feet and the storage capacity from 37–39 billion gallons to 52 billion gallons.

18 Aug 1973

The Furama Hotel was constructed; it was opened for business on 03 December. Located at the former headquarters of Butterfield & Swire in Central, it had 32 floors, 600 rooms and a revolving restaurant on the 30th floor. The hotel was closed and demolished in November 2001.

26 Aug 1973

An estimated 500–1,000 people took part in a public rally at Victoria Park to "fight corruption and arrest Godber," organised by 13 community groups, including the Hong Kong Federation of Students, Hong Kong Federation of Catholic Students, *The 70's Biweekly*, *Daily War News*, Young Vanguard, Workers and Students United Front, and May Day Action Committee, among young workers. About 200 picketers distributed leaflets, rallying public support with a petition seeking the extradition of Peter Fitzroy Godber from the United Kingdom to Hong Kong on corruption charges; the rally ended peacefully. On 02 September, about 300 people taking part in an unapproved rally under light rain at Morse Park in Kowloon were not stopped by the police. (Figure 203)

28 Aug 1973

The six-storey, 100-bed Yan Chai Hospital became operational; it was officially opened on 24 October as a general hospital in Tsuen Wan District.

10 Sep 1973

The Post Office launched a commercial air mail and parcel service called Speedpost. Standard Chartered Bank became its first customer with London-bound mail on the same day.

22 Sep 1973

The House of 72 Tenants, a comedy adapted from a stage play of the Hong Kong Repertory Theatre, was released in a film directed by Chor Yuen (楚原) and distributed by Shaw Brothers Pictures. It was the first Cantonese film produced since 1972 and the highest-grossing film of the year in Hong Kong with revenue of over HK$5.4 million.

29 Sep 1973

Jardine Matheson made a proposal to acquire Theo H. Davies & Company, an American trading firm with businesses in the Philippines and Hawaii, in the form of a share swap worth $275 million. The transaction was concluded by the year's end in what was the first successful acquisition of a US-listed public entity by a Hong Kong-based company.

Sep 1973

The Hong Kong Youth Hostels Association was formed as a member of the International Youth Hostels Federation dedicated to international travel and inter-cultural exchange with a global network of youth hostels.

05 Oct 1973

The Education Department announced the adoption of the metric system in primary school curriculum while also retaining some English and Chinese units of measurement for practical learning and daily use.

14 Oct 1973

The first China Week—organised by the Hong Kong Federation of Students—was opened at Lee Theatre with a two-week programme of cultural events, including photo exhibitions, displays of Chinese antiquities, music and song performances, film screenings, seminars and lectures. The annual signature event, supported by the eight institutions of higher education in Hong Kong, aimed to enhance public understanding of China and was last held in 1978.

17 Oct 1973

The first night-time horse racing event in Hong Kong was held at the Happy Valley Racecourse. Tickets for all six races were sold out.

Oct 1973

The Training Council was established by the government, aiming to provide a comprehensive vocational and professional education and training. On 12 October, Ann Tse-kai (T. K. Ann) (安子介) was appointed Chairman of the Council.

01 Nov 1973

The government began the renewal of juvenile identity cards for children aged 11–18 upon the introduction of laminated identity cards. The new design was simultaneously adopted in adult identity cards on which fingerprints previously required were removed while adding the place of birth of the cardholder.

08 Nov 1973

About 5,000 metric tons of fuel leaked from the Shell oil depot in Ap Lei Chau during the night, contaminating a large sea area southwest of Hong Kong Island. On 13 November, a Commission of Inquiry was appointed by the governor for an investigation. On 10 February 1974, the commission report revealed a poor location of the depot and a crack caused by the heavy weight and pressure of fuel. It recommended more thorough review by the government before approving similar plans.

15 Nov 1973

The United Kingdom and China reached an agreement on restrictions with Mainland residents bound for Hong Kong. Arrivals immediately dropped from a daily high of over 600 to less than 100. About 46,000 people had entered Hong Kong from the Mainland so far this year.

23 Nov 1973

The third and last Festival of Hong Kong was opened in a ceremony at the Government Stadium, featuring more than 750 cultural events.

30 Nov 1973

The Betting Duty (Amendment) Ordinance 1973 was promulgated, allowing better service with off-course betting at branches of The Hong Kong Jockey Club. On 22 December, 11 branches in Hong Kong and Kowloon were opened for business, accepting bets on the Quartet.

01 Dec 1973

Rediffusion Television became a free wireless television station with Chinese and English channels. In 1982, Deacon Chiu Te-ken (邱德根) acquired Rediffusion Television and changed its name to Asia Television.

06 Dec 1973

The United Christian Hospital in Kwun Tong, founded by the Hong Kong Christian Council in conjunction with Alice Ho Miu Ling Nethersole Hospital, was opened as a general hospital equipped with 550 beds and emergency services, serving the area of Kowloon East.

07 Dec 1973

The Emergency (Control of Oil) Regulations 1973 was promulgated, effective 09 December, authorising the director of oil supplies to issue orders with respect to the storage, supply, acquisition, disposal and use of oil, as well as the supply and use of gas and electricity, amid the global oil crisis.

11 Dec 1973

The 31st Hong Kong Exhibition of Chinese Products began at Wan Chai Reclamation, featuring 1,166 exhibitors over 30 days. On 16 May 1974, discontinuation of the exhibition was announced by the Chinese Manufacturers' Association of Hong Kong, citing a lack of venue from the government. The exhibition was resumed in 1994.

28 Dec 1973

The Import and Export (General) Regulations (Amendment of First and Second Schedules) Order 1973 was promulgated, effective 01 January 1974, removing import controls on gold and diamonds and export controls on gold, diamonds and currencies.

30 Dec 1973

The Hong Kong government further tightened blackout measures, allowing commercial use of lights between 7 p.m. and 10:30 p.m. only, and suspending all floodlights at recreational and sport venues. The blackout was lifted on 24 May 1974.

The government re-introduced daylight saving time as a measure to cope with the oil crisis, advancing clocks by one hour (+ 1 hour) at 3:30 a.m. The measure ended on 20 October 1974.

Dec 1973

The Council for Recreation and Sport was established. It was an advisory body under the Home Affairs Department and Hong Kong's first official department dedicated to the development of sports under government support in collaboration with the Amateur Sports Federation and Olympic Committee of Hong Kong.

1973

The New Territories Development Department as a part of the Public Works Department was established to take charge of the New Town Programme, specifically with respect to the districts of Tsuen Wan, Sha Tin and Tuen Mun. Responsibilities included planning, compensation for land resumption, civil engineering and overall implementation.

The Hong Kong Chinese Orchestra, supported by the Urban Council, began under the conductorship of Wong Chun-tung (王震東). The first performance took place on 03 February 1974 at Hong Kong City Hall. In July 1977, under a rebrand by the Urban Council, it became Hong Kong's first professional Chinese orchestra, with Ng Tai-kong (吳大江) as conductor.

18 Jan 1974

Kerry Trading Company Limited was founded by Robert Kuok Hock-nien (郭鶴年) in Hong Kong as a headquarters for local and overseas investments.

15 Feb 1974

The Independent Commission Against Corruption Ordinance 1974 was promulgated, establishing the Independent Commission Against Corruption with Director of Home Affairs Jack Cater as its first commissioner. The ICAC was formed as an independent disciplined force and law enforcement agency directly accountable to the governor of Hong Kong, comprising an Administration Branch, Operations Department, Corruption Prevention Department and Community Relations Department. It aimed to combat corruption and promote integrity through a three-pronged strategy of enforcement, prevention and education.

The Securities Ordinance 1974 was promulgated, establishing a Securities Commission to enhance oversight of the securities market with measures starting 01 March. The Protection of Investors Ordinance 1974 was also enacted to specify penalties in relation to securities fraud. Both ordinances were designed to protect investors.

The Official Languages Ordinance 1974 was promulgated, making Chinese an official language in government communications and hearings with the Magistrates' Courts, Juvenile Court, Labour Tribunal, Tenancy Tribunal and Coroner's Court.

26 Feb 1974

The Arrangement Regarding International Trade in Textiles was signed by the British Consul in Geneva on behalf of Hong Kong, setting out restrictions on the quotas of textiles, including cotton, wool and artificial fibre.

08 Mar 1974

A 19-year-old unemployed was convicted and sentenced to a detention centre on charges of obtaining property by deception. It was the first case and conviction by the Independent Commission Against Corruption pursuant to Section 17 of the Theft Ordinance 1970.

13 Mar 1974

A white paper titled *The Problem of Dangerous Drugs in Hong Kong* was released by the government, estimating some 100,000 local drug abusers and an annual import of 35 tons of opium and 7–10 tons of morphine. It recommended stronger deterrents against drug trafficking with longer prison terms and larger fines under the Dangerous Drugs Ordinance 1969.

24 Mar 1974

The first board of directors with Szeto Wah (司徒華) as its first president was elected in the first general meeting of the Hong Kong Professional Teachers' Union, which emerged from the strike of certificate-qualified teachers.

29 Mar 1974

The District Commissioner of the New Territories was renamed "Secretary for the New Territories." Sir David Akers-Jones continued in the post responsible for new town development and issues with indigenous inhabitants as head of seven New Territories District Offices (Tai Po, Yuen Long, Tsuen Wan, Sai Kung, Sha Tin, Tuen Mun and the Outlying Islands).

02 Apr 1974

The Consumer Council under the chairmanship of Kan Yuet-keung (Y. K. Kan) (簡悅強) was established by the government for collecting, receiving and disseminating information concerning goods and services, handling public complaints and suggestions, and tendering advice to the government for protection of consumer rights. On 26 May, its authority was expanded covering all service sectors, excluding public utilities.

23 Apr 1974

As part of the United Nations' designation of the World Population Year of 1974, a World Population Conference was held at Hong Kong Hilton by the Family Planning Association of Hong Kong on the issues of local population growth.

29 Apr 1974

Hongkong Land announced a three-phase, ten-year redevelopment plan with its property in Central, namely Alexandra House, Gloucester Building, Lane Crawford House, Windsor House, Marina House and Edinburgh Building. On 07 May 1976, a topping-out ceremony was held at Alexandra House, marking the first building rebuilt under the plan.

14 May 1974

The first Hong Kong Certificate of Education Examination under the Education Department was held, following a consolidation of two examinations designed separately for Chinese- and English-curriculum schools. A total of 55,976 students took the consolidated examination; results were released on 14 August.

24 May 1974

In the afternoon, seven male and four female staff at Po Sang Bank (Mong Kok Branch) were taken hostage by a gunman in an attempted robbery; negotiation by the police was unsuccessful. It marked the first live news coverage with Television Broadcasts Limited showing live pictures every half hour and a telephone interview with the robber. The suspect was subdued by the hostages and arrested by the police the next morning. The hostages were safely evacuated and sent to a hospital for treatment.

30 May 1974

Six Form 6 students were struck by lightning at Lantau Peak while watching the sunrise. Three died and three were injured.

May 1974

The Hong Kong Police Force set up a Special Duties Unit, also known as the Flying Tigers, for responding to serious crimes and terrorism.

In Sha Tsui Village (on the High Island Reservoir construction site), ceramic shards and charred wooden boards dating back to the Ming Dynasty were unearthed by archaeologists of the Hong Kong Museum and Hong Kong Archaeological Society. From April to May 1977, wooden remnants of boats, glass beads, ancient coins and ceramic pieces from the Ming Dynasty were also found at the High Island Reservoir construction site.

02 Jun 1974

The Preventive Service intercepted a fishing boat near Cheung Chau carrying 119 illegal immigrants from South Vietnam. On 17 June, 118 of them were repatriated while one individual was allowed to stay in Hong Kong temporarily.

18 Jun 1974

Tai Chi, a Hong Kong-made replica of Han-style sailing ships, set sail from Hong Kong for South America across the Pacific Ocean in search of the historical ties of ancient China with the Americas. It crossed the Pacific Ocean by 14 September but sank in Alaskan waters on 09 October; all seven people on board were rescued but failed to reach their destination Ecuador.

28 Jun 1974

Hongkong International Terminals Ltd was incorporated in a partnership between Hongkong and Whampoa Dock Company and Kwan Yick Limited. It was to build Terminal 4 of Kwai Chung Container Terminals and became the largest operator at the terminals upon the opening of Terminal 4 in 1975.

17 Jul 1974

The government released a white paper titled *Further Development of Medical and Health Services in Hong Kong*, proposing a faculty of dentistry at The University of Hong Kong, a faculty of medicine at The Chinese University of Hong Kong, and additional hospitals and clinics in Sha Tin and Tuen Mun for an estimated cost of HK$914 million as part of a development plan of medical services for 1974–1984.

18 Jul 1974

The Hong Kong Federation of Stock Exchange was co-established by the Hong Kong Stock Exchange, Far East Exchange, Kam Ngan Stock Exchange and Kowloon Stock Exchange. Under a rotational basis with all four exchanges, Francis Zimmern, Chairman of the Hong Kong Stock Exchange, was elected the first chairman of the federation at the inaugural meeting the next day.

Jul 1974

Junior Police Call, a non-profit organisation under the Police Public Relations Branch was founded to encourage participation among teenagers in fighting crimes and promote crime prevention through television programmes and publicity campaigns.

09 Aug 1974

Officials of Hong Kong and representatives of Australia in Hong Kong reached a consensus on export restrictions regarding five types of garments from Hong Kong to Australia, effective 01 July.

16 Aug 1974

The Lands Tribunal Ordinance 1974 was promulgated, effective 01 December, establishing a Lands Tribunal for legal cases involving government compensation with respect to land resumption, reclamation, street modification, rates and land taxes.

The Companies (Amendment) Ordinance 1974 was promulgated, stipulating annual filing of accounts and directors' reports with the Companies Registry by auditors of private companies, including a true balance sheet and income statement as well as any information regarding the balance sheet, company status, share issue, and changes in fixed assets as outlined in the directors' report.

19 Aug 1974

An opening ceremony was held to mark the completion of a 25-mile water tunnel of the High Island Reservoir linking to the Lower Shing Mun Reservoir and Sha Tin Water Treatment Works.

23 Aug 1974

The Employment (Amendments) (No. 3) Ordinance 1974 was promulgated, granting the right to severance pay among manual labourers and non-labour employees (earning less than HK$2,000 monthly) under two or more years of continuous employment upon layoffs with no fault of their own.

04 Sep 1974

The Hong Kong Technical Teachers' College, founded by the Education Department, was opened as a dedicated teacher training institution in place of the Morrison Hill Technical Institute.

20 Sep 1974

Financial Secretary Philip Haddon-Cave indicated a need to borrow HK$2 billion amid an expected deficit in the next few years. On 24 September, the government drew on the reserves deposited in the United Kingdom to cover the fiscal deficit.

30 Sep 1974

Agreements on textile trade with the United States and Canada were simultaneously signed by the Hong Kong government, taking effective the following day. The overall US quotas on Hong Kong exports were to be raised, along with adjustable quotas on products of cotton and man-made fibre, over a three-year period. Canadian restrictions on cotton yarn, cotton towels and some cotton woven garments made in Hong Kong were lifted.

Sep 1974

The Visual Arts Society was formed by graduates of The University of Hong Kong's Department of Extra-Mural Studies, including Aser But (畢子融), Eddie Lui (呂豐雅), and Gaylord Chan (陳餘生). In 1994, it was renamed Hong Kong Visual Arts Society.

03 Oct 1974

The 12th Commonwealth Press Conference commenced as a three-day event with 124 representatives from 17 Commonwealth Nations in the first meeting held in Hong Kong, focusing on industry challenges and issues regarding press freedom and journalism.

05 Oct 1974

An induction ceremony was held at the High Court with Kenneth Kwok Hing-wai (郭慶偉) as the first graduate of HKU's Faculty of Law admitted for law practise in Hong Kong.

16 Oct 1974

A paper titled *Secondary Education in Hong Kong over the Next Decade* was submitted by the government to the Legislative Council, stating a goal of implementing nine years of free education for local children by 1979.

19 Oct 1974

The Hong Kong Observatory hoisted Storm Signal No. 9 for five and a half hours amid Typhoon Carmen. One person died; 16 were injured; and five ocean-going vessels sustained damage.

Oct 1974

Mei Tung Estate in Wong Tai Sin, Kowloon was completed as the first public housing estate developed by the Housing Authority.

01 Nov 1974

The Cheung Sha Wan Temporary Wholesale Poultry Market became operational with both imported or locally raised live chickens.

12 Nov 1974

The Police Narcotics Bureau conducted raids in more than 10 locations and arrested Ng Sik-ho (吳錫豪) (nicknamed Limpy Ho), an international drug lord and restaurant owner, on Kent Road in Kowloon Tong. He was charged with trafficking morphine and raw opium into Hong Kong between 01 January 1967 and 12 November 1974. On 15 May 1975, following a trial in the High Court, he and his assistant named Ng Chun-kwan (吳振坤) were sentenced to 30 and 25 years in prison, respectively, while seven other defendants were given between 7 and 15 years of prison terms. On 14 August 1991, Ng Sik-ho was released upon a special pardon granted by the governor of Hong Kong.

25 Nov 1974

The Hong Kong government announced that the Hong Kong dollar would be delinked from the US dollar and allowed to float freely amid a weakening US dollar.

26 Nov 1974

The China PR National Football Team won 5–2 in an exhibition game with Hong Kong League XI at the Government Stadium during its first visit to Hong Kong. The game was broadcast by Television Broadcasts Limited.

30 Nov 1974

A Hong Kong–Guangdong immigration agreement came into effect with repatriation of illegal immigrants upon entry. However, they were allowed to stay if they reached an urban centre (south of Boundary Street) and found accommodation with their relatives or otherwise in what became known as the Touch Base policy. On the first day, five illegal immigrants arriving at Tung Ping Chau were caught and repatriated to the Mainland via Man Kam To.

17 Dec 1974

The body of 16-year-old Pin Yuk-ying (卞玉瑛) was found in a cardboard box discarded on Wong Nai Chung Road in Happy Valley. On 03 November 1975, Au-yeung Ping-keung (歐陽炳強) was convicted of murder by the High Court and sentenced to death but was later commuted to life imprisonment. It was Hong Kong's first murder conviction based solely on circumstantial and scientific evidence.

1974

The government amended the *Colony Outline Plan* of 1970 based on the results of the 1971 census; it was renamed the *Hong Kong Outline Plan*. It served as an official guide to urban planning comprising two major parts, namely planning standards and development strategies. In 1979, it was approved and adopted by the Land Development Policy Committee.

The University of Hong Kong's Hung On-To Memorial Library was established as the world's largest library dedicated to materials on Hong Kong.

06 Jan 1975

The opening ceremony of the Clean Hong Kong Campaign of 1975, sponsored by the Urban Council, took place at Hong Kong City Hall. The Keep Hong Kong Clean Campaign Committee dubbed it the Year of Cleanliness with a new bunny mascot named "Siu Pak To" in a publicity drive for youngsters.

07 Jan 1975

Retired Chief Superintendent Peter Fitzroy Godber was extradited back to Hong Kong from the United Kingdom on charges of corruption under the escort of Independent Commission Against Corruption officers. On 17 February, he appeared before Judge Yang Ti-liang (楊鐵樑) in the Victoria District Court. On 25 February, Peter Fitzroy Godber was found guilty on two counts of corruption, sentenced concurrently to four years in prison on each count and ordered to pay back HK$25,000 of bribe.

13 Jan 1975

The Hong Kong deputies of the Guangdong delegation to the National People's Congress attended the First Session of the Fourth National People's Congress in Beijing as part of the Guangdong delegation. The number of Hong Kong deputies increased from two to 14.

20 Jan 1975

The Pik Uk Prison on Clear Water Bay Road was opened with a capacity of 600 people in a total of 12 dormitories divided into two blocks. It was also Hong Kong's first correctional centre housing 400 young offenders.

26 Jan 1975

The first McDonald's in Hong Kong was opened on Paterson Street in Causeway Bay; it was operated by McDonald's Restaurants (Hong Kong) Limited, a joint venture between Hong Kong businessmen, including Daniel Ng Yat-chiu (伍日照), and US-based McDonald's Corporation.

30 Jan 1975

Xi Xi (西西) began to serialise her novel *My City* in the *Express Daily* under her penname Ah Kwo (阿果). The serial was concluded on 30 June and was released as a stand-alone edition in 1979.

01 Feb 1975

The first Hong Kong Art Biennial Exhibition was launched under the Hong Kong Museum of Art as an open platform for local artists to showcase their work. In 2012, it was reorganised as the Hong Kong Contemporary Art Biennial Awards.

04 Feb 1975

The Botanic Garden in Central was renamed Hong Kong Zoological and Botanical Gardens. New aviary and mammal enclosures were opened for public viewing on 25 February.

07 Feb 1975

The Child Care Centres Ordinance 1975 was promulgated, establishing regulations on childcare services with respect to the fire and safety standards of facilities and professional qualifications of teachers.

A Commission of Inquiry was appointed by the governor to examine the status of Hong Kong Telephone Company Ltd following an application for charge increases. In the commission report released on 19 November, a 30% charge increase effective 01 March 1975 was agreed, subject to a reduction in telephone installation and relocation fees. The Commission also made 34 recommendations, including the appointment of officials to the board of directors, implementation of a control scheme, and allocation of profits to a development fund; most were adopted by the government.

14 Feb 1975

The Hong Kong Federation of Students began its three-day 17th Annual General Meeting. Issues for discussion included global perspectives, further engagement with the Mainland and students' rights.

25 Feb 1975

The Yim Tso Ha egretry in Sha Tau Kok in conjunction with the Shing Mun Fung Shui Woodlands became the first "Sites of Special Scientific Interest" in Hong Kong.

08 Mar 1975

Nine people (including a pregnant woman) were killed in an arson attack as a man set fire after locking up an apartment at Kin Tak House on Hip Wo Street in Kwun Tong. The suspect was arrested on the same day. He was found guilty of arson and murder and was sentenced to death by the High Court on 23 December; he was commuted to life in prison in November 1976.

11 Mar 1975

Bell Yung (榮鴻曾), a scholar in association with The Chinese University of Hong Kong, began recording songs by blind Naamyam singer Dou Wun (杜煥) at Fu Long Teahouse in Sheung Wan. During a three-month period, he recorded a total of 42 tracks from 16 repertoires, a collection deemed important to the preservation of the Naamyam culture.

14 Mar 1975

The Urban Council drew up the first "Hawker Permitted Places" in Hong Kong under the Hawker (Urban Council) By-laws 1972, covering 20 road sections in Kowloon where hawking was allowed activities during specified hours each day. (Figure 204)

Figure 204
The hawker permitted areas on Tung Choi Street in Mong Kok. (Photo taken in 1977 and courtesy of C. Y. Yu/South China Morning Post via Getty Image)

01 Apr 1975

The Bank of East Asia in conjunction with the Bank of America jointly issued the BEA-BOA Credit Card, making it the first Hong Kong-dollar credit card issued in Hong Kong.

04 Apr 1975

The *Spiranthes hongkongensis* plant was first discovered in Hong Kong by botanists Hu Shiu-ying (胡秀英) and Gloria Barretto.

13 Apr 1975

The Hong Kong Federation of Education Workers was established with its first general meeting under the presidency of Ng Hong-mun (吳康民). It aimed to promote the development of education.

14 Apr 1975

A group of 10 Kuomingtang (KMT) war criminals, under amnesty granted by the Supreme People's Court on 19 March, arrived in Hong Kong from Beijing with the plan of moving to Taiwan. On 29 April, at least six applied for entry to Taiwan through the Chinese Association for Relief and Ensuing Services. Following the suicide of Zhang Tieshi (張鐵石) on 04 June, others went on to live in the Mainland, Hong Kong and the US. The group of 10 was the last of 293 KMT war criminals given amnesty by the Chinese government.

04 May 1975

Queen Elizabeth II, accompanied by her husband, Prince Philip, Duke of Edinburgh, arrived in Hong Kong in the first visit by a British monarch. Over three days, she visited a public housing estate in Kowloon, made a tour at HKU, CUHK, Hong Kong City Hall and Happy Valley Racecourse, and officiated at the opening ceremony of Hung Hom Terminus. A statement was previously issued on 30 April by The University of Hong Kong Students' Union, calling for a boycott of the Queen's visit as head of a colonial power. (Figure 205)

The Denmark-registered cargo vessel *Clara Maersk*, carrying about 4,600 South Vietnamese refugees, arrived at Kwai Chung Container Terminal. The refugees were lodged in three barracks in the New Territories, marking the first group under formal arrangement by the Hong Kong government and the beginning of an influx of Vietnamese refugees.

09 May 1975

The Mass Transit Railway Corporation Ordinance 1975 was promulgated, replacing the Mass Transport Provisional Authority with the Mass Transit Railway Corporation which was formally established on 26 September as an entity wholly owned by the government.

18 Jul 1975

The Landlord and Tenant (Consolidation) (Amendment) (No. 3) Ordinance 1975 was promulgated, prohibiting pre-sale of projected flats by property developers before an exemption order was issued by the Land Office; property developers were otherwise subject to buyer compensation.

The Hong Kong Museum of History at Star House in Tsim Sha Tsui was opened as Hong Kong's first public museum. It came as a spinoff of the Hong Kong Art Gallery and Museum established in 1962 at Hong Kong City Hall.

Jul 1975

Lek Yuen Estate, built by the Housing Authority, was opened for occupancy. It was the first public housing estate in the new town of Sha Tin. (Figure 206)

01 Aug 1975

The Labour Relations Ordinance 1975 was promulgated, authorising the Commissioner for Labour to investigate labour disputes and facilitate settlement through negotiation, conciliation or arbitration. The Governor-in-Council could impose a 30-day cool-off period on either party as deemed necessary by the Commissioner to minimise the socio-economic impact of industrial actions.

Figure 205
Queen Elizabeth II on Graham Street in Central during her visit to Hong Kong in 1975. (Photo courtesy of George Freston/Fox Photos/Getty Images)

Figure 206
The Amah Rock (left) in the 1980s against the background of Sha Tin New Town. (Photo courtesy of Special Collections, The University of Hong Kong Libraries)

01 Aug 1975

The Betting Duty (Amendment) (No. 2) Ordinance 1975 was promulgated, establishing the Hong Kong Lotteries Board to issue new cash lotteries in place of the government lotteries and Hong Kong Jockey Club (HKJC) betting tickets. After tax, 80% of proceeds were allocated to the prize pool from which HKJC operating costs were drawn; remaining profits were returned to the lotteries fund.

15 Aug 1975

The Objectionable Publications Ordinance 1975 was promulgated, banning publications of obscene, indecent, repulsive or other objectionable material. It also forbade portrayal or depiction (in text or otherwise) provoking criminal acts, sexual assaults, violence, cruelty, torture, terror, contempt of law enforcement or self-depravation with juveniles.

Aug 1975

The twenty-cent and two-dollar coins went into circulation, followed by the five-dollar coin in August 1976.

01 Sep 1975

The Mark Six lottery, launched by the Hong Kong Lotteries Board and managed by The Hong Kong Jockey Club, made its debut. To win first prize, it took six numbers in the exact order they were drawn from a total of 14 numbers at a cost of HK$10 for each bet. The first draw took place on 05 September without a first prize winner under a betting turnover of HK$648,000. This iteration of the Mark Six held its 52nd and final draw on 09 July 1976.

The Hong Kong Convention Centre in Causeway Bay was unveiled. It became a major exhibition venue equipped with a parking lot, offices and the Palace Theatre Banquet Hall; it occupied six floors at the World Trade Centre redeveloped in the same year.

The 1975 Asia-Pacific Conference of the International Federation of Social Workers was held in Hong Kong with 387 participants from 22 countries and international organisations on the issues of social planning and urban development.

07 Sep 1975

Commercial Television (CTV), founded by Commercial Television Limited as the third free-to-air TV station in Hong Kong, broadcast its first programme *Greeting Programme to CTV* in the afternoon, followed by a special CTV Variety Show in the evening. The station was required to broadcast two hours of non-commercial programmes every evening from Monday to Friday as part of the licence agreement.

10 Sep 1975

The Industrial Investment Promotion Committee, chaired by the Secretary for Economic Services, was established by the government to liaise with the Commerce and Industry Department, Trade Development Council, and Hong Kong General Chamber of Commerce.

14 Oct 1975

The Hong Kong Observatory hoisted Hurricane Signal No. 10 for about three hours amid Typhoon Elsie—which left 46 people injured and seven ocean-going vessels and three fishing boats damaged.

15 Oct 1975

The desalination plant at Lok On Pai in Castle Peak became operational. It was built at a cost of approximately HK$480 million and was the world's largest at the time with a maximum daily capacity of 40 million gallons of fresh water (roughly 10%–15% of total local consumption). Seawater was turned into fresh water and stored at the Tai Lam Chung Reservoir. On 16 May 1982, it ceased operations; on 15 November 1992, it was demolished by a blasting method used for the first time in Hong Kong. (Figure 207)

20 Oct 1975

Princess Margaret Hospital in Lai Chi Kok was opened with an infectious diseases ward of 162 beds before it became fully operational with 1,300 beds. The Lai Chi Kok Hospital was converted from a hospital for infectious diseases into a convalescent hospital for people with chronic psychiatric illnesses and those suffering from leprosy.

24 Oct 1975

Thumb Weekly, a comprehensive literary journal, began publication; its last issue was published on 25 February 1987.

03 Nov 1975

The 15.6-kilometre MTR Modified Initial System, connecting Central and Kwun Tong, commenced construction on a HK$5.65 billion budget. It had 12 underground and three overhead stations running through the residential and industrial areas in Central and Kowloon.

Figure 207
The desalination plant at Lok On Pai in Castle Peak. (Photo taken in 1977 and courtesy of P. Y. Tang/South China Morning Post via Getty Images)

21 Nov 1975

The Inland Revenue (Amendment) (No. 6) Ordinance 1975 was promulgated, effective 01 April 1976, establishing an independent property tax register and introducing a reformed property tax based on assessable value instead of rateable value to bring it in line with market value.

26 Nov 1975

A two-day sea trade conference began at Hong Kong Convention Centre with 500 participants from 28 countries and regions.

29 Nov 1975

The Tsim Sha Tsui Terminus was decommissioned after its last northbound passenger train departed at 2:15 p.m., only the Clock Tower remained as a landmark. The new Hung Hom Terminus of the Kowloon-Canton Railway became operational the following day.

01 Dec 1975

A three-day international shipping conference, organised by the International General Chamber of Commerce, began in Hong Kong with more than 70 local and overseas participants on the future and challenges of the shipping industry.

19 Dec 1975

The Supreme Court Ordinance 1975 was promulgated, reconstituting the Supreme Court with the addition of the Court of Appeal and the Court of First Instance effective 20 February 1976. The Supreme Court also amended its legal Chinese name.

1975

The Education Department implemented a vetting process with primary school syllabus under which textbooks must be reviewed by the Curriculum Development Committee before they could be adopted in the Recommended Textbook List. For use of any textbook not included on the list, schools must apply for permission with the Education Department.

The Family Planning Association of Hong Kong launched the new slogan "Two is Enough," calling for a maximum of two children per family in a publicity campaign regarding birth control and population growth with ads on three local television stations.

01 Jan 1976

The Buildings Ordinance Office under the Public Works Department began accepting building plans in both metric and English units. From 01 April 1977, all building plans were formulated in metric units.

The Antiquities Advisory Board was established under the Antiquities and Monuments Ordinance 1971 as a statutory body and advisor to the Antiquities Authority on matters concerning antiquities and monuments. The Antiquities and Monuments Office was established in the same year.

07 Jan 1976

For Leung Wing-sang (梁榮生) who was sentenced to 20 years in prison for a homicide on 19 July 1973, his lawyer filed for a retrial under the claim that Leung only pleaded guilty on misguided advice from the police. On 06 February, a Commission of Inquiry was appointed by the Governor-in-Council after a consultation with the Attorney General, launching an investigation on whether Leung's arrest and prosecution involved any unjust or coercive interrogation. On 25 June, it was concluded in the investigation that Leung was not falsely accused and that there was no unjust prosecution or interrogation.

09 Jan 1976

The Deposit-taking Companies Ordinance 1976 was promulgated, requiring deposit-taking companies to register with the Commissioner of Banking. They must show a registered capital of no less than HK$5 million and paid-up capital of no less than HK$2.5 million. They were also forbidden from taking public deposits of less than HK$50,000 or providing savings and current account services.

09 Jan 1976

In memory of Premier Zhou Enlai (周恩來), who passed away the day before, flags were flown at half-mast at the Hong Kong Branch of Xinhua News Agency and Bank of China, as well as Hong Kong government institutions including the Government House, in addition to business organisations, including Hongkong and Shanghai Banking Corporation and Standard Chartered Bank, and newspaper bureaus, schools and community organisations. On 14 January, a memorial service organised by the Hong Kong Branch of Xinhua News Agency was held at the Bank of China building where about 20,000 Hong Kong citizens and foreign nationals paid their respects. (Figure 208)

23 Jan 1976

The Wild Animals Protection Ordinance 1976 was promulgated, establishing a list of protected wild animals and restricted areas in Hong Kong, including the *fung shui* woodlands at Yim Tso Ha Tsuen in Sha Tau Kok and the marshes in Mai Po. On 08 August 1980, an amendment to the ordinance was promulgated, prohibiting unauthorised hunting in Hong Kong effective 01 January 1981.

01 Feb 1976

The government stipulated that a land premium be paid by sellers when houses less than five years old under the Small House Policy were sold to non-indigenous residents. On 15 November 1977, all applications for small houses in Sai Kung were suspended by the New Territories District Office on the grounds that they violated the spirit of the Small House Policy. On 17 August 1978, following a meeting between the Secretary for the New Territories and representatives of Heung Yee Kuk, it was determined that land premiums be paid when selling small houses less than five years old and built on private land under a building licence, as well as small houses built on government land under private arrangement regardless of the age of the small house.

A five-alarm fire broke out in the squatter area at Aldrich Bay in Shau Kei Wan. More than 500 huts caught fire, affecting over 3,000 people. Two firemen and 10 residents sustained injuries.

09 Feb 1976

A seven-day meeting on multilateral trade, organised by the Economic and Social Commission for Asia and the Pacific under the British Foreign and Commonwealth Office, began in Hong Kong with representatives from about 20 developing countries. The negotiation focused on free trade in accordance with the General Agreement on Tariffs and Trade; it was Hong Kong's first time holding such a meeting.

Figure 208
People paid their respect in memory of Premier Zhou Enlai (周恩來) at the Bank of China building on 14 January 1976. (Photo courtesy of South China Morning Post Publishers Limited)

15 Feb 1976

Cheng Yuet-ying (鄭月英), wife of narcotics syndicate leader Ng Sik-ho (吳錫豪), was charged with two counts of conspiracy in drug trafficking. On 23 February, following a trial in the Supreme Court, she was sentenced to 16 years in prison and a record fine of HK$1 million payable within a year.

17 Feb 1976

The Silent Revolution premiered on Rediffusion Television (RTV) as the first drama series produced by the Independent Commission Against Corruption. The first episode was titled *Breakers.*

18 Feb 1976

The Waterfall Bay Park in Pok Fu Lam, managed by the Urban Council, was unveiled. Waterfall Bay was named one of eight most scenic views of Xin'an County in both the 1688 and 1819 editions of the *Xin'an County Local Chronicles.*

Feb 1976

Literature and Art began publication as a journal devoted to literary and artistic creation through special features, reviews and interviews. On 01 April 1977, it was renamed *Literature and Art Monthly*; on 10 March 1978, its last issue (Issue 12) was released.

02 Mar 1976

A seven-day conference organised by the International Planned Parenthood Federation began in Hong Kong with 47 representatives from 10 countries. It was Hong Kong's first time hosting such a meeting.

12 Mar 1976

The Country Parks Ordinance 1976 was promulgated, effective 16 August, establishing regulations on country parks and special areas. The Country and Marine Parks Board and the Country and Marine Parks Authority (chaired by the Director of Agriculture and Fisheries) were also established.

19 Mar 1976

The Hong Kong Institution of Engineers was founded as a professional body representing engineers and responsible for accreditation.

28 Mar 1976

Twelve teams took part in the first Hong Kong Rugby Sevens at the Hong Kong Football Club Stadium. Team New Zealand won the championship.

30 Mar 1976

The Hong Kong Teresa Teng Fan Club was established as the first pop singer fan club in Hong Kong.

09 Apr 1976

The Independent Commission Against Corruption (Amendment) Ordinance 1976 was promulgated, authorising ICAC officers to put suspects under immediate arrest and search premises upon a search warrant issued by a court of law.

12 Apr 1976

Commercial Television premiered its martial arts drama series *The Legend of the Condor Heroes*, a first TV adaption of novels authored by Louis Cha Leung-yung (查良鏞).

12 May 1976

The Hong Kong Air Cargo Terminal at Kai Tak Airport became operational with a fully automated system capable of handling 450,000 tons of cargo every year. On 21 March 1984, Hong Kong Air Cargo Terminal Phase II was also opened, bringing the annual cargo handling capacity to 680,000 tons.

16 May 1976

The Beijing Tiananmen forum was held in Victoria Park with over 100 members of four youth groups, namely Young Militant, Youth Socialist Group, Daily Combat Bulletin, and 70s Front, in solidarity with those arrested during the Tiananmen Incident in Beijing on 05 April. The forum attracted hundreds of onlookers; three people in disagreement with the organisers and suspected of threatening the press were detained by the police.

17 May 1976

The four-day third Community Chest Conference began in Hong Kong with 80 international representatives. It was Hong Kong's first time hosting such event.

The first Asian Amateur Singing Contest, organised by Rediffusion Television, held its final at the Palace Theatre. Of 11 contestants from around Asia, Lo Wai-cheong (盧維昌) of Hong Kong won the competition. The contest was last held in 1981.

02 Jun 1976

The first Hong Kong International Dragon Boat Race was held in the waters near Shau Kei Wan. The Nagasaki Peiron Dragon Boat Team of Japan was invited to compete with the Hong Kong Dragon Boat Team.

07 Jul 1976

In memory of Zhu De (朱德), Chairman of the National People's Congress Standing Committee who passed away the day before, flags were flown at half-mast at the Hong Kong Branch of Xinhua News Agency and Bank of China, as well as Hong Kong government institutions including the Government House, in addition to business organisations, including Hongkong and Shanghai Banking Corporation and Standard Chartered Bank, and newspaper bureaus, schools and community organisations. On 11 July, a memorial service organised by the Hong Kong Branch of Xinhua News Agency was held at the Bank of China building and attended by about 18,000 people.

09 Jul 1976

The Metrication Ordinance 1976 was promulgated, requiring the adoption of metric units in all legislations.

The Employment (Amendment) Ordinance 1976 was promulgated, effective 01 January 1977, increasing employees' annual statutory holidays from six to 10 days.

The revamped Mark Six lottery was launched with the first scheduled draw on 13 July. The first prize was won by picking six numbers drawn from 36 numbers. The numbers were drawn by the statutory body Hong Kong Lotteries Board, while bets were placed with The Hong Kong Jockey Club (HKJC). The Mark Six is the only legal lottery in Hong Kong and has been operated solely by HKJC Lotteries Limited since 2003.

11 Jul 1976

The 25th Miss Universe Grand Final was held at Lee Theatre where Miss Israel took the crown in a beauty pageant of 72 contestants. It was the first and only Miss Universe pageant ever held in Hong Kong.

12 Jul 1976

Chinese detective Sergeant Tai Fook (戴福) of the New Territories was convicted of possessing wealth disproportionate to his official position. He was sentenced to six years in prison and fined HK$100,000; HK$5.16 million in assets disproportionate to his income was confiscated.

06 Aug 1976

The Commodities Trading Ordinance 1976 was promulgated, establishing a Commodities Exchange and a Commodity Trading Commission to govern the trading of commodities futures and registration of dealers, trading advisors and representatives. The Hong Kong Commodity Exchange under the chairmanship of Peter Scales was established on 17 December and granted a government licence on 03 May 1977.

10 Aug 1976

The Police Narcotics Bureau conducted raids in 23 places across Kowloon and the New Territories, finding HK$20,000 worth of drugs and arresting eight people, including syndicate leader Chan Man-chiu (陳文超), nicknamed Sha Chan Chiu, meaning "cocky Chiu." On 25 May 1977, following a trial in the Supreme Court, he was found guilty of conspiracy in drug trafficking and sentenced to 18 years in prison. Four other defendants were also convicted and sentenced to 11 to 13 years in prison.

11 Aug 1976

The fourth-generation General Post Office Building at Connaught Place in Central was inaugurated. It was equipped with service counters, post office boxes, a sorting centre and a delivery office. (Figure 209)

18 Aug 1976

The eight-day Chinese Congress on World Evangelization under the theme "Renewal of Mission" was held at Kowloon City Baptist Church and attended by some 1,600 church leaders from 27 dioceses in what was the first international Christian conference ever organised by Chinese Christians.

Figure 209
The fourth-generation General Post Office Building at Connaught Place in Central. (Photo taken in 1980 and courtesy of HKSAR Government)

25 Aug 1976

Blocks 9, 15 and 16 of Lower Sau Mau Ping Estate sustained heavy damage from a landslide amidst heavy rain, resulting in 18 deaths. An Independent Review Panel comprising international experts was appointed by the governor for an investigation on the cause of the incident, especially in relation to fill slopes. On 10 February 1977, a panel report was released, concluding that the fill slopes were inadequately compacted causing a large amount of rainwater infiltration. Government compensation was provided to the victims, including those of the June 18 Rainstorm in 1972. A department dedicated to slope management and maintenance was formed to start remedial work on 11 slopes.

26 Aug 1976

The amendments to the Royal Instructions were promulgated, increasing the number of Unofficial Members of the Legislative Council from 15 to 23 and the number of Official Members from 10 to 18, excluding the governor and four other ex-officio members. Eight unofficial members and five official members were appointed by the governor on the same day, including Kowloon Motor Bus (KMB) Operations Director Wong Lam (王霖) as the first councillor of grassroots backgrounds. Other unofficial members included Lydia Selina Dunn (鄧蓮如) and Henry Hu Hung-lick (胡鴻烈). Beginning 01 September, the actual number of official members increased from 10 to 15 and the unofficial members from 15 to 22.

The Hong Kong government renamed its Colonial Secretary and Colonial Secretariat as Chief Secretary and Government Secretariat, respectively, in a bid to minimise the colonial nature of official titles.

01 Sep 1976

Catherine Joyce Symons (C. J. Symons), an Unofficial Member of the Legislative Council, became the first woman to serve on the Executive Council of Hong Kong.

09 Sep 1976

In memory of Mao Zedong (毛澤東), Chairman of the Central Committee of the Communist Party of China and Chairman of the Central Military Commission of the Communist Party of China, who passed away in Beijing on this day, flags were flown at half-mast for two consecutive days at the Hong Kong Branch of Xinhua News Agency and Bank of China, in addition to newspaper bureaus, schools and community organisations. The next day, flags were also flown at half-mast at Hong Kong government institutions, including the Government House; six cinemas were closed in mourning. On 16 September, a memorial service organised by the Hong Kong Branch of Xinhua News Agency was held at the Bank of China building, with 27,000 people in attendance, including Governor Murray MacLehose.

25 Sep 1976

Cosmos Books Limited was founded as a book publishing and retail business.

30 Sep 1976

The magazine *City* was founded by writer Chan Koon-chung (陳冠中) as a journal on lifestyle, culture and art.

The two-day Commonwealth Finance Ministers Meeting began at Hong Kong Convention Centre with 34 finance ministers and 164 delegates of different countries for a discussion on British pound reserves, commodity trading and the foreign debt of developing countries.

01 Oct 1976

The Small Claims Tribunal commenced operations as an arbitration platform for money claims of HK$3,000 or less under procedures different from ordinary courts whereby lawyers would not appear on behalf of litigant parties before the tribunal.

06 Oct 1976

The government-sponsored Home Ownership Scheme was launched to support home purchases among public housing tenants as well as low- and middle-income families by building 30,000 home units (5,000 units per year).

12 Oct 1976

Video Technology Limited, founded by Allan Wong (黃子欣) and Stephen Leung (梁棪華), was incorporated. It later became the world's largest manufacturer of e-learning products for infants, toddlers and pre-schoolers.

13 Oct 1976

A government white paper titled *The Further Development of Rehabilitation Services in Hong Kong* was released, recommending more services for people with disabilities and rehabilitation among school children with special needs upon early screening. On 12 October 1977, another government white paper titled *Integrating the Disabled into the Community: A United Effort* was released, proposing nine years of regular school education for disabled children and more school and vocational training places for those with special educational needs.

19 Oct 1976

The Jumbo Floating Restaurant in Aberdeen was opened for business. The three-storey restaurant built and decorated in the style of a Chinese palace could accommodate up to 2,000 diners.

29 Oct 1976

The Government Secretariat established a Monetary Affairs Branch in charge of government assets, debts, currency, foreign exchange and monetary policy. Director of the Treasury Douglas William Blye was appointed as Acting Secretary for Monetary Affairs.

05 Nov 1976

The Independent Commission Against Corruption issued a warrant for the arrest of former police sergeant Lui Lok (呂 樂) for allegedly possessing assets worth $500 million, disproportionate to his official income, in violation of Section 10 of the Prevention of Bribery Ordinance 1970. He died in Canada in 2010 having been "wanted" for 34 years.

10 Nov 1976

The first Festival of Asian Arts was hosted by the Urban Council, featuring an exhibition of works by Asian artists, as well as dance, music and drama performances by arts groups in Asia. The festival was held annually until 1988 and then biennially before it ended in 1998.

15 Nov 1976

The monthly magazine *Choice* was launched by the Consumer Council to facilitate informed choices among consumers by disseminating test results and surveys on products and services as the world's first Chinese-language consumer magazine.

26 Nov 1976

The Employment (Amendment) (No. 2) Ordinance 1976 was promulgated, effective 02 January 1976, mandating a rest day for every seven days (instead of four rest days per month) for all manual labourers and non-labour employees (earning less than HK$2,000 a month), thereby increasing the total number of required rest days from 48 to 52 days a year.

16 Dec 1976

The first residential building in Taikoo Shing, a development project at a former dockyard and sugar factory by Swire Properties, was completed. It was the first large-scale private housing estate on Island East, totalling 12,968 home units in 61 buildings.

22 Dec 1976

The first flight carrying 177 Hong Kong residents stranded in Vietnam arrived in Hong Kong. By 07 April 1979, a total of 32 special flights had been arranged by the government to pick up 4,782 Hong Kong residents; 5,827 residents returned from Ho Chi Minh City via Bangkok on Air France flights.

Dec 1976

The *Compass* was founded as a periodical for poems written by Hong Kong poets as well as translated poems of different languages. It ceased publication in December 1978.

1976

Private development of permanent cemeteries was halted in favour of cremation by the government.

A stone carving with a zoomorphic motif was discovered on Kau Sai Chau in Sai Kung. In 1979, it was declared a monument by the Antiquities and Monuments Office.

06 Jan 1977

Retired police sergeant Lai Man-yau (黎民佑) was questioned on his excessive assets relative to his income and ordered to surrender his travel documents in an investigation by the Independent Commission Against Corruption (ICAC). On 01 February, his assets were frozen. On 27 May, he filed a lawsuit on the claim that he was subject to neither the Prevention of Bribery Ordinance 1970 nor the ICAC formed after his retirement. On 11 July, in a High Court decision, he was overruled and ordered to provide an explanation on assets in possession from the effective date of the ordinance to the date of allegation. On 04 July 1979, he was convicted of possessing wealth disproportionate to his official income and sentenced to two years in prison; his assets worth $16 million were confiscated.

10 Jan 1977

Ocean Park Hong Kong, located in Wong Chuk Hang, held its opening ceremony. On 15 January, it was officially opened to the public. At a cost of $150 million funded by The Hong Kong Jockey Club on government land free of charge, it came equipped with three aquatic facilities. On 01 July 1987, Ocean Park Limited, a non-profit statutory organisation, was established to operate the theme park. It featured rides and games, exhibit of land and sea animals, and large-scale performances in two zones, namely Wong Chuk Hang and Nam Long Shan. (Figure 210)

17 Feb 1977

The Hong Kong Industrial Estates Corporation Ordinance 1977 was promulgated, forming the Hong Kong Industrial Estates Corporation as a statutory body responsible for the construction and management of industrial estates. On 01 March, it was formally established; Legislative Councillor Aubrey Li Fook-wo (李福和) was appointed as Chairman.

Figure 210
A show with dolphins at the Ocean Theatre on Ocean Park Hong Kong's opening day. (Photo courtesy of Yau Tin-kwai/South China Morning Post via Getty Images)

02 Mar 1977

The Hong Kong government released the 1977/78 Budget, announcing a reserve of HK$1.16 billion as of 01 April to meet short-term and cyclical deficits, accounting for about 15% of estimated expenditure in the coming fiscal year. The government stated that it must maintain such a ratio of account balance and increase the level of fiscal reserve according to the increase in expenditure.

12 Mar 1977

Hong Kong beat Singapore 1–0 and won the championship game in Singapore in the qualification round of Group 1 (Asian and Oceanian zone) of the 1978 FIFA World Cup, moving up to the final round of Asian qualifiers. It was the best result achieved by Team Hong Kong in the World Cup as of 2017.

16 Mar 1977

Team Hong Kong took part in the fourth Commonwealth Table Tennis Championships in St. Peter Port, Guernsey, winning gold medals for the first time. These included men's and women's singles, men's and mixed doubles, and men's and women's teams.

Mar 1977

The *Hong Kong Economic Journal Monthly* began publication, covering finance, economics, real estate and trade analysis.

The Medical Council of Hong Kong held its first medical licensing examination. Overseas physicians (including those from six designated Commonwealth countries) must pass the examination and undergo clinical training before they were licenced to practice in Hong Kong. From September 1996, it was required of all doctors trained abroad in addition to one-year residency in a public hospital.

01 Apr 1977

Leung Ping-kwan (梁秉鈞), known by his pen name Ye Si (也斯), began to release his serial novel *Paper Cut-outs* in the newspaper *Express,* ending on 14 May, followed by an offprint in 1982 as the first novel based on magical realism published in Hong Kong.

20 Apr 1977

Financial Secretary Philip Haddon-Cave noted in a Legislative Council meeting that Hong Kong was not confined to a fiscal policy of positive non-interventionism unconditionally, stressing a government responsibility for macro-economic regulation and control in the interest of citizens by intervening in the exchange market, promoting industrial and commercial development, and continuing with basic public services.

22 Apr 1977

The computer-aided traffic control system became operational in West Kowloon as the first of its kind in Hong Kong. The system was implemented on Hong Kong Island in 1989, in Tsuen Wan in 1995 and in Sha Tin in 1998.

Apr 1977

The Hong Kong Observatory developed a yellow-and-red landslide warning signal system for exclusive use with the emergency services.

03 May 1977

The Secondary School Entrance Examination was held for the last time in Hong Kong.

06 May 1977

The Hong Kong Examinations Authority Ordinance 1977 was promulgated, establishing the Hong Kong Examinations Authority. The Authority became a consolidated administrator of the Hong Kong Certificate of Education Examination in 1978 (previously under the Education Department), Hong Kong Advanced Level Examination in 1979 and 1980 (previously administered separately by The Chinese University of Hong Kong and The University of Hong Kong), and other local and international standardised tests.

09 May 1977

The Hong Kong Commodities Exchange was inaugurated, starting initially with cotton futures before expanding to soybeans, gold and property management rights.

13 May 1977

The government designated a 460-hectare area as the Tai Po Kau Nature Reserve, Hong Kong's first special area of unique ecological value. As of 2017, Hong Kong had 22 special designated areas, totalling 1,997 hectares; half of them were located in country parks.

09 Jun 1977

Students of Precious Blood Golden Jubilee Secondary School staged a sit-in, demanding an explanation on issues relating to school finances and teachers' contracts. On 16 June, Director of Education Kenneth Topley issued a written warning, stating that licences of teachers who had any direct or indirect involvement would be revoked if they staged another boycott.

24 Jun 1977

Shing Mun Country Park and Lion Rock Country Park were designated as Hong Kong's first country parks. As of 2017, there were 24 country parks, totalling 43,467 hectares, about 40% of Hong Kong's overall land area.

27 Jun 1977

The first Hong Kong International Film Festival, organised by the Urban Council, began at Hong Kong City Hall. Twenty international films were featured, including Hong Kong's *The Last Tempest*, directed by Li Han-hsiang（李翰祥）, and *A Touch of Zen*, directed by King Hu（胡金銓）.

30 Jun 1977

The Consumer Council Ordinance 1977 was promulgated, effective 15 July, making the Consumer Council a statutory body authorised to take legal action against any acts harmful to the rights and interests of consumers.

The Employment (Amendment) (No. 3) Ordinance 1977 was promulgated, requiring seven days of paid annual leave, in addition to statutory holidays, for all manual labourers and non-labour employees (earning a monthly salary of less than HK$2,000) upon 12 months of continued employment. The ordinance also stipulated pro-rata payment in compensation of untaken annual leave upon termination following an employment of 3–12 months.

Jun 1977

The Hong Kong Repertory Theatre, established by the Urban Council, became the first professional Western theatre group in Hong Kong. On 12 August, a debut show was staged at Hong Kong City Hall, featuring American writer Thornton Wilder's comedy *The Skin of Our Teeth*.

01 Jul 1977

Two deaths and 65 injuries resulted from the collapse of bamboo sheds at a motorcycle competition hosted by Television Broadcasts Limited (TVB) at Shek Kong Air Strip. On 07 September, a Commission of Inquiry was appointed by the governor for an investigation. On 29 April 1978, it was noted in the commission report that a large group of spectators climbed onto the bamboo shed designed only to hold lighting and filming devices, causing the collapse under heavy load. The report concluded that the organiser, TVB, should be held responsible and called for further regulation requiring organisers to apply for a permit with large-scale outdoor activities.

24 Jul 1977

The police raided a crime syndicate in connection with a robbery at the Yau Ma Tei fruit market on 11 July; six people were arrested. Stolen cash, along with US$700,000 worth of counterfeit banknotes and an electrotype device, were uncovered.

Jul 1977

The Geotechnical Engineering Office under the Public Works Department was established to take charge of landslide prevention and slope management across Hong Kong.

01 Aug 1977

The Preventive Service under the Commerce and Industry Department was renamed the Customs and Excise Department, in accordance with the Preventive Service (Amendment) Ordinance 1977.

The Mirror was founded by Tsui Sze-man (徐四民) as a monthly publication on political and economic reviews.

25 Aug 1977

The Police Narcotics Bureau arrested nine people who allegedly conspired with Ma Sik-yu (馬惜如) and Ma Sik-chun (馬惜珍), directors of *Oriental Daily News*, in drug trafficking from 1967 to 1973. On 27 August, Ma Sik-chun surrendered himself and was arrested by the police. In September 1978, he jumped bail and went to Taiwan. On 14 April 2014, his application for revoking the arrest warrant was denied in the High Court. The Attorney General noted that, due to the lack of evidence, no charges would be pressed against Ma Sik-chun, who died in Taiwan in 2015. During an early investigation, Ma Sik-yu also left for Taiwan where he passed away in 1998.

15 Sep 1977

With support from Urban Councillor Tsin Sai-nin (錢世年), boat dwellers in the Yau Ma Tei Typhoon Shelter held a press conference in protest of poor living conditions and demanded temporary housing from the Housing Department.

18 Sep 1977

The Independent Commission Against Corruption (ICAC) arrested more than 40 former junior constables of the Yau Ma Tei Police District over a period of two days. They were alleged to be covering up drug trafficking activities at the Yau Ma Tei Fruit Market. On 21 September, another 42 junior police officers were arrested by the ICAC.

30 Sep 1977

In the history of Hong Kong's judicial system established in the 19th century, a verdict in Chinese was released for the first time in a case of police blackmail at the Victoria District Court.

05 Oct 1977

The governor announced in the Legislative Council that free and compulsory secondary school education was to start a year early, beginning in the school year of 1978/79 instead of 1979/80. Correspondingly, the minimum legal age of 15 for non-industrial employment was adopted.

13 Oct 1977

The Hong Kong College of General Practitioners was established to facilitate further medical training and specialist examinations. Peter Lee Chung-yin (李仲賢) served as President. In 1997, it was renamed the Hong Kong College of Family Physicians.

15 Oct 1977

The Hong Kong Arts Centre, along with its Shouson Theatre as well as a concert hall, a mini theatre and two galleries, was opened on the waterfront in Wan Chai as an art venue to host exhibitions and performances by local and overseas artists.

25 Oct 1977

The Independent Commission Against Corruption (ICAC) arrested 34 current and retired police officers having served in the Mong Kok Police District for the last five years. The following day, over 100 junior police officers held a rally at the Kowloon Police Headquarters and formed a committee with two representatives from each police district. The committee made a petition with Police Commissioner Brian Francis Slevin in objection to ICAC's approach of investigation, demanding a meeting with the commissioner before 28 December and threatening further action if not met.

27 Oct 1977

About 5,000 police officers held an assembly at Flower Market Stadium on Boundary Street in Mong Kok, speaking about their experience under Independent Commission Against Corruption investigation and subsequently forming the Junior Police Officers' Association. On 09 December, the Police Force (Amendment) (No. 3) Ordinance 1977 was promulgated, stipulating the legal status of police associations (not as a trade union) to be recognised by the police commissioner.

Figure 211
The office of the Independent Commission Against Corruption's (ICAC)Operations Department was damaged during the violent clashes between the police and ICAC personnel. (Photo taken in 1977 and courtesy of South China Morning Post Publishers Limited)

28 Oct 1977

In the morning, about 5,000 police officers gathered at Edinburgh Place in Central and marched to the Wan Chai Police Headquarters. In a meeting with five police representatives, Police Commissioner Brian Francis Slevin accepted some of their demands. At noon, about 100 people, including police officers, stormed the main office of Independant Commission Against Corruption's (ICAC) Operations Department in Hutchison House, tearing down the ICAC plaque and injuring five ICAC staff. The Junior Police Officers' Association, disappointed with the police commissioner, announced on 04 November that it would take further action in the interest of junior police officers. (Figure 211)

02 Nov 1977

For two consecutive days, the highly extravagant Manchu-Han style banquet was held at the Ambassador Hotel with the first booking from the Japanese TV station Tokyo Broadcasting System (TBS) for a record $100,000 per table of 12.

05 Nov 1977

Pak Ka Publisher launched a political monthly called *Zhengming* (contending to speak), followed by the launch of a twin publication *The Trend* in 1978.

Governor Murray MacLehose granted a conditional amnesty, declaring that no investigation of corruption by the Independent Commission Against Corruption would be launched against police officers for allegations prior to 01 January 1977, except those already under prosecution or involved in serious crimes. Consequently, 83 cases under investigation were closed.

07 Nov 1977

The Police Force (Amendment) (No. 2) Ordinance 1977 was promulgated as passed by the Legislative Council on the same day, authorising the police commissioner to summarily dismiss police officers in defiance of lawful orders.

09 Nov 1977

The government published a document titled *Senior Secondary and Tertiary Education: A Development Programme for Hong Kong over the Next Decade*. It outlined reform measures aiming to provide 60% of 15-year-olds with subsidised senior secondary education by 1986, as well as a proposal to shorten the curriculum of The Chinese University of Hong Kong from four to three years so as to standardise the two-year matriculation courses in secondary schools. On 18 October 1978, a government document titled *The Development of Senior Secondary and Tertiary Education* was released, proposing a total of 57,000 subsidised senior high school places to cover 60% of junior secondary (Form 3) graduates by 1981.

11 Nov 1977

The *Green Paper on Services for the Elderly* was released by the government, proposing an additional public assistance programme called Old Age Supplement, a lower age of eligibility from 75 to 70 gradually under the Old Age Allowance scheme, and a network day-care and service centres for the elderly.

14 Nov 1977

A government green paper titled *Help for Those Least Able to Help Themselves: A Programme of Social Security Development* was released in a public consultation on employee medical and life insurance schemes. It also proposed additional allowances for public assistance recipients and expanding the Old Age Allowance and Disability Allowance schemes.

17 Nov 1977

Speaking in Guangzhou on Chinese migration to Hong Kong, Deng Xiaoping (鄧小平) noted, "The main reason for the exodus is the great gap in living standards. We can solve the problem by improving our production and livelihood."

18 Nov 1977

Boat dwellers of the Yau Ma Tei Typhoon Shelter petitioned at the Government House and the Government Secretariat Office (where some slept outside) to seek accommodation in the temporary housing area in Cheung Sha Wan. On 21 November, requests for collective relocation were denied by the Housing Department as arrangement would be made on a case-by-case basis.

22 Nov 1977

The Gascoigne Road Flyover was opened to traffic in the first phase of the West Kowloon Corridor project linking Gascoigne Road and Ferry Street. Upon the completion of Phase IV in 1997, a corridor linking Yau Ma Tei and Lai Chi Kok became fully operational.

25 Nov 1977

Government advisory committees comprising 92 Unofficial Members were formed in the seven administrative districts of the New Territories. The first meeting was held by the Tsuen Wan District Advisory Committee on 28 November. The advisory committees were reconstituted as district boards.

01 Dec 1977

The Complaints Committee of the Independent Commission Against Corruption (ICAC) was established to monitor and review all non-criminal complaints against the ICAC or its staff under the chairmanship of Senior Unofficial Member of the Executive Council Kan Yuet-keung (簡悅強).

04 Dec 1977

The first Hong Kong Marathon, organised by the Hong Kong Distance Runners Club, was held in Shek Kong with a total of 194 participants. A civil engineer of the Public Works Department won the race with a time of 2 hours, 30 minutes and 19 seconds. It marked the first post-Second World War marathon in Hong Kong; it was last held in 1991.

06 Dec 1977

The Hong Kong Academic Aptitude Test was inaugurated in place of the Secondary School Entrance Examination under the Education Department. Along with academic results during the second semester of Primary 5 and the year of Primary 6, it formed the basis upon which students were assigned secondary school places.

08 Dec 1977

A group of 200 students from the Hong Kong University Students' Union surveyed the living conditions of boat dwellers of the Yau Ma Tei Typhoon Shelter, agreeing to support their demand for relocation by the Housing Department. On 13 December, the Committee for Boat Dwellers was formed by the students who handed the Housing Department with 471 petition letters folded into paper boats.

19 Dec 1977

A merger between Hutchison International Limited and Hongkong and Whampoa Dock Company Limited was approved by the Supreme Court, forming Hutchison Whampoa Limited which became a publicly listed company in Hong Kong on 03 January 1978.

21 Dec 1977

The government announced a standard time zone of eight hours ahead of the Greenwich Mean Time (GMT+8), thereby eliminating the use of daylight saving in Hong Kong.

30 Dec 1977

The Metrication Committee was formed to promote and facilitate the use of the metric system.

1977

The Canadian Chamber of Commerce in Hong Kong was established as a business organisation of companies and members.

10 Jan 1978

The Hongkong and Shanghai Banking Corporation began issuing $1,000 banknotes for the first time in Hong Kong.

14 Jan 1978

More than 600 stable hands of the Sha Tin Racecourse took part in a strike in protest of a salary reduction, refusing to handle horses on the racecourse. Races in Happy Valley were cancelled three times as a result in what was the first cancellation due to labour disputes. The Hong Kong Jockey Club reached a consensus on compensation and benefits on 21 January. The Happy Valley Racecourse resumed normal operation the following day.

18 Jan 1978

The Second Lion Rock Tunnel was opened to traffic as a northbound, one-way, two-lane carriageway. The Lion Rock Tunnel, which first became operational in 1967, was changed from a two-way, two-lane carriageway to a southbound, one-way, two-lane carriageway.

27 Jan 1978

The Mercantile Bank Note Issue (Repeal) Ordinance 1978 and Hongkong and Shanghai Banking Corporation (Amendment) Ordinance 1978 were promulgated, transferring the issuing rights of banknotes from Mercantile Bank to The Hongkong and Shanghai Banking Corparation (which assumed control of banknotes in circulation previously issued by Mercantile Bank).

15 Feb 1978

Phase I of the Home Ownership Scheme, implemented by the Hong Kong Housing Authority, was open to applicants. Among the first batch of housing estates were Yuet Lai Court in Kwai Chung, Shun Chi Court in Kwun Tong, Shan Tsui Court in Chai Wan, Chun Man Court in Ho Man Tin, Yue Fai Court in Aberdeen, and Sui Wo Court in Sha Tin.

About 2,600 students and faculty members, including Vice Chancellor Li Choh-ming (李卓敏) and Deputy Vice Chancellor Ma Lin (馬臨) of The Chinese University of Hong Kong (CUHK) took part in an assembly, organised by the Student Union, opposing the government plan to make its undergraduate programme from four to three years. Vice Chancellor Li promised to defend CUHK's existing academic structure. In February 1981, then-Vice Chancellor Ma reported that it would remain unchanged in the next six years as reassured by the government.

17 Feb 1978

The Reserved Commodities Ordinance 1978 was promulgated, effective 01 November, empowering the Commerce and Industry Department to determine the price of rice and oversee registered rice importers and wholesalers.

26 Feb 1978

A group of 16 Hong Kong deputies of the Guangdong delegation to the National People's Congress attended the First Session of the Fifth National People's Congress in Beijing with an increase from 14 Hong Kong deputies.

27 Feb 1978

The Hong Kong Civil Servants General Union was incorporated, comprising 13 Hong Kong civil service staff associations with an initial membership of about 20,000.

05 Mar 1978

The Common Sense, a television programme produced by Radio Television Hong Kong, premiered; it was the longest-running, non-ending news documentary series on global affairs with a focus on the political, economic and social development of Hong Kong and the Mainland.

15 Mar 1978

The government announced that it would reconsider granting large foreign banks with local licences to enhance the competitiveness of Hong Kong's financial sector. On 24 May, nine new licences were issued by the government.

17 Mar 1978

The Insurance Companies (Capital Requirements) Ordinance 1978 was promulgated, requiring proof of issued capital of no less than HK$5 million from insurance companies before they were allowed to incorporate with the Registrar of Companies.

28 Mar 1978

The MacLehose Dental Centre was established as a public clinic with a dental nurse training programme and services for school children.

06 Apr 1978

The first Asian Foreign Exchange and Money Dealers Conference was held in Hong Kong.

07 Apr 1978

One customs inspector and 118 police officers were dismissed under Section 55 of the Colonial Regulations. The regulation stipulated that public servants and police officers in Hong Kong may be removed without special formalities by the Secretary of State for Foreign and Commonwealth Affairs under the order of the British Crown.

A group of 24 police officers, including four in retirement, and two customs inspectors were charged with conspiracy to pervert the course of justice in connection with a corruption case at the Yau Ma Tei Wholesale Fruit Market (formerly Kowloon Wholesale Fruit Market). Following trials in the Victoria District Court and the Kowloon District Court from December 1978 to January 1979, 17 police officers, including one retired officer, and two customs inspectors were convicted and sentenced to imprisonment ranging from one year seven months to five years.

17 Apr 1978

The State Council approved the Application for Reopening Jinan University and Huaqiao University—submitted by the Chinese Ministry of Education in conjunction with the State Council's Overseas Chinese Affairs Office—and issued provisions including admission of Chinese students overseas and those in Hong Kong, Macao and Taiwan. The opening ceremony of Jinan University was held on 16 October; 266 students from Hong Kong and Macao were admitted during the year.

18 Apr 1978

The Exhibition of Archaeological Finds was held in the Chinese Export Commodities Exhibition Hall of Star House in Tsim Sha Tsui. A number of national treasures excavated in the Mainland—including the Bronze Running Horse and Jade Suit Sewn with Gold Thread—were on display.

Figure 212
An aerial view of Tuen Mun Road. (Photo taken in 1979 and courtesy of HKSAR Government)

Figure 213
About 10,000 people held a rally at Victoria Park to condemn the Education Department's decision to shut down Precious Blood Golden Jubilee Secondary School. (Photo taken on 28 May 1978 and courtesy of South China Morning Post Publishers Limited)

25 Apr 1978

The second-generation China Building in Central was opened upon completion. The 23-storey high-grade office building was rebuilt by Woodhall Company Limited under a joint venture between The Hongkong and Shanghai Banking Corporation and CK Asset Holdings.

05 May 1978

Phase I of Tuen Mun Road was opened to traffic, linking Tuen Mun and Tsuen Wan on a 17-kilometre expressway as the first highway in Hong Kong with three lanes. (Figure 212)

Pre-sales of World-Wide House, an office building under development by MTR Corporation Ltd and CK Asset Holdings at the former third-generation General Post Office, was launched. Office units were sold out on the first day, with a single-day record turnover of HK$600 million.

09 May 1978

Teachers and parents of Precious Blood Golden Jubilee Secondary School presented a petition at the Government House and launched a months-long sit-in outside the residence of the Catholic Diocese's Bishop. On 11 May, petitioners made a request with the bishop's representatives to unsuspend the students who questioned the school's management.

10 May 1978

Three bun towers collapsed in the early morning as competitors began climbing in a rush at the Cheung Chau Bun Festival, resulting in 24 injuries. On 02 March 1979, after meeting with the Cheung Chau Rural Committee, Secretary for the New Territories David Akers-Jones announced the cancellation of the midnight bun-snatching competition due to safety concerns.

14 May 1978

The Education Department decided to shut down Precious Blood Golden Jubilee Secondary School and establish St. Teresa Secondary School on the premise to be run by the Catholic Diocese. On 28 May, eight organisations jointly held a rally at Victoria Park with about 10,000 people, demanding through a signature drive that the school should first be re-opened, followed by an independent investigation. (Figure 213)

07 Jun 1978

The Hung Hom Public Funeral Parlour was opened as Hong Kong's first and only public funeral parlour run by the Urban Council.

16 Jun 1978

The first symposium of religious leaders in Hong Kong, jointly organised by the Confucian, Buddhist, Taoist, Protestant, Catholic and Muslim communities locally, was held at Hong Kong Convention Centre. They discussed moral issues in the media and problems associated with the youth, emphasising the teaching of morals and ethics, and resolved that the symposium to be held biennially.

23 Jun 1978

An agreement—between Advancetex Int'l Trading (HK) Company Limited and China National Textiles Import & Export Corp (Guangdong Branch)—for a garment factory in Rongqi, Shunde was signed. It marked the first Three-plus-One scheme (value-added products made with imported material, processed according to imported design through assembly of parts plus compensation trade) shortly before China's reform and opening-up. In October, production began at the factory.

15 Jul 1978

The Commission of Inquiry into the Precious Blood Golden Jubilee Secondary School Incident, led by The University of Hong Kong Vice Chancellor Rayson Huang (黃麗松), released an interim report, proposing a replacement school (Ng Yuk Secondary School) for former teachers and students of Golden Jubilee and the withdrawal of a previous written warning issued to teachers by the Director of Education. The Education Department accepted both proposals, ending the sit-in and sleep-in outside the residence of the Catholic Bishop since 09 May.

20 Jul 1978

Wang Kuang (王匡) arrived in Hong Kong as President of Xinhua News Agency Hong Kong Branch Limited.

Hong Kong Cotton Mills announced its business reorganisation, laying off 1,399 workers and causing a labour dispute. On 04 August, following negotiation with the Hong Kong & Kowloon Spinning, Weaving & Dyeing Trade Workers General Union, it reached an agreement with workers on severance pay, payment in lieu of notice, and long service pay, totaling HK$12 million payable starting 18 August.

26 Jul 1978

Typhoon Agnes hit Hong Kong. The Hong Kong Observatory hoisted Storm Signal No. 8 from 9:15 a.m. to 1:30 p.m. on the following day, and again from 5:25 p.m. on 29 July to 7:10 a.m. on 30 July. It was the first time Signal No. 8 had been hoisted twice within such a short period. It left three people dead, 134 injured and 67 fishing boats damaged.

29 Jul 1978

Local banking licences were issued to seven foreign banks, namely the Bank of Montreal, BNP Paribas, Canadian Imperial Bank of Commerce, Commerzbank, Crédit Lyonnais, Société Générale, and State Bank of India.

09 Aug 1978

The Performing Arts Company of China arrived in Hong Kong for 19 shows in the period of 15–25 August. Performances included Chinese music, piano, dance and Peking Opera, attracting an audience of over 30,000.

13 Aug 1978

The Central Committee of the Communist Party of China approved the *Report on the Preparatory Meeting for the Hong Kong and Macau Working Conference*, establishing a working group with the Hong Kong and Macao Affairs Office of the State Council which was officially inaugurated on 13 September.

18 Aug 1978

The Inland Revenue (Amendment) (No. 3) Ordinance 1978 was promulgated, effective retroactively 01 April, imposing local taxes on profits earned from investment made with foreign capital in Hong Kong.

The term "new wave", describing a new genre of filmmaking based on location shooting with an emphasis on social issues under a generation of new directors in Hong Kong, was coined in a *Close Up* magazine article "A New Wave in Hong Kong Cinema: Revolutionaries Who Challenge Tradition."

22 Aug 1978

Commercial Television (CTV) announced that it would cease operations with immediate effect due to financial difficulties. On 07 September, former staff in a rally at Victoria Park called on the government to hold CTV accountable for its closure, retain a third TV station and protect the rights of laid-off workers. On 19 October, a liquidation order for CTV was issued by the High Court.

31 Aug 1978

The agreement on the first "compensation trade" enterprise was signed between China National Textiles Import & Export Corp (Guangdong Branch) and Novel Enterprises Ltd (and its subsidiary Macau Textile Ltd) owned by Hong Kong businessman Chao Kuang-piu (曹光彪). It formed a textile factory in Zhuhai called Xiang Zhou Woollen Mills where manufacturing began on 07 November 1979.

05 Sep 1978

The Corruption Prevention Department of the Independent Commission Against Corruption released a report *Civil Service Accountability,* proposing civil liability with heads of government departments for subordinates found guilty of corruption.

World-Wide Steamship Company Limited founder Pao Yue-kong (Y. K. Pao) (包玉剛) and his son-in-law Peter Woo (吳光正) joined the board of directors of Hong Kong and Kowloon Wharf and Godown Company Ltd as its largest shareholders. On 07 December 1979, Hongkong Land announced its acquisition of Wharf shares from Jardine Securities, taking a 20% stake, almost as much as those held by the Pao family.

15 Sep 1978

The Taiping Handbag Factory began production with the first Processing and Assembly Factory Business (PAFB) enterprise licence issued by the State Administration for Industry and Commerce. Previously, on 31 July, Hong Kong businessman Cheung Chi-mi (張子彌) had agreed to provide the factory with equipment imported from Hong Kong to Dongguan under the PAFB scheme.

26 Sep 1978

A committee comprising members of 10 community and post-secondary student groups, including the Hong Kong University Students' Union, was formed to assist boat dwellers of the Yau Ma Tei Typhoon Shelter in their fight for onshore rehousing.

Sep 1978

The nine-year compulsory free education programme was implemented for six years of primary and three years of junior secondary education.

The Hong Kong Music Academy was established, offering full-time music courses. It became part of the Hong Kong Academy for Performing Arts' School of Music in the 1985/86 academic year.

01 Oct 1978

The government introduced a monthly allowance of HK$100 for eligible Hong Kong residents aged 70 or above under the Old Age Allowance scheme, replacing the previous Old Age and Disability Allowance available only to those aged 75 or above.

07 Oct 1978

The Sha Tin Racecourse with a venue capacity of more than 83,000 spectators celebrated its opening day with six races. (Figure 214)

19 Oct 1978

The Travel Industry Council of Hong Kong was established to promote industry development through engagement with the government and other hospitality-related sectors including airlines.

Figure 214
The Sha Tin Racecourse was opened on 07 October 1978. (Photo courtesy of C. Y. Yu/South China Morning Post via Getty Images)

02 Nov 1978

The New World Centre in Tsim Sha Tsui began its opening in phases; it became fully operational in 1981. It consisted of office buildings, a large shopping mall, a hotel and serviced apartments. Starting in 2010, it was demolished and redeveloped in phases. The InterContinental Hong Kong remained.

16 Nov 1978

The Judicial Committee of the Privy Council (UK) ruled that the Independent Commission Against Corruption had the power to prosecute retired police sergeant Lai Man-yau (黎民佑), pursuant to the Prevention of Bribery Ordinance 1970, even though he was no longer a civil servant when the ordinance was enacted.

22 Nov 1978

The two-day International Maritime Trade Conference began for a discussion on the shipping industry of Hong Kong and the Mainland; over 400 participants from 30 countries and territories participated.

23 Nov 1978

The Hong Kong Examinations Authority announced a new prerequisite of the Hong Kong Higher Level Examination, requiring a grade E or above in Chinese and English obtained in the Hong Kong Certificate of Education Examination.

26 Nov 1978

Seven races were held at the Sha Tin Racecourse in the first Sunday race held since the end of the Second World War.

27 Nov 1978

The High Island Reservoir, constructed at a cost of HK$1.35 billion, was put into use as the largest reservoir in Hong Kong with a storage capacity of 273 million cubic metres. On 09 February 1980, an inaugural ceremony was held by the government. (Figure 215)

Figure 215
An aerial view of High Island Reservoir. (Photo taken in 1978 and courtesy of HKSAR Government)

28 Nov 1978

The Hong Kong Academy of Ballet was incorporated, offering a teacher diploma programme and full-time professional ballet courses.

05 Dec 1978

The 14th Asian Racing Conference was held in Hong Kong with over 400 participants from 11 countries who shared their experience in horse racing and visited the Sha Tin Racecourse.

08 Dec 1978

The Chinese Language Movement Committee was formed, comprising representatives from 32 education, culture and post-secondary student groups. It aimed to raise the status of Chinese as a language by making it a teaching medium in secondary schools, improving the Chinese language education, and making examination results in the subject of Chinese under the Hong Kong Certificate of Education Examination a criterium for sitting the Hong Kong Higher Level Examination and Hong Kong Advanced Level Examination.

09 Dec 1978

Team Hong Kong participated in the eighth Asian Games in Bangkok, Thailand, winning two silver and three bronze medals, including first-time medals in bowling and badminton.

14 Dec 1978

The government announced that it would establish a Standing Commission on Civil Service Salaries and Conditions of Service so as to review the civil service pay scale and advise the governor. The Commission comprised four to six non-civil servant members, including an unofficial member of the Legislative Council or the Executive Council. On 01 January 1979, it was formally established under the chairmanship of Kan Yuet-keung (簡悅強).

23 Dec 1978

The Panama-registered cargo vessel *Huey Fong*, carrying about 2,700 Vietnamese refugees from Bangkok to Kaohsiung, Taiwan, upon entering Hong Kong, was intercepted by a Hong Kong marine police vessel and a British naval vessel. It anchored in the open sea about one nautical mile south of Po Toi Island. On 19 January 1979, it was allowed to sail into Hong Kong waters and anchor just north of Kau Yi Chau. The government took in the refugees on humanitarian grounds, leading to an influx of Chinese-Vietnamese refugees.

24 Dec 1978

Amid poor living conditions without onshore rehousing, boat dwellers of the Yau Ma Tei Typhoon Shelter, in conjunction with the Joint Committee on the Boat People's Living Situation, held a rally at Blake Pier in Central. More than 200 people were barred by the police from marching to the Government Secretariat Office and presenting a petition to the governor.

1978

Liao Chengzhi (廖承志), Director of the Overseas Chinese Affairs Office of the State Council, convened a meeting in Beijing concerning Hong Kong and Macao. The Chinese Central Government's policy of taking a long-term view and making full use of Hong Kong was reaffirmed.

Kerry Properties Limited was founded by Robert Kuok Hock-nien (郭鶴年). It became a publicly listed company in Hong Kong in 1996.

The Institute of Medical and Health Care of Hong Kong Polytechnic began offering advanced diploma courses in occupational therapy and physiotherapy. It replaced the Medical and Health Department's Physiotherapy and Radiology Training School. It included training for physiotherapists, occupational therapists, radiotherapists, medical laboratory technicians and optometrists.

A rock carving of geometric, bird and animal motifs was discovered at Lung Ha Wan in Sai Kung. In 1983, it was declared a monument by the government.

01 Jan 1979

The Traffic Accident Victims (Assistance Fund) Ordinance 1978 was promulgated, providing victims of traffic accidents and their dependants with financial assistance through a Traffic Accident Assistance Fund.

07 Jan 1979

The boat dwellers of the Yau Ma Tei Typhoon Shelter and their advocates travelling in two coaches to present a petition at the Government House were stopped by the police on the Hong Kong side of the Cross-Harbour Tunnel. In total, 76 people, including boat dwellers, students and social workers, were arrested; 67 were charged with illegal assembly. On 13 February, all 67 people were found guilty; 11 were bound over for 18 months while 56 boat dwellers were released unconditionally.

11 Jan 1979

The magazine *City Entertainment* launched its first issue. Its last issue was published on 11 January 2007; it was the longest-running professional film publication in Hong Kong.

21 Jan 1979

The first Guangdong–Hong Kong Cup held its first-round soccer match at the Yuexiushan Stadium in Guangzhou; Guangdong won 1–0. The second-round match was held at the Hong Kong Stadium on 28 Jan; Guangdong won 3–1 and was crowned champion with a final score of 4–1.

26 Jan 1979

The Inland Revenue (Amendment) Ordinance 1979 was promulgated, effective 01 April, exempting all community organisations, chambers of commerce and professional groups, as well as clans, family and ancestral trusts, from property tax.

Jan 1979

The dragon rock carving on the island of Kau Sai Chau in Sai Kung was declared a monument as the earliest kind in Hong Kong depicted in the 1819 edition of *Xin'an County Local Chronicles*.

07 Feb 1979

The Panama-registered cargo vessel *Skyluck* arrived in Hong Kong waters off Sai Wan from Singapore, carrying about 2,700 Vietnamese refugees. The vessel was escorted by marine police to the waters near Lamma Island; vessel crew and passengers were informed on the 09 February that they were not allowed to disembark. On 29 June, it ran aground as refugees broke the anchor chain; petrol bombs were thrown at police officers climbing aboard for an investigation. A group of 12 refugees and 26 crew members were arrested while all other refugees were settled in Chi Ma Wan Prison. (Figure 216)

20 Feb 1979

Radio Television Hong Kong held its first Top Ten Chinese Gold Songs Award with locally produced Chinese pop music; it became the oldest award of its kind in Hong Kong. (Figure 217)

Figure 216
The cargo vessel *Skyluck*, carrying about 2,700 Vietnamese refugees, ran aground on Lamma Island. (Photo taken in 1979 and courtesy of Sing Tao News Corporation Limited)

Figure 217
Winners Roman Tam Pak-sin (羅文) (back row, first from left) and Adam Cheng Siu-chow (鄭少秋) (back row, fifth from left) at the first Top Ten Chinese Gold Songs Award Presentation Ceremony on 20 February 1979. Four songs were composed by Joseph Koo (顧嘉煇) (front row, third from right); lyrics of three songs were written by James Wong Jum-sum (黃霑) (front row, second from left). (Photo courtesy of Radio Television Hong Kong)

Figure 218
Deng Xiaoping (鄧小平) met with Governor Murray MacLehose in Beijing on 29 March 1979. (Photo courtesy of Xinhua News Agency)

26 Feb 1979

The 1979 Asia Regional Meeting of the Commonwealth Association of Surveying and Land Economy was held in Hong Kong, covering the topics of housing, urban development and the industry of surveying in Asia.

04 Mar 1979

Charles, Prince of Wales, officiated at the opening ceremony of HMS *Tamar* (British Forces Overseas Hong Kong Naval Base). On 21 July 1981, it was renamed the Prince of Wales Building.

08 Mar 1979

The 1979 Urban Council elections were held; six seats were open for direct election. A total of 12,425 electors cast their votes in a record turnout of 39.4%. Elsie Elliott, Maria Tam Wai-chu (譚惠珠), Denny Huang Mong-hwa (黃夢花), Cecilia Yeung Lai-yin (楊勵賢), Hilton Cheong-Leen (張有興) and Augustine Chung Shai-kit (鍾世傑) were elected.

28 Mar 1979

CLP Power Hong Kong Ltd and Guangdong Electric Power Development Company reached an agreement to supply Guangdong Province with electricity. CLP began its daily supply of one million kilowatts to Guangdong Province following a button-pressing ceremony at its control centre in Kwai Chung attended by both parties on 31 March.

29 Mar 1979

In an official meeting with Governor Murray MacLehose, Deng Xiaoping (鄧小平) pointed out: "We have long maintained that Hong Kong's sovereignty belongs to the People's Republic of China, but Hong Kong also has a special status. Hong Kong is a part of China; it is not up for discussion. But it can be certain that when this is resolved in 1997, we will respect the special status of Hong Kong…For a long time to come in the current and early next century, Hong Kong could remain capitalist while socialism continues in the Mainland." (Figure 218)

01 Apr 1979

The Hong Kong Association of Travel Agents implemented a Travel Bonding Scheme under which compensation up to 10% of the amount in a special fund could be made upon a successful ruling in a complaint filed with the association proving losses due to negligence of an affiliated travel agency.

Figure 219
The ribbon-cutting ceremony, officiated by Vice Minister of Railways Geng Zhenlin (耿振林) in the presence of Governor Murray MacLehose, on 04 April 1979 in Guangzhou to mark the relaunch of the Guangzhou–Kowloon Through Train. (Photo courtesy of Sing Tao News Corporation Limited)

04 Apr 1979

The Guangzhou–Kowloon Through Train resumed service after the suspension in 1949. Governor Murray MacLehose attended an inaugural ceremony at the Guangzhou Railway Station and took the first train back to Hong Kong. (Figure 219)

25 Apr 1979

A government white paper titled *Social Welfare into the 1980s* was released, proposing a disability allowance giving persons with disabilities at half of the standard amount provided under the Public Assistance Scheme, in addition to increasing the number of student places in the department of social work of The University of Hong Kong, The Chinese University of Hong Kong and Hong Kong Polytechnic.

27 Apr 1979

The Exchange Fund (Amendment) Ordinance 1979 was promulgated, effective 01 May, requiring 100% liquidity coverage ratio at local banks with respect to the short-term balance of any exchange fund which must not be leveraged to expand credit.

Apr 1979

A rock carving featuring an animal motif and a spiral motif in two parts at the south end of Po Toi Island was declared a monument.

09 May 1979

The government set out three principal policies regarding road infrastructure, public transport service and efficiency of road systems in a document titled *Keeping Hong Kong Moving: The White Paper on Internal Transport Policy*.

13 May 1979

Daylight saving time was implemented at 3:30 a.m., ending at 3:30 a.m. on 21 October, for the last time.

The Advertising, Display and Floodlighting (Restriction) Order 1979 was implemented in a bid to reduce energy consumption by restricting the use of advertising lighting, display lighting and floodlighting between 8 p.m. and 11:30 p.m. every evening. The order was revoked on 10 October.

19 May 1979

Chief Secretary Denys Roberts took office as Chief Justice of Hong Kong, followed by an official visit to the Mainland in October 1983 as the first chief justice to do so. He remained in office until 1988.

30 May 1979

The first tourism festival, organised by the Federation of Hong Kong Chinese Travel Agents, was inaugurated with two weeks of events on promotion of travel-related services and tourism industry networks.

01 Jun 1979

China Overseas Construction Engineering Company Limited was incorporated. On 23 July 1992, it was renamed China Overseas Land & Investment Ltd as a developer of residential property, real estate and infrastructure in Hong Kong and the Mainland.

Scriven Trading Limited was incorporated as the largest overseas enterprise formed by the People's Government of Beijing Municipality. In 1988, it became a "window company" in Hong Kong under the direct leadership of the People's Government of Beijing Municipality. On 09 April 1997, it was renamed Beijing Holdings Limited before becoming a direct wholly owned subsidiary of the Beijing Enterprises Group in January 2005.

02 Jun 1979

The Hong Kong International Women's League hosted the eighth Annual Conference of the Federation of Asian Women's Association in Hong Kong. Over 100 delegates from 11 countries and regions attended the conference on the topic of the challenges of the 1980s.

10 Jun 1979

The second World Badminton Federation Championships began in Hangzhou, China. Amy Chan Lim-chee（陳念慈）and Ng Chun-ching（吳俊盛）of Hong Kong won the gold medal in the mixed doubles; Chan Tin-cheung（陳天祥）and Ng Chun-ching won the bronze medal in the men's doubles. It marked Hong Kong's first medals in a world-class badminton tournament.

22 Jun 1979

The Immigration (Amendment) (No. 2) Ordinance 1979 was promulgated, giving the government additional power to deal with illegal immigrants from the Mainland and Vietnam. The Royal Hong Kong Regiment (The Volunteers) and Royal Hong Kong Auxiliary Air Force were authorised to arrest illegal immigrants. On the same day, the British government announced that it would reinforce the British Garrison in Hong Kong to help intercept illegal immigrants.

Jun 1979

The Chinese container ship *Lin Jiang*, operated by China Merchants Group, arrived at Terminal 6 of Hongkong International Terminals from Huangpu, Guangzhou. The Hong Kong–Huangpu route was the first regular container ship route operated by the China Merchants Group.

10 Jul 1979

The Guangdong Provincial Department of Public Security announced a simplified Mainland-bound travel arrangement, effective 01 August, replacing the single-entry "Home Return Certificate for Compatriots from Hong Kong and Macau" with the three-year, multiple-entry Home Return Permit issued and made available by the Department at the branches of China Travel Service in Hong Kong and Macao.

20 Jul 1979

Governor Murray MacLehose as a British representative joined a UN General Assembly conference in Geneva, Switzerland on the issue of refugees in Southeast Asia. The next day, an agreement among 65 countries was reached to take in Vietnamese refugees unconditionally with six designated ports of first asylum, including Hong Kong. The UN High Commissioner for Refugees promised to cover related expenses, while other countries agreed to resettle refugees arriving at these ports.

02 Aug 1979

The Hong Kong Observatory hoisted Typhoon Signal No. 10 for nearly four hours amid Typhoon Hope—which caused 12 deaths, 260 injures and damage to 29 ocean-going vessels and 374 fishing boats.

06 Aug 1979

Following Typhoon Hope, about 70 boat dwellers of the Yau Ma Tei Typhoon Shelter appealed for onshore rehousing without success and broke into the defunct Chatham Road Camp in Tsim Sha Tsui to stage a sit-in protest. The next day, boat dwellers demanded urban rehousing and refused temporary housing in Tuen Mun arranged by the Housing Department, but eventually accepted the offer and ended their protest on 12 August.

09 Aug 1979

The Chinese General Administration of Customs announced that, effective 01 August, only those with a Home Return Permit would be allowed to carry watches, TVs, recorders, radios, cameras, electric fans, bicycles or sewing machines. Subject to Chinese customs tax, each person may bring one item per year into the Mainland.

18 Aug 1979

The Housing Authority's Elderly Persons Priority Scheme was launched, giving eligible residents aged 60 or above an option to be assigned a public housing unit in groups of three regardless of kinship, generally within two years upon filing an application. The scheme was later extended to cover senior couples, senior singles, and families living with elderly relatives.

20 Aug 1979

Hong Kong Public Libraries, run by the Urban Council, held its first Chinese Literary Week and organised the first-ever Creative Chinese Writing Award. One winner in the essay category and two winners in the novel category were selected from 960 submissions.

29 Aug 1979

A 16-year-old boy was killed in a shark attack while swimming at Hoi Ha Wan in Sai Kung.

Aug 1979

Chung Ying Theatre Company, a professional theatre group established by the British Council, with a focus on promoting drama education in communities and schools, put on its first public performance at Hong Kong City Hall on 05 December.

02 Sep 1979

Staff of the Housing Department under police escort staff resumed seven buildings located at Sai Lau Kok in Tsuen Wan upon expiry of a removal order. Clashes broke out, causing injuries to seven residents and several police officers, and continued the following day, causing injuries to four police officers, two homeowners and a Housing Department staff. All occupants moved out following the mediation of Urban Councillors Elsie Elliott and Augustine Chung Shai-kit (鍾世傑) as the dispute was resolved.

03 Sep 1979

The Hong Kong Taoist Association (HKTA) Yuen Yuen Institute No.1 Secondary School was opened in a ceremony as the first secondary school founded by HKTA.

30 Sep 1979

Phase I of the MTR Modified Initial System was opened in a ceremony officiated by Governor Murray MacLehose at Shek Kip Mei Station, where he was accompanied by about 1,000 passengers on the first train to Kwun Tong Station and back in a 28-minute ride. The Kwun Tong-Skep Kip Mei line was officially operational the following day. (Figure 220)

Sep 1979

The *Ba-Fang Literary Journal* was founded as a journal of approximately 300,000 words in length per issue published periodically featuring writers of the Mainland, Hong Kong and Taiwan. It ceased publication in November 1990.

05 Oct 1979

China International Trust & Investment Corporation (CITIC) held its inaugural board meeting at the Great Hall of the People in Beijing under the chairmanship of Rong Yiren (榮毅仁). Three of the 44 directors were from Hong Kong: Wong Kwan-cheng (王寬誠), Henry Fok Ying-tung (霍英東) and Li Ka-shing (李嘉誠). A state-owned enterprise with capital assets of RMB 200 million directly under the State Council, CITIC aimed to attract foreign capital, introduce advanced technology and equipment, and promote national development.

Figure 220
The opening ceremony of MTR's Shek Kip Mei Station with the first passenger train on 30 September 1979. (Photo courtesy of MTR Corporation)

10 Oct 1979

The Association of Experts for Modernization Limited was established by professionals in the legal, accounting, surveying, architectural, planning and engineering sectors. Dorothy Liu Yiu-chu (廖瑤珠) was appointed president of the association dedicated to providing Chinese institutions and enterprises with industrial and commercial expertise in the modernisation of China.

The Hong Kong Council of Social Service held its first Senior Citizens' Day to promote care and respect for senior citizens through seminars, health consultations, games and community activities.

26 Oct 1979

The MacLehose Trail, named after Governor Murray MacLehose, was opened to the public as the first and longest (as of 2017) hiking trail in Hong Kong, stretching 100 kilometres divided into 10 sections across eight country parks between Pak Tam Chung in Sai Kung in the east and Tuen Mun in the west.

31 Oct 1979

Sha Lo Tung Development Company Limited was incorporated. It began buying land in Sha Lo Tung in Tai Po and also acquired much of the private land there from villagers by promising to build small houses for them at no charge. In 1982, it announced a development plan of low-density housing, small houses (for villagers) and a golf course; in 1986, an application was made with the Country Parks Authority. The development plan was amended to a large degree due to environmental concerns; construction of small houses was never realised.

14 Nov 1979

The Hong Kong Certificate of Identity became available as an international travel document (much like a passport) for Hong Kong residents (mostly immigrants) ineligible for British-issued passports.

24 Nov 1979

The Kwai Chung Crematorium was opened as the first one in the New Territories under the Urban Services Department.

Nov 1979

| The first edition of *Geotechnical Manual for Slopes* by the Geotechnical Engineering Office was released as a guide to the design, construction and maintenance of slopes as well as site formation.

| The City Contemporary Dance Company was formed as the first professional contemporary dance company in Hong Kong.

08 Dec 1979

| An inaugural hike along the entire MacLehose Trail, organised by the *Great Outdoors* magazine, kicked off at 9 p.m. In 18 hours 8 minutes, Yeung Chun-tak（楊振德）finished first in Hong Kong's first-ever long-distance cross country event.

11 Dec 1979

| Walter James Boxall, a property manager of a telecom company, was extradited from Britain to Hong Kong by the Independent Commission Against Corruption. The following day he was charged with conspiring with his subordinates in a corruption case in which contracts on maintenance, refurbishment and cleaning services were awarded for bribes totalling HK$2.5–HK$3 million between 1966 and 1978. On 15 May 1980, he was found guilty in the Kowloon District Court and sentenced to four years in prison on five counts of conspiracy to defraud and 12 counts of receiving benefits.

14 Dec 1979

| The *Report of the Advisory Committee on Diversification 1979* was published by the government, making 47 proposals on the development of Hong Kong as an international port, including further integration with the Pearl River Delta region, greater supply of industrial-designated land, development of financial sectors, establishment of an industrial training council and an industrial development committee. The report was prepared by the Advisory Committee on Diversification, formed in October 1977 and chaired by Financial Secretary Philip Haddon-Cave, responsible for assessment of the economic development and long-term competitiveness of Hong Kong.

| Organised by the Tung Wah Group of Hospitals in collaboration with Television Broadcasts Limited (TVB), *Tung Wah Charity Gala* made its debut as a dedicated charitable fundraiser show on TVB Jade (channel) in the evening.

16 Dec 1979

| The second-phase MTR Modified Initial System, running between Shek Kip Mei Station and Tsim Sha Tsui Station, was opened. The Yau Ma Tei Station and Mong Kok Station were put into service on 22 and 31 December, respectively.

1979

| The United Nations High Commissioner for Refugees established a permanent office in Hong Kong to support the handling of Vietnamese refugees in Hong Kong and Macao.

| The Hong Kong Ballet was formed.

02 Jan 1980

| The passenger ship *Gu Lang Yu* made its maiden voyage to Hong Kong upon the launch of the Hong Kong–Xiamen route. On 10 January, the passenger ship *Shanghai* arrived in Hong Kong upon resumption of the Hong Kong–Shanghai route. On 11 January, the passenger ship *Xing Hu* arrived in Hong Kong upon resumption of the Hong Kong–Guangzhou route. These ships berthed at the Tai Kok Tsui Ferry Pier.

18 Jan 1980

| The Marine Fish Culture Ordinance 1980 was promulgated, stipulating regulatory requirements in relation to marine fish culture and a licence to operate in the designated areas.

Jan 1980

| Filming began in Quanzhou, Fujian for the first Hong Kong–Mainland collaborative film *Intolerance* since the inception of China's reform and opening-up policy. It was co-produced by Hai Hua Cinema Company of Hong Kong and Fujian Film Studio of the Mainland and directed by Hong Kong director Yeung Gat-aau（楊吉爻）, starring Hong Kong actor Siu Yuk-lung（蕭玉龍）.

12 Feb 1980

The MTR Modified Initial System, Hong Kong's first cross-harbour railway, became fully operational upon the opening of the Tsim Sha Tsui to Central section.

15 Feb 1980

The Disposal Ordinance 1980 was promulgated, establishing regulations on the prohibition of unauthorised disposal of waste and a licensing system for waste collection services and disposal facilities under a waste disposal plan.

25 Feb 1980

The first Asian and Pacific Conference of Correctional Administrators began in Hong Kong with representatives from 14 countries and territories in a three-day discussion on issues related to correctional institutions in the Asia-Pacific region.

13 Mar 1980

Further to the Coroner's Court on police inspector John MacLennan who was found dead with multiple gunshot wounds in his police quarter on 15 January, a Commission of Inquiry was appointed on 09 July by Governor Murray MacLehose. On 29 September 1981, an investigation report was released by the government with the conclusion of a suicide.

28 Mar 1980

The Ap Lei Chau Bridge was opened to traffic as Hong Kong's first highway bridge connecting Hong Kong Island to another island.

08 Apr 1980

The Hongkong and Shanghai Banking Corporation marked the launch of its Electronic Teller Card with an initial network of 16 automatic teller machines (ATMs) in an inaugural ceremony at the HSBC Main Building in Central. It was Hong Kong's first ATM system, allowing customers to check their balance and withdraw or transfer money 24 hours a day.

09 Apr 1980

Admiralty Centre, a 32-storey twin-tower commercial complex above MTR's Admiralty Station, marked its completion in a topping-out ceremony; it was opened for business in November. On 23 May, World-Wide House, a 29-storey commercial building above MTR's Central Station, held its topping-out ceremony; it was opened in December. These were the first commercial projects above MTR stations jointly developed by MTR Corporation Limited and CK Asset Holdings.

21 Apr 1980

The Law Reform Commission of Hong Kong was established for consideration of reform with aspects of the law referred by the Attorney General or the Chief Justice. Commission members included the Attorney General as Chairman, the Chief Justice, the Law Draftsman and 10 members of the community.

01 May 1980

Beijing Air Catering Company Ltd commenced operation as a provider of in-flight meal services established in a joint venture between the Civic Aviation Administration of China and Air China Catering Ltd—a subsidiary of the Maxim's Group founded by James Tak Wu (伍沾德) in Hong Kong—upon receiving a certificate issued by the China Foreign Investment Administration Committee, making it the first joint venture since China's reform and opening-up.

12 May 1980

Famous Cantonese opera actress Hung Sin-nui (紅線女) arrived in Hong Kong with the Guangdong Cantonese Opera Troupe since her return to the Mainland in 1955. On 24 June, a two-night performance *Medley with Hong Kong–Guangdong Actors* took place at Sunbeam Theatre, featuring Hung Sin-nui and nearly 300 actors of Guangdong and Hong Kong.

14 May 1980

A supplementary agreement between the governments of Hong Kong and Guangdong was signed in Guangzhou, increasing the annual supply of East River (Dongjiang) water to Hong Kong from 220 million cubic metres in 1983 to an estimated 620 million cubic metres in 1995, by an annual increment of 30–35 million cubic metres.

19 May 1980

The Italian Association of Foreign Trade and Hong Kong Trade Development Council signed an agreement in Hong Kong, expanding bilateral trade and industrial cooperation between Hong Kong and Italy.

27 May 1980

The Yau Tong Centre held a topping-out ceremony. The first phase, developed by Great Eagle Holdings Limited, was completed and opened for occupancy in September as Hong Kong's first housing estate under the Private Sector Participation Scheme.

May 1980

The Tai Po Industrial Estate, managed by the Hong Kong Industrial Estates Corporation, was opened for industrial occupants, including Ying Kee Safe & Furniture Manufacturing and Man Yee Can Company (Hong Kong) Limited. In the same month, a government loan of HK$18 million was provided to the Hong Kong Industrial Estates Corporation for building a factory facility at the Tai Po Industrial Estate.

02 Jun 1980

Hong Kong Electronics Association Ltd (present-day Hong Kong Electronic Industries Association Limited) was established to promote industrial development of electronics and organise an annual Electronics Fair in Hong Kong.

03 Jun 1980

Guangdong Enterprises Ltd was incorporated in Hong Kong as a window company funded by the Guangdong Provincial Government to promote trade and business collaboration with Hong Kong. It was officially opened for business on 05 January 1981 and was renamed Guangdong Enterprises (Holdings) Ltd on 29 November 1985.

06 Jun 1980

A government green paper titled *A Pattern of District Administration in Hong Kong* was released in a public consultation on reform to the local administration of the 1980s. The *White Paper on District Administration in Hong Kong*, published by the government on 04 January 1981, called for 18 District Boards to oversee community affairs, each supported in policy development by a Management Committee, in addition to changing the representation in the Urban Council by drawing 15 constituencies across Hong Kong Island and Kowloon, with one representative in each directly elected by residents.

20 Jun 1980

Hongkong Land announced its acquisition of up to 31 million shares of Wharf Holdings at HK$100 per share, thereby increasing its stake from 20% to 49%. On 22 June, Pao Yue-kong (包玉剛) announced his purchase of 20 million additional shares of Wharf Holdings at HK$105 per share, increasing his stake to 49% on 23 June, followed by an announcement of no further purchases on 24 June. On the same day, Hongkong Land issued a statement cancelling its purchase of Wharf shares under a current stake of 13.3 million shares. The Pao family acquired control of Wharf (Holdings).

24 Jun 1980

The first batch of housing units at Telford Gardens in Kowloon Bay was opened for occupancy as the first residential project above an MTR station. By 1982, all 21 buildings were completed, providing nearly 5,000 housing units.

29 Jun 1980

The 66-storey, 216-metre-high Hopewell Centre in Wan Chai held its topping-out ceremony. With a revolving restaurant on the 62nd floor, it was then the tallest building in Hong Kong and East Asia.

Jun 1980

The Housing Authority's Tai Yuen Estate was opened for occupancy as the first public housing estate in Tai Po.

The journal *Su Yeh Literature* was launched to cover novels, poems, translated work and literary reviews; it ceased publication in December 2000.

01 Jul 1980

The monthly magazine *China Tourism* was launched, promoting Chinese tourism and culture with feature articles and photos of tourist attractions, geographic landscapes and folk customs in the Mainland.

07 Jul 1980

The Stock Exchange of Hong Kong Ltd was incorporated following a merger of four existing stock exchanges, namely the Hong Kong Stock Exchange, Far East Exchange Ltd, Kam Ngan Stock Exchange Ltd and Kowloon Stock Exchange Ltd. The Stock Exchanges Unification Ordinance 1980 was promulgated on 08 August, recognising the legal entity of the Hong Kong Stock Exchange following the merger.

11 Jul 1980

The Water Pollution Control Ordinance 1980 was promulgated, establishing a statutory framework regarding the water quality of rivers, streams and the marine environment. The government was responsible for demarcation of water control zones and quality indicators.

16 Jul 1980

The 20th International Conference on Social Welfare was held in Hong Kong with more than 1,000 representatives from over 70 countries and territories with a focus on social development in times of economic uncertainty.

13 Aug 1980

The Independent Commission Against Corruption arrested at least 10 employees of China Motor Bus Company on suspicion of corruption involving job rosters and route assignments between 30 January 1977 and 13 August 1980. On 18 February 1981, 10 bus drivers were convicted of bribery and were bound over for 12 months. On 29 June, the officer in charge of roster assignment and his assistant were convicted of conspiracy to accept pecuniary advantages and sentenced to four and a half years and four years in prison, respectively. On 28 October, they were commuted to one and a half years and one year in prison, respectively, following an appeal.

19 Aug 1980

Trading of gold futures was made accessible at the Hong Kong Commodities Exchange (presently Hong Kong Futures Exchange). It was suspended on 24 September 1999. Gold futures resumed under the Hong Kong Futures Exchange on 20 October 2008.

27 Aug 1980

The 13-storey Queen Elizabeth Stadium, located in Wan Chai, was unveiled as a major venue of sporting events, performances and exhibitions. With a capacity of 3,500 seats, it was the first multi-function indoor sports and entertainment venue in Hong Kong.

29 Aug 1980

The first International Table Tennis Federation Men's World Cup was held at Queen Elizabeth Stadium in Wan Chai, featuring only singles matches. Chinese team member Guo Yuehua (郭躍華) won the championship.

01 Sep 1980

The International Conference on Metrology under the Asia Pacific Metrology Programme of the Commonwealth Science Council began in Hong Kong. The four-day conference, organised by the Hong Kong Public Works Department, aimed to provide a comprehensive review of metrology with representatives of the United Nations Educational, Scientific and Cultural Organization and of seven Commonwealth and Asian countries and territories.

The World Association of Detectives held its 55th Global Detective Conference in Hong Kong as its first annual conference held in Asia over five days.

01 Sep 1980

The Chinese sailing junk *Keying II*, presented by Hong Kong-based Worldwide Shipping Group, marked its voyage in a launch ceremony in Hampshire, UK. The junk was exhibited beginning 20 September in celebration of the Hong Kong in London festival.

09 Sep 1980

China Reinsurance (Hong Kong) Company Limited was incorporated with HK$10 million in capital as the first Chinese insurance company registered in Hong Kong.

14 Sep 1980

A symposium in reflection of 30 years of literary development and publication in Hong Kong was hosted by the newspaper *New Evening Post* (with its cultural section *Starry Sea)*.

24 Sep 1980

Housing units in seven buildings of City One Shatin Site 1 were sold out in two hours in a sale at New World Centre in Tsim Sha Tsui. It was the first large-scale private residential estate in the New Territories, co-developed by CK Holdings, Henderson Land Development, Sun Hung Kai Properties, and New World Development.

26 Sep 1980

The Hang Seng School of Commerce, located at Siu Lek Yuen in Sha Tin, was inaugurated, offering a two-year business diploma programme. Ho Nga-ming (何雅明) served as its first president.

Huamin Company Limited was incorporated as a window company of the Fujian Provincial Government for trade and business in Hong Kong. It was registered as Fujian Enterprises (Holdings) Company Limited on 27 September 1985.

30 Sep 1980

Jardine, Matheson & Co. announced that it would issue HK$1 billion in bonds with a return of 9.5%, along with warrants; they would to be repaid between 1984 and 1995. The bond issuance was the largest capital-raising activity of the time and intended to cover short- and medium-term debt resulting from acquisition of additional shares of Hongkong Land.

Sep 1980

The International Mail Centre in Hung Hom was completed as a facility to handle international mail in and out of Hong Kong as well as local mail in Kowloon and the New Territories.

The University of Hong Kong inaugurated its faculty of dentistry as Hong Kong's first dental school with an initial class of 76 students.

03 Oct 1980

Huang Hua (黃華), Vice Premier of the State Council and Minister of Foreign Affairs, arrived in Hong Kong, followed by a meeting with Governor Murray MacLehose on curbing illegal immigrants.

04 Oct 1980

The government confirmed that an eight-year-old boy of On Po Village in Sheung Shui died of rabies on 30 September. It simultaneously announced an order prohibiting anyone from taking dogs into or out of the proximity without the written consent of the Agriculture and Fisheries Department in accordance with the Public Order Ordinance 1967. Department staff and police officers were dispatched to search for stray dogs in the area.

07 Oct 1980

The Hong Kong Space Museum was opened with a permanent astronomical and an Omnimax theatre. It was the first structure built on the site of the former Tsim Sha Tsui Railway Terminus. (Figure 221)

17 Oct 1980

The first group of patients from Castle Peak Hospital was transferred to Kwai Chung Hospital, which was officially opened on 15 October 1981 with a capacity of 1,336 beds for psychiatric services.

Figure 221
The Hong Kong Space Museum
with an iconic semi-circular shape
on the Tsim Sha Tsui waterfront.
(Photo taken in 1982 and courtesy
of HKSAR Government)

19 Oct 1980

Governor Murray MacLehose arrived in Guangzhou and met with Guangdong Vice Governor Liu Tianfu (劉田夫) in a seven-hour meeting the following day regarding illegal immigrants from the Mainland to Hong Kong. Upon reaching an agreement on curbing illegal immigration, Governor MacLehose returned to Hong Kong on 21 October.

23 Oct 1980

The Immigration (Amendment) (No. 2) Bill 1980 was passed following its third reading as an urgent issue in the Legislative Council. It 1) abolished the Touch Base Policy in effect since November 1974 with a 74-hour grace period (10 p.m. on 23 Oct–midnight on 26 October) for those already in Hong Kong to apply for an identity card (residency); 2) enacted the Repatriation Upon Arrest policy with immigrants arriving in Hong Kong illegally from the Mainland; 3) required residents aged 15 or above to carry an identification document in public starting 30 October; and 4) prohibited employment of undocumented individuals starting 03 November.

19 Nov 1980

The two-day Far East International Shipping Conference began in Hong Kong with 400 representatives from 36 countries and territories in a meeting on the development of the shipping industry in China and the Far East.

26 Nov 1980

The three-day Asian Regional Safety and Accident Prevention Congress began in Hong Kong to promote occupational safety awareness among governments, employers and employees.

05 Dec 1980

The Public Order (Amendment) Ordinance 1980 was promulgated, effective 08 May 1981, requiring notification with the commissioner of police seven days in advance, unless exempt otherwise, for public assemblies which may be rejected for reasons of security, and an application with the commissioner of police seven days in advance for public processions.

10 Dec 1980

The Motor Insurers' Bureau of Hong Kong was incorporated; it became operational on 01 February 1981, requiring mandatory membership of licenced underwriters of motor insurance. It established a compensation fund for third-party victims of traffic accidents.

11 Dec 1980

The originals and replicas of famous paintings and the "Four Treasures of the Study" of the Ming Dynasty and Qing Dynasty from the Palace Museum in Beijing were on display for the first time in Hong Kong at Chung Hwa Book Store in Yau Ma Tei.

15 Dec 1980

Landmark Hong Kong in Central, including its Atrium Mall and Gloucester Tower, was unveiled in a ceremony. It stood on the sites of the former Gloucester Building, Lane Crawford House and Windsor House.

24 Dec 1980

The Hong Kong Association of Banks Ordinance 1980 was promulgated, effective 12 January 1981, incorporating the Hong Kong Association of Banks to take over the Exchange Banks' Association and promote the interests (including interest settlement rates) of fully licenced banks in Hong Kong with mandatory membership.

28 Dec 1980

Chung Shan Hot Spring Resort in Zhongshan, Guangdong was unveiled in a ceremony officiated by Vice Chairman of the National People's Congress Standing Committee Yang Shangkun（楊尚昆）. It was the first hotel venture with foreign investment following China's reform and opening-up policy. It was designed by architect Mo Bozhi（莫伯治） and built by a company co-founded by Henry Fok Ying-tung（霍英東）, Ho Yin（何賢）, Stanley Ho Hung-sun（何鴻燊）and Ma Man-kei（馬萬祺）.

1980

Fishing restrictions on "bottom trawling" with motorboats in Nanhai District were implemented by the Nanhai Fishery Office, Ministry of Agriculture of China, prohibiting fishing in waters less than 40 metres deep in the South China Sea. These restrictions were applicable to Hong Kong fishermen operating in the area.

01 Jan 1981

Chairman of CK Asset Holdings Li Ka-shing（李嘉誠）became Chairman of Hutchison Whampoa Limited as the first Chinese chairman of a British conglomerate, following The Hongkong and Shanghai Banking Corporation's sale of a 22% stake in Hutchison Whampoa to CK Asset Holdings on 25 September 1979.

05 Jan 1981

Guangdong (Hong Kong) Tourist Company, a member of Guangdong Enterprises Limited, was established, promoting tourism to Guangdong Province among the people of Hong Kong.

08 Jan 1981

The first two-day Junior Secondary Education Assessment began and was taken by about 93,000 examinees. The examination, comprising the subjects of Chinese, English and Mathematics, together with examination scores in school, formed the criteria upon which Form 3 students were selected to continue their education in government and government-aided senior secondary schools.

09 Jan 1981

The Insurance Companies (Amendment) Ordinance 1981 and Fire and Marine Insurance Companies Deposit (Amendment) Ordinance 1981 were promulgated, requiring undertakers of marine/fire or life insurance to maintain a minimum of HK$5 million in issued capital (fully paid-up) with excess value of HK$2 million (HK$4 million for underwriters of marine, fire and life insurance) in asset above liability.

20 Jan 1981

A three-alarm fire caused by an explosion in an oven at Artistic Hair Products Company on Seven Sisters Road in North Point left 11 dead and 19 injured. A group of 66 labour unions convened a Joint Emergency Meeting of Hong Kong and Kowloon Labour Unions and demanded an investigation from the Labour Department and Hong Kong Fire Services Department.

Jan 1981

The Hong Kong Federation of Trade Unions Workers' Club established a continuing education centre, offering workers a chance to learn new skills and knowledge. The programme offered three-month courses, three semesters a year.

13 Feb 1981

The Offences against the Person (Amendment) Ordinance 1981 was promulgated, allowing a legal abortion to take place in cases with malformed foetus under the opinion of two registered medical practitioners formed in good faith.

27 Feb 1981

A five-alarm fire broke out in the squatter area at Tai Hom Woi Tsuen in Diamond Hill, destroying about 600 huts and affecting 7,390 people.

05 Mar 1981

Choi Kwok-ching (蔡國楨), Chan Chi-kwan (陳子鈞), Francis Chaine (陳肇川), Edmund Chow Wai-hung (鄒偉雄), Tsin Sai-nin (錢世年) and Chan Po-fun (陳普芬) won six direct seats in the 1981 Urban Council elections. On 01 April, Hilton Cheong-Leen (張有興) defeated Denny Huang Mong-hwa (黃夢花) and became the first Chinese chairman of the Urban Council, succeeding Arnaldo de Oliveira Sales.

The week-long Asian Composers Conference and Festival began in Hong Kong; it was attended by more than 150 composers, performers and musicians from all over the world.

06 Mar 1981

The 1981 government census began; it was concluded on 15 March. The findings showed 4,986,560 permanent residents, 13,906 mobile (non-permanent) residents, 20,600 Vietnamese refugees, and 123,252 residents absent from Hong Kong at the time of the census.

24 Mar 1981

The Prince Philip Dental Hospital in Sai Ying Pun was unveiled, becoming operational on 07 October as Hong Kong's first dedicated dental hospital and school.

25 Mar 1981

Reverend Peter Kwong Kong-kit (鄺廣傑) was ordained as the ninth Anglican Bishop of the Diocese of Hong Kong and Macao and the first Chinese bishop of the diocese.

27 Mar 1981

The Kwun Tong District Board as the first district board in Hong Kong was formed with 32 members appointed by the governor of Hong Kong, including 22 unofficial members, seven official members and three ex-officio members from the Urban Council. The first meeting was held on 02 April.

29 Mar 1981

The World Wildlife Fund Hong Kong was inaugurated as the first Hong Kong branch of an international, non-governmental environmental organisation. It began managing the Mai Po Nature Reserve in 1983.

01 Apr 1981

Eight district boards in the New Territories were formed, namely Tsuen Wan, Sha Tin, Tai Po, North District, Yuen Long, Sai Kung, Tuen Mun and Islands; 165 district board members were appointed by the governor of Hong Kong.

03 Apr 1981

Hong Kong's first 24-hour 7-Eleven convenience store was opened at the Happy Valley Tram Terminus.

21 Apr 1981

The Shiuying Bamboo, a species endemic to Hong Kong, in Eagle's Nest was discovered by—and named after—Hong Kong botanist Hu Shiu-ying (胡秀英).

22 Apr 1981

The 1.5-kilometre East Kowloon Way (commonly known as the East Kowloon Corridor) connecting Hung Hom and To Kwa Wan, was opened to traffic as part of present-day Route 5.

27 Apr 1981

The 2.3-kilometre double-track Beacon Hill Tunnel was opened to train traffic, replacing the original single-track tunnel in an upgrade for an electric train system of the Kowloon–Canton Railway.

01 May 1981

The Employment (Amendment) (No. 2) Ordinance 1981 was promulgated, mandating 10 weeks of paid maternity leave (based on two-thirds of daily wages) for pregnant women under employment for 40 weeks or more. It also made it a criminal offence for an employer to dismiss any pregnant employees.

05 May 1981

The three-day Pacific Economic Conference began in Hong Kong with representatives from five member states, including the United Kingdom, Canada, Japan, Australia and New Zealand, on international trade and economic cooperation.

15 May 1981

The Hong Kong Dance Company was established by the Urban Council as a professional group dedicated to the traditional Chinese folk dances.

20 May 1981

The fourth Asian Horological Trade and Industry Promotion Conference, in conjunction with the Asian Horological Products Exhibition, organised by the Federation of Hong Kong Watch Trades & Industries Limited, was held in Hong Kong and attended by over 400 representatives for a discussion on industry development.

29 May 1981

The Banking (Amendment) Ordinance 1981 and Deposit-taking Companies (Amendment) (No. 2) Ordinance 1981 were promulgated, establishing a three-tier system for licenced banks, licenced deposit-taking institutions, and registered deposit-taking institutions. A licenced bank could accept deposits of any maturity, subject to an interest rate agreement; a licenced deposit-taking institution could accept deposits of any maturity, subject to a minimum deposit of HK$500,000, but could not operate current accounts; and a registered deposit-taking institution could not accept deposits with a maturity of less than three months or an amount of less than HK$50,000. The new licencing system came into effect on 01 July 1983 following a two-year transition period.

15 Jun 1981

The financial magazine *Economic Digest* began publication as a journal featuring financial news, reports and interviews with financial professionals.

18 Jun 1981

The government announced a one-year joint review on local education in partnership with the Organisation for Economic Co-operation and Development; an advisory group comprising international consultants was appointed to conduct a survey and issue a report. In the same month, a government report titled *Overall Review of the Hong Kong Education System* was released, providing the advisory group with a reference on Hong Kong's education policy since 1963. On 29 March 1982, an exchange with Hong Kong's education sector was held with the advisory group. In November 1982, a report titled *A Perspective on Education in Hong Kong: Report by a Visiting Panel* was released to the government. Recommendations included an education commission, native-language teaching, enhanced language proficiency among teachers, less pressure on students, diverse post-secondary education, strengthened moral education and curriculum reform under a dedicated department.

21 Jun 1981

The Independent Commission Against Corruption (ICAC) arrested 22 staff of China Motor Bus and 11 individuals for conspiring to steal bus fares; HK$120,000 in cash and HK$40,000 in gold were recovered. The following year, the ICAC dismantled the entire syndicate by charging 69 people with corruption and theft; 62 were found guilty and nine were sentenced to immediate imprisonment.

25 Jun 1981

The first three routes of Hong Kong–China (Guangdong) Express Bus, operated by The Motor Transport Company of Guangdong & Hong Kong Limited, began services from Hong Kong to Huiyang, Shantou and Xingning.

Jun 1981

The first two blocks of City One Shatin Site 1 were opened for occupancy. The final block was opened on 28 October 1987. The residential complex, jointly developed by CK Holdings, Henderson Land Development, Sun Hung Kai Properties and New World Development, was the first large-scale private estate in the New Territories, consisting of 52 blocks with 10,642 housing units.

Shui Pin Wai Estate in Yuen Long, built by the Housing Authority, was opened for occupancy as the first public housing estate since Yuen Long was designated for new town development.

04 Jul 1981

The Independent Commission Against Corruption (ICAC) began broadcasting *ICAC Investigators* on Television Broadcasts Limited (TVB) in a new educational series of seven one-hour episodes based on real cases.

17 Jul 1981

Shanghai Industrial Investment Company Limited was incorporated as a window company of the Shanghai Municipal Government, facilitating business exchange and trade cooperation between Hong Kong and Shanghai. It was registered as Shanghai Industrial Investment (Holdings) Company Ltd on 03 June 1993.

22 Jul 1981

A government white paper titled *Primary Education and Pre-Primary Services* was released to the Legislative Council, establishing criteria of primary school admission at the age of six, kindergartens at the age of four, and childcare centre below four. The report also recommended improving the training of teachers, reducing the size of classes, and adopting activity-based teaching.

17 Aug 1981

During a hike along Cheung Tsui Path at Tai Long Wan in Sai Kung, six scouts and their instructor standing on rocks to watch the waves were swept away by rip currents, resulting in three deaths and four injuries.

20 Aug 1981

A five-alarm fire at On Lok Village in Sau Mau Ping destroyed 1,500 huts and left 6,500 people homeless.

21 Aug 1981

The environmental agency of Hong Kong was reorganised. The Transport Division and Lands Division (previously under the Environment Branch) were expanded as the Transport Branch and Lands and Works Branch, respectively. The Home Affairs Branch took over the responsibility of policymaking with respect to environmental protection.

Benton Cheung Yan-lung (張人龍), Selina Chow Liang Shuk-yee (周梁淑怡) and Maria Tam Wai-chu (譚惠珠) were appointed Unofficial Members of the Legislative Council as Oswald Victor Cheung (張奧偉) and Li Fook-wo (李福和) stepped down. The number of unofficial members of the Legislative Council increased from 26 to 27.

26 Aug 1981

The State Council approved the establishment of Shantou University co-founded by the Ministry of Education, Guangdong Provincial Government and the Li Ka Shing Foundation. Enrolment began in 1983.

01 Sep 1981

The Education Department was expanded and raised to a higher level with the status of a government branch under the Government Secretariat. Kenneth Topley, Head of the Education Department, was promoted as Director of Education, taking office on 02 October. The Education Department was responsible for execution of policy under the Education Branch.

05 Sep 1981

The charity fundraiser *All Star Challenge*—co-hosted by Po Leung Kuk and Television Broadcasts Limited (TVB)—was held at Lee Theatre and broadcast live on TVB Jade. The programme was renamed *Gala Spectacular* in 1989.

09 Sep 1981

East Lake Millie's Garden, a residential project in Shenzhen developed by Hong Kong-based company Millie's Group, held its opening ceremony. It was the first Hong Kong–Shenzhen joint venture in real estate for which Millie's Group Chairman Lau Tin-chao（劉天就）became one of the first Hong Kong investors in the Shenzhen Special Economic Zone.

21 Sep 1981

China Hong Kong International Travel Company Ltd commenced operations as an agency of China International Travel Service Limited for business in Hong Kong, including travel arrangement to China for foreign nationals.

28 Sep 1981

RCL Semiconductors Limited was inaugurated in a ceremony at Tai Po Industrial Estate. It was Hong Kong's first factory to produce silicon wafers used in integrated circuits.

Sep 1981

The Chinese University of Hong Kong's Faculty of Medicine began classes as the second medical school in Hong Kong.

01 Oct 1981

Cable and Wireless (Hong Kong) Limited, a government venture in conjunction with Cable & Wireless, began to operate under a 25-year licence (up to 2006) as a provider of international telecommunications in Hong Kong.

25 Oct 1981

The Urban Council launched another Keep Hong Kong Clean campaign depicting a pair of angry eyes under the slogan "Hong Kong Is Watching" to promote public hygiene.

30 Oct 1981

The British Nationality Act 1981 was promulgated by the British government under which Hong Kong was declared a British Dependent Territory and Hong Kong residents by birth, acquisition or registration (prior to the law) were given British Dependent Territories citizenship (BDTC). Those born in Hong Kong or as permanent residents (after the law came into effect) were also eligible for BDTC status (which did not include the right of abode in the United Kingdom).

31 Oct 1981

The Stock Exchange of Hong Kong held its first general meeting and committee election. Woo Hon-fai（胡漢輝）, Chairman of the former Kam Ngan Stock Exchange, was elected as the first chairman.

The Hong Kong Federation of Trade Unions, along with an independent union and a union representing civil servants, each won a seat in the 1982 election of employee representatives to the Labour Advisory Board. It marked the first time that pro-left trade unions had been allowed to take part in a government advisory body comprising employers and workers on labour issues.

08 Nov 1981

Hongkong Electric's power station on Lamma Island began supplying electricity to Hong Kong Island, Ap Lei Chau and Lamma Island. After 1990, it became Hongkong Electric's sole power plant.

13 Nov 1981

The Hong Kong government made compensation benefits available for married female civil servants on a par with their male counterparts. The initiative provided women civil servants and their immediate family with benefits on housing, medical and dental services, education and study abroad.

21 Nov 1981

A five-alarm fire in the squatter area of Lam Tin within five hours destroyed about 1,800 huts in Hin Mo Shan Village, Epworth Village and Nam Mei Village, affecting about 7,000 residents.

28 Nov 1981

The Guangdong Provincial Department of Public Security announced the launch of a new Home Return Permit scheme with a validity of 10 years instead of three years, effective 01 December, further facilitating the visits of Hong Kong and Macao residents to their hometowns.

01 Dec 1981

The City and New Territories Administration was formed under a merger of the City District Office and the New Territories District Office. All offices and principal officers were universally known as District Offices and District Officers, respectively, starting 01 October 1982.

12 Dec 1981

The first Pan-Pacific Special Olympics Games held in Hong Kong began at Wan Chai Sports Ground. Team Hong Kong won 147 medals, including 60 gold, 60 silver and 27 bronze during the two-day event.

20 Dec 1981

A riot broke out at the Vietnamese Refugee Detention Camp in Sesame Bay on Lantau Island. Staff of the Prisons Department were attacked while fire was set to the camp. Police were dispatched; 200 refugees were transferred to Stanley Prison. The incident caused injuries to 30 staff and three Vietnamese refugees.

25 Dec 1981

In the early morning of Christmas day, following a car accident near The Landmark in Central, a riot involving 1,000 people broke out, destroying cars on the street. Hundreds of the Police Tactical Unit were dispatched; 11 people were injured and 18 arrested.

27 Dec 1981

The Association for the Rights of Industrial Accident Victims was founded. It aimed to support victims of industrial accidents and their families, promote occupational safety, and advocate for more stringent government measures in protecting workers.

09 Jan 1982

Nanyang Commercial Bank opened a branch in Shenzhen as the first foreign bank to open a branch in the Mainland after 1949.

21 Jan 1982

The Shaolin Temple, starring Mainland actor Jet Li (李連杰) under Hong Kong director Cheung Sing-yim (張鑫炎), made its debut as the first Hong Kong–Mainland co-production since China's reform and opening-up.

25 Jan 1982

The first Lunar New Year Fireworks Display in Hong Kong took place over Victoria Harbour on the first night of Chinese New Year.

01 Feb 1982

The Prisons Department was renamed Correctional Services Department to reflect its multi-faceted role in punishment, crime prevention and rehabilitation.

12 Feb 1982

The Vocational Training Council Ordinance 1982 was promulgated, establishing the Vocational Training Council to support vocational education in place of the Training Council.

12 Feb 1982

The first Highest Honour Award was presented to Joseph Koo Ka-fai (顧嘉煇) at the third annual Top Ten Chinese Gold Songs Award organised by Radio Television Hong Kong. It was renamed the Golden Needle Award at the seventh annual Top Ten Chinese Gold Songs Award in 1985 as the most prestigious prize which was awarded irregularly.

The Council for the Performing Arts, a government advisory body under the Recreation and Culture Department, was established on policy regarding the development of the performing arts, including music, songs, dance, drama and opera in Hong Kong.

19 Feb 1982

Sun Hung Kai Finance was issued a government banking licence; it became Sun Hung Kai Bank Limited in March. It was the first bank licenced to take deposits after a new three-tier banking system was introduced in 1981.

26 Feb 1982

The Tolo Harbour and Channel Water Control Zone was marked the first water quality control zone in Hong Kong. Implementation came into effect on 01 April 1987.

04 Mar 1982

The first election of the New Territories District Board was held, with a voting turnout rate of over 50% in the direct elections of 56 seats. It was the first election after the implementation of the new district administration system in the previous year. (Figure 222)

09 Mar 1982

The first Hong Kong Film Awards, co-sponsored by *City Entertainment* magazine and Radio Television Hong Kong, was held. *Father and Son* directed by Allen Fong Yuk-ping (方育平) won Best Film and Best Director. Michael Hui Koon-man (許冠文) in *Security Unlimited* and Kara Wai Ying-hung (惠英紅) in *My Young Auntie* won Best Actor and Best Actress, respectively.

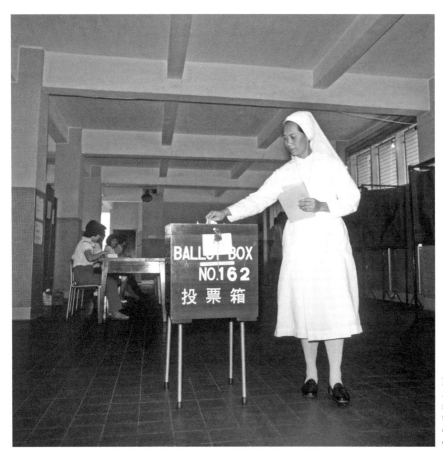

Figure 222
A nun cast her vote at a polling station in the first election of the District Board. (Photo taken on 04 March 1983 and courtesy of HKSAR Government)

12 Mar 1982

The northbound tube of the 1.9-kilometre Aberdeen Tunnel linking Wong Chuk Hang and Happy Valley was opened to traffic on a single-tube, two-way basis. On 14 March 1983, it became fully operational with the opening of the southbound tube.

18 Mar 1982

The Central and Western District Board was established with an inaugural meeting. It was the last district board established by the government under the 1981 *White Paper on District Administration in Hong Kong.*

30 Mar 1982

The Man Kam To Control Point became operational as a vehicular border checkpoint mostly for passengers on the Hong Kong–Guangdong Express Bus.

Mar 1982

Choi Yuen Estate, developed by the Housing Authority, was opened for occupancy as the first public housing estate in the development of Fanling and Sheung Shui.

A red tide at the shores of Tai Fu Kok and Lap Sap Chau in Sai Kung killed approximately 1.4 tons of fish under marine culture, causing losses of about HK$100,000.

The quarterly magazine *Literature and Art* was launched as a publication on religious, cultural, artistic and literary pieces; it ceased publication in June 1986.

01 Apr 1982

The Public Works Department was replaced by the Lands and Works Branch for government projects and public works. The Building Development Department, Engineering Development Department, New Territories Development Department, and Water Supplies Department—all formerly under the Public Works Department—became independent departments, with the addition of a new Lands Department under the Lands and Works Branch. The Electrical and Mechanical Services Department (formerly the Electrical and Mechanical Engineering Division of the Public Works Department) also became an independent department under the Lands and Work Branch.

12 Apr 1982

The first Hong Kong Open Badminton Championship Final was held at Queen Elizabeth Stadium in Wan Chai.

15 Apr 1982

South China and Caroline Hill FC tied 0–0 in a match of the Hong Kong First Division Football League at the Government Stadium where South China's qualification as a first division team was at stake. More than 3,000 frustrated fans gathered at the exit and started a riot along Caroline Hill Road, setting fire and destroying traffic lights, shop windows and parked cars. Police arrived to disperse the crowd and arrested six people before the riot ended by midnight.

26 Apr 1982

A Civil Aviation Administration of China airliner flying from Guangzhou to Guilin crashed in Gongcheng County near Guilin, killing all 112 people on board, including 50 passengers from Hong Kong after a layover in Guangzhou. About half of the 50 passengers were in the catering industry, including the director of the Hong Kong and Kowloon Catering Industry Mutual Aid Research Association.

27 Apr 1982

Speaking about Hong Kong during a meeting with North Korean leader Kim Il-sung in Pyongyang, Deng Xiaoping (鄧 小 平) said: "In China, no one in power would agree to an extended lease in the New Territories. Upon the founding of the People's Republic of China, we repudiated the unequal treaty on Hong Kong. Betrayal is not an option. As such, we told the British that China will take back Hong Kong Island, Kowloon peninsula and the New Territories in 1997, but will allow Hong Kong to maintain its status as a free port and international financial centre. The social system of Hong Kong will remain unchanged, and so will its way of life. Hong Kong will be administered by a local government comprising local people as a special administrative region of China."

Figure 223
The Kowloon–Canton Railway's first-generation electric train, commonly known as the yellow-head train. (Photo courtesy of MTR Corporation)

01 May 1982

A fight broke out between refugees from North and South Vietnam at the North Kai Tak Refugee Camp in Kowloon over a commemoration marking the end of the Vietnam War. On 03 May, the camp was set on fire. The next day, police entered the camp to quell the riot and avoided further factional conflicts by transferring about 900 South Vietnamese refugees to a camp on Argyle Street.

06 May 1982

The first electric section of the Kowloon–Canton Railway, connecting Hung Hom and Sha Tin, became operational, running a 12-minute ride every 10 minutes. Diesel trains continued running between Hung Hom and Lo Wu once every hour. On 15 July 1983, it became entirely electric, reducing travel time to 36 minutes. (Figure 223)

10 May 1982

The MTR section between Tsuen Wan to Lai King was opened to traffic. On 17 May, with the section between Lai King to Prince Edward in service, Tsuen Wan Line became fully operational.

13 May 1982

Sun Hung Kai Centre in Wan Chai was opened as a skyscraper with 51 floors, including 40 floors of office space.

20 May 1982

Edward Youde took office as the 26th Governor of Hong Kong. He died of illness in Beijing during his term of office on 05 December 1986, followed by a period of public mourning.

29 May 1982

Continuous heavy rain in Hong Kong caused several landslides and cases of flooding. As of 05 June, 25 people died; four were missing; at least 50 were injured; and more than 8,000 were affected.

01 Jun 1982

The Hong Kong government announced the end of all earlier water-rationing measures and resumed full-day water supply.

02 Jun 1982

Two people were killed and five were injured when a tornado hit multiple areas in the New Territories, including Lau Fau Shan, Tin Shui Wai, Wang Chau and Yuen Long.

03 Jun 1982

A mentally disturbed man killed his mother and sister in his home at Un Chau Estate in Sham Shui Po and subsequently stabbed children with a knife at nearby Anne Anne Kindergarten. Six people were killed and 42 were injured. The suspect was arrested upon the arrival of police.

29 Jun 1982

The Airport Tunnel underneath Kai Tak Airport connecting Kowloon City and Kowloon Bay as part of Route 5 was opened to traffic as the world's first tunnel constructed under an operational airport and the first toll-free tunnel in Hong Kong. On 04 May 2006, it was renamed the Kai Tak Tunnel.

Jun 1982

Exploration Theatre comprising young artists as a local production group was established. It was Hong Kong's first professional theatre transformed from an amateur group with government funding.

02 Jul 1982

The Hong Kong government donated £2 million to the South Atlantic Fund in support of the British military personnel, including those of Chinese descent and their families, wounded in the Falklands War.

The Immigration (Amendment) Ordinance 1982 was promulgated, stipulating that Vietnamese refugees arriving in Hong Kong on and after this day be put in detention camps under the Correctional Services Department. The Chi Ma Wan Detention Centre became the first designated detention camp.

09 Jul 1982

The Marine Fish Culture Ordinance 1980 was enacted, designating 24 fish culture zones in eastern New Territories, including Sai Kung, Tolo Harbour and Yan Chau Tong. As of 2017, Hong Kong had 26 fish culture zones, covering 209 hectares.

16 Jul 1982

The Wonderful World of Whimsy Limited was incorporated, becoming Hong Kong's first indoor arcade chain. It closed in February 1999.

18 Jul 1982

Anita Mui Yim-fong (梅艷芳) won the first New Talent Singing Championship, co-organised by Television Broadcasts Limited (TVB) and Capital Artists Limited, in a talent contest specifically for local entrants. The championship was mainly sponsored by TVB starting 1997 and was open to Chinese contestants around the world as the International Chinese New Talent Singing Championship.

28 Jul 1982

A group of 22 representatives from six student organisations staged a rally at the Consulate General of Japan in protest of the distorted account of the Japanese invasion of China in textbooks approved by the Japanese Ministry of Education, Sports, Science and Culture. On 05 August, the Hong Kong Federation of Education Workers released a statement of protest. On 15 August, the Hong Kong Federation of Students initiated a signature campaign across five districts. On 29 August, 13 organisations, including the Hong Kong Federation of Trade Unions and Hong Kong Federation of Education Workers, held a rally with over 1,000 people from 138 organisations.

29 Jul 1982

The government bought back approximately 488 hectares of land in Tin Shui Wai for HK$2.258 billion and reached an agreement with Mightycity Company (majority owned by state-owned China Resources Group) for joint development of public and private housing accommodating 135,000 people in Tin Shui Wai.

30 Jul 1982

The Smoking (Public Health) Ordinance 1982 was promulgated, effective in phases from 15 November 1982 to 15 August 1983, prohibiting smoking in designated public areas, all public lifts and lower decks of land-based public transport. In addition to labelling the tar content on packets, it required the notice "HK Government Health Warning: Cigarette Smoking is Dangerous to Your Health" in all advertisements and packets.

01 Aug 1982

The Trade and Industry Branch was established under the Government Secretariat, overseeing matters concerning trade, industry, and consumer protection. The Trade, Industry, and Customs Department was decentralised into three separate and independent departments, namely Trade, Industry, and Customs and Excise.

10 Aug 1982

In a meeting on Hong Kong with Chinese American scientists, Deng Xiaoping (鄧小平), Chairman of the Central Military Commission of the Communist Party of China, said: "After reunification, Hong Kong will function as a special administrative region; its system and way of life will remain unchanged, and we will strive to maintain its present status as an international trade and financial centre. Hong Kong will fly the People's Republic of China flag and be known as 'Hong Kong, China.' Hong Kong will be governed not by people from Beijing, but by those elected by local people, who should be patriots."

18 Aug 1982

Lam Kor-wan (林過雲), his brother and father were arrested on suspected involvement in a serial case murdering and dismembering teenage girls; police conducted a search for evidence at their residence in To Kwa Wan. On 27 October, Lam Kor-wan was found guilty of prima facie murder in a trial at the San Po Kong Magistracy; on 08 April 1983, he was convicted of murder and sentenced to death by the Supreme Court; on 29 August 1984, his sentence was commuted to life imprisonment by Governor Edward Youde. Lam was known as the "Rainy Night Butcher."

30 Aug 1982

The Hong Kong Observatory recorded a minor earthquake of magnitude 1.5 on the Richter scale at 4:23 a.m. in the waters east of Lantau Island.

Aug 1982

British archaeologist Brian A. V. Peacock was commissioned to conduct the first government archaeological survey across Hong Kong. It was completed in October 1985 with the releases of *The Investigation Report on Archaeological Resources in Hong Kong* and *The Hong Kong Archaeological Survey: Subsurface Investigation Reports*.

01 Sep 1982

Guangdong Province implemented a new immigration measure, requiring a Permit for Proceeding to Hong Kong and Macao (commonly known as a One-way Permit) with Chinese residents permanently settling in Hong Kong or Macao under an initial daily quota of 75 people, and an Exit-Entry Permit for Travelling to and from Hong Kong and Macao (commonly known as a Two-way Permit) with Chinese residents temporarily visiting Hong Kong or Macao.

The social literature magazine *New Bloom* was founded; it ceased publication in August 1988.

06 Sep 1982

Che Lee Yuen Jewellery & Goldsmith Company ceased operations. Customers were unable to withdraw their gold or cash cheques issued by the company. On the same day, Hang Lung Bank issued a statement denying rumours that it took significant losses resulting from the closure of Che Lee Yuen. The next day, the bank took out HK$600 million in banknotes to meet a bank run at its Yuen Long Branch.

11 Sep 1982

The Hong Kong Young Writers Association was established; Chan Kam-cheong (陳錦昌) was appointed as Chairman. It aimed to promote literature and art by working with organisations to nurture young writers in Hong Kong.

Figure 224
The meeting between Deng Xiaoping (鄧小平) and UK Prime Minister Margaret Thatcher at the Great Hall of the People in Beijing on 24 September 1982. (Photo courtesy of STR/AFP via Getty Images)

16 Sep 1982

The Hong Kong Exhibition Centre was opened on the third and fourth floors of the annex building of China Resources Building (Lower Block) in Wan Chai as the largest exhibition venue at 36,000 square feet. On 18 September, it held its first exhibition with the Fujian Export Commodities Fair.

18 Sep 1982

Six organisations, including the Hong Kong Federation of Students, Hong Kong Professional Teachers' Union and Hong Kong Federation of Trade Unions, held a 10,000-strong rally at Victoria Park in memory of the Japanese invasion of Manchuria and in protest of the distorted historical accounts in textbooks approved by Japanese Ministry of Education, Sports, Science and Culture. A two-day boycott of Japanese goods was initiated by the Hong Kong Federation of Students. A small home-made bomb was detonated inside the Matsuzakaya department store in Causeway Bay, causing minor injuries to a salesperson and the closing of three Japanese department stores (including Matsuzakaya) for three hours. On 23 September, two student representatives of The University of Hong Kong departed for Beijing with a petition signed by some 500 faculty members and students, asking for a strong stance by the Chinese government on Japan.

22 Sep 1982

British Prime Minister Margaret Thatcher arrived in Beijing to begin the first formal negotiation on the future of Hong Kong. On 24 September, in a meeting with Margaret Thatcher, Deng Xiaoping (鄧小平) said: "Sovereignty is non-negotiable. It should clearly be stated that it is time China take back Hong Kong in 1997, not only the New Territories but also Hong Kong Island and Kowloon." It was concluded in the meeting that further negotiation through diplomatic channels should continue. (Figure 224)

23 Sep 1982

The first elections of the Urban District Board were held, with 76 directly elected seats across 10 districts in Hong Kong and Kowloon. The voter turnout was 35.5%.

26 Sep 1982

British Prime Minister Margaret Thatcher arrived in Hong Kong for a three-day visit. The next day, Margaret Thatcher said in a press conference that the Sino-British treaties on Hong Kong should be modified by both parties rather than annulled. Students of The Chinese University of Hong Kong and Hong Kong Polytechnic demonstrated outside the venue, holding banners reading "Fight against Unequal Treaties" and "Reject Treaties on Aggression against China" and submitted a letter of protest. That evening, student unions affiliated with the Hong Kong Federation of Students launched a boycott, refusing to attend a reception at the Government House in honour of Margaret Thatcher.

28 Sep 1982

Plant A of CLP Power's Castle Peak Power Station became operational, followed by the opening of Plant B in 1986 as Hong Kong's largest power station with a total capacity of 4,108 MW.

Sep 1982

The Institute of Language in Education located on Dundas Street in Mong Kok was opened as a government institution, offering 16-week training courses to improve the language proficiency of teachers. The first batch of trainees included about 100 diploma-qualified teachers of English and Chinese in primary and secondary schools.

05 Oct 1982

Following Margaret Thatcher's visit to China, British and Chinese officials held their first meeting in Beijing on the fundamental principles and procedures of negotiation regarding Hong Kong with Chinese Vice Foreign Minister Zhang Wenjin (章文晉) and British Ambassador to China Percy Cradock on behalf of each side. By February 1983, five rounds of discussions had been held.

07 Oct 1982

The Hong Kong Observatory recorded a minor earthquake of magnitude 1.5 on the Richter scale at 10:13 p.m. in the waters east of Lantau Island.

31 Oct 1982

The Jubilee Sports Centre, built on 41 acres of land donated by The Hong Kong Jockey Club, was inaugurated in a ceremony as Hong Kong's first athletic training facility of international standards under a board of directors established in July 1977. On 01 April 1991, it was renamed the Hong Kong Sports Institute as a centre for athletic training, accreditation of trainers, and scientific research. (Figure 225)

01 Nov 1982

The Prince of Wales Hospital in Sha Tin was unveiled as Hong Kong's first fully air-conditioned public hospital with 1,448 beds, a specialist clinic, a nursing school and staff quarters, providing hospital services in New Territories East. The hospital became operational in 1984.

19 Nov 1982

Team Hong Kong took part in the nineth Asian Games in New Delhi, India, winning a silver and a bronze medal, including its first medal in windsurfing.

Figure 225
An aerial view of the Jubilee Sports Centre in Sha Tin. (Photo taken in 1982 and courtesy of HKSAR Government)

20 Nov 1982

Vice Chairman of the National People's Congress Standing Committee Liao Chengzhi (廖承志) told delegates of the Chinese Manufacturers' Association (CMA) of Hong Kong during a meeting in Beijing that China will resume sovereignty over Hong Kong as a Special Administrative Region governed by local people and retain Hong Kong's social and legal system. In the same month, CMA President Wong Kwan-cheng (王寬誠) said in a press interview in Beijing that "horse racing and dancing will go on," implying an unchanged way of life in Hong Kong after 1997.

23 Nov 1982

Harbour City in Tsim Sha Tsui, developed by Wharf Holdings Limited, was opened as Hong Kong's largest complex of shopping malls, office buildings, hotels and serviced apartments with a capacity of 600 stores and over two million square feet of office space.

04 Dec 1982

Amendments to the Constitution of the People's Republic of China with Article 31 and Paragraph 13 of Article 62 were adopted by the Fifth Session of the Fifth National People's Congress, giving the state authority to establish special administrative regions where necessary and the National People's Congress to determine where to establish such regions and what system of governance to be instituted. The amendments provided a constitutional framework on the issue of Hong Kong.

22 Dec 1982

The Hong Kong and Chinese governments reached an agreement that Mainland visitors must leave Hong Kong before the expiry of their Two-way Permits, effective 23 December.

24 Dec 1982

The Employees' Compensation (Amendment) Ordinance 1982 was promulgated, requiring insurance and work-related injury compensation for employees by employers. The Employees' Compensation Assessment Board was also established to provide assessment on work-related injuries.

27 Dec 1982

The fourth International Conference on Science Education began in Hong Kong for the first time in a five-day symposium with 390 representatives from over 20 countries and territories.

29 Dec 1982

Lo Fu (羅 孚), Editor-in-Chief of *New Evening Post* and a member of the Chinese People's Political Consultative Conference, was arrested in Beijing on charges of being a spy. In April 1983, he was convicted of espionage and sentenced to 10 years in prison by the Intermediate People's Court of Beijing Municipality. He was released on parole a month later and returned to Hong Kong in January 1993 with permission from the Chinese government.

1982

The Land Development Policy Committee agreed to a confined set of planning standards and guidelines under the *Hong Kong Outline Plan* (subsequently renamed *Hong Kong Planning Standards and Guidelines*), specifying basic criteria of land use and designation to meet social and economic development.

The professional theatre troupe Zuni Icosahedron was founded, emphasising alternative theatre and multimedia performances in support of drama education and international cultural exchange in Hong Kong.

09 Jan 1983

Meeting Point, a political organisation chaired by Lau Nai-keung (劉迺強), was founded. On the same day, it published a proposal on the future of Hong Kong, calling Hong Kong an inseparable part of China with unquestionable sovereignty and suggesting further public participation in political reform.

10 Jan 1983

The Agriculture and Fisheries Department reported on the withering of pine trees (especially Chinese red pines) under an infestation of pine wood nematodes starting in the summer of 1982. The government embarked on a sustained, large-scale campaign to replace infected pine trees with broad-leaved trees to mitigate further infestation.

28 Jan 1983

During a meeting in London with government officials and Governor Edward Youde regarding Hong Kong, Prime Minister Margaret Thatcher proposed that "in the absence of progress in the [Sino-British] talks, we should develop the democratic structure in Hong Kong as though it was our aim to achieve independence or self-government within a short period, as we have done with Singapore."

29 Jan 1983

The first Fringe Festival was opened, featuring 32 arts programmes (including dance, drama, painting and music programmes) and 22 exhibitions. Starting in 1999, it became known as the City Festival.

31 Jan 1983

The Exhibition of Ancient Chinese Bronzes in the Collection of Shanghai Museum was opened at Hong Kong City Hall. It was a collaboration between Hong Kong's Urban Council and Shanghai Museum and was curated by the Hong Kong Museum of Art. It was also the first exhibition of cultural relics at a public museum in partnership with the Mainland.

Jan 1983

The Bank of China Group was formed by the Bank of China (Hong Kong) in conjunction with 13 banks in Hong Kong and Macao, namely Yien Yieh Commercial Bank, Kwangtung Provincial Bank, China & South Sea Bank, Bank of Communications, Kincheng Banking Corporation, China State Bank Limited, National Commercial Bank Limited, Sin Hua Bank, Chiyu Banking Corporation Limited, Po Sang Bank, Nanyang Commercial Bank, Nan Tung Bank and Hua Chiao Commercial Bank.

01 Feb 1983

The Education Branch was renamed Education and Manpower Branch; Director of Education became Secretary for Education and Manpower. The Social Services Branch was renamed Health and Welfare Branch; Secretary for Social Services became Secretary for Health and Welfare.

06 Feb 1983

The White Swan Hotel in Guangzhou was opened for business under a joint development by Henry Fok Ying-tung (霍英東), George Pang Kwok-chan (彭國珍) and the Tourism Administration of Guangdong Province with a total investment of HK$200 million. It was the first five-star joint venture hotel following China's reform and opening-up.

11 Feb 1983

The Insurance Companies Ordinance 1983 was promulgated, effective 30 June, requiring a capital amount of no less than HK$5 million with all insurance companies and a capital amount of no less than HK$10 million with providers of life insurance, general insurance and statutory insurance.

08 Mar 1983

The first district-based elections of the Urban Council were held; one member was elected in each of 15 constituencies across Hong Kong Island and Kowloon. Voter turnout was 22.25%. The newly elected Urban Council comprised 39 members, including 15 unofficial members appointed by the government, 15 directly elected members, and nine representatives from District Boards.

10 Mar 1983

British Prime Minister Margaret Thatcher wrote to Premier Zhao Ziyang (趙紫陽) of the State Council of the People's Republic of China, stating: "Provided that an agreement can be reached between the two sides on administrative arrangements for Hong Kong to guarantee the future prosperity and stability of Hong Kong and is acceptable to the British Parliament and to the people of Hong Kong as well as to the Chinese Government, I would be prepared to recommend to the Parliament that sovereignty over the entire Hong Kong would be returned to China."

11 Mar 1983

The Inland Revenue (Amendment) Ordinance 1983 was promulgated, requiring property tax be based on the actual rental income of the landlord and management fees paid by the tenants for the landlord. It also required landlords to keep a record on rental incomes of their properties.

13 Mar 1983

Vice Minister of Water Resources and Power Li Peng (李鵬) led a delegation to Hong Kong for a meeting with British Under Secretary for Industrial Development Gordon Manzie regarding the construction of Daya Bay Nuclear Power Plant in Guangdong, followed by a meeting with Governor Edward Youde and a visit to CLP Power's Castle Peak Power Station.

28 Mar 1983

The Hong Kong government began issuing first-generation computerised identity cards which featured an anti-forgery watermark and were computer printed.

29 Mar 1983

The Ko Shan Theatre, located at Ko Shan Road Park in To Kwa Wan, was opened with an area of 2,500 square metres and a capacity of 3,000 seats.

Mar 1983

The first Hong Kong Children's Literature Festival, a five-month event organised by the Hong Kong Children's Arts Society, began for a series of activities designed for children, including novel-writing competitions, academic seminars, poster design competitions, book fairs and film screenings.

06 Apr 1983

Hilton Cheong-Leen (張有興) and Hugh Moss Gerald Forsgate were re-elected as Chairman and Vice Chairman of the Urban Council, respectively.

12 Apr 1983

Teddy Wang Teh-huei (王德輝), Chairman of Chinachem Group, was kidnapped on Bluff Path at the Peak. He was released on 20 April after his wife Nina Wang Kung Yu-sum (龔如心) paid a ransom of US$11 million.

20 Apr 1983

The Hong Kong Observatory launched a new warning signal system to alert the public in cases where there is a high risk of landslip and flooding.

27 Apr 1983

The Hong Kong Coliseum in Hung Hom was opened with a capacity of 12,500 seats and an area of over 1,600 square metres. Taking the shape of an inverted pyramid, it was designed as a venue for sporting events, concerts and recreational activities. (Figure 226)

Figure 226
The Hong Kong Coliseum in Hung Hom.
(Photo taken in 1983 and courtesy of Sing Tao News Corporation Limited)

29 Apr 1983

The Air Pollution Control Ordinance 1983 was promulgated, replacing the Clean Air Ordinance 1959 with updated regulations on air pollution in Hong Kong.

Apr 1983

The 47-storey Edinburgh Tower, an office building as a part of Landmark Hong Kong, was completed in the last phase of a redevelopment project in Central District by Hongkong Land.

05 May 1983

Sam Hui Koon-kit (許冠傑) starred in a concert for three days at Hong Kong Coliseum as the first singer to hold a show at the new facility.

10 May 1983

Violight Industry Company Limited, founded by Wang Guangying (王光英), was incorporated. It was opened for business on 18 August and was renamed China Everbright Holdings Company Limited on 31 July 1984, focusing on foreign trade and industrial investment.

19 May 1983

Xu Jiatun (許家屯) was appointed as President of Xinhua News Agency (Hong Kong Branch). He arrived in Hong Kong on 30 June to take office.

27 May 1983

Shum Yip (SZ) Trading Company Limited was incorporated in Hong Kong as the first overseas entity originating from the Shenzhen Special Economic Zone established to promote economic cooperation and facilitate exchanges between Shenzhen and the rest of the world, including Hong Kong. It was registered as Shum Yip Holdings Company Ltd on 08 February 1985.

May 1983

Asia Television's *The Legendary Fok* was released on Guangdong Television. On 06 May 1984, it aired on prime-time television with China Central Television, followed by other stations, becoming the first Hong Kong drama series broadcast across the Mainland.

01 Jun 1983

The Urban Council launched an ex-gratia payment scheme under which cooked food stall licencees were provided a payment of HK$36,000 in exchange for their licences.

10 Jun 1983

The Exchange Fund (Amendment) Ordinance 1983 was promulgated. The Exchange Fund of Hong Kong was authorised to influence the exchange rate of the Hong Kong dollar through direct or indirect means, thereby allowing the government to ensure a stable Hong Kong dollar in the foreign exchange market.

20 Jun 1983

The Hong Kong Government Office in New York was established to promote Hong Kong's economic interests in 31 eastern states of the United States. Former Secretary for Trade and Industry William Dorward was appointed as Commissioner of Hong Kong Economic Affairs, New York.

22 Jun 1983

The Chinese National College Entrance Examination (Gaokao) was made available in Hong Kong and taken by about 450 local students.

24 Jun 1983

The Hong Kong Branch of Xinhua News Agency held a service in memory of Liao Chengzhi (廖承志), Vice Chairman of the National People's Congress Standing Committee and former Director of the State Council's Hong Kong and Macao Affairs Office, who died of illness in Beijing on 10 June. More than 3,000 people attended the ceremony, including Chief Secretary Sir Philip Haddon-Cave and Political Advisor Robin McLaren.

01 Jul 1983

The Hong Kong Tourist Association inaugurated a nine-month courtesy campaign to encourage visitors to recognise outstanding service staff in conjunction with a service training programme to enhance Hong Kong's tourism industry.

07 Jul 1983

Edward Youde indicated his intention of attending the second phase of Sino-British negotiations on the issue of Hong Kong in Beijing on 12 July in his capacity as Governor of Hong Kong. The following day, an objection was raised by the Ministry of Foreign Affairs on the grounds that he represented a local government subordinate to the British government and could only appear as a member of the British delegation.

12 Jul 1983

The first round of talks in the second phase of Sino-British negotiations over the future of Hong Kong took place in Beijing between Chinese Vice Minister of Foreign Affairs Yao Guang (姚廣) and British Ambassador to China Percy Cradock. By 23 September, four rounds of talks had been held. (Figure 227)

27 Jul 1983

Amendments to the Standing Orders of the Legislative Council of Hong Kong 1968 were passed by the Legislative Council (LegCo). These included the removal of the word "colony" from the Standing Orders, authority to increase the time limit of debate at the discretion of the LegCo president, and disclosure of the government budget by the LegCo Finance Committee.

Figure 227
The meeting between Chinese Vice Minister of Foreign Affairs Yao Guang (姚廣), third from right, and British Ambassador to China Percy Cradock, third from left, in Beijing on 25 July 1983 during a second round of the second phase of Sino-British talks on Hong Kong. (Photo courtesy of Xinhua News Agency)

26 Aug 1983

Lee Quo-wei (利國偉), Chen Shou-lum (陳壽霖), and Maria Tam Wai-chu (譚惠珠) were appointed as Unofficial Members of the Executive Council. Chan Ying-lun (陳英麟), Rita Fan Hsu Lai-tai (范徐麗泰), Pauline Ng Chow Mei-lin (伍周美蓮), Peter Poon Wing-cheung (潘永祥) and Yeung Po-kwan (楊寶坤) were appointed as Unofficial Members of the Legislative Council. Maria Tam Wai-chu became the first person to take part in four different representative councils concurrently as a member of the Executive Council, Legislative Council, Urban Council and a District Board.

01 Sep 1983

The JETCO Automatic Service System commenced service with the Bank of East Asia, Chekiang First Bank, Wing Lung Bank and Shanghai Commercial Bank under the Joint Electronic Teller Services Limited co-founded by the four banks in conjunction with the Bank of China in 1982.

09 Sep 1983

The Hong Kong Observatory hoisted Hurricane Signal No. 10 for eight hours amid Typhoon Ellen—which left 10 people dead, 12 missing and 333 injured, as well as 44 ocean-going vessels and 360 fishing boats with damage.

10 Sep 1983

In a meeting with former British Prime Minister Edward Heath, Deng Xiaoping (鄧小平) said that the British idea of "returning sovereignty in exchange for the right to govern" was not feasible, urging a change of direction before China was made to deliver a unilateral plan on the issue of Hong Kong.

24 Sep 1983

A crisis of confidence emerged in Hong Kong following the unfruitful conclusion of the fourth round of talks in the second phase of Sino-British negotiations on the issue of Hong Kong on 23 September. The effective exchange rate index of the Hong Kong dollar fell by five percentage points within three hours upon market opening. The Hong Kong dollar ultimately reached an all-time low at HK$9.60 to US$1 in the so-called "Black Saturday" crisis as people flocked to exchange for US dollar and stock up on rice and daily necessities.

28 Sep 1983

The government assumed control of Hang Lung Bank on the brink of bankruptcy in the interest of consumers. Senior executives and directors of The Hongkong and Shanghai Banking Corporation were assigned to manage the bank's businesses under the Secretary for Monetary Affairs. On 30 September 1989, Dao Heng Group reached an agreement with the Financial Secretary Incorporated to acquire Hang Lung Bank for HK$600 million.

02 Oct 1983

Carrian Group Chairman George Tan Soon-gin (陳松青) was arrested on suspicion of theft and falsifying business reports, followed by a trial on 04 October. On 15 September 1987, after 281 days of trial in the Supreme Court, he and five other defendants were found not guilty due to insufficient evidence and questionable testimony. The investigation initiated in 1985 by the Independent Commission Against Corruption and related court proceedings on alleged corruption and fraud continued as of then.

05 Oct 1983

The German Chamber of Commerce in Hong Kong was formed, promoting bilateral trade and investment between Hong Kong and Germany in support of member interests in Hong Kong, the Mainland and Germany.

08 Oct 1983

Bankers Trust New York Corporation filed a petition with the Supreme Court for liquidation of Carrian Investments on the grounds of insolvency. Petitions for liquidation of Carrian Group and Carrian Investments were also filed by Bumiputra Malaysia Finance Limited and European Alliance Finance Company. On 07 November, liquidation of Carrian Group and Carrian Investments were approved by the Supreme Court.

15 Oct 1983

The government announced two measures to stabilise the Hong Kong dollar: (1) replacing the free-floating exchange rate with a peg to the US dollar; and (2) abolishing tax on interest earned from deposits in Hong Kong dollar.

17 Oct 1983

The linked exchange rate system with an official rate of HK$7.8 to US$1 was formally implemented. It required note-issuing banks to deposit reserves in US dollar with the Exchange Fund when issuing currency in Hong Kong dollar. Note-issuing banks may also exchange Hong Kong dollars for US dollars with the Exchange Fund. The system remains in place today.

19 Oct 1983

In the fifth round of the second phase of Sino-British negotiations in Beijing on the future of Hong Kong, Vice Minister of Foreign Affairs Yao Guang (姚廣) noted a message from Prime Minister Margaret Thatcher brought forward by British Ambassador to China Percy Cradock on 14 October. The message stating Britain's willingness to accept China's proposal as a basis for further negotiation was welcomed by China; China stressed that further negotiation must be based on the resumption of Chinese sovereignty over all of Hong Kong. The sixth round of talks began on 14 November. During these talks, Britain no longer insisted on British governance of Hong Kong post-1997.

23 Oct 1983

Urban Councillor Pao Ping-wing (浦炳榮) was named one of the "Ten Outstanding Young Persons of the World" by the Junior Chamber International as the first Hong Kong citizen to receive the award.

15 Nov 1983

The first Guangdong group of 25 tourists, organised by Guangdong (HK) Tours Company Limited, arrived in Hong Kong as the first group of Mainland sightseers in 30 years, making a visit to the Peak, Ocean Park, Jumbo Floating Restaurant, among other tourist attractions.

20 Nov 1983

Mother Teresa arrived in Hong Kong from India for a three-day visit during which she spoke at the third International Federation for Family Life Promotion Conference.

06 Dec 1983

The Hong Kong Observatory recorded a minor earthquake of magnitude 2.8 on the Richter scale at 10:26 p.m. in Mai Po.

18 Dec 1983

The China Hotel Guangzhou was partially opened for business; it became fully operational following an opening ceremony on 10 June 1984. It came as a joint venture between Hong Kong Shin Ho Ch'eng Development Limited and Guangzhou Yangcheng Service Company for a total investment of US$100 million. Major investors of Shin Ho Ch'eng Company included Fung King-hey (馮景禧), Li Ka-shing (李嘉誠), Kwok Tak-seng (郭得勝), Cheng Yu-tung (鄭裕彤), Gordon Wu Ying-sheung (胡應湘) and Lee Shau-kee (李兆基).

1983

The Antiquities and Monuments Office received reports from a Wong Chuk Hang resident on rock carvings with three spiral patterns located about a kilometre inland from the shore. In 1984, the rock carvings were declared monuments by the government.

01 Jan 1984

The City Polytechnic of Hong Kong was founded in accordance with the City Polytechnic of Hong Kong Ordinance 1983. Chung Sze-yuen (S. Y. Chung) (鍾士元) was appointed as Chairman of its Board of Directors. The institution was officially opened in a ceremony on 22 October with a temporary campus in central Mong Kok, offering courses in accounting, business management, computer programming and social administration under Founding Director Dr David Johns.

Figure 228
Urban taxi drivers during a strike on
11 January 1984. (Photo courtesy of
Sing Tao News Corporation Limited)

11 Jan 1984

The government announced an increase of taxi licence and registration fees as well as the suspension of issuance of urban tax licences, effective immediately, in addition to a 17% increase in taxi fares beginning 01 February. The next day, 12 urban taxi associations launched a protest by parking thousands of taxis or slowly driving down major roads across Hong Kong, resulting in serious traffic congestion. (Figure 228)

13 Jan 1984

Representatives of urban taxi associations demanded taxi licence and registration fee increases proposed by the government be withdrawn in a meeting with Vice President of the Hong Kong Branch of Xinhua News Agency Qi Feng (祁烽), Hong Kong Chief Secretary for Administration David Akers-Jones, and unofficial members of the Legislative and Executive Councils. At 9 p.m., crowds of young people went on a rampage in Mong Kok by blocking traffic, setting fire to garbage cans, throwing stones at a police station and looting stores. Riot police were deployed, firing tear gas for the first time since 1959. At least 30 people were injured in the conflict; 172 were arrested by 15 January. On 18 January, proposed fee increases were rejected in the Legislative Council.

16 Jan 1984

Communication Services Limited, a subsidiary of Hong Kong Telecom, was granted a government licence as the first provider of mobile radio telephone services, enabling local and international calls through mobile phone devices installed in cars.

25 Jan 1984

The Standing Committee on Company Law Reform was formed by the government to provide regular review and suggestion with the Financial Secretary on the Companies Ordinance, Securities Ordinance and Protection of Investors Ordinance.

27 Jan 1984

The Companies (Amendment) Ordinance 1984 was promulgated, taking effect on 31 August. It 1) reduced the minimum number of persons required to incorporate a public company to two, 2) governed the way companies were allowed to amend memorandums, 3) prohibited transfer of shares from a holding company to a subsidiary, 4) regulated matters regarding contracts prior to company incorporation, and 5) authorised the Registrar of Companies to reject companies with misleading names.

28 Jan 1984

Nine pop singers won in the inaugural Jade Solid Gold Best Ten Music Awards Presentation (1983) hosted by Television Broadcasts Limited (TVB). Anita Mui Yim-fong (梅艷芳) won two awards for her hit songs "Red Doubts" and "Hand over My Heart."

31 Jan 1984

Four armed robbers escaped with 134 million yen (about HK$4.6 million) taken from an armoured truck at the Central Branch of Po Sang Bank as a gunfight with the police broke out, leading to one death and two injuries. On 05 February, all four were captured following a gunfight as police broke into their hideout at Wun Sha Tower in Causeway Bay where weapons and narcotics were uncovered.

01 Feb 1984

Hong Kong singers Cheung Ming-man (張明敏) and Stella Chee (奚秀蘭) made a special appearance, along with actress Chen Sisi (陳思思) as one of the masters of ceremony, at the 1984 CCTV Spring Festival (Chinese New Year) Gala in Beijing. It was the first time that Hong Kong artists participated in the annual gala.

15 Feb 1984

A government paper titled *Further Development of Local Administration* was released, proposing 1) a gradual increase in the number of elected seats in District Boards beginning in the following year to reach a ratio of 2–1 in terms of elected and appointed members, 2) expanded functions of District Boards, and 3) a new Regional Council (resembling the Urban Council) for cultural, recreational and environmental affairs in the New Territories, supported by representatives of Heung Yee Kuk as ex-officio members.

21 Feb 1984

The Hong Kong Affairs Society was formed as a political commentary group consisting of working professionals including scholars, lawyers and business executives. Huang Chen-ya (黃震遐) was the founding president.

29 Feb 1984

A sweater factory in an industrial building in San Po Kong was burglarised. The safe-deposit box and more than 100 pieces of jewellery, with a total value of about HK$120 million, were stolen, making it the largest burglary case in Hong Kong.

01 Mar 1984

The Contemporary Open Air Sculpture Exhibition, co-organised by the Urban Council in conjunction with Hong Kong Sculptors Association and curated by the Hong Kong Museum of Art, was opened at the Hong Kong Coliseum piazza where over 30 pieces of artwork by sculptors of the Association and from around Asia were presented.

05 Mar 1984

The rebuilt Chinese Manufacturers Association Building was opened upon completion.

14 Mar 1984

The Legislative Council passed a non-binding motion proposed by Roger Lobo, an Unofficial Member of the Council, asking that any proposal regarding the future of Hong Kong be debated in the Legislative Council before any final agreement could be reached. China opposed the Lobo Motion and deemed it another British attempt to include Hong Kong as a third party in the Sino-British negotiations.

26 Mar 1984

The 11th round of talks in the second phase of Sino-British negotiations on the future of Hong Kong was held in Beijing. Britain proposed 1) that a "maximum degree of autonomy" replace a "high degree of autonomy" asserted by China, 2) that Chinese troops not to be stationed in Hong Kong, and 3) that a representative body of "British commissioners" (distinct from general consuls) be stationed in Hong Kong, different from the consulates of other countries in Hong Kong. These were all firmly opposed by China. By this point, negotiation on the first agenda item with respect to the post-1997 arrangement in Hong Kong was essentially complete.

28 Mar 1984

Jardine Matheson Holdings announced its re-incorporation in Bermuda, effective 14 May, making it the first British conglomerate to do so since the beginning of the Sino-British negotiation over the future of Hong Kong.

11 Apr 1984

The 12th round of talks in the second phase of Sino-British negotiations on the future of Hong Kong was held in Beijing. Up until the 22nd round on 06 September, discussion covered matters relating to the transition period and transfer of power.

14 Apr 1984

World Vision Hong Kong held its first "30-Hour Famine" fundraiser at St. Stephen's College in Stanley, where more than 4,000 people took part in a fasting without solid food for 30 hours, raising HK$330,000 by the end of the following day.

16 Apr 1984

The Hong Kong University Students' Union released a Declaration on the Future of Hong Kong, reiterating Chinese sovereignty over Hong Kong under a high degree of autonomy with a proposal on democratisation in the transition period and public participation in drafting the Basic Law. The following day, the Declaration was presented to the Government House and the Hong Kong Branch of Xinhua News Agency.

20 Apr 1984

Upon arrival in Hong Kong from Beijing, British Secretary of State for Foreign and Commonwealth Affairs Geoffrey Howe announced in a press conference that Britain would give up its sovereignty and rule over Hong Kong after 1997 and that China and Britain would study and find a way to ensure a high degree of autonomy in Hong Kong under Chinese sovereignty.

23 Apr 1984

Deputy Director of Hong Kong and Macao Affairs Office of the State Council Li Hou (李後) and Advisor to the Department of West European Affairs of the Ministry of Foreign Affairs Lu Ping (魯平) met with 14 members of Hong Kong's Urban Council and District Boards in Beijing. Li Hou was quoted as saying that HKSAR would remain financially independent and would not be required to contribute to any military expenses while citizens would not be subject to military service.

09 May 1984

Nine unofficial members of the Executive and Legislative Councils formed a delegation to Britain, stressing the will of Hong Kong in the Sino-British negotiations. Prior to departure, they released a Statement on the Future of Hong Kong, appealing for a full understanding of the Basic Law in detail by the British government prior to any agreement with China. On 11 May, Xinhua News Agency said that the statement was an attempt of obstruction detrimental to the long-term prosperity and stability of Hong Kong.

25 May 1984

In a meeting with Hong Kong and Macao deputies of the National People's Congress and the Chinese People's Political Consultative Conference, Deng Xiaoping (鄧小平), Chairman of the Central Military Commission of the Communist Party of China, said: "The Chinese government has the right to station troops in Hong Kong upon resuming sovereignty over Hong Kong. It is a symbol of safeguarding the People's Republic of China, a symbol of national sovereignty, and a guarantee of Hong Kong's stability and prosperity."

22 Jun 1984

In meetings with Hong Kong's business leaders and prominent individuals over two days, Deng Xiaoping (鄧小平) said: "Our adoption of 'One Country, Two Systems' on the issue of Hong Kong…is a pragmatic approach with full consideration of Hong Kong's historical and current circumstances…we need to believe that Chinese in Hong Kong can govern Hong Kong…the key to local governance by Hong Kong people is that Hong Kong should be governed by local patriots."

01 Jul 1984

The Hong Kong Academy for Performing Arts was established in accordance with the Hong Kong Academy for Performing Arts Ordinance 1984, followed by the opening of the main building on 18 September 1985. The Academy was constructed on land granted by the government with funding of HK$300 million from The Hong Kong Jockey Club. As Hong Kong's only public specialist institution in performing arts, it began with departments dedicated to dance, drama, music and technical arts under its first president Basil Deane.

02 Jul 1984

The government released an urban planning framework *Territorial Development Strategy*, outlining two models of urban development with a focus on reclamation around Victoria Harbour (near West Kowloon, Hung Hom Bay, Central and Wan Chai) to create 1,000 hectares of land at an estimated cost of HK$190 billion.

05 Jul 1984

The Yuen Long Industrial Estate, Hong Kong's second industrial estate designed with flats of factory units, was opened in a ceremony.

18 Jul 1984

The *Green Paper on the Further Development of Representative Government in Hong Kong* was released, proposing an electoral system of indirectly electing a portion of unofficial members (not by virtue of government office) of the Legislative Council by geographic and functional constituencies. On 21 November, a subsequent government white paper was released, indicating a public conviction in support of the green paper and suggesting that 24 of the 56 members of the Legislative Council be selected by indirect elections beginning in 1985 with the elimination of one appointed member and three official members.

08 Aug 1984

Kornhill Garden went on sale as the first major residential project on top of a station of MTR's Island Line under a joint venture of MTR Corporation, Hang Lung Properties and New World Development for an investment of HK$4 billion. Construction of 6,640 apartment units in 32 buildings began on 03 May 1984 and was completed in phases between 1986 and 1987.

17 Aug 1984

Amendments to the Royal Instructions were promulgated, effective 01 September, increasing the number of unofficial members in the Legislative Council from 29 to 32.

04 Sep 1984

An international medical technology fair was held at the Hong Kong Exhibition Centre to showcase products of medical equipment manufacturers and facilitate exchange among medical professionals and practitioners.

14 Sep 1984

Nearly 90 exhibitors from different countries took part in the first international eyewear exhibition in Hong Kong, organised by the Business & Industrial Trade Fairs Limited, showing different types of spectacles, lens production materials and equipment.

26 Sep 1984

The Joint Declaration of the Government of the United Kingdom of Great Britain and Northern Ireland and the Government of the People's Republic of China on the Question of Hong Kong, along with Annex I (Elaboration by the government of the People's Republic of China of its basic policies regarding Hong Kong), Annex II (Sino-British Joint Liaison Group) and Annex III (Land Leases), was initialled by British Ambassador to China Richard Evans and Chinese Vice Minister of Foreign Affairs Zhou Nan (周南) in Beijing. The People's Republic of China declared it would resume the exercise of sovereignty over Hong Kong while the United Kingdom declared it would restore Hong Kong to the People's Republic of China with effect from 01 July 1997.

10 Oct 1984

Yip Kai-foon (葉繼歡) and three other culprits took more than HK$930,000 worth of jewellery and watches in an armed robbery of King Fook Jewellery in Tsim Sha Tsui, followed by another armed robbery at Dickson Watch and Jewellery at Landmark in Central on 27 October, snatching about HK$8 million worth of jewellery and watches. Yip was arrested by undercover policemen posing as buyers on 28 December; he was found guilty of possessing arms without a licence and handling stolen goods and sentenced to 18 years in prison by the Supreme Court on 08 October 1985.

13 Oct 1984

The Hong Kong Institute of Surveyors was established for the development of industry standards in surveying.

Oct 1984

The Hong Kong Housing Authority formed a committee on housing subsidy to tenants of public housing with measures for assessment of tenant eligibility and a proposal to reduce subsidy with tenants whose income exceeded a given threshold. On 05 May 1985, a green paper titled *Housing Subsidy to Tenants of Public Housing* was released, proposing double rent for tenants of 10 years or more under improved personal finances unless proven otherwise.

01 Nov 1984

The Hong Kong Federation of Drama Societies was formed as an association of local theatre groups and performers to promote industry development and international exchange.

11 Nov 1984

The Federation of Hong Kong and Kowloon Labour Unions was formed as an integrated platform of 17 trade unions with over 15,000 members under the chairmanship of Chan Bun (陳彬).

12 Nov 1984

Banca Commerciale Italiana opened its first branch in Hong Kong where it used to have a representative office only.

15 Nov 1984

The Hong Kong branch of China Life Insurance Company Limited was opened.

23 Nov 1984

The Community Service Orders Ordinance 1984 was promulgated, making community service orders available to offenders aged 14 or above found guilty of an offence punishable by imprisonment. A court of law may issue an order for community service not more than 240 hours in lieu of imprisonment completely or partially.

26 Nov 1984

The Pacific City Bank of the United States, having acquired a controlling stake in the Bank of Canton in 1971, announced an approval granted by the Supreme Court of Hong Kong to acquire the remaining minority stake for US$46 million, making the Bank of Canton a wholly owned subsidiary.

04 Dec 1984

The 70-km Lantau Trail, a trail loop around South Lantau with a start and end point at Mui Wu, was opened as the first long distance hiking trail on Lantau Island.

Figure 229
On 19 December 1984, China and Britain formally signed the Sino-British Joint Declaration. (Photo courtesy of Xinhua News Agency)

08 Dec 1984

In the Centenary Cup Race, held by The Hong Kong Jockey Club at Sha Tin Racecourse, a horse named Silver Star suddenly stumbled while crossing the finishing line, causing the fall of British jockey Brian Taylor who died two days later from serious injuries in the first race-related death of a professional jockey in Hong Kong.

09 Dec 1984

Yaohan, a Japanese-owned department store, opened its first outlet at New Town Plaza in Sha Tin. On 21 November 1997, all nine outlets in Hong Kong were closed.

The Kowloon Mosque in Tsim Sha Tsui was re-opened under The Incorporated Trustees of the Islamic Community Fund of Hong Kong upon renovation with a four-storey building designed with a peach-shaped dome as the largest mosque in Hong Kong.

19 Dec 1984

The Sino-British Joint Declaration was formally signed by Chinese Premier Zhao Ziyang (趙紫陽) and British Prime Minister Margaret Thatcher in the presence of Chairman of the CPC Central Advisory Commission Deng Xiaoping (鄧小平) and President of the People's Republic of China Li Xiannian (李先念) at the West Hall of the Great Hall of the People in Beijing. The People's Republic of China announced resumption of sovereignty over Hong Kong while Britain declared restoration of Hong Kong to the People's Republic of China effective 01 July 1997. The Chinese government also outlined its basic policies regarding Hong Kong in the Joint Declaration. (Figure 229)

28 Dec 1984

Yue Xiu Enterprise Limited was incorporated as a business arm of the Guangzhou municipal government in Hong Kong responsible for attracting capital, technology, talent and management expertise from the international market including Hong Kong. On 08 September 1992, it was registered as Yue Xiu Enterprise (Holdings) Limited.

Dec 1984

The novella *Rouge* was released by writer Lilian Lee Pik-wah (李碧華). In March 1987, filming began for an adaptation; it won six awards at the 24th Taiwan Golden Horse Awards (1987), placed first at the 10th Nantes Three Continents Festival (1988), and won seven awards (including Best Film, Best Screenwriter and Best Director) at the eighth Hong Kong Film Awards (1989).

1984

The *Guide to the Kindergarten Curriculum*, prepared by the Curriculum Development Council, was released to provide guidelines with respect to one- and two-year kindergarten programmes, emphasising play-based learning and exposure relevant to the everyday life of children.

1984

Tin Ka Ping No. 1 Secondary School in Dapu County, Guangdong Province was opened for classes as the first secondary school in the Mainland funded by the Tin Ka Ping Foundation.

05 Jan 1985

Hong Kong Literary was founded under the editorship of Liu Yichang (劉以鬯). It was the longest-running literary journal in Hong Kong as of 2017.

09 Jan 1985

The Education Commission published *Report No. 1*, proposing to phase out the Junior Secondary Education Assessment while providing greater access to senior secondary education among Form 3 students.

13 Jan 1985

The Housing Department completed a structural investigation of 11 public housing blocks at Kwai Fong Estate and announced that all the buildings were structurally safe but in need of maintenance. Block 5 would be demolished and rebuilt due to economic considerations. On 23 January, the Housing Department announced that Blocks 9, 10 and 11 would be demolished and rebuilt; affected residents were to be relocated to new housing estates in Tsuen Wan, Ngau Tau Kok and Sha Tin. This was the first large-scale redevelopment and maintenance operation of a public housing estate in Hong Kong.

18 Jan 1985

A contract-signing ceremony was held in Beijing to mark the Guangdong Nuclear Power Joint Venture—a partnership between Hong Kong Nuclear Investment Company Limited (a wholly owned subsidiary of CLP Holdings Limited) and Guangdong Nuclear Investment Company Limited—under which CLP was to take a 25% stake and purchase 70% of electricity upon operation of the nuclear power plant.

22 Jan 1985

Hutchison Whampoa Ltd acquired a 34.6% stake in Hongkong Electric from Hongkong Land for HK$6.40 per share, totalling HK$2.9 billion, making it a substantial shareholder in Hongkong Electric. Hutchison Whampoa Ltd Chairman Li Ka-shing (李嘉誠) said the deal demonstrated the company's confidence in the future of Hong Kong.

23 Jan 1985

The Fu Shan Crematorium and Columbaria in Sha Tin—equipped with the first four new computer-controlled cremators in Hong Kong—became operational under the management of the Regional Services Department.

Jan 1985

The Hongkong and Shanghai Banking Corporation and Standard Chartered Bank began simultaneously issuing new, smaller-sized banknotes in denominations of HK$100 and HK$1,000 on which the word "colony" was removed. The banknotes were also standardised in size for each denomination.

04 Feb 1985

The Asian headquarters of Wang Laboratories began operations in Hong Kong upon its relocation from the US state of Hawaii.

The Medical and Health Department announced Hong Kong's first suspected case of AIDS as the patient in question was being treated in isolation at Princess Margaret Hospital. On 17 February, the patient died of AIDS according to clinical diagnosis.

14 Feb 1985

The Progressive Hong Kong Society was formed under the chairmanship of Maria Tam Wai-chu (譚惠珠), comprising members mostly from the Executive Council, Legislative Council and Urban Council. The group was dedicated to raising awareness on the future of Hong Kong and encouraging public service and administrative participation; it merged with the Liberal Democratic Federation of Hong Kong in November 1990.

01 Mar 1985

The International Festival of Publications was held and attended by publishers from many countries. Exhibits included books, magazines, calligraphy and stationery.

07 Mar 1985

The second District Council election was held—with 237 elected seats and a turnout rate of 37.5%.

Mar 1985

The Beijing-Hong Kong Academic Exchange Centre, initiated by Franklin Yang Chen-ning (楊振寧), was established and registered in Hong Kong as a non-profit supporting group and liaison to facilitate international academic and technology exchange with the Mainland.

01 Apr 1985

The Provisional Regional Council, Municipal Services Branch, and Administration Branch were established by the government. The Provisional Regional Council was responsible for areas outside the jurisdiction of the Urban Council. The Municipal Services Branch was responsible for matters relating to municipal hygiene, recreation and cultural development. The Administration Branch was responsible for government information and public relations, registration of newspapers and periodicals, and oversight of gaming and large-scale public entertainment.

The Kwai Chung/Tsing Yi District Board was formed as a spinoff from the Tsuen Wan District Board, thereby increasing the total number of district boards to 19. Ho Tung-ching (何冬青) served as chairman of the newly formed district board; he was the first non-government-appointed chairman.

The Hong Kong Institute for the Promotion of Chinese Culture was established, aiming to promote Chinese culture and facilitate academic exchange between local and overseas intellectuals through cultural activities, educational initiatives and scholarships.

04 Apr 1985

Amendments to the Letters Patent and Royal Instructions were promulgated, authorising the governor of Hong Kong to enact laws regarding elections of the Legislative Council, supervise elections, suspend from the exercise of functions of any official or appointed members, and dissolve the Legislative Council.

The Queen signed the Hong Kong Act 1985, passed by the House of Commons and the House of Lords in the United Kingdom. It ratified the Sino-British Joint Declaration signed in Beijing in December 1984 and formally declared that Britain would cease ruling Hong Kong in 1997; it put into effect the British Memorandum in the Sino-British Joint Declaration. Instead of British Dependent Territories citizenship, residents of Hong Kong were to be given British National (Overseas) status, effective 01 July 1997.

The Protection of Wages on Insolvency Ordinance 1985 was promulgated, establishing a Protection of Wages on Insolvency Fund. In cases of employer insolvency or bankruptcy, employees could apply for ex-gratia payments (capped at four months' pay or HK$8,000). It was later expanded to cover payments in lieu of notice, as well as severance and outstanding annual leave and statutory holidays, subject to a compensation ceiling.

10 Apr 1985

The Sino-British Joint Declaration along with the decision to establish the Basic Law Drafting Committee were ratified by the Third Session of the Sixth National People's Congress.

12 Apr 1985

Malaysian government auditor-general Tan Sri Ahmad Noordin appointed representatives to cooperate with the Independent Commission Against Corruption on the alleged corruption of Bumiputra Malaysia Finance.

20 Apr 1985

A British teenage couple were murdered on Braemar Hill in North Point. In a ruling on 20 January 1987, all four defendants were found guilty of murder; three were initially sentenced to death. The sentences were commuted to life imprisonment in 1992.

24 Apr 1985

The 50-kilometre Hong Kong Trail—running from the Peak to Big Wave Bay in Shek O—was opened to the public as the first long-distance hiking trail on Hong Kong Island.

Apr 1985

The Neighbourhood and Workers Service Centre was founded by New Youth Study Society mentor and Kwai Tsing District Board member Leung Yiu-chung (梁耀忠); it became a registered organisation on 01 September 1986.

01 May 1985

Six masked robbers, including Kwai Ping-hung (季炳雄), took off with watches worth about HK$1.8 million in an armed robbery of the Time Watch Company in Tsim Sha Tsui and exchanged three rounds of fire with police officers before getting away; nine people were injured.

07 May 1985

The Hong Kong Commodity Exchange was renamed Hong Kong Futures Exchange to reflect the expanded coverage of trading in financial futures contracts.

19 May 1985

Hong Kong won 2–1 in a football match with the Mainland at the Workers' Stadium in Beijing. It was part of the East Asian Zone 4 of the 1986 World Cup qualification rounds.

24 May 1985

Hong Kong Dragon Airlines Ltd was incorporated; it was issued an air operator's certificate by the Civil Aviation Department on 23 July 1985. It made its maiden flight from Hong Kong to Malaysia on 26 July. It was the first Chinese-owned airline in Hong Kong and the second air carrier registered locally.

27 May 1985

The Sino-British Joint Declaration was officially effective as instruments of ratification and annexes were exchanged between the Chinese and the British governments in Beijing.

The Sino-British Joint Liaison Group in accordance with the Sino-British Joint Declaration was formed to support implementation and facilitate a smooth transition with the return of Hong Kong in 1997. It was to identify measures to be taken by both governments upon agreement with respect to the economic and social status of the HKSAR as a member of the international community. Meetings were to be held at least once a year respectively in Beijing, London and Hong Kong. The group was to be dissolved on 01 January 2000.

The Sino-British Land Commission was established in accordance with the Sino-British Joint Declaration, comprising British and Chinese representatives in equal measure. It was responsible for addressing the issue of land leases as prescribed in Annex III of the Sino-British Joint Declaration, including review of proposed land use measuring less than 50 hectares not intended for public housing and an increase of land supply as suggested by the government prior to 30 June 1997. The commission held 35 meetings and granted a total of 2,972 hectares of land, averaging 247.66 hectares per year, before it was dissolved on 30 June 1997.

31 May 1985

The MTR Island Line between Admiralty and Chai Wan became operational; it was further extended with the opening of Sheung Wan Station on 23 May 1986. Japanese department store SOGO Hong Kong in Causeway Bay was opened for business with 130,000 square feet of retail space over 10 storeys at a construction cost of HK$600 million. In 2000, businessmen Cheng Yu-tung (鄭裕彤) and Joseph Lau Luen-hung (劉鑾雄) jointly purchased the property and operating rights of SOGO Hong Kong. (Figure 230)

05 Jun 1985

Lydia Selina Dunn (鄧蓮如) was appointed as Senior Unofficial Member of the Legislative Council, becoming the first woman to hold the position.

Figure 230
Governor Edward Youde (second from left) on the first train of MTR's Island Line on 31 May 1985. (Photo courtesy of HKSAR Government)

Figure 231
CK Asset Holdings' chairman Li Ka-shing (李嘉誠), fourth from right, made an inaugural transaction of the Electronic Payment System at The Landmark in Central on 25 September 1985. (Photo courtesy of Sing Tao News Corporation Limited)

06 Jun 1985

The Overseas Trust Bank came under a government order for two days of operation suspension due to difficulty repaying debts and was subsequently subjected to an investigation by the Police Commercial Crime Bureau. The Overseas Trust Bank (Acquisition) Ordinance 1985 was promulgated on 08 June, authorising a government takeover of the bank. The government announced a capital injection of HK$2 billion (estimated) drawn from the Exchange Fund on 07 June. The bank resumed operations on 10 June. A government agreement on the sale of the bank was reached with Guoco Group on 31 July 1993; it was sold for HK$4.457 billion on 15 October 1993.

12 Jun 1985

Electronic Payment Services, also known as EPS and run by Electronic Payment Services Company (Hong Kong) Limited, became operational with 29 participating banks. (Figure 231)

18 Jun 1985

The Hong Kong Basic Law Drafting Committee and its list of 59 members were approved by the Eleventh Session of the Sixth National People's Congress Standing Committee. The Drafting Committee comprised 36 members from the Mainland and 23 from Hong Kong, including Chairman Ji Pengfei (姬鵬飛) and Vice Chairmen Ann Tse-kai (安子介), Pao Yue-kong (包玉剛), Xu Jiatun (許家屯), Fei Yimin (費彝民), Hu Sheng (胡繩), Fei Xiaotong (Fei Hsiao-tung) (費孝通), Wang Hanbin (王漢斌) and David Li Kwok-po (李國寶).

28 Jun 1985

The 52-storey One Exchange Square and 51-storey Two Exchange Square in Central, developed by Hongkong Land, were opened. The 33-storey Three Exchange Square building was completed in 1988. The Hong Kong Stock Exchange took occupancy on the first and second floors of One and Two Exchange Square.

01 Jul 1985

The Hong Kong Basic Law Drafting Committee held its first plenary meeting in Beijing to decide on committee protocols, outline a master plan for a draft of the Basic Law within four to five years, and establish a broadly representative Basic Law Consultative Committee. (Figure 232)

A housing scheme for elderly persons aiming to provide healthy persons aged 58 or above with hostel-type public rental housing was announced by the Housing Authority. The housing blocks were to be equipped with recreational facilities, shared kitchens and bathrooms supported by housekeepers on duty. In 1987, Heng On Estate in Ma On Shan was opened for occupancy with the first housing units. The scheme was renamed Housing for Senior Citizens on 05 September 1991 and ended in November 2000.

15 Jul 1985

China International Trust & Investment Corporation issued bonds worth HK$300 million with a five-year maturity; it was the first bond issuance by a Mainland enterprise in Hong Kong.

17 Jul 1985

The inaugural meeting of the Basic Law Consultative Committee was held with Hong Kong members of the Basic Law Drafting Committee. It was decided to enlist the support of the Hong Kong Branch of Xinhua News Agency in establishing an office and to draft a Consultative Committee charter under a sub-committee with Simon Li Fook-sean (李福善), Mo Kwan-nin (毛鈞年), Szeto Wah (司徒華), Martin Lee Chu-ming (李柱銘), Dorothy Liu Yiu-chu (廖瑤珠) and Maria Tam Wai-chu (譚惠珠). The Selection Method of Members of the Basic Law Consultative Committee and the Constituency and Composition of Committee Members were adopted in the fourth meeting on 28 September. (Figure 233)

26 Jul 1985

The Legislative Council (Powers and Privileges) Ordinance 1985 was promulgated, expanding the scope of powers of the Legislative Council and providing councillors with special privilege in the discharge of duty.

Figure 232
The HKSAR Basic Law Drafting Committee held its first meeting at the Great Hall of the People in Beijing on 01 July 1985. (Photo courtesy of Xinhua News Agency)

Figure 233
Hong Kong members of the Basic Law Drafting Committee held an inaugural Consultative Committee convenors' meeting at the China Resources Building on 17 July 1985. (Photo courtesy of South China Morning Post Publishers Limited)

09 Aug 1985

The Travel Agents Ordinance 1985 was promulgated, requiring travel agents to obtain a licence from the Travel Agents Registry before starting a business. The Travel Agents Reserve Fund was established as a compensation scheme for travellers affected by an insolvent agent.

11 Aug 1985

The Yellow River Music Festival, organised by the Hong Kong Institute for Promotion of Chinese Culture, began; it ended on 26 August. Among the programmes was a 1,000-person choral performance of *Yellow River Cantata* by the Chinese Central Orchestra Chorus in conjunction with choral groups from Hong Kong and Macao under the conductorship of Yan Liangkun (嚴良堃).

A group of 15 high school students from Guangzhou paid a two-day visit to Hong Kong as the first group of Guangzhou students in the era of national reform and opening-up to take part in a Hong Kong–Macao–Guangzhou exchange organised by Hok Yau Club.

28 Aug 1985

The Garden Hotel Guangzhou—designed by Hong Kong architect Szeto Wai (司徒惠) in a joint project between Hong Kong Garden Hotel (Holdings) Limited and Guangzhou Lingnan Development Company for HK$900 million—was opened for business with a capacity of more than 1,000 rooms as the biggest hotel hitherto in Guangzhou.

09 Sep 1985

The Kowloon Central Library was opened as Hong Kong's largest public library with a collection of 250,000 books, including four special categories dedicated to fine and performing arts, local historical information, early newspapers in Hong Kong, and the Hong Kong Branch of the Royal Asiatic Society.

13 Sep 1985

The United States Senate passed a legislation to increase the annual immigration quota for Hong Kong from 600 to 5,000 individuals.

24 Sep 1985

The Tolo Highway, connecting Sha Tin and Fanling, was unveiled in a ceremony; it was opened to traffic the next day as the main trunk road in eastern New Territories.

Figure 234
Chung Sze-yuen (鍾士元), Senior Unofficial Member of the Legislative Council, cast his vote in the first elections of the Legislative Council on 26 September 1985. (Photo courtesy of South China Morning Post Publishers Limited)

26 Sep 1985

For the first time, 24 members of the Legislative Council were elected—half by the electoral college and half by functional constituencies. The electoral college consisted of 12 groups, comprising members of the Urban Council, Provisional Regional Council and 10 District Boards, with 433 electors and a turnout rate of over 95%. The functional constituencies were divided into nine groups, totalling 46,645 registered voters with a turnout rate of 57.6%. Of 56 seats in the Legislative Council, 10 were official members by virtue of government office, while 22 were appointed by the governor. (Figure 234)

27 Sep 1985

The Hong Kong–Macau Ferry Terminal in Sheung Wan was officially opened; it became operational on 31 October.

28 Sep 1985

The Tai Po Civic Centre—a public venue for music, drama, dance, assembly and school activities under the Provisional Regional Council—was opened as the first civic centre in Hong Kong.

Sep 1985

The Hong Kong International Arbitration Centre, formed with HK$1.2 million of government funding, began services in dispute resolution for enterprises in the Asia Pacific region.

The Hongkong and Shanghai Banking Corporation was issued a licence by the Chinese government to open a branch in Shenzhen; it became the first British bank to be granted a banking licence in the Mainland after 1949.

01 Oct 1985

The Deputy Chief Secretary, a government position created in June, was reassigned to take charge of matters related to constitutional development and elections.

11 Oct 1985

Ng Ming-yam (吳明欽), an elected member of the Tuen Mun District Board, was attacked by a group of 10 assailants armed with iron pipes in the first of such incident. On 04 March 1986, two young men were found guilty of assault with intent to injure after accepting a pecuniary advantage and were sent to a detention centre.

14 Oct 1985

A draft of the Hong Kong (British Nationality) Order 1986 was published by the British government, setting out eligibility requirements for obtaining a British National (Overseas) passport in accordance with the Hong Kong Act 1985.

29 Oct 1985

China Travel Service (Holdings) Hong Kong Limited was incorporated to provide package tours to global destinations, including the Mainland, and process applications for Home Return Certificates.

Acting Premier of the State Council Wan Li (萬里) joined Pao Yue-kong (包玉剛) and his wife at a cornerstone laying ceremony at Ningbo University—an institution conceived and funded by Pao Yue-kong. It was opened in a ceremony on 26 November 1986.

30 Oct 1985

Governor Edward Youde officiated at the opening ceremony of the Legislative Council building (Legislative sessions were previously held in the Central Government Offices). New councillors were also sworn into office on the same day under a new protocol which no longer required the oath of allegiance to the Queen.

21 November 1985

The Housing Department announced that 22 buildings across 10 public housing estates be demolished. Along with four additional buildings at Kwai Fong Estate in an earlier announcement, a total of 26 public housing blocks found to be structurally problematic were to be taken down and redeveloped over a period of four years, affecting about 80,000 residents.

07 Dec 1985

Carrian Group's former chairman George Tan Soon-gin (陳松青) and former director Bentley Ho (何桂全) were arrested by the Independent Commission Against Corruption on suspicion of conspiracy to defraud and illegally providing benefits to two of the company's senior executives. Their decade-long trial began on this day.

18 Dec 1985

The Basic Law Consultative Committee, consisting of 180 members, held its inaugural meeting under the chairmanship of Ann Tse-kai (T. K. Ann) (安子介). It undertook the longest and largest public consultation in the history of Hong Kong before dissolving on 30 April 1990 upon the promulgation of the Basic Law.

1985

Caritas Francis Hsu College was opened as Hong Kong's first Catholic post-secondary institution, offering adult education courses.

The Hong Kong Archaeological Society unearthed Neolithic cord-marked and soft clay pottery, bone tools, shell scrapers and many shells and fish bones at the Po Yue Wan site on Cheung Chau.

The Hong Kong Prevocational Schools Council was established as an advisory body to the government on behalf of local prevocational schools.

01 Jan 1986

The Employment (Amendment) Ordinance 1985 came into effect, introducing long service payment upon termination of employees having served five to ten consecutive years and dismissed for reasons excluding serious misconduct or employee redundancy. The eligibility and amount of long service payment varied with the age of employees.

03 Jan 1986

Senior Unofficial Member of the Legislative Council Lydia Selina Dunn (鄧蓮如), on behalf of all unofficial members, made three written requests with the British House of Commons and House of Lords concerning the draft of the Hong Kong (British Nationality) Order 1986, including granting British National (Overseas) passport holders the right to travel freely to the United Kingdom. On 23 April, Secretary of State for the Home Office Douglas Hurd in the House of Commons agreed to allow BN(O) passport holders to travel to the UK without a visa.

08 Jan 1986

A three-alarm hill fire broke out in Shing Mun Country Park and spread rapidly to Tai Mo Shan, destroying 900 hectares of forest and 130,000 trees. It was extinguished on the following day after 35 hours upon the efforts of about 1,000 firefighters. The country parks in Shing Mun, Tai Mo Shan and Tai Lam, along with the Tai Po Kau Nature Reserve, were closed down on 11 January and were re-opened on 18 February.

17 Jan 1986

The Securities (Stock Exchange Listing) Rules 1986 was promulgated, effective 01 February, giving the Securities Commissioner greater power in overseeing public listing and information disclosure. It required a company going public to file with the commissioner a copy of its application, a set of true and complete supporting documents, and a copy of its letter of commitment with the stock exchange.

21 Jan 1986

Governor Edward Youde authorised the Independent Commission Against Corruption to be exempt from a 1977 governor amnesty concerning corruption cases before 1977 and to launch an investigation on alleged corruption with respect to 26 problematic public housing blocks.

Jan 1986

The Police Complaints Committee was established as a non-statutory body overseeing the Complaints Against Police Office, replacing the Office of the Unofficial Members of the Executive and Legislative Councils Police Group formed in 1977. The committee was renamed the Independent Police Complaints Council on 31 December 1994.

20 Feb 1986

The Independent Commission Against Corruption arrested 22 people in connection with several cases of horseracing fraud, including horse owner and mastermind Yang Yuan-loong (楊元龍). On 03 September, upon the conclusion of a trial in the Supreme Court, Yang who was charged with manipulating several horseracing results between 1985 and 1986 pleaded guilty to six counts of conspiracy to defraud; he was fined HK$5.4 million and sentenced to two years in prison and two years of probation.

06 Mar 1986

The first Regional Council elections were held in conjunction with the Urban Council elections for 12 and 15 seats, respectively, with a turnout rate of approximately 27%.

14 Mar 1986

The Regional Council (Amendment) Ordinance 1986 was promulgated, differentiating the Regional Council from the District Board with additional functions under an amended Chinese name to avoid public confusion between the two bodies.

25 Mar 1986

The government released a report titled *Delivery of Medical Services in Hospitals* (also known as the *Scott's Report)*, revealing an urgent need for an independent agency to improve administrative efficiency in the management of public hospitals.

27 Mar 1986

The four stock exchanges in Hong Kong—Hong Kong Stock Exchange, Far East Exchange, Kam Ngan Stock Exchange and Kowloon Stock Exchange—were closed. On 02 April, the Stock Exchange of Hong Kong was formed in a merger and opened on the second floor of Exchange Square in Central with an automated quotation and trading system. On 22 September, it became a member of the World Federation of Exchanges. (Figure 235)

Figure 235
Chairman Li Fook-shiu（李福兆）delivered a speech at the inaugural ceremony of Hong Kong Stock Exchange on 02 April 1986. (Photo courtesy of South China Morning Post Publishers Limited)

Mar 1986

A Police–Independent Commission Against Corruption (ICAC) joint task force was formed to launch an investigation on alleged conspiracy to defraud with senior executives of Overseas Trust Bank and Dominican Finance, following the bankruptcy of Overseas Trust Bank amid financial losses of nearly HK$700 million. Former chairman of Dominican Finance Simon Yip（葉椿齡）and former chairman of Overseas Trust Bank Huang Tiong-chan（黃長贊）were arrested in the US on 02 May and extradited to Hong Kong on 07 May for trial under the support of the Federal Bureau of Investigation. On 14 July, former chairman of Overseas Trust Bank Patrick Chang Chen-tsong（張承忠）was sentenced by the Supreme Court to three years in prison for conspiracy to defraud. Between December 1986 and June 1987, former managing director of Overseas Trust Bank Chung Chiu-fat（鍾朝發）, former general manager of the Macao Branch of Overseas Trust Bank Cheung Kai-man（張啟民）, along with Simon Yip and Huang Tiong-chan, were successively found guilty of conspiracy to defraud and sentenced to imprisonment from two to eight years. It marked the first successful case in Hong Kong under the joint efforts of the police and ICAC.

01 Apr 1986

The Regional Council was formally established; it held its inaugural meeting.

The Environmental Protection Department, headed by Director Stuart Reed, was established as a central coordinator of nearly all government agencies in tackling pollution.

07 Apr 1986

The fourth-generation HSBC Main Building at 1 Queen's Road Central was opened upon completion at a cost of HK$5.2 billion. The 178.8-metre, 52-storey building, designed by architect Norman Foster, could accommodate 5,000 employees.

16 Apr 1986

The Fight Crime Committee stated in a report that at least 50 triad groups existed in Hong Kong. The report recommended strengthening the witness protection programme, curbing triad activities and imposing heavier penalties.

18 Apr 1986

The Hong Kong Basic Law Drafting Committee held its second plenary session in Beijing where it approved the 1) Structure of the Basic Law of the Hong Kong Special Administrative Region of the People's Republic of China (Draft), 2) Working Rules of the Basic Law Drafting Committee of the Hong Kong Special Administrative Region of the People's Republic of China, and 3) Decisions on the Establishment of Sub-groups of the Basic Law Drafting Committee of the Hong Kong Special Administrative Region of the People's Republic of China. Issues covered in the five subgroups were: 1) relationship between the Central government and HKSAR; 2) rights and duties of residents; 3) political structure; 4) finance and economy; and 5) education, science, technology and culture.

23 Apr 1986

Hong Kong became the 91st signatory of the General Agreement on Tariffs and Trade (succeeded by the World Trade Organization). It allowed Hong Kong to conduct international trade as a separate customs territory with member countries and regions under the rules of free trade.

08 May 1986

The Social Welfare Department, in accordance with the Protection of Women and Juveniles Ordinance 1951, broke into a house at Kwai Hing Estate and rescued Kwok Ah-nui (郭 亞 女), a six-year-old girl in captivity since birth. On 29 July, a panel on social welfare under the Executive and Legislative Councils released a report. It recommended further amendment to the Protection of Women and Juveniles Ordinance 1951 and Mental Health Ordinance 1962, as well as an emergency response unit and expanded services.

14 May 1986

The Committee on the Promotion of Civic Education in Hong Kong was established with an inaugural meeting under the chairmanship of Rita Fan Hsu Lai-tai (范徐麗泰) as a non-statutory body to liaise with the government and community for civic awareness.

17 May 1986

The Civil Aviation Administration of China and Taiwan-based China Airlines held talks in Hong Kong regarding China Airlines Flight 334 in what was the first open dialogue between Mainland and Taiwan officials since 1949. The cargo plane was en route from Bangkok to Taipei via Hong Kong but was commandeered by Captain Wang Hsi-chueh (王錫爵) and flew directly to Guangzhou Baiyun International Airport. On 20 May, after four rounds of negotiation in Hong Kong, an agreement was reached on returning the plane. On 23 May, handover of the plane, its cargo and two crew members (excluding Wang Hsi-chueh) took place at Kai Tak Airport in Hong Kong.

21 May 1986

The third Annual International Leather Exhibition, hosted by the Hong Kong Trade Fair Limited, began in Hong Kong with representatives from 640 companies in 26 countries in an exhibition of half-finished and finished merchandise, related equipment and chemical products.

23 May 1986

The Education Bureau released its *Guidelines on Sex Education in Secondary Schools,* an advisory on gradual implementation of sex education in junior and senior secondary schools where talks and seminars would be held.

30 May 1986

The Banking Ordinance 1986 was promulgated in place of the Banking Ordinance 1982 and Deposit-taking Companies Ordinance 1982, putting all accredited institutions in a three-tier banking system supervised by the Office of the Commissioner of Banking. It aimed to protect depositors and strengthen the overall banking system.

23 Jun 1986

The first Contemporary Chinese Composers Festival began in Hong Kong with a seven-day programme comprising symposiums and nightly concerts held at the Hong Kong Academy for Performing Arts.

26 Jun 1986

The 1986 International Travel Exhibition was held at the Hong Kong Exhibition Centre. Exhibitors included 39 regional tourism administrations, 32 hotels, 23 travel agencies and 18 international airlines.

01 Jul 1986

Chiu Hin-kwong (招顯洸), Daniel Tse Chi-wai (謝志偉), Peter Wong Chak-cheong (王澤長) and William Purves were appointed to the Executive Council by Governor Edward Youde. Chiu Hin-kwong and Daniel Tse Chi-wai were the first two elected members of the Legislative Council to be also appointed to the Executive Council.

04 Jul 1986

The Landlord and Tenant (Consolidation) (Amendment) Ordinance 1986 was promulgated, effective 01 August, easing rent controls on regulated buildings constructed before the Second World War. Starting 19 December, rent for buildings completed after the Second World War could be increased as calculated by the difference between 60% of the prevailing market rent and the current rent paid.

25 Jul 1986

The fourth-round meetings of the Sino-British Joint Liaison Group was concluded with an agreement to establish a registrar of ships in Hong Kong. On 03 December 1990, the Hong Kong Shipping Register was established, allowing ships registered in Hong Kong to continue operations after the establishment of the HKSAR in 1997, in place of the previous shipping register, which was a subsidiary of the UK Ship Register.

02 Aug 1986

Hong Kong was pronounced a cholera-infected port by the Medical and Health Department. Local residents were required to carry proof of vaccination when travelling to restricted countries designated by the World Health Organization. On 19 August, Hong Kong was removed from the list of cholera-infected ports for the last time.

03 Aug 1986

Two Legislative Council delegations on nuclear power visited France, Austria, the US and Japan. On 30 August, a delegation report was released with recommendations to the Chinese Central Government, Hong Kong Government, Guangdong Nuclear Power Joint Venture Company and Hong Kong Nuclear Investment Company. The report supported a Hong Kong–Mainland agreement to enable Hong Kong to closely monitor radiation levels, exchange data and coordinate on contingency plans.

15 Aug 1986

The HKSAR Land Fund was established by the Chinese government in accordance with the Sino-British Joint Declaration for the purpose of holding and managing incomes from land premium in the form of a trust with the future government of the HKSAR.

17 Aug 1986

The first Hong Kong Food Festival, organised by the Hong Kong Tourist Association, was held to promote Hong Kong as a gourmet paradise.

19 Aug 1986

The Hong Kong Observatory hoisted Standby Signal No.1 amid Typhoon Wayne, followed by a No. 8 Northeast Gale or Storm Signal the next day. On 25 August, Typhoon Wayne headed back to Hong Kong where Standby Signal No.1 was hoisted. On 04 September, Typhoon Wayne hit Hong Kong again for which Strong Wind Signal No. 3 was hoisted. It was the first tropical cyclone for which warning signals were hoisted three times in one month.

20 Aug 1986

A petition signed by 1.04 million residents of Hong Kong was presented to the Hong Kong and Macao Affairs Office of the State Council by 12 representatives of the Hong Kong Joint Conference for Shelving the Daya Bay Nuclear Plant.

21 Aug 1986

A tornado hit Tap Mun in Sai Kung and swept two fishing boats up in the air and back into the waters, causing two deaths and two missing.

16 Sep 1986

The Education Commission released *Report No. 2*, proposing a standardised two-year pre-college matriculation programme and a unified tertiary admission system.

17 Sep 1986

The Agreement between the Government of Hong Kong and the Government of the Kingdom of the Netherlands Concerning Air Services was signed by officials of Hong Kong and the Netherlands in The Hague. Effective 26 June 1987 and applicable after the establishment of the HKSAR, it specified scheduled air services with designated airlines in the first agreement by Hong Kong under UK authorisation with another country. As of 01 July 2017, Hong Kong had such an agreement with 67 countries.

20 Sep 1986

In a meeting with Vice Premier of the State Council Li Peng (李鵬) in Beijing, a Legislative Council delegation on nuclear power made several suggestions, including the establishment of a consultative body on nuclear power safety, levies not higher than coal-fired power in Hong Kong, and recruitment of French experts to manage the power plant initially. Li Peng showed support for Hong Kong to take part in the consultation, expressing an understanding of concern regarding safety, and hoped to boost confidence by raising awareness through field trips, exhibitions and education campaigns.

Team Hong Kong participated in the 10th Asian Games in Seoul, South Korea, winning one gold, one silver and three bronze medals. The gold medal was Hong Kong's first in an Asian Games and awarded to Catherine Che Kuk-hung (車菊紅) in the bowling event (women's single) on 26 September.

Sep 1986

The Education Bureau incorporated Putonghua into the primary school (Years 4–6) curriculum.

08 Oct 1986

The word "unofficial" was removed from the titles of Unofficial Members of the Legislative and Executive Councils, making both "unofficial" and "official" members simply known as "members." The change was also applied to the names of the offices of unofficial members.

Leaking chemical fluids caused an explosion in a leather factory at Wing Loi Industrial Building in Kwai Chung, resulting in 14 deaths and 10 injuries.

21 Oct 1986

Queen Elizabeth II and her Royal Consort Prince Philip arrived in Hong Kong for a second time. During their three-day visit, they officiated at the ground-breaking ceremony of the Hong Kong Convention and Exhibition Centre.

26 Oct 1986

The Hong Kong Association for Democracy and People's Livelihood was established under the chairmanship of Ding Lik-kiu (陳立僑), advocating direct elections for a portion of the Legislative Council in 1988.

29 Oct 1986

The Au Tau Pumping Station in Yuen Long was opened in a ceremony as the first phase of an expanded water supply from the East River (Dongjiang). The project included additional water tunnels, pipes and pumping stations, allowing water to flow from Muk Wu Pumping Station near Lo Wu to Tai Lam Chung Reservoir via the new pumping station with a daily capacity of 518,000 cubic metres.

30 Oct 1986

The first phase of Heng Fa Chuen, developed on MTR Island Line's Chai Wan Depot in conjunction with reclamation, was completed. The first 400 units of the residential complex were sold out within an hour at the sale office in Central on 26 July 1985. Heng Fa Chuen was fully constructed in November 1989, comprising about 6,500 units across 48 buildings.

Figure 236
The funeral procession of Governor Edward Youde on 09 December 1986. (Photo courtesy of Hong Kong Museum of History)

02 Nov 1986

The Ko Shan Meeting, initiated by the Joint Committee on the Promotion of Democratic Government comprising 91 community groups under leaders Szeto Wah (司徒華) and Martin Lee Chu-ming (李柱銘), was held at Ko Shan Theatre where a manifesto was issued for a democratic political system with separation of powers, universal suffrage in the Chief Executive elections, and direct elections for a portion of the legislature under the principle of "Hong Kong people governing Hong Kong."

07 Nov 1986

The *South China Morning Post* was acquired by News Corporation, a company owned by Australian businessman Rupert Murdoch, marking the first-time ownership by a non-British syndicate since its inception in 1903.

09 Nov 1986

A branch of New York-based Asian Cultural Council was established in Hong Kong to promote training of talent and exchange between Asia and the US in visual arts, performing arts and art education through grants and special events.

12 Nov 1986

Sun Xing (孫興) was named winner in the final round of the first Mr TV Quest hosted by Asia Television at the Hong Kong Coliseum.

02 Dec 1986

The Hong Kong Trade Development Council's Beijing Office was inaugurated. The Hong Kong Products Exhibition began on the next day at the China International Exhibition Centre in Beijing; more than 2,500 products were exhibited by 70 Hong Kong manufacturers and companies.

03 Dec 1986

Wong Kwan-cheng (王寬誠) passed away in Beijing at the age of 80. He was a member of the Sixth Chinese People's Political Consultative Conference, Deputy Director of the Executive Committee of the Basic Law Consultative Committee, and founder of the K. C. Wong Education Foundation. On 10 December, his funeral was held at Beijing Hospital in the presence of over 500 people, including Premier of the State Council Zhao Ziyang (趙紫陽). He was buried at Babaoshan Revolutionary Cemetery in Beijing.

05 Dec 1986

Governor Edward Youde passed away at the age of 62 from a heart attack at the British Embassy in Beijing where he attended the opening ceremony of Hong Kong Trade Development Council's Beijing Office and that of the Hong Kong Products Exhibition. He was the only governor to die in office. (Figure 236)

The Tuen Mun Ferry Pier at Butterfly Beach was opened for a Tuen Mun-Central hover ferry service operated by The Hongkong and Yaumatei Ferry Company. The route ended on 17 July 2000; routes (bound for Tai O, Macao and Zhuhai) by other carriers continued.

12 Dec 1986

The Hong Kong Sanatorium and Hospital announced the birth of Hong Kong's first infant conceived through in-vitro fertilisation.

26 Dec 1986

A four-alarm fire in the Aberdeen Typhoon Shelter destroyed 170 boats and injured two people; 1,657 victims were registered. The government announced that 80% of the victims would be resettled in public housing units at Lei Tung Estate in Ap Lei Chau due for completion shortly.

1986

The Hong Kong Economic and Trade Office established a branch in San Francisco to promote economic and trade partnerships with 19 states of the western United States.

The Hong Kong Committee for the United Nations Children's Fund was established to support protection of children's rights through campaigns such as fundraising and collaborative efforts with other organisations.

Archaeological excavations at Penny's Bay on Lantau Island, undertaken by the Hong Kong Archaeological Society, yielded over 20,000 blue-and-white porcelain fragments. These were mostly manufactured in the town of Jingdezhen, Jiangxi Province during the reign years (1465–1521) between Emperor Chenghua (成化) and Emperor Zhengde (正德) of the Ming Dynasty. From September to October 1990, similar artefacts, as well as a few Southeast Asian pottery fragments, were discovered at the site in an excavation by the Antiquities and Monuments Office. From January to March 1991, relics from the site were exhibited for the first time at Hong Kong Museum.

06 Jan 1987

A police search in six locations across Hong Kong uncovered cannabis worth approximately HK$16.8 million in Tai Tam on Hong Kong Island; seven people were arrested. It was then the largest cannabis criminal case in Hong Kong.

08 Jan 1987

The Junior Secondary Education Assessment (a standardised examination for Form 3 students) was held for the last time over two days. Starting from the 1987 academic year, students were enrolled in Form 4 based on in-school academic assessment and availability of school places.

14 Jan 1987

A government plan to demolish the Kowloon Walled City and make it a public park was announced. The Chinese government issued a statement in support of the plan. About 40,000 residents were to be resettled in three batches over three years.

16 Jan 1987

The Kowloon–Canton Railway's Lo Wu Station was opened along with a nearby six-storey building as a Hong Kong immigration and customs checkpoint with a double-deck pedestrian bridge connecting to the Luohu Port Joint Inspection Building (operational since 14 June 1985) in Shenzhen.

20 Feb 1987

The Control of Obscene and Indecent Articles Ordinance 1987 was promulgated, establishing an Obscene Articles Tribunal on 01 September. It served to regulate articles deemed obscene or indecent (including material considered violent, depraved or repulsive), determine whether a public article was obscene or indecent, and classify articles as obscene or indecent or neither obscene nor indecent.

The Sha Tin Central Library was opened as the first public library under the Regional Council.

25 Feb 1987

The 1987/88 Budget was released, introducing measures regarding double taxation for taxpayers with local and overseas employment.

26 Feb 1987

The Fire Services Headquarters Building in Tsim Sha Tsui was opened as the first permanent department headquarters.

12 Mar 1987

Amy Chan Lim-chee (陳念慈), Hui So-hung (許素虹), Vong Iu-veng (黃耀榮), Chong Siao-chin (張小遷), Hung Chung-yam (洪松蔭) and Yuko Gordon were named winners of the first Hong Kong Sports Stars Awards, organised by Swire Coca-Cola Hong Kong Limited. The event was co-organised by the Hong Kong Council for Recreation and Sport starting 1992; it was hosted by the Sports Federation and Olympic Committee of Hong Kong, China (SF&OC) in conjunction with the Leisure and Cultural Services Department starting from November 2000 and was solely organised by the SF&OC from 2004 onwards.

13 Mar 1987

The Public Order (Amendment) Ordinance 1986 was promulgated, making it a criminal offence to spread false information, incite public panic or disrupt public order with a maximum penalty of a HK$100,000 fine and two years' imprisonment.

14 Mar 1987

The first Hong Kong Flower Show, organised by the Regional and Urban Councils, took place in Sha Tin Central Park; it became an annual event held alternately in Victoria Park and Sha Tin Central Park. In 2000, after the Urban Council and Regional Council were dissolved, it continued annually in Victoria Park organised by the Leisure and Cultural Services Department.

27 Mar 1987

The Official Languages (Amendment) Ordinance 1987 and Interpretation and General Clauses (Amendment) (No.3) Ordinance 1987 were promulgated, requiring bilingual publication of legislations in English and Chinese with equal legal status. The Bilingual Laws Advisory Committee was established to support the Governor-in-Council on related issues.

30 Mar 1987

Mongkok Workers' Night School was renamed Hong Kong College of Technology. It aimed to provide further education for students who underperformed in public examinations.

01 Apr 1987

The government began implementation of the Housing Subsidy Policy (also known as the Double Rent Policy) by charging double rent among public housing tenants of more than 10 years (inclusive) whose household incomes were more than double the limit allowed in the public housing waiting list.

Herpetologist Anthony Bogadek discovered a reptile endemic to Hong Kong—Bogadek's Burrowing Lizard (*Dibamus bogadeki*)—in Hei Ling Chau.

08 Apr 1987

The *Long-Term Housing Strategy: A Policy Statement* was released, outlining a government plan to build 40,000 public housing units annually, re-develop old housing estates and introduce a Home Purchase Loan Scheme in support of homeownership among low- and middle-income people.

09 Apr 1987

David Clive Wilson took office as the 27th Governor of Hong Kong; he remained in office until 03 July 1992.

16 Apr 1987

In a meeting with the Hong Kong Basic Law Drafting Committee at the Great Hall of the People in Beijing, Deng Xiaoping (鄧小平) stressed that Hong Kong would remain unchanged with a capitalist system for at least 50 years after the return of Hong Kong to China in 1997.

22 Apr 1987

The Shajiao B Power Plant in Dongguan was inaugurated in a button-pressing ceremony and began supplying electricity to Guangdong Province in a HK$4 billion joint venture between SEZ Power Development Company and Gordon Wu Ying-sheung's (胡應湘) Hong Kong Hopewell Power (China) Limited. An inauguration ceremony was held on 29 April 1988.

27 Apr 1987

The government announced amnesty with children under the age of 14 who arrived in Hong Kong illegally before 27 April. The next day, more than 300 children were registered with the Hong Kong Immigration Department.

Apr 1987

Photo Magazine, a monthly magazine on photography and camera equipment, was founded; it ceased publication in 2017.

06 May 1987

The Legislative Council's Finance Committee approved HK$7.2 million to support publishing houses in releasing Chinese textbooks in 16 designated secondary school subjects. Publishers were to provide three different sets of textbooks in each subject and were given a HK$150,000 bonus for every title adopted.

19 May 1987

The British Chamber of Commerce in Hong Kong was established with 103 founding members to promote British investment and Sino-British trade.

27 May 1987

The *Green Paper: 1987 Review of Developments in Representative Government* was released in a public consultation regarding the possibility of direct elections for a portion of the Legislative Council in 1988. On 04 November, survey results published by the government showed that 67% of respondents did not support direct elections. On 11 February 1988, a white paper called *The Development of Representative Government: The Way Forward* was released to announce the postponement of direct elections to 1991 given a lack of social consensus, stressing a gradual uptake of representative government.

29 May 1987

The Immigration (Amendment) (No. 2) Ordinance 1987 was promulgated, making all Chinese residents of seven consecutive years or more in Hong Kong, citizens of British Dependent Territories in accordance with the Hong Kong (British Nationality) Order 1986, and Commonwealth citizens with the right to land in Hong Kong before 01 January 1983 as "permanent residents" with the right of abode in Hong Kong where they may enter and stay freely and unconditionally and were exempt from repatriation or deportation.

05 Jun 1987

The Ocean Park Corporation was incorporated as a statutory body under the Hong Kong Ocean Park Corporation Ordinance 1987.

09 Jun 1987

The Police Regional Crime Unit (Kowloon) in Yau Ma Tei came under a bomb attack, causing part of the ceiling to collapse but no injuries as police officers were out of office. On 19 June, an explosion occurred at Tsim Sha Tsui Centre, causing one injury. On 08 July, another explosion occurred at Cityplaza, causing 14 injuries. A self-proclaimed Hong Kong-based terrorist organisation claimed responsibility. A man suspected of being involved in all three explosions was arrested the next day.

10 Jun 1987

The Hong Kong Writers' Association was established; its inaugural meeting was held the next day under the presidency of Ni Kuang (倪匡).

17 Jun 1987

Hong Kong and Swedish officials signed a five-year trade agreement to lift export restrictions gradually on three types of textile products from Hong Kong effective 01 September and bathrobe products starting from 1990.

Hong Kong Telecommunications (HKT) Limited was incorporated. A merger between Cable & Wireless and Hong Kong Telephone Company, followed by a complete acquisition of shares by HKT, was announced on 19 October. On 01 February 1988, HKT replaced Hong Kong Telephone Company as a publicly listed company.

25 Jun 1987

The Customs Co-operation Council (currently the World Customs Organization) held a conference in Ottawa, Canada where Hong Kong became an official council member.

26 Jun 1987

The Pension Benefits Ordinance 1987 was promulgated, effective 01 July, putting in place a new civil servant pension scheme as an entitlement programme with a mandatory retirement age at 60, except civil servants in the disciplined services.

01 Jul 1987

The Hong Kong (British Nationality) Order 1986 stipulated by the British government came into effect. The Hong Kong Immigration Department began to issue British National (Overseas) passports in which an official endorsement specified the right of abode in Hong Kong and the right to stay in the UK for six months without a visa. From 01 July 1997 onwards, BN(O) passports were issued by the British Consulate in Hong Kong; from 01 October 1997 onwards, first-time registrations were no longer accepted.

The government began issuing the second-generation computerised identity cards in a city-wide renewal scheme. These were to remain in use after the establishment of the HKSAR government on 01 July 1997. There were two types: Hong Kong permanent identity cards, which gave the holder the right of abode in Hong Kong, and Hong Kong identity cards.

10 Jul 1987

The Weights and Measures Ordinance 1987 was promulgated, effective 01 January 1989, specifying the units of measurement (length, area, volume, capacity, mass and weight) and the standards of measurement (metric, British or Chinese units). It also standardised weighing and measuring instruments for commercial purposes in a bid by the Customs and Excise Department to protect consumers from fraudulent transactions.

18 Jul 1987

The government sent the first batch of 70 local teachers to the UK as part of a study abroad programme in conjunction with the recruitment of 84 expatriate teachers through the British Council as teaching staff for the school year starting in September. This was a two-year pilot scheme aiming to raise the standards of English teaching in secondary schools.

23 Jul 1987

The Hong Kong Housing Authority was reorganised as an independent policy-making body with greater discretion in planning, developing and financing public housing. It was responsible for overseeing the implementation of the long-term housing strategy in coordination with private developers on supply. After reorganisation, it continued to be funded by the government with support from the Housing Department as an executive arm. It was no longer chaired by a government official; former Chief Secretary David Akers-Jones served as its first chairman.

29 Jul 1987

A red tide occurred in the marine fish culture zone at Shap Sze Heung in Sai Kung, killing 300,000 kilograms of fish for a loss of HK$14 million among 70 fishermen.

14 Aug 1987

The Hong Kong Artists' Guild was established; David Akers-Jones was its founding chairman.

01 Sep 1987

The Broadcasting Authority was established as a statutory body to supervise television and radio broadcasting and handle public complaints and suggestions under the chairmanship of Allen Lee Peng-fei (李鵬飛).

24 Sep 1987

The Housing Department launched the first-phase demolition of the squatter areas in Shau Kei Wan. By December 1989, six squatter areas, including Ma Shan Village, Holy Cross Path Village and O Pui Lung Village, were taken down while residents were relocated to Tsui Wan Estate in Chai Wan. The two largest squatter areas then in Hong Kong were located in Shau Kei Wan and Diamond Hill.

27 Sep 1987

The Joint Committee on the Promotion of Democratic Government held a rally known as the "Victoria Park Conference on Democratic Government" with about 8,000 people in Victoria Park; it issued a manifesto calling for direct elections of the Legislative Council in 1988.

14 Oct 1987

In protest of the Waste Disposal (Amendment) Bill 1987 adopted by the Legislative Council, over 1,000 farmers surrounded the Legislative Council Building for an hour and a half, trapping the governor and council members inside.

Hong Kong and China Gas Company Limited opened its main gasworks in Tai Po, replacing the Ma Tau Kok Gas Works in Kowloon. It became operational in phases by the end of 1986 for delivery of coal gas and natural gas through a network of pipes across Hong Kong.

16 Oct 1987

The Waste Disposal (Amendment) Ordinance 1987 was promulgated, effective 24 June 1988, banning livestock farms in all urban areas and new towns, as well as other areas where waste treatment did not meet statutory requirements, in a bid to further control water pollution.

The Prisoners (Release under Supervision) Ordinance 1987 was promulgated, empowering the governor to grant parole to prisoners having served half or 20 months (whichever was longer) of prison terms of three years or more (except life imprisonment) upon review by the Release under Supervision Board. The governor could also order early release of those with six more months to go in prison with a sentence of two years or more (except life imprisonment) as recommended by the Board. They were subject to continued supervision under government-run accommodations and were allowed to take up defined employment.

19 Oct 1987

The Hang Seng Index (HSI) plunged by 420 points to close at 3,362 points, down 11%, following a global sell-off on 16 October. It forced a trading halt of HSI futures.

20 Oct 1987

The Hong Kong Stock Exchange and Hong Kong Futures Exchange attempted to stabilise market sentiments with a four-day suspension on the trading of local stocks and futures until 26 October amid plunging stocks worldwide in what became known as the 1987 stock market crash.

25 Oct 1987

A loan of HK$2 billion—including HK$1 billion drawn from the HK Exchange Fund and HK$1 billion from futures brokers and investors—was made available to the Hong Kong Futures Guarantee Corporation Limited in an attempt to resume trading of Hang Seng Index futures.

26 Oct 1987

The Hang Seng Index plunged 1,120 points to close at 2,241, down 33%, as trading resumed. It was the largest single-day drop in the stock market of Hong Kong dubbed "Black Monday."

27 Oct 1987

The Hong Kong Futures Guarantee Corporation Limited was provided with another HK$2 billion loan—HK$1 billion drawn from the HK Exchange Fund and HK$1 billion collectively provided by the Bank of China, HSBC and Standard Chartered Bank—in support of market operation for Hang Seng Index futures.

02 Nov 1987

The five-day third International Anti-Corruption Conference began in Hong Kong with more than 100 participants from 76 organisations across 31 countries and regions in a meeting on international cooperation of fighting corruption.

The Independent Commission Against Corruption indicted three businessmen and seven former government officials on alleged corruption related to the discovery of 26 problematic public housing blocks in 1985. On 11 March 1988, Siu Hon-sum (蕭漢森), former proprietor of a construction company, was convicted of bribery, fined HK$325,000 and sentenced to two years and nine months in prison. On 12 April 1988, Poon Pak-shing (潘伯勝), former assistant manager of the construction company, was convicted of bribery, sentenced to one-year probation in lieu of three months in prison and fined HK$4,000. Other defendants were acquitted.

03 Nov 1987

China Travel Service (Hong Kong) began to process travel documents of Taiwan residents looking to visit their relatives in the Mainland.

11 Nov 1987

The Securities Review Committee, chaired by Ian Hay Davison, was formed to give a full report on the events in the stock and futures markets of 1987, make recommendations on improvement and provide contingency measures for investors. On 02 June 1988, in its report *The Operation and Regulation of the Hong Kong Securities Industry*, it suggested a reorganised management structure of the Hong Kong Stock Exchange and Hong Kong Futures Exchange, along with an independent commission to ensure market order and protect investors.

24 Nov 1987

A four-alarm fire broke out at the Asia Television Building on Broadcast Drive in Kowloon Tong. It lasted for eight hours and kept Asia Television off the air for 10 hours.

25 Nov 1987

The Hong Kong government revised its tobacco tax from a weight-based to a unit-based formula for HK$165 per 1,000 cigarettes.

Between 25 November and 01 December, more than 100 people in Sham Shui Po were admitted to the hospital for consumption of choy sum (a vegetable) which was later found to contain a toxic pesticide called methamidophos in a government lab test.

07 Dec 1987

The Judicial Committee of the Privy Council (UK) ruled that the Court of Appeal of the Supreme Court of Hong Kong had misled the jury during Yip Kai-foon's (葉繼歡) appeal against his conviction of handling stolen goods, thereby ordering a retrial. On 31 May 1988, his sentence was reduced from 18 to 16 years of imprisonment.

13 Dec 1987

The journal *Yazhou Zhoukan* was founded by Chief Editor Michael O'Neill and Managing Editor Thomas Hon Wing Polin (康榮) as a sister publication of the English-language magazine *Asiaweek* and the world's first international Chinese-language journal on current affairs.

18 Dec 1987

The Building Planning (Amendment) Regulations 1987 was promulgated. Effective 08 January 1988, it relaxed restrictions on building design, abolished the 1969 requirement of pitched roofs on buildings to accommodate street lighting, and set a minimum ceiling height of 2.5 metres in all buildings.

Dec 1987

Capital magazine was launched as a financial monthly on the local economy, stock and financial markets.

1987

From 1987 to 1989, a sequence of cultural development between the prehistoric and historical periods was discovered in three archaeological excavations at the Tung Wan site on Lantau, revealing the Neolithic Dongwan culture near the Pearl River estuary for the first time. The excavations were undertaken by The Chinese University of Hong Kong's Centre for Chinese Archaeology and Art in collaboration with Sun Yat-sen University's School of Anthropology in Guangzhou and Shenzhen Museum.

The novel *Last Romance* by Yi Shu (亦舒) was released; a film adaptation began shooting in 1988.

The journal *Readers* was launched as a periodical on book reviews and literary subjects; it ceased publication the following year, resumed on 08 March 1995 and ceased publication again in July 1997.

The Hong Kong Institute of Professional Photographers was established; it aimed to promote professional photography through conferences, exhibitions and contests as a platform among photographers.

02 Jan 1988

Senior staff of the Hong Kong Stock Exchange, including former chairmen Ronald Li Fook-shiu (李福兆), Sun Hon-kuen (辛漢權) and Tsang Tak-hung (曾德雄), were arrested by the Independent Commission Against Corruption on allegations of accepting bribes in exchange for approving listing applications in 1986 and 1987. On 18 October 1990, Li was convicted and sentenced to four years in prison; HK$865,365 in proceeds from his resale of shares were confiscated.

15 Jan 1988

The Land Development Corporation Ordinance 1987 was promulgated, establishing the Land Development Corporation (predecessor of the Urban Renewal Authority) as a statutory body for urban renewal projects under government funding and prudent business principles.

16 Jan 1988

The first tour arranged by Taiwan's Mainlander Homebound and Visiting Relatives Promotion Society made its way to the Mainland via Hong Kong.

22 Jan 1988

The New Territories Leases (Extension) Ordinance 1988 was promulgated, allowing land leases in the New Territories and New Kowloon due to expire before 30 June 1997 to be extended to 30 June 2047 without further premiums, except short-term leases, special leases and those under the Land Registry in the form of a memorandum.

26 Jan 1988

The *Hong Kong Economic Times* was founded as a daily financial newspaper.

28 Jan 1988

A search by 150 police officers in more than 20 locations across Hong Kong uncovered an illegal loan-shark syndicate from which 49 people were arrested. Some HK$100 million in shark loans, accounting for about 65% of illegal lending in Hong Kong, were made by the syndicate.

31 Jan 1988

The Hong Kong Writers Association was founded by 31 writers under the chairmanship of Tsang Man-chi (曾敏之) as a platform of local writers for literary development.

26 Feb 1988

Po Lam Estate, developed by the Housing Authority, was opened for occupancy as the first public housing complex in Tseung Kwan O New Town.

Figure 237
Chief Justice-appoint Yang Ti-liang (楊鐵樑) speaking in the ceremonial opening of the legal year at St. John's Cathedral on 11 January 1988. (Photo courtesy of South China Morning Post Publishers Limited)

26 Feb 1988

The Ten Years of Hong Kong Sculpture exhibition—a collaboration between the Hong Kong Sculptors Association and Hong Kong Arts Centre—was opened with a showcase of local sculptures from the past decade.

10 Mar 1988

The District Board held its third election for 264 elected seats; it had a voter turnout rate of 30.3%.

15 Mar 1988

Yang Ti-liang (楊鐵樑) was appointed as Chief Justice of Hong Kong, becoming the first Chinese chief judge. (Figure 237)

18 Mar 1988

The Hong Kong Publishing Professionals Society was formed, comprising senior executives and industry professionals as an advocacy group dedicated to driving sector advancement and talent development.

25 Mar 1988

Seventeen Hong Kong deputies as part of the Guangdong delegation to the National People's Congress attended the First Session of the Seventh National People's Congress in Beijing. The number of Hong Kong deputies increased from 16 to 17.

30 Mar 1988

C. P. Pokphand Company Limited was incorporated; it was publicly listed in Hong Kong on 28 April as a holding company of Charoen Pokphand Group's (a conglomerate in Thailand) operations in Hong Kong and the Mainland.

01 Apr 1988

Crown Solicitor Jeremy Fell Mathews was appointed as Attorney General, serving until 30 June 1997 as the last non-Chinese attorney general of Hong Kong before the establishment of the HKSAR.

The Hong Kong Institute of Landscape Architects was established as a professional group to develop industry standards, nurture talent and promote international exchange among landscape architects locally and abroad.

10 Apr 1988

The Hong Kong University of Science and Technology was founded under The Hong Kong University of Science and Technology Ordinance 1987. On 10 October 1991, it was officially opened as Hong Kong's third university with a focus on technology and professional disciplines, comprising four schools (Engineering, Science, Business and Management, and Humanities and Social Science) under the presidency of Woo Chia-wei (吳家瑋).

17 Apr 1988

Chow Ping (鄒　平) discovered a rare plant endemic to Hong Kong called *Asarum hongkongense* on Lantau Island. It was the only plant of the Asarum genus found in Hong Kong.

26 Apr 1988

The Hong Kong Basic Law Drafting Committee held its seventh plenary session, adopting two official documents in preparation for a public consultation in Hong Kong and the Mainland over a period of five months. These were: 1) The Draft Basic Law of the HKSAR of the People's Republic of China for Solicitation of Opinions and 2) The Methods for Collecting Opinions in Respect of The Draft Basic Law of the HKSAR of the People's Republic of China for Solicitation of Opinions. The former was promulgated in Hong Kong on 28 April.

06 May 1988

The British retail chain Marks & Spencer opened its first store in Hong Kong located at Ocean Centre in Tsim Sha Tsui, specialising in British foods and clothing.

13 May 1988

In the first government prosecution in accordance with the Immigration Ordinance, 67 Mainland workers under arrest for illegally staying and working in Hong Kong were sentenced to 15 to 18 months in prison.

20 May 1988

The Film Censorship Ordinance 1988 was promulgated, effective 10 November, requiring classification of films upon review by the government. Category III films (in a three-tier system) were restricted to persons aged 18 or above.

26 May 1988

The government announced its plan to redevelop the Tiu Keng Leng Cottage Area for public housing in the early 1990s as part of the Phase III development of Tseung Kwan O New Town. On 30 May, a committee was formed by the residents to discuss the plan which was largely opposed on the grounds that it violated the 1961 decision allowing registered residents to remain indefinitely. The residents indicated that they would strongly resist any demolition.

16 Jun 1988

A government screening policy with Vietnamese refugees was introduced at midnight. Vietnamese were no longer granted refugee status by default upon entry and were put through a screening process in accordance with the 1951 Convention Relating to the Status of Refugees before they were classified as refugees and made eligible for resettlement in a third country; non-refugees were to be repatriated back to Vietnam.

The Education Commission in its *Report No. 3* recommended a three-year programme with all local universities with admission only of students having completed two years of pre-college matriculation courses (Forms 6 & 7). It once again brought about a public discussion regarding the four-year curriculum of The Chinese University of Hong Kong.

24 Jun 1988

The Mental Health (Amendment) Ordinance 1988 was promulgated, stipulating supervisory care of those suffering from mental illnesses, including medical examination in a hospital when deemed necessary by the police. The Mental Health Review Tribunal was established for assessment of patients with respect to mandatory hospitalisation.

Sino United Publishing (Holdings) Limited was incorporated as Hong Kong's largest publishing conglomerate comprising more than 20 members in the publishing, printing and distribution businesses, including Joint Publishing, Chung Hwa Book Company (HK) Ltd, Commercial Press (HK) Ltd and Wan Li Book Company Ltd.

29 Jun 1988

John Baptist Wu (胡振中), Bishop of the Catholic Diocese of Hong Kong, was promoted to the rank of cardinal under Pope John Paul II and became the first cardinal of Hong Kong.

01 Jul 1988

The Tate's Cairn Tunnel Ordinance 1988 was promulgated, creating a 30-year franchise under Tate's Cairn Tunnel Company Limited. On 11 July, a tunnel ground-breaking ceremony was held. (Figure 238)

15 Jul 1988

The Monetary Affairs Branch reached an agreement with The Hongkong and Shanghai Banking Corporation (HSBC) as a clearing house of the Hong Kong Association of Banks. Under the agreement effective 18 July, HSBC was required to open an account with the HK Exchange Fund and maintain an account balance (in HK dollar) above the aggregate net balance of all local banks combined. The HK Exchange Fund became a last provider of liquidity in the Hong Kong interbank market, enabling a strengthened banking system and a more stable linked exchange rate system.

22 Jul 1988

The Noise Control Ordinance 1988 was promulgated, imposing restrictions on noise levels from devices in public places, construction sites as well as residential, industrial and commercial buildings.

25 Jul 1988

A fatal accident occurred during a trial run of the Light Rail Transit (LRT) developed by the Kowloon-Canton Railway (KCR) Corporation. A train collided with a van on Castle Peak Road in Yuen Long, killing an eight-year-old boy and injuring four others. The government ordered an immediate suspension of trial runs. On 30 July, a delay in opening the LRT was announced by the government and KCR.

08 Aug 1988

The Hong Kong Federation of Insurers was jointly established by the General Insurance Council of Hong Kong and Life Insurance Council of Hong Kong. Under Founding Chairman Michael Neale Somerville, it became the largest trade group of insurance companies in Hong Kong. It served as a self-regulatory organisation before the Office of the Commissioner of Insurance was formed in 1990.

12 Aug 1988

The Daya Bay Nuclear Safety Consultative Committee, chaired by Legislative Councillor Wong Po-yan (黃保欣), was established to provide a channel of communication with the Guangdong Nuclear Power Joint Venture.

13 Aug 1988

The government released a safety report on the Light Rail Transit (LRT) prepared by the UK Department for Transport. The report found the LRT to be safe and proposed further technical and operational measures to improve the system. The recommendations were accepted by the government and Kowloon–Canton Railway Corporation.

22 Aug 1988

The Occupational Safety & Health Council was established in accordance with the Occupational Safety and Health Ordinance 1988. The statutory body was designed to promote occupational safety through educational and training programmes.

Figure 238
An aerial view of the squatter area at Tai Hom Village in Diamond Hill in front of the Tate's Cairn Tunnel under construction in the 1980s. (Photo courtesy of Hong Kong Museum of History)

28 Aug 1988

The Luoxi Bridge located in Panyu County of Guangdong Province was opened to traffic between Luoxi in Panyu and Haizhu District in Guangzhou. Measuring 1,916 metres, it was then the longest highway bridge in Guangdong Province and a project supported by a contribution of HK$10 million from Hong Kong businessman Henry Fok Ying-tung (霍英東).

30 Aug 1988

Three senior-level appointments of local officials were made within the Government Secretariat, including Brian Chau Tak-hay (周德熙) as Secretary for Health and Welfare, John Chan Cho-chak (陳祖澤) as Secretary for Trade and Industry, and Yeung Kai-yin (楊啟彥) as Secretary for Education and Manpower. These marked local Chinese at the highest levels of government following a policy adopted in 1986 to do without expatriates aged 57 or above in civil service appointments.

31 Aug 1988

A Civil Aviation Administration of China airliner landing in Hong Kong from Guangzhou ran off the end of the runway at Kai Tak Airport, killing seven people and injuring 15 others, amid a thunderstorm warning issued by the Hong Kong Observatory.

07 Sep 1988

The government announced an end to the closed refugee camp policy, allowing Vietnamese refugees in Hong Kong to attend school and seek employment.

14 Sep 1988

The Bond Centre in Admiralty was opened, comprising two office buildings of 46 and 42 storeys with an octagonal concave-convex exterior design. It was renamed Lippo Centre on 04 November 1992.

18 Sep 1988

The Light Rail Transit (LRT) Phase I became operational between Tuen Mun with Yuen Long. The Tuen Mun Phase II extension was opened in February 1992. The Tin Shui Wai Phase III extension was opened on 10 January 1993. The LRT was the first railway system in the western New Territories along the major public and private housing estates in Tuen Mun, Yuen Long and Tin Shui Wai. (Figure 239)

20 Sep 1988

An agreement on Vietnamese boat people in Hong Kong was reached between Hong Kong and the United Nations High Commissioner for Refugees (UNHCR). The UNHCR recognised Hong Kong's screening policy adopted in June, agreeing to provide boat people classified as non-refugees with legal services in appeal proceedings and absorb the operating costs of detention centres.

Figure 239
The Light Rail running through downtown Yuen Long in 1989. (Photo courtesy of HKSAR Government)

Figure 240
An illustration of the Rose Garden Project. (Illustration by Hong Kong Chronicles Institute. Source of reference: the Hong Kong Airport Core Programme)

22 Sep 1988

In the 1988 Legislative Council elections, 12 members were elected by 12 electoral college constituencies with a turnout rate of 97.4%; 14 members were elected by 11 functional constituencies with a turnout rate of 54%.

Sep 1988

The Curriculum Development Committee was reconstituted as the Curriculum Development Council. Under the chairmanship of Andrew So Kwok-wing (蘇國榮), it consisted of a council, six coordinating committees and various subject committees, aiming to enhance the efficiency of curriculum development.

Peregrine International was incorporated by founders Philip Tose and Francis Leung (梁伯韜) as an investment bank and securities trader, taking a major role in the Hong Kong IPOs of Mainland companies and state-owned enterprises since 1992. By 1995, it became the largest securities firm in Hong Kong.

01 Oct 1988

The Social Welfare Department implemented a voluntary registration scheme with privately-run residential care homes for the elderly, applying a three-tier grading system (EA1, EA2 and EB3) to highlight the level of service quality in a prelude to enacting regulations on nursing homes.

12 Oct 1988

The new Legislative Council held an inaugural meeting in which all 19 new members and 12 re-elected members took the oath of office in serving the people of Hong Kong instead of the Queen.

Governor David Clive Wilson delivered his Policy Address, proposing a new international airport at Chek Lap Kok to replace Kai Tak Airport. On 11 October 1989, he released the *Port and Airport Development Strategy*, outlining 10 new airport-related projects in what later became known as the Hong Kong Airport Core Programme or more commonly known as the Rose Garden Project. (Figure 240)

21 Oct 1988

Chairman of Television Broadcasts Limited (TVB) Run Run Shaw (邵逸夫) officiated at a lighting ceremony to mark the opening of TVB City in Clearwater Bay.

22 Oct 1988

Hong Kong hosted the first International Society for Contemporary Music's World Music Day in the Asia Pacific region.

26 Oct 1988

Seventy-three people were hospitalised after eating choy sum bought from various wet markets in Kowloon. On 28 October, the government announced that choy sum samples were found to contain the pesticide methamidophos. On 01 November, Hong Kong and Shenzhen authorities required all vegetables exported from Shenzhen to Hong Kong to be labelled with the farm of origin, pesticide content and date of harvest. At least 450 hospital admissions had resulted from vegetable poisoning so far.

27 Oct 1988

The first annual artist award organised by the Hong Kong Artists' Guild was held in recognition of outstanding contributions in art and design, including painting, literature, fashion and music.

08 Nov 1988

The China Ferry Terminal in Tsim Sha Tsui became operational, providing cross-border passenger ferry services between Hong Kong, Macao and Guangdong.

11 Nov 1988

The Land Development Corporation signed a letter of intent with CK Asset Holdings, New World Development, Sun Hung Kai Properties and Great Eagle Holdings Ltd concerning eight urban renewal projects in Central, Sheung Wan, Wan Chai, Yau Ma Tei and Mong Kok, involving a total of about HK$12 billion.

15 Nov 1988

The Medical and Health Department began providing free hepatitis B vaccinations to all babies born in Hong Kong.

25 Nov 1988

The Hong Kong Convention and Exhibition Centre in Wan Chai was opened. Measuring 409,000 square metres in gross floor area and featuring two hotels and additional office buildings, it was the first large-scale complex in Asia dedicated to conventions and exhibitions. (Figure 241)

26 Nov 1988

The Hong Kong Institute for Promotion of Chinese Culture launched its first Competition of Study Projects on Hong Kong's History and Culture, followed by an award ceremony in November 1989. The Hong Kong Museum of History has been a co-organiser since 2002.

Figure 241
The first phase of Hong Kong Convention and Exhibition Centre. (Photo taken in 1988 and courtesy of South China Morning Post Publishers Limited)

28 Nov 1988

The Land Development Corporation was given approval by the Town Planning Board to begin urban renewal projects at five sites, including Queen Street in Sheung Wan, Gilman Street and Wing Shing Street in Central on Hong Kong Island, as well as Nelson Street in Mong Kok and Yunnan Lane in Yau Ma Tei, Kowloon.

01 Dec 1988

The Hong Kong Film Directors' Guild was established; Ng See-yuen (吳思遠) was its first president.

02 Dec 1988

More than 4,000 students and teaching staff of The Chinese University of Hong Kong went on strike on the last day of the first semester with a large rally at the University Mall, demanding the government to withdraw the Education Commission's proposal to change its undergraduate programme from four to three years. Student representatives from The University of Hong Kong, Lingnan College and Shue Yan College attended the event.

03 Dec 1988

Governor David Clive Wilson, Financial Secretary Piers Jacobs, Secretary for Monetary Affairs David Nendick and Deputy Secretary for Monetary Affairs Joseph Yam Chi-kwong (任志剛) met discreetly with Chinese representatives of the Sino-British Financial Matters Group at Fanling Lodge for a discussion on forming a monetary authority.

1988

The Independent Commission Against Corruption and the People's Procuratorate of Guangdong Province signed an agreement on a Mutual Case Assistance Scheme, enabling cross-border investigations on corruption and related crimes when mutually deemed necessary. The Supreme People's Procuratorate joined the scheme in 2000; jurisdiction was extended to the rest of the Mainland.

The Hong Kong Association of Sponsoring Bodies of Schools was established to promote exchange and cooperation and to provide the government with relevant advice on enhancing the overall quality of education.

01 Jan 1989

The five-cent coin in circulation since 1866 was discontinued as a legal tender.

09 Jan 1989

The Hong Kong Basic Law Drafting Committee in its eighth plenary session deliberated on the Revised Draft Basic Law for Solicitation of Opinions; it also adopted the Basic Law of the HKSAR of the People's Republic of China (Draft) and the Proposal for the Establishment of the Committee for the Basic Law of the HKSAR under the Standing Committee of the National People's Congress.

13 Jan 1989

The Public Order (Amendment) Ordinance 1989 was promulgated, abolishing Section 27 under which dissemination of false information was a criminal offence.

16 Jan 1989

The first annual Ultimate Song Chart Awards Presentation was hosted by Commercial Radio.

23 Jan 1989

The Cenotaph for Martyrs Against Japanese Militarism, located at Tsam Chuk Wan in Sai Kung, was unveiled in commemoration of those who sacrificed their lives to resist the Japanese occupation as part of the Hong Kong–Kowloon Brigade.

24 Jan 1989

Governor David Clive Wilson in conjunction with the Executive Council accepted the recommendation to standardise all government-affiliated tertiary institutions with a three-year undergraduate programme as proposed in *Report No. 3* by the Education Commission.

01 Feb 1989

The Office of the Ombudsman for Administrative Complaints was established in accordance with The Ombudsman Ordinance 1988. On 01 March, it began operating as a statutory body to monitor government bodies. It was given the power to launch an investigation on negligence or malpractice upon referrals from members of the Legislative Council.

17 Feb 1989

An enactment notice on the Noise Control Ordinance 1988 was promulgated, regulating noise in public places, construction sites, residential, industrial and commercial buildings. Control on construction noise was implemented in two phases, requiring a valid permit for use of motorised construction equipment at night and on holidays as of 17 August and a permit for percussive piling works (which could no longer be undertaken at night) as of 17 November.

21 Feb 1989

The Sixth Session of the Seventh NPC Standing Committee approved the Basic Law of the HKSAR of the People's Republic of China (Draft) and three annexes, as well as the Decision of the National People's Congress on the Method for the Formation of the First Government and the First Legislative Council of the HKSAR (Draft Substitute). These were subject to a five-month public consultation in Hong Kong and the Mainland.

01 Mar 1989

The Deputy Chief Secretary was renamed Secretary for Constitutional Affairs and was made in charge of matters relating to constitutional development, elections, and legislations of the Urban Council and Regional Council. Michael Suen Ming-yeung (孫明揚) was the first Secretary for Constitutional Affairs.

05 Mar 1989

The New Hong Kong Alliance was founded with a declaration calling for governance in the interest of Hong Kong based on the Sino-British Joint Declaration and Hong Kong Basic Law.

06 Mar 1989

Hong Kong Securities Clearing Company Ltd under the chairmanship of Ronald Carstairs was formed with a total guarantee fund of HK$60 million. Members included the Hong Kong Stock Exchange, Bank of China, Bank of East Asia, National City Bank of New York, Standard Chartered Bank, Hang Seng Bank, and Hongkong and Shanghai Banking Corporation.

09 Mar 1989

The 1989 elections of the Urban Council and Regional Council were held for 27 elected seats with a turnout rate of 17.6%.

17 Mar 1989

The Insurance Companies (Amendment) Ordinance 1989 was promulgated, raising the minimum required solvency margin among insurers.

01 Apr 1989

The Deputy Financial Secretary was renamed Secretary for the Treasury. Hamish Macleod was the first Secretary for the Treasury.

The Medical and Health Department was reorganised into the Hospital Services Department and Department of Health. The Hospital Services Department was advisory body responsible for government-subsidised hospitals; T. Y. Chau (周端彥) was its first director. The Department of Health was responsible for formulation of healthcare policies and health legislations; Lee Shiu-hung (李紹鴻) was its director.

04 Apr 1989

Headliner, a TV programme produced by Radio Television Hong Kong, made its broadcast debut on ATV Home, covering current news and newspaper editorials. It was later developed into a satirical current affairs programme.

05 Apr 1989

The Chinese Alliance for Commemoration of Sino-Japanese War Victims was founded by Tu Hok-fui (杜學魁) to fight for war reparations, prevent the resurrection of Japanese militarism, and conduct research on Sino-Japanese history.

14 Apr 1989

The Securities and Futures Commission Ordinance 1989 was promulgated, establishing a Securities and Futures Commission to regulate the securities and futures markets. It was also the first ordinance promulgated in both English and Chinese as the official languages of Hong Kong.

17 Apr 1989

The Hong Kong Branch of Xinhua News Agency held a service in memory of former General Secretary of the Central Committee of the Communist Party of China Hu Yaobang (胡耀邦), who passed away on 15 April. Another memorial service was held on 22 April.

The Central Policy Unit was formed as an advisory body on key government policies; it reported directly to the governor; Leo Goodstadt was Chief Advisor.

01 May 1989

The Securities and Futures Commission was established in place of the Securities Commission and Commodities Trading Commission. It was made responsible for overseeing the Hong Kong Stock Exchange, Futures Exchange, and activities related to the local stock market, corporate mergers and acquisitions, including capital-raising schemes and issuance of licences for securities and futures dealers in Hong Kong.

02 May 1989

The World Bank issued HK$500 million in bonds with six-year maturity at a minimum price of HK$50,000 through the Hong Kong Stock Exchange, marking the first bond issuance in Hong Kong dollars by a non-local institution.

21 May 1989

About 500,000 citizens took part in an eight-hour march on Hong Kong Island in support of the Beijing Student Movement. The Hong Kong Alliance in Support of the Patriotic Democratic Movements of China, chaired by Szeto Wah (司徒華), was formed at 5 p.m. in a rally at the Happy Valley Racecourse; it held a 12-hour marathon concert at the Happy Valley Racecourse on 27 May. The next day, more than a million people (estimated by the organisers) took part in another march on Hong Kong Island while the police estimated a participation of some 500,000 as of 2 p.m. at the start of the march.

31 May 1989

The Legislative Council began a two-day debate on the second draft of the Basic Law. Senior legislator Allen Lee Peng-fei (李鵬飛) noted a consensus with the Executive and Legislative Councils on the HKSAR's political system with a recommendation to introduce direct elections with 20 seats in the Legislative Council in 1991 followed by a gradual increase for a complete implementation by 2003 in what became known as the OMELCO Consensus. In response, China insisted on a gradual and orderly development, stipulating in the Basic Law and with the National People's Congress that HKSAR should embody a legislature comprising 60 members—of whom 20 will be directly elected in the first term, 24 in the second term, and 30 in the third term.

04 Jun 1989

Following the June Fourth Incident in Beijing, more than 200,000 people in Hong Kong took part in a sit-in at the Happy Valley Racecourse organised by the Hong Kong Alliance in Support of the Patriotic Democratic Movements of China. The Alliance organised a six-hour march on Hong Kong Island with over one million participants.

05 Jun 1989

A government white paper titled *Pollution in Hong Kong—A Time to Act* was released on World Environment Day, outlining two 10-year policies, namely the Strategic Sewage Disposal Scheme (later known as the Harbour Area Treatment Scheme) and Producer Responsibility (Polluter Pays) Scheme. It also planned to decommission the incineration plants in Lai Chi Kok, Kennedy Town and Kwai Chung, replaced by three landfills in the New Territories to treat solid waste in what was Hong Kong's first major environmental policy document.

The Hang Seng Index (HSI) dropped 581.77 points to close at 2,093, a loss of about HK$120 billion, from panic selling. Amid a run on some banks, HK$194 million were allocated from the Exchange Fund by the government to stabilise the banking system and local currency.

13 Jun 1989

During the UN International Refugee Conference in Geneva, Governor David Clive Wilson pointed out that Hong Kong's policy of port of first asylum was outmoded and incapable of accepting Vietnamese boat people any further, emphasising the importance of refugee screening and support from other countries.

20 Jun 1989

The Open Learning Institute of Hong Kong was founded; it became The Open University of Hong Kong on 20 May 1997 as the only self-accrediting and self-financing university founded by the government and the first post-secondary institution in Hong Kong to adopt a distance-learning model.

23 Jun 1989

The Ozone Layer Protection Ordinance 1989 was promulgated in response to international conventions, prohibiting the manufacturing of products containing ozone-depleting chlorofluorocarbons and halons in Hong Kong. The ordinance also restricted the import and export of these substances and related products commonly found in coolants, foaming agents, cleaning solvents and fire extinguishers.

Senior Member of the Executive Council Lydia Selina Dunn (鄧蓮如) and Senior Member of the Legislative Council Allen Lee Peng-fei (李鵬飛) sought the right of abode in the United Kingdom on behalf of Hong Kong in a meeting held in London with UK Prime Minister Margaret Thatcher and Secretary of State for Foreign and Commonwealth Affairs Geoffrey Howe.

03 Jul 1989

During his visit to Hong Kong, UK Secretary of State for Foreign and Commonwealth Affairs Geoffrey Howe said it was infeasible to grant 3.25 million British Dependent Territories citizens in Hong Kong the right of abode in the United Kingdom.

10 Jul 1989

The Singaporean government announced an expanded immigration quota of 25,000 for people of Hong Kong, including blue-collar workers, in the next five to eight years. The following day, over 1,000 people took application forms at the Consulate-General of the Republic of Singapore in Hong Kong.

14 Jul 1989

The Drug Trafficking (Recovery of Proceeds) Ordinance 1989 was promulgated, authorising a court of law to confiscate proceeds of drug traffickers and making it a criminal act to conspire to launder money for drug traffickers.

16 Aug 1989

Hong Kong signed a taxation agreement with the United States on incomes from international shipping to avoid double taxation and prevent tax evasion, marking Hong Kong's first bilateral agreement on double taxation.

24 Aug 1989

During his hospitalisation at Queen Mary Hospital, prisoner Yip Kai-foon (葉繼歡) escaped by holding a visitor hostage.

Figure 242
The Community Chest of Hong Kong held a "Walk for Millions" fundraiser on 27 August 1989 through the Eastern Harbour Crossing before it was officially opened to traffic. (Photo courtesy of HKSAR Government)

01 Sep 1989

The Government Secretariat's Lands and Works Branch was split into the Planning, Environment and Lands Branch and Works Branch. The former was responsible for policy in environmental protection and land affairs under the Chief Secretary; the latter was responsible for implementation and overseeing the newly established Drainage Services Department under the Financial Secretary. The Recreation and Culture Branch was also formed, responsible for affairs in culture, recreation, sports, antiquities and monuments, country park management, broadcasting and entertainment.

05 Sep 1989

The police seized 420kg of No. 4 heroin in Sai Kung with an estimated market value of more than HK$3.2 billion; four people were immediately arrested in what was the biggest seizure of No. 4 heroin in Hong Kong and the second biggest in the world.

11 Sep 1989

Flash Fax, a Television Broadcasts Limited (TVB) children's programme, premiered. With its last episode on 31 December 1999, it was the longest-running children's TV programme in Hong Kong as of 2017.

21 Sep 1989

The two-kilometre Eastern Harbour Crossing was opened to traffic, connecting Quarry Bay on Hong Kong Island and Cha Kwo Ling in Kowloon. It was designed with a dual carriageway for vehicles and a tube for an MTR line, making it Hong Kong's first road-railway tunnel. On 08 November, Charles, Prince of Wales, officiated at the opening ceremony. (Figure 242)

Sep 1989

A new class of financial product called covered warrants (commonly known as warrants) was introduced to the local market by Salomon Brothers International. They allowed investors to purchase shares, currencies and commodities at a lower cost for a potentially higher rate of return but also came with higher risks.

12 Oct 1989

The Island Eastern Corridor Phase III (Final Phase) was opened to traffic, connecting Causeway Bay and Chai Wan as the express section of the then-Route 8.

18 Oct 1989

The Heritage Foundation, a conservative US think tank, released a policy research report calling the US policy of non-interference in Hong Kong insufficient. It suggested that the US should relinquish its role of a passive onlooker, abandon its usual low-profile policy towards Hong Kong, and become more actively involved.

19 Oct 1989

The Canadian government announced that it would accept 175,000 immigrants in the following year, an increase of 15,000 people, and it welcomed applications from Hong Kong residents who were concerned about the establishment of the HKSAR in 1997.

27 Oct 1989

The Independent Commission Against Corruption arrested Warwick Reid, Deputy Director of Public Prosecutions (Legal Department), on charges of accepting bribes from a lawyer on behalf of his client. On 06 July 1991, in a Supreme Court ruling, Reid whose wealth was found to be disproportionate to his official income was sentenced to eight years in prison and HK$12 million in restitution. On 02 June 1992, two lawyers and a businessman suspected of bribing Reid were convicted and sentenced to seven years in prison by the Supreme Court.

The Hong Kong Democratic Foundation, chaired by Edward Leong Che-hung (梁智鴻), was established to promote democracy and protect human rights in Hong Kong.

31 Oct 1989

The Tenth Session of the Seventh National People's Congress's Standing Committee decided that "in consideration of the incompatible acts by Szeto Wah (司徒華) and Martin Lee Chu-ming (李柱銘) as members of the Basic Law Drafting Committee, they could no longer be part of the committee until their hostile stance towards the Chinese government and their contempt with the Sino-British Joint Declaration were abandoned."

03 Nov 1989

During a visit to Hong Kong by Japanese Foreign Minister Nakayama Taro, about 200 citizens marched from Chater Garden to the Japanese Consulate where a petition was presented, demanding compensation from the forced exchange of Hong Kong dollars for military yen during the Japanese occupation.

05 Nov 1989

The Hong Kong Cultural Centre in Tsim Sha Tsui under management of the Urban Council was opened with a grand theatre, a concert hall, a studio theatre and a total capacity of over 4,000 seats. On 08 November, Charles, Prince of Wales, and Diana, Princess of Wales, presided over the opening ceremony. (Figure 243)

Figure 243
The Hong Kong Cultural Centre under construction. (Photo taken in the late 1980s and courtesy of Hong Kong Museum of History)

07 Nov 1989

The presidents of Hong Kong trade associations established by the Hong Kong Trade Development Council in 11 countries began a four-day visit in Hong Kong where they met with high-level government officials and executives of local businesses.

12 Nov 1989

Hong Kong attended for the first time the Pacific Economic Cooperation Conference in Auckland, New Zealand as an observer in support of international economic partnerships.

01 Dec 1989

Li Kwan-ha (李君夏) was appointed as Commissioner of Police and became the first Chinese to hold the position.

12 Dec 1989

The Textile Council of Hong Kong Ltd was established as a platform bridging with the government. It comprised 11 textile associations with members accounting for 40% of the industry in Hong Kong.

20 Dec 1989

The British Nationality (Hong Kong) Selection Scheme was announced; it aimed to grant 50,000 Hong Kong families (about 225,000 people) British citizenship through a points-based system.

21 Dec 1989

The 1989 Water Supply Agreement between Hong Kong and Guangdong Province was signed, stipulating 690 million cubic metres of water from East River (Dongjiang) to Hong Kong in 1995 and a yearly increase by 30 million cubic metres thereafter until it reached 840 million cubic metres in 2000. After 2000, annual increases would be subject to negotiation based on Hong Kong's demand for water until it reached an annual target of 1.1 billion cubic metres by 2008.

The Tuen Mun Central Library was opened with a collection of nearly 220,000 books and pieces of audio-visual materials.

29 Dec 1989

The Lok Ma Chau Border Crossing was opened for cross-boundary lorries; it was opened to passenger vehicles on 08 August 1991.

30 Dec 1989

Regarding the British Nationality (Hong Kong) Selection Scheme announced on 20 December, a spokesperson of China's Ministry of Foreign Affairs called it Britain's breach of commitment causing divisive circumstances contradictory to a stable and prosperous Hong Kong. The Chinese government urged Britain to change its course of action for Hong Kong's wellbeing and cautioned the potential consequences as China remained committed to taking necessary measures in response.

Hong Kong Telecommunications Ltd standardised all local telephone numbers with a seven-digit format by doing away with the area codes for Hong Kong Island, Kowloon and the New Territories. With seven-digit numbers, area codes were simply omitted; with six-digit numbers, the area codes were prefixed to the number, converting them to seven-digit numbers.

1989

The Junk Bay Chinese Permanent Cemetery, measuring about 285,000 square metres, was opened as the largest cemetery under the Board of Management of the Chinese Permanent Cemeteries.

01 Jan 1990

The Planning Department was formed as part of the Planning, Environment and Lands Branch. It was responsible for assessing the framework prescribed in the Territorial Development Strategy Review and providing guidelines on land use and development for the government, including the Town Planning Board.

05 Jan 1990

The *Waste Disposal Plan for Hong Kong* was released. Over the next 10 years, three old urban incinerators built in the 1960s and 1970s were to be decommissioned and replaced with three strategic landfills and transfer stations in the west, the southeast, and the northeast of the New Territories. It was the first official planning document on solid waste disposal in Hong Kong.

15 Jan 1990

Zhou Nan（周南）was appointed as President of the Hong Kong Branch of Xinhua News Agency; he arrived to assume office on 05 February.

17 Jan 1990

Moving into the 21st Century: A White Paper on Transport Policy for Hong Kong was released with three guiding principles, namely improvement on transport infrastructure, improvement on public transport, and management on road use.

15 Feb 1990

The Commission on Youth, chaired by Rosanna Tam Wong Yick-ming（譚王䓸鳴）, was established as an advisory body to the Governor on youth affairs in Hong Kong.

16 Feb 1990

The Hong Kong Sports Development Board was established in accordance with the Hong Kong Sports Development Board Ordinance 1990. It was responsible for allocation of resources and development of athletes; it was dissolved on 01 October 2004 and replaced by the Hong Kong Sports Institute.

17 Feb 1990

At the ninth plenary session of the Hong Kong Basic Law Drafting Committee, Deng Xiaoping（鄧小平）said, "After nearly five years of hard work, you have written a law of historical and international significance. For historical significance, we not only mean the past, but also the present and the future; for international significance, we mean it has far-reaching significance not only for the Third World, but also for all mankind. It was a creative masterpiece. I thank you for your dedication and congratulate you on this document." The drafting of the Basic Law was concluded.

20 Feb 1990

The Insurance Claims Complaints Bureau was established along with an independent Insurance Claims Complaints Panel to handle insurance-related complaints and compensation disputes.

Feb 1990

The Environmental Campaign Committee was formed to raise public awareness on environmental protection through educational campaigns and community events by providing financial support to environmental groups and making policy recommendations.

08 Mar 1990

Tuen Mun Hospital was opened as a public general hospital serving residents of Tuen Mun New Town and northwestern New Territories.

15 Mar 1990

Next Magazine was founded by Jimmy Lai Chee-ying（黎智英）.

21 Mar 1990

The composition of the 1991 Legislative Council was announced. It included 18 councillors from nine geographical constituencies through direct elections under the framework of "two votes per voter," 21 councillors from 20 (increased from the original 13) functional constituencies, 17 (reduced from 20) governor-appointed councillors, and three ex-officio councillors (other official members would leave the Legislative Council). The position of a vice president in the Council was created to preside at meetings.

The Hong Kong Trade Development Council launched Hong Kong's first International Food Exhibition with 122 exhibitors and over 50,000 attendees. It was renamed the Food Expo the following year.

23 Mar 1990

The Hong Kong Council for Academic Accreditation was formed in accordance with the Hong Kong Council for Academic Accreditation Ordinance 1990. It aimed to ensure qualifications issued in Hong Kong were on par with international standards through a review system.

27 Mar 1990

The Hong Kong Fire Services Department Staffs General Association staged a 144-hour hunger strike with about 1,500 firefighters outside the Government Secretariat's office and across district fire stations, demanding a 48-hour work week. The hunger strike ended the following day upon a preliminary agreement with the Civil Service Branch; a working group was to be formed on 01 June to review the work hours and staff structure of firefighters.

01 Apr 1990

Separate taxation for married couples was implemented. Persons with assessable income were provided a basic allowance while their spouses without assessable income were given a married person's allowance.

04 Apr 1990

The Basic Law of the HKSAR of the People's Republic of China and three annexes were reviewed and approved by the Third Session of the Seventh National People's Congress. Decisions on the establishment of the HKSAR, its first government, legislature and establishment of a Basic Law Committee, as well as the regional flag and regional emblem of the HKSAR, were also approved. (Figure 244)

Figure 244
The HKSAR Basic Law was deliberated and approved by the Third Session of the Seventh National People's Congress on 01 April 1990. (Photo courtesy of Xinhua News Agency)

06 Apr 1990

The Provisional Airport Authority was established to plan, design and build a new airport in accordance with the Provisional Airport Authority Ordinance 1990.

07 Apr 1990

The communications satellite *AsiaSat 1* was successfully launched on board the *Changzheng* 3 rocket from Xichang, Sichuan Province, marking China's first successful commercial launch of the first commercial satellite designed specifically for the Asian region under the ownership of Asia Satellite Telecommunications Company Ltd—a joint venture with Hutchison Whampoa Ltd of Hong Kong, Cable & Wireless of the UK, and CITIC Group of China.

10 Apr 1990

Chinachem Group chairman Teddy Wang Teh-huei（王德輝）was kidnapped for the second time; his abductors demanded a ransom of US$1 billion. In the same month, his wife, Nina Wang Kung Yu-sum（龔如心）, paid a total of about HK$28 million by instalment. The kidnappers were found, arrested and sentenced by Hong Kong and Taiwan authorities between 1990 and 1993, while the kidnapped remained missing. On 23 September 1999, he was declared legally dead by the Supreme Court following a petition by his father Wang Din-sin（王廷歆）.

19 Apr 1990

The Shing Mun Tunnels with dual two-lane tubes between Sha Tin and Tsuen Wan on Route 5 were opened to traffic.

23 Apr 1990

The United Democrats of Hong Kong (predecessor of the Democratic Party), chaired by Martin Lee Chu-ming（李柱銘）, was founded.

30 Apr 1990

Former president of the Hong Kong Branch of Xinhua News Agency Xu Jiatun（許家屯）secretly left Hong Kong for the US, arriving the following day. On 04 March 1991, he was stripped of his official position with the CPC Central Advisory Commission and expelled from the Party by the CPC Central Commission for Discipline Inspection.

10 May 1990

The Direct Subsidy Scheme was implemented, making government subsidies available to eligible private schools to improve the quality of education while retaining autonomy.

14 May 1990

The first bone marrow transplant surgery in Hong Kong took place at Queen Mary Hospital.

17 May 1990

The Bank of China Tower in Central was unveiled. Construction began in April 1985; it was topped out on 08 August 1988. The 367.4-metre, 70-storey building cost HK$1.1 billion and was then the tallest building in Asia. The building, designed by renowned Chinese-American architect I. M. Pei (Ieoh Ming Pei)（貝聿銘）, took the shape of a three-dimensional geometric figure complete with a glass curtain wall and aluminium alloy to resemble growing bamboo. (Figure 245)

The Purple Mountain Observatory in Nanjing named the asteroid No. 2899, which was discovered in 1964, as "2899 Runrun Shaw." It marked the first asteroid named after a Hong Kong citizen.

18 May 1990

The Age of Majority (Related Provisions) Ordinance 1990 was promulgated, effective 01 October, lowering the age of majority from 21 to 18. Persons aged 18 or above were legally allowed to make wills, sign contracts and serve as company directors. The voting age in direct elections was still 21 or above.

Figure 245
The Bank of China Tower. (Photo taken in 1997 and courtesy of HKSAR Government)

20 May 1990

Standard Chartered Bank marked the opening of a new 191-metre, 45-storey head office building in Central at a cost of HK$600 million.

04 Jun 1990

The Hong Kong Alliance in Support of Patriotic Democratic Movements of China held a June Fourth candlelight vigil at Victoria Park, demanding accountability from the 1989 June Fourth Incident in Beijing. A similar event in Victoria Park was held every year thereafter.

16 Jun 1990

The Queen's Birthday Honours List was announced. Lydia Selina Dunn（鄧蓮如）was conferred as Baroness and became a member of the British House of Lords as the first ethnic Chinese to be given a life peerage.

22 Jun 1990

The first HKTDC Hong Kong Book and Publishing Fair began at Hong Kong Convention and Exhibition Centre; it became an annual event thereafter. In 1992, it was renamed the Hong Kong Book Fair.

02 Jul 1990

The Intellectual Property Department was established for registration of trademarks and patents; Alice Tai Footman （戴婉瑩）was the first commissioner.

10 Jul 1990

The Hong Kong–Guangdong Environmental Protection Liaison Group was formed in Hong Kong, comprising senior government officials from Guangdong and Hong Kong, providing a joint platform on environmental issues and pollution control in the Pearl River Delta region.

11 Jul 1990

Five robbers ran away with jewellery worth about HK$25 million in an armed robbery at Mabros Jewellery in Central.

27 Jul 1990

The Securities (Insider Dealing) Ordinance 1990 was promulgated, prohibiting insider trading with provisions on penalties.

03 Aug 1990

The government announced new arrangements for constituent districts and council compositions with respect to the 1991 District Board elections. Of the 19 districts, shifts in physical boundary and constituency would be made in 14 and 17 districts, respectively. The number of District Board constituencies would expand from 157 to 210, while the number of elected district board members would increase to 274.

11 Sep 1990

The King Ford Moon Restaurant and Mahjong Club on Gillies Avenue in Hung Hom was set ablaze with a firebomb by a triad member, killing six people and injuring 23, for refusing to pay a holiday fee.

A mudslide occurred on a natural slope in Castle Peak, Tuen Mun, covering a distance of one kilometre with 22,000 cubic metres of mud.

12 Sep 1990

The Independent Commission Against Corruption arrested 38 people, including two former and one incumbent licensing officers of the Television and Entertainment Licensing Authority and several game centre operators. They were charged with allegedly accepting and conferring benefits for game centre licence applications between May 1989 and September 1990. The officers were convicted of accepting benefits following a trial in the District Court on 30 January 1991; two former officers were sentenced to two years in prison while the incumbent officer was sentenced to 18 months in prison. Their bribes, totalling HK$292,675, were confiscated.

21 Sep 1990

Two robbers stole about HK$370,000 worth of goods from the residence of Police Commissioner Li Kwan-ha (李君夏). On 14 March 1991, they were each sentenced to five years in prison by the Supreme Court.

22 Sep 1990

Hong Kong won two silver and five bronze medals, including first-time medals in fencing and wushu (marital arts) at the 11th Asian Games in Beijing.

25 Sep 1990

The West Kowloon Reclamation Project began for the construction of a new Yaumatei Typhoon Shelter. The project involved reclaiming 340 hectares of land along the shore between Yau Ma Tei and Lai Chi Kok; it was completed in 2003 as the largest reclamation in the urban centre of Hong Kong.

29 Sep 1990

The Hong Kong Confederation of Trade Unions was formed by 25 member unions comprising 97,000 individual members. Lau Chin-shek (劉千石) was Executive Committee Chairman; Szeto Wah (司徒華) was Secretary General.

15 Oct 1990

The government provided details on the British Nationality Selection Scheme under which 50,000 families could move to the UK and be granted the right of abode. Applicants had to be British Dependent Territories citizens or British Nationals (Overseas), in addition to being working professionals, entrepreneurs or members of the disciplined or sensitive services, in a point system based on seniority and qualifications. On 20 November, selection criteria were confirmed in the British Nationality (Hong Kong) (Selection Scheme) Act 1990 signed by the Privy Council (UK) with effect from 01 December.

26 Oct 1990

A 25-metre-long unauthorised concrete canopy on the only industrial building in To Kwa Wan collapsed and hit 13 passers-by, killing nine of them.

28 Oct 1990

About 5,000 citizens took part in a public rally in defence of the Diaoyu Islands, opposing the Japanese flag painted on the island's beacon tower by Japanese right-wing groups, followed by a march to the Consulate General of Japan in Hong Kong with a letter of protest.

30 Oct 1990

Three residential blocks of Sceneway Garden above MTR's Lam Tin Station went on sale in a new approach recommended by the Consumer Council and industry trade groups. Details in the sales brochure were made available a week in advance; provisional deposits and refund handling charges were increased. On 20 December 1991, residents began occupancy in 4,112 units across 17 blocks of Sceneway Garden.

Oct 1990

The bimonthly magazine *Twenty-First Century* was inaugurated under the sponsorship of The Chinese University of Hong Kong's Institute of Chinese Studies. It published a variety of articles on humanities and social sciences and served as a global exchange platform among Chinese researchers.

Bauhinia Magazine was founded as a monthly covering international politics and economic development with a focus on the Mainland, Hong Kong, Macao and Taiwan, supplemented with articles on social, historical and cultural issues.

03 Nov 1990

The Liberal Democratic Federation of Hong Kong, chaired by Hu Fa-kuang (胡法光), was established.

09 Nov 1990

The Tseung Kwan O Tunnel with dual two-lane tubes between Kwun Tong and Tseung Kwan O was opened to traffic.

12 Nov 1990

The Cheung Chau Crematorium became operational as the only crematorium on an outlying island.

15 Nov 1990

Alfred Donald Yap (葉天養), President of the Law Society of Hong Kong, led a delegation to Beijing and Shanghai for an eight-day visit at the invitation of the All China Lawyers Association. The delegation met with Director Lu Ping (魯平), former Director Ji Pengfei (姬鵬飛) and former Deputy Director Li Hou (李後) of the Hong Kong & Macao Affairs Office of the State Council; it conducted exchanges with the Ministry of Justice, Legislative Affairs Commission of the National People's Congress Standing Committee, and Supreme People's Court. The Law Society agreed to the proposal by the Association for an annual six-lawyer delegation to Hong Kong starting from 1991 in support of the development of China's legal system.

16 Nov 1990

Four armed men held up a jewellery store in the underground shopping mall at Regent Hotel in Tsim Sha Tsui. They made off with about HK$20 million worth of jewellery; no one was hurt.

22 Nov 1990

The Education Commission published its *Report No. 4* recommending that local primary and secondary schools choose either Chinese or English as the medium of instruction to avoid mixing the two languages. The report also suggested the development of aptitude-based curriculum through target-oriented assessments in Primary 3, Primary 6 and Form 3.

Nov 1990

The Youth Council as a consultative body modelled after a district board on community affairs was established by the Shatin District Board. It was the first council made up of mainly young people, subsequently followed by others in Kwun Tong, Tai Po, Tsuen Wan and Sai Kung.

The Hong Kong Archaeological Society conducted a nine-month salvage excavation on Chek Lap Kok Island, uncovering ceramics, stone tools, bronzes and coins of several historical periods from pre-historic times at locations including Sham Wan Tsuen, Fu Tei Wan, Ha Law Wan, Kwo Lo Wan, etc.

The Chinese University of Hong Kong and Sun Yat-sen University in Guangzhou jointly conducted a two-month excavation at the Tai Wan site on Lamma Island. Ten tombs from the Shang Dynasty were uncovered; a *yazhang* blade and a set of string ornaments were unearthed from Tomb No. 6. The *yazhang* blade was deemed to be a treasure of Hong Kong by Mainland cultural and heritage expert Yang Boda (楊伯達).

01 Dec 1990

The Hong Kong government began accepting applications from Hong Kong residents for British citizenship under the British Nationality Selection Scheme. By 28 February 1991, it received over 65,000 applications.

The Hospital Authority, in accordance with the Hospital Authority Ordinance 1990, was established as a statutory body to manage all government hospitals, government-subsidised hospitals, speciality clinics, sanatoriums and related medical services starting from 01 December 1991. Government medical staff were retained while replacing the Hospital Services Department. On 01 July 2003, 59 outpatient clinics of the Department of Health were placed under the Hospital Authority.

13 Dec 1990

The Lai Chi Kok Incineration Plant was decommissioned and was replaced with the Kwai Chung Incineration Plant. The Kennedy Town Incineration Plant was closed in March 1993.

16 Dec 1990

The Hong Kong Chinese Medical Association was established as a professional group to promote government accreditation of Chinese medicine practitioners. Mui Ling-cheong (梅嶺昌) served as president.

17 Dec 1990

The Hongkong and Shanghai Banking Corporation (HSBC) announced the establishment of HSBC Holdings as a UK-registered entity headquartered in Hong Kong under which HSBC became a wholly owned subsidiary.

1990

The Central Moneymarkets Unit was launched to provide computerised clearing and settlement facilities for Exchange Fund Bills and Notes.

The Hong Kong Sinfonietta was established; it became a professional orchestra in 1999.

13 Jan 1991

An Etiquette Day was held by the Hong Kong Tourist Association in conjunction with Radio Television Hong Kong in a campaign to promote a tourist-friendly city. Park Lane Shopper's Boulevard was named Etiquette Avenue.

25 Jan 1991

The Town Planning (Amendment) Ordinance 1991 was promulgated, expanding the jurisdiction of the Town Planning Board to include rural areas in the New Territories. A primary goal was to prohibit the use of rural farmland as open storage spaces and mitigate further environmental and traffic issues.

08 Feb 1991

The Finance Committee of the Legislative Council approved an appropriation of HK$230 million to finance Britain's role in the Persian Gulf War. It was specified for logistical, medical and humanitarian purposes.

18 Feb 1991

The establishment of the Office of the Exchange Fund was announced for public finance and fund investment under the directorship of Senior Deputy for Monetary Affairs Joseph Yam Chi-kwong (任志剛).

03 Mar 1991

The fourth District Board elections were held for 274 elected seats with a turnout rate of 32.5%.

08 Mar 1991

The Hong Kong Chinese Enterprises Association was incorporated as a group of Mainland Chinese companies operating in Hong Kong to promote economic and trade relations among Mainland Chinese businesses in the region and globally, supporting a prosperous and stable Hong Kong.

13 Mar 1991

The government released a white paper titled *Social Welfare into the 1990s and Beyond*, announcing a plan to increase annual social welfare spending from HK$5.08 billion to HK$7.38 billion by 2000, promote social services with non-profit organisations, and study the feasibility of charging for social services.

15 Mar 1991

A government census began; it ended on 24 March. In October, results showed a population of 5,674,114 permanent residents, 35,823 mobile residents and 51,847 Vietnamese refugees in Hong Kong.

16 Mar 1991

Tang Yuen-ha (鄧宛霞), a Kunqu and Peking opera artist, won the eighth Plum Blossom Award for Chinese Theatre. She was the first Hong Kong artist to receive the honour.

18 Mar 1991

The Buildings and Lands Department launched Operation Appendages with a task force to conduct a survey on dangerous buildings, potentially dangerous buildings and illegal buildings in various districts and expand on prosecution in relation to unauthorised building works. It began with the inspection of areas where collapses had previously occurred and took down unauthorised structures, such as canopies, deemed dangerous or potentially dangerous. By the end of June, 3,078 removal orders involving 30 buildings were issued.

20 Mar 1991

The Education Commission's *School Management Initiative* was released, recommending that the roles of school management committees and principal personnel be clearly defined while making schools more autonomous in the allocation of resources to improve education quality.

01 Apr 1991

The age limit under the Old Age Allowance scheme was lowered from 70 to 65.

The Air Pollution Control (Motor Vehicle Fuel) (Amendment) Regulation 1990 was promulgated, requiring petrol stations to provide unleaded gasoline in a bid to reduce vehicle emissions and air pollution.

18 Apr 1991

The Hong Kong Science Museum in Tsim Sha Tsui was opened with four exhibition halls, namely Science, Life Science, Technology, and Children's Gallery. A 20-metre Energy Machine was on display to showcase the science of kinetic energy, marking the world's largest demonstration of its kind as of 2017.

05 May 1991

The 1991 Urban Council and Regional Council elections were held for 27 elected seats with a turnout rate of 23.03%.

10 May 1991

Metro Broadcast Corporation Limited (Metro Broadcast) was granted a commercial radio broadcasting licence, making it the second commercial radio station in Hong Kong. Its first channel, Metro News, was launched on 22 July.

The Hong Kong Institute of Planners, in accordance with The Hong Kong Institute of Planners Incorporation Ordinance 1991, was established as a statutory body to promote the professional standards of city planners.

16 May 1991

The Federation for the Stability of Hong Kong, chaired by Chan Yat-san (陳日新), was established; it was dissolved in June 2010.

20 May 1991

The British government amended Article VII of the Hong Kong Letters Patent with a new paragraph, Subsection (3), stipulating that the International Covenant on Civil and Political Rights, adopted by the UN General Assembly on 16 December 1966, would apply to Hong Kong and would be implemented through the laws of Hong Kong. On 05 June, the Hong Kong Bill of Rights Ordinance 1991 was passed after three readings in the Legislative Council, implementing provisions of the International Covenant applicable to Hong Kong, effective 08 May.

23 May 1991

The Hong Kong Park was opened with an aviary, an education centre, a conservatory, a waterfowl lake, and a sports centre, among other facilities, including the Museum of Tea Ware and the Visual Arts Centre.

27 May 1991

A Lauda Air airliner from Hong Kong to Vienna, Austria via Thailand exploded and crashed shortly after taking off from Don Mueang International Airport in Bangkok, killing all 223 people on board, including 46 Hong Kong citizens.

30 May 1991

Big Echo, Hong Kong's first karaoke chain, was established; it opened its first venue in Tsim Sha Tsui later in the year. The entire chain shut down during the SARS epidemic in 2003.

May 1991

Chinese representative Lu Ping (魯平) and British representative Percy Cradock began a four-day, closed-door meeting on building a new airport. Amid China's concern about the fiscal reserves of Hong Kong, Britain proposed raising the amount set aside for the future HKSAR government from HK$5 billion to HK$25 billion. China agreed to the British proposal under which a total of HK$100 billion (largely from the estimated income from the Land Fund as stipulated in the Sino-British Joint Declaration) was forecast.

06 Jun 1991

A spokesman of China's Ministry of Foreign Affairs noted that Britain's insistence on enacting a "Bill of Rights" in Hong Kong was regrettable and would impinge on the implementation of the Basic Law. China reserved the right to review the laws of Hong Kong, including the Bill of Rights, in accordance with the Basic Law after 1997. The Ministry reiterated China's policy of protecting the rights and freedoms of Hong Kong enshrined in the Sino-British Joint Declaration and in the Basic Law guaranteeing the rights and freedoms of Hong Kong.

09 Jun 1991

Five robbers in bullet-proof vests with Type 54 pistols and Type 56 assault rifles rampaged five gold stores on Mut Wah Street in Kwun Tong. They ran off with HK$6.5 million in jewellery after exchanging 54 shots with the police; six people, including two police officers, were injured in what was the first robbery involving military firearms in Hong Kong. On 10 June, HK$500,000 in cash rewards for information were offered by the police.

13 Jun 1991

The Business and Professionals Federation of Hong Kong, chaired by Vincent Lo Hong-shui (羅康瑞) with an executive committee comprising 28 business professionals, was established to bridge the gap between Hong Kong and the Mainland by focusing on economic policies.

16 Jun 1991

The HKU Alumni Association of the Mainland was inaugurated at Peace Hotel in Beijing; 80 people attended the ceremony, including former Deputy Director of the Hong Kong and Macao Affairs Office of the State Council Li Hou (李後), Chairman of the China International Culture Association Luo Hanxian (羅涵先), former HKU Vice Chancellor Rayson Huang (黃麗松) and HKU alumni Vincent Ko Hon-chiu (高漢釗) and Dexter Man Hung-cho (文洪磋). Hsu Nai-po (許乃波) served as the first chairman.

19 Jun 1991

The official Chinese titles of the Civil Service Branch and its principal officer under the Government Secretariat were amended to reflect the department's responsibilities.

20 Jun 1991

The Hong Kong Red Cross China Relief Fund was set up by Hong Kong Red Cross with a bank account at HSBC to support disaster relief efforts in the Mainland.

26 Jun 1991

Tate's Cairn Tunnel between Siu Lek Yuen in Sha Tin and Diamond Hill in Kowloon was opened to traffic as Hong Kong's longest tunnel with dual two-lane tubes measuring four kilometres each.

The Kwun Tong Bypass, upon completion of Phase III, was fully opened to traffic, connecting Lei Yue Mun Road and Tate's Cairn Tunnel. The six-kilometre bypass, a part of Route 2, was the first expressway in Kowloon and the only designated highway in Kowloon East.

08 Jul 1991

The Bank of Credit and Commerce International was ordered to cease operations in all local branches as a shutdown under the European and US governments began on 05 July amid allegations of commercial fraud and transnational criminal activities. On 17 July, a government petition was filed with the Supreme Court for liquidation of all branches in Hong Kong, followed by a sit-in protest on Queen's Road Central and a clash between the police and bank customers.

12 Jul 1991

Cheung Tze-keung (張子強) and three others fled with HK$160 million in cash after hijacking an armoured vehicle and taking the guards hostage outside Kai Tak Airport's Cargo Terminal involving the largest amount of money in an armed robbery as of 2017. In September, Cheung was arrested on suspicion of conspiracy to commit robbery and was sentenced to 18 years in prison. On 22 June 1995, following an appeal at the Supreme Court, he was acquitted due to insufficient evidence.

The Crimes (Amendment) Ordinance 1991 was promulgated, decriminalising homosexuality among men over the age of 21.

The Hong Kong government allocated HK$50 million for victims of flood in eastern China; a public donation of HK$450 million was raised by 23 July in support of disaster relief.

14 Jul 1991

The 1991/92 Keep Hong Kong Clean campaign was initiated by the government; a five-member "Dragon of Cleanliness Family" as campaign mascots was introduced by the Urban Council and the Regional Council.

27 Jul 1991

The Selfless Charity Show for flood relief in eastern China was held by performing artists at the Happy Valley Racecourse where more than 100,000 people attended, raising more than HK$110 million.

12 Aug 1991

Painter Lin Fengmian (林風眠), who was a former principal of the National Art School in Beiping and one of the founders of the National Academy of Art (present-day China Academy of Art), passed away in Hong Kong at the age of 91. On 17 August, his funeral was held at the Hong Kong Funeral Home.

03 Sep 1991

In Beijing, Premier of the State Council Li Peng (李鵬) and UK Prime Minister John Major signed the Memorandum of Understanding Concerning the Construction of the New Airport in Hong Kong and Related Questions. It required prior consent from China on airport franchises, contracts and repayment of debts in excess of HK$5 billion scheduled to continue beyond 30 June 1997. It mandated a minimum fiscal reserve of HK$25 billion upon the establishment of the HKSAR on 01 July 1997 and agreed to setting up an Airport Authority.

11 Sep 1991

Citybus Limited launched its first route, 12A, running between the old Hongkong-Macau Ferry Terminal in Central and MacDonnell Road in Mid-Levels, as the fourth franchised bus company in Hong Kong.

12 Sep 1991

A total of 22,883 voters (a turnout rate of 46.9%) took part in the elections of 21 functional constituencies of the Legislative Council. On 15 September, a total of 750,467 voters (a turnout rate of 39.1%) cast their votes in 18 geographical constituencies under direct elections from a pool of 54 candidates. The United Democrats of Hong Kong won 12 of the 18 directly elected seats.

13 Sep 1991

The Hong Kong Airport Committee was announced for negotiation on franchises, contracts and debt guarantees bound to go beyond 1997; it was co-chaired by Guo Fengmin (郭豐民) and Anthony Galsworthy who were principal delegates of the Sino-British Joint Liaison Group.

Figure 246
The Hong Kong Museum of Art—a four-storey building near the Hong Kong Space Museum and Hong Kong Cultural Centre. (Photo taken in 1991 and courtesy of HKSAR Government)

09 Oct 1991

Governor David Clive Wilson announced in his last Policy Address that all members of the Legislative Council were to be elected in 1995. At least one-third of the councillors were to be selected through direct elections; appointments by the governor were abolished; and the president of the Legislative Council was to be elected among council members.

28 Oct 1991

Prince Philip, Duke of Edinburgh, opened the fourth international conference of the Duke of Edinburgh's Award in Hong Kong. During the five-day conference, over 140 representatives from 54 countries and regions met to promote the award, youth advancement schemes and regional development models.

Oct 1991

The Hong Kong government began to implement the Orderly Repatriation Programme. The first batch of 59 Vietnamese boat people as illegal immigrants was repatriated on 09 November.

06 Nov 1991

Four blocks of Locwood Court under Phase 1 of Kingswood Villas, a large private housing estate in Tin Shui Wai, were opened for pre-sale registration. The new residential units officially went on sale on 13 November; occupancy began on 19 December. Kingswood Villas, developed in seven phases and completed in 1998, comprising 15,880 units in 58 residential buildings, became Hong Kong's largest private housing estate by number of units.

The Hong Kong government tackled property speculation by requiring a sale and purchase contract in every transaction involving uncompleted or second-hand flats and shortening the grace period with stamp duty to 30 days upon contract signing instead of payment after a formal transaction. The stamp duty rate was unchanged.

11 Nov 1991

The Children's Cancer Foundation was restructured from the Children's Cancer Fund under The Chinese University of Hong Kong, expanding service coverage to eight public hospitals besides Prince of Wales Hospital. It became Hong Kong's first voluntary organisation dedicated to serving young cancer patients. (Figure 246)

12 Nov 1991

Hong Kong was approved to become a member economy during the third ministerial meeting of the Asia-Pacific Economic Cooperation in Seoul, South Korea.

15 Nov 1991

Hong Kong Air Cargo Terminal 2 at Kai Tak Airport became operational, increasing the cargo handling capacity to 1.5 million metric tonnes per year.

The new Hong Kong Museum of Art, remodelled from the former City Hall established in 1962 on the Tsim Sha Tsui waterfront, was opened with six exhibition halls at a cost of HK$235 million, showcasing a collection of Chinese paintings and calligraphy, local artistic creations and historical paintings.

22 Nov 1991

The government released a blueprint called *Metroplan* regarding Hong Kong's future urban development. It proposed large-scale reclamation, redevelopment and infrastructure projects with a focus on a network of railways and highways to ease traffic congestion and improve the living environment of Hong Kong.

05 Dec 1991

Legislative Councillor Gilbert Leung Kam-ho (梁錦濠) was arrested by the Independent Commission Against Corruption on suspicion of bribing members of the Regional Council for votes in the functional constituency elections of the Legislative Council in September. On 01 June 1993, he was convicted on three counts of bribery and vote-buying and was sentenced to three years in prison; he was the first legislator to be imprisoned.

09 Dec 1991

The third Eco Asia Conference and Eco Expo Asia, organised by the Hong Kong Institution of Engineers, began in a five-day event focused on urban environmental protection, along with an exhibition featuring 20 organisations from 12 countries at the Hong Kong Convention and Exhibition Centre.

12 Dec 1991

The political think tank Co-operative Resources Centre, convened by Allen Lee Peng-fei (李鵬飛), comprising 21 appointed or elected (by functional constituency) members of the Legislative Council, was established; it was dissolved on 31 March 1993.

14 Dec 1991

Twelve representatives of a Tsing Yi residents' group went on a 24-hour hunger strike outside the Government Secretariat's office, opposing the construction of Container Terminal No. 9 in Tsing Yi. The hunger strike ended the following day; about 100 Tsing Yi residents remained in a spontaneous protest.

21 Dec 1991

The first Hong Kong Biennial Awards for Chinese Literature, in recognition of the outstanding achievements of local writers, was inaugurated by the Urban Council Public Libraries. Of 170 entries, four winners were named in four categories: essays, new poetry, fiction, and children's literature. The additional category "Literary Criticism" began at the fourth Awards in 1996.

1991

The Hong Kong Economic and Trade Office (Toronto) was established to promote bilateral economic, trade and cultural relations between Hong Kong and Canada.

The Chinese University of Hong Kong's Centre for Chinese Archaeology and Art began to conduct an archaeological investigation and trial excavation at over 30 sites along the north coast of Lantau as part of the development of a new airport. The exercise unearthed many cultural relics of the Neolithic period and Bronze Age, as well as ceramics and traces of livelihood from the Tang and Song dynasties to the Ming and Qing dynasties.

15 Jan 1992

More than 200 entertainment artists marched from Central to the Police Headquarters in Wan Chai, opposing extortion and violence by triad groups in the film industry.

31 Jan 1992

The Stamp Duty (Amendment) (No. 4) Ordinance 1991 was promulgated, requiring a progressive *ad valorem* stamp duty in the sale and purchase of residential buildings as a measure to curb speculative activity in the property market.

03 Feb 1992

A clash between South and North Vietnamese boat people at the Sek Kong Vietnamese Camp over the use of hot water led to a fire in the living quarters, killing 24 people and injuring about 120. It was the worst riot in a refugee camp since Hong Kong started accepting Vietnamese boat people in 1975. (Figure 247)

18 Feb 1992

The government launched a public consultation on the proposed Deposit Protection Scheme designed to protect small deposits with priority of claim in the event of a bank liquidation. The proposal called for coverage of either 75% or 100% of deposits up to HK$100,000 per account; large banks were expected to cover all related costs. On 12 January 1993, it was withdrawn by the government.

24 Feb 1992

Maggie Cheung Man-yuk (張曼玉) became the first Chinese actress to win the Silver Bear for Best Actress at the 42nd Berlin International Film Festival for her role in the film *Center Stage* (阮玲玉).

03 Mar 1992

The Supreme Court issued an order to liquidate the local branches of the Bank of Credit and Commerce International, which ceased operations in July 1991. On 14 September, the Supreme Court approved the bank's compensation scheme—deposits of HK$100,000 or less would be fully recovered while deposits of over HK$100,000 would be repaid by instalment or compensated with a lump sum of HK$100,000.

04 Mar 1992

Hong Kong's last British Financial Secretary Hamish Macleod released his first Budget, projecting a surplus of HK$4.7 billion in the 1992/93 fiscal year. It also raised profits tax to 17.5% and taxes with tobacco, alcohol and fuel oil by 10%, increased salaries tax allowance, abolished taxes on cinema tickets and non-alcoholic beverages. It was the first government budget since direct elections were introduced to the Legislative Council in 1991.

Figure 247
The Police Tactical Unit on guard at Shek Kong Vietnamese Camp as North Vietnamese boat people were relocated to Hei Ling Chau on 05 February 1992 after a riot. (Photo courtesy of South China Morning Post Publishers Limited)

11 Mar 1992

The first batch of 44 advisors on Hong Kong matters, jointly recruited by the Hong Kong and Macao Affairs Office of the State Council and the Hong Kong Branch of Xinhua News Agency, were presented with letters of appointment in Beijing for a two-year term in their individual capacity, followed by reappointments in 1994 and 1996 until 30 June 1997.

13 Mar 1992

An art exhibition called Wu Guanzhong（吳冠中）in the 1990s—organised by the Hong Kong Institute for the Promotion of Chinese Culture—began at Shun Tak Centre in Sheung Wan; it was concluded on 28 March.

28 Mar 1992

Hutchison's "TienDeySeen" mobile phone service commenced operations, becoming the first provider of the second-generation cordless telephone (CT2) technology in Hong Kong.

30 Mar 1992

China Harbour Engineering Company won the bid to develop Tung Chung New Town with a contract worth HK$736 million under the Tung Chung Phase I development project. It marked the first contract with a Chinese company under the Hong Kong Airport Core Programme.

09 Apr 1992

A topping-out ceremony was held to mark the 374-metre, 78-storey Central Plaza in Wan Chai North, jointly developed by Sino Land and Sun Hung Kai Properties. It was the highest building in Hong Kong and the fourth highest in the world complete with a four-bar neon clock atop.

13 Apr 1992

The Supreme Court in a judicial review filed by the Friends of the Earth ruled that the development project under Sha Lo Tung Development Company Limited approved by the Country Parks Authority was unlawful and issued an injunction prohibiting the development of a golf course in Sha Lo Tung.

23 Apr 1992

The 100th flight of the Voluntary Repatriation Programme took off, sending 126 Vietnamese boat people back to their country under the supervision of the UN High Commissioner for Refugees. Under the repatriation programme introduced in 1989, 17,466 boat people had gone back to Vietnam voluntarily or through the Orderly Repatriation Programme.

28 Apr 1992

The Hong Kong Visual Arts Centre, a branch of the Hong Kong Museum of Art, was opened at Hong Kong Park.

Apr 1992

Tin Yiu Estate, built by the Housing Authority, was opened for occupancy. The estate was fully completed in the following year, comprising over 10,000 units across 11 blocks of public housing and three blocks under the Home Ownership Scheme. It was the first public housing estate in Tin Shui Wai New Town.

The Antiquities and Monuments Office in conjunction with the Hong Kong Archaeological Society began a 12-month excavation at the Yung Long site in Tuen Mun, unearthing cultural deposits from the early and late Neolithic period. The cultural relics from the late Neolithic period were characteristic of the Shixia culture in northern Guangdong and Liangzhu culture in the lower reaches of the Yangtze River.

The Chinese University of Hong Kong in conjunction with the Shaanxi Provincial Institute of Archaeology conducted an excavation at the Pa Tau Kwu site on Lantau Island, uncovering the remains of a dozen dwellings from the Shang Dynasty.

The Curriculum Development Institute under the Education Bureau was established as the secretariat of the Curriculum Development Council. The institute, in addition to curriculum development, supported schools through the implementation of curriculum policies and reforms, publication of curriculum guides and syllabuses, and review of textbooks with a professional staff of civil servants and subject experts.

05 May 1992

Five armed robbers ran away with HK$2 million in cash and jewellery from a mahjong parlour in Mong Kok after exchanging fire with the police and throwing three grenades before fleeing by hijacking a bus, causing two deaths and 19 injuries.

11 May 1992

The Efficiency Unit was set up to provide various government departments with management consultancy services with a view to improving the overall administrative efficiency and service standards of the government.

12 May 1992

Cham Yik-Kai (湛易佳) became the first person from Hong Kong to climb and reach the summit of Mount Everest at 8,848 metres.

28 May 1992

The government announced the implementation of the Liquidity Adjustment Facility, effective 08 June, providing licenced banks with an additional means of overnight liquidity through the Exchange Fund with which banks may deposit their excess liquidity to earn interest. The Exchange Fund became a platform of interbank lending in support of a stable linked exchange rate.

02 Jun 1992

The Hong Kong Drama Awards was inaugurated by the Hong Kong Federation of Drama Societies in recognition of the contribution of local artists with more than ten award categories, including Best Overall Performance, Best Director, Best Actor and Best Actress.

17 Jun 1992

The Hong Kong Observatory launched a new rainstorm warning system with signals in four colours according to the severity of rainfall: (in ascending order) green, yellow, red and black. In cases of a red or black signal, public announcements were to be made and schools were to be closed as stipulated by the Education Bureau.

23 Jun 1992

The Education Commission published its *Report No. 5,* recommending a merger between the Institute of Language in Education and four other education colleges to create an Institute of Education, in addition to establishing an Advanced Teacher's Certificate programme to advance the professional qualification of non-degree teachers.

30 Jun 1992

The British government introduced the Official Secrets Act 1911–1989 in Hong Kong under an order of the Privy Council, making it an offence to disclose information regarding security, intelligence, defence, international relations, criminal activities and investigations without authorisation, or information entrusted in confidence to a regional, national or international organisation.

09 Jul 1992

Chris Patten was sworn in as the 28th and last governor of Hong Kong. He left office at the end of British rule over Hong Kong on 30 June 1997.

10 Jul 1992

The Democratic Alliance for the Betterment of Hong Kong was founded; it issued a manifesto as a democratic, patriotic and constructive political group. Jasper Tsang Yok-sing (曾鈺成) was its first chairman.

15 Jul 1992

Financial Secretary Hamish Macleod revealed a balance of HK$236.121 billion and an accumulated profit of HK$98.652 billion with the Exchange Fund as of the end of 1991 in an unprecedented announcement at a Legislative Council meeting; it marked the beginning of the annual disclosure of Exchange Fund figures.

15 Jul 1992

Haihong Group, a part of the China Merchants Group, was publicly listed in Hong Kong at HK$1.50 per share and closed at HK$4.225 on the first day, up by 181%. It was the first Hong Kong-registered entity under a China-affiliated holding company to launch an IPO in Hong Kong (known as a red chip). The public offering raised HK$82 million and was 373 times oversubscribed.

29 Jul 1992

The police seized HK$30 million worth of smuggled goods, including air conditioners and televisions, nearly twice the total value of smuggled goods seized in the entire year of 1991.

01 Aug 1992

The Hong Kong Academy of Medicine, in accordance with the Hong Kong Academy of Medicine Ordinance 1992, was established as a professional group dedicated to providing local practitioners with continued medical education, specialist training and enrichment of medical knowledge and skills.

02 Aug 1992

Sheung Wan Gala Point, an open area more commonly known as the poor man's nightclub, was closed to facilitate reclamation projects in Central and Wan Chai.

04 Aug 1992

CITIC Pacific Limited became the first Mainland Chinese company named as a constituent of the Hang Seng Index (HSI).

19 Aug 1992

Explorer Rebecca Lee Lok-sze (李樂詩) reached an altitude of about 6,000 metres in the Himalayas. Previously, she travelled to the South Pole in 1985 and the North Pole in 1993, making her the first person from Hong Kong to have explored all three poles of the Earth.

01 Sep 1992

The Education Bureau incorporated a summary of the Hong Kong Basic Law as part of Social Studies in junior secondary schools and General Studies in matriculation education, in addition to providing secondary schools with teaching guides on the Sino-British Joint Declaration and the Basic Law.

03 Sep 1992

Cosco Enterprises (HK) Limited, a Chinese state-owned enterprise, was incorporated; its businesses included shipping, container leasing and terminals services. In November 2016, it was renamed Cosco Shipping (Hong Kong) Company Limited.

26 Sep 1992

The government began hosting a month-long Festival Hong Kong in five Canadian cities. On 12 November, Governor Chris Patten officiated at the closing ceremony of the festival in Vancouver during his visit to Canada.

03 Oct 1992

The first Hong Kong Cricket Sixes began in a two-day tournament at the Kowloon Cricket Club where Team Pakistan won the championship. It continued as an annual event (except 2013–2016; it resumed in 2017).

05 Oct 1992

US President George Herbert Bush signed the United States–Hong Kong Policy Act of 1992 regarding US policy on Hong Kong after the establishment of the HKSAR in 1997. Under a high degree of autonomy in Hong Kong in accordance with the Sino-British Joint Declaration, it allowed the US to grant Hong Kong most favourable status in financial and cultural affairs, recognise Hong Kong as an independent customs territory and economy, and support Hong Kong's participation with international organisations and treaties. It also recognised Hong Kong's human rights, autonomy, political system and lifestyle under the framework of "One Country, Two Systems."

07 Oct 1992

In the morning, Governor Chris Patten informed the Executive Council that seven councillors with no party affiliations would be appointed, replacing Allen Lee Peng-fei (李鵬飛), Selina Chow Liang Shuk-yee (周梁淑怡), Rita Fan Hsu Lai-tai (范徐麗泰), Edward Ho Sing-tin (何承天), Hui Yin-fat (許賢發), Lau Wong-fat (劉皇發) and Wang Gung-wu (王賡武). The move was intended to give greater separation between the Executive Council and Legislative Council; Rita Fan also resigned from the Legislative Council.

In the afternoon, Governor Chris Patten delivered his first Policy Address on economy, livelihood and education with a focus on substantial political reform. His proposal included 20 directly elected legislative seats under a "single seat, single vote" system, a voting age at 18, nine additional functional constituencies, individual voting instead of corporate voting, termination of appointed seats with the District Board, Urban Council and Regional Council, and non-concurrent appointment of members between the Executive Council and Legislative Council. The Chinese government expressed its strong opposition to his political initiatives on the same day.

Governor Chris Patten noted in his first Policy Address that government departments and institutions must be committed to serving the public and held accountable to the community with service standards and public supervision. By 1993, customer liaison groups or similar committees were established in a minimum of 32 government departments to collect public feedback.

Governor Patten also announced changes to the Executive Council and Legislative Council. Secretary for Economic Services Anson Chan Fang On-sang (陳方安生), Secretary for Education and Manpower John Chan Cho-chak (陳祖澤) and Secretary for Constitutional Affairs Michael Sze Cho-cheung (施祖祥) were appointed to the Executive Council, replacing Commander of the British Forces in Hong Kong John Foley and Secretary for the Civil Service Barrie Wiggham. The presidency of the Legislative Council was no longer assumed by the governor and was chosen among members of the Council.

08 Oct 1992

A spokesman of the Hong Kong and Macao Affairs Office of the State Council noted China's support for gradual democratic development in Hong Kong. Governor Chris Patten's drastic political reform as revealed in his Policy Address was unilateral and exclusive of public opinion in Hong Kong, impairing the transition of the Legislative Council in 1997 for which an approach was to be decided by the Preparatory Committee for the HKSAR. It was emphasised that China would not take responsibility for any pre-1997 reform contradictory to the Basic Law.

16 Oct 1992

The Employees Retraining Ordinance 1992 was promulgated. It established the Employees Retraining Board in conjunction with the Employees Retraining Fund to support employment by retooling workers through training courses and providing subsistence allowances amid a shifting economic structure.

20 Oct 1992

China Insurance HK (Holdings) Company Limited was incorporated with endorsement from China Insurance Regulatory Commission's Hong Kong and Macao Office. It was a joint entity of four Chinese insurance groups, namely The People's Insurance Company of China, People's Insurance Company (Group) of China, China Taiping Insurance Holdings Company Limited, and China Life Insurance Company Limited. The company was renamed China Taiping Insurance Group (HK) Company Limited in June 2009.

22 Oct 1992

In a meeting with Governor Chris Patten in Beijing, Minister of Foreign Affairs Qian Qichen (錢其琛) pointed out the political reform outlined in the 1992 Policy Address was in violation of the Sino-British Joint Declaration and must be withdrawn. The following day, Director of the Hong Kong and Macao Affairs Office of the State Council Lu Ping (魯平) in a press conference called the unilateral political reform "triple violations" with reference to the Sino-British Joint Declaration, Hong Kong Basic Law, and previous agreements on transition acknowledged by the foreign ministers of China and Britain, dubbing Chris Patten a "sinner."

28 Oct 1992

A four-day meeting between China's Association for Relations Across the Taiwan Straits and Taiwan's Straits Exchange Foundation began in Hong Kong. No consensus was reached on how the "One China Policy" should be expressed.

Oct 1992

The Chinese University of Hong Kong, in collaboration with the Guangdong Provincial Institute of Cultural Relics & Archaeology and Sun Yat-sen University's School of Anthropology in Guangzhou, began a two-month excavation at the Pak Mong site on North Lantau Island. It uncovered cultural deposits from the Shang Dynasty, Spring and Autumn Period and Western Han Dynasty, providing important clues regarding the history of Hong Kong spanning from the Nanyue period to Western Han Dynasty.

02 Nov 1992

The Agreement between the Government of the Kingdom of the Netherlands and the Government of Hong Kong for the Surrender of Fugitive Offenders was signed in Hong Kong. It went into effect on 20 June 1997 as Hong Kong's first agreement on the surrender of fugitives. Hong Kong had 19 similar agreements with foreign governments as of 01 July 2017.

06 Nov 1992

The Toys and Children's Products Safety Ordinance 1992 was promulgated, requiring compliance with international standards in toys. It was Hong Kong's first legislation on toy safety.

15 Nov 1992

The 14-day second FIFA Futsal World Championship began in Hong Kong as a first-time host of tournaments under *Fédération Internationale de Football Association.* Brazil won the championship.

18 Nov 1992

The International Art Fair was held at the Hong Kong Convention and Exhibition Centre, showcasing more than 4,000 exhibits with a total value of over HK$1 billion, including the artworks of Picasso, Matisse and Van Gogh.

19 Nov 1992

The Agreement on the Encouragement and Protection of Investments between the Government of Hong Kong and the Government of the Kingdom of the Netherlands was signed. It went into effect on 01 September 1993 as Hong Kong's first agreement on foreign investment. Hong Kong had 18 similar agreements as of 01 July 2017.

30 Nov 1992

A spokesperson of the Hong Kong and Macao Affairs Office of the State Council stated that the current Hong Kong government had no authority in the affairs of the HKSAR post-1997. Except land leases according to Annex III of the Sino-British Joint Declaration, all contracts, leases and agreements signed without consent of the Chinese government were deemed invalid after 30 June 1997.

02 Dec 1992

The police special duties unit, nicknamed the Flying Tigers, was deployed to capture armed robbers at Kwangchow House in Tsuen Wan Centre. In a crossfire, a robber fleeing the scene threw a grenade from high above at police officers. Seven officers were injured; six robbers were arrested.

11 Dec 1992

The Exchange Fund (Amendment) Ordinance 1992 was promulgated. It established the Hong Kong Monetary Authority (HKMA) and expanded the function of the Exchange Fund in support of a sound and stable monetary and financial system. It authorised the Financial Secretary to appoint a HKMA chief executive in place of the Commissioner of Banking and Secretary for Monetary Affairs.

17 Dec 1992

Hong Kong Internet and Gateway Services Limited was incorporated as the first local provider of Internet services; it became operational in August 1993.

18 Dec 1992

The Lord Wilson Heritage Trust, in accordance with the Lord Wilson Heritage Trust Ordinance 1992, was established to support preservation of heritage through education and publicity initiatives as well as renovation and acquisition of historical buildings and monuments.

The first heart transplant in Hong Kong was successfully performed at Grantham Hospital.

Dec 1992

Balanophora hongkongensis, a plant endemic to Hong Kong, was discovered in Castle Peak by botanists Lau Kai-man (劉啟文), Li Ning-hon (李甯漢) and Hu Shiu-ying (胡秀英); it was identified as a new species in 2003.

1992

The Hong Kong Eye Hospital, a specialist medical facility with state-of-the-art ophthalmic equipment, became operational; it was officially opened on 15 September 1993.

The Shiu-ying Hu Award was established by the Holly Society of America in honour of botanist Hu Shiu-ying (胡秀英) who was the recipient of the inaugural award. It marked the first international academic award named after an individual from Hong Kong.

01 Jan 1993

About 20,000 people gathered at Lan Kwai Fong in Central at 12 a.m. for a countdown on New Year's Day. During the celebration, a stampede occurred, resulting in 21 deaths and more than 100 injuries in what became known as the Lan Kwai Fong Tragedy. On the same day, Governor Chris Patten commissioned an investigation with a non-statutory inquiry chaired by Justice Kemal Bokhary.

06 Jan 1993

Three robbers armed with AK-47 rifles grabbed HK$3.8 million worth of jewellery from Tse Sui Luen Jewellery on Nathan Road. More than 30 shots were fired in a gunfight with the police; a stray shot killed a pregnant nurse. All robbers were captured.

12 Jan 1993

A Commission of Inquiry into Witness Protection was appointed by the governor for an investigation into the refusal of a prosecution witness to testify in a murder at the Vietnamese boat people detention centre for safety reasons. On 16 July, an investigation report was released, recommending a government witness protection programme.

14 Jan 1993

The Independent Commission Against Corruption (ICAC) filed charges against former chairman Carrian Group George Tan Soon-gin (陳松青) on allegations of corruption and conspiracy to defraud. In a Supreme Court trial on 27 September 1996, he pleaded guilty to conspiracy to defraud US$238 million and was sentenced to three years in prison. The ICAC investigation began in 1985 and was the longest case as of 2017.

The Cathay Pacific Airways Flight Attendants Union launched a strike with 1,000 members in protest of the termination of three work-to-rule flight attendants. Seven rounds of negotiation followed in the same month but failed. On 29 January, the House Committee of the Legislative Council passed a non-binding motion requesting a report from the Commissioner for Labour to Governor Chris Patten. On the same day, a management proposal for establishing a platform on resolution on disciplinary issues was accepted by the union. The three employees were reinstated, ending the strike.

Jan 1993

New coins minted with Bauhinia, Hong Kong's floral emblem, were introduced in place of the original series with the British Crown. Five-dollar and two-dollar coins were launched in the same month, followed by the release of one-dollar, 50-cent and 20-cent coins in October. In November 1994, ten-dollar coins were released.

The Kunqu Opera Research and Promotion Group was formed by the Hong Kong Institute for the Promotion of Chinese Culture, followed by a lecture series with artists Yao Chuanxiang (姚傳薌), Zheng Chuanjian (鄭傳鑒) and Zhang Xian (張嫻). On 21 May 2004, a youthful adaptation of *Peony Pavilion*, in a collaboration with Kenneth Pai Hsien-yung (白先勇), premiered in Hong Kong.

09 Feb 1993

The Independent Commission Against Corruption arrested 13 people, including five customs officers, on allegations of bribery to smuggle luxury cars through the ports of Man Kam To and Lok Ma Chau to the Mainland since 1991; 20 cars worth HK$18 million were seized. On 20 February, a Customs and Excise senior inspector was found guilty of giving and receiving bribes and was sentenced to two years in prison. On 10 March, a customs officer was found guilty and sentenced to 20 months' imprisonment and a three-year probation; on 29 April, his sentence was changed to four years' imprisonment following an appeal by the prosecutor.

12 Feb 1993

The Air Pollution Control (Amendment) Ordinance 1993 was promulgated, regulating the use of asbestos and banning the use of amosite and crocidolite. On 01 May 1996, the Air Pollution Control (Asbestos) (Administration) Regulation 1996 was promulgated, requiring that all asbestos abatement works must be handled by qualified persons. The import and use of all types of asbestos were banned starting from 04 April 2014.

19 Feb 1993

John Joseph Swaine, an Unofficial Member of the Legislative Council, was elected president in an all-member council vote. It marked the end of the arrangement, in place since 1843, whereby the governor was also the president of the Legislative Council.

15 Mar 1993

A total of 29 Hong Kong deputies of the Guangdong delegation to the National People's Congress attended the First Session of the Eighth National People's Congress in Beijing, increasing the number of Hong Kong deputies from 17 to 29.

17 Mar 1993

The Urban Council announced that it would phase out itinerant hawkers in the urban area by 01 April 1996. Licencees were required to decide within three years to either surrender their licences or move to government-sponsored hawker bazaars.

23 Mar 1993

The government began demolition work at the Kowloon Walled City; it was completed in April 1994. (Figure 248)

25 Mar 1993

Hong Kong Supernet Limited was incorporated as a start-up company of The Hong Kong University of Science and Technology; it went into service in October.

Figure 248
The Kowloon Walled City. (Photo taken in 1987 and courtesy of Post Staff Photographer/South China Morning Post via Getty Image)

26 Mar 1993

Ann Tse-kai (T. K. Ann) (安子介) and Henry Fok Ying-tung (霍英東) were elected as Vice Chairmen of the Chinese People's Political Consultative Conference, becoming the first two people from Hong Kong in deputy state-level posts.

Mar 1993

The consultation paper *Arts Policy Review Report* was released; it initiated a public discussion regarding arts and culture along with a proposal to make visual and literary arts eligible for government funding.

01 Apr 1993

The Hong Kong Monetary Authority (HKMA) was formed by merging the Office of the Exchange Fund and the Office of the Commissioner of Banking. As a central banking institution, it was given mandate to maintain currency stability, promote the stability and integrity of the financial system, maintain Hong Kong's status as an international financial centre and manage the Exchange Fund. Joseph Yam Chi-kwong (任志剛) was appointed as the first Commissioner and subsequently as the Chief Executive of HKMA.

The Government Flying Service was established, succeeding the Royal Hong Kong Auxiliary Air Force disbanded on 31 March 1993. It was a 24-hour on-call disciplinary force for conducting search and rescue and supporting the government in logistics, patrol and reconnaissance, excluding armed conflicts.

02 Apr 1993

The second group of 49 Hong Kong Affairs Advisors, jointly appointed by the Hong Kong and Macao Affairs Office of the State Council and Hong Kong Branch of Xinhua News Agency, were presented with letters of appointment in Beijing to serve in their individual capacity for a two-year term between 1993–1995; 48 advisors were reappointed for another two-year term between 1995 to 30 June 1997.

16 Apr 1993

Wardley Limited and Healthy World-Corporation (HK) Limited were granted banking licences in the second licence issuance since 1982, thereby increasing the number of licenced banks in Hong Kong to 166.

22 Apr 1993

Chinese Assistant Minister of Foreign Affairs Jiang Enzhu (姜恩柱) and British Ambassador to China Robin McLaren met in Beijing for the first round of formal talks on the 1994/95 electoral arrangement in Hong Kong. By 26 November, 17 rounds of talks had been held; no consensus was reached.

23 Apr 1993

The Protection of Women and Juveniles (Amendment) Ordinance 1992 was promulgated. It outlined four pre-conditions upon which children were deemed in need of care and protection, empowered the Director of Social Welfare to take custody of children for concerns of safety, and expanded protection initially for women to all children and juveniles. It was later renamed the Protection of Children and Juveniles Ordinance 1993.

The Crimes (Amendment) (No. 3) Ordinance 1992 was promulgated, abolishing the death penalty and replacing it with life imprisonment.

27 Apr 1993

Two compartments of an MTR train became detached enroute from Tai Wo Hau to Tsuen Wan due to a faulty connection. The incident occurred during rush hour and affected about 30,000 people; no one was injured.

07 May 1993

The Building Management Ordinance 1993 was promulgated as a substantial revision of the Multi-storey Buildings (Owners Incorporation) Ordinance 1970. It aimed to facilitate the incorporation of owners of buildings and regulate the management of incorporated owners.

09 May 1993

Hong Kong won one gold, two silver and eight bronze medals at the East Asian Games held for the first time in Shanghai. Fay Ho Kim-fai (何劍暉) won a gold medal in the women's lightweight single sculls.

12 May 1993

Former UK Prime Minister Margaret Thatcher arrived in Hong Kong for a three-day visit; she met with Director of the Hong Kong Branch of Xinhua News Agency Zhou Nan（周南）the following day.

17 May 1993

The Hospital Authority implemented a system of eight clusters (Hong Kong West, Hong Kong East, Kowloon Central, Kowloon West, Kowloon East, New Territories South, New Territories East and New Territories North), allowing patients to receive one-stop medical services (from consultation to rehabilitation) in their local districts of residence.

The British naval base HMS Tamar was closed and relocated to Stonecutters Island. The Prince of Wales Building was retained as the headquarters of the British Forces Overseas Hong Kong.

24 May 1993

The film *Farewell My Concubine* was named winner of the Palme d'Or at the 46th Cannes Film Festival in France, becoming the first Chinese film to win the award. A Hong Kong–Mainland joint production, it was directed by Chen Kaige（陳凱歌）, starring Leslie Cheung Kwok-wing（張國榮）, Gong Li（鞏俐）and Zhang Fengyi（張豐毅）.

31 May 1993

Wharf Cable Television was granted a 12-year pay TV government licence; it began broadcasting on 31 October with eight channels as the only cable TV station in Hong Kong. It was renamed Cable Television on 29 October 1998.

May 1993

The Advisory Committee on Teacher Education and Qualifications was established as an advisory body to the government on policies, practices and measures regarding the professional development of teachers. On 01 June 2013, it was renamed as the Committee on Professional Development of Teachers and Principals, serving the additional functions of educational research and professional development.

The first Le French May, a French art and culture festival through art, music and film, was jointly held by Alliance Française de Hong Kong in conjunction with the Consulate General of France.

01 Jun 1993

A man died following a shark attack while swimming at Sheung Sze Wan in Sai Kung; another man was killed by a shark in the waters off the Silverstrand Beach in Sai Kung on 11 June. It was a rare occurrence with back-to-back shark attacks within 10 days.

02 Jun 1993

A construction hoist on Java Road in North Point fell from the 20th floor to the platform on the third floor, killing 12 workers inside.

08 Jun 1993

The Sandwich Class Housing Scheme was introduced for homeownership among families with household income exceeding the threshold for public and subsidised housing but insufficient for private home purchases. The scheme, implemented by the Hong Kong Housing Society, aimed to provide residential units built on government land and low-interest loans of up to HK$500,000. The scheme was discontinued in October 1998.

18 Jun 1993

The grand final of the first FIVB Volleyball World Grand Prix Women's Championship began in a three-day event at the Hong Kong Coliseum. Cuba beat China to win the championship.

19 Jun 1993

The China Securities Regulatory Commission, Hong Kong Stock Exchange, Hong Kong Securities and Futures Commission, Shanghai Stock Exchange and Shenzhen Stock Exchange jointly signed the Memorandum of Regulatory Cooperation in Beijing, allowing Mainland enterprises to be publicly listed in Hong Kong.

26 Jun 1993

The Liberal Party was formed upon a reorganisation of the Co-operative Resources Centre which was disbanded in March. Founding Chairman Allen Lee Peng-fei (李鵬飛) supported the smooth transfer of Hong Kong, implementation of "One Country, Two Systems" and governance by Hong Kong people.

27 Jun 1993

The Hong Kong Observatory hoisted No. 8 Gale or Storm Signal for about 12 hours amid Typhoon Koryn—which led to 183 injuries.

30 Jun 1993

Wong Ka-kui (黃家駒), lead vocalist of Hong Kong rock band Beyond, died in Tokyo at the age of 31 from injuries sustained from a fall onstage during a TV programme filming in the early morning of 24 June. On 05 July, his funeral was held at Hong Kong Funeral Home where 3,000 fans paid their respect.

01 Jul 1993

The daily quota of One-way Permit (permanent residency) for Mainland residents with relatives in Hong Kong increased from 75 to 105 under an agreement between Hong Kong and the Mainland.

The Comprehensive Social Security Assistance Scheme was implemented in place of the Public Assistance Scheme, combining public assistance benefits and social allowances for support in the daily living expenses of low-income individuals.

The Telecommunications Authority, a regulatory agency responsible for licensing telecommunications and broadcasting services and managing Hong Kong's radio frequency spectrum, was established. Alexander Arena was the first Director-General of Telecommunications. On 01 April 2012, it was incorporated into the newly established Office of the Communications Authority.

02 Jul 1993

The Landlord and Tenant (Consolidation) (Amendment) Ordinance 1993 was promulgated, allowing the increase of controlled rents to market levels and removing all rent control by 01 January 1997.

The Travel Agents (Amendment) Ordinance 1993 was promulgated, establishing a Travel Industry Compensation Fund on 15 October as a protection scheme for outbound travellers in cases of personal injury or bankruptcy of travel agencies.

The Preliminary Working Committee of the Preparatory Committee for the HKSAR, comprising 57 members (including 30 members from Hong Kong), was approved for establishment by the Second Session of the Eighth NPC Standing Committee. The first plenary meeting was held in Beijing on 16 July; committee membership was expanded to 69 (including 37 members from Hong Kong) on 12 May 1994. The final plenary meeting was held in Beijing on 07 December 1995.

05 Jul 1993

The first China Studies workshop, endorsed by the Hong Kong and Macao Affairs Office of the State Council and the Hong Kong Branch of Xinhua News Agency, began for a seven-week training course to provide Hong Kong's mid- and senior-level civil servants with a learning platform on the latest development of the Mainland. It was co-organised by the Hong Kong government and Tsinghua University and was held in Beijing.

09 Jul 1993

The Bank of China (Hong Kong) was given government approval to become the third note-issuing bank; it began issuing HK-dollar banknotes on 01 May 1994.

15 Jul 1993

Tsingtao Brewery was publicly listed in Hong Kong to raise HK$890 million in what became the first initial public offering in the form of H shares by a state-owned enterprise.

16 Jul 1993

The Amusement Game Centres Ordinance 1993 was promulgated, strengthening the regulation and licensing of video game centres by designating those for persons under 16 and those for persons aged 16 or older, in addition to applying specific restrictions in each license with conditions, including business hours, prohibition of entry of persons in school uniforms, and prohibition of establishment near schools.

17 Jul 1993

The Tsuen Wan Central Library was opened with the world's first bilingual automated catalogue system of library information and book collection.

23 Jul 1993

The Boundary and Election Commission was formed as a statutory body responsible for all levels of council elections in accordance with the Boundary and Election Commission Ordinance 1993. It advised on drawing geographical constituencies, arranged for voter registrations and elections, and supervised all related matters, including election campaigns, candidate advertising, polling, vote counting, and handling of complaints.

27 Jul 1993

China Aerospace International Holdings Limited was incorporated in Hong Kong as a Chinese enterprise in space technology, satellites and communications. Its Chinese name was amended in 2008.

Jul 1993

Kwai Chung Container Terminal No. 8 was opened in a joint operation by Modern Terminals Ltd, Hongkong International Terminals Ltd, and COSCO–HIT Terminals Ltd. It marked the first container terminal with investment from a Mainland enterprise.

05 Aug 1993

Rape suspect Lam Kwok-wai (林國偉) was arrested. On 12 August 1994, he was tried in the Tuen Mun Law Courts where he was charged on three counts of murder, eight counts of rape and seven counts of robbery. On 28 September, he was found guilty of all charges and was sentenced to life imprisonment.

20 Aug 1993

The film *Hard Target*, directed by John Woo Yu-sen (吳宇森), premiered in the US, making it the first Hollywood film with a director from Hong Kong.

06 Sep 1993

The Hong Kong Jockey Club founded its Charities Trust with an allocation of HK$3 billion to support charitable causes, youth affairs, elderly services, sports and recreation, as well as cultural and art development in Hong Kong.

17 Sep 1993

The Hong Kong Observatory hoisted No. 8 Gale or Storm Signal for about 12 hours amid Typhoon Becky—which caused one death and at least 130 injuries.

25 Sep 1993

Hong Kong athlete Lee Lai-shan (李麗珊) won the gold medal in the women's division at the 1993 Windsurfing World Championships in Kashiwazaki, Japan. It was Hong Kong's first-ever medal in the event.

27 Sep 1993

Ming Pao reporter Xi Yang (席揚) was detained in Beijing for investigation by the National Security Bureau. On 04 April 1994, he was sentenced to 12 years in prison by the Intermediate People's Court of Beijing Municipality for stealing state secrets. On 25 January 1997, he was released on parole and returned to Hong Kong.

Sep 1993

Central Reclamation Phase I began as a part of the Hong Kong Airport Core Programme. It entailed 20 hectares of reclaimed land for the construction of Hong Kong Station, Airport Express and an expanded Central Business District. The project was completed in June 1998.

01 Oct 1993

The Cheung Sha Wan Wholesale Food Market was opened as a part of the West Kowloon Reclamation project under the Hong Kong Airport Core Programme; it was the first constructed building of the programme.

15 Oct 1993

Pamela Youde Nethersole Eastern Hospital in Chai Wan was opened with 1,620 beds for patients mainly from Hong Kong Island East.

The Central Mid-Levels Escalator and Walkway System, measuring 800 metres between Des Voeux Road Central and Conduit Road, came into service as the world's longest escalator of its kind.

The Home Affairs Branch was formed upon a reorganisation of the City and New Territories Administration; it was a government body tasked with district administration and community affairs across Hong Kong, including human rights, public consultation, as well as religious and customary engagement, as a bridge between the government and district councils.

The Hong Kong office of the European Community (European Union) was established.

25 Oct 1993

The *Consultative Document on Civil Service Terms of Appointment and Conditions of Service* was published. For the first time, it proposed a unified civil service recruitment scheme with local and overseas persons in support of a localisation policy with the establishment of the HKSAR.

08 Nov 1993

The first foetal gender selection centre in Hong Kong was opened for commercial service.

10 Nov 1993

The Independent Commission Against Corruption (ICAC) summarily dismissed Deputy Director of Operations Alex Tsui Ka-kit (徐家傑), its highest-ranking Chinese officer, without explanation under the Independent Commission Against Corruption (Amendment) Ordinance 1992, raising public concern. On 02 November 1994, a report on the dismissal prepared by the Legislative Council's Panel on Security was released; it found the decision of ICAC Commissioner Bertrand de Speville to be reasonable and correct.

19 Nov 1993

The 110-hectare West New Territories Landfill at Nim Wan in Tuen Mun became operational as Hong Kong's first strategic landfill at a cost of HK$2.2 billion with an intake capacity of 61 million cubic metres of waste.

23 Nov 1993

The Hong Kong Science Museum opened an exhibition called "Dinosaur Alive!" It featured eight mechanical dinosaurs and multimedia information, etc. This was the first time that dinosaur models were exhibited at Hong Kong Science Museum.

29 Nov 1993

Secretary for the Civil Service Anson Chan Fang On-sang (陳方安生) took office as Chief Secretary; she was the first female and the first Chinese Chief Secretary of Hong Kong.

Nov 1993

The Antiquities and Monuments Office began an eight-month excavation in three phases at the Kowloon Walled City. Stone plaques with Chinese characters "Kowloon Walled City" and "South Gate" as well as remains of the gate, walls, roads and houses were unearthed.

01 Dec 1993

The Legislative Council approved a HK$50 million grant for a Disaster Relief Fund to provide disaster relief globally and accept public donations in accordance with the Public Finance (Amendment) Ordinance 1990. On 01 February 1994, the Disaster Relief Fund Advisory Committee was established as an advisory body on funding and operation.

02 Dec 1993

Governor Chris Patten announced in the Legislative Council a plan to gazette and submit parts of his proposed constitutional reform package for deliberation. The Hong Kong and Macao Affairs Office of the State Council issued a statement the next day, declaring that any institution resulting from the constitutional reform would not be recognised in the HKSAR. Instead, a separate political system would be put in place after June 1997 in accordance with the Basic Law.

10 Dec 1993

The Quarantine and Prevention of Disease (Amendment) Ordinance 1993 was promulgated for prevention of the spread of infectious diseases. It amended the principal list of infectious diseases in accordance with the International Health Regulations, and increased the penalty for noncompliance.

12 Dec 1993

The Ping Shan Heritage Trail in Yuen Long was unveiled as Hong Kong's first heritage trail running 1.6 kilometres between Hang Mei Tsuen and Sheung Cheung Wai along nine traditional Chinese architectural sites. As of 2017, it included 13 special attraction sites, including four declared monuments accessible to the public.

The Hong Kong Performing Artistes Guild was established; Michael Hui Koon-man (許冠文) was its first president.

24 Dec 1993

The Town Planning Board released the amended Kowloon Outline Zoning Plans for 16 districts, stipulating a maximum plot ratio of 7.5 for residential buildings and a ratio of 12 for commercial/industrial buildings.

29 Dec 1993

The Big Buddha at Ngong Ping on Lantau Island was unveiled in a consecration ceremony under the auspices of 13 eminent Buddhist monks from around the world. Constructed by Po Lin Monastery, it measured 34 metres in height and more than 250 metric tonnes in weight, making it the world's tallest outdoor-seated bronze Buddha. (Figure 249)

31 Dec 1993

The police enforced crowd control measures in Lan Kwai Fong on New Year's Eve with a limit of 5,000 people as recommended by Justice Kemal Bokhary in his investigation report *New Year's Stampede: Lan Kwai Fong 1993*. Other mitigatory measures were implemented, including MTR's overnight service, widened roads and additional railings along the sidewalk.

The Urban Council held the first large-scale New Year countdown party at Victoria Park with over 40,000 people; it was designed to help prevent a repeat of the Lan Kwai Fong stampede.

Dec 1993

The Certificate for Picking Up or Setting Down of Passengers with Disabilities in Restricted Zones was launched in a joint effort by the Transport Department, Police Force, and Hong Kong Council of Social Service. It allowed passengers with disabilities to board and alight from a taxi in restricted zones. The scheme was expanded to cover private cars in August 1996 and private buses and minibuses in May 1999.

1993

The first Masters Games, organised by the Urban Council, was held. It had 11 competitive events and 2,863 participants, allowing people aged 40 or above to enjoy the fun of sports.

The professional troupe Theatre Ensemble was established; it was renamed PIP Cultural Industries in 2008 and began to promote arts and culture commercially without government subsidies.

Figure 249
The opening and consecration ceremony of the Big Buddha on Lantau Island on 29 December 1993. (Photo courtesy of South China Morning Post Publishers Limited)

07 Jan 1994

The Hong Kong Industrial Technology Centre in Kowloon Tong was marked with a topping-out ceremony; it began providing support services for small hi-tech start-ups in August.

10 Jan 1994

A man set fire to an HSBC branch in Shek Kip Mei with flammable liquid, trapping 13 employees and killing 12. The Fire Safety (Commercial Premises) Ordinance 1997 was promulgated on 14 March 1997 to strengthen the fire safety standards of commercial buildings and prevent a recurrence of such incidents.

14 Jan 1994

The Noise Control (Amendment) Ordinance 1993 was promulgated, introducing strict regulations over high-noise construction equipment and noise levels of mechanical and manual construction work in densely populated areas during permitted working hours, in addition to heavier penalties for non-compliance.

The Urban Council signed a contract with Maritime Mechanic Ltd for a trial scheme involving anti-shark nets. Nets were first installed at Clear Water Bay Second Beach in Sai Kung and subsequently at Silverstrand Beach in Sai Kung and Kadoorie Beach in Tuen Mun.

23 Jan 1994

The Phase III extension project of the Dongjiang–Shenzhen Water Supply System became fully operational. It included a new pumping station and expanded artificial channels and natural watercourses for an annual water capacity of 1,743 million cubic metres; it supplied Hong Kong with 1.1 billion cubic metres of water each year, accounting for over 70% of annual local water consumption.

01 Feb 1994

The Daya Bay Nuclear Power Plant's Unit 1 became operational, followed by Unit 2 on 07 May, as China's first large nuclear power station through a joint venture with foreign capital, equipment and technology. On 18 July, a ceremony was held in Beijing to celebrate the start of full operation.

04 Feb 1994

The Hong Kong Sports Development Board became a statutory body under a merger with the Hong Kong Sports Institute in accordance with the Hong Kong Sports Development Board (Amendment) Ordinance 1993.

25 Feb 1994

The Electoral Provisions (Miscellaneous Amendments) (No. 2) Ordinance 1993 was promulgated. It stipulated a "single-seat, single-vote" system in all elections of the Legislative Council, Urban Council, Regional Council and District Boards starting in 1994 and 1995; it changed two seats in the Urban Council from appointment-based to election-based and made all District Boards election-based. The voting age was lowered from 21 to 18.

28 Feb 1994

The Ministry of Foreign Affairs of China released a document titled *Facts about a Few Important Aspects of Sino-British Talks on 1994/95 Electoral Arrangements in Hong Kong,* condemning Britain's breach of an early bilateral understanding, unilateral disclosure of negotiation details, "triple violations" in the proposed constitutional reform, and unwillingness to negotiate productively.

03 Mar 1994

The Hong Kong Publishing Federation was formed under a joint establishment with eight trade associations and publishing companies as an advocacy group comprising over 700 book publishers, distributors and retailers.

04 Mar 1994

The Hong Kong Branch of Xinhua News Agency held a ceremony of appointment with the first group of 274 Hong Kong Affairs Advisors. The second group of 263 advisors was conferred on 09 January 1995, followed by the third group of 133 advisors on 13 July 1995. In total, 670 advisors were appointed in their personal capacity to provide views on Hong Kong issues.

10 Mar 1994

Amendments to the New Territories Land (Exemption) Bill 1993 proposed by Legislative Councillor Christine Loh Kung-wai (陸 恭 蕙) were accepted, expanding the inheritance rights of female indigenous inhabitants of the New Territories from non-agricultural land to agricultural land. The proposal was opposed by the Hong Kong and Macao Affairs Office of the State Council on 29 March on the grounds that indigenous inhabitants were not consulted.

11 Mar 1994

The Hong Kong Stadium in Causeway Bay was opened in a ceremony with a laser show upon reconstruction financed by The Hong Kong Jockey Club with a donation of HK$850 million. With a capacity of 40,000 seats, it was the largest outdoor recreation and sports venue in Hong Kong as of 2017.

The Drainage Services Department's Sewage Services Trading Fund began overseeing government sewage levies to recoup the construction and running costs of infrastructure under the Strategic Sewage Disposal Scheme.

22 Mar 1994

Over 1,200 indigenous inhabitants of the New Territories rallied against the New Territories Land (Exemption) Bill 1993 on land inheritance rights outside the Legislative Council. The protesters argued with women's groups supporting the proposal and attacked members of the Legislative Council; no one was arrested. On 25 March, Headquarters for the Battle to Defend Our Home was formed by Heung Yee Kuk to oppose the legislative amendments.

23 Mar 1994

Jardine Matheson announced the relocation of second listings of its subsidiaries Jardine Strategic Holdings and Jardine Matheson Holdings from Hong Kong to Singapore; primary listings remained in London.

30 Mar 1994

The Administrative Affairs Sub-group under the Preliminary Working Commission of the Preparatory Committee for the HKSAR issued a statement at the sixth meeting in Beijing, noting that civil servants might continue to serve in the HKSAR government after 01 July 1997. They were required to remain politically neutral; knowledge of Putonghua was not mandatory. The civil service system in terms of recruitment, examination, discipline, training and management would be retained in accordance with Article 103 of the Basic Law; principal officials may not be foreign nationals or Hong Kong permanent residents with the right of abode in a foreign country.

Mar 1994

The Language Fund was established to implement proficiency projects with an initial government funding of HK$300 million in the form of a trust under the Education Bureau. On 01 October 1996, it came under the management of the newly formed Standing Committee on Language Education and Research.

01 Apr 1994

The Social Welfare Department launched a Senior Citizen Card scheme to promote care for those aged 65 or above with special privileges, including priority access to certain government services, public transport fare concessions and discounts from participating merchants.

09 Apr 1994

The first baby conceived through sperm microinjection in Hong Kong was born.

15 Apr 1994

Hong Kong took part with more than 120 countries in the signing of the Final Act Embodying the Results of the Uruguay Round of Multilateral Trade Negotiations in Marrakesh, Morocco for an agreement to establish the World Trade Organization.

25 Apr 1994

The Hong Kong Institute of Education was established in accordance with The Hong Kong Institute of Education Ordinance 1994. It was a merger of the Northcote College of Education, Grantham College of Education, Sir Robert Black College of Education, Hong Kong Technical Teachers' College, and Institute of Language in Education.

08 May 1994

Over 7,000 indigenous inhabitants of the New Territories joined a march organised by Heung Yee Kuk in protest of the proposed New Territories Land (Exemption) Bill 1993.

24 May 1994

Daniel R. Fung (馮華健) and Peter Nguyen Van Tu (阮雲道) were appointed as Solicitor General and Crown Prosecutor, respectively, becoming the first Chinese senior legal officers in the government as part of the localisation policy.

26 May 1994

The third group of 50 Hong Kong Affairs Advisors received their letters of appointment in Beijing for a two-year term under the Hong Kong and Macao Affairs Office of the State Council in conjunction with the Hong Kong Branch of Xinhua News Agency. Appointments were renewed on 13 April 1996 and expired on 30 June 1997.

Media Asia Entertainment Group was incorporated as a film producer and distributor. As of 2017, it had won a total of four Best Film awards at the Hong Kong Film Awards for *Beast Cops*, *Infernal Affairs*, *The Warlords* and *Trivisa*.

02 Jun 1994

The Hong Kong government accepted a proposal of the Boundary and Election Commission for establishing 32 and 27 constituencies in the March 1995 elections of the Urban Council and Regional Council, respectively.

08 Jun 1994

Physicist Franklin Yang Chen-ning (楊振寧), mathematician Yau Shing-tung (丘成桐) and engineer Leroy L. Chang (張立綱) were named in the first group of foreign academicians to the Chinese Academy of Sciences. As of 2017, seven foreign academicians were from Hong Kong.

09 Jun 1994

A donation of HK$2 million from the Disaster Relief Fund was made to Oxfam for refugees in Rwanda. It marked the first of five donations totalling HK$12 million in support of Rwanda through various charitable organisations during the year.

22 Jun 1994

The Construction Sites (Safety) (Amendment) (No. 2) Regulations 1994 was promulgated, prohibiting any person under the age of 18 from working on a construction site without having completed approved training.

24 Jun 1994

The New Territories Land (Exemption) Ordinance 1994 was promulgated, giving female indigenous inhabitants of the New Territories the right to inherit land or property in the absence of a will as with any land across Hong Kong.

The Ombudsman (Amendment) Ordinance 1994 was promulgated, effective 01 July. The Office of the Commissioner for Administrative Complaints became the Office of the Ombudsman. Its coverage of investigation expanded from government departments to statutory bodies while complaints may be lodged by the public; an investigation may be initiated when deemed necessary even without a public complaint.

29 Jun 1994

The Liberal Party proposed an amendment to adopt the 1994 Plan during the second reading of the Legislative Council (Electoral Provisions) (Amendment) Bill 1994. It entailed incorporating nine new functional constituencies, retaining corporate voting, reducing the number of eligible voters from more than two million (as proposed by the government) to 320,000, and making an election committee headed by four categories of broadly representative people. The motion was defeated by one vote. The government bill was passed (32–24 votes) at 2:30 a.m. the following day after the third reading; it was promulgated on 08 July for implementation of political reform proposed by Governor Chris Patten in his 1992 Policy Address.

30 Jun 1994

The UK and China reached an agreement on the future use of military sites in Hong Kong at the 29th meeting of the Sino-British Joint Liaison Group, followed by a formal exchange of confirmation in November. The UK government was required to transfer 14 sites of military value to the Chinese government without compensation on 01 July 1997; 25 sites were to be made available for social and economic development; and Hong Kong was responsible for relocating five military facilities, including the naval base on Stonecutters Island and the military hospital at Gun Club Hill Barracks.

06 Jul 1994

The first UK–China group meeting was held on Hong Kong's sewage disposal beyond 1997.

08 Jul 1994

The Consumer Council (Amendment) Ordinance 1994 was promulgated, providing the Consumer Council with greater authority over some franchises and public utilities.

An allocation of HK$20 million drawn from the Disaster Relief Fund was made available by the government for flood victims in southern China through Hong Kong Red Cross, World Vision Hong Kong and Médecins Sans Frontières.

11 Jul 1994

Twelve people contracted cholera after consumption of seafood raised in the Aberdeen Typhoon Shelter. The Urban Council and Regional Council announced that clean water must be used to keep live seafood in all retail outlets and restaurants. Henceforth, fishing in urban typhoon shelters, including the Aberdeen Typhoon Shelter, was prohibited.

12 Jul 1994

The government public consultation paper *Taking the Worry Out of Growing Old—An Old Age Pension Scheme for Hong Kong* was released on the implementation of a mandatory contribution retirement scheme. On 27 January 1995, it was announced that the project would be shelved because of divergent views in the community.

18 Jul 1994

The 122.8-km Guangzhou–Shenzhen Expressway was commissioned; it officially became operational on 01 July 1997. It was jointly developed by Gordon Wu Ying-sheung's (胡應湘) Hopewell Holdings and Guangdong Provincial Highway Construction Company Ltd, making it the first expressway project between Hong Kong and the Mainland. It connected Guangzhou, Shenzhen and the Huanggang Port along the border of Hong Kong.

24 Jul 1994

The Hong Kong Progressive Alliance was established; Ambrose Lau Hon-chuen (劉漢銓) served as chairman. On 26 May 1997, it announced a merger with the Liberal Democratic Federation of Hong Kong and retained its name.

28 Jul 1994

An amended conversion scheme for expatriate civil servants was announced, allowing the renewal of employment contracts due to expire before 01 September 1995 as local employees. To promote localisation, successful applicants would retain their existing compensation package but fall one rank below if suitable candidates were available under local terms.

01 Aug 1994

The Environment and Conservation Fund was established; its executive committee was responsible for funding non-profit environmental and conservation-related projects in Hong Kong.

08 Aug 1994

The Hang Seng China Enterprises Index was launched with 10 constituent stocks, gauging the overall performance of Mainland enterprises listed in Hong Kong.

31 Aug 1994

The Ninth Session of the Eighth National People's Congress Standing Committee decided to nullify Hong Kong's Legislative Council, Urban Council, Regional Council and District Board on 30 June 1997. It was decided that all matters regarding the establishment of the HKSAR, including its first Legislative Council, was to be undertaken by the Preparatory Committee for the HKSAR in accordance with the Decision on the Method for the Formation of the First Government and the First Legislative Council of the Hong Kong Special Administrative Region.

07 Sep 1994

The United Nations' Convention on the Rights of the Child was enacted in Hong Kong by the British government. On 10 June 1997, the Chinese government in a letter to the UN Secretary-General stated that the Convention would continue to apply after the establishment of the HKSAR on 01 July 1997.

13 Sep 1994

The Legislative Council approved the Hawker (Urban Council) (Amendment) (No. 3) Bylaw 1994, authorising the Urban Council to ban itinerant hawkers in urban areas, without specifying an effective date. On 02 May 1995, a licensee selling ice-cream bars objected and filed an application for judicial review, causing the Urban Council to shelve its plan.

16 Sep 1994

The Hong Kong Observatory recorded an earthquake in the southern Taiwan Strait at 2:20 p.m.; it measured 6.5 on the Richter scale without any reported casualty or damage. With an intensity of V to VI on the Modified Mercalli Scale, it was the strongest tremor in Hong Kong since the earthquake near Nan'ao Island off the shore of Shantou in 1918.

18 Sep 1994

The 1994 District Board elections were held; it had a turnout rate of 33.1% for a total of 346 directly elected seats and no appointed seats. In the nine District Boards of the New Territories, 27 ex-officio seats designated for chairmen of rural committees remained. The Yau Ma Tei and Tsim Sha Tsui District and Mong Kok District were merged into Yau Tsim Mong District on 01 October 1994, making a total of 18 District Boards (renamed District Councils in 1999) in Hong Kong.

23 Sep 1994

A cargo plane took off from Hong Kong en route to Jakarta, Indonesia and crashed into the sea near Kai Tak Airport, killing six people.

26 Sep 1994

A 10-year-old boy was abducted on Eastern Hospital Road in Causeway Bay. On 28 September, four kidnappers were arrested. The police found the boy's body in Tai Mo Shan Country Park the following day. On 04 October 1995, two of the kidnappers were convicted of murder and sentenced to life imprisonment.

The Southeast New Territories Landfill at Tai Chik Sha in Tseung Kwan O became operational at a cost of HK$2 billion. It was the second strategic landfill in Hong Kong and had a total surface and sea area of 100 hectares with a waste absorption capacity of 43 million cubic metres.

Sep 1994

The Chinese University of Hong Kong changed its undergraduate programme from four to three years, starting in the current academic year.

01 Oct 1994

The Hong Kong Association of Banks removed the interest rate cap on Hong Kong dollar time deposits with maturity of over a month. It marked the first step in the government's move to revoke the 30-year-old interest rate agreement in a bid to make the Hong Kong dollar more resilient under the linked exchange rate and promote a competitive banking industry.

02 Oct 1994

The Democratic Party was formed under a merger between the United Democrats of Hong Kong and Meeting Point; Martin Lee Chu-ming（李柱銘）was its first chairman.

Team Hong Kong won five silver and seven bronze medals at the 12th Asian Games in Hiroshima, Japan. These included Hong Kong's first medals in rowing and sailing.

03 Oct 1994

The High Court ruled in favour of Steven N.S. Cheung（張五常）, a professor of economics at The University of Hong Kong, in his libel suit against *Eastweek*. It was the first civil case tried with a jury since 1915.

10 Oct 1994

A Double Tenth celebration was held at the Cultural Centre in Tsim Sha Tsui by the Chinese Culture Association upon approval of venue leasing by the Urban Council. The Hong Kong Branch of Xinhua News Agency stated that it violated the principle of "One Country, Two Systems" and found the government at fault for approving the lease.

21 Oct 1994

The Organized and Serious Crimes Ordinance 1994 was promulgated, authorising the police to require persons with information to answer questions for investigation of organised crimes. It also empowered the court to confiscate proceeds from crimes as specified, and made money laundering in relation to these crimes a criminal offence.

The Residential Care Homes (Elderly Persons) Ordinance 1994 was promulgated, effective 01 April, stipulating that all private homes for the elderly must comply with government requirements on architectural structure, fire safety and hygiene standards before an operating licence or certificate of exemption could be issued.

The Consumer Goods Safety Ordinance 1994 was promulgated, stipulating that all manufacturers, importers and suppliers of consumer goods must meet general safety requirements, except those already under specific regulations.

25 Oct 1994

The Central Military Commission of the Communist Party of China announced the establishment of the People's Liberation Army Hong Kong Garrison in Shenzhen.

28 Oct 1994

The Independent Commission Against Corruption conducted a three-day raid on the Mong Kok Police District Special Duty Squad; it arrested 48 people, including nine police officers, for allegedly conspiring to receive benefits and provide protection to drug traffickers and vice establishment operators.

30 Oct 1994

Education Convergence was established under its founding chairman Tso Kai-lok（曹啟樂）. It aimed to promote the overall development of education—from early childhood to tertiary education—through advocacy, policy review, research and discussion.

03 Nov 1994

The Chinese Manufacturers' Association of Hong Kong celebrated its 60th anniversary and organised the 32nd Hong Kong Brands and Products Expo after a gap of 21 years. It was held at the Hong Kong Convention and Exhibition Centre with 400 exhibitors. From 2003 onwards, it continued at Victoria Park.

04 Nov 1994

The United Kingdom and China reached a financial agreement on the Hong Kong Airport Core Programme. The total estimated cost was HK$158.2 billion; Hong Kong government would contribute at least HK$60.3 billion while total debt to be borne by the HKSAR government would not exceed HK$23 billion. The agreement was reached after four British financial proposals following the Memorandum of Understanding Concerning the Construction of the New Airport in Hong Kong in September 1991.

11 Nov 1994

The Legislative Council approved a provision of HK$10 million to establish a Consumer Legal Action Fund under the Consumer Council (Trustee), giving consumers support in bringing lawsuits against unscrupulous businesses.

17 Nov 1994

The 29th meeting of the Sino-British Land Commission was concluded with an agreement to grant 1,248 hectares of land for a new airport at Chek Lap Kok. (Figures 250 and 251)

18 Nov 1994

Hong Kong Polytechnic, Hong Kong Baptist College and City Polytechnic of Hong Kong were granted approval to reinstitute with university status and were renamed Hong Kong Polytechnic University, Hong Kong Baptist University and City University of Hong Kong.

14 Dec 1994

The first *Railway Development Strategy* was published, outlining a plan with the local rail network and a proposal of district-based strategic development.

Legislative Councillor Lau Chin-shek（劉千石）announced his resignation during a council meeting, becoming the first to do so in the history of Hong Kong. The move was in protest of the government's decision to withdraw the Employment (Amendment) Bill 1994 after the meeting adopted his proposed amendments.

19 Dec 1994

A countdown clock in commemoration of China's resumption of exercise of sovereignty over Hong Kong was unveiled on the east side of Tiananmen Square in Beijing, showing 925 days until 01 July 1997.

29 Dec 1994

The Scheme of Open Competition for Civil Service Posts was announced, requiring local and expatriate civil servants in the promotion ranks on contract due to expire on or after 01 September 1995 to compete with those of one rank below. Additionally, contract renewals were only available to permanent residents.

1994

The Hong Kong Housing Authority allocated HK$400 million to improve the security of 938 public rental housing blocks.

Figure 250
Chek Lap Kok on Lantau Island in 1989 before construction of a new airport. (Photo courtesy of South China Morning Post Publishers Limited)

Figure 251
The islands Chek Lap Kok and Lam Chau were joined together through reclamation in 1996. (Photo courtesy of HKSAR Government)

01 Jan 1995

Telephone numbers in Hong Kong were amended from seven to eight digits. Prefixes "2," "7," and "9" were assigned to home phone, pager and mobile phone numbers, respectively.

The World Trade Organization was founded with its headquarters in Geneva, Switzerland. Hong Kong was one of its founding members.

12 Jan 1995

The Chinese newspaper *Overseas Wah Kiu Yat Po* (Chinese Daily News), founded in 1925, ceased publication upon its final issue on 12 January, making it the longest-running Chinese newspaper in Hong Kong as of 2017.

25 Jan 1995

At least eight robbers broke into a car park in Yuen Long at 11 p.m., tying up two workers on duty and driving off in batches with 27 left-hand drive vehicles worth more than HK$5 million.

06 Feb 1995

Peter Lai Hing-ling (黎慶寧) became the first Chinese to assume office as Secretary for Security.

13 Feb 1995

The final revised government compensation scheme for the clearance of Tiu Keng Leng was announced. The scheme provided residents with an ex-gratia allowance of HK$7,000 per square metre and a relocation allowance based on the number of family members. In addition, they could be allocated public housing or given priority in purchasing a flat under the Housing Department's Home Ownership Scheme.

20 Feb 1995

Josephine Siao Fong-fong (蕭芳芳) won the Silver Bear for Best Actress at the 45th Berlin Film Festival for her role in *Summer Snow.* On 09 December, she also won the 32nd Taiwanese Golden Horse Award for Best Leading Actress.

24 Feb 1995

The Human Organ Transplant Ordinance 1995 was promulgated, prohibiting the commercial trading of human organs intended for transplant, along with restrictions on organ transplant between living persons and the transplant of imported organs.

26 Feb 1995

The Tuen Mun Golf Centre was opened as the first public golf driving range in Hong Kong. The Jockey Club Kau Sai Chau Public Golf Course was opened in December, making it the first public golf course in Hong Kong.

05 Mar 1995

The 1995 elections of the Urban Council and Regional Council were held for a total of 59 directly elected seats with a voter turnout rate of 25.8%. It marked the first time that all members were directly elected and the last elections of the two councils.

27 Mar 1995

The high-speed Guangdong-Kowloon Through Train was inaugurated at Guangzhou Railway Station; it went into service the following day with a top speed of 160 km per hour and a reduced journey time by 40 minutes between Hong Kong and Guangzhou.

30 Mar 1995

The Budget Expert Group under the Sino-British Joint Liaison Group held its first meeting in Beijing. Together with the Hong Kong government, it was responsible for preparing the 1996/97 and 1997/98 Budgets; Hong Kong was required to seek approval from China and Britain before announcing the budgets.

Figure 252
Vietnamese boat people started a riot at Whitehead Detention Centre in Sha Tin on 20 May 1995. (Photo courtesy of Sing Tao News Corporation Limited)

01 Apr 1995

The government introduced a sewage service scheme in keeping with the principle "polluter pays," imposing a basic sewage charge and a trade effluent surcharge on all residential, industrial and commercial users in the public sewerage system to defray the cost of government-run sewage treatment services.

Tommy Chui To-yan (徐道仁), a witness in a major cigarette smuggling case under investigation by the Independent Commission Against Corruption since 1994, was confirmed to have been killed in Singapore. After a court trial, Cheung Wai-ming (張偉明) and Cheng Wui-yiu (鄭會耀), who were involved in the case, were convicted of conspiracy to commit murder in 1998 and 2004 and sentenced to 27 years' imprisonment and life imprisonment, respectively.

28 Apr 1995

The fourth and last group of 45 Hong Kong Affairs Advisors, appointed by the Hong Kong and Macau Affairs Office of the State Council and the Hong Kong Branch of Xinhua News Agency, received their appointment letters in Beijing. Their term of office ended on 30 June 1997.

The Central Witness Protection Unit was established as a paramilitary bodyguard unit of the Police Force for protection of witnesses, their families and undercover police officers deemed under threat, and as a policymaking unit regarding witness protection.

08 May 1995

Singer Jacky Cheung Hok-yau (張學友) was named Best Selling Chinese Singer and World's Best-Selling Asian Singer at the World Music Awards ceremony in Monte Carlo, becoming the first Hong Kong artist to win both awards.

09 May 1995

Central Ferry Pier No. 5 was opened for commercial traffic with the first arrival from Cheung Chau at 6 a.m., becoming the first operational pier as part of the resettlement of outlying islands ferry facilities. By March 1996, six piers had become operational for routes along the inner harbour and outlying islands.

11 May 1995

A Hong Kong–Shenzhen agreement on the Shenzhen River Regulation Project was signed to tackle the problem of flooding in northern New Territories. The first phase was undertaken by Shenzhen while the cost was equally shared. The main works included straightening the Liu Pok and Lok Ma Chau bends and widening and deepening the river channels. The project started on 17 May and was concluded in April 1997.

The Hong Kong Observatory recorded a minor earthquake of magnitude 2.4 on the Richter scale at 9:59 a.m. in the waters around east Lantau Island.

20 May 1995

Some 1,500 Vietnamese boat people at the Whitehead Detention Centre in Sha Tin clashed with about 2,000 uniformed officers as they refused to be relocated to the High Island Detention Centre. The police fired 3,520 canisters of tear gas; some 27 Vietnamese boat people, along with 168 Correctional Services Department staff and police officers, were injured. As of 2017, it was the largest amount of tear gas ever used by the police in a single incident. (Figure 252)

30 May 1995

The Hong Kong Policy Research Institute was established; Paul Yip Kwok-wah (葉國華) served as chairman. It aimed to promote the implementation of "One Country, Two Systems" and "Hong Kong people governing Hong Kong" through public policy research.

01 Jun 1995

The Obscene Articles Tribunal judged a statue in Kailey Tower to be a Class II (indecent) article and required its male sexual organs to be covered before it could be publicly displayed, causing widespread concern. On 11 August, the Supreme Court overturned the adjudication, stating that the Control of Obscene and Indecent Articles Ordinance did not cover works of art and that the statue could be displayed in its original form.

The Hong Kong Arts Development Council was established in accordance with the Hong Kong Arts Development Council Ordinance 1995. It replaced the Council for the Performing Arts as the statutory body for promoting the arts in 10 disciplines, namely dance, drama, opera, film and media, music, visual arts, literary arts, arts education, arts administration, and arts criticism. It had a membership system by which industry representatives could be elected to take part in policymaking and funding allocation.

The Marine Parks Ordinance 1995 was promulgated, authorising the directorship of the Country and Marine Parks Authority under the Agriculture and Fisheries Department. The authority, in consultation with the Country and Marine Park Board, could designate, manage and control the marine parks and reserves in Hong Kong.

The North East New Territories Landfill at Ta Kwu Ling was put into use at a cost of HK$1.1 billion as Hong Kong's third strategic landfill with a total surface and sea area of 61 hectares and a waste absorption capacity of 35 million cubic metres.

02 Jun 1995

A male swimmer died in a shark attack in the waters off Silverstrand Beach in Sai Kung. On 06 June, another male swimmer was killed by a shark in the vicinity. On 13 June, a female swimmer was killed by a shark at Clear Water Bay in Sai Kung. Three shark attacks in Hong Kong in 13 days raised widespread concern about beach safety.

07 Jun 1995

The Environmental Protection Department began publishing daily readings of the Air Pollution Index with four levels of indication ranging from "good" to "very unhealthy." On 15 June 1998, the Department changed its General Air Pollution Index with five levels of indication ranging from "minor" to "severe" and began publishing the newly established Roadside Air Quality Index.

08 Jun 1995

The Agreement between the British and Chinese sides on the Question of the Court of Final Appeal in Hong Kong was signed, stipulating that the Court of Final Appeal would be constituted by the HKSAR upon its establishment on 01 July 1997.

20 Jun 1995

Apple Daily, founded by Jimmy Lai Chee-ying (黎智英) went on sale. It was not a member of the Joint Conference of Chinese Newspapers and did not follow the Conference's resolution that all Hong Kong Chinese newspapers should have a uniform sale price of HK$5. It came with a HK$3 voucher during the first month, thus lowering the real price to HK$2; its sales volume became the second highest in Hong Kong during the year.

22 Jun 1995

Chinese Vice Premier Qian Qichen (錢其琛) delivered the Basic Principles and Policies of the Central People's Government in Handling Taiwan-related Matters in Hong Kong after 1997. It stipulated 1) economic, cultural and personnel exchanges between Hong Kong and Taiwan may continue after the establishment of the HKSAR on 01 July 1997 under the "One China" and "One Country, Two Systems" principles; 2) official exchanges between Hong Kong and Taiwan, including inter-governmental agreements and organisations, must be approved by the Central People's Government or by the Chief Executive of the HKSAR with specific authorisation; and 3) Taiwan's institutions and personnel in Hong Kong must strictly abide by the Basic Law.

23 Jun 1995

The government abolished three sets of subsidiary legislation of the Emergency Regulations Ordinance, keeping its primary legislation only as a basis to enact regulations on occasions of emergency or public danger. On 18 July, the Law Sub-group of the Preliminary Working Commission of the Preparatory Committee for the Hong Kong Special Administrative Region stated that such amendments without China's approval were in violation of the principle of keeping Hong Kong's existing laws as indicated in the Joint Declaration, undermining the integrity and continuity of Hong Kong's legal system.

27 Jun 1995

The Television (Programmes) (Amendment) Regulations 1995 was promulgated, repealing Section 4 of the original legislation which prohibited TV programmes serving the interests of foreign political organisations.

29 Jun 1995

The Hong Kong Housing Authority increased the interest-free loan amount under its Home Ownership Loan Scheme to a maximum of HK$600,000, in addition to a monthly subsidy of HK$5,100 available to 4,000 approved applicants during the 1995/96 and 1996/97 financial years. The measures aimed to promote purchases of subsidised housing and free up public housing units.

30 Jun 1995

The UK and China reached an agreement on financial arrangement with the Airport Express and Airport Authority Hong Kong, allowing capital raising in support of project tendering. The same day, Hong Kong Air Cargo Terminals Ltd and Asia Airfreight Terminal Company Ltd were awarded the air cargo franchise of the new airport.

01 Jul 1995

The daily quota on One-way Permit—which allowed permanent residency among Mainland people with relatives in Hong Kong—increased from 105 to 150.

The Special Branch of the Royal Hong Kong Police Force was disbanded and was largely replaced by the Police Crime and Security Wing.

The fixed telecommunication network market was deregulated; Hutchison Telecom (Hong Kong) Ltd, New T&T Hong Kong Ltd and New World Telephone Ltd were granted service licences to promote competition in a market previously dominated by the monopoly of Hong Kong Telecommunications Ltd.

07 Jul 1995

The Sex Discrimination Ordinance 1995 was promulgated, effective 20 May 1996, making certain types of gender discrimination, discrimination based on marital status or pregnancy, and sexual harassment unlawful.

18 Jul 1995

The Hong Kong General Chamber of Small and Medium Business was incorporated, serving small- and medium-sized business owners, professional services providers and academic researchers in related fields.

01 Aug 1995

The government began to phase in standard terms of civil servant employment, requiring all new hires on permanent and pensionable terms to meet Chinese language requirements (HKCEE's Chinese language examination or equivalent). From 01 August 1996, new recruits to the Civil Service were no longer eligible for Overseas Education Allowance.

04 Aug 1995

The Mandatory Provident Fund Schemes Ordinance 1995 was promulgated, specifying a basic framework to institute a formal system of retirement protection under the administration of a non-government institution, applicable to those aged 18–65 under continuous employment in any capacity for 60 days or more with a mandatory 5% contribution each from the employer and employee in the monthly salary bracket of HK$4,000–HK$20,000 (unless exempt under Hong Kong law).

The Disability Discrimination Ordinance 1995 was promulgated, effective 20 May 1996, making it unlawful to discriminate against or vilify people with disabilities.

04 Aug 1995

The Personal Data (Privacy) Ordinance 1995 was promulgated, allowing private organisations and government departments to collect personal data directly related to their functions or activities, provided such functions were legitimate with appropriate security measures. Individuals had the right to access and correct relevant data from such organisations. The Office of the Privacy Commissioner for Personal Data, Hong Kong was established on 01 August 1996; the ordinance came into effect on 20 December 1996.

18 Aug 1995

The Hong Kong Economic & Trade Office in Singapore was established.

A minivan on Tuen Mun Road was hit by a boulder that rolled downhill from a construction site, killing the driver instantly. On 24 August, the Kowloon traffic lane on the Tuen Mun Road was closed for emergency reinforcement work. The government launched a temporary ferry route from Tuen Mun to Tsuen Wan to divert traffic. On 09 September, the highway was re-opened; the temporary ferry route was closed.

01 Sep 1995

Donald Tsang Yam-kuen (曾蔭權) became the first Chinese to serve as Financial Secretary.

The Department of Health established a Student Health Service with annual physical and mental health checks for Primary 1 to 6 students. The service was extended to Secondary 1 to 7 students starting in September 1996.

04 Sep 1995

Pursuant to the Ramsar Convention of Wetlands of International Importance Especially as Waterfowl Habitats, the Mai Po and the Inner Deep Bay wetlands with a total area of 1,500 hectares were designated as "Wetland of International Importance," covering six types of wetland habitats as a diversified home to wildlife, including the black-faced Spoonbill (an endangered bird species).

05 Sep 1995

The Executive Council announced that it would replace the position of "Senior Member" by instituting a "Convenor" with equal status as other council members; Rosanna Wong Yick-ming (王䓤鳴) was the first convenor.

13 Sep 1995

The *Report of the Working Group on the Use of Chinese in the Civil Service* was published, requiring government officers and administrators, including expatriate officers, to learn and make greater use of Cantonese in public communication and Putonghua with Chinese officials after the establishment of the HKSAR through training for proficiency in two written (Chinese and English) and three spoken (Cantonese, Putonghua and English) languages.

17 Sep 1995

The 1995 Legislative Council elections were held for a total of 60 seats, including 20 directly elected seats, 30 functional constituency seats and 10 election committee seats, with a turnout rate of 35.79% in the direct elections and a turnout rate of 40.4% in functional constituencies. The election committee elections were undertaken by 283 members of the District Boards.

25 Sep 1995

The Better Hong Kong Foundation was established as a non-profit and non-political organisation founded by 20 local business and community leaders to improve public confidence, both locally and internationally, in the future of Hong Kong's economic and social development after the establishment of the HKSAR in 1997.

Sep 1995

The Kindergarten Subsidy Scheme was implemented in support of non-profit kindergartens with an annual allowance of HK$695 per student to improve education quality.

01 Oct 1995

The Hong Kong Economic and Trade Office in Sydney was founded.

01 Oct 1995

The one-cent currency note, first issued in 1941, was void and taken out of circulation. As of the end of 1995, HK$1.27 million worth of one-cent currency notes remained unrecalled.

06 Oct 1995

An office of the People's Construction Bank of China (presently China Construction Bank) was granted a banking licence. It officially became the first overseas branch of the bank in December.

16 Oct 1995

The Hong Kong and Macao Affairs Office of the State Council revealed sample HKSAR passports designed in accordance with the specifications of the International Civil Aviation Organization with a blue cover, a gold-stamped national emblem and writings in traditional Chinese and English. The passports, with a validity period of 10 years for adults and five years for children, were intended for Chinese citizens holding a Hong Kong Permanent Identity Card. On 15 November, implementation of issuance after the establishment of the HKSAR on 01 July 1997 was announced by the Ministry of Foreign Affairs of the People's Republic of China.

21 Oct 1995

The Society for Protection of the Harbour began a public signature campaign to oppose further government reclamation of Victoria Harbour. The campaign ended on 28 December with about 140,000 signatures.

31 Oct 1995

Legislative Councillor Christine Loh Kung-wai (陸恭蕙) filed the Protection of the Harbour Bill, drafted by Town Planning Board member Winston Chu Ka-sun (徐嘉慎) in his personal capacity, with the Legislative Council and Legal Department, proposing to make reclamation a means of last resort. The Bill was read for the first time in the Legislative Council on 04 December 1996.

02 Nov 1995

An inmate of Stanley Prison filed a suit against the Commissioner of Correctional Services for unlawfully removing the horseracing sections in newspapers. The Supreme Court ruled that censorship of horseracing information based on an internal practice lacked legal basis and violated the Hong Kong Bill of Rights Ordinance 1991.

03 Nov 1995

Che Chi-ming (支志明), a chemistry professor at The University of Hong Kong, was elected as the first academician of the Chinese Academy of Sciences from Hong Kong and Macao. There were 26 academicians based in Hong Kong as of 2017.

18 Nov 1995

Prince Joachim of Denmark and Alexandra Manley were married in Copenhagen, Denmark. She was the first person born in Hong Kong to become princess of another country.

20 Nov 1995

Singapore became the first country to announce visa-free entry for HKSAR passport holders.

22 Nov 1995

The Court of Appeal of the Supreme Court overturned the judgement of the Court of First Instance, ruling that the seven civil service localisation measures were detrimental to expatriate civil servants and were in violation of the Hong Kong Bill of Rights Ordinance 1991. On 23 December, an appeal to the Privy Council was ruled out; however, implementation of localisation was to continue under amended guidelines.

28 Nov 1995

The Sino-British Joint Liaison Group held its fifth subgroup meeting on budget preparation in Beijing. Concerned over a possible budget deficit in the HKSAR, China objected Britain's substantial increase in Hong Kong's social welfare spending, warning that "driving a race car at high speed on a rugged mountain road could end up in a crash not long after…Governor Chris Pattern is in the driver's seat."

01 Dec 1995

The Airport Authority was established pursuant to the Airport Authority Ordinance 1995, responsible for building, operating and developing a new airport at Chek Lap Kok.

05 Dec 1995

The Hong Kong Government Information Centre launched a website, providing easier access to information about government departments.

09 Dec 1995

Upon its 28th anniversary, *Oriental Daily* cut its price to HK$2 per issue. Between 10 and 12 December, *Sing Pao Daily News*, *Apple Daily*, *Hong Kong Daily News* and *Tin Tin Daily News* followed suit with price cuts ranging HK$1–HK$4. Between 12 and 16 December, *TV Daily News, Hong Kong United Daily News* and *Express* announced their termination of publication.

13 Dec 1995

The Supreme Court concluded the first-ever civil case trial conducted in Chinese (involving a family financial dispute) with a ruling delivered in Chinese. The District Court and Lands Tribunal were permitted to conduct trials in Chinese starting on 16 February 1996.

20 Dec 1995

Lui Kin-hong (呂健康), a British American Tobacco Company senior executive in Hong Kong, was arrested in Boston on charges of involvement in an HK$8.5 billion cigarette smuggling case. On 22 May 1997, he was extradited to Hong Kong; on 25 June 1998, he was convicted of conspiracy to accept a bribe and was sentenced to three years and eight months in prison with a fine of HK$500,000.

22 Dec 1995

The Kowloon Walled City Park, developed on the site of the former Kowloon Walled City, was opened to the public.

Dec 1995

Tivoli Garden in Tsing Yi was made available for sale upon completion, comprising 1,024 residential units in the first estate under Hong Kong Housing Society's Sandwich Class Housing Scheme.

1995

The first *Government Common Character Set* was developed to group together Chinese words and characters in common daily computerised usage with government departments. In September 1999, a revised edition called *Hong Kong Supplementary Character Set* was launched.

The Regional Services Department's Museums Section in conjunction with The Chinese University of Hong Kong's Institute of Chinese Studies began a joint excavation at the Wun Yiu Kiln site in Tai Po where a 30-metre historical dragon kiln, along with traces of a porcelain manufacturing process from mining to firing, was unearthed.

01 Jan 1996

The Bank of China assumed a chairmanship role with the Hong Kong Association of Banks (HKAB) for the first time, thereby joining HSBC and Standard Chartered as a note-issuing bank in serving as HKAB chairman and vice chairman rotationally.

04 Jan 1996

Vitasoy announced a recall of its soy-based beverages produced at its Shenzhen plant in response to a series of customer complaints regarding odour. On 09 January, suspension of production took place in both Shenzhen and Hong Kong with a worldwide recall, inspection and destruction of nearly 43 million boxes. On 24 January, investigation results were announced, confirming a mechanical failure and inadequate cleaning but posing no harm to health. In February, it resumed production.

09 Jan 1996

The Indian-born Secretary for Transport Haider Barma was appointed as Chairman of Public Service Commission; Gordon Siu Kwing-chue（蕭炯柱）took over as Secretary for Transport. Upon this appointment, all secretary-level officials were ethnic Chinese, except the Attorney General.

21 Jan 1996

The Wilson Trail, named after former Governor David Clive Wilson, was opened as the only long-distance hiking trail covering Hong Kong entirely from south to north. The 78-kilometre, 10-section trail—from Stanley Gap Road on Hong Kong Island in the south to Nam Chung in the New Territories in the north—stretched across eight country parks.

26 Jan 1996

The Preparatory Committee for the HKSAR under the National People's Congress was established in Beijing with its first plenary session. It comprised 150 members (94 from Hong Kong and 56 from the Mainland) under the chairmanship of Vice Premier Qian Qichen（錢其琛）.

28 Jan 1996

The State Council in conjunction with the Central Military Commission announced a complete assembly of the Chinese People's Liberation Army Hong Kong Garrison in preparation for troops to be stationed in Hong Kong starting on 01 July 1997. The following day, Vice Premier Qian Qichen（錢其琛）presided at a flag presentation ceremony to mark the debut of the garrison in Shenzhen.

01 Feb 1996

The Supplementary Labour Scheme was implemented, allowing employers to recruit immigrant workers (excluding 26 designated job categories, such as waiters, cashiers, clerks and haulers) to fill job vacancies under an initial quota of 2,000.

03 Feb 1996

An earthquake of magnitude 7 on the Richter scale hit Lijiang in Yunnan Province, causing substantial damage and hardship. The Hong Kong community donated a total of HK$166 million, RMB 52.2 million and US$103,000 in addition to 3,280 metric tonnes of supplies. On 01 July 1997, a memorial inscription expressing gratitude to Hong Kong compatriots was unveiled at Lijiang.

10 Feb 1996

A group of 49 students of HKCWC Fung Yiu King Memorial Secondary School led by five teachers on a "Golden Leg" hiking trip were caught in a wildfire at Pat Sin Leng in Tai Po. Two teachers and three students died; 13 students suffered from burn injuries of varying degrees of severity. On 12 March, the Spring Breeze Pavilion at Pat Sin Leng was unveiled to commemorate the two teachers, Chau Chi-chai（周志齊）and Wong Sau-mei（王秀媚）, who died protecting their students.

19 Feb 1996

The Hong Kong Tourist Association held its first Chinese New Year Parade on the Tsim Sha Tsui waterfront. (Figure 253)

28 Feb 1996

The Hong Kong government noted a plan to commence the Northwest Railway project in early 1998 in a briefing on railway development with Chinese officials. On 27 May, it was announced that construction would begin a year early. On 29 May, Chinese officials expressed objection to granting contracts unilaterally by Hong Kong and cautioned contract nullification upon the establishment of the HKSAR. In an elaboration on the same day, Hong Kong made clear that no final decision had been made and that consultation in advance with Chinese officials would follow.

Figure 253
The first Chinese New Year Parade was held on 19 February 1996 to mark the Year of the Rat. (Photo courtesy of South China Morning Post Publishers Limited)

29 Feb 1996

The Sino-British Joint Liaison Group held its subgroup meeting on mobile phone services; Chinese officials were given information on six bidding service providers due to continue beyond 1997. On 27 July, an agreement on a 10-year franchise was reached upon signing the meeting minutes, allowing Hong Kong to issue licences.

01 Mar 1996

The Beat Drugs Fund was established to provide non-government organisations with funding support for prevention, education and publicity of anti-drug programmes.

02 Mar 1996

UK Prime Minister John Major began a three-day visit to Hong Kong with an announcement on a visa-free programme giving HKSAR passport holders access to the UK after the establishment of the HKSAR in 1997 as an expression of continued British commitment to Hong Kong.

06 Mar 1996

Financial Secretary Donald Tsang Yam-kuen (曾蔭權) delivered his first annual budget and Hong Kong's last budget under full British discretion. Major budgetary measures included increasing the salaries tax allowance, providing tax deductions based on tuition fees for courses at accredited institutions, and reducing property taxes for low- and medium-priced properties.

07 Mar 1996

The Education Commission released its *Report No. 6*, proposing a Language Proficiency Assessment for Teachers, recruitment of native English and Putonghua teachers, and designation of Putonghua as a core subject in primary and secondary schools with new courses in Primary 1, Secondary 1 and Secondary 4.

23 Mar 1996

The Preparatory Committee for the HKSAR began its two-day second plenary meeting in Beijing. On 24 March, it adopted the Decision on the Establishment of the Provisional Legislative Council of the HKSAR, allowing the establishment of a Provisional Legislative Council after the election of HKSAR's first Chief Executive. The Council was to support formulation of legislation by amending and abolishing laws as required to facilitate the functions of the HKSAR, including appointment of Judges of the Court of Final Appeal and Chief Judge of the High Court. The Committee also adopted the 1) Decision on the Establishment of the Hong Kong Celebration Committee for the Reunification of Hong Kong with the Motherland, 2) Decision on the Arrangements for General Holidays for the Second Half of 1997 and the Whole Year of 1998, and 3) Proposal for the Interpretation on the Implementation of the Nationality Law of the People's Republic of China in the HKSAR.

25 Mar 1996

Hong Kong-based Phoenix Satellite Television Company Limited was established, seeking to reach a Chinese audience worldwide. On 31 March, it began broadcast with its Chinese channel.

27 Mar 1996

The Judicial Committee of the Privy Council (UK) ruled it unlawful to detain four Vietnamese boat people of Chinese descent with non-refugee status in Hong Kong amid a Vietnamese government policy of refusing to accept non-Vietnamese returnees. The four, along with their family members, totalling 15 people, were released and allowed to settle in Hong Kong. By 03 April, another 214 boat people were released.

28 Mar 1996

In line with EU's precautionary measures, Hong Kong suspended the import and sale of British frozen beef in consideration of public concerns over Mad Cow Disease.

30 Mar 1996

About 54,000 people applied for the British National (Overseas) Passport at the Immigration Tower in Wan Chai. Disputes and fights arose in the large waiting crowds.

Mar 1996

The Regional Council began installing anti-shark nets at all public beaches at an estimated cost of HK$1 million per set and an annual maintenance fee of HK$1 million.

01 Apr 1996

The Official Languages Agency was established as a government unit dedicated to providing translation and interpretation services, forming guidelines on official documents, and promoting the use of the Chinese language for a civil service proficient in two written languages (Chinese and English) and three spoken languages (Cantonese, Putonghua and English).

13 Apr 1996

The Preparatory Committee for the HKSAR began a two-day public consultation on forming a Selection Committee with the first government of the HKSAR.

Apr 1996

The Policy on Safeguarding Rational Allocation of Public Housing Resources (commonly known as the Well-off Tenants Policy) was implemented by the Hong Kong Housing Authority. It required biennial declaration of assets among tenants paying double rent. Tenants were required to pay rent under a market rate or move out if their household incomes and net assets exceeded the established limit.

01 May 1996

The Independent Commission Against Corruption began a three-day operation, arresting 41 people on suspicion of fraudulently providing false residential addresses with voter registration in the Tai Po District Board election of September 1994; 39 were prosecuted, including an election candidate. On 14 May 1997, candidate Lai Wai-cheong (黎 偉昌) was convicted of voter fraud and fined HK$8,000 by the District Court.

07 May 1996

Hong Kong hosted the 12th Asia-Pacific Economic Cooperation (APEC) Energy Working Group Meeting with 17 APEC members on regional energy issues.

13 May 1996

A group of 5–6 illegal immigrants with heavy firearms were intercepted by police officers as they disembarked near a slaughterhouse on Victoria Road in Western District. A gunfight broke out; fugitive Yip Kai-foon (葉繼歡) was shot and arrested.

15 May 1996

The Interpretation on Some Questions Concerning Implementation of the Nationality Law of the People's Republic of China in the Hong Kong Special Administrative Region was adopted by the 19th Session of the Eighth NPC Standing Committee. It defined any Hong Kong resident of Chinese descent born within China (including Hong Kong) a Chinese national, even with a British Dependent Territories Citizen or British National (Overseas) passport. It also stated that British citizenship granted in Hong Kong under the British Nationality Selection Scheme would not be recognised.

20 May 1996

The Board of Education, upon review of the *Report of the Sub-committee on Special Education*, suggested an allocation of HK$108 million in the next fiscal year for government subsidies with additional teachers, qualified therapists and care workers in special education services.

The Equal Opportunities Commission was established as a statutory body dedicated to eliminating discrimination and promoting equal opportunities and responsible for enforcement of the Sex Discrimination Ordinance 1995 and Disability Discrimination Ordinance 1995 with investigative powers.

23 May 1996

Victor Li Tzar-kuoi (李澤鉅), the eldest son of Hong Kong businessman Li Ka-shing (李嘉誠), was kidnapped near Deep Water Bay Road by Cheung Tze-keung (張子強) and six armed assailants; he was released after a ransom of HK$1.038 billion was paid.

24 May 1996

The third plenary session of the Preparatory Committee of the HKSAR began for a two-day meeting in Zhuhai. It adopted three schemes: the Resolution on the Principles and Assumptions of the Measures for the Formation of the Selection Committee, Resolution on the Erection of a Monument to Commemorate the Return of Hong Kong to China, and Resolution on Textbook Issues.

28 May 1996

The Hong Kong Federation of Journalists was established, providing media professionals with a better understanding of policies, legal systems and current affairs of the Mainland through training and workshops.

30 May 1996

Milkyway Image (HK) Ltd was founded by Johnnie To Kei-fung (杜琪峯) and Wai Ka-fai (韋家輝).

31 May 1996

The Immigration (Amendment) Ordinance 1996 was promulgated, stipulating that detainment of Vietnamese boat people in Hong Kong may continue, except those who were refused repatriation by the Vietnamese government.

03 Jun 1996

The Hong Kong US Tour 1996 began in New York; it continued onto Dallas and Los Angeles, ending on 11 June, in a promotional campaign of international relations and trade development.

Governor Chris Patten accepted Tung Chee-hwa's (董建華) resignation from the Executive Council.

01 Jul 1996

The TV documentary *Hong Kong Vicissitudes* was launched by China Central Television; it covered the major historical events of Hong Kong with 12 episodes in a two-part programme.

A large-scale photo exhibition, called Hong Kong's History and Development, was opened in Beijing under the joint sponsorship of the Hong Kong and Macao Affairs Office, State Council Information Office, and Ministry of Culture in the presence of National People's Congress Standing Committee Vice Chairman Wang Guangying (王光英), Hong Kong and Macao Affairs Office Director Lu Ping (魯平), and Director of the Hong Kong Branch of Xinhua News Agency Zhou Nan (周南). The photo exhibition continued in Hong Kong and began on 26 March 1997 at the Hong Kong Exhibition Centre.

Figure 254
Hong Kong athlete Lee Lai-shan (李麗珊) won the gold medal in women's windsurfing at the Olympic Games in Atlanta, Georgia, US on 29 July 1996. (Photo courtesy of South China Morning Post Publishers Limited)

Figure 255
A clash between villagers of Tiu Keng Leng and police officers on 30 July 1996 over a government demolition project in the area. (Photo courtesy of Sing Tao News Corporation Limted)

10 Jul 1996

The Legislative Council approved and adopted the Chinese edition of the Standing Orders of the Legislative Council of Hong Kong 1968, allowing council meetings to be conducted in Cantonese by the president starting 1996/97.

15 Jul 1996

The Marine Parks and Marine Reserves Regulations 1996 was promulgated, outlining the rules and regulations in marine parks and marine reserves, including the requirement of a permit for fishing in marine parks. In the same month, Hoi Ha Wan Marine Park, Yan Chau Tong Marine Park and Cape D'Aguilar Marine Reserve were established.

19 Jul 1996

The Prevention of Bribery (Miscellaneous Provisions) (No.2) Ordinance 1996 was promulgated, promoting greater transparency and accountability in the functions of the Independent Commission Against Corruption (ICAC). It made it unlawful for any person to reveal without authorisation targets of ICAC investigations and outlined six conditions in which cases may be disclosed by media outlets.

The Agreement between the Government of the People's Republic of China and the Government of the Independent State of Western Samoa on Mutual Visa Exemption between HKSAR and Western Samoa was signed in Apia, Western Samoa, effective 01 July 1997. It was the first agreement by the Chinese government with respect to visa exemptions for Hong Kong.

22 Jul 1996

The Hong Kong Federation of Education Workers and Hong Kong Professional Teachers' Union submitted a letter of protest at the Consulate General of Japan in Hong Kong, condemning the building of a lighthouse on Diaoyu Islands by Japanese right-wing groups as an infringement on Chinese sovereignty and calling upon the Japanese government for its removal.

29 Jul 1996

Lee Lai-shan (李麗珊) won the gold medal in women's windsurfing at the 26th Olympic Games in Atlanta, Georgia, US, marking Hong Kong's first medal since joining the Olympics in 1952. On 07 August, upon her return, a government celebration was held at the Hong Kong Cultural Centre. In December, MTR announced that the station located in the new reclamation area of Tai Kok Tsui would be named "Olympic." (Figure 254)

The world's first successful right-lobe liver transplant took place at Queen Mary Hospital.

30 Jul 1996

Demolition began in Tiu Keng Leng where hundreds of villagers clashed with the police over discontent with the government compensation scheme. On 29 August, amidst ongoing demolition work, as the last dwellers moved out, Tiu Keng Leng was reclaimed. (Figure 255)

09 Aug 1996

The Hong Kong Athletes Fund was established with an initial funding of HK$13 million, including HK$8 million in government grant and over HK$5 million in public donation. It aimed to provide active and retired athletes with training and education subsidies, in recognition of the achievements of local athletes at the Atlanta Olympic Games.

The Preparatory Committee for the HKSAR held its fourth plenary session over two days in Beijing. On the second day, it adopted the Decision on the Specific Methods for the Formation of the Selection Committee for the First Government of the HKSAR, stipulating a 400-member Selection Committee with Hong Kong permanent residents aged 18 or above, including community leaders, business professionals, religious figures, former politicians as well as Hong Kong NPC deputies and Hong Kong members of the Chinese People's Political Consultative Conference. It also adopted the Opinions on the Implementation of Article 24(2) of the Basic Law of the HKSAR and the Provisional Measures for the Use of the Regional Flag and Regional Emblem of the HKSAR.

16 Aug 1996

The 1996 Paralympic Games began in Atlanta, Georgia, US. Hong Kong won five gold, five silver and five bronze medals; fencer Benny Cheung Wai-leung (張偉良) became the first Hong Kong athlete to win four gold medals in a single Paralympic Games.

26 Aug 1996

The Frontier, a political group founded by Emily Lau Wai-hing (劉慧卿) (who served as spokesperson), Lau Chin-shek (劉千石), Lee Cheuk-yan (李卓人), Leung Yiu-chung (梁耀忠) and Elizabeth Wong Chien Chi-lien (黃錢其濂), held its inaugural meeting. On 23 November 2008, it adopted a resolution to merge with the Democratic Party.

01 Sep 1996

The 2,536-km Beijing-Kowloon Railway was opened for traffic between Beijing and Kowloon via Shenzhen, followed by the launch of the Beijing–Kowloon Through Train on 18 May 1997.

06 Sep 1996

The Alliance of Worldwide Chinese for Protection of the Diaoyu Islands was established under the convenorship of David Chan Yuk-cheung (陳毓祥) with more than 70 former participants of the Defending the Diaoyu Islands Movement during the 1970s.

The Bank for International Settlements' All Governors Meeting was held in Basel, Switzerland. The Hong Kong Monetary Authority was invited to become a member with other central banks.

18 Sep 1996

A silent protest with 500,000 teachers and students from over 600 schools across Hong Kong took place to mark the 65th anniversary of the Japanese invasion on 18 September 1931 and condemn the Japanese occupation of Diaoyu Islands.

22 Sep 1996

The maiden voyage of *Baodiao*, with 18 members of the Alliance of Worldwide Chinese for Protection of the Diaoyu Islands and 42 Chinese and foreign journalists, set sail to proclaim China's sovereignty by raising the Chinese national flag on Diaoyu Islands. David Chan Yuk-cheung (陳毓祥) drowned on 26 September in the attempt. Six Diaoyu Islands defence groups held a candlelight vigil in his memory on 29 September. (Figure 256)

Figure 256
David Chan Yuk-cheung (陳毓祥), leader of the Hong Kong Baodiao Movement (in defence of Diaoyu Islands) set sail on *Baodiao* bound for the islands on 22 September 1996. (Photo courtesy of South China Morning Post Publishers Limited)

23 Sep 1996

The Agreement on Mutual Legal Assistance in Criminal Matters between Hong Kong and Australia was signed; it aimed to provide greater effectiveness in crime prevention, investigation, and confiscation of criminal proceeds. It took effect on 06 November 1999 as Hong Kong's first agreement of this nature. As of 01 July 2017, Hong Kong had similar agreements with 30 countries.

28 Sep 1996

The first International Table Tennis Federation Women's World Cup began in Hong Kong with competitions in singles only; Chinese athlete Deng Yaping (鄧亞萍) won the championship.

05 Oct 1996

The Preparatory Committee for the HKSAR in its fifth plenary session adopted the Method for the Selection of the First Chief Executive of the HKSAR, stipulating the following prerequisites of candidacy: aged 40 or above, Chinese citizenship as Hong Kong permanent residents, no foreign passport or right of abode in a foreign country, residency of 20 consecutive years in Hong Kong, commitment to the Basic Law, allegiance to the HKSAR, and candidacy in personal capacity. Candidates would be first nominated and then elected (with a simple majority in a secret ballot) by members of the Selection Committee.

The Preparatory Committee for the HKSAR in its fifth plenary session adopted the Method for the Formation of the Provisional Legislative Council of the HKSAR, stipulating the following requirements of a 60-member Provisional Legislative Council: 1) Hong Kong permanent residents aged 18 or above; 2) less than 20% of members as non-Chinese citizens and those with the right of abode in another country; 3) commitment to the Basic Law; and 4) allegiance to the HKSAR. Candidates would be first nominated and then elected (60 candidates with the most votes in a secret ballot) by members of the Selection Committee. (Figure 257)

07 Oct 1996

Hong Kong activists Tsang Kin-shing (曾健成), Chan Yu-nam (陳裕南), Albert Ho Chun-yan (何俊仁) and Taiwanese activist Jin Jieshou (金介壽) sailed past the Japanese Coast Guard and landed on the Diaoyu Islands, where they raised the flags of the People's Republic of China and Taiwan along with a banner bearing "The Chinese Territory of Diaoyu Islands" before returning safely.

Figure 257
Rita Fan Hsu Lai-tai (范徐麗泰), centre front, President of the Provisional Legislative Council, with fellow provisional councillors at the Legislative Council Building on 08 October 1997. (Photo courtesy of HKSAR Government)

14 Oct 1996

The UN Convention on the Elimination of all Forms of Discrimination Against Women took effect in Hong Kong upon approval from China and Britain, aiming to protect women's rights and interests. Its continuation in the HKSAR from 01 July 1997 was reaffirmed in an official document from the Chinese government to the UN Secretary-General.

17 Oct 1996

The Kowloon Bay International Trade & Exhibition Centre, developed by Hopewell Holdings, was opened as the only large-scale exhibition venue in East Kowloon adjacent to the industrial area in Kowloon Bay.

18 Oct 1996

Tung Chee-hwa (董建華) announced his candidacy for the first HKSAR Chief Executive; he released a blueprint of governance on 22 October under the slogan that "China will do great if Hong Kong does well; Hong Kong will do even better if China does well."

28 Oct 1996

Vice-President of the Court of Appeal Noel Power was appointed as Acting Chief Justice of the Supreme Court, with effect until 30 June 1997, in place of Yang Ti-liang (楊鐵樑) who resigned to run in the election of the first HKSAR Chief Executive.

Oct 1996

The Personal Emergency Link Service, launched by the Senior Citizen Home Safety Association's Care-on-Call Service, began providing 24-hour free support and care services for recipients of Comprehensive Social Security Assistance aged 70 and above living alone and aged 60–69 living alone with critical illnesses or severe disabilities.

01 Nov 1996

The Telecommunication (Amendment) Ordinance 1996 was promulgated, repealing Section 13C(3)(a) which authorised the Broadcasting Authority to prohibit radio licencees from broadcasting certain programmes under certain circumstances. The government believed that the original section could be detrimental to the freedoms of the press and expression in the future.

02 Nov 1996

During the sixth plenary session of the Preparatory Committee for the HKSAR, 340 members, along with 26 Hong Kong National People's Congress deputies and 34 Hong Kong members of the Chinese People's Political Consultative Conference, were elected to the first 400-member HKSAR Selection Committee; a code of conduct for the Selection Committee was adopted.

The Preparatory Committee for the HKSAR in its sixth plenary session adopted the Decision on the Method for the Nomination of Candidates for the First Chief Executive and Related Matters and approved a list of eight candidates for Chief Executive. All members of the Selection Committee were required to make a nomination and vote for a final round of candidates who were confirmed upon receiving 50 or more votes.

13 Nov 1996

During a debate in the Legislative Council on the Chief Executive election, Councillor Leung Yiu-chung (梁耀忠) for his criticism "foul grass grows out of a foul ditch" was ordered to leave the chamber on the grounds of misconduct by Council President Andrew Wong Wang-fat (黃宏發); he became the first councillor in history to be expelled.

15 Nov 1996

Tung Chee-hwa (董建華), Peter Woo (吳光正) and Yang Ti-liang (楊鐵樑) formally became candidates for HKSAR's first Chief Executive; each candidate received 50 or more votes from the 400-member Selection Committee.

20 Nov 1996

A five-alarm fire at Garley Building in Yau Ma Tei continued for about 23 hours, causing 41 deaths, including that of a fireman, and 81 injuries. On 29 August 1997, a final government investigation report was released with multiple proposals to raise public awareness on safety and improve firefighting capabilities.

20 Nov 1996

The Broadway Cinematheque in Yau Ma Tei was opened for business as a large cinema showing art films.

Nov 1996

The government dedicated a graveyard named Gallant Garden at Wo Hop Shek Cemetery for civil servants who passed away in the line of duty. Senior Fireman Liu Chi-hung (廖熾鴻), who died in the Garley Building fire in 1996, was the first civil servant to be buried at Gallant Garden.

Sha Chau & Lung Kwu Chau Marine Park, covering a total sea area of about 1,200 hectares, was established as Hong Kong's third marine park; it became the first and largest marine park dedicated to the conservation of the endangered *Sousa Chinensis*, commonly known as pink dolphins.

The remains of two 6,000-year-old houses as the earliest of its kind in Hong Kong were unearthed in a nine-month, 250-square-metre excavation at the Tai Wan site on Lamma Island jointly conducted by The Chinese University of Hong Kong, Chinese Academy of Social Sciences' Institute of Archaeology, and Sun Yat-sen University's School of Anthropology in Guangzhou.

09 Dec 1996

The Hong Kong Monetary Authority (HKMA) launched its Real Time Gross Settlement system, allowing instant settlement of interbank transactions via an account at HKMA.

11 Dec 1996

The Selection Committee held its third plenary session at the Hong Kong Convention and Exhibition Centre to elect the first Chief Executive. Tung Chee-hwa (董建華) won the election with 320 votes; Yang Ti-liang (楊鐵樑) and Peter Woo (吳光正) received 42 votes and 36 votes, respectively.

12 Dec 1996

The Preparatory Committee for the HKSAR in its fourth plenary session in Shenzhen validated the first Chief Executive election and a list of 130 candidates of the Provisional Legislative Council. It also made clear its intention to declare with the NPC Standing Committee in accordance with Article 160 of the Basic Law that the proposed Crimes (Amendment) (No. 2) Ordinance 1996, if passed, would be in contradiction to Article 23 of the Basic Law regarding crimes of national security and would be nullified after 01 July 1997.

16 Dec 1996

Premier of the State Council Li Peng (李鵬) appointed Tung Chee-hwa (董建華) as the first Chief Executive of the Hong Kong Special Administrative Region.

21 Dec 1996

The 400-member Selection Committee elected 60 members of the Provisional Legislative Council in Shenzhen, including 33 incumbent councillors and eight former councillors.

23 Dec 1996

The Code on Access to Information was implemented for a framework on public access to government information applicable to all policy bureaus and departments, all registries and offices of courts, and tribunals under the Judiciary Administration, as well as the Hong Kong Monetary Authority and Independent Commission Against Corruption (ICAC); any person may request for information from any government department in accordance with the Code.

30 Dec 1996

The National People's Congress Standing Committee approved the Law of the People's Republic of China on the Garrisoning of the HKSAR, outlining the composition and function of the Hong Kong Garrison, its relationship with the HKSAR, its jurisdiction, its duties and responsibilities. The law came into effect in 01 July 1997.

1996

Kai Tak Airport handled 1.56 million tonnes of cargo during the year, surpassing Narita Airport in Japan with the highest cargo throughput for the first time; it recorded 29.5 million international passengers as the third highest in the world.

The Working Group on Kindergarten Education's Pre-primary Curriculum Guide was released as the first combined guide with Education Bureau's Kindergarten Curriculum Guide and Social Welfare Department's Activity Guidelines for Day Nursery.

The Antiquities and Monuments Offices began the first territory-wide survey of historic buildings, ending in 2000; it made documentation of about 8,800 historic buildings of which most were built before 1950.

04 Jan 1997

The first Hong Kong Literature Festival, organised by the Urban Council, began under the theme "50 Years of Literature" with a series of seminars and exhibitions at the City Hall Public Library.

17 Jan 1997

About 22.1 hectares of land, including the streams and banks of Sha Lo Tung, was designated as a Site of Special Scientific Interest by the Agriculture and Fisheries Department for ecological conservation. Sha Lo Tung was well known for rare dragonflies and home to about 70 species, including *Macromidia ellenae*, a unique species first discovered in the early 1990s.

24 Jan 1997

Chief Executive-elect Tung Chee-hwa announced a list of 15 members of the first HKSAR Executive Council, including the Chief Executive himself, three ex-officio members and 11 unofficial members. Unofficial Member Chung Sze-yuen (鍾士元) was also appointed as Council Convenor.

The government released its *Long Term Housing Strategy Review Consultative Document,* outlining a strategy to support families with affordable housing by facilitating home ownership, increasing the supply of housing, allowing a greater role in the private sector, and providing public housing for those in need.

25 Jan 1997

A triad-related arson attack on a karaoke bar on Prat Avenue in Tsim Sha Tsui triggered a three-alarm fire, causing 17 deaths and 13 injuries. Four of five suspects were sentenced to life imprisonment; one was sentenced to 11 years in prison.

The Provisional Legislative Council held its first meeting in Shenzhen; Rita Fan Hsu Lai-tai (范徐麗泰) was elected as Chairman. Zhou Nan (周南), Deputy Director of the Preparatory Committee for the HKSAR, noted at the meeting that the Provisional Legislative Council as HKSAR's legislature may commence immediately under the legal basis and authority from the National People's Congress and the Preparatory Committee for the HKSAR.

26 Jan 1997

The Post Office issued new stamps featuring Victoria Harbour in place of stamps printed with the portrait of Queen Elizabeth (which might be used until the establishment of the HKSAR on 01 July).

31 Jan 1997

The Preparatory Committee for the HKSAR began its eighth plenary session over two days in Beijing. It adopted the Decision for the first Chief Executive and Provisional Legislative Council of the HKSAR to Commence Work before 30 June 1997, Decision on the Establishment of the Provisional District Organisations of the HKSAR, and Treatment of Laws Previously in Force in Hong Kong.

Jan 1997

Tradelink Electronic Commerce Ltd launched the first government-sponsored e-commerce service SilkNet to assist the garment and textile industry in obtaining export licences for restricted textiles.

04 Feb 1997

UK Secretary of State for the Home Department Michael Howard announced a British citizenship eligibility scheme with 8,000 people of ethnic minorities in Hong Kong with British Nationals (Overseas) passports lest they became stateless after 30 June 1997. On 17 March, the British Nationality (Hong Kong) Act 1997 as announced was enacted.

05 Feb 1997

The Environmental Impact Assessment Ordinance 1997 was promulgated, effective 01 April, requiring designated projects to undergo assessment and obtain a government-issued permit before commencement in a bid to minimise adverse environmental impact.

16 Feb 1997

The first Standard Chartered Hong Kong Marathon was held with over 1,000 participants on a course running from Sheung Shui to Shenzhen. It became Hong Kong's largest annual long-distance race organised by the Hong Kong Amateur Athletic Association and sponsored by Standard Chartered Bank, earning the International Association of Athletics Federations' Gold Road Race Label in 2016.

20 Feb 1997

Chief Executive-elect Tung Chee-hwa (董建華) announced a list of 23 HKSAR principal officials under appointment by the Chinese Central Government, including Anson Chan (陳方安生) as Chief Secretary, Donald Tsang Yam-kuen (曾蔭權) as Financial Secretary and Elsie Leung Oi-sie (梁愛詩) as Secretary for Justice. The remaining officials were reappointed from the existing civil service team.

The West Kowloon Expressway and Kwai Chung Section of Route 3 were opened to traffic as part of the Hong Kong Airport Core Programme. On 22 May, Tsing Yi Section of Route 3 was opened; on 06 May 1998, Ting Kau Bridge was also opened, making a complete Route 3. (Figure 258)

The Hong Kong Branch of Xinhua News Agency flew its flag at half-mast in memory of Deng Xiaoping (鄧小平), Chairman of CPC Central Advisory Commission and Chairman of Central Military Commission of the Communist Party of China, who passed away in Beijing on 19 February; it held a memory service with about 1,000 people who paid their respect on the same day.

23 Feb 1997

The Decision of the NPC Standing Committee on Treatment of the Laws Previously in Force in Hong Kong in Accordance with Article 160 of the Basic Law of the HKSAR was approved by the 24th Session of the Eighth National People's Congress Standing Committee. It stipulated the following: 1) laws previously in force to be adopted, except those in contradiction to the Basic Law; 2) ordinances, subsidiary legislations or parts of legislations not adopted in the HKSAR to be listed in Annex I and Annex II; 3) modification, adaptation, restriction or exemption of adopted laws to be made as necessary to comply with the scope of the HKSAR and its Basic Law; 4) legal terms and interpretations of adopted laws in the HKSAR to comply with Annex III; and 5) adopted laws to be amended or nullified when found to be in contravention of the Basic Law.

Figure 258
The Ting Kau Bridge running between Tsing Yi and Ting Kau was opened to traffic. (Photo taken on 06 May 1998 and courtesy of South China Morning Post Publishers Limited)

26 Feb 1997

Beijing Enterprises Holdings Ltd was incorporated in Hong Kong; it became a publicly listed company on 29 May. It marked a record in terms of IPO fundraising, price-to-earnings multiples, and oversubscription of new shares in the Hong Kong stock market. In January 2005, it was reorganised as Beijing Enterprises Group Company Ltd with a business focus on public utilities in Beijing.

03 Mar 1997

The Hong Kong Mortgage Corporation Ltd was incorporated as a subsidiary of the government-owned Exchange Fund. It aimed to make insurance and pension funds a capital source in support of mortgage loans, thereby reducing the risks and reliance on short-term funds among banking institutions.

21 Mar 1997

The Rugby World Cup Sevens began for the first time in Hong Kong with a three-day tournament; it was held at the Hong Kong Stadium where Fiji defeated South Africa to take the championship.

24 Mar 1997

The Hong Kong Housing Authority announced that it would demolish 13 temporary housing areas and allocate HK$2.2 billion for 10,000 interim housing units to accommodate affected residents.

The Education Commission, following a review of the *Report on Review of 9-Year Compulsory Education,* proposed to retain the nine-year free and compulsory education for all school-age children and replace the Hong Kong Academic Aptitude Test with an assessment of students' linguistic and mathematical abilities, critical-thinking and problem-solving skills.

26 Mar 1997

The naval base on Stonecutters Island was completed; it was taken over by the Chinese People's Liberation Army Hong Kong Garrison on 01 July.

31 Mar 1997

Over 30,000 people bought tickets to visit the 48-year-old Lai Chi Kok Amusement Park on its last opening day.

Mar 1997

The Urban Council reintroduced a policy without a specified schedule to phase out itinerant hawker licences, which was provisionally shelved upon judicial review in 1995. On 01 January 2000, its policy remained as the Food and Environmental Hygiene Department took over the role of hawker management from the Urban Council and Regional Council.

The Education Bureau released its *Review of Prevocational and Secondary Technical Education*; it suggested that schools omit "technical" and "prevocational" from their names at discretion and implement an updated curricula with new subjects in information technology, design and commerce.

The Italian Chamber of Commerce in Hong Kong & Macao was established as a platform of exchange and trade promotion between Hong Kong, Macao and Italy.

01 Apr 1997

The Social Welfare Department introduced its Portable Comprehensive Social Security Assistance Scheme, allowing elderly recipients of three years or more to continue receiving social assistance while living in Guangdong Province.

15 Apr 1997

The HK–US Agreement on Transfer of Sentenced Persons was signed, allowing convicted persons to serve their sentences in their home territories–Hong Kong or the United States. It was Hong Kong's first bilateral agreement of this nature designed to minimise language and cultural barriers and make it easier for families to visit prisoners. As of 01 July 2017, Hong Kong had similar agreements with 15 countries.

17 Apr 1997

Chief Executive-elect Tung Chee-hwa (董建華), accompanied by Heung Yee Kuk Chairman Lau Wong-fat (劉皇 發), made a visit to the Ping Shan Heritage Trail and Tang Ancestral Hall. (Figure 259)

27 Apr 1997

The Lantau Link, connecting Lantau Island, Tsing Yi and Ma Wan via the Tsing Ma Bridge, Kap Shui Mun Bridge and Ma Wan Viaduct, was unveiled with dual three-lane carriageways and a double-track railway. Along with the North Lantau Highway, it was opened to traffic on 22 May. As of 2017, Tsing Ma Bridge was the world's longest span suspension bridge with both road and rail traffic. (Figure 260)

30 Apr 1997

The Western Harbour Crossing, a part of the Hong Kong Airport Core Programme, was opened to traffic as Hong Kong's third tunnel crossing under Victoria Harbour and Hong Kong's first three-lane dual-tube tunnel. (Figure 261)

02 May 1997

The Social Workers Registration Ordinance 1997 was promulgated, effective 06 June, establishing a registration mechanism under which no unregistered person was allowed to work as a social worker. On 16 January 1998, the Social Workers Registration Board was established for registration and disciplinary action on violations.

03 May 1997

The Justice Department's Law Drafting Division completed the Chinese translation of all 514 existing legislations originally enacted in English only; both the Chinese and English versions were legally binding.

07 May 1997

The official Map of the Hong Kong Special Administrative Region of the People's Republic of China was approved at the 56th Executive Meeting of the State Council. The map outlining the boundary of the HKSAR was formally launched on 01 July.

Figure 259
Chief Executive-elect Tung Chee-hwa (董建華) (front row, third from left), accompanied by Heung Yee Kuk Chairman Lau Wong-fat (劉皇發) (front row, second from left), made a visit to the Ping Shan Heritage Trail and Tang Ancestral Hall on 17 April 1997. (Photo taken at the Tang Ancestral Hall and courtesy of Tang Kwan-chi)

Figure 261
The construction site at the entrance of the Western Harbour Crossing as part of the West Kowloon Reclamation. (Photo taken in 1997 and courtesy of HKSAR Government)

Figure 260
About 80,000 local residents joined the Community Chest's "Walk for Millions" fundraiser on the Lantau Link. (Photo taken in 1997 and courtesy of HKSAR Government)

10 May 1997

The Holidays (1997 and 1998) Bill was adopted after a third reading by the Provisional Legislative Council; it marked the first bill adoption by the Council.

12 May 1997

The Hong Kong Hall at the Great Hall of the People in Beijing was completed in commemoration of China's resumption of sovereignty over Hong Kong.

14 May 1997

A 15-year-old boy was lured by a juvenile gang into a flat at Sau Mau Ping Estate, where he was tortured to death before an attempt to incinerate his body was made. The police arrested and charged 14 juvenile offenders with murder, grievous bodily harm, and unlawful disposal of a body. In January 1999, four were sentenced to life imprisonment in a High Court trial.

18 May 1997

Wong Kar-wai (王家衛) won Best Director at the 50th Cannes Film Festival for his film *Happy Together*; he was the first director from Hong Kong to win the award.

19 May 1997

Hong Kong, Taiwan, Singapore, South Korea and Israel were given the status of a developed economy on par with the Group of Seven (G7) by the International Monetary Fund.

22 May 1997

The Preparatory Committee for the HKSAR began its two-day ninth plenary session in Beijing; it adopted the decisions on matters relating to the first Legislative Council and appointment of government officials with respect to the oath of office.

The Cheung Tsing Tunnel, complete with dual three-lane carriageways between Cheung Tsing Bridge and North West Tsing Yi Interchange, was opened to traffic as part of the Hong Kong Airport Core Programme.

23 May 1997

The Occupational Safety and Health Ordinance 1997 was promulgated, safeguarding the wellbeing of workers in both industrial and non-industrial capacities.

May 1997

The Independent Commission Against Corruption (ICAC) established an ICAC Club to encourage public participation in activities for understanding the importance of anti-corruption and promotion of integrity towards a clean, fair, stable and prosperous community.

The Kwai Chung Incineration Plant was closed; it was the last of an old-style incineration facility in Hong Kong.

The Stonecutters Island Sewage Treatment Works was opened with a daily sewage capacity of 1.7 million cubic metres; it became fully operational in December 2001 as a core part of the Strategic Sewage Disposal Scheme Stage 1. It was Hong Kong's first and the world's largest and most efficient chemically enhanced primary treatment works.

01 Jun 1997

The 1997 Hong Kong–Beijing Relay began at Wan Chai Sports Ground; it continued through nine cities and reached Beijing on 01 July with a total of 30 Mainland and Hong Kong athletes. The event was organised by Chinese sports organisations as part of the celebration on the establishment of the HKSAR.

05 Jun 1997

The Home Ownership Scheme's Secondary Market Scheme was launched, allowing resale of subsidised housing units of 10 years old or more (from the date of initial sale) without paying a land premium if buyers were either current or prospective tenants of public rental housing. The selling prices were negotiable; buyers must pay a land premium upon selling on the open market in the future.

07 Jun 1997

The Urban Council (Amendment) Bill 1997, Regional Council (Amendment) Bill 1997 and District Council (Amendment) Bill 1997 were passed after a third reading by the Provisional Legislative Council. They stipulated a Provisional Urban Council and a Provisional Regional Council (each with no more than 50 members) and 18 Provisional District Boards (each with no more than 40 members) upon the establishment of the HKSAR on 01 July. All members were to be appointed by the Chief Executive for a term to 31 December 1999.

11 Jun 1997

The State Council announced 01 July 1997 as a national holiday in celebration of the establishment of the HKSAR.

12 Jun 1997

The British Embassy in Beijing notified the Chinese government on the appointment of Senior Trade Commissioner to Hong Kong Francis Cornish as the first British Consul-General in the HKSAR. On 19 June, China's Ministry of Foreign Affairs noted its agreement to the appointment.

13 Jun 1997

The Official Secrets Ordinance 1997 was promulgated, allowing non-contravening provisions of the British Official Secrets Act (1911–1989) to remain applicable in Hong Kong with respect to unauthorised access to, or disclosure of, official information.

14 Jun 1997

The National Flag and National Emblem Bill 1997, Regional Flag and Regional Emblem Bill 1997, Public Order (Amendment) Ordinance 1997, Societies (Amendment) Ordinance 1997 were adopted after a third reading by the Provisional Legislative Council. The concept of national security was applied to related legislations.

15 Jun 1997

The Hong Kong Jockey Club on its last race day before the establishment of the HKSAR received a total betting amount of HK$2.54 billion, including HK$670 million on "Triple Trio" with a world-record pool of HK$710 million. Crowds reached a record 112,069 at the Happy Valley Racecourse and Sha Tin Racecourse.

16 Jun 1997

Chief Executive-elect Tung Chee-hwa (董建華) of the HKSAR announced that all incumbents of the Urban Council, Regional Council and 18 District Boards would remain in office with the addition of nine, 11 and 96 members, respectively, after the establishment of the HKSAR on 01 July.

19 Jun 1997

The Memorandum on the Boundary between Hong Kong and Guangdong was signed, defining the land boundary between northern New Territories and Shenzhen and between Deep Bay and Mirs Bay, as well as the sea boundaries to the west, south and east of Hong Kong.

21 Jun 1997

Tung Chung New Town was officially opened as Hong Kong's ninth new town and the only one on an outlying island.

24 Jun 1997

The Executive Council under its original Chinese name was dissolved after convening for its last meeting; it was re-established under an amended Chinese name after the establishment of the HKSAR on 01 July.

25 Jun 1997

Tai Po Waterfront Park was opened to the public in an area of 22 hectares with an insect house, a botanical garden, a promenade and the Tai Po Lookout Tower. It was the Hong Kong's largest public park as of 2017.

27 Jun 1997

The Crimes (Amendment) (No. 2) Ordinance 1996 was promulgated without Chinese government approval. It excluded the proposed provisions on crimes of subversion and secession but retained the provisions on treason and sedition. The Office of the Chief Executive-elect refused to accept the amendments, suggesting the related issues be addressed by the first Legislative Council of the HKSAR.

The Declaration of Change of Titles (General Adaptation) Notice 1997 was promulgated, stipulating amended titles in Chinese and/or English with HKSAR government departments and principal officials on 01 July 1997. These included the current forms of the Chief Secretary for Administration, Financial Secretary and Secretary for Justice. All 13 policy and two other branches were renamed as bureaus under the directorship of bureau secretaries. Colonial association such as "Royal" and "Governor-appointed" were removed.

The Hang Seng Index (HSI) closed at a record 15,196.8 points on the last trading day before the establishment of the HKSAR.

28 Jun 1997

At 8:02 a.m., President of the Legislative Council Andrew Wong Wang-fat (黃宏發) announced "adjournment sine die." The Legislative Council was dissolved after its last meeting spanning five days from 23 June; it considered 31 bills over 72 hours in what became the longest session since its establishment in 1843. (Figure 262)

Figure 262
Members of the last Legislative Council before the establishment of the HKSAR in a group photo. (Photo courtesy of HKSAR Government)

30 Jun 1997

The Protection of the Harbour Ordinance 1997 was promulgated, banning reclamation projects in the central area of Victoria Harbour between Hung Hom and North Point in the east and Western Harbour Tunnel in the west.

At 4:10 p.m., Governor Chris Patten bid farewell at the Government House. At 6:15 p.m., Patten accompanied Prince Charles, UK Prime Minister Tony Blair and UK Foreign Secretary Robin Cook in the Hong Kong Handover Sunset Farewell Ceremony & Parade on the east ground of Tamar, where the Union Jack and British Hong Kong flag were lowered. At 8:55 p.m., British government representatives held a farewell banquet at the Hong Kong Convention and Exhibition Centre. (Figures 263, 264 and 265)

At 9 p.m., 509 troops of the People's Liberation Army Hong Kong Garrison in 39 vehicles entered Hong Kong through Huanggang Port to be stationed at various barracks starting midnight. Major General Liu Zhenwu (劉鎮武) was the first garrison commander. (Figures 266 and 267)

At 11:45 p.m., a ceremony began at Hong Kong Convention and Exhibition Centre's New Wing in the presence of Chinese President Jiang Zemin (江澤民), Premier Li Peng (李鵬), Prince Charles, UK Prime Minister Tony Blair and more than 4,000 Chinese and foreign dignitaries and guests. At 11:47 p.m., Prince Charles delivered a speech stating that Britain was returning Hong Kong to China in accordance with the Sino-British Joint Declaration. At 11:59 p.m., as the Union Jack and old Hong Kong flag were lowered under the British national anthem, it marked the end of 156 years of British rule over Hong Kong. (Figure 268)

01 Jul 1997

Upon midnight, following the raising of the People's Republic of China national flag and Hong Kong Special Administrative Region's regional flag, President Jiang Zemin (江澤民) in a speech marked the resumption of sovereignty over Hong Kong by the Chinese government. After the ceremony, Prince of Wales Charles, along with former Governor Chris Patten, departed from Hong Kong on Her Majesty's Yacht *Britannia*.

At midnight, Chinese People's Liberation Army Hong Kong Garrison officially assumed defence duty in Hong Kong with the arrival of 4,000 troops to be stationed 14 barracks and military installations.

Figure 263
Governor Chris Patten in a farewell ceremony at the Government House. (Photo courtesy of HKSAR Government)

Figures 264 and 265
The Hong Kong Armorial Bearings, a symbol of British rule, was removed from the Central Government Offices in the evening of 30 June 1997 and replaced with the Chinese national emblem at midnight. (Photos courtesy of Sing Tao News Corporation Limited)

Figure 266
The first troops of the Chinese People's Liberation Army Hong Kong Garrison arrived in Hong Kong via Huanggang Port. (Photo courtesy of Pool AVENTURIER/BUU/HIRES/Gamma-Rapho via Getty Image)

Figure 267
Armoured vehicles of the Chinese People's Liberation Army Hong Kong Garrison entered Hong Kong through Man Kam To Control Point; residents lined the street in the rain to welcome and salute the national flag. (Photo taken on 01 July 1997 and courtesy of South China Morning Post Publishers Limited)

Figure 268
A ceremony marked the official resumption of sovereignty at 0:00 a.m. on 01 July 1997 at Hong Kong Convention and Exhibition Centre's New Wing. (Photo courtesy of Xinhua News Agency)

01 Jul 1997

At 1:30 a.m., a ceremony took place at the Hong Kong Convention and Exhibition Centre to mark the establishment of the HKSAR with an oath of office among principal government officials, Executive Council and Provisional Legislative Council members, and judges of the Court of Final Appeal and High Court. Chief Executive Tung Chee-hwa (董建華) in his inaugural speech said: "We are here today to announce to the world, speaking in our language, that Hong Kong has entered a new era." (Figure 269)

At 2:45 a.m., Provisional Legislative Council held its first meeting. At 3:55 a.m., it passed the Hong Kong Reunification Bill after a third reading; it was signed into law with immediate effect by Chief Executive Tung Chee-hwa (董建華). The law made all legislations passed by the Provisional Legislative Council before the establishment of the HKSAR legally binding; it endorsed the appointments of the Chief Justice and Permanent Judges of the Court of Final Appeal and of the Chief Judge of the High Court; it established the High Court, District Court, Magistrates' Courts along with other tribunals and judiciary boards; it authorised the continuation of the existing laws, legal proceedings, judiciary, criminal justice system and civil service system in accordance with the Basic Law. (Figures 270 and 271)

At 10 a.m., a ceremony in celebration of the establishment of the HKSAR began at the Hong Kong Convention and Exhibition Centre (HKCEC) with remarks by President Jiang Zemin (江澤民) and Chief Executive Tung Chee-hwa (董建華). On behalf of the Chinese Central Government, Vice Premier Qian Qichen (錢其琛) authorised the transfer of ownership of HK$170 billion in assets with the Land Fund to make it a part of HKSAR's fiscal reserves. At 4 p.m., a HKSAR government reception was held with over 5,000 Chinese and foreign dignitaries and guests. The Forever Blooming Bauhinia gold-plated bronze sculpture (commonly known as the Golden Bauhinia) was unveiled at HKCEC's New Wing with compliments of the Chinese Central Government. (Figure 272)

The Order of the State Council of the People's Republic of China No. 221 was promulgated, defining the land and sea boundaries of the HKSAR in an official map.

The Hong Kong Reunification Ordinance was promulgated in the first HKSAR Government *Gazette Extraordinary* with an official list of key government officials, including the Chief Executive, principal officers, Executive Council and Provisional Legislative Council members, Chief Justice and Permanent Judges of the Court of Final Appeal and Chief Judge of the High Court. The Chief Executive also introduced the Stipulations for the Display and Use of the National Flag and National Emblem and the Regional Flag and Regional Emblem.

The Office of the Commissioner of the Ministry of Foreign Affairs of the People's Republic of China in the HKSAR was established. Deputy Director of the State Council's Information Office and former Ambassador to the United Kingdom Ma Yuzhen (馬毓真) was the first commissioner and remained in office until 12 April 2001.

Figure 269
Tung Chee-hwa (董建華) was sworn in as the first Chief Executive of the Hong Kong Special Administrative Region. (Photo courtesy of Yoshikazu Tsuno/AFP via Getty Images)

Figure 270
Tung Chee-hwa (董建華) signed the Hong Kong Reunification Bill ratified to maintain Hong Kong's judicial system. (Photo courtesy of HKSAR Government)

Figure 272
The Forever Blooming Bauhinia Sculpture—located at the Golden Bauhinia Square next to Hong Kong Convention and Exhibition Centre's New Wing—was a gift presented by the Chinese Central Government. (Photo taken in 2009 and courtesy of Gunter Fischer/Education Images/Universal Images Group via Getty Images)

Figure 271
The first Chief Executive and 23 principal officials of the Hong Kong Special Administrative Region (HKSAR). (Photo taken on 03 July 1997 and courtesy of HKSAR Government)

01 Jul 1997

The Court of Final Appeal was established under Article 19 of the Basic Law and in accordance with the Hong Kong Court of Final Appeal Ordinance. It assumed the function of the Judicial Committee of the Privy Council (UK) as the highest appellate court in the HKSAR with independent judicial power, including that of final adjudication.

The Committee for the Basic Law of the HKSAR was formed by the 26th Session of the Eighth National People's Congress Standing Committee. The committee comprised members from the Mainland and Hong Kong; Xiang Chunyi (項淳一) was its first Director.

The first eye hospital *Lifeline Express* bound for Fuyang, Anhui departed from Hong Kong to provide low-income patients suffering from cataracts with free treatment.

02 Jul 1997

In the first Honours and Awards Presentation Ceremony at the Government House, Chief Executive Tung Chee-hwa (董建華) presented 12 recipients with the Grand Bauhinia Medal (in recognition of contribution with the highest honour): Ann Tse-kai (T. K. Ann) (安子介), Elsie Tu (杜葉錫恩), Simon Li Fook-sean (李福善), Lee Quo-wei (利國偉), Cha Chi-ming (查濟民), Tsui Sze-man (徐四民), Wong Ker-lee (黃克立), Tsang Hin-chi (曾憲梓), Chuang Shih-ping (莊世平), Henry Fok Ying-tung (霍英東), Chung Sze-yuen (鍾士元) and Lo Tak-shing (羅德丞).

03 Jul 1997

About 500 people, including 200 Mainland illegal immigrants born to Hong Kong residents, staged a rally at the Immigration Headquarters in Wan Chai, demanding the right of abode in Hong Kong under Categories (2) and (3) of Paragraph 2 in Article 24 of the Basic Law.

The Immigration Department began issuing HKSAR passports.

The Hong Kong Observatory issued a Red rainstorm warning signal for nine and a half hours amid heavy rain which caused more than 220 cases of landslides and floods.

04 Jul 1997

The Promulgation of National Laws (No. 2) 1997 was announced following a resolution by the National People's Congress Standing Committee, effective 01 July, implementing five national laws as amendments to Annex III of the Basic Law, namely the 1) Law of the People's Republic of China on the National Flag; 2) Law of the People's Republic of China on the National Emblem; 3) Law of the People's Republic of China on the Territorial Sea and the Contiguous Zone; 4) Law of the People's Republic of China on the Garrisoning of the HKSAR; and 5) Regulations of the People's Republic of China Concerning Consular Privileges and Immunities.

05 Jul 1997

The Lookout Tower, located at Tai Po Waterfront Park where colonial officials first arrived following the lease of the New Territories, was unveiled in commemoration of the transfer of sovereignty of Hong Kong and in recognition of the contribution of New Territories villagers in resisting invasions of the British and Japanese, and supporting the development of the New Territories.

07 Jul 1997

Commissioner of the Ministry of Foreign Affairs in the HKSAR Ma Yuzhen (馬毓真) in his first official visit presented Chief Executive Tung Chee-hwa (董建華) with a letter from Vice Premier and Minister of Foreign Affairs Qian Qichen (錢其琛), authorising the HKSAR to engage other countries on bilateral agreements on the transit of aircraft, promotion of investment, repatriation of fugitives, transfer of sentenced persons, and legal assistance in criminal matters.

08 Jul 1997

The Chief Executive presided over the first meeting of the Executive Council; all councillors took an oath to observe the principles of confidentiality and collective responsibility. The issues of Mainland children born to Hong Kong residents and methods for the election of the first Legislative Council in 1998 were discussed.

10 Jul 1997

The Immigration (Amendment) (No. 5) Ordinance 1997 was promulgated, effective 01 July, authorising the Certificate of Entitlement Scheme under which the Immigration Department could grant permanent residency for Mainland children and issue repatriation orders to those deemed ineligible. It enabled eligible children to settle in Hong Kong in accordance with Articles 22, 23 and 24 of the Basic Law.

11 Jul 1997

The Public Service (Administration) Order 1997 was issued by the Chief Executive as the first executive order following the establishment of the HKSAR. It replaced the provisions of the Letters Patent and Colonial Regulations on the administration of civil servants with the Public Service (Disciplinary) Regulation.

The Preparatory Committee for the HKSAR during its final plenary session in Beijing announced the committee's conclusion in accordance with the National People's Congress Standing Committee.

15 Jul 1997

The Executive Council approved the HKSAR government's approach to handling land leases and related matters in accordance with Article 7 and Article 123 of the Basic Law. The new 50-year land leases were subject to an annual rent equivalent to 3% of the rateable value of the land.

The Immigration Department released a list of about 170 countries and regions eligible for visa-free entry into Hong Kong for a stay of seven days to six months, and a list of about 40 countries and regions with a visa requirement for visits to Hong Kong.

17 Jul 1997

The Hong Kong Economic and Trade Office, London was opened in place of the Hong Kong Government London Office previously established in 1946.

24 Jul 1997

The Chinese Central Government appointed Jiang Enzhu (姜恩柱) as President of Xinhua News Agency, Hong Kong Special Administrative Region Branch Limited.

25 Jul 1997

The Chinese Central Government gave the HKSAR authorisation to engage other countries on mutual visa exemptions. As of this day, HKSAR passport holders had visa-free access to 36 countries.

The first HKSAR air transport agreement—between Hong Kong and the United Kingdom—was signed.

27 Jul 1997

The *New Evening Post*, launched in 1950, ceased publication.

28 Jul 1997

The Department of Health launched a measles vaccination booster programme with free vaccination for non-vaccinated people aged one to 19 and those who had received only one dose.

The Chinese Central Government appointed Liao Hui (廖暉) as Director of the Hong Kong and Macao Affairs Office of the State Council. He remained in office until 08 October 2010.

29 Jul 1997

The Elderly Commission was established as a government coordinator on the planning and development of elderly services programmes.

In the criminal case involving barrister David Ma Wai-kwan (馬維騉) and two others alleged to have perverted the course of justice in 1995, it was ruled in the newly established Court of Appeal of the High Court that previous common law cases and instruments issued by the Provisional Legislative Council were constitutional, overturning the arguments made by the defence. It was also ruled that Hong Kong courts had no jurisdiction over resolutions and decisions approved by the National People's Congress Standing Committee.

02 Aug 1997

The Hong Kong Observatory hoisted Increasing Gale or Storm Signal No. 9 for about seven hours amid Typhoon Victor. Thomas Larmour, a British national, was swept away by a large wave and drowned at the Stanley seawall while trying to save two young people trapped in the sea. He was posthumously awarded the Medal for Bravery (Gold) on 01 July 1998, making him one of the first medal recipients.

04 Aug 1997

Blue Ridge (LCC-19), the flagship of the US Navy Seventh Fleet, arrived in Hong Kong as the first foreign warship approved by the Chinese Central Government to dock in Hong Kong after the establishment of the HKSAR.

11 Aug 1997

The HKSAR government contributed US$1 billion from the Exchange Fund to the International Monetary Fund's financing package for Thailand in support of the country's economic reforms.

20 Aug 1997

The Provisional Legislative Council passed a motion on the issue of Vietnamese boat people, urging the HKSAR government to cancel the port of first asylum policy, repatriate all Vietnamese boat people and illegal immigrants stranded in Hong Kong, negotiate with Vietnam for an agreement on immediate repatriation, and recoup a reimbursement of HK$1.1 billion in expenses from the UN High Commissioner for Refugees.

The Department of Health announced the world's first human case of influenza A virus (subtype H5N1, or the avian influenza, known in the past to infect only birds) in Hong Kong.

01 Sep 1997

The Octopus card and its contactless electronic payment system were launched in place of the MTR value-stored tickets; it initially supported fare payment in public transport and was later expanded to cover convenience stores and retail shops.

03 Sep 1997

Chief Executive Tung Chee-hwa (董建華) made his first official trip abroad in a four-day visit to Malaysia and Singapore for meetings with Prime Minister Mahathir Mohamad and Prime Minister Goh Chok Tong (吳作棟), respectively.

08 Sep 1997

Chief Executive Tung Chee-hwa (董建華) made a five-day visit to the United States where he met with US President Bill Clinton and officiated at the opening ceremony of the Hong Kong Economic and Trade Office in Washington, DC.

In a meeting with Chief Justice Andrew Li Kwok-nang (李國能), UK's Lord Chancellor Derry Irvine made a commitment to nominating two judges from the House of Lords in the appointment of non-permanent judges to the Court of Final Appeal of the HKSAR.

11 Sep 1997

The Court of Final Appeal completed its first trial, dismissing an appeal over an estate dispute.

12 Sep 1997

The Futures Exchange's Hang Seng China-Affiliated Corporations Index (Red Chip) was launched to provide a definition and benchmark for investors interested in Mainland companies incorporated overseas and listed in Hong Kong.

15 Sep 1997

Authorised by the National People's Congress Standing Committee, Hong Kong Immigration Department began to accept applications for Chinese nationality, including those for restoration of Chinese nationality previously renounced.

23 Sep 1997

The 52nd Annual Meetings of the Boards of Governors of the World Bank Group and the International Monetary Fund began in Hong Kong for three days in an opening ceremony with Premier Li Peng (李鵬) and Vice Premier Zhu Rongji (朱鎔基).

25 Sep 1997

The Education and Manpower Bureau issued its Medium of Instruction Guidance for Secondary Schools, requiring classroom teaching in Chinese with students of public and subsidised secondary schools, starting with Secondary 1 from the 1998/99 academic year, unless exempt otherwise in accordance with certain requirements.

29 Sep 1997

The Land Fund Trust was dissolved after 11 years of operation; funds were transferred to the Hong Kong Monetary Authority. On 01 November 1998, assets were brought into the Exchange Fund managed by the Hong Kong Monetary Authority.

Figure 273
Chief Executive Tung Chee-hwa (董建華) speaking at a press conference upon delivery of his first
Policy Address. (Photo taken on 08 October 1997 and courtesy of HKSAR Government)

29 Sep 1997

The Electoral Affairs Commission was established to replace the Boundary and Election Commission established in 1993; it was to ensure all public elections were conducted in an open, fair and honest manner.

Businessman Walter Kwok Ping-sheung (郭炳湘) was kidnapped by a criminal gang led by Cheung Tze-keung (張子強). He was released on 04 October upon a ransom of HK$600 million paid on 03 October.

30 Sep 1997

The HKSAR government announced that a daily national and regional flag-raising ceremony be held at the Golden Bauhinia Square outside the Hong Kong Convention and Exhibition Centre starting from 01 October.

01 Oct 1997

A national and regional flag-raising ceremony was held at the Golden Bauhinia Square on the first National Day after the establishment of the HKSAR, followed by a government reception. The Hong Kong Garrison barracks were opened to the public for the first time.

03 Oct 1997

The Legislative Council Ordinance was promulgated, authorising the operation of the first Legislative Council of the HKSAR from 01 July 1998. It comprised 20 members from geographical constituencies through direct elections, 30 members from functional constituencies and 10 members elected by the Election Committee.

06 Oct 1997

The English newspaper *China Daily* (Hong Kong Edition) began publication as the first Mainland newspaper in Hong Kong after the establishment of the HKSAR.

07 Oct 1997

The Education Commission's *Report No. 7* was released, proposing the establishment of a Quality Education Fund for school and community engagement in support of forward-thinking education plans and reform measures, including the implementation of school-based management in all schools by 2000.

08 Oct 1997

Chief Executive Tung Chee-hwa (董建華) in his first policy address *Building Hong Kong for a New Era* proposed three housing policy targets: 1) building no less than 85,000 public and private housing units each year, 2) enabling homeownership with 70% of families within 10 years, and 3) reducing the average waiting time for public housing to three years, in addition to a plan for a major rail system and road network. (Figure 273)

09 Oct 1997

The High Court ruled against four cases of judicial review regarding the right of abode involving five children born to Hong Kong residents and only accepted the case regarding the rights of children born in or out of wedlock. To legally settle in Hong Kong, a One-way Permit issued by the Mainland government and a Certificate of Entitlement to the Right of Abode issued by the Hong Kong Immigration Department were required.

12 Oct 1997

Team Hong Kong, China took part at the eighth National Games in Shanghai, marking the first participation in the National Games where cyclist Wong Kam-po (黃金寶) won a gold medal in the men's 180-kilometre road race on 15 October, becoming Hong Kong's first National Games medallist.

13 Oct 1997

The World Economic Forum's 1997 East Asia Economic Summit began for a three-day conference in Hong Kong.

15 Oct 1997

Chief Executive Tung Chee-hwa (董建華) arrived in Tokyo for a two-day visit and a meeting with Japanese Prime Minister Ryutaro Hashimoto.

16 Oct 1997

The Hong Kong–Mainland Cross Boundary Major Infrastructure Co-ordinating Committee was established with the first plenary session in Shenzhen. Based on the previous arrangement by a Hong Kong–Mainland committee on infrastructure before the establishment of the HKSAR, it formed four subgroups dedicated to the development of seaways, roads and bridges, a Huanggang-Lok Ma Chau crossing, and air traffic control.

19 Oct 1997

Chief Executive Tung Chee-hwa (董建華) began an official trip to Brussels and London, meeting with European Commission President Jacques Santer and British Prime Minister Tony Blair.

20 Oct 1997

Amid the Asian financial crisis, speculative trading led by American investor George Soros led to a rise in Hong Kong dollar interest rate, an outflow of foreign funds, and a one-day drop by 630 points of the Hang Seng Index, followed by three days of continuous decline in the Hong Kong stock market, ending with a plunge of more than 3,000 points to reach 10,426 points over four trading days.

23 Oct 1997

The Hong Kong Monetary Authority announced an amonnt of US$88.1 billion in foreign exchange reserves (including the Land Fund) as of the end of September 1997, ranking third in the world (behind Japan and the Mainland).

Financial Secretary Donald Tsang Yam-kuen (曾蔭權) expressed confidence in the Hong Kong dollar and its link to the US dollar. He explained recent market volatility was a result of large-scale market speculation by short selling the Hong Kong dollar with a "long" position in the US dollar before having to cover their short positions. The HKSAR government, in response, took the following measures: (1) buying blue chip stocks by leveraging the Land Fund; (2) buying Hong Kong dollars by leveraging the Exchange Fund along with punitive high interest rates on banks with low liquidity in Hong Kong dollars; and (3) suppressing further speculative trading by allowing a higher prime rate with HSBC, Standard Chartered Bank, and Hang Seng Bank.

28 Oct 1997

The Hang Seng Index plunged 1,438.31 points (13.7%) in a single day, closing at 9,059.89 points as the biggest one-day drop since the 1987 stock market crash. On 29 October, it rebounded sharply by 1,705.41 points (18.82%), closing at 10,765.3 points to mark the biggest one-day gain by percentage as of 01 July 2017.

29 Oct 1997

King Harald V of Norway and Queen Sonja arrived in Hong Kong for a three-day visit.

31 Oct 1997

The Employment and Labour Relations (Miscellaneous Amendments) Ordinance 1997 was promulgated, repealing the Employment (Amendment) (No. 4) Ordinance 1997 and Employee's Rights to Representation, Consultation and Collective Bargaining Ordinance. The Trade Unions (Amendment) (No. 2) Ordinance 1997 was amended to modernise regulations on trade unions.

01 Nov 1997

The Estate Agents Authority was established to regulate the conduct of estate agents, formulate a licensing system, handle complaints against estate agents, and conduct inspections.

05 Nov 1997

The HKSAR government, with authorisation from the Chinese Central Government, entered into two agreements with the United Kingdom on the transfer of fugitives and sentenced persons, marking the first such agreements by the HKSAR.

10 Nov 1997

The International Bank of Asia was confronted with a bank run upon rumours of financial problems. Statements of reassurance were issued by the bank and the HKSAR government, along with a pledge of funding support by the Hong Kong Monetary Authority. The next day, it stabilised following deposit withdrawal of HK$1.6 billion in two days.

20 Nov 1997

President of Poland Aleksander Kwaśniewski arrived in Hong Kong for a two-day visit.

22 Nov 1997

The Ministry of Foreign Affairs announced that the Chinese government would continue to provide the United Nations with status reports on Hong Kong with respect to the International Covenant on Civil and Political Rights and the International Covenant on Economic, Social and Cultural Rights.

24 Nov 1997

Representing Hong Kong, China for the first time, Chief Executive Tung Chee-hwa (董建華) took part in the two-day APEC Economic Leaders' Meeting in Vancouver in the first official capacity of Hong Kong, China.

25 Nov 1997

The 30th annual meeting of the UN Economic and Social Commission for Asia and the Pacific in conjunction with the World Meteorological Organization Typhoon Committee began in Hong Kong for the first time with more than 70 representatives from 12 member countries and regions in a seven-day session. Director of the Hong Kong Observatory Lam Hung-kwan (林鴻鋆) was elected as Committee Chairman and was presented with a committee award for natural disaster prevention.

30 Nov 1997

A government committee on land supply was formed to supervise the implementation of a five-year plan in support of meeting the target of supplying no less than 85,000 housing units annually starting in 1999.

Nov 1997

The Antiquities and Monuments Office in conjunction with the Chinese Academy of Social Sciences' Institute of Archaeology conducted an expedited excavation at Tung Wan Tsai North in Ma Wan; 20 tombs, including 15 with human archaeological remains, of the period spanning from the late Neolithic period to the late Bronze Age, were uncovered. It was recognised as one of China's top 10 new archaeological discoveries in 1997.

01 Dec 1997

Upon review by the Committee on Medium of Instruction (Guidance for Secondary Schools), 100 (later amended to 114) of 124 English schools were granted permission to continue classroom teaching of all subjects in English.

Figure 274
The Agriculture and Fisheries Department disposed of live chicken at a farm in Pak Sha Tsuen, Yuen Long in an attempt to eliminate sources of avian influenza. (Photo taken on 29 December 1997 and courtesy of HKSAR Government)

02 Dec 1997

The Sino-British Joint Liaison Group held its first plenary session since the establishment of the HKSAR for a two-day meeting in Beijing on the issues of Vietnamese boat people stranded in Hong Kong and UN human rights reports.

03 Dec 1997

An international academic symposium on Hong Kong and the Mainland, organised by the Chinese Academy of Social Sciences in conjunction with The University of Hong Kong, began in Hong Kong for a three-day conference with 135 scholars from the Mainland, Hong Kong, Macao, Taiwan, the US, Britain, Japan, Canada and Australia, among other countries and regions.

08 Dec 1997

A group of 36 Hong Kong deputies was elected to the ninth National People's Congress in a vote by 419 members of an election committee.

The Housing Authority launched a Tenants Purchase Scheme, giving tenants the option to purchase their current public housing units at 12% of the private market price. The first six public housing estates under the scheme were announced on 12 December.

09 Dec 1997

Chief Executive Tung Chee-hwa (董建華) made his first duty visit to Beijing to report on HKSAR's economic, financial and social development to President Jiang Zemin (江澤民) and Premier Li Peng (李鵬).

12 Dec 1997

The Provisional Legislative Council's Finance Committee approved a grant of HK$5 billion to establish a Quality Education Fund in support of promotion of education programmes. On 16 January 1998, a Quality Education Fund Steering Committee was formed to advise on policy and appropriation.

15 Dec 1997

A government task force was formed to tackle the spread of Influenza A virus (subtype H5N1, commonly known as avian influenza) On 14 December 1998, for successful government efforts in pandemic control, Hong Kong received commendations from the World Health Organization and 18 international organisations.

The National Treasures: Gems of China's Cultural Relics—an exhibition organised by the Hong Kong Museum of Art—began with 163 sets of national relics from the Neolithic period to the Qing Dynasty, including a *yazhang* blade unearthed at the Tai Wan site on Lamma Island.

23 Dec 1997

People's Liberation Army Chief of the General Staff Fu Quanyou (傅全有) arrived with a delegation of the Central Military Commission for a one-week inspection of the Hong Kong Garrison and a meeting with Chief Executive Tung Chee-hwa (董建華).

Hong Kong suspended the import of live chickens from the Mainland. On 29 December, an attempt to eliminate sources of avian influenza was made through disposal of chickens in local farms, wholesale markets and retail stalls. (Figure 274)

31 Dec 1997

As of today, HKSAR passport holders had visa-free access to 44 countries; passport holders of 170 countries had visa-free entry to Hong Kong.

1997

Professor Chen Qingquan (陳清泉) of The University of Hong Kong was elected as the first HKSAR Academician of the Chinese Academy of Engineering (CAE). As of 01 July 2017, Hong Kong had seven CAE academicians.

08 Jan 1998

The Basic Law Promotion Steering Committee held its first meeting to study ways to foster a greater understanding of the Basic Law among teachers, students and civil servants in the local community as well as the general public overseas.

09 Jan 1998

The HKSAR government abolished the port of first asylum policy—in place since July 1979 with Vietnamese boat people who were now given the same status as other illegal immigrants.

The Provisional Legislative Council's Finance Committee approved an appropriation of HK$18 billion with the Hong Kong Housing Society for a five-year Home Starter Loan Scheme. The scheme entailed HK$3.6 billion with 6,000 applicants annually for a household loan of up to HK$600,000 or 30% of the property price in support of first-time homeownership. Applications ran from 17 April 1998 to 31 March 2002.

12 Jan 1998

The Judiciary held its first Opening of the Legal Year after the establishment of the HKSAR.

The largest Chinese-owned securities firm in Hong Kong, Peregrine Group, announced its liquidation.

16 Jan 1998

The Commission on Strategic Development was established under the chairmanship of Chief Executive Tung Chee-hwa (董建華). Members included the Chief Secretary for Administration, Financial Secretary, professionals in the industrial, commercial and financial sectors, as well as the grass-root community, as an advisory group on long-term development.

21 Jan 1998

The Agriculture and Fisheries Department began an artificial reef project by sinking an old cement barge at Hoi Ha Wan in Sai Kung. The project's first phase called for artificial reefs with boat wreckage to be placed in Hoi Ha Wan Marine Park and Yan Chau Tong Marine Park to enrich aquatic habitats and resources.

25 Jan 1998

Secretary for Justice Elsie Leung Oi-sie (梁愛詩) filed a lawsuit against *Oriental Daily News* and Oriental Press Group for contempt of court. The newspaper was accused of stalking Justice of the Court of Appeal Gerald Godfrey and making malicious claims about persecution by the government. On 30 June, Editor-in-Chief Thomas Wong Yeung-ng (黃陽午) was found guilty and sentenced to four months in prison in a ruling by the High Court. It marked the first conviction of contempt of court with a newspaper editor.

26 Jan 1998

The Honours and Awards System under the Chief Executive was formally established to recognise outstanding achievements and acts of bravery. It included the Grand Bauhinia Medal, Bauhinia Star, Medal of Honour, Medal for Bravery and Chief Executive's Commendation. As of 2017, 92 individuals were awarded the Grand Bauhinia Medal.

The Futures Exchange extended its normal closing time from 3:55 p.m. to 4 p.m. in line with the trading hours of the Stock Exchange.

27 Jan 1998

The Hongkong and Yaumati Ferry Company marked the end of a 65-year-old public vehicular ferry service with the termination of the regular North Point–Kowloon City service (retaining transport service of dangerous goods only).

31 Jan 1998

The Metrication Committee was officially dissolved upon expiration of its tenure, marking the end of its 30-year history. Functions were delegated to the Trade and Industry Bureau.

07 Feb 1998

Hong Kong resumed the import of live chicken from the Mainland and applied new control measures. It allowed supply only from farms approved by the Animal and Plant Quarantine Administration of the People's Republic of China and required a five-day quarantine with live chicken in Hong Kong to eliminate the risk of the H5 virus.

11 Feb 1998

The Arrangement between the Mainland and HKSAR for the Avoidance of Double Taxation was signed. Under the arrangement, Hong Kong enterprises operating in the Mainland without permanent establishment were subject to profits tax in Hong Kong only.

14 Feb 1998

The white paper *Homes for Hong Kong People into the 21st Century* was released; it covered a long-term housing strategy in the first major policy paper of the HKSAR government; it proposed a 13-year housing programme for no less than 85,000 residential units every year.

18 Feb 1998

Financial Secretary Donald Tsang Yam-kuen (曾蔭權) delivered the first HKSAR government budget titled *Riding Out the Storm, Renewing Hong Kong Strengths*.

Feb 1998

The North District Hospital in Sheung Shui, New Territories was commissioned; its accident and emergency service unit became operational on 06 August. It marked the first hospital completely planned and developed by the Hospital Authority.

02 Mar 1998

Hong Kong deputies travelled to Beijing for the First Session of the Ninth National People's Congress as a first-time standalone delegation.

03 Mar 1998

The Chief Executive-in-Council passed a motion for a National Day firework display on 01 October starting in 1998.

05 Mar 1998

Chief Executive Tung Chee-hwa (董建華) attended the National People's Congress for the first time and was seated at the main row.

06 Mar 1998

The Provident Fund Schemes Legislation (Amendment) Ordinance was promulgated, requiring the implementation of a mandatory retirement protection scheme in Hong Kong by 01 December 2000.

11 Mar 1998

The Hong Kong Mortgage Corporation Limited's promissory notes with a maturity of three years, totalling HK$500 million, were tendered and oversubscribed 5.44 times. It was the first batch of a HK$20 billion issuance arranged and managed by the Hong Kong Monetary Authority to provide funding in the purchase of mortgage loans.

13 Mar 1998

The HKSAR government accepted a resolution made by the Committee on Medium of Instruction (Guidance for Secondary Schools), allowing 14 of 20 schools in an appeal to continue classroom instruction in English on top of 100 schools already authorised. The Education and Manpower Bureau also authorised additional support starting in September for schools with classroom instruction in Chinese to nurture students in written Chinese and English as well as spoken Cantonese, Putonghua and English in a campaign to promote mother-tongue education.

18 Mar 1998

The Hong Kong Mortgage Corporation Limited entered into agreements with Chase Bank and Dao Heng Bank for a fixed-rate mortgage pilot scheme to protect home buyers from market fluctuations.

19 Mar 1998

The High Court ruled in a judicial review regarding the resettlement of the residents of Tiu Keng Leng Cottage Area, which was due for redevelopment as part of Tseung Kwan O New Town, that an adjusted government compensation was necessary to cover the lost opportunity for infinite stay with low rent among villagers deemed eligible before June 1961.

20 Mar 1998

The HKSAR government announced a list of members of the Innovation and Technology Commission initiated by the Chief Executive in support of promoting local innovations.

26 Mar 1998

The Chief Executive-in-Council endorsed and accepted a 21st-century development proposal on land, transport and environmental protection in the final summary report *Territorial Development Strategy Review* based on a prospective economic relationship with nearby provinces and a population of 8.1 million in 2011.

30 Mar 1998

The Hong Kong/Guangdong Co-operation Joint Conference was inaugurated with its first meeting in Guangzhou on cross-boundary passenger and freight services and related infrastructure development. It became an official platform on economic, financial, environmental and technological cooperation; 19 meetings had been held as of 01 July 2017.

31 Mar 1998

Hong Kong Telecom International Limited surrendered its franchise licence eight and a half years ahead of the original date of expiry in October 2006. Hong Kong's services-based and facilities-based telecommunications markets were deregulated on 01 January 1999 and 01 January 2000, respectively.

01 Apr 1998

The Committee on Bilingual Legal System was formed as an advisory body on the long-term goal of legal bilingualism and related measures for implementation as an international trade and financial centre under the Basic Law. The Bilingual Legislation Programme in 1989 required all statutory laws to be promulgated in both Chinese and English with equal legal significance.

03 Apr 1998

The Fire Safety (Commercial Premises) (Amendment) Ordinance 1998 was promulgated, effective 01 June, requiring the installation of automatic sprinkler systems, emergency lights, fire hydrants, hose reels in all commercial buildings constructed on or before 01 March 1987.

08 Apr 1998

The Provisional Legislative Council adjourned upon its last meeting; members' appointment of office remained until 30 June.

09 Apr 1998

The Information Technology and Broadcasting Bureau was reinstituted as a government coordinator of policy and development of information technology in place of the Broadcasting, Culture and Sport Bureau.

17 Apr 1998

The Adaptation of Laws (Interpretative Provisions) Ordinance was promulgated, amending the provisions on disabuse, application and interpretation stipulated in the Interpretation and General Clauses Ordinance to ensure compliance with the Basic Law and Hong Kong's status as a Special Administrative Region of the People's Republic of China.

The Land (Compulsory Sale for Redevelopment) Ordinance was promulgated, effective 07 June, allowing the sale of land rights under the Lands Tribunal upon a collection of undivided shares (property ownership) of 90% or more.

23 Apr 1998

The Western Wholesale Food Market became operational as the first centralised slaughterhouse facility with ducks and other waterfowl in complement with measures on prevention of another outbreak of avian influenza by isolating different types of poultry.

The *Report on the Financial Market Review* was released with an impact assessment of the Asian financial turmoil on Hong Kong since October 1997. It noted the effectiveness of Hong Kong's linked exchange rate and suggested further implementation of Hong Kong Mortgage Corporation's fixed rate mortgage scheme to reduce the impact of interest rate fluctuations on home buyers.

26 Apr 1998

The Independent Commission Against Corruption cracked down on a large piracy syndicate, seizing HK$7 million worth of pirated disks and HK$650 million worth of equipment. An acting senior superintendent of the Customs and Excise Department was arrested and sentenced to four years in prison for taking bribes in connection with the criminal case.

06 May 1998

The Ting Kau Bridge as part of Route 3 connecting Tsing Yi and Ting Kau was opened. The Country Park Section of Route 3 (including Tai Lam Tunnel and Yuen Long Approach) was opened on 25 June.

Hong Kong Telecommunications Limited launched its Super Netvigator Home Broadband service as the first commercial provider of broadband network services for home use.

09 May 1998

The Housing Department's first residential building for the elderly at Tin Ping Estate in Lam Tin was opened.

13 May 1998

Commissioner of Police Eddie Hui Ki-on (許淇安) and his delegation met with Minister of Public Security Jia Chunwang (賈春旺) in the first exchange between the law enforcement agencies of Hong Kong and the Mainland since the establishment of the HKSAR.

16 May 1998

The HKSAR government dispatched two immigration officers to Jakarta for assistance with stranded Hong Kong residents amid the anti-Chinese riots in Indonesia.

20 May 1998

Chief Judge Patrick Chan Siu-oi (陳兆愷), Judges Gerald Paul Nazareth and John Barry Mortimer ruled in an appeal involving five children without residency permits that any child of a parent with the right of abode at the time of, rather than after, the child's birth may have the right of abode in accordance with Category (3) of Paragraph 2 of Article 24 of the Basic Law.

24 May 1998

The first Legislative Council elections of the HKSAR were held, returning 60 members, including 20 from geographical constituencies, 30 functional constituencies and 10 members elected by the Election Committee. The turnout rates were 53.29%, 63.5% and 98.75%, respectively.

Figure 275
Severe flooding at Tin Ping Shan Village in Sheung Shui following heavy rainstorms. (Photo taken on 24 May 1998 and courtesy of South China Morning Post Publishers Limited)

Figure 276
The Airport Express became operational on 21 June 1998. (Photo courtesy of MTR Corporation)

24 May 1998

The Hong Kong Observatory issued a Red warning signal amid heavy rainstorms. Discharge from the Shenzhen Reservoir caused severe flooding in northern New Territories; 42 floods and one landslide were reported. Rubber rafts and helicopters were deployed in Sheung Shui, Sha Tau Kok and Fanling, rescuing 113 people. (Figure 275)

26 May 1998

The High Island Detention Centre was officially closed; it was the last detention centre for Vietnamese boat people in Hong Kong.

27 May 1998

The Education Department issued its Guidelines for Display of the National Flag, providing a protocol (including the sequence and positioning) in displaying the national and regional flags, along with details on flag requirements, in all schools.

The Chinese University of Hong Kong's Department of Surgery performed the world's first infant laparoscopic colon surgery on a 12-day-old infant suffering from total colonic aganglionosis.

01 Jun 1998

The World Intellectual Property Organization's Asian Regional Symposium began in Hong Kong for a three-day conference on implementation of the Agreement on Trade-Related Aspects of Intellectual Property Rights, among other issues on intellectual rights. Hong Kong became a party of the agreement in 1996 and began enforcement on 01 January 2000.

08 Jun 1998

The Air Mail Centre of Hong Kong Post, located at Hong Kong (Chek Lap Kok) International Airport and capable of handling air mail with full automation, was completed at a cost of HK$566 million.

09 Jun 1998

Electrician Lee Ying-kwong (李仍光) drowned while attempting to save two children swept away in a flood at Quarry Bay Country Park during a Black rainstorm warning signal. He was posthumously awarded the Medal for Bravery (Gold) on 01 July as one of the first citizens to receive the medal.

12 Jun 1998

The Chief Executive-in-Council approved the permanent closure of Hong Lok Street (commonly known as Bird Street) in Mong Kok to facilitate urban redevelopment by the Land Development Corporation (presently Urban Renewal Authority). The Bird Market was preserved and relocated to the Yuen Po Street Bird Garden in Mong Kok.

14 Jun 1998

Chief Executive Tung Chee-hwa (董建華) made a five-day visit to Australia and New Zealand; he met with Prime Minister of Australia John Winston Howard and Prime Minister of New Zealand Jennifer Mary Shipley, and was a guest speaker at the Asia-Australia Institute in Sydney, the Australia Summit in Melbourne and the Asia 2000 Forum in Auckland.

21 Jun 1998

The MTR Airport Express Line began running between Hong Kong (Chek Lap Kok) International Airport and urban centres. The MTR Tung Chung Line connecting Tung Chung New Town and Hong Kong Island began on 22 June. (Figure 276)

01 Jul 1998

President Jiang Zemin (江澤民) arrived in Hong Kong for a ceremony upon the first anniversary of the establishment of the HKSAR. On 02 July, he reviewed the People's Liberation Army Hong Kong Garrison in a visit to the naval base on Stonecutters Island and officiated at the opening ceremony of Hong Kong (Chek Lap Kok) International Airport before his departure; he was the first head of state to depart from the new airport. (Figures 277 and 278)

Figure 277
President Jiang Zemin (江澤民), right, inspected troops of the People's Liberation Army (PLA) Hong Kong Garrison at the naval base on Stonecutters Island, accompanied by PLA Chief of Staff Fu Quanyou (傅全有), centre, and Commander of PLA Hong Kong Garrison Liu Zhenwu (劉鎮武), left. (Photo courtesy of HKSAR Government)

Figure 278
An aerial view of Hong Kong International Airport's passenger terminal under construction. (Photo taken in 1997 and courtesy of HKSAR Government)

02 Jul 1998

The first HKSAR Legislative Council began its first meeting; Rita Fan Hsu Lai-tai (范徐麗泰) was elected as President of the Council. The Rules of Procedure of the Legislative Council of HKSAR was adopted as its first resolution. (Figure 279)

US President Bill Clinton arrived in Hong Kong for a two-day visit as the first foreign head of state to visit the new Hong Kong (Chek Lap Kok) International Airport. He was hosted by Chief Executive Tung Chee-hwa (董建華) at the Government House.

06 Jul 1998

Kai Tak Airport was officially closed upon the departure of Cathay Pacific flight CX251 bound for London at 0:02 a.m.

Hong Kong (Chek Lap Kok) International Airport was officially opened; operations were chaotic on the first day. On July 21, a Commission of Inquiry was appointed for an investigation on reasons of operational breakdown. On 22 January 1999, it concluded in a report that issues were caused by a malfunction of the flight data display system and a breakdown of the cargo-handling system and that Airport Authority Hong Kong and Air Cargo Terminals were accountable.

A Hong Kong–Mainland scheme allowing a greater number of Chinese tourists in Hong Kong was implemented, raising a daily quota from 1,142 to 1,500.

10 Jul 1998

A Hong Kong–Guangdong agreement on Dongshen Water Supply Improvement Works was signed, providing Guangdong with a Hong Kong government loan of HK$2.364 billion for building a closed tunnel system to facilitate the supply of water from the East River (Dongjiang) to Hong Kong.

11 Jul 1998

The Bank for International Settlements opened its first overseas office in Hong Kong for businesses in the Asia-Pacific region.

23 Jul 1998

The Housing Authority launched a Mortgage Subsidy Scheme, providing public housing tenants affected under the Comprehensive Redevelopment Programme with a six-year monthly mortgage subsidy for purchases of a Home Ownership Scheme resident unit within a three-year period.

13 Aug 1998

The Hang Seng Index closed at 6,660.42 points, dropping from 10,096.37 points since 12 May following months of speculative attacks on the Hong Kong dollar and Hong Kong stock market.

14 Aug 1998

The HKSAR government bought significant amounts of Hong Kong dollar and Hang Seng Index constituent stocks with the Exchange Fund to stabilise the exchange rate at HK$7.75 to US$1 in response to speculative short selling. It successfully defended against speculative attacks in 15 days as of 28 August with the Hang Seng Index closing at 7,829.74 points (18% higher) and a record turnover of HK$79 billion in the trading of futures.

31 Aug 1998

The 65-year-old franchise of China Motor Bus ended following a decision of non-renewal by the Chief Executive-in-Council on 17 February. The following day, 88 bus routes were transferred to the new operators Citybus and New World First Bus.

Aug 1998

Hong Kong athlete with disabilities So Wa-wai (蘇樺偉) won gold medals in the men's 100m (T36) and 200m (T36) at the International Paralympic Committee Athletics World Championships in Birmingham, UK, breaking the world record in both events. He joined Chan Shing-chung (陳成忠), Cheung Yiu-cheung (張耀祥) and Chao Kwok-pang (趙國鵬) in winning the gold medal in the men's 4×100m relay (T36), setting another world record.

Figure 279
Rita Fan Hsu Lai-tai (范徐麗泰), who served as the first President of the Legislative Council of the HKSAR, in a council meeting. (Photo taken on 02 July 1998 and courtesy of South China Morning Post Publishers Limited)

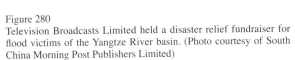

Figure 280
Television Broadcasts Limited held a disaster relief fundraiser for flood victims of the Yangtze River basin. (Photo courtesy of South China Morning Post Publishers Limited)

Aug 1998

The Disaster Relief Fund Advisory Committee of the HKSAR government approved HK$9 million for victims of floods in the Yangtze River basin which began in July. On 15 August, Television Broadcasts Limited launched a disaster relief fundraiser for the victims; Hong Kong raised the highest donation nationwide with a total of HK$680 million. (Figure 280)

03 Sep 1998

The South East Kowloon Development project was approved, calling for a plan to transform the former Kai Tak Airport in Kowloon Bay and its adjoining areas into a strategic growth area complete with housing, transport infrastructure and open spaces.

05 Sep 1998

The Hong Kong Monetary Authority announced seven measures, including guarantees with all licenced banks in Hong Kong for US dollars at a fixed rate of HK$7.75 to US$1, in an effort to reinforce the linked exchange rate and mitigate speculative activities.

07 Sep 1998

The HKSAR government introduced 30 measures for orderly operation in the securities and futures markets, including strict enforcement of "T+2" clearing and clampdown on non-compliant short selling.

09 Sep 1998

Legislator Chim Pui-chung (詹培忠) of the financial services functional constituency was discharged from duty in a vote by the Legislative Council; he was found guilty of conspiracy to forge documents and sentenced to three years' imprisonment in a ruling by the High Court on 03 August. He was the first legislator to be removed from office pursuant to Category (6) in Article 79 of the Basic Law.

10 Sep 1998

The Education Department in conjunction with the Committee on Respect Our Teachers Campaign and Radio Television Hong Kong held a reception at the Hong Kong Convention and Exhibition Centre in celebration of the first Teachers' Day—which was designated in the 1997 Policy Address.

11 Sep 1998

The Housing Authority began comprehensive asset assessment with applicants of public housing to ensure rational allocation of public resources; asset limits ranged from HK$220,000 in a one-person household to HK$700,000 in a household of eight or more.

17 Sep 1998

The Mandatory Provident Fund Schemes Authority (MPFA) was established as a statutory body to regulate and supervise the operation of MPF schemes.

28 Sep 1998

The Hong Kong Museum of History was relocated from Kowloon Park to its permanent home at 100 Chatham Road South in Tsim Sha Tsui. In partnership with the National Museum of Chinese History, it held an exhibition called Heavenly Creations: Gems of Ancient Chinese Inventions.

Sep 1998

The HKSAR government launched a Non-means-tested Loan Scheme in complement with the Financial Assistance Scheme for Post-secondary Students, providing local full-time post-secondary students with additional financial aid without assessment on incomes.

01 Oct 1998

The People's Liberation Army Hong Kong Garrison made public access available with the Shek Kong Airfield, Stonecutters Island Naval Base and Stanley Fort. It marked the first time that Shek Kong Airfield was opened to the public.

07 Oct 1998

The Council of International Advisors, comprising distinguished international business and corporate leaders, was established to advise the HKSAR government on the global and regional development trends affecting Hong Kong.

The Hong Kong Applied Science and Technology Research Institute (ASTRI) was conceived in a government plan to promote collaboration between academic and commercial entities as well as exchange with Chinese institutions for commercialisation of technology and innovation. The plan also called for an Innovation and Technology Fund with HK$5 billion of government funding. ASTRI was established in 2000.

09 Oct 1998

UK Prime Minister Tony Blair arrived in Hong Kong for a two-day visit as the last stop of his first trip to China.

14 Oct 1998

Phase I of the River Trade Terminal in Tuen Mun became operational; it was the first purpose-built container terminal for river cargo trade.

25 Oct 1998

The Hong Kong Sheng Kung Hui (Anglican Church) was established. Bishop Peter Kwong Kong-kit (鄺廣傑) was elected as the first Archbishop and Primate.

26 Oct 1998

The Kowloon-Canton Railway Corporation began construction of Phase I of the West Rail Line, a 30.5-kilometre rail between Kowloon and northwest New Territories with nine train stations.

28 Oct 1998

The HKSAR government held its first official ceremony to commemorate those who sacrificed their lives in defence of Hong Kong during the Second World War. Chief Executive Tung Chee-hwa (董建華) placed the names of 115 members of the Hong Kong Independent Battalion of East River (Dongjiang) Column, who died in service, alongside the list of fallen warriors at the City Hall Memorial Garden.

03 Nov 1998

The Hong Kong Museum of Art held an exhibition titled Egyptian Treasures from the British Museum with 105 ancient Egyptian artefacts.

04 Nov 1998

The National People's Congress Standing Committee embedded the Law on the Exclusive Economic Zone and the Continental Shelf of the People's Republic of China in Annex III of the Basic Law, making it a national law applicable in Hong Kong in accordance with Article 18 of the Basic Law. On 24 December, implementation of the national law was announced in a government gazette.

05 Nov 1998

The Environmental Protection Department launched its Waste Reduction Framework Plan for colour-designated recycling bins to collect used paper, plastics and metals across Hong Kong.

23 Nov 1998

An agreement between the Research Grants Council (Hong Kong) and the National Natural Science Foundation (the Mainland) was reached for collaborative research in science and technology, including a Joint Research Scheme to support research proposals jointly submitted by Hong Kong and Mainland researchers.

Nov 1998

Hong Kong entered a 68-month deflationary period, ending in August 2004.

05 Dec 1998

Hong Kong triad leader Cheung Tze-keung (張子強) was executed in a death sentence after he and his five accomplices were convicted of illegal arms trafficking by a court in Guangzhou. He was captured in January by Mainland authorities for kidnapping businessmen Victor Li Tzar-kuoi (李澤鉅) and Walter Kwok Ping-sheung (郭炳湘) in Hong Kong.

06 Dec 1998

Hong Kong took part in the 13th Asian Games in Bangkok as Team Hong Kong, China for the first time; it won five gold, five silver and five bronze medals, including first-time medals in snooker, squash and cycling.

18 Dec 1998

Lung Fu Shan Country Park was designated as the 23rd country park in Hong Kong; it was the smallest country park with an area of 47 hectares.

The two-day International Symposium on Lin Zexu: Opium War and Hong Kong—hosted by the Hong Kong Museum of History, Lin Zexu Foundation and Association of Chinese Historians—began at the museum. In attendance were Ling Qing (凌青), a fifth-generation grandson of Lin Zexu (林則徐) and former permanent representative of China to the United Nations, and scholars from Australia, Hong Kong and the Mainland. The Lin Zexu Foundation presented a stone statue of Lin Zexu to the museum.

31 Dec 1998

Measures of residential rent control under the Landlord and Tenant (Consolidation) Ordinance were lifted, allowing landlords to increase rents freely and repossess their properties upon the end of leases.

Dec 1998

The Independent Commission Against Corruption launched an investigation into a fraud case related to a letter of credit allegedly issued by Guangnan (Holdings); 23 people were prosecuted for getting letters of credit of HK$1.8 billion from banks through false accounts. By 29 July 2002, upon the end of the last trial, 15 people were convicted and sentenced to prison terms ranging from two to 10 years; another 23 suspects remained wanted.

1998

The Morningside Medal of Mathematics—in recognition of young Chinese mathematicians with outstanding achievements in pure and applied mathematics—was founded by Chairman of the International Congress of Chinese Mathematicians Yau Shing-tung (丘成桐) and Hong Kong entrepreneur Ronnie Chan Chi-chung (陳啟宗).

02 Jan 1999

Banks in Hong Kong began accepting deposits in Euro. On 04 January, Hong Kong made the first foreign exchange trading in Euros.

MTR Corporation Limited discontinued the use of stored value tickets, which were replaced with Octopus cards. (Figures 281 and 282)

06 Jan 1999

The third Ministers' Forum on Infrastructure Development in the Asia-Pacific Region began for a three-day conference in Hong Kong with representatives from 14 countries and regions.

14 Jan 1999

The Arrangement for Mutual Service of Judicial Documents in Civil and Commercial Proceedings between the Mainland and Hong Kong Courts was signed by the Chief Justice of Hong Kong and a representative of the Supreme People's Court; it came into force on 30 March.

15 Jan 1999

The Mainland Exit/Entry Permit for Hong Kong and Macao residents was launched in place of the Home Return Certificate first issued on 20 July 1979. (Figure 283)

Figure 281
MTR's common stored value ticket in use from 1984 to 1999. (Photo courtesy of MTR Corporation)

Figure 282
The first-generation "Octopus" smart payment cards. (Photo courtesy of Kim Lai Kit-ying)

Figure 283
The Home Return Permit shown at the bottom was a travel document with a validity of 10 years for Mainland entry/exit among residents of Hong Kong and Macao; it was replaced with a computer-readable card with enhanced security features (top) in use from 1999 to 2012. (Photo courtesy of South China Morning Post Publishers Limited)

18 Jan 1999

The Chinese Ministry of Finance issued US$1 billion in treasury bonds for the first time in Hong Kong through the Hong Kong Stock Exchange.

27 Jan 1999

The Film Development Fund, formed with HK$100 million in government funding, began accepting applications as an initiative to address the declining film market in Hong Kong.

28 Jan 1999

Chief Executive Tung Chee-hwa (董建華) attended the World Economic Forum Annual Meeting in Davos, Switzerland, participating as the first principal official of the HKSAR government.

29 Jan 1999

The Court of Final Appeal ruled in the case of Ng Ka-ling (吳嘉玲) that persons with the right of abode in Hong Kong were not considered "people from other parts of China" under the Basic Law and hence were not subject to repatriation. It also ruled that courts in the HKSAR were empowered to examine whether decisions by the National People's Congress and its Standing Committee were consistent with the Basic Law.

The Court of Final Appeal ruled in the case of Chan Kam-nga (陳錦雅) that the right of abode was applicable to persons born to Hong Kong residents who acquired permanent residency before or after the child's birth, making such persons eligible for the right to settle in Hong Kong.

04 Feb 1999

Secretary for Justice Elsie Leung Oi-sie (梁愛詩) issued a statement on non-prosecution due to insufficient evidence and public interest in a case against the chairman and majority shareholder of Sing Tao Group Sally Aw Sian (胡仙) over exaggerated claims on circulation numbers of newspaper *The Standard*.

05 Feb 1999

The Housing Authority implemented a new policy on public housing tenants, requiring asset review on family members upon household changes caused by death. Those with assets/income exceeding a certain limit must move out of public housing within 12 months.

The Air Pollution Control (Motor Vehicle Fuel) (Amendment) Regulation was promulgated, prohibiting the supply, sale and distribution of leaded gasoline and fuel additives containing lead.

20 Feb 1999

The United State government removed Hong Kong from the US Priority Watch List for intellectual property protection and enforcement for the first time since April 1996.

24 Feb 1999

The Director of Immigration filed a request with the Court of Final Appeal seeking clarification regarding the part on the National People's Congress (NPC) and its Standing Committee in the ruling of the Ng Ka-ling (吳嘉玲) case on 29 January. On 26 February, hearings began at the Court of Final Appeal which emphasised that NPC Standing Committee's right to interpret the Basic Law (under Article 158) or any power invested with the NPC and its Standing Committee pursuant to the Basic Law were by no means in question in the ruling on 29 January.

03 Mar 1999

The District Court ordered a defendant to pay HK$80,000 in damages and provide a written apology in Hong Kong's first sexual harassment complaint case assisted by the Equal Opportunities Commission.

The public consultation paper *Securities and Futures Market Reform* was released in a proposal on rectification of regulatory inadequacies with the establishment of an agile and modern regulatory agency in support of Hong Kong's competitiveness as an international financial centre.

04 Mar 1999

The Office of the HKSAR Government in Beijing was established; Leung Po-wing (梁寶榮) served as its first director.

11 Mar 1999

For the first time with compliments of the Chinese Central Government, two giant pandas, named An An and Jia Jia, arrived in Hong Kong and immediately took residence at the Ocean Park. The Hong Kong Jockey Club Giant Panda Habitat was opened on 17 May. (Figure 284)

12 Mar 1999

The District Councils Ordinance was promulgated, authorising the establishment, composition and election of District Councils with a list of requirements on eligibility and circumstances under which councillors may be disqualified.

18 Mar 1999

The Sun was launched with an introductory price of HK$2 per copy, triggering a price war as it was sold a few dollars cheaper than other daily newspapers. It ceased publication on 01 April 2016.

23 Mar 1999

Chairman of the Central Military Commission Jiang Zemin (江澤民) signed an order of appointment of Xiong Ziren (熊自仁) as Commander of the People's Liberation Army Hong Kong Garrison. Xiong served in the post until January 2003.

Mar 1999

The Hong Kong Mortgage Corporation Limited in conjunction with insurance companies launched a Mortgage Insurance Programme, enabling home buyers to secure mortgage loans up to 85% loan-to-value ratio in support of homeownership and a stable property market. A Master Mortgage Insurance Policy was signed with 26 approved sellers (commercial banks) on 31 March.

01 Apr 1999

The HKSAR government resumed scheduled auctions of land after a nine-month suspension and introduced an "Application List" land sale system.

02 Apr 1999

The first appointment ceremony and Scholar Achievement Awards of the Cheung Kong Scholars Programme were held at the Great Hall of the People in Beijing. The programme was established by the Li Ka-shing (李嘉誠) Foundation and the Chinese Ministry of Education to nurture talent and promote higher education reform.

Figure 284
Giant pandas An An, left, and Jia Jia, right, at Ocean Park's Hong Kong Jockey Club (HKJC) Giant Panda Habitat. (Photo taken on 17 May 1999 and courtesy of South China Morning Post Publishers Limited)

10 Apr 1999

The Housing Authority launched a Buy-or-Rent Option under which prospective tenants of public housing may rent according to the regular arrangement or purchase a public housing unit at a discount coupled with a subsidy of HK$160,000 in the first six years.

11 Apr 1999

Senior civil servants joined the first national studies workshop organised by the National School of Administration (later known as the Chinese Academy of Governance) in Beijing for a 14-day course to achieve a deeper understanding of national affairs and reform policies and strengthen their ties with senior officials in the Mainland.

30 Apr 1999

The HKSAR government approved a draft South Lantau Coast Outline Zoning Plan, covering an area of about 2,449 hectares with 1,565 hectares for a country park, 475 hectares for a green belt zone and 138 hectares for a coastal protection area.

01 May 1999

The International Labour Day became a statutory holiday in Hong Kong.

06 May 1999

The Legislative Council was given a government estimate that up to 1.675 million Mainlanders may be eligible for the right of abode in Hong Kong under the Court of Final Appeal ruling on 29 January.

18 May 1999

The HKSAR government decided to seek an interpretation on the right of abode in Hong Kong as stipulated in Paragraph 4 of Article 22 and Category (3) of Paragraph 2 of Article 24 of the Basic Law from the National People's Congress Standing Committee through the State Council.

21 May 1999

The Chinese Central Government refused to allow visits of US warships in Hong Kong. The Chinese Embassy in Yugoslavia was previously bombed by US–NATO warplanes on 08 May.

22 May 1999

Buddha's Birthday on the eighth day of the fourth lunar month became a public holiday in Hong Kong. The Hong Kong Buddhist Association made a request with the Chinese Central Government and the Buddhist Association of China to share the Buddha Tooth Relic for a seven-day worship ceremony in Hong Kong.

13 Jun 1999

A riot broke out at the Pillar Point Vietnamese Refugee Centre where tear gas was deployed by police officers; 17 people were injured.

21 Jun 1999

Exchange Fund Investment Limited launched a Hang Seng Index-linked unit trust to sell back local securities acquired by the HKSAR government in 1998. It was later named the Tracker Fund of Hong Kong; it went public on 12 November and became the first exchange traded fund in Hong Kong.

24 Jun 1999

Chief Executive Tung Chee-hwa (董建華) accepted a proposal prepared by the Working Group on Naming the Reunification Monument and Government House to rename (in Chinese) the Government House, effective 01 July.

The Court of First Instance affirmed the right of abode of non-Chinese nationals, given continuous residency of seven years or more in Hong Kong prior to the date of application.

26 Jun 1999

The National People's Congress Standing Committee, following an appeal submitted to the State Council by the Chief Executive for legal interpretation, held the Court of Final Appeal's failure to seek an interpretation on the Basic Law from the NPC Standing Committee and its own interpretation to be inconsistent with the original legislative intent. The NPC Standing Committee issued an interpretation on the following: 1) "persons of other parts of China" as stipulated in Paragraph 4 of Article 22 of the Basic Law, including children of Chinese nationality born in the Mainland to Hong Kong permanent residents, were required to go through legal formalities before entry into the HKSAR; and 2) "persons of Chinese nationality" as stipulated in Category (3) of Paragraph 2 of Article 24 of the Basic Law referred to those, at the time of birth, whose parents met the conditions set forth in Category (1) or Category (2) of Paragraph 2 of Article 24 of the Basic Law. These formed the basis upon which law courts of the HKSAR were to apply in relevant rulings going forward.

29 Jun 1999

The Court of First Instance ruled that voting restrictions on non-indigenous and married female inhabitants in the rural representative election of Shek Wu Tong Village on 02 March were in violation of the Hong Kong Bill of Rights Ordinance and the Sex Discrimination Ordinance, authorising a new election.

30 Jun 1999

The government-sponsored Innovation and Technology Fund was established with HK$5 billion to enhance Hong Kong's productivity and competitiveness through research and development and adoption of technology.

01 Jul 1999

The Reunification Monument, located at the Hong Kong Convention and Exhibition Centre, was unveiled.

Executive Councillor Leung Chun-ying (梁振英) became Council Convenor upon the retirement of his predecessor Chung Sze-yuen (鍾士元).

11 Jul 1999

The political group New Century Forum was established under the convenorship and deputy convenorship of Legislative Councillors Ng Ching-fai (吳清輝) and Ma Fung-kwok (馬逢國), respectively.

16 Jul 1999

The Legislative Council passed a resolution with respect to the right of abode proposed by the Secretary for Security with amendments to Schedule 1 of the Immigration Ordinance.

23 Jul 1999

The Chinese Medicine Ordinance 1999 was promulgated, establishing a Chinese Medicine Council as a statutory body responsible for regulatory measures on the trade of Chinese medicines.

The Factories and Industrial Undertakings (Amendment) Regulations 1999 was promulgated, effective 01 May 2001, requiring construction workers and container cargo handlers to receive basic safety training and hold a certificate (green card).

30 Jul 1999

Lingnan College was renamed Lingnan University; it became the first tertiary institution given a status upgrade since the establishment of the HKSAR.

17 Aug 1999

The Hong Kong Institute for Monetary and Financial Research was established by the Hong Kong Monetary Authority for research in the fields of monetary policy, banking and finance.

22 Aug 1999

The Hong Kong Observatory hoisted No. 8 Gale or Storm Signal for nearly 14.5 hours amid Typhoon Sam. During the typhoon, China Airlines fight CI642 from Bangkok crashed on landing, killing three people and injuring 203 others in the first fatal accident at the new airport. For gallantry in the evacuation, passengers Kwok Kam-ming (郭錦 明) and Tam Chung-keung (譚忠強) were awarded the Medal for Bravery (Gold) on 29 September.

26 Aug 1999

The Equal Opportunities Commission's *Formal Investigation Report on Secondary School Places Allocation System* was released, pressing the government on gender equality upon revealing systemic discrimination in the allocation system of secondary school places.

31 Aug 1999

The HKSAR government resumed ownership of the Cross-Harbour Tunnel upon expiry of a 30-year franchise; Hong Kong Tunnels and Highways Management Company Limited was appointed as an operator the following day.

16 Sep 1999

The Hong Kong Observatory hoisted No. 10 Hurricane Signal for nearly 11 hours amid Typhoon York which caused two deaths, over 500 injuries and 338 reports of fallen trees. It was the longest-running typhoon signal since the Second World War.

17 Sep 1999

The HKSAR government relaxed the one-branch-only rule applicable to foreign banks, allowing offices in a maximum of three different buildings without further restrictions on the number and location of back offices.

29 Sep 1999

Chief Executive Tung Chee-hwa（董建華）led a delegation of over 200 people to attend the 50th National Day celebration in Beijing.

Sep 1999

The government-sponsored Youth Employment and Training Programme was implemented in a six-month scheme of pre-employment training, work placement and career guidance to boost the employability of school leavers aged 15 to 19.

The University Grants Committee (UGC) launched a pilot scheme for yearly admission of 150 Mainland students in undergraduate programmes at UGC-funded tertiary institutions.

01 Oct 1999

In the celebration of the 50th anniversary of the founding of the People's Republic of China in Beijing, a group of Hong Kong delegates were invited to attend the ceremony at Tiananmen Tower. Floats from Hong Kong, Macao and Taiwan appeared for the first time in a National Day parade.

In the morning, a flag-raising ceremony in celebration of the 50th anniversary of the founding of the People's Republic of China was held at Golden Bauhinia Square officiated by Acting Chief Executive Elsie Leung Oi-sie（梁愛詩）in the presence of more than 400 guests, including Commissioner of the Ministry of Foreign Affairs in the HKSAR Ma Yuzhen（馬毓真）, Deputy Director of Xinhua News Agency (HKSAR Branch) Wang Fengchao（王鳳超）and Commander of Chinese People's Liberation Army Hong Kong Garrison Xiong Ziren（熊自仁）, among HKSAR officials, members of the Legislative Council and nearly 3,000 people in the audience. In the afternoon, Chief Executive Tung Chee-hwa（董建華）officiated at a celebration at the Hong Kong Stadium where military drills by the People's Liberation Army were performed for the first time outside the Mainland.

The Civil Aid Service established a command in an integration of three regional headquarters to enhance operational efficiency.

18 Oct 1999

The Post Office issued the first set of definitive stamps bearing the words "Hong Kong, China."

21 Oct 1999

Hong Kong joined the 13th General Meeting of the Pacific Economic Cooperation Council for a three-day conference in Manila, Philippines; Hong Kong was selected to host the 1999–2001 session.

Oct 1999

The HKSAR government conducted its first population survey on ethnic minority; results were released on 02 January 2000. Of the ethnic minority population of 280,000 in Hong Kong, Filipinos were the largest ethnic group at 158,000, accounting for 56.6%, followed by Indonesians at 40,000, accounting for 14.4%.

02 Nov 1999

The HKSAR government reached an agreement with The Walt Disney Company to build a theme park in Hong Kong with a total government investment of HK$22.45 billion. (Figure 285)

15 Nov 1999

The Hong Kong Stock Exchange's Growth Enterprise Market was established, providing an alternative avenue for emerging companies to raise funds outside the Main Board. Applicants were not required to meet the profitability requirements but to provide two years of business records.

16 Nov 1999

The HKSAR government began demolishing Shek Wu San Tsuen, a village in Sheung Shui, as part of the Ng Tung River improvement project. Groups of villagers, manufacturers and business owners, discontent with the Housing Department's compensation arrangement, formed a blockade and clashed with riot police, resulting in 10 injuries and 14 arrests.

17 Nov 1999

The University of Hong Kong's Vice Chancellor Cheng Yiu-chung (鄭耀宗), Acting Deputy Vice Chancellor Cheung Yau-kai (張佑啟), Professor of Ophthalmology So Kwok-fai (蘇國輝) and Director of the Institute of Molecular Biology Kung Hsiang-fu (孔祥復) and The Chinese University of Hong Kong's Professor of Chemistry Henry Wong Nai-ching (黃乃正) became the first five Hong Kong academicians elected to the Chinese Academy of Sciences since the establishment of the HKSAR.

28 Nov 1999

In the first District Council elections since the establishment of the HKSAR, 390 council members were elected (76 members were uncontested). The voter turnout rate was 35.82%. In addition, there were 102 appointed members; 27 ex-officio members were chairmen of Rural Committee. (Figure 286)

Figure 285
Chief Executive Tung Chee-hwa (董建華) announced an agreement with The Walt Disney Company to build a Disney theme park in Hong Kong. (Photo taken on 02 November 1999 and courtesy of HKSAR Government)

Figure 286
Chief Executive Tung Chee-hwa（董建華）opened the first ballot box at the Causeway Bay Community Centre. (Photo courtesy of Sing Tao News Corporation Limited)

Figure 287
British representative Alan Paul, left, and Chinese representative Wu Hongbo（吳紅波）, right, at the 47th meeting of the Sino-British Joint Liaison Group. (Photo courtesy of Sing Tao News Corporation Limited)

03 Dec 1999

The Court of Final Appeal ruled in *Lau Kong-yung*（劉港榕）*v. Director of Immigration* that relevant interpretation by the National People's Congress Standing Committee was legally binding in Hong Kong with effect from 01 July 1997.

04 Dec 1999

The 2.6-kilometre Lung Yeuk Tau Heritage Trail in Fanling was unveiled as the second heritage trail in the New Territories. It ran along historical buildings and sites, including the Tang Chung Ling Ancestral Hall, Tin Hau Temple, Lo Wai Walled Village and Shin Shut Study Hall.

10 Dec 1999

The Provision of Municipal Services (Reorganization) Ordinance was promulgated, establishing the provision of municipal services in place of the Provisional Regional Council and Provisional Urban Council (which ceased operation on 31 December).

15 Dec 1999

The Court of Final Appeal upheld a magistrate's decision to convict Ng Kung-siu（吳恭劭）and Lee Kin-yun （利建潤）for displaying defaced and damaged national and regional flags during a demonstration held by the Hong Kong Alliance in Support of Patriotic Democratic Movements of China on 01 January 1998. The Court ruled that Section 7 of the National Flag and National Emblem Ordinance and Section 7 of the Regional Flag and Regional Emblem Ordinance were consistent with the Basic Law.

17 Dec 1999

The HKSAR Admission of Talents Scheme was implemented to enhance Hong Kong's competitiveness by attracting and recruiting highly skilled or talented individuals under a quota system in which no employment contracts in advance were required.

21 Dec 1999

The Provisional Urban Council held its last meeting, followed by the last meeting of the Provisional Regional Council on 30 December.

The Sino-British Joint Liaison Group held its 47th and last meeting over two days at Government House before concluding on 01 January 2000 in accordance with the Sino-British Joint Declaration. (Figure 287)

23 Dec 1999

The Court of First Instance in a ruling affirmed the dissolution of the Provisional Urban Council and Provisional Regional Council was not in violation of Article 97 and Article 98 of the Basic Law.

31 Dec 1999

New Year celebrations were held across Hong Kong. Major events included Hong Kong Jockey Club's Millennium Extravaganza with the world's first horse race in the new millennium at the Happy Valley Racecourse starting at 0:45 a.m. on 01 January 2000 and the Municipal Councils' Millennium Carnival at Victoria Park (jointly presented by the Provisional Urban Council and Provisional Regional Council as their last event before dissolution).

The Central Coordinating Centre, established by the HKSAR government, was put into operation for contingency with potential problems arising from computer glitches at the beginning of the year 2000 (known as the Y2K bug). During the four days before and after New Year's Eve, an additional 13,000 civil servants were deployed as an emergency response unit. The Hong Kong Monetary Authority announced on 01 January 2000 that the banking system was under a smooth transition with the normal operation of ATMs, telephone banking services and credit card systems.

1999

The Hong Kong Direct Subsidy Scheme Schools Council was established to support member schools on the quality of education and autonomy on curriculum and school requirements.

01 Jan 2000

The Environment and Food Bureau was established to oversee newly established departments, namely the Food and Environmental Hygiene Department, the Agriculture, Fisheries and Conservation Department and the Environmental Protection Department. The Food and Environmental Hygiene Department assumed the functions of public hygiene, food safety and poultry inspection formerly with the Urban/Regional Service Department, Health Department, and Agriculture and Fisheries Department, respectively. On 01 July 2002, these functions were reinstituted with the Environment, Transport and Works Bureau and the Health, Welfare and Food Bureau.

The Home Affairs Bureau's Leisure and Cultural Services Department was established and made responsible for public recreational, sports, cultural facilities and related events.

07 Jan 2000

The Electronic Transactions Ordinance was promulgated, establishing a legal framework and a certification authority to facilitate commercial electronic transactions in support of e-business.

The first memorandum of understanding on the movement of waste was signed between the Environmental Protection Department (Hong Kong) and the State Environmental Protection Administration (the Mainland).

08 Jan 2000

The Housing Department suspended construction of two Home Ownership Scheme (HOS) residential buildings at Yuen Chau Kok in Shatin upon discovery of substandard (short) pilings. On 16 March, a decision by the Housing Authority called for demolition of the two buildings. Since 1999, substandard piling works had been uncovered at six construction sites of public rental and HOS housing.

15 Jan 2000

The 76-year franchise of Hongkong and Yaumati Ferry Company Limited ended; New World First Ferry Services Limited assumed eight of its routes.

18 Jan 2000

The HKSAR branch of Xinhua News Agency was renamed Liaison Office of the Central People's Government in the Hong Kong Special Administrative Region. President of the HKSAR branch of Xinhua News Agency Jiang Enzhu (姜恩柱) became its first director. In May 2001, it moved office from Queen's Road East in Happy Valley to The Westpoint, a high-rise in Sai Wan; its news division was assumed by Xinhua News Agency HKSAR Branch Limited. (Figure 288)

25 Jan 2000

The Federation of Hong Kong Filmmakers was founded, comprising 10 professional film associations; Jackie Chan (成龍) served as the founding convenor.

Figure 288
Jiang Enzhu (姜恩柱), former Director of the Hong Kong Branch of Xinhua News Agency, unveiled the Liaison Office of the Central People's Government in the HKSAR on Queen's Road East in Happy Valley and began serving as the first Director of the Liaison Office. (Photo taken on 18 January 2000 and courtesy of Xinhua News Agency)

Figure 289
Chief Executive Tung Chee-hwa (董建華), first left in front row, and Chairman of Hong Kong Exchanges and Clearing Limited (HKEX) Charles Lee Yeh-kwong (李業廣), second left in front row, in a ceremony marking the launch of HKEX as a publicly traded company. (Photo courtesy of South China Morning Post Publishers Limited)

27 Jan 2000

The Housing Authority released a consultation paper titled *Quality Housing: Partnering for Change*, outlining 40 recommendations for improvement on public housing, including the quality of piling works.

28 Jan 2000

The Organized and Serious Crimes Ordinance (Amendment) Ordinance 1999 was promulgated, strengthening the anti-money laundering efforts in Hong Kong.

10 Feb 2000

The HKSAR government announced a lump-sum grant model to replace the original funding and subsidy mechanism for social service organisations.

18 Feb 2000

Technology firm TOM Group became a publicly listed company on Hong Kong Stock Exchange's Growth Enterprise Market; it was 690 times oversubscribed amid a tech investment boom (dotcom stocks) in Hong Kong.

23 Feb 2000

The Widened Local Resettlement Scheme was implemented, allowing Vietnamese refugees and eligible Vietnamese boat people who had arrived and remained in Hong Kong before 09 January 1998 to apply for permanent resident status.

29 Feb 2000

Hong Kong-based Pacific Century CyberWorks Limited, owned by businessman Richard Li Tzar-kai (李澤楷), became the largest shareholder of Hong Kong Telecommunications Limited after acquiring a 54% stake from Cable & Wireless Group for US$35.9 billion.

03 Mar 2000

The Elections (Corrupt and Illegal Conduct) Ordinance was promulgated, ensuring fair and clean elections through regulations on campaign advertisements, contributions and expenses, including mandatory declaration on all donations.

06 Mar 2000

The Hong Kong Exchanges and Clearing Limited was established through the amalgamation of the Stock Exchange, Futures Exchange, and Securities Clearing Company Limited. On 27 June, Hong Kong Exchanges and Clearing Limited was listed on the Stock Exchange, becoming the first exchange company listed in Hong Kong. (Figure 289)

09 Mar 2000

| The Federation for Continuing Education in Tertiary Institutions' Project Yi Jin was launched, allowing Secondary 5 school leavers and adult learners to pursue higher education through a one-year full-time or two-year part-time bridging programme equivalent to a high school diploma upon completion. The programme began on 09 October.

21 Mar 2000

| The Hong Kong Direct Subsidy Scheme Schools Council was established to uphold the autonomy of direct subsidy scheme schools and improve the education quality of its member schools.

27 Mar 2000

| The Culture and Heritage Commission was established as an advisory body on government policies and funding priorities regarding the development of cultural affairs and the arts.

28 Mar 2000

| The HKSAR government announced an amount of HK$1,014.4 billion with the Exchange Fund as of 31 December 1999, an increase of 10.1% year-on-year, ranking third in the world after Japan and the Mainland.

Mar 2000

| The HKSAR government began downsizing the civil service—from 198,000 posts in 2000 to 172,000 posts in October 2002 and 160,000 posts in June 2005.

| The Sheung Shui Slaughterhouse became operational as one of the largest and most advanced in Asia at a cost of HK$1.8 billion.

| The Antiquities and Monuments Office in collaboration with Peking University's Department of Archaeology uncovered pottery of the Shang and Zhou dynasties, five-baht coins of the Han Dynasty and tombs of the Song and Ming dynasties in an excavation of the So Kwun Wat site in Tuen Mun. In 2008–2009, it partnered with Chinese Academy of Social Sciences' Institute of Archaeology for another excavation at the site where cultural deposits of the Shang Dynasty, Spring and Autumn Period, Eastern Han Dynasty and Ming Dynasty were discovered, including bronze ear cups, bronze plates and iron axes of the Eastern Han Dynasty in Tomb No. 6.

07 Apr 2000

| The Education and Manpower Bureau introduced a language benchmark test, requiring mandatory qualification with current and prospective teachers of English and Putonghua by a specified time and within the first year of employment, respectively. Teachers must pass the test before they were allowed to continue teaching in the respective subjects.

| Russell Street in Causeway Bay was designated as the first pedestrian-only avenue in a street improvement project.

22 Apr 2000

| The HKSAR government issued a statement on Taipei's Chung Hwa Travel Service in Hong Kong, emphasising Taiwanese organisations must operate in Hong Kong under the "One China" principle and in an unofficial capacity.

27 Apr 2000

| For the first time, Hong Kong hosted the meeting of the Asia-Pacific Economic Cooperation Tourism Working Group. It was held over two days, with representatives from 21 countries and regions and a focus on the drafting of a tourism charter.

30 Apr 2000

| The bronze-cast ox and monkey heads (of 12 Chinese zodiac animals) of the Old Summer Palace were put on auction by Christie's Hong Kong. The tiger head was auctioned off by Sotheby's Hong Kong on 02 May. These were bought by the China Poly Group Corporation and returned to the Chinese government.

Apr 2000

The Hong Kong Observatory issued four Red and one Black rainstorm signals amid a record total rainfall of 547.7 millimetres in the month of April since 1884.

Literary Century started publication as a journal of literature, interviews, book reviews and criticism; it suspended publication in December before resuming in January 2002.

01 May 2000

The Labour Day Golden Week was implemented with seven days of public holiday in the Mainland. In the first two days, 246 Mainland tour groups, totalling about 7,000 people, arrived in Hong Kong via Lo Wu in a new record.

05 May 2000

The Hong Kong Monetary Authority issued its first guidelines on virtual banks, requiring substantive services with physical presence in the form of an office and compliance with the principle of prudence applicable to traditional banks.

09 May 2000

The Agriculture, Fisheries and Conservation Department confiscated a pet monkey named Golden Eagle from owner Chan Yat-biu (also known as Uncle Chan) (陳日標) in violation of the Wild Animals Protection Ordinance. Golden Eagle was subsequently placed in the Sheung Shui Animal Management Centre. On 17 July, a discretion on humanitarian grounds was made in a ruling by the San Po Kong Magistracy, allowing Chan to keep Golden Eagle as the first licenced owner of a pet monkey in Hong Kong.

16 May 2000

The *Railway Development Strategy 2000* was released by the government as a blueprint leading up to 2016 for increasing rail coverage by 70% with the Island Line Extension, Shatin to Central Link, Kowloon Southern Link, Northern Link, Regional Express Line and Port Rail Line.

17 May 2000

The Cyberport Project Agreement was signed between Hong Kong Cyberport Management Company Limited (wholly owned by the HKSAR government) and Pacific Century CyberWorks Limited. Located in Telegraph Bay, Pok Fu Lam, Cyberport was a 24-hectare technology hub developed, managed and operated by Hong Kong Cyberport Management Company.

18 May 2000

The renovation of Chi Lin Nunnery, a Buddhist nunnery located in Diamond Hill, was completed. The main hall was built with traditional tongue-and-groove woodworking techniques; together with the adjacent Lotus Pond Garden, it formed a large Tang-style architectural complex.

22 May 2000

Tony Leung Chiu-wai (梁朝偉) became the first Hong Kong actor to win Best Actor at the 53rd Cannes Film Festival for his leading role in the film *In the Mood for Love*.

26 May 2000

The Road Traffic (Traffic Control) (Amendment) (No. 2) Regulation 2000 was promulgated, prohibiting the use of hand-held communication devices while driving.

27 May 2000

The Discovery Bay Tunnel was opened to traffic, connecting Discovery Bay, Tung Chung New Town and Hong Kong International Airport.

31 May 2000

Seven NASDAQ-listed companies—including Microsoft, Starbucks and Intel—started their first day of public trading on the Hong Kong Stock Exchange.

May 2000

The 277.2-metre Millennium Dragon Lantern, a giant traditional Chinese lantern specially made in celebration of the new millennium, was recognised by Guinness World Records as the largest dragon lantern ever made.

01 Jun 2000

The Pillar Point Vietnamese Refugees Centre in Tuen Mun as the last refugee camp in Hong Kong was officially closed. (Figure 290)

HKSAR began employing government workers with yearly contracts (renewable upon completion) and inaugurated a Civil Service Provident Fund Scheme in place of the previous pension system for permanent staff.

03 Jun 2000

Vice Chairman of the Chinese People's Political Consultative Conference Ann Tse-kai (T. K. Ann) (安子介) passed away at the age of 88. His funeral was held on 12 June, making him the first person from Hong Kong to be given a state funeral.

04 Jun 2000

A riot broke out at Hei Ling Chau Addiction Treatment Centre and lasted until the following morning; 33 detainees (including 13 Vietnamese), 24 members of the Correctional Services Department and eight police officers sustained injuries. Fifty-four detainees were later charged with rioting, arson, aggravated assault and criminal damage.

A Hong Kong horse, named Fairy King Prawn, won the Yasuda Kinen race in Tokyo, Japan; it became the first Hong Kong horse to win a race overseas.

18 Jun 2000

The Journalists' Code of Professional Ethics—requiring journalists to handle news materials in a fair and objective manner, ensure correct reporting, avoid obscenity, indecency and sensationalism, respect personal privacy and protect sources of information—was jointly formulated by the Hong Kong Journalists Association, Hong Kong News Executives' Association, Hong Kong Federation of Journalists, and Hong Kong Press Photographers Association.

Figure 290
Members of the Civil Aid Service placed a closing sign at the entrance of Pillar Point Vietnamese Refugees Centre in Tuen Mun in the early hours of 01 June 2000, ending 25 years of Vietnamese boat people in Hong Kong. (Photo courtesy of Sing Tao News Corporation Limited)

30 Jun 2000

The Court of First Instance ruled in a case regarding the right of abode of Mainlanders that the interpretation issued on 26 June 1999 by the National People's Congress Standing Committee in accordance with the Basic Law should form the basis of policy, except those cases already accepted by the Director of Immigration.

02 Jul 2000

A four-alarm fire broke out in stilt houses at Tai O on Lantau Island and lasted for five hours, destroying nearly 100 houses and affecting about 300 residents.

07 Jul 2000

The Broadcasting Ordinance was promulgated, establishing a fair, precise and business-friendly regulatory regime in the television industry.

The Intellectual Property (Miscellaneous Amendments) Ordinance 2000 was promulgated, effective 01 April 2001, expanding the coverage of copyright infringement stipulated in the Copyright Ordinance to the possession beyond dealings of infringed products. It also prohibited the possession of video recording equipment by unauthorised persons in cinemas or performance venues.

The University of Hong Kong's Public Opinion Programme Director Robert Chung Ting-yiu（鍾庭耀）in an article asserted that pressure was exerted by a government middleman to discourage further surveys on the Chief Executive and government performance. Following a three-member panel of inquiry appointed by the HKU Council, an investigation report was released on 01 September with a conclusion that the allegations could not be verified.

25 Jul 2000

The Hong Kong Press Council was founded with membership of 11 newspapers and two professional journalist groups. On 01 September, it began processing public complaints about violations of privacy by newspapers.

Jul 2000

The first Voluntary Retirement Scheme for civil servants was introduced, enabling staff of 59 grades with identified or anticipated staff surplus to retire voluntarily with pension benefits and compensation to reduce the number of civil servants.

02 Aug 2000

Room 1301 of the Immigration Tower in Wan Chai was set on fire by a group of protesters claiming the right of abode. Senior Immigration Officer Leung Kam-kwong（梁錦光）and a protester were killed while 46 people were injured in the most serious case of arson in a government department office. On 22 September, Leung was posthumously awarded the Gold Medal for Bravery. On 02 February 2002, in a Court of First Instance ruling, seven protesters were found guilty of murder and manslaughter and were sentenced to life imprisonment or 12–13 years in prison.

16 Aug 2000

The Chinese Medicine Council of Hong Kong began accepting applications for registration of Chinese medicine practitioners, closing on 30 December. On 29 November 2002, it announced a list of the first 2,384 registered Chinese medicine practitioners.

17 Aug 2000

PCCW was formed in a merger between Pacific Century CyberWorks Limited and Hong Kong Telecommunications Limited with a combined market value of US$47.6 billion as the fourth largest listed company by market value in Hong Kong.

A branch of Madame Tussauds London was opened at the Peak Tower in Hong Kong, featuring seven galleries and 100 wax statues of celebrities including Li Ka-shing（李嘉誠）, Lee Lai-shan（李麗珊）, Jackie Chan（成龍）and Michelle Yeoh（楊紫瓊）.

Figure 291
The *Shenzhou* spacecraft on display at Hong Kong Space Museum. (Photo taken on 22 August 2000 and courtesy of Sing Tao News Corporation Limited)

22 Aug 2000

The Chinese Aerospace Science and Technology Exhibition began at Hong Kong Science Museum, ending on 22 October. It dispayed a series of real models and replicas of launch rockets and satellites, including the *Shenzhou* spacecraft and a HKSAR regional flag following a trip to the orbit. (Figure 291)

23 Aug 2000

Vice Chairman of political party Democratic Alliance for the Betterment of Hong Kong Gary Cheng Kai-nam (程介南) was exposed for abuse of position and failing to declare his personal assets when he became a Legislative Councillor. On 19 September, he resigned from the Council and was removed from his political party. On 20 December 2001, he was convicted of misconduct in public office and accepting advantages, and was sentenced to 18 months in prison.

24 Aug 2000

Yu Man-hon (庾文翰), a teenager with learning difficulties, disappeared after leaving Hong Kong via the Lo Wu border crossing without an ID card. The incident raised public concern in both Hong Kong and the Mainland about insufficient immigration control and measures. In a phone conversation, Chief Executive Tung Chee-hwa (董建華) and his counterpart in Shenzhen pledged to locate the teenager who remained missing.

31 Aug 2000

The Hong Kong Museum of Coastal Defence, located at the Lei Yue Mun Fort built in 1887 in Shau Kei Wan, was opened to the public.

01 Sep 2000

The One School Social Worker for Each School policy was implemented in 450 secondary schools to provide more comprehensive student counselling.

08 Sep 2000

The 40-year-old *Tin Tin Daily News* ceased publication.

10 Sep 2000

The second Legislative Council elections were held, returning 60 members, including 24 from geographical constituencies, 30 from functional constituencies, and six by the Election Committee. The turnout rates were 43.57%, 56.5% and 95.53%, respectively.

12 Sep 2000

New arrangements were introduced to provide civil servants and citizens who died while performing exceptional acts of bravery with permanent burial grounds at Gallant Garden.

15 Sep 2000

Team Hong Kong, China took part in the 27th Summer Olympic Games in Sydney, Australia under the name Hong Kong, China for the first time in the Olympics.

25 Sep 2000

The Hong Kong Monetary Authority launched the world's first Real-Time Gross Settlement system for foreign exchange transactions, allowing timely settlement of US dollar-HK dollar transactions in the Asian time zone without a 12-hour wait for settlement in the New York time zone.

28 Sep 2000

The Education Commission released its *Reform Proposals for the Education System in Hong Kong*, proposing 1) "through-train" programmes between primary and secondary schools sharing a similar educational approach, 2) implementation of a three-year senior secondary school system, 3) provision of a diversified and career-related curriculum, and 4) introduction of assessment tests in Chinese, English and Mathematics in primary and junior secondary schools.

The Chinese government signed a memorandum of understanding with International Bank for Reconstruction and Development and International Finance Corporation—sister organisations of the World Bank Group—on establishing offices in Hong Kong.

04 Oct 2000

The second-term Legislative Council of the HKSAR held its first meeting; Rita Fan Hsu Lai-tai（范徐麗泰）was elected as President.

05 Oct 2000

The MTR Corporation Limited—under the majority ownership of the HKSAR government—was officially listed on the Hong Kong Stock Exchange.

13 Oct 2000

The Arrangements on the Establishment of a Reciprocal Notification Mechanism between the Mainland Public Security Authorities and the Hong Kong Police was signed, effective 01 January 2001, allowing notification between Hong Kong and the Mainland regarding compulsory measures (including prosecutions) against residents as well as unnatural deaths of residents of the other side.

14 Oct 2000

The District Football Teams Training Scheme was launched by the Leisure and Cultural Services Department in conjunction with the Hong Kong Football Association, establishing local football teams across the 18 districts of Hong Kong.

18 Oct 2000

Team Hong Kong, China participated in the 11th Paralympic Games in Sydney, Australia, winning eight gold, three silver and seven bronze medals.

23 Oct 2000

The Hong Kong Stock Exchange launched its third-generation Automatic Order Matching and Execution System, capable of handling 200 transactions per second, 1.6 times faster than its predecessor.

30 Oct 2000

The World Health Organization announced that poliomyelitis had been eradicated in the western Pacific region, including Hong Kong.

01 Nov 2000

The Immigration Department announced that Chinese passport holders were required only one year, instead of two years, of overseas residency before being allowed to work in Hong Kong. This change was to attract overseas Chinese nationals to Hong Kong.

05 Nov 2000

Chairman of the Chinese People's Political Consultative Conference Li Ruihuan（李瑞環）arrived in Hong Kong for a five-day visit and attended the 100th anniversary celebration of the Chinese General Chamber of Commerce.

11 Nov 2000

The Lingnan Garden, located at Lai Chi Kok Park in Kowloon, was opened to the public; it was the first Lingnan-style architectural design in Hong Kong.

25 Nov 2000

The Leisure and Cultural Services Department launched an exhibition called Contemporary Hong Kong Art 2000. It put on display 500 art pieces at Hong Kong Museum of Art until 27 December. These included sculptures, installations, graphic designs, Western paintings, seal carvings and Chinese calligraphy by Hong Kong artists Luis Chan Fok-sin（陳福善）, Lui Shou-kwan（呂壽琨）, Hon Chi-fun（韓志勳）, Cheung Yee（張義）, Van Lau（文樓）, Wucius Wong（王無邪）, Chu Hing-wah（朱興華）, Choi Yan-chi（蔡仞姿）, Lui Chun-kwong（呂振光）, Ho Siu-kee（何兆基）, Wong Shun-kit（王純傑）, Chan Yuk-keung（陳育強）and Kum Chi-keung（甘志強）.

Nov 2000

The Hong Kong Archaeological Society in conjunction with the Guangdong Provincial Institute of Cultural Relics and Archaeology began a two-month excavation at the Hok Chau Leng site of Mong Tseng Wai in Yuen Long. Pottery and flint tools from the Neolithic period, pieces of building structure from the Song Dynasty, as well as building components, ceramics and copper coins from the Ming Dynasty, were discovered.

01 Dec 2000

The Mandatory Provident Fund System was implemented, requiring contributions in a retirement scheme by employers and employees between the ages of 18 and 65 under permanent or temporary employment (including self-employment), unless exempt otherwise. It aimed to provide employees with retirement savings withdrawable upon the age of 65.

The European Union's Justice and Home Affairs Council agreed in principle to grant HKSAR passport holders visa-free access.

02 Dec 2000

The Ngau Tam Mei Water Treatment Works in Yuen Long became operational with a daily fresh water supply capacity of about 230,000 cubic metres for Yuen Long, Tin Shui Wai, Ngau Tam Mei, San Tin and Mai Po.

09 Dec 2000

The Electronic Service Delivery Scheme was launched, allowing access to more than 60 government services through the Internet, including payment of government bills, tax returns, voter registration, driving licence renewal, and change of personal particulars.

12 Dec 2000

The Chinese Culinary Institute was opened for full-time and part-time courses on Chinese cuisine and catering management.

16 Dec 2000

The Chinese University of Hong Kong's Faculty of Arts held its first presentation ceremony of the Global Youth Chinese Literary Award for the New Century.

The Hong Kong Heritage Museum in Sha Tin was opened as the largest public museum with six permanent exhibitions and six special galleries. The following day, Ceremony and Celebration: The Grand Weddings of the Qing Emperors was inaugurated in an exhibition of more than 100 artefacts of state banquets from the Palace Museum. As part of the celebration, restaurants in Hong Kong were invited to serve the imperial cuisine of the Qing Dynasty.

18 Dec 2000

The Hongkong and Shanghai Banking Corporation began issuing new HK$1,000 banknotes bearing enhanced security features, including a 3mm vertical shiny metal thread, a very bright watermark showing the number 1000, and red, blue and green fibres visible under ultraviolet light. Beginning 20 June 2001, new HK$1,000 banknotes with the same security features were also issued by the Bank of China (Hong Kong) and Standard Chartered Bank.

22 Dec 2000

The Court of Final Appeal ruled that restrictions on the voting rights and candidacies of non-indigenous inhabitants in village elections of the New Territories were in violation of Article 21(a) of the Hong Kong Bill of Rights Ordinance. The law stipulated that representation in the capacity of a village representative should apply to both indigenous and non-indigenous inhabitants.

2000

DJ Ray Cordeiro, commonly known as Uncle Ray, who began hosting music programmes on Radio Rediffusion and Radio Television Hong Kong in 1949 and 1964, respectively, in a career spanning 64 years by 2017, was named the World's Most Durable DJ by the Guinness World Records.

03 Jan 2001

The Hong Kong Film Archive in Sai Wan Ho was inaugurated; it was opened to the public on the following day. Built at a cost of HK$185 million, it housed over 3,800 films and more than 80,000 pieces of film memorabilia such as posters, film still shots, scripts and records of reviews.

11 Jan 2001

The International Monetary Fund (IMF) Office in Hong Kong was inaugurated as an affiliate of the IMF Beijing Office for economic surveillance and research in Hong Kong.

The China Mathematical Olympiad was held for the first time in Hong Kong where local contestants won a second-place prize and 14 third-place prizes.

12 Jan 2001

Chief Secretary for Administration Anson Chan Fang On-sang (陳方安生) announced her retirement effective the end of April with approval from the Chinese Central Government and the Chief Executive of the HKSAR. She was the first principal government official to resign since the establishment of the HKSAR.

15 Jan 2001

The Women's Commission was established as an advisory body on women's issues and long-term strategies in support of the advancement of women.

22 Jan 2001

Joyful Town, an amusement park formerly known as the Happy Dragon Recreation Park in Tai Wai, was closed to accommodate the expansion of Tai Wai Station.

23 Jan 2001

The Housing Authority relaxed the criteria of existing public housing tenants in terms of household size, allowing family members to live together or separately in public housing with greater flexibility. It aimed to provide relief for overcrowded households, provided they meet the household income and asset threshold.

06 Feb 2001

UN Human Rights Committee Vice Chairman Prafullachandra Natwarlal Bhagwati and member Christine Chanet arrived in Hong Kong for a five-day visit at the invitation of the HKSAR government. Bhagwati pointed out that the human rights in Hong Kong were satisfactory compared to many other places in the world.

09 Feb 2001

Permanent Representative of Hong Kong, China to the World Trade Organization (WTO) Stuart Harbinson was elected as 2001 Chairman of the General Council (WTO's highest decision-making body).

23 Feb 2001

The Hung Shing Temple on the island of Kau Sai Chau in Sai Kung was named an Outstanding Project in the UNESCO Asia-Pacific Awards for Cultural Heritage Conservation in 2000. It was the first heritage conservation project in Hong Kong to receive the award.

26 Feb 2001

The District Court ruled in favour of a plaintiff for pregnancy-related discrimination and ordered compensation for pecuniary losses resulting from her resignation. It marked the first pregnancy discrimination case upheld by a court of law in Hong Kong.

27 Feb 2001

The Buildings Department in conjunction with the Lands Department and Planning Department issued the guidelines on eco-friendly buildings, allowing exemption from restrictions on gross floor or covered areas stipulated in the Buildings Ordinance. The initiative aimed to promote environmentally friendly design in new buildings.

03 Mar 2001

The first Language Proficiency Assessment for Teachers in English and Putonghua was held for 650 test-takers.

14 Mar 2001

Police officer Tsui Po-ko (徐步高) slayed fellow officer Leung Shing-yan (梁成恩) and snatched his service revolver. Tsui used the revolver to rob the branch of Hang Seng Bank at Belvedere Garden in Tsuen Wan and killed Pakistani security guard Zafar Iqbal Khan. Leung was posthumously awarded the Medal for Bravery (Silver); Khan was awarded the Medal for Bravery (Gold).

15 Mar 2001

The first census since the establishment of the HKSAR began; it was concluded on 27 March. Results showed a total population of 6,708,389, including 6,523,851 usual (permanent) residents and 184,538 mobile (temporary) residents.

21 Mar 2001

Ji Peiding (吉佩定) was appointed as Commissioner of the Ministry of Foreign Affairs of the People's Republic of China in the HKSAR. He remained in the post until 25 July 2003.

26 Mar 2001

The film *Crouching Tiger, Hidden Dragon,* directed by Ang Lee (李安) and starring Chow Yun-fat (周潤發) and Michelle Yeoh (楊紫瓊), won four awards at the 73rd Academy Awards (Oscars), including Best Cinematography and Best Art Direction by Peter Pau (鮑德熹) and Timmy Yip (葉錦添), respectively, marking a record for a Chinese-language film. (Figures 292 and 293)

01 Apr 2001

Hong Kong Tourist Association was renamed as Hong Kong Tourism Board for a greater role in promoting Hong Kong as a world-class destination globally.

11 Apr 2001

The Development Bank of Singapore (DBS) acquired Dao Heng Bank and Overseas Trust Bank from Guoco Group for HK$44 billion. On 21 July 2003, a consolidation of Dao Heng Bank, Overseas Trust Bank and DBS's subsidiary Kwong On Bank was announced, forming DBS Bank (Hong Kong) Limited.

18 Apr 2001

For the first time, Hong Kong hosted six days of preliminary rounds of the ninth National Games and 2001 National Wushu & Sanda Championships at Queen Elizabeth Stadium.

25 Apr 2001

Hong Kong bowler Sunny Hui Cheung-kwok (許長國) won the first World Bowling Masters in Abu Dhabi, United Arab Emirates. He was ranked the world's top bowler.

01 May 2001

The Urban Renewal Authority was established in place of the Land Development Corporation. It released a 20-year master urban redevelopment plan with 25 projects still in progress and 200 new projects.

Figure 293
Hong Kong cinematographer Peter Pau Tak-hei (鮑德熹), centre, his actress sister Nina Paw Hee-ching (鮑 起 靜) and brother-in-law Henry Fong Ping (方平), after winning Best Cinematography at the 73rd Academy Awards. (Photo taken on 27 March 2001 and courtesy of South China Morning Post Publishers Limited)

Figure 292
Hong Kong art director Timmy Yip Kam-tim (葉錦添) won Best Art Direction at the 73rd Academy Awards. (Photo taken on 26 March 2001 and courtesy of Kevin Winter/Hulton Archive via Getty Images)

Figure 294
Financial Secretary Antony Leung Kam-chung (梁 錦 松) dotted the eyes of Brand Hong Kong's flying dragon logo at Whitty Street Depot. (Photo taken on 11 May 2001 and courtesy of South China Morning Post Publishers Limited)

08 May 2001

The seventh FORTUNE Global Forum began for a three-day conference at the Hong Kong Convention and Exhibition Centre with over 600 political and business leaders, including President of China Jiang Zemin(江澤民), former US President Bill Clinton and Prime Minister of Thailand Thaksin Shinawatra.

10 May 2001

Chief Executive Tung Chee-hwa (董建華) unveiled Brand Hong Kong at the closing ceremony of the seventh FORTUNE Global Forum. Its flying dragon logo, along with the slogan "Asia's World City," symbolised Hong Kong's ambitions and innovative thinking and remained in use for many years to come. (Figure 294)

The Hong Kong Jockey Club Institute of Chinese Medicine was established by the Hong Kong Applied Science and Technology Research Institute; it aimed to develop Hong Kong into a global Chinese medicine centre. It was dissolved on 28 September 2011.

11 May 2001

The Rehabilitation Centres Ordinance was promulgated for implementation of the Correctional Services Department's Rehabilitation Programme with young offenders aged 14–21. On 01 August 2002, Lai Chi Rehabilitation Centre on Lantau Island became operational and took in its first young offender.

15 May 2001

The Hong Kong University of Science and Technology's Institute of NanoMaterials and NanoTechnology was established as Hong Kong's first research facility on nanotechnology.

16 May 2001

The Hong Kong Central Library in Causeway Bay was inaugurated and opened for public access the following day. It became Hong Kong's largest and main public library, surpassing the City Hall Public Library, in terms of its size and book collection in a 12-storey building with a total floor area of 33,800 square metres at a cost of HK$690 million.

22 May 2001

Four robbers, including fugitive Kwai Ping-hung (季炳雄), opened fire on three officers of the Police Special Task Force on Waterloo Road in Mong Kok; two officers were critically wounded.

23 May 2001

The Legislative Council passed a motion condemning Japan's attempt to distort its history of military aggression in textbooks. It urged the Japanese government to renounce militarism, take responsibility for its past, make formal apologies and compensate victims of the Japanese invasion during the Second World War.

25 May 2001

The Council on Human Reproductive Technology was established to regulate the provision of reproductive technology procedures, including embryo research and surrogacy arrangement.

May 2001

Hong Kong was struck by the Influenza A virus (commonly known as avian influenza). On 18 May, a government order was issued to close all live chicken stalls for three days of disinfection and cleansing, and suspend the import of live chickens from the Mainland, followed by the disposal of all market-age chickens from local farms on 21 May. The import of live poultry was resumed on 15 June.

01 Jun 2001

The Admission of Mainland Professionals Scheme was launched in a government bid to enhance Hong Kong's competitiveness by attracting an inflow of qualified talent.

The Air Pollution Control (Vehicle Design Standards) (Emission) (Amendment) Regulation 2001 was promulgated, requiring all newly registered taxis to run on liquified petroleum gas or unleaded petrol starting 01 August.

04 Jun 2001

The World Association of Newspapers' 2001 Congress began at the Hong Kong Convention and Exhibition Centre.

06 Jun 2001

The 17th International Architecture Exhibition began in a four-day event at the Hong Kong Convention and Exhibition Centre.

07 Jun 2001

Hong Kong's first Super Cyber Centre, located in the Canton Road Government Offices, became operational in a joint arrangement by the Home Affairs Department, Information Technology and Broadcasting Bureau, and Information Technology Services Department. It was equipped with 100 Internet-connected personal computers for public access and spaces available for government and NGO workshops.

08 Jun 2001

Hong Kong participated for the first time in the 49th Venice Biennale, an exhibition of international contemporary art. Artists Oscar Ho Siu-Kee (何兆基), Leung Chi-Wo (梁志) and Ellen Pau (鮑藹倫) were invited by curator Chang Tsong-zung (張頌仁) for a showcase of Hong Kong's unique culture under the theme "Magic at Street Level."

22 Jun 2001

The High Court ruled that gender segregation in the allocation of secondary school places under the Education Department since 1978 was in violation of the Sex Discrimination Ordinance. On 25 April 2002, gender-inclusive allocation was implemented.

Jun 2001

The Hong Kong Paralympians Fund was established in support of athletes with disabilities by providing financial assistance during and after their career in sports. It was implemented on 02 March 2002.

03 Jul 2001

The final phase of deregulation of interest rate by the Hong Kong Monetary Authority covering Hong Kong dollar savings and current accounts took effect, allowing interest rates on all types of deposits to be determined by competitive market forces. Some banks responded by imposing minimum balance requirements.

06 Jul 2001

Hong Kong relaxed its entry requirements for undergraduate programmes at local universities among Mainland students. It no longer required a specified scholarship or admission scheme, thereby allowing study in Hong Kong with other private scholarship schemes or own funding.

09 Jul 2001

The Hong Kong Housing Authority launched a pilot Rent Allowance for the Elderly Scheme, providing 500 eligible persons waitlisted for public housing with financial support for private housing to help meet their immediate needs.

13 Jul 2001

The Curriculum Development Council's report *Learning to learn: The Way Forward in Curriculum Development* was released as a guideline on school curriculum over the next decade.

20 Jul 2001

The Court of Final Appeal ruled that Chong Fung-yuen (莊豐源), a Chinese citizen born in the HKSAR to non-residents of Hong Kong, had the right of abode in Hong Kong—a decision reached upon interpretation of Article 24(2)(1) of the Basic Law with reference to its legislative intent under the protocol of common law judicial interpretation—asserting that "Chinese citizens born in Hong Kong before or after the establishment of the HKSAR" shall be permanent residents. The Legislative Affairs Commission of the National People's Congress (NPC) Standing Committee expressed concern, citing inconsistency with previous interpretations by the NPC Standing Committee.

The Court of Final Appeal ruled in the case of Tam Nga-yin (談雅然) that Article 24(2)(3) of the Basic Law was not applicable to adopted children, causing widespread controversy. In October, she was issued a One-way Permit for the right of abode in Hong Kong by Mainland authorities.

The Chief Executive Election Ordinance was promulgated, providing for the term of office, temporary substitution and electoral arrangement with respect to the Chief Executive.

The Fixed Penalty (Public Cleanliness Offences) Ordinance was promulgated, effective 27 May 2002, allowing direct enforcement with a fixed fine of HK$600 for littering, spitting or other unhygienic conducts under a streamlined penal system in which court hearings were no longer necessary.

25 Jul 2001

The Hong Kong–Guangdong Co-operation Joint Conference held its fourth meeting at the Government House where a letter of intent was signed to signify collaborative efforts for industrial development in Nansha, Guangzhou. In addition, Hong Kong and Guangdong reached consensus on further cooperation regarding border control, environmental protection, quality of water supply, communication networks and a potential partnership between Hong Kong International Airport and Zhuhai International Airport.

The Food and Environmental Hygiene Department made its first monthly Rest-Day Clean-Up—in which stalls of live poultry were required to destroy all remaining stock and close by noon for facility sanitisation in the afternoon and evening.

15 Aug 2001

The Civil Aviation Department, for the first time, granted approval for three-month operation of an airship with aerial advertising and promotion in connection with a fundraising event.

21 Aug 2001

The Customs and Excise Department seized more than 4.1 million illicit cigarettes, worth HK$5.76 million and subject to import duties of about HK$3.31 million, at Kwai Chung Customhouse Cargo Examination Compound in the first capture of smuggled goods with mobile X-ray vehicle scanning systems.

24 Aug 2001

The last temporary housing area at Sha Kok Mei in Sai Kung was cleared, marking the end of 41 years of Hong Kong's temporary housing establishment.

30 Aug 2001

The Hong Kong Museum of History opened its permanent exhibition called The Hong Kong Story. It entailed a showcase of 400 million years of history, culture and change in the natural environment up until 30 June 1997 prior to the establishment of the HKSAR.

03 Sep 2001

Amid a slow recovery in the private property market, sales of residential flats under Housing Authority's Home Ownership Scheme (HOS) and Hong Kong Housing Society's Subsidised Housing Scheme were suspended until the end of June 2002. Sales of HOS flats resumed on 01 July 2002.

13 Sep 2001

The Global Summit of Women 2001 was held in Hong Kong with 400 delegates from 28 countries and regions on the topic of how women could use information technology to transcend boundaries.

18 Sep 2001

The Chief Executive-in-Council endorsed a Kowloon–Canton Railway proposal to adopt a tunnel option designed to preserve the Long Valley wetland in the construction of the Sheung Shui-Lok Ma Chau Spur Line.

24 Sep 2001

The All-China Journalists' Association issued an Arrangement of Hong Kong and Macau News Correspondents in the Mainland sanctioned by the Chinese Central Government, allowing media outlets of Hong Kong and Macao to establish Mainland bureaus.

28 Sep 2001

The Civil Aviation Department introduced new security measures in response to the 9/11 terrorist attacks in the United States, prohibiting air passengers from carrying knives or sharp objects in aircraft cabins or airport restricted areas where these items were also no longer available for sale in shops.

Sep 2001

The Guangdong Provincial Public Security Bureau's Entry and Exit Administration began accepting applications for residency in Hong Kong from people born out of wedlock to Hong Kong parents.

01 Oct 2001

The Bank of China Group restructured its businesses in Hong Kong, establishing Bank of China (Hong Kong) Limited through a consolidation of 10 Chinese banks, namely Bank of China Hong Kong Branch, seven Mainland-incorporated banks (Kwangtung Provincial Bank, Sin Hua Bank Limited, China & South Sea Bank, Kincheng Banking Corporation, China State Bank Limited, National Commercial Bank Limited and Yien Yieh Commercial Bank) and Hong Kong-incorporated Hua Chiao Commercial Bank and Po Sang Bank.

03 Oct 2001

The PayThruPost payment system became operational, allowing settlement of government fees and utility charges at 126 post offices across Hong Kong.

Figure 295
The People's Liberation Army Navy destroyer *Shenzhen* in an open visit at the naval base on Stonecutters Island. (Photo taken on 11 November 2001 and courtesy of South China Morning Post Publishers Limited)

18 Oct 2001

AXA, a French multinational insurance firm and one of the world's largest, inaugurated its Asia-Pacific headquarters in Hong Kong with an opening ceremony.

22 Oct 2001

CSL Mobile Limited, Hutchison 3 Hong Kong, SmarTone and SUNDAY Communications were issued government licences for third generation (3G) mobile services.

29 Oct 2001

An industrial building under demolition on Sze Shan Street in Yau Tong collapsed, causing six deaths and eight injuries.

Oct 2001

InvestHK Director-General Michael Rowse renounced his British nationality and was the first foreign official in Hong Kong to become a naturalised Chinese citizen.

The Antiquities and Monuments Office in collaboration with four institutes of archaeology (in Hebei, Henan, Shaanxi and Guangzhou) began a 12-month excavation at the Sha Ha site in Sai Kung, covering an area of about 3,000 square metres, where relics from the late Neolithic period to the Bronze Age were unearthed.

02 Nov 2001

Television Broadcasts Limited and China Central Television entered into an agreement in the first Hong Kong–Mainland media joint venture for business expansion domestically and internationally.

09 Nov 2001

The Electoral Procedure (Chief Executive Election) Regulation was promulgated, stipulating the arrangement in the second HKSAR Chief Executive election with respect to candidate nomination, campaign establishment, polling and vote counting.

10 Nov 2001

The People's Liberation Army Navy fleet arrived in Hong Kong for a four-day visit, berthing at the naval base on Stonecutters Island, marking the first visit since the establishment of the HKSAR. (Figure 295)

16 Nov 2001

The Police Training School's Tactical Training Complex in Wong Chuk Hang became operational as the first indoor training facility designed to resemble typical streets and buildings in Hong Kong.

22 Nov 2001

The Hong Kong Coalition of Professional Services was established, comprising 10 professional sectors, under the chairmanship of Executive Council Convenor Leung Chun-ying (梁振英).

28 Nov 2001

Hong Kong Cyberport's first office building was celebrated in a topping-out ceremony; it was officially opened on 27 June 2003.

01 Dec 2001

The opening hours of the Lo Wu and Lok Ma Chau Boundary Control Points were extended from 6:30 a.m. to midnight with immediate effect.

07 Dec 2001

The Ombudsman (Amendment) Ordinance 2001 was promulgated, making the Office of the Ombudsman independent from the government in addition to the expanded jurisdiction over the Equal Opportunities Commission and Office of the Privacy Commissioner for Personal Data.

10 Dec 2001

The Strategic Sewage Disposal Scheme (later known as the Harbour Area Treatment Scheme) Phase I was completed. Construction began in 1994 at a cost of HK$8.2 billion, comprising six underground tunnel systems connected to the Stonecutters Island Sewage Treatment Works and a discharge tunnel.

11 Dec 2001

The Hong Kong Logistics Development Council was established as an advisory body on government policy with respect to Hong Kong's position as a regional logistics hub.

14 Dec 2001

The Catholic Diocese of Hong Kong moved to provide 170 children awaiting the right of abode with free education (covering tuition, fees and transport fares) as audit students in two affiliated private schools.

20 Dec 2001

The Housing Department began demolition of Hong Kong's last cottage area located in Lai Chi Kok.

28 Dec 2001

The HKSAR government launched a 24-hour hotline known as the 1823 Citizen's Easy Link, allowing members of the public to enquire or complain about the services of participating departments.

2001

The Hong Kong Literature Research Centre—along with its "Special Collections," "Literature Database" and "Archives"—was established under The Chinese University of Hong Kong's Department of Chinese Language and Literature.

The Hong Kong Dietitians Association was established to support continued education and the development of an accreditation system for dietitians.

01 Jan 2002

Hong Kong's last signal station on Cheung Chau was decommissioned. Its function had been to provide alert manually in times of tropical cyclone or strong monsoon and night-time beacon lights.

The China National Tourism Administration lifted quota restrictions on Mainland travellers to Hong Kong and Macao while increasing the number of travel agencies approved for Hong Kong tour from the Mainland. The validity of multiple-entry business visas was extended from six months to a maximum of three years for a stay of up to 14 days per trip to Hong Kong.

10 Jan 2002

The Court of Final Appeal ruled in favour of only a small minority of 5,000 applicants seeking the right of abode in *Ng Siu-tung*（吳小彤）*v. Director of Immigration*. The Chinese authorities pledged not to pursue legal action against Mainlanders staying illegally in Hong Kong upon voluntary repatriation before 31 March. The HKSAR government also stated that it would not repatriate over-stayers before then.

25 Jan 2002

The HKSAR government began talks with the Ministry of Foreign Trade and Economic Cooperation on a proposal for a free trade zone in the Mainland. It became known as the Mainland and Hong Kong Closer Economic Partnership Arrangement (CEPA) on trade in goods and services as well as investments.

08 Feb 2002

Team Hong Kong, China participated in the 19th Winter Olympic Games in Salt Lake City, United States as a first-time participant in the Winter Games.

18 Feb 2002

Hong Kong Exchanges and Clearing Limited amended its Main Board Listing Rules and GEM Listing Rules, allowing stock issuers to provide a summary of financial reports in lieu of a full annual report.

28 Feb 2002

Chief Executive Tung Chee-hwa（董建華）was re-elected unopposed as Chief Executive of the HKSAR with 714 nominations from the Election Committee upon the conclusion of a two-week nomination period. On 04 March, Premier Zhu Rongji（朱鎔基）signed Order No. 347 of the State Council, appointing Tung Chee-hwa for a second term as the Chief Executive of the HKSAR.

06 Mar 2002

Financial Secretary Antony Leung Kam-chung（梁錦松）delivered his first Budget, proposing fiscal reserves be kept at a level equivalent to 12 months of government spending. It was the first time since the establishment of the HKSAR that a government target of fiscal reserves was proposed. To address the issue of fiscal deficit, three targets were laid out to be achieved by 2006/07, including a balanced operating account, a balanced consolidated account and a level of public expenditure to 20% or below of GDP.

19 Mar 2002

The Civil Aviation Department's first Air Operator's Certificate since the establishment of the HKSAR was issued to CR Airways (renamed Hong Kong Airlines in 2006).

26 Mar 2002

The University Grants Committee's report *Higher Education in Hong Kong*—prepared by University of Edinburgh Vice Chancellor Stewart Ross Sutherland—was released. The report proposed a funding strategy focused on a smaller number of institutions for greater competitiveness and a "Further Education Division" for the development of associate degree programmes.

28 Mar 2002

The Securities and Futures Ordinance was promulgated in place of 10 current securities-related ordinances for greater consumer protection with financial and investment products through up-to-date regulations in the securities and futures markets.

12 Apr 2002

Chief Executive Tung Chee-hwa（董建華）led a government delegation to attend the first annual Boao Forum for Asia in Hainan Province.

15 Apr 2002

Multinational media company Metro International launched its Hong Kong edition *Metro Daily,* a free newspaper distributed at MTR stations.

16 Apr 2002

The Hong Kong Public Libraries launched a lecture series on humanities, science and technology by eight renowned scholars, including Franklin Yang Chen-ning (楊振寧), Jao Tsung-i (饒宗頤) and Charles Kao Kuen (高錕).

19 Apr 2002

The Advisory Committee on Teacher Education and Qualifications reached a consensus on requiring prospective teachers of primary and secondary schools to be qualified in post-secondary education.

21 Apr 2002

Stephen Chow Sing-chi (周星馳) was named Best Actor, Best Director and Outstanding Young Director for *Shaolin Soccer* at the 21st Hong Kong Film Awards; he was the first actor to win all three awards.

22 Apr 2002

Hong Kong Internet Registration Corporation was established as a non-profit entity to administer the registration of Internet domain names under ".hk" and as a representative organisation at various international forums in place of the Joint Universities Computer Centre.

Apr 2002

The Social Welfare Department opened the first 15 Integrated Family Service Centres in a two-year trial run. In 2004/05, a reorganisation began to gradually divide these centres in 61 different locations.

08 May 2002

The HKSAR government began to arrest and repatriate people who were staying illegally in Hong Kong in accordance with the ruling by the Court of Final Appeal on 10 January.

12 May 2002

The Independent Commission Against Corruption launched a website dedicated to moral education with more than 600 sets of multimedia resources available to teachers on the values of honesty and integrity.

31 May 2002

The Hong Kong Court of Final Appeal (Amendment) Ordinance 2002 was promulgated, providing for civil appeals to be brought directly from the Court of First Instance to the Court of Final Appeal under specified circumstances.

01 Jun 2002

The HKSAR government's Continuing Education Fund was established; it began accepting applications for financial support and subsidies available through reimbursement of up to 80% of tuition or a maximum of HK$10,000 upon completion of an approved course.

20 Jun 2002

The HKSAR government released its *Review of the Institutional Framework for Public Housing*, highlighting a commitment to the long-term housing targets despite a weak private housing market in an economic downturn, as well as an achieved target of public housing subsidies provided to 1.3 million people since 1997, and a shortened average waiting period of 3.2 years for public housing.

22 Jun 2002

The Guangdong–Hong Kong Joint Clearing Facility for HK-dollar cheques became operational in a significant step towards facilitating financial flows and cooperation to streamline and speed up the process of cheque-clearing from anywhere between seven and 14 days to two working days.

27 Jun 2002

The Hong Kong Science Park was opened to facilitate development in technology and entrepreneurship in support of innovators locally and internationally.

28 Jun 2002

Chi Lin Nunnery was named winner of the first biennial Quality Building Award. The Award was co-founded by nine local professional groups and trade institutes in recognition of high-quality building projects and construction teams.

Jun 2002

The Hong Kong Observatory installed the world's first Light Detection and Ranging (LiDAR) System at the Hong Kong International Airport for enhanced capability to provide airport windshear alerts and warnings.

01 Jul 2002

A flag-raising ceremony was held at Hong Kong Convention and Exhibition Centre's Golden Bauhinia Square in celebration of the fifth anniversary of the establishment of the HKSAR. Chief Executive Tung Chee-hwa (董 建 華) and principal officials took the oath of office administered by President Jiang Zemin (江澤民), followed by the swearing-in of the Executive Council under the Chief Executive.

The Principal Officials Accountability System was introduced in the most significant government restructure since the establishment of the HKSAR. The Chief Secretary, Financial Secretary, Secretary for Justice and 11 bureau secretaries became political appointees (instead of civil servants) under greater accountability for administrative performance and were made Official Members of the Executive Council. (Figure 296)

The HKSAR government, in view of a changing economic and social environment, reorganised its policy bureaus. The Environment, Transport & Works Bureau and Health, Welfare & Food Bureau were established. The Economic Development & Labour Bureau, Housing, Planning & Lands Bureau, Commerce, Industry & Technology Bureau and Financial Services & the Treasury Bureau were formed after a reorganisation of bureau functions.

The Hong Kong Economic and Trade Office in Guangdong was established as the first one in the Mainland, aiming to foster greater Hong Kong–Guangdong economic and trade cooperation.

Figure 296
A group photo of Chief Executive Tung Chee-hwa (董建華) and principal government officials of the second HKSAR government. (Photo taken on 24 June 2002 and courtesy of HKSAR Government)

12 Jul 2002

| The Karaoke Establishments Ordinance was promulgated, effective 08 January 2003, requiring strict compliance with fire and safety standards in all karaoke bars before being allowed to continue doing business.

| The Fire Safety (Buildings) Ordinance was promulgated, effective 01 July 2007, stipulating greater fire safety standards and installations (automatic sprinklers, emergency lights, fire hydrants and hose reels in composite (multi-purpose) and domestic (residential) buildings constructed in or before 1987.

19 Jul 2002

| The Public Officers Pay Adjustment Ordinance was promulgated, effective 01 October, reducing civil service pay by 4.42%, 1.64% and 1.58% pertaining to civil servants of high, mid and low ranks, respectively, in the first civil service pay reduction by legislation since 1936.

| The Hong Kong Examinations Authority was renamed Hong Kong Examinations and Assessment Authority as a statutory body responsible for standardised tests and public examinations.

| A team of secondary school students participated in the 43rd International Mathematical Olympiad in the United Kingdom, winning Hong Kong's first gold medal as well as two silver and two bronze medals.

| The United Nations (Anti-Terrorism Measures) Ordinance was promulgated, implementing a decision of the UN Security Council for prevention of terrorist acts. It defined what constituted acts of terrorism, empowered the Chief Executive to specify terrorist groups by notice in the *Gazette*, and authorised the Secretary for Security to freeze terrorist assets.

25 Jul 2002

| The Hong Kong Exchanges and Clearing Limited (HKEX) released its *Consultation Paper on Proposed Amendments to the Listing Rules Relating to Initial Listing and Continuing Listing Eligibility and Cancellation of Listing Procedures,* proposing to delist companies with share prices persistently below 50 cents. It triggered a penny stock crash the following day; share prices of 577 (76%) of the 761 Main Board-listed stocks dropped. On 28 July, HKEX announced withdrawal of some proposed measures. On 10 September, a government report following an investigation was released, calling for an improved consultation process.

29 Jul 2002

| The University Grants Committee (UGC) announced its adoption of the International English Language Testing System (IELTS) for proficiency assessment with final-year university students of UGC-funded institutions.

30 Jul 2002

| An agreement on an exchange programme for civil servants between the HKSAR government and Shanghai municipal government was signed.

| The Court of Final Appeal ruled in *Gurung Kesh Bahadur v. Director of Immigration* that non-permanent residents had the right to enter or leave Hong Kong freely as stipulated in the Basic Law. This right could not be removed by local law; any limitation would have to be enacted according to an interpretation of the Basic Law and processed by a court of law.

02 Aug 2002

| The Customs & Excise Department (of HKSAR) and National Copyright Administration (of the Mainland) entered into the first cooperation agreement on protecting intellectual property rights and fighting optical disc piracy.

18 Aug 2002

| MTR's Tseung Kwan O Line, a 12.5-kilometre rail running between Tseung Kwan O and North Point, became operational; construction began on 24 April 1999 at a cost HK$18 billion.

19 Aug 2002

| The Education Bureau issued an attendance order to a parent for failing to send a child to school and insisting on home-schooling since February 2000. The parent was ordered to allow his/her 11-year-old daughter to return to school by 15 September.

21 Aug 2002

The Chinese Central Government appointed Gao Siren (高祀仁) as Director of the Liaison Office of the Central People's Government in the HKSAR. He remained in the post until 24 May 2009.

28 Aug 2002

China Merchants Bank opened a branch in Hong Kong for business expansion outside the Mainland.

Aug 2002

The National Radio and Television Administration granted permission for cable distribution of Asia Television's Home and World channels in the Pearl River Delta region of Guangdong.

13 Sep 2002

The Hong Kong Design Centre was inaugurated to create greater business value in design and to advance Hong Kong's status as an international centre of design excellence in Asia by promoting wider and more strategic use of design thinking.

The Civil Human Rights Front, comprising more than 30 social groups under the convenorship of Rose Wu Lo-sai (胡露茜), was established.

21 Sep 2002

The first local cases of dengue fever were detected in three workers at a construction site in Ma Wan.

23 Sep 2002

The Customs and Excise Department of Hong Kong and US Customs Service signed a Declaration of Principles with respect to the Container Security Initiative, a security regime to facilitate the exchange of intelligence and the identification of cargo posing a potential risk of terrorism.

24 Sep 2002

The HKSAR government released its Proposals to Implement Article 23 of the Basic Law on acts of treason, secession, subversion, sedition, theft of state secrets, and collusion with foreign political organisations. The proposal stipulated investigative power regarding search and seizure, financial investigation, and organised and serious crimes. The public consultation ended on 24 September with over 90,000 responses.

Sep 2002

The Task Force on Population Policy was formed. On 26 February 2003, it released its first report for a comprehensive long-term plan based on demographic trends and characteristics.

04 Oct 2002

Secretary for Education and Manpower Arthur Li Kwok-cheung (李國章) suggested a merger between The Chinese University of Hong Kong and The Hong Kong University of Science and Technology for a world-class institution to be formed in 2005. The plan was withdrawn in March 2004 amid public controversy.

06 Oct 2002

Team Hong Kong, China participated in the 14th Asian Games in Busan, South Korea, winning four gold, six silver and 11 bronze medals, including first-time medals in bodybuilding and karate.

01 Nov 2002

The Hong Kong Correctional Services Museum, a 480-square-metre, two-storey complex located at the Correctional Services Department Staff Training Institute in Stanley, was opened for public access to the history of Hong Kong's penal system.

03 Nov 2002

About 500 Hong Kong actors and artists staged a rally in front of the Central Government Offices in protest of *East Week* magazine's publication of nude photos taken forcefully, raising the issue of media ethics.

08 Nov 2002

The Home Affairs Bureau in a public consultation released its *Consultancy Study on the Provision of Regional/District Cultural and Performance Facilities in Hong Kong*. It proposed a reorganisation of city-wide and district-wide facilities with a focus on the West Kowloon Cultural District and privatisation of some public facilities to enhance Hong Kong's status as a cultural centre.

13 Nov 2002

Secretary for Housing, Planning and Lands Michael Suen Ming-yeung (孫明揚) announced nine measures to stabilise the housing market, including suspension of scheduled land auctions and of subsidised housing construction while continuing to provide housing subsidies for those in need. The Home Ownership Scheme and Private Sector Participation Scheme were put on hold starting 2003 while the Tenants Purchase Scheme was terminated.

15 Nov 2002

The Immigration (Amendment) Ordinance 2001 was promulgated, precluding Chinese officials stationed in Hong Kong from the status of ordinary residents, thereby ruling out their eligibility to become permanent residents upon seven years of continuous stay.

The Shaw Prize—founded by renowned film producer and philanthropist Run Run Shaw (邵逸夫)—was established to recognise outstanding contributions in academic and scientific research with profound impact on human life in the fields of Astronomy, Mathematical Sciences, and Life Science & Medicine with a prize of US$1.2 million each. The first award ceremony was held in Hong Kong on 07 September 2004.

18 Nov 2002

Premier Zhu Rongji (朱鎔基) arrived in Hong Kong to attend the 16th World Congress of Accountants the following day. Speaking during a welcome dinner at the Government House, he suggested that the HKSAR government could tackle its fiscal deficit by issuing bonds with 50-year maturity in the Mainland.

26 Nov 2002

Secretary for the Civil Service Joseph Wong Wing-ping (王永平) led a delegation of senior officials to Shanghai and Hangzhou for a three-day visit following the launch of the Hong Kong–Mainland Staff Exchange Programme.

27 Nov 2002

The HKSAR government released a development blueprint of higher education. It introduced a performance-based university funding model to promote excellence, redefined the limits on undergraduate programmes and non-local student places, and decoupled university staff compensation from the civil service pay-scale.

29 Nov 2002

A service charge of HK$100 was implemented for emergency room visits in public hospitals in a bid to clamp down on the misuse of emergency services that were previously free of charge.

30 Nov 2002

Businessman Harry Lam Hon-lit (林漢烈) was shot dead at close range by a hitman at Luk Yu Tea House in Central. Eight suspects, including the hitman and mastermind, were arrested in Shenzhen.

01 Dec 2002

The Sun Yat Sen Memorial Park was opened to the public; it was built on reclaimed land outside Sam Kok Wharf where Sun Yat-sen's (孫中山) ship was moored when he met with revolutionaries in Hong Kong after Hong Kong issued an expulsion order against him.

09 Dec 2002

The World Weather Information Service website, established by the Hong Kong Observatory under the UN World Meteorological Organization, was launched as the first website featuring official city forecasts issued by the respective official weather services.

18 Dec 2002

The Industrial and Commercial Bank of China launched Hong Kong's first dual-currency (Hong Kong dollar and renminbi) credit card.

30 Dec 2002

The Information Services Department launched its official website for dissemination of government information and news.

2002

The Ministry of Education in a circular authorised the recruitment of self-supporting Mainland students for undergraduate programmes by tertiary institutions in the Hong Kong SAR and Macao SAR.

01 Jan 2003

The Education Department became a part of the Education and Manpower Bureau through a merger in accordance with the Education Reorganization (Miscellaneous Amendments) Ordinance 2003.

The HKSAR government began deregulation of the local rice market and lifted quota restrictions on rice imports, exerting minimal control on the trade, except with respect to the registration of rice stockholders, reserve stock, and import quantity undertaken by registered rice stockholders—measures put in place to ensure a stable supply of rice in Hong Kong.

The fixed-line telecommunications market in Hong Kong was liberalised, allowing an open market without a limit on the number of licences or a timeframe on applying for a licence, in a bid to protect consumer interests through greater competition.

06 Jan 2003

The Hong Kong Archaeological Society in collaboration with Shenzhen Museum began a 24-day excavation at the Fu Tei Au site in Sheung Pak Nai, Yuen Long. Pieces of house foundations, drainage channels and tombs were discovered; two complete large *yue* axes, dating back some 4,000 years, were unearthed from Tomb No. 1, resembling the artefacts of the Shixia culture in northern Guangdong.

21 Jan 2003

The University of Hong Kong's School of Chinese Medicine marked its first graduating class in a ceremony, conferring 17 bachelor's degrees (Traditional Chinese Medicine) and 18 master's degrees (Acupuncture).

22 Jan 2003

The Legislative Council's Select Committee on Building Problems of Public Housing Units released its first investigation report on "short piles" in four public housing estates, namely Tin Chung Court, Shatin Area 14B Phase Two, Tung Chung Area 30 Phase Three, and Shek Yam Estate Phase Two Area Four. Recommendations included lessening the administrative burdens on non-official members of the Housing authority, bringing public housing under the Buildings Ordinance, and introducing a registration and accountability system with subcontractors.

The Independent Commission Against Corruption in collaboration with the International Criminal Police Organization began a three-day "Partnership Against Corruption" conference in Hong Kong with more than 500 representatives from 61 jurisdictions and eight international organisations.

23 Jan 2003

Chairman of the Central Military Commission Jiang Zemin (江澤民) signed an order appointing Wang Jitang (王繼堂) as Commander of the People's Liberation Army Hong Kong Garrison. Wang remained in the post until December 2007.

26 Jan 2003

Hong Kong served as a transit point in the first Spring Festival (Chinese New Year) charter flight from Shanghai to Taiwan.

27 Jan 2003

The Lok Ma Chau Control Point began providing 24-hour access for cross-border clearance.

11 Feb 2003

The Court of Final Appeal ruled in favour of an Indian national who was rejected for permanent resident status despite having lived in Hong Kong for seven years. The additional requirement regarding "currently living" in Hong Kong at the time of application was ruled a violation of Article 24 of the Basic Law that "persons not of Chinese nationality who have entered Hong Kong with valid travel documents, have ordinarily resided in Hong Kong for a continuous period of not less than seven years, and have taken Hong Kong as their place of permanent residence before or after the establishment of the HKSAR" shall be permanent residents.

14 Feb 2003

The National Security (Legislative Provisions) Bill 2003 was gazetted pursuant to the obligation imposed by Article 23 of the Basic Law, aiming for a legislation by amending the Crimes Ordinance, Official Secrets Ordinance and Societies Ordinance, among other provisions.

The Village Representative Election Ordinance was promulgated, allowing women and non-indigenous inhabitants to vote and run as candidates in the elections of village representatives under a new system in which a resident representative and an indigenous inhabitant representative were to be elected in an arrangement compliant with the Hong Kong Bill of Rights Ordinance and Sex Discrimination Ordinance. The first village representative election under the new rules was held on 12 July.

18 Feb 2003

The Employees Compensation Insurer Insolvency Bureau was established; on 01 April 2004, it began to manage cases with respect to liabilities arising from employee compensation insurance policies in the event of insurer insolvency.

21 Feb 2003

A retired professor of Sun Yat-sen University's Second Affiliated Hospital in Guangzhou stayed at Metropole Hotel (present-day Metropark Hotel Kowloon) in Hong Kong. The next day, he was hospitalised at Kwong Wah Hospital's Intensive Care Unit following an emergency room visit. He was identified as the index patient of the severe acute respiratory syndrome (SARS) in Hong Kong.

25 Feb 2003

In view of deflation, welfare benefits provided to "able-bodied" recipients under the Comprehensive Social Security Assistance programme were reduced by 11.1%; benefits for "non-able-bodied" recipients (with disabilities) were reduced by 6% in October 2003 and 5.1% in October 2004.

05 Mar 2003

The HKSAR government released its 2003/04 Budget, indicating a fiscal deficit of HK$70 billion in the 2002/03 financial year. It proposed reducing expenditure by HK$20 billion and increasing revenue by HK$20 billion for a balanced budget by 2006/07, along with an adjusted target of fiscal reserves.

10 Mar 2003

The Hospital Authority confirmed several cases of fever with symptoms of upper respiratory infection among the medical staff in Ward 8A at Prince of Wales Hospital in the past few days. The following day, 23 people with fever were admitted for observation in the hospital; eight patients showed symptoms of pneumonia.

13 Mar 2003

Henry Fok Ying-tung (霍英東) was elected as Vice Chairman of the 10th Chinese People's Political Consultative Conference.

The HKSAR government set up an expert task force for an investigation on the medical cases of viral respiratory infection diagnosed at Prince of Wales Hospital. A steering group, led by Secretary for Health, Welfare & Food Yeoh Eng-kiong (楊永強), was formed to implement control measures. The disease was named Severe Acute Respiratory Syndrome (SARS)—an atypical pneumonia proven to be fatal—on 15 March by the World Health Organization.

22 Mar 2003

The University of Hong Kong classified the SARS pathogen as a type of coronavirus.

Figure 297
The Department of Health delivered daily supplies to residents of Amoy Gardens' Block E under home quarantine during the SARS epidemic. (Photo taken on 31 March 2003 and courtesy of South China Morning Post Publishers Limited)

25 Mar 2003

A government steering committee on fighting SARS was formed with principal officials under the chairmanship of the Chief Executive.

26 Mar 2003

The Commission on Youth published its report *Continuing Development and Employment Opportunities for Youth*, recommending government measures to provide out-of-school youngsters with employment and development opportunities.

The Department of Health began an investigation on Block E of Amoy Gardens in Ngau Tau Kok, Kowloon where seven people in five families were infected with SARS. By 31 March, confirmed cases at the residential complex rose to 213.

Princess Margaret Hospital, which was the only infectious disease centre in Hong Kong, became a designated hospital to admit new SARS patients after 29 March. Its Accident and Emergency Department was closed from midnight.

27 Mar 2003

The HKSAR government announced anti-SARS measures, including suspension of classes in all kindergartens, primary and secondary schools for nine days starting from 29 March (until the end of April following several extensions). Persons having had contact with SARS patients were required to report to a Department of Health clinic every day for 10 days.

29 Mar 2003

The HKSAR government required all arriving passengers to fill out a health declaration form at the airport and all other border control points. The measure later became a standard procedure in times of potential outbreak of an infectious disease in Hong Kong.

31 Mar 2003

The Culture and Heritage Commission presented its *Culture and Heritage Commission Policy Recommendation Report*. Recommendations included preservation of Hong Kong's history and cultural information through a book series called Hong Kong Chronicles.

The Department of Health announced quarantine (until 09 April) of residents in Block E of Amoy Gardens where a high concentration of SARS cases was registered. The following day, relocation of residents began for quarantine at Lady MacLehose Holiday Village and Lei Yue Mun Park & Holiday Village. (Figure 297)

Mar 2003

The plan of a five-year herbarium project—between HKSAR's Agriculture, Fisheries and Conservation Department and Chinese Academy of Sciences' South China Institute of Botany—was finalised for a comprehensive review (and an updated *Check List of Hong Kong Plants*) on Hong Kong Herbarium's collection of 37,000 plant specimens.

01 Apr 2003

Famous singer and actor Leslie Cheung Kwok-wing (張國榮) died at the age of 46 after he jumped off the Mandarin Oriental Hotel in Central.

02 Apr 2003

The World Health Organization issued a warning against non-essential travel to Hong Kong. The warning was removed on 23 May.

10 Apr 2003

The HKSAR government implemented home quarantine measures, requiring people in close contact with SARS patients to undergo quarantine at home or a designated facility for a maximum of 10 days.

11 Apr 2003

In a meeting with the provincial government of Guangdong, Hong Kong reached an agreement on measures regarding SARS prevention and control, including data sharing, medical cooperation, reporting mechanism and cross-border quarantine, in addition to forming an expert task force.

12 Apr 2003

The Legislative Council's Bills Committee held its first public hearing on the National Security (Legislative Provisions) Bill.

15 Apr 2003

Johannes Chan Man-mun (陳文敏) became the first Honorary Senior Counsel of the HKSAR in an appointment by the Chief Justice of the Court of Final Appeal.

17 Apr 2003

The HKSAR government released findings of an investigation on the SARS outbreak in Amoy Gardens where 321 people became infected between 14 March and 15 April. The virus was found to have spread through the sewage system. By this day, approximately 1,300 SARS cases and a death toll of 65 were recorded in Hong Kong.

The Prevention of the Spread of Infectious Diseases (Amendment) Regulation 2003 was promulgated, requiring people arriving in and departing from Hong Kong to take body temperature and prohibiting those in close contact with SARS patients from leaving Hong Kong.

19 Apr 2003

Operation UNITE—initiated by six online media outlets and sponsored by The Hong Kong Jockey Club—began for a two-day territory-wide cleaning and public awareness campaign on SARS prevention. (Figure 298)

The HKSAR government kicked off a Territory-wide Cleansing Day in a two-day community-wide disinfection project across different districts and facilities in Hong Kong. Participants included government departments, district councils, non-government and charitable organisations, business groups and families of all cultures and backgrounds.

23 Apr 2003

The HKSAR government announced short-term relief measures with a HK$11.8 billion economic package in light of the SARS outbreak, including concessions on rates, water and sewage charges and effluent surcharges, rebate of salaries tax and a business loan guarantee scheme.

Figure 298
Secretary for Health, Welfare and Food Yeoh Eng-kiong (楊永強), second from left, marked a Territory-wide Cleansing Day at Wan Chai Market. (Photo taken on 19 April 2003 and courtesy of HKSAR Government)

24 Apr 2003

A team of World Health Organization experts arrived in Hong Kong to support an investigation on the SARS breakout in Amoy Gardens. On 16 May, investigation findings were published, attributing the unusual spread of SARS to a combination of environmental and hygiene factors.

26 Apr 2003

Nurse Lau Wing-kai (劉永佳) died of SARS while looking after SARS patients; he was the first medical personnel in Hong Kong to die of SARS in the line of duty. On 13 May, Dr Joanna Tse Yuen-man (謝婉雯) died of SARS at the age of 35 after volunteering to save SARS patients. A total of 386 medical staff were infected, resulting in eight deaths. On 30 June, Joanna Tse Yuen-man was awarded the Medal for Bravery (Gold). On the same day, Kate Cheng Ha-yan (鄭夏恩), Lau Wing-kai, Tang Heung-may (鄧香美), Lau Kam-yung (劉錦蓉) and Wong Kang-tai (王庚娣) were posthumously awarded the Medal for Bravery (Silver). (Figure 299)

Figure 299
Dr Joanna Tse Yuen-man (謝婉雯)—who died of SARS at the age of 35 after volunteering to save SARS patients—was laid to rest at Gallant Garden. (Photo taken on 22 May 2003 and courtesy of South China Morning Post Publishers Limited)

28 Apr 2003

The Hong Kong Monetary Authority launched a Euro Clearing System and appointed Standard Chartered Bank (Hong Kong) as the settlement institution, allowing real-time transactions of Euro settlement in the Asian time zone.

30 Apr 2003

The HK$50 million government Film Guarantee Fund in support of Hong Kong's film industry was open to applicants.

04 May 2003

The Hong Kong Federation of Trade Unions and Hong Kong Federation of Education Workers as part of a group of eight community organisations launched a city-wide campaign dedicated to "staying healthy, fighting SARS, promoting consumption and rejuvenating economic activities" in addition to fundraising for medical professionals.

05 May 2003

Team Clean—a government cross-departmental task force chaired by Chief Secretary for Administration Donald Tsang Yam-kuen (曾蔭權)—was established for sustainable, long-term measures on the hygiene standards in Hong Kong.

06 May 2003

The Customs and Excise Department and the Agriculture, Fisheries and Conservation Department were presented a certificate of appreciation for seizing 506 kilograms of illegal ivory in October 2002. It marked the first commendation by the Secretariat in Geneva overseeing the implementation of the Convention on International Trade in Endangered Species of Wild Fauna and Flora.

08 May 2003

Chief Executive Tung Chee-hwa (董建華) travelled to Huanggang in Shenzhen to receive the first batch of medical supplies from the Chinese Central Government. On 29 May, another batch of medical supplies from the Chinese Central Government arrived. (Figures 300 and 301)

12 May 2003

Hong Kong commenced a Container Security Initiative pilot scheme to enhance the security of cargo bound for the US in the wake of the 9/11 attacks.

20 May 2003

The Education Commission released its *Review of the Academic Structure of Senior Secondary Education*, noting that the curriculum in Secondary 6 and 7 (under the "5+2" academic structure with five years of secondary and two years of matriculation education) was too specialised. It recommended a senior secondary curriculum with four core subjects (Chinese, English, Math and Liberal Studies) and two electives under a "3+3" academic structure.

28 May 2003

The SARS Expert Committee—comprising seven international and two local experts under the chairmanship of Secretary for Health, Welfare and Food Yeoh Eng-kiong (楊永強)—was formed for a review on anti-SARS measures in Hong Kong. On 02 October, it released a report and noted a failure of Hong Kong's medical system in the early stage of the SARS outbreak; it made 46 recommendations, including the establishment of the Centre for Health Protection.

29 May 2003

The HKSAR government announced that the United Nations Framework Convention on Climate Change and Kyoto Protocol, adopted by the Chinese Central Government, were applicable to Hong Kong.

31 May 2003

At 4:45 a.m., Hong Kong amateur climber Chung Kin-man (鍾建民) reached the top of Mount Everest where the HKSAR flag was raised for the first time.

Figure 300
An official ceremony was held to mark the arrival of medical supplies from the Chinese Central Government for Hong Kong on 08 May 2003. (Photo courtesy of HKSAR Government)

Figure 301
The first batch of medical supplies bound for Hong Kong from the Chinese Central Government arrived in Shenzhen on 08 May 2003 during the SARS epidemic. (Photo courtesy of South China Morning Post Publishers Limited)

07 Jun 2003

Hong Kong animated film *My Life as McDull* in an entry representing China won the Grand Prix at the Annecy International Animation Film Festival in France.

11 Jun 2003

The last confirmed case of SARS was identified in Hong Kong where a total of 1,755 people were infected—of whom 299 died.

15 Jun 2003

Chief Executive Tung Chee-hwa（董建華）launched a HK$700 million employment scheme, aiming to tackle unemployment among the young and middle-aged by creating 32,000 new jobs and training opportunities.

18 Jun 2003

The Legislative Council passed a motion to recognise the Chinese Central Government's support for Hong Kong's fight against SARS.

23 Jun 2003

The World Health Organization removed Hong Kong, which had the second largest number of SARS cases and deaths after the Mainland, from the list of areas with recent local transmission of SARS.

28 Jun 2003

The Dongshen Water Supply Improvement Works—a project aiming to ensure the quality of fresh water supply from the East River (Dongjiang) to Shenzhen Reservoir (before reaching Hong Kong) with a sealed aqueduct system—was completed.

29 Jun 2003

Premier Wen Jiabao (溫家寶) arrived in Hong Kong for a three-day visit to commend the community-wide efforts in fighting SARS. The next day, he visited Amoy Gardens and Prince of Wales Hospital in Sha Tin, recognising the selfless sacrifice of medical personnel during the pandemic. (Figure 302)

The Mainland and Hong Kong Closer Economic Partnership Arrangement was signed in the presence of Premier Wen Jiabao (溫家寶) and Chief Executive Tung Chee-hwa (董建華), marking the first Hong Kong–Mainland free trade agreement in goods, services and investments. (Figure 303)

01 Jul 2003

A march organised by the Civil Human Rights Front in protest of the proposed legislations with respect to Article 23 of the Basic Law took place in the afternoon. It started from Victoria Park and ended at the Central Government Offices with a turnout of 500,000 and 350,000 people according to estimates by the organiser and police, respectively. (Figure 304)

04 Jul 2003

The Legislative Council (Amendment) Ordinance 2003 was promulgated. In a restructure of council composition, it abolished seats under the Election Committee and increased seats under geographical constituency (direct elections) to 30 in accordance with the Basic Law.

Figure 302
Premier of the State Council Wen Jiabao (溫家寶) presented medical professionals in Hong Kong with an appreciation card; pictured were Chung Sheung-chee (鍾尚志), second left in front row, Dean of CUHK's Faculty of Medicine, and Joseph Sung Jao-yiu (沈祖堯), middle in back row, Head of CUHK's Department of Medicine. (Photo taken on 30 June 2003 and courtesy of South China Morning Post Publishers Limited)

Figure 303
Financial Secretary Antony Leung Kam-chung (梁錦松), left, and Vice Minister of Commerce An Min (安民), right, signed the Mainland and Hong Kong Closer Economic Partnership Arrangement (CEPA). (Photo courtesy of Xinhua News Agency)

Figure 304
People gathered at Victoria Park in Causeway Bay for a march on 01 July 2003. (Photo courtesy of Mike Clarke/AFP via Getty Images)

05 Jul 2003

The HKSAR government announced three major amendments to the National Security (Legislative Provisions) Bill. These removed the ban on local organisations affiliated with Mainland organisations under sanction by the Chinese Central Government, added a public interest clause as a defence against unlawful disclosure of official secrets, and abolished the right to search and seizure without warrant authorised by a police officer at the rank of a chief superintendent or above. It also made a guarantee on the rights and freedoms of Hong Kong and moved forward with the bill's second reading on 09 July as scheduled.

06 Jul 2003

Prior to the second reading of the National Security (Legislative Provisions) Bill, Tien Pei-chun（田北俊）, Member of the Executive Council and Legislative Council, expressed his objection on behalf of the Liberal Party and resigned from the Executive Council, thereby making the bill short of enough votes for passage in the Legislative Council.

08 Jul 2003

Chinese imperial antiques, including wooden furniture, stationery and rock carvings, were sold at record-breaking prices at an auction by Christie's Hong Kong.

10 Jul 2003

A Kowloon Motor Bus double-decker fell from an overpass after colliding with a truck on Tuen Mun Road, causing 21 deaths and 20 injuries.

11 Jul 2003

The Betting Duty (Amendment) Ordinance 2003 was promulgated, effective 01 August, allowing football bets with The Hong Kong Jockey Club.

14 Jul 2003

A two-day conference dedicated to the revitalisation of tourism in Asia—co-hosed by the Boao Forum for Asia and World Tourism Organization—began in Hong Kong with more than 1,000 representatives from 30 countries and regions in what was the first major international conference held following the SARS pandemic.

15 Jul 2003

The Admission Scheme for Mainland Talents and Professionals was implemented in an open-ended, quota-free arrangement.

16 Jul 2003

Financial Secretary Antony Leung Kam-chung（梁錦松）resigned amid public criticism of his car purchase shortly before an increase of motor vehicle registration tax was announced in the 2003/04 Budget (released in mid-January). Chief Executive Tung Chee-hwa（董建華）accepted his resignation.

Secretary for Security Regina Ip Lau Suk-yee（葉劉淑儀）resigned; Chief Executive Tung Chee-hwa（董建華）accepted her resignation.

18 Jul 2003

The Chinese Central Government appointed Yang Wenchang（楊文昌）as Commissioner of the Ministry of Foreign Affairs of the People's Republic of China in the HKSAR. He remained in office until 15 February 2006.

22 Jul 2003

Container Terminal 9, located at southeast Tsing Yi, was opened for initial operation before it was fully constructed with six berths in 2005; it was jointly run by Hongkong International Terminals Limited and Modern Terminals Limited.

28 Jul 2003

The Individual Visit Scheme as a part of the Closer Economic Partnership Arrangement began for free travel to Hong Kong with tourists from Dongguan, Zhongshan, Jiangmen and Foshan. The scheme was later expanded to cover 49 Mainland cities, including 21 in Guangdong Province, as well as Beijing, Shanghai, Tianjin, Chongqing and other major cities.

01 Aug 2003

The Housing Department's Marking Scheme for Tenancy Enforcement in Public Housing Estates came into force to improve public hygiene with a points-based system, penalising eight and ten types of misconduct without and with warnings, respectively. The scheme was renamed in 2006 as Marking Scheme for Estate Management Enforcement in Public Housing Estates.

15 Aug 2003

In the first project under Hong Kong Housing Society's Senior Citizen Residences Scheme, 243 residential units of Jolly Place in Tseung Kwan O were open to applicants.

18 Aug 2003

The Census and Statistics Department released the latest data on the labour market, showing an unemployment rate of 8.7% as the highest on record as of 01 July 2017.

The Immigration Department launched a Territory-wide Identity Card Replacement Exercise for smart ID cards with 6.9 million residents of Hong Kong under an implementation schedule by year of birth.

26 Aug 2003

A Government Flying Service (GFS) helicopter crashed near Pak Kung Au on Lantau Road, killing two GFS pilots in the first fatal accident since the establishment of the service branch in 1993.

Aug 2003

The Guangdong/Hong Kong Expert Group on the Protection of Intellectual Property Rights was established, aiming to promote further cooperation in various aspects of IP protection. On 03 December, it held its first meeting in Hong Kong and inaugurated the Intellectual Property Database for Guangdong, Hong Kong and Macao.

01 Sep 2003

The Education and Manpower Bureau began requiring new kindergarten teachers to meet qualification standards under the Qualified Kindergarten Teacher scheme or equivalent.

05 Sep 2003

The HKSAR government announced putting aside the National Security (Legislative Provisions) Bill—which expired automatically at the end of the second Legislative Council session on 22 July 2004.

18 Sep 2003

Businessman Stanley Ho Hung-sun (何鴻燊) presented the Chinese government with the bronze-cast pig-head statue (one of 12 Chinese zodiac animals from the Old Summer Palace)—which he bought from an American collector for about RMB 6 million. The statue arrived in Hong Kong and was shipped to Beijing the following day. On 20 September 2007, he also bought and donated the horse-head statue for HK$69.1 million. (Figure 305)

26 Sep 2003

Now TV, a cable TV wholly owned by PCCW, began its inaugural broadcast.

28 Sep 2003

The first Asia Cultural Co-operation Forum began in Hong Kong for a three-day conference with government leaders from Indonesia, Japan, South Korea, Philippines, Singapore, Vietnam, and the Pearl River Delta region.

Figure 305
Entrepreneur Stanley Ho Hung-sun (何鴻燊) donated the bronze-cast "pig" head to the Chinese government in 2003. (Photo courtesy of cnsphoto)

Figure 306
Yang Liwei (楊利偉), China's first astronaut to go into space, attended a welcome ceremony at Hong Kong Stadium. (Photo taken on 01 November 2003 and courtesy of HKSAR Government)

29 Sep 2003

Six annexes to the Mainland and Hong Kong Closer Economic Partnership Arrangement were signed regarding zero-tariff trade in goods, rules of origin of goods, procedures for issuing certificates of origin, trade liberalisation with 18 service sectors, details on service providers, and measures to facilitate trade and investment.

15 Oct 2003

The HKSAR government announced several measures to stabilise the property market by: 1) resuming the Land Application List System in the following year; 2) allowing orderly sale of development projects of Mass Transit Railway and Kowloon–Canton Railway; and 3) suspending the sale of Home Ownership Scheme residential units until the end of 2006.

16 Oct 2003

The government-sponsored Hong Kong Harbour Fest was held at Tamar in a bid to revive the local economy and tourism industry after SARS. On 12 December, amid public concern about cost overrun, a Chief Executive-appointed independent inquiry was formed. On 15 May 2004, an investigation report was released, noting the inexperience of the event's proposer American Chamber of Commerce in Hong Kong, and the lack of scrutiny and supervision by the organisers. The report recommended that the government should appoint members to the planning committees and that similar events in the future should be organised through private-public funding.

On 15 May 2004, an investigation report was released, noting discrepancies with the event organiser American Chamber of Commerce in Hong Kong and a lack of scrutiny and supervision. The report suggested the inclusion of a committee and private-public funding in future events of a similar nature.

19 Oct 2003

Wang Chen (王晨) took first place at the 23rd Badminton Asia Championships in Jakarta, Indonesia; she became the first Hong Kong badminton player crowned champion since the establishment of the HKSAR.

27 Oct 2003

The Hong Kong/Shanghai Economic and Trade Cooperation Conference held its first meeting in Hong Kong under Chief Executive Tung Chee-hwa (董建華) and Mayor of Shanghai Han Zheng (韓正) for strengthened ties in eight areas, including investment and trade, financial services, and exchange among professionals.

29 Oct 2003

The Legislative Council appointed a committee of inquiry on the performance of the government (including the Hospital Authority) during the SARS epidemic. On 05 July 2004, a report was released, noting inadequate response by Secretary for Health, Welfare and Food Yeoh Eng-kiong (楊永強).

31 Oct 2003

China's first manned space flight crew, including astronaut Yang Liwei (楊利偉), arrived in Hong Kong for a six-day visit, participating in several public events. (Figure 306)

02 Nov 2003

The Education and Manpower Bureau held its first Chief Executive's Award for Teaching Excellence—sponsored by the Quality Education Fund in recognition of exemplary teachers.

A small crocodile was discovered at the Shan Pui River in Yuen Long; it was captured by the Agriculture, Fisheries and Conservation Department on 10 June 2004 and placed in the Kadoorie Farm & Botanic Garden, where it was given the name Pui Pui. On 15 August 2006, Pui Pui was relocated to the Hong Kong Wetland Park.

03 Nov 2003

Hong Kong was awarded the right to host the fifth East Asian Games in 2009.

07 Nov 2003

The Trust Fund for Severe Acute Respiratory Syndrome (SARS) with a government budget of HK$150 million was established to provide families of deceased SARS patients with special ex-gratia payments and recovered patients with financial assistance. On 13 November, it was open to applicants.

13 Nov 2003

The Basic Law Article 45 Concern Group—successor of the Basic Law Article 23 Concern Group—was established to promote universal suffrage in the 2007 Chief Executive election.

18 Nov 2003

The People's Bank of China, upon approval by the State Council, began a trial run of personal RMB businesses in Hong Kong, namely deposits, currency exchange, remittance and credit/debit cards, for closer Hong Kong–Mainland economic integration and tourism. On 24 December, Bank of China (Hong Kong) was appointed as the first settlement institution of RMB businesses in Hong Kong.

23 Nov 2003

In the second District Council elections, 400 councillors were elected (including 74 candidates who won uncontested). The voter turnout rate was 44.1%. In addition, there were 102 appointed members; 27 ex-officio members were chairmen of Rural Committees.

09 Dec 2003

The Splendid Chinese Culture website—a large-scale digital platform of Chinese history and culture established by the Academy of Chinese Studies (ACS)—was named winner of the 2003 UN World Summit Awards in Culture & Tourism. ACS was founded on 04 August 2000 in support of promoting a greater public understanding of Chinese history and culture.

The Mainland and Hong Kong Closer Tourism Cooperation Agreement was signed by the HKSAR government and China National Tourism Administration. It aimed to attract more tourists through greater cooperation including measures to protect tourists' rights.

The HKSAR government implemented a registration system of Chinese medicine. All proprietary Chinese medicines manufactured in or imported to Hong Kong must be registered with the Chinese Medicine Council of Hong Kong by 30 June 2004.

19 Dec 2003

The Public Officers Pay Adjustments (2004/2005) Ordinance was promulgated, effective 01 January 2004, stipulating a two-phase reduction in civil servant salaries to reach the level of 30 June 1997 by 01 January 2005.

20 Dec 2003

The Kowloon-Canton Railway's West Rail Line—measuring 30.5 kilometres with nine stations between Sham Shui Po in West Kowloon and Tuen Mun in the New Territories for an integrated rail network with the Mass Transit Railway and Light Rail Transit systems—was inaugurated. On 16 August 2009, it was extended to Hung Hom Station. (Figure 307)

Figure 307
A section of the West Rail Line in Yuen Long with the town of Tin Shui Wai in the background. (Photo courtesy of HKSAR Government)

24 Dec 2003

The police in an evening operation stormed a flat at Man King Building in Yau Ma Tei where Kwai Ping-hung (季炳雄) and an accomplice were arrested for possession of a large quantity of firearms. In a 2005 High Court trial, he was convicted of illegal possession of firearms and of resisting arrest with a firearm in 2001; he was sentenced to 24 years in prison.

Dec 2003

The Tung Chung Rural Committee was exposed by environmental groups for illegal quarry and ecological damage in the Tung Chung River in an attempt to supply 400 tonnes of pebbles in the construction of an artificial lake at Hong Kong Disneyland. On 14 April 2004, 12 people, including the Tung Chung Rural Committee chairman, were charged with corruption, bribery and fraud by the Independent Commission Against Corruption; four were convicted and sentenced to imprisonment ranging 11 months to two years.

2003

Tang Siu-pun (鄧紹斌) who had been paralysed and bedridden for 12 years from a gymnastic accident requested euthanasia in an open letter to Chief Executive Tung Chee-hwa (董建華) and Legislative Council. On 20 April 2004, the Chief Executive wrote back to encourage him to live an active life.

01 Jan 2004

The Closer Economic Partnership Arrangement was implemented, starting with zero-tariffs on 273 Hong Kong products deemed compliant with the rules of origin, and priority access of 18 Hong Kong service sectors in the Mainland. Seven areas of cooperation through a joint steering committee included: promotion of trade and investment, facilitation of customs clearance, commodity inspection and quarantine, e-commerce, transparency in laws and regulations, small and medium enterprises, and traditional Chinese medicine.

The Comprehensive Social Security Assistance Scheme was revised to include a new requirement that a person must be a Hong Kong resident for at least seven years to be eligible for entitlements.

05 Jan 2004

An MTR train en route from Tsim Sha Tsui to Admiralty was set on fire in the first arson attack since its inception in 1979, causing 14 injuries. Yim Kam-chung (嚴金鐘) was arrested and in 2006 was sentenced to life imprisonment.

07 Jan 2004

The Task Force on Constitutional Development, chaired by the Chief Secretary for Administration, was established as a platform to examine the relevant principles of the Basic Law, consult with related departments of the Chinese Central Government, and solicit public views on the issue.

10 Jan 2004

The Hong Kong Heritage Museum began a 16-day exhibition called Four Bronze Animal Heads from Yuanmingyuan. It displayed four of the 12 bronze-cast Chinese zodiac animal heads from the Old Summer Palace classified as top-grade national treasures. The pig-head statue made its debut in Hong Kong.

12 Jan 2004

The Steering Committee on Innovation and Technology was established as a government coordinator on formulation of tech-related policies and facilitation of greater synergy among different programmes. On 01 April 2015, it was re-established as the Advisory Committee on Innovation and Technology.

17 Jan 2004

A Symphony of Lights—a daily light and sound show synchronised with 33 buildings on shores of Victoria Harbour—was launched. On 21 November 2005, it made the *Guinness World Records* as the world's largest light and sound performance. (Figure 308)

Wing Lung Bank became the first Hong Kong bank to establish a branch in the Mainland (with approval by the China Banking Regulatory Commission) since the implementation of CEPA.

18 Jan 2004

RMB-denominated UnionPay cards issued by Mainland banks came into use in Hong Kong.

27 Jan 2004

Hutchison 3G HK, a telecommunications provider under Hutchison Whampoa, became the first operator to launch the third-generation mobile communication technology (3G) services.

09 Feb 2004

The HKSAR government reached an agreement with the developer of the Hunghom Peninsula Private Sector Participation Scheme project, allowing 2,470 Home Ownership Scheme flats to be sold in the open market under a modified Conditions of Sale for a premium of just $864 million. In face of public opposition to the demolition of the property, the developer announced on 10 December that the housing units would be preserved. In January 2008, the refurbished property, now renamed Harbour Place, went up for sale.

Figure 308
A Symphony of Lights—known to be the world's largest light and sound performance shown across Victoria Harbour every evening at 8 p.m. (Photo courtesy of HKSAR Government)

10 Feb 2004

Following a visit to Beijing (08–10 February) of the Constitutional Development Task Force headed by Chief Secretary for Administration Donald Tsang Yam-kuen (曾蔭權), Xinhua News Agency released a statement stressing that "One Country" preceded "Two Systems" and that "self-governance" required "patriotism." It marked the beginning of an emphasis on "patriotic governance."

13 Feb 2004

Soul of the City: International Symposium on Art and Public Space—a two-day conference organised by the Home Affairs Bureau—began as the first large-scale government conference on art-related topics.

25 Feb 2004

Banks in Hong Kong began providing personal RMB services, including deposit, currency exchange and remittance. From 30 April, RMB debit/credit cards issued in Hong Kong became available to Hong Kong residents for use in the Mainland.

26 Feb 2004

The HKSAR government presented the *Hong Kong Declaration on Sustainable Development for Cities* at the UN Asia-Pacific Leadership Forum on Sustainable Development for Cities—co-organised by the Chinese government and UN Department of Economic and Social Affairs.

28 Feb 2004

The Fine Dining—Exhibition on Ancient Chinese Culinary Wares was launched at Hong Kong Heritage Museum. It featured over 100 pieces of tableware, cooking utensils and drinking sets from the National Museum of China.

08 Mar 2004

The Women's Commission launched a Capacity Building Mileage Programme; it was the first large-scale platform on life-long learning and self-development among women.

Hong Kong neurobiologist Nancy Ip Yuk-yu (葉玉如) was named winner for her achievement in neurobiological research at the sixth annual L'Oréal-UNESCO for Women in Science Awards.

17 Mar 2004

Hong Kong Trade Development Council's CEPA Business Centre was opened as an information centre on Mainland business regulations and a consultancy platform with Mainland officials in support of Hong Kong businesses.

26 Mar 2004

The Antiquities and Monuments (Declaration of Historical Building) Notice 2004 was promulgated, making Morrison Building (formerly the Ta Teh Institute) a declared monument. It was the first time that the Antiquities and Monuments Ordinance was invoked to prohibit demolition in preservation of a private historic building.

30 Mar 2004

The Constitutional Development Task Force, headed by the Chief Secretary for Administration, presented its first report *Issues of Legislative Process in the Basic Law Relating to Constitutional Development* at a Shenzhen meeting with Chinese Central Government officials. It noted possible amendments to the "after 2007" provision stipulated in Article 7 of Annex I to the Basic Law with respect to the 2007 Chief Executive election.

01 Apr 2004

The Memorandum of Understanding on Cultural Cooperation between Singapore and HKSAR was signed for a formal framework on arts and culture, museums and libraries. It was Hong Kong's first bilateral agreement on cultural exchange and cooperation.

Figure 309
Jackie Chan（成龍）posed with
his handprint on Avenue of Stars
in Tsim Sha Tsui. (Photo courtesy
of HKSAR Government)

02 Apr 2004

The Copyright (Amendment) Ordinance 2003 was promulgated, lifting certain restrictions on parallel imports of computer software, including those for commercial, education or entertainment purposes, except products containing movies, television dramas, musical audio-visual recordings and e-books.

06 Apr 2004

The National People's Congress Standing Committee made its second interpretation of the Basic Law, namely provisions in Article 7 of Annex I and Article 3 of Annex II. It concluded: 1) "after 2007" included the year 2007; 2) "as necessary" meant that an amendment could be made; 3) as to whether an amendment was necessary, the Chief Executive should make a report to the NPC Standing Committee for a decision based on existing circumstances in accordance with Article 45 and Article 68 of the Basic Law and, if approved, for a legislation proposed by the HKSAR government and enacted by the Legislative Council; and 4) annexes remained in force if unamended.

15 Apr 2004

The Chief Executive presented to the National People's Congress Standing Committee a report on whether there remained a need to amend the methods for selecting the Chief Executive of HKSAR in 2007 and for forming the Legislative Council of the HKSAR in 2008, and a second report prepared by the Constitutional Development Task Force on issues of principle in the Basic Law relating to constitutional development.

19 Apr 2004

The HKSAR government issued securitised bond worth HK$6 billion backed by toll revenue from the Cross-Harbour Tunnel, Lion Rock Tunnel, Tseung Kwan O Tunnel, Aberdeen Tunnel, Shing Mun Tunnel and Lantau Link. It marked first and largest government issuance of securitised bonds.

26 Apr 2004

The National People's Congress Standing Committee reached its conclusion regarding the report on whether there remained a need to amend the methods for selecting the Chief Executive of HKSAR in 2007 and for forming the Legislative Council of the HKSAR in 2008 submitted by the Chief Executive on 15 April as follows: 1) neither election was to take place under universal suffrage while retaining the existing legislature composition and legislative protocols of the Legislative Council; and 2) amendments conforming to these decisions may be made in a gradual and stable manner in accordance with the Basic Law.

27 Apr 2004

The Avenue of Stars—a tourist attraction located on the Tsim Sha Tsui waterfront under a HK$40 million sponsorship by the New World Group and direct management by the government—was unveiled. It featured a line of commemorative plaques complete with the names, handprints and signatures of Hong Kong stars and directors in honour of their outstanding achievements. (Figure 309)

30 Apr 2004

The Bits of Old Hong Kong—an exhibition co-organised by the Hong Kong Museum of History—began at the National Museum of China; it ended on 29 July. It featured 150 cultural relics and 128 historical photographs of Hong Kong on loan for first time in an exhibition in the Mainland.

A People's Liberation Army naval fleet comprising eight warships and two helicopters arrived in Hong Kong for a six-day visit at the naval base on Stonecutters Island.

Apr 2004

Sixteen banks in Hong Kong were approved for full membership of China UnionPay by its Board of Directors, allowing Hong Kong to issue UnionPay cards.

11 May 2004

The Constitutional Development Task Force released its third report regarding "areas which may be considered for amendment in respect of the methods for selecting the Chief Executive in 2007 and for forming the Legislative Council in 2008." It suggested the possibility of expanding the Chief Executive Election Committee and increasing the total number of seats (and directly elected seats) in the Legislative Council.

18 May 2004

The Logistics Hong Kong International Conference and Exhibition began for a three-day forum; it was the first international logistics event organised by the Hong Kong Logistics Development Council.

23 May 2004

Hong Kong actress Maggie Cheung Man-yuk (張曼玉) won Best Actress at the Cannes Film Festival for her role in the French film *Clean.* She was the first Chinese actress to be given the honour.

01 Jun 2004

The first Pan-Pearl River Delta Regional Cooperation and Development Forum—a collaboration of Hong Kong SAR, Macao SAR and nine provinces and regions of the Mainland—was held in Hong Kong.

The Department of Health's Centre for Health Protection (CHP) was established to support disease prevention and control. Earlier on 01 April, Deputy Director of Health Leung Pak-yin (梁栢賢) was appointed as the first Controller of CHP.

05 Jun 2004

Peking University and Tsinghua University began a four-day examination-free student recruitment campaign in Hong Kong for admission of 50 local students each; more than 2,000 students showed up.

17 Jun 2004

The Memorandum on Closer Co-operation between Hong Kong and Shenzhen, along with eight other agreements on cooperation, was signed.

20 Jun 2004

The East Asian Games Planning Committee—chaired by President of the Sports Federation and Olympic Committee of Hong Kong, China (SF&OC) Timothy Fok Tsun-ting (霍震霆)—was established in preparation for the fifth East Asian Games in 2009.

21 Jun 2004

The Hong Kong Jockey Club Drug InfoCentre was opened as the first permanent anti-drug educational exhibition in Hong Kong and as the first resource centre on anti-drug abuse in the Asia-Pacific region.

24 Jun 2004

Ping An Insurance (Group) Company of China Limited was publicly listed in Hong Kong, becoming the first financial and insurance institution to be listed as a group outside the Mainland.

28 Jun 2004

Citibank (Hong Kong) Limited, a wholly owned subsidiary of US-based Citibank, became a restricted licence bank with approval from the Hong Kong Monetary Authority; it was eligible to participate in the Closer Economic Partnership Arrangement.

01 Jul 2004

The Hong Kong Deposit Protection Board was formed as an independent statutory body to oversee a scheme designed to protect deposits with local banks and promote a stable banking and financial system.

Standard Chartered incorporated its Hong Kong business to operate as a licenced bank in Hong Kong under Standard Chartered Bank (Hong Kong) Limited, a wholly owned subsidiary of Standard Chartered PLC.

02 Jul 2004

The Territory-wide System Assessment—commissioned by the Education and Manpower Bureau and administered by the Hong Kong Examinations and Assessment Authority—was implemented for Primary 3 students required to take subject examinations in Chinese, English and Mathematics. The assessment was extended to Primary 6 in 2005 and Secondary 3 in 2006.

05 Jul 2004

Fresh Fish Traders' School, following a special review by the Education and Manpower Bureau, was allowed to remain open. Earlier this year, it was ordered to suspend admission due to under-enrolment, followed by a protest of teachers and students. The primary school achieved sufficient enrolment of incoming Primary 1 students for the 2004/2005 school year that it could retain its programme.

11 Jul 2004

The Memorandum of Understanding between the Mainland and Hong Kong on Mutual Recognition of Academic Degrees in Higher Education was signed in Beijing between the Ministry of Education of the People's Republic of China and Education and the Manpower Bureau of the HKSAR. It provided a framework on reciprocal recognition of academic qualification for post-graduate studies.

13 Jul 2004

The Royal Institution of Chartered Surveyors established a local branch in Hong Kong for 4,000 professional members locally.

15 Jul 2004

The Council for Sustainable Development released its first paper *Sustainable Development: Making Choices for Our Future* in a public consultation on solid waste management, renewable energy, and urban living space.

16 Jul 2004

A team of Hong Kong students participated in the 35th International Physics Olympiad in South Korea, winning one gold, one silver and one bronze medals in addition to one honourable mention. The gold medallist also won the President's Award as a participant from a jurisdiction new to the Olympiad.

22 Jul 2004

The HKSAR government's $20 billion Global Bond Offering was completed for a non-recurring source of revenue to fund infrastructure and investment projects and promote the local bond market.

23 Jul 2004

The Education (Amendment) Ordinance 2004 was promulgated, effective 01 January 2005, requiring all subsidised schools to establish an incorporated management committee comprising teachers, parents and alumni by 01 July 2009.

01 Aug 2004

The People's Liberation Army (PLA) Hong Kong Garrison held its first public military parade with over 15,000 citizens at Shek Kong Barracks in celebration of the anniversary of the PLA's founding.

Figure 310
Hong Kong table tennis players Ko Lai-chak (高禮澤), left, and Li Ching (李靜), right, won silver medals at the 2004 Olympic Games. (Photo taken on 21 August 2004 and courtesy of Ramzi Haidar/AFP via Getty Images)

21 Aug 2004

Li Ching (李靜) and Ko Lai-chak (高禮澤) won a silver medal in table tennis men's doubles at the Athens Olympic Games. It marked the first Olympic medal of Team Hong Kong, China and the best result in table tennis at the Olympics. (Figure 310)

02 Sep 2004

The first plenary session of the Beijing-Hong Kong Economic and Trade Cooperation Conference began in Hong Kong. It established a three-tier exchange mechanism and identified seven areas for cooperation, namely Olympics economy, trade, professional exchanges, education, culture, tourism, and environmental protection.

06 Sep 2004

Fifty Chinese national athletes who won gold medals at the Athens Olympic Games arrived in Hong Kong for a three-day visit and made a special appearance in a performance at the Government Stadium.

12 Sep 2004

The HKSAR held its third Legislative Council elections with more than 3.2 million registered voters for 60 councillors, including 30 from geographical constituencies and 30 from functional constituencies. The voter turnout rates were 55.6% and 70.1%, respectively, higher than those of previous elections.

18 Sep 2004

A total of 396 people from Hong Kong took the National Judicial Examination for the first time after the implementation of the Closer Economic Partnership Arrangement.

20 Sep 2004

The Police Services Centre (Central District) became operational with 24-hour services for the public as the first police services centre in Hong Kong.

01 Oct 2004

The TV series *Our Home, Our Country*—produced by the Committee on the Promotion of Civic Education in conjunction with the Commission on Youth—made its debut. On 31 December, it began airing with the lyrics of the national anthem to promote greater public awareness.

02 Oct 2004

The Mei Foo branch of DBS Bank accidentally removed and lost 83 safety deposit boxes during a renovation in the first of such incidents in Hong Kong.

19 Oct 2004

Hong Kong Mortgage Corporation Limited issued US$3 billion in retail bonds, marking the first retail mortgage bond issued in Asia.

24 Oct 2004

The Kowloon–Canton Railway's Tsim Sha Tsui Extension—measuring one kilometre running between Hung Hom Station and East Tsim Sha Tsui Station—was opened for operation.

25 Oct 2004

The Judiciary published its *Guide to Judicial Conduct* to provide judges with practical assistance in dealing with matters relating to judicial conduct under three guiding principles, namely independence, impartiality, and integrity and propriety in all matters of conduct, both in and out of court.

27 Oct 2004

A supplement to the Closer Economic Partnership Arrangement was signed, effective 01 January 2005, adding 713 products to the tariff-free list while service markets in the legal, accounting, medical, audio-visual, construction, distribution, banking, securities, transport and freight forwarding sectors were further liberalised for Hong Kong.

29 Oct 2004

Hong Kong Science Park Phase I was opened with one million square feet of rentable space, attracting an inflow of more than 70 high-tech companies in the fields of applied research and product development.

01 Nov 2004

The Commercial Credit Reference Agency—operated by Dun & Bradstreet (HK) Limited in association with the Hong Kong Association of Banks (HKAB) and Hong Kong Association of Restricted Licence Banks and Deposit Taking Companies (DTCA)—was launched. It served to collect information about the indebtedness and credit history of small- and medium-sized enterprises (SMEs) and make such information available to members of HKAB and DTCA for the purpose of granting, reviewing or renewing SME credit lines.

09 Nov 2004

The Tai Hang Tung Storage began for use in preventing floods southward from Lion Rock to Mong Kok after heavy rainfall. It was the first underground flood storage tank in Hong Kong, with a capacity of 100,000 cubic metres.

11 Nov 2004

The Bank of East Asia's Luohu Sub-Branch was opened for business as the first sub-branch of a bank in Hong Kong established in Shenzhen after the signing of the Closer Economic Partnership Arrangement.

The HKSAR government's New Nature Conservation Policy was promulgated, identifying 12 sites, including Fung Yuen, Long Valley and Sha Lo Tung, for enhanced ecological conservation through Management Agreement and Public-Private Partnership schemes.

The Stockholm Convention on Persistent Organic Pollutants came into force, requiring the Mainland and Hong Kong to take measures to control or restrict the trade, production and use of 10 persistent organic pollutants.

Nov 2004

The Major Sports Events Committee launched its "M" Mark System and Support Packages to promote designated major sporting events in Hong Kong with additional support through publicity and interest-free loans.

The Hong Kong Archaeological Society in collaboration with Sun Yat-sen University and Chinese Academy of Sciences' Institute of Vertebrate Paleontology and Paleoanthropology began a three-month excavation at the Wong Tei Tung site in Sham Chung, Hong Kong. Stone artefacts unearthed were thought to have come from the Palaeolithic period. Scholars later pointed out that it was a Neolithic flint production site where adzes and flint tools were made.

06 Dec 2004

The Link Real Estate Investment Trust (The Link REIT)—a portfolio of retail and carparking facilities under the Housing Authority intended for divestment to tackle budgetary challenges—made its public debut as the first REIT listed on the Hong Kong.

15 Dec 2004

The Constitutional Development Task Force released its fourth report *Views and Proposals of Members of the Community on the Methods for Selecting the Chief Executive in 2007 and for Forming the Legislative Council in 2008*. It suggested a postponed decision on the timeframe regarding universal suffrage.

16 Dec 2004

The Immigration Department introduced its first self-service immigration clearance (e-Channel) at Lo Wu Control Point, followed by the launch of its first two Automated Vehicle Clearance Systems at Lok Ma Chau Control Point on 21 April 2005.

21 Dec 2004

The Kowloon–Canton Railway's Ma On Shan Line, measuring 11.4 kilometres with nine stations between Wu Kai Sha and Tai Wai, was opened for operation at a cost of about HK$10 billion.

27 Dec 2004

HKSAR government staff were dispatched to assist Hong Kong residents in Thailand affected by the tsunami in South Asia. On 01 January 2005, a government fundraiser was held, raising HK$33 million for victims in South Asia.

Dec 2004

The Education and Manpower Bureau introduced its voluntary Early Retirement Scheme to address a manpower surplus by allowing government primary school teachers under the age of 55 with at least 10 years of service to retire early with compensation.

01 Jan 2005

The Hong Kong Observatory recorded a morning temperature of 6.4°C in urban areas; it marked the lowest on a New Year's Day since 1962.

The Sports Commission was established as an advisory body on government policies and strategies regarding sports development in Hong Kong.

06 Jan 2005

The HKSAR government's Preparedness Plan for Influenza Pandemic was launched to provide public alerts amid an outbreak of avian influenza in Vietnam. A "yellow" response alert was issued the following day.

07 Jan 2005

The Crossing Borders Fundraising Show by Hong Kong performing artists ran for seven hours from 4–11 p.m. and raised over HK$36 million in support of tsunami victims in South Asia.

14 Jan 2005

The Drainage Services Department embarked on a 10-year nullah decking programme to improve sanitation by covering a total of 16 sections of nullahs (open sewage).

20 Jan 2005

A memorandum of understanding on Hong Kong Housing Society's HK$3 billion Building Management and Maintenance Scheme was signed to expedite the maintenance of old buildings.

25 Jan 2005

Langham Place in Mong Kok—a complex comprising commercial buildings, a shopping centre and a hotel—was officially opened upon completion of Hong Kong's largest redevelopment project jointly undertaken by the Urban Renewal Authority and Great Eagle Holdings.

05 Feb 2005

The Hong Kong Museum of Art began an exhibition called Impressionism: Treasures from the National Collection of France. It was a key programme of "The Year of France in China" in a cultural exchange between China and France with a tour to three major cities of China, namely Beijing, Shanghai and Hong Kong.

09 Feb 2005

The 2005 Carlsberg Cup (Lunar New Year Cup) was held on Chinese New Year's Day in a friendly football match between Hong Kong and Brazil, attracting over 23,000 spectators.

12 Feb 2005

A large branch of the Lam Tsuen Wishing Tree (a banyan tree frequented by tourists and locals alike) in Tai Po, New Territories broke off under a prolonged heavy load of oranges and joss paper (incense paper), causing two injuries. The customary practise of wish-making by throwing joss paper was banned and replaced with offerings on a wooden frame next to the tree.

16 Feb 2005

Democratic Alliance for the Betterment of Hong Kong (DAB) and Hong Kong Progressive Alliance merged to become a single political party called Democratic Alliance for the Betterment and Progress of Hong Kong (also abbreviated as DAB).

18 Feb 2005

The Commission on Poverty held its first meeting as an advisory body on government policy regarding alleviation of poverty.

10 Mar 2005

Chief Executive Tung Chee-hwa (董建華) in a press conference announced that he had notified the Chinese Central Government regarding his intention to resign from his capacity as Chief Executive for health reasons. He also expressed gratitude for a nomination by the Chinese People's Political Consultative Conference. On 12 March, he was appointed as Vice Chairman of the 10th Chinese People's Political Consultative Conference.

12 Mar 2005

Chief Executive Tung Chee-hwa (董建華) received approval for his resignation from the Chinese Central Government. Chief Secretary for Administration Donald Tsang Yam-kuen (曾蔭權) was appointed as Acting Chief Executive, followed by his announcement of candidacy in the Chief Executive election scheduled for 10 July in accordance with the Chief Executive Election Ordinance.

21 Mar 2005

The first Entertainment Expo Hong Kong began for a series of events to promote Hong Kong's entertainment industry, including film, digital entertainment, music and TV productions.

31 Mar 2005

An updated version of the Civil Servants' Guide to Good Practices was released; it came with a new chapter on misconduct in public office.

06 Apr 2005

Acting Chief Executive Donald Tsang Yam-kuen (曾蔭權) made a report to the State Council with a request for interpretation of Article 53(2) of the Basic Law regarding the term of office of a new Chief Executive elected to fill a vacancy. On 27 April, the National People's Congress (NPC) Standing Committee in its third interpretation of the Basic Law stated that a new Chief Executive shall be in office for the remainder of the previous five-year term.

24 Apr 2005

Hong Kong racehorse Silent Witness won the Queen's Silver Jubilee Cup to mark its 17th consecutive victory since debut; it was also the longest winning streak in Hong Kong, breaking the record of 16 consecutive wins by American racehorse Cigar in the 1990s. (Figure 311)

Figure 311
Hong Kong racehorse Silent Witness marked its 17th consecutive victory. (Photo taken on 25 April 2005 and courtesy of Kenneth Chan/South China Morning Post via Getty Images)

Figure 312
Contestants equipped with safety belts as a new measure at the Bun Snatching Competition. (Photo taken on 16 May 2016 and courtesy of HKSAR Government)

Figure 313
The traditional "Bun Snatching Competition" in 1963. (Photo courtesy of HKSAR Government)

Figure 314
Professor Jao Tsung-i (饒宗頤) during a meditation at The Wisdom Path. (Photo taken in 2008 and courtesy of Jao Tsung I Foundation)

05 May 2005

The Li Ka Shing Foundation announced a donation of HK$1 billion to The University of Hong Kong (HKU) for medical training and research. On 18 May, HKU's Council accepted the donation and announced its decision to rename its medical school as the Li Ka Shing Faculty of Medicine.

16 May 2005

The Bun Snatching Competition on Cheung Chau resumed after it was suspended for 26 years following an accident with the collapse of bun towers. For safety reasons, scaffolds were reinforced with a steel frame. It was rebranded as a sports event in which a maximum of 12 contestants were allowed to participate simultaneously in a competition. (Figures 312 and 313)

18 May 2005

The Hong Kong Monetary Authority announced three refinements to further support the Linked Exchange Rate System, including a strong-side convertibility undertaking to buy US dollars from licenced banks for HK$7.75, a shift in weak-side convertibility undertaking to sell US dollars to licenced banks from HK$7.80 to HK$7.85, and market operations within the defined convertibility zone intended to remove any market anomalies.

The Education and Manpower Bureau released its *New Academic Structure for Senior Secondary Education and Higher Education: Action Plan for Investing in the Future of Hong Kong*. It introduced a new academic structure with "3+3+4" years of junior secondary, senior secondary and university education. A New Senior Secondary curriculum with a focus on core subjects, electives and learning experiences was to be implemented in the 2009/10 school year; four-year undergraduate programmes were to be implemented in the 2012/13 school year.

20 May 2005

The Arrangement on Transfer of Sentenced Persons between Hong Kong and Macau was signed, allowing prisoners to serve sentences in the place of their origin.

The Wisdom Path on Lantau Island—featuring 38 timber columns of which 37 were inscribed with Professor Jao Tsung-i's (饒宗頤) calligraphy "Prajna Paramita Hrdaya Sutra" (Heart Sutra)—was opened to the public as the world's largest outdoor Buddhist wood scripture. (Figure 314)

24 May 2005

The HKSAR government released a report called *A First Sustainable Development Strategy for Hong Kong*. It proposed a year-on-year reduction of municipal solid waste by a minimum of 1% until 2014, 1%-2% of electricity generation from renewable sources by 2012, and urban redevelopment focused on more open space and preservation of local history and heritage.

26 May 2005

The MTR Corporation and Shenzhen Municipal Government entered into an agreement for a Build-Operate-Transfer (BOT) project with Phase 2 of Line 4 of the Shenzhen Metro System under a 30-year franchise.

The Environmental Protection Department of the HKSAR and State Environmental Protection Administration of China signed the Cooperation Agreement on Air Pollution Control and Prevention between the Mainland and HKSAR. Major areas of collaboration included air pollution control and monitoring, as well as research and exchange on related issues.

The Housing Authority introduced a scheme allowing change of ownership in the open market upon payment of land premium with government-subsidised housing units under the Home Ownership Scheme and Tenants Purchase Scheme upon expiry of the first assignment (self-occupancy) period.

27 May 2005

The Chief Executive Election (Amendment) (Term of Office of the Chief Executive) Bill was promulgated, stipulating that a new Chief Executive elected in a by-election would serve the remaining term of office of his/her predecessor.

16 Jun 2005

The Registration and Electoral Office announced that Donald Tsang Yam-kuen (曾蔭權) as the sole candidate was elected as Chief Executive of the HKSAR for the remaining term of office of his predecessor.

23 Jun 2005

The Bank of Communications became a public company as the first national shareholders-owned commercial bank listed on the Hong Kong Stock Exchange.

08 Jul 2005

The Beijing Organising Committee for the Games of the 29th Olympiad was given approval (from the International Olympic Committee) to host the 2008 Beijing Olympic and the Paralympic equestrian events in Hong Kong.

The Court of Final Appeal ruled in *Leung Kwok-hung* (梁國雄) *and Others v. HKSAR* that requirements of notification with the police prior to a public rally or assembly under the Public Order Ordinance were not in violation with the Basic Law on the grounds that police measures were necessary to enable a demonstration to proceed lawfully and peacefully.

12 Jul 2005

Sing Tao News Corporation launched its free newspaper *Headline Daily*.

13 Jul 2005

Registered nurse Sylvia Fung Yuk-kuen (馮玉娟) became the first recipient of the Florence Nightingale Medal in Hong Kong awarded by the International Red Cross.

The Court of Final Appeal ruled in *Secretary for Justice v. Lau Kwok-fai* (劉國輝) *and Another* that civil service pay adjustments enacted by the HKSAR government were not inconsistent with Article 103 of the Basic Law—which only required continuation of Hong Kong's previous system of recruitment, employment, assessment, discipline, training and management of civil services, excluding salaries and compensation packages.

16 Jul 2005

Asia Television's Mr. Asia Contest was inaugurated as the first male beauty pageant in Hong Kong open to contestants from Asia.

20 Jul 2005

The Court of Final Appeal ruled in *Lo Siu-lan* (盧少蘭) *vs. Hong Kong Housing Authority* (HKHA) that HKHA's divestment of its retail and carpark facilities in public rental housing estates to its affiliated real estate investment trust, The Link, was lawful. The decision on the appeal by a public housing tenant allowed The Link's initial public offering.

The first Military Summer Camp for Hong Kong Youth—jointly organised by the Education and Manpower Bureau and People's Liberation Army Hong Kong Garrison—was launched.

29 Jul 2005

The HKSAR government launched a Contingency Plan for Emergency Response Operations outside Hong Kong as a programme to assist Hong Kong residents in distress or a serious disaster while abroad.

30 Jul 2005

Centaline Group Chairman Shih Wing-ching (施永青) founded the free daily newspaper *am730*.

Jul 2005

The Legislative Council's Finance Committee approved a HK$520 million for implementation of an Early Retirement Scheme with teachers of government-subsidised secondary schools under the Education and Manpower Bureau between 2006/07 and 2008/09 in a bid to support a new curriculum and reduce overstaffing. The scheme was extended before conclusion following the 2012/13 school year.

01 Aug 2005

The MTR Disneyland Resort Line—measuring 3.5 kilometres between two stations (Sunny Bay and Disneyland Resort) on Lantau Island—became operational as the first fully automated rail line in Hong Kong.

The Social Welfare Department relaxed restrictions on eligibility in the Portable Comprehensive Social Security Assistance Scheme by expanding the annual permissible limit of absence from Hong Kong, allowing recipients on welfare for no less than one year (instead of three) to join, and expanding its coverage from Guangdong Province to Fujian Province.

04 Aug 2005

Sunbeam Theatre—a landmark Cantonese opera house—was renewed (and preserved) in an extended lease through January 2009 upon an agreement reached by the Secretary for Home Affairs and trade representatives with the property owner.

05 Aug 2005

The Law Enforcement (Covert Surveillance Procedures) Order was gazetted with effect from the following day. It resulted from an executive order issued on 30 July stipulating specific requirements with respect to covert surveillance.

A Voluntary Surrender Scheme was made available for licenced farmers, wholesalers and transporters of live poultry to surrender their licences in exchange for an ex-gratia payment.

24 Aug 2005

The High Court ruled in *Leung TC William Roy v. Secretary for Justice* that marginalisation of homosexual people under the age of 21 according to the Crimes Ordinance was discriminatory and inconsistent with Article 25 of the Basic Law and the Hong Kong Bill of Rights Ordinance.

26 Aug 2005

The Harmful Substances in Food (Amendment) Regulation 2005 was promulgated, banning the sale of food containing malachite green.

31 Aug 2005

Seven Swords and *Perhaps Love* were chosen as the opening and closing films, respectively, of the 62nd Venice International Film Festival. It was the first time that Hong Kong films were featured at the festival.

Figure 315
At the opening ceremony of Hong Kong Disneyland: (front row, from left) Chief Executive Donald Tsang Yam-kuen (曾蔭權), Chinese Vice President Zeng Qinghong (曾慶紅), The Walt Disney Company CEO Mike Eisner, and President and COO Robert Iger. (Photo courtesy of HKSAR Government)

Aug 2005

The Housing Authority launched the final phase of the Tenants Purchase Scheme open to eligible public housing tenants. It began with Nam Cheong Estate, followed by Cheung Fat Estate, Fu Shin Estate, Long Ping Estate and Tsui Lam Estate.

08 Sep 2005

The Hong Kong Maritime Museum, a non-profit private museum located at Murray House in Stanley, was opened to preserve and exhibit relics in relation to the history of maritime trade in Hong Kong and the Pearl River Delta. On 25 February 2013, it was relocated to Central Pier 8.

12 Sep 2005

Vice President of the People's Republic of China Zeng Qinghong (曾慶紅) officiated at the grand opening of Hong Kong Disneyland. It marked Disney's fifth theme park in the world, its second in Asia and its first in China—for which construction began on 12 January 2003. (Figure 315)

16 Sep 2005

The Court of Final Appeal ruled unanimously (5–0) in favour of businesswoman Nina Wang Kung Yu-Sum (龔如心) claiming probate in solemn form of a will dated 1990 by her late husband Teddy Wang Teh-huei (王德輝) for an estate of over HK$40 billion against her father-in-law Wang Din-shin (王廷歆).

25 Sep 2005

Chief Executive Donald Tsang Yam-kuen (曾蔭權) led a delegation with all legislative councillors, including pan-democratic legislators absent from the Mainland for more than a decade, in a two-day visit to the Pearl River Delta region, marking a trip of significance for improved relations with the Chinese Central Government.

Sep 2005

The Hong Kong Housing Authority launched its Comprehensive Structural Investigation Programme for a safety review of public rental housing estates aged 40 years or more and a viability study on further repair and maintenance.

04 Oct 2005

The first two State Key Laboratories of China in Hong Kong for "Emerging Infectious Diseases" and "Brain and Cognitive Sciences" were inaugurated at The University of Hong Kong.

18 Oct 2005

Supplement II to the Mainland and Hong Kong Closer Economic Partnership Arrangement (Phase III) was signed, effective 01 January 2006. It gave all products of Hong Kong tariff-free treatment (except prohibited goods), relaxed the rules of origin pertaining to wrist watches of Hong Kong brands, and introduced 23 liberalisation measures in 10 service areas.

19 Oct 2005

The Constitutional Development Task Force released its fifth report regarding the Chief Executive election in 2007 and Legislative Council elections in 2008. It recommended an expanded Election Committee and Legislative Council by increasing memberships from 800 to 1,600 and 60 to 70, respectively.

21 Oct 2005

The Health, Welfare and Food Bureau of the HKSAR, Ministry of Health of China, and Secretariat for Social Affairs and Culture of the Macao SAR entered into a Cooperation Agreement on Response Mechanism for Public Health Emergencies regarding support measures in the event of major public health crises in the Mainland, Hong Kong or Macao.

24 Oct 2005

A defendant was found guilty of illegal public distribution of movies through peer-to-peer file-sharing software BT. On 07 November, he was sentenced to three months in prison following a trial at the Tuen Mun Magistrates' Court, marking the first criminal case of its kind in Hong Kong.

27 Oct 2005

China Construction Bank was listed on the Hong Kong Stock Exchange, raising over HK$62 billion in an initial public offering.

29 Oct 2005

The Hong Kong Heritage Discovery Centre—located at Kowloon Park in Tsim Sha Tsui and housed in two of the former British Army's Whitfield Barracks (S61 and S62)—was opened with a gallery and other facilities dedicated to the preservation of heritage and education.

01 Nov 2005

The Customs and Excise Department implemented its Red and Green Channel System at entry ports across Hong Kong to expedite clearance of arriving passengers and ensure proper declaration of dutiable commodities.

Diamond Princess, Asia's luxurious cruise ship with a vessel displacement of over 110,000 tonnes, arrived at the Kwai Chung Container Terminal in its first visit to Hong Kong.

The number of Unofficial Members of the Executive Council increased from seven to 15.

The naming of asteroid 20780 ("Chanyikhei") after 16-year-old student Stark Chan Yik-hei (陳易希) was approved by the International Astronomical Union. He became the youngest person in Hong Kong after whom an asteroid was named.

03 Nov 2005

The Hong Kong Mortgage Corporation, along with six participating banks of the Mortgage Insurance Programme, launched its first 10-year fixed-rate mortgage scheme.

04 Nov 2005

Hong Kong Baptist University's Faculty of Arts launched a biennial Chinese literary global award called The Dream of the Red Chamber Award: The World's Distinguished Novel in Chinese, with a cash prize of HK$300,000. In the first ceremony on 13 September 2006, Jia Pingwa (賈平凹) was presented with the first prize for his book *Shaanxi Opera*, and Dung Kai-cheung (董啟章) was named winner of the Jury Award for his work *The History of the Adventures of Vivi and Vera*.

09 Nov 2005

The Home Affairs Bureau of the HKSAR and Ministry of Culture of China signed an Agreement on Closer Cultural Partnership Arrangement in Hong Kong on cultural exchange and collaboration in promoting arts and culture, as well as intellectual property protection.

11 Nov 2005

The Revenue (Abolition of Estate Duty) Ordinance 2005 was promulgated, abolishing estate duties.

12 Nov 2005

Team Hong Kong, China participated in the first Asian Indoor Games in Bangkok, Thailand. It won 12 gold, nine silver and five bronze medals, ranking fourth among 37 participating countries and regions, and made six new Hong Kong records in swimming.

16 Nov 2005

Hong Kong International Airport in partnership with Shenzhen's Shekou Port launched the world's first cross boundary check-in service, allowing passengers to obtain boarding passes and check in luggages at Shekou Port and board their flight immediately upon arrival at the airport by ferry.

18 Nov 2005

United International College in Zhuhai—jointly run by Hong Kong Baptist University and Beijing Normal University—was inaugurated in a cornerstone-laying ceremony as the first Hong Kong–Mainland institution of higher education.

27 Nov 2005

The bronze statue of Bruce Lee (李小龍) at the Avenue of Stars in Tsim Sha Tsui was unveiled in honour of what would have been his 65th birthday. (Figure 316)

Astronauts of the spacecraft *Shenzhou 6*, including Fei Junlong (費俊龍) and Nie Haisheng (聶海勝), arrived in Hong Kong for a three-day visit. (Figure 317)

The Cantonese Opera Development Fund was established to support professional Cantonese opera training, education and performances. The Secretary for Home Affairs served as its trustee.

30 Nov 2005

The Pearl River Delta Regional Air Quality Monitoring Network was launched for a daily air quality index in a joint effort between Hong Kong and Guangdong.

01 Dec 2005

The Construction Waste Disposal Charging Scheme came into effect, requiring waste producers to pay for the disposal of construction waste on a per-metric-tonne basis.

Figure 316
The two-metre bronze statue of Bruce Lee (李小龍) in an iconic pose from the film *Enter the Dragon* was unveiled on Avenue of Stars in Tsim Sha Tsui. (Photo taken on 27 November 2005 and courtesy of Sing Tao News Corporation Limited)

Figure 317
Astronauts of the spacecraft *Shenzhou 6* received a warm welcome at Hong Kong Stadium; pictured holding flowers were astronauts Fei Junlong (費俊龍) in the front and Nie Haisheng (聶海勝) in the back. (Photo taken on 28 November 2005 and courtesy of Sing Tao News Corporation Limited)

Figure 318
Chief Executive Donald Tsang Yam-kuen (曾蔭權) delivered a speech during the opening ceremony of the sixth World Trade Organization (WTO) Ministerial Conference at Hong Kong Convention and Exhibition Centre. (Photo taken on 13 December 2005 and courtesy of South China Morning Post Publishers Limited)

Figure 319
Groups of Korean farmers clashed with the police in a demonstration at the sixth World Trade Organization (WTO) Ministerial Conference. (Photo taken on 13 December 2005 and courtesy of South China Morning Post Publishers Limited)

13 Dec 2005

The sixth World Trade Organization Ministerial Conference began in Hong Kong for a five-day meeting, outlining a roadmap on the final agreement of the Doha Development Agenda regarding market access for agricultural and non-agricultural products. (Figure 318)

17 Dec 2005

Groups of Korean farmers staged a protest outside the sixth World Trade Organization Ministerial Conference and triggered a riot. The police dispersed the crowd with tear gas and arrested 1,153 people—14 of whom were charged with taking part in an unlawful assembly; charges were later dropped. (Figure 319)

21 Dec 2005

The government-proposed arrangement on the 2007 Chief Executive and 2008 Legislative Council elections was turned down in a vote (short of a two-thirds majority) by the Legislative Council.

AsiaWorld-Expo—Hong Kong's largest exhibition venue with 70,000 square metres of floor space and a 13,500-seat arena located northeast of the Hong Kong International Airport—was opened at a cost of HK$2.35 billion. (Figure 320)

Figure 320
The East entrance of AsiaWorld-Expo as Hong Kong's largest exhibition venue. (Photo courtesy of HKSAR Government)

23 Dec 2005

The Revenue (Personalized Vehicle Registration Marks) Ordinance 2005 was promulgated, allowing vehicle owners to customise their own licence plates under existing vehicle registration requirements enforced by the Transport Department.

2005

The eight universities in Hong Kong funded by the University Grants Committee were approved for admission of up to 10% of non-local students.

Hong Kong Movie City—a HK$1.1 billion joint project by Shaw Brothers, Shaw Property Holdings Limited and China Star Entertainment Limited—was opened in Tseung Kwan O Industrial Estate.

04 Jan 2006

Hong Kong director Wong Kar-wai (王家衞) became the first Asian director appointed as Jury President for the 59th Cannes Film Festival.

06 Jan 2006

The Hong Kong Police College was inaugurated as the only post-secondary academy of disciplined (uniformed) services.

09 Jan 2006

Professor Fan Sheung-tat (范上達) and his team at The University of Hong Kong's Department of Surgery were presented with a First-Class Award for "State Scientific and Technological Progress" at the State Science and Technology Awards of China ceremony. It was in recognition of an innovative surgical technique of liver transplant using the right liver graft from a living donor. It marked the first time that such an award was presented to a Hong Kong scholar.

12 Jan 2006

Chief Executive Donald Tsang Yam-kuen (曾蔭權) began his occupancy at the Government House. The Office of the Chief Executive became operational starting 16 January.

Figure 321
The Hong Kong Stock Exchange Trading Hall with a capacity of over 100 traders was made an exhibition hall following a renovation. (Photo taken on 06 March 2006 and courtesy of South China Morning Post Publishers Limited)

16 Jan 2006

Hong Kong Exchanges and Clearing Limited held a ceremony to mark the opening of its renovated Trading Hall located at Exchange Square in Central. (Figure 321)

21 Jan 2006

The first experimental poultry stall designed to distance customers from live chicken was opened in Yuen Long. Chicken upon slaughter were vacuum-packed for sale as a measure to prevent the spread of avian influenza.

26 Jan 2006

The High Court ordered four Internet service providers to share information with the International Federation of the Phonographic Industry on 22 Internet users for copyright violation in the world's first civil case of music copyright infringement.

08 Feb 2006

The Public Health (Animals and Birds) (Licencing of Livestock Keeping) Regulation and Waste Disposal Ordinance were promulgated, effective 13 February, imposing a ban on backyard poultry as a measure to reduce the risk of an avian influenza outbreak in Hong Kong.

12 Feb 2006

The United Nations Convention Against Corruption came into force in Hong Kong, providing a comprehensive global mechanism on anti-corruption measures.

15 Feb 2006

The Chinese Central Government appointed Lü Xinhua (呂新華) as Commissioner of the Ministry of Foreign Affairs of the People's Republic of China in the HKSAR. He remained in office until 12 April 2012.

18 Feb 2006

The ninth World Firefighters Games began in Hong Kong, ending on 25 February, with 3,300 firefighters from 35 countries and regions. Hong Kong took the top spot with 134 gold, 169 silver and 186 bronze medals.

19 Feb 2006

The franchises of Hong Kong's three public bus operators were renewed with the addition of fare adjustments.

Hong Kong musician Peter Kam Pui-tat (金培達) won a Silver Bear (Best Film Music) at the 56th Berlin International Film Festival for the film *Isabella*.

22 Feb 2006

Joseph Zen Ze-kiun (陳日君), Bishop of the Catholic Diocese of Hong Kong, was appointed as Cardinal by Pope Benedict XVI.

23 Feb 2006

Hongkong Electric commissioned the first commercial-scale wind turbine in Hong Kong, Lamma Winds, in Tai Ling on Lamma Island, producing on average about one million units of green electricity and offsetting 800 metric tonnes of carbon dioxide emissions each year.

27 Feb 2006

The Education and Manpower Bureau introduced measures in support of teachers by improving manpower and resources, adopting specialised teaching and increasing the number of permanent teachers in a bid to enhance the quality of teaching and learning.

05 Mar 2006

The State Council of the People's Republic of China released an outline of the 11th Five-Year Plan, emphasising its continued support for Hong Kong's status as a financial, trade and shipping centre.

06 Mar 2006

The Hong Kong Monetary Authority in conjunction with the Bank of China (Hong Kong) Limited launched a new RMB Settlement System. It included a clearing and settlement system with RMB cheques drawn from banks in Hong Kong for consumer spending in Guangdong, an automated system for remittance processing, card payments and RMB position-squaring, and a real-time enquiry service for participants.

Sheung Shui Heung held a once-every-60-years Tai Ping Qing Jiao (*Jiao* Festival)—a customary ritual wishing for "great peace" with the longest interval of its kind in Hong Kong. It attracted tens of thousands of villagers and spectators. (Figure 322)

10 Mar 2006

The Revenue (Profits Tax Exemption for Offshore Funds) Ordinance 2006 was promulgated, providing offshore funds with profits tax (17.5%) exemption intended to enhance Hong Kong's competitiveness as an international financial centre.

12 Mar 2006

Victoria Prison was decommissioned in a ceremony, marking the end of over 160 years of service as the first prison in Hong Kong.

14 Mar 2006

Kowloon–Canton Railway General Manager of Marketing Lai Kai-hin (黎啟憲) and 19 other senior executives publicly demanded the resignation of Chairman Michael Tien Puk-sun (田 北 辰). On the following day, Lai Kai-hin was summarily dismissed; others were issued warning letters. Acting CEO Samuel Lai Man-hay (黎文熹) resigned over the incident.

17 Mar 2006

Off-duty police officer Tsui Po-ko (徐步高) opened fire in Tsim Sha Tsui, killing police officer Tsang Kwok-hang (曾國恒) and seriously wounding police sergeant Sin Ka-keung (冼家強); Tsui was killed by Tsang during the shootout. On 04 April, Tsang was laid to rest at Gallant Garden in a funeral with full honours; on 01 July, he (posthumously) and Sin were awarded the Medal for Bravery (Gold).

18 Mar 2006

The Ngong Ping Sewage Treatment Works became fully operational as the first tertiary sewage treatment (removal of organic matters, filtration and disinfection) plant in Hong Kong.

19 Mar 2006

The Civic Party was inaugurated with members of the Article 45 Concern Group and several scholars. Kuan Hsin-chi (關信基) was its founding chairman; Audrey Eu Yuet-mee (余若薇) was party leader.

23 Mar 2006

The Pan-Pearl River Delta (PRD) Financial Services Forum began in Hong Kong with more than 600 government officials, including Chinese ministers, entrepreneurs and financial professionals. It was the first PRD-wide financial forum in Hong Kong.

24 Mar 2006

The Law Reform Commission published its report *Privacy: The Regulation of Covert Surveillance,* proposing legislation on surveillance as well as acquisition of personal information on private premises.

10 Apr 2006

Ocean Park's Sea Jelly Spectacular was inaugurated as the largest exhibit of jellyfish in Southeast Asia with nearly 1,000 jellyfish of 10 different species.

12 Apr 2006

The MTR Corporation Limited (together with its partners) and Beijing Municipal Government entered into a 30-year agreement on Beijing Metro Line 4 in the first urban rail project under a public-private partnership in the Mainland.

Figure 322
The opening ceremony of Tai Ping Qing Jiao (*Jiao* Festival) at Sheung Shui Heung—a showcase of cultural traditions, including dragon dance, flower plaques, bamboo scaffolding and the art of paper craft. (Photo taken on 08 March 2006 and courtesy of Sing Tao News Corporation Limited)

Figure 323
An aerial view of Hong Kong Wetland Park with its Wetland Discovery Centre pictured in the centre. (Photo taken on 10 December 2007 and courtesy of Oliver Tsang/South China Morning Post via Getty Images)

13 Apr 2006

The HKSAR government announced an agreement with Guangdong on fresh water from the East River (Dongjiang) in a three-year package deal for an annual lump sum HK$2.49 billion in exchange for a yearly supply of up to 820 million cubic metres of water to Hong Kong.

17 Apr 2006

The Interim Administrative Measures for Commercial Banks to Provide Overseas Financial Management Services— jointly issued by the People's Bank of China, China Banking Regulatory Commission, and State Administration of Foreign Exchange—was promulgated, allowing qualified Mainland institutions to make investment in Hong Kong and markets overseas.

20 Apr 2006

The Innovation and Technology Commission established five research and development centres for automotive, logistics and supply chain, information technology, nanotechnology, and textile and apparel. The initiative aimed to drive innovation and promote commercialisation.

The UN Convention for the Safeguarding of Intangible Cultural Heritage came into force. On 01 July 2008, the Intangible Cultural Heritage Advisory Committee was established as an advisory body on government policy regarding preservation of intangible cultural heritage in Hong Kong.

02 May 2006

The Food and Environmental Hygiene Department's Centre for Food Safety was formed to protect public health by ensuring the safety of food sold in Hong Kong.

The China Civic Education Promotion Association of Hong Kong was established to promote citizenship education and awareness.

12 May 2006

The Confucius Institute of Hong Kong was formed in collaboration with Hong Kong Polytechnic University as a platform of Chinese language and culture.

19 May 2006

The Hong Kong Wetland Park—a conservation, education and tourism facility located in Tin Shui Wai with a wetland reserve measuring 60 hectares and indoor exhibition halls measuring 10,000 square metres—was opened to showcase Hong Kong's diversified wetland ecosystem. The exhibition halls were opened on 29 December 2000. (Figure 323)

20 May 2006

The State Council of the People's Republic of China approved the inclusion of Cantonese opera and herbal tea—two intangible cultural heritage (ICH) items of Hong Kong, Macao and Guangdong—as part of the first national ICH list.

26 May 2006

Secondary Five graduate Chan Yik-hei (陳易希) was accepted by Hong Kong University of Science and Technology's Department of Electronics and Computer Engineering for a four-year undergraduate programme without taking any public examinations. It was the first direct admission of a student from a secondary school to a university in Hong Kong.

29 May 2006

Costa Crociere S.p.A., an international cruise operator, announced the establishment of its regional headquarters in Hong Kong.

01 Jun 2006

The HKSAR government introduced an incentive scheme with ex-gratia payment in exchange of pig farm licences, aiming to reduce public health risks and environmental pollution.

09 Jun 2006

Cathay Pacific Airways acquired a 100% stake in Dragonair, which became a wholly owned subsidiary (operationally independent) on 28 September.

12 Jun 2006

A new immigration arrangement was implemented allowing holders of a Mainland Travel Permit for Taiwan Residents to enter and stay in Hong Kong for seven days in lieu of an entry permit.

Callable Bull/Bear Contracts began trading on the platform of Hong Kong Exchanges and Clearing Limited.

World-renowned British physicist Stephen Hawking arrived in Hong Kong for a six-day visit.

16 Jun 2006

Chief Justice of the Court of Final Appeal Andrew Li Kwok-nang (李 國 能) issued the Guideline in relation to Part-time Judges and Participation in Political Activities, with respect to judicial independence and impartiality.

24 Jun 2006

The first General Aptitude Putonghua Shuiping Kaoshi—a Chinese proficiency test developed by Peking University's Chinese Language Education Institute—was held in Hong Kong under the approval of the Ministry of Education of China.

27 Jun 2006

Supplement III to the Mainland and Hong Kong Closer Economic Partnership Arrangement was signed, allowing Hong Kong residents with Mainland legal qualifications to represent Hong Kong-related matrimonial and succession cases in the capacity of a Mainland lawyer and for Hong Kong barristers to act as agents in civil litigation cases in the capacity of a citizen in the Mainland.

Chinese People's Political Consultative Conference Chairman Jia Qinglin (賈慶林) arrived in Hong Kong for a three-day visit.

28 Jun 2006

The Quality Migrant Admission Scheme was launched in a bid to attract highly skilled or talented individuals to live and work in Hong Kong through a points-based system with an annual quota of 1,000.

03 Jul 2006

The first phase of the civil servant five-day work week arrangement was implemented, extending service hours from Monday to Friday in place of office hours on Saturdays, except those on shifts and of the disciplined services.

08 Jul 2006

The Office of the Commissioner of the Ministry of Foreign Affairs in the HKSAR held its inaugural Open Day.

12 Jul 2006

The Court of Final Appeal ruled in a judicial review that the Law Enforcement (Covert Surveillance Procedures) Order was inconsistent with the Basic Law. It mandated a new government legislation within six months effective from the original High Court ruling on 09 February.

14 Jul 2006

The Arrangement on Reciprocal Recognition and Enforcement of the Decisions of Civil and Commercial Cases under Consensual Jurisdiction was signed by the Supreme People's Court of China and the HKSAR government, enabling reciprocal enforcement of court decisions.

21 Jul 2006

The Betting Duty (Amendment) Ordinance 2006 was promulgated, replacing turnover-based taxation with a system based on net stake receipts (gross profits) for The Hong Kong Jockey Club.

25 Jul 2006

Environmental Protection Department launched its Action Blue Sky campaign to improve air quality in Hong Kong.

26 Jul 2006

The Hong Kong Rope Skipping Association, China won four gold and seven silver medals, including its first-time win in the men's junior category, at the sixth World Rope Skipping Championships in Toronto, Canada.

06 Aug 2006

The MCL Cinema City in Nanshan, Shenzhen became the first Hong Kong-owned movie theatre to open in the Mainland under Phase II of the Closer Economic Partnership Arrangement.

07 Aug 2006

Hong Kong student Anna Pun Ying (潘瑛) won a gold medal at the China Girls Mathematical Olympiad in Urumqi, Xinjiang. It marked Hong Kong's first gold medal in addition to one silver and six bronze medals at the math competition.

09 Aug 2006

The Interception of Communications and Surveillance Ordinance was promulgated, prohibiting public officers from directly or indirectly engaging in the interception of communications or any covert surveillance, unless authorised, for protection of privacy and freedom of communication in Hong Kong.

26 Aug 2006

The world's largest online encyclopaedia, Wikipedia, began a two-day annual conference at The Chinese University of Hong Kong with respect to its Chinese edition.

01 Sep 2006

HKICC Lee Shau Kee School of Creativity—Hong Kong's first public secondary school dedicated to the arts and designed—began classes for students in Secondary 4–7.

06 Sep 2006

The HKSAR government began transition to its revamped website GovHK as a one-stop portal with comprehensive information and a user-friendly interface.

14 Sep 2006

The Hong Kong Observatory recorded an earthquake measuring 3.5 on the Richter scale in the sea near Dangan Island, approximately 36 km south-southeast of Hong Kong.

25 Sep 2006

Hong Kong Deposit Protection Board began providing protection of deposits in Hong Kong dollar and other currencies of up to HK$100,000 under its Deposit Protection Scheme.

28 Sep 2006

The Hong Kong Economic and Trade Office in Chengdu—covering Sichuan, Yunnan, Guizhou, Hunan, Shaanxi and Chongqing—was inaugurated.

Sep 2006

The Hong Kong Economic and Trade Office in Shanghai—covering Jiangsu, Zhejiang, Anhui and Hubei in addition to Shanghai—was inaugurated.

27 Oct 2006

Industrial and Commercial Bank of China became the first company to be listed simultaneously in Hong Kong (H Shares) and Shanghai (A Shares), marking the world's largest initial public offering by total capital raised (US$19.1 billion) and a record HK$425 billion in new stock subscriptions in Hong Kong.

Twenty-five torchbearers in Hong Kong completed a 4.5-kilometre torch relay of the 15th Asian Games (Doha).

The Hong Kong Monetary Authority announced its Banking (Capital) Rules and Banking (Disclosure) Rules regarding how capital adequacy ratio (CAR) of locally incorporated financial institutions should be calculated and what information on the state of affairs, profits and losses, and CAR should be publicly disclosed in compliance with a new capital adequacy framework known as Basel II.

The Smoking (Public Health) (Amendment) Ordinance 2005 was promulgated, effective 01 January 2007, mandating a smoke-free indoor environment in restaurants, bars, offices, schools, hospitals and markets.

28 Oct 2006

Henry Fok Ying-tung (霍英東), Vice Chairman of the Chinese People's Political Consultative Conference, passed away in Beijing at the age of 83. A public memorial service was held in Hong Kong on 07 November.

29 Oct 2006

The League of Social Democrats was established with its first general meeting; Wong Yuk-man (黃毓民) was its first chairman.

31 Oct 2006

The Decision of the Standing Committee of the National People's Congress on Authorizing the HKSAR to Exercise Jurisdiction over Its Port Zone within Shenzhen Bay Port was adopted, allowing port operation in Shenzhen under the laws of Hong Kong. The State Council on 30 December approved a designated zone of 41.565 hectares under a lease arrangement until 30 June 2047.

09 Nov 2006

Former Director of Health Margaret Chan Fung Fu-chun (陳馮富珍), following China's nomination, was elected as Director-General of the World Health Organization. In May 2012, she was reappointed for a second term ending June 2017.

The Ngong Ping 360 cable car became operational, running between the hilltop of Ngong Ping and downtown Tung Chung on Lantau Island.

11 Nov 2006

The 49-year-old Edinburgh Place Ferry Pier (also known as the Star Ferry Pier), along with Hong Kong's last mechanical clock tower, was decommissioned as part of the Central Reclamation Project; demolition began on 12 December. (Figure 324)

Figure 324
The old Star Ferry Pier in Central. (Photo taken on 28 August 2006 and courtesy of South China Morning Post Publishers Limited)

13 Nov 2006

Hong Kong, Macao and the Mainland held a joint cross-border exercise on infectious diseases in an evaluation of public health emergency preparedness, response and notification.

14 Nov 2006

The Nan Lian Garden—located at Diamond Hill in Kowloon and inspired by the garden design of the Tang Dynasty—was unveiled in a 3.5-hectare government project in collaboration with Chi Lin Nunnery.

18 Nov 2006

The Airbus A380, as the world's largest commercial aircraft, arrived at Hong Kong International Airport on a test flight and stayed for one day.

22 Nov 2006

The first Hong Kong Information and Communications Technology Awards—comprising seven award categories—was held in recognition of outstanding technology inventions and applications.

24 Nov 2006

Run Run Shaw (邵逸夫), founder of Shaw Brothers Pictures International Limited and one of the founders of the Asia-Pacific Film Festival, was named winner of the Lifetime Achievement award at the 51st Asia-Pacific Film Festival in Taipei.

01 Dec 2006

Team Hong Kong, China participated in the 15th Asian Games in Doha, Qatar, winning six gold, 12 silver and 10 bronze medals, including its first medals in triathlon and weightlifting.

03 Dec 2006

The ITU Telecom World 2006—an annual event with Olympics status in the tech industry—began at AsiaWorld-Expo in Hong Kong for a six-day exhibition, marking the first-time appearance outside of its headquarters in Geneva.

11 Dec 2006

The Dr Sun Yat-sen Museum located on Caine Road in Central was unveiled in a ceremony; it was opened to the public the following day. The premise was originally a residence built in 1914 known as the Kom Tong Hall; it was purchased by The Church of Jesus Christ of Latter-Day Saints before it was acquired in 2004 and made a declared monument in 2010 by the HKSAR government.

14 Dec 2006

A two-day international symposium with nine local tertiary institutions in celebration of Professor Jao Tsung-i's 90th birthday and his academic and artistic achievements began at The University of Hong Kong.

15 Dec 2006

The Prevention of Cruelty to Animals Ordinance 2006 was promulgated, increasing the maximum penalty to a fine of HK$200,000 and three years' imprisonment.

19 Dec 2006

A plot of residential land on Mount Kellett Road at the Peak was sold for a closing price of HK$1.8 billion, 1.3 times higher than the opening price of HK$768 million, in a public auction by the Lands Department, setting a world record of HK$42,149 per square foot of gross floor area.

The Chief Executive-in-Council approved Shue Yan College's status upgrade, making it Hong Kong's first privately funded university.

21 Dec 2006

The Hospital Authority launched measures to provide local pregnant women priority services in public hospitals, including higher charges for prenatal examination and childbirth delivery with non-residents and more effective triage through a central appointment system.

Hong Kong and Shenzhen signed a pact called Honest & Quality Hong Kong Tour, effective 01 January 2007, specifying fixed-price tours, adequate touring time and non-mandatory shopping arrangement for Mainland tourists in Hong Kong.

02 Jan 2007

The Housing Authority reintroduced the Home Ownership Scheme, making 3,056 government-subsidised housing units available for sale through a lucky draw on 12 February. (Figure 325)

03 Jan 2007

The Office of the Commissioner of the Ministry of Foreign Affairs in the HKSAR launched the first Hong Kong Cup Diplomatic Knowledge Contest, which ended in June. Nearly 50,000 secondary school students were enrolled in a competition on Chinese (including Hong Kong) diplomatic history and current affairs.

09 Jan 2007

The Hong Kong-Zhuhai-Macao Bridge Task Force—established under the National Development and Reform Commission of China—held its first meeting in Guangzhou on implementation of the infrastructure project.

11 Jan 2007

The RMB reached a higher value above the Hong Kong dollar (RMB 99.96 to HK$100) for the first time since it became a partially convertible currency.

24 Jan 2007

The film journal *City Entertainment*, founded in 1979 and once an organiser of the Hong Kong Film Awards, released its last issue (Issue 724) before ceasing publication.

14 Feb 2007

Hong Kong Memory—an online portal designed to capture Hong Kong's historical and cultural information—was launched in a five-year project supported by The Hong Kong Jockey Club in conjunction with the Leisure and Cultural Services Department under the leadership of Professor Elizabeth Sinn Yuk-yee (冼玉儀) and Professor Wong Siu-lun (黃紹倫), former deputy director and director, respectively, of HKU's Centre for Asian Studies.

15 Feb 2007

Chief Executive Donald Tsang Yam-kuen (曾蔭權) appointed a Commission of Inquiry on alleged attempts to reduce the number of places at the Hong Kong Institute of Education as a ploy to force a merger with The Chinese University of Hong Kong. On 20 June, an investigation report found the allegation to be unsubstantiated upon a lack of evidence of interference with academic independence from the Education and Manpower Bureau or any government officials.

Figure 325
Chairman of Housing Authority's Subsidised Housing Committee Michael Choi Ngai-min (蔡涯棉) officiated at a ballot draw for sale of surplus Home Ownership Scheme flats–2007 Phase I. (Photo taken on 12 February 2007 and courtesy of HKSAR Government)

Figure 326
Rita Fan Hsu Lai-tai (范徐麗泰), centre, served as a moderator of the Chief Executive Candidates Forum between Donald Tsang Yam-kuen (曾蔭權), left, and Alan Leong Kah-kit (梁家傑), right. (Photo courtesy of South China Morning Post Publishers Limited)

18 Feb 2007

The Hong Kong Observatory recorded a temperature of 25.3°C, making it the warmest Chinese New Year's Day in Hong Kong.

27 Feb 2007

Professor Che Chi-ming (支志明) of The University of Hong Kong's Department of Chemistry won a First Class Prize of the State Natural Science Award (2006) for his research in "reactive metal-ligand multiple bonded complexes." He was the first award recipient from Hong Kong.

Feb 2007

Hong Kong International Airport's Terminal 2 was partially opened as the centrepiece of the SKYCITY project; it became fully operational on 01 June with a total area of 140,000 square metres and 56 airline check-in counters.

01 Mar 2007

The third Chief Executive Candidate Forum, moderated by Legislative Council President Rita Fan Hsu Lai-tai (范徐麗泰), took place at the Hong Kong Convention and Exhibition Centre where candidates Donald Tsang Yam-kuen (曾蔭權) and Alan Leong Kah-kit (梁家傑) unveiled their campaign platforms in a televised debate. (Figure 326)

06 Mar 2007

Hong Kong film *Isabella* won the Best Film Award of the Orient Express Competition at the 27th Oporto International Film Festival. Isabella Leong Lok-sze (梁洛施) became the first Hong Kong actress to win Best Actress for her role in the film.

20 Mar 2007

Andy Lau Tak-wah (劉德華) and Josephine Siao Fong-fong (蕭芳芳) were awarded Box Office Star of Asia and Outstanding Contribution to Asian Cinema, respectively, at the first Asian Film Awards held in Hong Kong.

21 Mar 2007

Hong Kong International Airport introduced new security measures—allowing passengers to carry on board no more than 100 millilitre of liquid, gel or spray which must be placed in a sealed transparent plastic bag (with a capacity not exceeding one litre) upon inspection.

25 Mar 2007

Donald Tsang Yam-kuen (曾蔭權) defeated Alan Leong Kah-kit (梁家傑) in the third Chief Executive election (649 vs 123 votes) for a five-year term beginning 01 July 2007. On 02 April, Premier Wen Jiabao (溫家寶) made an official appointment by signing the Decree of the State Council of the People's Republic of China (No. 490).

28 Mar 2007

The *Report on Review of Public Service Broadcasting* was released, proposing a new government-funded public broadcasting company and a reconstitution of the 79-year-old Radio Television Hong Kong before continuing as a statutory public broadcaster.

30 Mar 2007

The Urban Renewal Authority's Kwun Tong Town Centre Redevelopment Project began along with a freezing survey on affected persons in the district.

31 Mar 2007

Hong Kong cyclist Wong Kam-po (黃金寶) won a gold medal in the 15-kilometre men's scratch at the UCI Track Cycling World Championships in Majorca, Spain. He was awarded the Rainbow Jersey and became the first Chinese national to win a cycling world championship.

01 Apr 2007

The Environmental Protection Department launched a HK$3.2 billion grant to tackle roadside air pollution through a subsidy scheme for replacement of pre-Euro and Euro I with Euro IV diesel-run commercial vehicles.

The Housing Department designated all common areas in public housing estates as non-smoking premises under the Marking Scheme for Estate Management Enforcement. Tenants were subject to a deduction of five merit points for each violation without prior warning.

The HKSAR government resumed recruitment of civil servants.

03 Apr 2007

The Hong Kong Local Records Office was established under Director Lau Chi-pang (劉智鵬) and Deputy Directors Joseph Ting Sun-pao (丁新豹) and Liu Shuyong (劉蜀永). It aimed to preserve and promote the local history and heritage of Hong Kong.

14 Apr 2007

The Hong Kong Film Development Council was established as an advisory body on government policy in support of the local film industry.

21 Apr 2007

The first Hong Kong Games was opened with 1,287 local athletes across 18 districts in four competitive sports, namely athletics, badminton, basketball and table tennis; it was concluded on 06 May.

25 Apr 2007

The Coroner's Court in its longest inquiry after 37 days of hearings ruled that police officer Tsui Po-ko (徐步高) committed illegal killings of police officers Leung Shing-yan (梁成恩) and Tsang Kwok-hang (曾國恒) and security guard Zafar Iqbal Khan.

26 Apr 2007

A pair of giant pandas named Le Le and Ying Ying arrived in Hong Kong with compliments of the Chinese Central Government in celebration of the 10th anniversary of the establishment of the HKSAR.

09 May 2007

The Antiquities Advisory Board declared the second-generation Queen's Pier, constructed in 1953, as a Grade 1 Historic Building. It had served as a landmark of official occasions, including the ceremonial arrivals of six governors since 1958.

11 May 2007

The China Banking Regulatory Commission authorised an expanded scope of offshore investment (shares of companies and funds listed in Hong Kong) in private wealth management for commercial banks in the Mainland.

15 May 2007

The Steering Group on Safe Food Supply to Hong Kong held its inaugural meeting in Beijing; it reaffirmed a regulatory mechanism on gatekeeping and a focus on random inspection of food items at source and destination.

21 May 2007

The High Court ruled in *The Democratic Party v. Secretary for Justice* that disclosure of political party memberships in accordance with the Companies Ordinance did not contravene freedom of association and privacy as outlined in Article 27 and Article 30 of the Basic Law.

25 May 2007

The Lantau Development Task Force released its revised *Concept Plan for Lantau*—a framework of sustainable development focused on urbanisation in the north and ecological conservation in the south of Lantau Island—outlining additional provisions on recreational facilities, including hiking trails, country parks and water sports venues.

29 May 2007

An international conference on climate change, organised by the HKSAR government, began at the Hong Kong Convention and Exhibition Centre.

01 Jun 2007

The Unsolicited Electronic Messages Ordinance was promulgated, criminalising illicit activities tied to commercial electronic messages with immediate effect. Starting from 22 December, it allowed the public to refuse receiving commercial messages.

02 Jun 2007

Chuang Shih-ping (莊世平), a former deputy of the National People's Congress, member of the Chinese People's Political Consultative Conference Standing Committee and founder of Nanyang Commercial Bank, passed away at the age of 97.

07 Jun 2007

The Professional Commons, a public policy group chaired by Albert Lai Kwong-tak (黎廣德), was established, comprising more than 100 members of the Election Committee.

18 Jun 2007

The Hong Kong Monetary Authority launched the RMB Real-Time Gross Settlement System for which Bank of China (Hong Kong) Limited was designated as a clearing bank.

22 Jun 2007

Princess Margaret Hospital's Infectious Disease Centre was opened with a capacity of 108 beds as the first designated centre in Hong Kong.

The Housing (Amendment) Bill 2007 was promulgated, introducing an adjustment mechanism in public housing rent based on the changing levels of tenant household income.

25 Jun 2007

The Transport Support Scheme was launched in a pilot programme to provide eligible persons living in Tuen Mun, Yuen Long, North District and the outlying islands with a monthly subsidy of up to HK$600.

Hong Kong Exchanges and Clearing Limited launched its Electronic Disclosure Project, requiring public companies listed on the Main Board to disclose information through the e-Submission System.

26 Jun 2007

China Development Bank issued the first batch of offshore RMB bonds in Hong Kong.

29 Jun 2007

President Hu Jintao（胡錦濤）arrived in Hong Kong for a three-day visit in celebration of the 10th anniversary of the establishment of the HKSAR. (Figure 327)

Supplement IV to the Mainland and Hong Kong Closer Economic Partnership Arrangement (CEPA) was signed. It expanded the coverage of CEPA's rules of origin to a total of 1,465 products as of 01 July 2007; 40 market-liberalisation measures were applicable to 28 service sectors, including 17 current and 11 new sectors, as of 01 January 2008.

The Pride of China: Masterpieces of Chinese Painting and Calligraphy of the Jin, Tang, Song and Yuan dynasties from the Palace Museum was launched at the Hong Kong Museum of Art. It was an exhibition of famous paintings, including the masterpiece *Along the River during the Qingming Festival* by Zhang Zeduan（張擇端）of the Northern Song Dynasty on display for the first time outside the Mainland. (Figure 328)

01 Jul 2007

President Hu Jintao（胡錦濤）administered the oath of office of Chief Executive Donald Tsang Yam-kuen（曾蔭權）and principal officials at the inauguration of the HKSAR's third government in a ceremony at the Hong Kong Convention and Exhibition Centre.

President Hu Jintao（胡錦濤）officiated at the opening ceremony of Shenzhen Bay Port and Hong Kong–Shenzhen Western Corridor. The Shenzhen Bay Port was the first co-location border control point. The 5.5-kilometre Hong Kong-Shenzhen Western Corridor was the fourth crossing between Hong Kong and Shenzhen. (Figure 329)

The Development Bureau and Environment Bureau were established in a restructure of the HKSAR government. Functions of the Labour and Welfare Bureau, Transport and Housing Bureau, Commerce and Economic Development Bureau and Food and Health Bureau were redesignated. The Constitutional Affairs Bureau was renamed Constitutional and Mainland Affairs Bureau; Education and Manpower Bureau was renamed Education Bureau.

09 Jul 2007

The polymer ten-dollar banknote, issued by the Hong Kong Monetary Authority, went into circulation.

Figure 327
President Hu Jintao（胡錦濤）spoke with two young table tennis players, Chiu Chung-hei（趙頌熙）, right, and Lee Ho-ching（李皓晴）, left, in a pep talk during a visit at Hong Kong Sports Institute. (Photo taken on 29 June 2007 and courtesy of Ricky Chung/South China Morning Post via Getty Images)

Figure 328
Visitors immersed in an exhibition of the historic painting *Along the River during the Qingming Festival*—a depiction of life in the capital city of Bianliang (also known as Kaifeng) during the Northern Song Dynasty. (Photo courtesy of Dustin Shum/South China Morning Post via Getty Images)

11 Jul 2007

The *Green Paper on Constitutional Development* was released in a public consultation, outlining a roadmap on the implementation of universal suffrage in future elections of the Chief Executive and Legislative Council.

24 Jul 2007

The Hong Kong Observatory issued a Very Hot Weather warning which remained in force for 286 hours and 10 minutes until 05 August, making it the longest hot weather warning as of 01 July 2017.

25 Jul 2007

The Hong Kong Museum of History began an exhibition called Major Archaeological Discoveries of China in Recent Years; it was concluded on 24 September. Relics from more than 20 archaeological sites in nine provinces and cities across China were on display.

27 Jul 2007

The State Administration of Radio, Film and Television of China eliminated the quota on Hong Kong-made films for the Guangdong market.

01 Aug 2007

The 82-year-old Queen's Pier and its surrounding government-owned land were designated for redevelopment as part of the Central Reclamation Phase III project.

02 Aug 2007

The HKSAR government announced a dedicated corridor and rail tracks in the Hong Kong section (between West Kowloon Terminus and the Hong Kong–Shenzhen border) of the Guangzhou-Shenzhen-Hong Kong Express Rail Link, further shortening the journey time between Hong Kong and Guangzhou.

08 Aug 2007

Steel fixers went on strike, demanding higher pay. On 12 September, an agreement was reached for a daily pay of HK$860 and eight-hour workdays, ending the 36-day strike.

Figure 329
President Hu Jintao (胡錦濤) in his presidential vehicle crossed the boundary between Shenzhen and Hong Kong in a ribbon-cutting ceremony, marking the official opening of Shenzhen Bay Bridge. (Photo courtesy of HKSAR Government)

10 Aug 2007

The High Court ruled in a judicial review that it was legal for the Antiquities Advisory Board not to list the Queen's Pier as a declared monument.

15 Aug 2007

The 7.4-kilometre Kowloon–Canton Railway Lok Ma Chau Spur Line, along with the Futian Checkpoint, was inaugurated as the second Shenzhen–Hong Kong cross-border rail, running between Sheung Shui Station and Futian Checkpoint at Lok Ma Chau.

23 Aug 2007

Nine-year-old prodigy March Tian Boedihardjo (沈詩鈞) was accepted to a five-year bachelor-master programme in mathematics under Hong Kong Baptist University's Faculty of Science, becoming the youngest university student in Hong Kong as of 01 July 2017.

03 Sep 2007

The 14th Asian Aerospace International Expo and Congress was opened, attracting over 500 exhibitors and more than 10,000 registered visitors from 83 countries in the event first held in Hong Kong.

10 Sep 2007

The Standard became the first free-of-charge English daily newspaper in Hong Kong.

14 Sep 2007

Hong Kong Science Park Phase II was opened.

15 Sep 2007

The Antiquities and Monuments (Declaration of Proposed Monument) (No. 45 Stubbs Road) Notice was promulgated, declaring King Yin Lei (demolition in progress) a proposed monument with a 12-month temporary ban on further demolition. On 25 April 2008, a government non-in-situ land exchange proposal was gazetted to preserve the historic mansion—built in 1937 in a mix of Chinese and Western architectural styles—including a traditional three-sided Lingnan-style courtyard house.

20 Sep 2007

The Expert Group on Preservation of Old and Valuable Trees was established, comprising a panel of arboriculture experts, as an advisory group in support of the Leisure and Cultural Services Department on the conservation of trees.

21 Sep 2007

The Asian Financial Forum—a government collaboration with the Hong Kong Trade Development Council—was opened for a conference with over 800 international financial professionals.

29 Sep 2007

The Fireboat Alexander Grantham Exhibition Gallery in Quarry Bay Park was opened. The *Alexander Grantham* was the first fireboat in Hong Kong and was restored as a heritage vessel. (Figure 330)

Sep 2007

The Education Bureau's Pre-primary Education Voucher Scheme was launched to provide students of non-profit private kindergartens with government subsidies.

02 Oct 2007

Team Hong Kong, China marked a record in the Special Olympics World Summer Games in Shanghai, winning 67 gold, 50 silver and 37 bronze medals in 10 competitive sports.

Figure 330
The permanent exhibition of fireboat *Alexander Grantham* at Quarry Bay Park as a museum on maritime firefighting in Hong Kong. (Photo courtesy of Sing Tao News Corporation Limited)

05 Oct 2007

The Housing Authority's Harmonious Families Priority Scheme was launched, allowing grown children of elderly tenants to live together in public housing as part of the elderly care policy "Ageing in Place."

11 Oct 2007

The Planning Department released its final report *Hong Kong 2030: Planning Vision and Strategy*, suggesting priority development of new towns in Kwu Tung North, Fanling North, Ping Che, Ta Kwu Ling and Hung Shui Kiu in view of a growing population.

22 Oct 2007

Marco Fu Ka-chun (傅家俊) became the first snooker player from Hong Kong to win the Royal London Watches Grand Prix.

Oct 2007

The Steering Committee on Population Policy, chaired by the Chief Secretary for Administration, was formed as a coordinator on formulation of government policy with respect to the local population.

06 Nov 2007

Alibaba, a Mainland e-commerce company, was listed on the Hong Kong Stock Exchange. It raised HK$11.6 billion and was over-subscribed 256 times for more than HK$450 billion, making it the largest Internet stock in Hong Kong as of 2017.

13 Nov 2007

The Hong Kong Taoist Association held an opening ceremony of the 12-day Great Ritual Offerings to the All-Embracing Heaven at Yuen Yuen Institute.

18 Nov 2007

In the third District Council elections, 405 councillors were elected (including 41 candidates who won uncontested). The voter turnout rate was 38.83%. In addition, there were 102 appointed members; 27 ex-officio members were chairmen of Rural Committees.

19 Nov 2007

The Hong Kong Institute of Archaeology began a two-month excavation at the Luk Keng Village site on Lantau Island, uncovering remains from the Bronze Age and Tang Dynasty. Stone cast for bronze-making and pottery with geometric patterns from the Xia and Shang periods were found, indicating the art of bronze casting in Hong Kong.

Figure 331
Crowds of people captured a special moment marking the merger of MTR Corporation and Kowloon–Canton Railway (KCR) Corporation as a new exit sign was raised at East Tsim Sha Tsui Station. (Photo courtesy of Sing Tao News Corporation Limited)

22 Nov 2007

Hang Seng Bank launched Hong Kong's first Islamic fund authorised by the Securities and Futures Commission.

02 Dec 2007

The Kowloon–Canton Railway Corporation ended its 97-year operation in a service concession (a merger of operation of two rail networks in Hong Kong) with MTR Corporation Limited. (Figure 331)

06 Dec 2007

The Minimal Access Surgery Training Centre at Pamela Youde Nethersole Eastern Hospital, Hong Kong East Cluster was opened with Hong Kong's first EndoLap (endoscopic and laparoscopic surgery) operating theatre.

11 Dec 2007

The first public Garden of Remembrance, located at Cape Collinson Crematorium, was opened for green burials as a designated area for scattering cremated ashes.

12 Dec 2007

Chief Executive Donald Tsang Yam-kuen (曾蔭權) submitted a report to the National People's Congress Standing Committee following a public consultation on the *Green Paper on Constitutional Development* in which he noted a public consensus for a timetable on universal suffrage. He proposed universal suffrage for Chief Executive elections no later than 2017 and for Legislative Council elections thereafter, further seeking confirmation whether electoral methods in 2012 were allowed for amendment.

16 Dec 2007

Shek Kip Mei Estate was re-opened upon reconstruction as the first public housing estate to adopt a barrier-free design with the objective of providing greater ease with accessibility for the elderly, the young and people with disabilities.

29 Dec 2007

The NPC Standing Committee in response to the Chief Executive report on 12 December made the following decisions: 1) electoral methods in the 2012 Chief Executive and Legislative Council elections might be amended as appropriate; 2) composition and power of the Legislative Council should remain; 3) universal suffrage could be adopted in the 2017 Chief Executive election; 4) universal suffrage might follow in the elections of the Legislative Council; 5) electoral methods and legislative powers would continue to apply if no amendments were made; and 6) an inclusive nomination committee must be formed in accordance with the Basic Law upon adoption of universal suffrage in the Chief Executive election.

Dec 2007

Chairman of the Central Military Commission Hu Jintao (胡錦濤) appointed Zhang Shibo (張仕波) as Commander of the People's Liberation Army Hong Kong Garrison who remained in the post until October 2012.

07 Jan 2008

A new Scheme of Control Agreement on electricity charges was signed with CLP Power and Hongkong Electric, prescribing a lower permitted rate of return from 13.5-15% to 9.99% coupled to environmental performance and emission control.

19 Jan 2008

The Hoi Ha Marine Life Centre—Hong Kong's first marine education facility supported by Hong Kong Jockey Club, Hongkong and The Shanghai Banking Corporation and World Wildlife Fund-Hong Kong—was opened.

24 Jan 2008

A 21-day cold spell with a daily low of 12°C began in the longest cold wave since 1968. The Hong Kong Observatory issued a Cold Weather warning which lasted for 594.5 hours until 18 February, marking the longest cold weather warning as of 01 July 2017.

25 Jan 2008

The Landfill Gas Utilisation Project at North East New Territories Landfill was commissioned as the largest utilisation programme in Hong Kong.

27 Jan 2008

Indecent photos of various Hong Kong actresses began circulating on the Internet, causing an uproar in the community. On 13 May 2009, a computer technician was convicted on three counts of obtaining access to a computer with dishonest intent and sentenced to eight and a half months in prison following a trial at the Kowloon City Magistrates' Courts.

01 Feb 2008

The Centre for Food Safety Rapid Alert System was launched to provide an intra-industry communication channel for dissemination of information.

22 Feb 2008

Batch I of the Revitalising Historic Buildings Through Partnership Scheme was launched.

10 Mar 2008

The Hong Kong–Shenzhen Joint Task Force on Boundary District Development held its first meeting in Shenzhen to explore co-development of land uses in the vicinity of the boundary between Hong Kong and Shenzhen.

11 Mar 2008

The World Ports Summit began for a two-day conference on the issues of port security, safety and environmental protection at the Hong Kong Convention and Exhibition Centre.

22 Mar 2008

The Ukrainian tugboat *Neftegaz-67* sank after colliding with a Mainland cargo ship east of Siu Mo To—an island located north of Lantau Island. A total of 18 crew members were killed; seven were rescued.

Mar 2008

The HK$1 billion HKSAR Government Scholarship Fund was established to recognise outstanding local and non-local students at public universities in Hong Kong.

03 Apr 2008

The Food and Drugs (Composition and Labelling) (Amendment: Requirements for Nutrition Labelling and Nutrition Claim) Regulation 2008 was promulgated, effective from 01 July 2010, requiring "1+7" nutrition labels in pre-packaged food products.

Figure 332
Hong Kong cyclist Wong Kam-po (黃金寶) arrived at the Golden Bauhinia Square in Wan Chai as the final torchbearer in the first leg of the 2008 Summer Olympic torch relay in China. (Photo courtesy of South China Morning Post Publishers Limited)

08 Apr 2008

The Regulations for Securities Investment Fund Management Companies to Set up Establishments in Hong Kong was issued by the China Securities Regulatory Commission, allowing Chinese financial institutions to operate in Hong Kong under Supplement IV to the Closer Economic Partnership Arrangement.

01 May 2008

A coach overturned near Nam Pin Wai in Sai Kung after speeding, killing 19 people and injuring 43.

02 May 2008

The first leg of the 2008 Summer Olympic torch relay in China began in Hong Kong with 119 torchbearers. The first and last torchbearers were athletes Lee Lai-shan (李麗珊) and Wong Kam-po (黃金寶). (Figure 332)

05 May 2008

The Education Bureau's Qualifications Framework was launched to promote a competitive workforce through continued learning in the academic, vocational and professional sectors.

09 May 2008

The Energy Efficiency (Labelling of Products) Ordinance was announced, effective 09 November 2009, requiring energy consumption labels on electrical appliances.

13 May 2008

The HKSAR government allocated HK$350 million from its Disaster Relief Fund, approved by the Legislative Council the following day, for victims of an earthquake measuring 8 on the Richter scale in Wenchuan, Sichuan Province on 12 May. At 2:28 p.m. on 19 May, marking the time of the earthquake, all government officials stood in silence for three minutes; flags were flown at half-mast across Hong Kong in a three-day remembrance.

14 May 2008

The first Hong Kong International Art Fair began in a five-day exhibition of modern and contemporary art from 102 international galleries at the Hong Kong Convention and Exhibition Centre.

20 May 2008

Chief Executive Donald Tsang Yam-kuen (曾蔭權) appointed the first group of eight under secretaries, followed by the first group of nine political assistants two days later.

26 May 2008

The Hong Kong Olympic Equestrian Venue in Sha Tin was completed in time for the equestrian events of the 2008 Olympic and Paralympic Games.

27 May 2008

The Hong Kong Construction Sector 5.12 Reconstruction Joint Conference was established to mobilise professional support and assistance in the reconstruction of earthquake-stricken areas in Wenchuan, Sichuan.

07 Jun 2008

The Hong Kong Observatory hoisted Black rainstorm warning for nearly five hours amid torrential rain causing landslides and traffic disruptions with two deaths and 16 injuries. A section of the highway leading to Tai O was covered in mud, cutting off traffic, water supply and mobile phone connections; nearly 6,000 residents in Tai O were affected.

20 Jun 2008

The National Aquatic Wildlife Conservation Association presented Ocean Park Hong Kong with the first batch of five Chinese sturgeons—an endangered species dubbed "living fossils in the water" native to China.

22 Jun 2008

The Government of Yunnan Province donated a Lufengosaur (one of the oldest dinosaurs in the Jurassic period) fossil for permanent display at the Hong Kong Science Museum. It was the first fossil unearthed in China on display outside the Mainland.

27 Jun 2008

The Food Business (Amendment) Regulation 2008 was promulgated, prohibiting overnight stocks of live poultry at retail outlets as a measure to prevent the outbreak of avian influenza.

04 Jul 2008

The Prevention of Bribery (Amendment) Ordinance 2008 was promulgated, applying Sections 4, 5 and 10 of the Prevention of Bribery Ordinance to the Chief Executive who became subject to regulations regarding "soliciting or accepting advantages" and "possession of unexplained property."

The Road Traffic Legislation (Amendment) Ordinance 2008 was promulgated, effective 09 February 2009, empowering police officers in uniform to impose alcohol breath tests at random in a move to combat drink-driving.

06 Jul 2008

Vice President Xi Jinping (習近平) arrived in Hong Kong for a three-day visit; he met with members of the Hong Kong rescue team mobilised to provide relief support following the Sichuan earthquake, inspected the 2008 Olympic equestrian venue, and visited homes of ordinary citizens.

10 Jul 2008

The Hospital Authority's Progress Report on Sentinel Events was released, covering 23 serious medical incidents in a six-month period from 01 October 2007 to 31 March 2008, following a policy of strengthened transparency and reporting.

11 Jul 2008

The West Kowloon Cultural District Authority Ordinance was promulgated, establishing a statutory body responsible for developing the West Kowloon Cultural District.

15 Jul 2008

The HKSAR government in conjunction with The Hong Kong Jockey Club announced a non-profit heritage conservation project called Tai Kwun—Centre for Heritage and Arts at the former Central Police Station. Renovation commenced in November 2011; operation began in phases starting from May 2018.

16 Jul 2008

The Bank of China (Hong Kong) Limited issued special HK$20 banknotes in commemoration of the 2008 Beijing Olympic Games. It marked the first banknotes dedicated to the modern Olympic Games.

18 Jul 2008

The Trust Fund in Support of Reconstruction in the Sichuan Earthquake Stricken Areas—a vehicle for government funding and public donation—was formed. It followed the establishment of the Steering Committee on the HKSAR's Support for Reconstruction in the Sichuan Earthquake Stricken Areas on 26 June. The HKSAR government had allocated HK$9 billion, along with a donation of HK$1 billion from The Hong Kong Jockey Club, as of 2010.

The Race Discrimination Ordinance was promulgated, effective 10 July 2009, rendering racial discrimination, harassment and vilification unlawful. The Equal Opportunities Commission was empowered to enforce the new law.

29 Jul 2008

Supplement V to the Mainland and Hong Kong Closer Economic Partnership Arrangement was signed for further liberalisation of Mainland market access in 17 service areas (including mining and exploration on top of 15 initial sectors such as banking, accounting and construction) with 29 specific measures starting from 01 January 2009.

03 Aug 2008

The Hong Kong Heritage Museum began an exhibition called The Ancient Olympic Games. It featured more than 110 Olympic treasures (medals, sculptures and coins) selected from the British Museum.

09 Aug 2008

The equestrian events of the 2008 Beijing Olympic Games began in Hong Kong as a first-time co-host of the Summer Olympics. (Figure 333)

10 Aug 2008

A five-alarm fire at Cornwall Court in Mong Kok killed four people—including Senior Fireman Siu Wing-fong (蕭 永方) and Fireman Chan Siu-lung (陳兆龍) who were posthumously awarded the Medal for Bravery (Gold) on 29 August—and injured 55 people. It was the first and only five-alarm fire in Hong Kong since 2000 as of 01 July 2017.

19 Aug 2008

The Memorandum of Understanding on Co-operation in the Wine-related Business was signed between Hong Kong and France, marking Hong Kong's first bilateral agreement on wine.

22 Aug 2008

The Hong Kong Observatory hoisted Increasing Gale or Storm Signal No. 9 for a record 11 hours amid Typhoon Nuri. The typhoon caused two deaths, over 112 injuries, 122 fallen trees and 39 collapsed signboards and scaffolds.

27 Aug 2008

An old coral tree in Stanley collapsed, killing one pedestrian and injuring two others.

01 Sep 2008

The Standing Committee on Language Education and Research launched a four-year, four-phase scheme to support Chinese teaching in Putonghua in 132 primary and 28 secondary schools.

07 Sep 2008

The fourth Legislative Council elections were held for 60 seats—30 geographical and 30 functional constituencies with turnout rates of 45.2% and 60.3%, respectively.

16 Sep 2008

The Hang Seng Index dropped 1,052.29 points following the collapse of US investment bank Lehman Brothers. Approximately HK$12.7 billion in collateralised debt obligations (minibonds) issued by Lehman Brothers in Hong Kong amid a drastic drop in value caused significant losses and subsequent claims. (Figure 334)

Figure 333
Hong Kong equestrian Lam Lap-shun (林立信) in the Individual Jumping Competition of the Beijing 2008 Summer Olympics. (Photo taken on 17 August 2008 and courtesy of South China Morning Post Publishers Limited)

Figure 334
Investors demanded accountability in a rally outside the Legislative Council following the collapse of Lehman Brothers. (Photo taken on 29 October 2008 and courtesy of South China Morning Post Publishers Limited)

20 Sep 2008

A three-and-a-half-year-old girl was diagnosed with kidney stones from the consumption of melamine-tainted milk imported from the Mainland. It was the first such case in Hong Kong.

23 Sep 2008

The Harmful Substances in Food (Amendment) Regulation 2008 was promulgated, prohibiting the sale of food containing excessive melamine.

24 Sep 2008

The third Asia Pacific Regional Conference of the Hague Conference on Private International Law began for a three-day meeting in Hong Kong with more than 100 delegates from 27 countries in the Asia Pacific region.

26 Sept 2008

The Jockey Club Creative Arts Centre—revitalised from the former Shek Kip Mei Factory Estate—was opened as a multi-disciplinary arts and cultural venue for local artists at below-market rent.

01 Oct 2008

The World Intellectual Property Organization Copyright Treaty and WIPO Performances and Phonograms Treaty on protection of IP rights came into force in Hong Kong.

08 Oct 2008

The inaugural meeting of the fourth Legislative Council began; Jasper Tsang Yok-sing (曾鈺成) of political party DAB was elected President.

10 Oct 2008

The Transport and Housing Bureau announced a standardised definition of "saleable area"—which included the residential unit, its balcony and utility platform, but not bay windows—as a requirement of the Lands Department Consent Scheme.

11 Oct 2008

The Cooperation Arrangement on Support of Restoration and Reconstruction in the Sichuan Earthquake Stricken Areas was signed. The HKSAR government—supported by the Trust Fund in Support of Reconstruction in the Sichuan Earthquake Stricken Areas—was committed to funding 20 reconstruction projects in the first stage.

14 Oct 2008

The HKSAR government introduced two measures to strengthen public confidence in the local banking system by providing a full guarantee of local deposits by leveraging the Exchange Fund and by establishing a Contingent Bank Capital Facility to make additional capital available to local banks.

20 Oct 2008

Hong Kong Exchange and Clearing Limited relaunched trading of gold futures since its suspension in 1999.

Oct 2008

Remnants of the Lung Tsun Stone Bridge, built between 1873 and 1875, were unearthed during an archaeological exploration—which ended in February 2009—as part of the Kai Tak Development project by the Civil Engineering and Development Department. The Town Planning Board on 26 August 2011 announced amendments to the Kai Tak Outline Zoning Plan in preservation of the bridge remnants, following a government proposal in May 2011.

11 Nov 2008

Wave Media Limited was granted a 12-year government licence to establish and maintain a new 24-hour Cantonese AM radio station.

12 Nov 2008

The Legislative Council formed a Subcommittee to Study Issues Arising from Lehman Brothers-related Minibonds and Structured Financial Products. In June 2012, it released two reports, recommending a regulatory regime comprising a single agency on structured products under the Securities and Futures Ordinance, a study on placing securities businesses of banks under the jurisdiction of the Securities and Futures Commission, and greater investor education.

19 Nov 2008

The International Chamber of Commerce established a branch of the Secretariat of its International Court of Arbitration in Hong Kong.

02 Dec 2008

The *Michelin Guide Hong Kong Macau 2009* was launched in the first bilingual edition (Chinese and English) on local restaurants and establishments by the French tyre company Michelin.

05 Dec 2008

A 40-member delegation of the *Shenzhou 7* manned space mission—including astronauts Zhai Zhigang (翟志剛), Liu Boming (劉伯明) and Jing Haipeng (景海鵬) in China's first spacewalk—arrived in Hong Kong for a four-day visit with a grand performance, a seminar and an exchange with students.

13 Dec 2008

Bottles of corrosive liquid were hurled from a building onto the pedestrian zone on Sai Yeung Choi Street in Mong Kok, injuring 46 people. On 16 May and 08 June 2009, a second and third incident repeated in the same area, resulting in 30 and 24 injuries, respectively. The cases remained unsolved as of 01 July 2017.

15 Dec 2008

The HKSAR government launched a Special Loan Guarantee Scheme to provide businesses with greater liquidity as a loan guarantor amid the 2008 global financial crisis. The application period ended on 31 December 2010.

20 Dec 2008

A man died of a heart attack due to a delay in paramedic support outside the Caritas Medical Centre. The Hospital Authority apologised for the incident and implemented improvement measures, including an enhanced emergency response mechanism within the vicinity of public hospitals and the installation of portable defibrillators.

Dec 2008

Agnes Lam Shun-ling (林舜玲) won a Special Mention for her English poem "Vanilla in the Stars" at the 24th Nosside International Poetry Prize. She was the first Chinese poet to win in the competition.

01 Jan 2009

The three-year Elderly Health Care Voucher Pilot Scheme was launched, providing residents aged 70 or above with medical vouchers worth HK$250 annually. The scheme was extended to 2014 and became a recurrent programme thereafter. In 2017, eligibility requirements were lowered to cover those aged 65 and above.

02 Jan 2009

A revised Code of Banking Practice was jointly issued by the Hong Kong Association of Banks and the Hong Kong Association of Restricted Licence Banks and Deposit-taking Companies for an enhanced regulatory regime on the financial and banking sectors in response to the 2008 global financial crisis.

09 Jan 2009

Benjamin Wong Chun-yu (王振宇) and Wang Jide (王繼德) of The University of Hong Kong's Li Ka Shing Faculty of Medicine (in conjunction with the Fourth Military Medical University of China) were named winners of a first-class award of the 2008 State Science and Technology Awards in recognition of the project called Discovery of Malignant Phenotype-Related Molecules and Establishment and Application of Sequential Prophylactic Strategy in Gastric Cancer.

15 Jan 2009

Wing Lung Bank became a wholly owned subsidiary of China Merchants Bank (CMB) and was renamed CMB Wing Lung Bank upon completion of a compulsory acquisition.

16 Jan 2009

Jao Tsung-i (饒宗頤) became the first Hong Kong scholar appointed as a fellow of the China Central Research Institute of Culture and History by the Premier of the State Council.

21 Jan 2009

Hong Kong Exchanges and Clearing Limited and Shanghai Stock Exchange signed a Closer Cooperation Agreement on further collaboration with respect to product development and constituent stocks.

The Education Bureau's Committee for a "Passing on the Torch" National Education Activity Series was inaugurated in a ceremony.

16 Feb 2009

The Census and Statistics Department announced a local population of 7,008,900 as of 31 December 2008, an increase by 56,100 from the end of 2007.

19 Feb 2009

The governments of Guangdong, Hong Kong and Macao held the first liaison meeting in jointly taking forward The Outline of the Plan for the Reform and Development of the Pearl River Delta.

09 Mar 2009

The Hong Kong Economic and Trade Office in Berlin was inaugurated to foster closer ties with Germany and seven other central and eastern European countries.

12 Mar 2009

The People's Bank of China and Hong Kong Monetary Authority signed a memorandum of understanding on Mainland–Hong Kong multi-currency cross-border payment arrangements scheduled for launch on 16 March 2009 in four currencies (HK dollar, US dollar, British pound and the euro).

18 Mar 2009

The Hong Kong Observatory reclassified typhoons into three categories—typhoon, severe typhoon and super typhoon—based on the central wind speed.

19 Mar 2009

The Antiquities Advisory Board announced results of the assessment of 1,444 historic buildings—of which 212 were designated with Grade 1 status; 366 with Grade 2 status; 576 with Grade 3 status; and 290 were designated non-graded buildings.

31 Mar 2009

The HKSAR government established a Task Force on Tree Management. On 29 June, it released the *Report of the Task Force on Tree Management: People, Trees, Harmony*. In March 2010, the Greening, Landscape and Tree Management Section (as a part of the Works Branch under the Development Bureau) was formed to implement an institutional framework in the context of an overall greening and landscape policy.

01 Apr 2009

The Chinese Central Government implemented a one-year, multiple-entry Individual Visit Scheme allowing eligible residents with Shenzhen household registration to apply for leisure travel to Hong Kong individually multiple times a year.

06 Apr 2009

The 16th Commonwealth Law Conference began in Hong Kong for the first time in a non-Commonwealth jurisdiction. The seventh Conference in 1983 was also held in Hong Kong.

23 Apr 2009

Hong Kong Science Park Biotech Centre was opened as a life science research and development laboratory with a biomedical technology support centre for pharmaceutical research.

27 Apr 2009

The HKSAR government made swine influenza (type A virus) (H1N1) one of the statutorily notifiable diseases under the Prevention and Control of Disease Ordinance in view of the outbreak of swine flu in Mexico and the United States.

30 Apr 2009

Ocean Park opened an attraction called Amazing Asian Animals. It was the world's first integrated indoor-outdoor exhibit in an area of approximately 25,000 square metres, featuring a variety of Asian animal species, including the giant panda, Chinese giant salamander and Chinese alligator.

Apr 2009

The Hong Kong Convention and Exhibition Centre completed its expansion project, followed by the opening of the Atrium Link Extension on 22 July.

01 May 2009

The first case of human swine influenza (type A virus) (H1N1) in Hong Kong and Asia—an imported case from Mexico—was confirmed. The Metropark Hotel in Wan Chai where the patient stayed was placed under an immediate lockdown; nearly 300 hotel guests and staff were quarantined in situ for seven days; pandemic alert level was raised to "emergency."

07 May 2009

The HKSAR government, in collaboration with Hong Kong Housing Society and Urban Renewal Authority, launched Operation Building Bright—a HK$1 billion, two-year subsidy scheme for maintenance of old buildings.

09 May 2009

Supplement VI to the Mainland and Hong Kong Closer Economic Partnership Arrangement was signed, providing Hong Kong suppliers in 42 service sectors with special Mainland market access. These included 29 new measures for further liberalisation in 20 service areas, including research & development and rail transport.

11 May 2009

The International Maritime Organization began a five-day conference in Hong Kong. The conference was held for the first time in Asia.

24 May 2009

The Chinese Central Government appointed Peng Qinghua (彭清華) as Director of the Liaison Office of the Central People's Government in the HKSAR. He remained in the post until 18 December 2012.

25 May 2009

Noah's Ark—an attraction with a garden, an exhibition hall and a hotel as part of Ma Wan Park and built to a style depicted in the Book of Genesis (Old Testament of the Bible)—was opened.

May 2009

The Mega Events Fund—a HK$100 million government subsidy scheme for arts, cultural and sporting events with local non-profit groups until March 2012—was established. In April 2012, it was extended for another five years (until March 2017) with an additional funding of HK$150 million.

01 Jun 2009

The Independent Police Complaints Council became a statutory body to observe, monitor and review investigations by the commissioner of police on reportable complaints against the police.

Create Hong Kong—an agency under the Commerce and Economic Development Bureau dedicated to driving the development of Hong Kong's creative economy—was established.

26 Jun 2009

The Voting by Imprisoned Persons Ordinance was promulgated, effective 30 October, removing restrictions on the right to vote among prisoners and those in custody.

30 Jun 2009

The HKSAR government reached an agreement with The Walt Disney Company for an expanded Hong Kong Disneyland. On 10 July, an increase in Hong Kong's equity in the joint venture through a HK$6.25 billion loan-to-equity conversion for a 52% stake in support of the expansion was approved by the Legislative Council.

01 Jul 2009

A total smoking ban in all indoor public places was implemented.

06 Jul 2009

Hong Kong became a designated offshore RMB centre according to the Measures for the Administration of Pilot RMB Settlement in Cross-border Trade—a notice announced by the People's Bank of China and other Mainland authorities on 01 July.

07 Jul 2009

The Environmental Levy Scheme on Plastic Shopping Bags was implemented.

10 Jul 2009

A Filipino man died of human swine influenza, marking the first death from the disease in Hong Kong.

22 Jul 2009

The Securities and Futures Commission, Hong Kong Monetary Authority and 16 distributing banks reached an agreement on repurchase of Lehman Brothers Minibonds from eligible customers at 60%–70% of the nominal value— a proposal rejected by the Alliance of Lehman Brothers Victims demanding full reimbursement. On 28 March 2011, bond receiver PricewaterhouseCoopers announced an increase in recoverable value of 85%–96.5% of initial investment among eligible bondholders.

24 Jul 2009

The animated film *McDull, Kung Fu Kindergarten* premiered in the Mainland. It was the first Hong Kong animated film financed by the Film Development Fund of the HKSAR government.

26 Jul 2009

The MTR Tseung Kwan O Line's LOHAS Park Station became the first rail station to open for traffic following the MTR-KCR merger.

Jul 2009

The HKSAR government began a three-month, cross-departmental pilot programme on plug-in hybrid electric vehicles.

04 Aug 2009

The Hong Kong Observatory hoisted No. 8 Gale or Storm Signal for six hours as Typhoon Goni swept past 100 kilometres southwest of Hong Kong. The typhoon caused four deaths and 11 injuries.

16 Aug 2009

The MTR West Rail Line's Austin Station was opened, marking the full operation of the Kowloon Southern Link.

19 Aug 2009

The Hong Kong-Guangdong Co-operation Joint Conference adopted an agreement to strengthen cooperation on reducing air pollution, improving water quality, developing a green industry, and promoting a Green Greater Pearl River Delta Quality Living Circle.

01 Sep 2009

Expanded free education (from nine to 12 years) in local public schools was implemented.

The Education Bureau began implementation of a New Academic Structure and a three-year Senior Secondary curriculum as a prerequisite for four-year undergraduate programmes.

03 Sep 2009

The HKSAR government issued its first batch of two-year institutional bonds with a total value of HK$3.5 billion.

13 Sep 2009

Six workers died in an industrial accident at the International Commerce Centre under construction above Kowloon Station. They were riding in a lift which fell from the 30th to the 10th floor.

14 Sep 2009

The Research Grants Council launched a Hong Kong PhD Fellowship Scheme to attract outstanding non-local students for postgraduate studies at University Grants Committee-funded universities.

17 Sep 2009

The Hong Kong Council for Testing and Certification was established as an advisory body on the development of the testing and certification sector—one of six focus industries designated by the Task Force on Economic Challenges.

Figure 335
Secretary for Home Affairs Tsang Tak-sing (曾德成) received a certificate of inscription of Cantonese opera onto the UNESCO Representative List of the Intangible Cultural Heritage of Humanity at a ceremony in Beijing with State Councillor Liu Yandong (劉延東), right, and Vice Minister of Education Hao Ping (郝平), left. (Photo taken on 19 August 2010 and courtesy of HKSAR Government)

Figure 336
A stage photo during the act "Departure" of the Cantonese opera classic Princess Chang Ping by Sin Fung Ming Opera Troupe. Performers included Yam Kim-fai (任劍輝), sitting in front row, Pak Suet-sin (白雪仙), kneeling in front row, Leung Sing-por (梁醒波), left in second row, and Lan Chi-pat (靚次伯), right in second row. (Photo courtesy of The Chinese University of Hong Kong Library)

21 Sep 2009

The 60th session of the World Health Organization Regional Committee for the Western Pacific began for a five-day meeting in Hong Kong with health officials from 37 countries and territories.

28 Sep 2009

Renminbi Sovereign Bond (totalling RMB 60 billion) was first issued in Hong Kong by the Ministry of Finance of China; Bank of China (Hong Kong) and Bank of Communications (Hong Kong Branch) were appointed as Joint Lead Manager and Bookrunner.

01 Oct 2009

Standard Chartered Bank began issuing HK$150 banknotes in commemoration of its 150th anniversary. It was the world's first 150-dollar denomination banknote.

02 Oct 2009

Cantonese opera—under a joint application by Guangdong, Hong Kong and Macao via the Chinese Central Government—was officially inscribed onto the UNESCO Representative List of the Intangible Cultural Heritage of Humanity. It was Hong Kong's first item of the world intangible cultural heritage. (Figures 335 and 336)

06 Oct 2009

Charles Kao Kuen (高錕), former Vice Chancellor of The Chinese University of Hong Kong, was awarded the Nobel Prize for Physics 2009 in recognition of his ground-breaking achievements in fibre-optic transmission.

16 Oct 2009

Cyclist Wong Kam-po (黃金寶) served as a torchbearer at the 11th National Games opening ceremony in Jinan, Shandong Province. He was the first National Games torchbearer from Hong Kong.

20 Oct 2009

The Chief Executive-in-Council approved construction of the Hong Kong section of Guangzhou–Shenzhen–Hong Kong Express Rail Link; an ex-gratia rehousing package was announced for affected villagers at Choi Yuen Tsuen in Shek Kong.

The Security Bureau's Outbound Travel Alert System—aiming to provide local travellers with an understanding of risk levels (amber, red and black) abroad—was implemented.

24 Oct 2009

Plaza Hollywood began offering six underground parking space with charging facilities as the first private car park dedicated to electric vehicles in Hong Kong.

29 Oct 2009

The World Intellectual Property Organisation Regional Symposium on Management of Intellectual Capital, Intellectual Assets and Intellectual Property began for a two-day conference in Hong Kong with over 200 regional representatives.

03 Nov 2009

The Hong Kong National Geopark—covering 5,000 hectares with eight geosites in two geological regions (Northeast New Territories Sedimentary Rock Region and Sai Kung Volcanic Rock Region)—was inaugurated and became a national geopark of China with approval from the Chinese Central Government. On 17 September 2011, it was listed as part of the UNESCO Global Geoparks Network and renamed Hong Kong Global Geopark of China. On 17 November 2015, it was renamed Hong Kong UNESCO Global Geopark.

09 Nov 2009

CLP Power's electric vehicle charging stations at Lung Cheung Mall Carpark and Fu Shing Building Carpark were inaugurated in a ceremony marking the start of the first batch of 21 charging stations in Kowloon and the New Territories activated by the end of the year.

30 Nov 2009

Hong Kong Design Institute held a topping-out ceremony at its Tiu Keng Leng campus—which was opened for classes in the 2010/11 academic year following a 2007 merger of design programmes of the Vocational Training Council in Kwai Chung, Tsing Yi, Kwun Tong and Sha Tin.

01 Dec 2009

The Guidelines on Sale of Uncompleted Residential Properties—formulated by the Real Estate Developers Association of Hong Kong—was implemented, requiring the use of "saleable area" in relation to the prices of residential property.

05 Dec 2009

The fifth East Asian Games in Hong Kong began in an opening ceremony officiated by International Olympic Committee President Jacques Rogge and State Councillor Liu Yandong (劉延東). Team Hong Kong, China had 383 participating athletes in all 22 sporting events, winning 26 gold, 31 silver and 53 bronze medals, including Hong Kong's first gold medal in football and all seven gold medals in squash. The Games was concluded in a closing ceremony at the Hong Kong Coliseum on 13 December. (Figures 337, 338 and 339)

18 Dec 2009

The Hong Kong Photographic Culture Association was established to promote the art of photography as an organiser of a biennial international photo festival.

20 Dec 2009

The Stonecutters Bridge—connecting Stonecutters Island with International Container Terminal No. 9 on Tsing Yi Island—was opened as the second longest cable-stayed bridge in the world, serving as the final section of Route 8.

24 Dec 2009

The Domestic Violence (Amendment) Ordinance 2009 was promulgated, enabling former and current cohabitants in gender-neutral (same sex) relationships to apply for court injunction against molestation.

2009

Hong Kong became the world's largest initial public offering market in terms of capitalisation for the first time; it retained the top spot for three consecutive years.

Figure 337
Hong Kong table tennis player Li Ching (李靜), middle in front row, took the oath on behalf of all athletes at the opening ceremony of the fifth East Asian Games. (Photo courtesy of HKSAR Government)

Figure 338
Hong Kong footballer Chan Siu-ki (陳肇麒), in red jersey, in a match with Team Korea during the East Asian Games. He hit a record of 37 goals in 2017 and became Team Hong Kong's all-time top scorer in international matches. (Photo taken on 03 December 2009 and courtesy of South China Morning Post Publishers Limited).

Figure 339
Hong Kong won seven gold medals in squash at the fifth East Asian Games. (Photo taken on 12 December 2009 and courtesy of South China Morning Post Publishers Limited)

05 Jan 2010

A group of young activists—collectively known as the Post 80s Anti-Express Rail Link Group (signifying those born in the 1980s)—began a four-day Prostrating Walk of the Five Districts (Legislative Council's five electoral districts) in protest of the construction (Hong Kong section) of the Guangzhou-Shenzhen-Hong Kong Express Rail Link.

11 Jan 2010

The Five-District Referendum—a de facto referendum on universal suffrage in the form of by-elections upon resignation of five legislative councillors—was co-initiated by the Civic Party and the League of Social Democrats. On 26 January, Tanya Chan (陳淑莊) of Hong Kong Island, Alan Leong Kah-kit (梁家傑) of Kowloon East, Wong Yuk-man (黃毓民) of Kowloon West, Leung Kwok-hung (梁國雄) of New Territories East, and Albert Chan Wai-yip (陳偉業) of New Territories West submitted their letters of resignation.

15 Jan 2010

The Hong Kong and Macao Affairs Office of the State Council in a statement stressed that any referendum was inconsistent with the Basic Law system and would be rendered unconstitutional in the HKSAR.

16 Jan 2010

The Legislative Council, following an appropriation of HK$66.9 billion for construction (Hong Kong section) of the Guangzhou–Shenzhen–Hong Kong Express Rail Link, was besieged by demonstrators in protest of the government's acquisition of land at Choi Yuen Tsuen in Shek Kong intended for a rail depot, ending in a clash with the police.

19 Jan 2010

The Memorandum of Understanding Concerning Advancing Hong Kong–Shanghai Financial Co-operation was signed by the HKSAR government and the Shanghai municipal government.

27 Jan 2010

The Guangzhou-Shenzhen-Hong Kong Express Rail Link's Hong Kong Section—about 26 kilometres in length with a dedicated tunnel system between West Kowloon Station in Hong Kong and Futian Station in Shenzhen connected to the national high-speed rail network—commenced construction. It was completed on 23 March 2018 and opened to traffic on 23 September 2018. The first train was named *Vibrant Express*.

29 Jan 2010

A five-storey tenement on Ma Tau Wai Road in To Kwa Wan collapsed, causing four deaths and two injuries; two neighbouring buildings were rendered structurally unsafe. (Figure 340)

The Central–Wan Chai Bypass and Island Eastern Corridor Link—a 4.5-km dual three-lane trunk road between the Rumsey Street Flyover in Central and Island Eastern Corridor in North Point as part of an east-west strategic route along the north shore of Hong Kong Island—began construction in a ground-breaking ceremony.

Jan 2010

The public housing redevelopment project of Lower Ngau Tau Kok (II) Estate marked the end of the Comprehensive Redevelopment Programme adopted in 1987 under the policy document *Long-Term Housing Strategy*.

01 Feb 2010

The principal office of the HSBC Group Chief Executive was relocated from London to Hong Kong; Michael Geoghegan was appointed as Asia-Pacific Chairman concurrently.

02 Feb 2010

The High Court ruled in favour of Chinachem Charitable Foundation Limited, pronouncing the estate will (made in July 2002) of deceased Chinachem Group chairman Nina Wang Kung Yu-Sum (龔如心) in solemn form. The will (made in 2006) submitted by Peter Chan Chun-chuen (陳振聰) was rendered invalid. On 05 July 2013, Chan was convicted of forgery and using a false document and sentenced to 12 years in prison.

Figure 340
Firefighters during a rescue mission following the collapse of a tenement building at 45 Ma Tau Wai Road, To Kwa Wan. (Photo taken on 29 January 2010 and courtesy of South China Morning Post Publishers Limited)

18 Feb 2010

The Hong Kong Observatory commissioned its Po Shan Seismograph Station—capable of early detection of seismic waves of earthquakes in the South China Sea through a broadband seismometer and a strong motion accelerometer. In May 2010, it joined the Global Seismographic Network.

21 Feb 2010

Echoes of the Rainbow—funded by the Film Development Fund of the HKSAR government—became the first Hong Kong film awarded a Crystal Bear for Best Feature Film (Generation Competition) at the 60th Berlin International Film Festival.

15 Mar 2010

The Hong Kong Certificate of Education Examination was last held; 16 candidates earned 10 distinctions each.

01 Apr 2010

The government revitalisation of industrial buildings scheme was implemented.

07 Apr 2010

The Framework Agreement on Hong Kong–Guangdong Co-operation, incorporating a list of economic initiatives, was signed in Beijing.

14 Apr 2010

The HKSAR government published its *Package of Proposals for the Methods for Selecting the Chief Executive and for Forming the Legislative Council in 2012*. It proposed expanding the 800-member Election Committee to 1,200-strong with 100 additional seats in each of the four sectors (including 75 seats for a total of 117 among directly elected district councillors), in addition to increasing the number of legislative councillors from 60 to 70 (35 under direct elections and 35 under functional constituencies).

Wong Fuk-wing (黃福榮)—a volunteer rescuer from Hong Kong following the Yushu earthquake in Qinghai Province—died in the line of duty. On 16 April, he was posthumously awarded the Medal for Bravery (Gold).

01 May 2010

Hong Kong unveiled its Hong Kong Pavilion and Urban Best Practices Area Exhibition at the Shanghai World Expo 2010.

07 May 2010

The Employment (Amendment) Ordinance 2010 was promulgated, effective 29 October. stipulating a fine of HK$350,000 and two years in prison among employers who wilfully and without reason defaulted on any sum ordered by the Labour Tribunal or Minor Employment Claims Adjudication Board (involving wages or other entitlements).

14 May 2010

Hang Seng School of Commerce was approved for an upgraded status as a self-financing post-secondary college; it was renamed Hang Seng Management College and began offering undergraduate programmes in September 2010.

16 May 2010

The Legislative Council by-election was held, returning all five legislative councillors who resigned in association with the Five-District Referendum. It marked the lowest voter turnout rate (17.19%) since the establishment of the HKSAR and the first election in which prisoners were given the right to vote.

24 May 2010

Democratic Party Chairman Albert Ho Chun-yan (何俊仁), Vice Chairman Emily Lau Wai-hing (劉慧卿) and Legislative Councillor Cheung Man-kwong (張文光) were invited for an unprecedented meeting at the Liaison Office of the CPG in the HKSAR with Deputy Director Li Gang (李剛), Minister of Justice Feng Wei (馮巍) and Deputy Minister Liu Chunhua (劉春華).

Figure 341
Chief Executive Donald Tsang Yam-kuen (曾蔭權) and principal government officials publicised the 2012 constitutional reform package during a promotional campaign. (Photo courtesy of HKSAR Government)

Figure 342
Chief Executive Donald Tsang Yam-kuen (曾蔭權), left, in a debate on constitutional reform with Legislative Councillor and Civic Party member Audrey Eu Yuet-mee (余若薇), right, with moderator Ng Ming-lam (吳明林), centre. (Photo courtesy of Daniel Sorabji /AFP via Getty Images)

27 May 2010

Supplement VII to the Mainland and Hong Kong Closer Economic Partnership Agreement was signed, effective 01 January 2011, covering 35 liberalisation measures on trade and investment in 19 areas, including 27 (eight first-time) measures in 14 service areas.

29 May 2010

Chief Executive Donald Tsang Yam-kuen (曾蔭權) and his principal officials met with the public in a campaign titled "Act Now"—which called for support in the 2012 constitutional reform package. (Figure 341)

01 Jun 2010

The HKSAR government introduced nine specific measures designed to enhance the transparency and fairness in the sales and transactions of first-hand residential properties, including requirements on sales brochures, price lists and show flats to be adopted by the Real Estate Developers Association of Hong Kong.

04 Jun 2010

The Leisure and Cultural Services Department held its first Chinese Opera Festival with 12 troupes, including the Peking Opera Theatre of Beijing and Xiaobaihua Yue Opera Troupe of Shaoxing.

17 Jun 2010

Chief Executive Donald Tsang Yam-kuen (曾蔭權) and Civic Party leader Audrey Eu Yuet-mee (余若薇) appeared in a televised debate on the constitutional reform package at the Central Government Offices. It marked the first public debate on constitutional issues by a Chief Executive. (Figure 342)

18 Jun 2010

The Waste Disposal (Clinical Waste) (General) Regulation, Waste Disposal (Charge for Disposal of Clinical Waste) Regulation and Waste Disposal (Amendment) Ordinance 2006 (Commencement) Notice 2010 were promulgated, effective 01 August 2011, introducing a fee-based licence scheme for treatment and disposal of medical waste in an environmentally sound and safe manner.

25 Jun 2010

Amendments to the methods for the selection of the Chief Executive and for the formation of the Legislative Council in 2012 were passed by a two-thirds majority in the Legislative Council. The number of Election Committee members—responsible for electing the HKSAR Chief Executive—was to increase from 800 to 1200 (150 required for nomination of a candidate); the number of Legislative Council members was to increase from 60 to 70—five new councillors through direct elections and five new councillors through new functional constituencies of District Councils to be elected by all registered voters who previously could not vote in functional constituencies.

Figure 343
Philippine police officers attempted to break into a hijacked bus in which a group of tourists from Hong Kong were being held hostage. (Photo taken on 23 August 2010 and courtesy of Ted Aljibe /AFP via Getty Images)

16 Jul 2010

The Agricultural Bank of China, following its A-share initial public offering on the Shanghai Stock Exchange on 15 July, became a H-share public company on the Hong Kong Stock Exchange at HK$3.20 per share. It was oversubscribed 4.87 times for over HK$26 billion. It marked the completion of A-share and H-share listings of the four major state-owned banks of the Mainland.

The Customs and Excise Department cracked the first case of a methamphetamine syndicate in Hong Kong, arresting five people and seizing HK$175 million worth of the illegal drug. It was the largest case of its kind as of 01 July 2017.

13 Aug 2010

The Hong Kong Monetary Authority introduced further risk-averse measures to ensure a stable banking system with a 60% maximum loan-to-value ratio on residential properties valued HK$12 million or above and those not intended for self-use, as well as a standardised limit on debt servicing ratios of borrowers to 50% coupled with a stress test on debt servicing abilities.

The Hong Kong Mortgage Corporation Limited revised its Mortgage Insurance Programme by suspending applications of mortgage loans exceeding 90% loan-to-value (LTV) ratio, lowering the maximum amount for mortgage loans of 90% or below LTV from HK$12 million to HK$7.2 million, and capping the maximum debt-to-income ratio at 50% for all income groups.

23 Aug 2010

Twenty-five people in a tour group of Hong Thai Travel Services from Hong Kong were taken hostage for over 12 hours in Manila, Philippines; eight were killed and seven were injured. The HKSAR government declared three days of condolences with flags flown at half-mast starting 24 August and issued its first "black" Outbound Travel Alert for the Philippines. On 01 July 2011, tour group members Fu Cheuk-yan (傅卓仁) and Leung Kam-wing (梁錦榮) and tour leader Masa Tse Ting-cheunn (謝廷駿) were posthumously awarded the Medal for Bravery (Gold). (Figure 343)

28 Aug 2010

The National People's Congress Standing Committee approved an amended Annex I of the Basic Law regarding the method for selecting the HKSAR Chief Executive and put on record an amended Annex II of the Basic Law regarding the method for forming the Legislative Council and its voting procedures.

01 Sep 2010

The Education Bureau began fine-tuning its medium of instruction policy in secondary schools starting with Secondary 1, taking a flexible approach to allowing classroom teaching in Chinese or English based on the ability of students.

02 Sep 2010

The Legislative Council held its first special meeting during adjournment under Rule 15(2) of the Rules of Procedure on the incident of a Hong Kong tour group being taken hostage in the Philippines. It approved a motion demanding a public apology and compensation to the deceased, injured and their family members from the Philippine government.

03 Sep 2010

Chief Judge of the High Court Geoffrey Ma Tao-li（馬道立）was sworn in as the second Chief Justice of the Court of Final Appeal of the HKSAR.

Hong Kong film director John Woo Yu-sen（吳宇森）was awarded a Golden Lion for Lifetime Achievement at the 67th Venice International Film Festival in Italy, making him the first Chinese director to receive the honour.

13 Sep 2010

The Hong Kong Mortgage Corporation announced its launch of a Premium Loan Guarantee Scheme in support of the government initiative to revitalise the Home Ownership Scheme secondary market by providing banks with guarantee on the portion of the premium loan over the 60% or 70% combined loan-to-value threshold and up to 90%.

15 Sep 2010

The first INTERPOL Information Security Conference began for a three-day meeting with over 300 representatives from 50 countries at the Hong Kong Police Headquarters.

08 Oct 2010

The Chinese Central Government appointed Wang Guangya（王光亞）as Director of the Hong Kong and Macao Affairs Office of the State Council. He remained in the post until 22 September 2017.

12 Oct 2010

The HKSAR government in conjunction with Hong Kong Housing Society introduced My Home Purchase Plan—a rent-and-buy scheme with small- and medium-sized flats for purchase of a MHPP home or private flat with a subsidy equivalent to half of the total rent paid. The first batch—comprising 1,000 flats at Greenview Villa in Tsing Yi—was scheduled for pre-letting in 2012 but was re-arranged for sale as announced in August 2012. The MHPP was scrapped in January 2013.

18 Oct 2010

The Office of the Privacy Commissioner for Personal Data released its investigation report regarding the collection and use of personal data of customers by electronic payment operator Octopus Cards Limited.

09 Nov 2010

An animated version of the treasured Chinese painting *Along the River during the Qingming Festival* began a three-week display at the AsiaWorld-Expo in Hong Kong. The panoramic painting was a star attraction at the China pavilion during the 2010 Shanghai World Expo.

11 Nov 2010

The Community Care Fund Steering Committee was established for people under financial difficulties but not covered by the social safety net. The HKSAR government in the following year allocated HK$5 billion and sought to raise another HK$5 billion from the business community.

Hong Kong reached the round of 16 in men's football at the 16th Asian Games in Guangzhou, marking its second time making the qualifying round since 1958.

12 Nov 2010

The Arbitration Ordinance was promulgated, stipulating a comprehensive regime on proceedings, interim measures and preliminary orders modelled after an internationally recognised framework.

12 Nov 2010

Team Hong Kong, China participated in the 16th Asian Games in Guangzhou, winning eight gold, 15 silver and 17 bronze medals, including first-time medals in the rugby sevens and equestrian events.

19 Nov 2010

The HKSAR government introduced a Special Stamp Duty to curb speculation with 5%–15% additional tax on residential properties resold within 24 months after acquisition, effective 20 November. The Hong Kong Monetary Authority, likewise, lowered the maximum loan-to-value ratio by 10% for residential properties with a value of HK$6 million or above. The Mortgage Insurance Programme became applicable to those with a value below HK$6.8 million.

An earthquake with a magnitude of 2.8 on the Richter Scale occurred in Deep Bay of Shenzhen; tremor was felt in Hong Kong.

26 Nov 2010

The HKSAR government gazetted its rail development plan for a Shatin-to-Central Link with a distance of 17 kilometres and 10 stations.

27 Nov 2010

The first Hong Kong International Photo Festival was launched by Hong Kong Photographic Culture Association. It attracted over 100 local and international master photographers and many more photography enthusiasts.

01 Dec 2010

In accordance with the Smoking (Public Health) (Designation of No Smoking Areas) (Amendment) Notice 2010, 131 open-air and covered public transport facilities were designated as non-smoking areas.

06 Dec 2010

The government launched its new account-based service delivery platform called MyGovHK, allowing users to access public information and services through a personalised webpage.

Dec 2010

The International Commerce Centre—a 108-storey commercial skyscraper located on top of MTR's Kowloon Station—was completed, marking the tallest and only building with more than 100 floors in Hong Kong, taller than the 88-storey Two International Finance Centre on Hong Kong Island.

09 Jan 2011

The New People's Party was founded under the chairmanship of Regina Ip Lau Suk-yee (葉劉淑儀).

23 Jan 2011

The political party People Power was founded under the chairmanship of Christopher Lau Gar-hung (劉嘉鴻).

25 Jan 2011

The Tamar Development Project—which included the new Government Headquarters and Legislative Council Complex—was marked with a topping-out ceremony; it was completed for occupancy in August 2011.

28 Jan 2011

The Antiquities and Monuments (Declaration of Proposed Monument) (Ho Tung Gardens) Notice was promulgated, declaring Ho Tung Gardens (constructed in 1927) a proposed historic monument for a period of 12 months. In December 2012, it was withdrawn due to failed negotiation with the owner on preservation; demolition work was completed in the following year.

11 Feb 2011

The Minimum Wage Commission was established to support implementation of a statutory minimum wage.

02 Mar 2011

The Scheme $6,000—Hong Kong's first non-recurring government tax rebate in the form of a cash pay-out—was announced for all permanent residents aged 18 or above.

03 Mar 2011

The University of Hong Kong Professor of Chemistry Vivian Yam Wing-wah (任詠華) was named Laureate of the 13th L'Oreal-UNESCO Women in Science Awards in recognition of her work in light-emitting materials and innovative ways of capturing solar energy.

09 Mar 2011

Residents of Choi Yuen Tsuen in Shek Kong—affected by the Hong Kong section of the Guangzhou-Shenzhen-Hong Kong Express Rail Link project—accepted MTR Corporation's offer on temporary housing nearby. On 24 April, villagers held a farewell party to thank supporters and began relocating to the temporary housing.

11 Mar 2011

The Motor Vehicle Idling (Fixed Penalty) Ordinance was promulgated, effective 15 December, prohibiting drivers from idling vehicle engines for more than three minutes in any 60-minute period in a bid to reduce environmental nuisances.

14 Mar 2011

The Outline of the 12th Five-Year Plan for National Economic and Social Development of the People's Republic of China—adopted by the Fourth Session of the 11th National People's Congress—marked a first-time individual chapter dedicated to Hong Kong and Macao affairs.

17 Mar 2011

A plane pull—jointly hosted by the Civil Aviation Department and local aviation industry in celebration of 100 years of aviation in Hong Kong—took place at the Hong Kong International Airport where a total of 360 participants manually pulled five different types of aircraft and set two Guinness World Records, namely the "heaviest amount of aircraft pulled simultaneously" and the "heaviest aircraft pulled over 100 metres by a team."

21 Mar 2011

The Urban Renewal Authority launched its Flat-for-Flat (FFF) Scheme, providing owner-occupiers affected by redevelopment projects with cash compensation and a choice of in-situ flats in the redeveloped estates, flats of another FFF redevelopment in the same district, or flats at a residential complex (later named De Novo) of the Kai Tak Development.

22 Mar 2011

Tung Wah College was reinstituted as a degree-granting tertiary institution offering undergraduate programmes.

01 Apr 2011

Under a new arrangement enacted by the Chinese Central Government and HKSAR, children aged over 14 (overage children) of Hong Kong permanent residents were eligible to apply for a One-way Permit to settle and reunite with their parents in Hong Kong.

08 Apr 2011

The Food Safety Ordinance was promulgated, effective 01 August, introducing a registration scheme for food importers and food distributors and a requirement for food traders to maintain proper transaction records to enhance food traceability.

18 Apr 2011

The Forum on the National 12th Five-Year Plan was held to promote a greater public understanding of national affairs and Hong Kong's efforts in supporting the Five-Year Plans.

01 May 2011

The Minimum Wage Ordinance came into effect with an initial statutory minimum wage of HK$28 per hour. It was raised to HK$30 on 01 May 2013, HK$32.50 on 01 May 2015 and HK$34.50 on 01 May 2017.

23 May 2011

The Bun Festival of Cheung Chau, Dragon Boat Water Parade of Tai O, Fire Dragon Dance of Tai Hang and Yu Lan Ghost Festival of the Hong Kong Chiu Chow Community were inscribed onto the Third National List of Intangible Cultural Heritage adopted by the State Council. (Figures 344, 345, 346 and 347)

May 2011

Caritas Francis Hsu College was renamed Caritas Institute of Higher Education; it was granted a degree-conferring status and began offering undergraduate programmes.

08 Jun 2011

The Court of Final Appeal made its first request with the National People's Congress Standing Committee for an interpretation of the Basic Law on diplomatic immunity in the Congo case.

10 Jun 2011

The Hong Kong Monetary Authority issued guidelines on strengthened risk management in residential mortgage lending, requiring banks to lower the maximum loan-to-value (LTV) ratio for properties valued HK$7–HK$12 million, decrease the maximum LTV ratio for those whose principal income was not derived from Hong Kong, and reduce the maximum LTV ratio for properties under a net worth-based mortgage.

Figure 344
People took to light incense sticks at the Fire Dragon Dance in Tai Hang, Causeway Bay—a ritual held every year during Mid-Autumn Festival praying for the riddance of diseases and epidemics. (Photo courtesy of HKSAR Government)

Figure 345
The bamboo sheds decorated with flowers in Sai Kung during the Yu Lan Ghost Festival—an annual ritual across Hong Kong dedicated to ancestral worship and the comforting of troubled spirits of the dead. (Photo courtesy of HKSAR Government)

Figure 346
The Bun Festival (*Jiao* Festival) of Cheung Chau on the eighth day of the fourth month in the lunar calendar—in gratitude to the deity of the North "Pak Tai" for bringing peace. Pictured was a parade of deities called "Piu Sik" in which children dressed as historical figures tour the streets on special stands. (Photo courtesy of HKSAR Government)

Figure 347
The Dragon Boat Water Parade of Tai O during the Tuen Ng Festival on the fourth day of the fifth month in the lunar calendar. Pictured was part of a ritual of receiving the gods Yeung Hou (楊侯), Tin Hau (天后), Kwan Tei (關帝) and Hung Shing (洪聖) from four temples in Tai O for worship in the morning before returning the sacred statues to their respective temples in the afternoon. (Photo courtesy of HKSAR Government)

Figure 348
The council chamber in the newly opened Legislative Council Complex. (Photo taken on 04 October 2011 and courtesy of South China Morning Post Publishers Limited)

30 Jun 2011

The 2011 Population Census began; it ended on 02 August. Results showed a total population of 7,071,576, including 6,859,341 usual (permanent) residents and 212,235 mobile (temporary) residents.

The Stamp Duty (Amendment) Ordinance 2011 was promulgated, imposing additional taxes on the sale of property to combat market speculation.

04 Jul 2011

The Social Welfare Advisory Committee released its *Report on Long-Term Social Welfare Planning in Hong Kong*, providing an analysis on the local demographic structure and change, social development as well as the provision of welfare services for a strategic direction regarding the future development of social welfare.

11 Jul 2011

The HKSAR government launched an inflation-linked retail bond, known as iBond, for public subscription in Hong Kong.

The Hong Kong Mortgage Corporation launched a pilot Reverse Mortgage Scheme designed to provide people aged 60 or above with monthly cash income by collateralising their homes (where they may continue to live) under a fixed-term agreement. Seven banks participated in the first round of the scheme.

12 Jul 2011

Hong Kong film director and producer Tsui Hark (徐克) won a Star Asia Lifetime Achievement Award at the 10th New York Asian Film Festival; he was named Asian Filmmaker of the Year at the 16th Busan International Film Festival in October.

18 Jul 2011

More than 150 current and former Legislative Council members bid farewell to the Legislative Council Building on Jackson Road and witnessed the unearthing of a time capsule. In September, the Legislative Council was relocated to a new complex at Tamar. (Figure 348)

25 Jul 2011

Hong Kong Exchanges and Clearing Limited introduced a "T+2 Finality" arrangement in the Central Clearing and Settlement System, requiring securities and money settlement to be finalised on T+2 (two business days after the trade).

08 Aug 2011

The Chief Executive's Office was relocated from the Government House to the new Government Headquarters at Tamar.

18 Aug 2011

The new Government Headquarters located at Tama and adjacent to the Legislative Council Complex, was completed with a design of "door always open." On 10 October, Tamar Park—part of the Tamar Development Project with an area of about 1.76 hectares—was opened under the concept of "land always green."

Figure 349
Participants of the New World Harbour Race 2011 at the starting point in Lei Yue Mun. (Photo taken on 16 October 2011 and courtesy of South China Morning Post Publishers Limited)

Figure 350
A group of 60 swimmers participated in the 66th Cross Harbour Race at the Tsim Sha Tsui waterfront in 1978. (Photo taken on 15 October 1978 and courtesy of South China Morning Post Publishers Limited)

23 Aug 2011

During the 14th Plenary of the Hong Kong–Guangdong Co-operation Joint Conference, HKSAR and Guangdong Province agreed to establish a Liaison Group on Combating Climate Change, with a view to controlling greenhouse gas emissions and promoting a low-carbon economy.

26 Aug 2011

The National People's Congress Standing Committee, in response to a request from the Court of Final Appeal, provided interpretations of Paragraph 1 of Article 13 and Article 19 of the Basic Law as follows: 1) The Central People's Government (CPG) was empowered to determine the rules or policies on state immunity applied in the HKSAR; 2) The HKSAR and its courts were obliged to apply (and must not depart from) the rules or policies on state immunity as determined by the CPG; 3) Acts of the State such as national defence and foreign affairs included the act of determination by the CPG as to the rules or policies on state immunity; and 4) laws of the HKSAR previously in force since 01 July 1997 must be subject to modifications, adaptations, limitations or exceptions as necessary for consistency with the rules or polices on state immunity as determined by the CPG.

11 Sep 2011

Deanie Ip Tak-han (葉德嫻) won a Volpi Cup for Best Actress at the 68th Venice International Film Festival for her role in the film *A Simple Life*. She was the first Hong Kong actress to receive the award.

03 Oct 2011

Ronald Joseph Arculli was appointed as Convenor of the Non-Official Members of the Executive Council in place of his predecessor Leung Chun-ying (梁振英) who resigned to run in the Chief Executive election.

12 Oct 2011

A resumed Home Ownership Scheme and an enhanced My Home Purchase Plan were announced in the Policy Address.

13 Oct 2011

The Court of Final Appeal dismissed an appeal by the Catholic Diocese of Hong Kong regarding the Education (Amendment) Ordinance 2004, ending a six-year litigation.

15 Oct 2011

More than 10 activist groups occupied the ground floor of the HSBC Main Building in Central, setting up tents and calling for the "defeat of financial hegemony," following the US Occupy Wall Street campaign.

16 Oct 2011

The Hong Kong Amateur Swimming Association in partnership with New World Group revived a harbour swim race last held in 1978. The New World Cross Harbour Race 2011 became a government-designated "M" Mark sporting event in 2012. (Figures 349 and 350)

28 Oct 2011

The Building (Inspection and Repair) Regulation, Building (Administration) (Amendment) Regulation 2011, Building (Minor Works) (Amendment) Regulation 2011 and Building (Amendment) Ordinance (Commencement) Notice 2011 were promulgated, effective 30 June 2012, implementing the Mandatory Building Inspection Scheme and the Mandatory Window Inspection Scheme.

06 Nov 2011

In the fourth District Council elections, 412 councillors were elected (including 76 candidates who won uncontested). The voter turnout rate was 41.49%. In addition, there were 68 appointed members; 27 ex-officio members were chairmen of Rural Committees.

23 Nov 2011

The Road Traffic (Amendment) Ordinance 2011 was promulgated, effective 15 March 2012, imposing stricter control over drug-driving with respect to six specified illicit drugs.

30 Nov 2011

An arson attack on hawker stalls on Fa Yuen Street in Mong Kok spread to buildings nearby and turned into a four-alarm blaze, killing nine people and injuring 34 others.

Nov 2011

The Chinese University of Hong Kong's Department of Anthropology began a month-long archaeological survey at San Tau and Tin Sum on Lantau Island—where 16 tombs dating back to the mid-to-late Tang Dynasty were identified through radar detection; seven tombs were presumed to have been those of soldiers or merchants from northern China.

13 Dec 2011

Supplement VIII to the Mainland and Hong Kong Closer Economic Partnership Arrangement was signed, effective 01 April 2012, providing 32 measures for liberalisation in services and facilitation of trade and investment (23 measures in 16 service sectors and others covering finance, tourism, innovation and technology). The origin criteria under trade in goods were enhanced; definitions and related requirements regarding Hong Kong service suppliers were relaxed.

14 Dec 2011

The Hong Kong–Zhuhai–Macao Bridge Hong Kong Boundary Crossing Facilities—located on an artificial island of about 150 hectares northeast of Hong Kong International Airport—commenced construction.

16 Dec 2011

Jao Tsung-i (饒宗頤) accepted his appointment as the seventh President of Xiling Seal Engravers' Society.

18 Dec 2011

The Labour Party was established under the chairmanship of Lee Cheuk-yan (李卓人).

19 Dec 2011

The Hong Kong Economic, Trade and Cultural Office in Taiwan was inaugurated to enable greater collaboration between Hong Kong and Taiwan.

03 Jan 2012

The Immigration Department made its Automated Passenger Clearance System (e-Channel) available to qualified frequent visitors from the Mainland.

06 Jan 2012

Bishop John Tong-hon (湯漢) of the Catholic Diocese of Hong Kong was appointed as the first cardinal in Hong Kong by Pope Benedict XVI.

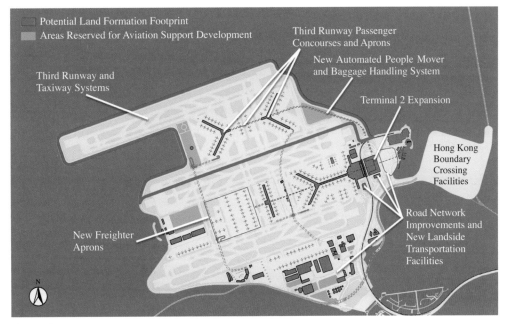

Figure 351
The Chief Executive-in-Council approved Hong Kong Airport Authority's proposal for a three-runway system on 20 March 2012, including the construction of a 3,800-metre runway, a new passenger terminal with 57 aircraft bays in an area of over 280,000 square metres and an expanded Terminal 2. (Illustration by Hong Kong Chronicles Institute. Source of reference: Airport Authority Hong Kong)

Jan 2012

The Securities and Futures Commission authorised the world's first renminbi-denominated gold exchange-traded fund.

13 Feb 2012

Chief Executive candidate Henry Tang Ying-yen（唐英年）admitted of unauthorised structures built in his house on York Road in Kowloon Tong.

15 Feb 2012

The HKSAR government began reducing the border restricted area, starting with 740 hectares of land (between Mai Po and Lok Ma Chau Control Point and between Lin Ma Hang and Sha Tau Kok) in the Frontier Closed Area where restrictions on road use were also lifted.

26 Feb 2012

Amid public concern following media reports regarding the Chief Executive's acceptance of hospitality offered by tycoons, Chief Executive Donald Tsang Yam-kuen（曾蔭權）announced an independent review committee—chaired by former Chief Justice of the Court of Final Appeal Andrew Li Kwok-nang（李國能）—on the regulatory framework and procedures for preventing conflicts of interests concerning the Chief Executive, Executive Council Non-Official Members and political appointees. On 31 May, a committee report was released, outlining 36 recommendations with a view to improving the current system and restoring public confidence.

07 Mar 2012

Centennial College, a member of The University of Hong Kong Group, was inaugurated as a self-financed, four-year undergraduate institution.

16 Mar 2012

Candidates of the fourth Chief Executive election—Leung Chun-ying (梁振英), Henry Tang Ying-yen (唐英年) and Albert Ho Chun-yan（何俊仁）—participated in a televised debate produced by Radio Television Hong Kong and carried live by 10 local online media outlets.

20 Mar 2012

The Chief Executive-in-Council adopted Hong Kong Airport Authority's proposal for a three-runway system. (Figure 351)

23 Mar 2012

The Air Pollution Control (Vehicle Design Standards) (Emission) (Amendment) Regulation 2012 was promulgated, requiring compliance with Euro V emission standards in all newly registered motor vehicles by 01 June (diesel light goods vehicles of design weight not more than 3.5 tonnes by 31 December).

The Hong Kong Advanced Level Examination was held for the last time and taken by a total of 31,666 students. On 29 June, examination results were released; four students earned a perfect score with six distinctions.

25 Mar 2012

Leung Chun-ying (梁振英) won in the fourth election of the HKSAR Chief Executive, defeating Henry Tang Ying-yen (唐英年) and Albert Ho Chun-yan (何俊仁) with 689 votes. On 10 April, Premier Wen Jiabao (溫家寶) signed an Order of the State Council, confirming Leung's appointment as Chief Executive of the HKSAR.

28 Mar 2012

The inaugural Hong Kong Diploma of Secondary Education Examination was administered. Scores ranged from the highest score "5**" to the lowest designated as "Unclassified."

30 Mar 2012

Phase I of the Ad Hoc Quota Trial Scheme for Cross Boundary Private Cars was open to applicants. Registered owners of private cars with a seating capacity of five or less could apply for a single-entry permit for a stay of no more than seven days in Guangdong through Shenzhen Bay Port.

China Minsheng Bank—the first national bank under a majority ownership of private enterprises in the Mainland—opened its first offshore branch in Hong Kong.

01 Apr 2012

The Buildings Department introduced a Reporting Scheme for Unauthorised Building Works in New Territories Exempted Houses, allowing owners of village houses to declare (by 31 December) and keep existing illegal housing structures temporarily upon safety inspection and certification.

The Communications Authority was established as a statutory body on broadcasting and telecommunications industries upon a merger of related agencies.

02 Apr 2012

The Court of Final Appeal ruled unanimously in *Fok Chun Wa & Anor v. Hospital Authority & Anor* that charging higher fees in public hospitals from non-eligible persons were not inconsistent with Article 25 of the Basic Law.

12 Apr 2012

The Chinese Central Government appointed Song Zhe (宋哲) as Commissioner of the Ministry of Foreign Affairs in the HKSAR. He remained in the post until 10 June 2017.

13 Apr 2012

The Road Traffic (Amendment) Ordinance 2012 was promulgated, requiring installation of an approved speed limiter in all public light buses coupled with a maximum speed limit of 80 km per hour.

25 Apr 2012

Buddha's parietal-bone relic—a national treasure of China—arrived in Hong Kong for public worship in a debut outside the Mainland since the time it was unearthed; Hong Kong became the only city to host the three great Buddhist relics of China, namely Buddha's tooth, Buddha's finger bone and Buddha's parietal bone.

30 Apr 2012

The Education Bureau accepted a refined Curriculum Guide of Moral and National Education. The Guide was prepared by the Curriculum Development Council to be adopted in primary and secondary schools in the 2012/13 and 2013/14 school years, respectively.

Figure 352
Bus enthusiasts snapped photos of KMB's last non-air-conditioned double-decker, commonly known as the hot dog bus, departing for the last time in regular service from Star Ferry Bus Terminus in Tsim Sha Tsui. (Photo courtesy of South China Morning Post Publishers Limited)

08 May 2012

Kowloon Motor Bus Company (1933) Limited decommissioned its last fleet of non-air-conditioned double-deck buses first introduced to Hong Kong in 1949. (Figure 352)

09 May 2012

The World Health Organizations Collaborating Centre for Traditional Medicine was established in Hong Kong as the first in the world focused on formulation of policies and regulatory standards for traditional medicine.

14 May 2012

The Hong Kong Science Museum began an exhibition called I Love Lyuba: Baby Mammoth of the Ice Age. It showcased the world's most well-preserved baby mammoth dating back more than 40,000 years along with several rare pieces of long-extinct Ice Age mammal skulls.

The Asian-Pacific Postal Union (APPU) Executive Council Meeting was held for the first time in Hong Kong with more than 160 delegates from 32 APPU member countries.

17 May 2012

President of the Legislative Council Jasper Tsang Yok-sing (曾鈺成) ended a 33-hour filibuster by imposing a three-hour limit (in accordance with Rule 92 of the Rules of Procedure) on closing remarks in a proposed amendment to the Legislative Council (Amendment) Bill 2012. It marked the first time that the rule was invoked to end a debate.

19 May 2012

The Hong Kong Heritage Museum began an exhibition called PICASSO: Masterpieces from Musée National Picasso, Paris. It featured 56 renowned paintings and sculptures and attracted nearly 300,000 visits before it ended on 22 July.

21 May 2012

The Sunbeam Theatre was renovated and re-opened as a venue for operatic performances.

08 Jun 2012

The Legislative Council (Amendment) Ordinance 2012 was promulgated, prohibiting council members from standing for council by-elections within six months after resignation.

15 Jun 2012

The Fisheries Protection Ordinance was promulgated, effective 31 December, banning destructive fishing practices such as the use of dredging, suction and trawling devices. In February 2013, a voluntary trawler licence buyout scheme was launched with a one-off grant and ex-gratia allowance.

21 Jun 2012

The Legislative Council vetoed (by one vote) a motion intended to give priority to a resolution on the reorganisation of the government secretariat—with the addition of a Deputy Chief Secretary for Administration, a Deputy Financial Secretary, a Secretary for Culture, and a Secretary for Technology and Communications. It was a proposal by Chief Executive-elect Leung Chun-ying（梁振英）for implementation on 01 July.

22 Jun 2012

The Competition Ordinance was promulgated, establishing a Competition Commission and a Competition Tribunal to prohibit conduct that would prevent, restrict or distort competition in Hong Kong. The ordinance came into full effect on 14 December 2015.

The Jao Tsung-i Academy—a cultural landmark located at the former Lai Chi Kok Hospital as one of the first projects under the Revitalising Historic Buildings Through Partnership Scheme—was opened for its Phase One Low Zone (one of three zones).

25 Jun 2012

The Hong Kong–Macao–Guangdong *Regional Cooperation Plan on Building a Quality Living Area* was released as the first joint regional plan on the greater Pearl River Delta region.

28 Jun 2012

Phase I of the Public Transport Fare Concession Scheme for the Elderly and Eligible Persons with Disabilities began for a concessionary fare of HK$2 per trip on the general Mass Transit Railway lines, franchised buses and ferries.

29 Jun 2012

Supplement IX to the Mainland and Hong Kong Closer Economic Partnership Agreement was signed, effective 01 January 2013, providing 43 measures for liberalisation in services and facilitation of trade and investment (including 37 measures in 22 service sectors) intended to facilitate further cooperation and promote mutual recognition of professional qualifications.

01 Jul 2012

President Hu Jintao（胡錦濤）attended the Celebrations of the 15th Anniversary of the Hong Kong's Return to the Motherland and Inauguration Ceremony of the Fourth HKSAR Government. He administered the oath of office to Chief Executive Leung Chun-ying（梁振英）and other principal officials.

Chief Executive Leung Chun-ying（梁振英）appointed Lam Woon-kwong（林煥光）as Convenor of the Non-official Members of the Executive Council.

04 Jul 2012

The Customs and Excise Department seized about 649 kilograms of cocaine, worth approximately HK$760 million, in a container arriving from Ecuador at the Kwai Chung Container Terminals. It was the largest case of its kind as of 01 July 2017.

06 Jul 2012

The Residential Properties (First-hand Sales) Ordinance was promulgated, effective 29 April 2013, providing greater consumer protection in the sales of new residential properties.

17 Jul 2012

The Yau Ma Tei Theatre—the only remaining Second World War-era theatre in Hong Kong—was re-opened upon renovation as a venue dedicated to Cantonese opera.

24 Jul 2012

The Hong Kong Observatory hoisted Hurricane Signal No. 10 for about three and a half hours amid Typhoon Vicente—which caused 138 injuries and 587 fallen trees.

The Hong Kong Museum of History began an exhibition called The Majesty of All Under Heaven: The Eternal Realm of China's First Emperor. It featured 120 Qin Dynasty relics, including terracotta figures, and attracted a record 420,000 visits.

27 Jul 2012

The Trade Descriptions (Unfair Trade Practices) (Amendment) Ordinance 2012 was promulgated, effective 19 July 2013, providing greater consumer protection against unfair trade practices by extending coverage from goods to services.

The Hong Kong Arts Development Council launched a Critic's Prize in recognition of outstanding critical writing on the arts in a bid to promote the discipline of arts criticism.

01 Aug 2012

Authorised institutions (banks) in Hong Kong began offering RMB services (including unlimited RMB currency exchange) to customers who were non-Hong Kong residents.

04 Aug 2012

Hong Kong cyclist Lee Wai-sze (李慧詩) won a bronze medal in the women's Keirin at the 30th Olympic Games in London, marking the third Olympic medal in the history of Hong Kong. (Figure 353)

10 Aug 2012

The Companies Ordinance was promulgated, effective 03 March 2014, aiming to enhance corporate governance, improve relevant regulations, facilitate further businesses and modernise the company law of Hong Kong. Provisions on corporate bankruptcy and liquidation were enacted through the Companies (Winding Up and Miscellaneous Provisions) Ordinance.

Figure 353
Lee Wai-sze (李慧詩) in celebration of her win in Women's Keirin at the London 2012 Olympic Games.
(Photo taken on 04 August 2012 and courtesy of South China Morning Post Publishers Limited)

15 Aug 2012

Seven Hong Kong activists aboard the fishing vessel *Kai Fung No. 2* broke through an encirclement of Japanese warships to reach the Diaoyu Islands where they sang the Chinese national anthem, marking the first protest for China's sovereignty on the islands since 1996. Fourteen people on board were detained by the Japanese police; they were released on 17 August.

21 Aug 2012

The HKSAR government launched a Universal Accessibility Programme to provide barrier-free access at public walkways with lifts and ramps in more than 230 locations.

22 Aug 2012

The Hong Kong West Drainage Tunnel was completed as the longest and widest drainage tunnel; it was the largest flood prevention project by the Drainage Services Department.

30 Aug 2012

Chief Executive Leung Chun-ying (梁振英) announced a package of 10 short-, medium- and long-term measures to increase the supply of land and housing, including the upfront sale of 1,000 subsidised housing units converted from My Home Purchase Plan, an additional 11,900 residential units by rezoning 36 government, institution and community sites, and a Long-Term Housing Strategy by an inter-departmental advisory group.

Student activist group Scholarism staged a rally at the Central Government Offices in protest of the government plan regarding Moral and National Education in schools.

06 Sep 2012

The HKSAR government introduced a Hong Kong Property for Hong Kong People policy, aiming to tackle housing issues by restricting sales and resales to local permanent residents in select housing estates within a 30-year period. Two residential sites of the Kai Tak Development were made available for public tender in a pilot programme on 19 March 2013 and were sold on 05 June.

08 Sep 2012

Chief Executive Leung Chun-ying (梁振英) suspended the introduction of moral and national education, allowing individual schools to decide whether to offer such curriculum. On 08 October, following a review by the Committee on Implementation of Moral and National Education, its curriculum guide was shelved.

09 Sep 2012

The fifth Legislative Council elections was held for 70 seats (35 geographical constituencies and 35 functional constituencies). The voter turnout rates were: 53% in direct elections, 52% in five District Council (second) functional constituencies, and 69.7% in functional constituencies.

13 Sep 2012

The Steering Committee on Long Term Housing Strategy was established as an advisory group responsible for making recommendations to address the issues of housing in support of the policy objectives outlined by the Chief Executive of the HKSAR.

14 Sep 2012

The Hong Kong Monetary Authority issued further measures on property mortgage loans to mitigate the risk of a market bubble, especially among borrowers with multiple outstanding mortgage loans, by lowering 1) the maximum stressed debt servicing ratio from 60% to 50% and 2) the loan-to-value ratio limit from 40% to 30% for property mortgage loans based on the net worth of mortgage applicants following an assessment.

15 Sep 2012

Nearly 100 demonstrators staged a rally near Sheung Shui Station chanting "Reclaim Sheung Shui Station" in protest of nuisance caused by buyers of parallel goods bound for the Mainland.

17 Sep 2012

Hong Kong Exchanges and Clearing Limited launched the USD/CNH (Hong Kong) futures, marking the world's first deliverable RMB currency futures product to be quoted, margined and settled in RMB.

28 Sep 2012

The Hong Kong Avenue of Comic Stars, located at Kowloon Park in Tsim Sha Tsui, was unveiled as the world's first comic walkway (100 metres long), featuring 30 polychromatic sculptures of Hong Kong classic comic characters and 10 bronze handprints of famous Hong Kong comic artists.

01 Oct 2012

The *Lamma IV*—a Hongkong Electric-owned vessel carrying 124 employees and their families on its way to the National Day commemorative firework in Central—sank near Lamma Island after colliding with the *Sea Smooth*—a passenger ferry operated by Hong Kong and Kowloon Ferry, causing 39 deaths and 92 injuries. The HKSAR government designated 04 October 2012 as a day of condolence in memory of those who died in the accident. (Figure 354)

07 Oct 2012

The Business and Professionals Alliance for Hong Kong was formed, comprising seven Legislative Council members-elect under the chairmanship of Andrew Leung Kwan-yuen (梁君彥).

11 Oct 2012

A trunk of a 100-year-old Chinese Banyan tree at Lam Tsuen San Tsuen in Tai Po collapsed, killing one person and injuring another, in an accident caused by structural problems of the tree.

22 Oct 2012

Chief Executive Leung Chun-ying (梁振英) appointed a Commission of Inquiry—chaired by Justice of Appeal of the Court of Appeal Michael Victor Lunn—to investigate the collision of vessels near Lamma Island on 01 October. An investigation report was submitted to the Chief Executive on 19 April 2013 and was partially released to the public on 30 April 2013. The Marine Department was held accountable for negligence and advised to implement institutional reform according to 13 recommendations.

24 Oct 2012

The Education Bureau under its Qualifications Framework introduced two major initiatives, namely the Award Titles Scheme and the use of academic credit, as a standardised indicator of attainment and adequacy in the academic, vocational and continuing education and training sectors.

Figure 354
The aftermath of a sunken ferry following a collision near Lamma Island on 01 October 2012. (Photo courtesy of Sing Tao News Corporation Limited)

Oct 2012

President of the Central Military Commission Hu Jintao (胡錦濤) signed an order appointing Wang Xiaojun (王曉軍) as Commander of the People's Liberation Army Hong Kong Garrison who remained in the post until July 2014.

09 Nov 2012

The Commission on Poverty was re-established with the objectives of preventing and alleviating poverty through analysis and review of relevant policies by drawing a poverty line and making full use of a Community Care Fund. On 10 December, it held its first meeting.

06 Dec 2012

Hong Kong Exchanges and Clearing Limited completed acquisition of the London Metal Exchange for HK$16.67 billion.

12 Dec 2012

It was announced that Primary 4 students in Hong Kong ranked first place for the first time in the Progress in International Reading Literacy Study 2011 and that Primary 4 and Secondary 2 students ranked among the top five in the world in the Trends in International Mathematics and Science Study 2011.

13 Dec 2012

The Hague Conference on Private International Law opened its new Asia Pacific Regional Office in Hong Kong.

16 Dec 2012

The Hong Kong Museum of Art began an exhibition called Andy Warhol: 15 Minutes Eternal. It featured 468 pieces from the Andy Warhol Museum (US) in the largest exhibition in Asia and attracted some 260,000 visits.

18 Dec 2012

The Chinese Central Government appointed Zhang Xiaoming (張曉明) as Director of the Liaison Office of the Central People's Government in the HKSAR. He remained in the post until 22 September 2017.

01 Jan 2013

The zero quota (parents as non-permanent resident of Hong Kong) policy—under which public and private hospitals must not accept bookings from non-local pregnant women for delivery in Hong Kong—came into force.

04 Jan 2013

The HKSAR government launched its Interim Scheme to Extend the Home Ownership Scheme (HOS) Secondary Market to White Form Buyers, providing 5,000 places for purchase of second-hand HOS flats without paying a land premium among eligible buyers of HOS subsidised housing (White Form). The scheme became a recurrent programme in 2018.

08 Jan 2013

The research paper Tumour Angiogenesis and Application in Anti-Angiogenesis Therapy—jointly published by Guan Xin-yuan (關新元) of The University of Hong Kong's Li Ka Shing Faculty of Medicine (Department of Clinical Oncology) and Kung Hsiang-fu (孔祥復) of The Chinese University of Hong Kong's Faculty of Medicine (Centre for Emerging Infectious Diseases) in conjunction with the Third Military Medical University of the Chinese People's Liberation Army, Peking University and Nanjing Medical University—was named winner of a First-class Award in the 2012 State Scientific and Technological Progress Awards.

09 Jan 2013

The Legislative Council defeated a motion to impeach Chief Executive Leung Chun-ying (梁振英); it was the first-ever attempt by a legislator to impeach a Chief Executive.

17 Jan 2013

The Chinese Medicine Development Committee was established as an advisory body on the long-term development of the Chinese medicine sector in Hong Kong.

The Economic Development Commission—comprising four working groups covering 1) transportation, 2) tourism, convention and exhibition, 3) manufacturing, innovation, cultural and creative services, and 4) professional services— was established to broaden Hong Kong's economic base and promote growth and development. It held its first meeting on 13 March.

The Financial Services Development Council was established as an advisory body on the sustainable growth and diversity of the financial services industry of Hong Kong.

29 Jan 2013

The Hong Kong Museum of History unveiled an exhibition called The Wonders of Ancient Mesopotamia. It showcased 170 treasures from the Department of the Middle East of the British Museum in a Hong Kong debut with 180,000 visits between 30 January and 13 May.

06 Feb 2013

Hong Kong Heritage Museum began an exhibition titled Fabergé—Legacy of Imperial Russia. It featured over 200 pieces of jewellery and adornments from the Moscow Kremlin Museums and the Fersman Mineralogical Museum in Russia.

21 Feb 2013

Cyclist Sarah Lee Wai-sze (李慧詩) won a gold medal in the women's 500m time-trial at the Union Cycliste Internationale's Track Cycling World Championships in Minsk, Belarus; she was awarded the rainbow jersey and became the first world champion in women's cycling from Hong Kong.

22 Feb 2013

Hong Kong Mortgage Corporation Limited announced that maximum coverage at 90% of loan-to-value ratio under its Mortgage Insurance Programme would apply only to loans of HK$4 million or less (instead of HK$6 million), effective 23 February.

The Import and Export (General) Regulation 2013 was promulgated, effective 01 March, prohibiting the export of powdered formula (made for infants/young children under 36 months old), including soy-based products, unless with a special licence.

The Hong Kong Observatory received a record 5,000 public reports on tremors from an earthquake of magnitude 4.8 on the Richter scale in Heyuan, Guangdong.

23 Feb 2013

The HKSAR government introduced further measures to combat property speculation by increasing stamp duty on sales of residential property to 1.5% (HK$2 million or less) and 8.5% (above HK$2 million). The Stamp Duty Ordinance, following an amendment, was made applicable to non-residential property.

28 Feb 2013

The HKSAR government announced that land sale under the Application Mechanism would be abolished starting from the 2013/14 financial year and that 46 residential sites (with a capacity of about 13,600 housing flats) would be made available under the 2013–14 Land Sale Programme.

18 Mar 2013

The Home Affairs Bureau launched a two-year pilot scheme to provide free legal advice for litigants in person who had commenced or were parties to legal proceedings in the District Court or other higher courts but had not been granted legal aid.

Figure 355
Dock workers on the second day of a labour strike at Kwai Chung Container Terminal. (Photo taken on 29 March 2013 and courtesy of South China Morning Post Publishers Limited)

21 Mar 2013

The Alliance for True Democracy was established, comprising 27 pan-democratic members of the Legislative Council and 12 political groups and trade unions under the convenorship of Joseph Cheng Yu-shek (鄭宇碩).

25 Mar 2013

The Court of Final Appeal ruled in *Vallejos and Domingo v. Commissioner of Registration* that foreign domestic helpers did not fall into the "ordinary resident" category for permanent residency stipulated in Categories (2) and (4) of Paragraph 2 in Article 24 of the Basic Law and must return to their place of origin according to their employment contracts.

27 Mar 2013

Benny Tai Yiu-ting (戴耀廷), Chan Kin-man (陳健民) and Chu Yiu-ming (朱耀明) jointly released the manifesto "Occupy Central with Love and Peace" in a campaign for universal suffrage in the 2017 Chief Executive election through non-violent civil disobedience.

28 Mar 2013

Over 100 dock workers of Hongkong International Terminals, a container terminal operator and a subsidiary of Hutchison Whampoa, went on strike, demanding a 20% pay increase. On 06 May, workers accepted a 9.8% pay-raise proposal from four vendors (their employers), ending a 40-day labour strike (the longest since the establishment of the HKSAR). (Figure 355)

Mar 2013

The Hong Kong Police Force began a field trial with body-worn video cameras to increase transparency in confrontational scenarios during public events where a breach of peace was likely to occur. In May 2017, another procurement was announced, aiming to equip all front-line officers by 2021.

02 Apr 2013

The Co-operation Agreement on the Development of a Digital Library in the Hong Kong Public Libraries was signed, allowing public access to the National Library of China and its collection of rare ancient books, local gazettes, stone carvings and paintings through the Hong Kong Public Libraries' Multimedia Information System.

05 Apr 2013

The HKSAR government rolled out its first Old Age Living Allowance as part of the Social Security Allowance Scheme, providing eligible elderly persons aged 65 or above with a monthly payment of HK$2,200.

08 Apr 2013

Hong Kong Exchanges and Clearing Limited began its After-Hours Futures Trading operation with the Hang Seng Index and H-shares Index futures from 5 p.m. to 11 p.m.

09 Apr 2013

The HKSAR government formed a Standard Working Hours Committee following the *Report of the Policy Study on Standard Working Hours* released by the Labour Department in November 2012.

23 Apr 2013

The Hong Kong: Our Home campaign was launched for a series of more 1,100 programmes and events designed to foster a strong community spirit with an emphasis on public involvement over a period of eight months.

02 May 2013

Chief Executive Leung Chun-ying (梁振英) established an Independent Review Committee on Independent Commission Against Corruption's (ICAC) Regulatory Systems and Procedures for handling Official Entertainment, Gifts and Duty Visits with respect to former ICAC Commissioner Timothy Tong Hin-ming's (湯顯明) handling of such issues. A report was filed on 02 September and made public on 12 September; it recommended ICAC officers to keep adequate documentation regarding social events, refrain from exchange of gifts, and avoid non-essential visits during official overseas trips.

13 May 2013

The Court of Final Appeal ruled in *W v. Registrar of Marriages* that provisions of the Matrimonial Causes Ordinance and Marriage Ordinance, which prohibited marriage of transgender persons, were in violation of Article 37 of the Basic Law and Paragraph 2 of Article 19 of the Hong Kong Bill of Rights Ordinance. On 17 July 2014, by a court order, it became effective that persons, after full sex re-assignment surgery, would be treated as being of the sex to which they were re-assigned for the purpose of marriage registration.

15 May 2013

Financial Secretary John Tsang Chun-wah (曾俊華) announced exemption from the First Registration Tax for electric vehicles at the unveiling ceremony of BYD's e6 electric taxis and e6 Premier electric cars.

18 May 2013

The Food Wise Hong Kong campaign was launched for public awareness on the issue of food waste and coordinated efforts in food waste reduction.

20 May 2013

The HKSAR government published *Hong Kong: Blueprint for Sustainable Use of Resources 2013–2022*, outlining a strategy to reduce per-capita disposal of municipal solid waste by 40% before 2022.

Edward Snowden, a former contractor of the US Central Intelligence Agency, arrived in Hong Kong seeking asylum after exposing US covert surveillance programmes on foreign nations. On 23 June, Snowden left Hong Kong legally via Hong Kong International Airport.

31 May 2013

The District Councils (Amendment) Ordinance 2013 was promulgated, abolishing all appointed seats in fifth District Councils starting from 01 January 2016.

10 Jun 2013

The HKSAR government began implementation of the second stage in reducing the Frontier Closed Area, covering more than 710 hectares of land between Lok Ma Chau Boundary Control Point and Ng Tung River. Restrictions on closed roads within the excised area were lifted.

12 Jun 2013

The Kai Tak Cruise Terminal—comprising two berths for ships up to a gross tonnage of 220,000 tonnes—was opened with the arrival of the vessel *Mariner of the Seas*. Construction began in May 2010 as part of the Kai Tak Development Phase 1; it was funded by the government at a cost of HK$8.2 billion and leased to a terminal operator. (Figure 356)

04 Jul 2013

The HKSAR government announced the results of its North East New Territories New Development Areas Planning and Engineering Study. It was an approach to increasing land supply through development in Kwu Tung North and Fanling North.

01 Aug 2013

The HKSAR government announced its Guangdong Scheme, effective 01 October, making Hong Kong residents aged 65 or above living in Guangdong eligible for monthly allowances under the Old Age Allowance without having to return to Hong Kong each year.

29 Aug 2013

Supplement X to the Mainland and Hong Kong Closer Economic Partnership Arrangement (CEPA) was signed, providing 73 liberalisation measures (65 on services and eight on finance, trade and investment) for a total of 403 CEPA liberalisation measures.

01 Sep 2013

The Second West-East Gas Pipeline—running from Khorgos in Xinjiang to Guangzhou in Guangdong through 14 provinces, municipalities and autonomous regions (connected to the Central Asia–China Gas Pipeline) was marked with the completion of its Hong Kong Branch Line for supplying natural gas to Hong Kong. Construction of the eastern part of the pipeline in Shenzhen began in 2009.

Figure 356
Royal Caribbean Cruises Limited's *Mariner of the Seas* upon arrival at the Kai Tak Cruise Terminal. (Photo taken on 12 June 2013 and courtesy of Dickson Lee/South China Morning Post via Getty Images)

03 Sep 2013

The Long-Term Housing Strategy Steering Committee released a public consultation paper titled *Building Consensus, Building Homes*, recommending a supply of 470,000 housing units over ten years.

The Tai O Heritage Hotel won an Award of Merit of the 2013 UNESCO Asia-Pacific Awards for Cultural Heritage Conservation, marking the first award in a project under Batch I of the Revitalising Historic Buildings Through Partnership Scheme.

16 Sep 2013

Upon the 16th Plenary of the Hong Kong–Guangdong Co-operation Joint Conference, co-chaired by Chief Executive Leung Chun-ying（梁振英）and Governor of Guangdong Province Zhu Xiaodan（朱小丹）, eight letters of intent and co-operation agreements were signed.

19 Sep 2013

The world's first self-service immigration clearance system (e-Channel) with voice navigation functions to accommodate visually impaired persons became operational at Lok Ma Chau Spur Line Control Point.

24 Sep 2013

North Lantau Hospital became operational as the first hospital on Lantau Island, providing eight hours of limited outpatient services daily. On 07 January 2014, it was expanded to offer 16-hour accident and emergency and in-patient services.

The West Kowloon Cultural District Authority held a ground-breaking ceremony in celebration of the Xiqu Centre, marking the first performing arts venue of the West Kowloon Cultural District.

28 Sep 2013

The Commission on Poverty announced the first official poverty line—defined as 50% of the median monthly household income before policy intervention (i.e. taxation and social welfare transfers). As of 2012, after policy interventions, 403,000 households with 1.018 million persons were defined as living in poverty (a poverty rate of 15.2%).

30 Sep 2013

The first home-grown hybrid light bus, as part of a trial scheme under the Pilot Green Transport Fund, was unveiled in a ceremony.

Sep 2013

The Antiquities and Monuments Office—upon discovery of over 500 Song Dynasty copper coins at To Kwa Wan Station (under construction) of the Shatin–Central Link—began a three-phase archaeological excavation (until May 2015), unearthing 81 relics in an area of 23,300 square metres. A total of 81 relics were uncovered at the site named the Sacred Hill Area, including 28 relics of stone walls, five building foundations and four ancient round- or square-shaped wells dating back to the Song, Yuan, Qing dynasties and Republican periods.

07 Oct 2013

During an APEC meeting in Indonesia, Chief Executive Leung Chun-ying（梁振英）and Philippine President Benigno Aquino III agreed to resolving the issue of the 2010 Manila hostage crisis. On 22 October, a resolution was passed by the Manila City Council for a formal apology to the HKSAR and victims.

15 Oct 2013

The Communications Authority approved Fantastic Television Limited and Hong Kong Television Entertainment Company Limited for the first domestic free television programme service licences in almost 40 years; Hong Kong Television Network Limited was rejected, causing an outcry.

Figure 357
(Left) Mei Ho House, Block 41 of Shek Kip Mei Estate—Hong Kong's first resettlement blocks constructed in 1954; (right) Mei Ho House Youth Hostel—an integrated multi-purpose cultural facility following a revitalisation project. (Photo taken on 29 January 2016 and courtesy of HKSAR Government)

21 Oct 2013

The heritage museum of Mei Ho House Youth Hostel—rebuilt from the first resettlement block in Hong Kong constructed in 1954—was opened as part of an integrated multi-purpose (accommodation, exhibition and heritage preservation) cultural facility under the Revitalising Historic Buildings Through Partnership Scheme. (Figure 357)

22 Oct 2013

The Association of Southeast Asian Nations Economic and Trade Cooperation Forum began in Hong Kong between HKSAR's Secretary for Commerce and Economic Development and trade ministers from 10 member states on further promotion of trade.

24 Oct 2013

The Steering Committee on Population Policy released a public consultation paper titled *Thoughts for Hong Kong*, proposing five strategies in addressing demographic challenges with a focus on the current population, including the issues of ageing and growth.

25 Oct 2013

The Air Pollution Control (Air Pollutant Emission) (Controlled Vehicles) Regulation was promulgated, effective 01 February 2014, mandating a gradual phase-out of pre-Euro IV diesel-run commercial vehicles and an introduction of a 15-year service limit on new commercial vehicles.

07 Nov 2013

The Hong Kong Science Museum began its largest dinosaur exhibition called Legends of the Giant Dinosaurs, with over 190 exhibits. It ran until 09 April 2014 and attracted more than 770,000 visits.

25 Nov 2013

OTC Clearing Hong Kong Limited—a subsidiary of Hong Kong Exchanges and Clearing Limited (HKEx) with 12 founding shareholders, including HSBC, Bank of China (Hong Kong), Standard Chartered Bank, Citibank, J.P. Morgan, China Construction Bank, and Industrial and Commercial Bank of China—was opened as a central counterparty for clearing and settlement services in over-the-counter derivatives.

02 Dec 2013

Hong Kong confirmed its first human case of avian influenza type A (H7N9), immediately raising the response level from "alert" to "serious" under the Preparedness Plan for Influenza Pandemic. The import of live chickens from Shenzhen was also suspended.

02 Dec 2013

The Government Laboratory celebrated its centenary with a four-day international conference with international experts on metrology, quality assurance, analytical chemistry and forensic science.

The China National Space Administration launched Chang'e No. 3 from Xichang Satellite Launch Center on a robotic lunar exploration mission equipped with a Camera Pointing System jointly developed by Hong Kong Polytechnic University and China Academy of Space Technology.

09 Dec 2013

Create Hong Kong (CreateHK) announced three winners in the inaugural First Feature Film Initiative, namely *Somewhere Beyond the Mist*, *Weeds on Fire* and *Mad World*. *Mad World* and *Weeds on Fire* won five awards at the 36th Hong Kong Film Awards in 2017.

17 Dec 2013

The Court of Final Appeal ruled that a seven-year residence eligibility requirement (since 01 January 2004) of the Comprehensive Social Security Assistance Scheme was in violation of the Basic Law; it ordered a one-year residence requirement be restored.

24 Dec 2013

The police issued alerts on high-quality counterfeit HK$1,000 banknotes in circulation mimicking banknotes issued by HSBC and Bank of China (Hong Kong) in 2003; some business owners refused to accept HK$1,000 banknotes altogether. On 08 January 2014, following inquiries by the Legislative Council, an initiative (in lieu of a recall) was announced by the government for exchange of the 2003 series HK$1,000 banknotes at licenced banks.

26 Dec 2013

Hong Kong film *A Simple Life* was named Outstanding Co-Produced Film; its leading actress Deanie Ip Tak-han (葉德嫻) won Outstanding Abroad Actress at the 15th China Huabiao Film Awards organised by the China Film Administration.

An 80-year-old man died of avian influenza A (H7N9), marking the first death from the disease in Hong Kong.

30 Dec 2013

The Hong Kong Velodrome—Hong Kong's first indoor cycling facility in Tseung Kwan O with a UCI-sanctioned 250-metre wooden cycling track—was completed; it was officially opened on 30 April 2014.

The Environmental Protection Department launched an Air Quality Health Index in place of the Air Pollution Index, providing more health-risk information based on the concentration of nitrogen dioxide, sulphur dioxide and particulate matter (PM10 and PM2.5).

15 Jan 2014

The HKSAR government announced the establishment of a Lantau Development Advisory Committee and appointed 19 non-official members two days later for advising the government through the Secretary for Development on the sustainable development and conservation of Lantau Island.

17 Jan 2014

The Road Traffic (Construction and Maintenance of Vehicles) (Amendment) Regulation 2014 was promulgated, effective 01 October, requiring the installation of vehicle backup cameras in new commercial vehicles, including goods vehicles, for greater safety.

05 Feb 2014

The HKSAR government suspended its 14-day visa-free arrangement for diplomatic and official passport holders of the Philippines, imposing a sanction amid the lack of a formal apology by the Philippine government following the Manila hostage crisis in 2010.

06 Feb 2014

A 2,000-pound bomb dropped by an American bomber during the Second World War was unearthed at a construction site on Queen's Road East in Wan Chai; it was the largest aerial bomb ever found in Hong Kong's urban centre. More than 2,200 people were evacuated; it took 18 hours to defuse and dismantle the bomb.

14 Feb 2014

Yuexiu Group of Guangzhou successfully acquired Chong Hing Bank for HK$11.644 billion at HK$35.69 per share in the first acquisition of a local bank by a non-financial institution since 1987.

22 Feb 2014

The Vietnamese cargo ship *Sunrise Orient* capsized near Cheung Chau; 17 crew members were rescued. It ran aground at Tung Wan Tsai in Cheung Chau and left a trail of fuel leak measuring 100 metres by three metres, polluting the sea and a nearby beach.

25 Feb 2014

The Chinese Central Government announced a rescheduled Asia-Pacific Economic Corporation Finance Ministers' Meeting—initially scheduled to take place from 10 to 12 September in Hong Kong—to be held in Beijing.

26 Feb 2014

Kevin Lau Chun-to (劉進圖), former Chief Editor of *Ming Pao* and Chief Operating Officer of MediaNet, was attacked by two assailants. On 09 March, two suspects were arrested in Dongguan by the Guangdong Provincial Public Security Department and were extradited to Hong Kong. On 21 August 2015, both defendants were convicted of wounding with intent and of two counts of theft and were sentenced to 19 years in prison by the High Court.

28 Feb 2014

The Stamp Duty (Amendment) Ordinance 2014 was promulgated, imposing a higher rate of special stamp duty (sell side) on sale of residential property acquired on or after 27 October 2012 within an extended period of 36 months, in addition to a buyer's stamp duty in property acquisitions on or after the same date by non-permanent residents of Hong Kong.

25 Mar 2014

The Hong Kong–United States Tax Information Exchange Agreement was signed, allowing free exchange of tax information between Hong Kong and the US. It was the first agreement of its kind signed by Hong Kong.

01 Apr 2014

The Hong Kong Economic and Trade Office in Wuhan became operational, followed by an official opening ceremony on 18 April 2015; it sought to promote closer links between Hong Kong and five provinces, namely Hubei, Hunan, Shanxi, Jiangxi and Henan.

Wing Hang Bank was acquired by Oversea-Chinese Banking Corporation (OCBC) Limited for HK$38.7 billion; it was renamed OCBC Wing Hang Bank on 01 October.

14 Apr 2014

Hong Kong Buddhist College was renamed Hong Kong Nang Yan College of Higher Education, becoming the 18th institution to offer undergraduate programmes in Hong Kong upon approval by the Education Bureau.

15 Apr 2014

The MTR Corporation announced a delayed opening of the Guangzhou–Shenzhen–Hong Kong Express Rail Link until 2017 and a cost overrun by HK$14.8 billion to reach HK$81.7 billion due to damage to boring machines from heavy flooding and difficulty with West Kowloon Terminus and Mai Po Wetland Park. On 29 April, MTR appointed an Independent Board Committee for a thorough review.

23 Apr 2014

The HKSAR and Philippine governments issued a joint statement on the 2010 Manila hostage crisis with a resolution on four demands made by the victims and their families: apology, compensation, sanctions against responsible officials and individuals, and tourist safety measures.

02 May 2014

The Education Bureau announced the first batch of e-textbooks approved under Phase I of the E-Textbook Market Development Scheme for implementation in the 2014/15 school year.

15 May 2014

The Environment Bureau began disposal of 28 tonnes of illegal ivory seized over the years.

16 May 2014

The HKSAR government appointed an Independent Expert Panel—chaired by Michael John Hartmann, a non-permanent judge of the Court of Final Appeal—on the cause and accountability regarding a substantial delay in the construction of the Guangzhou–Shenzhen–Hong Kong Express Rail Link (Hong Kong Section). On 16 July, an initial report was released on reasons of the delay. On 28 October, in a second report, two independent panelists outlined a set of recommendations on project schedule and cost estimates. On 30 January 2015, a full report was made public.

07 Jun 2014

Hong Kong Heritage Museum began an exhibition called The Extraordinary in the Ordinary: Chairs for Viewing the World through Time. It featured rare and ancient chairs designed for emperors, nobles and commoners from the collections of the Palace Museum, British Museum, and Metropolitan Museum of Art in New York.

09 Jun 2014

An exhibition of 1,600 pandas—made from recycled materials by French artist Paulo Grangeon—began in Hong Kong as part of a world tour and fundraiser in support of the World Wildlife Fund.

10 Jun 2014

The State Council Information Office issued *The Practice of the One Country, Two Systems Policy in the HKSAR*—a white paper on Hong Kong's return to China, its structure of governance as a Special Administrative Region, and accomplishments under the support of the Chinese Central Government. It emphasised the significant relationship between "One Country" and "Two Systems" and the authority of the Chinese Constitution and the Hong Kong Basic Law.

17 Jun 2014

The Leisure and Cultural Services Department announced Hong Kong's first Intangible Cultural Heritage Inventory. It comprised 480 items—based on a territory-wide survey (2009–2013) by Hong Kong University of Science and Technology's South China Research Center.

19 Jun 2014

The Hollywood film *Transformers: Age of Extinction*—partially filmed in Hong Kong—made its world premiere at Hong Kong Cultural Centre.

21 Jun 2014

PMQ—a revitalisation of the former Police Married Quarters (a Grade 3 historic building) on Hollywood Road and part of the government's Conserving Central initiative—was officially opened as a multi-purpose arts and designs exhibition venue.

11 Jul 2014

The first round of negotiation on a Free Trade Agreement with the Association of Southeast Asian Nations was held in Hong Kong.

15 Jul 2014

Chief Executive Leung Chun-ying (梁振英) submitted to the National People's Congress Standing Committee a report on whether there would be a need to amend the methods for selecting the Chief Executive of the HKSAR in 2017 and for forming the Legislative Council of the HKSAR in 2016.

19 Jul 2014

The Alliance for Peace and Democracy began a signature drive in opposition to the Occupy Central movement, receiving 1,504,839 signatures (online and offline) by 17 August. It held an anti-Occupy Central demonstration on 17 August with an estimated 193,000 people (111,800 people according to police estimates). (Figure 358)

28 Jul 2014

The World Rope Skipping Championships was held in Hong Kong where 159 local contestants won 29 gold, 30 silver and 33 bronze medals and broke three world records in the competition held for the first time in Asia.

Jul 2014

Chairman of the Central Military Commission Xi Jinping (習近平) signed an order appointing Tan Benhong (譚本宏) as Commander of the People's Liberation Army Hong Kong Garrison who remained in the post until April 2019.

05 Aug 2014

The HKSAR government launched Wi-Fi.HK to provide the public, including tourists, with wider free Internet access at available wi-fi hotspots without registration.

29 Aug 2014

The old Wan Chai Pier with a history spanning 46 years was decommissioned as part of the Central and Wan Chai Reclamation. The new Wan Chai Ferry Pier was opened the next day.

31 Aug 2014

The National People's Congress Standing Committee in response to the Chief Executive report submitted on 15 July issued its Decision on Issues Relating to the Selection of the Chief Executive of the HKSAR by Universal Suffrage and on the Method for Forming the Legislative Council of the HKSAR in the Year 2016 (8.31 Decision), stipulating that 1) Chief Executive elections might be implemented by universal suffrage starting 2017; 2) a broadly representative nominating committee in accordance with the provisions exercised in the fourth Chief Executive election should nominate 2-3 candidates (each candidate must be endorsed by a simple majority of committee members; 3) elections by universal suffrage should be prescribed through amending Annex I to the Hong Kong Basic Law; 4) existing election protocols would continue to apply if universal suffrage were not adopted; and 5) formation of the Legislative Council and its voting procedures would remain unchanged in 2016, followed by its adoption of universal suffrage upon such implementation in the Chief Executive elections.

01 Sep 2014

Deputy Secretary-General of the National People's Congress (NPC) Standing Committee Li Fei (李飛), Vice Chair of the NPC Standing Committee Legislative Affairs Commission Zhang Rongshun (張榮順) and Deputy Director of the Hong Kong and Macao Affairs Office of the State Council Feng Wei (馮巍) attended a briefing session in Hong Kong—jointly organised by the HKSAR government and Liaison Office of the Central People's Government in the HKSAR—on constitutional development regarding the 8.31 Decision. Members of the Legislative Council, chairmen and vice-chairmen of District Councils, Hong Kong deputies to the NPC, Hong Kong members of the Chinese People's Political Consultative Conference and community members were invited to attend.

The Online Voter Information Enquiry System was launched for individuals to access their own voter registration information.

11 Sep 2014

The HKSAR government launched the world's first US dollar-denominated Islamic bonds (sukuk) with an issuance size of US$1 billion and "AAA" S&P credit ratings.

Figure 358
The Alliance for Peace and Democracy launched a signature drive in Central. (Photo taken on 19 July 2014 and courtesy of South China Morning Post Publishers Limited)

Figure 359
Demonstrators occupied Harcourt Road in Admiralty during the Occupy Central movement. (Photo taken on 26 October 2014 and courtesy of South China Morning Post Publishers Limited)

17 Sep 2014

The HKSAR government announced its *Railway Development Strategy 2014*, recommending seven new rail projects (Northern Link and Kwu Tung Station, Tuen Mun South Extension, East Kowloon Line, Tung Chung West Extension, Hung Shui Kiu Station, South Island Line (West) and North Island Line be implemented by 2026 for a total investment of HK$110 billion.

19 Sep 2014

Team Hong Kong, China participated in the 17th Asian Games in Incheon, South Korea, winning six gold, 12 silver and 24 bronze medals, including first-time medals in gymnastics.

25 Sep 2014

Hong Kong Science and Technology Parks Phase III was inaugurated with the opening of three buildings, marking Asia's largest sustainable projects with an emphasis on energy efficiency.

28 Sep 2014

Benny Tai Yiu-ting（戴耀廷）, Chan Kin-man（陳健民）and Chu Yiu-ming（朱耀明）announced the beginning of the illegal Occupy Central sit-in campaign. Police officers began closing off the Central Government Offices in the morning; protesters occupied several major traffic sections, including Harcourt Road, in the afternoon. The police attempted to disperse crowds of protesters with tear gas and pepper spray in the evening; protesters had spread to Causeway Bay and Mong Kok by nightfall. (Figure 359)

28 Sep 2014

A spokesman of the Hong Kong and Macao Affairs Office of the State Council in a statement condemned the Occupy Central movement, denouncing any illegal acts poised to undermine the rule of law and stability in Hong Kong. The spokesman reiterated the legitimacy of the National People's Congress Standing Committee's decision on 31 August.

Sep 2014

Wong Pik-wan (黃碧雲) was presented a grand prize in a ceremony of the fifth Dream of the Red Chamber Award for her novel *Children of Darkness*; she was the first Hong Kong writer to win the award.

02 Oct 2014

Chief Executive Leung Chun-ying (梁振英) appointed Chief Secretary for Administration Carrie Lam Cheng Yuet-ngor (林鄭月娥) as a government representative in a dialogue on political reform with the Hong Kong Federation of Students.

06 Oct 2014

The Harbour Area Treatment Scheme Stage 2A—a project designed to improve the quality of seawater in Victoria Harbour by building a deep sewage tunnel and expanding the Stonecutters Island Sewage Treatment Works and eight preliminary treatment works on Hong Kong Island—was marked in a breakthrough ceremony. Construction began in 2009 at a cost of HK$17.1 billion.

09 Oct 2014

The Hong Kong–Chile Free Trade Agreement signed in 2012 came into effect, gradually removing tariffs on 98% of products and services originating from Hong Kong.

21 Oct 2014

Chief Secretary for Administration Carrie Lam Cheng Yuet-ngor (林鄭月娥), Secretary for Justice Rimsky Yuen Kwok-keung (袁國強), Secretary for Constitutional and Mainland Affairs Raymond Tam Chi-yuen (譚志源), Director of the Chief Executive's Office Edward Yau Tang-wah (邱騰華) and Under Secretary for Constitutional and Mainland Affairs Lau Kong-wah (劉江華) held a two-hour televised dialogue on political reform with the Hong Kong Federation of Students.

24 Oct 2014

The Antiquities Authority announced three historic buildings, namely Lin Fa Temple in Tai Hang, Hung Shing Temple on Ap Lei Chau and Hau Wong Temple in Kowloon City, as declared monuments in accordance with the Antiquities and Monuments Ordinance.

29 Oct 2014

James Tien Pei-chun (田北俊) was removed from duty as a member of the Chinese People's Political Consultative Conference (CPPCC) following a vote by its Standing Committee. He was the first Hong Kong CPPCC member to be expelled.

The Legislative Council passed a government resolution to establish an Innovation and Technology Bureau. The resolution, however, lapsed due to a delay in the vote for funding by the Finance Committee. On 03 June 2015, another resolution was passed in the Legislative Council; on 06 November, appropriation was approved by the Finance Committee.

03 Nov 2014

The Hong Kong Monetary Authority announced that seven banks were designated as Primary Liquidity Providers in the offshore renminbi market of Hong Kong (CNH market) for market-making activities with various CNH instruments.

Figure 360
Chief Executive Leung Chun-ying (梁振英), sixth from right, and Chairman of Hong Kong Exchanges and Clearing Limited Chow Chung-kong (周松崗), sixth from left, officiated at the opening ceremony of Shanghai-Hong Kong Stock Connect. (Photo courtesy of HKSAR Government)

10 Nov 2014

Tung Chee-hwa (董建華), Vice Chairman of the Chinese People's Political Consultative Conference and HKSAR's first Chief Executive, founded Our Hong Kong Foundation—a think tank committed to a stable, sustainable and prosperous Hong Kong by leveraging Hong Kong's competitiveness under "One Country, Two Systems" and seizing opportunities presented by the Mainland through multiple platforms under the support of more than 100 prominent community leaders as advisors. The Public Policy Institute, one of its key platforms, was established to provide research, analysis and advocacy on short-, medium- and long-term government policies.

11 Nov 2014

Hong Kong's traditional and cultural customs—including the arts of *Guqin* (the craft of Qin making), Quanzhen Temples Taoist Ritual Music, Hakka Unicorn Dance at Hang Hau in Sai Kung and Wong Tai Sin belief and customs— made the fourth National List of Intangible Cultural Heritage of the State Council.

The HKSAR government released an updated Nature Conservation Policy for sustainable development with respect to biodiversity.

17 Nov 2014

The Shanghai–Hong Kong Stock Connect—a mutual market access programme between Hong Kong Stock Exchange and Shanghai Stock Exchange allowing investment with eligible Shanghai-listed shares in Hong Kong and eligible Hong Kong-listed shares in Shanghai—was launched. (Figure 360)

The daily currency exchange limit of RMB 20,000 in Hong Kong was lifted.

19 Nov 2014

Hong Kong Television Network Limited commenced live Internet broadcast at 8 p.m.

The China Maritime Arbitration Commission inaugurated its first offshore arbitration centre in Hong Kong.

26 Nov 2014

In the morning, bailiffs under police escort began clearing obstacles on Argyle Street in Mong Kok in accordance with a High Court injunction issued on 20 October following a lawsuit filed by Chiu Luen Public Light Bus Company Limited. In the evening, demonstrators gathered and started a riot on Portland Street and Shantung Street in Mong Kok where 22 police officers were injured and 93 people were arrested.

01 Dec 2014

The High Court issued an interim injunction to prohibit demonstrators from blocking road sections in Admiralty, citing public interest and economic losses as outlined in a litigation filed by Kwoon Chung Motors Company Limited.

The HKSAR government released findings of the *Study on the Strategic Development Plan for Hong Kong Port 2030* and *Preliminary Feasibility Study for Container Terminal 10 at Southwest Tsing Yi*. It recommended an upgrade with the Stonecutters Island Public Cargo Working Area and Tuen Mun River Trade Terminal to accommodate ocean-going and river vessels simultaneously instead of planning for Container Terminal 10 before 2030.

04 Dec 2014

The Antiquities Advisory Board approved a plan to manually remove and restore an ancient well at the lowest possible cost of HK$10 million. The well, dating back to the Song Dynasty and Yuan Dynasty, was unearthed at Sacred Hill in Kowloon. This way, the construction of To Kwa Wan Station along the Sha Tin-to-Central Link could continue uninterrupted.

11 Dec 2014

Traffic resumed on Harcourt Road as bailiffs under police escort finished clearing the occupied areas of the Occupy Central movement in Admiralty. By 15 December, tram and bus service resumed on Yee Wo Street as occupied areas in Causeway Bay were cleared. The 79-day illegal Occupy Central movement came to an end.

13 Dec 2014

The HKSAR government held its first service at Hong Kong Museum of Coastal Defence in memory of the victims of the Nanjing Massacre and others who died during the Japanese invasion. (Figure 361)

16 Dec 2014

The HKSAR government released a new *Long Term Housing Strategy*—a strategic paper outlining a direction for a supply of 480,000 (60% public and 40% private) housing units from 2015 to 2025.

18 Dec 2014

The Agreement between the Mainland and Hong Kong on Achieving Basic Liberalisation of Trade in Services in Guangdong (under the framework of CEPA) was signed, effective 01 March 2015, providing Hong Kong with special access to 153 trade-in-services sub-sectors (about 95.6% of all trade-in-services sub-sectors) in Guangdong.

The HKSAR government established a Housing Reserve (by earmarking HK$27 billion from returns on government investment with fiscal reserves) designed to meet a 10-year public housing supply target.

Figure 361
The HKSAR government held its first service in memory of the victims who died during the Nanjing Massacre. (Photo courtesy of HKSAR Government)

19 Dec 2014

Former Chief Secretary for Administration Rafael Hui Si-yan (許仕仁) was convicted on five counts of misconduct in public office under the Prevention of Bribery Ordinance. He was sentenced to seven and a half years' imprisonment and ordered to return HK$11.182 million in bribes. Businessmen Thomas Kwok Ping-kwong (郭炳江) and Francis Kwan Hung-sang (關雄生) were sentenced to five years in prison; Chan Kui-yuen (陳鉅源) was sentenced to six years in prison and fined HK$500,000; Raymond Kwok Ping-luen (郭炳聯) was acquitted.

24 Dec 2014

Three boxes with HK$52 million in cash fell out of an armoured truck carrying HK$270 million on Gloucester Road in Wan Chai; passers-by scavenged HK$15.23 million worth of banknotes; some portions were returned but $7.3 million went missing.

28 Dec 2014

The MTR's Island Line extension—between Sheung Wan and Kennedy Town through Sai Ying Pun Station and HKU Station—became operational; Sai Ying Pun station was opened on 29 March 2015, making a complete Island Line.

30 Dec 2014

The Housing Authority launched a new phase of Home Ownership Scheme (HOS), putting on sale a total of 2,160 housing units from five residential estates in the first batch of new flats since HOS resumed in 2007. By the closing date on 12 January 2015, 41,000 applications were made, marking a record number of applicants since the resumption of sales of HOS flats.

04 Jan 2015

The Chinese Central Government in conjunction with the HKSAR government signed a Host Country Agreement and a Memorandum of Administrative Arrangements on the Conduct of Dispute Settlement Proceedings in Hong Kong with the Permanent Court of Arbitration (headquartered in The Hague, Netherlands) at a ceremony in Beijing.

09 Jan 2015

The Legislative Council Finance Committee approved funding of HK$19.2 billion for an incinerator project at Shek Kwu Chau.

14 Jan 2015

The HKSAR government released its 2015 Policy Address titled *Uphold the Rule of Law, Seize the Opportunities, Make the Right Choices, Pursue Democracy*. It condemned irrational concepts, including that of a Hong Kong nation promoted in *Undergrad* (a publication of HKU Students' Union) and by student leaders of the illegal Occupy Central movement.

18 Jan 2015

The Hong Kong Army Cadets Association was inaugurated as a uniformed group in a ceremony at the Stonecutters Island barracks. Chief Executive Leung Chun-ying (梁振英) and Director of the Liaison Office of the Central People's Government in the HKSAR Zhang Xiaoming (張曉明) served as honorary patrons; Regina Leung Tong Ching-yee (梁唐青儀), wife of Chief Executive Leung Chun-ying, served as Commander-in-Chief.

22 Jan 2015

HKSAR and Fujian officials signed an agreement on Strengthening Economic and Trade Co-operation and another agreement on Strengthening Financial Co-operation between Hong Kong and Fujian Province during the first Hong Kong-Fujian Co-operation Conference in Fuzhou.

08 Feb 2015

Lawmakers held a press conference on the sudden close-down of MyCoin, a Hong Kong-based bitcoin trading platform, in late 2014, involving some 3,000 investors and HK$3 billion.

13 Feb 2015

An agreement on surrender of fugitive offenders between Hong Kong and the Czech Republic came into effect. The HKSAR government had such agreement with 15 countries as of 01 July 2017.

14 Feb 2015

The HKU Students' Union Election Committee announced the ratification of the resolution for HKU Students' Union to withdraw from the Hong Kong Federation of Students (HKFS), marking the first such departure from HKFS. From April to May, student unions of Hong Kong Polytechnic University, Hong Kong Baptist University and City University of Hong Kong followed suit.

17 Feb 2015

The Administration Wing of the Chief Secretary for Administration's Office issued a government circular on the proper use of terminology, noting "Mainland–Hong Kong relations" instead of "China–Hong Kong relations."

27 Feb 2015

The Employment (Amendment) Ordinance 2014 was promulgated, effective immediately, providing eligible male employees with three days of paternity leave.

The Hong Kong Monetary Authority issued further measures on property mortgage, including a lowered maximum loan-to-value ratio from 70% to 60% for self-use residential properties with a value below HK$7 million.

Feb 2015

Localist organisations launched a series of "Recover" campaigns in Tuen Mun, Yuen Long and Sheung Shui, harassing Mainland customers and tourists. On the grounds of disturbance caused by parallel traders, they demanded cancellation of the one-year, multiple-entry Individual Visit Scheme. The campaigns lasted more than a month.

04 Mar 2015

The Hongkong and Shanghai Banking Corporation launched the issuance of two million HK$150 commemorative banknotes in celebration of its 150th anniversary in Hong Kong. On 08 September 2016, it announced a donation of HK$477 million in net proceeds from the campaign for charitable causes.

05 Mar 2015

The Drainage Services Department sludge vessel *Clean Harbour 1* made its maiden voyage delivering sludge from Stonecutters Island Sewage Treatment Works to another facility in Tuen Mun, minimising the impact arising from land transport.

17 Mar 2015

The Legislative Council received a government proposal on a desalination plant in Tseung Kwan O—with an initial daily capacity of 135,000 cubic metres at a cost of HK$154.6 million—for a sustained supply of fresh water in the age of climate change. The Tseung Kwan O Desalination Plant Phase I was approved by the Legislative Council's Finance Committee on 13 October 2017 and was granted funding on 01 November 2019.

23 Mar 2015

The Hong Kong Police fully implemented an Automatic Number Plate Recognition System capable of automatically scanning licence plates with a data link to the Transport Department, enabling police officers to pull over vehicles suspected of serious traffic contravention for further investigation.

29 Mar 2015

The HKSAR government expanded its Public Transport Fare Concession Scheme for the Elderly and Eligible Persons with Disabilities to cover green minibuses.

01 Apr 2015

The HKSAR government implemented a Plastic Shopping Bag Charging Scheme under which retailers must charge customers at least 50 cents for every plastic shopping bag, except those used for food hygiene reasons.

Figure 362
Members of the Task Force on Constitutional Development Task Force, including Carrie Lam Cheng Yuet-ngor (林鄭月娥), centre, Rimsky Yuen Kwok-keung (袁國強), right, and Raymond Tam Chi-yuen (譚志源), left, in a publicity campaign on universal suffrage in the 2017 Chief Executive election. (Photo courtesy of HKSAR Government)

01 Apr 2015

The Chief Executive-in-Council decided not to renew Asia Television's free-television licence due to expire on 01 April 2016 in the first case of TV licence non-renewal.

13 Apr 2015

The Chinese Central Government announced with immediate effect a new one-trip-per-week arrangement in place of the current multiple-entry Individual Visit Endorsements for Shenzhen residents travelling to Hong Kong.

17 Apr 2015

The Education Bureau announced revisions of the New Academic Structure Medium-Term Review, abolishing school-based assessments for seven elective subjects, namely Chinese History, History, Economics, Ethics and Religious Studies, Geography, Music, and Tourism & Hospitality Studies, starting with Secondary 4 students in September 2015.

21 Apr 2015

Hong Kong snooker player Ng On-yee (吳安儀) won the 2015 World Ladies Championship; she was the first Asian player to win the competition.

22 Apr 2015

The HKSAR government published its *Consultation Report and Proposals on the Method for Selecting the Chief Executive by Universal Suffrage* following the 8.31 Decision in 2014, proposing a maximum pool of 10 candidates (each endorsed by at least 120 members of the Election Committee) followed by a selection for 2–3 final candidates through a secret ballot by the 1,200-member Election Committee prior to a general election with five million eligible voters under the framework of "one person, one vote" and "first-past-the-post."

The Task Force on External Lighting in a report on light nuisance and energy waste introduced a voluntary charter scheme for businesses to switch off lighting installations of decorative, promotional or advertising purposes between 11 p.m. to 7 a.m. before a further review in two years' time regarding the need for legislation.

25 Apr 2015

The HKSAR government began a publicity campaign on constitutional reform. Chief Secretary for Administration Carrie Lam Cheng Yuet-ngor (林鄭月娥), Secretary for Justice Rimsky Yuen Kwok-keung (袁國強) and Secretary for Constitutional and Mainland Affairs Raymond Tam Chi-yuen (譚志源) met with the public in a bus tour through various districts, including Kennedy Town, Lok Fu and Tai Po. (Figure 362)

Queenie Law (羅君兒), granddaughter of Bossini (an apparel franchise) founder Law Ting-pong (羅定邦), was kidnapped from her house in Sai Kung following a burglary (in which HK$2 million worth of property were stolen). She was released upon a ransom of HK$28 million. The Hong Kong police along with Mainland authorities later arrested 10 suspects and recovered all ransom money. In June 2016, Zheng Xingwang (鄭興旺), arrested in Hong Kong, was sentenced to 12 years in prison by the High Court.

27 Apr 2015

The Liaoning Liaison Unit of the HKSAR government was inaugurated in Shenyang, Liaoning Province to promote government-to-government exchange and cooperation.

04 May 2015

The Immigration Department launched a pilot Admission Scheme for the Second Generation of Chinese Hong Kong Permanent Residents—an initiative designed to attract and retain talent, professionals and entrepreneurs for greater economic development without a quota limitation or requirements on prior job offers before entry.

18 May 2015

The Court of Final Appeal ruled with respect to the HK$83 billion estate of Nina Wang Kung Yu-Sum (龔如心) that Chinachem Charitable Foundation Limited should hold the entire estate as a trust for a plan to establish a Chinese prize of worldwide significance similar to that of the Nobel Prize in accordance with her will made on 28 July 2002.

26 May 2015

Tai Po Cambridge Nursing Home was exposed in a newspaper article for allegedly abusing elderly residents. On 16 June, its licence was renewed under a reduced capacity by the Social Welfare Department—which was heavily criticised for inadequate supervision and enforcement in an investigation report (released by the Office of the Ombudsman on 13 December 2018) titled *Social Welfare Department's Monitoring of Services of Residential Care Homes for the Elderly*.

31 May 2015

Officials of the Chinese Central Government met in Shenzhen with 54 members of the Legislative Council on the issue of constitutional reform. Li Fei (李飛), Chairman of the HKSAR Basic Law Committee under the National People's Congress Standing Committee, pointed out that the 8.31 Decision was made in accordance with the Basic Law and must be fully implemented, adding that implementation proposed by the HKSAR government was in compliance with the Basic Law and the 8.31 Decision in a democratic, open, fair and just manner most suitable for Hong Kong.

01 Jun 2015

The HKSAR government announced with immediate effect an extended retirement age to 65 and 60 among new recruits in civilian and disciplined services grades. Employment among serving civil servants may be extended through flexible measures.

Lau Ip-keung (劉業強) was elected as Chairman of Heung Yee Kuk for a four-year term in the first succession since his father, Lau Wong-fat (劉皇發), became Chairman in 1980.

05 Jun 2015

The Hong Kong Ladies Open began in a three-day tournament with 108 players at the Hong Kong Golf Club in Fanling; it marked the first world-class ladies' professional golf tournament in Hong Kong.

08 Jun 2015

Civic Party Co-founder and Legislative Councillor Ronny Tong Ka-wah (湯家驊) established a think tank called Path of Democracy in a bid to provide a new political horizon through a moderate approach. He resigned as a legislator and from the Civic Party on 22 June.

18 Jun 2015

The motion on government proposals regarding universal suffrage in the elections of the Chief Executive was vetoed (short of a two-thirds majority) in the Legislative Council.

19 Jun 2015

The Chief Executive-in-Council approved the Kwu Tung North Outline Zoning Plan and the Fanling North Outline Zoning Plan in association with the North East New Territories New Development Areas.

19 Jun 2015

The Hong Kong Stock Exchange published conclusions to its concept paper on weighted voting rights, noting support for a second stage consultation on proposed changes to the Listing Rules under a relaxed "one share, one vote" framework. On 25 June, a statement of objection on the grounds of public interest was issued by the Securities and Futures Commission (SFC). On 05 October, Hong Kong Stock Exchange published its decision to shelve its draft proposal on weighted voting rights in view of SFC's objection.

20 Jun 2015

The cruise ship *Quantum of the Seas* arrived at Kai Tak Cruise Terminal, marking the largest cruise ship to visit Hong Kong.

24 Jun 2015

The United Nations Conference on Trade and Development released its World Investment Report 2015 in which Hong Kong ranked second place in global foreign direct investment with an inflow of US$103 billion in 2014, second only to the Mainland.

27 Jun 2015

The Leisure and Cultural Service Department opened the first museum festival in Hong Kong called Transcend—Muse Fest HK 2015. It offered more than 70 cultural programmes supported by 22 exhibitors, including 14 public museums, over a period of 16 days.

05 Jul 2015

The Democratic Party of Hong Kong found excessive levels of lead (above World Health Organization standards) in tap water among some flats at Kai Ching Estate (under the Housing Authority) following the collection of samples in 13 public and private residential buildings in Kowloon West. On 18 July, government lab tests also revealed levels of lead content in tap water at Kai Ching Estate; blood tests among residents were normal.

17 Jul 2015

Chief Executive Leung Chun-ying（梁振英）appointed a Commission of Inquiry to ascertain the causes of excess lead found in drinking water in a review of the regulatory and monitoring system on water supply in Hong Kong. On 31 May 2016, a commission report was released, citing lead-based solders in water pipes as a major cause of excessive lead content; it also recommended thorough testing in all public housing estates and an independent agency to oversee the Water Supplies Department.

20 Jul 2015

Queen Mary Hospital successfully performed the world's first double liver transplant surgery with a liver combined from two donors.

24 Jul 2015

The HKSAR government established an Aviation Development and Three-runway System Advisory Committee on policy matters concerning civil aviation and the Hong Kong International Airport, including a three-runway system. The first committee meeting was held on 08 September.

28 Jul 2015

Ocean Park Hong Kong celebrated the Guinness World Records set by 37-year-old giant panda Jia Jia as the "Oldest panda ever in captivity" and "Oldest panda living in captivity."

29 Jul 2015

The United Nations Department of Economic and Social Affairs released its report *World Population Prospects: The 2015 Revision*, showing an average life expectancy of 83.74 years (80.91 years for men and 86.58 years for women were both highest in the world) for the first time in Hong Kong.

08 Aug 2015

The Hong Kong Observatory recorded a temperature of 36.3°C (with an average daily temperature of 24.2°C in 2015), marking two record highs as of 01 July 2017.

13 Aug 2015

The State Council declared a cenotaph at Wu Kau Tang Martyrs Memorial Garden in Tai Po as part of the second batch of State facilities and sites in remembrance of the War of Resistance against Japanese Aggression. (Figure 363)

03 Sep 2015

This day was designated as an additional, one-off statutory holiday under the General Holidays Ordinance and Employment Ordinance in commemoration of the 70th anniversary of the Victory of the Chinese People's War of Resistance against Japanese Aggression.

08 Sep 2015

Football fans booed during the national anthem and threw objects at the visiting team in a 2018 World Cup qualifier match between Hong Kong and Qatar. On 05 October, after a disciplinary investigation by FIFA, Hong Kong Football Association was fined 5,000 Swiss francs.

09 Sep 2015

Hong Kong Broadband Network Limited was fined HK$30,000 in the first conviction for failure to comply with a customer's request to refrain from using his personal data in direct marketing, an act in contravention of the Personal Data (Privacy) Ordinance 2012.

15 Sep 2015

Hong Kong Mortgage Corporation Limited announced its Premium Loan Insurance Scheme in collaboration with eight banks to help owners (aged 50 or above) of subsidised housing in land premium payment and facilitate a higher turnover of subsidised housing.

Figure 363
The cenotaph at the Wu Kau Tang Martyrs Memorial Garden in Tai Po—a national monument declared by the State Council in remembrance of the War of Resistance against Japanese Aggression. (Photo taken on 31 October 2013 and courtesy of Liu Shuyong)

20 Sep 2015

China Media Capital and Warner Bros. Entertainment entered into an agreement on a joint venture to form Flagship Entertainment Group Limited for global distribution of Chinese- and English-language films with a headquarters in Hong Kong.

22 Sep 2015

The Urban Renewal Authority announced a simplified design, including 1,000 square metres of open space in the atrium and entrance on Queen's Road Central, in the Central Market redevelopment project at a cost of HK$600 million.

25 Sep 2015

The Court of Final Appeal was opened in a ceremony upon relocation to the former Legislative Council Building on Jackson Road in Central.

10 Oct 2015

The Hong Kong Tourism Board launched its inaugural Cyclothon for two days of cycling fun and competition in a carnival.

11 Oct 2015

The Hong Kong Arts Development Council inaugurated its first Literary Festival with a series of lectures, workshops, film screenings and exhibitions. It was concluded in March 2016.

23 Oct 2015

The Kap Shui Mun Bridge was hit by a vessel in the evening and the bridge's seismic protection alarm went off. Consequently, the Kap Shui Mun Bridge and the Tsing Ma Bridge were closed for nearly two hours for inspection by engineering staff. The accident brought land traffic to a standstill on Lantau Island for the first time in the two bridges' 18-year history.

05 Nov 2015

Ocean Park Hong Kong held a ground-breaking ceremony to mark its waterpark project in Tai Shue Wan with 27 indoor and outdoor facilities in an area of approximately 6.63 hectares.

13 Nov 2015

The Payment Systems and Stored Value Facilities Ordinance was promulgated, establishing a regulatory regime and a licensing mechanism under the Hong Kong Monetary Authority for greater consumer protection with device-based and non-device based electronic payment systems.

17 Nov 2015

Football fans booed again during the national anthem in a 2018 World Cup qualifier match with the Chinese national team. On 14 January 2016, Hong Kong Football Association was fined 10,000 Swiss francs by FIFA.

19 Nov 2015

The Hong Kong International Arbitration Centre established a representative office in the Shanghai Free Trade Zone as the first branch of an international arbitration centre in the Mainland.

20 Nov 2015

The Innovation and Technology Bureau was formally established as a dedicated government body responsible for policymaking, promotion of public-private partnerships and coordination (government, industry, academia and R&D) with respect to innovation and technology.

Wu Siu-hong（胡兆康）won the gold medal (men's) at the 51st Bowling World Cup in Las Vegas, US; he was the first Hong Kong bowler to win the championship.

22 Nov 2015

In the fifth District Council elections, 431 councillor were elected (including 68 candidates who won uncontested). The voter turnout rate was 47.01%. In addition, 27 ex-officio members were chairmen of Rural Committees.

23 Nov 2015

The 30th annual meeting of the International Organization for Standardization Technical Committee began for an eight-day conference with 200 representatives from more than 40 countries and regions; it was the first time Hong Kong hosted the annual meeting.

27 Nov 2015

The Agreement on Trade in Services under the Mainland and Hong Kong Closer Economic Partnership Arrangement was signed, effective 01 June 2016, expanding liberalisation measures nationwide beyond Guangdong Province with 28 additional measures in cross-border services as well as telecommunications and cultural services.

30 Nov 2015

The HKSAR government and MTR Corporation reached an agreement on a revised schedule and budget of the Guangzhou–Shenzhen–Hong Kong Express Rail Link (Hong Kong Section). The anticipated date of completion was moved from Q4 2017 to Q3 2018 under an increased government funding from HK$65 billion to HK$84.42 billion (HK$880 million less than what was proposed in June 2015); any exceeding costs were to be borne by the MTR Corporation.

04 Dec 2015

The District Court found Full Wealthy Development Limited, a property developer, and 11 indigenous villagers of Sha Tin guilty on 22 counts of conspiracy to defraud the government by purchasing and selling, respectively, the rights to build small houses; they were sentenced to two and a half to three years in prison in the first case of this nature.

05 Dec 2015

The Hong Kong Academy of Sciences—a centre of scientific and technological excellence founded by 27 fellows under the presidency of Tsui Lap-chee (徐立之)—held its inaugural ceremony at the Government House.

06 Dec 2015

The 10th Anniversary of the Establishment of Partner State Key Laboratories in Hong Kong with a Plaque Awarding Ceremony for Hong Kong Branches of the Chinese National Engineering Research Centres was held in Hong Kong. As of 01 July 2017, there were 16 state key laboratories in Hong Kong.

07 Dec 2015

The Provisional Insurance Authority was established; it was renamed the Insurance Authority on 26 June 2017 and began its regulatory role in place of the Office of the Commissioner of Insurance while maintaining a close working relationship with regulators in the Mainland.

09 Dec 2015

The Mainland–Hong Kong Joint Mediation Center—a joint institution between the China Council for the Promotion of International Trade and the Hong Kong Mediation Centre—was established as a platform for resolving cross-boundary commercial disputes.

27 Dec 2015

The first batch of five single-deck electric buses commenced services as part of a two-year pilot programme fully subsidised by the government at a cost of HK$180 million for 36 single-deck electric buses and related charging facilities in a bid to improve roadside air quality.

28 Dec 2015

| The Hong Kong International Airport began a trial run of its HK$10-billion Midfield Concourse and auxiliary facilities upon completion; it became fully operational on 31 March 2016, providing 20 aircraft parking stands, including two dedicated to the Airbus A380.

Dec 2015

| The Hong Kong Archaeological Society began a two-month excavation at the Tung Lung Chau site where architectural remains, including porcelain fragments, tiles and bricks, dating to the Song Dynasty were uncovered.

01 Jan 2016

| The Hong Kong Jockey Club New Year Race at the Sha Tin Racecourse had a turnover of HK$1.549 billion and attendance with over 77,000 people, marking the highest numbers on a New Year's Day in 20 years.

| The HKSAR government formally launched a Future Fund—with an initial endowment of $219.7 billion notionally held against the Land Fund coupled with periodic top-ups—for higher investment returns as fiscal reserves to support government expenditure in case of a structural deficit.

04 Jan 2016

| The HKSAR government began implementation of the third stage in reducing the Frontier Closed Area, covering more than 900 hectares of land between Ng Tung River and Lin Ma Hang. Restrictions on closed roads within the excised area were lifted.

15 Jan 2016

| The UCI Track Cycling World Cup—hosted by the Cycling Association of Hong Kong, China Limited—began for three days of competition at Hong Kong Velodrome where more than 300 cyclists from 39 countries and regions took part. It marked Hong Kong's first time as host city and its 100th "M" Mark event.

16 Jan 2016

| Hong Kong witnessed the commencement of the Asian Infrastructure Investment Bank in Beijing as a participating member of the Chinese delegation at the opening ceremony and inaugural governors' meeting. On 13 June 2017, Hong Kong became an official member of the Bank.

24 Jan 2016

| Hong Kong Tramways Limited began services with its first-ever, open-top sightseeing tram, taking visitors on a TramOramic Tour through areas between Sheung Wan and Causeway Bay.

| The Hong Kong Observatory recorded a low urban temperature of 3.1°C, marking the coldest day since 1957 and the third coldest on record. Freezing rain and frost were observed at Tai Mo Shan where temperature reached -6°C.

25 Jan 2016

| The last two business owners of Nga Tsin Wai Tsuen, a walled village in Wong Tai Sin, Kowloon with a history spanning more than 600 years, agreed to leave the area on the day of a deadline under a removal order issued by the Urban Renewal Authority in December 2015, after they reached a compensation agreement in the previous evening, followed by a statement of departure issued by the Nga Tsin Wai Village Redevelopment Concern Group. It took nine years to acquire complete land ownership of the village in a conservation and redevelopment project.

01 Feb 2016

| The Mandatory Provident Fund (MPF) Schemes Authority began allowing withdrawal of MPF (retirement) benefits in a lump sum or by instalments upon the retirement age of 65 or early retirement at the age of 60.

Figure 364
Rioters jumped on the roof of a smashed taxi and threw objects at police officers during the Mong Kok riot in 2016. (Photo courtesy of Sing Tao News Corporation Limited)

08 Feb 2016

A riot broke out in the evening on Chinese New Year's Day as more than 200 by-standers overwhelmed staff of the Food and Environmental Hygiene Department dispatched to clear illegal cooked food vendors on Portland Street in Mong Kok. Rioters clashed with police officers and journalists and set fire in different locations until the following morning. More than 130 people, including five journalists and about 90 police officers were injured; 64 were arrested (25 of whom were later convicted). (Figure 364)

17 Feb 2016

American pop star Madonna began her first concert tour in Hong Kong.

19 Feb 2016

In response to the riot in Mong Kok, a police internal review committee under the chairmanship of the Deputy Commissioner of Police (Management) held its first meeting and established three sub-committees on assessment regarding "operations", "arms, equipment and training" and "support."

01 Mar 2016

The Hong Kong Jockey Club held a special extended edition of the Mark Six Draw in celebration of the 40th anniversary of the Mark Six lottery. It marked a record HK$100 million in first prize, HK$240 million in division prizes and HK$446 million in total betting turnover.

11 Mar 2016

The Legislative Council's Finance Committee approved an additional budget of HK$19.6 billion for a revised expenditure estimate of HK$86.4 billion in support of the Guangzhou–Shenzhen–Hong Kong Express Rail Link (Hong Kong Section). Opponents of the infrastructure project staged a protest at the Legislative Council Complex and were later cleared by the police.

13 Mar 2016

The Electronic Health Record Sharing System—introduced by the HKSAR government in July 2009 at a cost of HK$702 million—commenced services as a public-private platform of clinical information with patients' consent.

16 Mar 2016

The Fire and Ambulance Services Academy at Pak Shing Kok in Tseung Kwan O was formally opened as a personnel training facility in firefighting and rescue operations with advanced simulation.

18 Mar 2016

Hong Kong Science Museum opened an exhibition called Collider: Step inside the World's Greatest Experiment which was concluded on 25 May. It featured simulation of particle interaction through the world's largest and most powerful particle accelerator "Large Hadron Collider" while highlighting the research of scholars and scientists from Hong Kong at the European Organization for Nuclear Research.

24 Mar 2016

The Fixed Penalty (Public Cleanliness Offences) (Amendment) Ordinance 2016 was promulgated, effective 24 September, introducing a fixed penalty (a fine of HK$1,500) on top of summonses to be enforced by police officers and staff of the Food and Environmental Hygiene Department in tackling the problem of illegal shop front extensions and obstruction of public places. It was officially known as the Fixed Penalty (Public Cleanliness and Obstruction) Ordinance.

28 Mar 2016

The Hong Kong National Party—an advocate of separatism and local independence—was established. On 24 September 2018, it was officially declared an illegal organisation and banned from operation by the Secretary for Security on the grounds of national security and public safety.

30 Mar 2016

The Education Bureau established a Committee on Prevention of Student Suicides for a thorough examination of cases of the past three school years and preventive measures in the future. On 07 November, a final committee report was submitted, recommending early identification of mental health issues, strengthened education and support for parents and families, greater use of social media in supporting students, and the promotion of life-planning education.

01 Apr 2016

The Hong Kong Maritime and Port Board was established as a high-level policy platform pertaining to the development of Hong Kong's maritime industry and port facilities.

Asia Television Limited ceased transmission at midnight upon expiry of its domestic service licence, ending its 59 years of history of free television programmes. Radio Television Hong Kong was given an immediate transfer of ATV's two analogue channels and began to simulcast programmes of its digital TV channels.

06 Apr 2016

ViuTV, a subsidiary of HK Television Entertainment Company Limited, premiered with free television programmes.

13 Apr 2016

Hong Kong fencer Cheung Ka-long (張家朗) won a gold medal in the Men's Foil Individual at the 2016 Asian Fencing Championships in Wuxi, Jiangsu; he was the first gold medallist from Hong Kong in the category.

26 Apr 2016

The Chief Executive-in-Council approved a third airport runway as proposed in the draft Chek Lap Kok Outline Zoning Plan; construction began on 01 August.

A ground-breaking ceremony took place to mark the construction (Hong Kong section) of the cross-border bridge at the Liantang/Heung Yuen Wai Boundary Control Point—which was poised to become the seventh land-based control point between Hong Kong and Shenzhen.

06 May 2016

The Centre for Health Protection commissioned its Communicable Disease Information System for enhanced capability in surveillance and control of communicable diseases through a streamlined notification process designed to connect all control system components.

10 May 2016

The Hong Kong Jockey Club held a Super Mark Six draw with a record HK$169 million in first prize and two winning bets (about HK$84 million each as the third highest ever); it earned proceeds of about HK$21 million while government revenue in betting duty reached HK$87 million.

17 May 2016

National People's Congress Standing Committee Chairman Zhang Dejiang (張德江) arrived in Hong Kong for a three-day visit during which he attended a briefing by the HKSAR government at the Central Government Offices and made a tour at the Hong Kong Science Park to learn about Hong Kong's innovation and technology work.

18 May 2016

The HKSAR government hosted its first Belt and Road Summit with about 2,400 political leaders, policymakers, business executives and scholars from different countries geographically along the Belt and Road. In a keynote speech "Collaboration in Belt & Road for a Brighter Future by Riding on Hong Kong's Competitiveness," National People's Congress Standing Committee Chairman Zhang Dejiang (張德江) pointed out that Hong Kong could play a vital role with its strategic location, openness, professional services and gateway status.

19 May 2016

T. PARK—Hong Kong's first self-sustained sludge treatment facility located in Nim Wan, Tuen Mun—was opened as an integrated complex of sludge incinerators with a daily capacity of up to 2,000 tonnes of sludge, in addition to power generation, desalination, educational and ecological facilities.

23 May 2016

The Chinese Banking Association of Hong Kong, comprising six Chinese-owned banks in Hong Kong, was incorporated, followed by an inauguration ceremony on 27 June.

26 May 2016

Ken Tsang Kin-chiu (曾健超), who allegedly poured liquid on police officers and resisted arrest during the illegal Occupy Central movement in 2014, was found guilty on one count of assaulting police and two counts of resisting arrest; he was sentenced to five weeks in prison by the Kowloon City Magistrates' Courts.

27 May 2016

The Hong Kong Institute of Education was granted university status and was renamed The Education University of Hong Kong, making it the 10th university and eighth publicly funded university in Hong Kong.

06 Jun 2016

Hong Kong Tramways launched a Cooler Tram Pilot Programme with Tram No. 88 as the first tram equipped with an air-conditioning system.

12 Jun 2016

Amateur golfer Tiffany Chan Tsz-ching (陳芷澄) won the second EFG Hong Kong Ladies Open; she was the first Hong Kong golfer to take the championship and qualify for an Olympic golf tournament (2016).

13 Jun 2016

The Hong Kong Economic & Trade Office opened a temporary office in Jakarta; it became fully operational on 26 July 2017 for trade relations with Indonesia, Malaysia, Brunei and the Philippines.

18 Jun 2016

The Hong Kong Intangible Cultural Heritage Centre—as a part of Sam Tung Uk Museum in Tsuen Wan—was opened to enhance public awareness and understanding of intangible cultural heritage through a wide range of education and promotion activities.

19 Jun 2016

The Hong Kong Observatory issued a Very Hot weather warning—in force for 205 hours and 35 minutes until 27 June–marking the second longest very hot warning in a record year (2016) with 38 such very hot days as of 01 July 2017.

21 Jun 2016

A four-alarm fire broke out in a mini storage located at Amoycan Industrial Centre in Ngau Tau Kok; it lasted for 108 hours until 25 June, killing two firemen and injuring 10 people. On 28 June, amid public concerns about the lack of fire installations in old industrial buildings, a city-wide survey and inspection began under the Fire Services Department, Buildings Department, Lands Department, and Labour Department. On 01 July, Senior Station Officer Thomas Cheung Yiu-sing (張耀升) and Senior Fireman Samuel Hui Chi-kit (許志傑) who died in the line of duty were posthumously awarded the Medal for Bravery (Gold).

11 Jul 2016

Hong Kong played host to the 57th International Mathematical Olympiad in a five-day competition with a record 602 contestants from 109 countries or regions. Hong Kang achieved the best results so far, ranking ninth overall upon winning three gold, two silver and one bronze medals.

14 Jul 2016

The Electoral Affairs Commission brought forward a confirmation arrangement, requiring candidates in Legislative Council elections to pledge allegiance to the HKSAR and uphold the Basic Law, specifically Articles 1, 12 and 159.

20 Jul 2016

The Hong Kong Monetary Authority in conjunction with the Guangzhou branch of the People's Bank of China launched a joint e-Cheque clearing platform for next-day settlement of e-cheques issued by banks in Hong Kong and deposited with banks in Guangdong Province.

24 Jul 2016

Hong Kong contestants participated in the World Rope Skipping Championships 2016 in Sweden where they won 79 medals, defended the title of Group Demo Cup, and set a new record in Double Dutch Speed Relay. Chow Wing-lok (周永樂) became the first athlete from Hong Kong to win a gold medal in Men's Individual Freestyle.

26 Jul 2016

The HKSAR government made the first tranche of silver bonds—with a maturity of three years and coupon payment every six months—available for subscription by Hong Kong residents aged 65 or above. The subscription ended on 03 August with 76,009 applications and a principal amount of HK$8.9 billion for a final issuance size of HK$3 billion.

30 Jul 2016

Hong Kong National Party convenor Andy Chan Ho-tin (陳浩天) was disqualified as a candidate (New Territories West) in the Legislative Council elections upon a ruling by the Electoral Affairs Commission in the first of such case since the establishment of the HKSAR.

01 Aug 2016

The Commerce and Economic Development Bureau established a Belt and Road Office to advise the HKSAR Chief Executive on government coordination in support of the Belt and Road Initiative.

The Hong Kong International Airport began construction of its third runway with reclamation of 650 hectares of land north of the airport and introduction of an airport construction fee levied through air tickets from departing passengers.

02 Aug 2016

Edward Leung Tin-kei (梁天琦) was disqualified from his candidacy (New Territories East) in the Legislative Council elections upon failure to prove a genuine change of political stance in view of his association with the political group called Hong Kong Indigenous and known for localist and militant tendencies.

07 Aug 2016

The HKSAR government resumed ownership and operation of the Eastern Harbour Crossing upon expiry of a 30-year franchise at midnight.

25 Aug 2016

The Hong Kong Monetary Authority granted the first batch of Stored Value Facilities licences to five operators, namely Alipay Financial Services, HKT Payment (Tap & Go), Money Data (WeChat Pay HK), TNG Asia, and Octopus Cards.

28 Aug 2016

The first locally made and registered aircraft *Inspiration* took off from Hong Kong International Airport under the command of Captain Hank Cheng Chor-hang (鄭楚衡) for a 55,000-km flight journey around the world in 78 days, landing at 45 airports across 20 countries before returning to Hong Kong on 13 November. (Figure 365)

Aug 2016

The *Compendium of Hong Kong Literature 1919–1949*—a 12-volume compilation of prose, fiction, criticism, new poetry, drama, old-style literature, popular literature, children's literature and literary sources—was published.

04 Sep 2016

The sixth Legislative Council elections were held for 70 seats, including 35 geographical and 35 functional constituencies. The voter turnout rates were 58.28%, 57.09% and 74.3% in the geographical constituency, District Council (second) functional constituency and functional constituency, respectively.

21 Sep 2016

The Regional Verification Commission for Measles Elimination in the Western Pacific Region of the World Health Organization confirmed that the transmission of endemic measles virus had ceased in Hong Kong.

08 Oct 2016

The 2016 FIA Formula E HKT Hong Kong ePrix—as part of the world's first fully-electric vehicle racing series—began for a two-day competition with 10 professional teams and 20 racing cars at the Victoria Harbour waterfront in Central. It was the first such international motorsports event in Hong Kong and incurred a cost of HK$20 million on road preparation.

Figure 365
Hank Cheng Chor-hang (鄭楚衡), left, landed safely at Hong Kong International Airport after a 55,000-km flight journey around the world. (Photo taken on 14 November 2016 and courtesy of HKSAR Government)

12 Oct 2016

At the inaugural meeting of the sixth Legislative Council, Secretary-General Kenneth Chen Wei-on (陳維安) invalidated the oath of office taken by councillors-elect Edward Yiu Chung-yim (姚松炎), Sixtus Leung Chung-hang (梁頌恒) and Yau Wai-ching (游蕙禎) for alteration with political statements and slogans insulting Chinese sovereignty. Twelve other members also altered the oath of office with political remarks to varying degrees.

15 Oct 2016

Digital Broadcasting Corporation Hong Kong Limited's sound broadcasting licence was terminated following an approval by the Chief Executive-in-Council.

16 Oct 2016

Jia Jia–the world's oldest giant panda in captivity—passed away at Ocean Park Hong Kong; she was 38 years old (estimated to be about 114 years old in human age).

18 Oct 2016

In the morning, President of the Legislative Council Andrew Leung Kwan-yuen (梁君彥) issued a ruling invalidating the oaths taken on 12 October by councillors-elect Edward Yiu Chung-yim (姚松炎), Sixtus Leung Chung-hang (梁頌恒), Yau Wai-ching (游蕙禎), Lau Siu-lai (劉小麗) and Wong Ting-kwong (黃定光) and granted them permission for retaking the oath on following day. In the afternoon, Chief Executive Leung Chun-ying (梁振英) and Secretary for Justice Rimsky Yuen Kwok-keung (袁國強) mounted a legal challenge seeking to disqualify Sixtus Leung Chung-hang and Yau Wai-ching. At 9 p.m., the High Court in an emergency hearing granted permission for a judicial review; it denied an interim injunction to prohibit elected councillors from retaking an oath.

20 Oct 2016

King Tai Court in San Po Kong—a part of the Housing Authority's Green Form Subsidised Home Ownership Pilot Scheme—was open to applicants. It comprised 857 housing units at 40% discounts off market value; all units were sold by February 2017.

23 Oct 2016

The MTR Kwun Tong Line Extension went into operation upon the opening of Ho Man Tin Station and Whampoa Station.

03 Nov 2016

The Clearwater Bay Open began for a four-day golf tournament, marking the first PGA Tour Series-China event in Hong Kong.

04 Nov 2016

The Marine Parks (Designation) (Amendment) Order 2016 was promulgated, marking a designated marine park with 970 hectares of waters near The Brothers (islands) found to be an important habitat of Chinese white dolphins. As of 2017, Hong Kong had five designated marine parks and one marine reserve.

05 Nov 2016

The *ad valorem* stamp duty on residential property transactions increased to a flat rate of 15% (except first-time homebuyers with permanent resident status) in a bid to cool down the housing market.

07 Nov 2016

The National People's Congress Standing Committee made its fifth interpretation of the Basic Law with respect to public office as stipulated in Article 104, stating that 1) no public office should be assumed without taking a lawful oath; 2) an oath must be taken and read accurately, completely and solemnly with respect to its form and content, including the phrase "will uphold the Basic Law of the Hong Kong Special Administrative Region of the People's Republic of China, bear allegiance to the Hong Kong Special Administrative Region of the People's Republic of China" and 3) non-conforming oaths would be determined invalid without further arrangement for a re-take.

10 Nov 2016

The MTR Academy in Hung Hom was inaugurated as Hong Kong's first in-house training facility of railway operation and management.

12 Nov 2016

The Metro Broadcast Corporation ceased its broadcast of digital radio with approval from the Chief Executive-in-Council, marking the end of all private digital broadcast services.

13 Nov 2016

Jackie Chan (成龍) received an Academy Honorary Award from the Academy of Motion Picture Arts and Sciences; he was the first Chinese recipient of the lifetime achievement award.

14 Nov 2016

The Civil Aviation Department commissioned a new Air Traffic Management System capable of handling 8,000 flight plans daily and monitoring 1,500 air or ground targets (five times and 1.5 times the original system, respectively) in anticipation of future air traffic growth under a three-runway ystem.

15 Nov 2016

The Court of First Instance found the oaths taken by Sixtus Leung Chung-hang (梁頌恒) and Yau Wai-ching (游蕙禎) in the Legislative Council on 12 October inconsistent with the Oaths and Declarations Ordinance. Both councillors-elect were disqualified effective 12 October and were not allowed to re-take the oath before the president of the Legislative Council; their seats were left vacant.

The Tripartite Platform established by the HKSAR government, comprising doctors, advocates of patient and consumer rights and members of the Legislative Council, held its first meeting. It aimed to promote communication among the three parties with respect to the Medical Registration Ordinance and facilitate suggestions for amendments.

20 Nov 2016

The Hong Kong Maritime and Port Board launched its first Hong Kong Maritime Industry Week with a series of 30 conferences, forums and seminars in eight days, including the sixth Asian Logistics and Maritime Conference, Lloyd's List Maritime Briefing, and a seminar on maritime insurance law.

27 Nov 2016

Angus Ng Ka-long (伍家朗) took the men's singles title at Hong Kong Open Badminton Championships 2016. He was the first local winner of the tournament since it was launched 28 years ago.

30 Nov 2016

Hong Kong Heritage Museum began an exhibition called Ceremony and Celebration—The Grand Weddings of the Qing Emperors. It featured 153 rare items (jewellery, portraits, wedding accessories, court musical instruments and documents) related to the imperial weddings of Qing emperors in The Palace Museum collection.

01 Dec 2016

Hong Kong Eastern Football Club head coach Chan Yuen-ting (陳婉婷) was named Women's Coach of the Year by the Asian Football Confederation. She was the first award recipient from Hong Kong and the first female coach to lead a men's professional soccer team to championship in a top-flight competition.

02 Dec 2016

The HKSAR government, in view of a constitutional duty to uphold and enforce Article 104 of the Basic Law with respect to the legality of the oath of office for the Legislative Council and the harm to public interest caused by the oath-taking crisis, announced that it would petition the court to order the oaths taken by Lau Siu-lai (劉小麗), Edward Yiu Chung-yim (姚松炎), Nathan Law Kwun-chung (羅冠聰) and Leung Kwok-hung (梁國雄) as invalid and to declare their seats in the Council vacant.

05 Dec 2016

The Education Bureau issued a report titled *Promotion of STEM Education—Unleashing Potential in Innovation,* outlining a final set of recommendations in support of STEM (science, technology, engineering and mathematics) education in local primary and secondary schools.

The Shenzhen–Hong Kong Stock Connect (Shenzhen Connect) was launched, giving international and Hong Kong investors direct access to shares listed in Shenzhen and Mainland investors direct access to shares listed in Hong Kong.

08 Dec 2016

The foundation stone of the East Kowloon Cultural Centre was laid in a ceremony at the site of the former Lower Ngau Tau Kok Estate. This was another important cultural venue following the establishment of the West Kowloon Cultural District.

The State Theatre in North Point—a cinema of more than 60 years old with Asia's only parabolic concrete arch design on the rooftop built in the post-war era—was declared a Grade 1 Historic Building by the Antiquities Advisory Board.

09 Dec 2016

Chief Executive Leung Chun-ying（梁振英）announced his decision not to run for re-election and that he had notified the Chinese Central Government of this decision.

12 Dec 2016

Financial Secretary John Tsang Chun-wah（曾俊華）submitted his resignation in preparation for his candidacy in the 2017 Chief Executive election.

21 Dec 2016

The HKSAR government published Hong Kong's first *Biodiversity Strategy and Action Plan,* outlining a five-year roadmap with 67 measures for sustainable development in four focus areas, namely conservation, biodiversity, public awareness, and community involvement.

23 Dec 2016

Chief Secretary for Administration and Chairman of West Kowloon Cultural District Authority Chairman Carrie Lam Cheng Yuet-ngor（林鄭月娥）and Director of The Palace Museum Shan Jixiang（單霽翔）signed an agreement in Beijing on the development of a Hong Kong Palace Museum.

28 Dec 2016

The MTR South Island Line—a six-kilometre rail running along five stations (South Horizons, Lei Tung, Wong Chuk Hang, Ocean Park and Admiralty) between Ap Lei Chau and Admiralty on Hong Kong Island—became operational. It was the first fully automated line in Hong Kong. With this, a complete MTR network across all 18 districts in Hong Kong was realised.

Dec 2016

Rex Tso Sing-yu（曹星如）achieved a global top ranking in the World Boxing Organization's Super Flyweight (112–115 lbs) division, becoming the first Hong Kong boxer on the list of contenders.

03 Jan 2017

The Memorandum of Understanding on Jointly Developing the Lok Ma Chau Loop by Hong Kong and Shenzhen was signed to create a Hong Kong–Shenzhen Innovation and Technology Park in an 87-hectare loop as the largest tech-driven platform in Hong Kong.

09 Jan 2017

Tin Shui Wai Hospital was partially opened for service, providing three specialist outpatient clinics and day-care facilities, followed by the opening of its accident and emergency ward on 15 March.

The Chinese University of Hong Kong's Professor of Medicine and Therapeutics Szeto Cheuk-chun (司徒卓俊) and his team—in collaboration with the Chinese PLA General Hospital, Hangzhou Traditional Chinese Medicine Hospital, and Shanghai University of Traditional Chinese Medicine's Longhua Hospital on integrated Chinese and Western medicine in treating IgA nephropathy (Berger's disease)—won a first prize at the 2016 State Scientific and Technological Progress Awards.

12 Jan 2017

Chief Secretary for Administration Carrie Lam Cheng Yuet-ngor (林鄭月娥) submitted her resignation in preparation for her candidacy in the Chief Executive election.

18 Jan 2017

Chief Executive Leung Chun-ying (梁振英) delivered his fifth and final Policy Address *Make Best Use of Opportunities, Develop the Economy, Improve People's Livelihood, Build an Inclusive Society.* He highlighted the economic opportunities from the national 13th Five-Year Plan and the Belt and Road Initiative while emphasising re-industrialisation through innovation.

20 Jan 2017

The HKSAR government released *Hong Kong's Climate Action Plan 2030+* which entailed a long-term strategy formulated by the Steering Committee on Climate Change chaired by the Chief Secretary for Administration. The plan aimed to reduce Hong Kong's carbon intensity by 65% to 70% from its level in 2005 and carbon emissions per capita to 3.3–3.8 tonnes by 2030.

10 Feb 2017

A passenger set himself on fire in a train on the MTR Tsuen Wan Line en route from Admiralty to Tsim Sha Tsui. The arsonist died of his injuries while injuring 18 passengers. On 26 April, MTR published parts of an incident report prepared by an Executive Review Panel, recommending the installation of additional portable fire extinguishers in stations and train compartments with closed circuit television by the end of 2023.

14 Feb 2017

Seven police officers were found guilty of assault occasioning actual bodily harm and sentenced to two years in prison by the District Court. They were charged with alleged assault on Ken Tsang Kin-chiu (曾健超) during the illegal Occupy Central movement on 15 October 2014.

17 Feb 2017

Former Chief Executive Donald Tsang Yam-kuen (曾蔭權)—charged with one count of accepting advantages as Chief Executive and two counts of misconduct in public office by the Independent Commission Against Corruption (ICAC)—was found guilty on one count of misconduct in public office in a trial at the High Court. On 22 February, he was sentenced to 20 months' imprisonment, becoming the highest-ranking official in Hong Kong convicted of such an offence. On 24 April, he was released on bail pending an appeal; on 20 July 2018, the Court of Appeal dismissed his appeal but reduced his prison term to one year. In January 2019, he was released after serving the full term of his sentence. On 26 June 2019, the Court of Final Appeal ruled in favour of his appeal and quashed his conviction of misconduct in public office.

The Chief Executive-in-Council approved a draft Tung Chung Extension Area Outline Zoning Plan—covering about 216.67 hectares of land to expand Tung Chung into a town of 200,000 people.

24 Feb 2017

The Department of Justice launched a new electronic legislation database known as Hong Kong e-Legislation for free access to the laws of Hong Kong in Chinese and English.

Mainland developers Logan Property Holdings Company Limited and KWG Property Holding Limited jointly acquired a residential site on Lee Nam Road in Ap Lei Chau for HK$16.855 billion (HK$22,118 per square foot) in a record transaction since 1997.

27 Feb 2017

Hong Kong Exchanges and Clearing Limited announced that it achieved a total of 126 initial public offerings (IPOs) for a sum of HK$195.3 billion in 2016 as the world's top IPO market.

28 Feb 2017

Hong Kong Heritage Museum unveiled a permanent exhibition called Jin Yong Gallery and dedicated to the life of renowned martial arts novelist Louis Cha Leung-yung（查良鏞）. It featured more than 300 exhibits that reflected his early career and creative process as well as his impact on Hong Kong's popular culture.

Hong Kong experienced the warmest winter on record (December 2016–February 2017) with an average temperature of 18.4°C, exceeding the previous record of 17.4°C (December 1998–February 1999).

05 Mar 2017

Premier of the State Council Li Keqiang（李克強）in his annual government work report pledged the continued implementation of "One Country, Two Systems" in Hong Kong, stressing that "the notion of Hong Kong independence will lead nowhere." He also highlighted the role of Hong Kong and Macao in the Guangdong–Hong Kong–Macao Greater Bay Area with respect to national economic development.

11 Mar 2017

Hong Kong boxer Rex Tso Sing-yu（曹星如）defeated boxer Mukai Hirofumi in the Clash of Champions 2 held in Hong Kong. In addition to extending his winning streak to 21, he successfully defended his titles as World Boxing Organization's (WBO) International Champion and World Boxing Council's (WBC) Asia Champion—both in the Super Flyweight division—and claimed the gold belt as World Boxing Organization's Asia Pacific Champion against Mukai Hirofumi. (Figure 366)

13 Mar 2017

The Chinese People's Political Consultative Conference (CPPCC) endorsed the election of Chief Executive Leung Chun-ying（梁振英）as a CPPCC Vice Chairman with immediate effect.

The Antiquities and Monuments (Declaration of Proposed Monument) (Hung Lau) Notice was promulgated, provisionally declaring Hung Lau (a historic building located near Shek Kok Tsui Village in Castle Peak, Tuen Mun, New Territories) a proposed monument subject to preservation in view of the building's imminent demolition.

Figure 366
Hong Kong boxer Rex Tso Sing-yu（曹星如）, nicknamed The Wonder Kid, wrapped himself in the regional flag of the HKSAR after winning a match. (Photo courtesy of HKSAR Government)

17 Mar 2017

The District Court handed down its first verdict on the Mong Kok riots during Chinese New Year in 2016; three defendants were found guilty and sentenced to three years in prison.

26 Mar 2017

Carrie Lam Cheng Yuet-ngor（林鄭月娥）was elected as the fifth Chief Executive of the HKSAR; she won 777 votes, defeating John Tsang Chun-wah（曾俊華）and Woo Kwok-hing（胡國興）. On 11 April, she was received by President Xi Jinping（習近平）in Beijing where she accepted her appointment by the State Council as the fifth Chief Executive of the HKSAR.

27 Mar 2017

Organisers of the illegal Occupy Central movement in 2014—including Benny Tai Yiu-ting（戴耀廷）, Chan Kin-man（陳健民）, Chu Yiu-ming（朱耀明）, Tanya Chan（陳淑莊）, Shiu Ka-chun（邵家臻）, Tommy Cheung Sau-yin（張秀賢）, Eason Chung Yiu-wa（鍾耀華）, Lee Wing-tat（李永達）and Raphael Wong Ho-ming（黃浩銘）—were arrested and charged with conspiracy to commit public nuisance, inciting others to commit public nuisance and inciting others to incite public nuisance.

The Registration and Electoral Office found two of its laptop computers (containing information of 1,194 Election Committee members and some 3.78 million voters) missing from Asia World-Expo (a fall-back venue) following the Chief Executive election. The case remained unsolved.

28 Mar 2017

The Chief Executive-in-Council approved the termination of digital radio broadcast in Hong Kong, including Radio Television Hong Kong's existing programmes in six months' time.

08 Apr 2017

Hong Kong International Airport's new air traffic management system lost track of some flight information; all departing flights were temporarily suspended. The fallback system was activated for the first time since the new system's inception in November 2016.

10 Apr 2017

Hong Kong Mortgage Corporation Limited announced that its Board of Directors had approved the introduction of a life annuity scheme designed to provide immediate lifetime pay-outs to people aged 65 or above after a lump-sum premium payment. The scheme was officially launched on 05 July 2018.

11 Apr 2017

Hong Kong snooker player Ng On-yee（吳安儀）won the first World Women's 10-Red Championship shortly after winning the World Women's 6-Red Championship and World Women's Snooker Championship.

12 Apr 2017

The HKSAR government tightened property stamp duty exemption, introducing a 15% stamp duty for purchase of more than one residential property under a single instrument.

The UCI Track Cycling World Championships 2017 began for a five-day event at Hong Kong Velodrome. The annual cycling competition was held for the first time in Hong Kong and for the second time in Asia.

17 Apr 2017

Ocean Park Hong Kong welcomed the first golden snub-nosed monkey—an endangered species with a worldwide population of about 15,000 listed by the International Union for the Conservation of Nature—born in Hong Kong as an offspring of male golden monkey Qi Qi and female Le Le originally from Chengdu Zoo.

18 Apr 2017

The HKSAR government's Guangxi Liaison Unit in Nanning came into operation as a centre to promote economic, trade and cultural ties and support people and enterprises of Hong Kong in Guangxi.

Figure 367
The section of the Hong Kong–Zhuhai–Macao Bridge adjacent to Tai O. (Photo taken on 13 April 2017 and courtesy of HKSAR Government)

Figure 368
An aerial view of the Hong Kong–Zhuhai–Macao Bridge's (HZMB) Eastern Artificial Island under construction. (Photo taken by Qian Shicheng in June 2015 and courtesy of HZMB Authority)

25 Apr 2017

A new Scheme of Control Agreements on the supply of electricity with CLP Power and Hongkong Electric was signed for a 15-year term with a reduced permitted rate of return from 9.99% to 8% and a focus on energy efficiency and renewable energy.

26 Apr 2017

Hong Kong Heritage Museum launched an exhibition called Inventing le Louvre: From Palace to Museum over 800 Years. It featured a selection of paintings, drawings, artworks and sculptures from the collection of Louvre Museum of France.

01 May 2017

The HKSAR government relaxed the eligibility requirements of the Old Age Living Allowance by raising the asset limits among elderly singles and couples from HK$225,000 to HK$329,000 and from HK$341,000 to HK$499,000, respectively. It was also applied to those aged 65 to 69 (no financial assessment required for those aged 70 or above) under the Guangdong Scheme (Hong Kong residents living in Guangdong Province).

05 May 2017

The HKSAR government issued a notice regarding the resumption of 79 private lots (about 3.5 hectares of land) from the villages of Fung Chi Tsuen, Wing Ning Tsuen and Yeung Uk San Tsuen for development at Wang Chau (Phase 1) in Yuen Long.

12 May 2017

The West Kowloon Law Courts Building in Sham Shui Po—comprising the West Kowloon Magistrates' Courts, Small Claims Tribunal, Coroner's Court and Obscene Articles Tribunal—was opened in a ceremony.

14 May 2017

Fantastic Television Limited's free-to-air Fantastic TV Chinese Channel made its debut at 8 p.m.

16 May 2017

Henderson Land acquired the commercial site of Murray Road Multi-storey Carpark Building in Central for HK$23.28 billion (HK$50,064 per square foot) in a record transaction in terms of total price and price per square foot for commercial land.

The last precast tunnel module in the Hong Kong section of the Hong Kong–Zhuhai–Macao Bridge was successfully placed into position, marking the completion of the 12-km Hong Kong Link Road (comprising 9.4 kilometres of viaduct, one kilometre of tunnel and 1.6 kilometres of ground road) connecting the Main Bridge in Mainland waters with Hong Kong Port. (Figures 367 and 368)

16 May 2017

The People's Bank of China in conjunction with the Hong Kong Monetary Authority announced the establishment of a bond market (Bond Connect) between Hong Kong and the Mainland, giving overseas investors access to the China Interbank Bond Market through northbound trading initially, followed by southbound trading in due course; northbound trading began on 03 July.

The Independent Commission Against Corruption arrested 21 people for producing false concrete test reports on the Hong Kong–Zhuhai–Macao Bridge. In 2019, 12 people were convicted of conspiracy to defraud and were sentenced to two to 24 months' imprisonment or community service.

19 May 2017

The Hong Kong Monetary Authority introduced new measures on residential mortgage loans to reduce credit risk through 1) higher capital requirements, 2) lowered loan-to-value ratio by 10% among borrowers with one or more pre-existing mortgages, and 3) lowered debt service ratio by 10% among borrowers whose primary income came from outside of Hong Kong.

31 May 2017

The Lands Department announced that Rich Union Development Limited (a subsidiary of Nan Fung Development Limited) had won a tender for a commercial site at Kai Tak Area 1F Site 2 in Kowloon for approximately HK$24.7 billion (HK$12,863 per square foot). It exceeded the Murray Road Carpark site in Central on 16 May as the most expensive commercial land in Hong Kong as of 2017.

The Education Bureau issued an updated *Secondary Education Curriculum Guide*, requiring 51 hours of lesson on the Basic Law in junior secondary schools to provide students with a greater understanding of the Basic Law and the "One Country, Two Systems" framework.

02 Jun 2017

Hong Kong Science Museum began an exhibition called Eternal Life: Exploring Ancient Egypt. It featured more than 200 ancient Egyptian artefacts and computer tomography images of mummies, attracting over 850,000 visits with the highest attendance in an exhibition presented by the Leisure and Cultural Services Department.

03 Jun 2017

The HKSAR Government released its *Sustainable Lantau Blueprint*—mapping out the future direction of "Development in the North, Conservation for the South" on Lantau Island, including a proposed East Lantau Metropolis through reclamation of an area measuring 1,000 hectares near Kau Yi Chau. The plan envisioned a resident population of 700,000 to one million, and 470,000 jobs available on the island.

09 Jun 2017

The Census and Statistics Department released its *Thematic Report on Household Income Distribution in Hong Kong*, revealing widened income disparity with a record high Gini Coefficient of 0.539.

10 Jun 2017

The Chinese Central Government appointed Xie Feng (謝鋒) as Commissioner of the Ministry of Foreign Affairs in the HKSAR.

13 Jun 2017

Hong Kong became a new member of the Asian Infrastructure Investment Bank (AIIB). On 12 May, the Finance Committee of the Legislative Council approved Hong Kong's subscription of 7,651 shares in AIIB's capital, including 1,530 paid-up shares worth HK$1.2 billion and 6,121 callable shares.

18 Jun 2017

Emergency room charges in public hospitals increased from HK$100 to HK$180 per visit in a bid to further curb the abuse of accident and emergency services.

21 Jun 2017

The United Nations Department of Economic and Social Affairs released its *World Population Prospects: The 2017 Revision*—showing that people aged 60 or above accounted for 23% of Hong Kong's total population in a record high as of 2017.

23 Jun 2017

The Finance Committee of the Legislative Council approved a grant of HK$31.9 billion for the construction of Kai Tak Sports Park—an integrated venue comprising a main stadium with a capacity of 50,000 spectators, an indoor sports centre with 10,000 seats, and a public sports ground with 5,000 seats.

27 Jun 2017

The Guangzhou Branch of the People's Bank of China in conjunction with the Hong Kong Monetary Authority hosted a ceremony to mark the launch of cross-boundary electronic bill presentment and payment, enabling customers in Hong Kong to make bill payments in renminbi to merchants in Guangdong Province via the Internet or on mobile banking platforms.

28 Jun 2017

The Investment Agreement and Agreement on Economic and Technical Cooperation—under the framework of the Mainland and Hong Kong Closer Economic Partnership Arrangement (CEPA)—were signed to facilitate substantive obligations on admission of investments and provide an update to the arrangement set out in CEPA, respectively.

29 Jun 2017

President Xi Jinping (習近平) arrived in Hong Kong for a three-day visit during which he visited the West Kowloon Cultural District and witnessed the signing of an agreement of collaboration on the Hong Kong Palace Museum.

Hong Kong Heritage Museum began an exhibition called Hall of Mental Cultivation of The Palace Museum: Imperial Residence of Eight Emperors. It featured over 200 invaluable artefacts and furnishings of historical and cultural importance from the Qing Dynasty.

30 Jun 2017

Chinese President Xi Jinping (習近平) inspected troops of the People's Liberation Army Hong Kong Garrison at Shek Kong Barracks and visited the Junior Police Call Permanent Activity Centre and Integrated Youth Training Camp in Pat Heung.

01 Jul 2017

The fifth HKSAR government was inaugurated in a ceremony at the Hong Kong Convention and Exhibition Centre. President Xi Jinping (習近平) administered the oath of office to Chief Executive Carrie Lam Cheng Yuet-ngor (林鄭月娥) and other principal officials; he delivered an important speech in which he noted the implementation of "One Country, Two Systems" in Hong Kong was well recognised. He emphasised that the Chinese Central Government would unswervingly implement the policy of "One Country, Two Systems" and make sure that it was fully applied in Hong Kong without being bent or distorted, thus enabling continued advancement in the right direction. (Figures 369 and 370)

Chairman of the National Development and Reform Commission He Lifeng (何立峰), HKSAR Chief Executive Carrie Lam Cheng Yuet-ngor (林鄭月娥), Governor of Guangdong Province Ma Xingrui (馬興瑞) and Macao SAR Chief Executive Chui Sai-on (崔世安) in the presence of President Xi Jinping (習近平) signed the Framework Agreement on Deepening Guangdong–Hong Kong–Macao Cooperation in the Development of the Greater Bay Area.

President Xi Jinping (習近平) inspected the infrastructure projects at Chek Lap Kok, including the Hong Kong Link Road (a part of the Hong Kong–Zhuhai–Macao Bridge) and Three-runway System (3RS) under construction at Hong Kong International Airport.

The HKSAR government began a series of celebrations under the theme Together · Progress · Opportunity to mark the 20th anniversary of the establishment of the Hong Kong Special Administrative Region.

Figure 369
President Xi Jinping（習近平）administered the oath of office to Chief Executive-elect Carrie Lam Cheng Yuet-ngor（林鄭月娥）. (Photo courtesy of Anthony Wallace/AFP via Getty Images)

Figure 370
President Xi Jinping (習近平) administered the oath of office to principal officials of the fifth HKSAR government. (Photo courtesy of Keith Tsuji/Getty Images News via Getty Images)

Appendices

I Glossary of Personal Names and Their Chinese Equivalents

A	
Abbott, Harry	亞弼
Abercrombie, Patrick	亞柏康比
Adams, William Henry	亞當斯
Aguilar, José de	阿義拉
Akers-Jones, David	鍾逸傑
Alexandra, Princess of Denmark	文雅麗
Alfred, Prince (Duke of Edinburgh)	亞爾菲臘王子
Álvares, Jorge	歐維士
Amherst, William	阿美士德
Anderson, Alexander	安達臣
Andersson, Johan Gunnar	安特生
Andrade, Fernão Peres de	費爾南・安德拉德
Andrade, Simão de	西蒙・安德拉德
Anstey, Thomas Chisholm	晏士地
Aquino, Benigno, III	阿基諾三世
Arculli, Ronald Joseph	夏佳理
Arena, Alexander	艾維朗
Attlee, Clement	艾德禮

B	
Bain, William Neish	班欣
Bard, Solomon Matthew	白德
Barma, Haider	鮑文
Barretto, Gloria	白理桃
Bartholomew, Arthur Wollaston	巴度苗
Barty, Dermont Campbell	巴悌
Baudouin of Belgium (king)	博杜安
Belcher, Edward	卑路乍
Belilios, Emanuel Raphael	庇理羅士
Bell, Alison	鍾愛理遜
Bell-Irving, James Jardine	貝伊榮
Bennett, Joyce	班佐時
Bernacchi, Brook	貝納祺
Bevin, Ernest	貝文
Bianchi, Lorenzo	白英奇
Black, Agnes	碧克
Black, Robert	柏立基
Blackall, Henry	白樂高
Blair, Tony	貝理雅

Blair-Kerr, William Alexander	百里渠
Blake, Henry Arthur	卜力
Bland, Douglas	白連
Blye, Douglas William	白禮宜
Bogadek, Anthony	鮑嘉天
Boggs, Eli	博格斯
Bokhary, Kemal	包致金
Bonham, George	文咸
Borget, Auguste	奧古斯特・波塞爾
Bowen, George	寶雲
Bowring, John	寶寧
Boxall, Walter Richard	博素
Braga, John Vincent	布力架
Bray, Denis Campbell	黎敦義
Bremer, Gordon	伯麥
Brewin, Arthur Winbolt	蒲魯賢
Bridges, William Thomas	必列者士
Briggs, Geoffrey	貝理士
Brooke-Popham, Robert	樸芳
Brown, Samuel Robbins	布朗
Burlingham, Donald	寶靈翰
Burney, Edmund	賓尼
Bush, George Herbert	喬治・布殊
Butterfield, Richard	里察・巴特爾德
Butters, Henry Robert	畢特

C	
Caine, Sydney	金錫儀
Caine, William	威廉・堅
Caldecott, Andrew	郝德傑
Caldwell, Daniel Richard	高和爾
Carr, John	卡爾
Carrie, William James	卡麗
Carrington, John Worrell	賈靈頓
Cassian, Brigant	加斯恩
Cater, Jack	姬達
Chadwick, Osbert	查維克
Chaplin, Charles	差利・卓別靈
Charles I (king)	查理一世
Charles, Prince of Wales	查理斯王子

Chater, Catchick Paul	遮打		Eisner, Michael	邁克・艾斯納
Chennault, Claire Lee	陳納德		Eitel, Ernst Johann	歐德理
Chinnawat, Thaksin	他信		Elgin, 8th Earl of (James Bruce)	額爾金（詹姆斯・布魯士）
Chomley, Francis	孔萊		Eliot, Charles	儀禮
Churchill, Winston	邱吉爾		Elizabeth II (queen)	伊利沙伯二世
Ciccone, Madonna Louise	麥當娜		Elliot, Charles	義律
Clarke, Fielding	賈樂		Elliot, Elsie	葉錫恩
Clementi, Cecil	金文泰		Elliot, George	懿律
Clinton, Bill	克林頓		Elliott, Nell E.	黎理悅
Clinton, Hillary	希拉莉		Ernst, Fritz	恩斯特
Cochrane, Thomas	科克倫		**F**	
Collinson, Alfred Creighton	哥連臣		Farncomb, Edward	方甘士
Cook, Robin	郭偉邦		Fenton, William	芬頓
Cordeiro, Ray	郭利民		Finn, Daniel	芬戴禮
Cornish, Francis	酈富劭		Fisher, Geoffrey	費希爾
Coutinho, Martim Afonso de Melo	馬丁・阿豐索		Fisher, Norman George	菲莎
Cradock, Percy	柯利達		Foley, John	霍立賢
Crawford, Ninian	尼尼安・卡佛		Follows, Geoffrey	霍勞士
Cressall, Paul	祁樂壽		Forsgate, Hugh Moss Gerald	霍士傑
Cunningham, Alfred	克寧漢		Fox, Harry	霍士
D			Francis, John Joseph	法蘭些士
D'Aguilar, George Charles	德己立		Fraser, John Alexander	傅瑞憲
Dalkin, Roger	杜爾堅		Fraser-Smith, Robert	士蔑
Dalrymple, Alexander	達爾林普爾		Freeman, Kenneth John	弗里曼
Davis, David Frederick	大衛・戴維斯		Frost, B. L.	霍斯
Davis, John Francis	戴維斯		Fulton, John Scott	富爾敦
Davison, Ian Hay	戴維森		**G**	
De Speville, Bertrand	施百偉		Galsworthy, Anthony	高德年
Deane, Walter Meredith	迪恩		Gascoigne, William Julius	加士居
Derby, 16th Earl of (Frederick Stanley)	德比（腓特烈・史坦利）		Gaskell, William	加斯凱爾
Des Voeux, William	德輔		Gent, Edward	根特
Diana, Princess of Wales	戴安娜		Geoghegan, Michael Francis	紀勤
Doberck, William	杜伯克		George V (king)	喬治五世
Dodwell, Stanley Hudson	杜維爾		George VI (king)	喬治六世
Dorward, William	杜華		Gibb, Hugh Bold	吉布
Douglas-Home, Alexander	杜嘉菱		Gibson, Leslie Bertram	捷臣
Dunn, Stephen Troyte	鄧恩		Gilman, Richard James	機利文
E			Gimson, Franklin	詹遜
Edger, Joseph Frost	艾德格		Godber, Peter Fitzroy	葛柏
Edward VII (king)	愛德華七世		Godeaux, Napoleon-Ernest	葛篤
Edward, Prince (Later Edward VIII)	愛德華王子（後為英王愛德華八世）		Godfrey, Gerald	高奕暉
Eimbcke, Adolph Theodor	艾姆碧克		Gollan, Henry Cowper	歌倫
Eisenhower, Dwight	艾森豪威爾		Goodman, William Meigh	葛文

Goodstadt, Leo	顧汝德		Hulme, John Walter	曉吾
Grangeon, Paulo	葛蘭金		Humphreys, John David	堪富利士
Grantham, Alexander	葛量洪		Hunt, Ernest	韓德
Grayburn, Vandeleur Molyneux	祁禮賓		Hurd, Douglas	韓達德
Griffin, Winifred	龍福英		**I**	
Gützlaff, Charles	郭士立		Iger, Robert	羅伯特·艾格
H			Irvine, Derry	艾偉儀
Haddon-Cave, Philip	夏鼎基		Irving, Edward Alexander	伊榮
Hager, Charles Robert	喜嘉理		Irving, Rachel	艾惠珠
Hall, Henrietta	何顯理		**J**	
Hall, Ronald Owen	何明華		Jackson, Thomas	昃臣
Hallifax, Edwin Richard	夏理德		Jacobs, Piers	翟克誠
Hamberg, Theodore	韓山明		Jardine, Andrew	安德魯·渣甸
Hambro, Edvard	韓寶祿		Jardine, David	大衛·渣甸
Harald V of Norway (king)	哈拉爾五世		Jardine, William	威廉·渣甸
Harcourt, Cecil	夏慤		Jebsen, Jacob	雅各伯·捷成
Hartmann, Michael John	夏正民		Jessen, Henrich	亨利·珍臣
Haslewood, Clara Blanche	希士活夫人		Joachim, Prince of Denmark	約阿基姆王子
Hawking, Stephen	霍金		John Paul II (pope)	若望保祿二世
Hayter, George	海特		Johns, David	莊賢智
Heanley, Charles Montague	韓義理		Johnston, Alexander Robert	莊士敦
Heard, John	克德		Johnstone, Margaret Elizabeth	莊思端
Heath, Edward	希思		Jones, Arthur Creech	鍾斯
Hennesy, John Pope	軒尼詩		Jones, William Aneurin	瓊斯
Henningsen, Anker B.	海寧生		Joset, Theodore	若瑟
Herklots, Geoffrey	香樂思		**K**	
Hillier, Charles Batten	禧利		Kadoorie, Elly	埃利·嘉道理
Hồ Chí Minh	胡志明		Kadoorie, Horace	賀理士·嘉道理
Ho Tung, Irene	何艾齡		Kadoorie, Lawrence	羅蘭士·嘉道理
Ho Tung, Robert	何東		Keay, William Murray	威廉·基
Hodgson, Arthur	侯信		Kemp, Joseph Horsford	金培源
Hofman, Florentijn	霍夫曼		Kennedy, Arthur	堅尼地
Hogan, Michael Joseph	何瑾		Kerr, Donald W.	克爾
Holmes, David Ronald	何禮文		Keswick, James Johnstone	凱瑟克
Holyoak, Percy Hobson	何理玉		Kidd, Samuel Tedford	祁德
Homem, Pedro	別都盧		King, Thomas Henry	經亨利
Hope-Grant, James	克靈頓		King-Hall, William	霍爾
Hornell, William Woodward	康寧		Kotewall, Robert	羅旭龢
Horsburgh, James	霍士保		Kup, Antonie Wouter Pieter	古柏
Howard, John Winston	霍華德		Kwaśniewski, Aleksander	克瓦希涅夫斯基
Howard, Michael	夏偉明		Kyle, John	凱爾
Howe, Geoffrey	賀維		**L**	
Howe, Gerard Lewis	侯志律		Landale, David	蘭杜
Hughes, Arthur William	曉士		Landale, David Fortune	蘭代爾

Lane, Thomas	譚馬士·萊恩	Mathieson, Peter	馬斐森
Lanepart, Herbert Edward	連伯	Matisse, Henri Émile Benoît	馬諦斯
Lawson, John Kelburne	羅遜	May, Charles	梅理
Lechler, Auguste (Nordstadt), Lady	黎力基牧師夫人	May, Francis Henry	梅含理
Lee, Frederick	李輝德	McLaren, Robin	麥若彬
Legge, James	理雅各	Meacham, William	秦維廉
Leviton, Alan E.	萊維頓	Medhurst, Walter Henry	麥都思
Lightbody, Ian MacDonald	黎保德	Mercer, William Thomas	馬撒爾
Lister, Alfred	李斯特	Mitchell, William Henry	米徹爾
Lloyd, George Peter	羅以德	Mithaiwala, Dorabjee	米泰華拉
Lobo, Roger	羅保	Mody, Hormusjee Naorojee	麼地
Lobscheid, William	羅存德	Morgan, Frank Arthur	摩根
Lockhart, James Stewart	駱克	Morley, Denys Warwick	摩利
Louey, William Sui-tak	雷瑞德	Morrison, John Robert	馬儒翰
Lowson, James Alfred	勞森	Morse, Arthur	摩士
Lugard, Frederick	**盧嘉**	Moss, Albert James Robert	摩斯
Lund, Otto Marling	岳圖倫	Mother Teresa	德蘭修女
Lunn, Michael Victor	倫明高	Murdoch, Rupert	梅鐸
Lutz, Hans	陸漢思	Murrow, Yorick Jones	孖剌
Lyttelton, Oliver	列堤頓	Myers, George Sprague	美亞
M		N	
MacArthur, Douglas	麥克阿瑟	Napier, William John	律勞卑
Macartney, George	馬戛爾尼	Nathan, Matthew	彌敦
MacDonald, Claude Maxwell	**竇納樂**	Nendick, David	林定國
MacDonnell, Richard Graves	麥當奴	Newnham, Lanceray Arthur	紐臨
MacDougall, David Mercer	麥道高	Noble, Joseph Whittlesey	諾布爾
MacGregor, Atholl	麥理高	Noordin, Tan Sri Ahmad	諾丁
Macintosh, Duncan William	麥景陶	Noronha, Delfino	羅郎也
MacLehose, Murray	麥理浩	Northcote, Geoffry	羅富國
MacLennan, John	麥樂倫	O	
Macleod, Hamish	麥高樂	Old, Charles	區懷德
Mahathir Mohamad	馬哈蒂爾	O'Neill, Con Douglas Walter	歐念儒
Major, John	馬卓安	O'Neill, Michael	奧尼爾
Malcolm, George Alexander	麻恭	O'Rorke, Bridget	歐露芙
Malmesbury, 3rd Earl of (James Harris)	馬姆斯伯里（詹姆斯·哈里斯）	O'Sullivan, Ronnie	奧蘇利雲
		Overback, Gustave	奧弗貝克
Maltby, Christopher Michael	莫德庇	P	
Manson, Patrick	白文信	Pain, John	潘恩
Manuel I of Portugal (king)	曼努埃爾一世	Palmerston, 3rd Viscount (Henry John Temple)	巴麥尊（亨利·坦普爾）
Manzie, Gordon	孟思	Parkes, Harry Smith	巴夏禮
Martin, Robert Montgomery	馬丁	Patten, Chris	彭定康
Matheson, James	詹姆士·勿地臣	Paul VI (pope)	保祿六世
Mathews, Jeremy Fell	馬富善	Peacock, Brian A. V.	蒲國傑

Pedder, William	畢打	Scale, Peter	施彼德
Peel, William	貝璐	Schofield, Walter	施戈斐侶
Pelé, Edison Arantes do Nascimento	比利	Severn, Claud	施勳
Percival, Alexander	波斯富	Seymour, Horace James	薛穆
Pereira, Manoel	俾利喇	Shaftain, Frederick Frank Walter	修輔頓
Philip, Prince (Duke of Edinburgh)	菲臘親王	Shaw, George Bernard	蕭伯納
Phillippo, George	費立浦	Shellshear, Joseph Lexden	蕭思雅
Picasso, Pablo	畢加索	Sheridan, Terence	譚壽天
Piggott, Francis Taylor	碧葛	Shipley, Jennifer Mary	希普利
Pires, Tomé	皮萊資	Shortrede, Andrew	蕭德鋭
Polin, Thomas Hon Wing	康榮	Shuck, John Lewis	叔未士
Pope, Beatrice	寶興懌	Sirr, Henry Charles	錫爾
Ponte e Horta, José Maria da	柯邦迪	Slevin, Brian Francis	施禮榮
Pottinger, Henry	砵甸乍（璞鼎查）	Sloss, Duncan John	史羅司
Powell, Francis	鮑威爾	Smale, John Jackson	司馬理
Power, Noel	鮑偉華	Smith, Cecil Clementi	史密斯
Purves, William	浦偉士	Smith, George	施美夫
R		Smith, Lady Lydia	施美夫夫人
Raimondi, Timoleone	高雷門	Smith, Norman Lockhart	史美
Reed, Stuart	聶德	Smith, William McGregor	威廉‧史密夫
Rees-Davies, William	戴華士	Snowden, Edward	斯諾登
Reichelt, Karl Ludvig	艾香德	Soarez, Bartholameu	疏世利
Reid, Warwick	胡禮達	Somerville, Michael Neale	沈茂輝
Reina, Paolo Mem	雷納	Soros, George	索羅斯
Rennie, Alfred Herbert	連尼	Stanton, Vincent John	史丹頓
Ride, Lindsay Tasman	賴廉士	Staunton, George Thomas	士丹頓
Rigby, Ivo	李比	Sterling, Paul Ivy	史德靈
Ritchie, Neil	李芝	Stewart, Arthur Dudley	史超域
Roberts, Denys	羅弼時	Stewart, Frederick	史釗域
Robinson, William	羅便臣	Stubbs, Reginald Edward	司徒拔
Robson, James Jeavons	盧秉信	Sutherland, Stewart Ross	宋達能
Rogge, Jacques	羅格	Sutherland, Thomas	蘇石蘭
Romer, John	盧文	Swaine, John Joseph	施偉賢
Roosevelt, Franklin	羅斯福	Swire, George Warren	華倫‧施懷雅
Rosmead, 1st Baron (Hercules Robinson)	羅士敏（夏喬士‧羅便臣）	Swire, John Samuel	約翰‧施懷雅
Ross, Daniel	羅斯	Symons, Joyce	西門士夫人
Rowe, George Tippett	魯佐之	**T**	
Rowse, Michael	盧維思	Tagore, Rabindranath	泰戈爾
Russell, James	羅素	Talbot, Lee Merriam	戴爾博
Ruttonjee, Jehangir Hormusjee	傑汗智‧律敦治	Talbot, Martha	戴瑪黛
S		Taylor, Brian	戴萊
Sales, Arnaldo de Oliveira	沙理士	Taylor, Harry Alan	泰萊
Santer, Jacques	桑特	Thatcher, Margaret	戴卓爾夫人

Tonnochy, Malcolm Struan	杜老誌	Weddell, John	威德爾
Topley, Kenneth	陶建	Wiggham, Barrie	屈珩
Tose, Philip	杜輝廉	Wilder, Thornton	懷爾德
Trench, David	戴麟趾	Willauer, Whiting	魏勞爾
Truman, Harry S.	杜魯門	Williams, Gertrude Rosenblum	威廉斯夫人
V		Wilson, David	衛奕信（舊稱魏德巍）
Valtorta, Enrico	恩理覺	Wright, Norman	胡禮
Van den Born, Charles	溫德邦	X	
Van Gogh, Vincent	梵高	Xavier, Stephen	沙維亞
Van Straubenzee, Charles	史托賓斯	Y	
Victoria (queen)	維多利亞女王	Yersin, Alexandre	耶爾森
Volonteri, Simeone	西米安・獲朗他尼	Youde, Edward	尤德
W		Young, Mark	楊慕琦
Waldron, Thomas Westbrook	華德龍	Young-Herries, Michael Alexander Robert	郝禮士
Warhol, Andy	安迪・華荷		

▐▐ Glossary of Official Institutions and Titles

A	
Action Committee Against Narcotics	禁毒行動委員會
Administrative Officer	政務官
Administrator of Hong Kong	香港護理總督
Admiralty Court	海事法庭
Advisory Committee on Corruption	貪污事件審查委員會
Advisory Committee on Gambling Policy	賭博政策諮詢委員會
Agriculture and Fisheries Department	漁農處
Agriculture and Forestry Department	農林業管理處
Agriculture Department	農業部
Air Chief Marshal	空軍上將
Air Raid Precautions Department	防空署
Anti-Corruption Branch	反貪污部
Anti-Corruption Bureau	懲治貪污局
Antiquities Advisory Board	古物諮詢委員會
Assistant Superintendent of Police in the New Territories	新界助理警司
Assistant Under-Secretary for the Colonies	殖民地部助理次官
Attorney	代訴人
Attorney General	律政司
Auxiliary Fire Service Unit	後備消防隊
Auxiliary Medical Service Unit	醫療輔助隊

B	
Banking Advisory Committee	銀行業諮詢委員會 / 銀行諮詢委員會
Barrister	大律師
Board of Censors	檢查局
Board of Chinese Vernacular Primary Education	漢文教育組
Board of Education	教育諮詢委員會 / 教育委員會
Board of Examiners	考試委員會
Board of Management of the Chinese Permanent Cemeteries	華人永遠墳場管理委員會
Board of Trade (UK)	英國貿易委員會
Brigadier	准將
British Army Aid Group	英軍服務團
Building Section	屋宇建設處
Business Registration Office	商業登記署

C	
Cadet Officer	官學生
Canadian Immigration Office, Hong Kong	加拿大駐港辦事處
Captain	上尉
Captain Superintendent of Police	警察司
Census and Statistics Planning Office	戶口統計籌審處
Central Fire Station	中環消防總局
Central Magistracy	中央裁判司署
Chargé d'affaires to the People's Republic of China (UK)	英國駐華代辦

Chief Justice	正按察司
Chief Magistrate	總巡理府
Chief Superintendent of the Trade of British Subjects in China	英國駐華商務監督
Chiefs of Staff Committee (UK)	英國參謀長委員會
Chinese Constables	華人差役
Chinese Secretary	華文秘書
Chinese Studies Committee	中文科目委員會
City District Office	民政司署
Civil Aid Services	民眾安全服務隊
Civil Aviation Department	民航處
Civil Service Abuses Inquiry Commission	公務員瀆職委員會
Colonial Defence Committee (UK)	英國殖民地防務委員會
Colonial Office	殖民地部
Colonial Secretary	布政司
Colonial Surgeon	殖民地醫官
Colonial Treasurer	庫務司
Commander British Force in Hong Kong	駐港英軍總司令
Commander-in-Chief of British Forces in the First Anglo-Chinese War	英國赴華遠征軍總司令
Commander-in-Chief, Far East	遠東三軍司令
Commerce and Industry Department	工商業管理處 / 工商業管理署
Commission Appointed by His Excellency the Governor of Hong Kong to Enquire into the Causes and Effects of the Present Trade Depression in Hong Kong	經濟衰退研究專責委員會
Commission of Independent Examiners	考試局
Commission to Inquire into the Working and Organization of Tung Wah Hospital	調查東華醫院委員會
Commissioner for Housing	房屋管理處處長
Commissioner for Resettlement	徙置事務處處長
Commissioner of Banking	銀行監理專員
Commissioner of Police	警務處長
Commissioner of Rating and Valuation	差餉物業估價署署長
Committee of Higher Education	高等教育委員會
Committee on Chinese Law and Custom	中國法例及習慣研究委員會
Committee on Education, The	教育委員會
Commodore (Navy)	海軍准將
Commonwealth Office	聯邦事務部
Commonwealth Relations Office	聯邦關係部
Co-operative Development and Fisheries Department	合作專業及漁業管理處
Corporal	下士
Council for Recreation and Sport	康樂體育事務處
Criminal and Admiralty Court	駐華刑事和海事法庭
Criminal Court	刑事法庭
Criminal Investigation Department	刑事偵緝組
Curriculum Development Committee	課程發展委員會

D	
Defence Secretary	防衛司
Department of Agriculture, Fisheries and Forestry	農林漁業管理處
Department of Census and Statistics	戶口統計籌審司署
Department of Public Works	工務局
Department of Statistics	統計處
Department of Transport (UK)	英國運輸部
Deportation and Detention Advisory Tribunal	遞解及拘留諮詢審裁處
Deputy Commissioner of Police	警務處副處長
Deputy Superintendent of the Trade of British Subjects in China	英國駐華副商務監督
Development Secretariat	發展司署
Director of Broadcasting	廣播處長
Director of Education	教育司
Director of Home Affairs	民政司
Director of Public Works	工務司
District Council	區議會
District Court	地方法院
District Office	新界理民府
District Office (North)	北約理民府
District Office (South)	南約理民府
District Officer	理民官
District Officer (North)	北約理民官
District Officers	民政主任
District Watch Force	團防局
District Watchmen	更練

E	
Economic Services Department	經濟科
Education Board, The	教育委員會
Education Bureau, The	教育局
Educational Department	教育司署
Emergency Unit	衝鋒隊
Environment Branch	環境科
Envoy Extraordinary and Minister Plenipotentiary to Imperial China	英國駐華全權代表 / 英國駐華全權特使
Essential Commodities Board	基要商品委員會
Establishment Officer	銓敘司
European Economic Community	歐洲經濟共同體
Executive Council	行政局

F	
Family Planning Association of Hong Kong, The	香港家庭計劃指導會
Federation of Hong Kong Industries	香港工業總會
Fight Crime Committee	撲滅暴力罪行委員會
Finance Committee	財務委員會
Financial Secretary	財政司
Fire Services Department's Diving Team	政府蛙人隊伍

Fire Services Training School (Pat Heung)	八鄉消防訓練學校
Fish Marketing Organization	魚類統營處
Fisheries Department	漁務部 / 漁政司署 / 漁政署
Foreign and Commonwealth Office (UK)	英國外交及聯邦事務部
Foreign Office (UK)	英國外交部
Forestry Department	林務部

G	
General Post Office	郵政總局
Governadores da Índia Portuguesa	葡萄牙印度總督
Government Civil Hospital, The	國家醫院
Government Public Relations Office	公共關係辦事處
Government Rice Monopoly Board	食米專賣局
Government School Committee	皇家書館委員會
Government Secretariat	布政司署
Governor of Hong Kong, The	香港總督

H	
Harbour Department	船政廳署
Harbour Department and Directorate of Air Services	船政廳署暨航空事務處
Harbour Master	船政署
Health Inspector	衛生督察
Her Majesty's Treasury (UK)	英國財政部
Heung Yee Kuk	鄉議局
His Majesty's Inspector of Schools (UK)	英國皇家視學官
Home Affairs and Information Branch	民政及新聞科
Home Affairs Department	民政科
Hong Kong Auxiliary Air Force	香港輔助空軍
Hong Kong Auxiliary Police	香港輔助警察隊
Hong Kong Chinese Language Committee	公事上使用中文問題研究委員會
Hong Kong Chinese Regiment	華籍軍團
Hong Kong Commercial Counsellor, British Embassy Washington	英國駐美國大使館香港商貿事務參贊
Hong Kong Commercial Counsellor, UK Mission Geneva	英國駐日內瓦代表團香港商貿事務參贊
Hong Kong Defence Force	香港防衛軍
Hong Kong Economic and Trade Office, Brussel	香港駐布魯塞爾經貿辦
Hong Kong Economic and Trade Office, Geneva	香港駐日內瓦經貿辦
Hong Kong Economic and Trade Office, Tokyo	香港駐東京經貿辦
Hong Kong Economic and Trade Office, Washington DC	香港駐華盛頓經貿辦
Hong Kong Eugenics League, The	香港優生學會
Hong Kong Export Credit Insurance Corporation	香港出口信用保險局
Hong Kong Fire Brigade	消防隊
Hong Kong Fire Services Department	消防事務處 / 消防處

Hong Kong Housing Authority	香港屋宇建設委員會 / 香港房屋委員會
Hong Kong Housing Society	香港房屋協會
Hong Kong Naval Volunteer Force	皇家海軍預備隊
Hong Kong Observatory	香港天文台
Hong Kong Planning Unit	香港計劃小組
Hong Kong Police Training School	香港警察訓練學校
Hong Kong Productivity Council, The	香港生產力促進局
Hong Kong Regiment	香港軍團
Hong Kong Royal Naval Volunteer Reserve	香港皇家海軍志願後備隊
Hong Kong Shippers' Council, The	香港付貨人委員會
Hong Kong (Submarine Mining) Company	香港水雷炮連
Hong Kong Tourist Association	香港旅遊協會
Hong Kong Trade Development Council	貿易拓展委員會 / 香港貿易發展局
Hong Kong Volunteer Company	香港志願連
Hong Kong Volunteer Defence Corps	香港義勇防衛軍
Hong Kong Volunteers	香港義勇軍
House of Commons (UK)	英國下議院
Housing Branch	房屋科
Housing Commission	房屋委員會
Housing Department	房屋署
Hughesiliers	休士兵團

I

Immigration Control Office	警務處入境事務部
Immigration Department	人民入境事務處 / 入境事務處
Imports and Exports Office, The	出入口管理處
Independent Commission Against Corruption	總督特派廉政專員公署 / 廉政公署
Industrial Training Advisory Committee	工業訓練諮詢委員會
Industry Inspection Branch	工業視察組
Information Secretary	新聞事務司
Information Services Department	政府新聞處
Inland Revenue Department	稅務局
Inspector General of Chinese Maritime Customs	中國海關總稅務司
Inspector of Government Schools	皇家書館視學官
Inspector of Schools	視學官
Institute of Language in Education	語文教育學院
International Criminal Police Organization	國際刑警組織

J

Joint Planning Sub-committee, Chiefs of Staff Committee (UK)	英國參謀長委員會聯合計劃小組
Judge of Admiralty Court	海事法庭法官
Judicial Committee of the Privy Council (UK)	英國樞密院司法委員會
Judiciary, The	司法機構
Juror	陪審員

Justice of the Peace	太平紳士
Juvenile Court	少年法庭
Juvenile Delinquency Liaison Section, Hong Kong Police Force	少年罪犯調查組

K

Keep Hong Kong Clean Committee	保持香港清潔委員會
Kowloon Customs	九龍關
Kowloon Magistracy	九龍裁判署

L

Labour Advisory Board	勞工顧問委員會
Labour Department	勞工處
Labour Officer	勞工事務主任
Lands Tribunal	土地審裁處
Law Committee	法律委員會
Legal Aid Department	法律援助處
Legal Department	律政署
Legislative Council	立法局
Lieutenant (Navy)	海軍上尉
Lieutenant Colonel	中校
Lieutenant General	中將
Lieutenant Governor	副總督
London Office of the Hong Kong Government	香港政府駐倫敦辦事處

M

Major General	少將
Major-General (Navy)	海軍少將
Marine Department	海事處
Marine Police Headquarters	水警總部
Marine Region, Hong Kong Police Force	水警
Matriculation Board	大學入學考試委員會
Medical and Health Department	醫務衛生署
Medical Department	醫務署
Medical Officer	醫務官
Medical Officer for Schools	學校醫官
Municipal Council	市議會

N

National Archives (UK), The	英國國家檔案館
New Territories Development Department	新界拓展署
New Territories District Office, The	新界民政署

O

Office of the European Community to Hong Kong	歐洲共同體駐港辦事處
Official Member	官守議員

P

Parliament (UK)	英國國會
Petty Sessions	簡易法庭
Police Force	警務處
Police Magistrate	警察裁判官
Police Public Relations Branch	警察公共關係科

Police School	警察訓練學校
Police Tactical Unit	警察機動部隊
Police Training Contingent	警察訓練分遣隊
Police Training School	警察訓練學校
Post Office	郵政署
Preventive Service	緝私隊
Prime Minister (UK)	英國首相
Principal Assistant Colonial Secretary	首席助理布政司
Principal Crown Counsel	主任檢察官
Printing Department	政府印務局
Prisons Department	監獄署
Protector of Chinese Inhabitants	撫華道
Public Affairs Television Division	公共事務電視部
Public Notary	公證人
Public Relations Office	公共關係處
Public Service Commission	公務員敍用委員會
Public Works Committee	工務委員會
Public Works Department	工務司署
Puisne Judge	副按察司

R	
Radiation Board	輻射管理局
Radio Hong Kong	香港廣播電台
Rating and Valuation Department	差餉物業估價署
Registrar General	總登記官 / 華民政務司
Registrar General's Department	註冊總署
Registrar of Marriages	婚姻註冊官
Registrar of Societies	社團註冊官
Registration of Persons Office	人口登記局 / 人事登記處
Rent Control Committee	租務管制調查委員會
Resettlement Department	徙置事務處
Revenue Officer	緝私員
Royal Air Force	皇家空軍
Royal Rifles of Canada	皇家加拿大步槍團

S	
Sanitary Board	潔淨局
Secretariat for Chinese Affairs, The	華民政務司署
Secretary for Chinese Affairs, The	華民政務司
Secretary for Development	發展司
Secretary for Housing	房屋司
Secretary for Security	保安司
Secretary for the Environment	環境司
Secretary of State for Foreign Affairs (UK)	英國外交大臣
Secretary of State for the Colonies	殖民地事務大臣
Securities Advisory Council	證券事務諮詢委員會

Security Branch	保安科
Social Services Branch	社會福利科
Social Welfare Department	社會福利署
Social Welfare Office	社會局
Solicitor	執業律師
Special Branch, Hong Kong Police Force	香港警務處政治部
Special Committee on Housing	房屋管理處
Special Committees	特別委員會
Special Constabulary	特務警察隊
Special Police Reserve	特別警察後備隊
Standing Committee on Corruption	貪污問題常設委員會
Standing Committees	常設委員會
Superintendent of Fire Brigade	消防隊監督
Superintendent of Gaol	監獄獄長
Superintendent of Mines	礦務總監
Superintendent of the Botanical and Afforestation Department	植物及林務部監督
Superintendent of the Civil Aerodrome	機場監督
Supreme Commander of the Allied Powers	駐日盟軍總司令
Supreme Court	香港高等法院 / 香港最高法院
Surveyor General	總量地官

T	
Tai Po District Office	大埔理民府
Tenancy Bureau	租務調查處
Tenancy Tribunal	租務審裁處
Town Planning Board	城市設計委員會 / 城市規劃委員會
Training Council	香港訓練局

U	
University Grants Committee	大學教育資助委員會
Unofficial Member	非官守議員
Urban Council	市政局
Urban Services Council	市政衛生局
Urban Services Department	市政事務署

V	
Vegetable Marketing Organization	蔬菜統營處
Vice Consul of the Swiss Consulate in Hong Kong	瑞士駐港副領事

W	
Waterworks Office	水務局
Winnipeg Grenadiers	溫尼柏擲彈兵團

Y	
Yuen Long District Office	元朗理民府

III Glossary of Ordinances and Documents

A	
1963-1972 Development of Medical Services in Hongkong, The	香港醫療衛生服務發展報告書
A Pattern of District Administration in Hong Kong	綠皮書：香港地方行政的模式
A Perspective on Education in Hong Kong: Report by a Visiting Panel	香港教育透視：國際顧問團報告書
Activity Guidelines for Day Nursery	日間幼兒園活動指引
Adoption Ordinance 1956	1956 年領養條例
Advertising Display and Floodlighting (Restriction) Order 1979	1979 年廣告、陳列及泛光燈照明（限制）令
Age of Majority (Related Provisions) Ordinance 1990	1990 年成年歲數（有關條文）條例
Agreement between the Government of Hong Kong and the Admiralty	香港政府與海軍部所訂協議
Agreement between the Government of Hong Kong and the Government of the Kingdom of the Netherlands concerning Air Services	香港政府和荷蘭王國政府關於航班的協定
Agreement between the People's Council of Kwangtung Province and the Hongkong Authorities on the Supply of Water to Hongkong and Kowloon from the East River	關於從東江取水供給香港、九龍的協議
Agreement-made in pursuance of Article XXVI of the Treaty of Tientsin-containing Rules of Trade.	通商章程善後條約：海關稅則
Agricultural Products (Marketing) Ordinance 1952	1952 年農產品（統營）條例
Aims and Policy for Social Welfare in Hong Kong	香港社會福利目標及政策白皮書
Air Pollution Control Ordinance 1983	1983 年空氣污染管制條例
Air Pollution Control (Amendment) Ordinance 1993	1993 年空氣污染管制（修訂）條例
Air Pollution Control (Asbestos) (Administration) Regulation 1996	1996 年空氣污染管制（石棉）（行政管理）規例
Air Pollution Control (Motor Vehicle Fuel) (Amendment) Regulation 1990	1990 年空氣污染管制（汽車燃料）（修訂）規例
Air Transport (Licensing of Air Services) Regulations 1949	1949 年空運（航空服務牌照）規例
Airport Authority Ordinance 1995	1995 年機場管理局條例
Alien Enemies (Winding Up) Ordinance 1914	1914 年敵國人士（清盤）條例
Amusement Game Centres Ordinance 1993	1993 年遊戲機中心條例
Anti-British Feeling in China: Memorandum	中國人的反英情緒備忘錄
Antiquities and Monuments Ordinance 1971	1971 年古物及古蹟條例
Application of English Law Ordinance 1966	1966 年英國法律應用條例
Arrangement Regarding International Trade in Textiles	國際紡織品貿易協定
Auxiliary Police Force Ordinance 1871	1871 年輔助警察條例

B	
Banishment of Dangerous Characters Ordinance 1871	1871 年驅逐危險分子條例
Bank Notes and Certificates of Indebtedness Ordinance 1946	1946 年銀行紙幣及負債證明書條例
Bank Notes Issue Ordinance 1895	1895 年銀行紙幣發行條例
Bankers Cheques-False Pretence Ordinance 1860	1860 年銀行票據及詐騙法修訂條例
Banking Ordinance 1948, 1964, 1982, 1986	1948、1964、1982、1986 年銀行業條例
Banking (Amendment) Ordinance 1981	1981 年銀行業（修訂）條例
Bankruptcy Ordinance 1864, 1891	1864、1891 年破產條例
Betting Duty (Amendment) Ordinance 1973	1973 年博彩稅（修訂）條例
Betting Duty (Amendment) (No. 2) Ordinance 1975	1975 年博彩稅（修訂）（第 2 號）條例
Bill of Exchange Ordinance 1885	1885 年匯票條例
Bill of Sale Ordinance 1886	1886 年買賣憑據條例
Births and Deaths Registration Ordinance 1872, 1934	1872、1934 年生死登記條例
Block Crown Lease	集體官批
Boundary and Election Commission Ordinance 1993	1993 年選區分界及選舉事務委員會條例
British Nationality (Hong Kong) (Selection Scheme) Act 1990	1990 年英國國籍法（香港）（甄選計劃）令
British Nationality (Hong Kong) Act 1997	1997 年英國國籍（香港）令
British Nationality Act 1981	1981 年英國國籍法令
Building (Planning) (Amendment) (No. 2) Regulations 1962	1962 年建築物（規劃）（修訂）（第 2 號）規例
Building Management Ordinance 1993	1993 年建築物管理條例
Building Planning (Amendment) Regulations 1987	1987 年建築物設計（修訂）規例
Buildings (Amendment) (No. 2) Ordinance 1964	1964 年建築（修訂）（第 2 號）條例
Buildings Ordinance 1935	1935 年建築物條例
Business Registration Ordinance 1959	1959 年商業登記條例
Business Regulation Ordinance 1952	1952 年商業管理條例

C	
Census Ordinance 1881, 1931	1881、1931 年人口普查條例
Cheung Chau (Residence) Ordinance 1919	1919 年長洲（住宅區）條例
Child Care Centres Ordinance 1975	1975 年幼兒中心條例
China Coast Meteorological Register	中國沿海氣象紀錄
Chinese Burials and Nuisances Ordinance 1856	1856 年華人喪葬及滋擾條例
Chinese Emigrant Ship Fittings Ordinance 1873	1873 年華人移民船舶條例
Chinese Emigration Consolidation Ordinance 1874	1874 年華人移民整合條例

Chinese Extradition Ordinance 1889	1889 年華人引渡條例	Consumer Council (Amendment) Ordinance 1994	1994 年消費者委員會（修訂）條例
Chinese Hospital Incorporation Ordinance 1870	1870 年華人醫院則例	Consumer Goods Safety Ordinance 1994	1994 年消費品安全條例
Chinese Immigration Regulation Ordinance 1895	1895 年規管華人移民條例	Contagious Diseases Ordinance 1867	1867 年性病條例
Chinese Marriage Preservation Ordinance 1912	1912 年中國婚姻保存條例	Control of Obscene and Indecent Articles Ordinance 1987	1987 年淫褻及不雅物品管制條例
Chinese Passengers' Act 1855	1855 年華人乘客法令	Control of Publications Consolidation Ordinance 1951	1951 年刊物管制綜合條例
Chinese Peace Officers Regulation Ordinance 1844	1844 年華人保甲條例	Convention Between Great Britain and China Respecting an Extension of Hong Kong Territory, The	展拓香港界址專條
City Polytechnic of Hong Kong Ordinance 1983	1983 年香港城市理工學院條例	Convention of Peking	北京條約
Clean Air Ordinance 1959	1959 年保持空氣清潔條例	Convention of Wetlands of International Importance Especially as Waterfowl Habitats	拉姆薩爾公約
Code of Regulations for Educational Grants-in-Aid	補助學校計劃守則	Convention on the Elimination of all Forms of Discrimination Against Women	消除對婦女一切形式歧視公約
Code on Access to Information	公開資料守則		
Coinage Offences Ordinance 1865	1865 年偽造貨幣治罪條例	Convention on the Rights of the Child	兒童權利公約
Colonial Books (Preservation and Registration) Ordinance 1888	1888 年殖民地書籍（保存及註冊）條例	Convention Relating to the Status of Refugees	難民地位公約
Colonial Courts of Admiralty Act 1890	1890 年殖民地海事法庭法令	Corrupt and Illegal Practices Ordinance 1955	1955 年舞弊及非法行為條例
Colonial Development and Welfare Act 1945	1945 年殖民地發展和福利法令	Cost of Living Survey 1958–63/64	1958 年至 1963/1964 年生活費用調查
Colonial Regulations	殖民地規例	Country Parks Ordinance 1976	1976 年郊野公園條例
Colony Armorial Bearings (Protection) Ordinance 1959	1959 年香港盾徽（保護）條例	Countryside and the People, The	郊區與大眾
Colony Outline Plan	土地利用計劃書	Crimes (Amendment) Ordinance 1991	1991 年刑事罪行（修訂）條例
Commission of Inquiry Ordinance 1968	1968 年調查委員會條例	Crimes (Amendment) (No. 3) Ordinance 1992	1992 年刑事罪行（修訂）（第 3 號）條例
Commodities Trading Ordinance 1976	1976 年商品交易條例	Crimes (Amendment) (No. 2) Ordinance 1996	1996 年刑事罪行（修訂）（第 2 號）條例
Commodity Exchanges (Prohibition) Ordinance 1973	1973 年商品交易所（禁止經營）條例	Crown Lands Resumption Ordinance 1889	1889 年收回官地條例
Commonwealth Immigrant Act 1962	1962 年英聯邦移民法令		
Community Chest of Hong Kong Ordinance 1968	1968 年香港公益金條例	Crown Lands Resumption Amendment Ordinance 1922	1922 年收回官地修訂條例
Community Service Orders Ordinance 1984	1984 年社會服務令條例	Crown Rights (Re-entry etc.) Ordinance 1870	1870 年官地權（重收）條例
Companies Ordinance 1865, 1932	1865、1932 年公司條例	Currency Ordinance 1935	1935 年貨幣條例
Companies (Amendment) Ordinance 1972, 1974, 1984	1972、1974、1984 年公司（修訂）條例	Currency Amendment Ordinance 1937	1937 年貨幣修訂條例
Compulsory Service Ordinance 1939, 1951	1939、1951 年強制服役條例	D	
Conservation of the Hong Kong Countryside: Summary Report and Recommendation	香港保存自然景物問題：簡要報告及建議	Dangerous Drugs Ordinance 1923, 1969	1923、1969 年危險藥物條例
Construction Sites (Safety) (Amendment) (No. 2) Regulations 1994	1994 年建築地盤（安全）（修訂）（第 2 號）規例	Dangerous Goods Ordinance 1873	1873 年危險品條例
Consultation Paper: Arts Policy Review Report	藝術政策檢討報告諮詢文件	Declaration of Change of Titles (General Adaptation) Notice 1997	1997 年宣布更改職稱及名稱（一般適應）公告
Consultative Document on Civil Service Terms of Appointment and Conditions of Service	公務員聘用及服務條件諮詢文件	Declaration of Rights for Hongkong Citizens	香港居民人權宣言
		Declaration on the Granting of Independence to Colonial Countries and Peoples	關於對殖民地及人民給以獨立之宣言
Consumer Council Ordinance 1977	1977 年消費者委員會條例	Deed of Lease of Kowloon	租借九龍租約

Defamation and Libel Ordinance 1887	1887 年誹謗條例	Emergency (Deportation and Detention) Regulations 1962	1962 年緊急（驅逐出境及拘留）規例
Defence (Finance) Regulations 1939	1939 年防衛（金融）規例	Emergency (Detention Orders) Regulations 1956	1956 年緊急（拘留令）規例
Defence of Hong Kong: Report of Joint Planning Sub-Committee	香港防務報告	Emergency (Exportation) (Miscellaneous Provisions) Regulations 1951	1951 年緊急（出口）（雜項條款）規例
Defence Regulations 1939, 1940	1939、1940 年防衛規例	Emergency (Firework) Regulations 1967	1967 年緊急（爆竹煙花）規例
Defences Sketching Prevention Ordinance 1895	1895 年防止測繪防禦工事條例	Emergency (General Holiday) Regulations 1967	1967 年緊急（公眾假期）規例
Delimitation of Northern Frontier of New Territories	香港英新租界合同	Emergency (Immediate Resumption) (Application) Regulations 1953	1953 年緊急（立即收回官地）（通用）規例
Delivery of Medical Services in Hospitals	醫院提供的醫療服務	Emergency (Immigration (Control and Offences) Ordinance 1958) (Amendment) Regulations 1962	1962 年緊急（1958 年入境（管制及罪行）條例）（修訂）規例
Demolished Buildings (Re-development of Sites) (Amendment) Ordinance 1963	1963 年已拆卸建築物（原址重新發展）（修訂）條例	Emergency (Prevention of Inflammatory Posters) Regulations 1967	1967 年緊急（防止煽動性標語）規例
Deportation of Aliens Ordinance 1935	1935 年遞解外國人條例	Emergency (Prevention of Inflammatory Speeches) Regulations 1967	1967 年緊急（防止煽動性言論）規例
Deportation Ordinance 1917	1917 年遞解條例	Emergency (Principal) (Amendment) Regulations 1967	1967 年緊急（主體）（修訂）規例
Deposit-taking Companies Ordinance 1976, 1982	1976、1982 年接受存款公司條例	Emergency (Principal) Amendment (No. 2) Regulations 1950	1950 年緊急（主體）修訂（第 2 號）規例
Deposit-taking Companies (Amendment) (No. 2) Ordinance 1981	1981 年接受存款公司（修訂）（第 2 號）條例	Emergency (Principal) (Amendment) (No. 2) Regulations 1967	1967 年緊急（主體）（修訂）（第 2 號）規例
Development of Senior Secondary and Tertiary Education, The	高中及專上教育發展白皮書	Emergency (Principal) Regulations 1949	1949 年緊急（主體）規例
Diplomatic Privileges Ordinance 1948	1948 年外交特權條例	Emergency (Resettlement Areas) Regulations 1952	1952 年緊急（徙置區）規例
Disability Discrimination Ordinance 1995	1995 年殘疾歧視條例	Emergency Powers (Colonial Defence) Order in Council 1939	1939 年緊急情況權力樞密院頒令
District Watch Force Ordinance 1930	1930 年團防局條例	Emigration Passage Brokers Ordinance 1857	1857 年苦力掯客條例
Dogs and Cats Ordinance 1950	1950 年狗貓條例	Empire Preference Ordinance 1932	1932 年英聯邦特惠稅條例
Doing Business 2016	2016 年營商環境報告	Employees' Compensation (Amendment) Ordinance 1982	1982 年僱員賠償（修訂）條例
Dollar Currency Notes Ordinance 1935	1935 年一元紙幣條例	Employees Retraining Ordinance 1992	1992 年僱員再培訓條例
Draft Code of Model Standing Orders for Colonial Legislatures	殖民地立法機關會議常規範本草稿	Employers and Servants Ordinance 1902	1902 年僱主及傭工條例
Drug Regulations 1960	1960 年藥物規例	Employment Ordinance 1968	1968 年僱傭條例
Drug Trafficking (Recovery of Proceeds) Ordinance 1989	1989 年販毒（追討得益）條例	Employment (Amendment) Ordinance 1970, 1976, 1985	1970、1976、1985 年僱傭（修訂）條例
Dutiable Commodities (Amendment) Regulations 1957	1957 年應課稅品（修訂）條例	Employment (Amendment) (No. 2) Ordinance 1976, 1981	1976、1981 年僱傭（修訂）（第 2 號）條例
Dutiable Commodities (Marking and Colouring of Hydrocarbon Oils) Regulations 1963	1963 年應課稅品（輕質柴油染色）規例	Employment (Amendment) (No. 3) Ordinance 1974, 1977	1974、1977 年僱傭（修訂）（第 3 號）條例
E		Employment (Amendment) Bill 1994	1994 年僱傭（修訂）條例草案
Education Ordinance 1913, 1952, 1971	1913、1952、1971 年教育條例	English Schools Foundation Ordinance 1967	1967 年英基學校協會條例
Education (Amendment) Ordinance 1958	1958 年教育（修訂）條例	Environmental Impact Assessment Ordinance 1997	1997 年環境影響評估條例
Education Policy	教育政策白皮書	Essential Services Corps Ordinance 1949	1949 年基要服務團條例
Electoral Provisions (Miscellaneous Amendments) (No. 2) Ordinance 1993	1993 年選舉規定（雜項修訂）（第 2 號）條例		
Emergency Regulations Ordinance 1922	1922 年緊急情況規例條例		
Emergency Regulations 1931	1931 年緊急情況規例		
Emergency (Bank Control) Regulations 1965	1965 年緊急（銀行管制）規例		
Emergency (Closed Areas) Regulations 1967	1967 年緊急（禁區）規例		
Emergency (Control of Oil) Regulations 1973	1973 年緊急（管制石油）規例		

European District Reservation Ordinance 1888	1888 年保留歐人區條例
Exchange Fund (Amendment) Ordinance 1979, 1983, 1992	1979、1983、1992 年外匯基金（修訂）條例
Explosive Substances (Amendment) Ordinance 1966	1966 年爆炸品（修訂）條例
Export Control Order 1950	1950 年出口管制令
Exportation (Prohibition) (North Korea) Order 1950	1950 年輸出（禁止）（朝鮮）令
Exportation (Prohibition) (Specific Articles) (No. 2) Order 1950	1950 年出口（禁止）（特定物品）（第 2 號）令
Exportation (Prohibition) (Specific Articles) Order 1951	1951 年出口（禁止）（特定物品）令
Expulsion of Undesirables Ordinance 1949, The	1949 年驅逐不良分子出境條例
F	
Factories and Industrial Undertakings Ordinance 1955	1955 年工廠及工業經營條例
Factories and Industrial Undertakings (Amendment) Ordinance 1967	1967 年工廠及工業經營（修訂）條例
Factories and Industrial Undertakings (Amendment) Regulations 1967	1967 年工廠及工業經營（修訂）規例
Factories and Workshops Ordinance 1932	1932 年工廠及工場條例
Factory (Accidents) Ordinance 1927	1927 年工廠（意外）條例
Federation of Hong Kong Industries Ordinance 1960	1960 年香港工業總會條例
Female Domestic Service Ordinance 1923	1923 年家庭女役條例
Female Domestic Service Amendment Ordinance 1929	1929 年家庭女役修訂條例
Film Censorship Ordinance 1988	1988 年電影檢查條例
Film Censorship Regulations 1953	1953 年電影審查規例
Final Act Embodying the Results of the Uruguay Round of Multilateral Trade Negotiations	烏拉圭回合多邊貿易談判結果最後文件
Fire and Marine Insurance Companies Deposit (Amendment) Ordinance 1981	1981 年火險及水險保險公司保證金（修訂）條例
Fire Brigade Ordinance 1868	1868 年消防隊條例
Fire Safety (Commercial Premises) Ordinance 1997	1997 年消防安全（商業處所）條例
Five Year Plan for Social Welfare Development in Hong Kong 1973–78, The	社會福利未來五年發展計劃
Flogging Ordinance 1897	1897 年笞刑條例
Foreign Copper Coin Ordinance 1912	1912 年外國銅幣條例
Foreign Offenders Detention Ordinance 1872	1872 年外國罪犯拘留條例
Foreign Silver and Nickel Coin Ordinance 1913	1913 年外國銀鎳幣條例
Forests and Countryside Ordinance 2007	2007 年林區及郊區條例
Forts Protection Ordinance 1891	1891 年堡壘保護條例
Fraudulent Trustees and Etc. Ordinance 1860	1860 年受託人欺詐治罪條例
Frontier Closed Area Order 1951	1951 年邊境禁區令

Further Development of Local Administration	進一步發展地方行政的建議
Further Development of Medical and Health Services in Hong Kong, The	香港醫療衛生服務的進一步發展白皮書
Further Development of Rehabilitation Services in Hong Kong, The	香港康復服務的進一步發展綠皮書
G	
Gambling Ordinance 1891	1891 年賭博條例
Gambling (Amendment) Ordinance 1956	1956 年賭博（修訂）條例
General Agreement on Tariffs and Trade	關稅與貿易總協定
General Loan and Stock Ordinance 1952	1952 年一般借款及公債條例
General Order No. 1	一般命令第一號
General Regulations under which the British Trade is to be conducted at the Five Ports of Canton, Amoy, Foochow, Ningpo, and Shanghai	中英五口通商章程
Good Order and Cleanliness Ordinance 1844	1844 年維護良好秩序及潔淨條例
Government Lotteries Ordinance 1962	1962 年政府獎券條例
Grant Code	補助則例
Grantham Scholarships Fund Ordinance 1955	1955 年葛量洪獎學基金條例
Grant-in-Aid Scheme 1873	1873 年補助學校計劃
Green Paper on Services for the Elderly	老人福利服務綠皮書
Guide to the Kindergarten Curriculum	幼稚園課程指引
Guide to the Pre-primary Curriculum	學前教育課程指引
H	
Harbour of Refuge Ordinance 1909	1909 年建築避風塘條例
Hawker (Urban Council) By-laws 1972	1972 年小販（市政局）附例
Hawker (Urban Council) (Amendment) (No. 3) Bylaw 1994	1994 年小販（市政局）（修訂）（第 3 號）附例
Help for Those Least Able to Help Themselves: A Programme of Social Security Development	社會保障發展計劃綠皮書
Heung Yee Kuk Ordinance 1959	1959 年鄉議局條例
Hill District Reservation Ordinance 1904	1904 年山頂區保留條例
Hong Kong (British Nationality) Order 1986	1986 年香港（英國國籍）令
Hong Kong (Rehabilitation) Loan Ordinance 1947	1947 年香港（復興）公債條例
Hong Kong Academy for Performing Arts Ordinance 1984	1984 年演藝學院條例
Hong Kong Academy of Medicine Ordinance 1992	1992 年香港醫學專科學院條例
Hong Kong Act 1985	1985 年香港法令
Hong Kong Airport (Control of Obstructions) Ordinance 1957	1957 年香港機場（障礙管制）條例
Hong Kong Annual Report	香港年報
Hong Kong Archaeological Survey: Subsurface Investigation Reports, The	香港考古調查：試掘報告

Hong Kong Arts Development Council Ordinance 1995	1995 年香港藝術發展局條例	Hongkong Emigration Ordinance 1867	1867 年香港出洋移民條例
Hong Kong Association of Banks Ordinance 1980, The	1980 年香港銀行公會條例	Hongkong Pier and Godown Company Ordinance 1871	1871 年香港碼頭及貨倉公司條例
Hong Kong Auxiliary Police Force Ordinance 1959	1959 年香港輔助警隊條例	Household Expenditure Survey, 1963/64 and the Consumer Price Index, The	1963 年至 1964 年家庭消費支出統計與消費物價指數
Hong Kong Bill of Rights Bill 1991	1991 年香港人權法案條例草案	Hospital Authority Ordinance 1990	1990 年醫院管理局條例
Hong Kong Charter	香港憲章	Housing Ordinance 1954	1954 年房屋條例
Hong Kong Council for Academic Accreditation Ordinance 1990	1990 年香港學術評審局條例	Housing Subsidy to Tenants of Public Housing	公屋住戶房屋資助問題綠皮書
Hong Kong Defence Scheme 1936	1936 年香港防衛計劃	Human Organ Transplant Ordinance 1995	1995 年人體器官移植條例
Hong Kong Examinations Authority Ordinance 1977	1977 年考試局條例	I	
Hong Kong Industrial Estates Corporation Ordinance 1977	1977 年香港工業邨公司條例	Illegal Strikes and Lock-outs Ordinance 1927	1927 年非法罷工及閉廠條例
Hong Kong Institute of Education Ordinance 1994, The	1994 年香港教育學院條例	Illegal Strikes and Lock-outs Ordinance 1949	1949 年非法罷工及停工條例
Hong Kong Institute of Planners Incorporation Ordinance 1991, The	1991 年香港規劃師學會法團條例	Immigrants Control Ordinance 1949	1949 年移民管制條例
Hong Kong Long Term Road Study	香港長遠道路研究	Immigrants Control (Amendment) (No. 2) Regulations 1950	1950 年移民管制（修訂）（第 2 號）規例
Hong Kong Mass Transit Further Studies: Final Report	香港集體運輸計劃總報告書	Immigration Control Ordinance 1940	1940 年入境管制條例
Hong Kong Mass Transport Study	香港集體運輸研究	Immigration Ordinance 1971	1971 年人民入境條例
Hong Kong Mass Transport Study: Supplementary Report	香港集體運輸計劃研究補充報告	Immigration (Amendment) Ordinance 1982, 1996	1982、1996 年人民入境（修訂）條例
Hong Kong Ocean Park Corporation Ordinance 1987	1987 年海洋公園公司條例	Immigration (Amendment) (No. 2) Bill 1980	1980 年人民入境（修訂）（第 2 號）條例草案
Hong Kong Outline Plan	香港發展綱略	Immigration (Amendment) (No. 2) Ordinance 1979, 1987	1979、1987 年人民入境（修訂）（第 2 號）條例
Hong Kong Planning Standards and Guidelines	香港規劃標準與準則	Immigration (Control and Offences) Ordinance 1958	1958 年入境（管制及罪行）條例
Hong Kong Police Reserve Ordinance 1914	1914 年後備警察條例	Immigration Service Ordinance 1961	1961 年入境事務隊條例
Hong Kong Police Reserve Ordinance 1927	1927 年香港後備警察條例	Import and Export (General) Regulations (Amendment of First and Second Schedules) Order 1973	1973 年進出口（普通）規例（修訂第一及第二附表）令
Hong Kong Polytechnic Ordinance 1971	1971 年香港理工學院條例	Import Control Order 1947	1947 年進口統制令
Hong Kong Preliminary Planning Report 1948	1948 年香港初步規劃報告	Importation (Prohibition) (Specific Articles) Order 1951	1951 年進口（禁止）（特定物品）令
Hong Kong Sports Development Board Ordinance 1990	1990 年香港康體發展局條例	Importation and Exportation Ordinance 1915	1915 年出入口條例
Hong Kong Sports Development Board (Amendment) Ordinance 1993	1993 年香港康體發展局（修訂）條例	Independent Commission Against Corruption Ordinance 1974	1974 年總督特派廉政專員公署條例
Hong Kong Tourism Board Ordinance 1957	1957 年香港旅遊協會條例	Independent Commission Against Corruption (Amendment) Ordinance 1976, 1992	1976、1992 年總督特派廉政專員公署（修訂）條例
Hong Kong Trade Development Council Ordinance 1966	1966 年香港貿易發展局條例	Industrial Employment of Children Ordinance 1922	1922 年兒童工業僱傭條例
Hong Kong University of Science and Technology Ordinance 1987, The	1987 年香港科技大學條例	Industrial Employment of Women Young Persons and Children Amendment Ordinance 1929	1929 年女性、青年及兒童工業僱傭修訂條例
Hong Kong War Memorial Fund Ordinance 1947	1947 年香港國殤紀念基金條例	Inland Revenue Ordinance 1947	1947 年稅務條例
Hongkong and Shanghai Bank Ordinance 1866, The	1866 年香港上海滙豐銀行條例	Inland Revenue (Amendment) Ordinance 1964, 1970, 1979, 1983	1964、1970、1979、1983 年稅務（修訂）條例
Hongkong and Shanghai Banking Corporation (Amendment) Ordinance 1978, The	1978 年香港上海滙豐銀行（修訂）條例	Inland Revenue (Amendment) (No. 3) Ordinance 1978	1978 年稅務（修訂）（第 3 號）條例
Hongkong Code of Civil Procedure Ordinance 1873	1873 年香港民事訴訟程序條例	Inland Revenue (Amendment) (No. 6) Ordinance 1975	1975 年稅務（修訂）（第 6 號）條例

Insurance Companies (Amendment) Ordinance 1981	1981 年人壽保險公司（修訂）條例
Insurance Companies Ordinance 1983	1983 年保險公司條例
Insurance Companies (Amendment) Ordinance 1989	1989 年保險公司（修訂）條例
Insurance Companies (Capital Requirements) Ordinance 1978	1978 年保險公司（規定資本額）條例
International Covenant on Civil and Political Rights	公民權利和政治權利國際公約
International Union for Conservation of Nature Red List of Threatened Species	世界自然保育聯盟瀕危物種紅色名錄
Interpretation Ordinance 1950	1950 年釋義條例
Interpretation and General Clauses (Amendment) (No.3) Ordinance 1987	1987 年法律釋義及通則（修訂）（第 3 號）條例
Intestates' Estates Ordinance 1971	1971 年無遺囑者遺產條例
J	
J. E. Joseph Trust Fund Ordinance 1954	1954 年約瑟信託基金條例
Jurors Ordinance 1845	1845 年陪審團條例
Jury Amendment Ordinance 1947	1947 年陪審團修訂條例
Justices of the Peace Ordinance 1844	1844 年太平紳士條例
Juvenile Offenders Ordinance 1932	1932 年青少年犯條例
K	
Kadoorie Agricultural Aid Loan Fund Ordinance 1955	1955 年嘉道理農業貸款條例
Kellet Island Ordinance 1898	1898 年奇力島條例
Kowloon Order-in-Council	關於九龍的樞密院頒令
L	
Labour Relations Ordinance 1975	1975 年勞資關係條例
Labour Tribunal Ordinance 1972	1972 年勞資審裁處條例
Lancashire Pact	蘭開夏協定
Land Development Corporation Ordinance 1987	1987 年土地發展公司條例
Land Registration Ordinance 1844	1844 年土地註冊條例
Landlord and Tenant Ordinance 1947	1947 年業主與租客條例
Landlord and Tenant (Consolidation) (Amendment) Ordinance 1986, 1993	1986、1993 年業主與租客（綜合）（修訂）條例
Landlord and Tenant (Consolidation) (Amendment) (No. 3) Ordinance 1975	1975 年業主與租客（綜合）（修訂）（第 3 號）條例
Lands Tribunal Ordinance 1974	1974 年土地審裁處條例
Legal Aid Ordinance 1966	1966 年法律援助條例
Legal Officers Ordinance 1950	1950 年律政人員條例
Legal Practitioners Ordinance 1871	1871 年法律執業者條例
Legislative Council (Electoral Provisions) (Amendment) Bill 1994	1994 年立法局（選舉規定）（修訂）條例草案
Legislative Council (Powers and Privileges) Ordinance 1985	1985 年立法局（權力及特權）條例
Letters Patent	英皇制誥
Licensing Public Houses & c. Ordinance 1844	1844 年酒肆牌照條例
Life Insurance Companies Ordinance 1907	1907 年人壽保險公司條例
Lighting the City of Victoria Ordinance 1856	1856 年維多利亞城照明條例

Limitation Ordinance 1965	1965 年時效條例
Liquors Amendment Ordinance 1931	1931 年酒精修訂條例
Lis Pendens and Purchasers Ordinance 1856	1856 年購買地產條例
Long-Term Housing Strategy: A Policy Statement	長遠房屋策略
Long Term Housing Strategy Review Consultative Document	長遠房屋策略評議諮詢文件
Lord Wilson Heritage Trust Ordinance 1992	1992 年衛奕信勳爵文物信託條例
M	
Man Mo Temple Ordinance 1908	1908 年文武廟條例
Management of Hong Kong Opium Affairs Statute	管理香港洋藥事宜章程
Mandatory Provident Fund Schemes Ordinance 1995	1995 年強制性公積金計劃條例
Manifesto of the Anti-Mui Tsai Society	反對蓄婢會簡章
Marine Fish Culture Ordinance 1980	1980 年海魚養殖條例
Marine Parks and Marine Reserves Regulation 1996	1996 年海岸公園及海岸保護區規例
Marine Parks Ordinance 1995	1995 年海岸公園條例
Market Ordinance 1854	1854 年市場條例
Marriage Ordinance 1875	1875 年婚姻條例
Marriage Reform Ordinance 1970	1970 年婚姻制度改革條例
Marriages Ordinance 1852	1852 年婚姻條例
Married Women's Disposition of Property Ordinance 1885	1885 年已婚婦女財產處理條例
Mass Transit Railway Corporation Ordinance 1975	1975 年地下鐵路公司條例
Matrimonial Causes Ordinance 1966	1966 年婚姻訴訟條例
Medical Clinics Ordinance 1963	1963 年診療所條例
Medical Registration Ordinance 1884	1884 年醫生註冊條例
Medical Registration (Amendment) Ordinance 1957	1957 年醫生註冊（修訂）條例
Memorandum on Kowloon Peninsula Question	九龍半島問題備忘錄
Memorandum Signed in Hongkong on the 17th April 1948 in Connection with the Replacement of Certain Boundary Stones on the Anglo-Chinese Border at Sha Tau Kok	重豎沙頭角中英界石備忘錄
Mental Health Ordinance 1960, 1962	1960、1962 年精神健康條例
Mental Health (Amendment) Ordinance 1988	1988 年精神健康（修訂）條例
Mercantile Bank Note Issue (Repeal) Ordinance 1978	1978 年有利銀行發行紙幣（撤銷）條例
Mercantile Law Amendment Ordinance 1864	1864 年商貿修訂條例
Merchandise Marks Ordinance 1863	1863 年防止假冒商標條例
Merchant Shipping Ordinance 1844	1844 年商船管制條例
Metrication Ordinance 1976	1976 年十進制條例
Metroplan	都會計劃
Military Installations Closed Areas Order 1950	1950 年軍事設施禁區令

Military Service Ordinance 1917	1917 年兵役條例
Military Stores (Prohibition of Exportation) Ordinance 1862	1862 年軍事物資（禁止出口）條例
Mining Ordinance 1954	1954 年礦務條例
Miscellaneous Licences (Amendment) Ordinance 1965	1965 年各種牌照（修訂）條例
Misdemeanors Punishment Ordinance 1898	1898 年輕罪懲罰條例
Motor Vehicles Insurance (Third Party Risks) Ordinance 1951	1951 年汽車保險（第三者風險）條例
Mr. Chadwick's Reports on the Sanitary Condition of Hong Kong; with Appendices and Plans	查維克衞生調查報告書
Multi-fiber Arrangement Regarding International Trade in Textiles	多種纖維協定
Multi-storey Buildings (Owners Incorporation) Ordinance 1970	1970 年多層建築物（業主法團）條例

N

Naturalization Ordinance	歸化條例
Neutrality Ordinance 1855	1855 年中立條例
New System Referred to in the Report of the Board of Education for 1850, The	教育革新計劃
New Territories (Extension of Laws) Ordinance 1900	1900 年新界（法律延伸）條例
New Territories (Land Court) Ordinance 1900	1900 年新界（田土法庭）條例
New Territories Leases (Extension) Ordinance 1988	1988 年新界土地契約（續期）條例
New Territories Land (Exemption) Bill 1993	1993 年新界土地（豁免）條例草案
New Territories Land (Exemption) Ordinance 1994	1994 年新界土地（豁免）條例
Night Pass	夜間通行證
Noise Control Ordinance 1988, 1989	1988、1989 年噪音管制條例
Noise Control Ordinance 1988 (Commencement) Notice 1989	1989 年 1988 年噪音管制條例（開始生效）公告
Noise Control (Amendment) Ordinance 1993	1993 年噪音管制（修訂）條例
North-east Kowloon Development Scheme	九龍東北部發展草圖計劃

O

Objectionable Publications Ordinance 1975	1975 年不良刊物條例
Occupational Safety and Health Ordinance 1988, 1997	1988、1997 年職業安全健康局條例
Offences against the Person (Amendment) Ordinance 1972, 1981	1972、1981 年侵害人身罪（修訂）條例
Official Languages Ordinance 1974	1974 年法定語文條例
Official Languages (Amendment) Ordinance 1987	1987 年法定語文（修訂）條例
Official Secret Act 1911-1989	1911 年至 1989 年官方機密法令
Official Secrets Ordinance 1997	1997 年官方機密條例
Okinawa Reversion Agreement	沖繩歸還協定

Ombudsman Ordinance 1988, The	1988 年行政事務申訴專員條例
Ombudsman (Amendment) Ordinance 1994, The	1994 年行政事務申訴專員（修訂）條例
Operation and Regulation of the Hong Kong Securities Industry, The	香港證券業的運作與監察
Opium Ordinance 1909	1909 年鴉片條例
Order and Cleanliness Ordinance 1867	1867 年維持社會秩序及潔淨條例
Order in Council	樞密院頒令
Organized and Serious Crimes Ordinance 1994	1994 年有組織及嚴重罪行條例
Ottawa Agreement 1932	1932 年渥太華協議
Overall Review of the Hong Kong Education System	香港教育制度全面檢討
Overseas Trust Bank (Acquisition) Ordinance 1985	1985 年海外信託銀行（接收）條例
Ozone Layer Protection Ordinance 1989	1989 年保護臭氧層條例

P

Patents Ordinance 1862	1862 年發明創造專利條例
Peace of the Colony Ordinance 1857	1857 年殖民地社會安寧條例
Peace Preservation Ordinance 1884	1884 年維持治安條例
Peak District (Residence) Ordinance 1918	1918 年山頂（住宅區）條例
Pension Benefits Ordinance 1987	1987 年退休金利益條例
Pensions (Amendment) Ordinance 1967	1967 年退休金（修訂）條例
Personal Data (Privacy) Ordinance 1995	1995 年個人資料（私隱）條例
Petty Sessions Court Ordinance 1849	1849 年簡易法庭條例
Piece-Goods (Control) Order 1946	1946 年疋頭統制令
Places of Public Entertainment Regulation Ordinance 1919	1919 年公眾娛樂場所規例條例
Places of Public Entertainment Regulations 1934	1934 年公眾娛樂場所規例
Police Force Ordinance 1948	1948 年警隊條例
Police Force (Amendment) (No. 2) Ordinance 1977	1977 年警隊（修訂）（第 2 號）條例
Police Force (Amendment) (No. 3) Ordinance 1977	1977 年警隊（修訂）（第 3 號）條例
Police Force Regulation Ordinance 1844	1844 年警察條例
Port and Airport Development Strategy	港口及機場發展策略
Potsdam Declaration	波茨坦公告
Praya Reclamation Ordinance 1889	1889 年海旁填海條例
Preliminary Agreement of Canton Kowloon Railway	廣九鐵路草合同
Prepared Opium Ordinance 1858	1858 年熟鴉片條例
Prevention of Bribery Ordinance 1970	1970 年防止賄賂條例
Prevention of Bribery (Miscellaneous Provisions) (No.2) Ordinance 1996	1996 年防止賄賂（雜項條文）（第 2 號）條例
Prevention of Corruption Ordinance 1948	1948 年防止貪污條例
Prevention of Piracy Ordinance 1847	1847 年防治海盜條例

Preventive Service (Amendment) Ordinance 1977	1977 年緝私隊（修訂）條例		
Preventive Service Ordinance 1963	1963 年緝私隊條例		
Price Control Order 1946	1946 年物價管制令		
Primary Education and Pre-Primary Services	小學教育及學前教育服務白皮書		
Printers and Publishers Ordinance 1886	1886 年印刷業及出版業條例		
Printing Regulation Ordinance 1844	1844 年書刊出版條例		
Prisoners (Release under Supervision) Ordinance 1987	1987 年囚犯（監管下釋放）條例		
Problem of Narcotic Drugs in Hong Kong, The	香港毒品問題白皮書		
Professional Accountants Ordinance 1972	1972 年專業會計師條例		
Protected Places Order 1950	1950 年受保護區命令		
Protection of Children and Juveniles Ordinance 1993	1993 年保護兒童及少年條例		
Protection of Investors Ordinance 1974	1974 年保障投資者條例		
Protection of the Harbour Bill	保護海港條例草案		
Protection of the Harbour Ordinance 1997	1997 年保護海港條例		
Protection of Wages on Insolvency Ordinance 1985	1985 年破產欠薪保障條例		
Protection of Women and Girls Ordinance 1889	1889 年保護婦女及女童條例		
Protection of Women and Juveniles Ordinance 1951	1951 年保護婦孺條例		
Protection of Women and Juveniles (Amendment) Ordinance 1992	1992 年保護婦孺（修訂）條例		
Protection of Women-Emigration Abuses Ordinance 1873	1873 年保護華人婦女及華人移民條例		
Provisional Airport Authority Ordinance 1990	1990 年臨時機場管理局條例		
Public Assemblages (Regulation of Traffic) Ordinance 1869	1869 年公共集會（交通管制）條例		
Public Finance (Amendment) Ordinance 1990	1990 年公共財政（修訂）條例		
Public Gaming Ordinance 1844	1844 年禁止賭博條例		
Public Health and Buildings Ordinance 1903	1903 年公共衛生及建築物條例		
Public Health and Urban Services (Amendment) (No.4) Ordinance 1972	1972 年公眾衛生及市政（修訂）（第 4 號）條例		
Public Health Ordinance 1887	1887 年公共衛生條例		
Public Order Ordinance 1948, 1967	1948、1967 年公安條例		
Public Order (Amendment) Ordinance 1980, 1986, 1989	1980、1986、1989 年公安（修訂）條例		
Public Services Commission Ordinance 1950	1950 年公務員敘用委員會條例		
Public Transport Services (Hong Kong Island) (Amendment) Ordinance 1969	1969 年公共交通服務（香港島）（修訂）條例		
Public Transport Services (Kowloon and New Territories) (Amendment) Ordinance 1969	1969 年公共交通服務（九龍及新界）（修訂）條例		
Q			
Quarantine and Prevention of Disease (Amendment) Ordinance 1993	1993 年檢疫及防疫（修訂）條例		

R	
Radiation Ordinance 1957	1957 年輻射條例
Rating Ordinance 1845	1845 年徵收差餉條例
Rating (Amendment) Ordinance 1954	1954 年差餉（修訂）條例
Regional Council (Amendment) Ordinance 1986	1986 年區域議局（修訂）條例
Registration and Census Ordinance 1846	1846 年人口登記及戶口調查條例
Registration and Census Ordinance 1857	1857 年華人登記及調查戶口條例
Registration of Inhabitants Ordinance 1844	1844 年人口登記條例
Registration of Persons Ordinance 1949, 1960	1949、1960 年人事登記條例
Registration of Vessels Ordinance 1855	1855 年船舶註冊條例
Regulation of Chinese Ordinance 1888	1888 年管理華人條例
Rehabilitation—Integrating the Disabled into the Community	康復政策白皮書：群策群力協助弱能人士更生
Rendition of Chinese Ordinance 1850	1850 年華人罪犯遞解回籍條例
Rent Increases (Domestic Premises) Control Ordinance 1963	1963 年加租（住宅樓宇）管制條例
Report by Mr. Stewart Lockhart on the Extension of the Colony of Hong Kong	駱克先生香港殖民地展拓界址報告書
Report of Education Commission 1963	1963 年教育委員會報告書
Report of the Ad Hoc Committee on the Future Scope and Operation of the Urban Council	市政局未來範圍及工作報告書
Report of the Advisory Committee on Diversification 1979	1979 年經濟多元化諮詢委員會報告書
Report of the Board of Education on the Proposed Expansion of Secondary School Education in Hong Kong over the Next Decade	教育委員會對香港未來十年內中等教育擴展計劃報告書
Report of the Housing Commission 1935	1935 年房屋委員會報告
Report of the Sub-committee on Special Education	特殊教育小組報告書
Report of the Working Party on Social Security	社會保障的若干問題報告書
Report on Government Expenditure on Education in Hong Kong	1951 年香港教育研究報告
Report on Labour and Labour Conditions in Hong Kong	香港勞工和勞工狀況報告
Report on Review of 9-Year Compulsory Education	九年強迫教育檢討報告
Report on the Development of Post-Secondary Colleges	香港專上學院發展報告書
Report on the Feasibility of a Survey into Social Welfare Provision and Allied Topics in Hong Kong	就香港社會福利發展和相關課題進行調查研究的可行性報告
Report on the New Territories, 1899-1912	新界報告 1899-1912
Report on the Reform of Local Government	市政局地方政制改革報告書

Report on the Riots in Kowloon and Tsuen Wan	九龍及荃灣暴動報告書	*Social Welfare in Hong Kong—The Way Ahead*	社會福利白皮書
Reserved Commodities Ordinance 1978	1978 年儲備商品條例	Social Workers Registration Ordinance 1997	1997 年社會工作者註冊條例
Resettlement Ordinance 1958	1958 年徙置條例	Societies Ordinance 1911, 1920, 1949	1911、1920、1949 年社團條例
Residential Care Homes (Elderly Persons) Ordinance 1994	1994 年安老院條例	Societies (Amendment) Ordinance 1964	1964 年社團（修訂）條例
Review of Policies for Squatter Control, Resettlement and Government Low-Cost Housing	管制權宜住所居民、徙置及廉租屋宇政策之檢討白皮書	Stamp Ordinance 1866	1866 年印花稅條例
Review of Prevocational and Secondary Technical Education	職業先修及工業中學教育檢討報告書	Stamp Duty (Amendment) (No. 4) Ordinance 1991	1991 年印花稅（修訂）（第 4 號）條例
Rice Ordinance 1919	1919 年食米條例	Standing Orders of the Legislative Council of Hong Kong 1968	1968 年香港立法局會議常規
Road Traffic (Amendment) Ordinance 1960, 1969	1960、1969 年道路交通（修訂）條例	Standing Rules and Orders 1858, 1873	1858、1873 年會議常規及規則
Royal Charter	皇家特許狀	Standing Rules and Orders for the Legislative Council of Hong Kong 1884	1884 年香港立法局會議常規及規則
Royal Hong Kong Auxiliary Air Force Ordinance 1970	1970 年皇家香港輔助空軍條例	Stock Exchange Control Ordinance 1973	1973 年證券交易所管制條例
Royal Hong Kong Regiment Ordinance 1970	1970 年皇家香港軍團條例	Stock Exchanges Unification Ordinance 1980	1980 年證券交易所合併條例
Royal Instructions	皇室訓令	Stone Cutters' Island Ordinance 1889	1889 年昂船洲條例
Rule of the Bar	大律師辦案規則	Summary Jurisdiction Ordinance 1845	1845 年簡易司法管轄權條例
Rules and Regulations for Government Schools	皇家書館則例	Summary Offences Amendment Ordinance 1940	1940 年簡易程序罪行修訂條例
Rules and Regulations for the Executive and Legislative Councils	行政局立法局規則及規例	Summoning of Chinese Ordinance 1899	1899 年傳召華人條例
Rules for the Society for the Protection of Women and Children 1882	1882 年保良局條例	Sung Wong T'oi Reservation Ordinance 1899	1899 年保存宋王臺條例
S		Supreme Court Ordinance 1975	1975 年高等法院條例
Sale of Land by Auction Ordinance 1886	1886 年土地拍賣條例	**T**	
Salt, Opium Licensing & c. Ordinance 1844	1844 年售鹽、鴉片牌照稅條例	*Taking the Worry Out of Growing Old— An Old Age Pension Scheme for Hong Kong*	生活有保障、晚年可安享—香港的老年退休金計劃
School Management Initiative, The	學校管理新措施	Tate's Cairn Tunnel Ordinance 1988	1988 年大老山隧道條例
Secondary Education in Hong Kong over the Next Decade	香港未來十年內之中等教育白皮書	Telecommunication (Amendment) Ordinance 1996	1996 年電訊（修訂）條例
Securities Ordinance 1974	1974 年證券條例	Telephone Ordinance 1925	1925 年電話服務條例
Securities (Insider Dealing) Ordinance 1990	1990 年證券（內幕交易）條例	Television Ordinance 1964	1964 年電視條例
Securities (Stock Exchange Listing) Rules 1986	1986 年證券（證券交易所上市）規則	Television (Amendment) Ordinance 1973	1973 年電視（修訂）條例
Securities and Futures Commission Ordinance 1989	1989 年證券及期貨事務監察委員會條例	Television (Programmes) (Amendment) Regulations 1995	1995 年電視（節目）（修訂）規例
Seditious Publications Ordinance 1907	1907 年煽動性刊物條例	Tenancy (Prolonged Duration) Ordinance 1952	1952 年租約（延長期限）條例
Senior Secondary and Tertiary Education: A Development Programme for Hong Kong over the Next Decade	高中及專上教育綠皮書	*Territorial Development Strategy*	全港發展策略
Sex Discrimination Ordinance 1995	1995 年性別歧視條例	Theft Ordinance 1970	1970 年盜竊罪條例
Sir David Trench Trust Fund for Recreation Ordinance 1970	1970 年戴麟趾爵士康樂基金條例	To Her Britannic Majesty's Subjects	給女王陛下臣民的通知
Situation in the Far East in Event of Japanese Intervention against Us, The	1940 年遠東形勢研判	Tobacco Ordinance 1916	1916 年煙草條例
Slavery Ordinance 1844	1844 年奴隸條例	Town Planning Ordinance 1939	1939 年城市規劃條例
		Town Planning (Amendment) Ordinance 1991	1991 年城市規劃（修訂）條例
Smoking (Public Health) Ordinance 1982	1982 年吸煙（公眾衛生）條例	Toys and Children's Products Safety Ordinance 1992	1992 年玩具及兒童產品安全條例

Trade Unions and Trade Disputes Ordinance 1948	1948 年職工會及勞資糾紛條例	Vocational Training Council Ordinance 1982	1982 年職業訓練局條例
Trading with the Enemy Ordinance 1914	1914 年與敵貿易條例	Volunteers Ordinance 1862	1862 年義勇軍條例
Traffic Accident Victims (Assistance Fund) Ordinance 1978	1978 年交通意外傷亡者（援助基金）條例	**W**	
Tramways Ordinance 1882	1882 年電車條例	War Loan Ordinance 1916	1916 年戰爭債券條例
Travel Agents Ordinance 1985	1985 年旅行代理商條例	Washington Naval Treaty 1922	1922 年華盛頓公約
Travel Agents (Amendment) Ordinance 1993	1993 年旅行代理商（修訂）條例	Waste Disposal Ordinance 1980	1980 年廢物處置條例
Treaty of Nanking	南京條約	Waste Disposal (Amendment) Bill 1987	1987 年廢物處理（修訂）條例草案
Treaty of Peace with Japan	對日和平條約	Waste Disposal (Amendment) Ordinance 1987	1987 年廢物處理（修訂）條例
Treaty of Tientsin	天津條約	*Waste Disposal Plan for Hong Kong*	香港廢物處理計劃
Triad and Secret Societies Ordinance 1845	1845 年三合會及秘密社團條例	Water Pollution Control Ordinance 1980	1980 年水污染管制條例
Tsuen Wan and District Outline Development Plan	荃灣地區發展大綱草圖	Water-works Ordinance 1903	1903 年水務條例
U		Weights and Measures Ordinance 1885, 1987	1885、1987 年度量衡條例
U.S. Policy on Hong Kong	美國對香港政策	*White Paper on Chinese Marriage in Hong Kong*	香港華人婚姻問題白皮書
Uniform Ordinance 1895	1895 年制服條例	*White Paper on Defence 1966*	1966 年國防白皮書
United States–Hong Kong Policy Act of 1992	1992 年美國一香港政策法	*White Paper on District Administration in Hong Kong*	地方行政白皮書
University Ordinance 1911	1911 年大學條例	*White Paper: Social Welfare into the 1990's and beyond*	跨越九十年代香港社會福利白皮書
Urban Council Ordinance 1935	1935 年市政局條例	Wholesale (Kowloon) Marketing (Vegetables) Order 1946, The	1946 年批發（九龍）市場（蔬菜）令
Urban Council (Amendment) Ordinance 1956, 1965, 1966	1956、1965、1966 年市政局（修訂）條例	Wild Animals Protection Ordinance 1976	1976 年野生動物保護條例
Urban Council (Amendment) (No. 2) Ordinance 1953	1953 年市政局（修訂）（第 2 號）條例	Wills Act Amendment Ordinance 1886	1886 年遺囑法令修訂條例
Urban Council (Commissioner for Resettlement) Ordinance 1954	1954 年市政局（徙置事務處處長）條例	Wills Ordinance 1970	1970 年遺囑條例
V		Wireless Telegraphy Ordinance 1903	1903 年無線電報條例
Vaccination Ordinance 1888	1888 年接種疫苗條例	Wireless Telegraphy Ordinance 1926	1926 年無線電條例
Vehicle and Road Traffic (Amendment) (No. 2) Regulations 1950	1950 年汽車道路交通（修訂）（第 2 號）規例	Workmen's Compensation Ordinance 1953	1953 年工傷賠償條例
Venereal Disease Ordinance 1952	1952 年性病條例	*World Competitiveness Yearbook*	世界競爭力年報
Venereal Diseases Ordinance 1857	1857 年防止性病擴散條例		

A

A Contribution to the Prehistory of Hong Kong and the New Territories	《香港及新界史前史論稿》
A. S. Watson Co., Limited	屈臣氏大藥房
Abdoolally Ebrahim & Co.	衣巴剌謙洋行
Academy Awards (Oscars)	奧斯卡金像獎
Academy of Motion Picture Arts and Sciences	美國電影藝術與科學學院
Accident Insurance Association	香港意外保險公會
Aden	「伊敦輪號」
Agra & United Service Bank Limited	呵加剌匯理銀行
AIA	友邦保險
Air Force One	「空軍一號」
Air Raid Distress Fund	空襲救災基金
Albert	「亞爾勃號」
Alice Memorial Hospital	雅麗氏利濟醫院（雅麗氏紀念醫院）
Alice Memorial Maternity Hospital	雅麗氏紀念產科醫院
Alliance Bible Seminary	建道神學院
Alliance Française de Hong Kong	法國文化協會香港分會
American Board of Commissioners for Foreign Missions	美國公理會差會
American Club Hong Kong, The	美國會
American Express	美國運通銀行
American International Group	美國國際集團
American Presbyterians (North)	美北長老會
Amma International Limited	安美國際有限公司
Anglican Church	聖公會
Anti-Mui Tsai Society	反對蓄婢會
Apollo Telephone Answering Services Limited	太空電話通訊有限公司
Apostolic Vicariate	宗座代牧區
Apple Inc.	蘋果公司
Arnhold Karberg & Co.	瑞記洋行
Arrow	「亞羅號」
Asian Development Bank	亞洲開發銀行
Asian Games	亞洲運動會
Asian Infrastructure Investment Bank	亞洲基礎設施投資銀行
Asian Film Festival	亞洲影展
Asiatic Petroleum Company	亞細亞火油公司
Asile de la Sainte Enfance	聖童之家
Atlantic	「大西洋號」
Augustine Heard & Co.	瓊記洋行
AXA China Region Insurance Company Limited	AXA 國衛保險有限公司
AXA Hong Kong and Macau	安盛集團

B

Banca Commerciale Italiana	意大利商業銀行
Bank for International Settlements	國際清算銀行
Bank of America	美國銀行

Bank of Credit and Commerce International	國際商業信貸銀行
Bank of Hindustan, China and Japan Limited, The	慳度士丹中國日本匯理銀行
Bank of Korea	韓國銀行
Bank of Montreal	滿地可銀行
Bank of Tokyo, Limited, The	東京銀行
Banker Trust Company	美國信孚銀行
Banque de l'Indochine	東方匯理銀行
Banque De Paris et Des Pays-Bas	法國巴黎銀行
Banque Nationale pour le Commerce et l'Industrie	法國國家工商銀行
Baptist Convention of Hong Kong	香港基督教浸信會聯會
Barclays Bank International	巴克萊國際銀行有限公司
Barmen Mission	德國巴冕差會
Barretto & Co.	巴利圖洋行
Basel Charity school	巴色義學
Basel Mission	巴色差會
Beatles, The	披頭四樂隊
Belilios Public School	庇理羅士女子中學
Blue Ridge (LCC-19)	「藍嶺號」
Bokhara	「布哈拉號」
Boyd & Co.	和記洋行
Boys' & Girls' Clubs Association of Hong Kong, The	香港小童群益會
Britannia	「不列顛尼亞號」
British American Tobacco Company	英美煙草公司
British Council	英國文化協會
British East India Company	英國東印度公司
British Empire Games	英帝國運動會
British Overseas Airways Corporation, The	英國海外航空
Brothers of the Christian Schools	基督學校修士會
Bumiptura Malaysia Finance Limited	馬來西亞裕民銀行
Butterfield & Swire	太古洋行

C

C. P. Pokphand Company Limited	卜蜂國際有限公司
Calabi's Conjecture	卡拉比猜想
Calcutta	「加爾各答號」
California Fitness Centre	加州健身中心
Canadian Imperial Bank of Commerce	加拿大帝國商業銀行
Canadian Pacific Airlines	加拿大太平洋航空公司
Canadian Pacific Railway Co. & Steamship Co.	昌興輪船公司
Canossa Hospital (Caritas)	嘉諾撒醫院
Canossian Daughters of Charity	嘉諾撒仁愛女修會
Care U.S.A.	美國經濟援助協會
Caritas Internationalis	國際明愛
Caritas Medical Centre	明愛醫院

Caritas-Hong Kong	香港明愛
Carlowitz & Co.	禮和洋行
Castle Peak Hospital	青山醫院
Cathay Pacific Airways	國泰航空公司
Catholic Centre	公教進行社
Central School for Girls	中央女子書院
Ceylon	「錫蘭號」
Chartered Bank of India, Australia & China	印度新金山中國匯理銀行
Chartered Mercantile Bank of India, London and China	印度倫頓中國三處匯理銀行
Chase Bank	美國大通銀行
Chicago Mercantile Exchange	芝加哥商業交易所
China and Japan Telephone and Electric Company	中日電話電力公司
China Daily (Hong Kong Edition)	《中國日報》
China Light & Power Company Syndicate	中華電力有限公司
China Mail, The	《德臣西報》(《中國郵報》、《德臣報》)
Chinese Amateur Athletic Federation of Hong Kong, The	香港華人體育協進會
Chinese Banks' Association, The	香港華商銀行同業公會
Chinese Classics, The	《中國經典》
Chinese Lunatic Asylum	華人精神病院
Chinese Muslim Cultural and Fraternal Association, The	中華回教博愛社
Chinese Repository, The	《中國叢報》(《澳門月報》)
Chinese Writers, The	《中國作家》
Chinese YMCA of Hong Kong	香港中華基督教青年會
Ching Cheung	「禎祥號」
Christie's	佳士得拍賣行
Church Missionary Society	英國海外傳道會
Church World Service	基督教世界服務委員會
Citibank (Hong Kong) Limited	花旗銀行(香港)有限公司
Civil Air Transport Inc.	民航空運公司
Clara Maersk	「嘉娜馬士基號」
Clean	《錯的多美麗》
Club de Recreio	西洋波會
Club Germanta	德國會
Club Lusitano	西洋會所
Colorado	「科羅拉多號」
Commercial Bank Corporation of India & the East	印度東方商業銀行
Commerzbank	德國商業銀行
Commonwealth Games	英聯邦運動會
Communication Services Limited	香港流動通訊有限公司
Communist Party of Vietnam, The	越南共產黨
Compagnie des Messageries Maritimes	法國郵船公司
Cornwallis	「康華麗號」

Costa Crociere S.p.A.	歌詩達郵輪公司
Crédit Lyonnais	里昂信貸銀行

D	
Dairy Farm Co.	牛奶有限公司
Daiwa Securities International (HK)	大和證券國際(香港)
DBS Bank Limited	星展銀行
Deacons	的近律師行
Dent & Co.	寶順洋行(顛地洋行)
Deutsch-Asiatische Bank	德華銀行
Development Bank of Singapore	新加坡發展銀行
Devonshire	「地雲夏號」
Diocesan Boys' School	拔萃男書院
Diocesan Girls' School	拔萃女書院
Diocesan Home and Orphanage	曰字樓孤子院
Diocesan Native Female Training School	曰字樓女館
Dodwell, Carlill & Co.	天祥洋行
Dominican Order	道明會
Dorado	「多拉多號」
Douglas Lapraik & Co.	德忌利士洋行
Douglas Steamship Company	德忌利士輪船公司
Duke of Edinburgh Award	英國愛丁堡公爵獎勵計劃

E	
Eastern Extension Telegraph Company, The	大東電報公司
Electric Traction Company of Hongkong Limited	香港電力牽引有限公司
Electronic Payment Services Company (Hong Kong) Limited	迅通電子服務(香港)有限公司
Ellis Kadoorie School For Boys	育才書社
Emigrant	「伊米格蘭特號」
Employers' Federation of Hong Kong	香港僱主聯合會
English Schools Foundation	英基學校協會
European Economic Community	歐洲經濟共同體
European Union	歐洲聯盟

F	
Fairlea Girls' School	飛利女學校
Fame	「名譽號」
Family Planning Association of Hong Kong, The	家庭計劃指導會
Far East Exchange Limited	遠東交易所有限公司
Far Eastern Championship Games	遠東運動會
Far Eastern Economic Review	《遠東經濟評論》
Federation of Hong Kong Garment Manufacturers, The	香港製衣業總商會
Federation of Hong Kong Industries	香港工業總會
Federation of Motion Film Producers of Hong Kong	香港電影製片家協會
Festival de Cannes	康城影展
Festival Internacional de Cinema do Porto	葡萄牙波圖國際電影節

Festival International du Film d'Animation d'Annecy	安錫國際動畫電影節
Fields Medal	菲爾茲數學獎
First Hong Kong Troop, The	香港第一旅
Freeman Fox, Wilbur Smith and Associates	費爾文霍士及施偉拔顧問工程公司
Friend of China and Hong Kong Gazette, The	《中國之友與香港憲報》
Friend of China, The	《中國之友》(《華友西報》)

G

Galley of Lorne	「加利洛恩號」
Gibb, Livingston & Company	仁記洋行
Gilman & Co.	太平洋行
Goverment Lunatic Asylum	歐人精神病院
Government Central School	中央書院
Government Normal School, The	官立師範學堂
Government School	皇家書館
Government Trade School	官立高級工業學校
Government Training College	香港師資學院
Government Vernacular Middle School, The	官立漢文中學
Grant Schools Council	香港補助學校議會
Grantham Hospital	葛量洪醫院
Grantham Training College	葛量洪師範專科學校
Great Northern Telegraph Co. Limited	大北電報公司
Green Island Cement Company Limited	青洲英坭公司

H

Hague Conference on Private International Law	海牙國際私法會議
Heep Yunn School	協恩中學
Herald	「先驅號」
Hermes	「赫姆斯號」
Hildesheimer Blindenmission	信義宗喜迪堪會
Home for the Visually Impaired	心光盲人院
Hong Kong Aircraft Engineering Company Limited	香港飛機工程公司
Hong Kong Airways Limited	香港航空公司
Hong Kong and Canton Steam Packet Company, The	香港廣州郵船公司
Hong Kong and China Gas Company Limited, The	香港中華煤氣有限公司
Hong Kong and Kowloon Wharf and Godown Company Limited	香港九龍碼頭及貨倉有限公司
Hong Kong Anti-Cancer Society	香港防癌會
Hong Kong Anti-Tuberculosis Association	香港防癆會
Hong Kong Archaeological Society	香港考古學會
Hong Kong Art Club, The	香港美術會
Hong Kong Association for the Mentally Handicapped Children & Young Persons, The	香港低能兒童教育協進會
Hong Kong Association of Banks, The	香港銀行公會
Hong Kong Association of the Heads of Secondary Schools	香港中學校長會

Hong Kong Association of Travel Agents	香港旅行社協會
Hong Kong Automobile Association	香港汽車會
Hong Kong Badminton Association	香港羽毛球總會
Hong Kong Ballet Group, The	香港芭蕾舞學會
Hong Kong Baptist College	香港浸會書院
Hong Kong Baptist Hospital	浸會醫院
Hong Kong Bar Association	香港大律師公會
Hong Kong Bottlers Federal Inc.	香港汽水廠
Hong Kong Botanical Garden	香港植物公園
Hong Kong Branch of the Girl Guide Association	英國女童軍總會香港分會
Hong Kong Branch of the Society for the Prevention of Cruelty to Animals	防止虐待動物協會香港分會
Hong Kong Brewers and Distillers Limited	香港啤酒廠公司
Hong Kong Catholic Register, The	《香港天主教紀錄報》
Hong Kong Chinese Christian Churches Union, The	香港華人基督教聯會
Hong Kong Chinese Civil Servants' Association	香港政府華員會
Hong Kong Chinese Islamic Federation	香港中國回教協會
Hong Kong Chinese Medical Association, The	香港中華醫學會
Hong Kong Chinese Reform Association	香港華人革新協會
Hong Kong Chinese Women's Club	香港中國婦女會
Hong Kong Christian Council	香港基督教協進會
Hong Kong Christian Service	香港基督教服務處
Hong Kong Church World Service, The	香港基督教世界服務委員會
Hong Kong City Hall	香港大會堂
Hong Kong Civic Association	香港公民協會
Hong Kong College of Medicine	香港西醫書院
Hong Kong College of Medicine for Chinese, The	香港華人西醫書院
Hong Kong Committee for United Nations Children's Fund	聯合國兒童基金會香港委員會
Hong Kong Construction Association	香港建造商會
Hong Kong Corinthian Sailing Club	香港科林斯式航海會
Hong Kong Country Club	香港鄉村俱樂部
Hong Kong Cricket Club	香港木球會
Hong Kong Daily Press	《孖剌西報》(《每日雜報》、《剌報》、《孖剌沙西報》)
Hong Kong Daimaru Department Store	香港大丸百貨有限公司
Hong Kong Democratic Self-Government Party	香港民主自治黨
Hong Kong Dental Association	香港牙醫學會
Hong Kong Dispensary	香港藥房
Hong Kong Electric Company Limited	香港電燈有限公司
Hong Kong Eugenics League	香港優生學會
Hong Kong Exchange Banks' Association	香港外匯銀行公會
Hong Kong Federation of Students	香港專上學生聯會
Hong Kong Football Association	香港足球總會
Hong Kong Football Club	香港足球會

Hong Kong General Chamber of Commerce, The	香港總商會	*Hong Moh*	「香木號」
Hong Kong Girl Guides Association, The	香港女童軍總會	Hongkong and China Tramways Company Limited, The	香港中華電車有限公司
Hong Kong Golf Club	香港哥爾夫球會	Hongkong and Shanghai Banking Corporation, The	香港上海滙豐銀行
Hong Kong Government Gazette	《香港憲報》(《香港公報》、《香港轅門報》)	Hongkong and Whampoa Dock Company Limited	香港黃埔船塢公司
Hong Kong Hockey Association, The	香港曲棍球總會	Hongkong Canton & Macao Steamboat Company	省港澳輪船公司
Hong Kong Housing Authority	香港房屋委員會 / 香港屋宇建設委員會	Hongkong Fire Insurance Company	香港火燭保險公司
Hong Kong Institute of Architects, The	香港建築師學會	Hongkong Ice Company Limited	香港製冰公司
Hong Kong Institute of Chartered Secretaries, The	香港特許秘書公會	Hongkong International Terminals Limited	香港國際貨櫃碼頭有限公司
Hong Kong Internet and Gateway Services Limited	網聯國際有限公司	Hongkong Land Investment and Agency Company Limited	香港置地及代理有限公司
Hong Kong Jockey Club, The	香港賽馬會	*Hongkong Tiger Standard*, *Hong Kong iMail* (2000), *The Standard* (2002)	《虎報》(《英文虎報》)
Hong Kong Juvenile Care Centre	香港兒童安置所	Hongkong Tramway Electric Company Limited	香港電車電力有限公司
Hong Kong Lawn Tennis Association	香港草地網球協會		
Hong Kong Life Saving Society, The	香港拯溺總會	Hongkong Working Committee for Equal Pay, The	同工同酬委員會
Hong Kong Model Housing Society	香港模範屋宇會	HSBC Holdings plc	滙豐控股
Hong Kong Nudist Society	香港裸體運動會	*Huey Fong*	「匯豐號」
Hong Kong Philharmonic Orchestra	香港管弦樂團	Hutchison Whampoa Limited	和記黃埔有限公司
Hong Kong Playground Association	兒童遊樂場協會	*Hygeia*	「海之家」
Hong Kong Polytechnic University, The	香港理工大學	**I**	
Hong Kong Radio Society	香港廣播會 / 無線電協會	*Ianthe*	「伊安德號」
Hong Kong Red Cross	香港紅十字會	Imperial Airways	帝國航空公司
Hong Kong Red Swastika Society	香港紅卍字會	Imperial Brewing Company	帝國啤酒公司
Hong Kong Repertory Theatre	香港話劇團	Incorporated Trustees of the Islamic Community Fund of Hong Kong, The	香港回教信託基金總會
Hong Kong School for the Deaf	真鐸啟喑學校		
Hong Kong Settlers Housing Corporation	香港平民屋宇公司	Indian Recreation Club	印度遊樂會
Hong Kong Social Welfare Council	香港福利議會	Institute of Chartered Secretaries and Administrators	英國特許秘書公會
Hong Kong Society for Rehabilitation, The	香港復康會	Intel Corporation	英特爾公司
Hong Kong Society for the Protection of Children	香港保護兒童會	International Assurance Company, Limited	四海保險公司
Hong Kong Society of Architects, The	香港建築師公會	International Bank for Reconstruction and Development	國際復興開發銀行
Hong Kong St. John Ambulance	香港聖約翰救傷會		
Hong Kong St. John Ambulance Brigade	聖約翰救傷隊	International Criminal Police Organization	國際刑警組織
Hong Kong Stock Exchange	香港證券交易所	International Maritime Organization	國際海事組織
Hong Kong Sunbathing Society	香港日光浴會	International Monetary Fund	國際貨幣基金組織
Hong Kong Table Tennis Association	香港乒乓總會	International Organization for Standardization	國際標準化組織
Hong Kong Technical College	香港工業專門學院	International Women's League	國際婦女會
Hong Kong Technical Institute	官立技術專科學校	Internationale Filmfestspiele Berlin	柏林國際電影節
Hong Kong Telegraph, The	《士蔑西報》(《士蔑報》、《香港電訊報》、《士蔑新聞》、《士喪西報》)	Istituto per le Missioni Estere di Milano	米蘭外方傳教會
		J	
Hong Kong Telephone Company Limited	香港電話有限公司	Jamieson, How & Co.	占美臣洋行
Hong Kong Tramways Company Limited	香港電車有限公司	Jardine Aircraft Maintenance Company Limited	怡和飛機修理檢驗公司
Hong Kong True Light College	真光書院	Jardine, Matheson & Co.	怡和洋行
Hong Kong Tuberculosis, Chest and Heart Diseases Association	香港防癆心臟及胸病協會	Java-China-Japan Lijn	渣華中國日本荷蘭輪船公司
		Jebsen & Co.	捷成洋行
Hong Kong Young Women's Christian Association	中華基督教女青年會香港分會	JF Special Holdings Limited	怡富特別投資有限公司

John Calvin	「加爾文號」
Junior Chamber International	國際青年商會
Junior Technical School	初級工業學堂

K

Kadoorie Agricultural Aid Association	嘉道理農業輔助會
Kashmir Princess	「克什米爾公主號」
Kentucky Fried Chicken	肯德基家鄉雞
King George V School	英皇佐治五世學校
King's College	官立英皇書院
Kitchee Sports Club	傑志體育會
Koninklijke Java-China-Paketvaart Lijnen	渣華輪船公司
Kowloon Bowling Green Club	九龍草地滾球會
Kowloon British School	九龍英童學校
Kowloon Chamber of Commerce	九龍總商會
Kowloon Cricket Club	九龍木球會會所
Kowloon Ferry Company, The	九龍渡海小輪公司
Kowloon Hospital	九龍醫院
Kowloon Motor Bus Company Limited	九龍汽車有限公司
Kowloon Residents' Association	九龍居民協會

L

La Galissonnière	「拉加利桑尼亞爾號」
La Salle College	喇沙書院
Lady Maurine	「慕蓮夫人號」
Lady Mentague	「蒙塔古夫人號」
Lane Crawford	連卡佛公司
Law Society of Hong Kong, The	香港律師會
Lehman Brothers Holdings Inc.	雷曼兄弟控股公司
Leigh & Orange	利安顧問有限公司
Lions Club	獅子會
Lions Clubs International	國際獅子總會
Locarno Film Festival	瑞士洛迦諾電影節
London Metal Exchange	倫敦金屬交易所
Lutheran World Federation Department of World Service	世界信義宗香港社會服務處

M

M. Uritsky	「M 烏列斯基號」
Mannesmann	曼內斯曼
Manufacturers Life Insurance Company, The	宏利保險公司
Margaret Trench Medical Rehabilitation Centre	戴麟趾夫人復康院
Mariner of the Seas	「海洋水手號」
Marks & Spencer	馬莎百貨公司
Maryknoll Fathers' School	瑪利諾神父教會學校
McDonald's Restaurants (Hong Kong) Limited	麥當勞餐廳（香港）有限公司
McGregor & Company	麥奇利哥公司
McKinsey & Company	麥健時顧問公司
Medical Missionary Society	醫藥傳道會
Melchers & Co.	美最時洋行
Mercantile Bank Limited	有利銀行

Methodist Church	循道會
Microsoft Corporation	微軟股份有限公司
Miss Macao	「澳門小姐號」
Missions Etranges de Paris	法國巴黎外方傳教會
Modern Terminals Limited	現代貨箱有限公司
Mostra Internazionale d'Arte Cinematografica	威尼斯國際電影節

N

Naorojee & Co.	打笠治洋行
Nasdaq Stock Market, The	納斯達克證券市場
National City Bank of New York, The	萬國寶通銀行
National Mutual	澳洲國衞集團
Natural Foot Society	天足會
Nederlandsche Handel-Maatschappij	荷蘭小公銀行
Nethersole Clinic	那打素診所
Nethersole Hospital	那打素醫院
New Method College	新法書院
New Method English Tutorial School	新法英文專修書院
News Corp.	新聞出版有限公司
Newspaper Society of Hong Kong, The	香港報業公會
Northcote Training College	羅富國師範專科學校

O

Ohel Leah Synagogue	猶太教莉亞堂
Olympic Games	奧林匹克運動會
Organization for Economic Co-operation and Development	經濟合作及發展組織
Organization for Economic Cooperation and Development Trade Committee	經濟合作及發展組織貿易委員會
Oriental Bank, The	東藩匯理銀行
Oriental Brewery Limited	大東甑麥酒有限公司（東方啤酒）
Oriental Telephone and Electric Company	東方電話電力公司
Oversea-Chinese Banking Corporation Limited	華僑銀行

P

Pacific Air Maintenance and Supply Company Limited	太平洋航空維修供應公司
Pacific Mail Steamship Company	太平洋郵輪公司
Pacific Overseas Airlines	太平洋海外航空
Palmer & Turner	公和洋行（巴馬丹拿建築公司）
Pan American Airways	泛美航空公司
Pan American World Airways	泛美世界航空
Pathological Institute	香港病理學院
Peninsular and Oriental Steam Navigation Company	英國鐵行輪船公司
Pharmaceutical Society of Hong Kong, The	香港藥學會
Philippine Airlines	菲律賓航空
Philippine Clipper	「菲律賓飛剪號」
Pontificio Istituto Missioni Estere	宗座外方傳教會
Premier Congres des Prehistoriens d'Extreme-Orient	遠東史前學會

Privateer	「比里華沙號」	Sir Ellis Kadoorie Secondary School	官立嘉道理爵士中學
Q		Sir Robert Black Training College	柏立基師範專科學校（第三師範專科學院）
Quantum of the Seas	「海洋量子號」	Siri Guru Singh Sabha	星尊者協會
Queen Elizabeth	「伊利莎伯皇后號」	Sisters Announcers of the Lord	顯主女修會
Queen Elizabeth Hospital	伊利沙伯醫院	Sisters of St. Paul de Chartres	法國沙爾德聖保祿女修會
Queen Elizabeth II Youth Centre	伊利沙伯女王二世青年遊樂場館	Sisters of the Precious Blood	中華耶穌寶血女修會
Queen Elizabeth School	伊利沙伯中學	*Skyluck*	「天運號」
Queen Mary Hospital	瑪麗醫院	Societe Generale	法國興業銀行
Queen's College	皇仁書院	Society for the Aid and Rehabilitation of Drug Abusers, The	香港戒毒會
R		Society for the Protection of Chinese Servant Girls, The	防範虐婢會
Rainier International Bank	美國國際商業銀行	SOGO Hong Kong Company Limited	香港崇光百貨公司
Real Estate Developers Association of Hong Kong, The	香港地產建設商會	South China Athletic Association	南華體育會
Reform Club of Hong Kong	香港革新會	*South China Morning Post*	《南清早報》（後稱《南華早報》）
Rhenish Mission Society	德國禮賢會	South China Recreation Club	南華遊樂會
Rosary Church	玫瑰堂	Woman's Missionary Union, Southern Baptist Convention	美國南方浸信會女傳道會聯會
Rotary Club of Hong Kong, The	香港扶輪社	St. Anthony's Church	聖安多尼堂
Royal Hong Kong Yacht Club	皇家香港遊艇會	St. John's Cathedral	聖約翰大教堂
Royal Insurance Company Limited	英國皇家保險	St. Joseph's Church	聖若瑟堂
Rural Training College, The	官立鄉村師範專科學校	St. Joseph's College	聖若瑟書院
Russell & Co.	旗昌洋行	St. Louis Industrial School	聖類斯工藝學院
Ruttonjee Sanatorium	律敦治療養院	St. Louis School	聖類斯中學
Ruys	「羅斯號」	St. Paul's Church	聖保羅堂
S		St. Paul's Co-educational College	聖保羅男女子中學
Sacred Heart Canossian College	嘉諾撒聖心書院	St. Paul's College	聖保羅書院
Sacred Heart Church	聖心堂	St. Paul's Girls'College	聖保羅女書院
Salesians of Don Bosco	鮑思高慈幼會	St. Paul's Hospital	聖保祿醫院
Salomon Brothers International	美國所羅門兄弟投資銀行	St. Peter's Church	聖彼得教堂
Salvation Army, The	香港救世軍	St. Saviour's College	聖救世主書院
Samaritans, The	撒瑪利亞會	St. Stephen's Church	聖士提反堂
San Miguel Brewery Hong Kong Limited	生力啤酒公司	St. Stephen's College	聖士提反書院
Save the Children Fund	救助兒童基金會	St. Teresa's Church	聖德肋撒堂
School of General Nursing	伊利沙伯醫院普通科護士訓練學校	Standard Chartered Bank (Hong Kong) Limited	渣打銀行
Schroders & Chartered Limited	寶源投資	Standard Oil Company	標準石油
Schroders Limited	施羅德投資有限公司	Star Ferry Company, The	天星小輪公司
Scout Association of Hong Kong	香港童子軍總會	Starbucks Corporation	星巴克股份有限公司
Scout Association, The	英國童軍總會	State Bank of India	印度國家銀行
Seawise University	「海上學府」	Stockbrokers' Association of Hong Kong	香港股票經紀協會
Sentry Insurance Company Limited	美國先衛保險有限公司	*Sulphur*	「琉璜號」
Seventh-day Adventist Church	基督復臨安息日會	*Sungkiang*	「松江號」
Shanghai Tug & Lighter Co.	上海拖駁船有限公司	Sze Hai Tong Banking and Insurance Company Limited	四海通銀行保險有限公司
Shell	蜆殼石油公司	**T**	
Shewan, Tomes & Co.	新旗昌洋行	Taikoo Dockyard and Engineering Company of Hong Kong	太古船塢公司
Siam Air Transport	暹羅航空	Taikoo Royal Insurance Company Limited	太古皇家保險
Siemssen & Co.	禪臣洋行	*Takshing*	「德成號」
Sino British Club	中英學會		
Sino-British Orchestra	中英管弦樂團		
Sir Alexander	「葛量洪爵士號」		

Tang Shiu Kin Victoria Government Secondary School	鄧肇堅維多利亞官立中學	Vernacular Normal School for Women, The	官立漢文女子師範學堂
Thai Airways International	泰國國際航空公司	Victoria British School	維多利亞英童學校
Theo H. Davies & Co., Limited	戴維斯公司	Victoria Cinematograph	維多利亞影院
Thomas Cook & Son	英國通濟隆旅遊公司	Victoria Home and Orphanage	維多利亞女校
Thomas P	「湯馬斯 P 號」	Victoria Mental Hospital	域多利精神病院
Thracian	「色雷斯人號」	Victoria Park	維多利亞公園
Tokyo Bay	「東京灣號」	Victoria Recreation Club	域多利遊樂會
Travelers Life Insurance Company (Overseas) Limited	泰富壽險公司	Victoria Regatta Club	域多利賽艇會
True Light Middle School of Hong Kong	香港真光中學	*Visions of Hung-Siu-Tshuen, and Origin of the Kwang-Si Insurrection, The*	《洪秀全之異夢及廣西亂事之始末》（《太平天國起義記》）
Tudor Ice Company	丟杜公司		
Turner & Co.	香港端納洋行	**W**	
U		Walt Disney Company, The	華特迪士尼公司
Union Bank of Hong Kong	友聯銀行	Wang Laboratories	王安電腦公司
Union Chapel	愉寧堂	*War Drummer*	「戰鼓號」
Union Church	佑寧堂	Wardley Limited	獲多利有限公司
Union Dock Company	於仁船塢公司	Warner Brothers Entertainment, Inc.	華納兄弟娛樂公司
Union Insurance Society of Canton Limited	於仁燕梳公司	Welfare League	同仁會
United Nations	聯合國	Wellington College	威靈頓英文書院
United Nations Association	聯合國協會	Wesleyan Church	惠師禮會
United Nations Association of Hong Kong	聯合國香港協會	West Point Reformatory	西環養正院
United Nations Children's Fund	聯合國兒童基金會	Wheelock and Company Limited	會德豐有限公司
United Nations Economic Commission for Asia and the Far East	聯合國亞洲和遠東經濟委員會	Wheelock Marden Co.	會德豐洋行
United Nations Educational, Scientific and Cultural Organization	聯合國教科文組織	Wonderful World of Whimsy, The	歡樂天地有限公司
United Nations High Commissioner for Refugees	聯合國難民署	World Bank	世界銀行
		World Customs Organization	世界海關組織
United Nations International Children's Emergency Fund	聯合國國際兒童緊急救援基金	World Health Organization	世界衛生組織
		World Meteorological Organization	世界氣象組織
United Nations Relief and Rehabilitation Administration	聯合國善後救濟總署	World Table Tennis Championships	世界乒乓球錦標賽
United Services Recreation Club	三軍體育會所	World Trade Organization	世界貿易組織
Universal Postal Union	萬國郵政聯盟	**Y**	
Universe Campus	「宇宙學府」	Yaohan Department Store (H.K.) Limited	八佰伴（香港）百貨有限公司
University of Hong Kong, The	香港大學	*Yellow Dragon, The*	《黃龍報》
V		*Ying King*	「英京輪」
Vernacular Normal School for Men, The	官立漢文男子師範學堂	YMCA Canada	加拿大青年會
		Yokohama Specie Bank Limited	橫濱正金銀行

V Abbreviations

AAB	Antiquities Advisory Board		Dragonair	Hong Kong Dragon Airlines Limited
AAHK	Airport Authority Hong Kong		EAA	Estate Agents Authority
ACTEQ	Advisory Committee on Teacher Education and Qualifications		EAC	Electoral Affairs Commission
AFCD	Agriculture, Fisheries and Conservation Department		EAG	East Asian Games
			EC	Education Commission
AGF	Asian Games Federation		EMB	Education and Manpower Bureau
AIIB	Asian Infrastructure Investment Bank		EOC	Equal Opportunities Commission
AMO	Antiquities and Monuments Office		EPD	Environmental Protection Department
APEC	Asia-Pacific Economic Cooperation		ETO	Economic and Trade Office
ASF&OC	Amateur Sports Federation & Olympic Committee of Hong Kong		EU	European Union
			FEHD	Food and Environmental Hygiene Department
Asiad	Asian Games		FHB	Food and Health Bureau
ATV	Asia Television Limited		FPAHK	The Family Planning Association of Hong Kong
BA	Broadcasting Authority		GFS	Government Flying Service
BCCI	Bank of Credit and Commerce International		HA	Housing Authority
BEA	The Bank of East Asia, Limited		HA	Hospital Authority
BMCPC	The Board of Management of The Chinese Permanent Cemeteries		HAB	Home Affairs Bureau
			HAD	Home Affairs Department
BOCHK	Bank of China (Hong Kong) Limited		HD	Housing Department
CA	Communications Authority		HEC	Hongkong Electric Company, Limited
CAS	Civil Aid Service		Henderson Land	Henderson Land Development Company Limited
CATC	Central Air Transport Corporation			
CBRC	China Banking Regulatory Commission		HKADC	Hong Kong Arts Development Council
CDL	China Defence League		HKBN	Hong Kong Broadband Network
CEPA	Mainland and Hong Kong Closer Economic Partnership Arrangement		HKBPE	Exhibition of Hong Kong Products/Hong Kong Brands and Products Expo
CITIC	China International Trust & Investment Corporation		HKCEC	Hong Kong Convention and Exhibition Centre
			HKCSS	The Hong Kong Council of Social Service
CLP	China Light & Power Company Syndicate		HKEA	Hong Kong Examinations Authority
CMA	The Chinese Manufacturers' Association of Hong Kong		HKEAA	Hong Kong Examinations and Assessment Authority
CMB	China Motor Bus Company Limited		HKEX	Hong Kong Exchanges and Clearing Limited
CNAC	China National Aviation Corporation		HKFA	Hong Kong Football Association
Commercial Press	The Commercial Press (Hong Kong) Limited		HKFE	Hong Kong Futures Exchange
			HKFEW	Hong Kong Federation of Education Workers
CPPCC	Chinese People's Political Consultative Conference		HKFS	Hong Kong Federation of Students
			HKFTU	Hong Kong Federation of Trade Unions
CSL	Communication Services Limited/CSL Mobile Limited (Since 2014)		HKHS	Hong Kong Housing Society
			HKJC	The Hong Kong Jockey Club
CSSA	Comprehensive Social Security Assistance Scheme		HKL	Hongkong Land Investment and Agency Company Limited/The Hongkong Land Company, Limited (Since 1972)
CTSHK	China Travel Service (Holdings) Hong Kong Limited			
DAB	Democratic Alliance for Betterment of Hong Kong/Democratic Alliance for the Betterment and Progress of Hong Kong (Since 2005)		HKMA	Hong Kong Monetary Authority
			HKO	Hong Kong Observatory
			HKPA	The Hong Kong Progressive Alliance
			HKPF	Hong Kong Police Force
Dairy Farm	Dairy Farm Ice & Cold Storage Company Limited/Dairy Farm Company, Limited (Since 1983)		HKSAR	Hong Kong Special Administrative Region
			HKT	Hong Kong Telecommunications (HKT) Limited
DBS Bank	DBS Bank (Hong Kong) Limited		HKTB	Hong Kong Tourism Board

HKTDC	Hong Kong Trade Development Council
HKTV	Hong Kong Television Network Limited
HKTVE	HK Television Entertainment Company Limited
HMO	Hong Kong and Macao Affairs Office of the State Council
Home Return Permit	Home-Visiting Certificate for Compatriots from Hong Kong and Macau/Mainland Travel Permit for Hong Kong and Macau Residents (Since 1999)
Hong Kong Alliance	Hong Kong Alliance in Support of Patriotic Democratic Movements of China
Hong Kong-Kowloon Brigade	Hong Kong Independent Battalion of the Dongjiang Column
HOS	Home Ownership Scheme
HSBC	The Hongkong and Shanghai Banking Corporation Limited
HWFB	Health, Welfare and Food Bureau
HYF	The Hongkong and Yaumati Ferry Company, Limited
ICAC	Independent Commission Against Corruption
IMMD	Immigration Department
IPCC	Independent Police Complaints Council
JCPDG	Joint Committee on the Promotion of Democratic Government
Joint Publishing	Joint Publishing (Hong Kong) Company Limited
KMB	The Kowloon Motor Bus Company (1933) Limited
KWG	KWG Group Holdings Limited
LAB	Labour Advisory Board
LCSD	Leisure and Cultural Services Department
Link REIT	Link Real Estate Investment Trust
LOCPG	Liaison Office of the Central People's Government in the Hong Kong Special Administrative Region
LSD	League of Social Democrats
LWB	Labour and Welfare Bureau
MPF	Mandatory Provident Fund
MPFA	Mandatory Provident Fund Schemes Authority
MTR	Mass Transit Railway Corporation/MTR Corporation Limited (Since 2000)
NPC	National People's Congress
NWD	New World Development Company Limited
OAT	Obscene Articles Tribunal
One-way Permit	Permit for Proceeding to Hong Kong and Macau
OTB	Overseas Trust Bank
PA	Public Assistance Scheme

PCCW	Pacific Century CyberWorks Limited/PCCW Limited (Since 2002)
PLA	People's Liberation Army
PLC	Provisional Legislative Council
PTU	Hong Kong Professional Teachers' Union
RGC	Research Grants Council
RTV	Rediffusion Television Limited
SARS	Severe Acute Respiratory Syndrome
SCOLAR	Standing Committee on Language Education and Research
SEHK	The Stock Exchange of Hong Kong Limited
Selection Committee	Selection Committee for the First Government of the Hong Kong Special Administrative Region
SF&OC	Sports Federation & Olympic Committee of Hong Kong, China
SFC	Securities and Futures Commission
SHKP	Sun Hung Kai Properties Limited
Sino-British Joint Declaration	Joint Declaration of the Government of the United Kingdom of Great Britain and Northern Ireland and the Government of the People's Republic of China on the Question of Hong Kong
SmarTone	SmarTone Telecommunications Holdings Limited
Star Ferry	The "Star" Ferry Company, Limited
State Council	State Council of the People's Republic of China
SWD	Social Welfare Department
THB	Transport and Housing Bureau
Towngas	The Hong Kong and China Gas Company Limited
TPB	Town Planning Board
TPS	Tenants Purchase Scheme
TVB	Television Broadcasts Limited
Two-way Permit	Exit-entry Permit for Travelling to and from Hong Kong and Macau
UDHK	United Democrats of Hong Kong
UGC	University Grants Committee
UNESCO	United Nations Educational, Scientific and Cultural Organization
URA	Urban Renewal Authority
VTC	Vocational Training Council
Whampoa Dock	The Hong Kong and Whampoa Dock Company Limited
Wharf	Hong Kong and Kowloon Wharf and Godown Company Limited
WHO	World Health Organization
WTO	World Trade Organization

Bibliography

Official Documents and Reports

A Draft Agreement between the Government of the United Kingdom of Great Britain and Northern Ireland and the Government of the People's Republic of China on the Future of Hong Kong. 26 September 1984.

Administrative Report. Hong Kong: 1879–1883, 1908–1939.

Advisory Committee on Diversification. *Report of the Advisory Committee on Diversification, 1979.* Hong Kong: November 1979.

Board of Education. *Report of the Board of Education on the Proposed Expansion of Secondary School Education in Hong Kong over the Next Decade.* August 1973.

Burney, Edmund. *Report on Education in Hong Kong.* 1935.

Census and Statistics Department. *A Graphic Guide on Hong Kong's Development (1967–2007).*

———. *Hong Kong Statistics, 1947–1967.* Hong Kong: Census and Statistics Department, 1969.

Chen Hansheng, Lu Wendi, Peng Jiali, and Chen Zexian, eds. *Guanyu Huagong chuguo de Zhongwai zonghexing zhuzuo* [Chinese and Foreign Studies on Chinese Labourers Going Abroad]. In *Huagong chuguo shiliao huibian* [A Compilation of Historical Documents Concerning Chinese Labourers Overseas]. Vol. 4. Beijing: Zhonghua Book Company, 1981.

Cheung Wai-lam. *The Process of Appointment of Judges in Hong Kong since 1976.* Hong Kong: Research and Library Services Division of the Legislative Council Secretariat, 2001.

Chief Executive's Policy Address of the Hong Kong Special Administrative Region. 1997–2017.

China Investment Information Services Limited. *Guanyu fabu Gang gu tong gupiao mingdan de tongzhi* [Circular on Releasing the List of Stocks for Hong Kong Stock Connect]. 10 November 2014.

China Securities Regulatory Commission. *Guanyu zhengquan touzi jijin guanli gongsi zai Xianggang sheli jigou de guiding* [Regulations on Securities Investment & Fund Management Companies to Set up Establishments in Hong Kong]. 26 February 2014.

Civil Engineering and Development Department Kowloon Development Office. "Kai Tak Development Engineering Study cum Design and Construction of Advance Works—Investigation, Design and Construction: Further Archaeological Excavation Report." August 2009.

Colonial Office (CO) 129.

Colonial Office. *Mr. Chadwick's Reports on the Sanitary Condition of Hong Kong; with Appendices and Plans.* London: George E. B. Eyre and William Spottiswoode, 1882.

Commission of Inquiry into the Rainstorm Disasters. *Final Report of the Commission of Inquiry into the Rainstorm Disasters 1972.* November 1972.

Commission of Inquiry under Sir Alastair Blair-Kerr. *First Report of the Commission of Inquiry under Sir Alastair Blair-Kerr.* Hong Kong: Government Printer, 1973.

———. *Second Report of the Commission of Inquiry under Sir Alastair Blair-Kerr.* Hong Kong: Government Printer, 1973.

Commission on Youth. *Continuing Development and Employment Opportunities for Youth.* Hong Kong: March 2003.

Committee on the Review of the Institutional Framework for Public Housing. *The Report: Review of the Institutional Framework for Public Housing.* June 2002.

Constitution of the People's Republic of China (adopted at the Fifth Session of the Fifth National People's Congress on 04 December 1982).

Constitutional Development Task Force. *The Fifth Report of the Constitutional Development Task Force: Package of Proposals for the Methods for Selecting the Chief Executive in 2007 and for Forming the Legislative Council in 2008.* Hong Kong: October 2005.

———. *The First Report of the Constitutional Development Task Force: Issues of Legislative Process in the Basic Law Relating to Constitutional Development.* Hong Kong: March 2004.

———. *The Fourth Report of the Constitutional Development Task Force: Views and Proposals of Members of the Community on the Methods for Selecting the Chief Executive in 2007 and for Forming the Legislative Council in 2008*. Hong Kong: December 2004.

———. *The Second Report of the Constitutional Development Task Force: Issues of Principle in the Basic Law Relating to Constitutional Development*. Hong Kong: April 2004.

———. *The Third Report of the Constitutional Development Task Force: Areas Which May Be Considered for Amendment in Respect of the Methods for Selecting the Chief Executive in 2007 and for Forming the Legislative Council in 2008*. Hong Kong: May 2004.

Correspondence, Memorials, Orders in Council and Other Papers Respecting the Taiping Rebellion in China 1852-64. Shannon: Irish University Press, 1971.

Council Business Division of the Legislative Council Secretariat. *A Study of the Proposed Accountability System for Principal Officials and Related Issues*. Hong Kong: 06 May 2002.

Council for Sustainable Development. *Making Choices for Our Future: An Invitation and Response Document*. Hong Kong: July 2004.

———. *Making Choices for Our Future: Report on the Engagement Process for a First Sustainable Development Strategy*. Hong Kong: February 2005.

Decision of the Standing Committee of the National People's Congress on Issues Relating to the Selection of the Chief Executive of the Hong Kong Special Administrative Region by Universal Suffrage and on the Method for Forming the Legislative Council of the Hong Kong Special Administrative Region in the Year 2016. 31 August 2014.

Decision of the Standing Committee of the National People's Congress on Treatment of the Laws Previously in Force in Hong Kong in Accordance with Article 160 of the Basic Law of the Hong Kong Special Administrative Region of the People's Republic of China. 23 February 1997.

Donghua yiyuan 1893 niandu zhengxinlu [Annual Report of Tung Wah Hospital, 1893]. Hong Kong: Tung Wah Museum.

Drafting Committee for the Basic Law of the Hong Kong Special Administrative Region. *The Draft Basic Law of the Hong Kong Special Administrative Region of the People's Republic of China for Solicitation of Opinions*. April 1988.

———. *The Basic Law of the Hong Kong Special Administrative Region of the People's Republic of China (Draft)*. February 1989.

———. *The Basic Law of the Hong Kong Special Administrative Region of the People's Republic of China*. April 1990.

Drainage Services Department. *Sustainability Report 2014-2015*. Hong Kong: 2015.

"Early Arts Faculty Students, 1923 Graduates, Rachel Irving." Hong Kong University Archives.

Education and Manpower Bureau. *The New Academic Structure for Senior Secondary Education and Higher Education: Action Plan for Investing in the Future of Hong Kong*. May 2005.

Education Commission. *Education Commission Report No. 3*. June 1988.

———. *Learning for Life, Learning through Life: Reform Proposals for the Education System in Hong Kong*. September 2000.

———. *Education Commission Report No. 7: Quality School Education*. July 1997.

Eitel, E. J. "Annual Report on Government Education." 1880.

Fan Shuh-ching. *The Population of Hong Kong*. Hong Kong: Swindon Book Co., 1974.

Federation of Hong Kong Industries. "Hong Kong Week, 30th October-5th November, 1967." 1967.

First Historical Archives of China, ed. *Xianggang lishi wenti dang'an tulu* [An Illustrated Catalogue on the Historical Issues of Hong Kong]. Hong Kong: Joint Publishing, 1996.

———, ed. *Yapian zhanzheng dang'an shiliao* [Archival Materials on the Opium War]. Vol. 1. Tianjin: Tianjin guji chubanshe, 1992.

Fox, Freeman, and Partners. *Hong Kong Mass Transit Further Studies: Final Report*. Hong Kong: Government Printer, 1970.

Fox, Freeman, Smith Wilbur, and Associates, *Hong Kong Mass Transport Study*. Hong Kong: Government Printer, 1968.

Government Budget. Hong Kong: 1997–2017.

Government Civil Hospital. "Medical Report on the Epidemic of Bubonic Plague in 1894." 02 March 1895.

———. "The Colonial Surgeon's Report for 1885."

14 May 1886.

Government of the Hong Kong Special Administrative Region Gazette. 1997–2017.

Government of the Hong Kong Special Administrative Region. *2017 Make It Happen! Consultation Report and Proposals on the Method for Selecting the Chief Executive by Universal Suffrage.* April 2015.

———. *Hong Kong 2030: Planning Vision and Strategy: Final Report.* Hong Kong: Development Bureau and Planning Department, 2007.

———. Development Bureau, Civil Engineering and Development Department. *Sustainable Lantau Blueprint.* June 2017.

———. Environment Bureau. *Hong Kong Biodiversity Strategy and Action Plan 2016–2021.* December 2016.

———. Financial Secretary's Office. Economic Analysis and Business Facilitation Unit. Economic Analysis Division. *Economic Background and Prospects.* 2001–2017.

———. Financial Services Bureau. *Report on Financial Market Review.* April 1998.

———. Housing Bureau. *Homes for Hong Kong People into the 21st Century: A White Paper on Long Term Housing Strategy in Hong Kong.* Hong Kong: 1998.

———. Information Services Department. *Hong Kong In Brief.* 2008–2018.

———. Security Bureau. *Consultation Document on Proposals to Implement Article 23 of the Basic Law.* September 2002.

———. Transport Bureau. *Railway Development Strategy 2000.* May 2000.

Government Press Release. Hong Kong: 1997–2018.

Green Paper: The 1987 Review of Developments in Representative Government. May 1987.

Green Paper: The Further Development of Representative Government in Hong Kong. Hong Kong: Government Printer, 1984.

Guan Tianpei. *Chouhai chuji* [Collection of Materials on Maritime Affairs]. Edited by Wang Youli. Taipei: Huawen shuju, 1969.

Gugong bowuguan Ming Qing dang'an bu [Ming–Qing Archives Department of the Palace Museum], and Fujian shifan daxue lishi xi [Department of History of Fujian Normal University], eds. *Qingji Zhong wai shiling nianbiao* [Chronology of Chinese and Foreign Envoys in Late Qing Dynasty]. Beijing: Zhonghua Book Company, 1985.

Hertslet, Edward. *The Foreign Office List, Forming a Complete British Diplomatic and Consular Handbook: With Maps, Showing Where Her Majesty's Ambassadors, Ministers, Consuls, and others, Are Resident abroad; together with a List of Foreign Diplomatic and Consular Representatives Resident within the Queen's Dominions.* London: Harrison, 1865.

Historical and Statistical Abstract of the Colony of Hong Kong. Hong Kong: Noronha & Co., 1841–1940.

Hong Kong Annual Report. 1889–1938, 1946–1968.

Hong Kong Blue Book. 1844–1940.

"Hong Kong Declaration on Sustainable Development for Cities." 26 February 2004.

Hong Kong Government Gazette. 1853–1997.

Hong Kong Hansard. 1844–1941.

Hong Kong Monetary Authority. *Annual Report.* 1994–2018.

———. *Code of Banking Practice.* 02 January 2009.

Hong Kong Records Series (HKRS) 41, 58, 125, 156, 169-170, 276, 282, 352, 860.

Hong Kong Yearbook. 1970–2018.

Horsburgh, James. India *Directory, or, Directions for Sailing to and from the East Indies, China, New Holland, Cape of Good Hope, Brazil, and the Interjacent Ports: Compiled Chiefly from Original Journals at the East India House, and from Observations and Remarks, Made during Twenty-one Years Experience Navigating in Those Seas.* 1827.

Hospital Authority. *HA Annual Report.* Hong Kong: 2000–2019.

Independent Commission Against Corruption. *ICAC Annual Report.* Hong Kong: 1974–2017.

Independent Panel of Inquiry on the Harbour Fest. *Report of the Independent Panel of Inquiry on the Harbour Fest.* Hong Kong: May 2004.

Independent Review Committee for the Prevention and Handling of Potential Conflicts of Interests. *Report of the Independent Review Committee for the Prevention and Handling of Potential Conflicts of Interests.* Hong Kong: 31 May 2012.

Independent Review Committee on Independent Commission Against Corruption's Regulatory Systems and Procedures for Handling Official

Entertainment, Gifts and Duty Visits. *Report of the Independent Review Committee on ICAC's Regulatory Systems and Procedures for Handling Official Entertainment, Gifts and Duty Visits*. Hong Kong: September 2013.

Information Office of the State Council of the People's Republic of China. *White Paper: The Practice of the "One Country, Two Systems" Policy in the Hong Kong Special Administrative Region*. June 2014.

Institute of History and Philology, Academia Sinica, comp. *Ming shilu: Da Ming Taizu gao huangdi shilu* [Veritable Records of the Ming Dynasty: Veritable Records of Emperor Taizu]. Taipei: Institute of History and Philology, Academia Sinica, 1962.

———, comp. *Ming shilu: Da Ming Yingzong rui huangdi shilu* [Veritable Records of the Ming Dynasty: Veritable Records of Emperor Yingzong]. Taipei: Institute of History and Philology, Academia Sinica, 1962.

———, comp. *Ming shilu: Da Ming Shizong su huangdi shilu* [Veritable Records of the Ming Dynasty: Veritable Records of Emperor Shizong]. Taipei: Institute of History and Philology, Academia Sinica, 1962.

———, comp. *Ming shilu: Da Ming Shenzong xian huangdi shilu* [Veritable Records of the Ming Dynasty: Veritable Records of Emperor Shenzong]. Taipei: Institute of History and Philology, Academia Sinica, 1962.

"Interim Report on the Archaeological Watching Brief Findings in Harcourt Garden for South Island Line (East)." November 2012.

Interpretation by the Standing Committee of the National People's Congress Regarding Annex I (7) and Annex II (III) to the Basic Law of the Hong Kong Special Administrative Region of the People's Republic of China. 06 April 2004.

Interpretation by the Standing Committee of the National People's Congress Regarding Paragraph 4 in Article 22 and Category (3) of Paragraph 2 in Article 24 of the Basic Law of the Hong Kong Special Administrative Region of the People's Republic of China. 26 June 1999.

Interpretation by the Standing Committee of the National People's Congress Regarding the First Paragraph of Article 13 and Article 19 of the Basic Law of the Hong Kong Special Administrative Region of the People's Republic of China. 26 August 2011.

Judiciary of the Hong Kong Special Administrative Region. *Guide to Judicial Conduct*. October 2004.

Kotewall, Robert George, and Gordon C. K. Kwong. *Report of the Panel of Inquiry on the Penny Stocks Incident*. September 2002.

Kowloon Disturbances 1966: Report of Commission of Inquiry. Hong Kong: Government Printer, 1966.

Land Development Corporation. *LDC Annual Report*. Hong Kong: 1997–1998.

Lantau Development Task Force. *Revised Concept Plan for Lantau*. Hong Kong: Lantau Development Task Force, May 2007.

Legislative Council. Select Committee to Inquire into the Handling of the Severe Acute Respiratory Syndrome Outbreak by the Government and the Hospital Authority. *Report of the Select Committee to Inquire into the Handling of the Severe Acute Respiratory Syndrome Outbreak by the Government and the Hospital Authority*. Hong Kong: July 2004.

———. Subcommittee to Study Issues Arising from Lehman Brothers-related Minibonds and Structured Financial Products. *Report of the Subcommittee to Study Issues Arising from Lehman Brothers-related Minibonds and Structured Financial Products*. Hong Kong: June 2012.

Li, Andrew Kwok-nang. *Guideline in Relation to Part-time Judges and Participation in Political Activities*. 16 June 2006.

Liu Fang [Lau Fong], and Zhang Wenqin, eds. *Putaoya dong bo ta dang'an guancang Qingdai Aomen Zhongwen dang'an huibian* [Compilation of Chinese Archives about Macao during the Qing Dynasty]. Arquivo Nacional Torre do Tombo. Macao: Macao Foundation, 1999.

Liu Wensuo. "Shatin to Central Link — Tai Wai and Hung Hom Section Works Contract 1109: Stations and Tunnels of Kowloon City Section: Archaeological Excavation Report for Sacred Hill Area (Phases 1 to 3 Archaeological Works). Volume 1—Section 1 to 3." June 2017.

Lockhart, William. "Macao, to Lockhart's Father and Sister, Liverpool, July 1841." In the Lockhart Correspondence: Transcripts of Letters to and from Dr. William Lockhart and His Family (unpublished manuscript).

Long Term Housing Strategy. April 1987.

Lunn, Michael Victor, and Benjamin Tang. *Report of*

the Commission of Inquiry into the Collision of Vessels near Lamma Island on 1 October 2012. April 2013.

Mainland and Hong Kong Closer Economic Partnership Arrangement. Main Text and Six Annexes. 29 June 2003 and 29 September 2003.

Marine Court. *Loss of the s.s. "Seawise University" : Report of the Marine Court*. Hong Kong: Government Printer, 1972.

McKinsey & Company Inc. *The Machinery of Government: A New Framework for Expanding Services*. Hong Kong: Government Printer, 1973.

McKinsey Report on Strengthening the Machinery of Government of Hong Kong: Includes Summary of Report. 1973. FCO 40/410, The National Archives.

Ministry of Education of the People's Republic of China. *Jiaoyu bu bangong ting guanyu tongyi Xianggang, Aomen tequ gaodeng xuexiao zai neidi 17 ge sheng, zi zhi qu, zhi xia shi zhaoshou zifei sheng de tongzhi* [Circular of the General Office of the Ministry of Education on Approving Universities and Colleges in the Special Administrative Regions of Hong Kong and Macao to Recruit Self-funded Students of 17 Inland Provinces, Autonomous Regions and Municipalities Directly under the Central Government]. 25 April 2005.

MTR Corporation Limited. *Annual Report*. 2001–2017.

Official Record of Proceedings of the Legislative Council of Hong Kong. 1985–2017.

Official Record of Proceedings of the Provisional Legislative Council. 1997–1998.

People's Bank of China. *Zhongguo renmin yinhang gonggao (2003) di 16 hao* [Announcement No. 16 [2003] of the People's Bank of China]. 19 November 2003.

People's Bank of China, China Banking Regulatory Commission and State Administration of Foreign Exchange. *Zhongguo renmin yinhang, Zhongguo yinhangye jiandu guanli weiyuanhui, Guojia waihui guanli ju guanyu fabu "shangye yinhang kaiban daike jingwai licai yewu guanli zanxing banfa" de tongzhi* [Circular of the People's Bank of China, China Banking Regulatory Commission and State Administration of Foreign Exchange on Promulgating the Interim Administrative Measures for Commercial Banks to Provide Overseas Financial Management Services]. 17 April 2006.

"Plan of Victoria" , Hong Kong. In the Surveyor

General's Dept. WO 78/479, The National Archives.

Policy Address. Hong Kong: 1985–1996.

Pollution in Hong Kong: A Time to Act. Hong Kong: Government Printer, 1989.

Provisional Council for the Use and Conservation of the Countryside. *The Countryside and the People: Report of the Provisional Council for the Use and Conservation of the Countryside*. 1968.

Provisional Legislative Council. *Annual Report of the Provisional Legislative Council*. 1997–1998.

Qian Qichen. "Guanyu quanguo renda changweihui Xianggang tebie xingzhengqu choubei weiyuanhui yubei gongzuo weiyuanhui gongzuo qingkuang de huibao (zhaiyao)" [Report on Work of the Preliminary Working Commission of the Preparatory Committee for the Hong Kong Special Administrative Region under the Standing Committee of the National People's Congress (Summary)]. 26 December 1995.

Qing shilu: Shengzu ren huangdi shilu [Veritable Records of the Qing Dynasty: Veritable Records of Emperor Kangxi]. Beijing: Zhonghua Book Company, 1985.

Qing shilu: Xuanzong cheng huangdi shilu [Veritable Records of the Qing Dynasty: Veritable Records of Emperor Daoguang]. Beijing: Zhonghua Book Company, 1985.

Quanguo renmin daibiao dahui Xianggang tebie xingzhengqu choubei weiyuanhui guanyu sheli Xianggang tebie xingzhengqu linshi lifahui de jueding [Decision of the Preparatory Committee for the Hong Kong Special Administrative Region under the National People's Congress on the Establishment of the Provisional Legislative Council of the Hong Kong Special Administrative Region]. 24 March 1996.

Report of the Commission Appointed by His Excellency the Governor of Hong Kong to Enquire into the Causes and Effects of the Present Trade Depression in Hong Kong and Make Recommendations for the Amelioration of the Existing Position and for the Improvement of the Trade of the Colony. Hong Kong: Noronha & Co., 1934.

Report on the Riots in Kowloon and Tsuen Wan, October 10th to 12th, 1956, Together with Covering Despatch Dated the 23rd December, 1956, from The Governor of Hong Kong to the Secretary of State for the Colonies. Hong Kong: Government Printer, 1956.

Representative Government in Hong Kong. February 1994.

Robinson, William. *Governor's Despatch to the Secretary of State the Reference to the Plague*. 20 June 1894.

Secretary for Social Services. *Secondary Education in Hong Kong Over the Next Decade*. October 1974.

———. *Senior Secondary and Tertiary Education: A Development Programme for Hong Kong over the Next Decade*. November 1977.

Securities Review Committee. *The Operation and Regulation of the Hong Kong Securities Industry: Report of the Securities Review Committee*. Hong Kong: Government Printer, 1988.

Senate Minutes. 28 June 1921. Hong Kong University Archives.

State Council of the People's Republic of China. *Guowuyuan guanyu gongbu diyipi guojia ji fei wuzhi wenhua yichan minglu de tongzhi* [Circular of the State Council on the First Batch of the National List of Intangible Cultural Heritage]. 20 May 2006.

———. *Guowuyuan guanyu gongbu di si pi guojia ji fei wuzhi wenhua yichan daibiao xing xiangmu minglu de tongzhi* [Circular of the State Council on the Fourth Batch of the National List of the Representative Elements of Intangible Cultural Heritage]. 11 November 2014.

———. *Official Reply of the State Council Concerning the Area of the "Hong Kong Port Area at the Shenzhen Bay Port" over which the Hong Kong Special Administrative Region is Authorized to Exercise Jurisdiction and the Land Use Period*. 30 December 2006.

"Supplementary Treaty between Her Majesty and the Emperor of China, Signed at Hoomun-Chae, October 8, 1843, with Other Documents Relating Thereto." 1844.

Talbot, Lee M., and Martha H. Talbot. *Conservation of the Hong Kong Countryside: Summary Report and Recommendation*. April 1965.

Task Force on Constitutional Development. *Report on the Recent Community and Political Situation in Hong Kong*. Hong Kong: January 2015.

Task Force on External Lighting. *Report of the Task Force on External Lighting*. Hong Kong: April 2015.

Task Force on Tree Management. *Report of the Task Force on Tree Management: People, Trees, Harmony*. Hong Kong: June 2009.

The Chronicle & Directory for China, Corea, Japan, the Philippines, Cochin China, Annam, Tonquin, Siam, Borneo, Straits Settlements, Malay States, &c. for the Year 1885. Hong Kong: The Hong Kong Daily Press Office.

The Chronicle & Directory for China, Corea, Japan, the Philippines, Indo-China, Straits Settlements, Siam, Borneo, Malay States, &c. for the Year 1892. Hong Kong: The Hong Kong Daily Press Office.

The Directory & Chronicle for China, Japan, Corea, Indo-China, Straits Settlements, Malay States, Siam, Netherlands India, Borneo, the Philippines, &c. for the Year 1905. The Hong Kong Daily Press Office.

The Directory & Chronicle for China, Japan, Corea, Indo-China, Straits Settlements, Malay States, Siam, Netherlands India, Borneo, the Philippines, &c. for the year 1912. The Hong Kong Daily Press Office.

The Friend of China and Hong Kong Gazette. 1842–1848.

The Hongkong Almanack, and Directory for 1846: with an appendix. Hong Kong: Office of the China Mail, 1846.

The Letters Patent of 5 April 1843. Hong Kong: Legislative Council Library.

The North-China Herald and Supreme Court & Consular Gazette. Shanghai: North-China Herald, 1870–1941.

The Royal Instructions. 06 April 1843. Hong Kong: Legislative Council Library.

Treaties, Conventions, etc., between China and Foreign States, with a Chronological List of Treaties and of Regulations Based on Treaty Provisions, 1689–1886. Shanghai: Statistical Department of the Inspectorate General of Customs, 1887.

Tsang, Donald [Tsang Yam-kuen]. *Report on the Public Consultation on Constitutional Development and on Whether There Is a Need to Amend the Methods for Selecting the Chief Executive of the Hong Kong Special Administrative Region and for Forming the Legislative Council of the Hong Kong Special Administrative Region in 2012*. 12 December 2007.

U.K. Foreign and Commonwealth Office (FCO) 21.

———. Foreign Office (FO) 371.

U.S. House of Representatives. *Report upon the Commercial Relations between the United States with Foreign Nations for the Year 1878*. Washington: Government Printing Office, 1879.

U.S. Policy on Hong Kong. 17 July 1957. U.S. Department of State.

United Nations. Conference on Trade and Development. "World Investment Report 2015: Reforming International Investment Governance." 2015.

———. General Assembly. *Meeting on Refugees and Displaced Persons in South-East Asia, Convened by the Secretary-General of the United Nations at Geneva, on 20 and 21 July 1979, and Subsequent Developments: Report of the Secretary-General.* 7 November 1979.

———. Population Division of the Department of Economic and Social Affairs. "World Population Prospects: The 2015 Revision, Key Findings and Advance Tables." 2015.

Union Insurance Society of Canton Limited. "Brief Historical Record of the Union Insurance Society of Canton, Ltd." January 1952.

WD Scott & Co. Pty. Ltd. *The Delivery of Medical Services in Hospitals: A Report for the Hong Kong Government.* Hong Kong: Government Printer, 1985.

Wen Qing et al. *Chouban yiwu shimo* [The Complete Account of Management of Barbarian Affairs]. Beijing: Zhonghua Book Company, 1964.

White Paper: The Development of Representative Government: The Way Forward. Hong Kong: Government Printer, 1988.

White Paper: The Further Development of Representative Government in Hong Kong. Hong Kong: Government Printer, 1984.

Working Group on the Review of the Academic Structure for Senior Secondary Education and Interface with Higher Education. *Review of the Academic Structure of Senior Secondary Education.* May 2003.

World Health Organization. "Summary of Probable SARS Cases with Onset of Illness from 1 November 2002 to 31 July 2003." 21 April 2004.

Yeung Chun-kuen, and Lee Jark-pui. *Report of the Commission of Inquiry on Allegations Relating to The Hong Kong Institute of Education.* June 2007.

Newspapers and Periodicals

China Mail (1866–1961)

Hong Kong Commercial Daily (1997–2017)

Hong Kong Daily Press (1864–1941)

Hong Kong Sunday Herald (1929–1950)

Hong Kong Telegraph (1881–1951)

Hong Kong Weekly Press (1895–1909)

Huaqiao ribao (*Wah Kiu Yat Po*, or *Overseas Chinese Daily News*) (1947–1991)

Huazi ribao (*The Chinese Mail*) (1895–1940)

Huazi wanbao (*The Chinese Evening Post*) (1895–1940)

Illustrated London News (1873)

Kung Sheung Daily News (1926–1984)

Kung Sheung Evening News (1930–1984)

Ming Pao (1997–2017)

Sing Tao Daily (1997–2017)

South China Morning Post (1903–2017)

Ta Kung Pao (1938–2017)

The Chinese Repository (1842)

The Friend of China and Hong Kong Government Gazette (1842–1848)

The North-China Herald and Market Report (1868–1869)

The North-China Herald and Supreme Court & Consular Gazette (1870–1941)

Ting Kwong Pao (1933–1940)

Wen Wei Po (1997–2017)

Xia'er guanzhen (*The Chinese Serial*) (1853–1856)

Xianggang jingji ribao (*Hong Kong Economic Times*) (1997–2017)

Xianggang ribao (*The Hong Kong News*) (1942–945)

Xinbao caijing xinwen (*Hong Kong Economic Journal*) (1997–2017)

Xunhuan ribao (*Universal Circulating Herald*) (1874–1886)

Published Works

Alderson, G. L. D. *History of Royal Air Force Kai Tak.* Hong Kong: Royal Air Force Kai Tak, 1972.

Banham, Tony. *Not the Slightest Chance: The Defence of Hong Kong, 1941.* Hong Kong: Hong Kong University Press, 2003.

Bao liang ju [Po Leung Kuk], ed. *Baoliang ju 125*

zhounian tekan [A Special Issue for the Po Leung Kuk 125th Anniversary]. Hong Kong: Po Leung Kuk, 2004.

Bao Shaolin, Huang Zhaoqiang, and Ou Zhijian, eds. *Beixue nanyi: Gang Tai wen shi zhe suyuan. Xue ren juan* [Northern China Studies in the South: Origin of the Literature, History and Philosophy of Hong Kong and Taiwan, Volume Scholar II]. Taipei: Xiuwei zixun keji gufen youxiangongsi, 2015.

Bao'an xian Fenling Pengshi zupu [Genealogy of the Pang Clan in Fanling, Bao'an County].

Bao'an xian Yaqianwei Wushi zupu [Genealogy of the Ng Clan in Nga Tsin Wai, Bao'an County]. 1986.

"Bao'an wenshi congshu" bianzuan weiyuanhui [Editorial Board of Bao'an Literature and History Book Series], ed. *Kangxi Xin'an Xianzhi Jiao Zhu* [Annotated Edition of the Local Chronicles of Xin'an County during the Reign of Emperor Kangxi]. Beijing: Zhongguo dabaike quanshu chubanshe, 2006.

Bard, Solomon. *Traders of Hong Kong: Some Foreign Merchant Houses, 1841–1899*. Hong Kong: Urban Council, 1993.

Beiao laoweicun Zhangshi zupu [Genealogy of the Cheung Clan in Lo Wai Village, Pui O].

Beijing tushuguan [Beijing Library], ed. *Wenyuange siku quanshu yi bu: Ju wenjinge siku quanshu bu* [Addendum to Complete Library in Four Branches of Literature by the Belvedere of Literary Profundity: Based on Complete Library in Four Branches of Literature by the Literary Ford Library]. Beijing: Beijing tushuguan chubanshe, 1997.

Bentham, George. *Flora Hongkongensis: A Description of the Flowering Plants and Ferns of the Island of Hongkong*. London: Lovell Reeve, 1861.

Bickley, Gillian, ed. *A Magistrate's Court in Nineteenth Century Hong Kong*. Hong Kong: Proverse Hong Kong, 2005.

Board of Management of the Chinese Permanent Cemeteries. *Huayonghui bai zhounian tekan* [Special Issue on the Centenary of the Chinese Permanent Cemeteries]. Hong Kong: Board of Management of the Chinese Permanent Cemeteries, 2013.

Bōei Kenshūjo (Japan) Senshishitsu. *Honkon Chōsa sakusen* [Hong Kong–Changsha Operation]. Tokyo: Asagumo Shinbunsha, 1971.

Braga, José Maria. *Hong Kong Business Symposium: A Compilation of Authoritative Views on the Administration, Commerce and Resources of Britain's Far East Outpost*. Hong Kong: South China Morning Post Ltd., 1957.

Cai Luo, and Lu Quan. *Sheng Gang dabagong* [Canton–Hong Kong Strike]. Guangzhou: Guangdong renmin chubanshe, 1980.

Cai Rongfang [Tsai Jung-fang]. *Xianggang ren zhi Xianggang shi, 1841–1945* [Hong Kong People's History of Hong Kong, 1841–1945]. Hong Kong: Oxford University Press, 2001.

Cai Sixing [Henry Choi Sze-hang]. *Jianshaju haibin: Lishi, chengshi fazhan ji dazhong jiti jiyi* [Tsim Sha Tsui Seafront: History and Development of City and Collective Memory]. Hong Kong: City University of Hong Kong Press, 2019.

———. *Xianggang shi 100 jian da shi* [One Hundred Major Events in Hong Kong History]. 2 vols. Hong Kong: Chung Hwa Book Company, 2012–2013.

———. *Youpiao zhong de Xianggang shi* [Hong Kong History in Stamps]. Hong Kong: Chung Hwa Book Company, 2013.

Cai Sixing, and Liang Rongwu [Leung Wing-mo]. *Xianggang taifeng gushi* [Story of Hong Kong Typhoons]. Hong Kong: Chung Hwa Book Company, 2014.

Cai Zhixiang [Choi Chi-cheung]. *Da jiao: Xianggang de jieri he diyu shehui* [*Jiao* Festival: Festivals and Community Society in Hong Kong]. Hong Kong: Joint Publishing, 2000.

Cai Zhixiang, and Wei Jinxin, eds. *Yanxu yu biange: Xianggang shequ jianjiao chuantong de minzu zhi* [Continuity and Changes: Ethnographies of the Communal *Jiao* Festivals in Hong Kong]. Hong Kong: Chinese University Press, 2014.

Caritas Hong Kong, ed. *Caritas: Community Service 50th Anniversary 1953–2003*. Hong Kong: Caritas Hong Kong, 2003.

Carroll, John M. *A Concise History of Hong Kong*. Lanham: Rowman & Littlefield, 2007.

———. *Xianggang jianshi: Cong zhimindi zhi tebie xingzhengqu (A Concise History of Hong Kong)*. Translated by Lin Liwei [Willy Lam]. Hong Kong: Chung Hwa Book Company, 2013.

Carter, Thomas, comp. *Historical Record of the Forty-fourth, or the East Essex Regiment of Foot*. London: W. O. Mitchell, 1864.

Chalmers, Robert. *A History of Currency in the British Colonies*. London: Her Majesty's Stationery Office, 1893.

Chen Bangzhan, comp. *Song shi jishi benmo* [Historical Events of the Song Period in Their Entirety]. Beijing: Zhonghua Book Company, 2015.

Chen Daming. *Xianggang kang Ri youjidui* [The Anti-Japanese Guerrilla Force in Hong Kong]. Hong Kong: Huanqiu chuban youxian gongsi, 2000.

Chen Datong [Chan Tai-tung], ed. *Bai nian shangye* [A Century of Commerce]. Hong Kong: Guangming wenhua shiye gongshi, 1941.

Chen Dazhen et al., comps. *Dade Nanhai zhi* [Biography of the South China Sea during the Dade Year]. Edited by Qiu Xuanyu. Taipei: Lantai chubanshe, 1994.

Chen Dunde. *Balujun zhu Xianggang banshichu jishi* [Documentary of Eighth Route Army Stationed in Hong Kong Office]. Hong Kong: Chung Hwa Book Company, 2012.

———. *Xianggang wenti tanpan shimo* [Negotiation on the Hong Kong Issue from Beginning to End]. Hong Kong: Chung Hwa Book Company, 2009.

Chen Guocheng [Chan Kwok-shing], ed. *Xianggang diqu shi yanjiu zhi san: Fen Ling* [Hong Kong Regional Study Series: No. 3 Fanling]. Rev. ed. Hong Kong: Joint Publishing, 2019.

Chen Guoqiu, Chen Zhide [Chan Chi-tak] et al. *Xianggang wenxue daxi 1919–1949: Dao yan ji* [Grand Anthology of Hong Kong literature: A Collection of Introductory Remarks]. Hong Kong: Commercial Press, 2016.

Chen Hanxi. *Rao Zongyi: Dongfang wenhua zuobiao* [Jao Tsung-i: Coordinates of Oriental Cultures]. Hong Kong: Xianggang zhonghe chuban youxian gongsi, 2016.

Chen Hongyi [Albert Chen Hung-yee]. *Yiguo liangzhi xia Xianggang de fazhi tansuo* [Hong Kong's Explorations in the Rule of Law under One Country, Two Systems]. Hong Kong: Chung Hwa Book Company, 2014.

Chen Hongyi, and Zou Pingxue, eds. *Xianggang jibenfa mian mian guan* [Perspectives on the Hong Kong Basic Law]. Hong Kong: Joint Publishing, 2015.

Chen Huixun [Chan Wai-fan]. *Xianggang zaji (Wai yi zhong)* [A Miscellany of Hong Kong (Another Related Publication)]. Edited by Mo Shixiang [Mok Sai-cheung]. Hong Kong: Joint Publishing, 2018.

Chen Jiarong [Aaron Chen Jia-rong] et al. *Xianggang zhi Zhongguo lishi jiaoxue* [Teaching Chinese History in Hong Kong]. Hong Kong: Ling Kee Publishing Group, 1995.

Chen Jingxiang [Chan King-cheung], ed. *Xianggang jinrong fengyun 40 zai* [Forty Years of Hong Kong Finance]. Hong Kong: Hong Kong Economic Journal Company Limited, 2013.

Chen Kekun. *Xianggang fengwu manhua* [Random Talk about Hong Kong Heritage]. Hong Kong: Joint Publishing, 1994.

Chen Menglei, comp. *Gujin tushu jicheng* [Complete Collection of Illustrations from the Earliest to Current Times]. Shanghai: Zhonghua Book Company, 1934.

Chen Ming. *Xianggang baoye shigao (1841–1911)* [A History of the Press in Hong Kong (1841–1911)]. Hong Kong: Wah Kwong Newspaper Limited, 2005.

Chen Mingqiu [Chan Ming-kou], Liang Baolin [Apo Leung Po-lam], Liang Baolong [Leung Po-lung], Zhao Yongjia [Stephen Chiu Wing-kai], and Lu Feng'e [Luk Fung-ngor], eds. *Zhongguo yu Xianggang gongyun zongheng* [Dimensions of the Chinese and Hong Kong Labour Movement]. Hong Kong: Xianggang Jidu jiao gongye weiyuanhui, 1986.

Chen Ruizhang [Chan Shui-cheung]. *Dongjiang zongdui: Kangzhan qianhou de Xianggang youjidui* [East River Column: Hong Kong Guerrillas in the Second World War and Beyond]. Hong Kong: Hong Kong University Press, 2012.

Chen Tianquan [Anthony Chan Tin-kuen]. *Chengshi dibiao: Zhimindi shidai de xishi jianzhu* [Urban Landmarks: Western Architecture in the Colonial Era]. Hong Kong: Chung Hwa Book Company, 2019.

———. *Shensheng yu liyi kongjian: Xianggang Jidu zongjiao jianzhu* [Sacred and Liturgical Spaces: Christian Religious Architecture in Hong Kong]. Hong Kong: Chung Hwa Book Company, 2018.

Chen Xin, and Guo Zhikun, eds. *Xianggang quan jilu* [Illustrated Chronicle of Hong Kong]. 2 vols. Hong Kong: Chung Hwa Book Company, 1997–1998

Chen Yangyong. *Ku cheng wei ju: Zhou Enlai zai 1967* [Weathering the Storm: Zhou Enlai in 1967]. Beijing: Zhongyang wenxian chubanshe, 1999.

Chen Zhanyi [Chan Cham-yi], and Yang Yongxian [Yeung Wing-yin], eds. *Xianggang Riben guanxi nianbiao* [Chronology Table of Hong Kong and Japan Relations]. Hong Kong: Xianggang jiaoyu tushu gongsi Limited, 2004.

Chen Zhide [Chan Chi-tak]. *Bandang shidai de shuqing: Kangzhan shiqi de Xianggang yu wenxue* [Time of Turbulence: Hong Kong and Literature during Wartime]. Hong Kong: Chung Hwa Book Company, 2018.

Chen Zhihua [Chan Chi-wah], and Li Jianxin. *Xianggang bashi 90 nian* [Ninety Years of Hong Kong Buses]. Rev. ed. Hong Kong: Chung Hwa Book Company, 2015.

———. *Xianggang tielu 100 nian* [One Hundred Years of Hong Kong Railways]. Hong Kong: Chung Hwa Book Company, 2012.

Chen Zhihua, Li Qingyi, Lu Zhongling, and Huang Xiaofeng. *Xianggang haishang jiaotong 170 nian* [170 Years of Marine Traffic in Hong Kong]. Hong Kong: Chung Hwa Book Company, 2012.

Chen Ziyu [Danny C. Y. Chan]. *Xianggang bashi, 1933–2012* [Hong Kong Bus, 1933–2012]. Hong Kong: Joint Publishing, 2012.

Cheng Xiang [Ching Cheong]. *Xianggang liu qi baodong shimo: Jiedu Wu Dizhou* [Understanding the 1967 Riots: Reading the Diaries of Wu Dizhou]. Hong Kong: Oxford University Press, 2018.

Chesnoy, Jose. *Undersea Fiber Communication Systems*. San Diego: Academic Press, 2002.

Cheung, Gary Ka-wai. *Hong Kong's Watershed: The 1967 Riots*. Hong Kong: Hong Kong University Press, 2012.

China Construction Bank (Asia), and the Centre for Financial Innovation and Development of the Faculty of Business and Economics of The University of Hong Kong. *Xianggang Huazi yinhang bainian bianqian: Cong Guangdong yinhang dao Jianhang Yazhou* [A Century of Changes of Chinese Banks in Hong Kong: From the Bank of Canton to the China Construction Bank (Asia)]. Hong Kong: Chung Hwa Book Company, 2017.

China Resources (Holdings) Co., Ltd.: *Huarun sishi nian jinian tekan* [Special Issue on the Fortieth Anniversary of China Resources]. Hong Kong: China Resources (Holdings) Co., Ltd., 1988.

Collis, Maurice. *Zhonghua minguo shi ziliao conggao yigao: Huifeng: Xianggang Shanghai yinhang: Huifeng yinhang bainian shi* [The Translation Collection of Historical Documents during the Republic of China: HSBC: the Hongkong and Shanghai Banking Corporation (Centennial History of the Hongkong and Shanghai Banking Corporation)]. Translated by Li Zhouying, Gan Peigen, Bai Hong, Xu Xiongfei and Qian Zengwei. Edited by Lin Zhiqi and Li Zhouying. Beijing: Zhonghua Book Company, 1979.

Cooke, Charles Northcote. *The Rise, Progress, and Present Condition of Banking in India*. Calcutta: P. M. Cranenburgh, Bengal Print. Co., 1863.

Da gong bao bianji weiyuanhui [Editorial Board of Ta Kung Pao], ed. *Xianggang huigui shinian zhi* [Hong Kong: Ten Years after its Return to the Mainland]. Hong Kong: Ta Kung Pao, 2007.

Dai Wangshu. *Zainan de suiyue* [Disastrous Years]. Shanghai: Xingqun chubanshe, 1948.

Deng Cong [Tang Chung], Xiao Guojian [Siu Kwok-kin] et al. *Xianggang wenhua fazhan shi* [History of Cultural Development in Hong Kong]. Edited by Wang Guohua. Hong Kong: Chung Hwa Book Company, 2014.

Deng Jiazhou [Tang Ka-jau]. *Xianggang fojiao shi* [History of Hong Kong Buddhism]. Hong Kong: Chung Hwa Book Company, 2015.

Deng Kaisong, and Lu Xiaomin [Luk Hiu-man], eds. *Yue Gang guanxi shi, (1940–1984)* [History of Guangdong-Hong Kong Relations (1840–1984)]. Hong Kong: Qilin shuye youxian gongsi, 1997.

Deng Qipan zupu [Genealogy of Tang Kei Poon].

Deng Shengshi [Tang Shing-sze]. *Pingshan Deng zu qiannian shi tansuo* [Exploring the 1,000-year History of the Ping Shan Tang Clan]. Hong Kong: Tang Kwong-yin, 1999.

Deng Zhongxia. *Sheng Gang bagong gaiguan* [An Overview of the Canton–Hong Kong Strike]. Guangzhou: Zhonghua quanguo zong gonghui Sheng Gang bagong weiyuanhui xuanchuan bu, 1926.

Dengshi zupu [Genealogy of the Tang Clan].

Ding Jie [Ting Kit]. "*Huaqiao ribao*" *yu Xianggang Huaren shehui (1925–1995)* ["Overseas Chinese Daily News" and the Development of Chinese Society in Hong Kong (1925–1995)]. Hong Kong: Joint Publishing, 2014.

Ding Xinbao [Joseph Ting Sun-pao]. *Shanyu rentong: Yu Xianggang tongbu chengzhang de Donghua sanyuan, 1870–1997* [Charity Brings Happiness to the Giver: A Journey of Mutual Growth for TWGHs and Hong Kong (1870–1997)]. Hong Kong: Joint Publishing, 2010.

———, ed. *Xianggang lishi sanbu* [A Walking History of Hong Kong]. Rev. ed. Hong Kong: Commercial Press, 2009.

Ding Xinbao, and Lu Shuying [Lo Shuk-ying]. *Feiwo zuyi: Zhanqian Xianggang de waiji zuqun* [Not of My Kind: Foreign Communities in Hong Kong before World War II]. Hong Kong: Joint Publishing, 2014.

Dong Likun, ed. *Zhongguo neidi yu Xianggang diqu falü*

de chongtu yu xietiao [Conflict and Harmonisation of Laws in the Mainland of China and Hong Kong]. Hong Kong: Chung Hwa Book Company, 2016.

———, ed. *Zhongyang guanzhi quan yu Xianggang gaodu zizhi quan* [The Central Government's Right to Govern and Hong Kong's High Degree of Autonomy]. Hong Kong: Chung Hwa Book Company, 2015.

Drainage Services Department, ed. *Sewerage and Flood Protection: Drainage Services 1841–2008*. Hong Kong: Drainage Services Department, 2009.

Eitel, Ernest John. *Europe in China: The History of Hong Kong from the Beginning to the Year 1882*. London: Luzac & Company, 1895.

Empson, Hal. *Mapping Hong Kong: A Historical Atlas*. Hong Kong: Government Printer, 1992.

Endacott, G. B. *A Biographical Sketch-book of Early Hong Kong*. Hong Kong: Hong Kong University Press, 2005.

———. *A History of Hong Kong*. London: Oxford University Press, 1973.

England, Vaudine. *Kindred Spirits: A History of The Hong Kong Club*. Hong Kong: Hong Kong Club, 2016.

Evans, D. Morier, ed. *The Banking Almanac, Directory, Year Book and Diary for 1863; containing a Diary*. London: Richard Groombridge & Sons, 1864.

Fan Zhenru [Fan Chun-yu]. *Xianggang tebie xingzhengqu de xuanju zhidu* [The Electoral System of the Hong Kong Special Administrative Region]. Hong Kong: Joint Publishing, 2006.

Fang Hanqi, ed. *Zhongguo xinwen shiye tongshi* [General History of Chinese Journalism]. Beijing: China Renmin University Press, 1992.

Fang Jun, and Xiong Xianjun, eds. *Xianggang jiaoyu tongshi* [A History of Education in Hong Kong]. Hong Kong: Ling Kee Publishing Co., Ltd., 2008.

Fang Runhua [Henry Fong Yun-wah] et al., eds. *Xianggang Baoliangju shilue* [A Brief History of Hong Kong Po Leung Kuk]. Hong Kong: Po Leung Kuk, 1968.

Fang Xuanling et al., comps. *Jin shu* [Book of Jin]. Beijing: Zhonghua Book Company, 1974.

Faure, David, Lu Hongji [Bernard Luk Hung-kay], and Wu Lun Nixia [Ng Lun Ngai-ha], eds. *Xianggang beiming huibian* [Historical Inscriptions of Hong Kong]. Hong Kong: Urban Council, 1986.

Feng Bangyan. *Buduanchao yue, gengjia youxiu:*

Chuangxing yinhang maixiang qishi zhounian [Exceed · Excel: Seventieth Anniversary of Chong Hing Bank]. Hong Kong: Joint Publishing, 2018.

———. *Xianggang chanye jiegou zhuanxing* [Transformation of Hong Kong Industrial Structure]. Hong Kong: Joint Publishing, 2014.

———. *Xianggang dichanye bai nian* [A Century of Hong Kong Real Estate Development]. Hong Kong: Joint Publishing, 2001.

———. *Xianggang jinrong yu huobi zhidu* [Financial and Monetary Systems of Hong Kong]. Hong Kong: Joint Publishing, 2015.

———. *Xianggang jinrongye bai nian* [A Century of Hong Kong Financial Development]. Hong Kong: Joint Publishing, 2002.

———. *Xianggang qiye binggou jingdian* [Mergers and Acquisitions of Hong Kong Enterprises]. Hong Kong: Joint Publishing, 2013.

———. *Xianggang Ying zi cai tuan (1841–1996)* [British Enterprises in Hong Kong (1841–1996)]. Hong Kong: Joint Publishing, 1996.

———. *Zhuanxing shiqi de Xianggang jingji* [Hong Kong's Economy in Transition]. Hong Kong: Joint Publishing, 2017.

Feng Bangyan, and Rao Meijiao [Nyaw Mee-kau]. *Housheng liqun: Xianggang baoxian shi 1841-2008* [Enriching Lives: Insurance History of Hong Kong 1841–2008]. Hong Kong: Joint Publishing, 2009.

Feng Jinrong [Fung Kam-wing], Liu Runhe [Lau Yun-woo], and Chen Zhiming [Chan Chi-ming]. *Bilu lanlu, yiqi shanlin: Xianggang gongcheng fazhan 130 nian* [Upon the Plinth of a Barren Rock: 130 Years Engineering Development in Hong Kong]. Hong Kong: Chung Hwa Book Company, 2013.

Feng Keli [Fung Ho-lup]. *Pin er wu yuan nan: Xianggang minsheng fuli fazhan shi* [Poverty without Complaint: History of Hong Kong's Livelihood and Welfare Development]. Hong Kong: Chung Hwa Book Company, 2018.

Fenling Pengshi zupu [Genealogy of the Pang Clan in Fanling].

Fok Kai-cheong. *Lectures on Hong Kong History: Hong Kong's Role in Modern Chinese History*. Hong Kong: Commercial Press, 1990.

Fung Chi-ming. *Reluctant Heroes: Rickshaw Pullers in Hong Kong and Canton, 1874–1954*. Hong Kong: Hong Kong University Press, 2005.

Gaimushō Hyakunenshi Hensan Iinkai (Japan), ed.

Gaimushō no hyakunen [The Centennial History of the Ministry of Foreign Affairs]. Tokyo: Hara Shobo, 1971.

Gang Ao da baike quanshu bianwei hui [Editorial Board]. *Gang Ao da baike quanshu* [Encyclopaedia of Hong Kong and Macao]. Guangzhou: Huacheng chubanshe, 1993.

Gang Jiu duli dadui shi bianxie zu [Editorial Team]. *Gang Jiu duli dadui shi* [The History of the Hong Kong–Kowloon Brigade]. Guangzhou: Guangdong renmin chubanshe, 1989.

Gao Tianqiang [Ko Tim-keung], and Tang Zhuomin [Tong Cheuk-man]. *Xianggang Ri zhan shi qi* [Hong Kong under Japanese Occupation]. Hong Kong: Joint Publishing, 1995.

Government of the Hong Kong Special Administrative Region. *Tongxin chuang qianlu; Zhangwo xin jiyu: Xianggang tebie xingzhengqu chengli ershi zhounian* [Together, Progress, Opportunity: Twentieth Anniversary of the Establishment of the Hong Kong Special Administrative Region]. Hong Kong: Government Logistics Department, 2017.

———. Department of Health. Public Health Nursing Division. *Xianggang gonggong jiankang huli 65 zhounian (1954–2019) jinian zhuanji* [The Sixty-fifth Anniversary of Hong Kong Public Health Nursing Commemorative Album (1954–2019)]. Hong Kong: Public Health Nursing Division of the Department of Health of the Government of the Hong Kong Special Administrative Region, 2019.

Guangdong sheng difang shizhi bangongshi [Office of Local Chronicles of Guangdong Province], ed. *Guangdong lidai fangzhi jicheng* [The Complete Collection of Guangdong Local Chronicles in Past Dynasties]. Guangzhou: Lingnan meishu chubanshe, 2009.

Guangdong sheng zhexue shehui kexue yanjiusuo lishi yanjiu shi [Historical Research Unit of Guangdong Institute of Philosophy and Social Science], ed. *Sheng Gang da ba gong ziliao* [Materials on Canton–Hong Kong Strike]. Guangzhou: Guangdong renmin chubanshe, 1980.

Guangdong shengzhi bianzuan weiyuanhui [Editorial Board]. *Guangdong shengzhi dashiji* [Record of Major Events in Guangdong]. Beijing: Fangzhi chubanshe, 2014.

Guanghua yiyuan bai zhounian jinian tekan bianji weiyuanhui [Editorial Board], ed. *Guanghua baizai qing: Guanghua yiyuan bai zhounian jinian tekan* [Kwong Wah's 100-year History: One-hundredth Anniversary Special Issue of Kwong Wah Hospital]. Hong Kong: Kwong Wah Hospital, 2012.

Gudao bianweihui [Gudao Editorial Board], ed. *Qingdai dituji huibian* [Atlas of the Qing Dynasty]. Xi'an: Xi'an ditu chubanshe, 2005.

Guo Fei, comp. *Guangdong tong zhi* [Guangdong Annals]. Edition of the Thirtieth Year during the Reign of Emperor Wanli of the Ming Dynasty (1602).

Guo Shaotang [Kwok Siu-tong]. *Jianmin bainian: Nanhua tiyuhui 100 zhounian huiqing* [100 Years of Health Promotion: One-hundredth Anniversary of South China Athletic Association]. Hong Kong: Nanhua tiyuhui, 2010.

Guo Shaotang [Kwok Siu-tong], Yau Tsim Mong District Council, and the Community Culture Research Group of The Chinese University of Hong Kong, eds. *Zoujin shequ mi jiuqing: Xunzhao You Jian Wang jiuren jiushi* [Exploring the Historical Charm of Yau Tsim Mong]. Hong Kong: Yau Tsim Mong District Council, 2002.

Guo Zhikun, and Yu Zhisen, eds. *Xianggang quan jilu* [Illustrated Chronicle of Hong Kong]. Vol. 3. Shanghai: Shanghai renmin chubanshe, 2007.

Hamashita Takeshi, and Li Peide [Lee Pui-tak], eds. *Honkon toshi annai shūsei* [Complete Collection of Guidebooks on Urban Hong Kong]. 13 vols. Tokyo: Kabushiki Gaisha Yumani Shobō, 2013–2014.

Hamilton, Sheilah E. *Watching Over Hong Kong: Private Policing 1841–1941*. Hong Kong: Hong Kong University Press, 2008.

Han Haoxin [Hon Hou-jan], ed. *Xianggang huigui zuguo 20 zhounian zhi: Jinrong yu zhuanye* [The Twentieth Anniversary of Hong Kong's Reunification with the Motherland: Finance and Professionals]. Hong Kong: Xianggang shang bao youxian gongsi, 2017.

Harland, Kathleen. *The Royal Navy in Hong Kong, 1841-1980*. Hong Kong: Royal Navy, 1980.

Hase, Patrick H. *Bei yiwang de liuri zhanzheng: Yibajiujiu nian xinjie xiangmin yu Yingjun zhi zhan* (*The Six-day War of 1899: Hong Kong in the Age of Imperialism*). Translated by Lin Liwei [Willy Lam]. Hong Kong: Chung Hwa Book Company, 2014.

Hayes, James. *Xinjie bainian shi* (*The Great Difference: Hong Kong's New Territories and Its People 1898–2004*). Translated by Lin Liwei [Willy Lam]. Hong Kong: Chung Hwa Book Company, 2016.

He Bingxian [Ho Ping-hsien]. *Zhongguo de guoji maoyi* [International Trade in China]. Shanghai: Shanghai shudian, 1989.

He Chongzu. *Lujiang jun He shi jiaji* [Record of Ho's Family of Lujiang County].

He Jiaqi [Lawrence Ho Ka-ki], and Zhu Yaoquang [Chu Yiu-kong]. *Xianggang jingcha: Lishi jianzheng yu zhifa shengya* [Hong Kong Police: Historical Witness and a Life of Executing the Law]. Hong Kong: Joint Publishing, 2011.

He Peiran [Ho Pui-yin]. *Banmen zidi: Xianggang san hang gongren yu gonghui* [History of Three Trade Workers and Unions in Hong Kong]. Hong Kong: Joint Publishing, 2018.

———. *Yuan yu liu: Donghua yiyuan de chuangli yu yanjin* [Origins and Evolution: Establishment and Development of Tung Wah Hospital]. Hong Kong: Joint Publishing, 2009.

He Peiran, Peng Shumin [Pang Shuk-man] et al. *Xianggang wenhua daolun* [A Cultural Introduction to Hong Kong]. Edited by Wang Guohua. Hong Kong: Chung Hwa Book Company, 2014.

He Zhihui [Ho Chi-fai], ed. *Xianggang falü wenhua yanjiu* [Research on Legal Culture]. Hong Kong: Chung Hwa Book Company, 2017.

Ho Pui-yin. *Challenges for an Evolving City: 160 Years of Port and Land Development in Hong Kong*. Hong Kong: Commercial Press, 2004.

———. *The Administrative History of the Hong Kong Government Agencies, 1841–2002*. Hong Kong: Hong Kong University Press, 2004.

———. *Ways to Urbanisation: Post-War Road Development in Hong Kong*. Hong Kong: Hong Kong University Press, 2008.

———. *Weathering the Storm: Hong Kong Observatory and Social Development*. Hong Kong: Hong Kong University Press, 2003.

Hong Kong and China Gas Company Limited. *Lighting the Past Brightening the Future: 150 Years of Towngas*. Hong Kong: Hong Kong and China Gas Company Limited, 2012.

Hong Kong Federation of Students. *Xianggang xuesheng yundong huigu* [A Review of the Hong Kong Student Movement]. Hong Kong: Guangjiaojing chubanshe, 1983.

Hong Kong Federation of Trade Unions. *Gonglianhui yu nin tongxing: 65 zhounian lishi wenji* [A Historical Anthology for the Sixty-fifth Anniversary of the Federation of Trade Unions]. Hong Kong:

Chung Hwa Book Company, 2013.

Hong Kong Film Critics Society. *Wang Jiawei de yinghua shijie* [Film World of Wong Kar-wai]. Hong Kong: Joint Publishing, 2015.

Hong Kong Museum of History, ed. *A Century of Visitors: Prominent Visitors to Hong Kong in Its Early Years*. Hong Kong: Hong Kong Museum of History, 2017.

———, ed. *Jiawu zhanhou: Zuji Xinjie ji Weihaiwei* [The Aftermath of the First Sino-Japanese War: The Lease of the New Territories and Weihaiwei]. Hong Kong: Hong Kong Museum of History, 2014.

———, ed. *Xianggang huobi* [Hong Kong Currency]. Hong Kong: Hong Kong Museum of History, 2012.

Hong Kong Police Force. *Hong Kong Police Force 175th Anniversary: From Strength to Strength Serving with Pride and Care*. Hong Kong: Hong Kong Police Force, 2019.

Hongkong and Yaumati Ferry Company Limited. *Hongkong & Yaumati Ferry Company 70th Anniversary*. Hong Kong: Hongkong and Yaumati Ferry Company Limited, 1993.

Hongkong Land Limited. *Hongkong Land at 125*. Hong Kong: Hongkong Land Limited, 2014.

Huang Dicai [Richard Wong Tai-choi]. *Tushuo Xianggang lishi jianzhu 1841–1896* [Illustrating Hong Kong Historical Buildings 1841–1896]. Hong Kong: Chung Hwa Book Company, 2012.

Huang Dicai, Liu Liangguo [Prudence Lau Leung-kwok], and Hong Kong Museum of Education of the Education University of Hong Kong. *Yaolan di: Zhong xi qu jiao yu jin xi* [Cradle: Present and Past of Education in the Central and Western District]. Edited by Li Zijian, Zheng Baoying and Deng Yingyu. Hong Kong: Chung Hwa Book Company, 2020.

Huang Hai. *Shuli de renxin: Xianggang shehui sichao pingxi* [Estranged minds: Trend of Thoughts in Hong Kong Society]. Hong Kong: City University of Hong Kong Press, 2018.

———. *Xianggang shehui jieceng fenxi* [An Analysis of Social Class in Hong Kong]. Hong Kong: Commercial Press, 2017.

Huang Hongzhao, ed. *Xianggang jindai shi* [A Modern History of Hong Kong]. Hong Kong: Xuejin shudian, 2005.

Huang Jichi [Wong Kai-chee], Lu Weiluan [Lo Wai-luen], and Zheng Shusen [William Tay Shu-sam], eds. *Xianggang wenxue dashi nianbiao (1948–*

1969) [A Chronology of Major Literary Events in Hong Kong (1948–1969)]. Hong Kong: Chinese University Press, 1996.

Huang Luowen [Wong Lok-man]. *Baizai guanghui jiwang kailai: xianshi de gushi* [One Hundred Years and Growing: The Story of Sincere]. Hong Kong: Sincere Co. Ltd, 2000.

Huang Peijia. Xinjie fengtu mingsheng daguan [Landscapes and Landmarks of New Territories]. Edited by Shen Si. Hong Kong: Commercial Press, 2016.

Huang Zhaoqi [Wong Shao-kei], ed. *Xianggang huigui zuguo 20 zhounian zhi: Jijian yu dichan* [The Twentieth Anniversary of Hong Kong's Reunification with the Motherland: Infrastructure and Real Estate]. Hong Kong: Xianggang shang bao youxian gongsi, 2017.

Huang Zhenwei [Wong Chun-wai]. *Fanshu yu huanglong: Xianggang Huangren shuyuan Huaren jingying yu jindai Zhongguo* [English Lessons and the Yellow Dragon: Chinese Elites of Queen's College of Hong Kong and Modern China]. Hong Kong: Chung Hwa Book Company, 2019.

Huang Yaozhong [Wong Yiu-chung]. *Cong jiuji dao ronghe: Xianggang zhengfu de "Zhongguo nanmin zhengce" (1945–1980)* [From Relief to Integration: Hong Kong Government's Policy on Chinese Refugees]. Hong Kong: Joint Publishing, 2020.

Huaqiao ribao chuban bu [Wah kiu yat po], ed. *Xianggang nianjian* [Hong Kong Yearbook]. Hong Kong: Huaqiao ribao chuban bu, 1948–1994.

Huo Qichang [Fok Kai-cheong]. *Gang Ao dang'an zhong de Xinhai geming* [The 1911 Revolution in Hong Kong and Macao Archives]. Hong Kong: Commercial Press, 2011.

———. *Xianggang shi jiao xue can kao zi liao* [Reference for Teaching Hong Kong History]. Vol 1. Hong Kong: Joint Publishing, 1995.

———. *Xianggang yu jindai Zhongguo: Huo Qichang Xianggang shilun* [Hong Kong and Modern China: Fok Kai-cheong's Comments on Hong Kong History]. Hong Kong: Joint Publishing, 2019.

Hurley, R. C. *The Tourist's Guide to Hong Kong, with Short Trips to the Mainland of China*. Hong Kong: R. C. Hurley, 1897.

Institute of Modern History, Academia Sinica, ed. *Jindai Zhongguo dui xifang ji lieqiang renshi ziliao huibian* [Collected Material on China's Understanding of Western and Other Powers in Modern Times]. Vol.1, bk1. Taipei: Institute of Modern History, Academia Sinica, 1972.

Jiang Guansheng. *Zhonggong zai Xianggang (shang juan) (1921–1949)* [The Chinese Communist Party in Hong Kong (Vol. 1) (1921–1949)]. Hong Kong: Cosmos Books, 2011.

———. *Zhonggong zai Xianggang (xia juan) (1949-2012)* [The Chinese Communist Party in Hong Kong (Vol. 2) (1949–2012)]. Hong Kong: Cosmos Books, 2012.

Jiang Haiping, Zhang Chengliang, and Deng Kaisong. *Dong Jiang shui liangdi qing: Neidi yu Xianggang guanxi shiye zhong de Dong Jiang shui gong Xianggang wenti yanjiu* [A Study on the Supply of Dongjiang Water to Hong Kong from the Perspective of the Relationship between the Mainland and Hong Kong]. Guangzhou: Guangdong jiaoyu chubanshe, 2020.

Jiang Shigong. *Xianggang zhengzhi fazhan ziliao huibian (yi): Gang Ying shiqi ji qicao "Jiben Fa"* [Compendium of information on constitutional development in Hong Kong (I): The British–Hong Kong Period and the Drafting of the Basic Law]. Hong Kong: Joint Publishing, 2015.

———. *Xianggang zhengzhi fazhan ziliao huibian (er): 1997-2015 de zhengzhi fazhan* [Compendium of Information on Constitutional Development in Hong Kong (II): Constitutional Development between 1997–2005]. Hong Kong: Joint Publishing, 2015.

Jin Guoping. *Xi li dong jian: Zhong Pu zaoqi jiechu zhuixi* [Western Power in the East: Early Contact between China and Portugal]. Macao: Macao Foundation, 2000.

Jingji daobao she [Economic Bulletin Office]. *1953 nian jingji nianbao* [Annual Economic Report 1953]. Hong Kong: Jingji daobao she, 1953.

Jintian Dengshi Shijian tang jiapu [Lineage of the Tang Clan in Shijian Ancestral Hall, Kam Tin].

Jintian Dengshi zupu [Genealogy of the Tang Clan in Kam Tin].

Jiulong haiguan bianzhi bangongshi [Editorial Office], ed. *Jiulong haiguan zhi, 1887–1990* [The History of Kowloon Maritime Customs, 1887–1990]. Guangzhou: Guangdong renmin chubanshe, 1993.

Jiulong Pugangcun Linshi zupu [Genealogy of the Lam Clan in Po Kong Village, Kowloon].

Jiulong Yaqianwei Wushi chongxiu zupu [Revised Edition of the Genealogy of the Ng Clan in Nga Tsin Wai, Kowloon].

Jiulongcheng qu fengwuzhi bianzhuan xiaozu [Editorial Taskforce]. *Jiulongcheng qu fengwuzhi* [Heritage of Kowloon City District]. Hong Kong: Kowloon City District Council, 2015.

Kerr, Donald W. *Ke'er riji: Xianggang lunxian shiqi Dongjiang zongdui Yingjiu meijun feixingyuan jishi (I Bring You Home Now: A Memoir by Lt. Donald W. Kerr)*. Translated by Li Haiming [Lee Hoi-ming] and Han Bangkai. Hong Kong: Xianggang keji daxue Huanan yanjiu zhongxin, 2015.

Ko Tim-keung, and Jason Wordie. *Ruins of War: A Guide to Hong Kong's Battlefields and Wartime Sites*. Hong Kong: Joint Publishing, 1996.

Kobayashi Hideo, and Shibata Yoshimasa, *Riben junzheng xia de Xianggang* [Hong Kong under the Japanese Military Rule]. Translated by Tian Quan, Li Xi and Wei Yufang. Hong Kong: Commercial Press, 2016.

Kowloon City District Council and Kowloon City District Council Festive Celebration Planning Working Group. *Tracing the Transformation of Kowloon City*. 2nd ed. 2011.

Kuang Jianming [Kwong Kin-ming]. *Gang Ying shidai: Yingguo zhimin guanzhi shu* [British Hong Kong: Colonial Governance of Great Britain]. Rev. ed. Hong Kong: Tianchuang chubanshe youxian gongsi, 2019.

Kuang Zhiwen [Kwong Chi-man]. *Chongguang zhilu: Ri ju Xianggang yu Taiping Yang zhanzheng* [Road to Liberation: The Occupied Hong Kong and the Pacific War]. Hong Kong: Cosmos Books, 2015.

———. *Laobing busi: Xianggang Huaji Yingbing, 1857–1997* [Old Soldiers Never Die: Hong Kong Chinese Soldiers in the British Forces, 1857–1997]. Rev. ed. Hong Kong: Joint Publishing, 2018.

Kuang Zhiwen [Kwong Chi-man], and Cai Yaolun [Tsoi Yiu-lun]. *Dongfang baolei: Xianggang junshi shi, 1840–1970* [Eastern Fortress: A Military History of Hong Kong, 1840–1970]. Hong Kong: Chung Hwa Book Company, 2018.

———. *Gudu qianshao: Taiping Yang zhanzheng zhong de Xianggang zhanyi* [Exposed Outpost: The Battle of Hong Kong in the Pacific War]. Hong Kong: Cosmos Books, 2013.

Kwok Siu-tong. *Ever Onward: 60 Years of Sporting Excellence: Sports Federation and Olympic Committee of Hong Kong*. Hong Kong: Sports Federation & Olympic Committee of Hong Kong, China, 2011.

Kwun Tong District Council, and Kwun Tong District Office, eds. *Guantang miaoyu shilu* [Veritable Records of Temples in Kwun Tong]. Hong Kong: Kwun Tong District Council, 2010.

Labour Department. *The 60th Anniversary of the Labour Department, 1946–2006*. Hong Kong: Labour Department, 2007.

Lai Wenhui [Lai Man-fai]. *Jianming Xianggang zuqiu shi* [A Brief History of Hong Kong Football]. Hong Kong: Joint Publishing, 2018.

Law, Sophia Suk-mun. *The Invisible Citizens of Hong Kong: Art and Stories of Vietnamese Boat People*. Hong Kong: Chinese University Press, 2014.

Legge, James. *The Chinese Classics: with a Translation, Critical and Exegetical Notes, Prolegomena, and Copious Indexes. Vol. 1., Containing Confucian Analects, the Great Learning and the Doctrine of the Mean*. Hong Kong, 1861.

———. *The Chinese Classics: With a Translation, Critical and Exegetical Notes, Prolegomena, and Copious Indexes. Vol. 2., Containing the Works of Mencius*. Hong Kong, 1861.

Lei Jingxuan, and Shen Guoxiang, eds. *Xianggang xuanju ziliao huibian, 1982 nian–1994 nian* [Election Information Compilation for Hong Kong, 1982–1994]. Hong Kong: Hong Kong Institute of Asia-Pacific Studies of The Chinese University of Hong Kong, 1995.

Li Donghai [Leo Lee Tung-hai]. *Xianggang Donghua sanyuan yibai ershi wunian shilue* [A Brief History of 125 years of the Hong Kong Tung Wah Group of Hospitals]. Beijing: Zhongguo wenshi chubanshe, 1998.

Li Gucheng [Li Kwok-sing]. *Xianggang Zhongwen baoye fazhan shi* [History of the Chinese Press in Hong Kong]. Shanghai: Shanghai guji chubanshe, 2005.

Li Haiyan [Lee Hoi-yin], and Lin Xi'er [Lam Heyee]. *The Unspoken Dance: An Oral History of Hong Kong Dance 1950s–70s*. Hong Kong: City Contemporary Dance Company and International Association of Theatre Critics (Hong Kong) Limited, 2019.

Li Hong. *Xianggang da shi ji (gongyuan qian 214 nian–gongyuan 1987 nian)* [Hong Kong Chronicles (214 B.C.–A.D. 1987)]. Beijing: Renmin ribao chubanshe, 1988.

Li Hou. *Bai nian quru shi de zhongjie: Xianggang wenti shimo* [The End of the Hundred Years of Humiliation: The Complete Story of the Hong Kong Issue]. Beijing: Zhongyang wenxian chubanshe, 1997.

Li Jian. *Xianggang Yueju xulun* [Introduction to the Hong Kong Cantonese opera]. Edited by Zhang Li Shuznen [Estella Cham Lai Suk-ching]. Hong Kong: Joint Publishing, 2010.

Li Jifu, comp. *Yuanhe jun xian tuzhi* [Yuanhe Maps and Records of Prefectures and Counties]. Edited by He Cijun. Beijing: Zhonghua Book Company, 1983.

Li Jinqiang [Lee Kam-keung]. *Zhongshan xiansheng yu Gang Ao* [Dr. Sun Yat-sen and Hong Kong and Macao]. Taipei: Zhongguo wenshi chubanshe, 2012.

Li Jinwei. *Xianggang bainian shi (1948)* [A Hundred Years of Hong Kong (1984)]. Hong Kong: Xinyitang youxian gongsi, 2018.

Li Mingkun [Lee Ming-kwan] et al. *Tulu Xianggang da qushi* [Hong Kong in Focus 1997]. Hong Kong, Commercial Press, 1997.

Li Peide [Lee Pui-tak]. *Ji wang kai lai: Xianggang changshang 75 nian* [Seventy-five Years of Hong Kong Manufacturing]. Hong Kong: Commercial Press, 2009.

Li Pengguang [Li Pang-kwong]. *Guanzhi Xianggang: Yingguo jiemi dang'an de qishi* [Governing Hong Kong: Insights from the British Declassified Files]. Hong Kong: Oxford University Press, 2012.

Li Tao, comp. *Xu Zizhi tongjian changbian* [Extended continuation to the Comprehensive Mirror to Aid in Government]. Edited by Shanghai shi fan daxue guji zhengli yanjiusuo and Huadong shifan daxue guji zhengli yanjiusuo. Beijing: Zhonghua Book Company, 2004.

Li Ximi, Mao Huaxuan, Li Chengning, Zhang Jiaohua, Zhou Tian, Li Weimeng, and Dan Zhaowei, eds. *Tangda zhao ling ji bu bian* [Collection of Tang Dynasty Imperial Edicts and Orders (Supplements)]. Shanghai: Shanghai guji chubanshe, 2003.

Li Xinchuan, comp. *Jianyan yilai chao ye zaji* [Miscellaneous Notes on Inner and Outer politics since the Jianyan Reign Period]. Edited by Xu Gui. Beijing: Zhonghua Book Company, 2000.

Li Xingui, trans. *Chouhai tubian* [An Illustrated Compendium on Maritime Security]. Beijing: Zhonghua Book Company, 2017.

Li Zhigang. *Jidujiao zaoqi zai Hua chuanjiao shi* [History of Early Christian Missions in China]. Taipei: Commercial Press, 1985.

Lian Min'an. *Chuangkanhao xinbian, 1940's–1980's* [New Edition of Initial Issue 1940s–1980s]. Hong Kong: Chung Hwa Book Company, 2018.

Liang Baolong [Leung Po-lung]. *Hanxie weicheng: Xianggang zaoqi gongren yu gongyun* [A History of Early Hong Kong Workers and Labour Movements]. Hong Kong: Chung Hwa Book Company, 2017.

Liang Binghua [Leung Ping-wa]. *Chengzhai yu Zhong Ying waijiao* [The Walled City and the Sino-British Diplomacy]. Hong Kong: Qilin shuye youxian gongsi, 1995.

———. *Guantang fengwuzhi* [Heritage of Kwun Tong]. Hong Kong: Kwun Tong District Council, 2008.

———. *Nanqu fengwuzhi* [Heritage of the Southern District]. Rev. ed. Hong Kong: Southern District Council, 2009.

———. *Shenshuibu fengwuzhi* [Heritage of the Sham Shui Po District]. Hong Kong: Sham Shui Po District Council, 2011.

———, ed. *Xianggang Zhong Xi Qu difang zhanggu* [Anecdotes of the Central and Western District, Hong Kong]. Rev. ed. Hong Kong: Central & Western District Council, 2005.

———, ed. *Xianggang Zhong Xi Qu fengwuzhi* [Heritage of the Islands District, Hong Kong]. Hong Kong: Islands District Council, 2007.

———, ed. *Zhongxi qu fengwuzhi* [Heritage of the Central and Western District]. Rev. ed. Hong Kong: Central & Western District, 2011.

Liang Caoya [Leung Cho-nga], Ding Xinbao [Joseph Ting Sun-pao], Luo Tianyou [Joe Lo Tiu-yau], and Luo Huiyan [Lo Wai-yin]. *Jiaoyu yu chengchuan (2): Nanlai zhuxiao de koushu gushi* [Education and Heritage (II): Stories of Schools Relocated to Hong Kong from the North]. Hong Kong: Xianggang jiaoyu tushu gongsi, 2011.

Liang Caoya, and Luo Tianyou. *Kui Qing: Jiumao xinyan, chuancheng yu tupo* [Kwai Tsing: Past and Present, Inheritance and Breakthrough]. Rev. ed. Hong Kong: Kwai Tsing District Council, 2004.

———. *Xianggang kaoping wenhua de cheng yu bian: Cong qiangdiao shaixuan dao fanying nengli* [Inheritance and Changes in Hong Kong's Examination Assessment Culture: From Emphasising Screening to Reflecting Competence]. Hong Kong: Commercial Press, 2017.

Liang Gengyao. *Nan Song yan que: Shiyan chanxiao yu zhengfu kongzhi* [The Monopoly of Salt in the Southern Song Dynasty: Production and Sale under Government Control]. Rev. ed. Taipei: Taida chuban zhongxin, 2014.

Liang Qianwu, ed. *Guide to the Chinese Manufacturers' Products of Hong Kong*. Hong Kong: The Chinese Manufacturers' Association of Hong Kong, 1936.

Liang Shangyuan. *Zhong gong zai Xianggang* [The Communist Party of China in Hong Kong]. Hong Kong: Guangjiao jing chubanshe, 1989.

Liang Tingnan, comp. *Yifen wenji* [Record of Things Heard in the Company of Barbarians]. Edited by Shao Xunzheng. Beijing: Zhonghua Book Company, 1959.

Liao Disheng, Lu Zhanhong, and Hu Shiming. *Going the Extra Miles*. Hong Kong: Drainage Services Department, Government of Hong Kong Special Administrative Region, 2014.

Liaoshi zongzu pu [Genealogy of the Liu Clan].

Lin Tianwei [Lin Tien-wei], and Xiao Guojian [Siu Kwok-kin]. *Xianggang qiandai shilun ji* [Essays on Premodern Hong Kong]. Taipei: Commercial Press, 1985.

Lin Youlan. *Xianggang baoye fazhan shi* [History of the Newspaper Industry in Hong Kong]. Taipei: Shijie shuju, 1977.

———. *Xianggang shihua* [A Brief History of Hong Kong]. Hong Kong: Shanghai shuju, 1985.

Lin Zexu quanji bianji weiyuanhui [Editorial Board]. *Lin Zexu quan ji* [Anthology of Lin Zexu]. Fuzhou: Haixia wenyi chubanshe, 2002.

Lin Zhunxiang [Lam Chun-cheung]. *Xianggang, kaigang: Lishi xinbian* [Beginning of an Entrepot: Hong Kong Historical Revisit]. Hong Kong: Chung Hwa Book Company, 2019.

———. *Yin liu piao hui: Zhongguo zaoqi yinhangye yu Xianggang* [Hong Kong in the Early Banking of China]. Hong Kong: Chung Hwa Book Company, 2016.

Lin Xi'er [Lam Hayee]. *Pulse of the City: Riding on MTR for 40 Years*. Hong Kong: Joint Publishing, 2019.

Liu Cunkuan. *Xianggang shilun cong* [A Study of Hong Kong History]. Hong Kong: Qilin shuye youxian gongsi, 1998.

Liu Lin, Diao Zhongmin, Shu Dagang, and Yin Bo, ed. *Song hui yao ji gao* [Song Dynasty Manuscript Compendium]. Shanghai: Shanghai guji chubanshe, 2014.

Liu Runhe [Lau Yun-woo], Feng Jinrong [Fung Kam-

wing], Gao Tianqiang [Ko Tim-keung], and Zhou Jiajian [Chow Ka-kin]. *Jiulongchengqu fengwuzhi* [Heritage of Kowloon City District]. Hong Kong: Kowloon City District Council, 2005.

Liu Runhe [Lau Yun-woo]. *Xinjie jian shi* [A brief History of the New Territories]. Hong Kong: Joint Publishing, 1999.

Liu Shuyong. *Liu Shuyong Xianggang shiwenji* [Hong Kong History Anthology of Liu Shuyong]. Hong Kong: Chung Hwa Book Company, 2010.

———, ed. *Ershi shiji de Xianggang jingji* [Hong Kong's Economy in the Twentieth century]. Hong Kong: Joint Publishing, 2004.

———, ed. *Jianming Xianggang shi* [A Brief History of Hong Kong]. 3rd ed. Hong Kong: Joint Publishing, 2016.

———, ed. *Yizhi yiye zongguan qing* [Recollections of Hong Kong University Alumni]. Rev. ed. Hong Kong: Hong Kong University Press, 1999.

Liu Shuyong, and Su Wanxing [So Man-hing], eds. *Lianmakeng Cun zhi* [Annals of Lin Ma Hang Village]. Hong Kong: Chung Hwa Book Company, 2015.

Liu Shuyong, and Xiao Guojian [Siu Kwok-kin]. *Xianggang lishi tu shuo* [Illustrated History of Hong Kong]. Hong Kong: Qilin shuye youxian gongsi, 1998.

Liu Yizhang [Lau Yee-cheung], and Ji Chao [Kai Chiu]. *Gudao pianzhou: Jianzheng da shidai de Diaojingling* [The Lonely Island and the Small Boat: Witness Tiu Keng Leng in the Great Era]. Hong Kong: Joint Publishing, 2015.

Liu Yuxi, comp. *Liu Yuxi ji* [Poetic collection of Liu Yuxi]. Edited by "Liu Yuxi ji" zheng li zu, and Bian Xiaoxuan. Beijing: Zhonghua Book Company, 1990.

Liu Zesheng. *Xianggang gujin* [Ancient and Modern Hong Kong]. Guangzhou: Guangzhou weihua chubanshe, 1988.

Liu Zhipeng [Lau Chi-pang]. *Tunmen fengwuzhi* [Heritage of Tuen Mun]. Hong Kong, Tuen Mun District Council, 2003.

———. *Tunmen lishi yu wenhua* [Tuen Mun History and Culture]. Hong Kong, Tuen Mun District Council, 2007

———. *Xianggang Dade xueyuan: Zhongguo zhishi fenzi de zhuiqiu yu mingyun* [A Study of Ta Teh Institute of Hong Kong: Pursuit and Destiny of Chinese Intellects]. Hong Kong: Chung Hwa Book Company, 2011.

———, ed. *Zhantuo jiezhi: Ying zhi Xinjie zaoqi lishi tansuo* [Extension of Hong Kong Territory: Early Historical Exploration of New Territories under the British Rule]. Hong Kong: Chung Hwa Book Company, 2010.

Liu Zhipeng, and Ding Xinbao [Joseph Ting Sun-pao], eds. *Rijun zai Gang zhanzheng zuixing: Zhanfan shenpan jilu ji qi yanjiu* [Japanese War Crimes in Hong Kong: A Study of Trial Records of War Criminals]. Hong Kong: Chung Hwa Book Company, 2015.

Liu Zhipeng, and Huang Junjian [Kenneth Wong Kwan-kin]. *Huangzhukeng gushi: Cong hegu pingyuan dao Chuangxiefang* [The Story of Wong Chuk Hang: From River Valley to Genesis]. Hong Kong: Joint Publishing, 2015.

Liu Zhipeng, Huang Junjian, and Qian Haoxian [Raymond Chin Ho-yin]. *Tiankong xia de chuanqi: Cong Qide dao Chilajiao* [Legends under the Sky: From Kai Tak to Chek Lap Kok]. Hong Kong: Joint Publishing, 2014.

Liu Zhipeng, Huang Ling [Wong Ling], and Sun Xiao, eds. *Zhong Ying jie yu Shatoujiao jinqu* [Chung Ying Street and the Sha Tau Kok Closed Area]. Hong Kong: Heping tushu youxian gongsi, 2011.

Liu Zhipeng, and Liu Shuyong. *Hou Baozhang jiazu shi* [Professor Hou Pao-chang and His Family]. Rev. ed. Hong Kong: Heping tushu youxian gongsi, 2012.

———. *Xianggang diqushi yanjiu zhi si: Tuenmun* [A Study of District History of Hong Kong IV: Tuen Mun]. Hong Kong: Joint Publishing, 2012.

———. *Xianggang shi: Cong yuangu dao jiuqi* [A Brief History of Hong Kong from Ancient Times to 1997]. Hong Kong: City University of Hong Kong Press, 2019.

———, eds. *Fangzhi zhong de gudai Xianggang: "Xin'an xianzhi" Xianggang shiliao xuan* [Ancient Hong Kong in Local Chronicles: Selected Historical Materials of Hong Kong from the Local Chronicles of Xin'an County]. Hong Kong: Joint Publishing, 2020.

———, eds. *Xianggang Weihaiwei jingcha koushu lishi* [An Oral History of the Wei Hai Wei Police Force in Hong Kong]. Hong Kong: City University of Hong Kong Press, 2018.

———, eds. *"Xin'an Xianzhi" Xianggang shiliao xuan* [Selected Historical Materials of Hong Kong from the Local Chronicles of Xin'an County]. Hong Kong: Heping tushu youxian gongsi, 2007.

Liu Kwang-ching. *Anglo-American Steamship Rivalry in China, 1862–1874*. Cambridge: Harvard University Press, 1962.

Lok Sin Tong, Kowloon, ed. *Jiulong Leshantang bainian shishi: 1880–1980* [Centennial History of the Lok Sin Tong, Kowloon: 1880-1980]. Hong Kong: Lok Sin Tong, Kowloon, 1981.

Long Bingyi [David Lung Ping-yee]. *Xianggang gujin jianzhu* [Ancient and Modern Architecture in Hong Kong]. Hong Kong: Joint Publishing, 1992.

Longyuetou Wenshi zupu [Genealogy of the Wan Clan in Lung Yeuk Tau].

Lu Dale [Lui Tai-lok]. *Na siceng xiangshi de qishi niandai* [The 1970s We Seem to Know]. Hong Kong: Chung Hwa Book Company, 2012.

———. *Ningju liliang: Xianggang fei zhengfu jigou fazhan guiji* [Gathering Force: The Trajectory of Non-governmental Organisations in Hong Kong]. Hong Kong: Joint Publishing, 2010.

Lu Gonghui [Christine Loh Kung-wai]. *Dixia zhenxian: Zhong gong zai Xianggang de lishi* [Underground Front: Chinese Communist Party in Hong Kong]. Hong Kong: Hong Kong University Press, 2011.

Lu Hongji [Bernard Luk Hung-kay]. *Zuokan yunqi shi: Yiben Xianggang ren de jiao xie shi* [Watch the Rising Clouds: A People's History of the Hong Kong Professional Teachers' Union]. Hong Kong: City University of Hong Kong Press, 2016.

Lu Jin. *Jiulongcheng zhaijian shi* [A Concise History of Kowloon Walled City]. Hong Kong: Joint Publishing, 2018.

Lu Kun, Deng Tingzhen, and Wang Hongbin, eds. *Guangdong haifang huilan* [A Conspectus of Guangdong's Coastal Defence]. Shijiazhuang: Hebei renmin chubanshe, 2009.

Lu Shiqiang [Lu Shih-chiang]. *Zhongguo zaoqi de lunchuan jingying* [Vessel Operation in Early China]. Taipei: Institute of Modern History, Academia Sinica, 2015.

Lu Yan. *Xianggang zhanggu* [Hong Kong Anecdotes]. 13 vols. Hong Kong: Guangjiaojing chubanshe, 1977–1991.

Lujingcun Chenshi zupu [Genealogy of the Chan Clan in Luk Keng Village].

Luo Fu. *Xianggang wenhua manyou* [A Tour of Hong Kong Cultures]. Hong Kong: Chung Hwa Book Company, 1993.

Luo Wanxian [Law Yuen-han]. *Xianggang xiyi fazhan shi, 1842–1990* [History of Western Medicine in Hong Kong, 1842–1990]. Hong Kong: Chung Hwa Book Company, 2018.

Luo Xianglin [Lo Hsiang-lin] et al. *Yibasier nian yiqian zhi Xianggang ji qi duiwai jiaotong: Xianggang qiandai shi* [Hong Kong and Its External Communications before 1842: History of Hong Kong prior to British Arrival]. Hong Kong: Zhongguo xueshe, 1959.

Ma Duanlin, comp. *Wenxian tongkao* [Comprehensive Textual Research of Historical Documents]. Edited by Shanghai shifan daxue guji yanjiusuo, and Huadong shifan daxue guji yanjiusuo. Beijing: Zhonghua Book Company, 2011.

Ma Guanyao [Ma Koon-yiu]. *Che shui ma long: Xianggang zhanqian lushang jiaotong* [History of Pre-war Hong Kong Road Traffic]. Hong Kong: Joint Publishing, 2016.

———. *Xianggang gongcheng kao er: Sanshiyi tiao yi gongchengshi mingming de jiedao* [History of Hong Kong Engineering II: Thirty-one Streets Named after Engineers]. Hong Kong: Joint Publishing, 2014.

———. *Zhanqian Xianggang dianxun shi* [History of Telecommunications in Pre-war Hong Kong]. Hong Kong: Joint Publishing, 2020.

Ma Jinke, ed. *Zao qi Xianggang shi yan jiuzi liaoxuan ji* [A Selected Collection of the Studies in Hong Kong History]. Hong Kong: Joint Publishing, 2018.

Ma Muchi [Ma Muk-chi]. *Xigong lishi yu fengwu* [History and Heritage of Sai Kung]. Hong Kong: Sai Kung District Council, 2003.

Macmillan, Allister. *Seaports of the Far East: Historical and Descriptive, Commercial and Industrial, Facts, Figures, & Resources.* London: W. H. & L. Collingridge, 1923.

Mai Meisheng, ed. *Fandui xubi shilue* [A Brief History of the Anti-Mui Tsai Movement]. Hong Kong: Fuxing zhongxi yinwuji, 1933.

Mark Chi-kwan. *Lengzhan yu Xianggang: Ying Mei guanxi 1949–1957 (Hong Kong and the Cold War: Anglo-American relations 1949–1957).* Translated by Lin Liwei [Willy Lam]. Hong Kong: Chung Hwa Book Company, 2018.

Marquis-Who's Who, Inc. *Who's who in Commerce and Industry.* Chicago: Marquis Who's Who, 1957.

Matheson, Jardine. *Jardines: 175 Years of Looking to the Future.* Hong Kong: Jardines, 2007.

Meacham, William. *The Archaeology of Hong Kong.* Hong Kong: Hong Kong University Press, 2009.

Melson, Peter. *White Ensign-red Dragon: The History of the Royal Navy in Hong Kong 1841–1997.* Hong Kong: Edinburgh Financial Publishing Asia Ltd., 1997.

Meng Qingshun. *Xianggang lianzheng zhidu yanjiu* [A Study of the Integrity System in Hong Kong]. Hong Kong: Joint Publishing, 2017.

Miners, Norman. *The Government and Politics of Hong Kong.* Hong Kong: Oxford University Press, 1998.

Mo Shixiang, and Chen Hong. *Ri luo Xiangjiang: Xianggang dui Ri zuozhan jishi* [Sunset in Hong Kong: Chronicles of the War against Japan in Hong Kong]. Rev. ed. Hong Kong: Joint Publishing, 2015.

Morse, Hosea Ballou. *The Chronicles of the East India Company Trading to China, 1635–1834.* Oxford: Clarendon Press, 1929.

Munn, Christopher. *Anglo-China: Chinese People and British Rule in Hong Kong, 1841–1880.* New York: Routledge, 2013.

Ng Lun, Alice Ngai-ha. *Interactions of East and West: Development of Public Education in Early Hong Kong.* Hong Kong: Chinese University Press, 1984.

———, ed. *The Quest for Excellence: A History of The Chinese University of Hong Kong, 1963–1993.* Hong Kong: Chinese University Press, 1993.

Ng, Michael H. K., and John D Wong. *Civil Unrest and Governance in Hong Kong: Law and Order from Historical and Cultural Perspectives.* New York: Routledge, 2017.

Nihon Yūsen Kabushiki Kaisha. *Golden Jubilee History of Nippon Yusen Kaisha, 1885–1935.* Tokyo: Nippon yusen kaisha, 1935.

North District Council, ed. *Beiqu fengwuzhi* [Heritage of the North District]. Hong Kong: North District Council, 1994.

Norton-Kyshe, and James William. *The History of the Laws and Courts of Hong Kong from the Earliest Period to 1898.* Hong Kong: Vetch and Lee, 1971.

O'Connor, Paul. *Islam in Hong Kong: Muslims and Everyday Life in China's World City.* Hong Kong: Hong Kong University Press, 2020.

Ogura Hirokatsu. *Honkon* [Hong Kong]. Tokyo: Iwanami Shoten, 1942.

———. *Riju shiqi de Xianggang jian shi* [A Brief History of Hong Kong during Japanese Occupation]. Translated by Lin Chaochun. Hong Kong: Commercial Press, 2020.

Ou Muzhang, and Luo Wenhua. *Zhongguo yinhang ye fazhan shi: You wan Qing zhi dangxia* [The Evolution of Modern China's Banking Industry: From the Late Qing Dynasty to the Present]. Hong Kong: City University of Hong Kong Press, 2011.

Ou Zhijian [Au Chi-kin]. *Ma'anshan fengwuzhi: Kuangye xingshuai* [Heritage of Ma On Shan: Rise and Fall of the Mining Industry]. Hong Kong: Shatian quyi hui, 2002.

Ou Jiafa [Au Ka-fat]. *Yue Gang kaogu yu faxian* [Guangdong and Hong Kong Archaeology and Discoveries]. Hong Kong: Joint Publishing, 2004.

Ou Jialin [Allan Au Ka-lun], ed. *Xianggang dashi huigu quan jilu 1967–2016 daodu* [Hong Kong Review 1967–2006]. Hong Kong: TVB Publications Limited, 2007.

Ou Zhijian [Au Chi-kin], Chen Heshun [Alex Chan Wo-shun], and He Rongzong [Ho Wing-chung]. *Xianggang hai guan bai nian shi, 1909–2009* [Hong Kong Customs: A Centenary History, 1909–2009]. Hong Kong: Customs and Excise Department, 2009.

Ou Zhijian, Peng Shumin, and Cai Sixing. *Gaibian Xianggang lishi de liushi pian wenxian* [Sixty Documents that Changed the History of Hong Kong]. Hong Kong: Chung Hwa Book Company, 2011.

Ouchterlony, John. *The Chinese War: An Account of the Operations of the British Forces from the Commencement of the Treaty of Nanking*. London: Saunders and Otley, 1844.

Ouyang Xiu, and Song Qi, eds. *Xin Tang shu* [New History of the Tang Dynasty]. Beijing: Zhonghua Book Company, 1975.

Oxley, D. H., ed. *Victoria Barracks, 1842–1979*. Hong Kong: British Forces Hong Kong, 1979.

Pan Huilian [Pun Wai-lin]. *Xunzhao meirenyu Yang Xiuqiong: Xianggang yidai nü yongjiang kang Ri mixin* [In Search of the Mermaid Yeung Sau-king: Secret of a Generation of Hong Kong Female Swimmers' Resistance against Japanese Aggression]. Hong Kong: Pun Wai Lin, 2019.

Pan Shuhua [Poon Shuk-wah], and Huang Yonghao [Wong Wing-ho]. *Xianxia, haibin yu haiyu: Xiangjiang youyong shi* [Leisure, Seashore and Sea Bathing: History of Swimming in Hong Kong]. Hong Kong: Joint Publishing, 2014.

Peng Chong [Pang Chung]. *Zouguo Xianggang Aoyun lu* [Hong Kong's Road to the Olympics]. Hong Kong: South China Athletic Association, 2019.

Pinkstone, Mark, and David Booth. *Legislative Council Then and Now: A Journey to the New Complex*. Hong Kong: Legislative Council Commission, 2012.

Poon, S. W., and K. Y. Ma. *Report on the History of Quarrying in Hong Kong, 1840–1940*. Hong Kong: Lord Wilson Heritage Trust, 2010.

Poy, Vivienne. *A River Named Lee*. Scarborough: Calyan Publishing, 1995.

Public Affairs Branch of News and Information Division. *1967-2016 Xianggang dashi huigu quan jilu daodu* [Hong Kong Review 1967–2016]. Hong Kong: TVB Publications Limited, 2017.

Puga, Rogério Miguel. *The British Presence in Macau, 1635–1793*. Translated by Monica Andrade. Hong Kong: Hong Kong University Press, 2013.

"Putai Dao fengwuzhi" gongzuozu [Task Force]. *Putai Dao fengwuzhi* [Heritage of Po Toi Island]. Hong Kong: Chung Hwa Book Company, 2016.

Qian Liqun, Wen Rumin, and Wu Fuhui. *Zhongguo xiandai wenxue sanshi nian* [Thirty Years of Modern Chinese Literature]. Rev. ed. Taipei: Wunan tushu, 2002.

Qiu Dong [Yau Tung]. *Xinjie fengwu yu min qing* [Heritage of the New Territories and Its People]. Hong Kong: Joint Publishing, 1992.

Qu Dajun, comp. *Guangdong xin yu* [A New Account of Guangdong]. Beijing: Zhonghua Book Company, 1985.

Rao Jiucai [Iu Kow-choy]. *Shijiu ji ershi shiji de Xianggang yunongye chuancheng yu zhuanbian (shang ce nongye)* [Heritage and Change of Hong Kong's Fisheries and Agriculture in the Nineteenth and Twentieth Centuries (Volume I Fisheries)]. Hong Kong: Friends of the Country Parks; Cosmos Books, 2015.

———. *Shijiu ji ershi shiji de Xianggang yunongye chuancheng yu zhuanbian (Xiace nongye)* [Heritage and Change of Hong Kong's Fisheries and Agriculture in the Nineteenth and Twentieth Centuries (Volume II Agriculture)]. Hong Kong: Friends of the Country Parks; Cosmos Books, 2017.

———. *Xianggang de diming yu difang lishi (xia): xin jie* [Name of Places and History of Hong Kong (II): New Territories]. Hong Kong: Cosmos Books, 2012.

Rao Zongyi [Jao Tsung-i]. *Xianggang shi lun ji* [Research on Hong Kong History]. Edited by

Zheng Weiming [Cheng Wai-meng]. Hong Kong: Chung Hwa Book Company, 2019.

Rollo, Dennis. *The Guns and Gunners of Hong Kong*. Hong Kong: Gunners' Roll of Hong Kong, 1991.

Ruan Zhi [Yuen Chi]. *Rujing wenjin: Xianggang bianjing jinqu shi* [Prohibition on Entry: A History of the Frontier Closed Area in Hong Kong]. Hong Kong: Joint Publishing, 2014.

———. *Zhong Gang bianjie de bainian bianqian: Cong Shatoujiao Lianmakeng Cun shuo qi* [A Century of Changes at the Border between the Mainland of China and Hong Kong: From Lin Ma Hang Village in Sha Tau Kok]. Hong Kong: Joint Publishing, 2012.

Sayer, Geoffrey Robley. *Hong Kong 1841–1862: Birth, Adolescence and Coming of Age*. Hong Kong: Hong Kong University Press, 1980.

———, ed. *Hong Kong 1862–1919: Years of Discretion*. Hong Kong: Hong Kong University Press, 1975.

Sham Shui Po District Committee on Promotion of Civic Education, ed. *Cong Shenshuibu dao Shenshuipu* [From Sham Shui Po to Sham Shui Po]. Hong Kong: Sham Shui Po District Committee on Promotion of Civic Education, 1998.

Shang Zhitan. *Xianggang kaogu lunji* [Collected Essays on Hong Kong Archaeology]. Beijing: Wenwu chubanshe, 2000.

Shang Zhitan, and Wu Weihong [Steven Ng Wai-hung]. *Xianggang kaogu xue xu yan* [Documentation of Hong Kong Archaeological Research]. Beijing: Wenwu chubanshe, 2010.

Shanghai shudian chubanshe, ed. *Zhongguo difangzhi jicheng: Guangdong fuxian zhi ji* [A Collection of Local Chronicles in China: Local Chronicles of Prefectures and Counties in Guangdong Province]. Shanghai: Shanghai shudian chubanshe, 2003.

Shangshui Liaoshi Yueyougong jiapu [Lineage of Yuet Yau Kung of the Liu Clan in Sheung Shui].

Shangshui Liaoshi zupu [Genealogy of the Liu Clan in Sheung Shui].

Shangwu yinshuguan bianji bu, ed. *Tulu Xianggang daqushi (1993–1996)* [Hong Kong in Focus 1993–1996]. Hong Kong: Commercial Press, 1993–1996.

Shatian gujin fengmao bianji weiyuanhu [Editorial Board], ed. *Shatian gujin fengmao* [Shatin Then and Now]. Hong Kong: Sha Tin District Board, 1997.

Shenggang da bagong jiushi zhounian huigu lunwenji

bianji weiyuanhui [Editorial Board]. *Yue Gang gongren da ronghe: Sheng Gang da bagong jiushi zhounian huigu lunwenji* [The Great Integration of Guangdong and Hong Kong Workers: Collected Essays on the Ninetieth Anniversary of the Canton–Hong Kong Strike]. Hong Kong: Xianggang shehui baozhang xuehui; Xianggang gongyun shi yanjiu xiaozu, 2017.

Shi Minghui, ed. *Dayu Shan zhi* [Lantau Chronicle]. Hong Kong: Baolian chansi, 1958.

Sibitang Chenshi zupu zhi [Genealogy of the Chan Clan in Sei Bit Tong].

Silva, Beatriz Basto da. *Aomen biannian shi* [Chronicles of Macao]. Macao: Macao Foundation, 1995.

———. *Aomen biannian shi: Shijiu shiji* [Chronicles of Macao (Nineteenth Century)]. Macao: Macao Foundation, 1998.

Sima Qian. *Shi ji* [Records of the Grand Historian]. Beijing: Zhonghua Book Company, 1959.

Sinclair, Kevin. *Royal Hong Kong Police: 150th Anniversary Commemorative Publication, 1844–1994*. Hong Kong: Police Public Relations Branch of Royal Hong Kong Police Force, 1994.

Sinn, Elizabeth [Sinn Yuk-yee]. *Bank of East Asia: A Century of Innovation, Progress and Commitment 1919–2019*. Hong Kong: Bank of East Asia Limited, 2019.

———. *Chuansuo taipingyang: Jinshan meng, Huaren chuyang yu Xianggang de xingcheng (Pacific Crossing: California Gold, Chinese Migration, and the Making of Hong Kong)*. Translated by Lin Liwei [Willy Lam]. Hong Kong: Chung Hwa Book Company, 2019.

———. *Meeting Place: Encounters across Cultures in Hong Kong, 1841–1984*. Edited by Christopher Munn. Hong Kong: Hong Kong University Press, 2017.

Situ Hua [Szeto Wah]. *Dajiang dongqu: Situ Hua huiyilu* [The River of No Return: The Memoirs of Szeto Wah]. Hong Kong: Oxford University Press, 2011.

Sixteen Teachers from the Golden Jubilee Secondary School, eds. *Jin xi shijian: Cong chuangxiao dao fengxiao* [The Golden Jubilee Incident: From the Founding to the Closing of the School]. Hong Kong: Jiao yu xue zazhishe, 1978.

Smith, Carl T. *Chinese Christians: Elites, Middlemen, and the Church in Hong Kong*. Hong Kong: Hong Kong University Press, 2005.

Smith, D. Warren. *European Settlements in the Far East; China, Japan, Corea, Indo-China, Straits Settlements, Malay States, Siam, Netherlands, India, Borneo, the Philippines, etc.* London: Sampson Low, Marston & Company, 1900.

Song Lian et al., comps. *Yuan shi* [History of the Yuan Dynasty]. Beijing: Zhonghua Book Company, 1976.

Stokes, Gwenneth, and John Stokes. *Queen's College: Its History, 1862–1987*. Hong Kong: Queen's College Old Boys' Association, 1987.

Su Wanxing [So Man-hing]. *Yaqianwei: Xiaoshi zhong de shiqu zuihou weicun* [Nga Tsin Wai: The Last Village in the Disappearing Urban Area]. Hong Kong: Chung Hwa Book Company, 2013.

Sun Qin'an. *Mao Zedong yu guomindang zhuming jiangling* [Mao Zedong and Famous Kuomintang Generals]. Chongqing: Chongqing chubanshe, 2002.

Sun Yang. *Guomin zhengfu dui Xianggang wenti de chuzhi (1937-1949)* [The National Government's Handling of the Hong Kong Issue (1937–1949)]. Hong Kong: Joint Publishing, 2017.

Sun Yuxiu, ed. *Hanfen lou miji* [Secret Satchels of the Hanfen Studio]. Beijing: Beijing tushuguan chubanshe, 2000.

Sweeting, Anthony. *Education in Hong Kong Pre-1841 to 1941: Fact and Opinion*. Hong Kong: Hong Kong University Press, 1990.

Taikoo Dockyard & Engineering Company of Hong Kong. *Fifty Years of Shipbuilding and Repairing in the Far East*. London: Technical Advertising Service, 1953.

Tan Huizhu [Maria Tam Wai-chu], ed. *Jibenfa yu Xianggang: Huigui ershi zhounian* [The Basic Law and Hong Kong: The Twentieth Anniversary of Hong Kong's Reunification with the Motherland]. Hong Kong: Xianggang youhao xiejinhu, 2017.

Tan Chwee-huat. *Financial Sourcebook for Southeast Asia and Hong Kong*. Singapore: Singapore University Press, 2000.

Tanaka Kazunari. *Zhongguo de zongzu yu yanju: Huanan zongzu shehui zhong jisi zuzhi, yili ji qi yanju de xiangguan gouzao* [China, Clans and Drama: Structure of Sacrificial Organisations, Rituals and Drama in Southern Chinese Clan Societies]. Translated by Qian Hang and Ren Yubai. Hong Kong: Joint Publishing, 2019.

Tang Kaijian, Xiao Guojian [Siu Kwok-kin], and Chen Jiarong [Aaron Chen Jia-rong], eds. *Xianggang 6000 nian: yuan gu–1997*. [Hong Kong in 6,000 Years: From Ancient Times to 1997]. Hong Kong: Qilin shuye youxian gongsi, 1998.

Tōyō Keizai Shinpōsha, ed. *Gunseika no Honkon: Shinseishita Dai Tō-A no chūkaku* [Hong Kong under Military Administration]. Hong Kong: Honkon Tōyō Keizaisha, 1944.

Traver, Harold H., and Mark S. Gaylord, eds. *Drugs, Law and the State*. Hong Kong: Hong Kong University Press, 1992.

Tsang, Steve [Tsang Yui-sang]. *A Documentary History of Hong Kong: Government and Politics*. Hong Kong: Hong Kong University Press, 1995.

———. *A Modern History of Hong Kong*. Hong Kong: Hong Kong University Press, 2004.

Tu, Elsie Hume Elliot. *Wo yanzhong de zhimin shidai Xianggang* (*Colonial Hong Kong in the Eyes of Elsie Tu*). Translated by Sui Lijun. Hong Kong: Wen Wei Publishing, 2004.

Tuet, Alima, Yao Jide, and Ma Jianxiong, eds. *Xianggang Hui min shiliao gailan, 1917–2017* [Collection of Historical Archives of the Hui Muslim Community in Hong Kong, 1917–2017]. Hong Kong: Xianggang keji daxue Huanan yanjiu zhongxin, 2018.

Tuotuo et al., comps. *Song shi* [History of the Song Dynasty]. Beijing: Zhonghua Book Company, 1977.

U.S. Department of Treasury, comp. *Monetary Units and Coinage Systems of the Principal Countries of the World*. Washington: Government Printing Office, 1929.

Wang Cun, comp. *Yuanfeng jiuyu zhi* [Treatise of Nine Regions during the Yuanfeng Reign (1077–1085)]. Edited by Wang Wenchu and Wei Songshan. Beijing: Zhonghua Book Company, 1984.

Wang Gungwu, ed. *Xianggang shi xinbian* [Hong Kong History in New Perspectives]. Rev. ed. Hong Kong: Joint Publishing, 2017.

Wang Pu, comp. *Tang hui yao* [Essentials of the Tang]. Beijing: Zhonghua Book Company, 1955.

Wang Qile [Wong Chai-lok]. *Xianggang Zhongwen jiaoyu fazhan shi* [A History of the Development of Chinese Education in Hong Kong]. Hong Kong: Bowen shuju, 1983.

Wang Xiangzhi, comp. *Yudi Jisheng* [Records of Famous Places]. Beijing: Zhonghua Book Company, 1992.

Water Supplies Department. *Milestones of Hong Kong Water Supply*. Hong Kong: Water Supplies Department, 2011.

Watson, James L., and Rubie S. Watson. *Xiangtu Xianggang: Xinjie de zhengzhi, xingbie ji liyi (Village Life in Hong Kong: Politics, Gender, and Ritual in the New Territories)*. Translated by Cheung Yuen-lai and Shing Sze-wai. Hong Kong: Chinese University Press, 2011.

Wei Dingming [Ngai Ting-ming]. *Xian zong fo ji: Xianggang minjian xinyang bainian* [The Trail of Immortals and Buddhists: A Century of Folk Beliefs in Hong Kong]. Hong Kong: Joint Publishing, 2019.

———, ed. *Renji jin xi zhi* [History of Fifty Years of Yan Chai Hospital]. Hong Kong: Board of Yan Chai Hospital, 2017.

Wei Junzi. *Guangying li de langhua: Xianggang dianying mailuo huiyi* [Waves in Lights and Shadows: Memories about Hong Kong Films]. Hong Kong: Chung Hwa Book Company, 2019.

Wei Yuan, ed. *Haiguo tuzhi* [Records and Maps of the World]. Beijing: Wenwu chubanshe, 2017.

Welsh, Frank. *A History of Hong Kong*. London: Harper Collins, 1997.

Wen Wei Publishing, ed. *Jibenfa de dansheng* [The Birth of the Basic Law]. Hong Kong: Wen Wei Publishing Co., Ltd., 1990.

Wenshi zupu [Genealogy of the Man Clan].

Wesley-Smith, Peter. *Unequal Treaty, 1898–1997, China, Great Britain and Hong Kong's New Territories*. Hong Kong: Oxford University Press, 1980.

Whitefield, Andrew J. *Hong Kong, Empire and the Anglo-American Alliance at War, 1941–1945*. Hong Kong: Hong Kong University Press, 2001.

Wing On Department Stores Limited. *Wing On Department Stores Celebrating 100 Years of Retailing*. Hong Kong: Wing On Department Stores (Hong Kong) Limited, 2007.

Wright, Arnold, and H. A. Cartwright, eds. *Twentieth Impressions of Hong Kong, Shanghai and Other Treaty Ports of China: Their History, People, Commerce, Industries, and Resources*. London: Lloyd's Greater Britain Pub. Co, 1908.

Wu Baling [Ng Bar-ling]. *Xianggang zhanggu* [Hong Kong Anecdotes]. Hong Kong: Xianggang daxue Kong Andao jinian tushuguan, 1984.

Wu Bangmou [James Ng Bong-mau]. *Xianggang hangkong 125 nian* [Aviation in Hong Kong,

1891–2015]. Rev. ed. Hong Kong: Chung Hwa Book Company, 2016.

———. *Zai kan Qide: Cong Ri zhan shiqi shuo qi* [Another Look at Kai Tak: From the Time of Japanese Occupation]. Hong Kong: Zkoob Limited, 2009.

Wu Chongyao, ed. *Lingnan yishu*. Edition during the 11th–30th year of the reign of Emperor Daoguang of the Qing dynasty (1831–1863).

Wu Lanxiu, comp. *Nan Han ji* [History of Southern Han]. Edited by Wang Fu. Guangzhou: Guangdong gaodeng jiaoyu chubanshe, 1993.

Wu Renchen, comp. *Shiguo chunqiu* [Spring and Autumn Annals of the Ten Kingdoms]. Edited by Xu Minxia and Zhou Ying. Beijing: Zhonghua Book Company, 1983.

Wu Xiangxiang, ed. *Zhongshan wenxian* [Historical Documents on Zhongshan Country]. Taipei: Student Book Company, 1965.

Wu Zhiliang, Tang Kaijian, and Jin Guoping, eds. *Aomen biannianshi* [Chronicle of Macao]. Guangzhou: Guangdong renmin chubanshe, 2009.

Wulanmulun, ed. *Mai xiang 21 shiji de Xianggang jingji* [Hong Kong's Economy in the Twenty-first Century]. Beijing: Zhongguo caizheng jingji chubanshe, 1997.

Xia Qilong [Louis E. Keloon Ha]. *Xianggang Tianzhujiao chuanjiao shi, 1841–1894 (The Foundation of the Catholic Mission in Hong Kong, 1841-1894)*. Translated by Cai Diyun. Hong Kong: Joint Publishing, 2014.

———, ed. *Migao yu elong: shi jiu shiji Tianzhujiao fenchang yu Xianggang* [Michael and the Evil Dragon: The Nineteenth Century Catholic Cemetery and Hong Kong]. Hong Kong: Centre for Catholic Studies, The Chinese University of Hong Kong, 2008.

Xiacun Dengshi zupu [Genealogy of the Tang Clan in Ha Tsuen].

Xianggang jiaoyu ziliao zhongxin bianxie zu [Chinese Editorial Task Force for Hong Kong Education Materials]. *Xianggang jiaoyu fazhan licheng dashiji, 1075–2003* [A Chronology of Educational Development in Hong Kong, 1075–2003]. Hong Kong: Xianggang gejie wenhua cujinhui, 2004.

Xianggang laoxiao jiaoyu jigou [Hong Kong Workers' School Educational Organisation]. *Xianggang laoxiao 70 zhounian xiaoqing jinian tekan, 1946–2016* [Hong Kong Workers' School Seventieth Anniversary Commemorative Special Issue]. Hong

Kong: Laogong zidi zhongxue, 2016.

Xianggang Xinjie Jinqiancun Houshi zupu [Genealogy of the Hau Clan in Kam Tsin Village, New Territories, Hong Kong].

Xianggang yuandong xinwenshe [Hong Kong Far East News Agency], ed. *Gang Jiu qiao xiaoshi lue* [A Brief History of Overseas Chinese Schools in Hong Kong and Kowloon]. Hong Kong: Xianggang yuandong xinwenshe, 1946.

Xiao Guojian [Siu Kwok-kin]. *Dabu fengwuzhi* [Heritage of Tai Po]. Rev. ed. Hong Kong: Tai Po District Council, 2007.

———. *Qingdai Xianggang zhi haifang yu gulei* [Hong Kong's Maritime Defence and Old Forts during the Qing Dynasty]. Hong Kong: Xianchao shushi,1982.

———. *Tanben suowei: Xianggang zao qi lishi lunji* [Explore the Origins and Research the Details: Essays on the Early History of Hong Kong]. Hong Kong: Chung Hwa Book Company, 2015.

———. *Xianggang gudai shi xinbian* [A New Edition of the Ancient History of Hong Kong]. Hong Kong: Chung Hwa Book Company, 2019.

———. *Xianggang de lishi yu wenwu* [History and Cultural Relics of Hong Kong]. Hong Kong: Ming Pao Publications, 1997.

———. *Xianggang lidao shi ji zhi* [Records of Historical Sites on Hong Kong Outlying Islands]. Hong Kong: Xianzhao shushi, 1985.

———. *Xianggang lishi yu shehui* [Hong Kong History and Society]. Hong Kong: Xianggang jiaoyu tushu gongsi, 1994.

———. *Xianggang lishi diandi* [A History of Hong Kong]. Hong Kong: Xiandai jiaoyu yanjiushe, 1992.

———. *Xianggang lishi yanjiu* [A Study of Hong Kong History]. Hong Kong: Xianzhao shushi, 2004.

———, ed. *Youjianwangqu fengwuzhi* [Heritage of the Yau Tsim Mong District]. Hong Kong: Yau Tsim Mong District Council, 1999.

Xie Junjie [Brain Tse Chun-kit]. *Xianggang huobi jianshi: Cong zhanhou zhi kaibu 175 zai* [A Concise History of Hong Kong Currency: From Post-war Years to 2016]. Hong Kong: Chao meiti chuban youxian gongsi, 2016.

Xie Yongguang [Tse Wing-kwong]. *Xianggang zhanhou fengyunlu* [Post-war Years of Hong Kong]. Hong Kong: Ming Pao Publications, 2016.

Xu Jiatun. *Xu Jiatun Xianggang huiyilu* [Hong Kong Memoirs by Xu Jiatun]. Hong Kong: Xianggang lianhe bao youxian gongsi, 1993.

Xue Fengxuan [Victor Sit Fung-shuen]. *Xianggang fazhan ditu ji* [Hong Kong: 160 Years of Development in Maps]. 2nd ed. Hong Kong: Joint Publishing, 2010.

Xue Fengxuan, and Kuang Zhiwen [Kwong Chi-man]. *Xinjie xiangyiju shi: You zujiedi dao yiguo liangzhi* [History of Heung Yee Kuk N. T.: From Concession to One Country, Two Systems]. Hong Kong: Joint Publishing, 2011.

Xue Haoran [Kingsley Sit Ho-yin]. *Xinjie xiaoxing wuyu zhengce yanjiu: Lishi, xianzhuang yu qianzhan* [New Territories Small House Policy Study: Past, Present and Future]. Hong Kong: New Territories Heung Yee Kuk Research Centre, 2016.

"Xuxiu siku quanshu" Bianzuan Weiyuanhui [Editorial Board], ed. *Xuxiu siku quanshu* [Addendum to the Complete Works of the Four Treasuries]. Shanghai: Shanghai guji chubanshe, 2002.

Yang Guoxiong [Yeung Kwok-hung]. *Jiu shukan zhong de Xianggang shenshi* [Old Publications: Window of the Past]. Hong Kong: Joint Publishing, 2014.

Yang Peishan [Yeung Pui-shan], Ye Jianmin [Yep Kin-man], and Zhu Jialing [Chu Ka-ling]. *Yuenan chuanmin zai Xianggang* [Vietnamese Boat People in Hong Kong]. Hong Kong: Xianggang minzhu tongmeng, 1991.

Yang Qi, ed. *Xianggang gailun* [General Views on Hong Kong]. 2 vols. Hong Kong: Joint Publishing, 1990–1993.

———, ed. *Xianggang lunxian da yingjiu* [The Great Rescue after the Fall of Hong Kong]. Adapted by Yu Fei. Hong Kong: Joint Publishing, 2014.

Yang Ruwan [Yeung Yue-man], and Wang Jiaying [Wong Ka-ying], eds. *Xianggang gongying fangwu wushi nian: Jinxi huigu yu qianzhan* [Fifty Years of Public Housing in Hong Kong: A Golden Jubilee Review and Prospect]. Hong Kong: Chinese University Press, 2003.

Yang Wenxin [Yeung Man-shun], Huang Yudong [Wong Yuk-tung], Ming Rouyou [Ming Yau-yau], Xie Junye [Tse Chun-yip], and Chen Tianhao [Chan Tin-ho]. *Xiangjiang jiuwen: Shijiu shiji Xianggangren de shenghuo diandi* [Old News: Snapshots of Daily Life in Nineteenth-century Hong Kong]. Hong Kong: Chung Hwa Book Company, 2014.

Yao Yingjia. *Qunli sheng tian: Zhanqian Xianggang matou kuli yu Huaren shequ de guanzhi* [Grass-root Fighters: Hong Kong Stevedores and Colonial Governance over the Chinese before the War]. Hong Kong: Joint Publishing, 2015.

Yau, Kinnia Shuk-ting. *Japanese and Hong Kong Film Industries: Understanding the Origins of East Asian Film Networks*. London: Routledge, 2010.

Ye Jianmin [Ray Yep Kin-man]. *Jingmo geming: Xianggang lianzheng bainian gongye* [Silent Revolution: History of Anti-corruption Campaign in Hong Kong]. Hong Kong: Chung Hwa Book Company, 2014.

Ye Lingfeng. *Du shu sui bi* [Reading Notes]. 3 vols. Hong Kong: Joint Publishing, 2019.

———. *Ye Lingfeng wenji: Xianggang zhanggu* [The Collected Works of Ye Lingfeng: Hong Kong Anecdotes]. Guangzhou: Huacheng chubanshe, 1999.

Yeh, Emilie Yueh-yu, ed. *Early Film Culture in Hong Kong, Taiwan, and Republican China: Kaleidoscopic Histories*. Ann Arbor: University of Michigan Press, 2018.

Ying Jia, Ling Yunyi, and Liu Yaohui, eds. *Cangwu zongdu jun menzhi* [Records of Cangwu Military Principle]. Edited by Zhao Kesheng, and Li Ran. National Central Library in Taipei. Edition of Guangdong buzhengsi in the 9th year during the Reign of Emperor Wanli of the Ming Dynasty, 1581.

Yip Ka-che, Wong Man-kong, and Leung Yuen-sang, eds. *A Documentary History of Public Health in Hong Kong*. Hong Kong: Chinese University Press, 2018.

You Shaohua. *Xianggang sifa tizhi yange* [Evolution on Hong Kong's Organisational System of Judiciary]. Hong Kong: Commercial Press, 2012.

You Zi'an [Yau Tze-on], ed. *Huangdaxian qu fengwuzhi* [Heritage of Wong Tai Sin District]. Hong Kong: Wong Tai Sin District Council, 2002.

Yu Jiangqiang, ed. *Xianggang huigui zuguo 20 zhounian zhi: Lu you yu ling shou* [The Twentieth Anniversary of Hong Kong's Reunification with the Motherland: Tourism and Retail]. Hong Kong: Xianggang shang bao youxian gongsi, 2017.

Yu Ruxin. *Xianggang, 1967* [Hong Kong, 1967]. Hong Kong: Cosmos Books, 2012.

Yu Shengwu, Liu Cunkuan, and Liu Shuyong. *Xianggang lishi wenti ziliao xuan ping* [Selected Reviews of Hong Kong Historical Issues]. Hong Kong: Joint Publishing, 2008.

Yu Shengwu, and Liu Cunkuan, eds. *Shi jiu shiji de Xianggang* [Hong Kong in the Nineteenth Century]. Beijing: Zhonghua Book Company, 1994.

Yu Shengwu, and Liu Shuyong, eds. *Er shi shiji de Xianggang* [Hong Kong in the Twentieth Century]. Hong Kong: Qilin shuye youxian gongsi, 1995.

Yuan Qiushi. *Xianggang huigui dashiji, 1979–1997* [Chronology of Hong Kong's Return (1979–1997)]. Hong Kong: Joint Publishing, 1997.

———. *Xianggang huigui yilai da shi ji, 1997–2002* [Chronology of Hong Kong since Its Return, 1997–2002]. Hong Kong: Joint Publishing, 2003.

———. *Xianggang huigui yilai da shi ji, 2002–2007* [Chronology of Hong Kong since Its Return, 2002–2007]. Hong Kong: Joint Publishing, 2015.

Yuan Yonglun, comp. *Jing hai fen ji* [Record of the Pacification of Pirates]. Collection of the British Museum. Yangcheng Shangyuantang, 1830.

Yuehai jinrong konggu yanjiubu [Research Department of Guangdong Capital Holdings]. *Xianggang lianxi huilu baoweizhan* [Battle to Defend Hong Kong's Linked Exchange Rate System]. Hong Kong: Youth Literary Book Store, 1999.

Yung Wing. *My Life in China and America*. New York: Henry Holt and Company, 1909.

Zeng Ruisheng [Steve Tsang Yu-sang]. *Guanzhi Xianggang: Zhengwu guanyu lianghao guanzhi de jianli* [Governing Hong Kong: Administrative Officers and the Establishment of Sound Governance]. Hong Kong: Hong Kong University Press, 2007.

Zeng Zaozhuang, and Liu Lin, eds. *Quan Song wen* [Collected Works of the Song Dynasty]. Shanghai: Shanghai cishu chubanshe; Hefei: Anhui jiaoyu chubanshe, 2006.

Zhang Bingquan [Cheung Ping-kuen], and He Xingfeng [Carole Hoyan Hang-fung]. *Xianggang huaju koushu shi: Sanshi niandai zhi liushi niandai* [Oral History of Hong Kong Spoken Drama: 1930s to 1960s]. Hong Kong: Xianggang xiju gongcheng: Xianggang Zhongwen daxue Shao Yifu tang, 2001.

Zhang Huizhen [Cheung Wai-chun], and Kong Qiangsheng. *Cong shiyiwan dao sanqian: Lunxian shiqi Xianggang jiaoyu koushu lishi* [From 110,000 to 3,000: An Oral History of Hong Kong's Education under the Japanese Occupation]. Hong Kong: Oxford University Press, 2005.

Zhang Jiawei [Gary Cheung Ka-wai]. *Xianggang liu qi baodong neiqing* [Inside Story of 1967 Riots in Hong Kong]. Hong Kong: Taiping Yang shiji chubanshe, 2000.

Zhang Li. *Ershi shiji Xianggang shehui yu wenhua* [Hong Kong Society and Culture in the Twentieth Century]. Singapore: Mingchuang guoji, 2005.

Zhang Lianxing. *Xianggang ershiba zongdu* [The Twenty-eight British Governors of Hong Kong]. Hong Kong: Joint Publishing, 2012.

Zhang Rongfang, and Huang Miaozhang. *Nan Yue guo shi* [History of Southern Yue Kingdom]. 2nd ed. Guangzhou: Guangdong renmin chubanshe, 2008.

Zhang Ruiwei [Cheung Sui-wai]. *Chai Cun: Xiaoshi de Jiulong cunluo* [Village Dismantling: Demolished Villages in Kowloon]. Hong Kong: Joint Publishing, 2013.

Zhang Tingyu et al., comps. *Ming shi* [History of the Ming Dynasty]. Beijing: Zhonghua Book Company, 1974.

Zhang Xie, comp. *Dong xi yang kao* [A Study of the Eastern and Western Oceans]. Edited by Xie Fang. Beijing: Zhonghua Book Company, 2000.

Zhao Erxun et al., comps. *Qing shi gao* [Historical Manuscript of the Qing Dynasty]. Beijing: Zhonghua Book Company, 1977.

Zhao Weifang. *Xianggang dianying yishu shi* [A History of Hong Kong Film Art]. Beijing: Wenhua yishu chubanshe, 2017.

Zhao Xifang. *Baokan Xianggang: Lishi yujing yu wenxue changyu* [Newspapers in Hong Kong: Historical Context and Literary Field]. Hong Kong: Joint Publishing, 2019.

Zhao Yule [Chiu Yu-lok]. *Jindai nanlai wenren de Xianggang yinxiang yu guozu yishi* [The Literati Who Came to Hong Kong in Modern Times: Their Impression of Hong Kong and National Awareness]. 3-volume ed. Hong Kong: Joint Publishing, 2016.

Zhao Yule, Zhong Baoxian [Stephanie Chung Po-yin], and Li Ze'en [Lee Chak-yan]. *Xianggang yaolan (wai san zhong)* [A Guide to Hong Kong (Three Other Related Publications)]. Translated by Liang Yingjie, Gao Xiang, and Fan Minli. Hong Kong: Joint Publishing, 2017.

Zheng Baohong [Cheng Po-hung]. *Xianggang Hua yang hangye bainian. Maoyi yu jinrong pian* [A Century of Chinese-Western Industries in Hong Kong: Trade and Financial Industries]. Hong Kong: Commercial Press, 2016.

Zheng Hongtai [Victor Zheng Wan-tai], and Gao Hao. *Baishou xingjia: Xianggang jiazu yu shehui, 1841–1941* [Rags to Riches: Hong Kong Families and Society 1841–1941]. Hong Kong: Chung Hwa Book Company, 2016.

———. *Weishan zhewang: Cishan xintuo lishi yuan liuyu zhidu fenxi* [Philanthropy Is the King: An Analysis of the History and System of Charity Trusts]. Hong Kong: Chung Hwa Book Company, 2019.

Zheng Hongtai, and Huang Shaolun [Wong Siu-lun].

Xianggang gushi, 1841–1997 [A History of Hong Kong's Stock Market: 1841–1997]. Hong Kong: Joint Publishing, 2006.

———. *Xianggang miye shi* [A History of the Hong Kong Rice Trade]. Hong Kong: Joint Publishing, 2005.

———. *Xianggang shenfenzheng toushi* [A Look into Hong Kong Identity Card]. 2nd ed. Hong Kong: Joint Publishing, 2018.

Zheng Hongtai, and Lu Guanhao [Luk Koon-hoo]. *Dianshi chengjin: Dazao Xianggang jinrong zhongxin lichengbei* [Alchemy: Milestones of Hong Kong Financial Development]. Hong Kong: Chung Hwa Book Company, 2017

Zheng Hongtai, and Zhou Wengang, eds. *Dalang taosha: Jiazu qiye de yousheng liebai* [Waves Washing the sand: Why Some Family Businesses Succeed But Others Do Not]. Hong Kong: Chung Hwa Book Company, 2017.

———, eds. *Weiji guantou: Jiazu qiye de yingdui zhidao* [Coping with Crisis: Ways for Family Business to Survive and Thrive]. Hong Kong: Chung Hwa Book Company, 2015.

Zheng Huixin [Cheng Hwei-shing]. *Dong Haoyun riji* [Tung Hao-yun's Diary]. Hong Kong: Chinese University Press, 2004.

Zhong Baoxian [Stephanie Chung Po-yin]. *Xianggang yingshiye bainian* [A Hundred Years of Hong Kong Film and Television Industries]. Hong Kong: Joint Publishing, 2004.

Zhong Baoxian, and Gao Tianqiang [Ko Tim-keung]. *"Longjin qiao ji qi linjin quyu" lishi yanjiu* [A Research on Lung Tsun Stone Bridge and Its Surrounding Area]. Research Reports of the Antiquities and Monuments Office, 2012.

Zhong Shiyuan [Chung Sze-yuen]. *Xianggang huigui licheng: Zhong Shiyuan huiyi lu* [Hong Kong's Journey to Reunification: Memoirs of Sze-yuen Chung]. Hong Kong: Chinese University Press, 2001.

Zhong Zi [Chung Chi], ed. *Xianggang baoye chunqiu* [A Classic History of Hong Kong Press]. Guangzhou: Guangdong renmin chubanshe, 1991.

Zhonggong zhongyang wenxian yanjiushi [Literature Research Office of the Central Committee of the Communist Party of China], ed. *Deng Xiaoping nianpu (1975–1997)* [Chronicle of Deng Xiaoping (1975–1997)]. Beijing: Zhongyang wenxian chubanshe, 2004.

———, ed. *Mao Zedong nianpu (1893–1949)* [Chronicle of Mao Zedong (1893–1949)]. Rev. ed. Beijing: Zhongyang wenxian chubanshe, 2013.

———, ed. *Mao Zedong nianpu (1949–1976)* [Chronicle of Mao Zedong (1949–1976)]. Beijing: Zhongyang wenxian chubanshe, 2013.

———, ed. *Zhou Enlai nianpu (1898–1949)* [Chronicle of Zhou Enlai (1898–1949)]. Beijing: Zhongyang wenxian chubanshe, 1990.

———, ed. *Zhou Enlai nianpu (1949–1976)* [Chronicle of Zhou Enlai (1949–1976)]. Beijing: Zhongyang wenxian chubanshe, 1997.

———, ed. *Zhongguo minzhu tongmeng lishi wenxian (1941–1949)* [Historical Documents of the China Democratic League (1941–1949)]. Beijing: Wenshi ziliao chubanshe, 1983.

Zhou Chengren, and Li Yizhuan. *Zaoqi Xianggang dianying shi, 1897–1945* [History of Early Films in Hong Kong, 1875–1945]. Hong Kong: Joint Publishing, 2005.

Zhou Guang. *Guangdong kaogu jiyao* [Archaeological Abstracts of Guangdong]. Block-printed edition of 1893.

Zhou Guangzhen [Oliver Chou Kwong-chung]. *Xianggang yinyue de qianshi jinsheng: Xianggang zaoqi yinyue fazhan licheng (1930s–1950s)* [History of Hong Kong's Early Music Development (1930s–1950s)]. Hong Kong: Joint Publishing, 2017.

Zhou Jiarong [Chow Kai-wing]. *Xianggang Chaozhou shanghui jiu shi nian fazhan shi* [History of Ninety-Year Development of Chiu Chow Chamber of Commerce in Hong Kong]. Hong Kong: Chung Hwa Book Company, 2012.

———. *Xianggang tong shi: Yuangu zhi Qingdai* [General History of Hong Kong: From Ancient Times to the Qing Dynasty]. Hong Kong: Joint Publishing, 2017.

———, ed. *Bainian chuancheng: Xianggang xuezhe lun Zhonghua shuju* [The Festschrift of the One-hundredth Anniversary of Chung Hwa Book Company]. Hong Kong: Chung Hwa Book Company, 2012.

Zhou Jiarong [Chow Kai-wing], Huang Wenjiang [Wong Man-kong], and Mai Jingsheng [Mak King-sang]. *Xianggang jinhui daxue liu shi nian fazhan shi* [Sixty Years of Excellence at Hong Kong Baptist University]. Hong Kong: Joint Publishing, 2016.

Zhou Qufei. *Lingwai daida jiaozhu* [Annotations on the Land beyond the Passes]. Edited by Yang Wuquan. Beijing: Zhonghua Book Company, 1999.

Zhou Wang ergong shiji jinian zhuanji bianji weiyuanhui [Editorial Board]. *Zhou Wang er gong shiji jinian zhuanji* [Memorial Album of Chou

Wong Er Kung Historical Sites]. Hong Kong: Zhou Wang er yuan, 1982.

Zhou Yi [Chau Yick]. *Xianggang gongyun shi jianpian* [A Brief History of Hong Kong's Labour Movement]. Hong Kong: Li xun chubanshe, 2013.

———. *Xianggang yingxiong ernu: Dongjiang zongdui Gang Jiu dadui kang Ri zhanshi* [Hong Kong's Heroes: Wartime History of the Hong Kong–Kowloon Brigade of the East River Column]. Hong Kong: Liwen chuban, 2004.

Zhou Yongxin [Nelson Chow Wing-sun]. *Chuangjian gongping he guan'ai shehui: Xianggang minsheng zhengce de deyushi* [Creating a Fair and Caring Society: Pros and Cons of Hong Kong's Livelihood Policies]. Hong Kong: Chung Hwa Book Company, 2017.

———. *Zhenshi de pinqiong mianmao: Zongguan Xianggang shehui 60 nian* [The Reality of Poverty in Hong Kong: Examining Hong Kong Society in the Last 60 Years]. Hong Kong: Chung Hwa Book Company, 2014.

Zhu Jinde [Jackie C.T. Chu], and Chen Shili [Chan Sik-lap]. *Kuangshi juzhu: Xianggang kuangye shi* [Hong Kong Mining History]. Hong Kong: ProjecTerrae, 2015.

Zhu Qi. *Xianggang mei shu shi* [History of Hong Kong Fine Art]. Hong Kong: Joint Publishing, 2005.

Zhuang Haiyuan [Chuang Hoi-yuen], ed. *Xianggang huigui zuguo 20 zhounian zhi: Maoyi yu wuliu* [The Twentieth Anniversary of Hong Kong's Reunification with the Motherland: Trade and Logistics]. Hong Kong: Xianggang shang bao youxian gongsi, 2017.

Zi Yu [Chi Yu]. *Xianggang zhanggu* [Hong Kong Anecdotes]. Vol. 2. Hong Kong: Shanghai shudian, 1981.

Zou Xinghua [Chau Hing-wah], and Xiao Lijuan [Siu Lai-kuen], eds. *Cheng yu jiao: Xianggang yuzheng fazhan 1921–2011* [Custody and Correction: The Development of Hong Kong Penal System 1921–2011]. Hong Kong: Hong Kong Correctional Services Department, 2011.

Online Databases

Companies Registry, Hong Kong

Current and Past Meeting Records, Legislative

Council, Hong Kong

Database for the Study of Modern Chinese Thoughts and Literature, National Chengchi University

Government Records Service, Hong Kong

Gwulo: Old Hong Kong

Historical Laws of Hong Kong Online, The University of Hong Kong

Hong Kong Catholic Diocesan Archives

Hong Kong e-Legislation

Hong Kong Government Reports Online, The University of Hong Kong

Hong Kong Heritage Project, The

Hong Kong Legal Information Institute Database

Hong Kong Memory

House of Commons Hansard, UK Parliament

Industrial History of Hong Kong Group, The

Japan Centre for Asian Historical Records, National Archives of Japan

Kotenseki Sōgō Database [Japanese and Chinese Classics], Waseda University Library

LegCo Bills Database, Legislative Council Library, Hong Kong Special Administrative Region

LegCo Members Database, Legislative Council Library, Hong Kong Special Administrative Region

Memória de Macau

National Diet Library, Digital Special Collections, Japan

Sun Yat-sen Full Text Retrieval System

Websites

A. S. Watson Group

Abdoolally Ebrahim & Co (HK), Ltd.

Agriculture, Fisheries and Conservation Department, Government of the Hong Kong Special Administrative Region

Antiquities Advisory Board

Antiquities and Monuments Office

Asia Art Archive

Audit Commission, Government of the Hong Kong Special Administrative Region

Aviation Safety Network

Baptist Convention of Hong Kong (in Chinese only)

Beijing-Hong Kong Academic Exchange Centre

BNP Paribas

Board of Management of the Chinese Permanent Cemeteries (in Chinese only)

Bond Connect

Boys' & Girls' Clubs Association of Hong Kong, The

British Chinese Heritage Centre

British Council

C. Melchers GmbH & Co. KG

Cantonese Opera Advisory Committee & Cantonese Opera Development Fund

Caritas Hong Kong

Cathay Pacific Airways Limited

Catholic Diocese of Hong Kong

Census and Statistics Department, Government of the Hong Kong Special Administrative Region

Centre for Food Safety, Government of the Hong Kong Special Administrative Region

China Merchants Group

China Resources (Holdings) Co., Ltd.

China Travel Service (Hong Kong) Limited

Chinese Amateur Athletic Federation of Hong Kong, The

Chinese Artists Association of Hong Kong [Barwo] (in Chinese only)

Chinese Banking Association of Hong Kong

Chinese Banks' Association Limited, The

Chinese General Chamber of Commerce, Hong Kong, The

Chinese Gold and Silver Exchange

Chinese Manufacturers' Association of Hong Kong, The

Chinese Temples Committee

Chinese University of Hong Kong, The

Chinese YMCA of Hong Kong

Chung Sing Benevolent Society (in Chinese only)

Citibank

City University of Hong Kong

Civil Aid Service, Government of the Hong Kong Special Administrative Region

Civil Aviation Department, Government of the Hong Kong Special Administrative Region

Civil Engineering and Development Department, Government of the Hong Kong Special Administrative Region

Civil Service Bureau, Government of the Hong Kong Special Administrative Region

CK Hutchison Holdings Limited

CLP Holdings Limited

CLP Power Hong Kong Limited

Club Lusitano

College of Nursing Hong Kong

Commerce and Economic Development Bureau, Government of the Hong Kong Special Administrative Region

Community Care Fund

Conservancy Association, The

Conserve and Revitalise Hong Kong Heritage

Constitutional and Mainland Affairs Bureau, Government of the Hong Kong Special Administrative Region

Customs and Excise Department, Government of the Hong Kong Special Administrative Region

Cyberport

Dairy Farm

Department for Justice, Government of the Hong Kong Special Administrative Region

Department of Health, Government of the Hong Kong Special Administrative Region

Deutsche Bank in Hong Kong SAR

Dr Sun Yat-sen Museum

Drainage Services Department, Government of the Hong Kong Special Administrative Region

Education Bureau, Government of the Hong Kong Special Administrative Region

Education University of Hong Kong, The

Electoral Affairs Commission, Government of the Hong Kong Special Administrative Region

Electronic Health Record Sharing System

Employees Compensation Insurer Insolvency Bureau

Environmental Protection Department, Government of the Hong Kong Special Administrative Region

Equal Opportunities Commission

Family Planning Association of Hong Kong, The

Federation of Hong Kong Industries

Fire Services Department, Government of the Hong Kong Special Administrative Region

Food and Environmental Hygiene Department, Government of the Hong Kong Special Administrative Region

Foreign Correspondents' Club Hong Kong, The

Garden Company Limited, The

Gilman & Co.

Government Bonds, Government of the Hong Kong Special Administrative Region

Highways Department, Government of the Hong Kong Special Administrative Region

HK Electric

Hok Hoi Library (in Chinese only)

Home Affairs Bureau, Government of the Hong Kong Special Administrative Region

Hong Kong Academy for Performing Arts, The

Hong Kong Academy of Fine Arts

Hong Kong Aircraft Engineering Company Limited (HAECO Group)

Hong Kong Anti-Cancer Society

Hong Kong Applied Science and Technology Research Institute

Hong Kong Archaeological Society

Hong Kong Army Cadets Association

Hong Kong Arts Development Council

Hong Kong Association of Travel Agents

Hong Kong Buddhist Association, The

Hong Kong Buddhist Sangha Association (in Chinese only)

Hong Kong Catholic Cathedral of The Immaculate Conception, The

Hong Kong Cemetery

Hong Kong Chinese Christian Churches Union, The (in Chinese only)

Hong Kong Chinese Importers' and Exporters' Association, The

Hong Kong Christian Council

Hong Kong Christian Service

Hong Kong College of Technology

Hong Kong Correctional Services, Government of the Hong Kong Special Administrative Region

Hong Kong Court of Final Appeal

Hong Kong Cricket Club, The

Hong Kong Deposit Protection Board

Hong Kong Design Centre

Hong Kong Equestrian Association

Hong Kong Examinations and Assessment Authority

Hong Kong Exchanges and Clearing Limited

Hong Kong Export Credit Insurance Corporation

Hong Kong Federation of Trade Unions, The

Hong Kong Film Archive

Hong Kong Film Awards

Hong Kong Football Association

Hong Kong General Chamber of Commerce, The

Hong Kong Girl Guides Association, The

Hong Kong Golf Club

Hong Kong Herbarium

Hong Kong Heritage Museum

Hong Kong Hockey Association, The

Hong Kong Housing Authority and Housing Department, Government of the Hong Kong Special Administrative Region

Hong Kong Housing Society

Hong Kong International Airport

Hong Kong Jockey Club, The

Hong Kong Life Saving Society, The

Hong Kong Logistics Development Council

Hong Kong Medical Association, The

Hong Kong Monetary Authority

Hong Kong Mortgage Corporation Limited, The

Hong Kong Museum of Coastal Defence

Hong Kong Museum of History

Hong Kong Museum of Medical Sciences

Hong Kong Music Institute

Hong Kong Observatory, Government of the Hong Kong Special Administrative Region

Hong Kong Performing Artistes Guild

Hong Kong Police Force, Government of the Hong Kong Special Administrative Region

Hong Kong Polytechnic University, The

Hong Kong Red Cross Blood Transfusion Service

Hong Kong Science Museum

Hong Kong Science Park

Hong Kong Seamen's Union

Hong Kong Sheng Kung Hui

Hong Kong Society for Rehabilitation, The

Hong Kong Sports Institute

Hong Kong Standards and Testing Centre, The

Hong Kong Tourism Board

Hong Kong Trade Development Council

Hong Kong Tramways, Limited

Hong Kong Tuberculosis, Chest and Heart Diseases Association

Hong Kong UNESCO Global Geopark

Hong Kong University of Science and Technology, The

Hong Kong Yacht Club

Hong Kong Young Women's Christian Association

Hongkong Post, Government of the Hong Kong Special Administrative Region

Hospital Authority

HSBC Holdings plc

Hysan Development Company Limited

Incorporated Trustees of The Islamic Community Fund of Hong Kong, The

Independent Commission Against Corruption, Hong Kong Special Administrative Region

Indian Recreation Club

Inland Revenue Department, Government of the Hong Kong Special Administrative Region

Intangible Cultural Heritage Office

International Mathematical Olympiad

Investor and Financial Education Council

Jao Tsung-i Petite Ecole, The University of Hong Kong

Jardine, Matheson & Co.

Jebsen & Co.

Jockey Club Creative Arts Centre

John Swire & Sons (H.K.) Ltd

Kowloon Bowling Green Club

Labour Department, Government of the Hong Kong Special Administrative Region

Land Registry, Government of the Hong Kong Special Administrative Region, The

Lands Department, Government of the Hong Kong Special Administrative Region

Law Reform Commission of Hong Kong, The

Lee Kung Man Knitting Factory (HK) Limited

Leisure and Cultural Services Department, Government of the Hong Kong Special Administrative Region

Li Ka Shing Foundation

Lord Wilson Heritage Trust, The

Lung Fu Shan Environmental Education Centre

Mandatory Provident Fund Schemes Authority

Marine Department, Government of the Hong Kong Special Administrative Region

Mills, The

Minimum Wage Commission

Monitoring Committee on Implementation of the SARS Expert Committee Report's Recommendations, Government of the Hong Kong Special Administrative Region

MTR Corporation

Nam Pak Hong Association

Narcotics Division, Security Bureau, Government of the Hong Kong Special Administrative Region

National Archives of Japan

New Asia College, The Chinese University of Hong Kong

New Territories General Chamber of Commerce

Newspaper Society of Hong Kong, The

OCBC Wing Hang Bank Limited

Ocean Park Hong Kong

Office of the Communications Authority

Office of the Ombudsman, Hong Kong

Office of the Privacy Commissioner for Personal Data, Hong Kong

Our Hong Kong Foundation

P & O Heritage

Package of Proposals for the Methods for Selecting the Chief Executive and for Forming the Legislative Council in 2012

Pharmaceutical Society of Hong Kong, The

Planning Department, Government of the Hong Kong Special Administrative Region

Po Leung Kuk

Protocol Division Government Secretariat, Government of the Hong Kong Special Administrative Region

Qualifications Framework, Government of the Hong Kong Special Administrative Region

Radio Television Hong Kong

Rating and Valuation Department, Government of the Hong Kong Special Administrative Region

Rotary District 3450

Royal Museums Greenwich

Salvation Army, The

Samaritan Befrienders Hong Kong, The

School of Chinese, The University of Hong Kong

Scout Association of Hong Kong

Securities and Futures Commission

Shaw Studios

Sik Sik Yuen

Sikh Polis

South China Athletic Association

St. Paul's Hospital

Standard Chartered Hong Kong

"Star" Ferry Company Limited, The

State-owned Assets Supervision and Administration Commission of the State Council

Taikoo Sugar

Tao Fung Shan Christian Centre

Television Broadcasts Limited

Three Runway System, Hong Kong International Airport

Tourism Commission, Government of the Hong Kong Special Administrative Region

Tracker Fund of Hong Kong

Trade and Industry Development, Government of the Hong Kong Special Administrative Region

Transport Department, Government of the Hong Kong Special Administrative Region

Tung Wah Group of Hospitals

TWGHs Temple and Cultural Services

Two Girls, The House of Kwong Sang Hong Limited

University Hall Alumni Limited, The University of Hong Kong

University of Hong Kong, The

Urban Renewal Authority

Water Supplies Department, Government of the Hong Kong Special Administrative Region

West Kowloon Cultural District

World Bank Open Data

World Health Organization

World Wide Fund for Nature Hong Kong

Yuen Yuen Institute, The (in Chinese only)